A DICTIONARY
OF EUROPEAN
ANGLICISMS

A Usage Dictionary of Anglicisms
in Sixteen European Languages

Edited by

MANFRED GÖRLACH

OXFORD
UNIVERSITY PRESS

OXFORD
UNIVERSITY PRESS

Great Clarendon Street, Oxford OX2 6DP

Oxford University Press is a department of the University of Oxford.
It furthers the University's objective of excellence in research, scholarship,
and education by publishing worldwide in

Oxford New York

Auckland Cape Town Dar es Salaam Hong Kong Karachi
Kuala Lumpur Madrid Melbourne Mexico City Nairobi
New Delhi Shanghai Taipei Toronto

With offices in

Argentina Austria Brazil Chile Czech Republic France Greece
Guatemala Hungary Italy Japan Poland Portugal
Singapore South Korea Switzerland Thailand Turkey Ukraine Vietnam

Oxford is a registered trade mark of Oxford University Press
in the UK and in certain other countries

Published in the United States
by Oxford University Press Inc., New York

British Library Cataloguing in Publication Data

Data available

Library of Congress Cataloging in Publication Data

Data available

ISBN 0-19-823519-4   978-0-19-823519-4

ISBN 0-19-928306-0 (pbk.)   978-0-19-928306-4 (pbk.)

1 3 5 7 9 10 8 6 4 2

Typeset by SPI Publisher Services, Pondicherry, India
Printed in Great Britain
on acid-free paper by
Biddles Ltd, Kings Lynn, Norfolk

Contents

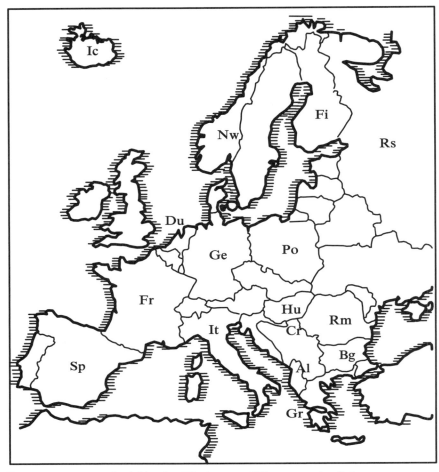

Languages covered within the *Dictionary of European Anglicisms*

FOREWORD

Standard histories of major European languages have always taken it to be self-evident that these languages have at various times been enriched, or at any rate have been enlarged, by the acquisition of words from other languages. Thus, for example, the Norman Conquest in the eleventh century brought in its wake layer upon layer of vocabulary from Old French into use in medieval English, words such as *baptism, council, govern, office, parliament, prince, victory*, and numerous others. Over a long period and especially since the seventeenth century the English language absorbed some of the central musical terminology of the Italian language, for example *allegro, concerto, diminuendo, fugato, moderato, oratorio*, and many others.

Since the seventeenth and eighteenth centuries the establishment of English-speaking colonies in North America, Australia, New Zealand, South Africa, and elsewhere has led to the emergence of numerous distinguishable varieties of English throughout the world. The settlers in each of these regions in their turn encountered and accepted many of the native inhabitants' names for their flora and fauna, and also many of the names of their tribal customs and beliefs. The new versions of English that resulted acquired in North America, for example, words such as *chipmunk, coyote* (via Mexican Spanish), *moccasin, pecan*, and *wigwam*. From the Aboriginal languages Australian English adopted such words as *boomerang, corroboree, didgeridoo, kangaroo*, and so on. From Maori New Zealand English acquired such words as *haka, katipo* (spider), *kiwi, marae* (meeting place), *pakeha*. From the languages of various inhabitants of South Africa English-speakers drew a wide variety of words, for example *dagga* (marijuana), *donga* (gully), *mawo* (an exclamation of astonishment). English-speaking colonists in South Africa also took into their everyday vocabulary a great many Afrikaans words such as *springbok* and *veld(t)*.

For more than a thousand years English has drawn words and phrases from many outside sources. Details of the movement of large quantities of such vocabulary have been extensively documented in dictionaries of various sizes and types from the 20-volume *Oxford English Dictionary* down to small pocket-sized dictionaries and minidictionaries.

At the same time, the donor languages, including those of the sixteen European languages selected for treatment by Manfred Görlach in this dictionary, were taking English words into their own languages. The pages that follow amply confirm that elements of the English language are being adopted in a spectacular fashion, though with varying frequency, in each of the European countries that Görlach and his fellow scholars chose to examine. This dictionary is a pioneer in a little-studied area of lexicography. It will be warmly welcomed and will encourage scholars throughout the world to look closely at the degree of the spread of English vocabulary into other European languages and into languages in other parts of the world, as, for example, in China, Japan, India, and Turkey.

R. W. Burchfield

ACKNOWLEDGEMENTS

I gratefully acknowledge the help I received from OUP, especially from Frances Morphy who assisted me throughout the dictionary's gestation phase, and from colleagues in various departments of the University of Cologne willing to answer individual points. My debt to the collaborators is infinite: they have patiently filled in data and given hundreds of writing hours for a project for which they could not expect any material rewards.

At Cologne, the intelligent and patient work of my research students made an impossible project possible. They include, at different times, but listed here in alphabetical order

Ursula Heister, Birgit Lensing, Katja Lenz, Ruth Möhlig, Maria Ninu-Stepanski, Marion Reudenbach, Kristina Ritter, Monika Schumacher, Anne Strauch, April Tedder, Corinna Tertel, Marcus Willemsen, and Friederike Wütscher.

I would particularly like to acknowledge the contribution of Prof. Dr Rudolf Filipović who died in December 2000 prior to the publication of this dictionary. His input on the Croatian language was invaluable and it is lamentable that he was not able to see the project through to fruition.

LIST OF CONTRIBUTORS

Al   Frau Tatiana & Dr. Rolf
     Ködderitzsch
     Noldestr. 37
     D-53340 Meckenheim
     GERMANY

Bg   Dr Nevena Alexieva
     English Department
     Sofia University
     Tsar Osvoboditel Blvd 15
     1000 Sofia BULGARIA

Cr   Prof. Dr Rudolf Filipović
     (deceased)

Du   Prof. Dr Amand
     Berteloot
     Institut für Niederländische
     Philologie
     Universität Münster
     Alter Steinweg 6–7
     D-48143 Münster
     GERMANY

Fi   Keith Battarbee
     Department of English
     University of Turku
     SF-20014 Turku FINLAND

Fr   Prof. John Humbley
     UFR EILA
     Université Paris 7 Denis Diderot
     F-75005 Paris
     FRANCE

Ge   Prof. Dr Manfred Görlach
     Handschuhsheimer
     Landstrasse 35
     D-69121 Heidelberg
     GERMANY

     Prof. Dr Ulrich Busse
     Institut für Anglistik und Am.
     Martin-Luther-Universität
     Halle-Wittenberg

     Dachritzstr. 12
     D-06099 Halle/Saale
     GERMANY

Gr   Ekaterini Stathi
     Messogion 73 B
     GR 15126 Athens
     GREECE

Hu   Dr Judit Farkas and
     Prof. Veronika Kniezsa
     Department of English
     Linguistics
     Eötvös Lorand University
     Ajtosi Dürer sor 19
     H 1146 Budapest
     HUNGARY

Ic   Prof. Dr Guðrún Kvaran and
     Ásta Svavarsdóttir
     Institute of Lexicography
     Neshagi 16
     Reykjavik IS 107 ICELAND

It   Dr Alessio Fontana
     Romanisches Seminar
     Universität zu Köln
     Albertus-Magnus-Platz 1
     D-50923 Köln
     GERMANY

     Prof. Virginia Pulcini
     Università degli Studi di Torino
     Facoltà di Lingue e Letterature
     Straniere
     Dipartimento di Scienze del
     Linguaggio
     Via S. Ottavio 20
     10124 Torino
     ITALY

Nw Dr art. Anne-Line Graedler
Dept. of British and American
  Studies, University of Oslo
PO Box 1003, Blindern
N-0315 Oslo NORWAY

Po Dr Elżbíeta Mańczak-Wohlfeld
Uniwersytet Jagielloński
Inst. Filologii Angielskiej
ul. Mickiewicza
PL-31-120 Kraków POLAND

Rm Ilinca Constantinescu and
  Dr Ariadna Ştefănescu
Institutul de Lingvistică
Calea 13 Septembrie Nr. 13
RO-76117 Bucureşti
ROMANIA

Dr Victoria Popovici
Institut für Romanistik
Fr.-Schiller-Universität Jena
D-07740 Jena
GERMANY

Rs Prof. T. V. Maximova
Department of English
University of Volgograd
2 Prodolnaya 30
40062 Volgograd
RUSSIA

Dr Sonja Heyl
Humboldt-Universität
Institut für Slawistik
Unter den Linden 6
D-10099 Berlin
GERMANY

Helen Pelikh
Department of English
University of Volgograd
RUSSIA

Sp Prof. Félix Rodriguez González
Departamento de Filología
  Inglesa
Universidad de Alicante
Ap. Correus 99
E-03080 Alicante SPAIN

ABBREVIATIONS AND SYMBOLS
USED IN THE DICTIONARY

Standard Abbreviations

abbrev	abbreviation	Fr	French
adj	adjective	Fris	Frisian
adv	adverb	Ge	German
Al	Albanian	Gmc	Germanic
Am Ind	American Indian	Gr	Greek
Am Sp	American Spanish	HGe	High German
Anglo Fr	Anglo French	Hindi	Hindi
Ar	Arabic	Hu	Hungarian
Austr	Australian	Ic	Icelandic
Bg	Bulgarian	i.e.	that is
Braz	Brazilian	imit	imitative
c	century	impers	impersonal
C	common noun	Ind	Indian
c.	circa	infl	inflected
Caribb	Caribbean	interj	interjection
Central Am	Central American	interrog	interrogative
cf	confer	intrans	intransitive
cm	centimetre	Ir	Irish
conj	conjunction	It	Italian
cp$^{1/2}$	compound	Jap	Japanese
Cr	Croatian	La	Latin
creat	creation	LGe	Low German
Dan	Danish	Lith	Lithuanian
Du	Dutch	M	Masculine
E	English	Mal	Malay
E.	East	ME	Middle English
e.g.	for example	mean	meaning
erron	erroneous	MLGe	Middle Low German
esp	especially	N	Neuter
etc	et cetera	N.	North
exc	except	n	noun
F	Feminine	neg	negative
Fi	Finnish	Nw	Norwegian
fig	figurative	OE	Old English

orig	original	spec	special
pers	person	specif	specific
pl	plural	subj	subject
Po	Polish	superl	superlative
Port	Portuguese	trans	transitive
pp	pages	trsl	translation
rend	rendition	Turk	Turkish
Rm	Romanian	uninfl.	uninflected
Rs	Russian	US	United States
sing	singular	usu	usually
Sp	Spanish		

DEA Abbreviations

acron	acronym	euph	euphemistic
admin	administration	fac	facetious
agric	agriculture	fash	fashion
Am footb	American football	femin	feminism
anatom	anatomy	footb	football
anthrop	anthropology	gen	general
arch	archaic	geog	geography
archaeol	archaeology	geol	geology
archit	architecture	geom	geometry
arith	arithmetics	golf	golf/golfing
astron	astronomy	gram	grammar/grammatical
attrib	attributive	high soc	high society
ball	ball games	hist	history/historical
ban	banned	horses	horses/horseracing
basketb	basketball	hortic	horticulture
biol	biology	hyperbol	hyperbolic
bot	botany	indus	industrial
box	boxing	jazz	jazz
cards	card games	joc	jocular
cars	automobiles	jour	journalese
chem	chemistry	ling	linguistics
cinema	cinematography	lit	literature/literary
coll	colloquial	math	mathematics
comput	computers/computing	mech	mechanical/mechanics
corresp	correspondence	med	medical/medicine
cosmet	cosmetics	mediev	medieval
cricket	cricket	metaph	metaphoric
dance	dancing	meteor	meteorology
derog	derogatory	mil	military
dimin	diminutive	mining	mining
eccles	ecclesiastical	mod	modish
ecol	ecology	money	money
econ	economy	mus	music/musical
educ	education	nat hist	natural history
electr	electricity	obs	obsolescent
eng	engineering	oil	oil
ety	etymology	pathol	pathology

pej	pejorative	sla	slang
pharm	pharmacology	sociol	sociology
philol	philology	space tech	space technology
photogr	photography	sport	sport
phys	physics	tech	technology/technical
physiol	physiology	telecom	telecommunications
planes	planes/aviation	teleg	telegraphy
polit	politics	tennis	tennis
predic	predicative	theat	theatre/theatrical
psychol	psychology	theol	theology
radio comm	radio communication	transp	transport
rare	rare/infrequent	vet	veterinary
reg	regional	vulg	vulgar
relig	religion/religious	writ	written
sci	science/scientific	you	youth
scifi	science fiction	zool	zoology

Symbols

>	more frequent than; develops into
<	less frequent than
=	equivalent of, equally frequent
Ø	zero morph (in pluralization); foreignism
↑	cross reference
/	alternatives
[ ]	phonetic transcription
' '	sense
a̱, a̱	primary, secondary stress
→	derivation

INTRODUCTION

The present dictionary is the first of its kind. After preparations of more than five years, the *Dictionary of European Anglicisms* project was effectively started in 1993 and has since become a truly European enterprise. The influence of English on other languages has been noticed (and often criticized) by individual speech communities before, and indeed documented in various national dictionaries of anglicisms, but there has never been an exhaustive comparative treatment of the phenomenon. The great Dutch scholar Zandvoort suggested compiling such a dictionary almost thirty years ago, but no dictionary of the type has ever been attempted. Thus, although there is an obvious need for such a compilation, methods first had to be developed for a reliable survey of the situation of anglicisms in sixteen selected European languages. At the time when I put forward the proposal to the publisher, I was insufficiently aware of the complexities which were bound to arise, not only from linguistic problems, but also from the organization of the scheme and the storage and proper analysis of huge masses of data. In all this, speed and efficiency were essential. Ever since the political division of Europe came to an end (1989–90) the intake of English lexis has been dramatic in the eastern countries in particular, and in order to avoid endless revisions necessitated by updating our data, we had to compile the dictionary quickly, with the aim of providing a necessarily provisional snapshot of the situation as it presented itself in the early 1990s. We hope that for all its limitations this survey in three volumes will provide a great amount of useful information. The lesson that one cannot aim for perfection in an enterprise like this was a hard one to come to terms with; however, we have tried to be as perfect as possible within the terms that we set for ourselves.

The *Dictionary of European Anglicisms* includes 16 European languages from different language families, but excluding those in close contact with English (e.g. Irish, Welsh, and Maltese). Data have been collected for four Germanic languages (Icelandic, Norwegian, Dutch, and German), four Slavic (Russian, Polish, Croatian, and Bulgarian), four Romance (French, Spanish, Italian, and Romanian) and four other languages (Finnish, Hungarian, Albanian, and Greek). These were selected partly because competent collaborators were willing to join the project and partly to allow the analysis of a maximal number of contrasts—purist vs. open speech communities, Western vs. Eastern countries, regional comparisons (Scandinavia, the Balkans), and the impact of mediating languages (French and German in particular).

Ic	Nw	Po	Rs
Du	Ge	Cr	Bg
Fr	It	Fi	Hu
Sp	Rm	Al	Gr

When I started, I was not aware of the beautiful iconicity of the languages represented: the final scheme looks like the result of careful planning when in fact it was partly fortuitous. The areal coverage is illustrated by the adjacent 'grid'.

Fig.1   The 16-language grid representing the DEA coverage

The four language groups roughly represent the North West (Germanic), the South West (Romance), the North East (Slavic), and the South East (others, mainly Balkanic). The 'geographical' arrangement is repeated in each of the four sections. I discuss the use of this grid below.

Aims and Restrictions

The *Dictionary of European Anglicisms* is intended as a documentation of the lexical input of English into European languages up to the early 1990s (with a cut-off date of 1995); earlier loans are included, but we have concentrated on the modern lexis imported after World War II. The situation is rapidly changing, so we have aimed deliberately to produce a 'snapshot' view of a particular point in time. Therefore, there was a need to get the dictionary data complete in much less time than is usually accorded to such projects.

The deadline has meant that some words which became popular only in 1996 or later had to be omitted. Thus, we *just* included the 'German non-word of 1996', *outsourcing*, which came second in a popular national competition of the 'nastiest' words. Its salience suggests its high degree of currency from the early 1990s, but I had not been aware of the word (and it is not listed in the most comprehensive recent dictionary, Carstensen and Busse 1993–5). Again, when in Italy in early 1997 I noticed the frequent use of *welfare (system)* on the front pages of daily papers—often not italicized and used without 'scare quotes'. The word, I was told, was old, but its popularity a very recent development.

In fields like computing it is difficult to pinpoint the year English terms came in and when they became reasonably current. There is no objective criterion to support the inclusion of some of these terms and not others. Since we depended on anglicisms being noted by collaborators, there were a few oversights, especially with regard to the most recent acquisitions (many of which are still of quite uncertain status).

The comparative method and the time schedule have also precluded basing our statements (including those on currency) on text corpora. There are doubts about the representativeness of corpora even for national dictionaries, and the methodological problems proliferate with any cross-linguistic analysis. Moreover, for many languages here included such corpora would have had to have been put together from scratch—so there was really no choice but to base statements about style and currency values on the introspection of the collaborators and their informants, combined with data in recent dictionaries.

Modern technology will make it possible—if there is any demand—to produce a second edition in a few years' time which will then include more recent acquisitions and permit contrastive analysis of the growth of this type of lexis. The European languages are likely to become more similar to each other in due course, but there will also be special developments, such as the consequences of recent French language legislation. Such diachronic analysis will in particular be feasible if the data are loaded to an electronic data bank (a possibility discussed but rejected so far because of the amount of time and money involved).

The *Dictionary of European Anglicisms* will not make redundant monographs devoted to contrastive analysis in specialist fields, such as the language of sports or music; the computerized form of the *Dictionary of European Anglicisms* database will facilitate such research. The dictionary is also likely to spark off sufficient interest among linguists and word-watchers and inspire them to supply additions and corrections. Finally, the data will be of interest to the compilers of bilingual dictionaries for the evidence they contain about *faux amis*: increasingly, anglicisms have moved away from their 'original meanings' (or at least connotations), with the result that an anglicism can often not be properly translated by its etymon.

Data Collection

In order to find out what anglicisms are shared by selected European languages, I drew up a first list of loanwords in German from various sources—dictionaries, newspaper texts and items that came to my mind or were suggested by colleagues and students. No attempt was made to establish the first list on the basis of a corpus or a specific source. This collection, made in 1988, yielded some 1200 items. It was checked for Polish by E. Mańczak-Wohlfeld who had just completed a dictionary of anglicisms in Polish; her additions brought the combined list to some 1500 items. After the number of contributors and languages was complete, I decided on a more formal procedure: specimen entries were written for selected words comprising data for a few languages. The collaborators were asked for information on a set of specified features, and I outlined to them the most desirable methods for gathering and describing the data. A pilot stage of the project made me aware of a few more problems, and additional features (for example the inclusion of the 'grids' and the 'wedges' < >) were discussed with and accepted by the publisher.

All the data collected were put on a computer by several generations of research students (listed above, p. ix) and printed out in five 'batches' (A–C, D–G, H–M, N–S, T–Z) which were sent to all contributors (and to second readers if available). The lists were returned with replies to every single headword—the minimal answer possible was to note the total absence of the item by means of a dash(—). Contributors were also asked to write provisional entries for words not covered so far—because they were unique to their language or a group of languages, because they counted as anglicisms in the collaborator's language (but were possibly internationalisms in others), or because they had been overlooked. This stage was followed by two more stages in which the data was circulated for checking and, where necessary, for correction and completion. In 1996 and 1997 separate lists of 'additions' were circulated; they contained late-comers which were first kept separate so that they might be treated with greater attention.

The number of books referred to during the compilation is very large; most are listed in the individual sections of the *Annotated Bibliography of Anglicisms (ABASEL)*, one of the two accompanying volumes to the *Dictionary of European Anglicisms*. Those which proved most helpful in the final editing process were: the *Concise Oxford Dictionary of Current English* (9th edn, 1995; henceforth *COD*), the *Shorter Oxford Dictionary* (1993), the *Barnhart Dictionary of English Etymology* (1988), and Carstensen and Busse's monumental *Anglizismenwörterbuch* (1993–5).

The Compilation of the Entries

The most recent edition of the *COD* (as of 1995) is used as a point of departure for *Dictionary of European Anglicisms* definitions. Each *Dictionary of European Anglicisms* entry includes a variety of information in a fixed sequence and in greatly condensed, but transparent form. The English etymon, as a headword, is followed by all the meanings recorded for loanwords in the various languages. For the more significant items, the data on the word's history and its spread across Europe are then summarized in a few sentences which flesh out the information given in the more condensed section which follows. The final, condensed section gives information for each individual language in which the loanword occurs, including spelling and pronunciation, gender attribution and pluralization (in nouns), approximate date of adoption, and, where relevant, the mediating language. The most important data follow: is the word part of the language, and how well integrated is it in terms of currency, style value, and acceptability? A native equivalent is given especially if it is a loan translation or other form of a calque; such replacements are frequent in purist languages. Non-English derivatives are nested in the same entry; derivatives which are also English words have separate entries.

The structure of the entries is set out and described in detail below. I conclude this introduction with a discussion of some of the principles underlying the inclusion and organization of the data in the entries.

The headword

A word is included in the dictionary if it is recognizably English in form (spelling, pronunciation, morphology) in at least one of the languages tested. This principle excludes in particular most internationalisms coined with Latin or Greek elements (*administration, telephone*) and many words from other languages transmitted through English (*avocado, anorak*). The principle allows the inclusion of words which, although clearly derived from English, are not themselves English words (*twen-, pulli*), or which are used in a non-English way (as a member of a different word class, e.g. *assembling* or in un-English compounds, e.g. *antibaby pill, baby-foot*). These classes of words are distinguished by an asterisk following the lemma in question. Derivatives which are also found in English and homonyms, especially those which involve different parts of speech, normally have separate entries.

The decision as to whether or not to include a particular word is partly a subjective one. Certain categories of words proved to be especially problematic. Many *names* have become generic nouns and are thus rightly included in 'proper' dictionaries; however, the process by which names become words is very different in individual languages and it was impossible to make clear-cut decisions. Readers will note the absence of such items as *Amnesty International, Greenpeace, International Monetary Fund, Weightwatchers*, and *World Wildlife Fund*.

Internationalisms also proved difficult. Words which are Latinate or neo-Greek and have nothing English in their form or pronunciation in any of the 16 languages are not included. Sometimes, however, an English pronunciation was attested in at least one language, making the word an anglicism and forcing its inclusion.

Words not known to the general educated reader formed the most problematic category. Specialists in computing, economics, various technologies and sports, popular music, and the drug culture could easily point to hundreds of items we have not included. These have not been missed or overlooked but rather intentionally omitted, even though it is impossible to state with any degree of precision why some items are included and others are not.

Part-of-speech labels

We have followed the conventions of the *COD* in assigning part-of-speech labels to the headwords. To their list we have added cp^1 and cp^2, to designate 'first/second part of a compound'. The *COD* often designates a cp^1 as 'adj.' (adjective): we do not follow this convention. Whereas some nouns occurring as loanwords are freely combined in compounds (e.g. *fan* $cp^{1/2}$), others are restricted to first or second position in N(oun)+N(oun) compounds (cp^1: *last-minute-, non-food-*; cp^2: *-shop,-look*). We are aware that this notation works better for Germanic languages (German, Dutch, Norwegian, and Icelandic) than for the others, but observe that this type of N+N compound is becoming increasingly accepted outside Germanic, thus creating a new type of word-formation for some languages.

Definitions

The conventions followed for numbering definitions are outlined in detail in 'Using this Dictionary' (p. xxi). The convention for marking definitions as 'additional' by inserting a (+) before the definition number works well for headwords that are lemmatized in the *COD*, since it provides the reader with an instant visual clue when the word has acquired additional, non-English meanings. Difficulties arise, however, with words which are indisputably English (and which appear as headwords in more comprehensive dictionaries such as the *OED*), but which are not lemmatized in the *COD*. In such cases the meanings are simply numbered sequentially.

The summary paragraph

The body of the entry (considered below) contains a great deal of information in a very condensed form. It is not always easy to abstract generalizations from that information. The summary paragraphs which accompany around 25 per cent of the entries are intended to elucidate for the reader significant generalizations that can be made about the history and distribution of the loanword.

The grid (*see Fig. 1*)

Summary paragraphs are usually accompanied by a grid, for which Fig. 1 serves as a template. The grid consists of a square showing the languages in language-family blocks: Germanic, Slavic, Romance, and 'other'. The blocks (and the languages within the blocks) are placed, more or less, as they are situated geographically in relationship to one another. Each individual language square is used to indicate the status of the word in that language in a simplified form. A completed grid thus provides the reader with an instant visual summary for individual languages, language-group-specific patterns, and regional clustering of traits. The language squares are coded as follows: white indicates that the word is fully accepted; shading indicates that the word is in restricted use, and black indicates that the word is not part of the language concerned. These categories represent a simplification of the 'degrees of acceptance' categories outlined on p. xxiv. White codes categories 3 and 2, shading codes category 1, and black codes categories—, 0, Ø, 4 and 5, i.e. all cases in which there is no loanword taken from English. Where restricted use combines with a high degree of formal indication (3 tech), shading is employed.

Presentation of the language-by-language data

The data for each language is presented sequentially, in the order outlined on p. xxii. Within the section on each individual language, if the data on different meanings (e.g. information on usage etc.) is identical, then the information is conflated. If it cannot be conflated, each meaning is treated in turn, and the information on each is separated from the next by a semi-colon. This most commonly occurs when a word has been borrowed more than once by the same language, and the two borrowings differ notably in form, meaning, and date of adoption; in such cases the data for the earlier borrowing are given first (see for example the entry for *baby*).

Route of transmission

Where evidence exists for indirect transmission of an anglicism via another language, the route of transmission is noted (e.g. via Fr). Such cases are distinguished carefully from those where the word in question is felt not to be an anglicism at all in a particular language: such cases are flagged by use of 'degree of acceptance' category 5 (e.g. (5Fr)). In some cases the etymological information needed to distinguish these two cases is not available: if there is doubt it is indicated by the use of (?), e.g. via Fr?, (5Fr?).

Using this Dictionary

The following pages illustrate the presentation of information in entries in the
dictionary. A full alphabetically-ordered list of the abbreviations used may be
found on pp. xii–xiv.

The lemma and its definitions

I   2   3
↓   ↓   ↓

baby *n.* , 4b *cp¹* 'a thing that is small, 5 'sweetheart', +8 'a
blue-striped, light overall worn by children to kindergarten or play-
school'

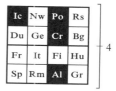

> This word is one of the earliest and most widespread anglicisms
> in Europe, although it has partly been handed on through French.
> Various suggested native alternatives have been reserved for offi-
> cial or formal purposes, but these remain impersonal and have not
> 4 ⊢ replaced this popular word which also seems to be phonoaestheti-
> cally perfect. Various metaphorical and metonymic usages have arisen independently, as
> have abbreviations of compounds (resulting in the +8 meaning). Note that in French the
> word has been borrowed in two forms, only one of which retains the English spelling and
> 'correct' pronunciation.

(1) English etymon (lemma):
  - appears in **bold, serif** font;
  - is followed by an asterisk (*) if it is not a word in English, although an
    Anglicism nevertheless (e.g. **twen-***, **pulli***);
  - is followed by a superscript numeral (¹) etc. if there is more than one
    Dictionary of European Anglicisms entry with the same lemma, and if the
    homographs belong to the same part of speech;
  - is followed by (1) etc. if there is more than one entry with the same lemma
    in the *COD*, providing a cross-reference to the relevant *COD* entry;
  - is followed by ™ if the word is or once was a proprietary name or
    trademark.

(2) Part of speech label:
  - appears in *italic*;
  - see 'List of Abbreviations' for the labels used, and see also the further
    discussion of parts of speech in the Introduction (p. xix).

(3) Meaning(s), numbered according to the following scheme:
  - where there is more than one meaning attested, the meanings are num-
    bered;
  - if the word appears in the *COD* with two or more numbered meanings
    then the numbers given to the meanings attested in *Dictionary of Eur-
    opean Anglicisms* correspond to the relevant numbers in the *COD* (e.g. 1,
    3, 4, where *COD* meaning 2 is not attested);
  - if the word has a meaning not recorded in the *COD* then the meaning
    number is preceded by a plus (+) sign. A meaning which is clearly related
    to a meaning given in the *COD* is assigned the *COD* number and a letter
    (e.g. +3a). A new meaning is assigned its own number, following sequen-

tially after all the *COD* meaning numbers (e.g. +9 if the *COD* lists 8 meanings);

- if the word is not lemmatized in the *COD* the numbering sequence (if more than one meaning is attested) starts at 1. This applies both to non-English (asterisked) words, and also to words which are English but which are not lemmatized in the *COD*;
- the 'definitions' appear between quotation marks. Where a *COD* definition exists it is used as a basis for the *Dictionary of European Anglicisms* definition, but is sometimes shortened or slightly altered in content;
- cross-references to other *Dictionary of European Anglicisms* entries are indicated by an upwards arrow followed by the italicized lemma (e.g. ↑ *fan*).

History and distribution

(4) Description and grid:
- for around 25 per cent of entries the word's history and its spread across Europe are summarized in a few sentences;
- the description is usually accompanied by a grid showing the distribution of the word across Europe (see p. xx of the Introduction for a more detailed discussion).

Language-by-language data

5   Ge [beːbi] N, pl. -*(ie)s*, mid19c, 1(2) > *Säugling*; 1960s, 4b(1 jour) 5(1 jour)   Du [beːbi]
    C, pl. -'s, 19c, 1(2) 4b(2) 5(1 arch)   Nw beːbi/bɶibi M, pl. -*er*, beg20c, 1(2) 4b(1) 5(1   7
6   sla)   Ic *beibi* [peiːpi] N pl. Ø, 1940s, 1(1 coll) 5(1 coll)   Fr *bébé* [bebe] M mid19c 1(3);
    baby [babi/bebi] M, pl. *babies/babys*, mid19c, ?(1); 1950s, 4b(1)   Sp *babi/baby* [babi] M,   8
9   pl. -*s* 1950s, +8 (3 > 2); [beibi] 1970s, 1(1 sla); 1990s, 4b(1 tech)   It [bebi] M, pl. Ø,
12 end19c, 1(2) 4b(1) 5(1 coll)   Rm < =E> M, [U], mid20c, 1(1) 4b(1) 5(1); *bebi* [bebi] M,   10
    pl. Ø, mid20c, 1(2 coll) 4b(1 jour) 5(2 coll); *bebe* [bebe/bebe] M, [U], 1940s, via Fr,   11
13 1(3)   Rs *bebi/bébi/beibi* N, uninfl., beg20c, 1(3) 5(2)   Po < =E> N, [U], beg20c, 1(1
    coll) < *dziecko*   Cr bebi F, pl. -Ø, mid20c, 1(1 coll)   Bg *beibi* N/F, pl. -*ta*/-Ø, end20c,
14 5(1 you sla); *bebe* N, pl. -*ta*, 20c, via Fr, 1(3) →-*shki* adj.   Fi < =E > /*beibi* [E], 5(coll/   16
    fac)   Hu *bébi* [E], pl. -*ik*, end19c/beg20c, 1(3) 5(3) = *baba*; *bébi* 4b(3)   Al *bebe* F, pl. Ø,
    mid19c, 1(1 reg)   Gr *bebis/beba* M/F, 1(3) = *moro* 5(0) < *moro nu*   15

(5) Language sigils:
- appear in a fixed sequence **Ge** (German), **Du** (Dutch), **Nw** (Norwegian), **Ic** (Icelandic), **Fr** (French), **Sp** (Spanish), **It** (Italian), **Rm** (Romanian), **Rs** (Russian), **Po** (Polish), **Cr** (Croatian), **Bg** (Bulgarian), **Fi** (Finnish), **Hu** (Hungarian), **Al** (Albanian), **Gr** (Greek);
- individual sigils are omitted if evidence of the particular anglicism in the relevant language, or at least of a calqued form, is lacking.

(6) Spelling:
- indicated as <=E> if the spelling is identical to that of the English etymon, and if this fact has information value (e.g. if it is one option, or if a language which is normally written in a non-Roman alphabet uses the English spelling);
- if the spelling (or one of the attested spellings) differs from that of the English etymon, then the word is cited in *italic*;
- for Russian, Bulgarian, and Greek, which have non-Latin alphabets,

items are always transliterated (in *italic*); since transliterations unambiguously reflect pronunciation no pronunciation guide is given, but stress is marked where relevant (see (7) below).

(7) Pronunciation:
  - indicated as [=E] if pronunciation is (near-) identical to that of English etymon;
  - if pronunciation is not predictable from the spelling and also differs from that of the English etymon, then the word is transcribed phonetically in the IPA (e.g. **Fr** [makintoʃ] for 'mackintosh');
  - if pronunciation is predictable from the spelling no pronunciation guide is given;
  - stress is indicated for words of more than one syllable;
  - main stress is indicated by a double underline and secondary stress (where present) by a single underline (e.g. **Du** [makadamize:r], **It** *macadamizzare* for 'macademize').

(8) Inflection (for nouns only):
  - for languages with gender distinctions nouns are marked for their gender, using the abbreviations F (feminine), M (masculine), N (neuter), C (common, where the language has a merger between M and N or M and F);
  - if alternatives exist this is indicated by the use of a slash (e.g. M/F).

(9) Pluralization (for nominals only):
  - where case differences exist the nominative form is given, preceded by 'pl.';
  - inflection is cited in *italic* (e.g. *-en*);
  - zero inflection is indicated by Ø;
  - uncountable nouns are marked [U];
  - uninflected nouns, adjectives and adverbs are labelled 'uninfl.'.

(10) Date
  - reflects the time when a term became frequently used or accepted rather than its first attestation in dictionaries;
  - year is usually specified for very recent loans (from *c.* 1985 on);
  - decade is usually specified for dates between 1900 and 1985 (e.g. 1970s);
  - part of century is usually specified for dates before 1900 (e.g. beg17c 'beginning of the seventeenth century'; mid18c 'middle of the eighteenth century'; end19c 'end of the nineteenth century'). Less specific dates (20c) are given where information is not sufficient.

(11) Route of transmission (if not directly borrowed from English):
  - where relevant this is indicated by 'via language X' (e.g. via Fr);
  - where doubt exists because of lack of conclusive evidence this is indicated by '?' (e.g. via Fr?).

(12) Meaning(s):
  - if the lemma has only one attested meaning, or if all the meanings listed are recorded for the individual language, this 'slot' is unfilled;
  - if the lemma has more than one attested meaning, this 'slot' is filled by

the number(s) of the meaning(s) attested in the particular language. For example if the lemma has attested meanings 1, 4b, 5 and +8, and meanings 1, 4b and 5 occur in the language in question, then those numbers will appear in this slot. See the Introduction (p. xxi) for a fuller explanation of how the information for each meaning is set out.

(13) Degree of acceptance:
  • appears within parentheses along with the contents of 'slot' 14 (see below), immediately following meaning number (if present), for example 2 (**1** tech);
  • the symbols indicate a cline of increasing integration (and often also of frequency and acceptability);
  • symbols found in this slot are:
    – the word is not known but a calque or another native equivalent is provided (see *gully* in all languages except German);
    o the word is known mainly to bilinguals and is felt to be English (e.g. *weekend* in German);
    Ø the word is known but is a foreignism—that is, it is used only with reference to British or American contexts (e.g. *earl, county*);
    1 the word is in restricted use in the language; the nature of the restriction is indicated in 'slot' 14 (see below);
    2 the word is fully accepted and found in many styles and registers, but is still marked as English in its spelling, pronunciation, or morphology;
    3 the word is not (or is no longer) recognized as English; English origin can only be established etymologically;
    4 the word is identical or nearly identical to an indigenous item in the receptor language, so that the borrowing takes the form of a semantic loan only (e.g. the computer-related sense of *mouse* is borrowed as an additional meaning for German *Maus*);
    5 The word, as far as the individual language is concerned, comes from a source other than English (e.g. 5La 'from Latin', 5Fr 'from French', etc.).

(14) Usage restrictions:
  • appear within parentheses with 'degree of acceptance' information;
  • are indicated using the following abbreviations:

Field	hist	= historical (referring to obsolete objects or concepts);
	lit	= literary;
	tech	= technical (used only in specialist vocabularies such as aviation, banking, computer technology, etc.);
Medium	writ	= written (used only in written media);
Region	reg	= regional (known to be restricted to national or regional varieties of the standard language, or to particular dialects);
Register	coll	= colloquial (informal, normally used only in spoken language);

	jour	= journalese;
	sla	= slang, non-standard;
	you	= youth (usage restricted to the younger generation);
Style	derog	= derogatory;
	euph	= euphemistic (used to avoid term tabooed in the native language;
	fac	= facetious (not meant to be serious; playful);
	pej	= pejorative;
Status	ban	= banned (usage restricted by legislation but still current, as for *franglais* items in French);
Currency	arch	= archaic (known but no longer used);
	mod	= modish, modern (fashionable jargon, not expected to last);
	obs	= obsolescent (possibly now going out of use, now rarer than a few years ago);
	rare	= rare, infrequently used;

- borderline cases are represented thus: (o > 1 mod) 'incoming modernism, not yet accepted', (1 tech > 2) 'technical term becoming common';
- uncertainty is represented thus: (1 tech?) 'technical term of doubtful status';
- restrictions may be combined, and are ordered as above (Field Medium Region Register Style Status Currency), for example (1 you obs) 'obsolescent youth language, (1 coll rare) 'rare colloquialism'; where two distinct usages exist they are separated by a slash, for example, (1 tech/you) 'most used as a technical term, but also an item of youth vocabulary'.

(15) Native (or non-English) equivalent:
- preceded by a 'wedge' indicating the comparative frequency and acceptability of the anglicism and its equivalent: '<' indicates that the non-English term is more frequent or acceptable, '>' indicates that the English term is more frequent or acceptable, '=' indicates that the two terms are equally acceptable;
- only one word is generally provided;
- if the word is clearly calqued on the English lemma it is preceded by one of the following labels: trans (translation), rend (rendition) or creat (creation);
- if only the meaning is borrowed (and added to a pre-existing word), the word is preceded by 'mean' (borrowed meaning);
- is only provided if English influence can be established.

(16) Derivative(s)
- preceded by →;
- listed only if not found in English, that is if it (they) could not have been borrowed wholesale;
- accompanied by part of speech label, but no further data;
- derivatives which are borrowed wholesale are given separate entries.

Criteria for Inclusion and Exclusion

In this dictionary a word or phrase qualifies for inclusion if it is from English (including items mediated through English) and retains an indication of this provenance *in its form*–i.e. in its spelling, pronunciation, the relationship of its spelling and pronunciation, or its inflexion – in at least one of the sixteen languages sampled. Pseudo-English items are accepted and marked by an asterisk. The following categories are excluded (cf. p.xix):

Obvious cases of codeswitching not intended as loanwords (marked by italics or inverted commas), items involving word-play, mistakes, and other ad-hoc uses;

1. Names (of persons, towns/countries, companies, products, etc.);
2. Obsolete loanwords no longer known;
3. Highly technical infrequent words known only to insiders;
4. Transparent compounds and derivations (esp. hybrids formed with one English element), unless taken over as units from English;
5. International items made from (neo-) Greek and Latin elements not containing any English features;
6. Calques (loan translations and semantic borrowings) unless forming part of an entry justified by the positive definition of an Anglicism.

Needless to say, all these categories provide many doubtful cases, and in consequence, subjective decisions – a problem magnified by the large number of collaborators.

Related Publications

Three books complementing the data and analysis comprised in the dictionary should be consulted. All are edited by Manfred Görlach.

An Annotated Bibliography of European Anglicisms (Oxford: OUP, 2002).

English in Europe (Oxford: OUP, 2002; paperback edition, 2004). This contains 17 chapters systematically detailing the impact of English words on the sampled languages.

English Words Abroad (Amsterdam: Benjamins, 2003). This contains systematic reflections on the methods developed for the *Dictionary of European Anglicisms*.

A

AA *abbr.* 2 'Alcoholics Anonymous'
Ge *AA* [a:a:] 1970s (3) < trsl *anonyme Alkoholiker* **Du** [a:a:] 1970s (2) **Nw** *AA* < *Anonyme Alkoholikere* **Ic** [a:a:] mid20c (3) = *AA-samtōkin* **Fr** *AA* < trsl *alcooliques anonymes* **It** *A.A.* 1970s (1) < trsl *alcolisti anonimi* **Rs** *eĭeĭ* 1990s (1 coll) < trsl *anonimnyĭ alkogolik* **Po** *A.A.* anonimowi alkoholicy [a:a:] **Bg** <=E> [=E] 1990s (1 coll) < *Anonimen alkokholik* **Fi** [a:a:] 1970s (3) < trsl *anonyymit alkoholistit* ar - < trsl *Anonymi Alkooliki*

about *adv.* 1a 'approximately'
Ic cp² *sirkabát* (*circa* + *about*) [=E] mid20c (2c) **Fi** [=E] (1 you coll)

absenteeism *n.* 1 'the practice of absenting oneself from work, school etc., esp. frequently or without permission'
Du *absenteisme* [apsɛnteismə] N [U] beg20c, via Fr (2 rare) → *absent* adj.; *absentie* n.; *absentenlijst* n. **Fr** *absentéisme* [apsãteism] M, mid19c (3) → *absentéiste* adj.; n. **Sp** *absentismo* M, end19c (3) → *absentista* **It** *assenteismo* [assɛnteizmo] M, pl. -*i*, beg 19c, via Fr (3) → *assenteista* n.; *assenteistico* adj. **Rm** *absenteism* N, beg20c (5Fr) **Rs** (5La) **Po** (5La) **Cr** (5La)

absorber *n.* 'a technical apparatus for absorbing, e.g. in a fridge'
The verb *absorb-* is old in many European languages, coming from French or Latin. The technical term *absorber*, now mainly known as a part of a cooling system, has been influenced by the morphology of individual languages, so that its character as an anglicism is no longer obvious.
Ge [apsorba] M, pl. -*Ø*, mid20c (3 tech) **Du** *absorbeur* (5Fr) **Nw** [apso:rber] M, pl. -*e*, mid20c (1 tech) **Fr** *absorbeur* [apsɔRbœR] M, mid20c (5Fr) **It** *assorbitore* [assorbitore] M, pl. -*i*, mid20c (3) **Rm** *absorbitor* N (5Fr/Rm) **Rs** *absorber* M, pl. -*y*, mid20c (3 tech) **Po** [apsorber] M, mid20c (1 tech) **Cr** *apsorber* M, pl. -*i*, end20c (1 tech) **Bg** *absorber* M, pl. -*al-i*, mid20c, via Ge (1 tech) **Hu** *abszorber* [absorber] pl. -*ek*, mid20c (1 tech) < *gázelnyelő* **Al** *absorbues* [apsorbues] M, pl. -*ë*, 1950s (3)

abstract *n.* 1 'a summary of the contents of a book, paper, etc.'
Ge [=E] M/N, pl. -*s*, 1980s (0 tech) < *Zusammenfassung* **Du** [=E] C, 1990s (1 tech) < *uittreksel, samenvatting* **Nw** <=E>/*abstrakt* [=E/apstrakt] N, pl. -*Ø*, mid20c (1 tech) **Ic** *abstrakt* [apstraxt] N, pl. -*strökt*, end20c, (1 tech coll) = *útdráttur* **Fr** [abstrakt] M, mid20c (1 tech, ban) < *résumé* **Sp** [=E] M, pl. -*Ø*, 1980s (1 tech) < *resumen, extracto* **It** [=E/abstrakt] M, pl. -*Ø*, 1970s (0>1 tech) **Rm** (0) **Po** [abstrakt] M, end20c (1 tech) **Cr** [apstrakt] M, pl. -*i*, end20c (1 tech) **Bg** *abstrakt* M, pl. -*al-i*, 1980s (1 tech rare) < *anotatsiya* **Fi** *abstrakti* (1 tech) = trsl *tiivistelmä* **Hu** [=E/abstrakt] pl. -*ok*/-*Ø*, end20c (1 tech) < *kivonat* **Gr** <=E> [=E] N, pl. -*Ø*/-*s*, 1980s (1 tech)

accelerator *n.* 3 'a substance that speeds up a chemical reaction'
Du [aksələra:tɔr] C, 1960s, (5La) **Ic** - < creat *hraðail* **Rs** (5La) **Po** (5La) **Cr** (5La) **Hu** (5La) **Gr** <=E> [=E] N [U] 1990s (1 tech)

accountant *n.* 'a keeper and inspector of accounts'
Ge [=E] M, pl. -*s*, 1970s (0 tech) < *Wirtschaftsprüfer*, cf. ↑*controller* **Du** [=E] C, beg20c (1 tech) **Nw** [=E] M, pl. -*s*, 1980s (1 tech)

account executive *n.* 'a business executive, esp. in advertising, who manages a client's account'
Ge [=E] M, pl. -*s*, 1960s (0 tech) **Du** [=E] C, 1970s (1 tech) **It** [=E/akaunt exɛkjutiv] M, pl. Ø 1980s (1 tech) < *funzionario commerciale*

ace *n.* 3a 'a service that is too good for the opponent to return' (tennis etc.) 3b 'a point scored with such a service'
Whereas the use of the term in dice or cards is old, as is the metaphorical extension to mean 'the best', the tennis term spread from Britain in the early twentieth century. Most languages added the new meaning to the existing term, but some borrowed it as a new word with (close to) English pronunciation.
Ge *As* (5La) **Du** [=E] pl. -*s* (1 tech) **Nw** *serve(ess)* via Ge (5La) **Fr** [as] M, 20c (1 tech ban) < trsl *as* **Sp** [=E] M, pl. -*s*, 1970s, 3b(1 tech) **It** [=E] 1990s (1 tech) **Rm** [=E] N, 1970s (2 tech) **Rs** *eĭs* M, pl. -*y*, 1990s (1 tech) **Cr** *as* M, pl. -*ovi*, mid20c, 3a(3) **Bg** *as* M, pl. -*al*[U] mid20c, 3(4 tech) **Hu** *ász* [a:z] 3b(5Ge) **Gr** - < mean *assos*

acid *n.* 3 'the drug LSD'
Ge [=E] N [U] 1970s (1 sla) **Du** [=E] C [U] 1970s (1 tech sla) **Nw** [=E] M [U] 1970s (1 sla) = trsl *syre* **Ic** [=E] N [U] 1970s (1 sla) < trsl *sýra* **Fr** *acide* [asid] M [U] 1970s (4 sla) **Sp** - < mean *ácido* **It** - < mean *acido* **Fi** [=E] 1980s (1 you) **Gr** *asid* N [U] end20c (1 sla)

acid house *n.* 1 'synthesized music with a simple

repetitive beat', 2 'youth culture associated with this music'

Ge *house* [=E] N [U] 1980s (1 you) **Du** [=E] C [U] 1980s (1 tech) **Nw** [=E] M [U] 1980s (1 tech/you) **Ic** [=E] 1990s (0 tech) **Fr** [=E] 1980s (1 you) **Sp** [asid haus/aθidaus] M, 1980s (1 you, obs) **It** [εsid aus] F, pl. *Ø*, 1980s (1 tech you) **Rs** (0) **Fi** [=E] [U] 1980s (1) **Gr** <=E> [asid/eisid] F [U] 1980s, 1 (1 you); <=E> [asid/eisid] N [U] 1980s, 2(1 you)

acid rock   *n.* 'a rock music genre'

A style of rock music characterized by high volume and ecstatic rhythm, with a drug-like effect (cf. *psychedelic rock*) which was popular in Western Europe in the 1970s but is now out of favour.

Ge [=E] M [U] 1970s (1 you obs) **Nw** [=E] M [U] 1970s (1 tech/you) **Ic** - < rend *sýrurukk* **Fr** [=E] 1970s (1 you) **Sp** [=E] M, 1960s (1 you, obs) **It** [=E] M [U] 1980s (1 tech) **Rm** [=E] N [U] 1970s (1 tech you); *rock acid* [rok ačid] N [U] (1 tech, you) **Rs** (0) **Cr** [=E] M [U] mid20c (1 tech) **Bg** *asid rok* M [U] 1990s (1 tech/you sla) **Fi** [=E] [U] 1980s (1) **Gr** <=E> [=E] N/F [U] 1970 (1 you, obs)

acre   *n.* 1 'a measure of land'

As a measure, normally used in referring to Britain or the USA; local terms are available for individual languages (whether pre-metric or metric). There may be some conflation with German *Acker* 'field' etc. in the form and meaning of the loans.

Ge (Ø) **Du** (Ø) **Nw** [=E] M, pl. -*s*/-*Ø* mid19c (Ø) **Ic** *ekra* [ɛ:kra] F, pl. -*ur*, end19c (4) **Fr** (Ø) **Sp** [akre] M, pl. -*s*, 1880s (Ø/3 tech) **It** *acro* M, pl. -*li*, end15c (3) **Rm** *acru* [akru] M, mid20c, via Fr (Ø) **Rs** *akr* M, pl. -*y*, mid19c (Ø) **Po** *akr* [akr] M, mid19c (3) → -*owy* adj. **Cr** [eikr] M, mid20c (Ø) **Bg** *akŭr* M, pl. *akra*/-*ri*, 20c (Ø) **Fi** *eekkeri* beg20c (Ø) **Hu** [e:kr] pl. [U] beg20c (Ø) **Al** *akër* [akër] F, pl. *akra*, end20c (1 rare) **Gr** *akr* N (Ø)

action   *n.* 5b 'exciting activity', +6c 'a fight, conflict', +6d 'a demonstration or other political action', +6e 'an action film'

The Latin-derived noun is very old and not covered here. This new loan is distinguished by its English pronunciation and restriction to very colloquial use in youth language.

Ge [ek(t)ʃn] F [U] 1960s, 5b (1 coll) **Du** *aktie/actie* [aksi] C, 1970s, +6D (5La) **Nw** [=E] M [U] 1960s, 5b, + 6e(2) **Ic** [axs-joun] F pl. -*ir*, 1970s, 5b(2 coll)+ 6d(2 sla) **Fr** (5La) **It** [ækʃon] F [U] 1970s, 5b, + 6c(1 mod) < mean *azione* **Rs** *ékshen* M [U] 1990s, 5b(1 coll, you) **Po** (5La) **Cr** (5La) **Bg** *ekshŭn* M, pl. -*al*-*i*,

1990s, 5b, + 6c, +6e (2 coll) **Fi** *äksön* [=E] 1980s, 5b, +6c(2 you, obs) **Hu** (5La) **Al** *aksion* [aksjon] M, pl. -*e*, 1950s, 5b, +6c, +6e (5Fr) **Gr** <=E>/*aktsion* F/ N [U] end20c, 5b, +6c(1 coll you) = *dhrasi*

action film   *n.* 'a film characterized by exciting action'

This lexical import from American English is characterized by English pronunciation; some languages (Italian, Romanian and Hungarian) have used the obvious calquing possibilities. Note that calquing is freer in Russian.

Ge [=E] M, pl. -*e*, 1960s (1 jour) **Du** *aktiefilm* [aksifilm] C, 1980s (4+5) **Nw** [=E] M, pl. -*er*, mid20c (2) **Ic** - < rend *aksjónmynd* **Fr** - < trsl *film d'action* **Sp** - < *film/película de acción* **It** [=E] M, pl. -*Ø* (1 tech, rare) < trsl *film d'azione, action movie* **Rm** -< trsl *film de acțiune* **Rs** (0) < rend *fil'm děistvie* **Po** (5) **Cr** (5)t **Bg** - < *ekshŭn* **Fi** *äksön filmi* [=E] 1980s (2 you, obs) **Hu** (0) < trsl *akció film*

AD   *acron.*↑ 'art director'

Du [=E] 1990s (1 mod) **Nw** [a:de] M, pl. -*er*, 1960s (3) **It** - < *art director* **Fi** [a:de:] 20c (3) **Gr** - < *art director*

adaptor/adapter   *n.* 1 'a device for making pieces of equipment compatible', 2 'a device for connecting electric plugs to a socket', +4 'a device for reloading batteries', +5 'a record-player'

Since the verb *adapt-* is old in many languages, this derivation is not always felt to be English, especially where -*er* is a native morpheme or is replaced by -*eur* etc.

Ge *adapter* [adapta] M, pl. -*Ø*, 1960s, 1, 2(3) **Du** *adapter/adaptor* [adaptər] C, pl. -*en*/-*s*, 1970s, 1, 2(2) +4(1 tech) < +4: *batterij-oplader* **Nw** *adapter* [adapter] M/N, pl. -*e*, 1960s, 1, 2(2 tech) **Fr** *adaptateur* M, 1, 2(5) **Sp** *adaptador* M, 2(5) **It** *adattatore* (5) **Rm** *adaptor* [adaptor] N, mid20c, 2(5Fr) **Rs** *adapter* M, pl. -*y*, mid20c, 1, 2, +4(3 tech) **Po** [adapter] M, mid20c, 2, +4(1 tech) +5(3) → -*owy* adj. **Cr** [adapter] M, mid20c, 1, 2(1 tech) **Bg** *adaptor* M, pl. -*al*-*i*, mid20c, 1, 2(3 tech) **Fi** *adapteri* 20c, 2(3) **Hu** (5La) **Al** *adaptor* M, pl. -*ë* (2 tech) **Gr** *adaptoras* M, mid20c, 1, 2, +4(3 tech); *adaptr* M (1 tech)

advantage   *n.* 4 'the next point won after deuce' (tennis)

Ge [=E] M, pl. -*s*, end19c/1980s (1 arch/mod) < *Vorteil* **Du** [=E] (1 tech) > *vooredel* **Nw** - < *fordel* **Sp** (0) < *ventaja* **Po** <=E> M, uninfl., beg20c (1 arch) **Cr** *edvantidž* 20c (1 tech) **Hu** [=E/adventid3] [U] end19c/ beg20c (1 tech, arch) < *előny* **Gr** *avadaz* N (5Fr)

Adventist   *n.* 'a member of a Christian sect'

This sect was founded by the preacher William Miller in the USA in 1831. Although the sect originated in the USA (where it is still based) the form of this term is easily connected with old *advent-* in most languages. Its status as an anglicism is therefore doubtful.

Ge (Ø) **Du** [atfəntist] C, mid20c (3 tech) **Nw** [adventist] M, pl. -*er*, beg20c (3) **Ic** *aðventisti* [aðvɛntʰɪstɪ/aðvɛntɪstɪ] M, pl. -ar, end19c, via Nw (3) **Fr** adventiste [advãtist] M/F, end19c (3) **Sp** adventista M/F (3) **It** avventista M/F, pl. -i/-e, 1930s (3 mod) **Rm** adventist [adventist/-ă] M/F/adj., 1930s, via Fr? (3) → adventism N **Rs** adventist M, pl. -y, beg20c (3) → -skiĭ adj. **Po** adwentysta [adventista] M, mid20c (2) **Cr** [=E] M, pl. -i, beg20c (3) **Bg** adventist M, pl. -i, beg20c (2) → -ki adj. **Fi** adventisti, 20c (5La) **Hu** (5La) **Gr** Adventistis/Adventistria M/F, 20c (5La/Ø)

adventure n. +5 'a type of computer game'
Ge [=E] N, pl. -s, end20c (1 tech) **Du** [=E] C, pl. -s, end20c (1 tech) **Fr** -< jeu d'aventure **It** [=E] F [U] end20c (1 tech) **Rm** (0) **Rs** (0) **Cr** (0) **Bg** <=E>/adventchūr M, pl. -a, 1990s (1 mod) **Hu** [=E] [U] end20c (1 tech)

aerobics n.pl. 'vigorous exercises designed to increase the body's oxygen intake'
Though the word was coined in American English as a term used in astronaut training in the 1960s, the activity was popular in the late 1970s and became a craze in the early 1980s. During the 1990s the frequency of this word seems to have decreased in the media and in conversation.
Ge [æːroːbiks] N [U] 1980s (2 obs) **Du** [=E] [U] 1980s (2) **Nw** <=E>/aerobic [eruː-bik(s)] M [U] sg., 1980s (2) **Ic** eróbik [ɛːroupɪk] N/F [U] 1980s (2) = rend polfimi **Fr** aérobic [aɛrɔbik] M/adj., 1980s (2) **Sp**

Ic	Nw	Po	Rs
Du	Ge	Cr	Bg
Fr	It	Fi	Hu
Sp	Rm	Al	Gr

aerobic [aerɔbik] M [U] 1980s (2) **It** aerobica [aɛrɔbika] F [U] 1980s (3) → aerobico adj. **Rm** aerobică [aerɔbikə] F, sg./adj., 1970s, via Fr (3) = gimnastică aerobică **Rs** aérobika F [U] end20c (3 you, mod) **Po** aerobik [aerobik] M, end20c (2) **Cr** aerobika F [U] 1980s (2) **Bg** aerobika F [U] 1980s (3); aerobik cp¹ (3) → aerobna adj. **Fi** aerobic [airɔbɪkː] 1980s (3) **Hu** aerobik [aerobik/eːrobik] [U] 1980s (2) **Al** ajrobik [ajroˈbik] M, pl. -e (1 you) **Gr** aerobik F/N usu. sg. [U] 1980s (2) > trsl aeroviki (ghymnastiki)/aeroviosi

Aerotank* n. 'a vessel for sewage disposal'
Rm aerotanc N, 1970s (1 tech) **Rs** aérotenk/aérotank M, pl. -i, mid20c (3 tech) **Cr** (0)

Afro- cp¹ 'characteristic of African/Afro-Caribbean/Afro-American culture' (music, fashion)
Ge [aːfro] 1980s (5) **Du** [=E] 1970s (2) **Nw** [a(ː)fru] 1960s (5) **Ic** afró-[aːfrou] 1970s (2 mod, obs) **Fr** [afro] adj., 1970s (1 you/mod) **Sp** [=E] cp²/adj. (2 tech) **It** [afro] 1970s (2) **Rm** - < afro [afro] adj./adv., uninfl., 1980s (1 mod) **Po** afro [afro] N [U] end20c (2 coll) **Rs** (0) **Po** (0) **Cr** [afro] 1970s (1 tech) **Bg** afro cp¹, 1980s (1 tech) **Fi** [aːfro] 1970s (2) **Hu** [afro] end20c (3/5) **Gr** afro, cp¹/², adj., end20c (1 tech, mod/5)

Afro-look* n. 'a hairstyle characterized by long and bushy locks'
This hairstyle was developed in the USA in the early

1970s and exported to Western Europe (and elsewhere). The short form Afro is the only one found in English (and this could be the source of French, Romanian, and Finnish borrowings); the distribution of the long form (German, Dutch, Italian, Croatian) points to borrowing from American English rather than a new coinage—although look is frequently used to form compounds.
Ge [=E] M [U] 1970s (1 you/obs) **Du** afrolook/afro look [=E] C [U] 1970s (1 tech) **Nw** afro [afru] M/N, pl. Ø, 1970s (1) **Ic** - < ↑Afro **Fr** - < coiffure afro **Sp** - < (estilo) afro **It** [afro luk] M, pl. Ø, 1970s (1 tech) **Rm** - < afro **Cr** [=E] M [U] 1980s (1 tech) **Fi** - < afro **Hu** [afroluk] [U] 1980s (1 tech, mod) **Gr** <=E> [=E] N, end20c (1 mod)

aftershave n. 'an astringent, often scented lotion for use after shaving'
The spread of this term is noteworthy since perfectly adequate terms exist in all the languages under consideration. This word has been adopted as a more fashionable synonym. Existing native equivalents were therefore not prompted by English. The word became strikingly frequent after the 1950s and is now current in nearly all the European languages. No calques have been formed, except when prompted by restrictive policies, as in French. The currency of the word is remarkable as the two parts of the compound are otherwise infrequent.
Ge [aːftaʃeːf] N, pl. -s, 1960s (1) = Rasierwasser **Du** after-shave [aːftərʃeːf] C, 1970s (2) **Nw** [=E] M, pl. -r, mid20c (2) = rend etterbarberingsvann **Ic** [aftershejv] N/M [U] mid20c (1 coll) < rakspíri **Fr** after-shave [aftœr-ʃɛv] M 1960s (1) > (lotion) après-rasage **Sp** [after ʃeif] M, pl. Ø/-s, mid20c (2) > loción para después de afeitarse, loción para después del afeitado **It** aftershave [after ʃeiv] M [U]/pl. Ø, 1960s (1 jour) < dopobarba **Rm** [=E] N, 1970s (2 mod) > loțiune după ras **Rs** (0) < creat los'on posle brit'ya **Po** - < trsl po goleniu **Cr** [=E] M, mid20c (2) **Bg** <=E>/aftŭrsheĭf M, pl. -ove, end20c (2 mod) < losion **Fi** [=E] (0) < partavesi **Hu** [=E] [U] 1980s (2 writ, jour, mod) < trsl borotválkozás utáni (hab/arcszesz) **Al** aftërshejv end20c (1) **Gr** <=E>/afterseif/afterseiv N, end20c (2)

after-ski* n./(cp¹) 1 '(relating to) clothes and footwear worn at ski resorts', 2 'social activities at ski resorts'
This expression looks like a translation of the French term après-ski, especially since it is itself not recorded in English; however, documentation appears to be lacking.
Ge - < après-ski **Du** - < après-ski **Nw** [=E] M, 1970s, 1, 2 (1 rare, mod) **Fr** - < après-ski(s) **It** - <

doposci **Rm** - < *apreski* **Po** - < trsl *po nartach* **Bg** - < *apreski* **Fi** *after-ski* 1980s (o) **Gr** (1 writ)

after sun* *n./(cp¹)* 'a cosmetic product used after sunbathing'

The English term is much less widespread than the French equivalent *après soleil* which may in fact be the source of both the English expression and other calques.

Du [=E] M/N, 1980s (1 tech) **Nw** [=E] C, 1980s (1 tech) **Ic** [=E] N [U] end2oc (1 coll) **Sp** *after sun/ aftersun* [aftersun] 1980s? (1 tech) **It** - < trsl *doposole* **Fi** [=E] 1980s (o) **Al** *aftërsan* end2oc (1 mod) **Gr** <=E> end 2oc (1 writ)

agreement *n.* 2 'mutual understanding', 3 'an arrangement between parties as to a course of action etc.' This term (more common in ↑*gentleman's*↓) has been adopted alongside native words and the older French *agrément* of diplomatic contexts. As a fashionable (and rather superfluous) synonym its status and future appear to be still in doubt in the languages that record the modernism.

Ge [=E] N, pl. *-s*, 1960s (1 mod) **Du** [=E] N, end2oc (1 mod) **Nw** (o) **Fr** (o) **Sp** - < *acuerdo* **It** [agriment] M, pl. Ø, 1930s, 3 (1 mod) < *accordo* **Rm** [=E] N, 1990s (o mod) < *agrement* [agrement] N (5Fr) **Po** (o) **Cr** (o) **Hu** [egri:ment] [U] mid2oc (1 coll) < *egyezség* **Al** *agriment* [agriment] M, pl. *-e*, end2oc (1 writ) **Gr** - < mean *symfonia*

ahoy *interj* (used aboard ship)

Ge *ahoi* 19c (3 tech/coll) **Nw** *ohoi* 19c (3) **Rm** *ahoi* [ahoj] (3 rare) **Rs** *akhoi* 19c (1 tech) **Cr** (o)

AIDS *n.* (acron. of) 'Acquired Immune Deficiency Syndrome'

AIDS was identified, and knowledge of it became immediately widespread, in the early 1980s (the first attestation in English was in 1982). The threat of the disease and world-wide media coverage made a name for it necessary within a very short time. This became, variously, the borrowed acronym pronounced as a word (in Ge, Du, Nw, Ic, Po, Cr, Hu, Gr) or as individual letters (as in It) or an acronym based on a translation (in Fr, Sp, Rm, Rs, Bg, Al, Gr) or a calque (as in Ic). The phonology and 'morphology' of *AIDS* have not allowed any derivations to be formed. Derivations are recorded for other new acronyms in French and Bulgarian.

Ge [eidz/e:ts] N [U] 1980s (2) **Du** [e:ts] C [U] 1980s (2) **Nw** <=E>/*aids* [eids/æids/ aids] M [U] 1980s (2) **Ic** [ei:ts] N [U] 1980s (2) < creat *eyðni, alnæmi* **Fr** -/(Ø) < trsl *sida* → *sidéen* N/adj.; *sidatique* adj. **Sp** - < trsl *SIDA/sida* **It** [aidz/aidiesse] M [U] 1980s (3) **Rm** (o) < trsl *SIDA, sida* **Rs** *éids* (1) < trsl *SPID (sindrom priobretënnogo immuno- defitsita)* **Po** [eits] M (2) **Cr** [=E] M [U] 1980s (2) < trsl *SIDA* **Bg** - < trsl *SPIN (sindrom na pridobita imunna nedostatŭchnost)* → *-ozen* adj. **Fi** [aids] 1980s (2) **Hu** [eidz]

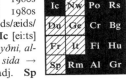

[U] 1980s (2>3) → *-es* adj. **Al** M [U] 1980s (3) > trsl *SIDI/SIDA* **Gr** <=E>/*eitz* N [U] 1980s (2) > trsl *SEAA (syndhromo epiktitis anosologhikis aneparkias)*

air bag *n.* 'a safety device that fills with air or nitrogen on impact to protect occupants of a vehicle in a collision'

Although this device was developed in the early 1970s it became well known only in the late 1980s when it became a regular feature in private cars. The linguistic consequences are diverse, and partly still fluid: use of the English term alone (in Du, Sp, It, Rm); the use of *air bag* alternating either with a less common native equivalent (as in Ge, Nw, Fr, Gr), or with a more common equivalent (as in Bg, Fi, Hu); or exclusive use of a native term (as in Ic).

Ge [e:rbek] M, pl. *-s*, 1970s (2 mod) > rend *Prallsack* **Du** [=E] C, 1990s (1 tech) **Nw** [e:rbæg] M, pl. *-er/-s*, 1990s (1 tech) > rend *kollisjonspute* **Ic** - < rend *loftpúði*; creat *öryggispúði, liknarbelgur* **Fr** <=E> M, 1990s (1 tech, ban) > rend *coussin gonflable, sac gonflable* **Sp** [eirbag/eabag/erbag] M, pl. Ø/-s, 1990s (2) **It** [erbeg/erbeg] M, pl. Ø, end2oc (2) **Rm** [erbeg] N, 1990s (1 tech) **Rs** (o) < creat *podushka bezopasnosti* **Po** - < rend *poduszka powietrzna* **Cr** [erbeg] M, 1990s (1 tech) > rend *zraini jastuk* **Bg** *eŭrbeg* M, pl. *-a/-ove*, 1990s (1 tech) < rend *vŭzdushna vŭzglavnitsa* **Fi** [airbæg] 1980s (2) < *turvatyyny* **Hu** [e:rbeg] [U] end2oc (1 tech) < trsl *légzsák* **Gr** <=E>/*erbag* N, pl. Ø/-s, 1980s (2 tech) > trsl *aerosakos*

airbagging* *n.* 'the action of (deliberately) causing an accident with a stolen car to make the airbag inflate' (↑*joyride*)

Ge [=E] N 1990s (1 you, mod), cf. ↑*joyride* **Du** [=E] C [U] 1990s (1 mod) **Sp** [=E] M, 1990s (o>1 mod)

airbrush *n.* 'an artist's device for spraying paint'

Ge [e:rbraʃ] M, pl. *-es*, 1980s (1 tech) → v.; *-ing* N **Du** [=E] C [U] 1980s (1 tech) **Nw** [=E] M, pl. *-er*, 1980s (1 tech) **Ic** [ɛ:rprœs:] cp¹, end2oc (1 tech) **Cr** [erbraʃ] M, end2oc (1 tech) **Fi** [=E] 1980s (1 tech) **Gr** <=E> [=E] N, end2oc (1 tech)

Airbus^TM *n.* 'an aircraft designed to carry a large number of passengers'

This term remains a product name although it is used more loosely in some languages. The second element is known from *omnibus* etc. and is pronounced accordingly, whereas *air* is marked as English for most languages (unless replaced by *aero-*); cf. other *air*-compounds.

Ge [e:rbus] M [U] 1960s (2) **Du** [ɛ:rbʏs] C, 1960s (1 tech) **Nw** [=E/-bus] M, pl. *-er*, 2oc (1 rare) **Sp** <=E>/*Aerobus* [erbus/airbus] M [U] 1970s (2>3) **It** <=E>/*aerobus* [erbas/ erbus/airbus] M, pl. Ø, 1980s (1 tech) **Rm** *aerobuz* [aerobuz] N, 1970s, via Fr (3 tech); *airbus* [erbys] N, 1960s (3); [erbas] N, 1990s (2 mod) **Rs** *aérobus* M, pl.

-*y*, end20c (3)   **Po** [erbus] M, end20c (2)   **Cr** [ẹrbus] M, pl. -*i*, end20c (2)   **Bg** eŭrbus /aerobus M, pl. -*al-i*, 1980s (1>2 tech)   **Fi** [=E]™ only   **Hu** [eːrbus] pl. -*ok*/Ø, 1980s (1 writ, jour, mod)   **Al** *aerobus* M, pl. -*e*, 1970s (1 reg)   **Gr** <=E>/*erbạs* N, end20c (2) > trsl *aeroleoforio*

air-conditioned 'equipped with air- conditioning'
     Like related words (see below) *air-conditioned* is dominated by partial adaptation of its ultimately Romance elements, or by proper translation. The status, and future, of these terms as anglicisms appears doubtful.
     Ge (o) < *vollklimatisiert*   **Du** [=E] 1980s (2 tech)   **Nw** *airkondisjonert*   **Ic** - < rend *loftkældur*   **Fr** - < trsl *air conditionné*   **Sp** - < rend *con aire acondicionado*   **It** - < rend *con aria condizionata*   **Rm** - < rend *cu aer condiţionat*   **Po** (o)   **Cr** (o)   **Hu** [=E] 1980s (1 tech, mod) < trsl *légkondicionált*   **Al** rend *ajër i kondicionuar*   **Gr** <=E> end20c (1 writ) < *klimatizete* v.

air-conditioner *n.* 'an air-conditioning apparatus'
     Du [=E] C, 1970s (2 tech)   **Nw** [=E] 1980s (1 rare) < creat *klimaanlegg*   **Ic** - < rend *loftkæling; loftkælitæki*   **Sp** - < trsl *acondicionador de aire*   **It** - < mean *condizionatore, climatizzatore*   **Rs** *konditsioner* M, pl. -*y*, 1970s (3)   **Po** (o)   **Cr** (o)   **Hu** - < trsl *légkondicionáló*   **Al** rend *kondinsioner i ajrit*   **Gr** <=E> end20c (1 writ)

air-condition(ing) *n.* 1 'a system for regulating the humidity, ventilation and temperature of a building etc.', 2 'the apparatus for this'
     Ge *air-condition* [=E] F; *air-conditioning* [=E] N [U] 1960s, 2(1 coll) < *Klimaanlage*   **Du** [airco(ndition-ing)/=E] C, 1945-(2)   **Nw** [=E] M [U] mid20c (2) < *klimaanlegg*   **Ic** - < rend *loftkæling*   **Fr** - < trsl *air conditionné* < *climatisation*   **Sp** - < trsl *aire acondicionado*   **It** - < 1: rend *aria condizionata*   **Rm** - < *aer condiţionat*   **Rs** - < *konditsionirovanie*   **Po** (o)   **Cr** ẹrkondišn M, mid20c, 1(2)   **Bg** ẹrkŭndishŭn M [U] 1970s, 2 (1 coll) < *klimatichna instalatsiya, klimatik*   **Hu** [=E] 1960s, 1(1 tech) < *légkondicionálás*   **Al** - <rend *kondinisioner i ajrit*   **Gr** <=E>/*erkodision* N, end20c, 1,2 (2) = *klimatismos/klimatistiko (mikhanima)*

Airedale (terrier) *n.* 2 'a breed of dog'
     One of the many breeds (and in particular ↑*terriers*) of dogs whose names have become more or less well known around Europe. The short form appears to be an option in most languages and is the exclusive form in Spanish, Italian, and Finnish (↑*Skye*, ↑*Yorkshire*).
     Ge [ẹːrdeːl tẹria] M, pl. Ø, beg20c (1 tech)   **Du** *airdale terriër* [=E] C, mid20c (tech)   **Nw** [ẹːrdeiltærjer] M, pl. -*e*, mid20c (1 tech)   **Ic** [=E] end20c (0 tech)   **Fr** [ɛʀdɛl] M, 1890s (1)   **Sp** *airdale* [ẹrdeil] M, beg20c (1 tech)

Ic	Nw	Po	Rs
Du	Ge	Cr	Bg
Fr	It	Fi	Hu
Sp	Rm	Al	Gr

It *airedale* [ẹ-/ẹːrdeil] M, pl. Ø, 1960s (1 tech)   **Rm** [=E] M, beg20c (1)   **Rs** *érdẹl' ter'er* M, pl. -*y*, end20c (2)   **Po** [erdeil terier] M, end20c (1 tech)   **Cr** ẹrdel *terijer* M, pl. -*i*, end20c (1 tech)   **Bg** ẹrdel *terier* M, pl. -*ral-ri*, end20c (1 tech)   **Fi** [airedale] 20c (3)   **Hu** [eːrdeːl (terrier)] pl. -*ek*, beg20c? (3)   **Gr** <=E> [=E+terie] N, 20c (1 tech)

airfresh* *n.* ™ 'a deodorant spray for rooms'
     Ge [ẹːr-] N [U] 1950s (1)   **Du** - < *luchtverfrisser*   **Nw** - < rend *luftfrisk(n)er*   **Ic** [ɛːrfres:] end20c (o)   **It** [erfreʃ] M, Ø, 1940s (1) < mean *deodorante*   **Hu** (o) < rend *légfrissítő*   **Gr** (1 writ)

air hostess *n.* 'a stewardess in a passenger aircraft'
     Du [=E] C, pl. -*en*, 1970s (2 tech) < *stewardess*   **Nw** - < *flyvertinne*   **Ic** - < creat *flugfreyja*   **Fr** - < trsl *hôtesse de l'air*   **Sp** - < *azafata*   **It** - < rend *assistente di volo*   **Rm** -< *stewardesă*   **Rs** - < *styuardẹssa*, rend *bort-provodnitsa*   **Po** (o)   **Cr** (o)   **Bg** - < *styuardesa*; rend *bordna domakinya*   **Hu** (o) < *stewardess*, rend *légikisasszony*   **Al** - < *stjuardesë*

airline *n.* 1 'an organization providing regular air transport'
     This term is widely known, but is not felt to be part of most of the languages under review. The 'modern' appeal of the term appears not to be strong enough for it to compete successfully with (or even replace) earlier native expressions.
     Ge [=E] F, pl. -*s*, 1970s (o>1 mod) < *Fluggesellschaft*   **Nw** (o) < *flyselskap*   **Ic** - < *flugfélag*   **Fr** - < trsl *ligne aérienne*   **Sp** - < trsl *línea aérea*   **It** [erlạin] F, pl. -*s*, 1970s (1 tech) < rend *compagnia aerea*   **Rm** -< rend *linie aeriană*   **Rs** - < trsl *aéroliniya*   **Cr** [=E] F, end20c (1 tech)   **Bg** *Airlines* (1 writ_{NAME}) < trsl *vŭzdushni linii, aviolinii*   **Hu** [=E] [U] end20c (1 tech, writ, jour)   **Al** - < trsl *linjë ajrore*   **Gr** <=E> [=E] pl. -*s*, end20c (1 writ, tech) < trsl *aeroghrammi, aeroporiki eteria*

airliner *n.* 'a large passenger aircraft'
     Slightly more widespread and acceptable than ↑*airline*, probably because it is more succinct than the paraphrase which would result from the translation of 'large passenger aircraft'.
     Ge [=E] M, pl. Ø, 1970s (o>1 mod)   **Fr** <=E>/*liner* 20c (1 ban) < *avion de ligne*   **It** - < *aereo di linea*   **Rm** - < *avion de linie* (5Fr)   **Rs** *aérolạiner* M, pl. -*y*, mid20c (3 mod)   **Bg** - < trsl *(vŭzdushen) lạiner*

airmail *n.* 2 'mail carried by air'
     This term is known mainly from international labels applied to envelopes and is apparently better known than French *par avion*. For internal uses it is unlikely to succeed in replacing native expressions (some of which may be calques).
     Ge (o) < *Luftpost*   **Du** [=E] C [U] 1970s (o) < *luchtpost*   **Nw** (o) < *luftpost*   **Ic** [=E] uninfl., mid20c (o tech) < rend *flugpóstur*   **Fr** - < *par avion*   **Sp** - < trsl *correo aéreo*   **It** - < (*per*) *via aerea*   **Rm** [=E] adj./adv., 1970s (1) < *par avion* (5Fr)   **Rs** - < trsl *aviapọchtalavia*   **Po** - < trsl *poczta lotnicza*   **Cr** (o)   **Bg** - < trsl *vŭzdushna poshta, par avion* (5Fr); rend *po vŭzdukha*   **Hu** [=E] mid20c < trsl *légiposta*   **Al** - < *postë ajrore*   **Gr** <=E> 20c (1 writ) < trsl *aeroporiko takhydhromio*

airport *n.* 'a complex of runways and buildings for the take-off, landing, and maintenance of civil aircraft'

This compound, made up of Romance elements, is native in French and Italian and is partly borrowed from these languages rather than from English. Germanic languages form calques or independent solutions. The word has a certain currency all over the world as a consequence of English being the international language of air traffic, but it does not appear to compete successfully with native terms.

Ge [eːrport] M, pl. *-s*, 1960s (0>1 mod) < *Flughafen* **Du** (Ø) **Nw** (0) < *flyplass*; trsl *lufthavn* **Ic** - < *flugstöð, flugvöllur* **Fr** *aéroport* M, 1920s (5La) **Sp** - < *aeropuerto* **It** - < trsl *aeroporto* **Rm** - < *aeroport* (5Fr) **Rs** *aéroport* M, pl. *-y*, mid20c (3) **Po** (0) **Cr** (0) < *aerodrom, zraina luka* **Bg** - < *aerogaral/letishte* **Hu** [eːrport] pl. Ø, end20c (1 mod) < *repülőtér* **Al** *aeroport* M, pl. *-e*, mid20c (3) **Gr** <=E> 20c (1 writ) < rend *aerodhromio*

alderman *n.* 2 'a member of an English city council'
Ge (0 arch) **Du** (Ø) **Nw** (0) **Fr** (Ø) **Sp** M (Ø> writ, rare) **Rs** *ol'dermen/oldermen* M, pl. *-y*, 19c (Ø) **Po** [aldermen] beg20c (Ø) **Cr** [alderman] M, end20c (1) **Bg** (Ø) **Fi** *oltermanni* via Sw (Ø) **Hu** [oldøːrman] pl. *-ok*, end-19c/beg20c (Ø/1 tech, arch) < *városi tanácsos* **Gr** (Ø)

ale *n.* 1 'British beer'
Some Germanic languages have the genetically related word which is used for native beers and sometimes also for British-style beers. In other cases *ale* is a foreignism, because the drink has not been successfully exported.

Ge (Ø) **Du** [ejl] C [U] 14c (4 arch) = *aal* [aːl] **Nw** [=E] N [U] mid19c (Ø) < *Øl* **Ic** - < *öl* (5) **Fr** (Ø) **Sp** [ale] F, end18c (Ø) **Rm** (Ø) **Rs** *él'* M [U] beg20c (Ø) **Cr** [=E] M, mid20c (Ø) **Bg** *el* M [U] end20c (Ø) **Fi** [=E] 1990s (2) **Hu** [eːl] [U] end19c (1 tech) < creat *világos angol sör* **Gr** (Ø)

all hands *n.* 1 'the entire crew of a ship', 2 'the entire workforce'
Du *allehens* [aləhɛns] beg20c (2 coll)

all-in *adj.* 'inclusive of all items, costs, etc.'
Du [=E] (1 tech)

all right 1 *pred. adj.* 'satisfactory, in good condition', 2 *adv.* 1 'satisfactorily, as desired', 3 *interj.* 'expressing consent or assent to a proposal or order'
This term exemplifies the ready adoption of expletives, used out of syntactic context, but it has been less widely adopted than ↑*OK*. (The adoption of two synonyms in some languages is noteworthy).

Ge (0 arch) **Du** [=E] beg20c (2) **Nw** <=E>/*ålreit* [olræit/oːlræit] beg20c (2/3) **Ic** *olræt* [=E] 1940s, 1,3(1 sla, arch) < 3: rend *allt í lagi* **It** [orrait/olrait] 1900s (1 coll, you) **Rm** [=E] 1980s (0>1 coll) **Rs** (0) **Cr** [=E] mid20c (2) **Bg** *olrajt* (0) < *okeĭ* **Fi** [=E] 1960s

(0) **Hu** [=E] end19c, 1,3(2) < *rendben* **Al** - < *okej, në rregull* **Gr** 3(0 coll, arch)

all-risk* *cp¹* 'against all risks' (in insurance)
Du [=E] 1950s (1 tech) **Ic** *allrisk*-[=E] 1960s (1 tech) < creat *altjóns-, alskaða-* **Fr** - < trsl *tous risques* **Sp** - < *a todo riesgo/conta todo riesgo* **Fi** [=E] mid20c (1 tech) **Gr** <=E> [=E] cp, end20c, (1 tech) < rend *kata pados kindhynu*

all-round *cp¹* 1 'versatile, qualified, on skilful in many respects', *n.* +1 'a speedskating competition involving any distance'
(Rarely) recorded in sports contexts in the 1930s, this term became popular and spread to other fields, mainly in Central Europe, from the 1960s onwards. There are few calques—other languages appear to make do with earlier native equivalents. Cf. the derivative ↑*all-rounder* and compound ↑ *-man* which are even more restricted in their currency.

Ge [=E] *cp¹*, 1960s, 1(2) **Du** [=E] *cp¹*/adj., mid20c, 1(2) **Nw** *allround* [=E/oːl-] *cp¹*, mid20c, 1, +1 (2) **Cr** [=E] mid20c, 1(2) **Bg** -< +1: *mnogoboĭ* **Hu** [=E] *cp¹*, end19c (2 arch) < *sokoldalú*

all-rounder *n.* 1 'a versatile person', +2 'a speedskater who participates in all distances'
Ge [ɔlraunda] M, pl. Ø, 1970s, 1(1 coll) < 1: *Allroundman* **Du** [=E] C, 1970s, 1(1 tech); [=E] C, 1980s, +2(1 tech) **Nw** [=E] M, pl. *-e* mid20c (2)

allround-man* *n.* 'a person trained or skilful in many trades'
Ge [=E] M, pl. *-men*, 1960s (1)

all-star *cp¹* 1 (of records, shows, etc.) 'composed wholly of outstanding performers'
Ge [=E] 1960s (1 obs) **Nw** [=E] 1960s (1 obs) **Ic** [=E] end20c (0 sla) < rend *stjörnu-* **Sp** [=E/olestar] 1990s (Ø<1 jour, mod) **It** [olstar] 1980s (1 jour, tech) **Rm** [=E] end20c (0>1 mod) **Cr** [=E] end20c (1) **Fi** *all-stars* end20c (1) **Hu** [=E] [U] end20c (0>1 jour, mod, writ) **Gr** (Ø) only in *all- star game*

American football *n.* 'a kind of football played with an oval ball'
When this sport became known in Europe, all languages used the existing term *football* and qualified it with the national equivalent of 'American', apart from German where only the English form is available. The term ↑*rugby* is much older and more widespread; it is often preferred as a synonym even though rugby and American football are different games.

Ge [=E] M [U] 1960s (Ø/1 tech) **Du** - < *Amerikaans voetbal* **Nw** (0) < *amerikansk fotball* **Ic** - < trsl *amerískur fótbolti* **Fr** - < trsl *football américain* **Sp** - < trsl *fútbol americano* **It** [=E] M [U] mid20c (2) < trsl *football americano* **Rm** - < trsl *fotbal american* **Rs** - < trsl *amerikanskiĭ futbol* **Po** - < trsl *amerykański futbol/futball* **Cr** (0) **Bg** - < trsl *amerikanski futbol* **Fi** - < trsl *amerikkalainen jalkapallo* **Hu** - < trsl *amerikai futball* **Al** *futbolli/futboll amerikan* M

[U] mid20c (1) **Gr** *amerikan futbol* N [U] mid20c (Ø/ 1 tech) < trsl *amerikaniko podhosfero*

American way of life *phr.* +1 'typical of American life'
Ge [=E] M [U] 1960s (Ø>1 mod) **Du** [=E] C [U] 1960s (Ø) **Nw** (Ø) **Fr** [amerikan wε ɔv lajf] 1950s (Ø) **Sp** [=E] M [U] 1960s (Ø/1 writ) > trsl *modo/estilo de vida americano* **Rm** - < rend *modul de viață american* **Rs** - < trsl *amerikanskiĭ obraz zhizni* **Cr** (o) **Bg** - < trsl *amerikanski nachin na zhivot* **Gr** (o mod) < trsl *amerikanikos tropos zois*

amplifier *n.* 1 'an electronic device for increasing the strength of electrical signals'
Ge (o) < *Verstärker* **Nw** (o) < *forsterker* *versterker* **Ic** - < rend *magnari* **Fr** - < *amplificateur* **Sp** - < *amplificador* **It** - < *amplificatore* **Rm** - < *amplificator* **Rs** (o) < trsl *usilitel'* **Po** (5La) **Cr** [=E] end20c (1 tech) **Bg** - < trsl *usilvatel* **Fi** - < *vahvistin* **Hu** [æmplifaiə] [U] mid20c (1 tech) < *hangerősítő* **Al** - < *amplifikator* **Gr** <=E> [=E] M, end20c (o>1 tech) < *eniskhytis*

angledozer *n.* 'a kind of bulldozer'
Fr [ãglədozœR] M, 1940s (1 tech, ban) > *bouteur biais* **Po** [angledozer] M, mid20c (1 tech)

antibaby pill* *n.* 'an oral contraceptive pill'
Since this term is not recorded for English the compound may well be a Continental coinage, but it is uncertain where the word was invented. Its distribution (in German, Spanish, Romanian, Croatian, and Hungarian) suggests a German origin. The contraceptive itself was invented by the American biologist Dr Gregory Pincus in 1967.
Ge *Antibabypille* F, pl. *-en*, 1960s (2+5) **Du** - < *anticonceptiepil* **Nw** (o) < *p-pille* **Fr** - < *la pillule* **Sp** *píldora antibaby* [antibeibi] F, 1960s (2 fac, obs) < trsl *la píldora* **It** - < rend *pillola anticoncezionale* **Rm** *(pilulă) antibaby* F, 1970s (2 coll/euph); *(pilulă)/anticonceptional(ă)* **Rs** - < *protivozachatochnye tabletki/konratseptivy* **Po** - < rend *pigułka antykoncepcyjna* **Cr** *antibebi-pilula* F, pl. *-e*, end20c (2) **Bg** - < rend *khapche antibebe* < *kontratseptiv* **Hu** - < trsl *antibébi tabletta* **Al** *pilula/hape antibebe* end20c (3) < *kontraceptiv* **Gr** - < rend *antisyliptiko khapi*

antidoping* *n., cp¹* '(a medical test in sport) designed to test whether illicit substances have been used'
Nw [antidu:ping] cp¹/M [U] 1980s (2) **Fr** *(contrôle) antidoping* [ãtidɔpin] 1960s < *(contrôle) antidopage* **Sp** [antidopin] M, pl. Ø, 1970s (2 tech) < *control antidoping;* = *control antidopaje* **It** [antidɔping] M [U] 1960s (1 tech>2) = *controllo antidoping* **Rm** [antidoping] cp² [U] 1970s (1 tech) **Rs** -→ *antidopingovyĭ(kontrol')* adj. **Po** *-antydopingowy (test)* adj. **Cr** *antidoping* M [U] 1980s (2) **Bg** *antidoping* M [U] end20c (3 tech) → *-ov* adj. **Fi** [=E] 1980s (2) **Al** *kontrolli antidoping* end20c (3) **Gr** only in *antidoping control* [=E] 1980s (2)

antidumping* *n./cp¹* 'protective measures against dumping'

This compound seems to be an extension of the earlier and more widespread ↑*dumping*. Some of the occurrences may be national coinages rather than borrowings.
Ge [antidampiŋ] 1920s (1 tech) **Nw** [antidumping, -dømpiŋ] M [U] mid20c (1) **Fr** [ãtidœmpiŋ] mid20c (1 tech) **Sp** [antidumpin] adj., 1960s (2 tech) **It** [antidampiŋ] M [U] mid20c (1 tech) < *dazio antidumping* **Rm** [antidumping/- damping] N/adj., 1960s, via Fr (3 tech) **Rs** -→ *antidempingovyĭ* adj. **Po** *antydumping* M [U] end20c (2 mod) **Cr** [antidamping] M [U] mid20c (1 tech) **Bg** - < *antidumpingov* adj. **Fi** [=E] (1 tech) **Hu** - < rend *antidömping* [U] mid20c (1 tech) **Al** *antidumping* M, pl. *-e*, 1980s (1 tech) **Gr** <=E> [=E] N [U] end20c (1 tech)

anti-establishment *n./cp¹* '(a person or body) opposed to the Establishment or established authority'
This term is part of the political (student) jargon of the late 1960s, and is possibly coined from the more widespread ↑*establishment* rather than being borrowed.
Ge [=E] 1960s (1 obs) **Nw** [antiëstæbliʃment] 1960s (1) **Sp** [=E] M, pl. Ø, 1960s (1 tech) **It** [anti:istebliʃment] M [U] 1960s (1) **Po** (o)

antifouling* *n.* 'measures taken against barnacles and other growth below the waterline of a boat' (cf. ↑*fouling*)
Ge [=E] N [U] 1960s (1 tech, rare) **Fr** *anti- fouling* M, 1960s (1 tech) **Po** (o) **Cr** *antifauling* F, mid20c (1 tech)

antifreeze *n.* 'a substance added to water to lower its freezing-point'
Ge - < *Frostschutz* **Du** *antivries* [antivri:s] C [U] 1960s (3) **Nw** - < *frostvæske* **Ic** - < *frostlögur* **Fr** - < trsl *antigel* **Sp** - < trsl *anticongleante* **It** - < trsl *antigelo* **Rm** - < *antigel* (5Fr) **Rs** *antifriz* M [U] mid20c (3 tech) **Cr** *antifriz* M [U] mid20c (3) **Bg** *antifriz* M [U] mid20c (2 tech) **Hu** - < rend *fagyásgátló* **Al** *antifriz* M, pl. *-e* (1 reg) **Gr** - < trsl *antipsyktiko (yghro)*

antiskating* *n.* 'a device mounted on record players to reduce the pressure exerted on the record'
Ge [=E] N [U] 1960s (1 tech) **Du** [=E] C, 1980s (1 tech) **Nw** [antiskeitiŋ] M [U] 1960s (1 tech, obs) **Fr** [ãtiskεtiŋ] M, 1970/80s (1 tech/ban) < *antiripage* **Sp** - < *antiskizante* **Po** (o) **Gr** <=E> [=E] N, mid20c (1 tech, obs)

apartment *n.* 1+2 'a room or suite of rooms, sometimes furnished, for rent'
This word competes with the early French loan which is almost identical in form and meaning. Only German and Norwegian appear to distinguish between the two; in other languages the English influence is restricted to fashionable use at best.
Ge [=E] N, pl. *-s*, 1970s (1 mod) = *Appartement* (5Fr) **Du** - < *appartement* (5Fr) **Nw** [=E] pl. *-s*, 1980s (1 mod) < *appartement* (5Fr) **Sp** - < *apartamento* **It** *appartamento* (5Fr) **Rm** - < *apartament* **Rs** (5Fr) **Po** (5Fr) **Cr** (5Fr) **Bg** - < *apartament* (5Fr) **Hu** (5Fr) **Al** *apartament* M, pl.

-e, 1960s (3/5Fr) **Gr** apar̲tment N, pl. Ø/-s, end20c (2 mod) > apart(e)ma̲n (5Fr)

appeal n. 4 'attractiveness; an appealing quality'

This word appears to have been channelled in by the widely popular ↑sex appeal. Since it has to compete with a large number of synonyms (and there is no real need for a loanword) its currency is, unsurprisingly, quite limited. Note that the earlier French-based appell- has possibly acquired the modern English sense in a number of languages.

Ge [=E] M [U] 1960s (1 coll) **Du** [=E] C [U] 1990s (1 tech) **Nw** (o) < appell **Sp** [=E] M [U] 1990s (1 writ, rare) **It** [=E] M [U] 1960s (2) < fascino **Cr** (o)

appeasement n. 'a policy of conciliation'

This term gained (limited) currency in the 1930s when it referred to soft-pedalling policies towards Hitler. It is rarely used to refer to modern political contexts, even in English.

Ge [=E] N [U] 1930s (1 tech, obs) < Beschwichtigungs-politik **Du** [=E] C [U] 1930s (1 tech) **Nw** (o) **Fr** (o) **It** [=E] M [U] 1950 (1) **Po** [episment] M [U] end20c (1 tech) **Cr** epi̲zment M [U] end20c (1 tech)

appetizer n. 'a small amount, esp. of food or drink, designed to stimulate the appetite'

Ge [=E] M, pl. Ø/-s, 1960s (1 tech, jour) < Vorspeise **Du** [=E] N, pl. -s, 20c (1 tech)

approach n. 5 'a stroke from the fairway to the green', (golf) +8 'a scholar's way of treating his or her material'.

This is a fashionable term in quasi-scholarly discussions where method is felt to be too weighty. It is restricted to a few Germanic languages (Ge, Du, Nw). French and Italian have the native equivalents with the modern English meanings added.

Ge [əpro̲ːtʃ] M, pl. -es, 1970s, +8(1 coll, tech) **Du** [=E] C, 1970s, +8(1 tech) **Nw** [=E] M, 1980s, +8(1 coll, tech) < tilnærmingsmåte **Fr** - < mean approche **Sp** [-o̲-/-e] 5(1 tech) **It** - < mean approccio **Bg** - < +8: trsl podkhod **Gr** - < mean prosegisi

aqualung n. 'a portable breathing apparatus for divers'

Du aqualong C, pl. -en, 1960s (3) **Nw** (o) **Rm** (o) **Rs** akvala̲ng M, pl. -i, mid20c (2 tech) **Po** akwalung [akvalunk] M, mid20c (1 tech) **Cr** a̲kvalung M, mid20c (1 tech) **Bg** akvala̲ng M, pl. -al-i, mid20c (2 tech) **Hu** (5Ge) **Al** akualang [akualan̲g] M, pl. -ë, end20c (1 tech)

aquaplaning n. 'a skid caused by a wet road surface'

This hybrid compound has been readily accepted in various languages (note the morphological adaption in French, where the English form is officially banned).
Ge [akvapla̲ːniŋ] N [U] 1970s (3) > rend Wasserglätte **Du** [akwaplaning] N [U] 1970s (2) **Nw** [a̲kvapla̲ːning] M [U] 1960s (1 obs) < trsl vannplaning **Fr** [akwaplaniŋ] M, 1970s (1 tech/ban) > aquaplanage **Sp** [akwaplan̲in] M [U] 1980s (1 tech) > hidroplaneo **It** [akwaple̲niŋ]

M [U] 1980s (1 tech) **Rs** (o) **Cr** akvaple̲ning M [U] end20c (1 tech) **Bg** akvapla̲ning M [U] 1980s (1 tech) **Hu** a̲kvapláning [akvapla̲ːniŋ] [U] end20c (1 tech) **Gr** <=E> [=E] N [U] end20c (1 tech) < ydhrolisthisi

Arizona* n. 'a type of jeans'

Fr (Ø) **Po** arizony [arizoni] pl., mid20c (1 tech) **Hu** <=E> [U] 1980s (1 writ)

arm-wrestling n. 'a trial of strength in which each party tries to force the other's arm down on to a table on which their elbows rest'

Du - < armworstelen **Nw** - < håndbak **Rs** armre̲stling M [U] end20c (2 tech) **Cr** (o) **Bg** - < creat kanadska borba

army n./(cp¹) 'a fashion style'

Nw [=E] 1980s (1 mod) **Rs** (o) **Po** (o) **Fi** <=E>/armi [=E] (1) **Hu** [a̲ːrmi] 1990s (Ø>1 mod) **Gr** <=E> [=E] cp¹, end20c (1 tech)

arrangement n. 'a composition arranged for performance by different instruments or voices' (music)

Modern English pronunciation of this term, which is used in pop music, competes poorly with the well-established French term used in very similar contexts.

Ge [=F/=E] N, pl. -s, 1980s (1 tech, rare) **Du** - < arrangement (5Fr) **Nw** (5Fr) **Ic** - < útsetning **Fr** (4) **Sp** - < arreglo **It** < arrangiamento (5Fr) **Rm** - < aranjament (muzical) [aranʒame̲nt] N, 1960s (5Fr) **Rs** (5Fr) **Cr** (5Fr) **Bg** - < aranzhime̲nt (5Fr) **Hu** (5Fr) **Al** < aranzhim

arrowroot n. 'a plant from which starch is obtained for nutritional and medicinal purposes'

This term has become more or less obsolete with the increasing rarity of the product, but in Norway it is now used more than previously (because there are now more imported products which contain it).
Ge [=E] N [U] mid19c (1 obs, tech) **Du** [=E] C/N, mid19c (1 tech) **Nw** [=E] M [U] 20c (1 tech) **Ic** - < örvarrót **Fr** arrow-root [aroru̲t] M, 19c (1 tech) **Sp** arrurruz M, 19c (3 tech) **Rs** arroru̲t M [U] end19c (1 tech, obs) **Po** [erorut] M [U] mid19c (1 tech) **Fi** arrowjuuri [arɔvjuːri] end20c (3 tech) **Hu** [e̲roruːt] [U] 20c (1 tech/o) **Gr** araruti N, 20c (3 reg, obs)

art director* n. 'a person in charge of layout, graphic design, etc. in advertising or publishing.'

Ge [=E] M, pl. -en/-s, 1970s (1 mod, tech) **Du** [=E] C, 1970s (1 tech) **Nw** [=E] M, pl. -er/-s 1970s (1 tech) **Fr** - < directeur artistique **Sp** - < trsl director artistico **It** [art dire̲ktor] M, pl. Ø, 1960s (1 tech) < trsl direttore artistico **Rm** - < director artistic **Rs** - < trsl khudo̲zhestvennyĭ dire̲ktor **Po** [art direktor] M, end20c (1 tech) < trsl ar̲t-direktor M, pl. -i, end20c (1 tech) < trsl umjetnički direktor **Bg** - < trsl khudozhestven direktor **Al** drejtor arti 1950s (4) **Gr** <=E> [=E] M/F, pl. Ø/-s, 1990s (1 tech, writ)

art cp² 'art style'

Although this item could also have come from

French the combinations in which it occurs are whole-sale borrowings mainly from modern (American) art styles. ↑*body* ~, *land* ~, *minimal*~, *op*~, *pop*~.
Du (Ø) **Nw** [=E] cp², 1960s (1) < *kunst* **It** [=E] mid20c (1) **Rs** *art* M [U] end20c (2 tech) **Po** [art] M [U] mid20c (2 tech) **Fi** (Ø) **Bg** *art* cp$^{1/2}$, end20c (2 jour) **Gr** <=E>/*art* (2)

art-house *n.* 'a cinema specializing in artistic rather than popular films'
Du [=E] N, 1970s (1 tech)

asdic *n.* 'an early form of echo- sounder' (acronym from Allied Submarine Detection Investigation Committee)
Du [=E] C, 1940s (1 tech) **Nw** [asdik] M, pl. -*er*, mid20c (1 tech) **Ic** *asdik(tæki)* [astɪk] N, pl. Ø, mid20c (1 tech) **Fr** [asdik] M, mid20c (1 tech) **Sp** [asdik] mid20c (1 tech) **It** [azdik] M, mid20c (1 tech) **Rm** [asdik] N, 1960s, via Fr (3 tech) **Po** *azdyk* M, mid20c (1 tech) **Hu** [=E] [U] beg20c (1 tech) < *szonár*

assembler *n.* 2b 'a programming language'
  This word exemplifies the international nature of more specific computer terminology (contrast ↑*computer* itself). It has been borrowed with minor adaptations in spelling, pronunciation and morphology.
Ge [=E] M [U] 1960s (1 tech) **Du** [=E] C, 1980s (1 tech) **Nw** [asembler] M, pl. -*e*, 1980s (1 tech) **Fr** *assembleur* [asãbloɛʀ] M, 1960s (1 tech) **Sp** [asembler] 1980s (1 tech) < *ensamblador* **It** [assembler] M [U] 1980s (1 tech) = trsl *assemblatore* **Rm** *asamblor* [asamblor] N, 1970s, via Fr (1 tech) **Rs** *assembler* M [U] end20c (1 tech) **Po** [asembler] M, end20c (1 tech) **Cr** *asembler* M, pl. -*i*, end20c (1 tech) **Bg** *asembler* M [U] end20c (1 tech) **Fi** *asembleri* **Hu** [=E] [U] end20c (1 tech) **Gr** <=E> [=E] N [U] end20c (1 tech)

assembling* *n.* 'amalgamation of industrial firms'
Ge [=E] N [U] 1980s (1 tech, rare) **Du** - < *assemblage*

attaché case *n.* 'a small case for carrying documents'
Du - < trsl *attachékoffer* **Nw** (0) **Ic** - < *stress-taska* **Fr** [ataʃekɛz] M, 1960s (1 mod) **Rs** *attashe-keïs* M, pl. -*y*, mid20c (1 jour, rare) **Bg** - < rend *diplomatichesko kufarche* **Fi** - < trsl *attaseasalkku* **Hu** - < trsl *diplomata táska* **Al** - < *çantë diplomatike*

auditing* *n.* 'an official examination of accounts, an audit'
It [ɔːditiŋ] M, pl. Ø, 1970s (1 tech) < *verifica contabile* **Rm** *audit* [audit] N, end20c (1 tech) → *auditare* F **Rs** *audit* M [U] 1990s (2 tech) → -*or*, M; -*skil'* adj. **Bg** *odit* M, pl. -*al-i*, end20c (1 tech)

audition *n.* 1 'an interview for a role as a singer, actor etc.'
Du - < *auditie* (5Fr) **Nw** [=E] M, pl. -*s/-er*, 1980s (2) **Ic** [=E/auːtɪsjoun] F, pl. -*ir*, 1960s (1 tech) < *prufa* **Fr** (5) **Sp** - < *audición, prueba* **It** - < *audizione* (5La) **Rm** - < *audiție* (5Fr) **Cr** - < *audicija* (5Fr) **Hu** (5La) **Al** *audicion* M, pl. -*e*, end20c, via/from Fr? (1 tech) **Gr** - < *odision* (5Fr)

auditor *n.* 1 'a person who conducts an audit'
Fr *auditeur* M, 1970s (4) < *réviseur* **Sp** [auditor] (3 tech/5La) **It** [=E] M, pl. Ø, 1960s (1 tech) **Rm** (0>1 tech) **Rs** *auditor* M, pl. -*y*, 1990s (1 tech) **Po** (5La) **Cr** (0) **Hu** (5La)

auto bank* *n.* 'an establishment for buying and selling used cars'
Gr <=E> [=E] F, 1990s (1 mod) → *autobanking* N

auto-camping* *n.* 'a mobile home'
Fr <=E> M, 1960/70s (5+2) **It** - < *autocampeggio* **Rs** *avtokemping* M, pl. -*i*, mid20c (2 tech) **Cr** (0)

autocar *n.* +2 'an omnibus', +3 'a fork-lift truck'
Ge [autoːkaːr] M, pl. -*s*, 20c, +2(1 reg) **Du** +2(5Fr) < +3: *vorkhef-truck*; +2: *touringcar* **Fr** [ɔtɔ-kaʀ/otokaʀ] M, end19c, +2(3) → *autocariste* M/F **Sp** [autokar] M, pl. -*es*, +2(3) **It** - < +3: *autocarro* **Rm** [autokar] N, mid20c, via Fr, +2(3) **Rs** *avtokar* M, pl. -*y*, mid20c, +3(3 tech) **Po** *autokar* [autokar] M, beg20c (3) **Bg** *avtokar* M, pl. -*al-i*, mid20c, +3(3 tech, arch) < *motokar* **Hu** [=E] pl. -*ok(?)*, beg20c, +2(1 arch) **Al** - < *autokarro* (5 It)

auto-caravan* *n.* 'a mobile home'
Fr [otokaʀavan] M, 1980s (5+4) < ↑*camping-car/mobile home/motor-home* **It** *autocaravan* F, pl. Ø, mid20c (1>2 tech) < *camper* **Po** (0) **Bg** - < *karavana* (5Fr) **Hu** *karaván* [karavaːn] pl. -*ok*, 1960s (2 tech, mod)

autocross *n.* 'cross-country motor racing'
  One of the many sports terms based on -*cross* referring to events off the track. This term is modelled on the more frequent and earlier *motocross*.
Ge [autoːkros] N [U] 1960s (1 obs) **Du** [=E] C, 1970s (1 tech) **Nw** [æutukros] M [U] mid20c (1 tech) **Ic** [auːtoukʰrɔsː] 1980s (1 tech) **Fr** (0) **Sp** *autocros(s)* [autokros] M, 1970s **It** [auto krɔs] M [U] 1980s (2) **Rm** - < *cros automobilistic* **Rs** *avtokross* M, pl. -*y*, mid20c (3 tech) **Po** [autokros] M [U] end20c (1 tech) **Cr** *auto-kros* M, mid20c (1 tech) **Bg** - < *motokros* **Hu** [=E] [U] 1980s (1 tech) **Al** *autokros* 20c, via It? (1 tech) **Gr** - < *motokros*

autorepeat* *n.* 'a device which automatically starts a tape from its beginning once it has ended'
Ge [autoːripiːt] M/N [U] 1980s (1 tech, rare) **Nw** [æuturipiːt] [U] 1980s (1 tech, jour) **Fr** (0) **Bg** *avtoripit* M [U] 1990s (1 tech/coll); <=E> (1 writ) **Hu** (0 writ) **Gr** <=E> 1980s (1 writ)

autoreverse* *n.* 'a device which automatically plays the other side of a tape'
  This is one of a host of terms introduced with the advent of tape recorders, and of limited currency among fans (note that ↑*autorepeat* has a more limited distribution); these terms are not found in *COD*, being too new or too specialized.
Ge [autoːrivöːrs] N [U] 1980s (1 tech) **Du** [=E] C [U] 1980s (1 tech) **Nw** *autorevers* [æutureværs] [U] 1980s (1 tech, jour) **Fr** [otorivɛrs/ -rəvɛrs] M, 1980s (1

tech)   **It** [autorevęrs] M [U] 1990s (1 tech) < creat *riavvolgimento automatico*   **Rm** <=E>/*autorevers* [autorevęrs] N [U] 1970s (1 tech)   **Rs** *avtorevers* M [U] end20c (1 tech)   **Po** [autorevers] M [U] end20c (1 tech)   **Cr** (0)   **Bg** *avtorivųrs*/ *autorevęrs* M [U] 1990s (1 tech/coll)   **Hu** (0 writ)   **Al** - < *khtimautomatik*   **Gr** <=E> [otorivęrs] N, [U] end20c (1 tech)

autoscooter*   *n.* 'an electric bumper car, a dodgem'
   This word was possibly coined on the Continent. Its limited distribution reflects the absence of this type of fairground ride from fun fairs in many countries.
   Ge [ąuto:skų:ta] M, pl. Ø, 1960s (2)   **Du** [=E] C, 1950s (2)   **Nw** - < *radiobil*   **Fr** - < *auto-tamponneuse*   **It** - < *autoscontro*   **Bg** - < *kolichka*   **Hu** - < *dodzsem*   **Gr** - < *sygruomena aftoknita*

autostop*   *n.* 'hitchhiking'
   Ge (per) *Ąutostop* M [U] 1950s, via Fr (3 obs) < *(per) Anhalter; Trampen*   **Du** [o̱:to:sto̱p] 1970s (1 reg,coll) < *lift*   **Fr** *(auto-)stop* [otosto̱p] M, 1950s (3) → *auto-*

stoppeur/se M/F   **Sp** <=E>/*autoestop* [autoesto̱p] M [U] 1960s, via Fr (2)   **It** [autosto̱p] M [U] mid20c (3)   **Rm** [awtosto̱p] N, 1970s, via Fr (3)   **Rs** *avtostop* M [U] end20c, via Fr (3 coll,you)   **Po** [auto-] M [U] mid20c (3 coll)   **Bg** *ąvtostop* M [U] mid20c, via Fr (3)   **Cr** *ąutostop* M [U] mid20c (3)   **Hu** *autóstop* [ąuto:ʃtop] [U] mid20c (3)   **Gr** *otosto̱p* N [U] mid20c, via Fr (2)

autotraining*   *n.* 'the method or action of bringing oneself to a desired mental or moral state'
   Auto- is here understood as an equivalent of ↑*self*. These are a number of comparable words in which neo-classical *auto*-replaces *self-*(*see* Picone 1996: 295).
   Du - < *autogene training*   **It** - < rend *training autogeno*   **Rs** *autotrening* M [U] end20c (3 tech)   **Po** *autotrening* [autotrenink] M, end20c (2)   **Cr** - < *autogenitrening*   **Bg** *ąvtotrening* M [U] end20c, via Rs (3 tech)   **Hu** *autotréning* [ąutotre:ning] [U] end20c (1 tech>2)

B

baby *n.* 1 'an infant', 4b cp[1] 'a thing that is small of its kind', 5 'a sweetheart', +8 'a blue-striped, light overall worn by children to kindergarten/play-school'

This word is one of the earliest and most widespread anglicisms in Europe, although it has partly been handed on through French. Various suggested native alternatives have been reserved for official or formal purposes, but these remain impersonal and have not replaced this popular word which also seems to be phonaesthetically perfect. Various metaphorical and metonymic usages have arisen independently, as have abbreviations of compounds (resulting in the +8 meaning). Note that in French the word has been borrowed in two forms, one of which retains the English spelling and 'correct' pronunciation.

Ge [beːbi] N, pl. -*(ie)s*, mid19c, 1(2) > *Säugling*; 1960s, 4b,5(1 jour) **Du** [beːbi] C, pl. -'s, 19c, 1(2) 4b(2) 5(1 arch) **Nw** [beːbi/bæibi] M, pl. -*er*, beg20c, 1(2) 4b(1) 5(1 sla) **Ic** *beibi* [pei:pi] N, pl. Ø, 1940s, 1,5(1 coll) **Fr** *bébé* [bebe] M, mid19c, 1(3); *baby* [babi/bebi] M, pl. *babies/babys*, mid19c (1); adj., 1950s, 4b(1) **Sp** *babi/baby* [beibi] 1970s, 1,5(1 sla); [babi] M, pl. -*s*, 1950s, +8(3>2); adj., 1990s (1 tech) **It** [bebi] M, pl. Ø, end19c, 1(2) 4b(1) 5(1 coll) **Rm** [=E] M [U] mid20c, 1,4b,5(1); *bebi* [bebi] M, pl. Ø, mid20c, 1,5(2 coll) 4b(1 jour); *bebe* [bebe/bebe] M [U] 1940s, via Fr, 1(3); *bebeluş* M, 20c (3) **Rs** *bebi/bebil beibi* M, uninfl., beg20c, 1(3) 5(2) **Po** N [U] beg20c, 1(1 coll) < *dziecko* **Cr** *bebi* F, sg./pl., mid20c, 1(1 coll) **Bg** *beĭbi* N/F, pl. -*ta*/Ø, end20c, 5(1 you, sla); *bebe* N, pl. -*ta*, 20c, via Fr, 1(3) → -*shki* adj. **Fi** <=E>/*beibi* [=E] 5(2 coll/fac) **Hu** *bébi* [=E] pl. -*ik*, end19c/beg20c, 1,5(3); *bébi* 4b(3) = 5: *baba* **Al** *bebe* F, pl. Ø, mid19c, 1(1 reg) **Gr** *bebis/beba* M/F, 1(3) *moro*; 5(0) < *moro mu*

baby boom *n.* 'a temporary marked increase in the birthrate'

Although both nouns are widely available for compounding in the individual languages (where N+N compounds are common) the idiomatic character of this compound suggests it is wholesale borrowing.

Ge [beːbiːbuːm] M [U] 1960s (2 coll) **Du** [beːbibuːm] C, 1960s (2 tech) → *babyboomer* n. **Nw** [beːbi- / bæibibum] M [U] 1980s (2) **Ic** [=E] N [U] end20c (1 coll) **Fr** *baby(-)boom* [babi-bum/bebi-] M, 1960s (2) → *baby-boomer* M **Sp** [beibi bum] M [U] 1960s (2) **It** [bebi bum] M, pl. Ø, 1970s (1 jour) **Rs** *bébi- bum* M [U] end20c (3 jour) **Po** (0) **Cr** [=E] M [U] end20c (2) **Bg** *beĭbi bum* M [U] 1996 (1 jour, rare) **Fi** [=E] (1) **Gr** *beibi bum*/<=E> N, 1960s (2)

babydoll* *n.* 1 'pyjamas consisting of a short shirt and matching shorts', 2 'a long dress style, imitating that of a schoolgirl'

'Baby doll' pyjamas became fashionable after Carol Baker wore them in the film *Baby Doll* (released in 1956). The term, borrowed as a noun rather than as an adjective qualifying 'pyjamas', became obsolete in the 1970s. Its distribution is significant: for social and political reasons it was never found in Romanian, Russian, Polish, Bulgarian, or Albanian.

Ge [beːbidol] N/M, pl. -*s*, 1960s, 1(1 arch) **Du** [beːbidɔl] C, 1960s, 1(2) **Nw** [beːbi-/bæibidol] M, pl. -*er*, 1960s, 1(2 obs) **Ic** [=E] uninfl., 1960s, 1(1 mod) **Fr** [bebidoɪ] M, 1960s, 1(1 obs) **Sp** *baby doll* [beibidol] 1990s, 1(2 tech) 2(1 tech) = 1: *picardías, camisola, picardia* **It** [bebi dol] M, pl. Ø, 1960s, 1(2) **Po** mid20c, 1(1 tech) **Cr** [=E] F, mid20c, 1(1 obs) **Fi** [=E] 1970s, 1(1) **Hu** [=E] pl. -*ok*, mid20c, 1(2/3) **Gr** [beibidol] N, via Fr, 1(2)

baby face *n.* 'a person with a childish and innocent face'

Ge (0) **Du** [=E] C, 1980s (2) **Nw** (0) **Ic** [=E] N, pl. Ø, end20c (1 sla) **It** [bebi fes] F, pl. Ø, mid20c (1 jour) **Po** < rend *twarz dziecinna* **Cr** (0) **Fi** [=E] (1 you) **Gr** *beibi feis* N [U] end20c (1 coll)

baby-foot* *n.* 'table football'

Fr [babifut] M, 1950s (2)

babysitter *n.* 1 'a person who looks after a child or children when the parents are out', +2 'an electronic device for listening to a baby while in another room', +3 'a chair designed for babies'

This compound was adopted along with a new lifestyle after 1950, following the earlier adoption of ↑*baby*; the metaphorical senses and the noun ↑*babysitting* followed later. The delay in Eastern

European languages is unmistakable (morphological problems did not allow the backformed verb, which is mainly restricted to Germanic languages). Note that calques are rare.

Ge [beːbisita] M, pl. Ø, 1950s, 1(2) → *babysitten* v. **Du** *babysit (ter)* [beːbisɪt(ər)] C, mid20c, 1, +3(2) → *-ten* v. **Nw** [=E] M, pl. *-e*, mid20c, 1(Ø) +2(1 tech) +3(1) < 1: *barnevakt* **Ic** [=E] (uninfl.) mid20c, 1(0) < 1: rend *barnapía*; +2: creat *barnagaumi* **Fr** [babisitœr/bebi-] M, mid20c, 1(2) **Sp** [beibisiter] M/F, end20c (1 rare) < *canguro* **It** [beːbisitter] F, pl. Ø, 1950s (2>3) **Rm** [=E] M/F, pl. Ø, end20c, 1(1 mod) **Rs** *bebisitter* M, pl. *-y*, end20c, 1(2 jour, mod) **Po** [beibisiter] M, end20c (2) → *-ka* F, v. **Cr** *bebisiter* M/F, pl. *-i*, mid20c (2) → *-ical-ka* F **Fi** [=E] 1(1 mod>0); *beibisitteri* +3(1 mod>0) **Hu** [=E] pl. *-ek*, end20c, 1(2 mod) **Gr** *beibisiter/<=E>* M/F, end20c, 1(2)

babysitting *n.* 'the work of looking after a child or children when the parents are out'

Ge [=E] N, 1960s (1 rare) < *Babysitten* **Du** *babysit* [beibisɪt] C, mid20c (2) **Fr** *baby-sitting* M, 1960s **Sp** [=E] M [U] 1990s (1 rare) **It** [bebi sitting] M [U] 1950s (2) > *baby-sitteraggio* **Rm** (Ø) **Po** [beibisitink] N, end20c (2) **Cr** [=E] M [U] mid20c (2) **Gr** <=E>/*beibisiting* N [U] end20c (2)

back¹ (1) *n.* 4b 'defence' (football)

A first wave of football terms was accepted in the late 19th or early 20th century and was variously affected by purist measures to establish native equivalents. (In German-speaking countries English words were regionally restricted to Austria and Switzerland; cf. ↑*corner*, ↑*goal*). Names of positions were of course affected by footballing changes of strategy in the 1970s/1980s.

Ge [bek] M, pl. *-s*, 19c (1 reg) < *Verteidiger* **Du** [bεk] C, 1940s (1 tech) **Nw** [bek] M, pl. *-er*, beg20c (2) > *bakspiller* **Ic** *bakk* [pahk] M, pl. *-ar*, mid20c (1 tech) = creat *bakvörður* → *bakkari* M, pl. *-ar* **Fr** - < trsl *arrière* (=player) **Sp** - < *defensa* **Rm** *bec* [bek] M, beg20c (1 obs) **Rs** *bék* M, pl. *-i*, beg20c, 4(3 tech, obs) < trsl *zashchitnik* **Po** [bek] M [U] beg20c (1 tech) **Cr** *bek* M, pl. *-ovi*, beg20c (2) **Bg** *bek* M, pl. *begove*, beg20c (1 tech) = trsl *zashtitnik* **Hu** *bekk* [bek] M, pl. *-ek*/Ø, end19c/beg20c (1 tech, arch) < *hátvéd* → *bekkel* v. **Al** *bek* ['bek] M, pl. *-e*, 1930s (1 reg) **Gr** *bak* M/N, beg20c (1 tech)

back² (1) *n.* +6 'the reserve gear of a car'

Ic *bakk* [pahk] M/N [U] 1940s (2 coll) = creat *bakkgír*; *(afturá)bakgír* **Cr** (0) **Fi** *pakki* beg20c (3)

back *v.* 1a 'give moral or financial support to', 2 '(cause to) move backwards', +2a 'turn the sails of a ship to decrease its speed'

Du *backen* [bεkə(n)] 1960s, 1a(0) 2(1 tech) **Nw**

bakke/bake [bake/bæke] beg20c, 1a(2/3); *bakke* [bake] beg20c, 2(3) **Ic** *bakka* [pahka] 1920s, via Da, 2(3) +2a(3 tech) → *bakk* adv.

backboard *n.* +2a 'the left-hand side (looking forward) of a ship, etc.'

This noun was adopted early on, along with other nautical terms. The word is now "Sc., rare or obs." in English.

Ge *Backbord* N [U] 18c (3) **Du** *bakboord* N [U] 17c (5) **Nw** - < *bakbord* **Ic** *bakborði* M (5) **Fr** *bâbord* 15c (5Du) **It** *babordo* M [U] beg19c, via Fr (3/5Du) **Rm** *babord* [babord] N [U] beg19c, via Fr (3) **Cr** (0) **Fi** *paapuri* (5Sw) **Hu** (5Ge)

backgammon *n.* 1 'a game for two played on a board'

This word has largely remained a foreignism: the game has a restricted distribution on the Continent.

Ge [=E] N [U] 1980s (1 tech) **Du** [=E] N [U] 1980s (1 tech) **Nw** [=E] [U] 1980s (1 tech) **Ic** [pahkam:on] N [U] end20c (1 coll) < *kotra* (5 arch) **Fr** [bakgamon] M, mid19c (1 tech) **Sp** [bagamon] M, 1970s (1 tech) **It** [bεkgεmon] M [U] 1930s (1 tech, obs) **Cr** [=E] M [U] end20c (1 tech) **Bg** - < *tabla* (5Turk) **Fi** [=E] (1) **Gr** - < *tavli*

background *n.* 1 'the part of a scene, picture or description that serves as a setting to the chief figures or objects and foreground', 3 'a person's family education, etc.' (mus., film, advert., soc.)

Of the many applications of the English word only the use in music (jazz, etc.) has become current, but is even here a minority form compared with native (and more polysemous) terms.

Ge [=E] M [U] 1960s, 1(1 tech, coll) 3(1 jour) < *Hintergrund* **Du** [=E] C [U] 1980s, 1(1 tech) 3(1 coll) < *achtergrond* **Nw** (0) < *bakgrunn* **Ic** [pahkraunt] N/cp¹, end20c, 1(1 sla) = *bakgrunn-ur*, *bakgrunns-* **Fr** [bakgʀaund] M, 1950s (1 mod, rare) < rend *arrière-plan* **Sp** [bagraun/bakraun] M [U] 1970s (1 tech>2) **It** [bεkgraund] M [U] 1960s (1 tech) **Rm** [=E] N, 1970s (1 tech>2) **Rs** *békgraund* M [U] end20c (1 tech, coll) **Po** [bekgraunt] M [U] end20c, 3(1 tech) **Cr** *bekgraund* M, beg20c, 1(1 tech) **Bg** *bekgraund* M [U] end20c, 3(1 tech, rare) **Hu** [=E] [U] end20c, 3(1 mod) **Al** - < *prapaskenë* **Gr** <=E>/*ba(k)ʀaund* N [U] end20c (1 tech, coll)

backhand *n.* 1 'a stroke played with the back of the hand turned towards the opponent' (tennis)

This is one of the various tennis terms accepted with the game in the nineteenth century, but variously affected by purist measures, in Western Europe. It was introduced much later (with no calquing) into Eastern Europe.

Ge [=E] F [U] end19c (1 reg, obs) < trsl *Rückhand*

Du [bɛkhənt] C [U] 1970s (1
tech) **Nw** [-hæ:n(d)] M [U]
mid20c (1 tech) **Ic** bakhönd F
[U] mid/end20c (4 tech) = bak-
handarhögg **Fr** - < mean revers
Sp - < mean revés **It** - < mean
rovescio **Rm** backhand/bechend

[=E] N, beg20c (2 tech) = rever **Rs** békkhend [U] M,
mid20c (1 tech) **Po** bekhend [bekhent] M, mid20c (1
tech) **Cr** bekend M, pl. -i, beg20c (2) **Bg** bekhend M
[U] mid20c (1 tech); bethend (1 tech, coll) **Hu** [=E]
[U] end19c/beg20c (1 tech) < fonákütés **Gr** bakkhad
N [U] end20c (1 tech)

backing n./cp[1] 1a 'support', 2 'a musical accompaniment, esp. to a singer'
  Marginally attested in the Germanic languages
mainly as a technical term in modern music.
  Ge [=E] N/cp[1], 1970s, 2(1 tech, rare) **Du** [=E] C [U]
1980s (1 tech) **Nw** [=E] M [U] 1960s (1 tech) **Rs**
(0) **Bg** beking M [U] end20c, 2(1 tech)

backlash n. 1 'an excessive or marked adverse reaction'
  Marginally attested in the Germanic languages as a
recent adoption in journalese and political jargon.
  Ge [beklɛʃ] M [U] 1960s (1 jour, mod) < Gegenreak-
tion **Du** [=E] C, 1980s (1 tech) **Nw** [=E] M/N [U]
1960s (1 jour) = tilbakeslag **Ic** [=E] N [U] 1990s (0
sla) < bakslag

backlist n. 'a publisher's list of books published before the current season and still in print'
  Ge (0) **Du** [=E] C, pl. -en, 1980s (1 tech) **Nw**
<=E>/backliste [=E] M, pl. -(e)r, 1980s (1 tech)

back-seat driver n. 'a person who is eager to advise
without assuming responsibility (orig. of a passenger
in a car etc.)'
  Ic [=E] mid20c (1 coll)

backstage adj./adv. 1 'out of view of the audience'
(theatr.), 2 'not known to the public'
  Ge [=E] [U] 1980s, 1(1 tech/jour) **Du** [=E] 1990s (1
tech) **Nw** [=E] end20c (1) **Fr** (Ø) **Sp** [baksteitʃ]
M, end20c (1 tech) < bastidores **It** [=E] M, pl. Ø,
1980s (1 tech) < retroscena **Rs** (0) **Cr** [bekstejdʒ]
adj., 1(1 tech) **Fi** [=E] 1970s (1) **Gr** <=E> [=E]
1990s (1 coll, mod)

back to prep. +1 (basics, the 50s/60s etc., our roots,
. . .) 'esp. applied to fashion, pop music, etc.'
  Nw [=E] 1960s (1 jour, you) **Fi** [=E] mid20c (0) **Gr**
<=E> [=E] mid20c (1 coll/you)

back-up n. 1 'moral or technical support', +1a 'musical accompaniment', 2 'a reserve', 3a 'a copy of data'
(comput.) 3b 'the procedure for making security copies of data' (comput.)
  Ge [=E] N, pl. -s, 1980s, 3a,b(1 tech) **Du** back-up
[=E] C, 1980s, 3a,b(1 tech) **Nw** [=E] M [U] 1980s,
1(1c) +1a,2,3a,b(1 tech) **Ic** [pahkœhp] N, pl. Ø,
end20c, 3b(1 tech) = creat öryggisafrit, geymslu-
afrit **Fr** back-up [bakœp] M, 1980s, 3a(1 tech, ban)
< de secours, sauvegarde **Sp** [bakap/bakap] M, pl. -s,
1980s, 2,3a,b(1 tech) < 3b: copia de seguridad/reser-

va **It** [bɛkap] M, pl. Ø, 1970s, +1a,3a,b(1 tech) =
copia **Rm** [=E] N [U] end20c, 3a,b(1 tech) **Rs**
bekap M [U] 1990s, +1a,3a,b(1 tech) **Cr** [bekap] M,
end20c, +1a,3a(1 tech) **Bg** bekŭp M [U] end20c,
3a,b(1 tech) **Fi** [=E] 1980s, 3a,b(0) **Hu** [=E] [U]
end20c, 3a,b(1 tech) **Gr** <=E>/bakap [=E] end20c,
3a,b(1 tech)

back up v. 1 'give support to', 2 'make a spare copy
of data' (comput.), +6 'accompany' (music)
  Nw bakke opp/backe opp [bake/bæke-] 1960s (2+5) →
oppbacking C **Ic** bakka (e-n) upp [pahka ʏhp] 1960s,
1(3 coll) +6(3 tech) **It** [bɛk ap] M, pl. Ø, mid20c, 1(1
tech) 2(1 tech) **Gr** bakaparo 2(3 tech)

bacon n. 1 'cured meat from the back or sides of a
pig', +2 'smoked pork fillet'.
  It is difficult to explain why this word was ever
borrowed into European languages since perfectly
adequate native terms exist. And indeed it is margin-
alized in many languages.
  Ge [be:-] M [U] mid20c, 1(1 tech,
rare) **Du** [be:kən] N/C [U]
mid20c, 1(2 tech) **Nw** [=E/bæi-
ken] N [U] beg20c (2 tech) **Ic** beikon
[pei:kon] N [U] mid20c, 1(2) **Fr**
[bekɔn] M, 19c/beg20c, +2(2) **Sp**
bacon/beicon [béikon] M [U]

mid20c, 1(2<3) **It** [bɛkon] M [U] 1940s, +2(1) <
pancetta di maiale affumicata **Rm** [=E] N [U]
beg20c (2) **Rs** bekon M [U] mid20c, 1(3) → -nyĭ
adj. **Po** bekon [bekon] M [U] mid20c, 1(2) **Cr**
bekon M [U] mid20c, 1(2) → -ski adj. **Bg** bekon M
[U] mid20c, via Rs, 1(3 rare) **Fi** pekoni (3) **Hu** [=E/
bakon] [U] beg20c (2) < angol szalonna **Gr** beikon N,
end20c, 1(2)

badge n. 1 'a distinctive emblem worn as a mark of
office etc.', +3 'a small emblem bearing a slogan', +4 'a
plastic card', +5 'a magnetic ID card'
  British English badge is less current on the Continent than its American English counterpart ↑button.
Note the restriction to 'a small emblem bearing a
slogan' and various individually developed senses in
French and Romanian.
  Ge [betʃ] M, pl. -s, 1980s, +3(0
you) < Button **Du** [bɛtʃ] C/N,
1970s (1 tech) **Nw** [=E] M, pl.
-r, mid20c, +3(1 rare) **Fr** [bad]
M, beg20c, +3,+5(2) **It** [bedʒ]
M, pl. Ø, 1980s, 1(1 tech) **Rm**
[=E] N [U] 1990s, +4(1 coll,
you) **Rs** bedzh M, pl. -i, 1990s, +3,+5(1 jour,
rare) **Cr** bedž M, pl. -ovi, end20c, 1(2) **Bg** badzh
M, pl. -a/-ove, 1990s, 1(1 tech, mod) → badzhovka
F **Gr** badz N, end20c, 1(1 rare)

badlands n. 'extensive uncultivable eroded arid
areas'
  Ge (Ø rare) **Du** (Ø) **Fr** [badlãs] F, pl., 1960s (1
tech) **Sp** [=E] M, pl., 20c (Ø/1 tech) **Rm** [=E] N,
pl., 20c (1 tech) **Rs** bedlend M, pl. -y, beg20c (1 tech,
obs) **Cr** (0)

badminton *n.* 1 'a game played with rackets in which a shuttlecock is sent back and forth across a net'
  This term was adopted with the game in the early to mid-twentieth century. The German calque, borrowed into Bulgarian, now denotes a more leisurely form of the sport (cf. ↑*basketball/korbball*).
  Ge [bedmintən] N [U] 1930s (1 tech) > creat *Federball* **Du** [=E] N [U] mid20c (2 tech) → *-ner* n; *-nen* v. **Nw** [=E] M [U] beg20c (2) **Ic** [patminton/papminton] N [U] 1930s (2) > creat *fjaðraknattleikur, hnit* **Fr** [badmintən] M, end19c?/1930s (2) **Sp** [badminton] M [U] 1980s (2 tech) **It** [bedminton] M [U] 1950s (1 tech) < mean *volàno* **Rm** [=E/bedminton] N [U] 1970s (2) **Rs** *badminton* M [U] mid20c (3) **Po** [betminton] M [U] mid20c (2) → *-ista* M; *-istka* F; *-owy* adj. **Cr** [=E] M [U] mid20c (2) → *-ski* adj. **Bg** *badminton* M [U] mid20c (1 tech) < *federbal* (5 Ge) **Fi** - < *sulkapallo* **Hu** (0) < *tollaslabda* **Al** *badminton* M [U] 1970s (1 reg) **Gr** *badminton* N [U] mid20c (1 tech)

	Ic	Nw	Po	Rs
Du	Ge	Cr	Bg	
Fr	It	Fi	Hu	
Sp	Rm	Al	Gr	

bad-taste party* *n.* 'a party where people dress up in "bad taste" '
  Ge [=E] F, pl. *(-ie)s*, 1990s (1 you) **Nw** [=E] N, pl. *-erl-ies*, 1980s (1 you)

baffle *n.* +2b 'a part of a loudspeaker system used to limit the emission of sound'
  Fr [bafl] M, 1950s (1 tech, ban) < *enceinte acoustique/ écran* **Sp** <=E>/*bafle* [bafle] M, pl. *-s*, 1980s (2>3) > *pantalla (acústica)*

bag *n./cp²* 1 'a receptacle of flexible material with an opening at the top (used for shopping etc.)', +10 'a measure (for grain etc.)'
  Ge [bek] M, pl. *-s*, end19c, +10(1 tech, rare); 1970s, 1(0>1 mod) **Du** [=E] C, 1980s, 1(1 coll) < *tas* **Nw** [=E] M, pl. *-(g)er*, mid20c (2) **It** [beg] M, pl. Ø, 1980s, 1(1 tech) **Po** [bek] M, end20c, 1(1 mod) **Fi** [bægi] cp², 1980s (0) **Hu** cp², 1(0 writ)

bagpipe *n.* 'a musical instrument'
  Ge (0) < *Dudelsack* **Du** - < *doedelzak* **Nw** (0) < *sekkepipe* **Ic** - < *sekk(ja)pípa, belg(ja)pípa* **Fr** (Ø) < *cornemuse* **It** [begpaip] F, beg20c (1 obs) < *zampogna, cornamusa* **Rm** - < *cimpoi* **Rs** - < *volynka* **Po** (0) **Bg** *begpaip* M, pl. *-al-i*, 20c (1 tech, rare) < *shotlandska gaïda* **Fi** - < trsl *säkkipilli* **Gr** - < rend *askaulos*

baking powder *n.* 'a mixture of sodium bicarbonate, cream of tartar, etc., used instead of yeast in baking'
  Ge - < trsl? *Backpulver* **Du** - < *bakpoeder* **Nw** - < *bakepulver* **Ic** - < *lyftiduft* **Rm** - < rend *praf de copt* **Po** - < rend *proszek do pieczenia* **Cr** (0) **Bg** - < *bakpulver* (5Ge) **Fi** - < trsl? *leivinjauhe* **Gr** *be(i)kin pauder* N [U] 20c (2)

baking soda *n.* 'sodium bicarbonate, used in making tooth-paste'
  Al - < *sodë buke* **Gr** [=E] F, 1990s (1 tech)

ballpoint (pen) *n.* 'a pen with a tiny ball as its writing point'
  Ge - < *Kugelschreiber* **Du** [=E] C, 1970s (2 tech) < *balpen* **Nw** (0) < *kulepenn* **Ic** - < trsl *kúlupenni* **Fr** - < *stylo (à) bille* **It** - < *penna biro* **Rs** - < trsl *sharikovaya avtoruchka* **Bg** - < *khimikalka* **Fi** - < trsl *kuulakärkikynä* **Hu** - < rend *golyóstoll*

ballroom (dancing) *n.* 1 'formal social dancing', +2 'a particular style or set of dances in dancing contests etc.'
  Du *ballroom dancing* [=E] N [U] (1 tech); *ballroomdans* [=E+dans] C [U] 1980s (1 tech) **Nw** [=E] M [U] 1970s (1 tech) **Ic** *ballroom* [=E] end20c, +2(0 tech) **It** - < *ballo liscio* **Po** (0) **Bg** - < +2: rend *balni tantsi*

ball-trap* *n.* 'clay pigeon shooting'
  Fr [baltrap] M, end19c (2)

ballyhoo *n.* 2 'extravagant or sensational publicity'
  Ge [=E] N [U] 1970s (1 jour, rare) **Nw** (0)

banana split *n.* 'a sweet dish made of banana, ice-cream, etc.'
  Ge *Bananensplit*, M, pl. *-s*, 1960s (5+2) **Du** [=E] C, 1990s (2) **Nw** <=E>/*banansplit* [bana:n(a)split] M, pl. Ø, 1970s (2) **Ic** *bananasplitt(i)* [pa:nanasplıht(ı)] N, pl. Ø, 1950s (3) **Fr** [banana split] 1960s (0) **Sp** [banana esplit] M, pl. Ø, end20c (Ø jour, rare) **It** [banana split] F, pl. Ø, 1980s (2) **Rm** (0) **Po** (0) **Cr** (0) **Fi** [=E] (0) **Gr** <=E> [=E] N, end20c (2)

band *n.* 1a 'a group of musicians', 1b 'a group of musicians, playing jazz, pop or dance music' (cf. ↑*jazzband*)
  Although jazz bands were popular from the 1920s onwards, this word was adopted only after 1945, its meaning being restricted to jazz and pop music. In this specialized sense it is one of the most successful modern loans.
  Ge [bent] F, pl. *-s*, 1940s (2) > *(Tanz)kapelle* **Du** [=E] C, 1950s (2) **Nw** [bæ:n/ban] N, pl. Ø, 1940s (2) **Ic** *band* [pant] N, pl. *bönd*, 1920s (4 coll) < *hljómsveit* **Fr** (0) **Sp** - < *banda* **It** [bend] F, pl. Ø, 1950 (2) **Rm** [=E] N [U] 1970s (1 you, mod) **Rs** *bénd/banda* M/F, pl. *-y*, beg20c (1 mod) **Po** [bent] M [U] end20c *bend* (1 mod) **Cr** M, mid20c (2) **Bg** *banda* F, pl. *-ndi*, mid20c (3 tech) = 1b: *-bend* M ↑*bigband* **Fi** [bændı] 1970s (3) **Hu** [=E] pl. *-ek/Ø*, 20c (2) **Al** *bandë* F, pl. *-a*, 1950s (1 reg) **Gr** *bada* F, mid20c (3 tech)

bandleader *n.* 'the leader of a band'
  This term is notably more restricted than its two elements, both of which have been widely accepted.
  Ge [bentli:da] M, pl. Ø, 1960s (0>1 mod) **Du** *bandleider* (2+5) **Nw** (0) **Ic** [=E] M, mid20c (1 tech, sla) < rend *hljómsveitarstjóri* **Fr** (0) **It** [bendlider] pl. Ø, 1980s (1 mod) **Rm** [bandlider/=E] M, 1970s (1 mod, you) **Po** [bentlider] M, end20c (1 tech) **Cr** *bendlider* M, pl. *-i*, mid20c (1 tech) **Bg** - < *lider* **Gr** - < *lider*

bandwagon *n.* 1 'a wagon used to carry'
  Po [bentvagon] M, end20c (1 tech) **Cr** (0)

bandy *n.* 'a kind of hockey'

Although not listed in *COD* this term for a variant of hockey is still used in some regions of Great Britain. **Ge** [bɛndi] N [U] beg20c (1 arch) **Du** [bɛndi] N [U] 1970s (1 tech) **Nw** [=E] M [U] beg20c (2) **Ic** *bandi* [panti] N [U] 1970s, via Da (1 tech) **Fr** [bãdi] M, beg20c (1 arch) **Rm** [bɛndi] N [U] 1970s (1 tech) **Rs** *bɛndi* M [U] uninfl., beg20c (1 arch) **Po** [bɛndi] N, uninfl., mid20c (1 tech) **Cr** *bɛndi* M, mid20c (1 tech) **Fi** [=E] 1980s (3) **Hu** [=E] [U] 20c (1 tech, obs) < *jéglabda* **Gr** (Ø)

bang *interj./n.* 1a 'a loud short sound'

Du [baŋ] interj., 1950s (4) **Nw** [baŋ] interj., 20c (3) **Ic** *bang* [paiŋ] interj., mid20c (2 you) **Fr** [bãg] interj./M, uninfl., 1950s (1) **Sp** [baŋ] M, interj. (1) **It** [baŋg/bɛŋg] 1950s (2) **Rm** *bɑŋg* interj. (5) **Po** (0) **Cr** (0)

banjo *n.* 'a musical instrument resembling a round-bodied guitar'

This term, originally designating a musical instrument used by Afro-American slaves in the USA, spread through Europe from the 1920s onwards, retaining its (near-)English pronunciation in some, but not all languages. **Ge** [banjo:/=E] N, pl. -*s*, beg20c (3) **Du** [banjo:] C, mid20c (3) **Nw** [banju] M, pl. -*er*, beg20c (3) **Ic** *banjó* [panjou] N, pl. Ø, beg20c (2) **Fr** [bã(d)ʒo] M, mid19c (2) **Sp** [banxo/banjo] M, pl. -*s*, 1930s (2 tech) **It** [bɛndʒo] M, pl. Ø, 1900s (2 tech) **Rm** [bɛndʒo] N, end19c, via Fr (3) **Rs** *bandʒho* N, uninfl., beg20c (1 tech) **Po** *bandʒo/<=E>* [bandʒo] N [U] beg20c (1 tech) **Cr** *bendʒo* M, beg20c (2 tech) **Bg** *bandʒho* N, pl. -*dʒhita*, 20c (Ø/2 tech) **Fi** [=E] end20c (3) **Hu** *bendʒsó* [=E] pl. -*k*, end19c/beg20c, from Portug./Engl. (3 tech) **Gr** *bantzo* N, beg20c (2 tech)

banker (1) *n.* 1 'a person who owns or manages a bank', 3 'a result forecast identically in several football-pool entries on one coupon', +4 'a favourite horse, team etc. in the pools, a sure bet'

This term exhibits a complex linguistic history: *bank* is from Italian and has, with the derivative *banquier* 'banker' spread further in Europe; *banker* is a new term adding a modish touch to the traditional concept (this is also true of ↑*banking*).

Ge [=E] M, pl. -*s*, 1970s (1 mod) < *Bankier* **Du** - < *bankier* **Nw** <=E>/*bankers* [banker(s)] M [U] 20c, 1(0) 3(1) +4(2) **Sp** - < *banquero* **Rm** - <*bancher* (5Fr/It) **Rs** (5Ge<Fr) **Po** (5It) **Cr** (5It) < *bankar* **Bg** *banker* M, 1(5Fr) **Fi** *pankkiiri* via Sw? 1(5Fr) **Hu** (5Fr) **Al** - < *bankier*

banking *n.* 'bank management'

Ge [=E] cp²/N [U] 1980s (1 coll) **Nw** (0) **It** [bɛŋiŋg] M, pl. Ø, end20c (1 tech) **Po** (0) **Cr** (0) **Bg** - < rend *bankovo delo* **Gr** <=E>/*bankin(g)* N [U] 1990s (1 tech, mod)

bantam *n.* 1 'a breed of domestic fowl', +3 'a weight class in boxing'

The name of the fowl (after a town in Java) goes back to the eighteenth century, and could have been borrowed independently (especially in Dutch). The weight class is named from the fighting quality of bantam cocks. Both etymology and morphology make the classification as an anglicism questionable. **Ge** [bantam] N [U] beg20c (3 tech) **Du** *bantammer* C, beg20c, 1(1 tech); *bantamgewicht* [bantam-] N [U] mid20c, +3(1 tech) **Nw** *bantamvekt/bantamhøns* [bantam-] cp¹, beg20c, 1,+3(1 tech) → *bantamer* M **Ic** *bantamvigt* [pantam-] F [U] mid20c, +3(1 tech) = rend *dvergvigt* **Fr** - < *(poids) coq* **Sp** - < *peso gallo* **It** [bantam] M [U] 1950s < +3: *peso gallo* **Rm** *(rasă) bantam* [bantam] N/adj., 1930s, via Fr, 1(3 tech) **Rs** *bentamka* F, pl. -*i*, beg20c, 1(3 tech) **Po** *bantamki* [bantamki] pl., mid20c, 1(1 tech) **Cr** <=E> M, mid20c, 3(1 tech) → -*aš* M **Bg** - < +3: rend *kategoriya "petel"* **Fi** [=E] 1(1) **Hu** [=E/*bantam*] [U] end19c/beg20c, +3(1 tech) < *légsúly* **Gr** +3(0 tech) < *khatighoria fteru*

bar[1] *n.* 4a 'a counter in a public house, restaurant of café', 4b 'a room in a public house in which customers may sit and drink', +8 'a nightclub', +9 'an item of furniture used to store alcohol', +10 'a counter in a shop where articles are sold, or services offered'

This early loan is remarkable for its universal spread, the few equivalents available for it, and the restriction to one group of senses of this notably polysemous item. A number of related senses have developed which are not always easy to distinguish from the original English ones. Note the compound ↑*drink bar**.

Ge [ba:r] F, pl. -*s*, 19c, 4a,b(3); 1960s, cp^{1,2}, +9,+10(3) **Du** [ba:r] C, beg20c, 4a,b,+9(3); [ba:r] cp², beg20c, +10(3) > 4a: *tapkast, buffet*; = 4b: *café*; **Nw** [ba:r] M, pl. -*er*, beg20c, 4a,b(3) +9(2) < 4a = *bardisk* **Ic** [pa:r] M, pl. -*ir*, mid20c, 4a,b, +9(3) **Fr** [baʀ] M, mid19c, 4a,b,+8,+9(3) **Sp** *barra* F, 4a(4); M, pl -*es*, end19c, 4b(3) **It** [bar] M, pl. Ø, beg20c, 4b(3) → *barista* (↑*barman*) **Rm** [bar] N, 1930s, via Fr, 4a,b,+8,+9(3) → *bărulet* N dim. **Rs** *bar* M, pl. -*y*, beg20c, 4a,b,+9(3) 3 **Po** [bar] M, beg20c, 4a,b(3); *barek* M, +9(3) → -*owy* adj. **Cr** [ba:r] M, pl. -*ovi*, beg20c, 4b,+8,+9(3) → -*ski* adj. **Bg** *bar* M, pl. -*al-ove*, mid20c, 4a,b,(2); via Ge +8(3); < +9: *barche* → -*ovets* M; -*ovski* adj. **Fi** *baari*, end20c (3) **Hu** [=E] pl. -*ok*, end19c (3) **Al** *bar* M, pl. -*e*, beg20c, 4a,b(3) **Gr** *bar/<=E>* N, pl. Ø/-*s*, beg20c, 4a,b,+8(3)

barbecue *n.* 1a 'a meal grilled out of doors on a metal appliance', 1b 'a party at which such a meal is eaten', 2a 'the metal appliance used for the preparation of a barbecue'

Sporadically attested from the eighteenth century onwards, this term became popular after 1945. It has, however, remained marginal compared with ↑*garden party* and ↑*grill*

Ge [=E] N [U] 1960s, 1b(0>1 mod) < *Grillparty* **Du** [barbəkju] C, 1960s, 1a,b,2a(2) **Nw** [=E] M, pl. -*r/-s*, 1960s, 1b(1 rare) < *grillparty, -fest, grill* **Ic**

[parpekju] 1a,b(Ø) < *grill(-)*   **Fr**
[baʀbəkju/-ky]   mid20c,   1b,
2a(1)   **Sp** - < *barbacoa*   **It** [bar-
beky/barbekju] M, pl. Ø, 1960s,
1b,2a(2) < 1b: *grigliata* < 2a: *griglia*   **Rm** (0)   **Rs** *barbekyu/k'yu*
N, uninfl., 1990s, 1a,b(1 mod)
Po [barbekju] N, uninfl., end20c, 1b,2a(2)   **Cr** [=E]
M, mid20c (2)   **Bg** *barbekyu* N, pl. *-ta*, 1990s, 1b,2a(1
mod) < *skara*   **Gr** *barbikiu/barbekiu/<=E>* N, 1b,
2a(2)

barber-shop   *n./cp¹* 'a popular style of close harmony singing'
   Ge [=E] cp¹, end20c (1 tech, rare)   **Nw** [=E] M [U]
1970s (1 tech)   **Ic** [=E] (Ø) > trsl *rakarastofusöngur,
rakarakvartett*   **Fi** [=E] (0)

barkeeper   *n.* 2 'a person serving drinks in a bar'
   This word competes with the synonymous loan
↑*barman*. It is more frequent in German and Norwegian but *barman* is the commoner word in most other
languages.
   Ge [ba:rki:pa] M, pl. Ø, mid20c
(1 coll)   **Du** *barkeeper* [ba:r-
ki:pər] C, mid20c (1) = 1: *barman,
buffethouder*   **Nw** [=E] M, pl. *-e*,
mid20c (1) < *bartender*   **Ic** - <
trsl *barþjónn*   **Sp** - < *barman, ca-
merero*   **It** - < *barista, barman*
Rm - < *barman*   **Rs** - < *barmen*   **Po** [barkiper] M,
end20c (1 tech)   **Cr** (0)   **Bg** - < *barman*   **Hu** - < trsl
bártulajdonos   **Gr** <=E> [=E] M, mid20c (1 coll)

barmaid   *n.* 'a woman serving behind the bar of a
public house'
   This word is notably more restricted than ↑*barman*;
local coinages individually compounded from *bar* +
'girl' predominate.
   Ge (0) < *Bardame*   **Du** - < *barmeisje, -meid, -juffrouw*
(3+5)   **Nw** (0)   **Fr** [baʀmɛd] F, end19c (1)   **It** [bar-
meid] F, pl. Ø, mid20c (1 tech) < *barista*   **Rm** - <
barmaniţă   **Rs** - < *barmensha*   **Cr** (0)   **Bg** - < *bar-
manka* (3)   **Gr** (0) < *barwoman*

barman   *n.* 1 'a man serving behind the bar of a
public house', +2 'the owner of a bar'
   This word often appears to be a more recent acquisition, together with a new lifestyle, in languages
which had not earlier borrowed ↑*barkeeper*.
   Ge (0)   **Du** [ba:rman] C, pl.
-nen/-men, mid20c, 1(3)   **Nw** (0)
< *bar-keeper, bartender*   **Ic** - <
barþjónn   **Fr** [baʀman] M, pl.
barmen/barmans, end19c (2)
Sp *barmen* [barman] M, pl. *-s/-
mans/-men*, beg20c (2) < *camar-
ero (de barra)*   **It** [barman] M, pl. Ø, 1900s (3)   **Rm**
[barman] M, 1960s (2) → *barmaniţă* F   **Rs** *barmen*
M, pl. *-y*, mid20c, 1(3) → *-sha* F   **Po** [barman] M,
mid20c (2) → *-ka* F   **Cr** [=E] M, pl. *-i*, mid20c (2)
Bg *barman* M, pl. *-i*, mid20c, 1(2) → *-ka* F; *-ski*
adj.   **Hu** [=E] pl. *-ek*, 1920s, 1(1 tech)   **Al** *barmen*

M, pl. *-ë*, mid19c (1 reg)   **Gr** *barman* M, pl. Ø/-en,
end20c (2)

barmixer*   *n.* 'a person who mixes cocktails'
   Ge [ba:rmiksa] M, pl. Ø, 1930s (1 rare)   **Po** (0)   **Cr**
(0)   **Hu** [=E] pl. *-ek*, 1920s (1 tech>2 tech)

barrel   *n.* 3 'a measure of liquid capacity'
   This term competes with native words for 'cask' etc.
and appears to have been adopted mainly as a measure for crude oil, as in German.
   Ge [=E] N, pl. *-s*, 1945-(1 tech_OIL)   **Du** (Ø)   **Nw** (Ø)
< *fat*   **Ic** [=E] mid20c (1 tech, obs_OIL) < *(olíu)fat,
tunna*   **Fr** - < trsl *baril*   **Sp** - < *barril*   **It** - < *barile*
Rm - < *baril* (5Fr)   **Rs** *barrel'* M, pl. *-i*, beg20c, via
Fr (Ø)   **Po** [barel] M, mid20c (Ø)   **Cr** [=E] M, pl.
-i, mid20c (1 tech)   **Bg** *barel* M, pl. *-a*, end20c (1
tech_OIL); *varel* (5Gr)   **Fi** *barreli* 20c (1 tech)   **Hu**
[beril] pl. *-ek*, 17/18c (Ø)   **Al** *barelë* F, pl. *-a*,
mid20c, via It? (1 tech)   **Gr** - < *vareli*

bartender   *n.* 'a person serving behind the bar of a
public house'
   The frequency of the word is notably lower than
those of the synonymous ↑*barkeeper* and ↑*barman*.
   Du [ba:rtendər] C, 1970s (1 tech/mod)   **Nw** [ba:rten-
der] M, pl. *-e*, mid20c (2) > *barkeeper*   **Ic** - < trsl
barþjónn   **It** - < *barman*   **Rm** - < *barman*   **Rs** - <
barmen   **Po** [bartender] M, end20c (1 tech, rare)   **Cr**
(0)   **Bg** - < *barman*   **Gr** <=E> [=E] M, pl. Ø/-s,
end20c (1 tech)

barter   *n.* 1 'trade by exchange of goods without
money', +2 (fig.) 'commercial exchange'
   This word is a modernistic adoption with very restricted use in the field of economic jargon. Native
equivalents predominate throughout.
   Ge [=E] M [U] 1960s (1 tech,
rare) < *Tauschhandel*   **Du** [=E]
C [U] 1970s (1 tech) < *ruilhan-
del*   **Nw** [=E] 20c (1 tech) < *byt-
tehandel*   **Fr** <=E> 20c (1
tech)   **Sp** [barter] M [U] end20c
(1 tech, rare) = *trueque*   **Rm**
[barter] N [U] end20c (1 tech)   **Rs** *barter* M [U]
end20c (3 tech) → *-nyĭ* adj.   **Po** [barter] M [U]
end20c (2) → *-owy* adj.   **Cr** <=E> M, mid20c (2)
Bg *barter* M [U] end20c, 1(1 tech) +2(2) → *-en* adj.
Hu [=E] [U] 20c (1 tech)

base¹   *n.* 3 'a place from which an operation or activity is directed' (milit.), +3a 'a place where a military
force is stationed, (a complex of) barracks'
   This word occurs as an element in the names of
various US military bases, but is not current as a
proper word, the Neo-Greek form being used instead.
   Du - < *basis*   **Nw** [ba:se] M, pl. *-r*, mid20c, 3,
+3a(3)   **Ic** *beis* [pei:s] M, pl. *-ar*, 1950s, +3a(1 sla);
basi [pa:sɪ] +3a(3 sla) = *herstöð*   **Fr** - < 3: mean
base   **Sp** - < mean *base*   **It** - < mean *base*   **Rm**
bază (militară) [bazə] F, end19c, 3(5Fr)   **Rs**
(5Fr)   **Po** 3(5Gr)   **Cr** - < *baza*   **Bg** *baza* F, +3a
(5Fr)   **Hu** - < mean *bázis*   **Al** *bazë* F, pl. *-a*,
mid20c, 3(3)   **Gr** - < mean *vasi*

baseball *n.* 1 'a team game played esp. in the USA, in which players score points by completing a circuit of four bases after hitting the ball', 2 'the ball used in this game', +3 'a game modelled on American baseball'

This term was adopted along with terms for other ball games in the late nineteenth or twentieth century but has remained a foreignism until recently (and thus has not sparked off calques).

Ge [=E] M [U] end19c, 1,2(Ø/1 tech, rare) **Du** <=E> [beːsbɔːl] N [U] 1940s, 1(2 tech) → -*en* v. < *honkbal* **Nw** [=E/basebal] M [U] mid20c (Ø/1 tech) **Ic** [=E] M [U] mid/end20c, 1(Ø) = trsl *hafnabolti* **Fr** *base-ball/baseball* [bɛzbol] M, end19c, 1(1 tech) **Sp** *baseball* [beisbol] M [U] beg20c, 1(1 tech) > trsl *pelota base*; *beisbol* end20c (2>3) → -*ista*; -*ero*; *istico* **It** [bɛzbol/bɛzbol] M [U] end19c, 1(2) **Rm** *base-ball* [=E] N [U] end19c, 1(1 tech) → -*ist* M **Rs** *beísbol* M [U] beg20c, 1(Ø/1 tech) → -'*nyǐ* adj.; -*ist* M, -*ka* F **Po** M [U] beg20c, 1(1 tech) → -*owy* adj. **Cr** *bejzbol* M [U] end20c, 1(1 tech) → -*aš* M; -*ski* adj. **Bg** *beǐzbol* M [U] mid20c, 1(Ø/2 tech) → -*en* adj. **Fi** <=E>/*amerikkalainen pesäpallo* [=E] 1a(0); *pesäpallo* +3(3 tech) **Hu** [=E] [U] end19c/beg20c (1 tech>2 tech) **Al** *bejsboll* [bejsbol] M [U] mid20c, 1,+1a,2(1 tech/3) **Gr** *beizboll*/<=E> N [U] mid20c, 1(Ø)

baseline *n.* 2 'the line marking each end of the court' (tennis, baseb)

Ge - < trsl *Grundlinie* **Du** [=E] C, 1980s (1 tech) **Nw** - < *grunnlinje* **Fr** - < *ligne de fond, ligne de base* **Sp** - < *linea de saque* **It** [beizlɛn] F, pl. Ø (1 tech) < *linea di fondo* **Rm** - < *linie de tuşă* **Rs** (0) < trsl *zadnyaya liniya* **Bg** *beǐzlaïn* M, pl. -*a*, end20c (1 tech, sla) < trsl *osnovna liniya* → -*er* M **Hu** [=E] [U] 20c < *alapvonal* **Gr** <=E> [=E] F, 20c (1 tech) < rend *teliki ghrammi*

BASIC™ *n.* 'a computer programming language', (acron. of) Beginners All-Purpose Symbolic Instruction Code

Note that the clever acronym (invented by J. G. Kemeny and T. E. Kurtz in 1964) has all but replaced the earlier one in BASIC English, developed by C. K. Ogden and I. A. Richards in 1934 (acron. of British American Scientific International Commercial).

Ge [=E] N [U] 1970s (1 tech) **Du** [=E] N, 1980s (1 tech) **Nw** [=E] 1980s (1 tech) **Ic** [=E] end20c (1 tech) **Fr** [bazik] 1960s (1 tech) **Sp** [=E] M [U] 1980s (1 tech) **It** [bɛzik] M [U] 1970s (1 tech) **Rm** [=E] N [U] 1980s (1 tech) **Rs** *beǐsik* M [U] end20c (3 tech) **Po** M [U] end20c (1 tech) **Cr** [=E] M [U] end20c (1 tech) **Bg**<=E>/*BEǏSIK* M [U] end20c (1 tech) **Fi** [=E] **Hu** [=E] [U] 1980s (1 tech) **Gr** <=E> [beizik] F [U] end20c (1 tech)

basket *n.* 4 'a goal scored in basketball', +7 'sneakers, basketball shoes', +8 'the game of basketball'

Ge - < 4: mean *Korb* **Du** [=E] C, 1980s, 4(1 tech) **Nw** [=E] M, mid20c, +7?,+8(2) **Ic** - < 4,+8: trsl *karfa* **Fr** [baskɛt] F, 1950s, +7(2); M, 1900s, +8(2) **Sp** [basket] M, 1980s, +7(1 you) **It** [basket] M,

1920s, +8(3) = *pallacanestro* **Rm** *baschet* [basket] N [U] beg20c, +8(3); M, mid20c, +7(3) **Rs** *basket* M [U] mid20c, +8(3 coll, you) **Po** M [U] beg20c, +8(2 mod) < *koszykówka* **Cr** M [U] end20c, +8(2 tech) **Bg** *basket* M, pl. -*a*/[U] mid20c, 4(2 tech) +8(3 coll) **Gr** *basket* N [U] beg20c, +8(2)

basketball *n.* 1 'a team game in which goals are scored by throwing a large ball through a net fixed above the ground', 2 'the ball used in this game'

The game was invented in 1891 and named in 1892. The term was adopted in Europe during the late nineteenth and early twentieth century (cf. various calques), but remained marginal until 1936 when it became an Olympic discipline. As with ↑*badminton*, the calques now often refer to less competitive ways of playing the game. *COD* has an entry for *korfball* 'a game like basketball played by two teams consisting of six men and six women each'. This is a reimported Dutch calque.

Ge [baːsketbal] M [U] 1940s (2+5) > trsl *Korbball* → -*er* M **Du** *basketbal* [baːskət-] N [U] 1940s, 1 (1 tech); C, pl. -*len*, 2(1 tech) > 1: trsl *korfbal* **Nw** [=E/bal] M [U] mid20c (2) > trsl *kurvball* **Ic** - < trsl *körfubolti* **Fr** *basket- ball/basket* [baskɛt(bol)] M, beg20c (2) → *basketteur, basketteuse* **Sp** *basketball/basketboll/basquetboll/basket* M [U] 1930s (2) < trsl *baloncesto* → *basquetista* **It** [basketbol] M [U] 1920s, 1(2 tech) < *basket, pallacanestro* **Rm** *baschetball/baschetbol* [basketbal/-bol] N [U] beg20c (2) 1: < *baschet* →; 2:*minge de baschet baschebalist/-istă* M/F **Rs** *basketbol* M [U] beg20c, 1(3 tech) → '*nyǐ* adj.; -*ist* M; -*istka* F **Cr** *basketbol* M [U] end20c, 1(1 tech) **Bg** *basketbol* M [U] beg20c, 1(2) → -*ist* M; -*en* adj. **Fi** - < trsl *koripallo* **Hu** [=E] [U] 1(1 tech) < trsl *kosárlabda* **Al** *basketboll* M [U] 1950s, 1,2(1 tech) **Gr** *basketbol* M [U] beg20c, 1(2) < *basket* > rend *kalathosferisi* → *basketbolistas/-stria* M/F

basset *n.* 'a breed of short-legged dog'

The word was borrowed into English from French in the seventeenth century; the pronunciation indicates an English source for some languages and adoption from French in others. Note that German has the term from both sources.

Ge *Basset* [=E] M, pl. -*s*, 20c (1 tech, rare); [basɛ] (5Fr) **Du** [=E] C, pl. -*s*, 20c (1 tech) **Nw** [=E] M, pl. -*er*, 20c (1 tech) **Fr** (5) **Sp** (5Fr); *basset hound* [=E] M, 20c (1 tech) **It** *bassotto* (5Fr) **Rm** *baset* [basɛt] M, mid20c, via Fr (3) **Rs** *basset* M, pl. -*y*, end20c (1 tech) **Po** (5Fr) **Cr** (0) **Bg** *baset* M, pl. -*al-i*, end20c (1 tech) **Fi** *bassetti* 20c (1 tech)

bat(1) *n.* 1 'an implement for hitting balls in games', 3 'a batsman' (cricket, baseball)

Du [=E] N, beg20c (1 tech) **Fr** *batte* F (5 tech) **Sp** *bate* M, pl. -*s*, mid20c, 1(3 tech) **Rm** - < *batman* **Cr** *bat* M, mid20c (1 tech)

batch *n.* 4 (*cp¹*) 'using or dealt with in batches, not as a continuous flow', 5 'a group of records processed as a single unit' (comput.)

Ge [betʃ] M? [U] 1980s, 4(1 tech) **Du** [=E] C, pl. -*es*, 1980s (1 tech) **Nw** [=E] M, 1960s (1 tech) **Fr** <=E> 20c, 5 (1 tech, obs) **Sp** [=E] N, 1980s (1 tech) **It** [betʃ] 1970s (1 tech) = *elaborazione a lotti/ interattiva* **Rm** [=E] N [U] 1970s, 5(1 tech) **Rs** (0) **Bg** *bech/bach/bat* M, pl. -*al-ove*, 1990s, 5(1 tech) < trsl *paket* **Hu** [=E] N [U] 1980s, 5(1 tech) **Gr** <=E> [bats] [U] end20c, 5(1 tech)

Batman *n.* 'the batlike superhero known from comics/film'

The comic-strip character was invented in 1939, and first became popular in Europe in the 1960s. The name has sparked off playful imitations with the suffix -*man* (**Ge** *Genschman* = the politician Genscher); it is not as widespread as ↑*Superman*, however.

Ge [batman] M [U] 1960s (1 you) **Du** [=E] C, pl. *men*, 1980s (1 you) **Nw** [=E] M, 1980s (1 you) = *Lynvingen* **Ic** *Batman* [pahtman] M, end20c (2 you) = *Leðurblökumaðurinn* **Fr** (1 you_NAME) **Sp** [batman] (1_NAME) **It** [batman] M [U] 1960s (2_NAME) **Rm** [=E] M, end20c (1 you) **Rs** *bétmen* M, pl. -*y*, 1990s (1 you, mod) **Po** [batman] M̄ [U] end20c (2 mod) **Cr** [batman] M [U] end20c (1 you) **Bg** *batman* M, pl. -*i*, 1993 (1 mod) **Fi** *Batman* [=E] [U] 1980s (2 jour_NAME) **Hu** *Batman* [=E] [U] 1980s (1 jour) **Al** *betmen* M [U] 1993 (1 you) **Gr** *batman* M [U] end20c (1 you)

batsman *n.* 1 'a person who bats' (cricket)

Ge (Ø) **Du** [=E] C, pl. -*men*, 1940s (1 tech) **Nw** (Ø) **Sp** - < *bateador* **It** - < *battitore* **Rm** *batman* [batman] M, 1970s (1 tech) < *apărător* **Cr** (0) **Rs** *batsmen* M, pl. -*y*, mid20c (1 tech) **Gr** *batsman* M, pl. Ø/-*en*, 20c (Ø)

batten *n.* 1 'a strip of wood or metal used to hold something in place', 3 'a strip of wood or metal for securing a tarpaulin over a ship's hatchway' (naut.)

Rs *batensy*, pl., beg20c, 3(1 tech) **Bg** *batensi*, pl., beg20c, via Rs, 3(3 tech) **Fi** - < *pattinki* (5Sw)

battle *n./cp¹* +3 '(a garment) of or belonging to battle-dress uniform' (often fashion)

Nw [=E] cp¹, 1980s (1 mod)

battledress *n.* +2 'a soldier's jacket'

Du [=E] C, pl. -*en/-es*, 1940s (1 tech) **Nw** [=E] M, pl. -*er*, 1940s (1) **Fr** *battledress* [batœldʀɛs] M [U] mid20c (1 tech) **Po** [bateldres] M, mid20c (1 tech) **Cr** (0)

Ic	Nw	Po	Rs
Du	Ge	Cr	Bg
Fr	It	Fi	Hu
Sp	Rm	Al	Gr

bay rum *n.* 1 'a perfume, esp. for the hair, distilled orig. from bayberry leaves in rum', +1a 'such a perfume drunk as alcohol'

Du - < *pimentawater/lotion* **Nw** - < *karnapp(vindu)* **Ic** *bæromm/bæron* [pai:rom/pai:ron] N [U] mid/end20c, +1a (1 sla) **Cr** (0) **Fi** - < *bay-öljy* **Hu** [=E] [U] end19/beg20c, 1(1 obs)

bay window *n.* 'a window built into an outward projection in a wall'

Fr *bay-window* [bɛwindo]/*bow-window* F, 17c/19c (1 tech) > *oriel* **It** *bow-window/bovindo* [bou windou] M, pl. Ø, 20c (1 tech) **Rm** *bovindou* [bovindow] N, mid20c, via Fr (3 tech) **Cr** (0)

bazooka *n.* 1 'a short-range rocket-launcher'

Invented in World War II (and named after a brass instrument of similar shape), the term was widely known in the period between the 1950s and the 1970s, but appears now to be obsolescent.

Ge [=E] F, pl. -*s*, 1950s (1 tech, obs) **Du** [bazu:ka] C, pl. -'*s*, 1945-(1 tech, arch) **Nw** [basu:ka] M, pl. -*er*, mid20c (1 tech) **Fr** [bazuka] M, mid20c (1 tech) **Sp** *bazooka/bazuca* M, pl. -*s*, mid20c (1 tech, obs) **It** <=E>/*bazuka* [badzuka/badʒuka] M, pl. Ø, 1940s (1 tech) **Rm** [bazuka] F, pl. Ø, mid20c (1 tech, obs) **Rs** *bazuka* F, pl. -*i*, mid20c (3 tech, obs) **Po** [bazuka] F, mid20c (1 tech) **Cr** *bazuka* F, pl. -*e*, mid20c (1 tech) **Bg** *bazuka* F, pl. -*ki*, mid20c (1 tech, obs) **Fi** [=E] (1 tech) < *sinko* **Hu** [=E] [U] mid20c (1 tech) **Al** *bazukë* [bazuk] F, pl. -*a*, mid20c (1 tech) **Gr** *bazuka* N, pl. Ø/-*s*, mid20c (1 tech)

beachcomber *n.* 1 'a vagrant who lives by searching beaches for articles of value', +1a 'a pilferer',

Du - < *strandjutter* **Nw** [=E] M, pl. -*e*, 1950s, 1 (Ø/1 obs) **Ic** *bísi* [pi:si] M, pl. -*ar*, mid20c, via Nw/Sw, +1a (3 sla) → *bísari* M; *bíseri* N; *bísa* v.

beach volleyball *n.* 'a type of volleyball played on sand'

It is too early to assess the actual currency of this term (and possible calques); the admission of the game into the programme of the Atlanta Olympics certainly boosted its popularity.

Ge [bi:tʃvoli: bal] M [U] 1993 (1 tech, mod+5) > trsl *Strandprellball* **Du** *beach volleybal* [=E] C [U] 1980s (1 tech) = *strandvolleybal* **Nw** [=E] M [U] 1990s (1 tech) < rend *sandvolleyball* **Fr** *beach volley* [bitʃuɔle] M, 1990s (1 tech) **Sp** - < trsl *voley playa* **It** *beach volley* [bitʃ vɔli] M [U] 1990s (1>2) **Rm** *beach volley* [=E + voley] N [U] end20c (1 tech) = rend *volei pe plajă* **Rs** - < trsl *plyazhnyi voleibol* **Po** - < rend *koszykówka plazowa* **Cr** (0) **Bg** - < trsl *plazhen voleibol* **Fi** [=E] 1990s (1) **Al** - < rend *volejboll në rërë* end20c **Gr** <=E>/*bits volei* N [U] 1990s (2 mod)

beagle *n.* 1 'a breed of hound'

Adopted together with many other terms for breeds of dog, *beagle* has never been very popular and is little known outside specialist circles.

Ge [=E] M, pl. -*s*, 20c (1 tech, rare) **Du** [bi:gəl] C, 1980s (1 tech) < *brak* **Nw** [=E] M, pl. -*r*, 20c (1 tech) **Ic** [=E] (0 tech) **Fr** <=E>/*bigle* [bigl] M, 16c/mid19c (2/1 tech) **Sp** [bigel] M [U] 1970s (1 tech) **It** [bi:gəl/bigel] M, pl. Ø, 1980s (1 tech) **Rm** [=E] M [U] beg20c (1 tech) **Rs** *bigl'* M, pl. -*i*, 20c (1 tech, rare) **Cr** [=E] M, pl. -*ovi*, 20c (1 tech) **Fi** [bi:gle] 20c (3) **Bg** *bigul* M, pl. -*al-i*, end20c (1 tech) **Hu** [=E] pl. -*ek/-ök*, 20c (1 tech) **Gr** (0)

beam *v. intr.* 3a (scifi) 'travel from one point to another along an invisible beam of energy' (a term used in the *Star Trek* films and TV series)

Ge *beamen* [i:] 1970s (1 mod)   **Nw** *beame* [bi:mə] end20c (1 mod)   **Ic** *bíma* [pi:ma] end20c (1 sla)   **Cr** (0)

beat   *n.* 1a 'a main accent or rhythmic unit in music or verse', 1c (jazz) 'a strong rhythm', (jazz) +1e 'music characterized by this rhythm'

This term became popular after 1945 and was finally defined by *beat music* as 'invented' in Great Britain in 1962, whence it became a central concept in modern music. In America, *beat* is connected with jazz and an alternative lifestyle: an aspect of the ↑*beat generation* of the 1960s (cf. ↑*beatnik*).

Ge [=E] M [U] 1960s, 1a, c (1 tech); 1970s, +1e(2) → *beaten* v.   **Du** [bi:t] C, 1960s (2 tech)   **Nw** [=E] M [U] 1960s (1 tech)   **Ic** *bít* [pi:t] N [U] mid/end20c, 1a(2 tech, sla) 1c,+1e(2 sla)   **Fr** [bit] 1960s (1 tech)   **Sp** [=E/bit] M [U] 1960s/70s (1 tech)   **It** [bi:t] M [U] 1960s, 1c(1 tech) +1e(2)   **Rm** [bit] N [U] 1970s, 1c, +1e(1 tech)   **Rs** *bit* M [U] mid20c (3 tech)   **Po** [bit] M [U] mid20c (2) → *-owy* adj.   **Cr** *bit* M [U] mid20c, 1a,c(1 tech)   **Bg** *biĭt* M [U] mid20c, 1a,c(1 tech)   **Fi** [=E] (2)   **Hu** [=E] [U] 1960s, +1e(2)   **Gr** *bit* N, mid20c (1 tech)

beat generation   *n.* 'a movement of young people in the 1950s who rejected conventional society' (term coined by Jack Kerouac)

Ge [bi:t+Ge] F [U] 1960s (1 obs)   **Du** [=E] C [U] 1980s (1 tech)   **Nw** [=E/bi:t+Nw] M [U] 1950s (1)   **Ic** - < rend *bítkynslóð(in)*   **Fr** (Ø)   **Sp** [=E] 1960s (Ø) = trsl *generación beat*   **It** [=E] F, pl. Ø, 1960s (1) < trsl *generazione beat*   **Rm** (0) < trsl *generaţia beat* 1970s (1 tech, mod)   **Rs** - < rend *razocharovannoe pokolenie*   **Po** - < rend *generacja beatowa*   **Cr** (0)   **Bg** - < rend *pokolenieto na bitnitsite*   **Fi** (Ø)   **Hu** [=E] [U] 1960s (4) < trsl *beat generáció*   **Gr** <=E> [=E] F [U] 1960s (1 obs)

Beatle   *n.* 1 'one of the four Beatles', +2 'a member of any pop group resembling the Beatles', +3 'a long-haired youth'

The most popular music group of the 1960s created a lifestyle for which their name became partly generic (for a type of musician, but also for a style of dress and a hair style). Note that no singular was developed in some languages, but derivations occur. The spelling similarity with ↑*beat* is secondary (originally the group named themselves the *Silver Beetles*).

Ge [=E] M, pl. -*s*, 1960s, 1(2); 1970s, +3(2 obs)   **Du** [=E] C, 1960s, 1(2), +3(2 fac, rare)   **Nw** [=E] M [U] 1960s, 1(1)   **Ic** *Bítill* M, pl. *Bitlar(nir)* 1960s, 1(3); *bítill/bítli* [pi:tɪtl/pihtlɪ] M, pl. -*ar*, +2, +3 (3 you, obs)   **Fr** (Ø)   **Sp** [bitel] M, pl. -*s*, 1960s, 1(2) → *beatleliano, biteliano*   **It** [bitel] M, 1960s, 1(2)   **Rm** <=E> [bɪtlɪʃj/=E] M, 1960s, 1(2) -*z/-y/žy*, mid20c (2 coll)   **Po** *bitels, beatles* [bitels] M, mid20c (2) → *-owski* adj.   **Cr** *bitlz* M, pl. -*i*, mid20c (2) → *-ica* F; *-ovski* adj.   **Bg** *Biĭtŭls* pl., 1960s, 1(Ø); *bitŭls* M, pl. -*i*, 1(3)   **Fi** Ø   **Hu** [=E] [U] 1960s, 1 (0>1); *beatles* [bitlis] pl. -*ek*, +2, +3 (2)   **Al** *bitëlls* M, pl. -*a*, 1970s (1 jour)   **Gr** *bitl* M, pl. -*s*, 1960s, 1(2)

beatnik   *n.* 1 'a member of the beat generation', +2 'a nonconformist youth characterized by dress and hair style'

The original American English meaning appears to have remained a foreignism; European languages adopted the term for youth who adopted the usual characteristics of a nonconformist lifestyle. The term became obsolete after 1980.

Ge [=E] M, pl. -*s*, 1960s, 1 (Ø) +2(1 obs)   **Du** [=E] C, 1960s (2 obs)   **Nw** [=E] M, pl. -*s*/-*er*, 1950s (1)   **Ic** *bitnik(k)* [pihtnɪ(h)k] M, pl. -*ar*, 1960s, 1(Ø)   **Fr** [bitnik] M, 1960s, 1(Ø) +2(1 obs)   **Sp** [=E/bitnik] M, pl. -*s*, 1960s, 1(Ø obs)   **It** [bi:tnik] M, pl. Ø, 1960s (2)   **Rm** *beatnic* [=E] M, 1960s (1 obs)   **Rs** *bitnik* M, pl. -*i*, mid20c (3 obs) → *-ovskiĭ* adj.   **Po** *bitnik*/ <=E> [bitnik] M, 20c (3) → *-owski* adj.   **Cr** *bitnik* M, pl. -*ici*, mid20c, 1(Ø) +2(2 obs)   **Bg** *bitnik* M, pl. *bitnitsi*, mid20c, 1(Ø)   **Fi** [=E] (Ø)   **Hu** [=E] pl. -*ek*, 1960s, via Rs (2/3 obs)   **Gr** <=E>/*bitnik* M/F, pl. -*s*/ Ø, 1(1 obs) +2(1 coll)

beauty   *n.* 3 'a beautiful woman (or person)'

Ge (0)   **Du** [=E] C, pl. -'*s*, beg20c (2 coll) = *beauté*   **Nw** (0)   **Ic** [=E] N, pl. Ø, 1950s (1 sla)   **Sp** [=E] F, pl. -*ies*, 1910s (1 jour, rare)   **Cr** (0)   **Hu** (5Fr)

beauty box*   *n.* 'a box or small case for make-up, a vanity case' (cf. ↑*beauty case*)

Ge [bju:tiboks/=E] F, pl. -*en*, 1970s (1 obs) < *beauty case*   **Du** - < *beauty case*   **Nw** [bju:tiboks/=E] M, pl. -*er*, 1960s (1 obs) < *beauty bag*   **Ic** [=E] N, pl. Ø, 1960s (1 coll)   **Sp** *biutibox* [=E] 1990s (1 jour, rare)   **Fi** [=E] 20c (1)   **Gr** <=E> [=E] N, 1990s (1 mod)

beauty case   *n.* 'a small case or bag for holding cosmetics, a vanity case'

Ge [=E] M/F, pl. -*s*, 1960s (1 mod) > *beauty box*   **Du** [=E] C, 1970s (2)   **Fr** (0)   **It** [bjuti keis] M, pl. Ø, 1960s (2)   **Cr** (0)   **Gr** <=E> [=E] N, 1990s (1 mod)

beauty farm*   *n.* 'a health farm, a health spa'

Ge [=E] F, pl. -*en*, 1960s (1 obs) < *Schönheitsfarm*   **Du** [bju:ti farm] C, 1990s (1 mod)   **Nw** (0)   **It** [=E] F, pl. Ø, 1980s (1) < *beauty center, istituto di bellezza*   **Cr** - < *beauty centar*   **Hu** [=E] pl. -*ok*/Ø, 1980s (2 mod)   **Gr** - < trsl *farma omorfias*

bebop   *n.* 1 'a type of jazz originating in the 1940s and characterized by complex harmony and rhythms', +2 'a dance'

Ge [=E] M [U] 1950s (1 arch)   **Du** [bi:bɔp] C [U] 1940s (1 tech)   **Nw** *bop*/<=E> [=E] M [U] 1940s (1 tech) → *boppe* v.   **Ic** *bíbopp* [pi:pohp] N [U] mid20c, 1(2 tech) → *biboppari*   **Fr** *be-bop* [bibɔp] M, 1940s (1 obs)   **Sp** [=E/bipɔp] M [U] mid 20c (1 tech)   **It** [bi:bɔp/bibap] M [U] 1950s (1 tech)   **Rm** *bop/be-bop* [=E] N [U] 1970s, 1(1 tech)   **Rs** *bibop* M [U] mid20c (1 tech, obs)   **Po** *bop*/<=E> [bop/bibop] M [U] mid20c, 1(1 tech)   **Cr** *bibap* M [U] mid20c, 1(1 tech)   **Bg** *bibop* M [U] mid20c (1 tech)   **Fi** [=E] (0)   **Hu** <=E>/*bop* [=E] [U] 19/20c, 1(1 tech)   **Gr** *bibop* N [U] 1950s (1 obs)

because   *conj./prep.* 'for the reason that'

Fr <=E>/*bicause* [bikɔz] prep./conj., 1920s/50s (1 fac)

bed and breakfast *n.* 2 'an establishment that provides one night's lodging and breakfast'
Ge (Ø) **Du** (o) **Nw** [=E] M/cp¹ [U] 1970s (1 mod) **Ic** [=E] (Ø) **Fr** [bɛdandbrɛkfast] M, mid20c (1 tech) < *chambre d'hôte* **Sp** [=E] M [U] (Ø) **It** [=E] M [U] mid20c (Ø) **Po** (o) **Cr** (o) **Fi** [=E] (Ø) **Hu** (o) **Gr** (Ø)

bedlam *n.* 1 'a scene of uproar and confusion'
Rs *bedlam* M [U] beg20c (2 coll)

beefsteak *n.* 1 'a thick slice of lean beef, esp. from the rump, usu. for grilling or frying', +2 'a fried meatball, a minced meat schnitzel'
One of the most current early anglicisms, transmitted (with *roastbeef*) through French and partly through German. The form has frequently been reanglicized and the term has occasionally also been transferred to ersatz substitutes (+2).
Ge [biːfsteːk/bɛfstek] N, pl. *-s*, beg19c, 1(2) +2(2 obs) **Du** *biefstuk* [bifstʏk] C/cp¹, pl. *-en*, 19c, 1(3) +2(3) **Nw** *biff* [bif] M, pl. *-er*, mid19c, 1(3) **Ic** [piːfsteiːk] F [U] end20c, 1(0 coll); *buff* N, pl. Ø, mid19c, via Da, 1(3) > rend *bauti, bautasteik* **Fr** *bifteck/beefsteak* [biftɛk] M, beg19c (3) **Sp** *bisté(c)* [biste(k)] mid19c, via Fr (3) **It** *bistecca* F, pl. *-cche*, (3) **Rm** *biftec* [biftek] N, mid19c, via Fr, 1(3) **Rs** *bifshteks* M, pl. *-y*, 19c, via Fr and Ge (3) **Po** *befsztyk* [befʃtik] M, mid19c, via Ge (3); *befsztyczek* M → *-owy* adj. **Cr** *biftek* M, pl. *-i*, mid19c, 1(3) **Bg** *biftek* M, pl. *-a/-teksi*, end19c, via Fr, 1,+2(3) **Fi** *pihvi* 19c, via Sw (3) **Hu** <=E>/*bifsztek* [=E] pl. *-ek*, end18c (2) **Al** *biftek* [bif'tek] M, pl. *-ë*, 19c, via Fr, 1(3) **Gr** *bifteki* N, 19c, via Fr, +2(3)

beep *n.* 2 'a high-pitched noise'
Du [biːp] C, 1980s (1 tech_COMPUT) **Nw** [=E] N, pl. Ø, end20c (1) **Ic** *bib(b)* [piːp/piːp:] N [U] mid20c (3 you) **Fr** *bip* [bip] M, 1990s (1 mod) **Sp** <=E>/*bip* [=E/bip] 1990s (1 tech) **It** *bip* [bip] M, pl. Ø, 1990s (1 tech) **Rm** [bip] N, end20c (1 tech, mod) **Rs** *bip* M [U] mid20c (2 tech, coll) **Po** [bip] M, end20c (1 tech) **Fi** - < *piip* **Gr** *bip* N, end20c (1 tech)

beeper *n.* 'a small portable electronic device which emits beeps when the wearer is contacted'
This term is spreading with the device, which is widely used in hospitals to call doctors on duty etc.
Ge [biːpa] M, pl. Ø, 1990s (1 mod) < *Piepser* **Du** [biːpər] C, 1990s (1 tech) **Nw** [=E] M, pl. *-e*, 1990s (1 rare) < *personsøker* **Ic** - < creat *píptæki*; rend *símboði, friðþjófur* **Fr** *bip* [bip] M, 1990s (1 mod) **Sp** - < *busca(personas)* **It** [biper] M, pl. Ø, 1990s (1 tech) < *cercapersone* **Rs** *biper* M, pl. *-y*, 1990s (2 tech) **Po** [bíper] M, end20c (1 mod) → *-niecie* N **Cr** *biper* M, pl. *-i*, 1990s (1 tech) **Gr** *biper* N, 1990s (1 tech, mod)

behaviourism *n.* 1 'the theory that human behaviour is determined by conditioning'
This psychological theory, created in 1913, has spread to other disciplines (e.g. linguistics) but has

remained a scientific term. The hybrid character of the word is still felt in the pronunciation and morphology of the loan in most languages, the first part remaining unmistakably English.
Ge *-ismus* [eː/ei] M [U] beg20c (3 tech) **Du** *-isme* [bɪheːvij ɔrɪsmə] N [U] mid20c (1 tech) **Nw** *behaviorisme* [behaviurɪsme/biheiviorɪsme] M [U] mid20c (3 tech) **Ic** *-ismi* [piːheivjorɪsmɪ] M [U] mid20c (1 tech) = rend *atferlisstefna* **Fr** *behavio(u)risme/béhaviorisme* [bievjɔrɪsm/beavjɔrɪsm] M, mid20c (2 tech) → *béhavioriste/be-/behaviouriste* M/F/adj. **Sp** *behavio(u)rismo* M [U] 1920s (1 tech) < trsl *conductismo* **It** *behaviorismo* M [U] 1940s (3 tech) < trsl *comportamentismo* → *comportamentistico* adj. **Rm** *behaviorism* [behaviorɪsm/=E] N [U] 1960s (2 tech) → *behaviorist* M; *-ă* F/adj. **Rs** *bikheviorizm* M [U] mid20c (2 tech) **Po** *behavioryzm* [bexaviorizm] M [U] mid20c (1 tech) → *behaviorysta* M; *behaviorystka* F; *behaviorystyczny* adj. **Cr** *bihejviorizam* M [U] beg20c (3 tech) **Bg** *bikhejviorizŭm* M [U] mid20c (1 tech) **Fi** *behaviorismi* 20c (3) **Hu** *behaviorizmus* [behaviorizmuʃ] [U] 20c (1 tech) **Al** *biheviorizëm* [biheviorizëm] M [U] 1970s (1 tech) **Gr** *bikheiviorismos/bekha-/bikha-* M [U] beg20c (3 tech) = trsl *syberiforismos*

bel *n.* 'a unit used in the comparison of power levels in electrical communication or intensities of sound'
The term (more frequent in its compound form *decibel*) was appropriately derived from the name of Alexander Graham Bell (1847–1922), who is most famous for the invention of the telephone (patent granted in 1876).
Ge [=E] N, pl. Ø, 20c (3 tech) < *decibel* **Du** [bɛl] C, mid20c (1 tech) **Nw** [=E] M, pl. Ø, 20c (1 tech) **Ic** [pɛːl] N, pl. Ø, mid20c (2 tech) < *desibel* **Fr** [bɛl] M, 20c (1 tech) **Sp** [=E] (1 tech) = *belio* < *decibelio* **It** [=E] M, pl. Ø, 1950s (1 tech) < *decibel* **Rm** [=E] M, mid20c, via Fr (3 tech) **Rs** *bel* M, pl. *-y*, beg20c (1 tech) < *detsibél* **Po** M, mid20c (1 tech) **Cr** *decibel* M, mid20c (1 tech) **Bg** *bel* M, pl. *-a*, mid20c (1 tech) < *detsibel* **Fi** - < *desibeli* **Hu** [=E] [U] 20c (1 tech) **Al** *bel* M [U] 1960s (1 reg) **Gr** - < *desibel*

benchmark (test) *n.* 'a test using a standard or point of reference'
Ge [=E] M, pl. *-s*, end20c (1tech) **Du** [=E] C, 1980s (1 tech) **Nw** *benchmarking* [=E] M [U] 1990s (1 tech) **Fr** [bɛntʃmaʀk] M, 1980s (1 tech, ban) < *test de performance* **Sp** [=E] pl. *-s*, 1980s (1 tech) > *?programa de pruebas* **Cr** (o) **Fi** *benchmarking* [=E] 1980s (1 tech) **Hu** [bentʃmaːrk] [U] end20c (1 tech) < *teljesítménymutató*

Bermudas/Bermuda shorts *n. pl.* 1 'close-fitting knee-length shorts', +1a 'loose-fitting knee-length shorts'
This term has filled an obvious lexical gap. Its acceptability was certainly increased by its non-English form and its 'holiday' connotations.
Ge <=E>/*Bermuda-Shorts* [bermuːdas] pl., 1970s (3) **Du** *bermuda* [bɛrmyda] C, pl. *-'s*, 1970s

(2) **Nw** <=E>/*bermuda/bermudashorts* [bærmu̱:-da(s)] M, sg., 1960s (2) **Ic** *bermúdabuxur* F, pl., 1960s, +1a (3 mod) **Fr** *bermuda* [bɛʀmyda] M [U] 1960s (2) **Sp** *(pantalones) bermudas* [bermúdas] F, pl., mid20c (3) **It** *bermuda* [bermu̱da] M, pl. Ø, 1950s (3) **Rm** *bermude* F, pl., 1970s, via Fr (3 mod) = rend *pantaloni bermude* **Rs** *bermu̱dy* pl., mid20c (3 mod) **Po** *bermudy* [bermudi] pl., mid20c (2) **Cr** *bermuda (hlače)* M, pl., mid20c, +1a(2) **Bg** *bermu̱d(k)i* pl., 1980s (3) **Fi** *bermudat/bermuda shortsit* pl., 20c, +1a(3) **Hu** *bermuda (nadrág)* [bermuda] end20c (3 mod) **Gr** *vermu̱dha* F, mid20c, +1a(3)

Bessemer-   *n./cp¹* 'a process used to remove impurities from pig-iron to render it suitable for making steel' (invented by Henry Bessemer in 1855)

The name of the English inventor Sir Henry Bessemer (1813–98) usually occurs as a cp¹ in combination with 'process' or 'converter'. His method of converting cast iron into steel by a blast of air greatly reduced the cost of production and was quickly adopted by all industrialized nations soon after its invention in 1855. **Ge** *-stahl* 19c (3 tech) → *bessemern* v. **Du** *bessemer (proces)* cp¹, 19c (3 tech) → *bessemeren* v. **Nw** [=E] cp¹, end19c (1 tech) **Fr** *bessemer* [bɛsmɛʀ] M, 19c (1 tech) **Sp** *Bessemer* M, 20c (1 tech) **It** *(convertitore) Bessemer* M, pl. Ø, 19c (1 tech) **Rm** [besmer] N/cp² [U], end19c, via Fr (2 tech) **Rs** - → *bessemerovanie* N [U] → *bessemerovskiĭ* adj. **Po** - → [besemerovate] → *besemerować* v.; *besemerowanie* N; *besemerowania* F; *besemerowski* adj. **Cr** *besemer (čelik)* M, beg20c (1 tech) **Bg** - → *besemerov* adj. **Fi** - → *bessemermellotus* **Hu** [=E] [U] end19c (1 tech)

best in show   +1 'first-prize winner' (in a cat or dog show, etc.)

Nw [=E] 1970s (1) **Rs** *best in show* M, uninfl., 1990s (1 tech/jour) < creat *pobeditel' na vystavke* **Fi** <=E>/*BIS* [=E/bɪs] 20c (0 tech)

best of, the   *phr.* 1 'used of an album containing a collection of an artist's most popular songs', +1a 'a ranking applied to objects, and persons'

Ge [=E] F, pl -s/Ø, end20c, 1 (1 tech, you) **Nw** [=E] 1970s, 1(1) **Ic** (0) **Fr** <=E> end 20c, 1(1) **It** [=E] end20c, 1(1 jour, rare) **Rm** [=E] end20c, 1(1 you, mod) **Po** (0) **Cr** (0) **Bg** *dube̱st* 1990s (1 you, sla); <=E> (1 writ) **Gr** <=E> [=E] end20c (1 tech)

best-seller   *n.* 1 'a book or other item that has sold in large numbers'

This term has been universally adopted for successful books and individually transferred to other products (though much less frequently); analogous formations (*long seller, steady seller*) are rare. **Ge** *Bestseller* [=E] M, pl. Ø, mid20c (2) **Du** [=E] C, mid20c (2) **Nw** [=E] M, mid20c (4) < trsl *bestselger* **Ic** [=E] M, pl. -ar, 1960s (0) < trsl *metsölu-* **Fr** [=E/beseler] M, pl. -s, mid20c (2) **Sp** [beseler] M, pl. -s, mid20c (2) → *-iano*; *-ista*; *-ero* **It** [=E] M, pl. Ø, mid20c (2 tech) **Rm** *bestseller/best seller* [=E] N, 1970s (2) **Rs** *bestse̱ler* M, pl. -y, mid20c (2) **Po** *bestseller* [-er] M, mid20c (2) **Cr** *bestse̱ler* M [U]

mid20c (2) **Bg** *be̱stselŭr* M, pl. -al-i, end20c (2) **Fi** *bestselleri* 20c (0) **Hu** [=E] pl. -a < *legjobban eladható* **Al** *bestseler* [bestse̱ler] M [U] 1990s/mid20c (1 reg) **Gr** *best se̱ler/bestse̱ler* N, pl. Ø/-s, mid/end20c (2)

big band   *n.* 'a large jazz or pop orchestra' **Ge** [bikbent] F, pl. -s, mid20c (2) **Du** [bigbent] C, mid20c (2) **Nw** [=E] N, pl. Ø, mid20c (1) < trsl *storband* **Ic** *biggband* N, pl. -bönd, mid20c (2 coll) = trsl *stórsveit* **Fr** (0) **Sp** [=E/bigband] F, pl. -s, 1970s (1 tech, mod) **It** [bigbend] F, pl. Ø, mid20c (1 tech, you) **Rm** [=E] N, 1970s (1 tech, mod) **Rs** *big be̱nd* M, pl. -y, 1970s (1 tech) → *-owy* adj. **Cr** *big-bend* M, mid20c (1 tech) **Bg** *big-be̱nd* M, pl. -al-ove, mid20c (1 tech) **Fi** [=E] 20c (0) **Hu** [=E] pl. -ek/Ø, mid20c (2 mod)

big bang (theory)   *n.* 1 'the explosion of dense matter, postulated as the origin of the universe', 2 'the introduction in 1986 of important changes in the regulations and procedures for trading on the Stock Exchange', +3 (fig.) 'renovation'

Ge [=E] M, 1980s, 1(1 tech, rare) 2(Ø>1 tech) < 1: *Urknall* **Du** *big bang* [bigbɛng] C [U] 1980s, 1(1 tech) < *oerknal* **Nw** *big bang-teori* [big bæ(:)ŋ] mid 20c, 1(1 tech) **Ic** - < trsl *Miklihvellur* **Fr** *big(-)bang* [bigbãg] M, mid20c, 1(1 tech); 1990s, +3(1 mod) **Sp** [=E/big ban] M [U] mid20c, 1(1 tech); 1990s, +3(1 jour) **It** *(teoria del) big bang* [big bɛng] 1970s, 1(1 tech) **Rm** *big bang* [=E] N [U] 1980s, 1(1 tech) < rend *teo̱riya vzryva* **Po** *big bang* [bik benk] M [U] end20c, 1(1 tech) **Cr** [=E] M [U] end20c, 1(1 tech) **Bg** - < rend *teoriya za golemiya vzriv* **Fi** - < trsl *suuri (alku) pamaus* **Hu** [=E] [U] 20c, 1(1 tech) < *ősrobbanás* **Gr** <=E> [=E] N [U] 1990s, 1 (1 tech)

Big Brother   *n.* 1 'an all-powerful and inescapable dictator', +2 'the USSR'

The term comes from Orwell's *1984*, in which it personifies the power of a totalitarian regime. It has come to denote a great number of uneven power relations. It is frequently modified, sometimes playfully. Unsurprisingly, the term is not so common in Eastern Europe, where the book was not available until recently.

Ge [bik bra̱za] M [U] 1980s, 1(1 coll) = trsl *der große Bruder* **Du** [=E] C [U] 1980s, 1(1 writ, coll, jour) **Nw** [=E] M [U] 1980s (1) < trsl *storebror* **Ic** - < trsl *stóri bró̱ðir* **Fr** 1(0) **Sp** [=E] M [U] 1980s (1 jour) < trsl *Gran Hermano/Hermano Mayor* **It** - < trsl *Grande Fratello* **Rm** +2(0) < trsl *starshiĭ brat* **Po** - < trsl *Wielki Brat* **Cr** - < *veliki brat* **Bg** - < +2: trsl *golemiya brat* **Gr** - < trsl *meghalos adhelfos*

big business   *n* 'large-scale financial dealings, esp, when perceived as sinister or exploitative'

This term, as might be expected, is being accepted more slowly than the word *business* (which partly denotes the same phenomenon). It is working its way into Europe through the Germanic North-West.

Ge [=E] N [U] 1960s (1 mod) **Du** [=E] C, end20c (1 coll, jour) **Nw** [=E] M [U] 1980s (1) **Ic** [=E] M [U] mid/end20c (0 sla) **Fr** (0) **Sp** (0) **It** [big biznes] M, pl. Ø, end20c (1 tech) **Rs** *big biznes* M [U] 1990s (1 tech) < trsl *bol'shoĭ biznes* **Po** [bik biznes] M, end20c (2 mod) **Cr** (0) **Bg** - < trsl *edriya biznes* **Hu** [=E] [U] end20c (1 tech, mod) < trsl *nagy üzlet* **Gr** <=E> [=E] N [U] end20c (1 tech, mod)

big deal *interj.* 'I am not impressed'
Du [=E] 1980s (1 sla, mod) **Nw** [=E] 1980s (1 sla) **Ic** [=E] end20c (1 sla) **Rm** (0) **Cr** (0) **Fi** [=E] 1990s (1 sla)

Big Mac™ *n.* 'a type of hamburger sold at MacDonald's'

This term appears to be on its way to becoming generic in various European languages, but it is difficult to compare these developments cross-linguistically.

Ge [=E] M, pl. -*s*, 1980s (1 coll) **Du** [brɪymɛk] C, 1980s (2) **Nw** [bigmæk] M, pl. -*s*, 1980s (1) **Fr** <=E> end20c (1 you) **Sp** [big mak] M, end20c (1 you) **It** [=E] M, pl. Ø, end20c (1™) **Rm** (0) **Rs** *big mak* M, pl. -*i*, end20c (2 coll, mod) **Po** [bik] M, end20c (2 coll) **Cr** [=E] M [U] end20c (1 you) **Bg** *big mak* M, pl. -*al-ove*, 1995 (1 mod) **Fi** [=E] end20c (2) **Hu** [=E] [U] 1990s (Ø >2) **Gr** <=E> [=E] N, end20c (1 tech, you)

bike *n./cp²* 'a (motor) cycle'
Ge [=E] N, pl. -*s*, 1980s (0>1 mod) **Nw** [=E] M/cp², pl. -*r*, 1980s (1 mod) < *motorsykkel* **Sp** [baik] F, end20c (1 tech, you) < *motocicleta* **It** [baik] M, pl. Ø, 1980s (1 you, mod) < *motocicletta* **Rs** *baĭk* M, pl. -*i*, 1990s (3 coll, you) **Po** (0) **Cr** (0) **Bg** *baĭk* M, pl. -*al-ove*, 1990s (1 tech, mod) **Gr** <=E> [=E] N, pl. Ø/-*s*, 1990s (0>1 mod)

biker *n.* 1 'a motorcyclist', +2 'a mountain biker'
Ge [=E] M, pl. Ø, 1980s, 1(1 coll, rare) +2(1 mod) **Nw** [=E] M, pl. -*e*, 1980s, 1(1 you) **Sp** [baiker] M, pl. -*s*, end20c, 1,+2(1 you, mod) **It** [baiker] M, pl. Ø, 1980s, 1(1 you, mod) < *motociclista* **Rs** *baĭker* M, pl. -*y*, 1990s (2 coll, you) **Po** [baĭk¹/M, 1990s, 1(1 mod)

bikini *n.* 1 'a two-piece swimsuit for women', +2 'small panties, scanty briefs'

Although this item of clothing was invented in America and its name was transmitted through English the form has no English characteristics. Its status as an anglicism is therefore in doubt.

Ge [=E] M, pl. -*s*, 1950s (3) **Du** [=E] C, pl. *'s*, 1950s, 1(3) **Nw** [=E] M, pl. -*er*, 1960s, 1(3) **Ic** *bikini* [pɪ-

cʰɪni] N, pl. Ø, 1960s, 1(2) **Fr** [bikini] M, mid20c (3) **Sp** <=E>/*biquini* [bikini] 1960s, 1(3) **It** [bikini] M, pl. Ø, 1940s, 1(3) = *due pezzi* **Rm** [=E] N/M, pl. Ø (3) **Rs** *bikini* N, uninfl., 1970s 1, +2(3) **Po** <=E> N, uninfl., mid20c (3) → -*arstwo* N; -*arz* M; -*arski* adj. **Cr** [=E] M, mid20c, 1(3) **Bg** *bikini* pl., 1970s, 1(2) +2(3) **Fi** [=E] 1960s, 1(3) **Hu** [=E] pl. -*k*, 1960s, 1(3); [=E] cp¹, 1960s, +2(3) **Al** *bikini* M, pl. Ø, 1980s (1 jour/you) **Gr** *bikini* N, mid20c, via Fr (2/3)

bilge *n.* 2a 'the lowest internal section of a ship's hull'
Ge [bilgə] F, pl. -*n*, end19c (3 tech) **Du** [=E] C, 1950s < *kim* **Bg** *bildzh* M [U] 20c (1 tech) **Fi** *pilssi* 20c, via Sw (3)

bill (1) *n.* 2 'a draft of a proposed law'
Ge (0 arch) **Du** (Ø) **Nw** (0) **Fr** [bil] M, end17c (2) **Sp** [=E] M, pl. -*s*, mid19c (Ø tech) **Rm** *bil* [=E] N, mid19c, via Fr (2 arch, rare) **Rs** *bill'* M, pl. -*i*, 19c (Ø) **Po** M, beg19c (1 tech, arch) **Cr** (0) **Bg** *bil* M, pl. -*a*, 20c (Ø) **Hu** [=E] end19c (1 tech, arch) < *törvényjavaslat*

billboard *n.* 'a large outdoor board for advertisements etc.'
Du [=E] N, pl. -*s* (1 tech) **Nw** *board(s)* [bo:rd] M/N, pl. Ø/-*s*, 1980s (1) **Po** [-t] M, 1990s (1 jour) **Bg** *bilbord* M, pl. -*al-ove*, 1995 (1 tech)

binder *n.* +5 'a paper clip'
Nw *binders* sg. [binders] M, pl. -*er*, Ø, beg20c (3)

bingo *n.* 'a popular gambling game'

This game of chance has become (marginally) known in continental Europe since the 1980s, under its English name. Its form, however, suggests a non-English provenance and in consequence pronunciation is largely according to national conventions.

Ge [biŋgo:] N [U] 1980s (3 tech) **Du** [biŋgo] N, pl. -'s, 1960s (2>3) **Nw** [biŋgu] M [U] 1950s (3) **Ic** *bingó* [piŋkou] N, pl. Ø, 1960s (2) **Fr** [biŋgo] M, 1940s/60s (1) **Sp** [biŋgo] M [U] 1970s (3) → *binguero* **It** [biŋgo] M [U] 1960s (3) **Rm** [biŋgo] N [U] 1990s (1 you) **Rs** *bingo* N, uninfl., 1980s (2 tech mod) **Po** [-go] N [U] end20c (2 mod) **Cr** [=E] M [U] end20c (3 tech) **Bg** *bingo* N [U] 1990s (2) **Fi** [biŋɔ] (3) **Hu** [=E] pl. Ø, 1990s (2 mod) **Gr** *bingo* N [U] 1990s (2 tech, mod)

bingo *interj.* 'expressing surprise, sudden satisfaction, etc., as in winning at bingo'
Ge [biŋgo:] 1980s (3 sla) **Du** [=E] 1980s (1 sla) **Nw** [biŋgu] 1960s (3 coll) **Ic** *bingó* [piŋkou] 1960s (2 sla) **Sp** [biŋgo] 1980s (3 sla) **It** [biŋgo] 1990s (1 coll, you) **Rm** [biŋgo] 1990s (1 you) **Gr** *bingo* 1990s (1 sla)

biofeedback *n.* 'the technique of using the feedback of a normally automatic bodily response to a stimulus, in order to gain voluntary control of that response' (biol, med.)
Ge [=E] N [U] 1970s (1 tech) **Hu** [=E] [U] end20c (1 tech)

birdie *n.* 2 'a score of one stroke less than par' (golf)
All golfing terms (except for *golf* itself) tend to be

known to specialists only, which supports near-English pronunciation (as does the snob value of the terms).
Ge [=E] N, pl. -s, 1970s (1 tech)   **Du** [=E] C, 1980s (1 tech)   **Nw** [=E] M, pl. -s, end20c (1 tech)   **Ic** [=E] mid20c (1 tech)   **Fr** <=E> M, 20c (1 tech/ban) > *oiselet, moins-un*   **Sp** [bi̯rdi] M, 1970s (1 tech)   **It** [bœrdi] M, pl. Ø, 1990s (1 tech)   **Fi** [=E] end20c (1)   **Gr** <=E> [=E] N, pl. Ø/-s, end20c (1 tech)

biro™   *n. cp¹·²* 'a kind of ballpoint pen'

The ball-point pen was invented in 1938 by the Hungarian journalist László Biro. It was widely used by the British Royal Air Force (because it worked at high altitudes) and became very popular. The use of the eponym by itself is restricted to British English.
Ic *birópenni* [piːrouphɛnːɪ] M, pl. -ar, 1950s (2+5) = *kúlupenni*   **It** (*penna*) *biro* [bi̯ro] F, pl. Ø, 1940s   **Cr** (0)

birth control   *n.* 'the control of the number of children one conceives, esp. by contraception'
Ge - < trsl *Geburtenkontrolle*   **Du** - < *geboortebeperking*   **Fr** [=E]? M, 1930s (1 arch) < trsl *contrôle des naissances*   **Sp** - < trsl *control de la natalidad*   **It** - < trsl *controllo delle nascite*   **Rm** - < rend *controlul nașterilor*   **Rs** - < trsl *kontrol' rozhdaemosti*   **Po** - < *kontrola uródzen'*   **Cr** (0)   **Bg** - < creat *ogranichavane na razhdaemostta*   **Hu** [=E] [U] end20c (Ø > 1 tech) < trsl *születésszabályozás*   **Gr** - < trsl *eleghkos ghenniseon*

bit (4)   *n.* 'a basic unit of information expressed as a choice between one and zero' (comput.) (from b̲inary dig̲it̲)

Taken over as a term of computing, the form of *bit* is not analysed as an acronym, nor is there a perception of closeness to *bit* 'small quantity', as there is in English.
Ge [=E] N, pl. -s, 1970s (1 tech)   **Du** [=E] C, 1960s (1 tech)   **Nw** [=E] M, pl. -er/-s, 1960s (1 tech)   **Ic** [=E] N, pl. Ø, 1970s (1 tech) < rend *biti*   **Fr** [bit] M, 1960s (1 tech)   **Sp** M, pl. -s, 1970s (1 tech) → *bítico*   **It** [bit] M, pl. Ø, 1960s (1 tech)   **Rm** [=E] M, 1980s (1 tech)   **Rs** *bit* M, pl. -y, mid20c (2 tech)   **Po** <=E> M, mid20c (2 tech) → *-owy* adj.   **Cr** <=E> M, mid20c (2 tech) → *-ni* adj.   **Bg** *bit* M, pl. -a, end20c (1 tech) → *-ov* cp²/adj.   **Fi** *bitti* [bɪtːɪ] 1980s (2 tech)   **Hu** [=E] [U] 1950s (1 tech)   **Gr** <=E> [=E] N, pl. Ø/-s, end20c (1 tech)

bitter   *n.* 2 'a liquor with a bitter flavour, used as an additive in cocktails'
Ge - < *Magenbitter* (5)   **Du** (5)   **Nw** [=E] M [U] end19c (4)   **Ic** [pɪhter] M, pl. -ar, mid/end19c (5Da)   **Fr** [bitɛʀ] M, 19c, via Du (1 tech)   **Sp** <=E>/*biter* M, end19c (3)   **It** [bitter] M, pl. Ø, end19c (3)   **Rm** <=E>/*biter* [=E] N, mid20c, via Fr/Ge (3)   **Po** [-er] M, end20c (1 tech)   **Bg** *biter* M [U] mid20c (1 tech)   **Fi** [=E] (1)   **Hu** (5Ge)

bitter lemon   *n.* 'a non-alcoholic drink'

The status of this term characteristically wavers between that of a foreignism and that of a modern adoption in regions where the drink is known (it is not known in much of Eastern and Southern Europe).
Ge [=E] N/F, pl. -s, 1970s (1 tech)   **Du** [=E] C, 1970s (2)   **Nw** [=E] M [U] mid20c (2)   **Fr** (0)   **Sp** [bi̯terlemon] M [U] end20c (1 tech)   **Rm** - < *bitter/(biter) citro* N, 1970s (3 obs)   **Rs** (0)   **Po** (0)   **Cr** [=E] M, end20c (1 tech)   **Bg** - < trsl *biter limon* M, 1970s (1)   **Hu** [=E] [U] 1990s (1 writ, mod)   **Gr** *biter lemon* N, end20c (1 tech)

black box   *n.* 1 'a flight-recorder', 2 'any complex piece of equipment, usu. a unit in an electronic system, with contents which are mysterious to the user'
Ge [=E] F, pl. -es, 1960s, 1(1 tech); 1970s, 2(1 tech, rare) < 1: *Flugschreiber*   **Du** [=E] C, pl. -es, end20c, 1(1 tech)   **Nw** [=E] M, pl. -er, 1970s (1 tech) < 1: *ferdsskriver*   **Ic** - < trsl *svarti kassinn*   **Fr** - < trsl *boîte noire*   **Sp** - < trsl *caja negra*   **It** - < trsl *scatola nera*   **Rm** - < rend *cutie neagră*   **Rs** *blék boks* M [U] 1990s (1 tech) < trsl *chërnyi ya̱shchik*   **Po** - < trsl *czarna skrzynka*   **Cr** - < trsl *crna kutija*   **Bg** - < 1: trsl *cherna kutiya*   **Fi** - < trsl *musta laatikko*   **Hu** - < trsl *fekete doboz*   **Gr** <=E>/*bla̱k box* N, end20c (1 tech) < trsl *mavro kuti*

blackjack (1)   *n.* 1 'a card-game similar to pontoon'
Ge (0) < *Siebzehn-und-vier*   **Du** [=E] N [U] 1970s (2 tech) = *eenentwintig*   **Nw** - < *tjueett*   **Ic** - < *tuttugu og einn*   **Fr** [blak-(d)ʒak] M, 1980s (1 tech)   **Sp** [blakjak] M, 1970s (1 tech)   **It** [blɛk dʒɛk] M [U] mid20c (1)   **Rm** [=E] N [U] 1990s (1 tech) = *douăzeci și unu*   **Rs** [blɛk dzhek] M [U] 1980s (1 tech)   **Po** [blekdʒek] M [U] end20c (2 tech)   **Cr** [blekdʒek] M [U] end20c (2 tech)   **Bg** *blekdzhek* M [U] end20c (1 tech)   **Gr** <=E>/*blaktza̱k* N [U] end20c (2) < *ikosiena*

black light   *n.* 'ultraviolet light'
Ge - < trsl *Schwarzlicht*   **Du** [=E] C, 1990s (1 mod)   **Nw** [=E] N [U] 1960s (1/2)   **Ic** [=E] N, pl. Ø, 1980s (1 tech)   **Fr** - < trsl *lumière noire*   **Rm** - < rend *lumină neagră*

blackmail   *n.* 1a 'the extortion of payment in return for not disclosing discreditable information, a secret, etc.', 1b 'a payment extorted in this way', 2 'the use of threats or moral pressure'
Du [=E] C, 1990s, 1a, b(1 jour, mod)   **Nw** [=E] [U] end20c (1 coll)   **Ic** [=E] N [U] mid20c, 1a, 2(1 sla) < *fjárkúgun*

blackmail   *v.* 1 '(try to) extort money etc. (from a person) by blackmail', 2 'coerce with threats or moral pressure'
Nw [blæ̱kmeilə]   **Ic** *blakkmeila* [plahkmeila] mid20c (1 sla)

blackout *n.* 1 'a temporary or complete loss of vision, consciousness or memory', 2 'a loss of electric power', 3 'a compulsory period of darkness as a precaution against air raids', 5 'a sudden darkening of a theatre stage', +6 'censorship', +7 'keeping mum'

This term is remarkable for the great variety of senses apparently borrowed from English (rather than independently developed). The chronological sequence and the process of mediation through other languages are opaque.

Ge [bl<u>e</u>kaut] M, pl. -*s*, 1970s, 1(1 coll) 2(1 coll, rare) 5(1 tech) < 2: *Stromausfall*   **Du** [=E] C, 1940s, 1, 2, 3(1 coll)   **Nw** [=E] M, pl. -*er*/-*s*, 1a (1 coll) 2(1) 5(1 tech)   **Ic** [plahkaut] N [U] 1960s, 1 (1 sla) 5 (1 tech)   **Fr** *black-out* [blakaut] M, 1940s, 3, 5(2) +7(1)   **Sp** [blakau(t)] M [U] 1970s, 2, 3, +6(1 tech, jour, rare)   **It** [bl<u>e</u>kaut] M, pl. Ø, 1970s, 1, 2(2)   **Rm** [=E] N, 1990s, 2,5(1 tech)   **Rs** *blék<u>a</u>ut* M, pl. -*y*, 1990s, 5(3 tech)   **Po** *blekaut* M [U] end20c, 5(1 tech)   **Cr** [=E] M, [U] end20c, 2(1 tech)   **Bg** *blek<u>a</u>ut* M, pl. -*al*-*i*, end20c, 1(1 tech) 2 (1 tech_{NAUT})   **Gr** *blak<u>a</u>ut* N, end20c, 1(2 coll) 2,3(2)

blah-blah *n.* 'pretentious nonsense'

This imitative and highly colloquial term may derive from native onomatopoeia. While borrowing is possible, it is usually not sufficiently attested.

Ge *Bla-bla* N [U] 1960s (3 coll)   **Du** *blabla* 20c, via Fr (3)   **Nw** *bla-bla* [bla:bl<u>a</u>:] 1950s (3 coll)   **Ic** *bla-bla* int. [=E] end20c (3 coll)   **Fr** *blablabla* (5)   **Sp** *bla, bla, bla* (5)   **It** *blablà*/*blablablà* M, pl. Ø, 1970s (3)   **Rm** *bla bla* (5Fr)   **Po** *bla bla* [bla bla] N, end20c (2c)   **Cr** (0)   **Fi** - < *päläpälä*   **Hu** <=E>/*blabla* [=E] [U] mid20c, via Fr (3) → *blabláz* v.   **Gr** *bla bl<u>a</u>* N [U] mid20c (5Fr)

blank *n.* 1b 'a document having blank spaces to be filled in', 3 'an empty space or period of time', +3a 'a space of the size of one character' (comput.)

Ge [=E] M, pl. -*s*, 1970s, 3, +3a (0>1 tech); < 1b: *Blankoformular*   **Sp** - < 3: *espacio en blanco*   **Rm** *blanc* [bla<u>n</u>k] N, 20c, 1b(5Fr); end20c, +3a(4)   **Rs** *blank* pl. -*i*, mid20c, 1b(3)   **Bg** *bl<u>a</u>nka* F, pl. -*ki*, mid20c, via Rs, 1b(3)   **Fi** - < *blanketti* 1b < *lomate*   **Hu** 1b(5Ge)

blanket *n.* 1 'a large woollen bed-covering or wrap'   **Nw** *blankis* [bl<u>a</u>ŋkis] M, sg., beg20c (3 arch)

blank verse *n.* 'unrhymed verse, esp. iambic pentameters'

Ge [bl<u>a</u>ŋkfers] M, pl. -*e*, 18c (3 tech)   **Du** *blanke verzen*, beg19c (3+5)   **Nw** - < trsl *blankvers* (3)   **Ic** - < rend *stakhenda*   **Sp** - < *verso blanco*   **It** [blaŋk v<u>ə</u>:rs] M, pl. Ø, beg20c (1 tech) < rend *verso sciolto*   **Rm** - < trsl *vers alb*   **Rs** - < rend *b<u>e</u>lyĭ stikh*   **Cr** [=E] M, mid20c (2)   **Bg** - < rend *beli stikhove*   **Hu** *blankvers* [=E/bl<u>a</u>nkverʃ] [U] 18/19c (1 tech)

blazer *n.* 2 'a man's (dark blue) summer jacket', +2a 'a woman's summer jacket, +3' 'a knitted jacket fastening down the front, usu. with long sleeves'

This is one of the most widespread exports as far as dress is concerned. The sense of a man's dark blue jacket still predominates, but some languages have developed independent senses.

Ge [bl<u>e</u>:za] M, pl. Ø, beg20c, 2, +2a(2)   **Du** [bl<u>e</u>:zər] C, mid20c, 2(2)   **Nw** <=E>/*bleser* [ble:ser] M, pl. -*e*, mid20c, 2, +2a(2)   **Ic** *bleiser(jakki)* [plei:ser] M, pl. -*ar*, mid20c, 2(2 coll)   **Fr** [blazeR/-eR] M, 1920s, 2, +2a(2)   **Sp** [bl<u>a</u>ser/bleisier/bleisier] M, 1920s, 2(2 tech)   **It** [bl<u>e</u>zer] M, pl. Ø, 1930s, 2, +2a(2)   **Rm** *blazer* [bl<u>e</u>jzə/bl<u>e</u>zər] N, 1970s, via Fr?, 2, +2a (3 mod)   **Rs** *bl<u>e</u>izer*/*bl<u>a</u>zer* M, pl. -*y*, mid20c, 2, +2a (3 mod)   **Po** *blezer* [blezer] M, mid20c, +3(2)   **Cr** *blejzer* M, pl. -*i*, mid20c, 2, +2a(2)   **Bg** *bl<u>e</u>izer* M, pl. -*al*-*i*, 1970s, 2, +2a(2) → -*che* N   **Fi** *bleiseri* [bleɪserɪ] +2a(3)   **Hu** *blézer* [bl<u>e</u>:zer] pl. -*ek*, 1960s, 2,+2a(3)   **Gr** *bl<u>e</u>izer* N, end20c, 2,+2a(2)

blend *n.* 1a 'a mixture', (of tobacco, drinks), 1b 'a combination' (of qualities)

Ge [blent] M/N [U] 20c (1 tech>2)   **Du** (Ø)   **Nw** [=E] M [U] mid20c (1 tech)   **It** [=E] M/F, pl. Ø, 20c (1) < *miscela*   **Rs** (0)   **Po** (0)   **Cr** (0)   **Bg** *bl<u>e</u>nda* F, pl. -*di*, 1990s, 1b(1 tech_{MUS})   **Fi** (0)   **Hu** [=E] pl. -*ek*/Ø, mid20c (2/3 writ, jour) < *keverék*   **Gr** <=E>/*bled* [=E] N, pl. -*s*/Ø, end20c (1 tech>2)

blender *n.* 1 'a mixing machine used in food preparation'

Du [=E] C, 1950s (1 tech)   **Ic** [=E] M, pl. -*ar*, mid20c, via Da (1 coll) < creat *blandari*   **Rs** *bl<u>e</u>nder* M, pl. -*y*, 1990s (1 tech)   **Cr** (0)   **Gr** *bl<u>e</u>der* mid20c (2)

blind date *n.* 1 'a social engagement between a man and a woman who have not previously met'

Ge [=E] N, pl. -*s*, 1990s (Ø>1 you)   **Du** [blaint+E] C, pl. -*s*, 1990s (1 you)   **Cr** (0)   **Po** < trsl *randka w ciemno*   **Fi** - < trsl *sokkotreffit*   **Hu** [=E] [U] end20c (Ø>1 writ, jour)   **Gr** (0)

blinker *n.* 1 'either of a pair of screens attached to a horse's bridle to prevent it from seeing sideways', 2 'a device that blinks, esp. a vehicle's indicator lights'

Ge 2(5)   **Du** 2(5)   **Nw** <=E>/*blinkers* [=E] M, sg., pl. -*er*, beg20c (1 tech)   **It** [bl<u>i</u>ŋker] M, pl. Ø, 1980s, 2 (1 tech) < *lampeggiatore*   **Rs** *bl<u>e</u>nker*/*bl<u>i</u>nker* M, pl. -*y*, mid20c, 2(1 tech)   **Hu** 2 (5Ge)

blister *n.* 2 'a bubble-like swelling on any surface', +5 'a blister pack'

Ge [=E] M, pl. Ø, +5(1 tech, rare)   **Du** [=E] C, 1990s, +5(1 tech)   **Sp** [bl<u>i</u>ster] M, pl. -*s*, 1980s, +5(1 tech)   **It** [=E] M, end20c, +5(1 tech)   **Rs** *blister* M, pl. -*y*, mid20c, +5(3 tech) → -*nyĭ* adj.   **Cr** (0)   **Bg** *blister* M, pl. -*al*-*i*, end20c, +5(1 tech)

blister pack *n.* 'a bubble pack'

Ge *Blister(verpackung)* M, 1970s (1 tech, rare)   **Du** *blisterverpakking* [=E+Du] C, 1960s (1 tech)   **Nw**

blisterpakning [=E+Nw] C, pl. *-er*, 1980s (1 tech)   **Fr**
blister(-pack) [blistɛʀ] M, 1980s (1 tech, ban) < *habil-*
lage (transparent) **Sp** (*envase*) *blister* M, 1980s (1
tech)   **It** - < ↑*blister*   **Rs** - < *blịster*   **Cr** (o)   **Bg** -
< ↑*blister*

blizzard   *n.* 'a severe snow-storm'
   Ge [=E] M, pl. *-s*, 19c (Ø)   **Du** [=E] C, beg20c (1 tech
   also metaphorical)   **Nw** [=E] M, pl. *-er*, 20c (Ø/1
   tech)   **Fr** [blizaʀ] M, 19c (1 tech)   **It** [blịdzard] M,
   pl. Ø, 1920s (1 tech)   **Po** [-art] M [U] beg20c (1
   tech)   **Cr** [=E] M, mid20c (Ø)   **Hu** [=E] [U] beg20c
   (1 tech/Ø)

block   *v.* 1a 'obstruct', (a passage etc.), +5a 'stop a
ball' (sport, esp. basketball)
   Ge - < *blockieren* (5Fr)   **Du** *blokken* [blɔkə(n)] 1970s,
   +5a(1 tech); *blokkeren* via Fr 1(5)   **Nw** *blokke* [blɔkə]
   1980s, +5a(3 tech); *blokkere* 1a(5Ge/Fr)   **Ic** *blokka*
   [plɔhka] end20c, +5a(3 tech)   **Fr** *bloquer* (4)   **Sp** *blo-*
   car +5a(5Fr)   **It** *bloccare* (5Fr)   **Rm** *bloca* 1a,
   5a(5Fr)   **Rs** *blokịrovat'* mid20c, 1a(3) +5a(3 tech) →
   -irovanie N   **Po** (5Fr)   **Cr** (o)   **Bg** *blokiram* mid20c,
   1a(3)   **Hu** *blokkol* (5Ge/Fr)   **Al** *bllokoj* 1950s (3)
   Gr *blokạro/blokạrisma* 1a(3) +5a(3 tech)

blocking*   *n.* 'a blocking action' (sport)
   Nw *blokk* [blok] M, pl. *-er*, 1980s (3 tech)   **Sp** - <
   blocage   **It** - < *bloccaggio*   **Rm** - < *blocaj*   **Rs** - <
   blokịrovanie   **Po** *bloking* [-nk] M, mid20c (1
   tech)   **Bg** - < *blok*, *blokạda*, *blokạzh*   **Al** *bllokịm* M
   [U] mid20c (3)   **Gr** *blok* N, beg20c (1 tech) →
   blokạrisma N

block-note*   *n.* 'a notebook'
   Du *blocnote/bloknote/bloknoot* [blokno:t] C, 1970s,
   via Fr (2) < *kladblok*   **Fr** *bloc-notes* [blɔknɔt] M,
   end19c (3)   **Sp** - < *bloc (de notas)* (5Fr)   **It**
   bloc(k)-notes [blɔknọtes] M, pl. Ø, mid20c, via Fr
   (3) = *taccuino*   **Rm** *blocnotes* [bloknọtes/-nọtes] N,
   mid20c (5Fr)   **Rs** (5Fr)   **Cr** (o)   **Gr** *blok* N, 20c (2)
   → *blokaki*

bloke   *n.* 'a man, a fellow'
   Ic *blók* [plou:k] F, pl. *blækur*, 1920s (3 coll)

Bloody Mary   *n.* 'a drink composed of vodka and
tomato juice'
   A large number of cocktails are commonly known
under their English names; *Bloody Mary* is here documented to represent this type of anglicism. The reference to Mary Tudor (1516–58) is likely to be facetious,
prompted by the colour of the drink.
   Ge [=E] F, pl. *-s*, end20c (1 tech)   **Du** [=E] C, pl. *-'s*,
   1980s (2)   **Nw** [=E] M, pl. *-s*, 20c (1)   **Ic** [=E] mid/
   end20c (2)   **Fr** [blɔdimaʀi] M, mid20c/1980s (1
   mod)   **Sp** [blạdi mẹri/blọdi mẹri] M [U] 1980s (1
   you, mod)   **It** [blạdi mẹri] M, pl. Ø, mid20c (1
   tech)   **Rm** [=E] N, pl. Ø, 1980s (1 mod)   **Rs** - < trsl
   krovạvaya mẹri   **Po** [-eri] F, end20c (2 coll)   **Cr** *bla-*
   dimẹri M, end20c (2)   **Bg** *blŭdi mẹri* F/N, pl. Ø/-*rita*,
   end20c (1 coll)   **Fi** [=E] (2)   **Hu** [=E] [U] 1970/80s
   (2)   **Gr** <=E> [=E] N, end20c (2)

bloomer(s)   *n.* 1 'women's knickers', 3 'women's
loose-fitting trousers', +4 'babies' knickers'

Turkish-style trousers were part of a reform of women's dress instigated by Amelia Bloomer (1818–94),
a famous fighter for women's rights and writer on
education and social reform (although the invention
of the *bloomer suit* may in fact be credited to Elizabeth
Smith Miller).
   Ge [blu:ma] M?, pl. *-s*, 1970s, 3(1 rare, obs) < *Pump-*
   hose   **Fr** *bloomer* [blumœr] M, 1930s, +4(1 tech)   **Sp**
   <=E>/*blumers* M, pl., 1920s, 3(1arch)   **Po** [-ers] pl.,
   beg20c (1 tech) → *bloomeryzm* M; *bloomerystka* F

blooming*   *n.* 'the making of iron into blooms' (steel
production)
   Fr [blumiŋ] M (1 tech)   **It** - < *blumo*   **Rm** *bluming*
   [=E] N, mid20c, via Fr? (2>3 tech)   **Rs** *blyuming* M
   [U] beg20c (1 tech)   **Po** *bluming* M, mid20c (1 tech)
   Cr *bluming* M [U] mid20c (1 tech)   **Bg** *bluming* M [U]
   beg20c (1 tech)

blow-out   *n.* 4 'an uncontrolled uprush of oil or gas
from a well'
   Ge [blo:aut] M, pl. *-s*, 1970s (1 tech, obs)   **Nw** [=E]
   M, pl. *-er/-s*, 1970s (1 obs) < trsl *utblåsning*   **Fr** (1
   obs)

blow-up   *n.* 1 'an enlargement of a photograph', 2 'an
explosion'
   Ge [=E] N/M, pl. *-s*, 1970s (o>1 mod)   **Du** [=E] C,
   1980s, 1(1 tech)   **It** [blou/blo ạp] M, 1970s, 1(1 tech)

blue   *adj.* 1 'having a colour like that of a clear sky', 2
'sad, depressed', 3 'indecent, pornographic', 5 'polit-
ically conservative'
   Nw *blå* [blo:] 5(4)   **Ic** [plu:] uninfl., end20c, 2(1 sla);
   blár mid20c,   3,5(4)   **It** *blu* uninfl.,   mid19c,
   1(5Fr)   **Po** [blu] uninfl., end20c, 1(1 mod)   **Al** *blu*
   beg20c, 1(5Fr)   **Gr** *blu-* cp¹, end20c, 1(2)

blue baby   *n.* 'a baby with a blue complexion from
lack of oxygen in the blood due to a congenital defect
of the heart or major blood vessels'
   Ge [=E] N, pl. *-(ie)s*, 1960s (1 tech_MED)   **Nw** [=E]
   M, pl. *-ies*, end20c (1 tech_MED)

blueback*   *n.* '(the skin of) a newborn hooded seal'
   Nw [=E] M, pl. *-er*, 20c(1 tech)

blue-beat   *n.* 'a Jamaican music style'
   Nw [=E] M [U] 1980s (1 tech)   **Rs** (o)

blue box   *n./cp²* 1 'an electronic device used to access
long-distance telephone lines illegally', +3 'a device
used in filming for special effects' (film)
   Ge [=E] F, pl. *-es/en*, 1980s, +3(1 tech, rare)   **Fr**
   méthode blue-box cp², 1990s, +3 (1 tech)   **Cr** (o)
   Bg *bluboks* M, pl. *-al-ove*, end20c, 1(1 tech)   **Hu**
   [=E] pl. Ø, 20c, +3(1 tech)

blue-chip   *n./cp¹* 'a reliable investment' (applied to
shares)
   Ge [=E] pl., 1980s (1 tech, rare)   **Du** [=E] C, 1980s (1
   tech)   **Nw** [=E] pl. *-s*, 1980s (1 tech)   **Fr** [=E] M,
   1980s (1 tech, ban) < *valeur de premier ordre*   **Sp**
   [blu tʃip] M, pl. *-s*, 1980s (1 tech) < *valor puntero*   **It**
   [=E] F, pl. Ø, 1980s (1 tech)

bluegrass   *n.* 1 'an American grass' 2 'a type of country music'
   Ge [=E] N [U] 1970s, 2(1 tech)   **Du** *blue-grass* C [U]

1980s, 2(1 tech)　**Nw** [=E] M [U] end2oc, 2(1 tech) > trsl *blágras, blágresi*　**Ic** [=E] N [U] end2oc, 2(1 tech) > trsl *blágras*; trsl *blágresi*　**Fr** (o)　**Sp** *blue grass/* <=E> [blu̱gras] M [U] end2oc, 2(Ø1 jour)　**Rm** [=E] N [U]

1970s, 2(1 tech)　**Rs** *blu̱gras* M [U] end2oc, 2(1 tech, mod)　**Po** [blugras] M [U] end2oc, 2(1 mod) → *-owy* adj.　**Cr** [=E] M [U] end2oc, 2 (1 tech) < *plava trava*　**Bg** *blu̱gras* M [U] end2oc, 2(1 tech)　**Gr** 2 (Ø)

blue jeans　*n.* 'denim trousers'

One of the most popular post-war loans, this word was first recorded in American English in 1901. The word has been spreading since 1955, notably unadapted, but is now more common in the shorter form ↑*jeans* and is normally untranslated (alternatives like **Ge** *Nietenhose* etc. have remained marginal).

Ge [=E] pl., 1950s (2 obs) < *Jeans*　**Du** [=E] pl., 1970s (1 arch) < *jeans*　**Nw** [=E] M, pl. Ø, 1960s (2 mod) < *jeans*　**Ic** - < *gallabuxur*　**Fr** *blue-jean(s)* [blud3in(s)] M, 1960s (1 obs) < *jeans* **Sp** [blujiṉs] M, pl., 1960s

(1 tech) < *jeans* < *vaqueros, tejanos*　**It** [blu d3inz] M, sg./pl., 1950s (3) < *jeans*　**Rm** *blugi* [blu̱d3i] M, pl., 1970s (2 coll); *blue jeans* [=E] M, pl., 1970s (1 rare) > *jeans*　**Rs** - < *dzhinsy*　**Po** [- d3ins] pl., end2oc (2 coll)　**Cr** *blu̱- džins* M, pl., end2oc (2 coll)　**Bg** *blu̱- dzhins* M, pl. Ø, 1990s (1) < *du̱nki*　**Hu** [=E] pl. *-ek*, mid2oc (2/3) < *farmer*　**Al** *bluxhins* M, pl. *-e*, 1970s (1 jour)　**Gr** *blu tzin/ blutziṉ* N, usu. sg., pl. Ø, mid2oc, via Fr (2)

blue line　*n.* 'either of the two lines midway between the centre of the rink and each goal' (ice hockey)

Nw [=E] M, pl. *-r*, 2oc (1 tech)　**Fr** - < trsl *ligne bleue*　**It** - < *linea blu*　**Rm** - < rend *linie albastră*　**Rs** - < trsl *sinyaya liniya*　**Bg** - < trsl *sinya liniya*　**Fi** - < trsl *siniviiva*　**Hu** [=E] (1 tech) < trsl *kékvonal*　**Gr** - < trsl *ble ghrammi*

blueprint　*n.* +1a 'a photographic print of the final stage of a book, in white on a blue background'

Ge - < rend *Blaupause*　**Du** [=E] C [U] 1990s (1 mod) < trsl *blauwdruk*　**Nw** - < rend *blåkopi*　**Ic** [=E] N, pl. Ø, mid/end2oc (o tech) < trsl *bláprent*

blue yodel* *n.* 'an American folk music style'

Nw [=E] M [U] 1980s (1 tech, reg)　**Gr** (Ø)

blues[1]　*n.* 'a bout of depression'

Ge (o)　**Du** [blu:s] 2oc (1 coll)　**Nw** (o)　**Ic** *blús* [plu:s] M [U] end2oc (1 sla) → *blúsa* v.; *blúsaður* adj.; *blúsari* M　**Fr** *(avoir le) blues/coup de blues* [bluz] 1980s (1 jour)　**Fi** [=E] 2oc (1)

blues[2]　*n.* (*pl.*) 2a (often treated as sg.) 'melancholic music of Black American folk origin', 2b (treated as sg.) 'a piece of such music', +3 'a slow-paced dance', +4 'slow jazz'

This term, popular since the 1920s in all European countries, has remained associated with Black American folk music, although the element 'melancholic' has occasionally led to its application to other types of music of a similar character.

Ge [blu:s] M, sg. [U] 1920s, 2a, b (1 tech)　**Du** [blu:s] C [U] beg2oc (2 tech)　**Nw** [=E] M, sg. [U] mid2oc, 2a, b(2) → *bluesete* adj.　**Ic** *blús* [plu:s] M, mid2oc, 2a(2); pl. *-ar*, mid2oc, 2b(2) → *blúsa* v.; *blúsaður* adj.; *blúsari* M; *blúsisti* M　**Fr** M [U] 1920s, 2,+4(2 tech)　**Sp** [blus] M [U] 1920s, 2a,+4(2 tech); pl. Ø, 2b(2 tech) → *blu(e)sero, blu(e)sista* adj.　**It** [=E] M, sg., 1930s, 2a(3); 1960s 2b,+3,+4(2)　**Rm** [bluz] N, 1960s (2)　**Rs** *blyuz* M, pl. *-y*, beg2oc, 2b,+3(2 tech, obs); sg. [U] 2a(2 obs)　**Po** [blus] M [U] beg2oc, 2a(2) → *-owy* adj.　**Cr** [=E] M, sg. [U] mid2oc, 2a, b,+3(1 tech)　**Bg** *blus* M, [U]/pl. *-a*, mid2oc, 2a,b,+3(2) → *-ov* adj.　**Fi** [=E] 2oc, 2(2)　**Hu** [=E] [U] 1920s (2/3)　**Al** *bluz* M [U] mid2oc, 2a,b(1 tech)　**Gr** *bluz* F/N [U] mid2oc, 2a,+3,+4(2)

bluesman*　*n.* 'a man who plays the blues'

The remarkable distribution of this term, which is restricted to Southern and Eastern Europe, suggests at least partial mediation through Russian. The term also illustrates the development of the loan-morpheme *-man* (as in ↑*tennisman*).

Fr (o)　**Sp** [blu̱sman] M, pl. *-men*, end2oc (1 tech) < *blusista*　**It** [blu̱zman] M, pl. Ø, 1930s (1)　**Rm** [blu̱zmen] M, 1970s (1 tech, jour)　**Rs** *blyuzmen* M, pl. *-y*, mid2oc (1 tech, arch)　**Po** [blusmen] M, end2oc (1 mod)

Cr [=E] M, mid2oc (1 tech)　**Bg** < *blusa̱r* M, pl. *-i*, mid2oc (1 tech) → *-ski*　**Gr** <=E>/*blu̱zman* M, pl. Ø/*-men*, end2oc (1 tech)

blueswoman*　*n.* 'a woman who sings or plays the blues'

Fr [bluzwuman] F, 2oc (1 tech, rare)　**Sp** [=E]/*blus wo̱man] F, end2oc (1 tech)　**It** [=E] F, pl. *-women*, end2oc (1 tech)　**Rm** (o/1 tech)　**Gr** *bluzghu̱man* F, 2oc (1 tech, rare)

bluff (1)　*n.* 1 'an act of bluffing, a show of confidence intended to deceive', +1a 'a trick in poker and other games', +2 'a card game'

An early loan transmitted through French into German etc. around 1900, whence it spread in its un-English pronunciation. Corresponding verbs were probably derived independently.

Ge [blöf] M, pl. *-s*, beg2oc, 1(3)　**Du** *bluf* [blyf] C [U] 1950s, 1(4); 19c, +2(4)　**Nw** *bløff* [blöf] M, pl. *-er*, beg2oc (3)　**Ic** *blöff* [plœf:] N, pl. Ø, 1920s, via Da, 1(2 coll) +1a(2 tech)　**Fr** [blœf] M, mid19c (2) → *bluffeur/-euse* M　**Sp** [bluf] M, pl. *-s*, beg2oc (2); *blofear* (1 reg)　**It** [blɛf/blœf/blaf] M, pl. Ø, 1910s (3) → *bluffare, bleffare* v.　**Rm** *bluf* [blœf/blaf/bluf] N, 1960s, 1(3 coll)　**Rs** *blef* M [U] beg2oc, 1(3) +1a(1 tech)　**Po** *blef* [blef] M [U] beg2oc, 1(3)　**Cr** *blef* M, pl. *-ovi*, beg2oc, via Ge, 1, +1a(3) → *-er* M　**Bg** *blüf* M, pl. *-al-ove*, mid2oc, 1(2) +1a(2 tech) → *blüfyo̱r* M　**Fi** *bluffi* [bluffi] 1980, 1, +2(o)　**Hu**

blöff [blœf] pl. *-ök*, beg20c, 1,+1a(3)   **Al** *blofg* M, pl. *-e*, 1980s (3)   **Gr** *blofa* F, beg20c, 1,+1a(3)

bluff (1)   *v.* 1 'make a pretence of strength or confidence to gain an advantage', 2 'mislead by bluffing'   **Ge** [blöfən] beg20c (3)   **Du** *bluffen* [blyfə(n)] 19c, 1,2(4)   **Nw** *bløffe* [bløfə] beg20c, pl. *-er* (3)   **Ic** *blöffa* [plæf:a] beg/mid20c, via Da (2 coll)   **Fr** *bluffer* mid19c (2)   **Sp** *blufear* beg20c (3a)   **It** *bluffare/bleffare* 1910s (3)   **Rs** *blefovat* beg20c (3)   **Po** *blefować* [blefovats] beg20c, 1(2) → *zablefować*   **Cr** *blefirati* beg20c, 1,2(3)   **Bg** *blüfiram* 20c, 1(3)   **Fi** *bluffata* 20c, 1,2(2)   **Hu** *blöfföl* [blœffœl] 1,2(3) → *-és* n.   **Al** *blofoj* 1980s (3 jour)   **Gr** *blofaro* beg20c (3)

blunder   *n.* 'a clumsy or foolish mistake'   **Du** [=E] C, 19c (3)   **Nw** [=E/blunder] M, pl. *-e*, mid20c (2)   **Fi** *blunderi* [blunderı] 20c (0)

blush   *n.* +3 'rouge, red powder for the cheeks'   **Du** [blʏʃ] C [U] (1 tech)   **Fr** [blœʃ] M, 1960s (1 tech)   **Sp** [bluʃ] M [U] end20c (1 tech)

board[1]   *n.* 4 'the directors of a company', 6 'the side of a ship', +6a 'the side of a lorry'

Since this word is shared by all Germanic languages (and early Anglo-French), its character as an anglicism is impossible to determine for most languages.   **Ge** *Bord* 6(5)   **Du** *boord* 6(5); *boord* [=E] C, 1990s, 4 (1 tech)   **Nw** *bord* 6(5)   **Ic** *borð* 6(5)   **Fr** *bord* 6(5)   **Sp** - < *bordo*   **It** [bɔrd] M, pl. Ø, end20c, 4(1 tech); *bordo* 6(5Fr)   **Rm** *bord* [bord] N, end19c, 6(5Fr/Ge/It); 1990s, 4(1 mod)   **Rs** *bort* M, pl. *-y*, beg20c, 6, +6a (3 tech)   **Po** *bord* [bort] M, beg20c, 6 (1 tech)   **Bg** *bord* M, pl. *-al-ove*, end20c, 4(2 tech) → *-en* adj.   **Al** *bord* M, pl. *-e*, beg20c, 4, 6(1 tech)

board[2]   *n.* +7 'a large outdoor advertisement board'   **Du** *bord* (4)   **Nw** <=E>/*boards* [=E] M, sg., 1980s (1 tech)   **Po** [bort] M, 1990s (2 jour)   **Bg** - < ↑*bilbord*

boarding   *cp*[1] 'having to do with the boarding of an aeroplane'   **Nw** [=E] 1980s (1)   **Po** (0)   **Bg** *bording* M [U] end20c (1 sla)   **Hu** [=E] 20c (1 tech)   **Gr** (0 tech/1 writ)

boarding card   *n.* 'a ticket needed to board an aeroplane'   **Ge** [=E] F, pl. *-s*, 1980s (1 tech) < *Bordkarte*   **Nw** [=E] N, pl. *-s*, 1970s (1) < trsl *ombord stigningskort*   **Ic** [=E] N [U] end20c (1 coll) < rend *brottfararspjald*   **Fr** - < trsl *carte d'embarquement*   **Sp** - < *tarjeta de embarque*   **It** - < trsl *carta d'imbarco*   **Rm** - < rend *ticket de bord/tichet de îmbarcare*   **Rs** - < trsl *posadochnyĭ talon*   **Po** *boarding* [bordink kart] F, end20c (1 tech)   **Cr** [=E] F, mid20c (1 tech)   **Bg** - < trsl *bordna karta*   **Fi** [=E] 20c (2)   **Hu** [=E] end20c (1 tech) < trsl *beszállókártya*   **Gr** (0/1 writ) < trsl *karta epivivasis*

boat   *n.* 1 'a small vessel for travelling on water'   **Ge** *Boot* N, pl. *-e*, 12c (3)   **Du** *boot* [bo:t] C, pl. *boten*, 15c (4)   **Nw** *båt* (4)   **Ic** *bátur* M (4)   **Fr** *bateau* [bato] M, 12c (3)   **Sp** *bote* M, 18c (3)   **Rs** *bot* M, pl. *-y*, 18c (1 tech) → *-ik* M   **Po** (0)   **Cr** (0)

boat people   *n.* 'refugees who have left a country by sea'   **Ge** [=E] pl., 1970s (Ø) < rend *Bootsflüchtlinge*   **Du** [=E] C [U] 1980s (1 jour)   **Nw** - < *båtflyktninger*   **Ic** - < trsl *bátafólk*   **Fr** [botpipœl] M, 1980s (1 jour)   **Sp** [=E/bout pipol] pl., 1970s (1 jour) < *balsero* (Cuba)   **It** [bɔt pi:pol] pl., 1970s (0 jour) > *profughi*   **Po** [-pipl] pl., end20c (1 tech)   **Cr** [=E] pl., end20c (Ø)

bob[1] (1)   *n.* 1 'a short hairstyle for women and children', +1a 'a haircut in this style'   **Ge** *Bob/Bobschnitt* [=E(+Ge)], M [U] beg20c/1980s, 1(1 tech); pl. *-s*, +1a (tech)   **Nw** [=E] M [U] 20c (1 tech)   **Sp** M [U] end20c (1 tech)   **Fi** - → *bobbaus* v.

bob[2] (2)   *n.* 3 'a bobsleigh' (sports)   **Ge** *Bob* [bop] M, pl. *-s*, end19c (3)   **Du** [=E] C, pl. *-s*, beg20c (3) → *bobben* v.   **Nw** *bob* [=E] M, beg20c (2)   **Fr** M, end19c (1 tech) → *bobeur*   **Sp** [bob/bobe] M, pl *-s*, 1920s (1 tech)   **It** [bɔb] M, pl. Ø, 1930s (3 tech) → *bobbista* n.   **Rm** [=E] N, beg20c (3 tech)   **Rs** *bob* M, pl. *-y*, end20c (1 tech)   **Cr** M, beg20c (1 tech)   **Bg** *bob* M, pl. *-al-ove*, 1970s (1 tech)   **Fi** (Ø)   **Hu** [=E] pl. *-ok*, end19c/beg20c (3 tech)   **Gr** *bob* N, end20c (1 tech)

bob[3]*   *n.* 'a game similar to billiards'   **Ic** *bobb* [pɔp:] N [U] 1950s (3)

bobbin   *n.* 1b 'a spool or reel for films', +3 (naut.) 'a big steel ball on a rope that rolls against the bottom of the sea'   **Ic** [pɔp:ıns] M, beg20c, +3 (1 tech); *bobbingur* [pɔp:ıŋkyr] M, pl. *-ar*, 1920s, +3(3 tech) = *botnvaltra*   **Rm** (5Fr)   **Rs** *bobina* F, pl. *-y*, beg20c, via Fr (3 tech)   **Cr** (0)   **Bg** *bobina* (5Fr)   **Hu** (5Fr) 20c, 1b (1 tech)   **Al** *bobinë* [bobin] F, pl. *-a*, beg20c, +3 (3 tech)   **Gr** *bobina* F, 20c, via Fr, 1b(3 tech)

bobbinet   *n.* 'machine-made cotton net'   **Ge** *bobinet* M, pl. *-s*, end19c (1 tech, arch)   **Du** [bobinıt] N [U] beg20c (1 tech)   **Nw** *bobinett* [bobinet] M [U] mid20c (1 obs)   **Ic** *bobínet(t)* [pɔbb:ine(h)t] N, pl. Ø, end19c (1 arch, mod)   **Fi** (0 tech)   **Hu** *bobinet (csipke)* [bobine(t)] [U] 20c? (1 tech/5Fr)

bobby (1)   *n.* 'a (British) policeman'   **Ge** (Ø)   **Du** (Ø)   **Nw** (Ø)   **Fr** (Ø)   **Sp** [bobi] pl. *-ies*, mid20c (Ø)   **It** [bɔbi] M, pl. Ø, mid20c (Ø)   **Rs** *bobbi* M, uninfl., mid20c (Ø)   **Po** *bobl* <=E> [bop/=E] mid20c (Ø)   **Cr** *bobi* M, pl. *-ji*, beg20c (Ø)   **Bg** *bobi* M/N, pl. *-ta*, mid20c (Ø)   **Fi** (Ø)   **Hu** [=E] pl. *-ik*, end19c/beg20c (Ø)   **Gr** (Ø)

bobsled   *n.* 'a bobsleigh'   **Ic** *bobsleði* [pɔp:-] M, 1970s (2+5 tech)   **Sp** (0)   **Po** (0) **Fi** (Ø)

bobsleigh   *n.* 1 'a sledge used for racing down an ice-covered run', +1a 'the sport of racing in these'

A popular sports term adopted in the late nineteenth century, soon shortened to its first element in many languages. The alternative ↑*bobsled* appears to have been comparatively rarely used, but shortening to ↑*bob* is common.   **Ge** [=E] end 19c (0 arch)   **Du** *bobslee* [bɔpsle:] C, pl. *-ën*, end19c, 1 (3) → *bobsleeën* v.   **Nw** [=E] M, pl. *-er/-s*, mid20c (1 tech) **Ic** *bobsleði* [pop:-] M, 1970s (2+5) **Fr** [bɔbslɛg] M, beg20c (1 tech) **Sp** [bob/bo(b)slei] M, pl. *-s*, beg20c (1 tech) **It** - < *bob* **Rm** *bobslei* [bobslej] N, beg20c (3 tech, arch) **Rs** *bobslei* M [U]

mid20c, +1a(3 tech) → *bobsleist* M **Po** bobslej [bopslej] beg20c (2) → *-owy* adj. **Bg** *bobslei* M [U] 1970s, +1a(3 tech) → *-ist* M **Fi** 1 (Ø) **Hu** [=E] pl. *-ek*, end19c/beg20c, 1(1 tech) **Al** *bobslej* M, pl. Ø, mid20c (1 reg) **Gr** - < *bob*

bobtail *n.* 1 'a docked tail' (of dog or horse), +2a 'a breed of dog'
Ge [=E] M, pl. *-s*, end20c, +2a(1 tech) **Du** [bɔpte:l] C, 1940s, +2a(2) **Fr** [bɔbtɛl] M, 1920s < *queue écourtée* **Sp** [bobtail/-ei-] pl. *-s*, 20c, +2a (2 tech) **It** [bɔbteil] C, 20c, +2a(2) **Rs** *bobtei'l* M, pl. *-i*, end20c (2 tech) **Bg** *bobtei̇l* M, pl. *-al-i*, end20c, +2a(1 tech) **Fi** [=E] 20c, +2a(2) **Hu** [=E] pl. *-ek*, 20c, +2a(2/3)

body *n.* 1 'the physical structure of a person', 3a 'the main or central part of a thing' (esp. a car), 9 'a bodysuit', +10 'a bodyguard' +11 'a well-built woman',
The shortened form *body* for 'body stocking' appears to have spread rapidly during the mid-1980s. The full form is rarer: *stocking* may have seemed descriptively misleading. *Body* also occurs as cp[1] referring to the human body mainly in relation to cosmetics (see ↑*bodylotion*).
Ge [bodi:] M, pl. *-(ie)s*, 1980s, 1(2 sla) 9(2) **Nw** [=E] M, pl. *-er*, 1980s, 9(2) **Ic** *boddí* [pɔt:i] N, pl. Ø, 1930s, 3a(2 coll) +11 (2 sla) → *boddíbíll* M **Fr** [bɔdi] M, pl. *-ys/-ies*, mid20c, 9(1 tech) **Sp** [bodi] pl. *bodys/bodies*, 1980s, 9,

+11(2) **It** [b[ɔ]di] M, pl. Ø, 1980s, 9(3) **Rm** [=E] N, 1990s, +9(1 tech[FASH]) **Rs** *bodi* N, uninfl., end20c, 9(1 mod) **Po** *body* N, uninfl., end20c, 9(1 mod) **Cr** *bodi* M, end20c, 9(1 mod) **Bg** *bodi* N/M, pl. Ø/-*ta*, 1990s, 1(1 coll, fac) 9, +10(1>2 mod) **Fi** *bodi* [bodi] 1980s, 9(2) **Hu** [=E] pl. *-ik*, 1990s, 9(2 mod) **Al** *bodi* M, pl. *-e*, 1990s, 9(1 you) **Gr** *bodi/ body* N, pl. Ø/-s, end20c, +11(1 jour); 9(2) < *rend kormaki*

body-art *n.* 'artwork on the human body'
Ge [=E] F [U] 1970s (1 tech, arch) **Du** [=E] C [U] 1970s (1 tech) **Nw** [=E] M [U] 1980s (1 tech) **Sp** [=E] M [U] 1970s (1 tech) **It** [bodi art] F, 1970s (1 tech) **Rs** (0) **Po** (0) **Cr** [=E] M [U] end20c (1 tech) **Bg** *bodiart* M [U] 1990s (1 tech, mod) **Fi** [=E] 1980 (1) **Hu** [bodia:rt] [U] end20c (1 tech) **Gr** (0)

bodybuilder *n.* 'a person who practises body-building'
Ge [=E] M, pl. Ø, 1960s (2) **Du** [=E] C, 1970s (2) **Nw** [=E] M, pl. *-e*, 1970s (2) > trsl *kroppsbygger* **Ic** [=E] M, 1970s (1 coll) < trsl *vaxtarræktar-*

maður **Fr** *bodybuildé* **Sp** - < *culturista* **It** - < *culturista* **Cr** [=E] M, pl. *-i*, 1980s (2 tech) **Fi** [bodibilderi] 1980s (0) **Hu** [=E] 1960s (2 tech) < *testépítő* **Gr** *bodybilder/bodibilder* M/F, 1980s (2)→ *bodibilderas/-u* M/F (3 sla)

body-building *n.* 1 'the practice of strengthening the body, esp. by shaping and enlarging the muscles, by exercise'
The phenomenon and the English term spread quickly in (Western) Europe from the 1960s onwards; note alternatives with (the potentially misleading) *cultur-*. The agent noun ↑*body builder* is rarer (apparently created by back formation) and the morphologically awkward verb is rarer still.
Ge [=E] N [U] 1960s (2) → *bodybuilden* v. **Du** [=E] C [U] 1940s (2) **Nw** [=E] M [U] 1970s (2) > trsl *kroppsbygging* **Ic** [=E] 1970s (1 coll) < trsl *vaxtarrækt* **Fr** *bodybuilding* [bodibildiŋ] M, 1980s (2) → *bodybuildé(e)* adj.

Sp [bodi bildin] M [U] end20c (1 tech, mod) < *culturismo* **It** [bɔdibildiŋ (g)] M [U] 1980s (2 tech) > *culturismo* **Rm** [=E] N [U] end20c (1 tech, mod) < *culturism* **Rs** *bodibilding* M [U] end20c (1 tech, mod) < *kul'turizm* **Po** [-ink] N, uninfl., end20c (1 tech) **Cr** *bodi-bilding* M [U] end20c (2 tech) **Bg** *bodibilding* M [U] 1990s (1 tech, mod) **Fi** [=E] 1980s (0) < *bodaus* → *bodata* v. **Hu** [=E] [U] 1950s (2 tech) < trsl *testépítés* → *bodizás* v. **Al** *bodibillding* M [U] 1990s (3) **Gr** *body bilding/bodi bilding* N [U] 1980s (2)

body-check *n.* 'a deliberate obstruction of one player by another' (sport)
Ge [=E] M, pl. *-s*, 1960s (1 tech) **Du** [=E] C, end20c (1 tech) **Nw** [=E] M, pl. *-s*, 1980s (1 tech, rare) **Fr** M, mid20c (1 tech) **It** [=E] M [U] end20c (1 tech) **Rm** *bodicec* [=E] N, 1960s (2 tech) → *bodiceca* v.

Cr *bodi-ček* M, mid20c (3 tech) **Bg** *bodichek* M, pl. *-al- chetsi*, mid20c (1 tech) **Hu** [=E] *bodicsek* [boditʃek] [U] 1950s (1 tech) **Gr** *body tsek/bodi tsek* N [U] end20c (1 tech)

bodyguard *n.* 1 'a person escorting and protecting another person' (politicians etc.), +1a 'a stout and strong-looking fellow', +2 'a special device for ensuring personal safety'
This word is still marginal, the concept being covered by native terms. Where it does occur, mostly in journalese, it has negative overtones.
Ge [=E] M, pl. *-s*, end20c, 1(1 mod) = trsl *Leibwächter* **Du** [=E] C, end20c, 1(1 mod) < trsl *lijfwacht* **Nw** [=E] M, pl. *-er/-s*, mid20c, 1(1) > *livvakt* **Ic** [=E] M [U] end20c, 1 (1 coll) +1a(1 sla) < trsl *lifvörður* **Fr** - < 1:

trsl *garde de corps, gorille* **Sp** - < I: rend *guardaespal-das* **It** - < I: trsl *guardia del corpo* **Rm** <=E>/*badigard* [b<u>o</u>digard/b<u>a</u>digard] M, end20c, I(2 mod) = rend *gardă de corp, gorilă* **Rs** b<u>o</u>digard M, pl. -*y*, 1990s, I(2) +2(3) < trsl I: *telokhranitel*; trsl +2: *telovhranitel'* **Cr** [bodigard] M, end20c, I(I mod) = trsl *tjelok-ranitelj* **Bg** b<u>o</u>digard/gard M, pl. -*ove*, 1990s, I(2) > ↑*body* **Fi** [=E] I(0) **Hu** I(0) < *testőr* **Al** *badigard* M, pl. -*ë*, 1990s (I) **Gr** I(0) < trsl *somatofylakas*

body lotion *n.* 'a lotion for the whole body'
Ge [=E] F, pl. -*s*, 1970s (I tech, rare) **Du** [=E] C, 1970s (2) **Nw** [=E] M, pl. -*er*/-*s*, 1970s (2) **Ic** [=E] N [U] mid20c (I coll) **Sp** - < *body-milk* **It** [b<u>o</u>di l<u>o</u>ſon] F, pl. Ø, 1970s (I) < *lozione per il corpo* **Rm** - < rend *loţiune (de corp)* **Rs** - < rend *los'on dlya tela* **Po** (0) **Cr** (0) **Bg** - < rend *losion za tyalo* **Fi** [bodilotion] [=E] 20c (0) **Hu** [=E] [U] end20c (I writ, mod) **Al** - < *locion përtrupin* **Gr** (I writ) < *ghalaktoma*

body-shirt* *n.* 'a body-stocking, a bodysuit'
Ge - < *Body* **Nw** [=E] M, pl. -*s*, 1960s (I obs) < *body* **Sp** - < *body* **It** - < *body* **Rs** - < *bodi* **Po** (0) **Cr** - < b<u>o</u>di M **Bg** - < b<u>o</u>di **Hu** - < *body, bodi* **Gr** - < b<u>o</u>dy/*bodi*

body stocking *n.* 'a woman's undergarment covering the trunk and legs'
Ge [=E] M, pl. -*s*, 1970s (I obs) < *Body* **Du** [=E] C, 1970s (I) **Nw** [=E] M, pl. -*s*, 1970s (I) < *body* **Ic** - < rend *samfella* **Fr** - < *body* **Sp** - < *body* **It** - < *body* **Rs** - < *bodi* **Po** - < *body* **Bg** - < b<u>o</u>di **Fi** *body* [=E] (2) **Gr** - < b<u>o</u>dy/*bodi*

bodysuit *n.* 'a close-fitting one-piece stretch garment for women'
Ge [=E] M, pl. -*s*, 1970s (I obs) **Nw** [=E] M, pl. -*s*, 1970s (I obs) < *body* **Sp** [=E] pl. -*s*, 1980s (I jour, rare) < *body* **Po** - < *body* **Gr** - < b<u>o</u>dy/-*i*/*kormaki*

bogey (I) *n.* 'a score of one stroke more than par' (golf) (cf. ↑*birdie*)
Ge [=E] M, pl. -*s*, 1980s (I tech, rare) **Nw** [=E] M, pl. -*s*, 1980s (I tech) **Ic** [pou:ci] N [U] mid20c (I tech) **Fr** <=E> M, mid20c (I tech) **Sp** [b<u>o</u>gi] 1930s (I tech) **Fi** (I tech) **Gr** <=E> [=E] N, pl. Ø/-*s*, end20c (I tech)

boghead *n.* 'a type of coal'
Fr [bogɛd] M, 19c (I tech) **Rm** [b<u>o</u>ghed] N [U] end19c (I tech) **Rs** b<u>o</u>gkhed M [U] beg20c (I tech) **Po** [bokhet] M [U] end20c (I tech) **Bg** b<u>o</u>gkhed M [U] mid20c (I tech) **Fi** (Ø)

bogie *n.* I 'a wheeled undercarriage pivoted below the end of a rail vehicle', 2 'a small truck used for carrying coal, rubble, etc.'
Du [=E] C, 19c, I(I tech) **Nw** *boggi* [b<u>o</u>gi] M, pl. -*er*, mid20c, I(2 tech) **Fr** *bogie/boggie* [b<u>ɔ</u>gi] mid19c, I(2 tech) **Sp** <=E>/*boje* M, pl. -*s*/*boggies*, end19c, I(2 tech) 2(I tech) **Rm** *boghiu* [bogjiu] N, beg20c, via Fr, I(3 tech) **Rs** b<u>a</u>ggi M, uninfl., mid20c, I(I tech) → -*ist* M

boiler *n.* I 'an apparatus for heating water', +5 'a man's pot belly'
The first sense has replaced an earlier, more technical sense designating part of a steam engine. Throughout Europe, native equivalents have retained connotations of clumsy officialese.
Ge [=E] M, pl. Ø, mid20c, I(2) > *Warmwasserbereiter* **Du** [b<u>ɔ</u>jlər] C, mid20c (2) > *heetwaterketel, warmwatertoestel, warmwaterreservoir* **Nw** (0) < I: *varmtvannsbereder* **Ic** - < I: *hitakútur* **Sp** [boiler] M, mid20c (I arch) < *caldera* **It** [b<u>o</u>iler] M, pl. Ø, 1960, I(3) < *scaldabagno* **Rm** [b<u>o</u>jler] N, 1940s, via Ge, I(3)

Rs b<u>o</u>iler M, pl. -*y*, mid20c, I(I tech) → *naya; nyĉ* adj. **Po** *bojler* [boiler] M, mid20c, I(2) **Cr** *bojler* M, pl. -*i*, mid20c, I(3) **Bg** b<u>o</u>iler M, pl. -*al-i*, mid20c, I(2) +5(3 coll, fac) → -*en* adj. **Fi** *boileri* [b<u>ɔ</u>ileri] I(3) **Hu** b<u>o</u>jler [=E] pl. -*ek*, 1920s–1950s, I(3) **Al** *bojler* M, pl. -*ë*, mid20c, I(I reg) **Gr** b<u>o</u>iler N, mid20c, I(I rare)

bolt *n.* 2 'a large pin with a head, used to hold things together'
Ge - < *Bolzen* (4) **Du** - < *bout* (4) **Nw** *bolt* (5Low-Ge) **Ic** *bolti* [p<u>o</u>lti] M, beg/mid20c, via Da? (4) **Rm** *bolţ* [bolts] N, beg20c (5Ge) **Rs** *bolt* M, pl. -*y*, beg20c (3 tech) **Cr** (0) **Bg** *bolt* M, pl. -*al-ove*, beg20c (2 tech) → -*ov* adj. **Fi** *pultti*, 20c (5Sw)

bond *n.* 4a 'a certificate issued by a government or a public company as a means of obtaining credit'
Ge [bont] M, pl. -*s*, end19c (I tech) < *Schuldverschreibung* **Du** [bont] C, 1990s (I tech) < *obligatie* **Nw** (0) < *obligasjon* **Fr** (Ø) **Sp** - < *bono, oblicación* **It** [bond] M, pl. Ø, end20c (I tech) < *titolo obbligazionario* **Rm** [=E] N, 1990s (I tech) **Rs** *bond* M, pl. -*y*, mid20c (I tech) < *obligatsiya* **Bg** - < *obligatsiya* **Fi** (Ø) **Hu** [=E] [U]/pl. Ø, mid20c (I tech) **Al** - < *bono, obligacion* **Gr** <=E>/*bod* N, pl. -*s*, 1990s (I tech, mod, rare) < *omologho*

booby trap *n.* 2 'an apparently harmless explosive device intended to kill or injure anyone touching it'
Du [=E] C, 1950s (I tech) **Nw** [=E] M, pl. -*s*, 20c (I tech, rare) **Fr** *booby-trap* [b<u>u</u>bitrap] M, 1940s (I tech, ban, obs) < *piège*

boogie *n.* 2 'a dance to pop music', +3 'a style of music' (cf. ↑*boogie woogie*)
Ge [=E] M [U] 1950s (2 obs) **Du** [=E] C [U] 1950s, 2(2 obs) **Nw** [b<u>u</u>gi/=E] M [U] 1960s, 2(I obs) +3(I tech) **Fr** [bugi] M [U] M, mid20c (I tech) **Sp** [b<u>u</u>gi] M, end20c (I tech) **It** [=E] M [U] 1940s (2) **Rm** [=E] N [U] 1960s (I obs) **Rs** - < *bugi vugi* **Po** - < *boogie woogie* **Cr** - < *boogie woogie* **Bg** - < *bugi vugi* **Fi** - < *boogie woogie* **Hu** [=E] 1930 (2a)

boogie-woogie *n.* I 'a style of playing blues or jazz on the piano', +2 'a dance (esp. children's) to a particular tune and words'.
The rhythmical piano blues style and the associated dance spread rapidly through Europe in the 1950s.

The exotic form of the word with its internal rhyme was no obstacle to its ready adoption. **Ge** [bugi: vʊgi:] M, pl. -s, 1950s (1 obs) **Du** [=E] C, mid20c (2) **Nw** <=E>/boogie [bʊgivʊgi/- vʊgi] M [U] mid20c (2) **Ic** [pu:ci vu:ci] N [U] mid20c, 1(2 tech) +2(2 you) **Fr** [bugiwugi] M, 1950s (1 obs) **Sp** <=E> [=E] M [U] mid20c (1 obs) **It** [bughivugi] M [U] 1940s (2) < *boogie-boogie* **Rm** [bugi ugi] N [U] 1960s, 1(1 obs) **Rs** *bugi-vugi* M, uninfl., mid20c (2 tech, obs) **Po** [bugiwugi] N, uninfl., end20c (1 obs) **Cr** *bugi-vugi* M [U] mid20c, +2(1 obs) **Bg** *bugi-vugi* N [U] mid20c (2 tech) **Fi** [=E] mid20c +2(2) **Hu** *bugi-vugi* [U] 1960s (2/3 obs) **Gr** <=E>/*bugi vugi* N [U] 1990s, +2(1 obs)

booing   *n.* 'an utterance of *boo*, esp. as an expression of disapproval made to a performer'

It is clearly difficult to prove that this onomatopoeic word was indeed borrowed, but its limited distribution may support this assumption.
Ge - < *Buhruf, Ausbuhen* **Du** - < *boe- geroep* **Nw** *buing* [bʉ:ing] C, 20c (3) **Fi** - < *buuata*

book   *v.* la (trans.) 'reserve', 4(intrans.) 'make a reservation'
Ge - < trsl *buchen* **Du** *boeken* (4) **Nw** *booke* (inn) [buke/bʉke] 1950s (2) → *fullbooket* **Ic** *bóka* [pou:ka] mid/end20c (4) **Sp** - < *reservar* **Po** *bukować* [bukowats] mid20c (1 tech) → *za-*v. **Cr** *bukirati* mid20c (2 tech) → *pre-*v. **Bg** - < *rezerviram* **Fi** *buukata* (2) **Hu** *bukkol* [bukkol] 1960s (1 tech) < *helyet foglal* **Al** - < *reservoj* **Gr** - < *kano booking*

booking   *n.* 'the act or an instance of booking or making a reservation'
Ge - < trsl *Buchung* **Du** - < *boeking* (5) **Nw** [=E] M, pl. -er, mid20c (2) **Ic** - < *bókun* **Sp** - < *reserva* **Rm** [=E] N [U] 1990s (1 tech, rare) **Po** (0) **Cr** *buking* M [U] end20c (2) **Bg** *buking* adj, uninfl., end20c (1 tech_{NAUT}) < *rezervatsiya* **Fi** *buukkaus* (2) **Hu** *bukkolás* [bukkola:ʃ] 1960s (1 tech) < *helyfoglalás* **Gr** <=E>/*bukin(g)* N [U] 1990s (1 tech) < *kratisi*

bookmaker   *n.* 'an agent who takes bets, calculates odds, and pays out winnings'

This term is associated mainly with horse-racing, a field which was dominated by the English language in the nineteenth century. It was occasionally transferred to other forms of betting. Note the scarcity of calques.
Ge (0 arch) < trsl *Buchmacher* **Du** [bukme:kər] C, beg20c (1 tech) **Nw** [=E/ma:kər] M, pl. -e, 20c (1 tech) **Ic** - < *veðmangari* **Fr** <=E>/*book* [bukmekœr] M, mid19c (1 tech) **Sp** [bukmeiker] M, pl. -s, beg20c (Ø/1 tech) **It** [bukmeiker] M, pl. Ø, end19c (1) = *allibratore* **Rm** [=E] M, end19c (1 tech) **Rs** *bukmeker* M, pl. -y, beg20c (1 tech) **Po** *bukmacher/bookmacher* [bukmaxer] M, beg20c, via Ge (1 tech) → -*ski* adj. **Cr** *bukmejker* M, pl. -i, end20c (1 tech) → -*ski* adj. **Bg** *bukmeikŭr* M, pl. -i, end20c (1 tech, mod) →

-*ski* adj. **Hu** *bukméker* [bukme:ker] pl. -*ek*, end19c/beg20c (1 tech/2) **Gr** <=E> [=E] M, pl. -s/*books*, end20c (1 tech)

boom (2)   *n.* 1 'a period of prosperity', +2 'a sudden increase', +3 'a school-/surprise party'

The spread of this term all over Europe is remarkable since it competes with both French *hausse* and native equivalents. Note the infrequency of the related verb (which may have been independently derived in German). An earlier meaning in German, 'aggressive advertisement', is now obsolete.
Ge [=E] M [U] beg20c (2) > *Hausse* → -*en* v. **Du** [=E] C, beg20c (2) > *hausse* **Nw** [=E] M, pl. -er, mid20c (2) **Ic** *búmm* [pum:] N [U] end20c, 1(1 sla) < *uppgangur* **Fr** [bum] M, end19c/beg20c, 1,+2(2 ban); 1950s, +3(2 sla) > 1,+2: *boum* **Sp** [bum] M [U] 1920s, 1,+2(2) **It** [bum] M [U] 1930s, 1,+2(2>3) **Rm** [bum] N [U] 1970s, 1,+2(1 jour) **Rs** *bum* M [U] mid20c, 1,+2(2) **Po** *bum*/<=E> [bum] M [U] end20c, 1,+2(2) **Cr** *bum* M [U] mid20c, 1,+2(1 tech) **Bg** *bum* M [U] 1970s, 1,+2(2) **Fi** *buumi* [bu:mɪ] 1,+2(2) **Hu** [=E] [U] mid20c, 1,+2(1 tech) < *fellendülés* **Al** *bum* M, pl. -e, end20c, 1(1 writ/3) **Gr** *bum*/<=E> N [U] end20c, 1,+2(1 tech)

boomerang   *n.* 1 'a curved flat hardwood missile which returns to the thrower', 2 'a plan that recoils on its originator', +3 'an object or person that returns quickly'

This foreignism (for the Australian Aboriginal weapon) is universal, with English mediation still apparent in its form. Various metaphorical usages may have been borrowed or may have evolved independently.
Ge *Bumerang* [buməraŋ] M, pl. -s, 19c, 1(1 tech); mid20c, 2(2) **Du** *boemerang* [bu:mərang] C, beg20c, 1,2(2 tech) **Nw** *bumerang* [bʉ:meraŋ] M, beg20c, 1,2(2), +3(1) **Ic** *búmerang(ur)* [pu:meran/pu:meraŋkʏr] M, pl. -*ar*, 20c, 1(Ø) > rend *bjúgverpill* **Fr** [bumrãg] M, mid19c, 1(1 tech) 2(2) **Sp** <=E>/*bumerán* M, pl. -s, end19c, 1(1 tech) 2(2) **It** <=E>/*bumerang* [bumeraŋ] M, pl. Ø, mid19c, 1,2(3) **Rm** *bumerang* [-raŋk] N, end19c, via Fr/Ge?, 1(3) **Rs** *bumerang* M, pl. -i, beg20c, 1(2) 3(2/1jour) **Po** *bumerang* [bumerank] M, beg20c, 1(1) 3(2) → -*owy* adj. **Cr** *bumerang* M, pl. -i, beg20c, 1,2(2) **Bg** *bumerang* M, pl. -a/-i, beg20c, 1(Ø tech) 2(2) → -*ov* adj. **Fi** *bumerangi* [bumeraŋɪ] 1(3), +3(1) **Hu** *bumeráng* [bumera:ng] pl. -*ok*, end19c/beg20, 1,2(2/3) **Al** *bumerang* [bumeran] M [U] mid20c, 1,2(1 you) **Gr** *bumerang* N, beg20c, 1(1 tech) 2(2)

boost   *v.* +2c 'raise the voltage of a particular frequency' (mus./tech.)
Ic *bústa* [pusta] end20c (1 tech) **Cr** (0)

booster   *n.* 1 'a device for increasing electrical power or voltage', 2 'an auxiliary rocket'

This term is spread evenly throughout Europe, obviously in its two senses, as part of an unambiguous technical jargon. Note French attempts to replace the international word.

Ge [=E] M, pl. Ø, 1970s (1 tech)   **Du** [=E] C, end20c
(2 tech)   **Nw** [=E] M, pl. -e (1 tech)   **Fr** [bustœr] M,
1940s (1 tech, ban) > 1: *suramplificateur*; 2: *accéléra-
teur/propulseur   secondaire/auxiliaire/pousseur*   **Sp**
[buster] M, pl. -s, 1980s (1 tech)   **It** [buster] M, pl.
Ø, 1940s (1 tech) = *amplificatore*   **Rm** [bustər] N,
1940s (1 tech)   **Rs** buster M, pl. -y, mid 20c, 1(1
tech) → nyi adj.   **Po** buster [buster] M, mid20c, 1(1
tech)   **Cr** buster M, pl. -i, end20c, 2(1 tech)   **Bg** buster M, pl. -al- i, mid20c, 1(1 tech)   **Fi** boosteri [bu:s-
teri] (3) < *vahvistin*   **Hu** búszter [bu:ster] pl. Ø, 1(1
tech); búszterrakéta [bu:sterrake:ta] 20c, 2(1
tech)   **Gr** buster N, end20c, 1(1 tech)

boot (1)   *n*. 1 'an outer covering for the foot, reaching
above the ankles', +1a 'a particular type of boot', +8
'the initial loading of a floppy disk' (comput.)
Ge [=E] pl., 1970s, 1,+1a(0>1 mod)   **Nw** boots [=E]
M, sg., 1970s, 1,+1a(2)   **Ic** only in ↑moonboots   **Fr**
boots [buts] M, pl., 1970s, 1(1 mod)   **Sp** booting
[butin] M, end20c, +8(1 tech) = *carga inicial*   **It**
[=E] M, pl. Ø, 1980s, +8(1 tech) < avvio   **Rs** butsy
F, pl., mid20c, +1a(3)   **Po** but [but] 1,+1a(5)   **Cr**
buce pl., end20c, 1,+1a(2)   **Bg** but M [U] 1990s,
+8(1 tech); boti pl., via Fr, +1a(3)   **Fi** buutsi [bu:tsɪ]
20c, +1a(2)   **Gr** <=E> [=E] N, pl. -s, end20c, 1(1
mod) +8(1 tech)

boot (up)   *v*. 3 'put a computer in a state of readiness'
(comput.)
Ge (hoch)booten [=E] 1980s (1 tech)   **Du** booten
[=E] 1980s (1 tech)   **Nw** boote [bu:tə] 1980s (1
tech)   **Fr** booter [bute] 1980s (1 tech, sla) < *amorcer,
lancer*   **It** - < *fare il boot up, avviare*   **Rm** buta [buta]
1980s (1 tech)   **Po** [but] end20c (1 tech)   **Cr** (0)   **Fi**
bootata [bu:tata] 1980s (1 tech, coll)   **Hu** [=E] end20c
(1 tech) → -ol v.

bootleg   *n./adj.* '(denoting) an illegal copy of a music
cassette, record or CD'
Ge [=E] N, pl. -s, 1970s (1 tech, rare)   **Du** → boot-
legging C   **Nw** [=E] M, pl. -es, 1980s (1 tech)   **Ic**
búttlegg [puhtlɛk:] N, pl. Ø; búttleggur [puhtlɛk:ʏr]
M, pl. -ar/-ir, end20c (1 tech, sla) = rend *sjóræning-
jaútgáfa*   **It** [butlɛg] M, pl. Ø, 1980s (1 tech) < *copia
pirata*   **Po** (0)   **Cr** [=E] M, pl. Ø, 1990s (1 tech)   **Bg**
- < *piratsko kopie*   **Fi** (Ø)   **Gr** butleg N, pl. Ø/-s,
end20c (1 tech, rare)

bootlegger   *n*. 1 'a smuggler', 2 'a person who copies
sound recordings illegally'
   This word shows an interesting diachronic development: the earlier adoption 'smuggler of illicit alcohol' is
a foreignism and widespread (but obsolescent or obsolete); the term for the more recent illegal copying of
recordings has not yet reached most of Eastern Europe.
Ge [=E] M, pl. Ø, beg20c, 1(1 arch); 1980s, 2(1
mod)   **Nw** [=E] M, pl. -e, beg20c, 1(1 arch); mid/
end20c, 2(1 tech)   **Fr** (Ø)   **Rs** butleger M, pl. -y,
beg20c, 1(Ø); 1990s, 2(1 jour)   **Po** butleger/<=E>
[butleger] M, beg20c, 1(1 you)   **Cr** butleger M, pl. -i,
beg20c, 1(1 arch)   **Bg** - < 1: *kontrabandist*, 2: *pirat*   **Fi** (Ø)   **Hu** [=E] pl. -ek, 19c, 1(Ø/2 obs)

bootstrap   *n*. 2 'the technique of loading a program
by means of a few initial instructions which make
possible the introduction of the rest of the program
from an input device' (comput.)
Du [=E] C, 1990s (1 tech)   **Nw** [=E] 1980s (1 tech)
Fr [butstrap] M, 1980s (1 tech,coll) → *système auto-
entretien*   **Sp** (0)   **It** [bu:tstrɛp] M, pl. Ø, 1980s (1
tech) = *caricamento del sistema*   **Rs** (0)   **Cr** (0)   **Bg**
(0)   **Hu** bootstrapprogram [bu:tstrep-] cp¹ [U] 1980s
(1 tech)

booze   *n*. 1 'alcoholic drink'
Nw [=E] M [U] mid20c (Ø/1 rare)   **Ic** bús [pu:s] N [U]
1950s (2 sla) → búsa v.; búsari M   **Cr** (0)

bop (1)   *n*. 1 'bebop, a type of jazz'
Du [=E] C, 1960s (1 tech) = *bebop*   **Nw** [=E] M [U]
1950s (1 tech)   **Ic** bopp [pɔhp] N [U] mid20c (3
tech)   **Sp** [=E] M [U] end20c (1 jour, rare)   **It** [bɔp]
M [U] 1950s (1 tech)   **Rm** [=E] N [U] 1970s (1
tech)   **Rs** bop M [U] 20c (1 tech)   **Po** M [U] mid20c
(1 tech)   **Cr** bap M [U] mid20c (1 tech)   **Bg** bop M
[U] mid20c (1 tech)   **Fi** - < *bebop*   **Hu** [=E] [U] 1940s
(3 tech)

bopper   *n*. 'a jazz musician who plays bebop'
Du [=E] C, 1970s (1 tech)   **Nw** [=E] M, pl. -e, mid20c
(1)   **Ic** boppari [pɔhparɪ] M, pl. -ar, mid20c (3
tech)   **Sp** [boper] M, pl. -s, end20c (1 jour, rare)
Rm [=E] M, 1970s (1 tech)   **Rs** (0)   **Cr** (0)

bord-case*   *n*. 'hand-luggage'
Ge [bɔrtke:s] M/N, pl. -s, 1960s (1 mod)   **Rs** - < rend
ruchnoi bagazh

borderline   *n*. (usu. *cp¹*) 1 'the line dividing two conditions' (esp. psychol.)
Ge [=E] F, pl. -s, 1980s (1 tech)   **Du** [=E] 1980s
(1)   **Nw** [=E] 1980s (1 tech)   **Ic** - < *jaðar*-   **Sp** [bor-
derlain/borderline] M/attr. [U] end20c (1 tech)   **It**
[bɔrdɛrlain] M/F, pl. Ø, 1980s (1 tech)   **Rm** [=E] N/
cp² [U] 1980s (1 tech)   **Bg** - < rend *granichen*
adj.   **Gr** <=E> [=E] N [U] end20c (1 tech)

boss (1)   *n*. 1 'a person in charge, an employer, manager or overseer', +2a 'leader'
   This word appears to be colloquial and often negative (except in Icelandic), thus complementing more
neutral terms (such as German *Chef*). Note the delayed borrowing in Eastern Europe, and the scarcity
of derivatives.
Ge [=E] M, pl. -e, beg20c, 1(3 pej)   **Du** baas 1(5) but
big boss [=E] C, pl. -es, 1980s (1 mod)   **Nw** [=E] M,
pl. -er, mid20c, 1(3) → bosse v.   **Ic** [pɔs:] M, usu. not
in pl., 1(2 coll)   **Fr** [bɔs] M, pl. Ø, end19c, 1(1 sla) →
bossisme?   **Sp** M, mid20c, 1(1 fac)   **It** [bɔs] M, pl. Ø,
1910s, 1(3)   **Rm** boss/bos [=E] M, 1960s, 1(2
coll)   **Rs** boss M, pl. -y, beg20c (2 pej)   **Po** bos/
<=E> M, beg20c (1 coll)   **Cr** bos M, pl. -ovi,
mid20c, 1(1 coll)   **Bg** bos M, pl. -ove, 1980s (2
coll)   **Fi** bosse [bɔsse] 20c, 1(1) < *pomo*   **Hu** [=E]
pl. Ø [U] end20c, 1(1 sla, mod)   **Al** bos M, pl. -ë,
mid20c, 1(1 you)   **Gr** bos M/N [U] end20c, 1(1 coll,
pej) +2a(1 sla)

boston   *n*. 1 'a dance', 2 'a card game', 3 'a type of dark woollen cloth for suits', 4 'a kind of cake filled with jam'

Both the card game and the dance were once widespread but now appear to be largely obsolete.

Ge [=E] M [U] 1910s, 1,2(1 arch) **Du** [bǫstɔn] N [U] beg20c, 1,2,3(1 arch) **Nw** [bǫston] mid19c, 1,2(1 arch) **Ic** [pɔston] N [U] end19c, via Da, 1,2(2 arch) **Fr** [bɔstõ] M, 19c, 1,2(1 arch) **Sp** [bǫston] M, 19c, 1,2(1 arch) **It** [bǎston] M [U] end19c, 1,2(1 arch) **Rm** [bǫston/boston] N [U] end19c, via Fr, 1,2(3 arch) **Rs** *bostǫn* M [U] beg20c, 1,2,3(1 arch) **Po** [-on] M, beg20c, 1,2,3(1 arch) → *-owy* adj. **Cr** M [U] beg20c, 1,2(1 arch) **Bg** *bostǫn* M, [U] beg20c, 1,2,3(1tech, arch) **Fi** [=E] beg20c, 2(1) 4(3) **Hu** *bǫszton* [boston] [U] 19c, 1,2(2 arch) **Gr** *bǫston* N [U] beg20c, 3(1 tech)

bottleneck *n.* 1 'a place where the flow of traffic, production, etc. is constricted', 2 'an obstruction to the flow of sth.', 3b 'a style of playing the guitar using a device worn on the player's finger'

Ge 2(0); 1970s, 3b(1 tech, rare) < 2: *Engpaß*; trsl *Flaschenhals* **Du** [=E] C, 1950s (1 tech) **Nw** (0) < trsl *flaskehals* **Ic** - < trsl *flöskuháls* **Fr** - < 1,2: rend *goulot d'étranglement* **Sp** [=E] M, end20c, 2(1 tech) **It** - < 1: *imbottigliamento* **Fi** - < trsl *pullonkaula* **Cr** - < trsl *usko grlo* **Gr** - < 1: creat *botiliarisma*

bottle party *n.* 'a party to which the guests bring drinks'

Ge [=E] F, pl. *-(ie)s*, 1950s (1 coll) **Po** (0)

bottom-up *n./cp¹* 'a type of analysis which starts at a detailed level and moves towards a more general level' (cf. ↑*top-down*)

Ge [=E] 1980s (1 tech, rare) **Du** [=E] 1980s (1 tech) **Nw** [=E] 1980s (1 tech) **It** [bǎttom ʌp] adj./adv., 1980s (1 tech) = *dal basso in alto* **Rm** [=E] 1990s (1 tech) **Fi** [=E] 1990s (1 tech)

bourbon *n.* 'an American whiskey distilled from maize and rye'

Ge [börbən] M [U] 1970s (1 tech) **Du** [=E] C [U] 1980s (2) **Nw** [=E] M [U] 1980s (1) **Ic** [purpo(u)n] N [U] mid20c (1) = *búrbónviskí* **Fr** [buʀbõ] M, mid20c (1 tech/2?) **Sp** [bųrbon] M, pl. *-s*, 1970s (1 tech) **It** [burbǫn/barbon] M [U] 1960s (1>2) **Rm** *burbon* [burbǫn] N [U] 1970s, via Fr (3) **Rs** *burbǫn* M [U] 1970s, via Fr (3 tech) **Po** (5Fr) **Cr** *burbon* M [U] mid20c (2) **Bg** *burbǫn* M [U] mid20c, via Fr (3 tech); *bųrbŭn* end20c (1 tech) **Fi** (0) **Hu** [=E] [U] 20c (1 tech/5Fr) **Gr** *berbon* N [U] mid20c (1 tech)

bowden-* *cp¹* 'a wire mechanism used to transmit tractive power' (named after its inventor Sir H. Bowden, 1880–1960)

Ge *Bowdenzug* [bau-] M, 1940s (2+5) **Du** *bowdenkabel* [bǫudən-] C, 1960s (2+5) **Rs** *boudenovskiĭ (tros), tros Boudena* **Hu** *bovden* [bǫuden] pl. Ø, end19c (3 tech)

bowie- *cp¹* 'a type of knife'

James Bowie (1799–1836) is a hero of American folklore, as one of the leaders of the Texan rebellion.

He was killed at the Alamo. He was the reputed inventor of this particular type of knife which became widely known, partly through literary references.

Ge *-messer* [bǫ:wi] 19c (1 obs+5) **Du** *bowiemes* [bǫ:wi-] N, beg20c (name+5) **Nw** *bowie-kniv* [=E+Nw] 19c (1 tech) **Ic** *bowiehnífur* M, 1870s (Ø) **Fr** - < trsl *couteau Bowie*, 19c (1 tech, reg) **Hu** [=E] [U] 19c (1 arch)

bowl *n.* 1 'a usu. round deep basin used for food or liquid', +5 'punch', +6 'vessel for punch'

The Continental development of this term led from the vessel used for mixing punch (18c) to the drink itself (*c.* 1850s). This is a famous *faux ami* which causes difficulties for English speakers.

Ge *Bowle* [bǫ:lə] F, pl. *-en*, 18c, +5,+6(3) **Du** [bo:l] 19c, +5, +6(2) **Nw** *bowle/båle* [bǫ:l(e)] M, pl. *-r*, mid19c, +5(3) **Ic** *bolla* [pɔl:a] F [U] beg20c, via Da, +5(3) **Fr** *(punch)bowl* 18c, +6(1 arch) **Sp** *bol* M, pl. *-es*, end19c, via Fr, 1(1 arch) **Rm** [=E] N [U] end19c, +5,+6(1 obs) **Cr** *bǫla* F, pl. *-e*, end19c, +5(3) **Bg** *bole* N [U] end20c, via Hu, +5(3 tech) +5(3) **Hu** *bólé* [bǫ:le:] pl. *-k/Ø*, via Ge, 19c, +5,+6(3) **Gr** *bol* N, via Fr, mid20c, +6(2)

Ic	Nw	Po	Rs
Du	Ge	Cr	Bg
Fr	It	Fi	Hu
Sp	Rm	Al	Gr

bowl *v.* 1b 'play bowls or skittles'

Ge [bǫ:lən] 1970s (1 rare) **Du** [bǫ:lən] C, beg20c (2) **Nw** *bowle* [bǫvle] mid20c (2) → *bowler* M **Rm** (Ø) **Fi** (Ø)

bowler (2) *n./cp¹* 'a man's hard felt hat with a round, dome-shaped crown'

The name comes from the nineteenth-century hatmakers Thomas and William Bowler. A similar hard roundish-brimmed hat is known in America as the 'derby'.

Ge (Ø) < *Melone* **Nw** *bowlerhatt* [bǫvler-] M, 20c (1) **Ic** [=E/pou:ler-] M, often cp¹, pl. *-ar*, beg20c (1 coll) = rend *(harð)kúluhattur* **Fr** - < *chapeau melon* **Sp** - < *bombín* **Bg** - < *bombe*

bowling *n.* 1 'British lawn bowls', +3 'the American form of skittles', +4 'a building containing bowling-alleys'

The American game is a recent import and is similar to the Continental form of skittles (German *Kegeln*). The American term serves to distinguish the two games where necessary. The British game was more widespread in the nineteenth century (cf. ↑*bowling green*) but has failed to compete with similar local forms (for example, French *boule* and Italian *boccia*).

Ge [bo:lɪŋ] N [U] 1960s, +3(2); 19c, 1(Ø) **Du** [bǫ:ling] N [U] 1960s, 1,+3,+4 (2 tech) < +3, +4: *kegelen* → *bowler* n.; *bowlen* v. **Nw** [=E/bǫvling] M [U] 1950s, +3, +4(2) **Ic** [pou:lɪŋ] N/F [U] mid/end20c, +3(1 coll) =

Ic	Nw	Po	Rs
Du	Ge	Cr	Bg
Fr	It	Fi	Hu
Sp	Rm	Al	Gr

creat *keila, keiluspil* **Fr** [bulɪŋ] M, 1950s, +3, +4(2) **Sp** [bǫulin] M [U] 1980s, +3, +4(1) < +3:

bolos; < +4: *bolera* **It** [b̪uliŋ] M [U] 1960s, +3(2) 1(Ø) **Rm** [b̪awling/b̪ow-] N [U] 1970s, +3, +4(2) **Rs** *b̪ouling* M [U] mid20c, +3, 1(Ø) **Cr** *b̪ovling* M [U] mid20c, +3 (1 tech) → *-aš* M **Bg** *b̪ouling* M [U] 1980s, +3, +4(1 tech, mod) < *kegli* **Fi** (Ø) **Hu** [bo:ling] [U] mid20c, 1, +3(1 tech) < *tekézés* **Gr** *b̪ouling* N [U] end20c (2)

bowling green *n.* 1 'a smooth green used for playing bowls', +2 'a lawn surrounded by garden beds'
Ge [=E]/*boulingrin* [=Fr] N, pl. *-s*, 19c, via Fr, 1(1 arch) **Nw** 1(o) **Fr** *boulingrin* [bulãgrɛ̃] M, 17c, +2(1 arch/tech) **Rm** [=E] N [U] end19c, 1(Ø/1 arch)

box (1) *n.* 1 'a container', 3 'a separate compartment', +3a 'a compartment for coal in the hold of a ship', +3b 'an isolation ward in a hospital', +3c 'a compartment for keeping a car in a garage', +3d 'an isolation compartment for working with radioactive substances', 4 'an enclosure or receptacle for a special purpose' (money ~, telephone ~), 12 'the penalty area' (south), +15 'a music loudspeaker', +16 'a simple camera', +17 'a kitchenette', +18 'a small flat', +19 'a playpen'
This word was first adopted as a horse-racing term, with a great number of other meanings borrowed later or developed independently, possibly supported by genetically related words from La *buxis* < Gr *pyxis*. The interdependence of meanings in European languages needs further investigation.
Ge [=E] F, pl. *-en*, 19c, 1(2) 3(1 tech_HORSES,CARS); 20c, +15(1 tech) +16(2) **Du** [=E] C, pl. *-en*, 19c, 3(1 tech); 20c, +15(3 tech) +19(3); end19c, +16(2 tech) **Nw** *boks* [=E] M, pl. *-er*, end19c, 1,3,4(3) **Ic** *box* [poxs] N, pl. Ø, end18c, 1(3) +3a(3 tech, arch) 4(3 arch) +15(1 tech)< 1,+3a,4: rend *-hólf*; < 12: rend *vítateigur*, +15:*hátalari* **Fr** [boks] M, end19c, 3(2 ban) < *compartiment* **Sp** M, pl. *-es*, 1920s, 3(1 tech_HORSES,CARS); 1980s, +3b(1 tech) **It** [boks] M, pl. Ø, end19c, 3,4(2) +3c(3) **Rm** *boxă* [boksə] F, end19c, via Fr, 1,3,+15(3); *box/bax* [baks] N, end20c, 1(2 mod) **Rs** *boks* M, pl. *-y*, mid20c, 3,+3b,+3c,+3d(1 tech) **Po** *boks* M, mid20c, 3(2) **Cr** *boks* M, pl. *-ovi*, mid20c, 3(1 tech) **Bg** *boks* M, pl. *-al-ove*, mid20c, 3,+3b, +3d(2) +17(3) → *-ov* adj.; *-onĕra* F **Fi** *boksi* [boksɪ 3(2) +15(1) +18(3 coll) **Hu** *boksz* [boks] pl. *-ok*, end19c/beg20c, 3(2/3 tech/Ø); [=E] 20c, +16(1 tech) **Al** *boks* M, pl. Ø, 1960s, 3,4(1 reg)

box (2) *v.* 1a 'fight (an opponent) at boxing' (↑*boxer*)
Ge *boxen*, 18c (3) → *Boxen* n. **Du** *boksen* [boksən] 19c (3) **Nw** *bokse* [boksə] mid19c (3) → *bokser* M; *boksing* C **Ic** *boxa* [poxsa] end19c, via Da (3) → *box* N = rend *hnefaleikar* **Fr** *boxer* [bokse] 18c (2) **Sp** *boxear* 19c (3) **It** *boxare* mid19c (3) **Rm** *boxa* [boksa] end19c, via Fr (3) **Rs** *boksirovat'* mid19c (3) **Po** *boksować* mid19c (3) **Cr** *boksati* end19c (3) **Bg** *boksiram (se)* beg20c (3) **Hu** *bokszol* [boksol] 17/18c (3) **Al** *bëj boks* mid20c (3)

box-calf *n.* 'a kind of leather'
Ge *Boxkalf* N [U] beg20c (3 tech) > trsl *Boxkalb* **Du** *bokscalf* [=E] N [U] mid20c (3 tech) **Nw** *bokskalv*

[=E+Nw] M, beg20c (1+5) **Ic** *boxkalf-*/*boxkálf-* cp¹, beg20c (1 tech) **Fr** *boxcalf/box* [boks] M, beg20c (1 tech, obs) **Sp** *boxcalf/boscal* [boscal] M, pl. Ø/-*s*, 1920s (1 tech) **Rm** *box* [boks] N [U] mid20c (3 tech) **Po** *boks* M [U] mid20c (1 tech) **Cr** *boks* M [U] beg20c (1 tech) **Bg** *boks* beg20c, via Fr (1 tech) **Hu** *boksz(bőr)* [boksbør] pl. *-ök*, end19c/beg20c (3 tech) **Al** *boks* M, pl. Ø, mid20c (1 tech) **Gr** *-* < (*dherma*) *box*

boxer¹ (1) *n.* 1 'a person who practises boxing'
This term for the sportsman was borrowed by all European languages at an early date; the verb was also borrowed, or adapted through backformation.
Ge [boksa] M, pl. Ø, 19c (3) **Du** *bokser* [boksər] C, 19c (3) **Nw** *bokser* [bokser] M, pl. *-e*, 19c (3) **Ic** *boxari* [poxsari] M, pl. *-ar*, 1900s, via Da (3) = rend *hnefaleikari* **Fr** *boxeur* [boksœr] M, 18c (3) **Sp** *boxeador* M, 19c (3) **It** *boxeur*, 19c, via Fr (3) < *pugile* **Rm** *boxer* [bokser/boksœr] M, beg20c, via Fr (3) **Rs** *boksër* M, pl. *-y*, 19c, via Fr (3) → *-skiĭ* adj. **Po** *bokser* [-er] M, mid19c (2) → *-ski* adj. **Cr** *bokser* M, pl. *-i*, end19c (3) → *-ski* adj. (3) **Bg** *boksyor* M, pl. *-i*, beg20c, via Fr (3) → *-ski* adj. **Hu** *bokszoló* [boksolo:] pl. *-k*, 17/18c (3) **Al** *boksier* [boksjer] M, pl. *-ë*, 1940s (1 sla) **Gr** *boxer* M, beg20c, via Fr (2) = *pyghmakhos*

boxer² (2) *n.* 2 'a dog with a smooth brown coat and puglike face'
Ge [boksa] M, pl. Ø, 19c (3) **Du** [boksər] C, 19c (3) **Nw** *bokser/boxer* [bokser] M, pl. *-e*, 19c (3) **Ic** [=E] M, end20c (1 tech) **Fr** *boxer* [boksɛr] M, 1920s, 2(2) **Sp** *boxer* M, beg20c, 2(2) **It** [bokser] M, pl. Ø, 1930s (2) **Rm** [=E] M, 20c, via Fr (3); *box* [boks] M, 1880s (3 arch) **Rs** *boksër* M, pl. *-y*, beg20c (2) **Po** *bokser* [-er] M, mid20c (2) → *-ski* adj. **Cr** *bokser* M, pl. *-i*, mid20c (3) → *-ski* adj. (3) **Bg** *bokser* M, pl. *-al-i*, end20c (2 tech) **Fi** *bokseri* [bokserɪ] (3) **Hu** *bokszer* [bokser] pl. *-ek*, 19c (3) **Gr** *boxer* N, end20c (2)

boxer-³* *n.* cp¹ (*-motor*) 'an opposed cylinder engine'
Ge *-motor* 20c (3 tech+5) **Du** *boxermotor* [=E] C, mid20c (2 tech) **Nw** *boksermotor* [=E+Nw] M, 1950s (1) **Ic** *boxermótor* M, mid20c (1 tech) = creat *boxervél*, *boxari* **Sp** (*motor*) *boxer* M, 20c (1 tech) **It** *motore -* [bokser] M, pl. Ø, mid20c (1 tech) **Po** (o) **Cr** (o) **Bg** *boksermotor* M, pl. *-al-i*, mid20c (1 tech) **Fi** *bokseri* (3) **Hu** *bokszer (motor)* [bokser-] pl. *-ok*, 20c (1 tech) **Gr** *boxer motor* N/M, 20c (1 tech) < trsl *kinitiras boxer; mikhani boxer*

boxer shorts *n.* 'men's (less frequently, women's) underpants similar to shorts'
This term rapidly became popular in the 1980s but remained restricted to 'Western' Europe; its currency contrasts with the more widely known ↑*shorts*. With reference to a single item, a new singular form *short* is frequently found.

Ge [=E] pl., 1980s (2) Du *box-ershort* C, 1980s (1 tech) < *box-er* Nw [=E] M, sg., 1980s (1 mod) Ic *boxerbuxur* F, pl., end20c (1 coll) = trsl *boxara-buxur* Fr *boxer(short)* [bɔk-sœrʃɔrt] M, 1960s (1 tech)

Sp *(calzoncillos/pantalón) boxer* M, pl. *-s*, end20c (1 tech) It *boxer (shorts)* [bɔkser] M, pl., 1980s (2) Bg *bokseri/bokserki* pl., 1990s (3 mod) Fi *bok-serit* pl., 1980s (3) Gr *boxer (sorts)* N, pl. *-s*, end20c (2) < *boxeraki*

boxing *n.* 'the practice of fighting with the fists, esp. in padded gloves, as a sport'
Ge - < *Boxen* Du - < *boksen* (3) Nw *boksing* [boks-ing] (3) Fr - < *boxe* F Sp - < *boxeo* It - < *boxe* F = *pugilato* Rm *box* N Rs - < *boks* M → *-irovanie* N Po - < *boks* M → *-owanie* N [U] Cr - < *boks* M Bg - < *boks* M → *-irane* N; *-ov* adj. Hu - < *bokszolás* Al - < *boks* M Gr - < *box* N = *pyghmakhia*

box office *n.* 1 'an office for booking seats and buying tickets at a theatre, cinema etc.', +3 'an entertainment popular enough to attract large paying audiences'
Du [=E] 1990s, 1(1 tech) Nw (0) Ic - < *miðasala* Fr [boksɔfis] M, 1950s (1) Sp [=E] M [U] end20c, 1(1 tech, jour, rare) It [bɔks ɔfis/ɔffis] M, pl. Ø, 1980s, 1(1) Rm [=E] N [U] 1970s, +3(1 jour)

boy *n.* 1 'a male child or youth', +2a 'an attractive young man' (homosexual), +3a 'a male servant at a hotel or in an office', +3b 'a native servant', +5 'a male music-hall dancer', +6 (*cp²*) 'an instrument for facilitating housework', +7 'a husky, provocative man'
    This term, apparently first adopted as a foreignism (cf. ↑*lady* etc.), came to be current in ↑*lift-boy* etc. in the late nineteenth century. There are various later extensions (mostly also found in English) with reference to the American army, and pop, and gay culture. Only the metaphorical(?) sense 'household aid' is clearly restricted to German (1960s).
Ge [=E] M, pl. *-s*, 19c, +3a(1 tech/arch); 1960s, +6(2) Du [=E] C, beg20c, 1(coll, reg) +3b(1 arch); 1980s, +2a(1) Nw [=E] M, pl. *-er/-s*, beg20c, +3b(Ø/1) Fr [bɔj] M, mid19c, +3b(1 arch); mid20c, +5(1 tech) Sp M, pl. *-s*, end19c, 1(1 fac), +3a(1 arch); 1920s, +3b(1 arch); 1930s, +5(1 jour); end20c, +2a(euph) It [=E] M, pl. Ø, beg20c, +3a(1) +5(2) Rm [=E] M, pl. Ø, 1970s, 1(Ø) +3a,b(1) Rs *boĭ* M, pl. *boi*, beg20c, +3a(1 coll, rare) Po *boj* M, beg20c, +3a(2) Cr *boj* M, beg20c, +3a(2) Bg *boĭ* M, pl. *boyove*, 1990s, +7(1 you, sla) Fi +3a(Ø) Hu [=E] pl. *-ok*, end19c, 1,+3a(3 tech)

boycott *n.* 'the refusal of social and commercial relations as a punishment or means of coercion'
    Charles Cunningham Boycott (1832–97), a retired officer employed as an agent for estates in Co. Mayo, was 'boycotted' by the Irish Land League. This is one of the early loans which had spread through Europe by 1900, often mediated through French. It is still very

frequent, with a host of derivatives in individual languages.
Ge [boikot] M, pl. *-e*, end19c (2) → *-ieren* v.; *-eur* M Du *boycot* [=E] C, pl. *-en/-s*, beg20c (2) → *-en* v. Nw *boikott* [=E] M, pl. *-er*, end19c (2) → *boikotte* v. Fr [bɔjkɔt] M, end19c (2) → *boycottage; boycotter* v.; *boycotteur* M; *boycotteuse* F Sp *boicot/boicoteo* M, beg20c, via Fr (3) → *-ear* v. It *boicottaggio* M, pl. *-i*, end19c, via Fr (3) Rm *boicot* [bojkɔt] N, end19c, via Fr (3) Rs *boĭkot* M, pl. *-y*, beg20c (2) Po *bojkot* M [U] beg20c (2) → *-owanie* N [U]; *-ujcy* M; *-owy* adj. Cr *bojkot* M [U] beg20c (2) → *-irati* v.; *-aš* M Bg *boĭkot* M, pl. *-al-i*, beg20c (2) Fi *boikotti*, 20c (3) Hu *bojkott* [bojkot] pl. Ø, end19c (2/3) → *-ál* v. Al *bojkotim/bojkot* [bojko'tim] M, pl. *-e*, mid20c (3) Gr *boikotaz* N, beg20c, via Fr (2) → *boikotarisma* N

boycott *v.* 1 'combine in refusing social or commercial relations with (a person, group, country, etc.) usu. as a punishment or means of coercion'
Ge *boycottieren*, end 19c (3) Du *boycotten* [bɔikətə(n)] end19c (2) → *boycotting* N Nw *boikotte* [boikotə] end19c (2) Ic *bojkotta/boykotta* [pojkˀ(h)ɔhta] end19c, via Da (1 tech, sla) Sp *boicotear* beg20c (3) It *boicottare* end19c (3) → *boicottatore* M Rm *boicota* [bojkotɑ] end19c, via Fr (3) → *-are* F Rs *boĭkotirovat'* 19c (3) → *boĭkotirovanie* Po *bojkotować* beg20c → *z-* v. Cr *bojkotirati* 20c (3) Bg *boĭkotiram* (3) → *-tirane* N Fi *boikotoida* 20c (3) Hu *bojkottál* [bojkotta:l] end19c (2/3) Al *bojkotoj* mid20c (3) Gr *boikotaro* 20c (3)

boyfriend *n.* 'a person's regular male companion'
Nw [=E] M, pl. *-s*, end20c (1 rare) Fr Ø Sp [=E] M, 1960s (1 fac, arch) It [=E] M, pl. Ø, 1940s (2) Rm [=E] M [U] end20c (0) Rs *boĭfrend* M, pl. *-y*, end20c (1 coll, you) Po M, end20c (1 coll) Cr [=E] M, end20c (1 coll, you) Bg *(boĭ)frend* M, pl. *-ove*, 1990s (1 you, mod) Hu [=E] pl. Ø, end20c (1 you, mod) < *fiú(barát)* Gr <=E> [=E] M, 1990s (0>1 coll, fac)

Boy Scout *n.* 'a scout' (cf. ↑*scout*.)
Ge (Ø) < *Pfadfinder* Nw (0) < *speider* Ic - < *scout* Fr [bɔj-skut] M, 1910s (1 sla/arch) Sp <=E>/*scout* [bojeskau(t)] M, pl. *-s*, beg20c (2) < *explorador* It [=E] M, pl. Ø, 1910s (3) → *scoutismo* n.; *scoutistico* adj. Rm (Ø) < *cercetaş* Rs *boĭskaut* M, pl. *-y*, end20c (1 coll) < *skaut* Po - < *skaut* Cr - < *skaut* Bg *(boĭ)skaut* M, pl. *-i*, end20c (1 tech) Hu [=E] pl. *-ok*, end19c/beg20c (1 arch, rare) < *cserkész*

boysenberry *n.* 1 'a hybrid of several species of bramble', 2 'the fruit of this plant'
Ge *Boysenbeere*, 20c (1+5) Nw boysenbær [=E+Nw] (1+5) Fr - < trsl *mûre de Boysen* (1 tech/

reg) **Rs** - < trsl *boĭzenova yagoda*   **Fi** *boysenmarja*, 20c (3+5)

brain   *n.* +4c 'a clever person'
Ic [=E] N, pl. Ø, end20c (1 sla)

brain drain   *n.* 'the loss of skilled personnel through emigration'

This term became popular from the late 1960s onwards, languages being neatly divided between borrowers and calquers. Initially coined for the loss of scientists to America, it now refers to any migration to another industrialized nation which has better jobs to offer.

Ge [=E] M [U] 1960s (1 tech) **Du** [=E] C, 1970s (1 tech) **Nw** [=E] M [U] 1960s (1 tech) **Ic** - < rend *atgervisflótti* **Fr** *brain drain* [brɛndrɛn] M (1 jour, obs) < *fuite des cerveaux* **Sp** M [U] 1970s (1 tech, jour, rare) < *fuga de cerebros* **It** [=E] M [U] 1970s (1 jour) < rend *fuga dei cervelli* **Rm** [=E] N [U] 1970s (1 jour) **Rs** *breĭn dreĭn* M, 1960s (1 jour) < rend *utechka mozgov* **Po** - < rend *drenaż mózgów* **Cr** [=E] M [U] 1970s (1 tech) < *odljev mozgova* **Bg** - < rend *iztichane na mozŭtsi* **Hu** [=E] [U] mid20c (1 tech) **Gr** (0)

brainstorming   *n.* 'a concerted, collective intellectual treatment of a problem'

This term appears to have been popularized in advertising circles. It is interesting to see that its restricted currency is divided between 'colloquial' and 'technical' uses, with few calques available.

Ge [=E] N [U] 1960s (1 coll) **Du** [brɛːnstɔrmɪŋ] C [U] 1960s (2) → *brainstormen* v. **Nw** [=E] M [U] 1960s (1) → *idédugnad* **Ic** [=E]/*brainstormur* M [U] 1970s (1 tech, sla) > creat *heilarok* **Fr** [brɛnstɔrmiŋ] M, mid20c

(1 tech, ban) = rend *remue-méninges* **Sp** [breinstormin] M [U] end20c (1 tech) > *tormenta de ideas* **It** [breinstorminŋ] M [U] 1980s (1 tech) **Rm** [=E] N [U] 1970s (1 tech) **Rs** (0) **Po** [-ormink] M [U] end20c (1 tech) **Cr** [brejnstorming] M [U] end20c (1 tech) > *moždana okuja* **Bg** - < trsl *mozŭchen shturm* **Fi** - < *aivoriiki* **Hu** [=E] [U] mid20c (1 tech) < trsl *ötletgyártás*

brain(s) trust   *n.* 'a group of expert advisers'

Coined for the group of economic experts convened to advise President Roosevelt, the word soon came to designate any advisory group of specialists; this general meaning was borrowed as a technical term (with a journalistic flavour) from the 1960s onwards. There are only a few calques, since the sense can be covered by existing words with a similar meaning.

Ge [brɛːntrast] M, pl. -*s*, 1960s (1 tech) > trsl *Gehirntrust* → -*er* M   **Du** [=E] C, 1960s (1 tech) = *vertrouwensraad* **Nw** <=E>/*hjernetrust* [=E+-trøst] M [U] mid20c (1 tech) **Fr** *brain-trust* [brɛntRœst] M, mid20c (1 tech/obs) **Sp** M, 1970s (Ø tech, jour) **It**

[=E] M, pl. Ø, 1930s (1 tech) < trsl *trust dei cervelli* **Rm** [=E] N, end20c (0>1 tech) **Rs** - < trsl *mozgovoĭ trest* **Po** - < rend *trust mozgow* **Cr** [=E] M, mid20c (1 tech) > trsl *trust mozgova* **Bg** - < trsl *mozŭchen trŭst* **Fi** - < *aivotrusti* **Hu** - < trsl *agytröszt*

brainwashing   *n.* 'the process by which ideas other than and at variance with those already held are implanted in someone's mind'

This concept has world-wide currency as a form of treatment of political prisoners (and is used rarely and metaphorically outside this context). The English term is said to be a calque on a Chinese expression of the 1950s. It provided the source for further calquing in individual languages, which is apparently much preferred to straightforward borrowing.

Ge - < trsl *Gehirnwäsche* **Du** [=E] C, 1970s (1 tech) < trsl *hersenspoeling* **Nw** (0) < trsl *hjernevask* **Ic** - < trsl *heilapvottur* **Fr** - < trsl *lavage de cerveau* **Sp** - < trsl *lavado de cerebro* **It** [=E] M [U] mid20c

(1 tech) < trsl *lavaggio del cervello* **Rm** (0) < rend *spălarea creierelor* **Rs** - < rend *promyvanie mozgov* **Po** - < rend *pranie mózgu* **Cr** [=E] M, mid20c (1 tech) < trsl *pranje mozgova* **Bg** - < rend *promivane na mozŭtsi* **Fi** - < trsl *aivopesu* **Hu** [=E] [U] mid20c (0) < trsl *agymosás* **Gr** - < trsl *plysi egefalu*

brainy   *adj.* 'intellectually clever or active'
Ic [=E] end20c (1 sla)

brakevan   *n.* 'a railway coach from which the train's brakes can be controlled'
Nw *brekkvogn* [brek-+Nw] end19c (4+5)

branding   *n.* +2 'a kind of tattooing'
Ge [=E] N [U] 1990s (1 tech)

brand new   *adj.* 'completely new'
Ge - < trsl *brandneu* (3>4+5) **Du** - < *brandnieuw* (5) **Nw** (0) **Gr** (0)

brandy   *n.* 1 'a strong alcoholic spirit distilled from wine or fermented fruit juice'

This term was borrowed from Dutch into English and shortened, then re-exported into European languages where it is now more or less equivalent to earlier native terms. It is more frequent in some compounds like ↑*cherry brandy.*

Ge [brendi] M [U] end19c (2 tech) < *Weinbrand* **Du** [brɛndi] C [U] beg20c (1 tech) = *brandewijn* **Nw** [=E] M [U] mid20c (1) **Ic** *brandi* [=E] N [U] beg20c, via Da (2) **Fr** [brãdi] M, pl. *brandys*, beg19c (1 tech) **Sp** M, pl. *-ies/-ys*, end20c (2) **It** [brendi] M [U] beg19c, 1(3) **Rm** [brendi] N, pl. Ø, 20c (2) **Rs** *brendi* M [U] beg20c (2) **Po** [-e-] N, uninfl., beg20c (2) **Cr** *brendi* M [U] beg20c (2) **Bg** *brendi* N [U]/pl. -*ta*, mid20c (2) **Fi** [=E] 20c (Ø) **Hu** *brendy* [=E] pl. -*ik*, end19c (2/3) **Al** *brandi* [brɛndi] M [U] 1960s (3/1 reg) **Gr** *brɑdi* N 20c (2) < *koniak*

brass *n.* 3 'brass wind instruments forming a band or section of an orchestra'
Nw [bras] M [U] 1970s/80s (2)   **Ic** [pras:] N [U] mid/end20c (2 tech) < *málmblásturshljóðfæri*   **Rm** [=E] 1970s (1 rare)   **Fi** (0)

brass band *n.* 'a group of musicians playing brass instruments'
Du [=E] C, 1970s (1 tech)   **Nw** [brạsban] N, pl. Ø, 1970s (2)   **Ic** *brassband* [pras:pant] N, pl. *-bönd*, mid/end20c (2 coll)   **Bg** *brạsbend* M, pl. *-al-ove*, 1990s (1 tech)   **Fi** [=E] (0)

break *n.* 2 'an interval; a pause in work', +3a 'a sudden breakthrough from a defence position', (sport) 4a 'a piece of good luck; a fair chance', +6c 'a point scored while one's opponent is serving' (tennis), 7 'a short unaccompanied passage for a soloist' (jazz), +9 (abbr.) 'breakdance', +10 'CB radio telephone', +11 'an estate car with a large rear door, esp. in French cars'
The use of *break* 'wagonette' (from *brake*), popular in the late nineteenth century, has long been obsolete. The word was reborrowed in the 1950s, as a jazz term, and to denote a sudden attack in team games. It was borrowed again in the 1980s as a tennis term, and this sense (+6c) is now certainly the most frequently used. From the 1980s, the word also became the preferred or sole form for 'breakdance' in French, Spanish, Romanian, Russian, Bulgarian, and Hungarian. The distributions of +10 'CB radio telephone' and of +11 'estate car' are not quite clear.
Ge [bre:k] N, pl. *-s*, 1980s, +3a(1 tech, rare) +6a(1 tech) +10,+11(1 rare); *Bräke* 7(1 tech) > +10: *Breake* → *-en* v.   **Du** [bre:k] C, 1970s, 2,+6a,+11(1 tech)   **Nw** [=E] N, pl. Ø/-s, mid20c, +3a,+6a,7,+9(1 tech)   **Ic** *breik* [=E] N, pl. Ø, mid20c, 2,4a(1 sla) 7(1 tech, sla) +9(1 you, mod)   **Fr** [brεk] M, beg20c, +6a(1 tech, ban); 1920s/80s, 7(1 tech); 1980s, +9 (1 mod) 19c+1950s, +11(2) > *brèche*   **Sp** [=E/brek] M, pl. *-s*, end20c, 2(1 fac, rare) +6a,7(1 tech, obs); 1970s, +11(1 tech) < *ranchera*   **It** [brεk] M, pl. Ø, 1940s, 2(1>2); +3a,+6a(1 tech); +11(0>1 tech, obs)   **Rm** *brec/break* [brek/=E] N, mid20c, +6a,7(2 tech); cp², +11(2); 1980s, +9(2 you, mod)   **Rs** *breïk* M, pl *-i*, mid20c, +6a(2 tech); [U] end20c, +9(2 you, mod)   **Po** M [U] mid20c, 2,+3a,+6a(1 tech)   **Cr** [=E] M, mid20c, +6a,7(1 tech)   **Bg** *brek* M, mid20c, +6c(3 tech); *breïk* M, pl. *-al-ove*, mid20c, 7(1 tech); [U] 1980s, +9(3 tech)   **Fi** [=E] 7(1 mod)   **Hu** [=E] pl. *-ek*, end19c/beg20c, +6a,7(1 tech); 1980s, +9(2 mod, you) → *-el* v.   **Al** *brejk* M, pl. *-ë*, 1980s, +6a(1 tech)   **Gr** *breịk* N, pl. Ø/-s, 20c, 2(1 jour, mod); 1990s, +6a(1 tech) 7(1 tech)

break *v.* 2b 'have an interval between spells of work', 20 'win a game against an opponent's service' (tennis), 21 'come out of a clinch', (box.) +21a *interj.* 'referee's command to separate' (box.)
Ge [bre:kən] mid20c, 20(1 tech) +21a(1 tech, rare)   **Nw** *breake* [breikə] end20c, 21,+21a(0)   **Ic** *breika* [prei:ka] end20c, 2b(1 sla)   **Sp** <=E> mid20c, +21a

(1 tech)   **It** [brεk] M, pl. Ø, 1940, 21(3) +21a(3)   **Rm** *brec/break* [brek/=E] beg20c, +21a(2>1 tech)   **Rs** *breïk* mid20c, +21a(3 tech)   **Po** mid20c, +21a(2 tech)   **Bg** *brek* mid20c, +21a(3 tech)

breakage *n.* 2b 'damage caused by breaking' (esp. for goods, merchandise)
Ge [=E] N, pl. *-s*, beg20c (0 tech, arch)   **Nw** *brekkasje* [brekạ:ʃje] M, pl. *-r*, 20c (4)

breakdance *n.* 'an acrobatic street dance of the 1980s' (cf. ↑ break +9)
As a name for a spectacular and much popularized acrobatic dance, this term quickly spread with the craze, but it was already felt to be obsolescent or historical in 1995. Note the frequent short forms, which occur despite the fact that national equivalents of *dance* would have been available for partial translation.
Ge [brε:kdans] M [U] 1980s (1 mod, obs) → *breakdancer* M; *breaker* M   **Du** [=E] C [U] 1980s (1 obs)   **Nw** *breakdans* [=E+Nw], 1980s (1 mod) → *breakdanser* M; *breake* v.   **Ic** *breikdans* [=E] M [U] 1980s (1 you, mod)   **Fr** - < *break* M   **Sp** <=E>/*break* [breikdans/breịk/brek/breạk?] M/(F) 1980s (1 mod)   **It** [brεkdεns] F [U] 1980s (1 tech)   **Rm** ↑*break*   **Rs** *breïk/breịkdans* M [U] 1980s (2 mod) → *-ovyï* adj.   **Po** [-a-] M [U] end20c (1 jour, mod)   **Cr** [=E] M, end20c (1 mod) → *-r* M   **Bg** - < *breïk*   **Fi** [=E] 1980s (2)   **Hu** - < *break* → *-el* v.   **Gr** *breịkdans* N [U] 1980s (1 mod, obs)

breakdown *n.* 1b 'a loss of mental health and strength', +4 'an electrical failure', +5 'a chemical disintegration'
Ge [=E] M [U] 1980s, 1b(0>1 coll) < *Zusammenbruch*   **Du** [=E] C, 1970s (1 mod) < *instorting, inzinking*   **Nw** [=E] N, pl. Ø/-s (1) < *sammenbrudd*   **Ic** [=E] N [U] 1960s, 1b(1 sla) < *taugaáfall*   **Fr** (0)   **It** [breikdaun/brεkdaun] M, pl. Ø, end20c, +4(1) < *arresto*   **Rm** [=E] N [U] 1980s, 1b(1 tech)   **Gr** <=E>/*breikdaun* N, end20c, +4(1 rare) < *blackout*

break even *v.* 'emerge from a transaction with neither profit or loss'
Nw *gå break even* [=E] 1980s (1 tech)

break-even (point) *n.* 'the point at which profits and losses are balanced'
Ge [=E] M, pl. *-s*, 1980s (0 tech)   **Du** [=E] N [U] 1980s (1 tech)   **Nw** *break even* [=E] 1980s (1 tech)   **Sp** <=E>/*break even* [=E] M (1 tech) < *punto de equilibrio, punto muerto*   **It** [breikị:ven/brek ịven] M, pl. Ø, end20c (1 tech) < *pareggio di bilancio*

breakfast *n.* 'the first meal of the day'
Ge (Ø)   **Nw** (0)   **Fr** [brεkfœst] M, mid19c (2)   **Sp** [=E] M, end19c (0>1)   **Rm** (Ø>1)   **Gr** (0)

breeches *n.* 1 'short trousers fastened below the knee', +1a 'women's saddlebags'
This term, borrowed together with horse-racing and riding fashions of the late nineteenth century, was apparently restricted to Central Europe (possibly transmitted through German?).
Ge [brị:tʃis] pl., 19c (1 tech) < *Reit(er)hosen*   **Du**

[=E] pl., mid20c (1 tech) < *rij-broek* **Sp** [britʃes] beg20c, 1(1 tech, obs) **Rs** *bridzhi* pl., mid20c (3 tech/you) **Po** *bryczesy* [britʃesi] pl., mid20c, 1(1 coll) **Cr** *bričesi* pl., beg20c (1 obs) **Bg** *brich* M, pl. *-a/-ove*, beg20c, 1(3); *brichove* +1a(3) **Fi** (Ø) **Hu** *bricsesz* [britʃes] pl. Ø, end19c/beg20c, 1(2/30bs) > *csizmanadrág*

breeder reactor   *n.* 'a nuclear reactor'

    Ge - < trsl *Brüter* **Du** - < *kweekreactor* **Nw** *brider-(reaktor)* [briːder+Nw] M, 1970s (1 tech) **Fr** - < *surgénérateur* **Sp** - < *reactor reproductor* **It** *breeder* [briːder] M, pl. Ø, 1970s (1 tech) **Cr** (o) **Bg** *brüder reaktor* M, pl. *-ora/-ori*, end20c (1 tech) **Al** - < *reaktor bērthamor*

breeding   *n.* 1 'the process of developing or propagating animals or plants'

    It [briːdiŋ] M [U] 1950s (1 tech)

bridge¹   *n.* 5 'a dental structure used to cover a gap, supported by teeth on either side'

    Ge - < mean *Brücke* **Du** - < mean *brug* **Nw** - < mean *bru* **Ic** - < mean *brú* **Fr** [bʀidʒ] M, beg20c [=E] (1 tech) **Sp** - < mean *puente* **It** - < mean *ponte* **Rm** [=E] N [U] 1930s (1 tech, arch) < mean *punte* **Rs** - < mean *most* **Po** - < trsl *mostek* **Cr** - < mean *most* **Bg** - < mean *most* **Fi** - < mean *silta* **Al** - < mean *urë* **Gr** - < mean *ghefyra*

bridge²   *n.* 1 'a card game derived from whist'

    This card game (first recorded in the Near East in the 1870s) became popular throughout (upper-class) Europe after 1900; it is notable that—in contrast to the dental term—no calques have apparently been prompted (this is also the case for ↑*whist* and ↑*poker*).

    Ge [britsch] N [U] beg20c (2) **Du** [=E] N [U] mid20c (2 tech) → *-en* v. **Nw** [briʃ] M [U] beg20c (2) **Ic** *bridge/bridds* [prɪts] N/M [U] beg20c, via Da (2) > trsl *brú* **Fr** M, beg20c (2) **Sp** [britʃ] M [U] beg20c (1 tech) **It** [bridʒ] M [U] 1900s, 1(3) **Rm** [=E] N, 1930s, via Fr (2); → *-ist* M; *-istă* F; *-istic* adj. **Rs** *bridzh* M [U] beg20c (2) **Po** *brydż* M [U] beg20c (3) → *-yk* M; *-ysta* M; *-ystka* F; *-owy* adj. **Cr** *bridž* M [U] beg20c (3) **Bg** *bridzh* M [U] beg20c (2) → *-yor* M **Fi** [=E/brɪdge] (2) **Hu** *bridzs* [=E] [U] beg20c (2>3) → *-el* v. **Al** *brixh* [bridʒ] M [U] mid20c (2/3) **Gr** *britz* N [U] beg20c (2)

briefing   *n.* 1 'a meeting for giving information' (usually to journalists or within the military)

    This term was (marginally) adopted from military contexts, aviation and journalism, but has only very slowly been transferred to more general topics—again, predominantly in journalese.

    Ge [=E] N, pl. *-s*, 1970s (1 tech) → *briefen* v. **Du** [=E] C, 1970s (1 tech) **Nw** *brifing* [=E/ briːfiŋ] M [U] 1950s (2) → *briefe* v. **Fr** [bʀifiŋ] N, mid20c (1 jour) < *bref* → *briefer* v. **Sp** [brifiŋ] M [U] 1970s (1 tech) **It** [briːfiŋ] M, pl. Ø, 1970s (1 tech) **Rm** [=E] N, 1990s (1 tech, jour) **Rs** *brifing* M, pl. *-i*, end20c (1

jour) **Po** [brifink] M, end20c (1 jour) **Cr** *brifing* M, end20c (1 tech) → *brifirati* v., *brifiranje* M **Bg** *brifing* M, pl. *-al-i*, 1990s (2 jour) **Fi** - < *briiffaus* **Gr** *brifin(g)* N, pl. Øl-s, 1990s (1 tech, jour)

brig (1)   *n.* 1 'a two-masted square-rigged ship'

    The Romance *brigantine* was shortened in English to *brig* c. 1720 and thence borrowed into many European languages. Its age and non-distinctive form make it difficult or impossible to identify it as an anglicism (possibly felt to be from Dutch?).

    Ge *Brigg* pl. *-s*, end18c (3) **Du** *brik* C, pl. *-ken*, 18c (3) **Nw** *brigg* [=E] M, pl. *-er*, mid19c (3) **Ic** *brigg* [prɪk:] N, pl. Ø; *briggur* [prɪk:ʏr] M, pl. *-ir*, end18c, via Da; F, pl. *-ur* = creat *briggskip* **Fr** *brick* [bʀik] M, end 18c (1 tech) **Sp** *brick* M, pl. *-s*, mid19c (1 arch) < *bergantín* **It** - < *brigantino* **Rm** *bric* [brik] N, end19c, via Fr (3) **Rs** *brig* M, pl. *-i*, 18c (1 tech) **Po** *bryg* [brik] M, mid19c (1 tech) **Cr** <=E> M, pl. *-i*, mid19c (3) **Bg** *brig* M, pl. *-a/-ove*, end19c (1 tech) **Fi** - <*brigantiini* F **Hu** *brigg* [brigg] pl. *-ek*, beg20c (1 tech) **Gr** *briki* N, end19/beg20c (3 rare)

bright   *adj.* 3 'clever, talented, quick-witted'

    Du [=E] 1990s (1 sla, mod) **Nw** [=E] 20c (1 sla) **Ic** [prait] mid20c, 3(1 sla)

brinkmanship   *n.* 'the art or policy of pursuing a dangerous course to the brink of catastrophe before desisting' (esp. of international politics)

    Ge [=E] F [U] 1960s (1 tech, rare) **Du** [=E] N [U] 1950s (1 tech)

Bristol board   *n.* 1 'a kind of pasteboard for drawing on', +2 'a visiting card'

    Ge *Bristolkarton* M, pl. *-s*, beg20c, 1(1 tech, rare) **Du** *bristol* [brɪstɔl] N, beg20c, 1(1 tech) → *-karton* n.; *-papier* n. **Fr** *bristol* [bʀistɔl] M, mid19c, 1(1 tech) +2(3) **Sp** - < *cartulina/papel Bristol* **It** *bristol* [bristol] M, pl. Ø, 1(1 tech) **Rm** *bristol* [bristol] N, end19c, via Fr, 1(1 tech) **Rs** *bristol'* M [U] beg20c, 1(3 tech) < trsl *bristol'skiĭ karton* **Po** *brystol* M, mid19c, 1(3) **Bg** *bristol* M [U] beg20c (3 tech) **Fi** *Bristolin kartonki* 20c, 1(1) **Hu** *brisztolkarton* [bristolkarton] pl. *-ok*, 19c, 1(1 tech) **Gr** *khartoni Bristol* N, 20c, 1(3+1 tech); *bristol* N, via Fr (1 tech)

broiler   *n.* 1 'a chicken raised for broiling or roasting'

    This term is a rare case in having an almost exclusively Eastern European distribution, mediated through Russian (and Bulgarian). It is now quickly becoming obsolete in Eastern Germany.

    Ge [=E] M, 1960s (1 reg, obs) < *Brathähnchen* **Nw** [=E] M, pl. *-e*, 1960s (2 obs) **Rm** [=E] M/cp², end20c (1 tech) **Rs** *broïler* M, pl. *-y*, end20c, 1(3) → *-nyĭ* adj. **Po** *brojler* [-er] M, mid20c (2) → *-owiec* M **Cr** *brojler* M, pl. *-i*, mid20c (2) **Bg** *broĭler* M, pl. *-al-i*, mid20c (2) → *-ov* adj. **Fi** *broileri* [brɔileri] 20c (3) **Hu** <=E>/*broyler* [=E] M, 1960s (1 tech)

broke   *adj.* 'having no money; financially ruined'

    Ic *brók* [prou:k] uninfl., mid20c (1 sla) **Cr** (o)

broker *n.* 2 'a person dealing in stocks and shares'

This term used to be a foreignism (complementing the native *Makler*, *courtier* etc.), but appears to be gaining ground in Eastern Europe—and elsewhere as a fashionable alternative.

Ge [bro̱:ka] M, pl. Ø, 1960s (Ø>1 tech, mod) < *Makler* **Du** [=E] C, 1970s (1 tech) **Nw** [=E] M, pl. *-e*, 1980s (1 mod) < *mekler* **Ic** - < rend *miðlari* **Fr** [brɔkœʀ] M, 1980s (1 tech, ban) > *courtier* **Sp** [bro̱ker] M, pl. *-s*, 1930s (1 tech) < *corredor, intermediario financiero*; → *-ismo* n. **It** [brɔker] M, pl. Ø, 1960s (1 tech) > *mediatore* **Rm** [=E] M, end20c (1 tech) **Rs** *bro̱ker* M, pl. *-y*, end20c (1 tech) → *-skiĭ* adj. **Po** [broker] M, beg20c (1 tech) **Cr** *bro̱ker* M, pl. *-i*, mid20c (1 tech) → *-ski* adj. **Bg** *bro̱ker* M, pl. *-i*, 1990s (1 tech) → *-ski* adj. **Fi** (Ø) **Hu** *bróker* [bro̱:ker] pl. *-ek*, 20c (1 tech) **Gr** *bro̱ker* M, pl. Ø/*-s*, end20c (1 tech, mod)

brokerage *n.* 1 'the action or service of a broker', 3 'a broker's fee or commission'

It [brɔkera3] M, pl. Ø, 1970s, 1(1 tech) = *brokeraggio* **Rm** *brokeraj* [brokəra3] N [U] 1990s, 1(3 tech); cp², 3(3 tech) **Rs** *brokera̱zh* M [U] end20c, via Fr, 3 (1 tech) **Cr** (0) **Bg** *brokera̱zh* M [U] mid20c, via Fr, 1(1 tech_NAUT)

-brothers *cp²* (used with a proper name) 'a group of close relatives working together' (show-business, sports, etc.)

Ge [bra̱zas] pl., 1960s (1 jour) **Du** (0) **Nw** (0) **Fr** <=E> 20c (1 fac) **It** [bra̱derz] M, pl., 1960s (1) **Rm** (Ø) **Bg** - < trsl *Bratya* **Gr** <=E> [=E] pl., 20c (1/Ø)

browning (orig.™) *n.* 'a type of pistol'

Named after the inventor John Moses Browning (1855–1926), who together with his two brothers produced three types of firearms, of which the automatic pistol became especially popular. The name was well-known in the early twentieth century but is now probably obsolete in most languages.

Ge [=E] M, pl. *-s*, beg20c (2 tech, obs) **Du** [=E] C, beg20c (1 tech) **Nw** [bro̱wniŋ] M, pl. *-er*, 20c (1 tech) **Ic** [=E] (Ø) **Fr** [bʀoniŋ] M, beg20c (1 tech) **Sp** [bra̱unin/bro̱unin] F, pl. Ø, 1920s (1 tech) **It** [bra̱uniŋ] F, pl. Ø, 1920s (1 tech) **Rm** [bra̱wning] N, 1920s, via Fr (2 tech) **Rs** *bra̱uning* M, pl. *-i*, beg20c (3 tech) **Po** *brauning/*<=E> [- nk] M, beg20c (2 tech) **Cr** *bra̱uning/*<=E> M, pl. *-zi*, beg20c (2) **Bg** *bra̱uning/bro̱uning* M, pl. *-al-i*, beg20c (1 tech) **Fi** *brovninki* [brɔvnɪŋkɪ] 20c (1 tech) **Hu** [=E] pl. *-ok*, end19c (2 obs) **Gr** *bra̱uning* N, 20c (1 tech)

brunch *n.* 'a late-morning meal eaten as the first meal of the day'

This word is still quite marginal apart from fashionable or facetious uses. In Europe generally having a late breakfast as a first meal at around 11 o'clock is unusual and does not urgently require a designation.

Ge [=E] N, pl. *-s*, 1970s (1 mod) → *-en* v. **Du** [=E] C,

pl. *-esl-en*, 1960s (2 coll) → *brunchen* v. **Nw** [brønʃ] M, pl. *-er*, 1960s (1) **Ic** [prœns] M [U] end20c (1 coll) **Fr** [brœnʃ] M, pl. *-sl-es*, 1970s (1 mod) **Sp** [brantʃ] M, 1980s (Ø/1 jour, fac) **It** [brantʃ] M, pl. Ø, end20c (1 mod) **Rm** (0) **Rs** *branch* (0) **Cr** [=E] M, pl. *-evi*, end20c (1) **Fi** *brunssi* 1980s (2) **Hu** [=E] pl. Ø, 1990s (1 writ, jour, mod) **Gr** <=E>/ *brants* N, 1990s (2 mod)

brush *n.* +1a 'a brush used to curl the hair'
Du - < *brusje* **Nw** [brøʃ] M, pl. *-er*, 1980s (1 tech)

brushing *n.* 1 (orig.™) 'a hairdressing technique of cutting hair after rolling it onto a round brush'
Du [=E] C, 1970s (1 tech) **Fr** [brœʃiŋ] M, 1960s (1 tech) > 1: *mèche-à-mèche* **Sp** [braʃin/broʃin] M [U] end20c, via Fr (1>2 tech) **Cr** (0) **Gr** *bra̱sing* N, mid20c, via Fr (1 tech)

bubble *n.* +5 'goods that are worth nothing'
Po *buble* [buble] pl., mid20c (3)

bubble bath *n.* 1 'a preparation for adding to bath-water to make it foam'
Du *bubbelbad* [by̱bəlbɑt] N, pl. *-en*, 1970s (2 tech) **Ic** *bubblebað* [pœp:el-] N, 1960s (1+5 coll) < trsl *freyðibað* **Hu** - < trsl *habfürdő* **Gr** - < rend *afrolutro*

bubblegum *n.* 'chewing-gum that can be blown into bubbles'
Ge [ba̱bəlgam] N, pl. *-s*, 1970s (1 jour, you) **Du** *bubbelgum* [by̱bəlɣym] C [U] 1970s (2) **Nw** (0) < trsl *bobletyggegummi* **Ic** [puplekum] N, mid20c (1 coll, you) < creat *blöðrutyggjó, kúlutyggjó* **Fr** M, 1970s (1 you) **It** [bu̱bblɛ gum/=E] M, pl. Ø, mid20c (1 jour, you) **Rm** [=E] N [U] end20c (1 you) **Rs** *ba̱bl' gam/bubl' gum* M [U] 1980s (1 coll, mod) **Po** (0) **Cr** [=E] M, end20c (1 you) **Bg** (0) < rend *dǔvka za baloni* **Hu** (0 writ) **Gr** (1 writ) < trsl *tsikhlofuska*

buckram *n.* 1 'a type of cloth used in book-binding' **Ge** [bu̱kram] M [U] beg20c (3 arch) **Du** [by̱kram] N [U] 1940s (1 tech) **Fi** [=E] (1 tech)

buckskin *n.* 2 'a thick smooth cotton or woollen cloth'
Ge [bu̱kskin] M [U] mid19c (1 tech, obs) **Nw** [=E] M [U] mid19c (1 obs) **Ic** *búkk- /bokkskinn* [puhk-/pɔhkscɪn:] N [U] mid19c, via Da, 2(2 obs) **Fi** [=E] 19c? (1 tech) **Hu** [bu̱kskin] [U] end19c (1 tech, obs)

budget *n.* 1 'money needed or available for a person or project', 2a 'national revenue and expenditure', 2b 'an estimate or plan of expenditure in relation to income', 3 (*cp¹*) 'cheap'

This early loanword appears to have been exclusively mediated through nineteenth-century French. It is certainly not felt to be an anglicism

Ge [bydʒeː] N, pl. -s, via Fr, 2a(3 tech) = *Etat*   **Du** [bʏdʒɛt] N, pl. -s/-en, beg19c, 2a,b(2 tech) 3(3) → -*tair* adj.; -*eren* v.; -*ering* n.   **Nw** *budsjett* [bʉdʃɛt] N, pl. -*er*, mid19c, 2a,b(3)   **Ic** [putsjeht] N [U] end20c, via Da, 1,2b(1 coll) < 2b: rend *fjárhagsáætlun*   **Fr** [bydʒɛ] M, 18c, 2a(3); 19c, 2b(3) → *budgétaire* adj.; *budgétiser* v.   **Sp** [baˈdjet] M, beg20c, 1(o arch); mid20c, via Fr 2a(o arch) < 2a: *presupuesto*   **It** [baˈdʒɛt/bydʒe] M, pl. Ø, 18c (2)   **Rm** *buget* [buˈdʒɛt] N, end19c, via Fr, 2a,b(3) → -*ar* adj.; -*ivor* adj.   **Rs** *byudzhet* M, via Fr, 2a,b(3) → -*nyĭ* adj.   **Po** *budżet* M, beg19c, 1,2a,b(2) → -*owanie* N; -*owy* adj.   **Cr** *budžet* M, pl. -*i*, 2a(3) → -*ski* adj.; -*irati* v.   **Bg** *byudzhet* M, pl. -*a/-i*, end19c, via Fr, 1,2a,b(3) → -*en* adj.   **Fi** *budjetti*, 19c, via Sw, 2a(3)   **Hu** *büdzsé* [bydʒeː] pl. Ø, 17/18c, via Fr, 1,2a(1 tech)   **Al** *buxhet* [budʒet] M, pl. -*e*, 1920s, 1,2a(1 tech)   **Gr** <=E>/*batzet* N, pl. Ø/-s, 1990s, 1,2a,b(1 tech, mod)

buffer (1)   *n.* 1b 'a railway device that protects against or reduces the effect of an impact', 3 'a temporary memory area to aid data transfer between programs operating at different speeds etc.' (comput.)

This word is one of a set of railway terms exported, along with the products, to most European countries. Note that in most early loans the written form appears to have been borrowed.

Ge - < 1b: *Puffer*   **Du** [bʏfər] C, 19c(3)   **Nw** <=E>/*buffert* [buˈfer(t)] M, pl. -*er*, beg20c, 1b(3); 1980s, 3(1 tech)   **Ic** [=E] M [U] end20c, 3(1 tech) < rend *bið-minni*   **Fr** - < mean *tampon*   **Sp** [bufer] M, pl. -s, 1980s, 3(1 tech)   **It** [bɪfer] M, pl. Ø, 1980s, 3(1 tech) = *tampone*   **Rs** *bufer* M, pl. -*y*, beg20c(3) → *nyĭ*   **Po** *bufor* M, beg20c (2) → -*owy* adj.   **Cr** *bafer*/<=E> M, pl. -*i*, beg20c (3)   **Bg** *bufer* M, pl. -*a/-i*, beg20c (2 tech) → -*en* adj.   **Fi** *buffertti* 20c (1 tech)   **Gr** <=E>/*bafer* N, end20c, 3(1 tech)

bug   *n.* 3 'a concealed microphone', 4 'an error in computer program or system'

Ge [=E] M, pl. -s, end20c, 4(1 tech)   **Du** [=E] C, 1980s, 4(1 tech)   **Nw** [=E] M, pl. -s, 1980s, 4(1 tech)   **Ic** *bögg* [pœːk:] N, pl. Ø, end20c, 4(1 tech) = trsl *lús*   **Fr** [bœg] M, 1970s, 4(1 tech, ban) < *bogue*   **It** [bʌg] M, pl. Ø, 1980s, 4(1 tech) = *baco, errore di programma*   **Rm** [=E] N, end20c, 4(1 tech)   **Rs** *bag* M, pl. -*z*, 1980s, 3(1 tech)   **Po** [bak] M, end20c, 4(1 tech)   **Cr** *bag* M, pl. -*ovi*, end20c, 4(1 tech)   **Bg** *bŭg* M, pl. -*a/-ove*, end20c, 4(1 tech)   **Fi** (Ø)   **Hu** [=E] 1970s, 4(1 tech)   **Gr** <=E>[=E] N [U] end20c (1 tech)

bug   *v.* 1 'conceal a microphone in' (esp. a building or room), 2 'annoy, bother'

Nw *bugge* [bøggə] 1980s, 1(1 tech)   **Ic** *bögga* [pœk:a] end20c (2 sla) → *bögg* N; *böggaður* adj.   **Rs** - → *bagging* M [U] 1990s, 1(1 tech)   **Cr** (o)

buggy   *n.* 1 'a horse-drawn cart', 2 'an open, small, sturdy car with its chassis reduced in size', 3 'a pram', +4 'casual/sports clothes'

This term was borrowed for the (American) horse-drawn cart in the nineteenth century, mainly as a foreignism. The vehicle is now obsolete (outside groups like the Old Amish etc.) and with it, this sense of the term. The term was then transferred to *beach buggies* etc. and so is marginally used as a loan-word. Slightly more current, however, is the adoption of *(baby) buggy* from American English of the 1980s.

Ge [bagi] M, pl. -(*ie*)*s*, 1980s, 2(1 tech) 3(2)   **Du** [bagi] C, pl. - 's, beg20c (1 tech)   **Nw** (o)   **Fr** [bygi/bœge] M, beg19c, 1,2(1 arch) > *boghei/boguet*   **Sp** [bugi] M, pl. -*ies*, 20c, 1(1 tech, obs) 2(1 tech, rare)   **It** [bagi] M, pl. Ø, 1980s, 2(1 tech)   **Rm** [bagi] N, end19c, 1,2(1 tech, rare)   **Bg** *bŭgi* N, pl. -*ta*, 1980s, 2(1 tech)   **Hu** [bugi] pl. -*k*, end19c, 1,2(1 arch)   **Gr** *bagi* N, pl. -s, end20c, 2(1 tech)

bugle-horn   *n.* 1 'a brass instrument used by huntsmen and for military signals', +1a (*pl.*) 'generic name for wind instruments'

Ge *Bügelhorn* 1(4+5)   **Du** *bugel* [bʏɣəl] C, beg20c, 1(1 tech, arch)   **Nw** 1(o) < *signalhorn*   **Fr** *bugle* [bygl] M, 19c, 1(1 tech)   **Rm** *buglă* [buglə] F, 1970s, via Fr, 1,+1a(3 tech)   **Po** [bjuklhorn] M, end20c, 1(1 tech)

building   *n./cp²* 1 'a permanent fixed structure forming an enclosure and protecting against the elements', +1a 'a skyscraper'

Ge (o)   **Du** [bɪlding] C, 1970s, +1a(1 reg) < *flatgebouw*   **Nw** (o)   **Fr** [b(y)ildiŋ] M, end19c, +1a(2)   **Sp** M, 1920s, +1a(1 tech rare/obs) < *rascacielos, torre*   **Rm** [bilding] N, 1970s, 1(1 jour/Ø)   **Rs** (o)   **Bg** *bilding* M, pl. -*a/-i*, end20c, via Fr, +1a(Ø/1 jour, rare)   **Gr** cp² (o/1 writ)

bulk   *n./cp¹* 5 'a ship's cargo'

Ge [=E] cp¹, 20c (1 tech)   **Du** [bʏlk] C [U] 1940s (3 tech)   **Nw** [bølk/bʉlk] cp¹, 20c (2 tech/3tech)   **Bg** *bŭlk* M [U] mid20c (1 tech)

bulk carrier   *n.* 'a ship equipped for loading and unloading in bulk'

Ge [=E] M, pl. Ø, 1960s (1 tech, rare)   **Du** [bʏlk+=E] C, 1960s (3 tech)   **Nw** [bølk-/bʉlk-+=E] M, pl. -*e*, 20c (1)   **Fr** [=E] M, mid20c (1 tech, ban) < *vraquier*   **Sp** *bulkcarrier* M, 1960s (1 tech) = (*buque*) *granelero*   **Cr** *balkarijer* M, pl. -*i*, mid20c (1 tech)   **Bg** *bŭlkerier/bŭlker* M, pl. -*a/-i*, mid20c (1/3 tech)

bulldog   *n.* 1a 'a dog of a sturdy powerful breed with large head and smooth hair', +3 'a single-cylinder tractor' (orig.™).

The dog's name became popular along with those of other British breeds in the late nineteenth century when it spread over (almost) all of Europe. The +3 sense is an obvious metaphorical extension based on physical strength.

Ge *Bulldog* M, via Fr?, 1a(1 arch); *Bulldogge* F, pl. *-n*, 19c, 1a(3); [=E] M, pl. *-s*, 20c, +3(2 tech) **Du** *buldog* [b<u>y</u>ldɔɣ] C, pl. *-gen*, beg20c(2) **Nw** *bulldogg* [b<u>u</u>ldog] M, pl. *-er*, end19c, 1a(3) **Ic** [=E] mid20c, 1a(0 tech) < rend *bolabitur* **Fr** *bouledogue* [buldɔg] M, 18c, 1a(3) **Sp** [=E/buldog] M, pl. *-s*, end19c, 1a(2) **It** [buldɔg] M, pl. Ø, mid19c, 1a(2) **Rm** *buldog* [b<u>u</u>ldog/buldog] M, end19c, via Fr, 1a(3) **Rs** *bul'd<u>o</u>g* M, pl. *-i*, beg20c, 1a(2) **Po** *buldog* [-k] M, mid19c, 1a(3) → *buldozek* M **Cr** *b<u>u</u>ldog* M, pl. *-zi*, beg20c, 1a(3) **Bg** *buld<u>o</u>g* M, pl. *-al-<u>o</u>tsi*, beg20c, 1a(2) **Fi** *bulldoggi* 20c (5) **Hu** *buldog* [b<u>u</u>ldog] pl. *-ok*, end19c, 1a(3) **Al** *buldog* M, pl. *-ë*, 1960s, 1a (1 reg) **Gr** *buld<u>o</u>g* N, beg20c, via Fr, 1a(2)

bulldozer *n.* 1 'a powerful tractor with a broad upright blade at the front for clearing ground', 2 'a forceful and domineering person'

The literal meaning is recorded in American English in 1930 and the term spread through Europe starting in the 1950s; apparently in both E and W Europe only few calques, if any, were coined.

Ge [b<u>u</u>ldo:za] M, pl. Ø, 1950s, 1(2) 2(1 jour) = 1: *Planierraupe* **Du** [b<u>u</u>ldo:zər/b<u>y</u>ldo:zər] C, mid20c (2 tech) **Nw** *bulldoser* [b<u>u</u>ldu:sər] M, pl. *-e*, 1940s (3) **Ic** - < rend *jarðýta* **Fr** [byldozɛʀ/buldozœʀ] M, 1930s (2 ban) > *bouteur* **Sp** [b<u>u</u>ldoθer/buld<u>o</u>ser] M, pl. *-s*, mid20c (1>2 tech) **It** [buldɔdzer] M, pl. Ø, 1940, 1(2) **Rm** *buldozer* [buld<u>o</u>zer] N, 1940s, via Fr (3); → *-ist* M; *-istă* F **Rs** *bul'd<u>o</u>zer* M, pl. *-y*, mid20c (3) → *-ist* N = *nyĭ* adj.; *-ka* F **Po** *buldożer* [buldozer] M, mid20c, 1(3) **Cr** *buld<u>o</u>žer* M, pl. *-i*, mid20c, 1(2) **Bg** *buld<u>o</u>zer* M, pl. *-al-i*, mid20c (2) → *-ist* M **Hu** *buldózer* [b<u>u</u>ld<u>o</u>:zer] pl. *-ek*, 1960s (3 tech) → *-es* n. **Al** *buldozer* [buldo'zere] M, pl. *-ë*, mid20c (1 tech) **Gr** *buld<u>o</u>za* F, mid20c, 1(3)

bull's-eye *n.* 3 'a thick disc of glass in a ship's deck or side to admit light'

Ge - < trsl *Bullauge* **Nw** - < *kuøye* **Po** *bulaj* [bulai] M, mid20c (1 tech)

bullshit *n.* 1 'nonsense', 2 'trivial or insincere talk or writing'

Du [=E] C [U] 1970s, 1(1 sla) **Nw** [b<u>u</u>lʃit] M [U] 1980s, 1(1 coll, sla) **Ic** [pulsjiht] mostly interj., end20c (1 sla) **Rm** 1(0) **Po** [=E] end20c, 1(1 sla) **Gr** 1(0 sla)

bull terrier *n.* 1 'a breed of short-haired dog'

Adopted through French along with names for other British breeds in the nineteenth century. The French pronunciation partly affected pronunciation in other languages.

Ge [b<u>u</u>lteria] M, pl. Ø, 19c (3) **Du** *bul-terriër* [bulterijər] C, beg20c (2 tech) **Nw** [b<u>u</u>lterjer] M, pl. *-e*, 20c (1 tech) **Ic** [=E] end20c (0 tech) **Fr** [bultɛʀje] M, 19c (1) **Sp** *bullterrier* [bulteri<u>e</u>r] M, beg20c (1 tech) **It** [bulterrier/bulteri<u>e</u>] M, pl. Ø, 19c (2) **Rm** [=E] M, 1930s, via Fr (1 tech) **Rs** *bul'ter'<u>e</u>r* M, pl. *-y*,

beg20c (2) **Po** *bulterrier* [-er] M, beg20c (2) → *-ek* M **Cr** [=E] M, pl. *-i*, beg20c (2) → *-ka* F **Bg** *b<u>u</u>lter-ier* M, pl. *-al-i*, mid20c (2 tech) **Fi** *bullterrieri* 20c (3) **Hu** [b<u>u</u>lterier] pl. *-ek*, 19c (3 tech) **Gr** *bulteri<u>e</u>* N, 20c, via Fr (2)

bully (3) *n.* 1 'The start of play in (ice-) hockey', +2 'a Volkswagen van'

This sports term is one of several adopted from hockey terminology. By contrast, the origin of its applications to the VW van is obscure (and is restricted to German and Dutch).

Ge [b<u>u</u>li:] N, pl. *-(ie)s*, 1970s, 1(1 tech); M, +2(3) **Du** [b<u>u</u>li] C, pl. *-'s*, mid20c (1 tech) **Fr** M, mid20c (1 tech) **Rm** [=E] N [U] 20c, 1(1 tech) **Hu** *buli* [b<u>u</u>li] [U] 20c, 1(1 tech) **Gr** *b<u>a</u>li* N, 20c (1 tech)

bum (2) *n.* 2 'a habitual loafer', +3 'someone who lives at others' expense'.

Nw *boms* sg. [bums] M [U]/pl. *-er*, beg20c, 2(3) **Ic** *bömm* [=E] N, pl. Ø, end20c, 2(1 sla) **Fi** *pummi* +3(3)

bummer *n.* 2 'an unfortunate or unpleasant occurrence', +2a 'depression'

Ic *bömmer* [pœm:er] M [U] 1970s (1 sla) → *bömmerast* v.; *bömmeraður* adj.

bumper *n.* 1 'a horizontal bar at the front or back of a motor vehicle to reduce damage in a collision or as a trim', +5 'a device for stopping quick movement'

As with other motor-car terms, this concept is normally expressed in native terms or earlier French borrowings. The earlier loanword *bumper* 'cup' appears to be obsolete. Note that the English compound *Bumper car* has not been borrowed—the Continental term is ↑*autoscooter*.

Ge [=E] M, pl. Ø, end20c, +5(1 tech_{SPORT}) < 1: *Stoßstange* **Du** [b<u>y</u>mper] C, 1940s (3) **Nw** (0) < 1: *støfanger* **Ic** - < 1: *stuðari* **It** - < 1: *paraurti* **Rs** *b<u>a</u>mper* M, pl. *-y*, mid20c, 1(2 tech) **Po** - < 1: trsl *zderzak* **Bg** - < 1: *bronya*; +5: *bufer* **Fi** - < 1: *puskuri* **Hu** - < 1: *lökhárító*

bunch *n.* 2 'a collection; a set or lot'

Du (Ø) **Ic** [pœns] N [U] end20c (1 sla)

bungalow *n.* 1 'a one-storeyed house', +2 'a house for holiday-makers'

Borrowed as a foreignism designating 'a lightly-built house for Europeans in India', this term came to be used for 'a single-storeyed house with a flat roof', mostly in dormitory towns. This modern sense has spread, with small local differences, all over Europe—as real-estate advertisements amply document.

Ge <=E>/*bangalo* [b<u>u</u>ngalo:] M, pl. *-s*, beg20c, 1(2) **Du** [b<u>y</u>nggalo:/b<u>y</u>ngɣalo] C, beg20c, 1,+2(2) **Nw** [b<u>u</u>ngalov/bønga-] M, pl. *-er*, mid20c (Ø) **Ic** [punkalou:(1)] M, pl. *-ar*, mid20c, 1(1 coll, obs) **Fr** [bɑ̃galo] M, 19c, 1(Ø) +2(2) **Sp** [b<u>u</u>ngalo/bungal<u>o</u>] M, pl. *-s*, beg20c (2) **It** [bungalov/b<u>a</u>ngalo] M, pl. *-s*, mid19c (2) **Rm** *bungalou* [bungal<u>o</u>w] N, 1960s, 1(1 lit) **Rs** *b<u>u</u>ngalo* N, uninfl., mid20c, 1,+2(1 coll) **Po** [bungalov/-ou] M, beg20c, 1(1 tech) +2(2) **Cr** *bungalov* M, pl. *-i*, mid20c, +2(2) **Bg** *bungal<u>o</u>* N, pl. *-la*, mid20c, +2(3) **Fi** [=E] (Ø) **Hu** *bungaló* [b<u>u</u>ngal<u>o</u>:] pl. *-k*,

end19c/beg20c, 1(3); mid20c, +2(3) **Gr** *bangalou*/
<=E> N, pl. Ø/-s, mid20c, 1,+2(2)

bungee jumping *n.* 'the sport of jumping from a
height while secured by a bungee'

The distribution of this recent fashion, and its English designation, illustrate that North-West Europe
still represents the focal area for the adoption of anglicisms.

Ge [=E] N [U] 1991 (1 mod)
Du [=E/bɪnʒi dʒʏmpɪŋ] N, 1990s
(1 mod) **Nw** 1990s (1 mod) <
rend *strikkhopping* **Ic** - < rend
teygjustökk **Fr** *benji* [bɛnʒi] M,
1980s (1 mod) **Sp** [=E] M [U] (1
mod, rare) < *puenting* **It** [bangi
dʒampiŋ] M [U] 1990s (1 tech) < creat *salto con
l'elastico* **Rs** *bandzi-dzhamping* M [U] 1990s (1
mod) **Bg** *bǔndzhi skok* 1990s (1 mod+5) **Fi** *benji-
hyppy* 1990s (1+5) **Gr** *bantzi* N [U] 1990s (1 mod)

bunker *n.* 1 'a large container for fuel', 2 'a rein-
forced underground shelter for use in wartime', 3 'a
sand-filled hollow, used as an obstacle in a golf-
course'

A rare case of inter-European exchange is represented here. The 'storage' sense was borrowed from
English as a naval term for *bunkers* in harbours etc.
During the 1915–18 period it was extended to mean 'a
dug-out fortification' and later 'an air-raid shelter' in
German, and this meaning was then borrowed back
into English. The new golfing sense may therefore be
borrowed from English or German (the latter being
more likely).

Ge [buŋka] M, pl. Ø, beg20c, 1(1 tech) 2(3); 1940s, 3(1
tech) → -*n* v. **Du** [bʏŋkər] C, beg20c, 1(2); 1940s,
2(2) **Nw** <=E>/*bunkers* [buŋker(s)] M, pl. -*e*/
bunkre/-*s*, mid20c, 1(2 tech) 2(3) 3(1 tech) **Ic**
[puŋker-] cp¹, mid20c, 1(1 tech, obs) **Fr** [bunkœʀ/
bunkɛʀ] M, 1940s, via Ge, 2(2 ban); [bœnkœʀ] 1990s,
3(1 tech/ban) > 2: *fortin*, 3: *ensable, fosse de sable* **Sp**
[buŋker] M, pl. -*s*, 1940s, 2(2/5Ge); 1980s, 1,3(1
tech) **It** [buŋker] M, pl. Ø, 1940s, 2(2) 3(1 tech) = 2:
rifugio **Rm** *buncăr* [buŋkər] N, 1940s, via Ge, 1(2
tech) 2(2) **Rs** *bunker* M, pl. -*y*, beg20c, 1,2(3) **Po**
bunkier [bunkier] M, pl. -*kry*, mid20c, via Ge, 1(1 tech)
2(2) **Cr** *bunker* M, pl. -*i*, mid20c, 1(1 tech) 2(2) **Bg**
bunker M, pl. -*al-i*, beg20c, via Ge, 1(3 tech) 2(3) → -*en*
adj.; -*azh* M; -*ovam* v.; -*ovŭchen* adj. **Fi** *bunkkeri* 20c,
1,2(1 tech) **Hu** [bunker] pl. -*ek*, beg20c, via Ge, 1(1
tech) 2(5Ge) **Al** *bunker* [bun'ker] M, pl. -*ë*, mid20c (1
tech)

bunker coal *n.* 'a kind of coal'

Nw *bunkers* [buŋkers] M [U] beg20c (2) → *bunkre*
v. **Rm** - < trsl *cărbune de buncăr* **Po** *bunker* [bun-
ker] M [U] beg20c (1 tech) **Bg** - < trsl *bunkerovŭchni
vǔglishta*

bunny *n.* 3 'a club hostess, waitress, etc. in a skimpy
costume with ears and a tail suggestive of a rabbit'

This term has largely remained a foreignism; it is
attested only for the Germanic languages, and (with

the closure of the playboy clubs) has become obsolete
since the 1980s.

Ge [bani] N, pl. -*(ie)s*, 1970s (1 coll, obs) >
Häschen **Du** [=E/bʏni] C, 1980s (1 coll) **Nw**
(Ø) **Ic** [=E], 1960s (Ø obs) < trsl *kanína* **Fr**
(0) **Sp** (0) **It** - < trsl *coniglietta* **Po** (0)

Burberryᵀᴹ *cp¹/n.* 1 'a distinctive type of raincoat'ᵀᴹ, +2 'a kind of cloth'

Ge <=E/-*Mantel*> [=E] 20c, 1(1 rare) **Du** [bʏr+E]
C, pl. 's, 20c (1 rare) **Nw** [=E] M, 20c (1 mod,
rare) **Ic** [=E] cp¹, 1970s, 1(1 mod) **Fr** (0) **Sp** [bur-
beri] M, 20c, +2(1 mod, for trousers) **It** [=E/burberi/
barberi] M, pl. Ø, end20c, 1(1 tech_NAME) **Po** [ber-
beri] N [U] end19c (1 tech) **Cr** *berberi* M, pl. -*ji*,
end20c, 1(2) **Hu** *börberi* [bø:rberi] [U] end19/
beg20c, +2(3 obs)

burger *n.* 1 'a hamburger', 2 'a hamburger of a particular type or with specified additions, +3 'a fast food
restaurant'

After reanalysis of *ham + burger*, and new compounds formed in American English (*cheese-, meat-*
etc.), these food items, along with their names, were
exported into European languages as a marker of a
modern lifestyle. The term is rare by itself, usually
occurring in combination (but cf. the business name
Burger King). Non-English compounds, many of
them playful, were coined in the 1980s.

Ge only cp² [börga] M, pl. Ø, 1970s, 1,2(2) **Du**
[bʏrxər] cp², C, 1980s, 1,2(2) **Nw** [burger] M, pl. -*e*,
1980s, 1,2(2) **Ic** - < 1,2: creat -*borgari* **Fr** (O) **Sp**
[burger] M, pl. -*s*/Ø, 1980s, +3(2) **It** [burgɛr] M, pl.
Ø, end20, 1,2(1) **Rm** [=E] M [U] end20c, 1,2(1 mod
< Ø) **Rs** *burger* cp²/M, pl. -*y*, 1990s, 1,2(2) **Po**
[berger/burger] M, end20c, 1,2(2 mod) **Cr** *burger*
M, pl. -*i*, end20c, 1(2) **Bg** *burger* cp²/M, pl. -*al- i*,
1990s, 2(1) **Fi** *burgeri* 1,2(0) **Hu** [burger] pl. -*ek*,
1980s, 1,2(2) **Al** *hamburg* M, pl. Ø, 1980s, 1,2(3)
Gr <=E> [=E] N/cp², end20c, 1,2(2)

burn-out *n.* 1 'physical or emotional exhaustion', +3
'development of friction and smoke between car
tyre and paving when the driver steps on accelerator and brakes at the same time', +4 'nuclear burn-
out'

Ge [=E] cp¹ in *Burn-out Syndrom*, end20c, 1(1 tech)
Nw [bø:rnaut] M, pl. -*s*, 1970s, 1(1 tech) < trsl *ut-
brenthet*, +3(1 sla) **Ic** - < creat *útbrunninn* adj. **Fr**
<=E> 1980s, +4(1 tech, ban) < *caléfaction* **Fi** [=E]
1980s, 1(2) **Gr** <=E> [=E] N [U] end20c, +3(1 tech)

burning* *n.* = ↑*burn-out*

Nw [bø̞rniŋ] C, 1970s (1 sla)

bush (1) *n.* 3 'a wild uncultivated district (esp. in
Africa and Australia)'

The English meaning is colonial, whether derived
from the equivalent South African Dutch word or
independently developed. In Germanic languages it
could, then, be independent of English, or an additional meaning to an existing cognate word. Most
languages apparently did not even borrow the term
as a foreignism.

Ge *Busch* (4) **Du** [=E] C [U] end20c (1 coll) < *oerwoud, rimboe, bush-bush* **Nw** [buʃ] M [U] beg20c (3) **Fr** [buʃ] M, 19c (1 tech) **Rs** *bush* M [U] beg20c (Ø) **Po** *busz* M [U] mid20c (2)

bushel *n.* 1, 2 'a measure of capacity used for grain'
This term is mainly a foreignism, and if used at all, only as a measurement for grain etc. Native equivalents are available, but in reduced currency due to competition from metric terms.
Ge (Ø) < *Scheffel* **Du** (o) **Nw** (Ø) < *skjeppe* **Fr** (o) **Sp** M (Ø rare) **It** [buʃel] M, pl. Ø, 1930s (1 tech) **Rm** *buşell/bushel* [buʃel] M, mid20c (1<2 tech) **Rs** *bushel'* M, pl. *-i*, mid19c (Ø) **Po** *buszel* [-el] M, mid19c (Ø) **Cr** *bušel* M, end19c (Ø) **Bg** *bushel* M, pl. *-a*, 20c (Ø) **Fi** *buššeli* (1 tech) **Hu** [buʃel] [U] 19/20c? (Ø>1 tech) **Gr** *busel* N (Ø)

bushman *n.* 2a 'a member of a South African aboriginal people', +3 'a primitive person'
Since the term was first coined in (Cape) Dutch, but later partially transmitted through English, the etymology of the word is largely uncertain in many languages. The English and Dutch forms are very similar.
Ge *Buschmann* 2a(3 tech/5Du?) **Du** *Bosjesman* 2a(5) **Nw** - < trsl *buskmann* **Ic** - < *búskmaður* **Fr** *bochiman(s)* M (1 tech/5Du) **Sp** Ø **It** *boscimano* (5Du) **Rm** *boşiman* [boʃiman] M, 1960s (5Fr) **Rs** *bushmen* M, pl. *-y*, mid20c, 2a(Ø) +3(3) → *-skiĭ* adj. **Po** *buszmen* [-en] M, mid20c, 2a (1 tech) +3(2) → *buszmeński* adj. **Cr** *bušman* M, pl. *-i*, 20c, 2a(2) → *-ski* adj. **Bg** *bushmen* M, pl. *-i*, mid20c, 2a(Ø) +3(2) **Fi** *busmanni*, 20c, 2a (3 tech) **Hu** *busman* [buʃman] pl. *-ok*, 2a(5 Afrikaans) **Gr** *vusmanos* M, 20c, 2a(3)

business *n.* 1 'trade' (often pejorative), 7 'buying and selling', +7a 'a trade of a specified kind'
This term was added to a variety of native expressions in the late nineteenth or early twentieth century in most languages, suggesting unscrupulous or treacherous forms of trade. Its main currency appears to have developed since the 1960s, supported by compounds like ↑*show* ~ and ↑*businessman*.
Ge [=E] N [U] end19c, 1, 7(2 coll, pej) < 1: *Geschäft*; 7: *Handel* **Du** [=E] C [U] end20c, 1(1 coll) often as cp² abbr. *-biz* **Nw** [=E] M [U] mid20c (1 coll) **Ic** *bisness* [pɪsnes:] M [U] 1920s, 1(2 sla) 7(2 coll) < 7: rend *viðskipti* **Fr** *business/bizness(s)* [biznɛs] end19c/beg20c, 1(1) **Sp** M, usu. pl., 20c, 1(2) **It** [biznis/biznes] M, pl. Ø, end19c (2) **Rm** [biznis] N, 1960s, 1(1 coll); *bişniţă* [biʃnitsə] F, 1970s, 1(3 sla); → *bişniţar* M **Rs** *biznes* M [U] beg20c, 1,+7a(3) **Po** *biznes/* <=E> [-es] M, beg20c (2) → v.; *-owy* adj. **Cr** *biznis* M [U] beg20c, 1(2) **Bg** *biznes* M/cp^{1,2} [U] mid20c, 1,+7a(2) **Fi** *bisnes* (2) **Hu** *biznisz* [=E] pl. Ø, end19c/beg20c, 1(2 tech, fac) **Al** *biznes* [biznes] M [U] 1970s, 1(1 euph) **Gr** <=E>/*biznes* F/N [U] end20c, 1(1 coll/fac) 7(1 coll, mod) +7a(1 jour, mod)

business class *n.* 'a class of accommodation on board aeroplanes'
One of a set of air-travel terms which airlines do not care to translate—possibly to facilitate international comprehensibility (calques, if offered, might well not be accepted by customers).
Ge [=E] F [U] 1980s (1 mod) **Du** [=E] C [U] 1980s (1 mod) **Nw** <=E>/*business-klasse* [=E+ Nw] M [U] 1980s (2+5) **Ic** *bisnessklassi* M [U] end20c (2 tech+5) **Fr** <=E> F, 1980s (1 tech) > *classe affaires* **Sp** [bisnis klas] F, 1980s (1 tech) **It** [biznis/biznes klas] F [U] end20c (1 tech) **Rm** (o) **Rs** *biznes klass* M [U] end20c (1 tech) **Po** [-esklas] F, end20c (1 tech) **Cr** [=E] F [U] 1980s (1 tech) **Bg** *biznes klasa* F [U] end20c (1 tech+3) **Fi** [=E] (o) **Hu** [=E] pl. Ø, end20c (1 tech, jour, mod) **Al** *biznes klas* 1980s (2) **Gr** <=E> [=E] F [U] end20c (1 mod)

businessman *n.* 1 'a person engaged in trade' (often pejorative) (cf. ↑*businesswoman*)
This term was added to native expressions either to stress the internationality of the person's trade or to intimate the ruthlessness or morally dubious character of his dealings. The positive and negative senses both survive (with the balance possibly tilted to the negative interpretation).
Ge [=E] M, pl. *-men*, beg20c (1 coll) < *Geschäftsmann* **Du** - < *zakenman* **Nw** <=E>/*-mann* [=E] M, pl. *-men(n)*, mid20c (1) < *forretningsmann* **Ic** *bisnessmaður* [pɪsnes-] M, pl. *-menn*, 1920s (2+5 coll) **Fr** <=E>/*biznessman* [biznesman] M, pl. *businessmans/businessmen*, end19c (1 obs) **Sp** M, beg20c (Ø/ rare) **It** [biznismen] M, pl. Ø, 1900s, 1(2) < *uomo d'affari* **Rm** [biznismen] M, 1960s (1 coll) < rend *om de afaceri* **Rs** *biznesmen* M, pl. *-y*, mid20c (2) **Po** *biznesmen/*<=E> [-es-] M, mid20c (2) → *-ka* F **Cr** *biznismen* M, pl. *-i*, mid20c (2) → *-ka* F; *-ski* adj. **Bg** *biznesmen* M, pl. *-i*, mid20c (2) → *-ski* adj.; *-ka* F **Fi** (Ø) > trsl *bisnesmies, liikemies* **Hu** [=E] pl. Ø, end20c (1 tech) < trsl *üzletember* **Al** *biznesmen* M, pl. *-e*, 1960s (1 reg) **Gr** *biznesman* M, pl. Ø/*-men* end20c (1 coll, fac) < *epikhirimatias*

business plan *n.* 'a plan setting out how to develop an enterprise'
Rm [=E] N [U] end20c (Ø/1 tech, mod) **Rs** *biznes plan* M, pl. *-y*, end20c (1 tech) **Po** [-es -an] M, end20c (1 mod)

businesswoman *n.* 1 'a female person engaged in trade'
The distribution of this term is remarkably more restricted than that of its male counterpart, possibly because the phenomenon is more recent, or less common.
Ge - < *Geschäftsfrau* **Du** - < *zakenvrouw* **Nw** [=E] M, pl. *-women*, 1980s (1) < *forretningskvinne* **Ic** *bis-*

nesskona F, pl. *-ur*, mid/end20c (2+5 coll) **Fr** (0) **It** [biznis wuman/-wumen] F, pl. Ø, end20c (1 tech) < *donna d'affari* **Rm** - < rend *femeie de afaceri* **Rs** *biznesvumen* F, uninfl., 1990s (1 fac/jour/rare) < trsl *delovaya zhenshchina* **Po** *bisneswoman/biznes-woman/businesswoman/*<=E> [bizneswumen] F, pl. -en, end20c (2 mod) **Bg** - < *biznesmenka, biznesdama* **Al** - < *biznesmene* **Gr** *biznesghuman/biznes ghuman* F, end20c (1 coll, fac) < *epikhirimatias*

bust (2) *n.* 1 'a (sudden) failure; a bankruptcy', 2 'a police raid'
  Ic [=E] N, pl. Ø, end20c, 1(1 sla) 2(1 tech, sla) **Gr** *bast* N, end20c, 2(1 sla)

bust *v.* 3a 'raid, search', +4 'swindle'
  Ic *bösta* [pœsta] end20c (1 sla)

busy *adj.* 1 'occupied or engaged in work etc.; with the attention concentrated'
  Du (Ø) **Nw** [=E] mid20c (1 sla, obs) **Ic** *bissí* [pɪsi:] uninfl., mid20c (1 sla) **Bg** *bizi* uninfl., end20c (1 sla)

butler *n.* 'the principal man-servant of a household'
  This term started out as a foreignism, and has remained so for many languages, although the word has a certain euphemistic snob appeal. Earlier pronunciation, and the time of its first adoption, point to French mediation.
  Ge [bötla/batla] M, pl. Ø, 19c (Ø/1 arch) **Du** [bytlər] C, mid20c (2) **Nw** [bøtler] M, pl. *-e*, beg20c (1) < *hovmester* **Ic** [pæhtler] M, pl. *-ar*, beg/mid20c (Ø) **Fr** (0) **Sp** - < *mayordomo* **It** - < *maggiordomo* **Cr** *batler* M, pl. *-i*, beg20c (2) **Fi** *butleri* 20c (Ø) **Hu** [=E] pl. Ø, 19c (Ø) < *főinas* **Gr** *batler* M, beg20c (2)

butterfly *n.* 4 'a stroke in swimming', +5 'a split jump in figure skating', +6 'a somersault in gymnastics', +7 'a body-building instrument', +8 'a transfusion needle'
  The swimming style was developed from the breast-stroke in 1935, the term being derived from the flapping movement of the arms. The uses in skating and gymnastics terminology are highly technical and restricted to these fields.
  Ge [=E] M [U] 1950s, 4(2 tech) = mean *Schmetterling(sstil)*; 1970s, +5,+6,+7(1 tech, rare) **Du** - < *vlinderslag* **Nw** [=E] M [U] mid20c, 4(1 tech) **Ic** - < 4: rend *flugsund* **Fr** - < mean *papillon, brasse papillon* **Sp** - < mean *mariposa* **It** - < mean *farfalla, stile (a) farfalla* **Rm** - < mean *fluture* **Rs** *batterflyai* M [U] mid20c, 4(2 tech); end20c, +5,+6,+7(1 tech, rare) → *-yaist* M **Po** *baterflaj* [baterflaj] M, 4,+5,+6(1 tech) **Cr** *baterflaj* M [U] end20c, 4(1 tech) = mean *leptiv* **Bg** *büterflaï* M [U] mid20c, 4(2

tech); *büterflaïka* F, pl. *-ki*, mid20c, +8(3 tech MED) **Fi** - < 4: mean *perhosuinti* **Al** *baterflaj* M [U] end20c; 4(1 reg) **Gr** - < 4: mean *petaludha*

button *n.* 1 'a badge (bearing a slogan)'
  The meaning arose in the USA in the (political) youth culture of the late 1960s. It is more frequent than the synonymous ↑*badge*, and is restricted to Germanic.
  Ge [batn] M, pl. *-s*, 1960s (2) **Du** [=E] C, end20c (2) **Nw** [=E] M, pl. *-s*, 1960s (2)

button-down *cp[1]/n.* 'applied to a collar whose points are buttoned to the shirt'
  Ge cp[1] [=E] 1980s (1 tech, rare) **Du** cp[1] [=E] 1980s (1 tech) **Nw** [=E] 1980s (1 tech) **Fr** - < *(à) col boutonné* **It** [boton daun] M, pl. Ø, end20c (1 tech)

buyout *n.* 'the purchase of a controlling share in a company etc.' (= ↑*management buyout*)
  Ge [=E] M/N, pl. *-s*, 1980s (1 tech, mod) **Nw** [=E] M, pl. *-s*, end20c (1 tech) **Sp** M, 1990s (1 tech) **It** [bai aut] M, pl. Ø, end20c (1 tech) < *acquisto*

bye, bye-bye *interj.* 'goodbye'
  Ge [=E] end20c (1 coll) **Du** [=E] 1970s (2 coll) **Nw** (0) **Ic** *bæ(-bæ)* [pai:(pai:)] 1930s (2 coll) < *bless* → *bæjó* interj. **Fr** [bajbaj] 1940s (1 coll) **Sp** [baibai] 1980s (1 fac) **It** [=E] 1930s (2 mod) **Rm** [=E] end20c (1 coll) **Rs** *baï-baï* end20c (1 coll, you) **Po** (0) **Cr** (0) **Bg** *baï-baï* mid20c (2 coll, you) **Hu** [=E] 20c (1 coll, fac) **Gr** [=E] end20c (1 coll)

by night *adv.* 'at night-time'
  Du [=E] 1960s (2 coll, obs) **Nw** [=E] 1970s (1 fac) **Fr** [=E] 1970s (1 rare) only *Paris-by-night* **Sp** <=E> end20c (1 tech, rare) **It** [bai nait] mid20c (2) = *di notte* **Rm** (0) **Po** <=E> end20c (2 coll) **Fi** (0) **Cr** [=E] end20c (2 coll) **Hu** [=E] 20c (1 coll, jour, mod) **Gr** <=E> [=E] mid20c (2 writ, coll)

bypass *n.* 1 'a road passing round a town', +1a 'a traffic diversion', 2b 'an alternative passage for the circulation of blood', +2c 'a secondary pipe' (in plumbing)
  Of the various English senses, only the modern medical one is truly international, adopted with the technique which was developed in the USA in 1970. For other senses native equivalents are available (type 1 **Ge** *Umgehungsstraße*).
  Ge [=E] M, pl. *-pässel-es*, 1970s, 2b(1 tech>2) **Du** [=E] C, end20c, 2b(1 tech) **Nw** (usu. cp[1]) [=E] M, 1980s, 2b,+2c(1 tech) → *bypasse* v. **Ic** [pai:pʰas:] N [U] end20c, 2b(1 tech) < trsl *hjáveita* **Fr** *by-pass* [bajpas] M, 1920s, +1a,2b,+2c(1 tech) < 2b: *pontage*; +2c: *dérivation* **Sp** *by pass/by-pass* [baipas/bipas] M, pl. Ø, end20c, 1(1 tech); 1970s, 2b(2) < *puente*; end20c, +2c(1 tech) **It** [baipas] M, pl. Ø, 1970s, 2b(2) +2c(1

tech) → *bypassare* v.   **Rm** *by-pass/baipas* [=E] N, 1970s, 2b(1 tech)   **Rs** *baipas* M [U] end20c, 2b(1 tech)   **Po** [-pas] M, 2b(2 tech)   **Cr** *bajpas* M [U] end20c, 2b(1 tech)   **Bg** *baipas* M, pl. *-al-i*, end20c, 2b(2 tech)   **Hu** [=E] [U] end20c, 2b(1 tech)   **Gr** *baipas* N, end20c, 2b(1 tech>2)

byte   *n.* 'a unit of information (= 8 bits)' (comput.)

This computer term manifests the expected stylistic homogeneity (1 tech) and non-adaptation of form throughout Europe.

Ge [=E] N, pl. *-s*, 1970s (1 tech)   **Du** [=E] C, 1970s (1 tech)   **Nw** [=E] M, pl. *-s*, 1970s (1 tech)   **Ic** *bæt(i)* [pai:t(ı)] N, pl. Ø, end20c (3 tech)   **Fr** [bajt] M, 1970s (1 tech, ban) < *octet*   **Sp** [bait] pl. *-s*, 1980s (1 tech)   **It** [bait] M, pl. Ø, 1970s (1 tech)   **Rm** *bait* [bajt] M, 1980s (2 tech)   **Rs** *bait* M, pl. *-y*, end20c (2 tech)   **Po** *bajt* M, end20c (2 tech)   **Cr** *bajt* M, pl. *-ovi*, end20c (1 tech)   **Bg** *bait* M, pl. *-a*, end20c (1 tech) → *-ov* cp²/adj.   **Fi** (Ø) < *tavu*   **Hu** *bájt* [=E] pl. Ø, end20c (1 tech)   **Gr** <=E>/*bait* N, pl. Ø/*-s*, end20c (1 tech)

C

c&w* *n.* 'country and western music'
  Nw [se:ove:] M [U] 1980s (1 tech, writ, jour) **Gr** <=E> end20c (1 writ)

cab *n.* 1 'a taxi', 3 'a hackney carriage'
  In Western Europe, this term is archaic or a foreignism at best: *taxi* is now the common word. In German *cabby* and *cabman* are listed for the driver *c.* 1900.
  Ge [kɛp] N, pl. *-s*, mid19c (1 arch) **Du** [kɛp] C, beg20c, 1(1 tech, arch) **Nw** (Ø) **Fr** [kab] M, mid19c, 3(1 arch) **Sp** [kab] M, 1980s, 1(Ø/writ, rare); beg20c, 3(Ø arch) **It** [kɛb] M, pl. Ø, mid19c, 3(1 arch) **Rm** [keb/kab] N, beg20c, 3(1 obs) **Rs** *keb* M, pl. *-y*, beg20c (Ø) **Hu** [=E] 19c, 3(1 arch)

cabin cruiser *n.* 'a large motor boat with living accommodation'
  Nw [=E] M, pl. *-e*, end20c (1) **Fr** [kabinкʀuzœʀ] M, mid20c (1 tech) **It** - < ↑*cruiser*

cableman* *n.* 'a technician in charge of cables' (film, TV)
  Fr [kablman] M, 1960s (1 tech, ban) > rend *câbliste* **It** - < rend *cablatore*

CAD *n.* 'computer-aided design' (acron.)
  Ge [tse:a:de:/ket] N [U] 1980s (1 tech) **Du** *CAD/ C.A.D.* [kɛt] 1980s (1 tech) **Nw** [se:a:de:/kœd] M [U] 1980s (1 tech) > trsl *DAK* (*dataassistert konstruksjon*) **Ic** [=E] end20c (1 tech) **Fr** - < trsl *C.A.O.* (*conception assistée par ordinateur*) **Sp** M [U] end20c (1 tech) **It** [=E] M, 1970s (1 tech) **Rm** [kad] 1990s (1 tech) > *PAC* (*proiectare asistată de calculator*) **Rs** *KAD* M [U] end20c (1 tech) **Po** M, end20c (1 tech) **Bg** <=E>/*KAD* M [U] end20c (1 tech) **Fi** [=E] 1990s (1 tech) **Hu** [kad] [U] end20c (1 tech) **Gr** *CAD* [kad] N [U] end20c (1 tech)

caddie *n.* 1 'a helper in golf', +2 'a light trolley or cart for golf clubs', +3 'a trolley (in supermarkets etc.)'
  This term exemplifies typical European adaptation. It was adopted as a foreignism or specialist term for the person in the 1930s, the abbreviated form *caddie car(t)* came to be used later for the cart. A metaphorical extension to supermarket trolleys developed, this originally being a trade name in Dutch and French.
  Ge [kedi:] M, pl. *-s*, 1930s, 1(tech, rare); 1980s, +2(1 tech) **Du** [=E] C, 1940s, 1,+2(1 tech) +3(2) **Nw** [=E] M, pl. *-er*, mid20c, 1(1 tech) **Ic** [kʰat:i] M,

pl. *-ar*, mid20c, 1(1 tech) **Fr** <=E>/*caddy* [kadi] M, pl. *-ies/-ys*, end19c/1900s (1 tech, ban); 1950s, +3(2) >1: *cadet, cadette* **Sp** [kadi] M, pl. *-s*, beg20c, 1(1 tech) **It** [kɛddi] M, pl. Ø, mid20c 1(1 tech) < *portabastoni* **Po** [ke-] M [U] end20c, 1(1 tech) **Fi** [=E] 1(0)

caddy (trousers)* *n.* 'a kind of trousers'
  Ge *Caddyhose* F, pl. *-en*, 1970s (1 tech, obs+5) **Po** *caddy* [ke-] pl., beg20c (1 arch)

cajun *n.* +2 'French-American folk music'
  Du [=E] C [U] 1970s (2 tech) = *cajunmuziek* **Nw** [=E] M [U] 1970s (1 tech) **Ic** [=E] end20c (1 tech) **Fr** [kaʒɛ̃] M/adj., uninfl., end19c > *acadien/cadjin/-ine* **It** [kaʒun] M/F, pl. Ø, end20c (1 tech) **Fi** [=E] (Ø) **Gr** (0)

cake *n./cp*$^{1/2}$ 1a 'a sweet pastry', +3a 'a cosmetic product in flat, compact form' (cosmetics), +5 'a cookie, a biscuit'
  This term was first adopted with incorrectly interpreted *-s* and the deviant meaning 'biscuit' during the 19c resulting in *Keks*. This German loanword was then handed on to various other languages. (The grid is here used to illustrate this specific influence.) Almost simultaneously, there was a more marginal word close to English in form and meaning used as a fashionable alternative to native equivalents, which has since become obsolete or been readopted.
  Ge *Keks* [ke:ks] M, pl. *-e*, end19c, +5(3); [=E] end19c, 1a(1 arch) **Du** [ke:k] C, beg20c, 1a(2) **Nw** *kjeks* [çjeks] M, pl. Ø, 19c, +5(3) **Ic** *kex* [cʰexs] N, pl. Ø, mid19c, via Da, +5(3); *kökucp*^{1}, mid20c, +3a(4) **Fr** [kɛk]

M/cp^2, end19c, 1a(2) +3a(1) **Sp** [=E] M, pl. *-s*, end19, 1a(1 jour, rare) **It** [keik/kɛik] M/cp^2, pl. Ø, mid20c, 1a(1 arch) **Rm** *chec* [kek] N, mid20c?, 1a(3); *keks* [keks] N, end19c, via Ge, +5(3 reg) **Rs** *keks* M, pl. *-y*, beg20c, +5(3) **Po** *keks* M, beg20c, 1a,+5(3) → *-ik* M **Cr** *keks* M, pl. *-i*, end19c, +5(3) **Bg** *keks* M, pl. *-al-ove*, end19c, via Ge, +5(3); *keik* M, pl. *-al-ove*, end20c, 1a(2 mod) → *-ov* adj. **Fi** *keksi* 19c, +5(3) **Hu** *keksz* [keks] pl. *-ek*, end19c, via Ge, +5(3) **Al** *keks* M, pl. *-e*, beg20c, 1a,+5(1 reg) **Gr** *keik/kek* N, end19c, via Fr, 1a(2)

cakewalk *n.* 1 'an old dance', 3 'a form of fairground entertainment'

Ge [=E] M [U] beg20c, 1(1 obs) **Du** [=E] C, beg20c, 1(1 tech, obs) 3(1 tech) **Nw** [keikvo:k] M, pl. -*s*, beg20c, 1(1 arch) **Fr** [kekwɔk] M, end19c/beg20c, 1(1 arch) **Sp** [=E/kakewal] M, beg20c, 1(1 arch) **It** [kei/keik wɔlk] M, pl. Ø, beg20c, 1(1 obs) **Rm** [=E] 20c, 1(Ø) **Rs** *kekuok* M [U] beg20c, 1(1 tech, arch) **Po** [- ok] M [U] beg20c, 1(1 obs) **Cr** [=E] M [U] beg20c, 1(1 obs) **Bg** *keikuok* M [U] beg20c, 1(1 tech, arch) **Hu** *kék-vók* [=E] [U] end19c, 1(1 arch)

call *v.* 3a 'bring to one's presence by calling, summon, etc.'
 Nw *calle* [kɔ:le] 1980s (2) **It** [kɔl/kol] M, pl. Ø, end20c (1 tech) **Gr** (0)

callanetics *n.* (orig.^{TM}) 'gymnastics accompanied by music'
 Ge [=E] pl., 1990s (1 tech, rare) **Du** [=E] pl., 1990s (1 tech) **Nw** [=E] M [U] 1990s (1 tech, rare) **Rs** *kalanetika* F [U] 1990s (3 tech, mod) **Po** [kalanetiks] M [U] 1980s (2 mod) **Bg** *kalanetika* F [U] 1990s (3 tech, mod) **Fi** [=E] 1990s (0) **Hu** [=E] [U] 1990s (1 tech) **Gr** <=E>/*kalanetiks* N, pl., 1990s (2 mod)

call-boy *n.* 2 'a male prostitute who accepts appointments by telephone'
 The origin of this term (being either American English or German), which is based on the more frequent ↑*call-girl*, is disputed. Its distribution is limited and clearly depends on the pre-existence of *call-girl*.
 Ge [=E] M, pl. -*s*, 1970s (1 euph, mod) **Du** [=E] C, 1970s (1 euph) **Nw** [=E] M, pl. -*s*, end20c (1 fac) **Fr** (0) **It** [kɔl/kɔl bɔi] M, pl. Ø, end20c (1 mod, jour) **Po** (0) **Cr** (0) **Gr** *kɔl boi* N, end20c (1 sla)

call-girl *n.* 'a female prostitute who accepts appointments by telephone'
 This term became popular in the 1960s, e.g. through the Profumo affair, but was delayed in Eastern and Southern Europe. The lexical field is well-stocked with native terms, so the restricted acceptance was determined by euphemistic considerations.
 Ge [=E] N, pl. -*s*, 1960s (1 euph) **Du** [=E] C, 1960s (1 euph) **Nw** [=E] M, pl. -*s*, 1960s (1 euph) **Fr** [kolgœrl] F, 1960s (1) **Sp** [kɔl gel] F, pl. -*s*, 1970s (1 tech) **It** [kɔl gərl/gerl] F, pl. Ø, 1950s (1) < trsl *ragazza squillo* **Rm** [=E] 1990s (0) **Rs** *kol-g3:l* F, uninfl., 1995 (1 coll) < creat *devushka po vyzovu* **Po** [kol gerl] M, pl. -*sy*, end20c (1 mod) **Cr** *kolgerl* F, pl. -*e*, end20c (1 euph) **Bg** *kolgŭrla* F, pl. -*i*, 1990s (1 mod) **Hu** [=E] pl. -*ök*, mid20c (1 euph) **Gr** *kɔl gerl* N, end20c (1 sla)

calling *n.* +3 'an intercom, a door telephone'
 Nw [=E] M, 1970s (2) **Ic** - < *kallkerfi, dyrasími*

cambric *n.* 'linen or cotton fabric'
 Ge *Kambrik* [a] M [U] mid19c (3 tech) **Nw** [keimbrik] M [U] beg20c (1 tech) **It** *cambrì* M [U] 1900s (1 tech) **Rm** *chembricǎ* [kembrikə] F [U] end19c (1 obs) < *batist* **Rs** *kembrik* M [U] mid20c (1 tech) < *batist* **Po** *kambryk* [kambrik] M [U] mid20c (1 tech) **Cr**

kambrik M [U] mid20c (1 tech) **Fi** *kambriikki* (1) **Al** *kambrik* [kambrik] M [U] mid20c (3)

camcorder *n.* 'a combined video camera and video recorder'
 Ge [kemkorda] M, pl. Ø, 1980s (1 tech) **Du** [=E] C, 1980s (1 tech) **Nw** [=E] M, pl. -*e*, 1980s (1) **Fr** *camrecorder*/<=E> (1 tech, ban) < *caméscope* **It** [kamkordɛr/kemkɔ] F, pl. Ø, 1980s (1 tech) < creat *telecamera*

Rs *kamkorder* M, pl. -*y*, 1990s (1 tech) **Cr** [=E] M, pl. -*i*, end20c (1 tech) **Bg** *kamkorder* M, pl. -*al-i*, end20c (1 tech) **Hu** [=E] pl. -*ek*, end20c (1 tech)

cameraman *n.* 1 'a person whose job is operating a camera'
 This term is international, but recognized as an anglicism only outside the Germanic languages. Note purist reactions mainly in Romance languages.
 Ge *Kameramann* M, pl. -*männer/-leute*, beg20c (3 = trsl?) **Du** [ka:məraman] C, pl. -*mannen/-lieden/-lui*, mid20c (3) **Nw** *kameramann* (3) **Ic** *kamerumaður* M, pl. -*menn*, 1960s (2+5 tech) = rend *tökumaður* **Fr** *caméraman*/<=E> [kameʀaman] M, pl. *caméramans/cameramen* M, beg20c (2 ban) < *cadreur* **Sp** [kameraman] M, pl. -*men,- s*, 1920s (2 obs) < *cámara, operador* [kameraman] M, pl. Ø, 1960s (2 tech) > *operatore televisivo* **Rm** [kameraman] M, end20c (1 tech) < *operator de imagine* **Rs** - < *operator* **Po** *kameraman* [-men] M, end20c (1 tech) **Cr** *kamerman* M, pl. -*i*, mid20c (1 tech) → -*ski* adj. **Bg** *kamermen* M, pl. -*i*, 1995 (1 jour, rare) < *operator* **Hu** *kameraman* [kameraman] pl. Ø, end20c, via Ge (1 tech) **Al** *kameraman* M, pl. -*ë*, mid20c (3) **Gr** *kameraman*/*kameraman* M (2) > *ikonoliptis, khiristis kameras*

camp *n.* 1a 'a place where troops are lodged and trained', +1c 'a former military camp where civilians live', +1d 'a prisoner-of-war camp', 2 'temporary overnight lodging in tents etc. in the open',
 Ge [kemp] N, pl., -*s*, 1960s, 2(1 mod); 1940s, +1d(1 obs) **Du** *kamp* 1a,+1d,2(5Fr) **Nw** [=E] M, pl. -*s*, mid20c, 2(1) < *campingplass* **Ic** *kampur* [kʰampyr] M, pl. -*ar*, 1940s, 1a, +1c(4 coll) **Fr** (5) **It** - < 1a, +1d: *campo*; 2: *campeggio* **Po** (0) **Cr** *kamp* M, pl. -*ovi*, mid20c, 2(3) → -*er* M **Hu** [=E] pl. Ø, end19c, 1a(1 tech) < *tábor* **Al** *kamp* M, pl. -*e*, 1940s, 1a, +1d,2(5Fr/3)

camp *adj.* 2 'homosexual', 3 'done in an exaggerated way for effect (esp. using old-fashioned or bad taste objects)'
 Ge [kemp] 1980s (1 sla, rare) → -*y* adj. **Du** [=E] 1970s (1 sla) **Nw** [=E] 1980s, 3(1) → *ucamp* **Sp** [kamp] 1960s, 3(1) **It** [kemp] adj., pl. Ø, end20c (1 mod, sla, you)

camp *v.* 'lodge in temporary quarters in the open'
 Ge *campen*, mid20c (2); *kampieren* 19c (3) **Du** *kamperen* (5) **Nw** *campe* [kæmpe] 1950s (2) → *camper* M **Fr** *camper* (5) **Sp** *acampar* (5) **It** *accamparsi* (5) **Rm** *campa* [kampa] beg19c (5Fr) **Po** (0) **Cr**

kampirati mid2oc (3)   **Bg** *kŭmpiram/kŭmpinguvam* mid2oc (3 tech)   **Hu** *kempingezik* [ke̯mpingezik] mid2oc (2>3)

camper   *n.* 1 'a person who camps out', 2 'a large motor vehicle with accommodation for camping out'

The derivation of the various *camp-* words is uncertain (and may be different for individual languages). It is likely that the early loanword *camping* led to back-formation (or new borrowing) of a related verb which could have produced the agent noun (and the name for the vehicle). There may also be inter-European connections.

Ge [kempa] M, pl. Ø, 1960s, 1(2); 1980s, 2(2)   **Du** [=E] C, 1970s, 2(2 tech) > *kampeerwagen*   **Nw** [kæmper] M, pl. *-e*, 1960s, 1(2); [kæmpər] 1980s, 2(1) < *bobil*   **Fr** *campeur* (5)   **Sp** [kamper] M, 1990s, 2(1 tech, rare); - < 1: *campista*   **It** [kampɛr] M, pl. Ø, 1960s, 2(3)   **Rs** *kemper* M, pl. *-y*, 1990s, 2(2 tech)   **Po** (o)   **Cr** [kamper] M, pl. *-i*, mid2oc 1(3); end2oc, 2(1)   **Bg** - < 1: *kŭmpingar* (3)   **Hu** - < *kempingező* [ke̯mpingezø:] pl. *-k*, mid2oc (2>3)   **Al** - < *kampist* M, pl. *-ë*, mid2oc, 1(3)

camping   *n.* 1 'a place providing temporary accommodation', 2 'the action of camping'

This English word was readily accepted to denote modern motorized holidays with accommodation in tents or campers/caravans. It spread throughout Europe in the 1950s. *Camping site* was frequently abbreviated on the basis of the 'French' model to produce a non-English homonym. This term forms the root for a large family of words by compounding, back-formation, etc.

Ge [kempiŋ] N [U] 1950s, 2(2) → *-platz*   **Du** [kempɪg] C, end2oc, 1(2) 2(1 tech) < 2: *kamperen*   **Nw** [kampiŋ/kæm-] M [U] mid2oc, 1(1 coll) 2(2)   **Fr** [kãpiŋ] M, beg2oc, 1, 2(2)   **Sp** [kampin] M, pl. *-s*, 1920s 1, 2(2)   **It** [kempiŋ] M [U]/pl. Ø, 1930s, 1(2) 2(1) = 1: *campeggio* M, 2: *andare in campeggio*   **Rm** [kempiŋ] N, mid2oc, 1(2)   **Rs** *kemping* M, pl. *-i*, end2oc, 1(2) → *-ovyĭ* adj.   **Po** *kemping/<=E>* [ke-] M, end2oc, 1(2) → *-owanie* N [U]; *-ować* v.; *-owy* adj.   **Cr** *kamping* M, pl. *-zi*, mid2oc, via Fr, 1(3) → *-ar* M; *-uvane* N; *-ov* adj.   **Bg** *kŭmping* M, pl. *-al/-i*, mid2oc, via Fr, 1(3) → *-ar* M; *-uvane* N; *-ov* adj.   **Fi** [=E] (1)   **Hu** *kemping* [ke̯mping] pl. *-ek*, mid2oc, 1(2>3); *kempingezés* [ke̯mpingeze:ʃ] [U] 2(2>3)   **Al** *kamping* M [U] mid2oc, 1(1 reg)   **Gr** *kampin(g)* N, 2oc, via Fr, 1, 2(2)

camping car*   *n.* 'a motor home'

Ge (o)   **Du** - < *kampeerwagen*   **Nw** - < *camping-vogn*   **Fr** *camping-car* [kãpiŋkaʁ] M, 1970s (1 tech, ban) < *autocaravane*   **Po** (o)   **Cr** (o)   **Bg** - < *kara-vana*   **Hu** - < trsl *kemping autó*

camping-gas*   *n.* 'a cooker with one burner and a butane container'

Du *campinggas* (2+5)   **Fr** *camping-gaz* [kãpiŋgaz] M, 1960s (orig.™)   **Sp** [kampin gas] M, 1960s (2)   **It** [kɛmpiŋ(g) gas] M, pl. Ø, mid2oc (1 tech) < *fornello da*

campeggio   **Po** (o)   **Cr** (o)   **Bg** - < *gazov ko-tlon*   **Hu** *kempinggáz* [kemping ga:z] pl. Ø, mid2oc (2>3)   **Gr** <=E> 2oc (1 writ)

camp-mobil*   *n.* 'a van customized for camping'

Ge [ke̯mpmobi:l] N, pl. *-e*, 1970s (1 tech, obs)   **Po** (o)   **Cr** (o)

campus   *n.* 'the grounds of a university' (esp. outside the city)'

The origin of this term is clearly American English, but its Latin form makes it an anglicism only where this is indicated in its pronunciation, as in Norwegian; elsewhere, the word would have to be classified as (5La).

Ge [kampus] M [U] 1960s (Ø, 5La)   **Du** [kampʏs] C, pl. *-sen*, mid2oc (1 reg)   **Nw** [kampus/kæmpus] M, pl. *-er*, 1960s (1 tech)   **Ic** [kʰampʏs] M, pl. *-ar*, mid/end2oc (Ø)   **Fr** [kãpʏs] M, end19c/beg2oc (2)   **Sp** [kampus] M, pl. Ø, 1920s (2>3)   **It** [kampus] M, pl. Ø, 1950s (Ø>1 tech)   **Rm** [kampus] N, 1970s, via Fr? (1 mod)   **Rs** (o)   **Po** (5La)   **Cr** *kampus* M, pl. *-i*, mid2oc (Ø tech)   **Bg** (o)   **Fi** (5La)   **Hu** [=E/kampus] pl. *-ok*, 2oc (Ø >1 mod)   **Gr** *kampus* N, end2oc (Ø/1 tech) < *panepistimiupoli*

cancel   *v.* 1a 'withdraw or revoke (a previous arrangement)', 4 'annul (a flight etc.)'

Ge *canceln* [ke̯ntsəln] 1980s, 4(1 mod)   **Du** *cancellen* [kensələ(n)] 1970s, 4(1 tech)   **Nw** *kansellere* [kanse-le:rə] 2oc (5Fr)   **Ic** *kansellera* [kʰansel:era] end2oc, 1a(1 coll)   **Sp** *cancelar* (5La)   **It** *cancellare* (5La)   **Cr** (o)   **Bg** *kantseliram* mid2oc, 4(3 tech) → *-irane* N   **Gr** *kanselaro* 1990s, 4(1 tech)

cancelling*   *n.* 'a countermand' (in ship-building and the ship trade)

Rm [=E] N, 1970s (1 tech)   **Bg** *kantseling* M [U] end2oc (1 tech)

candid-camera   *n.* 'a small camera for taking informal photographs of people, often without their knowledge'

Du [=E] C, pl. *'s*, 1980s (2 tech)   **It** [=E] F, 1960s (2 jour)   **Hu** *kandi kamera* pl. *-ák*, mid2oc (3)   **Gr** (o)

cannel (coal)   *n.* 'bituminous coal'

Ge *Kännelkohle* F, 19c (3 tech, rare)   **Nw** [=E] 19c (1 tech, arch)   **Ic** *kannelkol* N, end19c (2 tech, arch)   **Fr** *cannel-coal* M, 19c (1 tech, arch)   **Rm** [=E?] N [U] beg2oc (2 tech)   **Rs** *kennel'* M [U] beg2oc (1 tech) → *-skiĭ* adj.   **Po** *kenel* [kenel] M [U] mid2oc (1 tech) → *-ski* adj.   **Bg** - < *rend kenelski vŭglishta*   **Fi** *kan-nelhiili* (1)   **Hu** *kennel* [ke̯nnel] [U] 19c/2oc (1 tech)

canoe   *n.* 1 'a small narrow boat propelled by paddling'

Since this term originally came from a Caribbean language through Spanish, the mediating function of English is not obvious in a number of languages. For others this derivation is obvious only because it is indicated in dictionaries.

Ge *Kanu* N, pl. *-s*, 19c (3) → *-tel-tin* M/F   **Du** *canol kano* [ka:no] C, 19c, 1(5Carib.) → *-ën* v.   **Nw** *kano* [ka:nu] 2oc(3)   **Ic** *kanó* M, pl. *-ar*, mid2oc, via Da (2 tech) = *eintrjáningur*   **Fr** *canoë* [kanɔe] M, mid19c (3)

→ *canoéiste, canoéisme, canoeing* M **Sp** - < *canoa* (5) **It** - < *canoa* (5Sp) **Rm** [kan<u>o</u>e] F, pl. Ø, 1940s, via Fr, 1(3) **Rs** *kano<u>é</u>* N, uninfl., mid19c, via Sp (3 tech) **Po** *kanoe*/<=E> [kanu] N [U] mid20c (1 tech) **Cr** *k<u>a</u>nu* M, pl. *-i*, beg20c, 1(2) **Bg** *kan<u>u</u>* N, pl. *-ta*, mid20c (2 tech) **Fi** *kanootti* (3) **Hu** *k<u>e</u>nu* [k<u>e</u>nu] pl. *-k*, 17/18c (3) **Al** *kanoe* F [U] **Gr** *kan<u>o</u>* N, beg20c, via Fr (2)

canter *n./cp¹* 'a gentle gallop'

Adopted with other horse-racing terms in the nineteenth century, this word has remained technical and its distribution is patchy. The phrase *in a canter* meaning 'easy' (victory) survives in a few languages (German *Kantersieg*).

Ge *K<u>a</u>nter* M [U] 19c (3 tech) **Fr** [kãtɛr] M, mid19c (1 tech) **Sp** [k<u>a</u>nter] M, 1920s (1 arch) **It** [k<u>e</u>nter/ k<u>a</u>nter] M [U] 1900s (1 tech) **Rm** [k<u>a</u>nter] N, beg20c, via Fr? (3 tech) **Rs** *k<u>e</u>nter* M [U] beg20c (1 tech) **Fi** *kantteri*, 20c (1) **Hu** *kenter* [k<u>e</u>nter] [U] end19c/beg20c (1 tech)

canvas *n.* 1a 'a strong coarse kind of cloth', 3 'a kind of canvas used as a basis for tapestry and embroidery', +3a 'an open kind of canvas used as a lining etc.'

Ge [k<u>e</u>nvəs] M/N [U] 1970s, 1a(1 tech, rare) **Du** [k<u>a</u>nvas] N [U] beg20c, 1a(3) **Nw** [k<u>a</u>nvas] M [U] 20c, 1a(1 tech) < *strie, stramei* **Ic** *kanvas* N [U] end19c, 1a, +3(5Da) < *strigi* **Fr** *canevas* 1a(5) **It** *canapa* (5La) **Rm** *canava* [kanav<u>a</u>] F, 18c, 3(5Fr) **Rs** *kanv<u>a</u>* F [U] beg20c, 3(3 rare) **Bg** *kanav<u>a</u>* (5Fr) **Fi** [=E] 1a(3) **Hu** *k<u>a</u>navász* (5Ge<Fr) **Al** *kanavacë* [kanav<u>a</u>c] F, pl. Ø, 1920s, 1a(1 tech) **Gr** *kamv<u>a</u>s* M, beg20c (5Fr)

canvassing *n.* 1 'the soliciting of votes'

Ge [=E] N [U] 1960s (1 tech, rare) **Du** [kanvasiŋ] N [U] beg20c (1 tech) > *kanvas* → *canvassen* v. **Nw** [k<u>a</u>nvasiŋ] M [U] 20c (1 tech) **It** [k<u>e</u>nvassiŋ] M, pl. Ø, 1950s (1 tech)

canyon *n.* 'a deep gorge, often containing a stream or river'

This Spanish term became well-known through American English mediation, with reference to canyons in Arizona etc. Whether the term is felt to be an anglicism depends on both spelling and pronunciation (Spanish *cañón* [kaniõ]). There is a rare derivation with *~ing* meaning 'canoeing in canyons' (**Ge** 1 tech, mod, Fr 1990s)

Ge (Ø) **Du** (0) **Nw** [=E] M, pl. *-er/-s*, 20c (1 tech) **Fr** (Ø) **Sp** *cañon* (4) **It** [k<u>e</u>njon] M, pl. Ø, 20c (2) **Rm** *canion* [kanj<u>o</u>n] N, beg20c (5Sp) **Rs** *kan'<u>o</u>n* M, pl. *-y* (5Sp) **Po** (5Sp) **Cr** *k<u>a</u>njon* M, pl. *-i*, beg20c (1 tech) → *-ski* adj. **Bg** *kany<u>o</u>n* M, pl. *-al-i*, 20c (5Sp) **Fi** *kanjoni* (5Sp) **Hu** *kanyon* (5Sp) **Al** *kanion* M, pl. *-e*, mid20c (3/5Sp) **Gr** *k<u>a</u>nion* N (Ø)

cap *n.* 1a 'a soft head-covering with a peak', 1b 'a head-covering worn by those engaged in a particular profession', +1f 'a rider's cap'

Du [=E] C, 1970s (1 tech) **Nw** *caps* [=E] M, pl. *-er*, 1970s (2) **Ic** *kappi* M, pl. *-ar*, beg19c, 1a,b(5Da) **It** [k<u>e</u>p] M, pl. Ø, beg20c, +1f(1 tech) **Rs** *k<u>e</u>pka* F, pl. *-i*, beg20c, 1a,+1f(3) **Bg** *k<u>e</u>pe* N, pl. *-ta*, beg20c, via Fr? 1a(3)

cape *n.* 1 'a sleeveless cloak', +1a 'a short sleeveless lady's cloak, usu. made of fur'

Ge [ke:p] N, pl. *-s*, 19c, 1(2) **Du** [ke:p] C, beg20c, 1(2) **Nw** [ke:p] M, pl. *-r*, beg20c, 1(2) **Ic** *keip* [kʰei:p] N, pl. Ø; *keipur* [kʰei:pʏr] M, pl. *-ar*, 1930s, via Da, +1a(2 coll) **Fr** 1(5) **Sp** *capa* (5La) **It** *cappa* (5La) < *mantella* **Rm**

cap<u>ă</u> [kapə] F, 1920s, 1,+1a (5Fr) **Cr** *kep* M, pl. *-ovi*, beg20c, 1(3) **Hu** *kepp* [kepp] pl. *-ek*, end19c/beg20c, 1(2/3) **Gr** *k<u>a</u>pa* F, beg20c (5/1t)

capsize *v.* 2 'be overturned (of a boat)'

Du *kapseizen* [kapsɛizən] mid19c (3) **Nw** *kapseise* [kapsæise] 19c (3)

car *n.* +1a 'an elegant automobile', +6 'a coach for holiday excursions', +7 'a fork-lift truck', +8 *cp²* as in *side car* etc.

Ge [=E] M, pl. *-s*, 1970s, via Fr, +6(1 reg) < +6: *Reisebus*; = 6: *autocar* **Nw** (0) **Ic** [kʰa:r] N, mid/ end20c, +1a(1 sla) **Fr** [=E] (abbrev.) +6(3) = *autocar* **Sp** +8(1) **It** [kar] M, pl. Ø, 1910s, +8(1) **Rs** *kar* M, pl. *-y*, mid20c, +1a,+7(3 tech) **Po** (0) **Bg** *kar* M/cp², pl. *-al-i*, mid20c, +7(3) → *-en* adj. **Fi** *kaara* +1a(0) **Al** *kerr* +1(1 reg) **Gr** +8(1 tech)

caravan *n.* 1a (British English) 'a vehicle equipped for living in, usu. towed by a motor vehicle' 1b (American English) 'a covered wagon or lorry', +4 'a station wagon'

The meaning of this loanword in individual languages is uncertain because of the British/American English distinction.

Ge [k<u>a</u>rava:n] M, pl. *-s*, 1960s, 1a(1 mod) < *Wohnanhänger*, *Wohnwagen* → *Caravaner* M **Du** [=E] [karav<u>a</u>n] C, 1950s, 1a,b(2>3) → *caravannen* v.; *caravaner* n. **Nw** [k<u>a</u>ravan] M, pl. *-sl-er*, 1a,b(2) = *campingvogn* → *caravanisme* M, *caravanist* M **Ic** *karavan(i)* [kʰa:ravan(ı)] M, pl. *-ar*, beg20c, 1a(5Da) < rend *húsbíll* **Fr** *caravane* [karav<u>a</u>n] F, mid20c, 1a(4) **Sp** *caravana* F, mid20c, 1a,b(3) < *roulotte* **It** [k<u>a</u>ravan] M, pl. Ø, 1960s, 1a(2) < *roulotte* **Po** *karawan* [karav<u>a</u>n] M, mid20c (1 coll) **Cr** *kar<u>a</u>van* M, pl. *-i*, mid20c, 1b(1 tech) **Bg** *karav<u>a</u>na* F, pl. *-ni*, mid20c, via Fr, 1a(3) **Fi** *karavaanila* 1a,b(5) → *karavaanari* **Hu** *k<u>a</u>rav128n* [karava:n] pl. *-ok*, mid20c, 1a(2 mod) **Gr** *k<u>a</u>ravan* N, mid20c, +4(2)

caravanning *n.* +2 'the practice of travelling or living in a caravan on holidays'

Ge [=E] N [U] 1960s (1 tech, rare) < *Camping* **Du** [=E/karav<u>a</u>niŋ] C [U] 1970s (2) **Nw** - < *camping* **Fr** *caravaning* [kaʀavaniŋ] 20c (1 ban) > *caravanage, tourisme en caravane* **Sp** *caravaning* [karabanin] M (1 tech, writ) > *camping caravaning* **It** [k<u>a</u>ravaniŋ] M

[U] 1930s (1 tech) **Po** *karawaning/<=E>* [karava-nink] M, mid20c (2 mod) → *-owy* adj.

card *n./cp²* 9 'a plastic card for various uses, esp. cashless payment'

This term has been used since the 1980s, typically as cp², for various types of plastic card: for identification, telephones, parking, hotel rooms and cashless banking etc. A detailed survey of what English+English or hybrid compounds exist for what types of cards would be desirable; cf. ↑*credit card, smart card*, etc.

Ge [=E], often cp², F, pl. *-s*, 1980s (2) = *Karte* **Du** [=E], 1980s (2) = *pasje* **Nw** [=E] N, pl. *-s*, 1980s (1) < *kort* **Ic** *kort* N, pl. Ø, 1980s (4) **Sp** - < *tarjeta (de crédito)* **It** [kard] F, pl. Ø, 1980s (2) = trsl *carta* **Rm** [=E] N, 1990s (1 tech) **Rs** *kart* M/cp², pl. *-y*, 1990s (3 tech) < rend *kartochka* **Po** (5La) **Cr** < mean *kartica* **Bg** k̲a̲rta (5Fr/Ge); cp² only in *fono*- **Fi** *kortii* (5Sw) **Hu** (0 writ) **Al** *kartë*, F, pl. *-a*, 1994 (3) **Gr** *<=E>/kard* F/cp², 1990s (2) < *karta*

Cardiff (coal)* *n.* 'a kind of coal'

Rs *kardiff* M [U] beg20c (1 tech, arch) **Po** *kardyf* M [U] beg20c (1 tech) → *-owy* adj. **Bg** k̲ardi̲f M [U] 20c (Ø/3 tech) **Gr** K̲ardif N [U] beg20c (1 tech)

cardigan *n.* 'a knitted jacket fastening down the front'

The waistcoat was named after James Thomas Brudenell, seventh Earl of Cardigan (1797–1868) who led the Light Brigade in the battle of Balaclava in 1854. The item became widely known in connection with the reports of the Crimean War which drew considerable contemporary attention.

Ge [=E] M, pl. *-s*, 1950s (1 obs) **Du** [=E/k̲ardi̲ɣan] C, 1940s (1 tech) **Nw** *<=E>/kardigan* [k̲a:rdigan] M, pl. *-er/- s*, 1950s (2) **Fr** [kaʀdig̲ã] M, 1930s (1 obs) **Sp** [k̲ardigan] M, pl. *-s*, 1950s (2>3) **It** [k̲ardigan] M, pl. Ø 1960s (2) **Rm** [k̲ardigan] N, 1960s, via Fr (3 obs) **Rs** *kardig̲an* M, pl. *-y*, 1990s (2) **Po** *kardigan* [kardigan] M, end20c (2) **Cr** k̲ardigan M, pl. *-i*, mid20c (2) **Hu** k̲ardig̲án [k̲ardiga:n] pl. *-ok*, end20c (3) **Gr** k̲ardig̲an N, end20c (2)

CARE *acron.* 'Cooperative for American Relief Everywhere'

Ge [ke:r] (cp¹, freq. in *Care-Paket*) 1940s (1 obs) **Nw** (0) **Fr** (0) **Sp** (0) **Po** [ker] end20c (1 mod) **Cr** [ker] M, mid20c (1) **Gr** (Ø)

care *n.* 4a 'protection, charge' (esp. *cp²*, e.g. intensive care)

Du [=E] C [U] 1980s (1 tech) **Gr** (0/1 writ)

care of *phr.* 'at the address of'

Ge *c/o* 1940s (1 writ, rare) **Nw** [s̲e̲:u̲:] 20c (1>2) **Fi** *c/o* (1 rare) **Gr** *c/o* (1 writ)

car ferry *n.* 'a ferry equipped for the transport of cars'

Ge - < trsl? *Autofähre* **Nw** - < *bilferge* **Ic** - < *bil(a)ferja* **Fr** [karferi/kaʀfeʀe] M, 1960s (2rare) < *transbordeur, navire transbordeur* **It** - < *traghet*-

to **Po** (o) **Cr** [=E] M, mid20c (1 tech) **Hu** - < trsl *autókomp*

cargo *n.* 1a 'goods carried on a ship or aircraft', +3 'a boat or aircraft designed to take freight'

Du *<=E>/carga*, 1a(5Sp) **Nw** [k̲argu] M [U] 20c, 1a(1 tech) **Ic** [kʰarkou] N [U] mid20c, 1a(1 tech) < *farmur* **Sp** - < *carga* **It** [k̲argo] M, beg20c, +3(3); - < 1a: *carico* **Rm** [k̲argo̲] N [U] mid20c, 1a(1 tech) = *caric* **Rs** (5Sp) **Po** [kargo] N [U] end20c, 1a(1 tech) **Cr** [k̲argo] M [U] mid20c, 1a(1 tech) **Bg** *kargo* N [U] mid20c, 1a(5Sp) **Hu** *kargó* 1a(5Sp) **Gr** *k̲argo/<=E>* N [U] end20c (1 tech)

cargo boat *n.* 'a boat designed to take freight'

Du *cargo* [karxo] C, end19c, via Sp (1 tech) **Fr** *cargo* [kargo] M, beg20c (3) **Sp** - < *barco de carga, car-guero* **Rm** *cargou/cargobot* [karg̲ow/kargobo̲t] N, beg20c, via Fr (3) **Po** (0) **Cr** *kargo* M, beg20c (1 tech) **Al** *kargo* F, pl. Ø, 1960s (1 reg)

cargoliner* *n.* 'a cargo boat'

Nw [k̲argulainer] M, pl. *-e*, 20c (1) **Cr** *kargo* M, 20c (1 tech) **Bg** k̲argola̲iner M, pl. *-al-i*, mid20c (1 tech)

carpet *n.* +3 'a mat'

Du *karpet* [karpɛt] N, pl. *-ten*, 1910s, via Fr (3) **Fr** *carpette* [karpɛt] F, mid19c (3) **Rm** *carpetă* [karpe̲tə] F, 20c, via Fr (3)

carpool* *n.* 'an arrangement by which cars are shared, esp. for going to work'

Ge [k̲a:rpu:l] M, pl. *-s*, 1980s (1 mod) < *Fahrgemeinschaft* **Du** [=E] 1970s (2) → *carpoolen* v. **Nw** (0) **Fr** [kaʀpul] M, 1980s (1 mod) > *covoiturage* **It** [kar pu:l/poul] M, pl. Ø, end20c (1 mod)

carport *n.* 'a shelter for a car'

Ge [k̲a:rport] M, pl. *-s*, 1980s (1 mod) **Du** [k̲arpɔrt] C, 1970s (1 tech) **Nw** [k̲a:rport] M, pl. *-er*, 1960s (1)

carrier *n.* 2 'a company undertaking to convey goods or passengers for payment', 6 'an aircraft-carrier'

Ge [k̲eria] M, pl. Ø, 1970s, 2(Ø/1 tech, rare) **Du** [=E] C, 1940s (1 tech) **Nw** [=E] M, pl. *-s*, 1970s (1) **Sp** [karrier] M/cp², end20c (1 tech) **Cr** M, pl. Ø, end20c, 2(1 tech) **Bg** - < rend *samoletonosach*

car-sharing *n.* 'an arrangement whereby several people use one car in order to divide the expense'

Ge *Car-Sharing* [k̲a:ʃe: rɪŋ] N [U] 1980s (1 mod)

cart *n.* +5 'a small sports car' (cf. ↑*go-cart*)

Ge *Kart* [=E] M/N 1980s, abbrev. (1 tech, rare) → *karting* (cf. ↑*go-cart*) **Du** [kart] C, 1970s (1 tech) **Nw** *<=E>/kart* [=E] M, pl. *-er*, 1970s (1 tech) **Fr** *kart* [kaʀt] M, 1960s (1 tech) → *karting* (cf. ↑*go-cart*) **Sp** *kart* [kart] M, pl. *-s*, mid20c (1 tech) → *karting* (cf. ↑*go-cart*) **Rm** *<=E>/kart* [kart] N, 1960s, via Fr? (3 tech) **Rs** *kart* M, pl. *-y*, mid20c (1 tech) **Po** *kart* [kart] M, mid20c (1 tech) **Cr** (0) **Bg** - < *karting* **Fi** *kartti*, 20c (3 sla) **Gr** *kart* N, pl. Ø/-s, end20c (1 tech)

carter* *n.* 'a gear case' (named after the inventor, Harrison Carter)

Du [=E] N, 1940s (1 tech) **Fr** [kaʀtɛʀ] end19c (3 tech) **Sp** *cárter* M, beg20c, via Fr (3 tech) **It** [karter] M, pl. Ø, beg20c (3 tech) **Rm** *carter* [kartər] N, 1970s (1 tech) **Rs** k<u>a</u>rter M, pl. -*y*, mid20c (1 tech) **Cr** *karter* M, pl. Ø, mid20c (1 tech) **Bg** k<u>a</u>rter M, pl. -*al-i*, mid20c (1 tech) **Hu** *karter* [k<u>a</u>rter] pl. Ø, beg20c (3 tech)

carting* *n.* 1 'a place for cart races', 2 'cart races', 3 'a go-cart'

Ge <=E>/*Karting*, 1980s, via Fr? 1,2(1 tech, rare) **Fr** <=E>/*karting* [kaʀtiŋ] M, 1960s, 2(1 tech) **Sp** *karting* [k<u>a</u>rtin] M [U] mid20c, 2(1 tech); 1: *pista de karts, kartódromo* **Rm** <=E>/*karting* [k<u>a</u>rtiŋ] N [U] mid20c (1 tech) **Rs** k<u>a</u>rting, M [U] mid20c, 1,2(2 tech) → -*ist* M **Po** *karting* M, end20c, 1,2(1 mod) **Cr** *karting* [kartink] M [U] end20c, 2(1 tech) **Bg** k<u>a</u>rting M, pl. -*al-i*, mid20c, 3(3 tech); [U] 2(3 tech) **Fi** *kartting-ajot* mid20c (1 tech) **Gr** k<u>a</u>rting N [U] 1980s, 1,2(1 tech, mod)

cartoon *n.* 1 'a humorous drawing in a newspaper etc.', 2 'a sequence of drawings telling a story', 3 'a filmed sequence of drawings using the technique of animation'

The earliest meaning borrowed, that of a single parodic drawing, is the most widespread, even though the difference from a series of drawings is not always clear. By contrast, the loanword rarely refers to films. This word and its derivatives compete with the earlier *caricature* which appears more frequently and has a wider application.

Ge [kartuːn] M, pl. -*s*, 1960s, 1(2) < *Karikatur* → -*ist* M **Du** [=E] C, 1950s, 1(2) < *spotprent* → -*ist* n. **Nw** - < *tegneserie, karikatur* **Ic** - < 1: *skopmynd*; 2: *teiknimyndasaga* **Fr** [kartun] M, 1930s, 3(1 tech) < *dessin animé* → *cartooniste* M **Sp** [kart<u>u</u>n] M, pl., end20c, 1,2(1 tech); 1930s, 3(1 tech) < *dibujos animados* → *cartoonista* M, *cartoonesco* adj. **It** [kartuːn] M, pl. Ø, 1950s, 3(1) < trsl *cartone animato* **Rm** - < *desen animat* **Rs** - < *karikatura* **Cr** (0) **Bg** - < *karikatura* **Al** *karton* (5It) < 3: *film me kartona* **Gr** *kartun*/<=E> N, pl. Ø/-*s*, mid20c, 3(0) < creat *kinumena skhedhia*

cartridge *n.* +4a 'an ink-container for insertion into a printer', +4b 'a toner-container for a photocopying machine', +5 'a video-game cassette'

Du [=E] C, 1990s, +4a(1 tech) **Sp** - < *cartucho* **It** - < *cartuccia* **Rm** [=E] N, 1990s, +4a(0>1 tech) **Rs** k<u>a</u>rtridzh M, pl. -*i*, 1990s (3 tech) **Po** [kartridʒ] M, end20c (1 tech) **Cr** (0) **Hu** -*disk* [=E] pl. Ø, end20c,

+4a(1 tech) **Gr** <=E> [=E] N, end20c, +4a,b(1 tech)

car wash *n.* 1 'an establishment containing equipment for washing vehicles automatically'

Ge [=E] end20c (1 writ, mod) < *Autowaschanlage* **Du** [=E] (1 writ) = *autowasstation* **Fr** - < *lave-auto* **Po** M, uninfl., 1990s (1 coll) **Bg** - < *avtomivka* **Hu** [=E] end20c (1 writ, mod)

case[1] *n.* 1 'an instance of sth. occurring' (used as examples in problem solving), 3a 'an instance of a person receiving professional guidance, e.g. from a doctor', 3b 'such a person or the circumstances involved'

Du [=E] C, 1970s (1 tech) **Nw** [=E] M, pl. -*s/-er*, 1980s (1 tech) **Ic** [kʰei:s/cʰei:s] N, pl. Ø, end20c, 3a,b(1 sla/tech) **Sp** *caso* (5La) **It** *caso* (5La) **Bg** - < mean *sluchaĭ* **Fi** <=E>/*keissi* [=E] end20c (1 coll) **Hu** (5La)

case[2] *n.* +1a 'a superstructure on the back part of a trawler, esp. over the machine-room'

Ic *keis* [kʰei:s] M, pl. -*ar*, mid20c (2 tech)

case history *n.* 'information about a person for use in professional treatment'

Nw <=E>/*case-historie* [=E] M, pl. -*ies/-(e)r*, 1980s (1 tech, obs) **It** [k<u>e</u>is hist<u>o</u>ri] F, 1970s (1 tech) < trsl *storia del caso*

case study *n.* 3 'a study or account of a particular instance used as an exemplar of general principles'

Ge - < trsl *Fallstudie* **Du** [=E] C, pl. '*s*, 1980s (1 tech) **Nw** <=E>/*case-studie* [=E] M, pl. -*ies/-(e)r*, 1980s (1 tech) **Fr** - < trsl *étude de cas* **It** [k<u>e</u>is st<u>a</u>di] M, 1980s (1 tech) < trsl *studio del caso* **Rm** - < trsl *studiu de caz* **Cr** [=E] M, end20c (1 tech) **Fi** *keissitutkimus/keissi* end20c (1 coll) **Hu** [k<u>e</u>:sst<u>a</u>di] [U] end20c (1 tech_SCIEN_)

casework *n.* 'social work concerned with individuals'

Du [=E] N [U] 1970s (1 tech) **Nw** [=E] N [U] 1970s (1 tech) **It** [k<u>e</u>is w<u>o</u>rk] M, 1970s (1 tech)

caseworker *n.* 'a social worker doing casework'

Nw [=E] M, pl. -*e*, 1970s (1 tech) **It** [k<u>e</u>isw<u>o</u>rker] M, 1970s (1 tech)

cash *n.* 1 'money in coins or notes'

This term arrived in a well-supplied lexical field, and where accepted, carried negative or at least highly colloquial connotations (except for neutral modern developments such as ↑*electronic cash*). Unsurprisingly, the distribution of the word has recently extended to Eastern Europe. Note the infrequency of derivatives.

Ge [keʃ] N [U] beg20c, 1970s (1 coll) < *Bar(geld)* **Du** [=E] C [U] mid20c (1 mod) < *contant geld* **Nw** [=E] M [U] end20c (1 coll) → *cashe* v.; *cashe (ut)* v. **Ic** [kʰas:] N [U] end20c (1 sla) < *reiðufé* **Fr** [kaʃ] 1920s (1 coll) only in *payer cash* < *payer comptant* **Sp** [kaʃ] M/adv., 1980s (1 coll/mod) **It** [kɛʃ] M [U] mid20c (1 tech) < *contanti*　**Rm** [keʃ] adv., 1980s (1 mod)　**Rs** *késh* M [U] 1990s (1 mod)　**Po** *kesz* F [U] 1990s (1 mod)　**Cr** *keš* M [U] end20c (1 coll)　**Bg** *kesh* M [U] 1990s (2 tech/coll) → -*ov* adj.　**Hu** [=E] [U] mid20c (1 tech)　**Al** *kesh* 1993 (1 mod)　**Gr** *kas* adv., end20c (2 coll) < *metritis*

cash and carry- (c&c) *phr./cp¹* 2 'a wholesale store'

This term is an example of a linguistic fashion of the 1960s which became obsolete before it reached Eastern Europe.

Ge [keʃenkɛri:] 1960s (1 obs)　**Du** [kɛʃ ɛn kɛri] C, pl. -'s, 1980s (1 mod)　**Nw** [=E] 1960s (1 obs)　**Fr** <=E> M [U] mid20c (1 obs, ban) > *payer-prendre* **Sp** [=E] M, pl. Ø, end20c (1 obs)　**It** [keʃenkɛrri] M [U] 1950s (1 tech)　**Rs** *késh-énd-kéri* 1990s (1 mod)　**Po** 1990s (1 mod)　**Cr** (o)　**Hu** [=E] 20c (1 tech)　**Gr** <=E> [kas end kari] end20c (1 mod)

cashew- *n., cp¹* 2 'the edible nut of the cashew tree'

Although this word dates from 1703 in English, the word (and the nut) appears to have been adopted only relatively recently in Continental languages.

Ge *Cashewnuβ* [keʃu:] 20c (1>2+5)　**Du** *cashewnoot* [kɛʃju-] 1970s (2 tech+5)　**Nw** *kassjunøtt/cashew-* [kæʃu/kaʃu:] 1980s (1 tech+5)　**Ic** *kasjúhneta* [kʰa:sju-] F, 1980s (1 coll+5)　**Fr** *cachou* [=E] 1990s (0)　**Rs** *kesh'yu* M, uninfl., 1990s (1 tech)　**Bg** *kashu* N [U] end20c (5Port)　**Fi** [=E] (0)　**Hu** *kesu* [keʃu] [U] 20c (1 tech)　**Gr** *kasiu* N, pl. -*s*, end20c (1>2)

cash flow *n.* 'the movement of money into and out of a business'

The distribution appears to be typical of a modern financial term: known only to experts, and not yet affecting Eastern Europe.

Ge [keʃflo:] M [U] 1970s (0>1 tech)　**Du** [=E] C [U] 1970s (1 tech)　**Nw** [=E] M [U] 1980s (1 tech)　**Fr** *cash-flow* [kaʃflo] M, 1960s(1tech)<*margebruted'autofinancement* **Sp** [kaʃflo] M, 1970s (1 tech) < trsl *flujo de caja* **It**

[kɛʃ flou] M, pl. Ø, 1970s (1 tech) > creat *autofinanziamento* **Rm** [=E] N [U] 1990s (1 tech)　**Po** - < trsl *przeptyev pieniędzy* **Bg** - < trsl *parichen potok* **Hu** [=E] end20c (1 tech, jour)　**Gr** <=E>/*kas flou* N [U] 1990s (1 tech)

cash in (on) *v.* 2 'profit from, take advantage of sth.'　**Nw** *cashe inn (på)* [kæʃe] 1980s (1 coll)

cashmere *n./cp¹* 1 'fine soft wool', 2 'a material made from this'

The great variation in spelling points to different periods of adoption and degrees of integration; reanglicization is possible, as in the frequent spelling *cashmere* in present-day German.

Ge *Kaschmir*-cp¹, 19c (3); *Cashmere* [=E] M [U] end20c (1 mod)　**Du** *kasjmier* (5Ind)　**Nw** *kasjmir* [kaʃmi:r] M [U] beg20c, via Ge (1 tech)　**Ic** *kasmír* [kʰasmir] cp¹/M [U] mid19c, via Da (3)　**Fr** M, 1960s

(1 tech) > *cachemire* (5)　**Sp** [kaʃmir] M [U] end20c (1>2 tech) < *cachemir* **It** *cachemire/<=E>* [kaʃmir] M [U] beg19c (2)　**Rm** *caşmir* [kaʃmir] end19c, via Fr (3)　**Rs** *kashemir* M [U] 19c, 2(3) → -*ovyi* adj.　**Po** *kaszmir* [kaʃmir] M [U] mid20c (2) → -*owy* adj.　**Cr** *kašmir* M [U] beg20c, 2(3)　**Bg** *kashmir* M [U] beg20c, via Fr, 2(3) → -*en* adj.　**Fi** *kasmir* (2)　**Hu** *kasmir* [kaʃmi:r] adj./n., 17/18c (3)　**Al** *kazmir/kashmir* M [U] 1930s, 1,2(1 reg)　**Gr** *kasmiri* N, end19c/beg20c, via Fr and Turk (3)

cash on delivery *n.* 'a system whereby a carrier is paid for goods when they are delivered'

Ge <=E>/*c.o.d.* [=E] N [U] 20c (1 tech)　**Nw** <=E>/*c.o.d.* [=E] (1 tech)　**Ic** - < *póstkrafa* **It** *C.O.D.* [=E] 1940s (1 tech) < trsl *pagamento alla consegna* **Rm** (0)　**Cr** (0)　**Bg** - < trsl *plashtane pri dostavka* **Fi** *c.o.d.* [=E/se:o:de:] (1 tech)

cast *v.* 3 'throw out (a fishing line) into the water', 9b 'allocate roles in a play, film, etc', +13 'produce sound' (of music loudspeakers)'

Du [=E] C, 1960s, 9b(2 tech)　**Nw** 9b(0)　**Ic** *kasta* mid20c, 3(4) +13(4 tech, sla)

cast *n.* 6 'the actors taking part in a play, film, etc.'

Du [=E] C, pl. -*s*, end20c (1 tech)　**Ic** [=E] N [U] end20c (1 tech)　**Fr** [=E] M, pl. -*s*, 1980 (1 tech)　**Sp** [=E] M [U] 1980s (1 tech)　**It** [=E] M, pl. Ø, 1940s (2 tech)

casting *n.* +2 'the sport of casting with a fishing-rod', +3 'test filming in order to allocate roles in a film, etc.'

This word exemplifies the phenomenon whereby anglicisms known to distinct groups of specialists only are adopted independently, resulting in their having a very low frequency in all the languages affected.

Ge [=E] N [U] 1990s, +2(1 tech/mod); 1980s, +3(1 tech)　**Du** [=E] C, 1960s (2 tech)　**Nw** [=E] M [U] 20c, +2(1 tech); M, pl. -*er*, 1980s, +3(1 tech)　**Fr** [=E] M [U] 1970s?, +3(1 mod/ban) > *distribution artistique* **Sp** [kastin] M,

pl. -*s*, 1980s (1 tech)　**It** [kastiŋ] M [U] 1980s, +3(1 tech)　**Rs** *kasting* M [U] 1990s (1 tech)　**Po** [kastink] M [U] end20c, +3(1 tech)　**Bg** *kasting* M [U] end20c, +2(1 tech); 1990s, +3(3 tech, mod)　**Gr** *kasting* N [U] 1990s, +3(1 tech)

casuals *n.* 2 'informal clothes'

Du [=E] C [U] 1990s (1 jour)　**It** *casual* [kɛʒual] M/adj. [U] 1980s (2)　**Cr** (o)　**Gr** *casual/kazual* adj./N [U] 1980s (2)

catch *v.* +13 'wrestle' (as practised in *catch-as-catch-can*)

Ge [ketʃən] 1960s (2 obs)　**Du** *catchen* [kɛtʃən] 1970s (1 coll, obs)　**Fr** *catcher* [katʃe] 20c　**Po** (0)　**Gr** - < *kano kats*

catch *n.* +6 'wrestling'

The word appears to be infrequent by itself; it is likely to be an abbreviation of ↑*catch-as-catch-can*.

Ge [=E] N [U] (1 tech, rare) < *Catchen* **Du** [kɛtʃ] C [U] 1970s (1 tech)　**Fr** *catch* [katʃ] M, mid20c (2)　**Sp**

[=E] M [U] 1930s (1 tech, arch)   **It** [kɛtʃ] M [U] 1930s (1 tech)   **Rm** *catch/checi* [=E] mid20c, via Fr (1 tech)   **Rs** *kéch* M [U] mid20c (3 tech)   **Po** (0)   **Cr** (0)   **Bg** *kech* M [U] mid20c (3 tech) < ↑*catch-as-catch-can* → *-adzhiya* M   **Gr** *kats* N [U] end20c, via Fr (1 tech)

catch-as-catch-can   *phr.* 1 'wrestling', +2 'any other free-style procedure'

This once very popular 'sport' appears to be less widespread today, and with it, its designation. Note the smaller number of verbs and agent nouns, both probably back-formed, in Southern and Eastern Europe. The contest was recently revived as ↑*wrestling*.

Ge [kɛtʃesketchkẹn] N [U] 1950s (1 obs)   **Du** [kɛtʃ ɛs ketʃ kẹːn] N [U] 1970s (1 tech)   **Nw** [=E] M [U] mid20c (1 obs)   **Fr** - < *catch* **Sp** [=E] M [U] 1920s (1 tech, arch)   **Rm** <=E>/*catch-can* [=E] N [U] mid20c, via Fr?, 1(1 tech)   **Rs** - < *kéch* M   **Po** [ketʃ es ketʃ ken] mid20c, 1(1 tech)   **Cr** *kecheskecken* M [U] mid20c (1 tech)   **Bg** *kecheskechkẹn* M [U] mid20c, 1(1 tech, rare)   **Hu** *kecsezkecsken* [=E] [U] end19/beg20c (1 tech)   **Gr** - < *kats*

catcher[1]   *n.* 2 'the fielder who stands behind the batter' (baseb.), +3 'a type of wrestler' (in ↑*catch-as-catch-can* contests)

Ge [ketʃa] M, pl. Ø, 1950s, +3(2 obs)   **Du** [=E] C, 1970s (1 tech)   **Nw** (Ø)   **Fr** *catcheur/catcheuse* [katʃœʀ/-øz] M/F, mid20c, +3(2 tech)   **Sp** [katʃer] M, end20c, 2(1 tech)   **It** [kɛtʃer] M, pl. Ø, 1960s (1 tech) < 2: *ricevitore*; < +3: *lottatore*   **Rs** *kétcher* M, pl. -*y*, end20c, +3(1 tech) = *kechist*   **Po** *keczer* [ketʃer] M, end20c, +3(1 tech)   **Cr** *kečer* M, pl. -*i*, end20c, +3(1 tech)   **Bg** *kechŭr* M, pl. -*i*, end20c, 2(1 tech)   **Gr** <=E>/*katser* M, pl. Ø/-*s*, end20c, 2,+3(1 tech); *katser* M, via Fr, +3(1 tech)

catcher[2]   *n.* 'a fishing net with a frame and a handle'
Ge *Kescher* M, pl. Ø, end19c (3 tech)

catering   *n.* (orig.[TM] 'the practice of supplying food for planes, schools or parties'

This term appears to have spread mainly in connection with airlines (where it did not necessarily originate).

Ge [kẹːtəriŋk] N [U] 1970s (1 tech, mod)   **Du** [kẹːtəriŋ] C [U] 1970s (1 tech)   **Nw** [=E] M [U] 1960s (2)   **Fr** <=E> M, 1980s (1 tech, ban) > *ravitaillement*   **Sp** [katerin] M, pl. Ø, 1970s (1 tech)   **It** [keiteriŋ(g)] M

[U] 1970s (1 tech)   **Rm** [=E/katering] 1990s (1 tech)   **Rs** (0)   **Po** [keterink] M [U] end20c (1 mod)   **Cr** [=E] M [U] mid20c (1 tech)   **Bg** *ketŭring* M [U] end20c (1 tech)   **Hu** [=E] M [U] beg20c (1 tech)   **Gr** <=E>/*ketering* N [U] end20c (2)

caterpillar   *n.* 2b 'a vehicle with caterpillar tracks'
Ge - < rend *Planierraupe* **Nw** [=E] M, pl. -*er*, mid20c (1 tech/Ø)   **Ic** *Caterpillar* M (1[TM]) < rend *jarðýta*   **Fr** M, 1930s (1 tech/obs) < mean? *chenille*   **Sp** [katerpilar] M, 1970s (1 tech, obs)   **It** [katerpillar] M, pl. Ø, 1930s (2)   **Rm** [katerpilar] N, mid20c (1 tech)   **Rs** *katerpiller* M, pl. -*y*, mid20c (2 tech)   **Po** (0)   **Cr** [katerpilar] M, pl. -*i*, mid20c (1 tech)   **Bg** - < trsl *gŭsenichen*   **Fi** *katerpillari* 20c (3)   **Hu** [=E] pl. Ø, 20c (1 tech) < *hernyótalpas vontató*   **Gr** *katerpilar* N, mid20c (1 tech)

catgut   *n.* 'strong thread made of the twisted intestines of sheep etc.'

This loanword appears to be used exclusively in surgery (and not for strings of musical instruments). The misleading term (it is *not* made from cats' guts) was translated literally into French, but is opaque in the other languages.

Ge *Katgut* [katgut] N [U] end19c (3 tech)   **Du** [kẹtgat] N [U] beg20c (1 tech)   **Nw** <=E>/*katgut* [katgut/=E] M [U] 20c (1 tech)   **Ic** *katgút* beg20c, via Da (1 tech) < *(saum)girni*   **Fr** [katgyt] M, beg20c (1 tech) < trsl

boyau de chat   **Sp** [katgut] M, beg20c (1 tech)   **It** [kɛtgʌt/kɛtgat] M [U] end19c (1 tech)   **Rm** [katgut] N [U] end19c, via Fr (3 tech)   **Rs** *ketgut* M [U] beg20c (1 tech)   **Po** *ketgut/katgut* [ketgut/ka-] M, beg20c (1 tech)   **Cr** *ketgut* M [U] mid20c (1 tech)   **Bg** *kyatgut/-gŭt* M [U]/pl. -*a*, beg20c (1 tech)   **Hu** *katgut* [katgut] [U] end19/beg20c (1 tech)

Cattleya (plant)   *n.* 'an orchid'
Fr *cattleya/catleya* M, 1900 (3 tech)   **Rs** *kattleya* F, pl. -*ei*, mid20c (1 tech)   **Po** *katleja* [katleja] F, mid20c (1 tech)   **Cr** (0)

CB (radio)   *n.* 'citizens' band'
Ge *CB* [tse:be:] uninfl., 1970s (3 tech, obs) = *CB-Funk*   **Du** - < *MC*   **Nw** (0)   **Fr** *C.B.* [sibi] F, 1970s (1 tech, ban) < *bande de fréquences banalisée, bande de fréquences publique* > *cébiste* → *cibiste* M   **Sp** *CB* [θebe] F, end20c (1 tech) < *banda ciudadana* → *cebeísta* n.   **It** *citizens' band* [sitizenz bend] F, pl. Ø, 1990s (1 tech) < trsl *banda cittadina*   **Po** [-radjo] N, end20c (2 mod)   **Cr** *CB* [cẹbe] M, end20c (1 tech) → *-aš* M; *-aški* adj.   **Hu** [tse: be:] pl. -*k*, end20c (2>3 mod)   **Gr** *CB/Si Bi* N, end20c (1 tech) < *walkie talkie; asyrmatos*

CD   *abbr.* 1 'compact disc', +4 'a CD drive'

This term has mostly been adopted in its abbreviated form and is pronounced according to national conventions. The long form is Latinate; therefore its form is not commonly felt to be English, and integration presents no problem.

Ge [tse:dẹ:] F, pl. Ø/-*s*, 1980s, 1(3)   **Du** [se:de:] C, 1980s, 1(3)   **Nw** [sẹ:de:] M, pl. -*er*, 1980s, 1(3) > *kompaktplate*   **Ic** [=E] 1980s, 1(1 coll) < rend *geisladiskur*   **Fr** [sede] M, 1980s, 1(2 ban) < *disque compact*   **Sp** [θedẹ] M, pl. -*s*, 1980s, 1(2) < *compact disc*   **It** [tʃi di/si di] M, pl. Ø, 1980s, 1(2) > *compact* *disc, disco compatto* **Rm** [sidi/tʃede] N, 1990s, 1(1 mod) **Rs** *si di* M, uninfl., 1980s, 1(1 tech, coll, you) < *kompakt disk* **Po** - < *kompakt disk* M = rend *pïyta kompaktowa* **Cr** [cede] M [U] end20c, 1(1 tech) **Bg** <=E> [sidi/tsede], pl. Ø/-ta, 1990s, 1(1 tech, coll) +4(3 tech) **Fi** [se:de:] 1980s, 1(3) **Hu** [tse: de:] pl. -k, end20c, 1(2 mod) **Al** - < *kompakt disk* **Gr** CD/si di N, end20c, 1(2) > creat *psifiakos dhiskos*

CD-player   *n.* 'a player for compact discs'

     This term came with ↑*CD*; note the reduced number of calques, which may be indicative of its late adoption—or of the fact that the first part tends not to be translated.

Ge [tse:de:ple:a] M, pl. Ø, 1980s (2) > *CD-Spieler* **Du** (0) < *c.d.-speler* [se:de:-] 1980s (2) **Nw** (0) < *CD-spiller* **Ic** - < rend *geislaspilari* **Fr** - < trsl *lecteur de CD, lecteur de disques compacts* **Sp** - < *lector de CD/compact disc* **It**

[tʃi di pleier] M, pl. Ø, 1980s (1 tech) < creat *lettore di CD* **Rm** [=E] 1990s (0 > 1 mod) **Rs** *CD- pleier* M, pl. -y, 1980s (1 tech/you) **Po** (0) **Cr** [cede pleier] M, end20c (1 tech) **Bg** CD/si-di pleŭr M, pl. -ra/-ri, 1980s (1 tech) < pleier **Fi** - < CD-soitin **Hu** (0) < CD- lejátszó **Gr** si di pleier N/M, 1980s (2)

CD-ROM   *n.* (*abbrev.*) 1 'compact-disc read-only memory for retrieval of data on a VDU screen', 2 'a CD-ROM drive'

     As a technical term, the frequency of the English pronunciation is more common than in the preceding item, but the source of the acronym is opaque in both English and the recipient languages.

Ge [=E/tse:de:rom] F, pl. Ø/-s, 1980s (1 tech) **Du** *CD ROM* [se:de:ʀom] 1980s, 1(1 tech) **Nw** [se:de:rum/se:de:rum] M [U] 1980s, 1(2) **Ic** [=E] uninfl., 1980s, 1(1 tech) = rend *geisladiskur, geisladrif* **Fr** [sedeʀɔm] 1980s, 1 (1 ban) > *disque optique compact/DOC* **Sp** <=E>/cederrón [θederon] M, pl. Ø, 1980s, 1(2 tech) **It** [tʃidirɔm/sidirɔm] M, pl. Ø, 1980s, 1(2) **Rm** [=E] N, 1990s (1 tech) **Rs** si-di-rom M, pl. -y, 1990s, 1(1 tech) **Po** <=E> M, end20c (1 tech) **Cr** [cederom] M, pl. -i, 1980s, 1(1 tech) **Bg** <=E> [si-di rom] M [U]/pl. -ma, 1990s, 1(1 tech) 2(3 tech) **Fi** [se:de:rɔm] **Hu** [tse: de: rom] [U] end20c (1 tech) **Gr** <=E> [si di rom] N, end20c (1 tech)

celebrity   *n.* 1 'a well-known person'

Du - < *celebriteit* **Nw** - < *celebritet* **Fr** - < *célébrité* (5) **Sp** - < *celebridad* **It** - < *celebrità* (5La) **Rm** - < *celebritate* **Po** F [U] end20c (1 jour) **Hu** - < *celebritás* (5La) **Gr** (0)

cellophane   *n.* (orig.™) 'thin transparent wrapping material'

     This term was coined from Latin/Greek roots (c. 1912, and possibly first in French) and is no longer felt to be English; the same applies to ↑*celluloid*.

Ge *Zellophan* N [U] beg20c (3) **Du** *cellofaan* N [U] 1970s (3) **Nw** *cellofan* [selufa:n] M [U] 20c (3) **Ic** *sellófan* [sɛl:oufan] N [U] mid20c, via Da (2) **Fr**

[selɔfan] F, beg20c (3) **Sp** *celofán* [θelofan] M [U] mid20c (5Fr) **It** <=E>/*cellofan* [tʃelofan] M [U] 1930s (3) **Rm** *celofan* [tʃelofan] N, 1940s, via Fr (3) **Rs** *tsellofan* M [U] mid20c → -ovyĭ adj. **Po** (5Gr+La) **Cr** *celofan* M [U] 20c (3) → -ski adj. **Bg** *tselofan* M [U] mid20c, via Ge (3) → -en adj. **Fi** *sellofaani* (3) **Hu** *celofán* [tselofa:n] pl. Ø (3) **Al** *celofan* M, pl. Ø, 1960s (3) **Gr** *zelofan/selofan* N, via Fr, mid20c (3)

cellotape*   *n.* 'adhesive tape'

Sp - < *celo/cello* **It** - < ↑*Scotch* **Cr** [selotejp] M [U] mid20c (3) **Gr** *seloteipl/ zeloteip* N, mid20c (2)

celluloid   *n.* 1 'transparent flammable plastic'

     This term was first coined in American English in 1871, and came to be connected with films in the 1930s.

Ge *Zelluloid* N [U] beg20c (3) **Du** [sɪlylɔjt] N [U] beg20c (2) **Nw** [selɵlui:d] M [U] 20c (1 arch) **Ic** *sellúlóið* N [U] end19c (1 tech) **Fr** *celluloïd* [selyloid] M, end19c (3 tech) **Sp** *celuloide* M [U] beg20c (3) **It** *celluloide* F [U] end19c (3) **Rm** *celuloid* [tʃeluloid] N [U] end19c, via Fr (3) **Rs** *tsellюloid* M [U] beg20c (1 arch) → -nyĭ adj. **Po** *celuloid* [celuloit] M [U] beg20c (2 tech) **Cr** *celuloid* M [U] 20c (3) **Bg** *tseluloid* M [U] mid20c, via Ge (3) → -en adj. **Fi** *selluloidi* (3) **Hu** [tsellюloid] [U] 20c (3 tech) **Al** *celuloid* M, pl. Ø, mid20c (3) **Gr** *seluloid* N [U] 20c (1 tech)

center/centre   *n.* 1 'a middle point', 3a 'a place or group of buildings forming a central point or the main area for a particular activity', 7a 'a middle player in some field games'

     This term competes with Latin *centrum*, French *centre*, and other native expressions. It is now most frequently found in combinations like *city-* and *shopping-* (also used absolutely) or in new coinages like *eros-*, *fitness-* in which the spelling *center* is preferred (German). In football it is short for ↑*centre forward* (7a).

Ge [senta] cp²/N, pl. Ø/-s, 1960s, 3a(1 mod) 7a(1 tech) < 3a: *Zentrum* **Du** cp² [=E] N, 1980s, 3a(2); *centrum* C, 7a(1 tech) < 1: *centre* **Nw** <=E>/*senter* [senter] N, pl. Ø/sentre, 1960s (3) **Ic** *senter* [sɛnter] M, pl. -ar, beg20c, 7a(1 tech, sla) = rend *framherji* **Fr** -*center* [sɑ̃tœr] cp²/M, 1990s (1 mod) **Sp** M, 1990s, 7a(Ø/1 tech) = *pivot* **It** [senter] M/cp², pl. Ø, 1960s, 3a(1>2) < *centro* **Rm** - < 2,3a: *centru* (5La); 7a: rend *mijlocaş* **Rs** *tsentr* M, pl. -y, mid20c (3) → -al'nyĭ adj.; -ovoĭ adj. **Po** (5Fr) **Cr** *centar* M, beg20c, 7a(3) **Bg** *tsentŭr* M, pl. -al-trove, beg20c, via Rs, 1,3a(5Ge) 7a(4 tech, coll) → *tsentralen* adj. **Fi** *center* [sent:er1] end20c, 3a(2) **Hu** 1,3a(5La); [tsenter] pl. -ek, end19c, 7a(1 tech) < 7a: *középcsatár*; → -ez v. **Al** *qendër* [tʃendēr] F, pl. -ra, beg20c, 1,3a(3) **Gr** - < *kentro* 1(5); *center* [sɛnter] cp²/N, end20c, 3a(1 mod); *seder* N, 7a(1 tech) = 3a: *kentro*

center-back*   *n.* 'a middle player or position in a backline' (sports)

Nw *senterback* [=E] M, pl. -er/-s, 20c (1 obs) **Fr** - < trsl *arrière-centre* **Sp** - < trsl *defensa central* **Rm** -

< rend *fundaş central* **Rs** - < trsl *tsentral'nyĭ zash-chitnik* **Bg** - < trsl *tsentralen zashtitnik* **Hu** *center-bekk* [tsenter-bek] pl. *-ek*, end19c (1 tech, arch) < *középhátvéd* **Al** *qendërbek* M, pl. *-ë*, 1930s (1 tech/3) **Gr** *sederbak/sederbak* M/N, beg20c (1 tech)

centercourt* *n.* 'a court for a tennis match' (cf. ↑*court*)

Ge [=E] M, pl. *-s*, end20c (1 tech) **Du** *centre court* [=E] N, 1980s (1 tech) **Nw** [=E] M, pl. *-er*, 20c (1) **Fr** - < trsl *court central* **Rs** *senterkort* M, pl. *-y*, end20c (1 tech) > trsl *tsentral'nyi kort* **Hu** [tsenter-ko:rt] [U] 20c (1 tech) **Gr** *senterkort* N, end20c (1 tech)

central locking *n.* 'a locking system in motor vehicles whereby the locks of several doors can be operated from a single lock'

Ge - < trsl *Zentralverriegelung* **Nw** - < rend *sentrallås* **Ic** - < rend *samlæsing* **Fr** - < trsl *fermeture centralisée* **Sp** - < trsl *cierre centralizado* **It** - < trsl *chiusura centralizzata* **Bg** - < trsl *tsentralno zaklyuchvane* **Fi** - < trsl *keskilukitus* **Gr** <=E>/*sentral loking* N [U] 1990s (1 tech>2)

centre *v.* 5 'kick or hit the ball to the centre of the pitch', +5a 'send the ball to another player'

Du *centeren* mid20c (1 tech) **Nw** *sentre* [sentre] 1950s (3) → *sentring* C **Ic** *sentra* [sentra] beg20c, 5,+5a(1 tech, sla) **Sp** - < mean *centrar* **Rm** *centra* [tʃentra] (5Fr) **Cr** *centrirati* beg20c, 5,+5a(3) **Bg** *tsentriram* 3 **Hu** *centerez* [tsenterez] end19c (2 tech) **Al** *centroj* 1920s (3) **Gr** *sedraro* → *sedrarisma* M; *sedra* F

centreboard *n.* 'a board for lowering through a boat's keel to prevent leeway'

Du *centerboard* N, beg20c (1 tech) < *middenzwaard* **Nw** *senterbord*/<=E> [=E/-bu:r] N, pl. Ø, 20c (1 tech+5)

centre forward *n.* 'a middle player or position in a forward line' (sport)

This term was adopted with the spread of football, but has been replaced by calques, together with other related terms, in many languages.

Ge [=E] end19c (1 reg, obs) < trsl *Mittelstürmer* **Nw** *senterforward*/<=E> [=E] M, pl. *-s/-er*, beg20c (1 obs) > trsl *senterløper* **Ic** - < rend *framherji* **Fr** - < *avant-centre* **Sp** - < trsl *delantero centro* **It** - < trsl *centravanti, centrattacco* **Rm** - < rend *centru înaintaş* **Rs** *tsentrforvard* M, pl. *-y*, beg20c (1 tech) < trsl *tsentral'nyĭ napadayushchiĭ* **Po** - < creat *napastnik środkowy* **Cr** *centarfor/centar* M, beg20c (1 tech) **Bg** - < trsl *tsentŭr napadatel* **Fi** - < trsl *keskushyökkääjä* **Hu** [tsenter-] end19c (1 tech_FOOTB) **Al** - < *qëndër sulmues* **Gr** *seder for/sederfor* M, beg20c (1 tech_FOOTB); *forghuord* M, beg20c (1 tech_BASKETB)

centre half *n.* 'a middle player or position in a defensive line' (sport) (cf. ↑*stopper*)

Ge [=E] end19c (1 reg, obs) < rend *Mittelläufer* **Du**

center half C (1 obs) < *middenspeler* **Nw** *senterhalf*/<=E> [=E] M, pl. *-er*, beg20c (1 obs) < *midtstopper* **Ic** [ha:fsent] M, beg/mid20c (1 tech, sla) < rend *miðvörður* **Fr** - < trsl *demi-centre* **Sp** - < trsl *medio centro* **It** - < rend *centromediano* **Rm** *half centru* [half tʃentru] M, mid20c (1+5) < rend *mijlocaş centru* < *stoper* **Rs** - < *tsentral'nyĭ poluzashchitnik, stopper* **Po** - < *stoper* **Cr** *centarhalf* M, beg20c (1 tech) **Bg** *tsentŭr half* 20c (3 tech) **Hu** [tsenter-half] end19c (1 tech_FOOTB) **Al** - < trsl *mesfushor* **Gr** *seder haf/sederhaf* M, beg20c (1 tech)

chairman *n.* 'a person chosen to preside over a meeting'

A somewhat modish import of uncertain permanence—especially since the word is under pressure in English by *chairperson* (which has not yet been recorded as a potential loanword).

Ge [=E] M, pl. *-men*, 1980s (1 coll) < *Vorsitzender* **Du** [=E] C, pl. *-men*, 1990s (1 jour, mod) < *voorzitter* **Nw** (0) < *møteleder* **Fr** (Ø) **Sp** [=E] M, 1930s (Ø tech, writ) < *presidente* **It** [tʃɛarmɛn] M, pl. Ø, 1980s (1 tech) < *presidente* **Po** (0) **Cr** (0) **Al** - < *president* **Gr** (0) < *proedhros*

challenge *n./cp¹* 1a 'a summons to take part in a contest or trial of strength etc.', 2 'a demanding or difficult task', +7 'a contest'

This word appears to be very marginal. So far it competes with little success against native terms in sports, and is even less common in the sense of a 'demanding task'; cf. ↑*challenger* (with unexplained differences in distribution)

Ge [=E] F, 1980s, +7(1 coll, rare) < mean *Herausforderung* **Du** [=E] C, 1970s, +7(1 mod) < *uitdaging* **Nw** (0) < *utfordring* **Ic** [t(s)jal:ens] uninfl., end20c, 1a,2(0 sla) < *áskorendaeinvígi* **Fr** [ʃalãʒ/tʃalɛndʒ] M, end19c, 2,+7(2 ban) < *défi* → *challenger, challengeur* n. **Sp** [tʃalenʃ] F, end20c, +7(1 tech, rare) **It** [tʃelindʒ] F, pl. Ø, 1930s, 2,+7(1 tech) < *sfida* **Rm** [=E] cp¹, 1990s, +7(0>1 mod) **Po** [-elen-] M, uninfl., mid20c, +7(1 tech) **Hu** - < trsl *kihívás napja* **Al** - < *sfidë*

challenger *n.* 'a person taking part in a contest'

Nw (0) < *utfordrer* **Fr** *challenger/challengeur* [tʃalɛndʒœr/ʃalãʒœr] end19c/beg20c (1 tech) = *défiens* **Sp** [tʃalenjer] M, 1920s (1 tech_BOX) < *aspirante* **It** [tʃelindʒer] M, pl. Ø, 1930s (1 tech) < trsl *sfidante* **Rm** *şalanger* [ʃalandʒer] M, mid20c?, via Fr (3) **Po** [tʃelendʒer] M, end20c (1 mod) **Cr** *čelendžer* M, pl. *-i*, mid20c (1 tech)

champ *n.* (abbrev.) ↑*champion*

Ge [ʃemp] M, pl. *-s*, 1970s (1 coll, rare) < *Champion*

champion *n.* 1 'a person or animal who has defeated all rivals in a competition etc.'

Since the earlier loan from French is identical in spelling, written sources are ambiguous. It seems that English pronunciation has ousted French during the course of the twentieth century, whereas *championat* (where available) remains French.

Ge [ʃempion] M, pl. -s, end19c (1 coll) **Du** *kampioen* [kampiu̯:n] C, pl. -en, 15c (5) **Nw** [ʃæmpien] M, pl. -s, 20c (1) → *championat* N (5Fr) **Fr** *champion*/-*ionne* (5) **Sp** - < *campeón*/*ona* (5/It) **It** [tʃempion] M, pl. Ø, mid20c (1 mod) < *campione, campionessa* **Rm** *campion* [kampjon] M/*campioană* [kampjoanə] F, mid19c (5It) **Rs** *chempion* M, pl. -y, beg20c (3/5Fr) → -*skiĭ* adj.; -*ka* F; -*at* M **Po** *czempion*/<=E> [tʃempion] M, beg20c (5Fr) → -*ka* F **Cr** *šampion* M, pl. -i, mid20c, (5Fr) **Bg** *shampion* M, pl. -i, beg20c (5Fr) → -*ski* adj.; -*at* M; -*ka* F **Hu** (5Fr) **Al** *kampion* M, pl. -ë, mid20c (5It) **Gr** *tsabion* M, pl. Ø/-s (1 jour) < *protathlitis*/-*tria, nikitis*/-*tria* M/F

chance *n.* 2 'a risk', 4 'an opportunity', +4a 'an opportunity to have success with the opposite sex'

The word was widely accepted from 18/19c French; it is uncertain how far the identical English word has affected the pronunciation of the loanword and led to its being interpreted as an anglicism.

Ge 4(5Fr) **Du** 4(5Fr) < *kans* **Nw** *sjans*/*kjangs*/*tjangs* 4; *få sjans* [ʃaŋs/ʃans/çaŋs] M, pl. -er, 20c, +4a(3 coll) → *sjanse* v. **Ic** *séns*/*sjans* [sjɛns/sjans] M, pl. -ar, mid20c, partly from Da, 2,4(2 coll) +4a(2 sla) → *sénsast* v. **Fr** *chance* (5) **Sp** [tʃans/tʃanθe] F, pl. -s, 1920s, 4(2>3/5Fr) **It** (5Fr) **Rm** *șansă* [ʃansə] F, end19c, 4(5Fr) **Rs** (5Fr) **Bg** *shans* M, pl. -al-ove, beg20c, 4(5Fr) **Hu** 4(5Fr) **Al** *shans* M, pl. -e, mid20c, 4(5Fr)

change *n.*/*cp¹* 2a 'money given in exchange for money in larger units or a different currency', 4a 'exchange'

A typical word spreading with international tourism etc., often exclusively known in written form (and in Latin script, in Russian, Greek), in shop displays (writ). There are few compounds and derivatives—the corresponding verb is almost totally native.

Du [tʃe:nӡ] C, beg20c (1 writ) **Nw** [=E] 20c, 2a(o) < *veksel* **Fr** 2a(5) **Sp** - < *cambio* **It** - < *cambio* **Rm** [=E] 2a(o writ) < (*casă de*) *schimb* **Rs** *cheĭndzh*/*chendzh* M [U] 1990s, 2a(2 coll) 4a(1 writ) **Po** <=E>/*exchange* F [U] beg20c (1 coll) **Cr** 2a(o) **Bg** <=E> 4a(2 writ); *cheĭndzh*/*chench* cp¹/M [U] 1970s, 2a(2 coll, pej); 1990s, 4a(2) → -*adzhiya* M; *cheĭndzh-byuro* N **Fi** <=E> 1980s, 2a(1 writ) **Hu** [=E] [U] mid/end20c, 2a(1 tech, writ/5Fr) **Gr** 2a(o writ)

change *v.* 3b 'exchange'

Nw *kingse* [çiṇse] 20c (3 coll, sla) **Fr** (5) **It** - < *cambio* **Po** (o) **Bg** *chencha se* refl. (3 sla) **Al** - < *shkëmbej*

charleston *n.* 'a lively American dance of the 1920s'

One of the most fashionable dances of the 1920s, which is why this word is still (passively) known in many languages.

Ge [ʃa:rlston] M [U] 1920s (1 obs) **Du** [=E] C, 1920s (1 obs) **Nw** [ʃa:ston] M [U] 1920s (1 obs) **Ic** [sjarleston/tʰjal:eston] M [U] 1920s, via Da (2) **Fr** [ʃaʀlɛstɔn] M, 1920s (1 obs) **Sp** *charlestón* M [U] 1920s (3) **It** [tʃarleston] M [U] 1920s (2 obs) **Rm** [tʃarleston/ʃarleston] N [U] beg20c, via Fr (1 obs) **Rs** *charl'ston* M [U] beg20c (1 arch) **Po** [tʃarlston] M [U] beg20c (1 arch) **Cr** *čarlston* M [U] beg20c (2 obs) **Bg** *charlston* M [U] beg20c (2 obs) **Fi** [=E] beg20c (1) **Hu** [=E] [U] beg20c (2 obs) **Al** *çerleston* M [U] 1920s (2/3) **Gr** *tsarleston* N [U] beg20c (1 obs)

Charl(e)y* *n.* +2 'a Briton or the British in general' **Ic** *tjalli* [tʰjal:ı] M, pl. -ar, beg/mid20c (3 coll, pej)

chart *n.* 2 'a sheet of information in the form of a table, graph, or diagram'

Ge [=E] N, pl. -s (1 tech) **Du** [=E] C, pl. -s (1 tech) **Nw** [=E/ʃa:t] N, pl. Ø (1 tech, rare) **Sp** [tʃart] M, pl. -s, end20c (1 tech) → *chartista* n., *chartismo* n. **It** - < ↑*flowchart* **Rs** *chart* M, pl. -y, 1995 (1 tech, rare) **Cr** (o) **Bg** *chart* M, pl. -al-ove, 1990s (1 tech, coll)

chart(s) *n.* 3 'a list and rating of the currently most popular songs' (mostly pl.)

Ge [ʃa:rts] pl., 1980s (1 you, mod) > *Hitliste, Hitparade* **Nw** - < *hitliste* **Ic** - < *vinsældalisti* **Fr** <=E> M/F?, 1980s (1 mod) **Sp** [tʃart] M, pl. (1 tech, you) < *hit parade* → *chartear* **Rm** *charts* N, end20c (1 mod) < *top* **Rs** *charty* pl. end20c (1 you) **Bg** *chart* M, pl. -al-ove, 1990s (1 jour, you) < *toplista, khitlista* **Gr** *tsarts*/<=E> N, pl., end20c (1 tech, you, mod)

charter¹ *n.* 1b 'a written constitution or description of an organization's functions etc.'

Du *charter* (5) **Nw** [ʃa:rter] N, pl. Ø/*chartre*, 20c (2) **Sp** - < *carta* (5La) **It** - < *carta* (5La) **Rm** - < *cartă* [kartə] F, 20c (5Fr/La) **Rs** *khartiya* F (5Gr) **Bg** - < *kharta* (5Gr) **Hu** (5Gr) **Al** - < *kartë* (5La) **Gr** - < *khartis*

charter² *cp¹/²* 2 'a contract to hire an aircraft, ship, etc.'

The noun and verb became common commercial terms for the hiring of ships for special purposes in the nineteenth century. A second wave of influence came in with mass tourism and the distinction between regular scheduled and charter flights—from which both noun and verb are spreading into the hiring of other objects or persons.

Ge [ʃa:ta] M, pl. Ø, -s, 1960s (2 tech) **Du** [ʃɑ rtər] C, 1950s, 2a(1 tech) **Nw** [ʃa:rter] N, usu. cp¹, 1940s (2) **Fr** [ʃaʀteʀ] M/adj., 1950s, 2(2ban) > *vol nolisé*; *vol affrété, fréter* → *chartériser* v. **Sp** *chárter* [tʃarter] M, pl. -s, 1950s (2); adj. (3) **It** esp. *volo charter* [tʃarter] M [U] end19c (1 tech) **Rm** [=E] N/cp²,

1970s (1 tech)   **Rs** *ch*<u>a</u>*rter* M [U] mid20c (2) → *-ny*ï
adj.   **Po** *czarter* [tʃarter] M, mid20c (2) → *-owy*
adj.   **Cr** *č*<u>a</u>*rter* M, pl. *-i*, mid20c (1 tech)   **Bg** *ch*<u>a</u>*rt*<u>ŭ</u>*r*
M [U] 1970s (2 tech) → *-en* adj.; *chartyor* M   **Fi** [=E]
1970s (1)   **Hu** [=E] 1980s (1 tech)   **Al** çarter M [U]
1970s, 2(reg)   **Gr** *ts*<u>a</u>*rter* cp² [U] end20c (2)

charter   *v.* 2 'hire' (esp. a ship, plane, bus, car)
Ge [ʃ<u>a</u>(r)tan] 19c/1960s (2 tech) → *Charterer* M   **Du**
charteren 19c (3)   **Nw** *chartre* [ʃ<u>a</u>:rtre] 1960s (2) →
chartring M   **Fr** *chartériser* (1 ban) > *affréter, noli-*
ser   **It** - < *noleggiare, charterizzare*   **Po** *czarterować*
[tʃarterovats] mid20c (2) → *wy*-v.; *za*-v.   **Cr** *čartirati*
mid20c (2 tech)   **Bg** *chart*<u>i</u>*ram* 20c (2tech)

chatterton('s compound)*   *n.* 'insulating tape'
Fr *chatterton* [ʃatɛʀtɔn] M, mid19c (2 tech)   **Fi** *Chat-*
tertonin massa 20c? (1 tech)

cheap   *adj.* 4a 'costing little effort or acquired by discreditable means and hence of little value', 4b 'contemptible, despicable'
Nw *kjip* [çi:p] 1960s, 4b(3 coll, sla)   **Ic** [=E] uninfl.,
end20c, 4a,b(1 sla) < trsl *ódýr*   **Fr** [tʃip] 1980s (1
mod)   **It** [tʃi:p] 1960s, 4a,b(1 obs, rare)

check   *n.* 1 'a means or act of testing, etc. (e.g. in
safety precautions)', +2d (in ice-hockey) '(permitted)
barging'
The earlier loans from *cheque* are usually differentiated in spelling and not confused; however, the nom-
inal and verbal borrowings meaning 'control' and
'stop' have produced a wealth of senses and applications ranging from technical uses to highly colloquial
ones, in which semantic borrowing and independent
development are not easy to distinguish. The word's
currency is supported by *check in*, and less frequently
check out, terms commonly used in airports and hotels.
Ge [ʃek] M, pl. *-s*, 1970s, 1(1 tech, mod); [(t)ʃek] 1960s,
+2d(1 tech) < 1: *Überprüfung*   **Du** [=E] C, 1990s, 1(1
mod)   **Nw** *sjekk* [ʃek] M, pl. *-er*, mid20c, 1(3)   **Ic**
tékk [tʰjɛhk] N, pl. Ø, end20c, 1(1 coll) = *skoðun*   **Sp**
chequeo M, 20c, 1(2>3) < *control, revisión*   **It** [tʃɛk]
M, pl. Ø, 1980s (1 tech) < *controllo*   **Hu** [tʃekk] [U]
end20c, 1(1 tech) < *ellenőrzés*   **Gr** *tsek*<u>a</u>*risma* N, 1(3
coll) < *elegkhos*

check   *v.* 1a 'examine the accuracy, quality, or condition of', 1b 'make sure, verify', 6 (US) 'deposit luggage
for storage or dispatch', +8 'grasp, comprehend', +9
'pick up a partner'
Ge [ʃekən] 1970s, 1a,b(1 coll); 1970s, +8(2 sla) → *ab-*,
durch-   **Du** *checken* [tʃ<u>ɛ</u>kə(n)] end20c, 1a,b(1
tech)   **Nw** *sjekke* [ʃ<u>ɛ</u>ke] 1950s, 1a,b(3) +8(3 coll, sla)
+9(c) → *sjekker* M   **Ic** *tékka* [tʰjɛhka] 1970s, 1a(2
coll)   **Sp** *chequear* mid20c, 1a,b(3) < *examinar, revi-*
sar etc.   **Cr** *ček*<u>i</u>*rati*, end20c, 1a,b(1 tech)   **Fi** *tsekata*
end20c, 1a,b(3 coll)   **Hu** [=E+-el/-ol] 20c, 1a,b(2
tech)   **Gr** *tsek*<u>a</u>*ro* end20c, 1a,b(2 coll, jour)

check-in   *n.* 'an act of checking in or a place designated for this'
Ge [=E] N/M, pl. *-s*, 1970s (1 mod)   **Du** *inchecken*
[ɪntʃɪkə(n)] N [U] 1970s (2)   **Nw**
<=E>/*sjekk-inn* [ʃekin] M [U] 1970s (2)   **Ic** [tʰjɛhkɪn:]

N [U] end20c (1 coll)   **Sp** M [U]
end20c (1 tech) < *mostrador de*
facturación   **It** [tʃɛk <u>i</u>n] 1970s (2
tech) < *accettazione*   **Rm** [=E]
N [U] end20c (1 tech)   **Po**
<=E> M, uninfl., end20c (1
mod, tech)   **Cr** *č*<u>e</u>*k in* M [U]
end20c (1 tech)   **Bg** *chek-in*/<=E> M [U] end20c (1
tech_{PLANES})   **Hu** [=E] [U] 20c (1 tech)   **Gr** <=E>/
tsek <u>i</u>n N, end20c[U] (2)

check in   *v.* 1 'register (at an airport, hotel, etc.)' 2
'record the arrival of'
Ge *einchecken* 1970s (2)   **Du** *inchecken* end20c, 1(1
coll)   **Nw** *sjekke inn* [ʃeke] 1950s (3+5) → *innsjekking*
M; *innsjekket* adj.   **Ic** *tékka (sig) inn* end20c, 1(2 coll)
It - < *fare il 'check-in'*   **Po** (0)   **Cr** *ček*<u>i</u>*rati* end20c,
1(1 tech)   **Bg** *chek*<u>i</u>*ram* end20c, 1(3 tech) → *-ane* N

checklist   *n.* 'a list of necessary items, actions, etc.,
consulted to ensure that nothing is missing'
Ge *Checkliste* [ʃ<u>e</u>-] F, pl. *-en*, 1970s (1 coll+5)   **Du**
[=E] C, pl. *-en*, 1970s (1 tech, coll) < *controlelijst*   **Nw**
sjekkleste [ʃek-+Nw] 20c (3)   **Ic** *tékklisti* M, pl. *-ar*,
end20c (2 coll) > rend *gátlisti*   **Fr** *check-list* [(t)ʃek-
list] F, mid20c (1 tech, ban) > *liste de vérification*   **Sp**
<=E> M, pl. *-s*, end20c (1 tech, rare)   **It** [tʃ<u>ɛ</u>kl<u>i</u>st] M,
pl. Ø, end20c (1 tech) < trsl *lista di controllo*   **Rm** [=E]
1980s (0)   **Rs** (0)   **Bg** *cheklist* M, pl. *-al-ove*,
mid20c (1 tech_{NAUT})   **Hu** [=E] [U] end20c (1 tech)

check out   *v.* 1 'leave a hotel etc. with due formal-
ities', 2 'investigate, examine for authenticity or suit-
ability'
Ge *auschecken* 1980s, 1(1 tech, rare)   **Du** *uitchecken*
[œytʃɪkən] N [U] 1970s (2)   **Nw** *sjekke ut* [ʃeke] 1970s
(3+5) → *utsjekket* adj.   **Ic** *tékka (sig) út* end20c, 1(2
coll)   **Po** (0)

checkpoint   *n.* 'a place where documents etc. are
inspected'
Use of this term was apparently sparked off by
Checkpoint Charlie, the popular name of the Berlin
border control after the Wall was built in 1961. The
term has limited currency, and the chances of its survival are in no doubt.
Ge [=E] M, pl. *-s*, 1960s (1 tech) < *Kontrollpunkt*   **Du**
- < *controlepost, Checkpoint Charly*   **Nw** (0)   **Fr**
<=E> M, mid20c (1 ban) < *point de vérification*   **It**
[tʃɛkp<u>ɔ</u>int] M, pl. Ø, 1950s (1 tech) < rend *posto di*
controllo   **Rm** - < rend *punct de control*   **Rs** - <
*control'ny*ï *punkt*   **Po** - < rend *punkt kontrolny*   **Cr**
[=E] M, pl. Ø, end20c (1 tech) < *kontrolua točka*   **Bg** -
< *kontrolen punkt*

check-up   *n.* 'a thorough (medical) examination'
Ge [=E] M, pl. *-s*, 1970s (1 mod)
< *(Vorsorge) Untersuchung*
Du *check up* [=E] C, 1990s (1
mod)   **Nw** (0) < *sjekk*   **Ic** *tékk-*
öpp [tʰjɛhkœhp] N, pl. Ø, end20c
(1 coll) < *(læknis) skoðun*   **Fr**
[(t)ʃekœp] M, 1960s (1 ban) >
bilan de santé   **Sp** - < *chequeo = reconocimiento*

médico, revisión médica **It** [tʃɛkap] M, pl. Ø, 1960s (2 tech) **Hu** [=E] [U] end20c (Ø>1 tech) **Gr** <=E>/tsek ap/tsekap N, end20c (2) > *gheniki iatriki exetasi*

check up *v.* 1 'ascertain, verify, make sure', +2 'pick up a partner'

Ge *abchecken* [aptʃekən] 1970s (3 coll) **Nw** *sjekke opp* [ʃeke] 1970s (3 coll+5) **Sp** - < *chequear* 1(2>3) **Gr** *kano tsekap*

Cheddar *n.* 'a type of cheese' (cf. ↑*Chester*)

This word, like others of its kind, wavers between a foreignism and the designation of an imported, or even locally produced, type of cheese. Since the cheese varies in popularity it is not likely to become a full loanword, at least not in Western Europe.

Ge [=E] M [U] beg20c (Ø) **Du** [=E] C [U] 1950s (2 tech) **Nw** [ʃedar] M [U] mid20c (1) **Ic** [=E] M (Ø) **Fr** [ʃedaʀ] M, end19/beg20c (Ø) **Sp** (*queso*) *cheddar* M [U] end20c (Ø1 tech, rare) **Rm** [tʃedar] N [U] 1970s (1 tech) **Rs** *chedder* M [U] mid20c (3) **Po** *cheddar* [tʃedar] M, end20c (2) **Cr** (o) **Bg** *chedŭr* M [U] end20c (Ø mod) **Fi** [=E] [U] (Ø) **Gr** *tsedar* N [U] end20c (1>2)

cheeks *n.* 4c 'either of the side pieces of various parts of machines'

Rs *chiksy* pl., beg20c (1 tech)

cheerio *interj.* 'expressing good wishes on parting'

Ge (0) **Du** [=E] 1950s (1 coll) **Nw** (0) **Rs** (0) **Po** (0) **Hu** *csirió* 20c (1 coll, sla, fac)

cheerleader *n.* 'a person who leads cheers or applause'

Ge <=E> [-li:da] F/M, pl. -*s*, 20c (Ø>1 techSPORTS) **Du** [=E] C, pl. -*s*, (1 tech) **Nw** [=E] M, pl. -*s*, 1980s (1 tech) **Sp** [E/tʃierlider] F, pl. -*s*, end20c (1 tech) **Fi** [=E] (Ø) **Gr** <=E> [=E] F, pl. -*s*, end20c (1 tech)

cheeseburger *n.* 'a beefburger with a slice of cheese in it'

Arguably the most common burger after its model, ↑*hamburger*. The term is slowly spreading through Europe, but is confined to items sold in the street or in certain fast food chains.

Ge [ʃi:sbörga] M, pl. Ø/-*s*, 1970s (1 coll) **Du** [=E] C, end20c, 1(1 tech, coll) **Nw** [(t)ʃi:sburger] M, pl. -*e*, end20c (2) > *osteburger* **Ic** - < rend *ostborgari* **Fr** [(t)ʃizbœrgœr/tʃizburgœr] M, end20c (1 coll) **Sp** - < rend *hamburgesa con queso* **It** [tʃizburger] M, pl. Ø, end20c (1) **Rm** [=E] M, end20c (o) **Rs** *chizburger* M, pl. -*y*, end20c (1 mod, you) **Po** [tʃisberger/-urger] M, end20c (2 coll) **Cr** *čizburger* M, end20c (1 coll) **Bg** *chizburger* M, pl. -*al-i*, 1990s (1 mod) **Fi** [=E] 1990s (o) < trsl *juusto(ham)purilainen* **Hu** [=E] pl. -*ek*, 1990s (2 mod) < trsl *sajtburger* **Al** *çisburger* 1994 (1 mod) **Gr** *tsizberger* N, end20c (2)

cheesecake *n.* 1 'a tart filled with sweetened curds etc.'

The English word may have been calqued on German *Käsekuchen*; the word has apparently not caught on in the sense of 'portrayal of women in a sexually attractive manner'

Ge - < *Käsekuchen* **Nw** (0) < *ostekake* **Ic** - < creat *ostakaka* **Fr** [(t)ʃizkɛk] M, 1980s, (1 mod) **Gr** <=E>/*tsizkeik* N, 1980s (2)

cheque *n.* 'a written order to a bank to pay a stated sum to a stated recipient'

Cheque, coined in England in 1706 (from *exchequer*), was widely transmitted through French as a banking term in the nineteenth century, its spelling taken to be French. The word is now fully integrated in all languages, apparently no calques having developed in contrast to the compound ↑*traveller's cheque*.

Ge *Scheck* M, pl. -*s*, 19c (3) **Du** [ʃɪk] C, beg20c, via Fr (3) **Nw** *sjekk* [ʃek] M, pl. -*er*, 19c (3) → *sjekkis* n. **Ic** *tékki/tékkur* [thjɛhci/thjɛhkʏr] M, pl. -*ar*, beg20c, via Da (2 coll) < *ávísun* **Fr** *chèque* [ʃek] M, mid19c (3) **Sp** [tʃeke] M, end19c (3) → *chequera* **It** [ʃek/tʃek] M, pl. Ø, mid19c (3) < *assegno* **Rm** *cec* [tʃek] N, mid19c, via Fr? (3) **Rs** *chek* M, pl. -*i*, 19c (3) → -*ovyǐ* adj. **Po** *czek* M, mid19c (3) **Cr** *ček* M, pl. -*ovi*, beg20c (3) **Bg** *chek* M, pl. -*al-ove*, beg20c (3) **Fi** *shekki* [ʃekki] (3) **Hu** *csekk* [=E] pl. -*ek*, beg19c (3) **Al** *çek* M, pl. -*ë*, end19c (3) **Gr** *tsek*/ <=E> N, end20c (2) = *trapeziki epitaghi*

cherry brandy *n.* 'an alcoholic drink'

This term has been used for a liqueur since the nineteenth century, originally as a foreignism; for the brandy proper, *Kirsch* (German Alsatian, spread through French) has limited currency beside native terms.

Ge [ʃeri:brendi:] M, pl. -*(ie)s*, end19c (2) **Du** [=E] C, 1950s (2 tech) **Nw** [=E/ʃæri-] M [U] (1) **Ic** - < trsl *kirsuberjabrennivín* **Fr** *cherry* [ʃeri] M, end19c (1 arch) **It** [tʃɛrri brendi] M [U] 1920s (1) **Rm** [ʃeri brendi/tʃeri

brendi] N, mid20c (1 rare) **Rs** *cherri-brendi* M, uninfl., end19c (2) **Po** [-endi] N, uninfl., end20c (1 tech) **Cr** *čeri-brendi* M [U] end19c (2) **Hu** *sherry brandy* [ʃeribrendi] [U] end19c/beg20c (2>3) **Al** *sheri brandi* M [U] mid20c (2) **Gr** *cherry/tseri/tsery* N, beg20c (2)

Chester* *n.* 'a kind of cheese' (cf. ↑*Cheddar*)

The same as *Cheshire (cheese); Chester* is not recorded in English dictionaries, and *Cheshire* is not found as a loanword.

Ge *Chester* [ʃesta] M [U] 19c (Ø) < *Chesterkäse* **Du** [=E] C [U] mid20c (2 tech) **Ic** [=E] M (Ø) **Fr** [ʃesteʀ] M, mid19c (Ø) **Sp** [tʃester] M, end19c (1 tech, rare) **Rm** [ʃester] N [U] mid20c, via Fr (1 tech) **Po** *czester*/<=E> [-er] M, mid19c (2) **Cr** (o) **Hu** [=E] [U] [U] (Ø) **Gr** <=E>/*tsester* N, end20c (1 tech)

chesterfield *n./cp¹* 'a sofa' (name) 2 'a man's plain overcoat', +3 'a brand of cigarette'

Philip Dormer Stanhope, the fourth Earl of Chesterfield (1694–1773) is well-known for the eponyms for the overcoat and the sofa – and for the letters to his son. The name of the cigarette appears to have remained a trademark only.

Ge [=E?] M, beg20c, 2(1 arch) **Du** [tʃistərfiːlt] C, 1960s 1,2(1 tech) **Nw** [=E] cp¹, 20c, 1(1 tech, jour) **Ic** [(t)sjɛsterfilt] N [U] 1940s, 1(1 tech) +3(1 coll) **Sp** [tʃesterfild] M, 1960s, 1(1 tech) 2(1 tech, rare); *chester* mid20c, +3(2) **It** [tʃɛsterfild] M, pl. Ø, end19c, 2(1 obs) **Rm** [=E] N [U] mid20c, +3(ᵀᴹ only) **Rs** *chesterfild* M [U] end20c, +3(1 mod) **Po** [tʃesterfilt] end20c, 2,+3(1 tech) **Cr** [=E] M, end20c, +3(1 tech) **Bg** *chestŭrfild* M [U] end20c, +3(1 mod) **Hu** [=E] pl. Ø, 20c, +3(1>2 tech) **Al** *Çesterfild* +3(1ᵀᴹ) **Gr** <=E> [=E] end20c, 1(1 tech); *kanapes chesterfield* +3(1 tech)

cheviot *n.* 2 'a type of woollen cloth'
Ge [=E] M [U] end19c (1 tech) **Du** [=E] C/N, end19c (1 tech) **Nw** *sjeviot* [ʃɛviot/tʃeviot] M [U] beg20c (1 tech) **Ic** *sivjot/sevjot* [sɪvjo(h)t/sɛvjo(h)t] N [U] mid20c, via Da (2 arch) **Fr** *cheviotte* [ʃɛvjɔt] F, end19c (1 tech) **Sp** <=E>/*cheviò* M [U] end19c (3) **It** [tʃeviot] M [U] 1870s (1 tech) **Rm** *ṣeviot* [ʃeviot] N [U] end19c, via Fr (3) **Rs** *sheviot* M [U] 19c, via Fr (2 tech, arch) → *-ovyĭ* adj. **Po** *szewiot* [ʃeviot] M [U] beg20c, via Fr (1 tech) **Cr** *ṣeviot* M, beg20c (1 tech) **Bg** *sheviot* M [U] beg20c, via Fr (3) **Fi** *seviotti*, 20c (3) **Hu** *ṣeviot* [ʃeviot] [U] end19c, via Fr (1 tech/5) **Gr** *seviot* N [U] via Fr, beg20c (1 tech)

chewing gum *n.* 'flavoured gum for chewing'
Though invented in the 1870s this item became well known under its English name in Western Europe only after 1945. The term was soon to be replaced by calques in all the languages affected.

Ge (0) < trsl *Kaugummi* **Du** [=E] C/N [U] 1940s (1 obs) < trsl *kauwgom* **Nw** - < trsl *tyggegummi* **Ic** - < creat *tyggigúmmí* **Fr** [ʃuiŋɔm] M, beg20c (1) > *gomme à mâcher* (Québec) **Sp** - < trsl *goma de mascar* < *chicle*

It [tʃuiŋ gam] M, pl. Ø, 1920s (2) < trsl *gomma da masticare, cingomma* **Rm** [=E] N [U] 1950s (0) < *ciungă*; rend *gumă de mestecat* **Rs** *chuingam* M [U] end20c (1 coll) < trsl *zhevatel'naya rezinka* **Po** - < rend *guma do żucia* **Cr** (0) **Bg** (0) < *dŭvka* **Fi** - < trsl *purukumi* **Hu** (0 writ, jour) < trsl *rágógumi* **Gr** <=E> 20c (1 writ)

chief *n./cp¹* 1a 'a leader or ruler', 2 'the head of a department, the highest official', +2a 'a chief engineer on a ship'
Ge [=E] cp¹ 1960s, 1a(1 jour, rare); 1950s, +2a(1 tech, rare) **Nw** <=E>/*kjif* [çi̯ːf] +2a(1 tech, obs) **Ic** *séff(i)* [sjɛːf:(ɪ)] M, pl. *-ar*, end19c, 2(2 coll, fac) **Rm** (5Fr) **Rs** (5Fr) **Po** M [U] +2a(0) **Cr** *čif* M, mid20c (1 tech) **Bg** - < *shef* (5Fr) **Hu** [=E] pl. Ø, 20c, 1a,2(1 tech, mod) < *főnök, parancsnok*

chime *v.* 1a 'ring' (of bells)
Nw *kime* [çi̯ːme] 19c (3)
chimes *n.* 1c 'a set of attuned bells'
Du [=E] pl., 1970s (1 tech)
chintz *n.* 'printed cotton fabric with a glazed finish'
Ge *Schintz* [=E/ʃints] M [U] mid20c (1 tech) **Du** [ʃints] N [U] 1980s (1 tech) **Nw** [ʃints] M [U] mid20c (1 tech) **Fr** [ʃints] M, mid20c (1 tech) **Sp** [=E] M [U] mid20c (1 tech) **It** [tʃints] M [U] 1960s (1 tech) **Rm** *cinz* [tʃinz] N, mid20c, via Fr (1 tech, obs) **Po** M [U] mid20c (1 tech) **Fi** *sintsi* [sıntsı] (3) **Gr** <=E>/*tsints* N [U] 20c (1 tech)

chip *n.* 1 'a splinter or small piece (of wood etc.)', 4 'a counter in gambling games, roulette', 5 'a micro-chip'
While this word has limited currency in sense 4 it is internationally accepted as a computing term, mostly in the form *microchip*. For the potato-based food ↑*chips* is used, but is not felt to be related.
Ge [ʃip] M, pl. *-s*, 4,5(1 tech>2) = 4: *Jeton*; < 5: *Mikrochip* **Du** [=E] C, 1970s, 4,5(2 tech) **Nw** <=E>/*chips* (sg.) [(t)ʃip] M, pl. *-s*, 1970s, 5(1 tech) **Ic** - < 5: *kubbur* **Fr** [ʃip] M, 1980s, 5(0/1 tech) < *puce* (> *microplaquette, pastille*) **Sp** <=E> M, pl. *-s*, 1970s, 5(2 tech) **It** *cip* M, pl. Ø, 1930s, 4(1); M, pl. Ø, 1970s, 5(1 tech) **Rm** <=E>/*cip* [=E] N, 1970s, 5(1 tech) **Rs** *chip* M, pl. *-y*, end20c, 5(1 tech) **Po** M, end20c, 5(1 tech) **Cr** *čip* M, pl. *-ovi*, end20c, 5(1 tech) **Bg** *chip* M, pl. *-a/-ove*, mid20c, 4(2 tech); 1970s, 5(1 tech) **Hu** <=E>/*csip* [=E] pl. Ø, end20c, 5(1 tech) **Gr** *tsip* N, end20c, 5(1 tech)

Chippendale *n.* 1 'a style of furniture'
Thomas Chippendale (1718?–79) was a designer of drawing-room furniture. The elegant style was widely copied, but the name never became generic, still referring to a historical fashion (and a foreignism outside Britain).
Ge [=E] N [U] mid20c (1 tech) **Du** [=E] N [U] (1 tech) **Nw** [=E] M [U] end19c (1 tech) **Ic** [=E] 20c (0 tech) **Fr** *chippendale* [ʃipɛndal] adj., uninfl., mid20c (1 tech) **Sp** M beg20c (1 tech) → *estilo chippendale* adj. **It** [tʃipɛndeil] M [U] 1910s (1 tech) **Rm** [=E] N [U] beg20c (1 tech) **Rs** *chippendeil* M [U] beg20c (1 tech) **Po** *chippendale* [tʃipendale] pl., end19c (1 tech) **Cr** [=E] M [U] end19c (1 tech) **Fi** [=E] beg20c (2) **Hu** [=E] [U] end18/beg19c (1 tech) **Gr** <=E> [=E] N [U] 20c (1 tech)

chips *n.* 3a (BrE) 'deep-fried potatoes, pommes frites', 3b (AmE) 'potato crisps', +3c 'a pack of crisps'
The American English: British English opposition has led to complex patterns. It is normal for European languages to have *pommes frites* (*friture, Fritten* etc.; note the English terms *french fried potatoes/fries*) for the meal eaten warm, complemented by the dry, crisp item sold in packs (=*chips*). However, not all languages appear to distinguish between the two.
Ge [=E] pl., 1960s, 3b(2) **Du** [=E] pl., mid20c, 3b(2) **Nw**

Ic	Nw	Po	Rs
Du	Ge	Cr	Bg
Fr	It	Fi	Hu
Sp	Rm	Al	Gr

[(t)ʃips] M [U] mid20c, 3a(1) 3b(2) <3a: *pommes frites*:
< 3b: *potetgull* **Ic** [=E/sjɪhps] uninfl., mid20c, 3a(0
coll) only in *fish and chips* < 3a: *franskar (kartöflur)*; <
3b: *(kartöflu)flögur* **Fr** [ʃips] F, pl./sg., beg20c,
3b(2) **Sp** *patatas chips* [=E] F, pl. end20c, 3b(1) **It**
[tʃips] F, beg20c, 3b(2); < 3a: *patatine fritte* **Rm** [=E]
end20c, 3a,b(0) **Rs** *chipsy* pl., mid20c, 3b(1 coll/
mod) **Po** *czips/<=E>* M, end20c, 3b(2) **Cr** *čips*
M, sg. & pl., end20c, 3a,b(2) **Bg** *chips* M [U]/pl. *-a/
-ove*, 1980s, 3b(2) +3c(2) **Fi** *sipsit* pl., end20c, 3b(3
coll); 3a: < rend *ranskalaiset perunat* **Hu** [=E] [U]
end20c, 3b(2 mod) **Al** *çips* M, pl. *-e*, end20c
(3) **Gr** *tsips* N, pl., end20c 3b(2)

chisel *n.* 'a hand tool with a squared bevelled blade
for shaping wood, soil, stone or metal'
   Fr [ʃizɛl] M, 1980s (1 tech) **Rs** *chizel'* M, pl. *-i*,
mid20c (1 tech)

chive *n.* 'a small culinary herb (Allium schoenopra-
sum) allied to onion and leek'
   Gr *tsaivs* N (1 tech)

choke *n.* 1 'a device to enrich fuel mixture', +3 'the
narrowed part of a gun'
   As a motoring term this is quite widespread, but
occasionally confused with *shock* (as German etc);
derivatives for the verb and the choke-button in a
car are much less frequent.
   Ge *Schock*/<=E> M, pl. *-s*, 1970s, 1(3 tech) → *Choker*
M **Du** [ʃoːk] C, 1970s, 1(2) → *choken* v. **Nw** [ʃoːk]
M, pl. *-er*, mid20c, 1(2) → *choke* v. **Ic** - < 1: *inn-
sog* **Fr** [(t)ʃok] M, end19c, 1(1 tech, ban) < *enrichis-
seur*; +3 = *choke-bore* (1 tech) **It** [tʃok] M, pl. Ø,
mid20c, 1(2 tech) **Rs** *chok(bor)* M, pl. *-y*, mid20c,
+3(1 tech) **Po** *czok* [tʃok] M, mid20c, +3(1 tech) **Cr**
čok M, mid20c, 1(1 tech) **Gr** *tsok* N, mid20c, 1(1 tech)

choke *v.* 8 'enrich the fuel mixture in an internal-
combustion engine by reducing the intake of air'
   Du *choken* [ʃoːkə(n)] 1970s, 8(2) **Nw** [ʃoke] 20c (1) <
gi choke

choker *n.* 1 'a close-fitting necklace', +2 'a scarf worn
underneath an open collar'
   Ge [ʃoːka] M, pl. Ø, 1930s, 1(1 tech, rare) **Du** *choker*
[=E] C, +2(2 tech) **Nw** [ʃoukər] M pl. *-e*, 20c, 1(1
tech, rare) **Rs** *choker* M, pl. *-y*, end20c (1 coll, rare)

chop *n.* 2 'a thick slice of meat', 3 'a stroke in tennis'
   Fr [tʃop] M, mid20c, 2(1 mod) = *mutton-chop*; 1920s,
3(1 tech) **Sp** M, 1980s?, 3(1 tech) **Rs** 3(0)

chopper *n.* 4 'a type of motorbike with high handlebars' (cf. ↑*easy rider*)
   Ge [=E] M, pl. Ø, 1980s (1 tech,
you) **Du** [=E] C, 1970s (1 tech)
Nw [=E] M, pl. *-s/-e*, 1970s (1)
Fr [ʃopœR] M, 1970s (1 tech) **Sp**
[tʃoper] F, pl. *-s*, end20c (1 tech,
you) → *-ero* M **It** [tʃopper] M,
pl. Ø, 1970s (1 tech) **Rs** *chopper*

M, pl. *-y*, end20c (1 tech, you) **Cr** *čoper* M, pl. *-i*,
end20c (1 tech) **Bg** *chopŭr* M, pl. *-al-i*, end20c (1
tech/you) **Fi** *chopperipyörä* (0) < *harrikka* **Gr** *tsoper* N, 1980s (1 tech, you) → *tsoperia* F; *tsoperaki* N

chow-chow *n.* 1 'a dog of a Chinese breed with long
hair and bluish-black tongue'
   This term was adopted along with many others for
breeds of dogs in the (early) twentieth century. Note
that it is always reduplicated, whereas in English the
short form is preferred for the dogs, while the longer
form is reserved for 'preserve of ginger, orange peel
etc.' and 'mixed vegetable pickle' (not found as loanwords).
   Ge [ʃauʃau] M, pl. *-s*, beg20c (2)

Du [=E] C, mid20c (2 tech) **Nw**
[ʃorʃor] M, pl. *-er*, mid20c (1
tech) **Ic** [=E] (0 tech) **Fr**
[ʃoʃo] M, pl. *chows-chows*,
beg20c (1 tech, arch) **Sp** [=E]
M, pl. Ø, beg20c (1 tech) **It**
[tʃautʃau/ tʃoutʃou] M, pl. Ø, 1950s (2) **Rm** [ʃuʃu/
=E] M, pl. Ø, mid20c (1 tech) **Rs** *chau-chau* M/F,
uninfl., end20c (1 tech) **Po** M, uninfl., mid20c (2)
Bg *chau-chau* N, pl. Ø, mid20c (1 tech) **Fi** [=E] 20c
(2) **Hu** *csau-csau* [tʃautʃau] pl. *-k*, 20c (3) **Gr** (0)

Christian Science *n.* 'the beliefs and practices of
the Church of Christ Scientist'
   Ge [=E] F [U] 20c (1 tech) < trsl *Christliche Wis-
senschaft* **Du** [krɪstjən sajəns] C [U] beg20c (1
tech) **Nw** [=E] M [U] mid20c (1 tech) **Fr** < trsl
science chrétienne

chuck *n.* 2 'a device for holding a workpiece in a lathe
or a tool in a drill'
   Nw <=E>/*kjoks* M, pl. *-er*, 20c (1 tech)

chutney *n.* 'a pungent Indian condiment'
   Ge [tʃatni:] N, pl. *-s*, end20c (1 tech) **Du** (0) **Nw**
[ʃøtni] M [U] 20c (1 tech) **Ic** [=E] end20c (0 tech)
Fr [ʃœtnɛ] M, mid20c (1 tech) **Gr** <=E>/*tsatnei* N,
end20c (0 tech)

c.i.f *abbrev,* 'cost, insurance, freight'
   Ge *cif* [(t)sif] [U] 19c (1 tech, rare) **Du** *cif* [sif] C,
end19c (1 tech) **Nw** <=E>/*cif* beg20c (1 tech) **Ic**
[sɪf:] mid20c (1 tech) **Fr** *C.I.F.* [seiɛf], adj./adv., 20c
(1 tech) > *C.A.F.* (*Coût Assurance, Fret*) **Sp** [θif] adj.
[U] 1970s (1 tech) **It** *C.I.F.* [tʃif] 19c (1 tech) **Rm**
[tʃif] beg20c (1 tech) = *CAF* **Rs** *sif* M [U] mid20c (1
tech) **Po** [cif] beg20c (1 tech) **Cr** [cif] mid20c (1
tech) **Bg** *SIF* M [U] mid20c (1 tech) **Fi** [sɪf] 20c
(1) **Hu** *cif* [tsif] 19/20c (1 tech)

cinder *n.* 1 'the residue of coal or wood that has
stopped giving off flames'
   Ge *Zinder* M [U] 19c (0 arch) **Du** - < *sintel* (5) **Nw**
sinders [sɪnders] M [U] 19c (3 arch)

cinemascope* *n.*ᵀᴹ 'a system for showing wide-
screen-format films' (orig.ᵀᴹ)
   Both *cinemascope* and ↑*cinerama* started out as
trade marks, coined from Greek roots; their 'Englishness' depends on the American company names and
the (partly) close-to-English pronunciation. The
terms are largely obsolete today.
   Ge [sinemaskoːp] N [U] mid20c (2 tech) < *Breit-
wand* **Du** [sinəmaskoːp] C [U] 1950s (1 tech) **Nw**
[sinemaskuːp] N [U] mid20c (1 tech, obs) **Ic**

[si:nɛmaskou:p] uninfl., 1960s (0 tech) **Fr** *cinéma-scope* [sinemaskɔp] M, mid20c (3 tech) **Sp** [θinemas-kope] M [U] mid20c (2 tech) **It** [tʃinemaskop(e)] M [U] 1950s (2 tech, obs) **Rm** *cinemascop* [tʃinemas-kop] N, 1950s, via Fr/It (3 tech) **Cr** *sinemaskop* M [U] mid20c (1 tech) **Hu** *kinemaszkóp* [kinemasko:p] [U] 20c (1 tech) **Al** *kinemaskop* M, pl. *-ë*, 1960s (reg) **Gr** *sinemaskop* N [U] 20c (5Fr)

cinerama* *n.* 'an American system for showing 3-D films' (orig.™)

Ge [sinera:ma] N [U] mid20c (2 tech, obs) < *Breit-wand* **Du** [sinəra:ma] N, pl. *-'s*, 1950s (1 tech) **Nw** [sinera:ma] N [U] mid20c (1 tech, obs) **Fr** *cinérama* [sinerama] M, mid20c (1 tech) **Sp** [θinerama] M [U] mid20c (2 tech) **It** [tʃinerama] M [U] 1950s (1 tech) **Rm** *cineramă* [tʃinerama] F, 1950s, via Fr/It (3 tech) **Rs** *sinerama* F [U] mid20c (1 tech/arch) **Po** <=E> F [U] mid20c (1 tech) **Cr** *sinerama* F [U] mid20c (1 tech) **Hu** [=E] [U] mid20c (1 tech) **Gr** *sinerama* N [U] mid20c (1 tech)

city *n./cp¹/² 1a* 'a large town', *2a* 'the part of London governed by the Lord Mayor and the Corporation', *+2d* 'the commercial area of a large town', *+2e* 'a town centre', *+4* 'a type of designer drug'

This foreignism referring to the commercial centre of London is a nineteenth-century borrowing. The word was re-adopted in the 1960s with reference to the area of the city where shops and theatres are found, making some progress against native terms because of its short form and fashionable appeal. From the 1980s on, it is also frequently found as cp¹, with little meaning beyond imparting a certain mod-ishness (*-bag, -bike, -shirt,* ↑ *-shorts* etc.).

Ge [siti:] F, pl. *-(ie)s*, 20c, +2e(1 mod) < *Innenstadt* **Du** [=E] C, beg20c, 2a,+2e(2) **Nw** [=E] [U] beg20c, 2a(∅) +2d,e(1 coll) **Fr** [siti] F, 2a(∅) **Sp** [θiti] F [U] end19c, 2a(1 tech); 1970s, +2d(1 tech); 1980s, +2e(1 fac, mod) +4(1 tech, rare) **It** [siti] F, pl. ∅, 18c, 2a,+2e,+2d(1 jour) **Rm** [=E] M [U] end19c, 2a,+2d(∅) **Rs** *siti* M, uninfl., mid19c, 2a(∅); mid20c, +2d(1 fac, rare) **Po** <=E> N, uninfl., mid19c, 2a(1 tech) **Cr** *siti* M [U] mid20c, 2a,+2d,e(2) **Bg** *siti* M [U] 2a(∅) 1a,+2d,+2e(2 jour) **Fi** [=E] 1980s 2d,+2e(2) **Hu** [=E] pl. ∅/-k, end19c, 2a(0) +2d(1 tech) +2e(1 mod>2) **Gr** <=E>/*siti* cp², end20c, +2a,e(0)

city dress* *n.* 'a man's suit composed of a black jacket and waistcoat and striped trousers'

Ic [sɪhti trɛs:] N, pl. ∅, beg20c, via Da (1 coll, arch)

cityshorts* *n.* 'dressy (wide) knee-length shorts'

Nw [=E] sg./pl., M, pl. ∅, 1980s (2 mod) **Fi** [=E] 1990s (2)

civil servant *n.* 'a member of the civil service'

Du (∅) **Nw** (∅) **Po** [-servent] M [U] end20c (1 jour)

civil service *n.* 'State administration'

Du (∅) **Nw** (∅) **Po** [-serv-] F [U] end20c (1 jour) **Al** - < trsl *shërbim civil*

claim *n. 1a* 'a demand', *6* 'a piece of land allotted' (mining)

Ge [=E] M, pl. *-s*, end19c, 6(∅/1 tech); 1960s, 1a(1 coll, rare) **Du** [kle:m] C, beg20c (1 tech) → *-en* v. **Fr** <=E> M, 19c, 6(1 tech, obs)

clan *n. 1* 'a group of people with a common ancestor, esp. in the Scottish Highlands', *3* 'a group with a strong common interest'

This term was common as a foreignism from the nineteenth century onwards. It developed in the 1930s to include the sense 'political party' (now obsolete) and since the 1960s it is frequently found, (also as cp²) with pejorative connotations, referring to a group of people ruthlessly devoted to their common interests.

Ge [kla:n] M, pl. *-s*, 19c, 1(1 tech); 1960s, 3(1 coll, pej) **Du** [=E] C, 1950s, 1(2) **Nw** [kla:n] M, pl. *-er*, end19c, 1(∅) 3(2) **Ic** [kʰla:n] N [U] end20c, 3(1 sla) **Fr** [klã] M, 18c, 1(1 tech/∅) 3(2); beg19c, 3(3) → *clanisme* **Sp** <=E> M, pl. ∅, 1(∅/3 tech) 3(3) **It** [klan] M, pl. ∅, 18c, 1(2) 2(3) **Rm** [klan] N, beg20c, via Fr (3) **Rs** *klan* M, pl. *-y*, mid19c, 1(∅); mid20c, 3(2 jour, pej) → *-ovyĭ* adj. **Po** *klan* M, mid19c, 1,3(2) → *-owy* adj. **Cr** *klan* M, pl. *-ovi*, beg20c, 1(1 tech) 3(2) **Bg** *klan* M, pl. *-al-ove*, beg20c, 1(∅/2) 3(2 pej) → *-ov* adj. **Fi** *klaani* [kla:nɪ] 20c, 1(3) **Hu** *klán* [kla:n] beg19c, 1(1 tech) 3(2 coll) → *klán-szellem* **Al** *klan* M, pl. *-e*, beg20c (3)

clanvocation* *n.* 'a gathering of people with common interests'

Rs *klanvokeĭshn* M [U] end20c (1 coll/jour)

clarkia *n.* 'a plant with showy white, pink, or purple flowers'

Fr [klarkja] F, end19c (1 tech) **Rs** *klarkiya* F, pl. *-kii*, end19c (1 tech) **Po** *klarkia* [klarkia] F, mid20c (1 tech)

clash *n. +1c* 'a car crash', *2a* 'a conflict'

Du [=E] C, pl. *-es*, 1980s (1 coll) **Nw** [=E] N/M, pl. ∅, 1970s, 2a(1 coll) → *clashe* v. **Fr** [klaʃ] M, 1970s, 2a(1)

clean *adj 10a* 'free from any record of a crime or offence', *+13* 'free from drugs', *+14* 'clean cut, sharply outlined'

Ge [=E] 1970s, +13(1 sla) < *sau-ber* **Du** [=E] 1970s, +13(1 coll) **Nw** [=E] 1970s, +13(1 sla) **Ic** [=E] end20c, 10a,+13(1 sla) **Fr** [klin] 1980s, +13,+14(1 you) **It** [klin] end20c, 10a,+13(0>1) < *pulito* **Gr** *klin*, end20c, +13(1 sla) = *katharos*

clearing *n. +3* 'a transaction not involving money', *+4* 'the balancing of cheques and bills between banks', *+5* 'a department in a bank where this is done'

Although universal throughout Europe since the early twentieth century as a banking term, this word is rarely used and unknown outside specialist circles.

Ge [=E] N [U] 1960s, +3,+4(1 tech) **Du** [=E] C [U] beg20c, +3(1 tech) **Nw** [=E] M [U] beg20c, +3(1 tech) **Ic** *klíring* [kʰli:riŋk] F [U] mid20c, +4,+5(1

tech, sla) < creat *kröfuskipti, reikningsskil* **Fr** [kliʀiŋ]
M, beg20c, +3,+4(1 tech, ban) > (*chambre de*) *compensation* **Sp** M, 1960s, +3(1 tech, rare) < *compensación* **It** [kliriŋ] M, pl. Ø, 1930s, +3,+4(1 tech/
jour) **Rm** *cliring/<=E>/clirin* [kliriŋ/kliriŋ] N [U]
beg20c, via Fr?, +3(1 tech/jour) **Rs** *kliring* M [U]
beg20c (1 tech) → *-ovyĭ* adj. **Po** *kliring <=E>* M,
beg20c, +3,+4(1 tech) → *-owy* adj. **Cr** *kliring* M [U]
mid20c, +3(1 tech) → *-ški* adj. **Bg** *kliring* M [U]
mid20c, +3,+4(1 tech) → *-ov* adj. **Fi** [=E] +3(0)
Hu *kliring* [kliːriŋ] [U] end19/beg20c, +3(1 tech,
obs) **Al** *klering* M [U] 20c (1 tech) **Gr** *kliring* N
[U] mid20c, +3(1 tech)

clearing house *n.* 'a bankers' establishment where
cheques and bills from member banks are exchanged'
Ge *Clearing-Stelle* 1960s (1 tech+5) **Du** *clearing-
bank, -instituut* 1920s (1 tech+5) **Nw** [=E] N, pl. *-s*,
beg20c (1 tech) **Fr** *clearing-house* 19c (1 ban) <
chambre de compensation **Sp** [=E] F, pl. *-s*, 1920s
(Ø>1 tech, arch?) < *cámara de compensación (ban-
caria)* **It** [=E] M, pl. Ø, end19c (1 tech) **Rm** - <
rend *oficiu de cliring* **Po** (0) **Cr** (0) **Bg** - < rend
kliringova kŭshta **Hu** *clairinghouse* [U] 19c (1 tech,
arch) **Gr** *kliring (khauz)* N, beg20c, via Fr (1 tech)

clergyman *n.* 1 'an Anglican minister', +2 'his vest-
ments'
Du [=E] C, 1970s, 1(Ø) +2(1 tech) **Fr** [klɛʀʒiman]
M, pl. *des clergymans/clergymen*, 19c, 1(Ø) +2(1
tech) **Sp** [kleriman/kledʒiman] M, pl. *-men*, end19c,
1(Ø arch); mid20c, +2(2) **It** [klɛrdʒimɛn] M, pl. Ø,
1950s, 1(0) +2(1 obs)

clever *adj.* 1a 'skilful, talented; quick to understand
and learn', 2 'adroit, dextrous', 3 'cunning'
   The restricted distribution of *clever/-ness* is noteworthy for a German for whom the terms are among
the best-established loanwords (cf. ↑*fit/-ness*), neatly
filling a pejorative niche, which is often best done by a
loanword (cf. ↑*smart* which is more widespread).
Ge [klɛva] 1950s, 2,3(2 coll) → *Cleverle* N **Du**
[klɛvər] end20c (2 coll) **Nw** 2,3(0) **Ic** [kʰlɛvːer]
uninfl., end20c, 1a(0 sla)

cleverness *n.* 'cunning'
Ge [=E] F [U] 1950s (1 coll) **Nw** (0)

cliffhanger *n.* 'a story with a strong element of sus-
pense; a suspenseful ending to an episode of a serial'
Ge [=E] M, pl. Ø (0>1) **Nw** (0)

clinch *n.* 3 'an action or state in which participants
become too closely engaged' (boxing, wrestling) +4 'a
quarrel'
   One of the most widespread boxing terms, it is used
in a more general, colloquial meaning only in the
Germanic group.
Ge [=E] M [U] beg20c, 3(1 tech);
im ~ 1960s, +4(2 coll) **Du** [klinʃ]
C, pl. *-es/-en*, 1950s, 3(1 tech)
+4(1 coll) **Nw** *<=E>/klinsj*
[klinʃ] M, pl. *-er*, beg20c, 3,+4(1
tech/coll) → *clinche* v. **Fr**
<=E> M, 20c (1 tech) < *corps à*

Ic	Nw	Po	Rs
Du	Ge	Cr	Bg
Fr	It	Fi	Hu
Sp	Rm	Al	Gr

corps **Sp** [=E] M, pl. Ø, 1970, (1 tech) < *cuerpo a
cuerpo* **It** [klintʃ] M [U] 1910s, 3(1 arch) < *corpo a
corpo* **Rm** *clincil/clincin* [klintʃ/klintʃin] N, mid20c,
3(1 tech) **Rs** *klinch* M [U] beg20c, 3(1 tech) **Po**
klincz M [U] beg20c, 3(1 tech) → *-owanie* N [U];
-owy adj. **Cr** *klinč* M [U] beg20c, 3(1 tech) **Bg**
klinch M [U] mid20c, 3(1 tech) **Hu** [=E] [U] end19/
beg20c, 3(1 tech) **Gr** [=E] N [U] 20c, 3(1 tech)

clip(s)[1](1) *n.* 1 'a device for holding things together',
+1a 'this as used in surgery', 2a 'a piece of jewellery
fastened by a clip', +4 'a clip for holding the hair'
   The distribution does not reflect how long an
adopted meaning has been in existence: the term is
most restricted in the sense '(paper)clip'; it is well
attested for 'piece of jewellery'; and universal for *videoclip* (often preferred in its full form) – the last being
both of universal interest and untranslatable. 1 and 2a
are often mistakenly used in their pl. form.
Ge *<=E>/Klip(s)/Klipp(s)* [=E] M, pl. *-s*, beg20c,
1(2); 1960s, 2a(2); 1980s, +4(1 tech, mod) **Du** [=E]
C, mid20c, 1,2a(2) **Nw** *klips/clips* [=E] M/N, pl. Ø,
end20c, 1(1) 2a(3); *klipp* +4(4) **Ic** [klɪfs] N, pl. Ø,
mid20c, via Da, +5(2 coll) **Fr** [klip] M, mid20c,
1,+1a(1 tech, ban) 2a(3) < 1: *agrafe* **Sp** [=E] M, pl.
-s, 1960s, 1(2); 1930s, 2a(2 arch) **It** [klip(s)] M, pl.
Ø/-s, 1930s, 1,2a(2) **Rm** *clips* [klips] N, pl. *clipsuri*
[klipsurj], 1945, 2a(3) **Rs** *klipsy* F, pl., *klipsa*,
mid20c, 2a(3/2) **Po** *klips* M, mid20c, 1,2a(3) **Cr**
klipsa F, pl. *-e*, mid20c, 2a(3) **Bg** *klips* M, pl. *-al-
ove*, mid20c, 2a(3) **Fi** *klipsi* 1(1) **Hu** *klipsz* [=E] pl.
-ek, mid20c, 2a(3) **Gr** *klip/klips* N, pl. *-s/Ø*, 1,2a(2)

clip[2](2) *n.* 3 'a short excerpt from a film or video'
Ge *Clip* 1980s (1 tech, mod) **Du** [=E] C, mid20c
(2) **Ic** *klipp* [kʰlɪhp] N, pl. Ø, end20c (3) **Fr** 1980s
(2) < *vidéoclip, clip vidéo* **Sp** *<=E>* 1980s (2) **It**
[klip(s)] M, pl. Ø/-s, 1930s (2) **Rm** *clip* [=E] N,
1980s (2) **Rs** *klip* M, pl. *-y*, end20c (2) **Po** *video-
clip* M, mid20c (2 mod) **Bg** *(video)klip* M, pl. *-al
-ove*, end20c (2) **Hu** *klipp* [=E] pl. *-ek*, end20c (1
mod) **Al** *klip* (1 you) **Gr** *klip* N, pl. *-s/Ø* (2)

clipmaker* *n.* 'a person who produces videoclips'
Rs *klipmeĭker* M, pl. *-y*, 1990s (3 tech)

clipper *n.* 2 'a fast sailing-ship', +4 'a long-distance
jet', +5 'intermittent light'
   Technological progress is reflected in both the English term and the anglicisms – with the ship becoming
less important, the metaphorical extension to the air
travel was inevitable. (The two meanings are distinguished in spelling in German K-: C-)
Ge *K-*[=E] M, pl. Ø, end19c, 2(3 tech); *C-*1950s, +4(1
tech) **Du** *klipper* [klɪpər] C, mid20c, 2(3 tech);
[klipər] C, end20c, +4(1 tech) **Nw** *klipper* M, pl. *-e*,
mid19c, 2(1 tech); 20c, +4(1 tech) **Ic** *klipper* [kʰlɪh-
per] M, pl. *-ar*, end19c, 2(1 tech, arch) **Fr** [klipœr] M,
mid19c, 2(1 arch) +4(1 obs) **Sp** [kliper] M, end19c,
2(1 arch) 1930s, +4(1 arch) **It** [klipper] M, pl. Ø,
mid19c (1 tech) **Rm** *cliper* [kliper] N, 1930s, 2(1
tech); mid20c, +4(1 tech); 1970s, +5(1 rare) **Rs** *klipper* M, pl. *-y*, beg20c (1 tech) **Po** *kliper* [-er] M,

beg20c, 2(1 tech) → -*owy* adj.   **Cr** *kliper* M, mid20c,
+4(1 tech)   **Bg** *kliper* M, pl. -*al*-*i*, beg20c, via Rs, 2(1
tech)   **Fi** *klipperi* [klɪpperɪ] beg20c? 2(3)   **Hu** *klipper*
[klipper] 19c/20c, 2(1 arch) +4(1 mod)   **Al** *kliper* M
[U] 2(1 reg)

clivia*   *n.* 'a flowering houseplant'
   Ge *Klivie* [klịːviə] F, pl. -*n*, beg20c (3)   **Du** [klịːvija]
C, pl. - 's, beg20c (1 tech)   **Nw** [klịːvia] M, pl. -*er* (1
tech)   **Fr** [klivja] M (1 tech)   **Sp** [klịvja] F (3 tech)
It [klịvia] F, end19c (3)   **Rs** *klịviya* F, pl. -*vii*, beg20c
(1 tech)   **Po** *kliwia* F, mid20c (1 tech)   **Bg** *klịviya* F,
pl. -*vii*, 20c (3 tech)   **Fi** *kliivia* [kliːvɪa]   **Hu** *klịivia*
[kliːvia] pl. -*ák*, beg20c (3)   **Gr** *klịvia* F, 20c (3)

clogs   *n. pl.* 1 'shoes with wooden soles'
   Ge [kloks] pl., 1970s (1 tech, mod)   **Nw** (0) < *tres-
ko*   **Ic** - < *klossar*   **Po** (0)

clone   *n.* 1a 'a group of organisms produced asexually
from one stock or ancestor', 1b 'one such organism', 2
'a person or thing regarded as identical with another'
   Ge *Klon* [=E/kloːn] M, pl. -*e*, 1980s, 1a,b(3 tech) →
klonen v.   **Du** <=E>/*kloon* [=E] C, pl. -*en*, 1b(4)
Nw *klon* [kluːn] M, pl. -*er*, 1940s (3) → *klone* v.;
kloning n.   **Ic** *klón* [kʰlouːn] N, pl. Ø, end20c, 1a,b(2
tech) → *klóna* v.; *klónun* n.   **Fr** [klɔn] M, 1920s (3) →
cloner v., *clonage* M   **Sp** *clon* M, 1980s (3 tech) →
clonar v.; *clonage* M.; *clónico* adj.   **It** [klọne] M, pl. -*i*,
1930s (3 tech) → *clonale* adj.; *clonare* v.; *clonazione*
F.   **Rm** *clon*/*clonă* [klon/klọnə] N/F, 1970s, 1a(1
tech)   **Rs** *klon* M, pl. -*y*, mid20c, 1a,b(1 tech) →
-*irovanie* N   **Po** (5Gr)   **Cr** *klon* M, pl. -*ovi*, end20c,
1a,b(1 tech)   **Bg** *klon* M, pl. -*al*-*ove*, 1990s, 1b(1 tech,
rare); *klọning* n., pl. -*al*-*i*, end20c, 1b,2(3 tech) →
-*ov* adj; *kloniram* v.; -*irane* N   **Fi** *klooni*, 20c
(3)   **Hu** *klón* (5Gr)   **Gr** *klonos* M (5) → *klonopio*
v., *klonopiisi* F

close   *adv.* 1 'at only a short distance or interval'
   Du [=E] adv./pred.adj., 1980s (2 mod)   **Nw** *kloss*
[klos] 19c (3)   **Ic** [=E] end20c (0 sla)

close combat   *n.* 'fighting body to body without
weapons'
   Fr *close-combat* [klozkõba] M, 1970s (1 tech)

closed shop   *phr.*/*cp*[1] 1 'a place of work etc. where all
employees must belong to an agreed trade union', 2
'this system', +3 'a place of work with limited access'
   Ge [=E] cp[1], 1970s 1,2(1 tech, rare)   **Du** [=E] C [U]
1980s, 2(1 tech)   **Sp** <=E> M [U] 1980s, 1,2(Ø> 1
tech)   **It** [klọzdʃɔp] M, pl. Ø, 1970s (1 tech, rare)
Cr (0)   **Hu** [=E] end20c (1 tech_COMPUT_)

close race   *n.* 'a race where two or more competitors
finish at about the same time' (also used metaphorically)
   Nw [=E] N [U] 20c (2)

closet   *n.* 3 'a water closet', +3a 'the room holding
this' (cf. ↑*WC*)
   This originally euphemistic word was borrowed as
WC, water closet and *closet* (the shortening being possibly independent in some languages; further abbreviated in German to *Klo* (3 coll). Note that nineteenth-
century *closet* also meant *chambre séparée* (German)

Ge *Klosẹtt* N, pl. -*s*, mid19c, via Fr? (3); *Klo* N, pl. -*s*,
19c (3 coll) = *Toilette*   **Du** <=E>/*kloset* [klozɪt] N,
19c (2) < *toilet, WC, plee*   **Nw** *(vann)klosett* [klosẹt]
N, pl. -*er*, mid19c (2 obs)   **Ic** *klósett* [kʰlouːseht] N,
pl. Ø, beg20c, via Da (2 coll) > rend *salerni* → *kló* N
Fr - < *water kloset(s)*, *W.-C.*   **Sp** - < *water closet* <
WC   **It** - < *water closet*/*WC* < *gabinetto*   **Rm** [klo-
sẹt] N, end19c, via Fr/Ge? (3 obs) < *WC, toaletă*   **Rs**
klozẹt M, pl. -*y*, beg20c, 3(3 coll)   **Po** *klozet* M,
beg20c, 3(1 coll) → *klozecik* M; -*owy* adj.   **Cr** *klozet*
M, pl. -*i*, beg20c, 3(2 coll) → -*ski* adj.   **Bg** *klozẹt* M,
pl. -*al*-*i*, beg20c, 3(3 coll) < *toalẹtna* → -*en*
adj.   **Fi** *klosetti* [klɔsettɪ] (2)   **Hu** *klọzett* [klọzett] pl.
-*ek*, 19c, via Ge (3)   **Al** - < *WC, tualet*

close-up   *n.* 1 'a photograph taken at close range', 2
'an intimate description'
   Du [=E+yp] C, 1940s, 1(1 tech)   **Nw** [=E] M, pl. -*s*,
mid20c (1 rare)   **Ic** [=E] N, pl. Ø, end20c (0 tech, sla)
< *nærmynd*   **Sp** M, 1920s, 1(1 tech, rare) < *primer
plano*   **It** [klɔzʌp] M, pl. Ø, beg20c, 1(1 tech) <
primo piano   **Fi** [=E] 20c (1 tech)   **Hu** [=E] [U]
mid20c, 1(1 tech)

cloth   *n.* +6 'dense satin fabric'
   Ge [=E] N/M [U] end19c (1 tech, obs)   **Po** *klot* [klot]
M, mid20c, (1 tech)   **Hu** *klott*/*glott* [klott/glott] [U]
end19/beg20c (3 obs)

clown   *n.* 1 'a comic entertainer, esp. in a circus'
   Said to have been popularized on the Continent
through Shakespeare's plays during the eighteenth
century, and replacing *bajazzo* as a circus clown in
the nineteenth century. The metaphorical extension
to 'person that makes a fool of himself, . . . that cannot
be taken seriously' is obvious and may be independent. Re-anglicization of spelling and pronunciation is
frequent (German).
   Ge [kloːn] (1 reg/obs); [klaun], M, pl. -*s*, beg19c (2>3)
→ -*isch* adj.; -*erei* F; -*erie* F   **Du** <=E>/*klown* [=E] C,
beg20c (2)   **Nw** *klovn* [klovn] M, pl. -*er*, mid19c (3) →
klovneri N; *klovnaktig* adj., *klovne* v.   **Ic** - < *trúður*
Fr [klun] M, beg20c (2) → -*erie* n.; -*esque* adj.   **Sp**
<=E>/*clon* [kloun/klaun] M, pl. -*s*/-*es*, mid19c (1 tech)
< *payaso* → *clownesco* adj. (rare)   **It** [klaun] M, pl. Ø,
beg19c (3) > *pagliaccio* → *clownesco*/*claunesco*
adj.   **Rm** *clovn*/*claun* [klovn/klạun] M, end19c (3) →
clovnesc adj.; *clovnerie* F   **Rs** *kloun* M, pl. -*y*, 19c (3)
→ -*ạda* F; -*skiĭ* adj.   **Po** *klaun*/<=E> M, beg20c (2) →
-*ada* F; -*owski* adj.   **Cr** *klạun* M, pl. -*ovi*, beg20c (2) →
-*ijada* F; -*ovski* adj.   **Bg** *klọun* M, pl. -*i*, beg20c, via Rs
(3) → -*ski* adj.; -*ada* F   **Fi** *clown(i)*/*klouni* [klɔunɪ]
(3)   **Hu** [=E] pl. Ø, beg19c (2 coll, obs)   **Al** *kloun*
M, pl. -*ë*, beg20c (3/2)   **Gr** *klọun* M (2)

cloze test   *n.* 'an exercise of supplying words that
have been omitted from a passage as a test of read-
ability or comprehension'
   Nw [=E/klọss] M, pl. -*er*, 1970s (1 tech)   **Fr** [kloz] M,
1970s (1 tech)   **It** [klọːz test] M, pl. Ø, 1970s (1
tech)   **Cr** (0)   **Bg** *test klouz*/<=E> M, pl. *testa*,
1980s (1 tech)   **Fi** *cloze-testaus* [=E] 1970s (1 tech)
club   *n.* +1a 'a policeman's baton', 2 'a stick used in a

game, esp. one with a head used in golf', 4 'an association of people united by a common interest', 6 'an organization offering subscribers special deals', +10 'a discotheque'

This foreignism has been known in Western Europe since the eighteenth century, with the political sense developing during the French Revolution. Recent developments have led to its application to all kinds of society, company or association, and their meeting places. (The sense 'baton' is found only in Greek).
Ge *Klub*/<=E> [klup] M, pl. -*s*, 19c, 4,6(3) < 4: *Verein* **Du** <=E>/*klub* [klʌp] C, 19c, 2(1 tech) 4,6(3) **Nw** *klubb* [klub] M, pl. -*er*, mid19c, 4,6(3) **Ic** *klúbbur* [kʰlup:ʏr] M, pl. -*ar*, beg19c, via Da, 4,6(3) **Fr** [klœb] M, 18c, 4,6(2); 19c, 2(1) → *clubiste* M **Sp** <=E> M, pl -*sl*-*es*, 18c, 2(1 tech) 4(2>3) → *clubista* n. **It** [klɛb/klæb/klab] M, pl. Ø, 18c, 4,6(3) **Rm** [klub] N, beg19c, viaFr/Ge, 4,6(3) **Rs** *klub* M, pl. -*y*, 18/19c, 4,6(3) → -*nyï* adj. **Po** *klub* [klub] M, 18/19c, 4,6(3) → -*ik* M; -*ista* M; -*istka* F; -*owiec* M; -*owy* adj. **Cr** *klub* M, pl. -*ovi*, end19c, 4(3) → -*ski* adj. **Bg** *klub* M, pl. -*al*-*ove*, beg20c, via Rs, 4,6(3) → -*en* adj. **Fi** *klubi* 19c, 4(2) **Hu** *klub* [klub] pl. -*ok*, 17/18c, 4,6(3) **Al** *klub* M, pl. -*e*, beg20c, 4(3) **Gr** <=E>/*klab* N, pl. Ø/-*s*, end20c, 4,6,+10(2); *klob* N, mid20c, 1a,2(1 tech) → *clubbing*

clubhouse *n.* 'the premises used by a club'
Ge *Klubhaus* N, pl. -*häuser*, 19c (3+5) **Du** *clubhuis* (3+5) **Nw** *klubbhus* (3+5) **Ic** *klúbbhús* N, pl. Ø, mid19c, via Da (3+5 rare) **Fr** [klœbaus] M, mid20c (1 tech, ban) < *pavillon, maison de club* **It** - < *club* **Rm** - < *club* **Rs** - < *klub* **Po** (0) **Cr** (0) **Bg** - < *klub* **Hu** - < trsl *klubház*

clubman *n.* 'a member of a club'
Fr <=E> M, 20c (1 tech) **Sp** <=E> M, end20c (1 tech) < *clubista* M/F **Rm** *clubman*/*clubmen* [klubman/klubmen] M, mid20c (1 jour>mod) → *clubmană* F **Po** *klubman* [klubmen] M, end20c (Ø)

clump *n.* 1 'a cluster of plants, esp. trees or shrubs'
Po *klomb* [klomp] M, mid19c (3) → -*ik* M; -*owy* adj.

cluster *n./adj.* 1 'a close group of similar things' (in various technical uses), +4 'a statistical method'

This term is a recent adoption: in linguistics (3 'a group of successive consonants or vowels'); in music ('a complex of sounds produced simultaneously on a piano', as in Cage or Ligeti); in nuclear physics; in astronomy; and in medicine ('several organs transplanted together').
Ge [=E] M, pl. Ø, 1970s, (1 tech, rare) **Du** [=E] C, 1970s, 1(1 tech) → *clusteren* v. **Nw** [kløster] M/N, pl. -*sl*-*e*, 1970s (1 tech) **Ic** - < *klasi* **Fr** [klœstœr] M, 1970s (1 tech) **Sp** [kluster] M, pl. -*s*, end20c (1 tech) **It** [klaster] M, pl. Ø, beg20c, 1(1 tech PHYS/ASTRON) **Rs** *klaster* M, pl. -*y*, end20c (1 tech) → *nyï* **Bg** *klŭstŭren* adj., 1970s, +4(1 tech) **Hu** [klaster] [U] end20c, 1(1 tech SCIEN)

clutch *n.* 3a 'a device for connecting and disconnecting a vehicle's engine and transmission', 3b 'the pedal operating this'
Nw <=E>/*kløtsj* [kløtʃ] M, pl. -*er*, 20c(2) → *clutching* C; *clutche*/*kløtsje* v.

coach[1] *n.* 4a 'a trainer in sport'

This term originated in mid-nineteenth-century university slang and was adopted more or less as a synonym of the earlier *trainer*; *coach* is still much less frequent, but is often used in variation or because of its shorter form. Similarly *coach* v. is much rarer than *train* v.
Ge [=E] M [U] end19c (1 tech, coll) < *Trainer* **Du** [=E] C, pl. -*es*, mid20c (1 tech) **Nw** [=E] M, pl. -*er*, 1980s (1 tech) < *trener* **Ic** - < *þjálfari* **Fr** [kotʃ] M, mid20c (1 tech, ban) < *entraîneur, -euse* **Sp** [koutʃ] M [U] end20c (1 tech, jour, rare) < *entrenador* **It** [ko:tʃ] M, pl. Ø, end20c (1 tech) < *allenatore* **Rm** [kotʃi] M, 1970s (1 tech, rare) < *antrenor* **Rs** *kouch* M, pl. -*i*, end20c (1 tech, coll) < *trener* **Po** (0) **Cr** *kouč* M. pl. -*evi*, mid20c (1 tech) **Fi** [=E] 1980s (1 coll) < *valmentaja* **Al** - < *trajner* **Gr** *kouts* M, end20c (1 tech, coll, jour) < *proponitis*

coach[2] *n.* 1 'an overland bus', 2 'a railway carriage'

This word is very marginal, the original sense of a horse-drawn carriage being borrowed straight from Hungarian, or replaced by native terms (after some modish use in the late nineteenth century)
Ge (0 arch) **Du** [=E] C, 1950s, 1(1 tech) **Fr** <=E> 20c 2(1 tech) **Rm** [kotʃi] N, 1970s, 1(1 rare) < *autobuz, cursă* **Po** M, mid20c (1 tech)

coach *v.* 1a 'train a pupil, team, or crew'
Ge [ko:tʃən] 1970s (1 jour/tech, rare) < *trainieren* **Du** *coachen* [ko:tʃə(n)] 1950s (2 tech) **Nw** *coache* [kowtʃe] end20c (1 coll) < *trene* **Ic** - < *þjálfa* **Sp** - < *entrenar* **It** - < *allenare* **Po** (0) **Gr** *koutsaro* (1 tech, coll, jour) < *propono*

coaming *n.* 'a raised border round the hatches of a ship'
Rs *komings* M, pl. -*y*, 18c (1 tech) **Bg** *komingsi* pl., beg20c, via Rs (3 tech)

coaster *n.* 'a ship that travels along the coast from port to port'
Du [=E] C, 1950s (1 tech) < *kustvaarder* **Ic** - < *strandferðaskip* **Rm** - < creat *navă de coastă*

coat *n./cp*[2] 1 'a long overcoat'

This word is frequent as cp[2], with a few early compounds taken over from English (*cover-, duffle-, trench-*), but also occasionally used for new coinages, e.g. in (rare) German *Autocoat*.
Ge [ko:t] M, pl. -*s*, 20c (2) **Nw** [=E] M/cp[2], pl. -*s*, 20c (1/2) **Ic** - < only in *duffel-coat* **Rm** [cot] cp[2], mid20c (1 rare) **Rs** *kot* cp[2], M, beg20c (2) **Po** (0) **Cr** (0) **Gr** [kout, kot] cp[2] (2)

coating *n.* 1 'a thin layer or covering of paint etc.', 2 'material for making coats'

Ge [koːtiŋk] M/N, pl. -s, 1970s, 1(1 tech, rare); beg20c, 2(1 tech, obs) Du [=E] C, 1970s (1 tech, jour) → *coaten* v. It [koːtiŋ(g)] M [U] beg19c, 2(1 arch)

cobbler n. 2 'an iced drink of wine etc., sugar and lemon'

Ge [=E] M, pl. Ø/-s, end19c (0 arch) Du [koblər] C [U] beg20c (1 obs) Hu [kobler] [U] beg20c? (1 arch)

coca-cola n. 'a carbonated non-alcoholic drink'(™)

The phonology of this word has no English basis, but its provenance from the USA is, of course, universally known. The word is pronounced as if Latin or Italian, and is frequently shortened to one of its elements. (*-cola* also functions in other tradenames)

Ge [koːka koːla] F/N, pl. -s, 1950s (3) < *Cola* Du C, pl. *coca cola's*, mid20c (3) Nw [kukakuːla] M, pl. -er, mid20c (2) < *cola* Ic [kʰouːka kʰouːla] N [U] mid20c Fr [kɔkakɔla] M, mid20c (2) = *coca* Sp [koka kola] F, mid20c (3) > *coca* It [koka kola] F, pl. *coca-cole*, 1940s (3) Rm [koka kola] F, 1960s (3) < *coca* Rs koka kola F [U] mid20c (3) Po kola/ <=E> [koka kola] F, mid20c (2 coll) Cr kokakola F [U] end20c (3) Bg koka kola F, pl. -oli, mid20c (2); kola F, 1970s (3 coll) Fi kokakola, mid20c (3) Hu [=E] pl. -ák, beg20c (2) Al koka kola F [U] end20c (3/2) Gr koka kola F (3)

cocker (spaniel) n. 1 'a small breed of dog with a silky coat'

Adopted along with the names of other breeds of dog in the nineteenth century in Western Europe (and partly handed on via German); the English abbreviation to *cocker* is rare (French, Romanian, Polish, Bulgarian).

Ge [kokaʃpaːniəl] M, pl. -s, 19c (2>3) Du [kɔkər spɛnjəl/- spaːnjəl] C, mid20c (2) Nw [kokerspaːnjel] M, pl. -er, mid19c (2) Ic [=E] end20c (0 tech) Fr cocker [kɔkɛʀ] M, mid19c (2) Sp [koker ispaniel] M, pl. -s, mid20c? (2) < *cocker* (2) It [koker spaniel] M, pl. Ø, mid19c (2) Rm cocker (spaniel) (2) = *cocker spaniol* Rs koker spaniel' M, pl. -i, mid20c (2) Po koker/ <=E> [-er] M, mid20c (2) → -ek M Cr koker španijel M, pl. -i, mid20c (2) → -ka F Bg koker (shpanyol) M, pl. -al-i, mid20c (2 tech) → -che N. Fi [kɔkker spanɛlɪ] 20c (3) Hu mainly *spaniel* [=E] [ʃpaːniel] pl. -ek, beg20c (3) Gr koker spaniel N, end20c (2)

cockpit n. 1a 'a compartment for the pilot of an aircraft or spacecraft (earlier also a similar compartment in boats)', 1b 'a similar compartment for the driver in a racing car'

This term shows various stages of adoption: the original sense and associated metaphorical uses (*COD* 2,3) have not been taken over. The earliest borrowing was in the sense of a pilot's cabin on a boat, which then later transferred to that on a plane (but was rarely used for racing-cars or spacecraft). Where this word is recent only the sense associated with aeroplanes has been adopted. The origin of the compound is opaque.

Ge [kokpit] N, pl. -s, beg20c/1960s, 1a(2); 1960s,

1a(2); 1960s, 1b(2 mod) Du [kɔkpit] C, mid20c, 1a(2) Nw [=E] M, pl. -er, beg20c, 1a(2) Ic [kʰɔhkpɪht(ʏr)] M, end20c, 1a(1 tech,sla) < rend *flugstjórnarklefi* Fr [kɔkpit] M, end19c (1 tech, ban) > *poste de pilotage, habitacle du pilote, cabine* Sp [=E] M, end20c, 1a(1 tech, rare) It [kɔkpit] M, pl. Ø, 1970s, 1a(1 tech) < *cabina di pilotaggio, abitacolo* Rm coc(k)pit [kokpit] N, mid20c, 1a(1 tech>2) Rs kokpit M, pl. -y, beg20c, 1a(1 tech) Po kokpit/ <=E> M, 20c, 1a(1 tech) Cr kokpit M, pl. -i, end20c, 1a(1 tech) Bg - < *kabina* Fi [=E] mid20c, 1a(0) < trsl *ohjaamo* Hu [=E] [U] 20c, 1a(1 tech) Gr kokpit N, end20c (1 tech) = *pilotirio*

cocktail n. 1 'a mixed alcoholic drink', 2 'a dish of mixed ingredients', +4 'a milk shake', +5 any other form of mixture (cf. ↑*Molotov~*), +6 'a cocktail-party'

This fashionable term was adopted early on in the sense of a drink, to be used later (1960s) for other mixtures (fruit etc.). The term ↑*Molotov~* (a petrol-filled bottle) is said to have originated during the Spanish civil war or (more likely) with reference to an anti-tank weapon in Finland (1939–40), but did not gain widespread currency before the 1950s. *Cocktail* is sometimes used as a short form for ↑*cocktail party*, and found in various combinations as a cp[1] (for dresses, drinks, or food connected with cocktail parties).

Ge [kokteːl] M, pl. -s, mid19c, 1(2); 1960s, +5(2) +6(1 reg) Du [=E] C, mid20c (2) Nw [kokteil/-tæil] M, pl. -er/-s, beg20c, 1,2(2) +5(1) Ic kok(k)teill [kʰɔxteitl] M, pl. -ar, 1930s, via Da, 1,2,+6(2) > 1,+6: creat *hanastél* Fr [kɔktɛl] M, end19c, 1,+5,+6(2) Sp [koktel] M, pl. -s, end19c, 1,+5(2); mid20c, +6(2) < *cóctel*, pl. -es (3) → *coctelera, cocteleria* It [koktel] M, pl. Ø, end19c, 1(3); 1930s, +6(2) < *rinfresco* Rm [=E] N, beg20c, 1,+5,+6(2); *cocteil* [=E/kɔktejl] N, via Fr, 1,+5,+6(2>3) Rs koktei̯l' M, pl. -i, beg20c, 1,+4,+5(2) Po koktajl/coctajl/koktail/coctail/ <=E> [koktajl] M, beg20c, 1,+4,+6(2) → -ik M, -owy adj. Cr koktel M; pl. -i, mid20c, 1,+6(2) Bg kokteȋl M, pl. -al-i, mid20c, 1,+5(2) +6(3) → -en adj. Fi [=E]/koktaili, mid20c, 1,+5(2) Hu koktél [kokteːl] pl. -ok, end19c/beg20c, 1,+5,+6(3) Al koktej M, pl. -e, mid20c, 1(2) Gr kokteil N, pl. -Ø/-s, 19c, via Fr, 1(2); mid20c, +5(1 tech) +6(1 mod)

cocktail bar n. 1 'a place for drinks', +2 'a place for non-alcoholic drinks'

Ge [kokteːlbaːr] F, pl. -s, beg20c, 1(2) Du *cocktailbar* [=E] C, beg20c, 1(2) Nw [=E] M, pl. -er, 20c, 1(2) Fr <=E> 20c, 1(1) It [kokteil bar] M, pl. Ø, mid20c, 1(1) Rm - < *bar* Rs koktei̯l'bar M, pl. -y, end20c (2) Po [koktajl bar] M, mid20c, +2(1) Cr koktel-bar M, pl. -ovi, end20c, 1(2) Bg kokteȋl-bar M, pl. -ral-rove, end20c, 1(2 mod) Fi [=E] mid20c, 1(1 you) Hu koktél-bár [kokteːlbaːr] pl. -ok, beg20c, 1(2>3) Gr kokteil bar N, 20c, 1(1)

cocktail dress   *n.* 'a usu. short evening dress'
Ge *-kleid* 1950s (2+5)   **Du** *cocktailjurk*, 20c (2+5)   **Nw** *cocktailkjole* (2+5)   **Ic** *kokkteilkjóll* M, pl. *-ar*, mid20c (2+5 mod, obs)   **Fr** - < rend *robe de cocktail*   **Sp** - < rend *vestido de cóctel*   **It** - < rend *abito da cocktail* M   **Rm** - < rend *rochie de cocteil*   **Po** **Cr** - < trsl *koktel haljina*   **Bg** - < rend *roklya za kokteil*   **Fi** *cocktailasu* mid20c (2+5)   **Hu** *koktél-ruha* mid20c (2+5)

cocktail party   *n.* 'a relaxed early-evening party'
Ge [kọkte:lpạ:rti:] F, pl. *-(ie)s*, 1950s (2)   **Du** *cock-tail-party* [=E] C, 1970s (2) < *cocktail-partij*   **Nw** [=E] M, pl. *-er/-ies*, 1960s (1)   **Ic** *kokkteilpartí* [kʰɔx-teilpʰạrti] N, pl. Ø, mid20c (2 coll)   **Fr** *cocktail* [kɔk-tɛl] (2)   **Sp** M, mid20c (1 jour, rare) < *cocktail* (2) *cóctel* (3)   **It** [kɔ̞kteil pạrti] M, pl. Ø, 1930s (1>2) < *ricevimento*, *rinfresco*   **Rm** - < ↑*cocktail*   **Rs** *kọkteil'* pạrti F, uninfl., end20c (1 coll)   **Po** [koktajl parti] N, uninfl., end20c (2)   **Cr** *kọktel pạrti* F, uninfl., mid20c (2)   **Bg** *koktẹil* M, pl. *-al/-i*, mid20c (3)   **Fi** *cocktail-tilaisuus* mid20c (2+5)   **Hu** *koktél-parti* [kọkte:lparti] pl. *-k*, end19c/beg20c (2>3)   **Al** *koktej* M, pl. *-e*, mid20c (2) < *pritje*   **Gr** *koktẹil pạrti/-i* N, mid20c (1 rare)

cocooning*   *n.* 'a new way of life involving voluntary isolation and spending most of one's time at home'

The term was coined by the US economist Faith Popcorn in 1987 and has since spread to psychologists' jargon.
Ge [=E] N [U] 1990s (0>1 mod)   **Du** [=E] C [U] 1990s (1 mod)   **Nw** [=E] M [U] 1990s (1 mod)   **Fr** [kɔkuniŋ] M, 1990s (1 mod)   **Sp** [kokụnin] M [U] 1990s (1 mod)   **Cr** (0)   **Gr** <=E> [=E] N [U] 1990s (1 mod)

cod   *n.* 'a type of large marine fish'
Nw (0)   **Rm** [=E] M, mid20c (1)

code   *n.* 1,2 'a system of words, letters, figures, symbols, or signals used to represent others for secrecy or brevity' (information, military intelligence, linguistics, genetics), 3 'a piece of program text' (comput.), +6 'a set of (secret) numbers or letters used to gain admission to sth.'

Nineteenth-century adoptions of this word are likely to be from French, but more recent ones come directly from English. They are normally merged, however, since the native pronunciation does not distinguish between the English and the French vowel quality.
Ge *C-/K-*[o/ou] M, pl. *-s*, 20c, 1,2(1 tech) → *kodieren* v.   **Du** [kọ:də] C, beg20c, 1,2(3)   **Nw** *kode* [kụ:de] M, pl. *-r*, 20c, 1,2,+6(3) → *kode* v.   **Ic** *kódi/kóti/kóði* [kʰou:tɪ/kʰou:ðɪ] M, pl. *-ar*, 20c, 1,2,3(5 tech Da) +6(5 coll Da)   **Fr** [kɔd] M, 1,2(5)   **Sp** - < *código*   **It** - < *codice*   **Rm** *cod* [kod] N, beg20c, 1,2,+6(4/5Fr)   **Rs** *kod* M, pl. *-y*, beg20c (3) → *-irovat'* v.; *-irovanie* N   **Po** *kod* [-t] M, 1,2,+6(3)   **Cr** *kọd* M, pl. *-ovi*, beg20c, 1,2(3)   **Bg** *kod* M, pl. *-al-ove*, beg20c, 1,2,+6(5Fr) 3(4 tech) → *-iram* v.; *-ov* adj.;

-iran adj.   **Fi** *koodi* 20c (3)   **Hu** *kód* [ko:d] 1,2(5Fr) → *-ol* v.   **Al** *kod* M, pl. *-e*, mid20c, 1,2(1 tech)   **Gr** <=E> [=E] M, end20c, 3(1 tech); *kodhikas* M, 1,2(5); *kodhikos* M, +6(5)

coder*   *n.* 'a coding-machine in information technology'
Fr *codeur* [kɔdœʀ] M, 1960s (4/5)   **Rs** *coder* M, pl. *-y*, 1980s (1 tech)   **Po** *koder* [koder] M, mid20c (2)   **Cr** *koder* M, pl. *-i*, end20c (1 tech)   **Bg** *koder* M, pl. *-al-i*, mid20c (1 tech)   **Fi** *kooderi*, 20c (2) = trsl *koodaa-ja*   **Hu** *kóder* [ko:der] pl. *-ek*, mid20c (1 tech)

coffee shop   *n.* 1 'a small, informal restaurant' +2 'a place where drugs can be bought'
Ge [=E] M, pl. *-s*, 1980s, 2(0>1 mod, sla)   **Du** <=E>/ *koffie-shop* [=E] C, 1970s (2)   **Nw** [=E] M, pl. *-er*, 1980s, 1(1mod) < *kafé*   **Sp** [=E] M, pl. *-s*, 1980s, +2(Ø/1 jour)   **Po** (0)   **Cr** (0)   **Bg** - < 1: *kafe*   **Fi** [=E] (0)   **Gr** <=E> [kọfisop] N, beg20c, 1(1 writ, coll)

coffer-dam   *n.* 1 'a watertight enclosure pumped dry to permit work below the waterline (building bridges, repairing ships)', +2 'a watertight case for repairing ships', +3 'a room on a ship dividing oil tanks from water tanks and living quarters' +4 'a piece of rubber used to keep a tooth dry during dental treatment'
Ge *Kofferdamm* M, 20c (3 tech, rare)   **Du** [=E+dam] C, pl. *-men*, 1940s, 1,+2(1 tech); beg20c, +3(1 tech)   **Nw** *kofferdam* [kọferdam] M, pl. *-er*, 20c (1 tech)   **Fr** [kɔfɛrdam] M, 20c, 1(1 tech, ban) = *bâtar-deau*   **Rm** *coferdam* [koferdam] N, beg20c, +3(3 tech)   **Rs** *kọfferdam* M, pl. *-y*, 20c, +3(1 tech)   **Bg** *kọferdam* M, pl. *-al-i*, mid20c, 1,+2(1 tech) → *-en* adj.

coil   *n.* 6 'a device for converting low voltage to high voltage (esp. with respect to the internal-combustion engine)' (electr.), 7 'a piece of wire, piping, etc. wound in circles or spirals'
Ge [=E] N, pl. *-s*, 1960s, 7(1 tech, rare)   **Nw** [=E] M, pl. *-er/-s*, 20c (1 tech)   **Sp** M, 1970s, 7(1 tech)   **Gr** (0 tech)

coke¹ (1)   *n.* 1 'a solid substance left after the gases have been extracted from coal'

One of the early loans of the Industrial Revolution. The plural form was interpreted as a mass noun in German (and handed on to neighbouring languages thus).
Ge *Koks* [ko:ks] M [U] beg19c (3) → *Kokerei* F   **Du** *cokes/kooks* C [U] 19c (3)   **Nw** *koks* [koks] M [U] end19c (3)   **Ic** *koks* [kʰɔxs] N [U] end19c, via Da (2)   **Fr** [kɔk] M, 19c, 1(1 tech, arch) → *cokéfaction* F, 1920s; *cokéfier* v., 1910s; *cokerie* F, 1880s   **Sp** *cok* M, pl. Ø, end19c, 1(1 tech)   **It** [kɔ:k] M [U] mid19c, in *carbone coke* (3)   **Rm** *cocs* [koks] N, mid19c, via Ge (3)   **Rs** *koks* M [U] mid19c, via Ge (3 tech) → *-ovanie* N; *ovyi* adj.; *-irovat'* v.   **Po** *koks* [koks] M [U] mid19c, (3) → *-ik* M; *-iak* M; *-iarnia* F; *-iarz* M; *-owanie* N; *-ownia* F; *-ownik* M; *-ownictwo* N; v. *-owyl-owniczy* adj.   **Cr** *kọks* M [U] 19c (3) → *-ara* F; *-ni* adj.; *-irati* v.   **Bg** *koks* M [U] beg20c, via Ge (3 tech) → *-uvam* v., *-iram* v., *-ov* adj.   **Fi** *koksi* end19c

(3) **Hu** *koksz/kox* [koks] pl. Ø, 18c?, 1(3) **Al** *koks* M [U] beg20c (1 tech) **Gr** *kok* N [U] end19c (1 tech)

coke² (2) *n.* 'cocaine' The drug ↑*coke* in English is short for *cocaine*, which is homophonous with the earlier word and was notably borrowed mainly into the Germanic languages which extended the meaning on the English pattern.

Ge *Koks* [ko:ks] M [U] 1980s (1 you) → *koksen* v. **Du** [=E] C, 1970s (2 coll) **Nw** [=E] [U] end20c (1 rare) < *kokain* **Ic** *kók* [kʰouːk] N [U] end20c (3 sla) **Fr** *coco* (5) = *cocaïne* **Sp** - < *coca* (5) **It** - < *coca* **Rs** *koka* F [U] end20c (1 coll, you) < *kokain* **Po** *koks* [koks] M [U] end20c (1 coll) **Bg** *koka* F [U] end20c (1 tech, sla) **Fi** *koka* end20c (1 you) **Hu** *koksz/kox* [koks] pl. [U] 20c(1 tech, coll SPORT) → *kokszol* v. **Al** *koks* M [U] end20c (1 tech/3) < *kokain*

coke³ *n.* '↑ coca cola'

Ge [=E] F, pl. -*s*, 1970s (1 coll, you) < *Cola* **Du** [=E] C, end20c (1 coll) **Nw** [=E] mid20c (1 rare) < *cola* **Ic** *kók* [kʰouːk] N [U] mid20c (3) **Fr** (0) < *coca* **Sp** - < *coca, cola* **It** *coca* [koka] F, pl. Ø **Rm** - < *coca cola, coca* **Rs** *koka* F [U] end20c (2) < *koka kola* **Po** *koka* [koka] F, mid20c (2 coll) **Cr** - < *kokakola* **Bg** *koka* F, pl. *koki*, end20c (1 coll) < *kola* **Fi** *kokis* [kɔkɪs] end20c, via Sw? (3) **Hu** [=E]/*kók* end20c (1 you) < *kóla* **Al** - < *koka-kola* **Gr** - < *koka*

coke⁴ *n.* 'a sweet pastry of round shape and coated with chocolate'

Gr *kok* N (2)

cold cream *n.* 'an ointment for cleansing and softening the skin'

The currency of this term has remained marginal, although it has been attested for more than a hundred years in many languages; note, however, the infrequency of calques.

Ge [=E] F/N, pl. -*s*, 19c (1 tech) **Du** *coldcream* [=E] C, end20c (1 tech) **Nw** - < trsl *koldkrem* **Ic** - < trsl *kalt krem* **Fr** *cold-cream* [kɔldkʀim] M, 1830s (1 arch) **Sp** [kolkren] M, pl. Ø, end19c (1 arch) **It** [kol kriːm] M [U] end19c (1 arch) < *crema cosmetica* **Rm** *coldcremă* [koldkremə] F, end19c (1+5 rare) **Rs** *kol'dkrem* M [U] beg20c (1 tech, arch) **Po** [kolt krim] M, beg20c (1 tech) **Cr** *cold cream* [kold kriːm] F, pl. Ø, beg20c (1 tech) **Bg** *koldkrem* M [U]/pl. -*a*, end20c (3 tech) **Hu** [=E] pl. Ø, end19/beg20c (1 tech) **Al** *gold-krem* M [U] 1950s (1 obs)

cold turkey *n.* 1 'abrupt withdrawal from addictive drugs; the symptoms of this'

Ge [ko:ltörki] M [U] 1980s (1 sla, rare) **Du** [=E] C [U] 1980s (1 sla) **Ic** [=E] end20c, 1(osla) **Sp** - < trsl *pavo (frío)*

collector's item *n.* 'a valuable object, esp. one of interest to collectors'

Ge - < *Sammlerstück* **Du** [=E] N, pl. -*s*, end20c (1 tech) **Nw** *item*, [=E] N, pl. -*er*, end20c (1 tech, rare) < *samleobjekt*

college *n./cp^{1/2}* 1,2 'an establishment for higher and further or specialized education'

The data are ambiguous since Latin and French forms yield identical loanwords, and it is difficult to establish how far the true English term has remained a foreignism. (But contrast the cp¹ distribution).

Ge [=E] N, pl. -*s*, end19c (Ø) **Du** (Ø) **Nw** [=E] N, pl. Ø/-*rectel*-*s*, mid19c (Ø/1 tech) **Ic** [=E] mid20c (Ø) **Fr** (4) **Sp** [=E] M, pl. -*s*, 1980s (Ø/1 tech) **It** [kɔledʒ] M, pl. Ø, end19c (Ø) **Rm** - < *colegiu* **Rs** *kolledzh* M, pl. -*i*, end20c (2) **Po** *koledż/*<=E> [-e-] M, beg20c (2 tech) **Cr** *koledž* M, pl. -*i*, beg20c (1 tech/Ø) **Bg** *kolezh* M, pl. -*al*-*i*, beg20c, via Fr (3); *kolidzh* (o>1 mod) → -*anin* M; -*anka* F; -*anski* adj. **Fi** [=E] (Ø) **Hu** [=E] pl. -*ok*, 19/20c (Ø) **Al** *kolegj* F, pl. -*e*, mid20c (1 tech) **Gr** <=E> [=E] N/ cp², end20c (Ø/2 mod) < *kolleghio* N (3/Ø)

college- *n./cp¹* +7 'thought to be typical of a college', +8 'a sweatshirt, sweatshirt material'

Ge -*mappel*-*shorts/*-*stil, etc.* [=E] 1970s, +7(2) **Du** *college* (5Fr) **Nw** -*genser* [=E] 1970s (2) **Ic** - < rend *háskóla*- **It** *(scarpe) college* [kɔlledʒ] M, pl. Ø, 1980s, +7(1) **Po** (0) **Fi** [kɔlɪts] +8(2) **Gr** *kolleghiakol*-*i* N/F, +8(3)

collie *n.* 'a sheepdog orig. of a Scottish breed'

Ge [koli] M, pl. -*s*, end19c (1 tech) **Du** [=E] C, 19c (2 tech) **Nw** [=E] M, pl. -*r*, mid20c (1 tech) **Ic** *kollí (hundur)* [kʰɔlːiː-] M, end20c (1 tech) **Fr** *colley* [kɔlɛ] M, 19c (1 tech) **Sp** M, pl. -*s*, end19c (1 tech) **It** [kɔlli] M, pl. Ø, mid19c (2 tech) **Rm** [koli] M, pl. Ø, mid20c (2) **Rs** *kolli* M/F, uninfl., beg20c (2) **Po** M, uninfl., beg20c (2) **Cr** *koli* M, uninfl., mid20c (2) **Bg** *koli* N, pl. -*ta*, mid20c (1 tech) **Fi** [kɔlːie] (3) **Hu** *collier*, 20c, via Fr (3) **Gr** *kolei* N, 20c, via Fr (1 tech)

Colorado beetle *n.* 'a kind of beetle the larva of which is highly destructive to the potato plant'.

The term was used in English from the mid-nineteenth century, but spread to other languages only in the twentieth; calques predominate.

Ge *Koloradokäfer* (1 arch+5) < *Kartoffelkäfer* **Du** *coloradokever* (name+5) **Nw** *koloradobille* (name+5) **Ic** *kólóradóbjalla* F, pl. -*björlur*, end20c (2 tech+5) = rend *kartöflubjalla* **Fr** - < rend *tique du Colorado* < *donyphore* **Rm** - < rend *gândac de Colorado* **Rs** - < trsl *koloradskii zhuk* **Po** *kolorado* [kolorado] N [U] mid20c (1 tech) **Bg** - < trsl *koloradski brŭmbar* **Fi** - < trsl *koloradokoppakuoriainen* **Hu** - < trsl *kolorádóbogár* = *burgonyabogár*

colt *n.* +3 'a type of revolver'

Samuel Colt (1814–62) patented his 'six-shooter' *colt* in 1835. It was later adopted by the US army, where it became widely used in the Mexican War of 1846–8, and well-known through reports of the Wild West and western films. The use of the term is often extended to include all types of revolvers.

Ge [kolt] M, pl. -*s*, 20c (1 tech) < *Revolver* **Du** [=E] C,

1970s (1 tech) **Nw** [kolt] M, pl. -*er*, 20c (1 tech) **Ic** [kʰɔ]t] M, mid/end20c (Ø) **Fr** [kɔlt] M, 19c (1 tech) **Sp** <=E> M, 1930s (1) < *revólver* **It** [kɔlt] F, pl. Ø, mid20c (1) < *pistola, rivoltella, revolver* **Rm** [kolt] N, mid20c (1 tech) **Rs** *kol't* M, pl. -*y*, 19c (2 tech) **Po** *kolt/*<=E> [kolt] M, mid20c (2 tech) **Cr** *kolt* M, pl. -*i*, mid20c (1 tech) **Bg** *kolt* M, pl. -*al-ove*, mid20c (1 tech) < *revólver* **Fi** [=E] 20c (1) **Hu** [=E] pl. -*ok*, beg20c (2 tech, arch) **Gr** *kolt* N, 20c (1 tech)

column *n.* 5 'part of a newspaper devoted to a special subject'

Ge *Kolumne* (5La) **Du** [kɔlym] C, 1970s (2 jour) **Nw** (0) < *spalte* **Ic** - < *dálkur* **Sp** - < mean *columna* **It** - < *colonna* (5La) **Po** (5La) **Cr** *kolumna* F, pl -*e*, end20c (2) **Bg** *kolona* F, pl. -*ni*, beg20c (5It) -*nka* **Fi** *kolumni* (5) **Hu** *kolumna* from La (5) **Al** *kolonë* F, pl. -*a*, beg20c (5It) **Gr** - < mean *stili*

columnist *n.* 'a journalist contributing regularly to a newspaper'

Ge (5La) **Du** [kɔlymnist] C, pl. -*en*, 1970s (2 jour) **Nw** *kolumnist* [kolumnist] M, pl. -*er*, end20c (3 tech, mod/5La) **Ic** - < *dálkahöfundur* **It** [kɔlumnist] M, pl. 1950s (1 tech) > *colonnista, opinionista* **Rm** [kolumnist] M, 1970s (3 tech, rare) **Cr** *kolumnist* M, pl. -*i*, end20c (2) **Fi** *kolumnisti* beg20c (3) **Gr** *koliumnist* M, 1980s (1 jour)

combine *n.* +1a 'an illicit arrangement to fix the result of a sporting event', 2 'a combine harvester', +3 'musical equipment', +4 'kitchen equipment'

One of the few terms widely transmitted in its non-English short form through Russian and consequently more common in Eastern Europe, where the word has occasionally been interpreted as an internationalism of Romance provenance. Note the large number of derivatives.

Ge [kombain] F, pl. -*s*, 20c, via Rs, 2(1 tech/reg) < *Mähdrescher* **Du** [kɔmbajn/=E] C, 1940s, 2(1 tech) < *maaidorser* **Nw** *combiner* [combainer] M, pl. -*e*, 20c, 2(1 rare) < *skurtresker* **It** [kɔmbin] F, pl. Ø, 1930s, +1a(1 tech) **Rm** *combină* [kombinə] F, mid20c, via Rs, 2,+3(3); *combaină* [kombajnə] F, 2(1 obs) → *combiner* M; *combainist* M **Rs** *kombain* M, pl. -*y*, mid20c, 2,+4(3) → -*ër* M; *ërsha* F; -*ovyĭ* adj. **Po** *kombajn* M, mid20c, via Rs, 2(2) → -*ista* M; -*istka* F; -*er* M; -*izacja* F; -*owy* adj. **Cr** *kombajn* M, pl. -*i*, mid20c, 2(2) → -*er* M **Bg** *kombaĭn* M, mid20c, via Rs, 2(2) +3,+4(3 tech); *kombaĭna* F, pl. -*ni*, 2(2 tech, reg) → -*er* M; -*erka* F; -*erski* adj. **Hu** *kombájn* pl. -*ok*, beg20c, via Rs, 2(5) **Al** *kombajnë* [kombajn] F, pl. -*a*, mid20c, via Rs, 2(1 tech) **Gr** *kobina* F, 20c, +1a(5Fr) 2(3 tech)

combo *n.* 1 'a small jazz or dance band'

Ge [kɔmbo] F, pl. -*s*, end20c (1 tech) **Du** [=E] C/N, pl. -'*s*, end20c (1 tech) **Nw** [=E/kumbu] M, pl. -*er/-s*, 1970s (1 tech) **Ic** *kombó* [kʰɔmpou] N, pl. Ø, 1970s (1 coll) **Fr** <=E> M mid20c (1 tech) **Sp** [kɔmbo] M,

1980s (1 tech) **Rm** [kɔmbo] N, 1970s (1 tech, rare) **Po** [-bo] N, uninfl., end20c (1 tech) **Bg** *kombo* N, pl. Ø, end20c (1 tech) **Fi** [kombo] end20c (1) **Hu** [=E] [U] 20c (1 tech)

comeback *n.* 1 'a return to a previous state of success or fame'

This word was apparently borrowed in relation to film stars just after 1945 in Western Europe and later extended to the careers of other prominent people (cf. the slogan, of limited currency as a loan phrase applied to boxers, *They never come back*).

Ge [kambɛk] N, pl. -*s*, 1940s (2) **Du** [=E] C, mid20c (2) **Nw** [kombæk] M, pl. Ø, mid20c (2) **Ic** [kʰɔm:pahk] N [U] 1970s (0 coll) **Fr** *come-back* [kɔmbak] M, uninfl., 1960s (2 jour, ban) < *retour, rentrée* **It** [kambɛk] M, pl. Ø, end20c (1) < *ritorno alla ribalta* **Rm** [=E] N, 1960s(1 jour) < *rend întoarcere* **Rs** *kam- b'ek* M [U] 1990s (1 jour) **Po** [kambek] M [U] end20c (1 jour) **Cr** [=E] M [U] end20c (1 tech) **Bg** *kŭmbek* M, pl. -*a*, 1990s (1 tech_MUS) **Gr** *kambak* N [U] end20c (1 coll/jour)

come on *v.* 8 (as imperat.) 'expressing encouragement'

Ge [=E] 1990s (1 sla, you) **Du** [=E] 1990s (1 sla, mod) < *kom op* **Nw** - < *kom an* **Ic** [kʰɔm:on] interj., mid/end20c (1 sla, you) **Rm** (0) **Rs** (0) **Cr** (0) **Bg** *kŭmon* 1990s (1 you, coll)

come out *v.* 3b 'openly declare that one is a homosexual' (cf. ↑*coming out.*)

Nw - < *stå fram* **Ic** *koma út (úr skápnum)* 1980s (4 sla) **It** - < *rend uscire allo scoperto*

comfort *n.* 2a 'physical well-being', +2c 'mental well-being', +6 'luxury'

Although originally English, this word was so strongly influenced by French transmission from the nineteenth century onwards that it is hardly felt to be an anglicism in any of the languages concerned; there seems to have been no re-anglicization (cf. ↑*budget*).

Ge *K-*[komfo:r] M [U] 19c, via Fr, +6(3) → -*abel* adj. **Du** [kɔmfɔrt] N, 19c, +6(5Fr) → -*abel* adj. **Nw** *komfort* [komfo:r] M [U] beg20c, via Fr, +6(3) **Fr** *confort* [kɔ̃fɔʀ] M, beg19c, 2a(4) **Sp** *confort* [konfɔr(t)] M [U] mid19c, 2a,+6(3/5Fr) → *confortable* **It** [kɔmfort/kɔmfort] M, pl. Ø, beg19c, +6(3) > mean *conforto* **Rm** *confort* [konfort] N [U] mid19c, 2,+2c(4/5Fr) **Rs** *komfort* M [U] mid19c, 2a,+2c,+6(3) → -*nyĭ* adj.; -*abel'nyĭ* adj.; -*nost'* F; -*no* adv./ *dis-* **Po** *komfort* M pl. Ø, mid19c, 2a,+2c,+6(2) → -*owy* adj.; -*owo* adv. **Cr** *komfor* M [U] beg20c, +6(2) → -*an* adj. **Bg** *komfort* M [U] beg20c, via Ge, +2c(2 tech) +6(3) → *dis-*M; -*en* adj. **Hu** *komfort* [komfort] beg19c, 2a,+6(3) **Al** *komfor/konfort* M [U] 1950s, +6(1 reg) **Gr** *komfor* N, pl. Ø, usu. pl., via Fr, +6(2) < *anesis*

comic(s) *n.* 2a,b 'a periodical, mainly in the form of comic strips', 2c 'comic strips'

The distinction between the individual strip and the complete periodical (usu. *comic* in English) appears to have been retained in many languages.
Ge *Comic* [=E] M, pl. *-s*, 1950s, 2a,b(2) **Du** [k<u>o</u>mik] C, end20c; 2a,b(2 tech) < *stripverhaal* **Nw** (0) < *tegneserie* **Fr** *comics* M, pl., mid20c, 2a,b(1 tech) > *bande dessinée* **Sp** [k<u>o</u>mik] M, pl. *-s*, mid20c (2) > 2a,b: *tebeo, historietas* > 2c: *tira cómica → comiquero* **It** [komik] M, pl. *-s*, 1950s, 2a,b(1) < *fum<u>e</u>tto* **Rm** *comics* [=E] N, 1970s, 2a,b(1 coll>jour) < *bandă desenată* **Rs** k<u>o</u>*miks* M, pl. *-y*, mid20c (2) **Po** *komiks* M, mid20c, 2a,b(2) → *-owy* adj.; *-owo* adv. **Cr** (0) **Bg** k<u>o</u>*miks* M, pl. *-al-i*, mid20c, 2a,b(3); k<u>o</u>*miksi* pl., 2c(3) **Hu** [=E] 20c (1 tech) < *képregény* **Al** *komik* M, pl. *-ë*, 1990s, 2a,b(1 tech)/ - < *fumete* **Gr** k<u>o</u>*mik* N, pl. *-s*, mid20c (2)

comic strip *n.* 'a sequence of drawings telling a story'
Ge *Comic Strip* [=E] M, pl. *-s*, 1950s (2) **Du** - < *stripverhaal* **Nw** [=E] M, pl. *-s*, 1980s (1) **Sp** - < trsl *tira cómica* **It** *comic* [k<u>o</u>mic] M, pl. *-s*, 1950s < *fumetto* **Rs** - < *komics* **Cr** (0) **Bg** - < *komiksi* **Hu** in pl. *-s*, [=E] [U] 20c (1 tech)

comingman* *n.* 'a man destined or expected to be important or successful'
Du [=E] C, 1990s (1 mod) **Nw** *coming man* [=E] M, pl. *-men*, 20c (1) **Fr** <=E> M, 20c (2 ban) > *espoir*

coming out *n.* 'an open confession' (mainly in: declaring one's homosexuality)
Ge [=E] N, pl. *-s*, 1980s (1 mod) **Du** [=E] N, 1990s (1 coll, jour, mod) **Nw** [=E] [U] 1980s (1 mod) **It** [=E] M, pl. Ø, end20c (1) < *uscita allo scoperto*

comingwoman* *n.* 'a woman destined or expected to be important or successful'
Nw *coming woman* [=E] M, pl. *-women*, 20c (1) **Fr** <=E> F, 20c (2 ban) > *espoir*

command car* *n.* 'an armoured military vehicle'
Fr *command-car* [kɔmãdkaʀ] M, mid20c (1 tech)

commercial *n.* 'a television or radio advertisement'
Ge [=E] N/M, pl. *-s*, 1980s (0>1 mod) < *Werbung/ Werbefilm/Werbespot* **Du** [=E] C, 1970s (2 tech) **Nw** (0) < *reklamesnutt* **It** - < *pubblicità* **Rs** *komm<u>e</u>rshialz* pl., end20c (1 coll) < *reklama* **Po** (5La)

commodity *n.* 1 'a commercial article or raw material'
Ge [=E] F, pl. *-(ie)s*, 1960s (1 tech, rare) **Du** [=E] C, 1990s (1 tech) **Sp** [=E] M, pl. *-ies*, 1990s (1 tech, rare)

commodore *n.* 1 'a naval officer'
Although the form is English (derived from French *commandeur*, cf. English *commander*) it is not felt to be an anglicism in any of the receiving languages.
Ge *K-* [komod<u>o:</u>rə] M, pl. *-s*, 19c (3 tech) **Du** [kɔmodo:r] C, 20c (2 tech) **Nw** (0) **Fr** [kɔmɔdɔʀ] M, 18c (Ø) **Sp** *comodoro* (5) **It** *commodoro* M, pl. *-i* (3 rare) **Rm** *comodor* [komod<u>o</u>r] M, mid20c, via Fr (Ø) **Rs** k<u>o</u>*mmodor* M, pl. *-y*, 19c (1 tech) **Po** *komo-*

dor [komodor] M, beg20c (2 tech) **Cr** *komodor* M, pl. *-i*, beg20c (3) **Fi** *kommodori* 20c (1 tech) **Hu** [=E] 19c (1 tech)

common law *n.* 'law derived from custom and judicial precedent'
Nw (0) **Fr** (Ø) **Sp** [=E] M, 1920s (Ø/1 rare) = *derecho consuetudinario* **Rs** k<u>o</u>*men lo* N, uninfl., 1990s (1 jour) < trsl *obychnoe pravo* **Po** <=E> N, uninfl., beg20c (Ø) **Bg** - < trsl *obichaĭno pravo* **Fi** (Ø) **Hu** [=E] [U] 19c (Ø) **Gr** (Ø) < trsl *kino dhikeo*

common sense *n.* 'sound practical sense'
Ge [=E] M [U] 19c (1 coll) < *gesunder Menschenverstand* **Du** [=E] C, 1980s (1 coll, jour) **Nw** [k<u>o</u>monsens] often cp[1], M [U] 20c (1) < *sunn fornuft* **Ic** [=E] uninfl., end20c (0 sla) < *heilbrigð skynsemi* **Sp** [k<u>o</u>mon s<u>e</u>ns] M [U] end20c (Ø/1 rare) = *sentido com<u>u</u>n* **It** - < trsl *senso comune, buons<u>e</u>nso* **Rs** k<u>o</u>*men sens* M, uninfl., 1990s (1 jour) < trsl *zdravyĭ smysl* **Po** <=E> M, uninfl., beg20c (1 tech) **Cr** [=E] M [U] beg20c (1 tech) < *zdrav razum* **Hu** [=E] [U] 19c (1 tech) < trsl *józan ész*

commuter *n.* 1 'a person travelling some distance to work', +2 'a short haul plane'
Ge - < *Pendler* **Nw** - < *pendler* **Fr** [kɔmytœʀ] M, 1990s (1 tech, ban) < 1: *navetteur*; < +2: *avion de transport régional* **Sp** [kom<u>u</u>ter] M, 1990s, 1(1 tech, rare) **It** - < *pendol<u>a</u>re*

compact disc *n.* 1 'a disc on which information or sound is recorded digitally and reproduced by reflection of laser light' (cf. ↑*CD*)
Ge [=E] F, pl. *-s*, 1980s (1 tech) < (cf. ↑*CD*) *CD* **Du** [=E] C, end20c (1 tech) < *c.d.* (3) > *compactplaat* **Nw** [=E/kump<u>a</u>kt-] M, pl. *-s*, 1980s (1 obs) < (cf. ↑*CD*) *CD* (= trsl *kompaktplate*) **Ic** - < *geisladiskur* **Fr** *compact-disc* 1980s (1 tech, ban) < *disque compact, disque laser, C.D.* **Sp** <=E>/*compact* [k<u>o</u>mpakd<u>i</u>sk] M, pl. *-s*, 1980s (2) < (cf. ↑*CD*) *CD* **It** *compact (disc)* [k<u>o</u>mpakt disk] M, pl. Ø, 1980s (2) < (cf. ↑*CD*) *CD* **Rm** [komp<u>a</u>kt disk] N, end1980s (2>3) > trsl *disc compact* **Rs** *komp<u>a</u>kt disk* M, pl. *-i*, 1980s (2) **Po** *komp<u>a</u>kt* M (2 mod) = trsl *płyta kompaktowa → -owy* adj. **Cr** [=E] M [U] (1 tech) < (cf. ↑*CD*) *CD* **Bg** *(komp<u>a</u>kt)disk* M, pl. *-al-ove*, 1980s (2 tech) **Fi** (0) **Hu** [=E] pl. Ø, end20c (1 tech, writ) < (cf. ↑*CD*) *CD* **Al** *kompaktdisk* M, pl. *-e*, end20c (2 you) **Gr** k<u>o</u>*mpakt d<u>i</u>sk* N, 1980s (2) < (cf. ↑*CD*) *CD* > rend *psifiakos dhiskos*

company *n.* 2 'the state of being a companion, being together with someone; companionship', 3a 'a commercial business', 3b 'usu. the partner(s) not named in the title'
It is uncertain how far the English word has affected the currency of the universal French term and equivalents like *Firma, (Handels-) Gesellschaft* etc.
Du [=E] C, end20c, 3a(1 coll, mod) **Nw** *kompani* [kumpani:] 3a,b(5Fr) **Ic** *kompani* [kʰɔmpani] N, pl.

Ø, end19c, 2,3a(2 coll); & *Co* [o: 'kʰou:] 3b(2) **Sp** - <
mean *compañia* F, 20c, 3a = *firma; and company* [=E]
3b(1 sla) **It** [=E] F, pl. Ø, mid20c, 3b(2) < 3b: *e soci;*
< 3a: *compagnia* **Rm** *companie;* & *Co.* [endkompani/
etkompani] 3b(2) **Rs** *kompaniya* F, pl. *-nii,* beg20c,
via Fr, 2,3a,b(2) **Po** [kompani] F, uninfl., end20c,
3a(2) < *firma* **Cr** *kompanija* F, pl. *-e,* beg20c, 23a
Bg *kompaniya* F, pl. *-nii,* beg20c, via Rs, 2,3a(5Fr) <
3a: *firma* **Fi** *kumppani* 19c, via Sw, 3b(2); &*kumppa-
nit* 19c, 3b(3 obs) **Hu** [=E] [U] 1980s, 3a(1 tech,
jour) **Al** *kompani* F, pl. Ø, beg20c, 3a(3) **Gr** 3a(0)
3b(0 writ)

compost   *n.* 1a 'mixed manure, esp. of organic origin'
    This word, having come from Romance into Eng-
lish to be transmitted again through French in the
nineteenth century, is largely not felt to be an anglicism.
Ge *Kompost* M [U] 19c (3) → *kompostieren* v. **Du**
<=E> *kompost* [kɔmpɔst] C [U] end19c (3) → *compos-
teren* v. **Nw** *kompost* [kumpost] M [U] 19c (3)
Fr [kɔmpɔst] M, 18c (3) **Sp** [kompost] M, 1970s,
via Fr (2 tech) → *compostage* **It** [=E] M [U] 20c (1
tech) < *composta* **Rm** [kompost] N, end19c, via Fr (3
tech) **Rs** *kompost* M [U] 19c (3 tech/5Ge) **Po** (5La)
Cr (5La) **Bg** *kompost* M [U] beg20c, via Rs (1
tech) **Fi** *komposti* 19c (3) **Hu** (5La)

compound-*   *n.* /cp¹ᐟ²/ 'a steam engine'
Ge *-maschine* [=E] cp¹, end19c (1 tech+5) **Du** [=E]
beg20c (1 tech) **Fr** *machine compound* [kɔ̃pund] adj.,
uninfl./F, 19c (1 tech, arch) **Sp** *maquina-*[=E] cp²,
end19c (1 tech, arch) **It** [=E] cp², end19c (1 tech)
Rm *locomotivă compound* [lokomotivə kompawnd]
uninfl., beg20c, via Fr (2 tech) **Rs** *kompaund-ma-
shina* F/cp¹, pl. *-y,* 19c (1 tech, arch) **Po** *kompaund*
[-nt] M, beg20c (1 tech) **Hu** *kompaund-* [kompaund-]
beg20c (1 tech) **Gr** (0 tech)

compound   *v.* +8 'connect' (electr./mech.)
Rm *compounda* [kompawnda] beg20c (1 tech) → *com-
poundare* F; *compoundat* adj.

computer   *n.* 1 'an electronic device for storing and
processing data'
    This term spread very rapidly during the 1950s and
1960s, but has been successfully replaced by native
equivalents, particularly in some Romance languages;
in others, the replacements are felt to be somewhat
clumsy or imprecise.
Ge [=E] M, pl. Ø, 1960s (2) =
Rechner **Du** [kɔmpjutər] C,
1960s (2) **Nw** [kompju:ter] M,
pl. *-el-s,* 1960s (1 obs) < rend *datamaskin* **Ic** - < rend *tölva* **Fr**
<=E> M, 1950s (1 tech, ban, obs)
< *ordinateur* **Sp** [kompiuter] M,

pl. *-s,* 1960s (1 tech, rare) < *ordenador, computador,
computadora* → *computerismo; computomanía* **It**
[kompjuter] M, pl. Ø, 1960s (3) > *calcolatore/elabor-
atore (elettronico)/cervello elettronico* → *-iale* adj.;
-istico adj. **Rm** [=E] N 1970s, 1(2) = *calculator* >
ordinator **Rs** *komp'yuter* M, pl. *-y,* mid20c (3) →

-chshik M; *-nyi* adj.; *-izatsiya* F **Po** *komputer* [kom-
puter] M, mid20c (2) → *-ek* M; *-owiec* M; *-yzacja* F;
-owy adj.; *-owo* adv. **Cr** *kompjutor* M, pl. *-i,* mid20c
(2) → *-ski* adj.; *-izirati* v.; *-izacija* F **Bg** *kompyutŭr*
M, pl. *-al-tri,* 1970s (2) → *-en* adj.; *-dzhiya* M **Fi** [=E]
1980s (0) < *tietokone* **Hu** *komputer* [kompju:ter] pl.
-ek, mid20c (2) **Al** *kompjuter* M, pl. Ø, 1970s
(3) **Gr** <=E>/*kompiuter/kobiuter* M/N, pl. Ø/*-s,*
end20c (2) = creat *ilektronikos ypologhistis*

computerize   *v.* 1 'equip with a computer', 2 'store,
perform, or produce by computer'
Ge *komputerisieren* 1960s (2 tech) **Du** *computerise-
ren* [kɔmpjutərisɛrən] 1970s (2 rare) < *automati-
seren* **Ic** - < rend 1: *tölvuvæða;* 2: *tölvuvinna* **Fr** - <
informatiser **Sp** *computerizar* < *informatizar* **It**
computerizzare 1960s (3) < *informatizzare* → *-izzato*
adj.; *-izzazione* n.; *-izzabile* adj. **Rm** *computeriza*
[komputeriza] 1980s (2) → *computerizare* F; *compu-
terizat* adj. **Rs** *komp'yuterizirovat'* end20c, 1(3 tech/
2) **Po** *komputerować* [komputerovats] end20c, 1(2)
→ *s-* v. **Cr** *kompjuterizirati* end20c, 1(2) **Bg** *kom-
pyutriziram* (3) → *-trizatsiya* F **Hu** *komputerizál*
[kopjuteriza:l] mid20c (2) → *-ás* n. **Al** *kompjuterizoj*
1970s (2/3)

concealer   *n.* 'a cosmetic used to cover pimples'
Rs *konsiler* M [U] 1990s (1 tech) **Gr** <=E>/*konsiler*
N, 1980s (1 tech)

concern   *n.* 'a business, a firm'
Ge *Konzern* M, pl. *-e,* 19c, via Fr (3) **Du** [kɔnsɛrn]
N, 1940s (2) **Nw** *konsern* [konsæ:rn/-sø:rn] N, pl.
-er, 1920s (2) **Rm** [kontʃern] M, mid20c (3) **Rs**
kontsern M, pl. *-y,* beg20c (3) **Po** *koncern* [kontsern]
M, mid20c (2) **Cr** *koncern* M, pl. *-i,* beg20c (2) **Bg**
kontsern M, pl. *-al-i,* beg20c, via Ge (3) **Fi** *konserni*
[kɔnsernı] (5Ge) **Hu** *konszern* [konsern] pl. *-ek,*
1920s (1 tech, obs) **Al** *koncern* M, pl. Ø, mid20c
(3) **Gr** (0)

concise   *n.* +2 'a dental filling'
Nw [=E] M [U] end20c (1 tech) **Rs** *konsaiz* M [U]
end20c (1 tech) **Po** <=E> M, end20c (2 tech)

condenser   *n.* 1 'an apparatus or vessel for condens-
ing vapour', 2 'a device for storing an electric charge'
Ge - < *Kondensator* (5La) **Du** condensor, 1(5La);
condensator C, 1970s, 2(1 tech) < 1: *condensor, conden-
sator* **Nw** *kondenser, kondensator* [kundenser/-densa:tur] M, pl. *-e,* 20c (1 tech) **Fr** *condenseur* M (5)
Sp - < *condensador* **It** - < *condensatore* **Rm** - <
condensator **Rs** - < *kondensator* (5La) **Po** (5La)
Cr - < *kondenzator* **Bg** - < *kondenzator* **Fi** - < *kon-
densaattori* **Hu** - < *kondenzátor* **Al** - < *kondensator*

conditioner   *n.* 'a lotion applied to hair after shampooing to improve condition'
Ge [=E] M, pl. Ø, 1980s (1 tech, rare) **Du** [=E] C,
1980s (1 jour) **Nw** [=E] M, pl. *-e,* 1980s (1 mod) <
(hår)balsam **Ic** - < rend *(hår)næring* **Sp** - < *acon-
dicionador* **Rs** *konditsioner* M [U] 1990s (2 **Po**
[-er] M, end20c (2 mod) **Cr** *kondišener* M, pl. *-i,*
end20c (2) **Bg** *kŭndishŭnŭr* M, pl. *-al-i,* 1990s (1
tech, mod) **Hu** *kondicionáló* (5La) **Al** *kondinsioner*

M, pl. -*ë*, 1980s (3 you)   **Gr** <=E>/*kodisioner* N, 1980s (2) = *krema malion*

condom   *n.* 'a rubber sheath used as a contraceptive'
Ge C-/K- [kondo:m] N/M, pl. -*e*, 1980s (3)   **Du** *condoom*, end20c, via Fr ? (3)   **Nw** *kondom* [kundu:m] N, pl. -*er*, 20c (3)   **Ic** - < *verja, smokkur*   **Fr** [kɔ̃dɔm] M, 18c (5 obs) /link with E uncertain/ > *capotè* (*anglaise*)   **Sp** - < *condón*   **It** [kɔndɔm] M, pl. Ø, 1980s (1) < *preservativo*   **Rm** [=E] N, 1990s (1 rare) < *prezervativ*   **Rs** *kondom* M, pl. -*y*, beg20c (2 rare) < *prezervativ, kontratseptivy*   **Po** *kondom* M, mid20c (2)   **Cr** *kondom* M, pl. -*i*, beg20c (3)   **Bg** *kondom* M, pl. -*al*-*i*, end20c (1 tech) < *prezervativ*   **Fi** *kondomi* 1960s (3)   **Hu** [=E] [U] end20c (1 tech, writ) < *koton*   **Al** *kondom* M, pl. -*e*, end20c (1 euph) < *presevotio*

connection   *n.* 6 (often in pl.) 'a relative or associate, esp. one with influence', +6a 'a racket, an illicit organization'
Ge *Connection* [=E] F, pl. -*s* (1 mod)   **Ic** - < trsl *sambönd*   **Fr** *connexion* (5)   **It** [=E] F, pl. Ø, end20c, +6a(1 jour) esp. in *pizza connection*   **Po** (5La)   **Cr** (0)   **Hu** (0)   **Gr** [konektsions] N, pl., end20c, 6(1 coll)

consort   *n.* 'a small orchestra, a group of singers'
Ge [=E] N, pl. -*s*, 20c (1 tech)   **Nw** [=E] end20c (1 tech, rare)   **Hu** [=E] pl. Ø, 20c (2 tech)

constable   *n.* 1a 'a police(wo)man'
Ge - < cf. *Konstabler* mid19c, via Fr (3 arch)   **Nw** *konstabel* [kunsta:bel] M, pl. -*er*, beg20c, via Ge (3)   **Fr** [kɔ̃stabl] M, 18c (Ø)   **Rs** *konstebl'* M, pl. -*i*, mid19c   **Po** *konstabl* M, end20c (1/Ø)   **Cr** *konstebl* M/F, end20c (1/Ø)   **Fi** *konstaapeli* end19c (3)   **Hu** *konsztábler* [konsta:bler] pl. -*ek*, beg19c, via Ge (Ø arch)

consulting   *n./cp¹* 1 'giving professional advice', +2 *cp¹* 'a firm giving advice on investments'
The word is a typical specimen of modern economic jargon; it is still marginal compared to native terms, but has gained ground quite rapidly in Eastern Europe after 1989. The agent noun *consultant* is even rarer.
Ge [=E] N/*cp¹* [U] 1960s (1 tech, mod)   **Nw** [=E] *cp¹*/ M, 1980/90s (1 tech)   **Fr** - < *consultant* (5)   **Sp** <=E> M/*cp¹*, pl. Ø, 1970s (1 tech)   **It** - < 1: *consulenza*   **Rm** [=E] N, end20c, 1(1 tech, jour>2) > *consultanţă*   **Rs** *konsalting* M [U] end20c, 1(1 tech) → -*ovyĭ* adj.   **Po** *konsulting*/<=E> [- sultink] M, end20c (2) → -*owy* adj.   **Cr** *konzalting* M, end20c (1 tech)   **Bg** *konsulting* M [U] end20c, 1(1 tech)   **Fi** *konsultointi* 1980s (3) → *konsulti* n.   **Hu** - < *konzultáció* (5La)   **Al** *konsultim* M, pl. -*e*, end20c (3)   **Gr** (0) < +2: trsl *symvuleftiki epikhirisi*

consumerism   *n.* 1 'the protection or promotion of consumers' interests'
Nw *konsumerisme* [konsɯ:merisme] M [U] 1970s (3 tech)   **Fr** *consumérisme* [kɔ̃symeʀism] M, 1970s (3) → *consumériste* adj.   **Rs** *konsyumerizm* M [U] 1990s (1 tech)   **Gr** *konsumerismos* M, end20c (5Fr)

container   *n.* 1 'a vessel, a box', 2 'a large boxlike receptacle for the transport of goods', +3 'a public

skip for the collection of rubbish, glass, paper; a bottle bank'
This term was borrowed into the major languages as the shipment of goods in prepacked containers on ships, planes, and lorries became common during the 1960s. The similar size and function of public skips for presorted waste has led to a new sense which is now possibly better known than (2) among ordinary speakers.
Ge [konte:na] M, pl. Ø, 1960s, 2(1 tech); 1970s, +3(2)   **Du** [kɔnte:nər] C, mid20c (2)   **Nw** [kontæiner] M, pl. -*e*, 1950s, 2,+3(2)   **Ic** [=E] 1970s, 2(0 obs) < 2,+3: rend *gámur*   **Fr** [kɔ̃teneʀ] M, 20c, 2(1 ban) < *conteneur*   **Sp** [konteiner] M, 2,+3(2) < trsl *contenedor* (3)   **It** [kɔntainer/=E] M, pl. Ø, 1930s, 2(2)   **Rm** <=E>/*container* [kontajner/kontejner] N, 1940s, 2,+3(2>3)   **Rs** *konteiner* M, pl. -*y*, mid20c (3) → -*nyĭ* adj.; -*ovoz* M   **Po** *kontejner/kontener* [kontener/-ej-] M, mid20c (2) → -*owiec* M; -*ek* M; -*yzacja* F [U]; -*owy* adj.; s-+ -*owany* adj.   **Cr** *kontejner* M, pl. -*i*, mid20c, 2,+3(2) → -*ski* adj.   **Bg** *konteiner* M, pl. -*al*-*i*, mid20c, 1,2,+3(2) → -*en* adj.; -*izatsiya* F; -*ovoz* M   **Fi** *kontti* 1970s, 2(4)   **Hu** *konténer* [konte:ner] pl. -*ek* mid20c, 2,+3(2) → -*ez* v.   **Al** *kontejner* M [U] mid20c, 1,2(1 reg)   **Gr** *konteiner* N, pl. Ø/-*s*, end20c (1 tech)

containerize   *v.* 1 'pack in or transport by container'
Du *containeriseren* [kɔntenəriseʀən] 1980s (2 rare)   **Rm** *containeriza* [kontajneriza] 1970s (3 rare) → *containerizare* F   **Hu** *konténerez* [konte:nerez] 20c (3 tech)

containment   *n.* 1 'the action or policy of preventing the expansion of a hostile country or influence', +2 'the outer shell of an atomic reactor',
Ge [=E] N [U] 1950s, 1(1 tech, jour); pl. -*s*, 1980s, +2(1 tech, rare)   **Du** (Ø)   **Nw** [=E] M [U] 1950s, 1(1 tech)   **Sp** - < 1: *contención*

controller   *n* +2a 'a person responsible for finance & efficiency planning', +3 'an electronic device'
The English word has been adopted (marginally) as a term of business management, in addition to the much earlier and more widespread French term. Where the two merge, identification of the anglicism is no longer possible (cf. next item, which is even rarer).
Ge [=E] M, pl. Ø, 1960s, +2a(1 tech) < *Kontrolleur*   **Du** [kɔntro:lər] C, end20c (1 tech)   **Nw** <=E>/*kuntroller* [kuntroler] M, pl. -*els*, 1980s (1 tech)   **Fr** *contrôleur* [kɔ̃tʀolœʀ] M (4) → *contrôleuse* F   **Sp** [kontroler] M, +2a(1 tech); - < +3: *controlador*   **It** [kontroller] M, pl. Ø, beg20c (1 tech) < 2a: *revisore* < +3: *controllore*   **Rs** *kontroër* M, pl. -*y*, mid20c, +3(1 tech)   **Po** (5Fr)   **Cr** (5Fr)   **Bg** *kontrolyor* +2a(5Fr); *kontroler* M, pl. -*al*-*i*, mid20c, +3(1 tech)   **Hu** *kontrollőr* from Fr, +2a(5); *kontroller* [kontroller] pl. Ø, 20c, +3a(1 tech)   **Al** *kontrollor* M, pl. -*ë*, mid20c (3)

controlling***   *n.* 'industrial management'
Ge [=E] N [U] 1960s (1 tech)   **Rs** *kontrolling* M [U]

1990s (1 tech)   **Po** [-nk] N [U] end20c (1 mod)   **Gr** > *controlling* N, end20c (1 tech) < *kontrol*

converter   *n.* 2a 'an electrical apparatus for the inter-conversion of alternating current and direct current', 2b 'an electrical apparatus for converting a signal from one frequency to another', 3 'a reaction vessel used in making steel'

Ge K- [konvęrta] M, pl. Ø, beg20c, 3(3 tech)   **Du** [=E] C, end20c, 2b(1 tech_COMPUT)   **Nw** *konverter* [=E, kunværter] M, pl. -e, 20c, 2b,3(1 tech) < 3: *omformer*   **Ic** - < rend (*spennu-/straum- /tíðni-)breytir*   **Fr** - < *convertisseur*   **Sp** - < *convertidor* M   **It** [kɔnvęrter] M, pl. Ø, 1910s (1 tech) < *convertitore*   **Rm** *convertor* [konvertor] N, mid20c, 2b(3 tech) = *convertizor* (5Fr)   **Rs** *konverter* M, pl. -y, mid20c (1 tech)   **Po** *konwertor* [konvertor] M, mid20c, 2b(1 tech); *konvertor* M, mid20c, 3(1 tech) → -*ownia* F; -*owy* adj.   **Cr** *konverter* M, pl. -i, mid20c, 2b(1 tech)   **Bg** *convertor/ konverter* M, pl. -a/-i, mid20c, 2b,3(3/1 tech)   **Fi** *konvertteri* mid20c, 3(3); - < 2a,b: *muuntaja*   **Hu** *konverter* [konverter] pl. -ek, beg20c (1 tech)   **Al** - < *konvertitor* (5 lt)   **Gr** *konverter* M/N, mid20c (1 tech)

conveyor (belt)   *n.* 'an endless moving belt for conveying articles or materials, esp. in a factory'

The distribution of the term is almost restricted to Eastern Europe where the word, abbreviated to its first element, was transmitted through Russian.

Ge - < *Fließband*   **Du** - < *transportband*   **Nw** - < *samlebånd*   **Ic** - < *færiband*   **It** [kɔnvęior] M, pl. Ø, 1960s (1 tech) < trsl *nastro trasportatore*   **Rm** *conveier/conveior* [konvęjer/konvejor] N, mid20c, via Rs (3 tech)   **Rs** *konvęier* M, pl. -y, mid20c (2 tech)   **Po** *konwejer* [-er] M, mid20c, via Rs (1 tech)   **Cr** *konvęjer* M, pl. -i, mid20c (1 tech)   **Bg** *konvęyer* M, pl. -a/-i, mid20c, via Rs (3)   **Hu** *konvejor* [konvejor] pl. Ø, 1920s (1 tech) < *futószalag*   **Al** *konvejer* M, pl. -ë, mid20c (1 tech)

cook   *n.* 1a 'a person who cooks, esp. professionally or in a specified way', +1b 'a person who cooks on board a ship'

Nw *kokk*, 1a(5); +1b: - < *stuert*   **Ic** *kokkur* [kʰɔhkʏr] M, pl. -ar, 16c (5Da) > 1a: *matreiðslumaður*; > 1b: *matsveinn*   **It** - < *cuoco*   **Rs** *kok* M, pl. -i, beg20c, +1b(3 tech)   **Po** *kuk* M, mid20c, +1b(1 tech)   **Bg** *kok* M, pl. -ove, beg20c, via Rs, +1b(3 tech, rare)

cook's mate   *n.* 'the assistant of a ship's cook'

Du - < *koksmaat* (5)   **Nw** *kokksmat* [kɔksmat] M, 19c (3 arch)

cool   *adj* 3 'unexcited, calm', 6 (jazz) 'restrained', 9 'excellent, marvellous'

Whereas *cool (jazz)* was adopted as a specialist term in the 1950s, the word was re-adopted as a youth term (with 3 followed later by 9, as in English) at least in Western languages. Note that derivatives have been borrowed much more reluctantly (↑*coolness*, etc.).

Ge [=E] 1970s, 3(1 you) 6(1 tech) 9(1 sla)   **Du** [=E] 1990s, 3,9(1 you); cp[1] 1980s, 6(1 tech)   **Nw** <=E> *kul* [kʉːl] mid20c (possibly influenced by Sw *kul* 'fun') 3(2) 6(1) 9(1 coll, sla) → *u-kul* adj.   **Ic** *kúl* [kʰuːl] uninfl., 1970s, 3,9(1 sla) 6(1 tech) = trsl *svalur*   **Fr** [kul] mid20c, 3(1 you) 6(1 tech); *cool* interj. (1 you)   **Sp** [kul] M, end20c, 3(1 tech); 1980s, +9(1 mod); end20c, 6(1 tech)   **It** [kuːl] uninfl., 1950s, 6(1 tech)   **Rm** [kuːl] uninfl., 6(1 tech)   **Rs** (0)   **Po** [kul] uninfl., end20c, 3,6(1 tech)   **Cr** [=E] end20c, 3,6(1 tech)   **Bg** *kul* uninfl., mid20c, 6(1 tech); end20c, 9(1 sla, you)   **Hu** [=E] mid20c, 6(1 tech)   **Gr** <=E>/*kul* uninfl., end20c, 3,9(1 coll, you) 6(1 tech) → *kulatos* adj.; *kularo* v.

cool down   *v.* 'make or become cool, calm'

Nw *coole/kule* (*ned*) [kʉːle] 1970s (1 coll)   **Ic** [=E] interj. end20c (0 sla)   **Gr** *kularo* (1 coll, you)

coolie   *n.* 1 'an unskilled native labourer in India, China, etc.', +2 'an apparatus for transporting sth.', +3 'a badly paid worker'

This word is one of the best known South Asian terms borrowed through English. Originally a foreignism, it has come to be widely applied to servants in particularly disgraceful working conditions. The extension to a device for the transport of suitcases etc. is found in German and Hungarian only.

Ge *Kuli* [=E] M, pl. -s, 19c, 1(3 tech); *Kofferkuli* etc., 20c, +2(2)   **Du** *koelie* C, 17c, 1(5Malay)   **Nw** *kuli* [kʉːli] M, pl. -er, beg20c, 1(Ø)   **Ic** *kúli(i)* M, pl. -ar, beg20c, 1(Ø)   **Fr** [kuli] M, mid19c, 1(1 tech)   **Sp** [kuli/kulij] M, end19c, 1(Ø/1 obs)   **It** [kuːli] M, pl. Ø, mid19c, 1(Ø obs)   **Rm** *culi* [=E] M, 20c, 1(Ø)   **Rs** *kuli* M, uninfl., beg20c, 1(Ø)   **Po** *kulis* [kulis] M, 1(1 tech)   **Cr** *kuli* M, end20c, 1(1 tech)   **Bg** *kuli* M, pl. Ø, 20c, 1(Ø)   **Fi** *kuli* beg20c, 1(1)   **Hu** *kuli (kocsi)* mid20c, +2(3) = *kofferkuli* → -*zik* v.

cool it   *v.* 'relax, calm down'

Nw *coole/kule'n* [kʉːle(n)] 1970s (1 coll, sla)   **Rm** (0)

cool jazz*   *n.* 'a jazz style that was developed in the 1950s, succeeding bebop'

Ge [=E] M [U] mid20c (1 tech)   **Nw** [=E] M [U] mid20c (1 tech, arch)   **Sp** [=E] M [U] end20c (1 tech)   **Po** [kul-] M [U] mid20c (1 tech)   **Bg** *kul* M [U] mid20c (3 tech)   **Fi** [=E] M [U] mid20c (1 tech)   **Hu** [=E] [U] 1940s (1 tech, arch) < *cool*   **Gr** <=E> [=E] F [U] mid20c (1 tech)

coolly   *adv.* 'in a cool way'

Nw <=E>/*kuli* [=E/kʉːli] mid20c (1 coll)

coolness   *n.* 'lack of excitement, calmness, distance'

Ge [=E] F [U] 1960s (1 you)   **Nw** (0)

co-producer   *n.* 'a person sharing responsibility for the production of a film or a play with another producer'

Ge - < *Co-/Ko-Produzent*   **Du** - < *coproducent*   **Nw** [kuːprudjʉːser]/*co-produsent* M, 1980s (1 tech)   **Ic** - < trsl *meðframleiðandi*   **Fr** - < *coproducteur*   **Sp** - < *coproductor*   **It** - < *coproduttore*   **Rm** - < *coproducător*   **Po** (0)   **Bg** - < *koprodutsent*   **Hu** *koproducer* [k*o*produtser] pl. *-ek*, 20c (3 tech/5La)   **Al** - < *bashkë prodhues* **Gr** (0/1 writ) < trsl *symparaghoghos*

copyright   *n.* 'the exclusive legal right over a work held by author or publisher'

As a technical term in publishing, *c.* has been used since the nineteenth century, variously supplemented by calques which are not always completely equivalent from a legal point of view, as in German and French.

Ge [=E] N, pl. *-s*, beg20c (2 tech) > *Urheberrecht* **Du** [=E] N, end20c (1 tech) < *auteursrecht* **Nw** [=E] M, pl. *-er*, 20c (1 tech) **Ic** [=E] uninfl., mid20c (0 tech) < rend *höfundarréttur* **Fr** [k*o*pir*a*jt] M, 19c (1 tech) < *droit d'auteur, de copie, de reproduction* **Sp** [kopirr*a*i(t)] M, beg20c (2 tech) = *derechos de autor* **It** [=E] M [U] end19c (2 tech) = rend *diritti d'autore* **Rm** [=E] N, 1970s (1 tech) **Rs** *kopir*a*it* M [U] end20c (1 tech) > rend *avtorskoe pravo* **Po** <=E> M [U] beg20c (1 tech) **Cr** *k*o*pirajt* M [U] beg20c (1 tech) **Bg** *k*o*pir*a*it* M [U] 1990s (1 tech) < rend *avtorsko pravo* **Fi** [=E] 19c (0) **Hu** [=E] M [U] beg20c (1 tech) **Al** - < *e drejtë e autorit* **Gr** *kopyr*a*it/kopir*a*it* N [U] 20c (2)

copy-shop*   *n.* 'a shop in which photocopies are made (often self-service)'

Ge [k*o*pi∫op] M, pl. *-s*, 1980s (2) **It** [k*o*pi∫op] M, pl. Ø, end20c (1) < *copisteria* **Hu** [=E] [U] 1990s (2 writ, mod)

cord(uroy)   *n.* 1 'thick cotton fabric with velvety ribs'

The long form is first attested in American English in 1780; it may be derived from British English *cord.* The two words may have spread independently through Europe with other terms for cloths, or *cord* may have been seen as the abbreviated form. Note that the word is not attested for French (and Spanish, Italian) – the French form is misleading.

Ge *C-/K* -[kort] M [U] mid19c (2) **Du** *corduroy* [=E] N [U] mid20c (1 tech) < *ribfluweel, koordfluweel, koord* **Nw** *cord-fløyel/kord* [kord-] M [U] mid20c (2/3) **Ic** - < *rifflað flauel* **Sp** - < *pana* **Rm** [kord] N [U] mid20c (3 tech) **Po** *kort* [kort] M [U] mid20c (1 arch) **Cr** *k*o*rd* M [U] mid20c (1 tech) **Hu** *kord* [kord] [U] 19c (3)

corned-beef   *n.* 'processed beef, often tinned'

This term was adopted into French at a very early date and thence transmitted to other European languages, along with the product. Although the product is known internationally, the anglicism is apparently not found throughout.

Ge [k*o*rnetbef] (2 obs)/[-bif/=E]

N [U] beg19c, via Fr (2) **Du** [=E] N [U] beg20c (2) **Nw** [k*o*:rn(d)bif] M [U] end20c (1) **Ic** [=E] N, 1950s (0 obs) < rend *saxbauti* **Fr** [k*ɔ*rn*ɛ*dbif/k*ɔ*rnbif] M, 18c (2 obs) > *singe(s)* **Sp** <=E> M, 1980s (1 arch) **Po** [korntbif] M, uninfl., end20c (1 mod) **Cr** [=E] M [U] end20c (1) **Hu** [=E] [U] end20c (1 tech, writ) **Gr** *kornbif* N, 19c, via Fr (1 rare)

corner   *n.* 8a 'an angle of the ring' (box, etc.), 9 'a free kick or hit from a corner' (footb. and hockey)

Adopted for various sports (boxing, ball games), around 1900 the term was frequently replaced by obvious native equivalents, but remained available locally (e.g. for German in Austria) or as a fashionable alternative. The compound *corner-kick* was also widespread in the early twentieth century.

Ge *C-/K-* [=E] M, pl. Ø, beg20c, 8a(1 mod), 9(1 reg, obs) < 8a: *Ecke* < 9: *Eckball* **Du** [=E] C, mid20c, 8a,9(1 tech) < *hoekschop* **Nw** [=E] M, pl. *-e*, beg20c, 9(2) = trsl *hjørne(spark)* **Ic** - < trsl *horn, hornspyrna* **Fr** [k*ɔ*rn*ɛ*r] M, beg20c, 9(2 tech, ban) > *jet de coin* (hockey, handball); *tir d'angle, coup du coin* (football) **Sp** *córner* [k*ɔ*rner] M, pl. *-s*, 9(2>3) = *saque de esquina* **It** [k*ɔ*rner] M, pl. Ø, 1920s (2 tech) = 9: *calcio d'angolo*, 8a: *angolo* **Rm** [k*ɔ*rnər] N, 1920s, 9(2) = 8a: *colţ* = 9: *lovitură de colţ* **Rs** *korner* M, pl. *-y*, beg20c, 9(1 tech, rare) < trsl *uglovoǐ udar* **Po** *korner/*<=E> [korner] M, beg20c(2) **Cr** *korner* M, pl. *-i*, beg20c, 9(2) **Bg** *k*o*rner* M, pl. *-a/-i*, beg20c, 9(1 tech/coll) < rend *ǔglov udar* **Hu** *korner* [korner] [U] end19/beg20c, 9(1 tech) < trsl *szöglet* **Al** *korner* M, pl. Ø, mid20c (1 reg) **Gr** *k*o*rner* N, beg20c, 9(1 tech)

cornflakes   *n.* pl. 1 'a type of breakfast cereal'

Recorded from the 1930s (but rare; cf. earlier ↑*quaker oats* with a similar meaning) the cereal became well-known from the 1960s onwards; it is remarkable how few calques have been tried (or have successfully competed against the loanword).

Ge [kornfle:ks] pl., 1960s (2) **Du** [k*ɔ*rnfle:ks] pl., mid20c (2) **Nw** [k*o*:rnfle(i)ks] M, sg. [U] mid20c (2) **Ic** *kornfleks* [k^h*ɔ*(r)tnfl*ɛ*xs] N, sg. [U] beg/mid20c (2 coll) > trsl *kornflögur* **Fr** *corn-flakes/*<=E> [k*ɔ*rn*ɛ*ks] M, mid20c (2) **Sp** [k*ɔ*nfl*ɛ*ks/k*ɔ*rfleks] M, 1960 (2) = *cereales* **It** [k*ɔ*rnfl*ɛ*iks M, 1960s (2) > trsl *fiocchi di grano* **Rm** [k*ɔ*rnfleks] N pl., 1970s (1 obs) < rend *fulgi (de porumb)* **Rs** *kornfleiks/kornfl*ě*ksy* M end20c (1 mod) < trsl *kukuruznye khlop'ya* **Po** *cornfleksy* <=E> [kornfleksi/=E] end20c (1 mod) **Cr** *k*o*rnfljks* M sg./pl., end20c (2) **Bg** - < rend *zǔrneni yadki* **Fi** <=E>/*cornflakesit* [=E] pl., mid20c (2) > trsl *maissihiutaleet* **Hu** [=E] [U] end20c (2) **Gr** *kornfleiks* N, end20c (1 tech)

cornflour   *n.* 2 'flour of rice or other grain'

Gr *kornfl*a*ur* N [U] mid20c, 2(2) > trsl *anthos aravositu*

corny   *adj.* 1d 'old-fashioned; out of date', +1e 'crazy, funny, peculiar'

Nw [=E] 1980s, +1e(1 coll) **Ic** [k^h*ɔ*rni] uninfl., mid20c, 1d(1 sla) **Fi** *korni* 1990s (1)

corporate identity   *n.* 'the image created by large businesses of their business policy'
Ge [=E] F, pl. *-(ie)s*, end20c (1 tech)   **Du** [=E] C, pl. *-is*, end20c (1 tech)

cosy (corner)   *n.* 2 'a canopied corner seat for two'
Du *cosy-corner* [=E] C, 1940s (1 tech, jour)   **Ic** *kósihorn* N, pl. Ø, end20c (2+5 coll)   **Fr** [kozi] M, 1940s (1 obs)

cosy   *adj.* 1 'comfortable and warm'
Du [=E] uninfl., 1990s, 1(1 mod)   **Ic** *kósí* [kʰouːsi] uninfl., mid20c (2 coll) → *kósilegur* adj.   **Fr** [kozi] beg20c (1 arch)

cottage   *n.* 1 'a small simple house, esp. in the country', +4 'a house with a small garden'
    This term appears to have been adopted as an element of fashionable English life around 1900, but is now only locally applied to houses in the respective country (e.g. in Vienna); otherwise it is known as a foreignism.
Ge [=E] N, pl. *-s*, end19c, 1(1 reg, obs)   **Du** [=E] C, beg20c, 1(1 tech)   **Nw** (0)   **Fr** [kɔtɛdʒ/kɔtaʒ] M, mid18c, 1(1 obs)
Sp [kotidʒ] M, pl. *-s*, end19c (Ø rare)   **It** [kɔttedʒ] M, pl. Ø, 17c, 1(2)   **Rm** (Ø)   **Rs** *kottedzh* M,

pl. *-i*, end19c, 1(3); end20c, +4(3 mod)   **Po** F, uninfl., 1(1 tech)   **Bg** (0)   **Hu** [=E] pl. Ø, 17/18c, 1(Ø/1 arch, rare)   **Gr** (Ø)

cottage cheese   *n.* 'soft white cheese'
Ge [=E] M [U] 1970s (Ø>1 tech) = trsl *Hüttenkäse* **Nw** [=E] 1960s (2) > trsl *hytteost* **Ic** - < rend *kotasæla* **Fr** *cottage* [kɔtɛdʒ/kɔtaʒ] 1980s (0) **Po** (0) **Fi** (Ø) **Gr** *tyri kotatz* N (5+1 tech); *kotatz tsiz* N [U] end20c (1 tech)

cotton   *n.* 3 'thread or cloth made from cotton fibre'
    The history of this term is complex: the earlier *kattun*, etc. (in German, Dutch, Norwegian) came through Arabic and only partly through English. C. was partly re-adopted recently, but the two lines of transmission cannot be distinguished in many languages.
Ge [kotən] M/N [U] 1960s (1 mod) < *Baumwolle* **Nw** (0) < *bomull* **Ic** *kot(t)ún/kat(t)ún* N [U] mid17c, via Da (5 obs Da) < *bómull, baðmull* **Fr** *coton* (5) **It** *cotone* (5) **Rm** *coton* [koton] N [U] (5Fr) **Rs** *kotton* M [U] 19c (1 tech) **Po** [-on] M [U] end20c (2) **Bg** *koton* (5Fr) **Hu** [=E] [U] 19c (1 tech) **Gr** *koton* N [U] 20c, via Fr (1 tech) < *vamvaki* N, *vamvakero* adj.

couch   *n.* 1 'an upholstered piece of furniture for several people'
    As one of many terms for upholstered pieces of furniture, *c.* has become really current only in a few languages (partly through German?). It is slightly more widespread with reference to a psychiatrist's couch, through Freud's use of it. Modern *couch potato* does not appear to have been borrowed so far.

Ge *C-/Kautsch* [=E] F, pl. *-es/en*, beg20c (2) = *Sofa*; M (reg) **Du** [=E] C, pl. *-es*, end20c (2 tech_PSYCHOL) < *sofa, ligbank, divan* **Nw** (0) < *sofa* **Ic** - < *sófi* **It** - < *divano, sofà* **Rs** (5Fr) **Cr** *kauč* M, pl. *-evi*, beg20c (2) < *sofa*

countdown   *n.* 1a 'an act of counting at the launching of a rocket', 2 'the period and activities, leading up to a significant event'
    For the aeronautical term, the languages are neatly divided between those using loanwords, those with calques, and those with no term. The transfer to use in more general contexts is even rarer.
Ge [=E] M/N pl. *-s*, 1960s, 1(1 tech) 2(1 coll) **Du** [=E] C, end20c (1 tech, mod) **Nw** (0) < rend *nedtelling* **Fr** - < trsl *compte à rebours* **Sp** - < trsl *cuenta atrás* **It** [kauntdaun] M [U] 1970s (1 jour) < rend *conto*

alla rovescia **Rm** - < rend *numărătoare inversă* **Rs** *kauntdaun* M [U] end20c (1 tech) **Po** <=E> M [U] end20c, 1a(1 tech) **Bg** *kauntdaun* M [U] 1990s, 1a(1 jour, rare) **Fi** (0) **Hu** [=E] [U] 20c, 1a(1 tech) 2(2 mod, sla) < rend *visszaszámlálás* **Gr** 1a(0 tech) < trsl *adistrofi metrisi*

counter   *n.* +3 'a defensive blow' (box.)
Ge *Konter* M [U] 1970s (3 tech) **Du** [=E] C, 1970s (2) **Rm** - < *contră* **Rs** - < trsl *kontrudar* **Bg** - < rend *kontrirasht udar*

counter   *v.* 3 'give a return blow' (box.)
Ge *kontern* 1970s (3 tech) **Du** *counteren* [kauntərən] 1970s (2) **Rm** - < *contra* **Po** *kontra* (5La) **Bg** - < *kontriram*

counterfeit   *n.* +1c 'a pirate copy of a record or tape, esp. with a forged cover'
Du [=E] C, 1970s (1 tech) **Nw** [=E] M, 1980s (1 tech)

country and western   *n./cp^1/2* +1c 'a style of rural or cowboy songs originating in the US' (cf. ↑*c&w*)
Ge [=E] cp¹, 1970s (1 tech) **Du** [=E] C [U] 1970s (2) < *country, countrymuziek* **Nw** [=E] M [U] 1960s (2) **Ic** [=E] N 1950s (0 tech) **Fr** - < *country, folk* **Sp** [=E/kountri an western] M [U] 1980s (1 tech) < *country* **It** *country* [kauntri] cp², 1970s (1<2) **Rm** *country* [=E] end20c (0) = rend *muzică country* **Rs** (0) **Po** [-ern] M [U] 1970s (2) **Cr** *kantri-end-vestern* M [U] mid20c (2) **Bg** *kuntri* N [U] 1980s (3 tech, coll) **Fi** [=E] (0); *kantri* 1970s (2) **Gr** <=E> [=E] F [U] mid20c (1 tech)

country dance   *n.* 'a traditional type of dance'
    Early transmission through French has made the provenance from English opaque; the term is therefore not felt to be an anglicism.
Ge *Kontertanz* M, 18c, via Fr (3) **Du** *contradans/contredans* C, via Fr (1 arch, tech+5) **Nw** *kontradans* via Fr (1 arch) **Ic** [=E] M, end20c (1 mod); *kontradans* M, end18c (3 obs) **Fr** *contredanse* [kɔ̃trədɑ̃s] F,

17c (3) **Sp** *contradanza* F, 18c, via Fr (3 tech, arch) **It** [kauntri dens] F [U] 18c, via Fr (1 obs) = *contraddanza* **Rm** *contradans* [kontradans] N, end18c, via Fr/Ge (3 arch) **Rs** *kontrdans* M [U] 19c (1 tech, arch) **Bg** *kontradans* M, [U] via Fr (3 tech) **Hu** *kontratánc* [kontrata:nts] [U] before20c (3 arch)

country (music) *n.* 'a style of rural or cowboy songs originating in the US'

This term has largely replaced the earlier ↑*hillbilly* and ↑*bluegrass* for the rural music style from the Southern USA accompanied by a guitar, banjo, etc. This compound may have been the source for other cp¹ uses meaning 'rural, unsophisticated' (esp. with reference to dress).

Ge -*Musik* [=E+Ge] F [U] 1970s (2 tech+5) **Du** *countrymuziek* [kantri] 1970s (2+5) **Nw** <=E>/*køntri* [kontri/køn-/kawn-] M [U] 1960s (2) **Ic** *kántrí (tónlist)* [khauntri(-)] N (F) [U] 1950s (2 tech+5) < trsl *sveitatónlist* **Fr** [kuntri] M/F, 1970s (1 tech) **Sp** [kóuntri] adj., uninfl., 1960s (1 tech) **It** [kauntri] M [U] 1970s (1 tech) **Rm** N [U]/adj., uninfl., end20c (2) **Rs** *kantri* N, uninfl., 1970s (1 tech) **Po** *country* N, uninfl., adj. uninfl., end20c (2) **Cr** [=E] F [U] end20c (2) **Bg** *kuntri* N [U] 1980s (3 tech, coll); *kuntrimuzika* F [U] (2+5) **Fi** *kantrimusiikki*, 20c (3) **Hu** [=E] [U] 1970s (2) **Al** *muzik(ë) kantri* end20c (1 you) **Gr** *kantry/-i (musiki)* F [U] mid20c (1 tech)

course *n.* 2b 'a person's or thing's correct or intended direction', 2c 'the direction taken by a ship or aircraft', 4a 'a series of lectures, lessons, etc.'

Most loanwords appear to come straight from Latin, or have the meanings of native words extended; the impact of the English word is difficult to establish.

Ge (5La) **Du** [=E] C, 1990s, 4a(1 mod) **Nw** *kos* [ku:s] M, 19c, 2b(3) **Ic** *kúrs* [khurs] M, pl. -*ar*, beg19c, 2c(5 coll, tech Da); mid20c, 4a(5 coll Da) **Sp** - < *curso* (5La) **It** - < *corso* (5La) **Rm** - < *curs* (4) **Rs** (5La) **Po** 2b,2c,4a(5La) **Bg** *kurs* M, pl. -*al-ove*, beg20c (5Fr) **Fi** *kurssi* 19c, via Sw (5La) **Al** *kurs* M, pl. -*e*, mid20(3)

court *n.* 2a 'a tennis court'

Along with other tennis terminology, this term was adopted early (at the end of the nineteenth century) in W. Europe, where, however, it has been largely replaced by native equivalents. It is now spreading again to other languages, and is a fashionable equivalent for native terms, as a consequence of the recent popularity of tennis. (cf. ↑*centercourt*)

Ge [kort] M, pl. -*s*, 1960s (1 tech, mod/arch) < *Tennisplatz* **Du** [=E] C, 1990s (1 tech) **Nw** (0) < *tennisbane* **Fr** [kur] M, end19c (3) **Sp** <=E> M, pl. -*s*, beg20c (1 arch) < *pista* **It** - < *campo* **Rm** [=E] N, end20c (0>1 jour) **Rs** *kort* M, pl. -*y*, beg20c (2) **Po** *kort* [kort] M, beg20c (3) **Bg** *kort* M, pl. -*al-ove*, beg20c (2 tech) **Gr** *kort* N, 20c (1 tech) < *ghipedo (tou) ten(n)is*

cover *n.* +1g 'an album cover (record, CD etc.)', +1h 'something that protects the seats of a car', 4a 'a pretence; a screen'

Ge [kava] N, pl. Ø/-*s*, 1970s, +1g(1 tech) < *Plattenhülle* **Du** [=E] C/N, end20c, +1g(1 tech) 4a(1 tech) < *(platen)hoes* **Nw** [kover] N, pl. -*e*, 1970s, +1g(2) **Ic** [khou:ver/khɔv:er] N, pl. Ø, 1970s, +1g(1 sla) +1h(1 coll) 4a(0 sla) **Sp** [kober] F, pl. -*s*, 1970s (1 tech); ↑*cover version* **Rs** (0) **Cr** [=E] M, end20c, +1g(1 tech)

cover *v.* 6a 'report' (journ.), 12 'make a cover version of (a song etc.)', +14 'add new profile to a tyre', +15 'put a sole on a shoe', +16 'vulcanize',

Ge *covern* 1980s, 12(1 mod) **Du** *coveren* [kavərə(n)] 1980s, 6a(1 tech); 1960s, +14,+15(1 tech); 1970s, 12(1 tech); 1980s, +16(1 tech) **Fr** *couvrir* 1960s, 6a(4) **Gr** - < 6a: mean *kalypto*

cover charge *n.* 'an extra charge levied per head in a restaurant, nightclub, etc.'

Nw [=E] M [U] 1980s (2)

covercoat* *n.* 'a type of coat'

The term *cover(t)coat* was widespread in Europe in the early twentieth century, but appears now to be obsolete everywhere (in contrast to ↑*trenchcoat*).

Ge [kavako:t] M, pl. -*s*, beg20c (1 arch) **Du** [=E] N [U] 1940s (1 tech) **Fr** *cover-coat* M, beg20c (1 tech, arch) **Sp** <=E> M, beg20c (1 arch) **Rm** *covercot* [koverkot] N, mid20c (3 obs) **Rs** *koverkotovoe pal'to* N, uninfl., beg20c (1 arch) **Po** *kowerkot* [koverkot] M, beg20c (1 obs) **Cr** *koverkot* M, pl. -*i*, beg20c (1 arch) **Hu** *koverkó* [koverko:] pl. Ø, end19/beg20c (1 arch)

cover girl *n.* 'a female model whose picture appears on magazine covers etc.'

This term refers to scantily dressed girls on the front covers of magazines; it came in during the 1960s, but does not seem to have achieved the popularity of the earlier ↑*pinup girl*.

Ge [kavagörl] N, pl. -*s*, 1960s (1 jour) **Du** [=E] C, 1970s (1 tech, jour) **Nw** [kovergø:rl] M, pl. -*s*, 1980s (1) = *forsidepike* **Ic** - < trsl *forsíðustúlka* **Fr** *cover-girl* [kɔvœrgœrl] F, mid20c (1 tech) > *modéle pin up* **Sp** [kober gel] F, 1970s (1 tech) = *chica de portada* **It** [kɔver gœrl] F, pl. Ø, 1950s (1) < trsl *ragazza copertina* **Rm** 1980s (0) **Rs** *kavé gël* F, uninfl., 1990s (1 jour) **Po** [-er gerl] F, uninfl., pl. -*sy*, end20c(1 jour) **Cr** [=E] F, pl. -*e*, end20c(1 jour) **Hu** [kavergørl] pl. -*ök*, end20c (1 jour, mod) **Gr** *kover gerl* N, 1980s (1 coll, mod) < *exofyllo*

cover story *n.* 'a news story in a magazine, illustrated or advertised on the front page'

Ge [kavərsto:ri] F, pl. -*(ie)s*, 1960s (1 jour) < *Titelgeschichte* **Du** [=E] C, pl. -*s*, 1970s (1 jour) **Nw** [=E] M, pl. -*ies*, 1980s (1 jour) **Ic** - < trsl *forsíðu-*

frétt **It** [kɔvɛr stɔri] F, pl. Ø, 1980s (1 jour) **Rs** (0) **Cr** (0)

cover version *n.* 'a recording of a previously re-corded song'

Ge *Coverversion* [kavəvɛrzjoːn] F, pl. -en, 1970s (1 tech + 5La) **Du** *coverversie* [kavɛrvɛrsiː] C, 1990s (1 tech) **Nw** -versjon, cover [=E] M, 1980s (1 tech) **Ic** [=E] end20c (0 tech) **Sp** *cover* [koḇer] M, pl. -s, 1970s (1 tech) **Bg** *kaḇŭrversiya* F, pl. -sii, 1990s (1+4 tech); *kaḇŭr* M, pl. -al-i (3 tech)

cowboy *n.* 1 'a person who herds and tends cattle, esp. in the western USA', 2 'this as a conventional figure in American folklore', 3 'an unscrupulous person'

One of the best-known nineteenth-century foreign-isms, this term came to be applied to attitudes and manners thought of as typical of the American West, but never to native cowherds. It has been variously re-anglicized where early loans were un-English in pro-nunciation, but rarely translated. Names for the fe-male equivalent are rare and mostly facetious.

Ge [=E] M, pl. -s, 19c, 1,2(2); 1970s, 3(2 pej/euph) **Du** [=E] C, beg20c, 1,2(2) **Nw** [koboi] M, pl. -er, end19c, 1,2(2); 3(1) **Ic** <=E>/káboj/kabboj [kʰau:poj/kʰap:oj] M, pl. -ar, 1950s, 2(2 coll, you) = rend *kúreki* **Fr** *cow-boy* [kobɔj/kaobɔj] M, end19c, 1,2(2) **Sp** [kauboi] M, pl. -s, beg20c, 1,2(2 arch) > *vaquero* **It** [=E] M, pl. Ø, end19c, 1,2(2) **Rm** [=E] M, pl. Ø, beg20c, 1,2(2) **Rs** *kovboĭ* M, pl. -i, beg20c, 1,2(2) →-ka F; -skiĭ adj. **Po** *kowboj*/<=E> [kovboj] M, beg20c, 1,2 (2) → -ki n. pl.; -ski adj. **Cr** *kaḇoj* M, pl. -i, beg20c, 2(2) → -ski adj. **Bg** *kaḇoĭ*/*kovboĭ* M, pl. -boi, end19/beg20c (2/3) → -ski adj. **Fi** 1,2(Ø) **Hu** [=E] pl. -ok, 19c, 1,2(Ø); [kovboi] 20c(2) **Al** *kauboj* M, pl. Ø, mid20c, 1,2(3) **Gr** *kau-bois* M, beg20c, 1,2(3); *kauḇoi* M, 1,2(2) → *kauḇoissa* F

cowgirl *n.* 'a female cowboy'

Ge [kaugörl] N, pl. -s, 1960s (1 reg) **Nw** [kawgø:l] M, pl. -s, 1980s (1 fac) **Fr** (Ø) **Sp** [kaugel] F, pl. -s, end20c (1 tech, rare) **It** [kaugœrl] F, pl. Ø, 1980s (1 rare) **Po** (0) **Cr** (0) **Gr** - < *kauḇoissa*

cowper-* *n.* 'a wind heater in steel-making'

The device is named after the inventor E.A. Cowper (1819–93)

The word is widespread as a technical term, but completely unknown to non-specialists.

Ge <=E>+-*Apparat* [kau-+Ge] mid20c (1 tech+5) **Du** *cowpertoren* [kaupər-] 1970s (1 tech+5) **Fr** M (1 tech) **It** [kauper] M, pl. Ø, 1930s (1 tech) **Rm** *cauper* [kawper] N, mid20c, via Rs? (3 tech) = *preîn-călzitor Cowper* **Rs** *kauper* M, pl. -y, end19c (1 tech) **Po** *kauper* [kauper] M, mid20c (1 tech) **Bg** *kauper* M, pl. -al-i, beg20c, via Rs (3 tech) → -en adj. **Hu** [=E/ku:per] pl. Ø, 20c (1 tech) **Gr** (0 tech)

cox *n.* 'a coxswain of a racing boat'

Nw [=E] M, pl. -er, 20c (1 tech) **Hu** *koksz*, 20c, via Ge? (1 tech/5)

cox *v.* 'act as a cox'

Nw *coxe* [koḵse] 20c (1 tech)

Cox (apple) *n.* 'a variety of eating apple'

Named after the English breeder R. Cox.

Ge [koks] M, [U]/pl. -e, 1970s (2) < *Cox Orange* **Du** [kɔks] C, pl. -en, 1980s (3) **Fr** *cox* [kɔks] F (1 tech) **Rs** (1 obs) **Po** *koksa* [koksa] F, mid20c (3) **Gr** <=E>/koks uninfl., end20c (1 rare)

crack[1] *n.* 7 'a first-rate player, etc.', +10 'a car accid-ent', +11 'a financial crash'

This term was first adopted for race-horses, but soon transferred to eminent sportsmen and later to other people of outstanding talents. Much rarer is the adoption of *crack (up)*, in the sense of +10; the origin of the un-English sense +11 (more likely to be ↑*crash*? and possibly influenced by confusion with German *Krach* of identical meaning) is likely to have been through extension from +10.

Ge [krek] M, pl. -s, beg20c, 7(1 coll) **Du** [krɛk] C, mid20c, 7(2) **Nw** *krakk* [krak] N, pl. Ø, 1920s, +11(5 Ge) **Ic** *krakk* [kʰrahk] N [U] 1920s, +11(5Da) < *hrun* **Fr** [krak] M, 19c, 7(1) **Sp** [krak] M, pl. -s, 1920s/1970s, 7(1 tech); end19c, +11(2 tech) **It** *crac* [krak] M, pl. Ø, end19c, 7,+10(0) +11(3) < +11: *fallimento, bancarotta* **Rs** *krakh* +11(5Ge) **Po** *kraksa* [kraksa] F, mid20c, +10(3) **Bg** *krakh* +11(5Ge) **Hu** *krekk* [krekk] end19/beg20c, 7(1 tech, obs); *krach* +11(5Ge) **Gr** *krakh* N, beg20c, + 11 (5 Ge)

crack[2] *n.* 9 'a potent hard crystalline form of cocaine'

This word, associated with the drug scene in the 1980s, spread very quickly. The political division of Europe is largely reflected in the dates of the adoption.

Ge [krek] N/M [U] 1980s (1 sla) **Du** [=E] C [U] 1980s (1 sla, you) **Nw** [=E] M [U] 1980s (1) **Ic** *krakk* [kʰrahk] N [U] 1990s (2 tech, sla) **Fr** [krak] M, 1990s (1 tech) **Sp** <=E> M, pl. Ø, 1980s (1 you) **It** [krak] M, pl. Ø, 1980s (1 sla) **Rs** *krék* M [U] end20c (1 sla) **Po** [-e-] M [U] 1990s (1 sla) **Cr** [krek] M [U] 1990s (1 sla) **Bg** *krek*/*krak* M [U] 1990s (1 sla) **Fi** [=E] 1990s (2) **Hu** [=E] [U] end20c (1 tech, mod) **Gr** *krak* N [U] end20c (1 sla)

crack *v.* 4 'give way or cause to give way; yield', 9 'decompose (heavy oils)' (also cp[1]), +11 'crash finan-cially; go bankrupt'

Ge *cracken* [krekən] 1970s, 9(1 tech) **Nw** *krakke* [krake] 1970s, 9(1 tech) **Ic** *krakka* [kʰrahka] mid20c, 4,+11(1 sla) **Fr** *craquer* 1960s, 9(1 tech) **Sp** *craquear* 1960s, 9(1 tech); *hacer crack* 4,+11 (1 tech) **Rm** *craca* [kraka̱] mid20c, via Fr, 9(3 tech) → *cracare* F **Rs** *krekirovat'* M, mid20c, 9(3 tech) **Bg** *krekiniram* mid20c, 9(3 tech) **Hu** *krakkol* [krakkol] beg20c, 9(1 tech)

cracker *n.* 2 'a firework', 4a 'a thin dry biscuit'

The food-related term apparently spread with the word printed on the packages, and its adoption was probably assisted by its onomatopoeic quality. The lesser frequency of the firework term is likely to reflect the more restricted export of the item (and the pre-existence of native terms, cf. German *Kracher*).

Ge *Kräcker* M, pl. Ø, 1980s, 4a(2)   **Du** [krɛkər] C, mid20c, 4a(2)   **Nw** 4a(0) < *kjeks*   **Fr** [krakœr/krakɛr] M, 1970s (0)   **Sp** [kraker] F, pl. *-s*, beg20c, 4a(1 tech)   **It** [krɛker] M, pl. Ø, 1950s, 4a(2)   **Rs** *kreker* M, pl. *-y*, end20c, 4a(2)   **Po** *krakers* M, end20c, 4a(2)   **Cr** *kreker* M, pl. *-i*, end20c, 4a(2)   **Bg** *kreker* M, usu. sg., 1990s, 4a(1 mod)   **Hu** *kréker* [krɛːker] [Ø] 20c, 4a(3)   **Gr** *kraker* N, pl. Ø/-s, end20c, 4a(2)

Ic	Nw	Po	Rs
Du	Ge	Cr	Bg
Fr	It	Fi	Hu
Sp	Rm	Al	Gr

cracking* *n.* 1 'a process in steel-making', 9 'the application of specific temperatures of intense heat to crude oil during refinement in order to separate various derivative products' (oil)

An international term, but restricted to specialist jargon, as a technical term in steel, and later, oil production. The related verb is frequent, but other derivatives are not.

Ge [krɛkiŋ] N [U] 20c, 2(1 obs) < *Cracken*   **Nw** *krakking* [krakiŋ] M [U] 1950s, 1,9(1 tech)   **Fr** [krakiŋ] 1920s, 9(1 tech, ban) < *craquage*   **Sp** [krákin] M [U] 1920s (1 tech) = *craqueo*   **It** [krɛkiŋ] M [U] 1940s (1 tech)   **Rm** - < *cracaj*   **Rs** *kreking* M [U] mid20c, 9(1 tech) → *-ovyĭ* adj.   **Po** *kraking/krakowanie* [-nk/kra-kovanie] N/M [U] mid20c, 9(1 tech) → *krakingowy* adj.   **Cr** *kreking* M [U] mid20c, 1(1 tech)   **Bg** *kreking* M [U] mid20c, 1(1 tech), via Rs, 9(1 tech) → *-ov* adj. → *krekiniram* v.   **Fi** *krakkaus* 20c (2 tech)   **Hu** *krakkolás* [krakkolaːʃ] [U] beg20c, 9(1 tech); [=E] 20c, 1(1 tech)   **Al** *kreking* M [U] mid20c, 9(1 reg)

cranberry *n.* 2 'a small red berry used in cooking and as a source of fruit juice'

Du [=E] C, pl. *-ies*, 1970s (2)   **Nw** (0)   **Fr** (Ø)

crank *n.* 1 'part of an axle or shaft (bicycles)'

Du [=E] C, 1960s (2 tech) < *krenk*   **Nw** *krank* [kraŋk] M, pl. *-er*, 20c (3 tech)

crash *n.* 1a 'a loud and sudden smashing noise', 2a 'a violent collision (of a vehicle)', 3 'financial ruin', 4 'a sudden failure which puts a system out of action' (comput.)

This word was adopted as a term of financial exchange and of air travel, and variously transferred to similar contexts, assisted by its onomatopoeic qualities (note the similarity with the unrelated German *Krach* 'loud noise, conflict' which may have borrowed senses from English, and was in turn reborrowed). The related verb is again less frequently adopted.

Ge [krɛʃ] M [U] 1970s, 2a(1 mod) 3(1 tech, mod) < 3: *Börsen-krach*   **Du** [=E] C, pl. *-es*, 1970s, 2a,3(2 tech)   **Nw** <=E>/*krasj/kræsj* [=E/kraʃ] N, pl. Ø, 1960s (2/3)   **Fr** [kraʃ] M, pl. *des crashs/crashes*, 1960s, 2a(1 ban,

Ic	Nw	Po	Rs
Du	Ge	Cr	Bg
Fr	It	Fi	Hu
Sp	Rm	Al	Gr

mod) < *écrasement* (plane) → *se crasher* v.   **Sp** [=E] M, pl. Ø, 1980s, 3(1 tech)   **It** [kraʃ] M [U] 1960s, 1a,2a,4(2) = 4: *crollo del sistema*   **Rm** - < 3: *crah* (5Ge)   **Rs** *krakh* (5Ge)   **Po** - < *krach* (5Ge)   **Hu** - < *krach* (5Ge)   **Gr** <=E> [=E] N, end20c, 4(1 tech) < 3: *krakh* (5Ge)

crash *v.* 2 'fall, etc. with a loud smashing noise', 3a 'collide violently with another vehicle', 3b 'fall on to the land or into the sea', 4 'collide violently', 5 'undergo financial ruin', 6 'enter without permission', 8 'fail suddenly' (comput.)

Ge *crashen*, end20c, 3a(1 sla, you)   **Du** *crashen* 1970s, 3a,b,4,8(1 mod) 5(1 tech)   **Nw** *krasje/kræsje/crashe* [kræʃe/kraʃe] 2,3a,b,4,5,8(2/3) 6(1 rare)   **Ic** [kʰras:a] end20c, 2,3a,b(1 sla, you)   **Fr** *(se)crasher*, 20c, 3b (1ban) < *s'écraser*

crash boat* *n.* 'a fast boat'

Ge *Crashboot* [=E] end20c (1 tech+5)   **Nw** *krasjbåt* [kræʃ- /kraʃ-] 1960s (1+5)

crash course *n.* 'a period of intensive training'

Ge *Crashkurs* [=E] M, pl. *-e*, 1970s (1 tech+5)   **Nw** *crashkurs/-program* [kræʃ- /kræʃ-] 1970s (1+5)

crash test* *n.* 'a controlled crash used in accident research' (mainly motor cars)

Ge [=E] M, pl. *-s*, 1970s (2 tech)   **Nw** [=E] M, pl. *-er*, 1980s (1 tech)   **Fr** [kraʃ təst] (1 tech, ban) < *rend essai de choc*   **It** [kraʃtɛst] M, pl. Ø, 1980s (1 tech)   **Cr** [=E] M, end20c (2 tech)   **Gr** <=E>/*kras tɛst* N, end20c (1 tech) = trsl *dhokimi sygrusis*

crawl *n.* 3 'a high-speed swimming style'

This sporting term was widely adopted during the early twentieth-century; it competes with native equivalents meaning 'free style' – which are not strictly synonymous, although the free choice of the fastest style is normally equivalent to *crawl*.

Ge *Kraul(en)* N [U] beg20c (3) → *Krauler*; *-schwim-mer*   **Du** [krɔ:l] C [U] mid20c (2)   **Nw** <=E>/*krål* [kro:l] M [U] beg20c (2)   **Ic** *krol(l)* [kʰrɔ:l/kʰrɔl:] [U] mid20c (1 tech, obs) < rend *skriðsund*   **Fr** [krol] M, beg20c (2)   **Sp** <=E>/*crol* [krol] M, 1920s (1 tech) → *crolista*   **It** [=E] M [U] 1930s (1 tech) < *stile libero* → *crawlista* n.   **Rm** *craul* [krawl] N [U] beg20c (3) < *(stil) liber*   **Rs** *krol'* M [U] beg20c (1 tech) → *krolist* M   **Po** *kraul*<=E> M [U] beg20c (2)   **Cr** *kraul* M [U] 20c (3)   **Bg** *kroul* M [U] beg20c (2 tech); *krol* (2 coll) → *-ist* M   **Fi** *krooli* 20c (3)   **Hu** *kallózás/craw-lozás* [kallo:zaːʃ/ krɔːloza:ʃ] [U] end19/beg20c (3 tech)   **Al** *krol* M [U] beg20c (3)   **Gr** *krol* N [U] (1 tech) < *elefthero*

crawl *v.* 7 'swim with a crawl stroke'

Ge *kraul(en)* beg20c (3)   **Du** *crawlen* [krɔːlən] 1950s (2)   **Nw** *crawle/kråle* [krɔ:le] beg20c (2)   **Ic** [kʰrɔ:la] mid20c (1 tech, obs)   **Fr** *crawler* [krole] 1930s (1 tech) → *crawlé*; *crawleur* M; *crawleuse* F   **Sp** - < *nadar a crol* → *crolista* M/F   **Rs** - < *plavat' krolem*   **Po** (0)   **Cr** *kraulati* 20c (3)   **Bg** - < *pluvam krol/kroul*   **Fi** *kroo-lata* 20c (3)   **Hu** - < *kallózik* [kallo:zik]

crazy *adj.* 1 'insane, mad' (esp. about humour), 2 'extremely enthusiastic', 3b 'excellent'

Du [=E] 1970s, 1(2 mod) < *gek*   **Nw** [=E] 1980s, 1(1)   **Ic** [kʰrei:si] uninfl., 1960s, 1,3b(1 sla)   **Rm** [=E] end2oc, 1(o)   **Rs** *creĩzi* uninfl., 1990s, 1,2(1 sla, you)   **Bg** *kreĩzi* uninfl., end2oc, 1(2 sla, you) → *iz-kreĩzvam* v.   **Fi** *kreisi* end2oc (o coll, you)   **Gr** 1(o)

cream   *n./cp²* 4 'a creamlike preparation, esp. a cosmetic'

The word is quite frequent with reference to cosmetic products (but many languages prefer the older French loanword *crème*, like German)

Ge [=E] F, pl. -*s*, 1960s (1 mod) < *Krem* (5Fr)   **Nw** [=E] M, end2oc (1 mod, rare)   **Sp** - < mean *crema*   **Rs** *krem* (5Fr)   **Bg** *krem* (5Fr)   **Hu** (o) < *krém* (5Fr)   **Al** *krem* (5Fr)   **Gr** - < mean *krema*

creamer   *n.* 3 'a cream or milk substitute for adding to coffee and tea'
Du [=E] C, pl. -*s* (2)

credit card   *n.* 'a card from a bank etc., authorizing the obtaining of goods on credit'

Since the two elements of the compound are available in all the languages sampled, calques are the rule, and borrowing an exception.

Ge - < trsl *Kreditkarte*   **Du** [=E] C, 1970s (2) = trsl *krediet-kaart*   **Nw** - < trsl *kredittkort*   **Ic** - < trsl *kreditkort* N, pl. Ø, 1980s (2) = creat *krítarkort*   **Fr** - < trsl *carte de crédit*   **Sp** - < trsl *tarjeta de crédito*   **It** [kredit kard] F, pl. Ø, 1990s (1 mod) < trsl *carta di credito*   **Rm** [=E] N, 1990s (1 tech>o) < trsl *carte de credit*   **Rs** - < trsl *kreditnaya kartochka*   **Po** < trsl *karta kredytowa*   **Cr** - < trsl *kreditna kartica*   **Bg** - < trsl *kreditna karta*   **Fi** - < ↑*card*   **Hu** [=E] Ø end2oc (1 writ) < trsl *hitelkártya*   **Al** - < trsl *kreditkartë* 1990s (2)   **Gr** - < trsl *pistotiki karta*

crew   *n.* 1b 'a body of people managing a ship or aircraft', 1c 'a body of people working together'

This word was frequent as a naval term from the late nineteenth century on, and came to be transferred to other groups of people working together, but was never used as freely and loosely as the partial synonym ↑*team*. The word has encroached on the meaning covered by the earlier French *équipage*, still widespread in European languages.

Ge [kru:] F, pl. -*s*, end19c/1960s, 1b(1 tech); 1960s, 1c(1 jour) < 1b: *Mannschaft*, = 1c: *team*   **Du** [kru:] C, end2oc, 1b(1 tech) = *bemanning*   **Nw** [kru:] N, pl. Ø, 2oc (1 tech)   **Ic** [=E] N/F, pl. Ø, end2oc, 1b(o tech, sla) < *áhöfn*

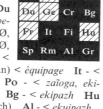

Ic	Nw	Po	Rs
Du	Ge	Cr	Bg
Fr	It	Fi	Hu
Sp	Rm	Al	Gr

Fr <=E> 2oc, 1b(1 ban) < *équipage*   **It** - < *equipaggio*   **Po** - < *zaĩoga, ekipa*   **Cr** - < *posada* 1b(1 tech)   **Bg** - < *ekipazh*   **Hu** [=E] [U] end19/beg2oc, 1b(1 tech)   **Al** - < *ekuipazh*

crew-cut   *n./adj.* 'a very short (man's) haircut'
Ge (o)   **Du** [=E] C [U] 1970s (1 mod)   **Nw** [=E] M, pl. -*s*, 1950s (1 mod)   **Ic** [=E] adj., uninfl., mid2oc (o sla) < *burstaklipptur* adj.; -*klipping* F

cricket   *n.* 'a sport played on a grass pitch'
This game never caught on in Continental Europe.

Although it is universally known by its English name, the term is a foreignism, strictly speaking.

Ge *C-/K-*[=E] N [U] end19c (Ø>2 tech)   **Du** [krikət] N [U] end19c (1 tech) → -*en* v.; -*er* n.   **Nw** [=E] M [U] beg2oc (Ø)   **Ic** *krikket* [kʰrıhket] N [U] end19c, via Da (Ø)   **Fr** [kʁiket] M, 18c (Ø)   **Sp** <=E>/*críquet* [kríket] M [U] end19c (2 tech)   **It** [kriket] M [U] end19c (2 tech)   **Rm** *crichet* [kriket/kriket] N [U] beg2oc, via Fr? (1 tech)   **Rs** *kriket* M [U] beg2oc (Ø) → -*nyĩ* adj.   **Po** *krykiet* M [U] beg2oc (1 tech) → -*owy* adj.   **Cr** *kriket* M [U] mid2oc (1 tech) → -*ski* adj.; -*aš* M   **Bg** *kriket* M [U] mid2oc (Ø/2 tech)   **Fi** *kriketti* 2oc (Ø)   **Hu** *krikett* [kriket] [U] 19/2oc (2 tech)   **Al** *kriket* M [U] mid2oc (2 tech)   **Gr** *kriket* N [U] 2oc (1 tech)

cringle   *n.* 'an eye of rope containing a thimble for another rope to pass through' (naut.)
Rs *krengel's* M, pl. -*y*, 18c (1 tech)   **Bg** *krengels* M, pl. -*al*-*i*, 2oc, via Rs (3 tech)

crinkle   *n. cp¹* 'a crease in cloth'
Ge [=E] cp¹/N? [U] 1980s (1 tech, rare)   **Nw** (o)

cromlech   *n.* 2 'a prehistoric stone circle'
Ge (Ø)   **Du** [=E] C, 1970s (1 tech)   **Nw** (Ø)   **Fr** [kʁɔmlɛk] M, 18c (1 tech)   **Sp** <=E>/*crónlech* M, 2oc (1 tech)   **It** [krɔmlek] M, pl. Ø, 1930s (1 tech, obs)   **Rm** *cromleh* [kromleh] N [U] mid2oc, via Fr (1 tech)   **Rs** *kromlekh* M, pl. -*i*, 19c (1 tech)   **Po** *kromlech* [-ex] M [U] beg2oc (1 tech)   **Cr** *kromlek* M, pl. -*ci*, mid2oc (1 tech)   **Bg** *kromlekhi* pl., 2oc, via Rs (3 tech)   **Gr** *kromlekh* N [U] 2oc (1 tech)

croon   *v.* 'sing, esp. in a sentimental manner'
Du *croonen* [kru:nə(n)] 1940s (1 obs)   **Nw** *croone* [krune] mid2oc (1 obs)   **Ic** *krúna* [kʰru:na] mid/end2oc (1 tech)

crooner   *n.* 'a (male) sentimental popular singer'
Ge [=E] M, pl. Ø, 1970s (o>1 tech, jour)   **Du** [=E] C, 1940s (1 obs)   **Nw** [=E] M, mid2oc (1 obs)   **Ic** [=E] M, pl. -*ar*, mid/end2oc (1 tech)   **Fr** [krunœʁ] M, 1950s < *chanteur de charme*   **Sp** [kruner] M, pl. -*s*, 1970s (1 tech)   **Rm** [=E] M, 1970s (1 rare) -*i*, end2oc (1)   **Cr** *kruner* M, pl.

croquet   *n.* 1 'a game played on a lawn with balls knocked through hoops'

This game appears to have enjoyed limited popularity in early twentieth-century Europe, but is rarely played on the Continent today. Although the word is still widely known, it is so with reference to a foreign or historic diversion.

Ge *Krocket* N [U] end19c (Ø/1 tech)   **Du** [=E] N [U] beg2oc (1 tech)   **Nw** *krokket* [kroke(r)t] M [U] beg2oc (2)   **Ic** *krokket* [kʰrɔhket] N [U] end19c, via Da (2)   **Fr** [kʁɔkɛ] M, 19c (3)   **Sp** [kroket] M, beg2oc (1 arch, obs)   **It** [krɔket] M [U] end19c, via Fr (1 tech)   **Rm** *crochet* [-ket] N [U] mid2oc (2 arch)   **Rs** *kroket* M [U] beg2oc (Ø)   **Po** *krokiet* [-iet] M [U] beg2oc (1 arch) → -*owy* adj.   **Cr** *kroket* M [U] beg2oc (1 arch)   **Bg** *kroket* M [U] beg2oc, via Ge (Ø tech)   **Fi** *kroketti* 2oc (3)   **Hu** *krokett* [kroket] [U] end19/beg 2oc (1 tech)   **Al** *kroket* M [U] mid2oc (1 reg)   **Gr** *kroke* N [U] 2oc (Ø/1 tech)

cross *n.* 8b 'a pass of the ball towards the centre' (footb.), 8c 'a blow with a crosswise movement of the fist' (box.) +8d 'a stroke in tennis', +10 'a cross-country race', +10a 'an athletic race'

This word is widespread only as a shortened form of ↑*cross-country* (*race*) which can refer to athletics, cycling, motor-cycling or car racing (the reference is often identified by compounding). Note the comparatively few calques and verbal uses.

Ge [=E] M, pl. -*el*-*es*, 1980s, +8d(1 tech, rare); 1960s, +10(1 tech) < *Querfeldein* (-*lauf, -rennen*) **Du** *cross-bal* +8d(1 tech+5); [krɔs] C, pl. -*esl*-*en*, 1970s, +10(1 tech) **Nw** <=E>/*crossball* [=E] usu. cp¹, 1980s, 8b(2+5); M [U] mid20c, +10(2) **Fr** [krɔs] M, end19c, +10(2) **Sp** [kros] M, pl. Ø, 1920s, 8c,+10(2) > *campo a través → crosero* **It** [kros] M, pl. Ø, 1920s, 8b(3) 8c,+8d(1 tech) +10(2) = 8b: rend *traversone*; < 8c: *gancio*; < +8d: *colpo incrociato* **Rm** *cros* [=E] N, mid20c, 8c(1 tech) +8d(1 rare) +10(3) → *crosistl-ă* M/ F **Rs** *kross* M [U] mid20c, +8d(1 tech)+10(3) → -*ovki* pl. **Po** *kros*/<=E> M, uninfl., mid20c, 8b,+10(1 tech) → -*owiec* M; -*owy* adj. **Cr** [kros] M, pl. -*ovi*, mid20c, +10(1 tech) → -*ist* M **Bg** *kros* M, pl. -*al*-*ove*, mid20c, 8c(1 tech) +10,+10a(3 tech) → -*ov* adj.; -*che* N **Fi** *krossi*, 20c, +10(2) **Hu** - < +10: *cross-country* **Al** *kros* M, pl. -*e*, mid20c, 8b,+10(3 tech) **Gr** *kros* N [U] cp² usu. in *moto cross*, +10(1 tech)

cross *v.* +11 'take part in a cross-country event', +12 'drive as in a cross-country race'

Du *crossen* [krɔsə(n)] 1970s **Nw** *crosse* [krɔse] 1960s, +12(1/2) **Bg** - < *pravya kros*

cross-breeding *n.* 'the process of producing a breed of animal or plant by crossing'

Rs *krossbriding* M [U] 20c (1 tech) **Bg** *krosbriding* M [U] 20c (1 tech) → -*ov* adj.

cross-country *n./cp¹* 1,2 '(a race etc) taking place across fields etc., not keeping to main roads'

Ge [=E] N/cp¹, beg20c (1 tech) < rend *Querfeldein-* **Du** [=E] C, pl. -'*s*, 1940s (1 tech) = *veldrit* **Nw** (0) < *terreng-* **Fr** *cross* (*-country*) [krɔskuntʀi] M, end19c (2) < *cross*; also *cyclo-cross, moto-cross* **Sp** [kros kountri] M, beg20c (1 tech) < *campo a través* **It** [kros kauntri] cp², end19c (1 tech) **Rs** - < *kross* **Po** N, uninfl., mid20c (1 tech) **Cr** *kros-kontri* M [U] mid20c (1 tech) **Bg** - < *kros* **Hu** [=E] end19/beg20c (1 tech ꜱᴘᴏʀᴛ) **Al** - < rend *kros në natyrë* **Gr** <=E>/ *kros kantri* N/cp², 20c (1 tech) < rend *anomalu dhromu*

crosser* *n.* 1 'a cross-country runner', 2 'bicycle cross-racing'

Du *crosser* [=E] C, 1980s, 1,+2(2) **Fr** - < *crossman/ crosswoman* M/F **Rs** - < *krossmen*

crossing *n.* 5 'mating' (biolog.)

Rs *krosing* M [U] 19c (1 tech) **Bg** *krosing* M [U] 20c (1 tech)

crossing over *n.* 'an exchange of genes between homologous chromosomes'

Fr [krɔsiŋ ɔvœʀ] M, 1930s (1 tech) > *recombinaison* **Sp** [krosinober] M, mid20c (1 tech) **It** [=E] M [U] 1930s (1 tech) **Rm** [=E] N [U] 20c (1 tech) > *încrucişare/schimb* **Bg** (0) **Hu** [krɔssiŋ oːver] [U] 20c (1 tech)

crossword *n.* 'a puzzle consisting of a grid of squares and blanks into which words have to be filled from clues'

Ge - < trsl *Kreuzworträtsel* **Nw** - < trsl *kryssord* **Ic** - < *krossgáta* **Fr** - < *mots croisés* **Sp** - < rend *crucigrama* **It** - < rend *parole crociate* **Rs** *krossvord* M, pl. -*y*, 20c (3) **Bg** - < trsl *krŭstoslovitsa* **Fi** - < rend *sanaristikko* **Al** - < trsl *fjalëkryq* **Gr** - < trsl *stavrolexo*

croup *n.* 'inflammation of the larynx in children'

One of the few early medical terms adopted from English, now no longer identified as English in most languages and current mainly in the combination *pseudo~*.

Ge *Krupp* M [U] 19c (3 tech) **Du** *kroep* [krup] C [U] 19c, via Fr (3 tech) **Nw** *krupp* [krʉp] M [U] beg20c (3) (usu. *falsk krupp*) **Fr** [krup] M, 18c (1 obs) except *faux croup* **Sp** *crup* [krup] M, mid19c, via Fr (2 tech) → *crupal, cruposo* adj. **Rm** *crup* [=E] N [U] end19c, via Fr (3 tech); *crup fals* N [U] end19c, via Fr (3 tech) **Rs** *krup* M [U] beg20c (1 tech) **Po** *krup* [krup] M [U] beg20c (3 obs) **Bg** *krup* M [U] mid20c (1 tech) **Hu** *krupp* [krupp] beg19c **Al** *krup* M [U] mid20c (1 reg)

crown glass *n.* 'glass made without lead or iron'

Ge *Kronglas* N [U] beg20c (3 tech+5) **Du** *crownglas* [kraun-] C, pl. -*glazen*, 1940s (3 tech) < *kroonglas* **Nw** - < *kroneglass* **Ic** - < *krónugler* **Fr** *crown-glass* [kʀonglas] M, 18c (1 tech) **Sp** <=E> M, mid20c (1 tech) = *vidrio crown* **It** [kraun] M [U] 1970s (1 tech) **Rm** *crown* [=E] N [U] beg20c (1 tech) **Rs** (5Ge) **Po** *kron* M [U] beg20c (1 tech) → -*owy* adj. **Bg** *kronglas* M [U] 20c, via Ge (3 tech) **Fi** *kruunulasi*, 20c (3 tech) **Hu** [=E] [U] 19c (1 tech, arch) < trsl *koronaüveg*

cruise *n.* 'a journey by sea, esp. as a holiday'

Ge - < rend *Kreuzfahrt* **Du** [=E] C, 1960s (2 tech) **Nw** [=E] N, pl. Ø, 1960s (2) **Sp** - < rend *crucero* **It** - < rend *crociera* **Rs** *kruiz* M, pl. -*y*, mid20c (3) **Po** (0) **Cr** - < rend *kružno putovanje* **Bg** *kruiz* M, pl. -*al*-*i*, end20c, via Rs (3 mod) → -*en* adj. **Fi** - < *kruisaily* < mean *risteily* **Gr** - < *kruaziera*

cruise *v.* 1 'make a journey by sea', 3b (of a vehicle or driver) 'travel with no fixed destination esp. slowly'

Du *cruisen*, 20c (2) **Nw** [krʉːse] 1960s, 1(2) 3b(1 coll) **Ic** *krúsa/krjúsa* [kʰr(j)uːsa] end20c, 3b(1 sla) **Fi** *kruisailla* 1980s (1 sla, you)

cruise control *n.* 'a device which maintains a motor vehicle at a preset constant speed'

Nw <=E>/*cruise-kontroll* [krʉskuntrɔl] 1980s (1 tech+5) **Gr** <=E> [=E] N, end20c (1 tech)

cruise missile *n.* 'a missile able to fly at a low altitude and guide itself by reference to the features of the region it traverses'

Ge [=BrE] N, pl. -s, 1970s (1 jour) < creat *Marschflugkörper* **Du** *cruise-missile* [=E] C, 1980s (2 tech) < *kruisraket* **Nw** [=E] M, pl. -r, end20c (1 tech) < rend *krysserrakett* **Fr** *missile cruise* end20c (1 tech, ban) < rend *missile de croisière* **Sp** - < rend *misil de crucero* **It** *missile cruise* M, pl. -i, 1970s (1 tech) **Rm** (o) < *rachetă cruise*; rend *rachetă de croazieră* **Rs** (o) < creat *krylataya raketa* **Cr** - < rend *krstareća raketa* **Bg** - < rend *raketa kruz* **Fi** - < rend *risteilyohjus* **Gr** <=E> [=E] N, pl. Ø, end20c (1 tech); < trsl *pyravlos kruz* (5+1 tech)

cruiser *n.* 1 'a class of warship of high speed', 2 'a large motorboat with living accommodation'
Ge - < 1: mean *Kreuzer* **Du** - < *cruiseschip* (2 tech+5) **Nw** [=E] M, pl. -e, 1960s (2) **Fr** [kruzœr] M, end19c (1) **It** [kru:zer] M, pl. Ø, 1930s (1 tech) **Cr** *kruzer* M, end20c (2) **Fi** - < trsl *risteilijä* **Gr** <=E>/*kruzer* N, end20c (1 tech) < *ghiot*

cruiserweight *n.* 'light heavyweight' (box.)
Ge - < *Halbschwergewicht* **Du** - < *halfzwaargewicht* **Nw** *cruiservekt* [=E] 20c (1 tech+5) **Ic** - < rend *léttpungavigt* **It** - < *mediomassimo* **Rs** - < rend *polutyazhëlyi ves* **Bg** - < *polutezhka kategoriya* **Al** - < *peshat e mesme* **Gr** - < *mesea katighoria*

cuckoo *adj.* 'crazy, foolish'
Nw *ko-ko* (3/5) **Ic** *kúkú* [=E] uninfl., end20c (1 sla) **Bg** *kuku* uninfl. (5)

cue *n.* 1a 'the last word of an actor's speech, serving as a signal to another actor to enter or speak', 1b 'a similar signal to a singer or musician etc.', 2c 'a hint on how to behave in particular circumstances'
Du [=E] C 1980s, 1 a,b(1 tech, sla) **Ic** [=E] N, pl. Ø, end20c, 1a,b(1 tech, sla) 2c(0)

cue *v.* 1 'give a cue to', 2 'put (a piece of audio equipment) in readiness to play a particular part'
Du *cuen* [kjuǝ(n)] 1990s (1 tech) **Ic** *kjúa* [cʰju:a] end20c, 1(1 sla) 2(1 tech)

cue in *v.* 1 'insert a cue for'
Ic *kjúa inn* end20c (1 sla)

culvert *n.* 1 'an underground channel carrying water', +3 'the cover/bridge over this'
Nw *kulvert* [kulvert] M, pl. -er, 20c, 1(1 tech) **Fi** *kulvertti* 20c, +3(3)

Cumberland sauce* *n.* 'a sauce made with redcurrants'
Ge [kambalent zo:sǝ] F, pl. -en, mid20c (2 tech+5) **Nw** *cumberland-saus*, 20c (1+5) **Ic** *Cumberlandsósa* [=E+sou:sa] F [U] mid20c (1+5) **Fr** (Ø) **Po** *cumberland* [kumberlant] M [U] beg20c (1 tech) → *-zki* adj. **Hu** *cumberland-mártás* [=E+Hu] [U] (2 tech+5) **Gr** (o tech)

cummerbund *n.* 'a waist sash, originally Indian'
Ge *Kummerbund* [kumabunt] M, pl. -el-bünde?, end19c (3 tech)

cup *n.* 4 'a drink of flavoured wine, cider etc.', 5 'an ornamental cup-shaped trophy', +5a 'a sports contest' (often cp²), +5b 'the prize', 7 'either of the two cup-shaped parts of a brassière'

This word was rarely borrowed in its original sense (5b), the prize for the winner; but is more frequent for the competition itself (where it was obviously abstracted from combinations like *America's Cup, World Cup*, etc. – still the only use in French, Italian. Native terms appear to predominate in all languages. Note the euphemistic use for 'part of bra'.

Ge [kap] M, pl. -s, beg20c, 5,+5a(1 tech); 1960s, 7(1 tech) < 5, +5a: *Pokal*, = 7: *Körbchen* **Du** [kʏp] C, end20c, 5(2) 7(2 tech) < *beker* **Nw** [køp] M, pl. -er, 20c, 5,+5a,b(2) 7 (1 tech) **Ic** - < 5a,b: trsl *bikar(keppni)*, 7: *skál* **Fr** *coupe* [=E/kup] M, 1920s, 4 (1 tech) < 5: trsl *copa* **It** [kap] F, pl. Ø, mid20c, +5b(2) < *coppa* **Rm** *cupă* [kupǝ] F, mid20c, 5,+5a,b,7(4) **Rs** *kubok* M, pl. -i, mid20c, 5,+5a,+5b(3 tech) **Po** [kup] M [U] beg20c, 5,+5a(1 mod) **Cr** *kup* M, pl. -ovi, beg20c, 5,+5a(1 tech) **Bg** *kupa* F, pl. -pi, mid20c, 5,+5a(5Fr) **Fi** [=E] mid20c, 5,+5a(2) **Hu** [=E] [U] end19/beg20c, 5,+5a,+5b (1 tech) < *kupa* **Al** *kupë* F, pl. -a, mid20c, 5,+5b(3) **Gr** (o) < 5,+5a,b: mean *kypelo*; 7(1 writ)

cupola(-furnace) *n.* 3 'a furnace for melting metals'
Ge *Kuppelofen*, mid19c (3 tech, +5) **Nw** *kupolovn* [kupo:l-] 19c(3 tech+5) **Hu** *kupolakemence* via Ge(5)

curl *v.* 4 'play curling'
Nw *curle* [kø:rle] 20c (1) **Bg** - < *igraya kürling*

curler *n.* 2 'a player in the game of curling'
Nw [=E] M, pl. -e, 20c (1) **Bg** - < *igrach na kürling*

curling *n.* 'a game played on ice'
Adopted along with many other sporting terms in the late nineteenth or early twentieth century, and mildly productive by backformation; the fact that the sport itself is not really popular (and never was) has limited the currency, however widely attested the word is.
Ge [körliŋ] N [U] 1930s (1 tech) **Du** [=E] N [U] 1970s (1 tech) **Nw** [kø:rliŋ] M [U] 1940s (1 tech) **Fr** [kœrliŋ] M, end19c (1 tech) **Sp** <=E> M, end20c (1 tech, rare) **It** [kœrliŋ] M [U] 1910s (1 tech) **Rm** [=E] N [U] end20c (Ø) **Rs** *kerling* M [U] beg20c (Ø) **Po** [kerlink] M [U] beg20c (1 tech) **Cr** *kerling* M [U] beg20c (1 tech) **Bg** *kürling* M [U] 1980s (1 tech) **Fi** [=E] 20c (Ø) **Hu** [=E] [U] end20c (1 tech) **Gr** *kerling* N [U] end20c (Ø)

curry *n.* 1 'a dish of meat, vegetables, etc., cooked in a sauce of hot-tasting spices', +2 'an orig. Indian blend of spices'
This word was adopted as a foreignism from Indian cuisine but since the spices have become widely used (with rice, sausages, etc.) the word has become quite popular. The pronunciation of the stressed vowel reflects early [æ, u] and late [a] adoption.
Ge [köri] M/N [U] end19c, +2(2) **Du** *kerrie* C [U] +2(5) **Nw** *karri* [kari] M [U] end19c, +2(3), 1(1

rare) **Ic** *karrí* [kʰarːi] N [U] beg19c, via Da, +2(3); cp¹ 1(3) **Fr** [kyʀi] M, 1820s, +2(2) **Sp** [kurri/kari] M, pl. -s, end19c (2<3) **It** [kærri] M, beg19c, +2(1) **Rm** [kari] N [U] end20c, +2(1 tech, rare) **Rs** *kérri/karri* N, uninfl., 1990s, +2(2 tech) **Po** <=E> N, uninfl., end20c, +2(1 mod) **Cr** [=E] M [U] end20c, +2(1 tech) **Bg** *kúri* N [U] mid20c (1 tech) **Fi** [=E] 20c, +2(3) **Hu** [=E] [U] beg20c, +2(2 tech) **Gr** *kari* N [U] 20c, +2(2)

cursor *n.* 'a movable indicator on a VDU screen' (comput.)
Ge [=E] M, pl. -s, 1980s (1 tech) **Nw** <=E>/*kursor* [=E] M, pl. -er, 1980s (1 tech) < *srivemente* **Du** [=E] C, pl. -s/-en, 1980s (2 tech) **Ic** - < rend *bendill* **Fr** - < *curseur* **Sp** [kursor] M, pl. -es, 1980s (4 tech) **It** - < mean *cursore* **Rm** [kursor] N, 1980s (4 tech/Fr) **Rs** *kursor* M, pl. -y, end20c (1 tech) **Po** *kursor* [kursor] M, 1980s (1 tech) **Cr** *kursor* M, pl. -i, 1980s (1 tech) **Bg** *kursor* M, pl. -al-i, 1980s (1 tech) **Fi** *kursori* 1980s (3) > creat *kohdistin* **Hu** *kurzor* [kurzor] pl. Ø, 1980s (2 tech) **Al** *kursor* M, pl. -ë, 1992 (3) **Gr** <=E>/*kersor* M, pl. -es, end20c (2 tech); *kersoras* M (3 tech)

customizing *n.* 'the making to order of modifications according to individual requirements'
Ge [=E] N [U] 1980s (1 tech, rare) **Sp** - < *customización* **Fi** - < *kustomoida*

cut *v.* 2 'divide or be divided with a knife etc.' 3b 'detach all or the significant part of (flowers, corns, etc.) by cutting', 6a 'reduce (wages, etc.)', 6b 'reduce or cease (services, etc.)', 14a 'edit (a film or tape)', 14b 'stop filming or recording', +22 (usu. with negation) '(not) be able to'
Du *cutten* [kʏtə(n)] 1980s, 14a(1 tech) **Nw** *kutte* [kʉte] end19c, 2,6a,b,14b(3) **Ic** *kútta* [kʰuhta] 1940s, via Da, 3b(1 tech); *kötta* [kʰœhta] end20c, 14b(1 tech) +22(1 sla)

cut(away) *n.* +2a 'a man's formal dress'
Ge [köt] M, pl. -s, end19c (1 obs) **Du** *cutaway* [=E] C, 19c, +2a(1 tech) **Nw** *cutaway* [=E] M, pl. -s, 19c (1 arch) **Po** [kate-wej] M, mid20c (1 arch)

cute *adj.* +1c 'sweet, pretty' (esp. about girls and children)
Du [=E] 1990s (1 sla, mod) **Ic** *kjút* [=E] uninfl., mid20c (1 coll, arch)

cutter¹ *n.* 3a 'a small sailing-ship'
This term for the ship was borrowed early on (and partly through its written form); the motivation ('a ship cuts along the coast') is lost in English and not reconstructable in loanwords.
Ge *K-* [kuta] M, pl. Ø, 19c (3) **Du** *kotter* [kɔtər] C, 18c (3) **Nw** *kutter* [kʉter] M, pl. -e, end19c (1 tech) **Ic** *kútter/kúttari* [kʰuhter/kʰuhtarı] M, pl. -ar, beg19c, via Da (2) **Fr** [kœtœr/kytɛr] M, 19c (1 tech,

arch) **Sp** <=E>/*cuter* [kuter] M, mid19c (1 arch) **It** [katter] M, pl. Ø, 18c (1 tech) **Rm** *cuter* [kuter] N, beg20c (3 tech) **Rs** *kater* M, pl. -y, 18c (3) **Po** *kuter* [kuter] M, mid18c (3) **Cr** *kuter* M, pl. -i, 19c (3) **Bg** *kater* M, pl. -al-i, beg20c, via Rs (3) **Fi** *kutteri* (3) **Hu** *kutter* [kutter] 19/20c (3 tech) **Gr** *kot(t)ero* N, beg20c, via It (3)

cutter² *n.* +1a 'a person who cuts films', +6 'a machine for cutting meat', +7 'a tool for cutting part of a plane', +8 'shavings', +9 'a cutting device with a razor blade used in lay-out work'
Ge [köta/kata] M, pl. Ø, mid20c, +1a, +6 (1 tech); 1980s, +9(1 tech) → -*in* F **Du** [k[ʏ]tər] C, mid20c, +1a(1 tech) **Nw** *kutter* [kuter] M, pl. -e, end19c, +7(3 tech); *kutter(-flis)* +8(3 tech) **Fr** *cutter/cutteur* [kœtœr/kytɛr] M, 1980s, +9(1 tech) **Sp** <=E>/*cuter* [kuter] M, 1980s, +9(2<3) **Rm** *cutter* [kuter] [=E] N, end20c, +6(1 tech, rare) **Rs** *kutter* M, mid20c, +6(1 tech) → -*ovanie* N **Po** *kuter* [kuter] M, mid20c, +6(1 tech) **Hu** *cutter* [=E] 20c, +1a(1 tech) < *vágó*

cutting *n.* +4 'a haircut with short, straight-cut hair', +5 'small fragments of rock brought up in (oil) drilling' (cf. Nw)
Nw [kɔtiŋ] M [U] 20c (1 tech) < +5: *borkaks, grus som følger med boreslam* **It** [kating] M, pl. Ø, 1970s, +5 (1 tech)

cyberspace *n.* 'virtual reality (generated by computer)'
The term was coined by US author William Gibson; it is one of the many recent compounds with *cyber-*(*-art*, etc.), all of uncertain permanence.
Ge [=E] M [U] 1990s (1 mod) **Du** [=E] C [U] 1990s (1 jour, mod) **Nw** [=E] [=U] 1990s (1) > *datarom* **Ic** - < rend *sýndarveruleiki* **Sp** - < trsl *ciberespacio* **It** [saiberspeis] M [U] 1990s (1 mod) < trsl *ciberspazio* **Po** - < rend *przestrzen cybernetyczna* **Cr** (0) **Bg** *saĭbŭrspeĭs* M [U] 1990s (1 jour, rare) **Fi** - < trsl *cyberavaruus* [kyber-] **Gr** <=E> [=E] N [U] 1990s (1 mod) = trsl *kyvernokhoros*

cyborg *n.* 'a person whose physical abilities are extended beyond normal limitations by machine technology' (scifi)
Ge [=E] M, pl. -s, 1990s (0>1 mod) **Du** [=E] C, 1990s (1 mod) **Nw** *kyborg* [kyborg] M, pl. -er, 1970s (1) **Sp** [θibor] pl. -s, 1990s (1 mod) **It** [saiborg] C, pl. Ø, 1970s (1 mod) **Rm** [siborg] M, 1980s (1 mod) **Rs** *kiborg* M, pl. -i, end20c (1 mod) **Cr** (0) **Bg** *kiborg* M, pl. -i, 1990s (1 mod) **Fi** <=E>/*kyborgi* 1980s (1 mod)

D

daddy *n.* I 'father'
Ge [dɛdi:] M, pl. *-(ie)s*, end20c (I coll) **Nw** [=E]
(o) **Fr** (o) **Cr** (o) **Hu** (o) **Gr** <=E>/*dadis* M,
mid20c (I coll/3 coll, rare)

dagger *n.* I 'a short stabbing-weapon like a knife'
Du *dag(ge)* (5Fr) **Nw** *daggert* [dagert] M, pl. *-er*,
19c (3 arch) **Ic** *daggarður* [tak:arðvr] M, pl. *-ar*,
mid16c, via Da (3 arch)

daltonian* *adj.* 'colour blind'
Fr *daltonien/ne* [daltɔnjẽ/-jɛn] mid19c (3) **Sp** *dalto-
niano/-a/daltónico* **It** *daltonico,a* end19c (3) **Rm**
daltonian [daltonjan] 1970s (5Fr) < *daltonist* **Rs** - <
dal'tonik **Cr** (o) **Po** (o) **Bg** - < *daltonist* **Al** - <
daltonist **Gr** *dhaltonios, -a, -o* 20c (3 tech)

daltonism *n.* 'colour blindness'
John Dalton (1766–1844), a pioneer of atomic theory, suffered from colour-blindness, which he described in detail in 1794, and which came to be
named after him. Descriptive terms equivalent to English *colour-blindness* appear to be more popular than
this term in European languages.
Ge *Daltonismus* (o tech) **Du** *daltonisme* N [U] 19c (I
tech) **Fr** *daltonisme* [daltɔnism] M, 1840s > *achro-
matopsie, dyschromatopsie* **Sp** *daltonismo* M [U] 19c
(3 tech) **It** *daltonismo* M [U] end19c (3) **Rm** [dal-
tonism] N, beg20c (5Fr) **Rs** *dal'tonizm* M [U] beg20c
(3) **Po** *daltonizm* M [U] beg20c (3 tech) → *daltonista*
M **Cr** *daltonizam* M [U] beg20c (I tech) → *daltonist*
M, pl. *-i* **Bg** *daltonizŭm* M [U] beg20c (5Fr) → *daltonist* M **Hu** *daltonizmus* [daltonizmuʃ] 19c (3
tech) **Al** *daltonizëm* M[U] beg20c(3) **Gr** *dhaltonis-
mos* M [U] 20c, via Fr (3 tech)

dance *n./cp'* +4a 'a style of disco music'
Du [=E] C [U] 1990s (I tech, you) **Nw** [=E] M [U]
1990s (I tech, you) **Sp** [dans] M [U] 1990s (I tech,
you, mod) **It** *disco dance* [=E] F [U] 1970s (2) **Rm**
[=E] N [U] 1990s (I tech/you, mod) **Rs** *déns* M [U]
1990s (I tech/you, mod) **Po** [dens] M, 1990s (I coll,
mod) **Bg** *dens* M [U] 1990s (I tech/you, mod)

dance floor *n.* I 'a usu. uncarpeted area of floor
reserved for dancing', +2 'pop music for dancing'
Ge *Dancefloor* [=E] M [U] 1990s, I(I mod); *dance floor
(music)* [=E] F [U] 1990s, +2(I mod) **Du** *dancefloor*
[=E] C [U] (I mod) **Gr** <=E>/*dansflor* F/N [U]
1990s, +2(I tech)

dancing *n.* +3a 'a social gathering', +6 'a dancehall',
+7 'a dancefloor'

This loanword is probably an abbreviation of a
compound like *dancing-room*. Although this form of
clipping is possible in other languages, the modern
distribution is mostly due to French mediation, affecting the Germanic area only marginally.
Ge [=E] N, pl. *-s*, 1950s, via Fr (I
reg) < *Tanzlokal* **Du** [dɛnsing]
C, beg20c, +6(I tech) **Nw** [=E]
M [U] 20c, +6(I tech) **Fr**
[dãsiŋ] M, beg20c, +6(I obs) <
boîte, discothèque **Sp** [dansiŋ]
M, pl. *-s*, 1920s, +3a,+6(I ar-
ch) **It** [dɛnsiŋ] M, pl. Ø, 1900s, +6(2) < *sala da
ballo* **Rm** [=E] N, beg20c, via Fr, +3a,+6(I arch)
Rs *dansing* M [U] beg20c, +3a,+6 (3 mod/you) **Po**
dansing/<=E> [dansink] M, beg20c, via Fr, +3a(3) →
-owy adj. **Cr** *dansing* M, pl. *-zi*, beg20c, +6(2) **Bg**
dansing M, pl. *-a/-i*, mid20c, via Fr, +7(3) **Hu** [dan-
sing/dantzing] pl. Ø, beg20c, +3a(I arch) +6(I arch) <
tánc; < +6: táncterem **Al** *dansing* M, pl. *-e*, mid20c (I
reg) **Gr** *dansing* N, mid20c, via Fr, +6(I arch)

dandy *n.* I 'a man unduly concerned with style and
fashion in dress and appearance'

This word is a cultural shibboleth of nineteenth-
century British society, in vogue in London during
1813–19. It spread throughout the Continent, but is
now obsolescent or historical, although it is still well-
known (seldom used to refer to present-day dandies).
Ge [dendi] M, pl. *(-ie)s*, beg19c
(2 obs) **Du** [dendi:] C, 19c (2)
Nw [=E] M, pl. *-er*, mid19c (2)
Ic *dandi* [tanti] M, pl. *-ar*, 19c
(2 coll) → *dandílegur* adj. **Fr**
[dãdi] M, beg19c (I obs) → *dan-
dysme* M **Sp** <=E>/*dandi*
[dandi] M, pl. *-s*, mid19c (2<3) → *dandismo* M, *dand-
ístico* adj. **It** [dendi] M, pl. Ø, beg19c (2) **Rm**
dandi [dendi/-a-] M, end19c, via Fr (I obs) **Rs**
dendi M, uninfl., 19c (I fac/obs) **Po** *dandys* M,
mid19c (2) → *-ek* M; *-owaty* adj. **Cr** *dendi* M, pl. *-i*,
19c (2) → *-jevski* adj. **Bg** *dendi* M, pl. Ø, beg20c (I
lit) **Hu** *dendi* [=E] pl. *-k*, beg19c (2 arch) **Gr**
dhandhis M, 19c, via Fr (3 obs); *dandy-/<=E>* cp',
end20c (I tech)

dark *n./cp'* +5 'a kind of pop music of the 1980s', +6
'someone belonging to a youth movement, wearing
black clothes'

It [dark] M, pl. Ø, 1980s, +6(1 sla, mod)   **Bg** *dark* M [U]/adj., uninfl./cp¹, 1980s (3 tech/you)

dark horse   *n.* 'a little-known person who becomes successful or prominent'

Du [=E] C, 1990s (1 jour/mod)   **Nw** [=E] M, pl. *-s*, mid20c (1 jour)   **It** [dark h<u>o</u>rs] M, pl. Ø/-s, end19c (1 jour, rare)   **Po** [dark hors] M, uninfl., end20c (1 tech)   **Fi** - < creat *musta hevonen*   **Hu** [=E] [U] 20c (1 mod, rare)

dark room   *n.* +2 'a darkened room where people meet for anonymous sex' (esp. in homosexual subculture)

Ge [=E] M, pl. *-s* (1 sla, you)

darling   *n.* 1 'a beloved or lovable person' (cf. ↑*everybody's darling*.)

This term is widely known as a (facetious) form of address, but less widespread (in journalese) as a commonly used word. Its currency is too recent to judge its status with certainty.

Ge [d<u>a</u>rlıŋ] M, pl. *-s*, 1970s (1 mod)   **Du** [=E] C, 1990s (1 coll)   **Nw** [=E] M, pl. *-s*, 20c (1 coll, fac)   **Ic** [=E] uninfl., mid20c (0 coll, mod)   **Fr** (0)   **Sp** [d<u>a</u>rlin] M/F, end20c (1 fac, mod/ rare)   **It** [d<u>a</u>rlıŋ] M/F, pl. Ø,

1930s (1 coll, fac)   **Rm** [darling] M/F [U] 1970s (1 you, mod)   **Rs** *darling* [M/F] sg., 1990s (1 fac)   **Po** (0)   **Cr** [darling] F/M [U] mid20c (3)   **Bg** d<u>a</u>rling M [U] end20c (1 coll, you)   **Hu** [=E] pl. Ø, beg20c (2 fac)   **Al** (0)   **Gr** [=E] M/F/N, end20c (1 mod, coll)

dart(s)   *n.* 2a 'a small pointed missile used in a game', 2b (in pl.) 'an indoor game where darts are thrown at a target'

This game played in pubs and at home has caught on very slowly on the Continent, so that the words for the game and the arrows are quite marginal – again with a notable East-West cline. Calques (like German *Wurfpfeil*,...) appear to have been unsuccessful.

Ge [=E] N, pl. *-s*, 1980s (1 tech, mod) > 2b: *Wurfpfeil(spiel)*   **Du** [darts] N [U] 1980s (1 tech)   **Nw** <=E> *darts* sg. [=E] M [U] 1980s, 2b(2) < *pilkast*   **Ic** - < rend *pila, pilukast*   **Rm** *darts* [=E] N, 1990s, 2b(0>1 jour)   **Rs**

darts M [U] 1990s, 2b(1 tech, mod) → *-lend* M   **Po** (0)   **Bg** *darts* M [U] 1990s, 2b(1 tech, mod)   **Fi** *dart-sit*, end20c (2)   **Hu** [=E] [U] 1980/90s (1 tech)   **Gr** *darts* N, pl., end20c (1 tech, mod)

dashboard   *n.* 1 'a surface below the windscreen of a motor vehicle containing instruments and controls'

Du [=E] N, mid20c (2) = *instrumentenbord*   **Nw** *dashbord* [=E+Nw] N, pl. Ø, mid20c (2)

data   *n.* 1 'known facts', 2 'quantities or characters operated on by a computer'

Since the Latin loan (usually referring to the calendar) is old, the computer term is usually integrated as an extended meaning. The status of this Latin-derived

loanword as an anglicism is doubtful; contrast ↑*date* which is always English.

Ge *Daten* pl., 1960s (5 La)   **Du** [d<u>a</u>ta] (5La)   **Nw** [da:ta] sg., M, pl. Ø, mid20c, 2(3); 1 (5La)   **Ic** [=E/ ta:ta] N, 1970s (1 tech, coll) < rend *gögn*   **Fr** <=E> 20c 2(1 ban, obs) > *donnée(s)*   **Sp** - < *datos* (5La)   **It** [data/de<u>i</u>ta] M, pl. Ø, 1960s (1 tech) < trsl *dati*   **Rm** *date* [d<u>a</u>te] F, pl., 19c (5)   **Rs** (0) < *dannye* pl.   **Po** - < trsl *dane*   **Cr** (0)   **Bg** - < trsl *danni*   **Fi** [d<u>a</u>ta] 2(3) = *tieto(ja)*   **Hu** 1(5La)   **Gr** <=E> [=E/d<u>a</u>ta] N, pl., end20c (1 tech) = trsl *dhedhomena* N

data bank   *n.* 1 'a store or source of data'

Since the two elements were available in most languages, the natural method of filling the lexical gap was to employ the native forms to form a compound – which can be classified as a translation or as an anglicism with its form adapted to the individual language.

Ge - < trsl *Datenbank*   **Du** - < trsl *databank*   **Nw** - trsl *databank*   **Ic** - < trsl *gagnabanki*   **Fr** - < trsl *banque de donné*   **Sp** - < trsl *banco de datos*   **It** [=E] F, pl. Ø, 1960s (1 tech) < trsl *banca dati*   **Rm** - < rend *bancă de date*   **Po** < trsl *bank danych*   **Cr** (0)   **Hu** [d<u>a</u>:ta bank] pl. *-ok*, end20c (1 tech>2) < *data base*; trsl *data-bank*   **Gr** - < *trapeza dhedhomenon*

database   *n.* 'a structured set of data held in a computer, esp. one that is accessible in various ways'

Ge [=E] F, pl. *-s*, 1980s (0>1 tech) < trsl *Datenbasis*   **Du** [=E] C, 1970s (1 tech)   **Nw** [da:taba:se/da:- tabase] M, pl. *-r*, 1980s (1 tech)   **Ic** <=E> [=E/ ta:tapei:s] M, pl. *-ar*, 1970s (0/1 tech, coll) < creat *gagnagrunnur*   **Fr** - < *base de don- nées*   **Sp** - < *base de datos*   **It** [d<u>a</u>tabeis/de<u>i</u>tabeis] M, pl. Ø, 1960s (2 tech) = rend *base di dati*   **Rm** - < rend *bază de date*   **Rs** (0) < trsl *baza dannykh*   **Cr** - < trsl *baza podataka*   **Bg** - < trsl *deïta baza*; rend *baza danni*   **Fi** - < creat *tietokanta*   **Hu** *data base* [=E] pl. Ø, end20c (1 tech)   **Gr** <=E> [=E] F [U] end20c (1 tech) = trsl *vasi dhedhomenon*

date   *n.* 6a 'an engagement or appointment (esp. with a person of the opposite sex)'

This term derives from American youth culture, but has not caught on outside certain sections of the younger population – and then only in Germanic countries.

Ge [de:t] N, pl. *-s*, 1980s (1 you) < *Rendezvous, Ver- abredung*   **Du** [=E] 1980s (1 coll/mod)   **Nw** [=E] M, pl. *-s*, 1980s (1 sla, you)   **Ic** [=E] uninfl., mid20c (Ø) < *stefnumót*

davit   *n.* 'a small crane on board a ship'

Ge [d<u>e</u>:vit/<u>a</u>:] M, pl. *-s*, 19c (1 tech, obs)   **Du** [d<u>e</u>:vıt] C, 19c (1 tech)   **Nw** [d<u>a</u>:vit] M, pl. *-er*, beg20c (1 tech)   **Ic** *davíða* [ta:viða] F, pl. *-ur*, 1930s, via Da (3 tech) = Great *bátsugla*   **Hu** [=E] pl. Ø/-*ok*, 19c (1 tech_{NAUT})

day hospital*   *n.* 'a health establishment providing one-day therapies'

Fr - < trsl *hôpital de jour*   **It** [dei <u>o</u>spital] M [U] 1980s (2)

DCC*   *abbrev* 'digital cassette'

Du [=E] C, 1990s (1 tech) **Rs** *di si si* F/N, 1990s (1 tech) **Fi** [de:se:se:] **Gr** *DCC* [disisi] N/F, 1990s (1 tech)

D-Day *n.* 1 '6 June 1944', 2 'the day on which an important operation is to begin'

The individual languages use native expressions to designate 'day of a decisive event'; whether any of these can be identified as a calque is doubtful. The English term is thus mostly restricted to '6 June 1944', its use being purely historical and little used outside anniversaries (as in 1994).

Ge [=E] M [U] 1960s, 1(Ø/1 tech) < 2: *Tag X* **Du** *D-day* [=E] C, 1980s (1 tech) < *d-dag* **Nw** [=E] M, mid20c (Ø) < trsl *D-dag* **Fr** M, 1(Ø) < 2: *Jour J* **Sp** - < *Día D* **It** [didɛi] M, pl. Ø, mid20c (1 jour) < *ora x* **Rm** - < rend *ziua Z* **Po** M, end20c (1 tech) **Cr** [diḏej] M [U] mid20c, 1(1 tech) **Fi** - < rend *H-hetki* **Hu** 1(0)

dead heat *n.* 1 'a race in which two or more competitors finish exactly level'

This term was adopted with horse-racing and was fashionable in the late nineteenth century, but has come to be replaced by translations or paraphrases in most languages.

Ge - < rend *totes Rennen* **Du** *deadheat* [=E] C, 1980s (1 tech) **Nw** - < rend *dødt løp* **Fr** *dead-heat* [dɛd(h)it] M, mid19c (1 tech) **Rm** - < creat *sosire cap la cap* **Po** [dedhit] M [U] beg20c (1 tech) **Hu** - < trsl *holtverseny*

deadline *n.* 1 'a time limit for the completion of an activity etc.'

Although native equivalents have of course always been available, this word has made some impact as a fashionable alternative since the 1970s, esp. in commercial and university contexts. Note the infrequency of calques.

Ge [detlain] F, pl. *-s*, 1970s (1 jour) < *Frist* **Du** [=E] C, 1970s (2) **Nw** [=E] M, pl. *-s*, mid20c (2) < *(tids)frist*; > trsl *dødlinje, dødstrek* **Ic** [=E] uninfl., end20c (0 sla) **Fr** (0) **It** [ded-lain] F, pl. Ø, end20c (1 jour) < *termine ultimo* **Rm** [=E] N/F [U] 1990s (0) **Po** (0) **Fi** [=E] end20c (2 coll) **Gr** [=E] F/N, end20c (0>1 tech) < *prothesmia* F

dead weight *n.* 3 'the total weight carried on a ship' (cf. ↑*dwt*)

Du *deadweight* [=E] N [U] 1950s (1 tech) **Nw** [=E] M [U] 20c (1 tech) < trsl *dødvekt* **Rm** [dḏḏwajt/=E] N, 20c (1 tech) **Rs** *deḏveit* M [U] 20c (1 tech) **Cr** [ded-vejt] M [U] mid20c (1 tech) **Bg** *deḏueit/deḏveit* M [U] 20c, via Rs (1/3 tech) **Fi** - < creat *kuollut paino* **Hu** - < trsl *holt súly* **Gr** <=E> [=E] N, end20c (1 tech)

deadwood *n.* +2 'the lower part of a ship'

Rm [=E] N, 20c (1 tech) < rend

lemn mort **Rs** *deḏvud* M, pl. *-y*, beg20c (1 tech, rare) **Po** *dejwud* [deivut] M, mid20c (1 tech) **Cr** *deḏvud* M, mid20c (1 tech) **Bg** *deḏvud* M [U] beg20c, via Rs (3 tech)

deal *v.* 1a 'take measures concerning a problem, person, etc., esp. in order to put something right', +1e 'arrange for or come to an agreement about something', 2 'be engaged in commerce', +2a 'trade in drugs'

These loanwords (noun, verb, and derivatives) complement native words for 'trade': (a) covering slightly illegal or immoral transactions, (b) specifically relating to the drug trade, and (c) occasionally referring to jobbers on the stock exchange. The term for the person, notably the drug dealer, is most widespread.

Ge [=E] *dealen* [iː] 1970s, +2a(1 tech, coll) **Du** *dealen* [diːlə(n)] C, 1970s, 2,+2a(1 coll) **Nw** *deale* ["diːle] 20c, 2,+2a(1 tech) **Ic** *díla* [tiːla] 1970s, +2a(1 sla) **Fr** *dealer* [dile] 1980s, +2a(1 tech) **Sp** *dilear* 1980s, +2a(1 sla) **Po** (0) **Cr** [=E] M, pl. *-ovi*, 1970s, 2,+2a(1 coll) **Gr** *dilaro* end20c, +2a (3 sla)

deal *n.* 2 'a business arrangement, a transaction', +2a 'the buying and/or selling of drugs', +2b 'slightly immoral or unconventional business'

Ge [=E] M, pl. *-s*, 1970s, +2a,b(1 coll) **Du** [=E] C, 1970s, 2(1 coll) **Nw** [=E] M, pl. *-er*, 20c, 2(1 coll) +2a(1 tech) **Ic** *dill* [titl] M, pl. *dílar*, 1970s, 2,+2a(1 sla) **Fr** [=E] M, 1980s, 2,+2a(1 jour/tech) **Po** (0) **Fi** *diili* 2, +2a(2 coll) **Gr** *dil* N, end20c, +2a(1 mod, jour)

dealer *n.* 1 'a person dealing in (retail) goods', 3 'a jobber on the Stock Exchange', +4 'a person trading in drugs'

Ge [diːla] M, 1970s, +4(1 tech, coll) **Du** [diːlər] C, 1940s [1]/1970s (1 tech) **Nw** [=E/diːlər] M, pl. *-e*, 20c, 3,+4(1 tech) **Ic** *díler* [tiːler] M, pl. *-ar*, 1970s, +4(1 sla) → *dílerí* N **Fr** <=E>/*dealeur* [dilœR] M, 1970s, +4(1) **Sp** *dealer* > *diler* [diler] M, pl. *-s*, 1980s, 3(1 tech); +4(1 tech) < *camello* **It** [diːler] M, pl. Ø, 1980s, 1,3(1 tech) < 1:*grossista*; 3: *agente di borsa* **Rm** [=E] M, 1990s, 1(1 mod) 3(1 tech, jour) +4(0) **Rs** *diler* M, pl. *-y*, end20c (1 tech) → *-skii* adj. **Po** [diler] M, pl. *-rzy*, end20c (1 mod) → *-ski* adj. **Cr** *diler* M, pl. *-i*, end20c, 3(2 tech) **Fi** *diileri* 1980s, +4(2 coll) **Hu** [diːler] pl. *-ek*, end20c, 1(1 tech) +4(1 tech/euph) **Gr** *diler* M/F, 1(2 tech) +4(1 tech)

dealings *n.pl.* 'contacts or transactions, esp. in business'

Ic *dilingar* F, pl., 1970s (1 sla) **Gr** *diling* N, pl. Ø/-s, 1990s (1 tech, jour)

debit card *n.* 'a card from a bank used to pay for goods, services, etc., the amount being drawn electronically from the holder's account'

Du [=E] C, 1990s (1 rare) **Ic** *debitkort* [tɛ:pitkʰɔɾt]
N, pl. Ø, 1990s (2) **Rm** [=E] N, 1990s (1
tech>o) **Cr** - < *debitna kartica* **Bg** - < *debitna karta* **Gr** <=E>/*de̱bit kard* F, 1990s (1 tech) < trsl
khreostiki karta

debrief *v.* 'interrogate (a person) about a completed
mission or undertaking'
Du *debriefen* [=E] end20c (1 tech) **Nw** *debriefe*
[de̱:bri:fe] end20c (1 tech) **Fr** *débriefer* [debʀife]
1980s (1 tech)

debriefing *n.* 'a meeting held after a completed operation in order to discuss the outcome'
Nw [=E/de:-] M [U] mid20c (1 tech) **Fr** *débriefing*
[debrifiŋ] M, 1980s (1 mod/ban) < *critique* → *débriefer*
v. **Po** (0)

debug *v.* 2 'identify and remove defects from a computer program, a machine, etc.'
Ge - → *debugging* N, 1980s (1 tech, rare) **Du** *debug-
gen* [deby̱gə(n)] 1980s (1 tech) **Nw** *debugge* [di̱:bøge]
1980s (1 tech) **Ic** [=E] 1970s (0 tech) < trsl *aflúsa*;
rend *kemba* **Fr** - < *déboguer* **It** - → *debugging* M
[U] 1970s (1 tech) **Po** [debuk] end20c (1 tech) **Bg**
debu̱gvam end20c (3 tech) **Fi** *debugata* end20c (1
tech/sla) **Hu** [=E] 1980s (1 tech) → -*ging* n.; -*ger*
n. **Gr** - → -*ging* [=E] N, end20c (1 tech)

debugger *n.* 'a program for debugging other programs' (comput.)
It [di:ba̱ger] M, pl. Ø, 1970s (1 tech) **Rs** (0) **Po**
[debuger] M, end20c (1 tech) **Cr** (0) **Bg** *debu̱g* M
[U] end20c (3 tech) **Hu** [di̱bʌgger] pl. Ø, 1980s (1
tech) **Gr** (0 tech)

deck *n.* 1a 'a platform in a ship', 1b 'the accommodation on a particular deck', 3 'a component or unit in
sound-reproduction equipment that incorporates a
playing or recording mechanism for discs, tapes,
etc.', +7 'in agricultural mechanisms'
    The nautical use is first found in England, c.1500,
but the word may in fact be Dutch. Either language could have supplied this loanword, though most
languages appear to have borrowed it from England. To
complicate matters, (Low) German mediation is also
possible. A modern wave of influence came with the
spread of radio/tape recording equipment, an industry
largely dominated by the USA.
Ge [=E] N, pl. -*s*, 19c/1970s, 1a(4
LowGe) 3(4) **Du** *dek* N, pl.
-*ken*/-*s*, 1a(5); *deck* [=E] N,
end20c, 3(1 tech) **Nw** *dekk*
[=E] N, pl. Ø, 19c, 1a(5LowGe);
deck 1980s, 3(1) **Ic** *dekk* [tɛhk]
N, pl. Ø, end18c, 1a,b(5Da) <
þilfar **It** [dɛk] M, pl. Ø, 1980s, 3(1) < *piastra di
registrazione* **Rm** [=E] N, 1980s, 3(1 jour,
mod) **Rs** *dek* M, pl. -*i*, 19c, 1a(1 tech); *de̱ka* F, pl.
-*i*, end20c, 3(2 tech); mid20c, +7(1 tech) **Po**
(5Ge) **Cr** *dek* M, 20c, 1a(1 tech) **Bg** *dek* M, pl.
-*al-ove*, end20c, 3(2 tech) → -*ov* adj. **Fi** *dekki*
3(3) **Hu** [=E] pl. Ø, end20c, 3(1 tech) **Gr** *dek* N,
20c, 1a(1 tech) 3(1 tech) < *katastroma* N

decode *v.* 'convert (a coded message) into intelligible
language'
    For the verb, it is not strictly possible to distinguish
between English and French; for the derivatives, a
decision can be based on whether -*er* and -*ing* are
available as native morphemes (in which case the
derivatives may be independently coined). Note com-
plications arising from morpheme replacement of -*er*
in Romance languages.
Ge *dekodie̱ren* 1980s (3) **Du** *decoderen* (5Fr) **Nw**
dekode [de̱:ku:de] 20c (3 tech) **Fr** *décoder* (5) **Sp** - <
descodificar **It** - < *decodifica̱re* 1970s (3) **Rm** *de-
coda* [dekoda̱] mid20c (5Fr) **Rs** *dekodi̱rovat'* mid20c
(3 tech) **Cr** *dekodi̱rati* mid20c (3
tech) **Bg** *dekodi̱ram* 20c (3 tech) **Fi** *dekoodata*
1980s (2 tech, rare) > *purkaa* **Hu** *dekódol* [de̱ko:dol]
20c (3 tech) → *dekódolás* n. **Al** *dekodoj* mid20c (3)

decoder *n.* 2 'an electronic device for decoding signals (e.g. in a TV set)'
Ge [deko:da] M, pl. Ø, 1970s (1 tech) **Du** [deko̱:dər]
C, 1970s (1 tech) **Nw** *dekoder* [de̱:kuder] M, pl. -*e*, 20c
(1 tech) **Fr** *décodeur* [dekɔdœʀ] M, 1960s (1 tech, ban,
obs) **Sp** - < *descodificador* **It** [deko̱der] M, pl. Ø,
1970s (2) < trsl *decodificatore* **Rm** <=E>/*decodor*
[dekoder/dekodo̱r] N, 1970s (5Fr) **Rs** *deko̱der* M,
pl. -*y*, end20c (2 tech) **Po** (5Fr) **Cr** *dekoder* M, pl.
-*i*, mid20c (3 tech) **Bg** *dekode̱r* M, pl. -*al-i*, mid20c (1
tech) **Fi** *dekooderi* end20c (2 tech) **Hu** *dekóder* [de-
ko:der] pl. -*ek*, mid20c (1 tech) **Gr** *dikoder/dekoder*
M/N, end20c (1 tech) = trsl *apokodhikopiitis*

decoding *n.* 'conversion into an intelligible message'
Ge [de:ko̱:diŋ] N [U] 20c (1 tech) < *Dekodieren* **Nw**
dekoding [de̱:ku:diŋ] C [U] 20c (1 tech) **Fr** - < *déco-
dage* **Sp** - < *descodificación* **It** - < *decodificazio̱ne*
Rm - < *decodaj, decodare* **Rs** - < *dekodirovanie* N
Po (0) **Cr** - < *dekodi̱ranje* N **Bg** - < *dekodi̱rane*
Fi - < *dekoodaus* > *purku* **Hu** - < *dekódolás* **Gr** (0
tech)

deep cleaner* *n.* 'a cosmetic lotion (esp. for the
face)'
Nw - < rend *dyprens* **Ic** - < trsl *djúphreinsi* **Po** [dip
kliner] M, end20c (1 coll) **Hu** [=E] [U] end20c (1
tech/mod) < *mélytisztító* **Gr** <=E> end20c (1 writ)

defroster *n.* 'a spray or electric device for de-icing
car windows and defrosting fridges'
    This loanword was obviously more readily accepted
into Germanic languages which share the word *frost*.
(It may be that the term is interpreted as a native
formation.)
Ge [defro̱sta] M [U] 1960s (1
tech) **Du** [defrɔstər] C, 1980s
(1 tech) **Nw** [defro̱ster] M [U]
1960s (1 tech) **Ic** [=E] M [U]
1960s (0 tech, obs) < rend *isvari*
Fr - < *dégivreur* **Sp** - < *descon-
gelante* **It** - < rend *scongela-
tore* **Rs** *defro̱ster* M [U] mid20c (1 tech) **Po**
(0) **Cr** *defroster* M, pl. -*i*, mid20c (1 tech) **Hu** *de̱-
froszter* [=E] [U] mid20c (1 tech)

delete *v.* 1 'remove or obliterate written or printed matter'

Ge [=E] (1 tech_COMPUT) **Du** *deleten* [dili:tən] 1980s (1 tech) **Nw** [dili̱te] 1980s (1 tech, rare) < *slette* **Ic** *deletera* [dɛ:letera] end20c (1 tech_COMPUT) < trsl *eyða* **Fr** (0) **It** [dili:t] 1980s (1 tech) < *eliminare* **Po** [dilit] 1980s (1 tech) **Bg** *deli̱tvam* end20c (3 tech) **Fi** *deletoida* < mean *pyyhkkiä/poistaa* **Hu** [=E] end20c (1 tech_COMPUT) **Gr** - < *kano dili̱t*

demijohn *n.* 'a bulbous narrow-necked bottle holding from 3 to 10 gallons and usu. in a wicker cover' Ge [=E] M, pl. -s, 18c (1 arch) **Bg** *damadzha̱na*, via lt (3) **Hu** *demizson* [de̱mizon] pl. -ok, end19c/beg20c (3)

demo *n.*[1] 'a public meeting, march, etc., for a political or moral purpose', 2 *cp*[1] 'a demonstration of the capabilities of computer software, a group of musicians, etc.' (*demo software; demo tape*)

The status of this word is uncertain: the shortened forms may derive from earlier *demonstration* (5La) in the individual languages. It does not appear to contain any trace of English pronunciation.

Ge [de̱:mo:] F, 1960s, 1(5La); N, 1980s, 2(1 tech, rare) **Du** *demo(bandje)* [de̱:mo:] C, 1970s, 2(4) **Nw** [de̱:mu] M, pl. -er, 1960s, 1(5La); 1980s, 2(1 tech) **Ic** *demó* [tɛ:mou] N, pl. Ø, 1970s, 1(1 sla) 2(1 tech) **Fr** [demo] F, 2(1 tech/5) **Sp** <=E> M, pl. -s, end20c, 2(1 tech) **It** [de̱mo] F, pl. Ø, 1980s (1 tech) **Rm** (0) **Rs** (0) **Cr** [de̱:mo:] M [U] 1980s, 2(1 tech) **Bg** *de̱mo* cp[1] (in: *demoalbum*) 1990s, 2(1 tech) **Fi** [de̱mɔ] 2(3) **Gr** <=E>/*demo* F/N, end20c, 2(1 tech)

demo-party* *n.* 'a demonstration party, a gathering of computer enthusiasts where new computer software is introduced and demonstrated' **Nw** [de̱:mu-] N, pl. Ø/-ies, 1980s (1 tech, you) **Rs** (0)

demo-tape *n.* 'a demonstration tape (of rock or pop bands) sent to record companies as a sample' Ge [=E] N, 1980s (1 tech, rare) < *Demoband* **Du** - < *demo(bandje)* **Nw** [de̱:mu-] M, pl. -r, 1980s (1 tech) **Ic** - < *demó* **Sp** - < *cinta de demonstración* **Rs** (0) **Cr** - < *de̱motraka/de̱movrpca* **Bg** - < trsl *de̱mo-kaseta* **Fi** - < *demonauha* **Hu** - < rend *de̱molemez* **Gr** *de̱mo* F/N, end20c (1 tech)

demurrage *n.* 1a 'money paid to a shipowner by a charterer for failing to fulfil a contract' **Fr** (0) < *surestaries* **Rs** *demerredzh* M [U] mid20c (1 tech) **Po** [demuradʒ] M [U] mid20c (1 tech) **Bg** *demyureı̆dzh/dima̱ridzh* M [U] mid20c (1 tech)

denim *n.* 1 'a usu. blue hard-wearing cotton used for jeans' Ge [=E] M/N [U] 1970s (1 tech) **Du** [de̱:nɪm] N [U] 1950s (2) **Nw** [=E/deni:m] M [U] 1970s (3) **Ic** *dením* [tɛ:nim] N [U] end19c (2) **Fr** [dɔnim] M, 1970s (1 tech) **Sp** [=E] M, pl. -s, 1930s (1 tech) **It** [de̱nim] M, pl. 1960s (1 tech) **Rs** (0) **Po** (0) **Cr** [=E] M [U] end20c (1 tech) **Bg** (0) **Fi** [=E] (2) < creat *farkkukangas* **Hu** [=E] [U] mid20c (1 tech/writ) **Gr** *de̱nim* N [U] 20c (1 tech)

deodorant *n.* 'a substance sprayed or rubbed onto the body to remove or conceal unwanted smells'

Although the provenance of this term is clearly English its neo-Latin form makes its classification as an anglicism doubtful: all languages appear to pronounce the word according to native rules, often shortening it to the first two syllables.

Ge [de:o:do:ra̱nt] N, pl. -s/-e, 1960s (3) < *Deo* **Du** *deodorant/deodorans* (5La) **Nw** [deudura̱nt] M, pl. -er, 1960s (3) **Ic** [tɛ:outou:ra̱ntɬ]/*déo* M/N, pl./[U] 1960s (1 coll) = rend *svitasprey, svitalyktareyðir* **Fr** *déodorant* [deɔdɔrã] M/adj., mid20c (3) **Sp** - < *desodorante* M **It** *deodora̱nte* M, pl. -i, 1900s (3) **Rm** [deodora̱nt] N, 1970s, via Fr (3) > *dezodorizant, dezodorant* **Rs** *dezodora̱nt* M [U] end20c (3) **Po** (5Fr) **Cr** *deodora̱nt* M, pl. -i, mid20c (3) **Bg** *dezodora̱nt* M, pl. -al-i, 1960s, via Rs (3) **Fi** *deodorantti* (3); *dödö* (3 fac) **Hu** [=E] [U] 20c (1 tech/writ) < *de̱zodor* (4) → -ál v. **Al** *deodorant* [deodora̱nt] M, pl. -e, 1960s (3) **Gr** (1 writ) <=E> 20c < *aposmitiko*

derby *n./cp*[1] 1 'a horse-race', 2a 'any important sporting contest', 2b 'a local derby', 3 (derby) 'a bowler hat', +4 'a kind of shoe'

The name of the race founded by Edward Stanley, twelfth Earl of Derby (1752–1834) in 1780 quickly became a generic term and was exported along with other horse-racing terms in the nineteenth century (often transmitted through French or German). The transfer to other sporting events occurred in the twentieth century, but the almost universal spread of the term to football (where it is now more widespread than in its original senses) remains to be documented.

Ge [derbi/dörbi] N, pl. -(ie)s, end19c, 1(1 tech); 1960s, 2a,b(2) **Du** [dy̱:rbi:] C, 1960s, 1,2b(2) 3(1 tech); *derbyschoen* +4(1 tech +5) **Nw** [=E/dæ:rbi/dɔ:rbi] N, pl. Ø, 20c, 1,2a,b(1 tech) **Ic** [=E/tɛrpi] uninfl.,

1(Ø); freq. cp[1], *derbyhattur* 3(1 coll) **Fr** [dɛʀbi] M, 19c, 1(1 tech); beg20c, 2a(1 tech_FOOTB); end19c, +4(1 tech) **Sp** <=E>/*derbi* [derbi] M, pl. -s, end19c, 1(1 tech, rare); 1960s, 2a,b(2<3) **It** [de̱rbi] M, pl. Ø, end19c, 1,2a,b(3) **Rm** [=E]/*derbi* [derbi] N, beg20c, 1,2a(2>3) **Rs** *de̱rbi* N, uninfl., beg20c, 1,2a(1 tech) **Po** *derby* [derbi/=E] N, uninfl., beg20c, 1,2a(1 tech) **Cr** *derbi* N [U] mid20c, 1(1 tech) 2a(3) **Bg** *derbi* N, pl. -ta, mid20c, 1,2a,b(1 tech) **Hu** *derby/-i* [derbi] pl. -k, end19c, 1(3) 2a(3) **Al** *derbi* [derbi] M [U] 1,2a(1 reg) **Gr** *derbi/-y* N, beg20c, 2a(2)

derrick *n./cp*[1] 1 'a crane for heavy weights', 2 'a framework over an oil well'

This word is derived from the name of a famous Elizabethan hangman, the structure being reminiscent of a gallows. Its spread is a notable case of the prominent position of Britain in nineteenth-century technology and shipbuilding.

Ge [=E] M, pl. -s, 20c, 1(3 tech) < *Derrickkran* **Du** [dɛrɪk] C, mid20c, 2(1 tech) **Nw** *derrik* [dærik] M, pl.

Ic	Nw	Po	Rs
Du	Ge	Cr	Bg
Fr	It	**Fi**	Hu
Sp	Rm	Al	Gr

-*er*, beg20c (1 tech)   **Fr** [deʀik] mid19c (1 tech/ban) < *tour de forage* **Sp** [derrik] M, 20c, 1(1 tech) 2(1 tech) < 1: *grúa derrick*; 2: *torre de perforción* **It** [=E] M, pl. Ø, 1930s (1 tech)   **Rm** [=E] N, beg20c (1 tech) = *macara învârtitoare* **Rs** *derrik* M, pl. -*i*, beg20c, 1(1 tech)   **Cr** *derik* M, pl. -*i*, beg20c (1 tech)   **Bg** *derikkran* cp[1], M, mid20c, 1(1+5 tech)   **Hu** <=E>/ *Derrick-daru*, pl. -*k* (1 tech+5); [=E] [U] 1930s, 1,2(1 tech, arch) < *oszlopdaru*

design   *n.* 1a 'a preliminary plan or sketch for the making or production of a building, machine, garment, etc.', 1b 'the art or profession of producing these', +4c 'the shape of a product (in fashion, arts & crafts)'

The three related senses of this word spread in Europe from the 1960s onwards; the English word was hindered by the existence of widespread French-derived *dessin* (of a slightly different meaning). It was adopted even where the actual design(er)s were French or Italian (in fashion, cars etc.). The verb, often back-derived, is notably rarer than the two nouns. The pronunciation has remained close to English even where (Romance) reinterpretation of -*sign*- would have been obvious.

Ge [=E] N, pl. -s, 1960s, +4c(2) **Du** [=E] N [U] 1980s, +4c(2) (also as cp[1]) **Nw** [=E/de-] M/ N, pl. -*er*/Ø/-*s*, 1950s, 1b,+4c(2) → *designe* v. **Ic** [=E] 1960s, 1a,+4c(0 tech, coll) < mean *hönnun* **Fr** [dizajn/dezajn] M, 1960s, +4c(2 ban) > *stilique, conception* **Sp** - < *diseño* **It** [dizain] M [U] 1960s, 1b,+4c(2) **Rm** [=E] N, 1970s, +4c(2) **Rs** *dizaĭn* M [U] 20c (2) **Po** <=E> M, 20c, 1a,+4c(1 tech) **Cr** *dizajn* M, pl. -*i*, 20c, +4c(2) → -*irati* v. **Bg** *dizajn* M [U]/pl. -*al-i*, end20c, 1b,+4c(2) **Fi** [=E] 1960s, 1b,+4c(2) **Hu** [=E] [U] 1970s, +4c(2) > *ipari formatervezés* **Al** - < *dizenjo* (5It) **Gr** *dizain* N [U] end20c, 1b(2) +4c(2)

design   *v.* 1 'produce a design for (a building, garment, etc.)'

Ge *designen* [dizainən] 1970s (1 mod) < *entwerfen* **Du** -< *ontwerpen* **Nw** *designe* [desaine] 1970s (2) **Ic** - < mean *hanna* **Sp** - < *diseñar* **It** - < *disegnare* (5) **Po** (0) **Cr** *dizajnirati* 20c (2)

designer   *n.* 1 'a person who makes artistic designs or plans for buildings, machines, garments, etc.'

Ge [dizaina] M, pl. Ø, 1960s (2) → -*in* F **Du** [=E] C, 1980s (2) **Nw** [=E/de-] M, pl. -*e*, 1950s (2) **Ic** - < trsl *hönnuður* **Fr** [dizajnœʀ/dezajnœʀ] M/F, 1970s (1 tech, ban) > *créateur, dessinateur, styliste* **Sp** - < *diseñador* **It** [=E] M, pl. Ø, 1960s (2) **Rm** [=E] M, 1970s (2) **Rs** *dizaĭner* M, pl. -*y*, end20c (2) **Po**

[-er] M, pl. -*rzy*, end20c (1 tech, mod) → -*ski* adj.   **Cr** *dizajner* M, pl. -*i*, 20c (2) → -*ski* adj. **Bg** *dizaĭner* M, pl. -*i*, end20c (2) → -*ka* F; -*ski* adj. **Fi** [=E] 20c (1) **Hu** [=E] [U] end20c (1 tech) < *fromatervező* **Al** *dizajner* M/F, end20c (2) < *skhedhiastis/skhedhiastria*

designer drug   *n.* 'a synthetic analogue of an illegal drug, esp. one not itself illegal

Ge *Designerdroge* F, pl. -*en*, 1980s (2+5) **Nw** <=E>/ *designerdroge* M, pl. -*s*/-*r*, 1980s (1 tech) **Sp** - < trsl *droga de diseño*

desk   *n.* 1 'a piece of furniture with a surface for writing, reading, etc. on', 2 'a counter in a hotel etc.', 3 'a section of a newspaper office etc. dealing with a specified topic'

Du [dæsk] C, 1970s, 1(2) 2(2) = 1: *bureau*; = 2: *balie* **Nw** [=E] M, usu. def. form *desken*, pl. -*er*, mid20c, 3(3 tech) **Ic** [=E] N, pl. Ø, end20c, 2(0 coll) **Fr** [desk] M, 1970s, 3(1 tech) **Cr** *desk* M, pl. Ø, end20c, 3(3 tech) **Fi** *tiski* 2(4)

desktop   *n.* +1b 'a computer menu that imitates the working surface of a desk or an office', cp[1] 2 'a computer suitable for use at an ordinary desk'

This word illustrates the acceptance of new computer technology; few calques appear to have been suggested. There is a West-East cline probably explained by economic conditions.

Ge [=E] M/N? [U] 1980s, 2(1 tech) **Du** [=E] C, 1980s, 2(1 tech) **Nw** [=E] 1980s, 2(1 tech) > trsl *skrivebords-* **Ic** [=E] end20c, +1b(0 tech) **Fr** <=E> 1980s, 2(1 ban) > *ordinateur de table* **It** [=E] M, pl. Ø, 1990s (1 tech) **Rm** <=E> 1990s, 2(0>1 tech) **Rs** *desktop* M [U] 1990s, +1b(1 tech) **Po** (0) **Cr** *desktop* M [U] 1990s, 2(1 tech) **Bg** *desktop* M [U]/pl. -*al-ove*, [U] 1990s (1 tech) **Fi** [=E] 2(2 coll) > creat *pöytäkone* **Hu** [=E] end20c (1 tech>2) **Gr** <=E> [=E] N/cp[1/2], end20c (1 tech)

desktop publishing   *n.* 'the production of printed matter with a desktop computer and printer'

Ge [=E] N [U] 1980s (1 tech) = *D.T.P.* **Du** [dɪsktɔp pʏblɪʃiŋ] C [U] 1980s (1 tech) **Nw** [=E] M [U] 1980s (1 tech) > trsl *skrivebordstrykking* → *desktoppe* v. **Fr** (0 ban) < *micorédition, éditique* **Sp** - < *autoedicición, edición electrónica* **It** [=E] M [U] 1990s (1 tech) **Rm** <=E> N [U] 1990s (0>1 tech) **Cr** [=E] N [U] 1990s (1 tech) **Bg** *desktop* M [U] 1990s (3 tech) **Fi** <=E>/*DTP* [=E] (2 coll) **Hu** [=E] *DTP* [U] [de:te:pe:] end20c (1 tech) **Gr** <=E> [=E] N [U] end20c (1 tech)

destroyer   *n.* 2 'a fast warship with guns and torpedoes'

This term was widely translated into European languages if the word was indeed first used in English for this type of ship. Its present-day distribution is noteworthy as it is found in two, more marginal, languages, Croatian and Albanian (possibly as a relic – the word is also found as an old loan in Turkish).

Ge - < trsl *Zerstörer* **Du** [=E] C, 1970s (1 tech) < *torpedobootjager* **Nw** [=E/de-] M, pl. -*e*, beg20c (1 tech) **Ic** - < *tundurspillir* **Fr** [dɛstʀwaje/dɛstɔjœʀ] M, beg20c (1 arch) **Sp** [destrojer] M, pl. -*s*, end19c (1 tech) < trsl *destructor* **Rm** - < trsl *distrugător* **Cr** *destrojer* M, mid20c (1 tech) < *razaraé* **Bg** - < trsl *razrushitel* **Fi** - < trsl *hävittäjä* **Hu** - < *torpedó-romboló* **Al** *destrojer* [destrojer] M, pl. -*ë*, mid20c (1 tech)

detec-* *abbrev* 'detective'
Nw *detek* [dɛtek-] cp[1] + *time* 1960s (3)

detective *n.* 1 'a person, esp. a member of a police force, employed to investigate crime', +2 'a genre of fiction'

The status of this and the following word as an anglicism is doubtful, the pronunciation being according to national conventions, as is usual for neo-Latin items. Nineteenth-century evidence shows the word came from English, but was pronounced as an internationalism from the beginning.

Ge [de:tekti̯:v] M, pl. -*e*, beg20c, 1(5Fr) **Du** [=E/detɪktivə] C, beg20c (2) **Nw** *detektiv* [dɛtekti:v] M, pl. -*er*, beg20c, 1(3) **Ic** - < 1: rend *leynilögreglumaður, spæjari*; +2: *leynilögreglusaga; reyfari* **Fr** *détective* [detɛktiv] M, end19c (3) **Sp** M, beg20c (3) → *detectivesco* adj. **It** [detɛktiv] M, pl. Ø, end19c (3) = *investigatore* **Rm** *detectiv* [detektiv] M, end19c, via Fr, 1(3) **Rs** *detektiv* M, pl. -*y*, beg20c, via Fr, 1(3); [U] +2(3) → -*nyĭ* adj. **Po** *detektyw* [detektiv] M, beg20c, 1(3) → -*istyczny* adj. **Cr** *detektiv* M, pl. -*i*, beg20c, 1(3) **Bg** *detektiv/dedektiv* M, pl. -*i*, beg20c, via Fr, 1(3) → -*ski* adj. **Hu** *detektív* [detekti:v] pl. -*ek*, end19/beg20c, 1(3 obs) < *nyomozó*; only in cp[1] e.g. *detektívregény* (-novel) +2(3+5) **Al** *detektiv* [detektiv] M, pl. -*ë*, beg20c (3) **Gr** *dedektiv/detektiv/dedektiv* M, 20c, 1(2)

detector *n.* 1 'a thing that detects', 2 'a device for the detection or demodulation of signals'

Ge *Detektor* M, pl. -*en* (5La) **Du** (5La) **Nw** *detektor* [detektu:r] M, pl. -*er*, beg20c (3 tech) **Fr** - < *détecteur* **Sp** M (3 tech/5La) **It** [detektor] M, pl. Ø, 1950s (1 tech) < *rivelatore* **Rm** [detektor] N, mid20c (5Fr) **Rs** *detektor* M, pl. -*y*, mid20c (3 tech) **Po** (5La) **Cr** *detektor* M, pl. -*i*, mid20c (3 tech) **Bg** *detektor* M, pl. -*a/-i*, mid20c, via Ge (2 tech) → -*en* adj. **Hu** *detektor* [detektor] pl. -*ok*, 20c (3 tech) **Al** *detektor* [detektor] M, pl. -*ë*, mid20c (3 tech)

deuce *n.* 2 'a score of forty all' (lawn tennis)
Ge [=E] N [U] beg20c/1980s (1 tech, rare) < *Einstand* **Du** [dju:s] N [U] 1970s (1 tech) **Nw** [=E] M [U] 20c (1 tech) **Fr** (0 ban) < *égalité* **Sp** [dius/jus] M [U] 1960s (1 tech) = *(cuarenta) iguales* **It** [diu:s] M [U] 1960s (1 tech) < *pareggio, paritá* **Rm** [=E] N [U] 1970s (1 tech) < *egalitate* **Rs** *d'yus* M [U] end20c (1 tech) **Po** <=E> N [U] beg20c (1 obs) **Cr** [=E] M [U] beg20c (1 tech) **Bg** *dyus* M [U] end20c (1 tech) **Hu** <=E>/*gyúsz* [dju:s] [U] end19c (1 tech, arch) **Gr** [=E] end20c (1 tech)

Devon(ian) *n./cp[1]* 1 'the fourth period of the Palaeozoic era' (geol).
Ge *Devon* [devo̯:n] N [U] 19c (3 tech) **Du** *Devoon*

[de:vo̯:n] N [U] mid20c (1 tech) **Nw** *devon* [devu̯:n] [U] beg20c (3 tech) **Ic** *devon* [tɛ:von] N [U] more freq. cp[1], 1870s, via Da (2 tech) **Fr** *dévonien* [devɔnjã] M/adj, 19c (1 tech) **Sp** *deónico* M/adj., 19c (3 tech) **It** *devoniano* M [U] 1870s (1 tech) < rend *periodo devoniano, periodo devonico* **Rm** *devonian* N/adj. [U] beg20c, via Fr (3 tech) **Rs** *devon* M [U] 19c (1 tech) → -*skiĭ* adj. **Po** *dewon* [devon] M [U] beg20c (1 tech) → *dewoński* adj. **Cr** *devon* M [U] beg20c (1 tech) **Bg** *devon* M [U] 20c, via Rs/Ge (3 tech) → -*ski* adj. **Fi** *devonikausi* **Hu** *devonkorszak* (3+5); *devon* [=E] [U] 19c (3 tech) **Al** *Devoniani* [devonjani] M [U] beg20c (3 tech)

dibble *v.* 1 'sow with the help of a dibber'
Ge *dibbeln* beg20c (3 tech) **Du** *dibbelen* beg20c (3 tech) **Po** (0) **Cr** *diblovati* end20c (1 tech)

diet *cp[1]* +2b 'low in sugar or fat'
Ge (5Gr) **Nw** (0) **Ic** [=E] 1980s (2) **Fr** (0) **Sp** (0) **It** [=E] 1990s (1 jour, mod) < ↑*light* **Rs** (5Ge) **Po** (5La) **Cr** (0) **Hu** [=E/die:t] 1980s (2 writ, jour)

differ *v.* +3 'have an effect or influence on a situation; make a difference'
Ic *diffa* [tɪf:a:] (in *(það) diffar engu*) end20c (1 sla) **Fr** - < *différer* **Sp** *diferir* (5La) **It** (5La) **Hu** (5La)

dig *v.* 6 'like, appreciate, understand'
Nw *digge* ["di̯ge] 1960s (3 sla) → *digger* M; *diggbar* adj.; *digg* adj./N **Ic** *digga* [tɪk:a] end20c (1 sla) **Fi** *digata* 1960s (2 sla)

digest *n.* 1a 'a summary', 2 'a synopsis of literature'
This loanword is quite marginal, native terms being available. Its distribution was certainly influenced by the best-selling *Readers Digest* publication.
Ge [=E] M/N, pl. -*s*, 1960s, 1a(1 jour, rare) **Nw** (0) **Fr** [daj3-ɛst/di3est] M, 1930s, 1a(1 ban) < *condensé* **Sp** [da̯ijest/dijest] M, mid20c (1 jour, rare) **It** [da̯id3-est] M, pl. Ø, 1950s, 2(1 tech) **Rs** *da̯idzhest* M [U] end20c (1 jour, rare) → -*irovanie* N **Po** (0) **Cr** *dajdžest* M, mid20c, 1a(2) → -*irati* v. **Bg** *da̯idzhest* M, pl. -*a/-i*, end20c, 2(1 jour/rare) **Hu** [=E] [U] 1970s, 1a(1 jour) < *válogatás*

digger *n.* 1 'a person that digs', 2 'a miner'
This term (more frequent in the compound *gold digger*) was common on the Continent with reference to American adventurers, but is rare now even as a foreignism.
Ge 2(0 arch) **Nw** ["diger] M, pl. -*e*, 1960s, 1(3 sla) **Fr** (Ø) **Rs** *digger* M, pl. -*y*, 1990s, 1(1 jour) → -*stvo*; -*skiĭ* adj. **Po** *diggerzy* pl. Ø, mid20c, 2(1 tech) **Cr** *diger* M, mid20c, 2(1 tech) **Hu** [digger] pl. -*ek*, 2(1 tech, hist/Ø)

digit *n.* 1 'any numeral from 0 to 9, esp. when forming part of a number'
Nw [=E] M, pl. -*s*, 1980s (1 tech, rare) **Fr** [di3it] M, 1970s (1 tech) > *chiffre, bit, digital, caractère* **Sp** *digito* (5La) **Rm** [=E] M, 1980s (1 tech) **Po** (0) **Hu** [=E/di̯git] [U] end20c (1 tech_INFO)

digital I 'of or using a digit or digits', 2 (of a clock, watch, etc.) 'giving a reading by means of displayed digits as opposed to hands', +3 (of a computer) 'operating on data represented as a series of usu. binary digits or in similar discrete form', +4 'a mode of digital recording'
Ge (5La) **Du** (5Fr) **Nw** [digita:l] 1960s (1 tech) **Ic** [tɪc:tʰal] end20c, 2,+3,+4(0 tech) < trsl *stafrænn* **Fr** [diʒital] 1960s, 2,+3(4) < *numérique* → *-iser* v.; *-seur* M **Sp** *digital* [dixital] (3 tech/5La) **It** *digitale* 1960s (3 tech) → *-izzare* v.; *-izzatore* n.; *-izzazione* n. **Rm** *digital* [didʒital] 1970s (1 tech) **Rs** *didzhital'* 1990s (3 tech); *digital'nyi* adj., end20c (3 tech) **Po** (0) **Cr** *digitalan* (1 tech) → *digitalizirati* v. **Bg** *digitalen* (3 tech) → *digitalizirane* N **Fi** *digitaalinen* (3) **Hu** *digitális* [digita:liʃ] 1,2,+3(1 tech>2) **Al** *dischitale* 1,2(1 tech) **Gr** *ditzital* adj. uninfl., 1,2(2) +3,+4(1 tech) = *psifiakos, -i, -o*

digitizer n. 'a computer accessory that converts data into digital form'
Sp - < *digitalizador* **Rm** *digitizor* [didʒitizor] N, 1990s (1 tech) **Rs** *digitaizer* M, pl. *-y*, 1990s (1 tech) **Bg** *digitaizer* M, pl. *-al- i*, 1990s (1 tech)

dildo n. 1 'an object shaped like an erect penis and used, esp. by women, for sexual stimulation'
Ge [dɪldo] M, pl. *-s*, 1980s (3) **Du** [dildo] M, pl. *-'s*, 1970s (3) **Nw** [dildu:] M, pl. *-er*, 1980s (3) **Rs** (0) **Cr** (0) **Fi** [dildo] end20c (2 tech) **Hu** [dildo:] pl. Ø, end20c (3)

dim v. +1a 'reduce the brightness of electric light', 2 'dip (headlights)'
Ge *dimmen* 1960s, +1a(3) **Du** *dimmen* [dɪmə(n)] beg20c (3) **Nw** *dimme* ["dime] 1970s (3 tech) → *dimming* C **Ic** *dimma* 1970s, +1a(4)

dimmer n. 1 'a device for varying the brightness of on electric light'
The restriction of this term to Northern/Central Europe may well reflect the spread of the technological innovation.
Ge [dima] M, pl. Ø, 1960s (3) > creat *Helligkeitsregler* **Du** [dɪmər] C, 1970s (2 tech) **Nw** [dimər] M, pl. *-e*, 1970s (1 tech) **Ic** [tɪm:er]/*dimmari* [-arı] M, pl. *-ar*, 1970s (2 tech) **Fr** - < *variateur* **It** [dimmer] M, pl. Ø, mid20c (tech) **Rs** *dimmer* M, pl. *-y*, end20c (1 tech) **Po** - < *ściemniecz*

dinghy n. 1 'a small boat', 3 'a small inflatable rubber boat'
This word is from Hindi, but was transmitted through English. Its currency is restricted as a technical term in rowing, even though it is (as *Finn-dinghy*) an Olympic discipline.
Ge *Dingi* [=E] N, pl. *-(ie)s*, beg20c, 1(1 tech) **Du** [=E] C, pl. *-'s*, 1970s (1 tech) **Fr** <=E>/*dinghie* [diŋgi] M, 1930s,

1(1 tech); - < 3: *canot pneumatique* **Sp** *dingui* M, pl. *-s*, 20c (1 tech) **It** <=E>/*dingo* [=E] M, pl. Ø, 1920s, 1(1 tech) **Rm** *dinghi* [=E] N, 20c, via Fr, 1(1 tech) **Rs** *dingi* N, uninfl., mid20c, 1(1 tech) **Po** *dingi* N [U] mid20c (1 tech) **Cr** *dingi* M, mid20c, 1(3) **Bg** *dingi* N, pl. *-ta*, mid20c, 3(1 tech) **Hu** *dingi* [=E] pl. *-k*, beg20c, 1(1 tech) **Gr** *dingyi/-i* N, 20c, 1(1 tech)

dingo n. 1 'a wild or half-domesticated Australian dog'
Since the word designates an Australian animal and is not English in form, its status as an anglicism is questionable.
Ge [dingo:] M, pl. *-s*, beg20c (Ø) **Du** (Ø) **Nw** [dingu] M, pl. *-er*, 20c (Ø) **Ic** *dingó(/hundur)* [tiŋkou] M, pl. *-ar*, 1930s (1 tech) **Fr** [dēgo] M, 19c (Ø) **Sp** [dingo] M, pl. *-s*, 20c (1 tech) **It** [=E] M, pl. Ø/-ghi, end19c (3) **Rm** [dingo] M, pl. Ø, 20c, via Fr (Ø) **Rs** *dingo* M/N, uninfl., mid20c (2) **Po** [-o] M, uninfl., mid20c (2) **Cr** *dingo* M, pl. *-i*, 20c (2) **Bg** *dingo* N, pl. Ø, 20c (Ø) **Fi** [dıŋgɔ] (Ø) **Hu** *dingó* [=E] pl. *-k*, 19c? (Ø) **Gr** (Ø)

dinner n. 2 'an evening meal', +2a (short for ↑*dinner music*) 'music played during a dinner'
Ge [dina] N, pl. *-s*, beg20c, 2(Ø/1 arch) < *Abendessen* **Du** - < *diner* (5Fr) **Nw** 2(0) **Ic** [=E] M [U] mid20c, 2(0) +2a(1 tech, sla) **It** - < *cena* **Rm** - < *dineu* **Rs** 2(0) **Po** 2(0) **Cr** 2(0) **Hu** [diner] [U] 19c, 2(Ø) < *estebéd* **Gr** 2(0>1 mod)

dinner jacket n. 'a man's short usu. black formal jacket for evening wear'
Ge [dinadzekit] N, pl. *-s*, 1970s (1 mod) < *Smoking* **Du** [=E] C (1 tech) **Nw** - < *smoking* **Ic** *dinnerjakki* M, pl. *-ar*, mid20c (2+5 coll) **Sp** - < *smoking* **It** - < *smoking* **Po** - < *smoking* **Cr** (0) **Bg** - < *smoking* **Fi** -< *smokki* **Al** - < *smoking*

dinner music n. 1a 'music played during a dinner', 1b 'the type of music that is typical of such occasions'
Ic *dinnermúsik* N, mid20c (2 coll) = *dinnertónlist*

dip n. 5 'a sauce or dressing into which food is dipped before eating'
This is one of the fashionable terms created by the food industry. It is still marginal as far as regional distribution and frequency/stylistic acceptability are concerned.
Ge [=E] M, pl. *-s*, 1960s (1 mod) < *Soße* → *dippen* v. **Du** *dip (saus)* [dɪp-] C, pl. *-pen, dipsausen/- sauzen* 1970s (2 tech +5) **Nw** <=E>/*dipp* [=E] M, pl. *-er*, 1960s (1/2) → *dippe* v. **Ic** *dipp* [tɪhp] N [U] 1970s, 5(1 coll) < rend *idýfa* **Bg** (0) **Fi** *dippi(kastike)* 20c (2) → *dipata* v. **Gr** *dip* N, end20c (2 mod)

dip v. 1 'let down briefly into liquid', +7a 'lower a flag in salute', (naut.), 10 'wash sheep by immersion in a vermin-killing liquid'
Ge *dippen* 1960s, 1(1 jour, mod); beg20c, +7a(1 tech,

rare) **Du** *dippen* 1970s, 1(5) **Nw** *dippe* ["dipe]
1980s, 1(1 mod) **Fi** *idipata* 1(1)

diplexer* *n.* 'an instrument preventing interference
between signals of different frequencies'
It *diplexer* [diplekser] M, pl. Ø, 1970s (1 tech) **Rs**
diplekser M, pl. -*y*, mid20c (1 tech) **Bg** *diplekser* M,
pl. -*al*-*i*, mid20c (3 tech) **Fi** *diplekseri* (2 tech) **Hu**
[diplekser] pl. -*ek*/Ø, end20c (1 tech)

direct mail *n.* '(a method of distributing) advertising
folders, requests for money, etc. as printed matter
through the mail'
Ge [=E] F [U] 1970s (1 tech, mod) **Du** [=E] 1990s (1
tech) **Nw** [=E] M [U] 1980s (1) **Fr** - < *publipostage* **Hu** [=E] [U] 1970s (1 tech)

direct marketing *n.* 'the practice of marketing and
selling goods through mail order'
Nw [=E] M [U] 1980s (1) **Du** [=E] C [U] 1990s (1
tech) **Fr** *marketing direct* 1990 (1 mod)

directory *n.* 2 'a computer file listing other files or
programs'
Ge [=E] N, pl. -*(ie)s*, end20c (1 tech) < *Verzeich-
nis* **Du** [=E] C, pl. -*ies*, 1990s (1 tech) **Nw** [=E] N,
pl. -*ies*, 1970s (1 tech) < *katalog* **Ic** [=E] N, pl. Ø,
end20c (1 tech) < *(efnis)skrá* **Fr** <=E> 20c (1 tech)
< *répertoire* **It** [dairektori/də-] F, pl. Ø, 1980s (1
tech) < mean *direttorio* **Rm** - < mean *director* **Rs**
direktoriya F, pl. -*i*, 1980s (3 tech) **Po** N [U] end20c
(1 tech) **Cr** (0) **Bg** *direktoriya* F, pl. -*rii*, 1980s (3
tech) **Fi** - < *hakemisto* **Hu** [=E] [U] end20c (1
tech) **Gr** <=E> [=E] N, pl. -*s*, end20c (1 tech) =
mean *kataloghos*

dirt track *n.* 'a course made of rolled cinders, soil,
etc., for motorcycling races or flat racing'
Ge [=E] beg20c (1 arch) < *Sandbahn(-)* **Nw** [=E] M,
pl. -*s*, 20c (1 tech) > *grusbane* **Ic** [=E] end20c (Ø)
Fr <=E> 1930s (1 tech/obs) → *tracker* (1 obs) **Sp**
[dirtrak] M, 1920s (1 tech) **Rm** [dirt trak] N [U]
mid20c (1 tech) **Bg** *dürttrek* M [U] end20c (1 tech)

dirty *adj.* 3 'sordid, lewd; morally illicit or questionable', 5 'dishonest, unfair'
Nw [=E] 1970s, 5(1 sla) **Ic** [tœrti] uninfl., end20c,
3,5(1 sla)

dirty dancing *n.* 'a dance style'
The limited currency of this item is noteworthy
considering the media coverage of the (short-lived)
dance style in 1990–91.
Ge [=E] N [U] 1990 (1 obs) **Du** [=E] N [U] 1990s (1
obs) **It** [=E] M [U] 1990s (1 obs) **Rm** (0) **Bg** - <
trsl *mrŭsen tants* **Hu** (Ø) **Gr** <=E> [=E] N [U]
1990 (1 obs)

dirty mind *n.* 'an inclination to interpret innocent
events etc. in a lewd way'
Du [dv:timajnd] C, 1980s (1 coll/2) **Nw** (0) **Ic** - →
dirty minded adj.

disc/disk *n.* 4a 'a computer storage device', 4b 'a
smooth non-magnetic disc with large storage capacity
for data recorded and read by laser', ↑**diskette**
Ge *Disk* F, pl. -*s*, 1960s, 4a(1 tech) < ↑*Diskette* **Du**
[dısk] C, 1980s, 4a(2 tech) **Nw** *disk* [=E] M, pl. -*er*,

1970s (3 tech) **Ic** *(geisla)diskur* M, pl. -*ar*, 1980s
(4) **Fr** *disque* (4) **Sp** - < ↑*floppy disk* **It** - < ↑*floppy
disk* **Rm** *disc* [disk] N, end20c (4 tech) **Rs** *disk* M,
pl. -*i*, 1980s (2 tech) **Po** *dysk* M, 1980s, 4a(2 tech)
Cr *disk* M, pl. -*ovi*, end20c, 4a(1 tech) **Bg** *disk* M, pl.
-*al*-*ove*, 1980s (3 tech) **Hu** *disk* [=E] pl. -*ek*, end20c (1
tech) **Al** *disk* M, pl. *disqe*, end20c (3 tech) **Gr**
<=E>/*disk* N, end20c (1 tech) < mean *dhiskos*

disc jockey *n.* 'a presenter of recorded popular
music'
The spread of this compound was certainly assisted
by the fact that the two components had already been
borrowed. The acronym ↑*DJ* is even less frequent –
though not in Italian and Bulgarian and is normally
pronounced the English way. There are few calques –
which probably sound too parochial for the trendy
subject matter.
Ge [diskjoki] M, pl. -*s*, 1960s (2)
> *Plattenjockey* > *Schallplatten-
unterhalter* (GDR) = ↑*DJ* **Du**
diskjockey [diskdʒɔki] C, 1960s
(2 tech) **Nw** *disk-jockey* [=E/-
jɔki] M, pl. -*er*/-*s*, 1950s (2) >
plateprater **Ic** - < rend *diskari,
plötusnúður* **Fr** *disque-jockey*/*disc-jockey* [dis-
k(ə)ʒɔkɛ] M, 1950s (2 ban) > *animateur* **Sp** [disjo-
kei/-ki] M, pl. -*s*, 1970s (2 tech, you) >
pinchadiscos **It** [disk dʒɔkei] M, pl. Ø/-*s*, 1950s (2)
< ↑*DJ* **Rm** [=E] M, pl. Ø, 1970s (2) → *disk jockeiţă*
F, 1990s (1 fac, rare) **Rs** *diskzhokei* M, pl. -*i*, end20c
(1 you) **Po** *dyskdżokej*/<=E> [-ei] M, mid20c (2
mod) **Cr** *disk-džokej* M, pl. -*i*, end20c (2) **Bg** - <
trsl *diskozhoker*/*diskovodesht* **Fi** - < rend *tiskijukka*
Hu [=E] M pl. -*ék*, 1970s (2) > trsl *lemezlovas* **Gr**
<=E>/ *disk tzokei* M/F, mid20c (2 you, mod)

Ic	**Nw**	**Po**	**Rs**
Du	**Ge**	**Cr**	**Bg**
Fr	**It**	**Fi**	**Hu**
Sp	**Rm**	**Al**	**Gr**

discman* *n.* (Sony™) 'a miniature compact disc
player' (cf. ↑*walkman*)
Ge [=E] M, pl. -*men*/-*mans*, 1990s (1 tech, rare) **Du**
[=E] C, 1990s (2 tech) **Nw** [=E] M, pl. -*er*, 1990s
(1) **Sp** M, pl. Ø, end20c (1 tech) > *compact disc
personal* **Rs** *diskmen* M, pl. -*y*, 1990s (2 tech) **Po**
[-en] M, 1990s (1 tech) **Gr** <=E> [=E] N, 1990s (1
tech, rare) < *forito cd-player*

disco *n.*/*cp*$^{1/2}$ 1 'a discotheque' (the abbrev. predominantly from English), 2 'a style of pop music', +3 'a
pocket-size cassette player with headphones'
Although the full form *discotheque* is French, the
shortened form arose in American English in 1964,
and spread rapidly with the music. Since its elements
are Greek, the status of the word as an anglicism is
doubtful.
Ge [disko:] F, pl. -*s*, 1970s, 1(3); [U] 1980s, 2(1
tech) **Du** [=E] C, pl. -'*s*, 1970s, 1,2(2); also
cp^{1} **Nw** <=E>/*disko* [disku] M/N, pl. -*er*/Ø, 1970s,
1(2); *cp*^{2}, +3(2) < 1: *diskotek* **Ic** *diskó* [=E] N/*cp*^{1} [U]
1970s, 2(2 tech); *vasadiskó cp*^{2}, +3 (2 coll) **Fr** [disko]
adj./M, 1970s, 2(1) **Sp** <=E> *cp*^{1}, 1970s, 1(3 coll);
M, uninfl., 2(3) < 1: *discoteca* **It** *discoteca* F, pl. -*che*,
1960s (3) **Rm** [=E] N [U] 1970s, 1,2(3 coll) <

discotecă **Rs** *di̱sko* N [U] 1970s, 2(2 you) **Po** *dys-koteka* F/*disko* <=E> N, uninfl., mid20c, via Fr, 1,2(2) **Cr** *di̱sko* M, mid20c, 1,2(2) **Bg** *di̱sko* N/cp[1] [U] end20c, 2(2 tech/you) **Fi** *disco*/*disko* 1970s, 1,2(3) **Hu** <=E> *di̱szkó* [=E] pl. *-k*, mid20c, 1(3 you); cp[1] *diszkózene* 2(3 you+5) **Al** *diskotek*/*disko* [diskote̱k] F, 1992, pl. *-a*, mid20c, 1,2(3) **Gr** *di̱sko* F, from *diskote̱k*, 1970s/80s, via Fr, 1(2) 2(1 obs)

discount *n.* 1 'a deduction from a bill or an amount due', +4 'a shop for cheap/wholesale goods'

Various forms of Italian and French provenance are in competition, but the [au] form clearly indicates that the commercial sense, which spread with chain stores from the 1950s onwards, is of American English provenance. Widespread in Western Europe, the term clearly shows the effects of a 'political lag'. Note that no verbal derivatives or borrowings are recorded.

Ge [diskau̱nt] M [U] 1960s (1 mod) = *-er*/*Diskonter* 'discount shop'; < 1: *Rabatt* **Du** [dis-kaunt/diskau̱nt] C, 1970s (2 tech) = *-er, -zaak, -winkel* **Nw** [=E] [U] 1990s, 1(1 obs, rare) **Fr** [diskunt/=E] M, 1960s, 1(2 tech, ban) +4(2 tech, ban) > 1: *ristourne, escompte*; +4: *magasin discompte* **Sp** (0) < 1: *descuento* **It** [diskau̱nt] M [U] 1980s, +4(2 tech) **Rm** <=E>/*discont* [=E/disko̱nt] N, 1990s, 1(0/1 tech) **Rs** (5It) **Cr** *di̱skont* M [U] end20c (2) → *-ni* adj. **Bg** - < 1: *sko̱nto* (5It) **Hu** - < *diszkont* [di̱skont] +4(5It) **Gr** <=E> [=E] N, 1980s, +4(1 mod)

discounter *n.* 1 'a person who deducts (esp. an amount from a bill)', 2 'a discount store' **Ge** [=E] M, pl. Ø, 1960s, 2(1 rare) **Du** [=E] C [U] 1980s, 2(2) < *discountzaak* **Fr** <=E>/*discounteur* [diskuntœr/diskauntœʀ] M, 1960s (1) = *discompteur* **Rs** *diskontë̱r* M, pl. *-y*, end20c (1 tech)

disk drive *n.* 'a mechanism for rotating a disk and reading or writing data from or to it' (comput.) **Ge** [=E] M/N, pl. *-s*, 1980s (1 tech) < *Laufwerk* **Du** [di̱skdrajv] C, 1980s (2 tech) **Nw** [=E] M, pl. *-s*, 1980s (1 tech, rare) < rend *diskettstasjon* **Ic** - < trsl *diskadrif* **Fr** *drive* [drajv] M (1 tech) = *gestionnaire périphérique* **Sp** - < *unidad de disco* **It** [=E] M, pl. Ø, 1970s (1 tech) **Rs** *di̱sk-drai̱ver*/*drai̱ver* M, pl. *-y*, 1980s (3 tech) **Po** <=E> M, end20c (1 tech) **Bg** *drai̱v* M, pl. *-a*/*-ove*, 1980s (3 tech) < rend *diskovo ustroĭstvo* **Fi** - < *levyasema* **Hu** [=E] [U] end20c (1 tech) **Gr** <=E> [=E] N, end20c (1 tech) > trsl *odhighos dhísku*

diskette *n.* 'a floppy disk'

The word has little English in its form, and may have been in existence in individual languages before the computer age (which would make it an extended meaning). Its status as an anglicism is open to doubt. **Ge** [diske̱tə] F, pl. *-n*, 1980s (3 tech) **Du** [diskɪtə] C, 1970s (1 tech) = *floppy, floppy-disk* **Nw** *diskett* [=E] M, pl. *-er*, 1980s (3 tech) **Ic** *disketta* [tɪskɛhta] F, pl. *-ur*, 1970s (2 tech, coll) > rend *disklingur* **Fr** <=E>

20c (1 ban) > *disquette* **Sp** *diskete*/*disquete*/*disquette* [diske̱t/diske̱te] M, pl. *-s*, 1970s (2) **It** *dischetto* [diske̱tto] M, pl. *-i*, 1960s (3) **Rm** *dischetă* [diske̱tə] F, end20c, via Fr (3 tech) **Rs** *diske̱ta* F, pl. *-y*, 1980s (3 tech) **Po** (5Fr) **Cr** *disketa* F, pl. *-e*, end20c (3 tech) **Bg** *diske̱ta* F, pl. *-ti*, 1980s, via Rs (3 tech) **Fi** *disketti* 1980s (3) = mean *levy*/*levyke* **Hu** *diszkett* [=E] pl. *-ek*, 1980s (1 tech/5Fr) < *floppy* **Al** *diskete̱* F, pl. *-a* (1 tech?) **Gr** *dhiske̱ta* F, end20c (3 tech)

Disneyland *n.* 1 'a showy reconstruction of a town based on theatrical make-believe, a fantastic world', 2 'proper name of a pleasure ground'

This term for a pleasure park named after Walt Disney (1901–66) seems to be becoming generic; its metaphorical meaning is difficult to document, and may in fact still be developing and not be fully conventional. **Ge** [di̱sne:lant] N [U] mid20c, 1(1 coll) 2(Ø) **Du** 2(Ø) **Nw** 2(Ø) **Ic** [=E] N [U] mid/end20c, 2(Ø) **Fr** (0) **Sp** *Disneylandia* F [U] end20c (Ø/2) **It** [disneilɛnd] M, mid20c, 2(2) **Rm** 2(Ø) **Rs** *disneĭlend* [U] end20c, 2(Ø) **Po** [-ejlent] M, end20c (2) **Cr** [=E] M [U] end20c, 2(2) **Bg** *Disnilend* M [U] 1990s (1 jour, rare) **Fi** 2(Ø) **Hu** [=E] M [U] pl. Ø, 1980s, 2(Ø) **Al** *disnejland* M [U] 1990, 2(you) **Gr** [di̱zneiland] F, mid20c, 2(Ø)

dispatch *n.* +4a 'a bonus for shipment', +5 'treatment of cargo' **Du** [=E] C [U] end20c, +5(1 tech) **Sp** - < *despachar* **Rs** *dispe̱tch* M [U] 20c, +4a (3 tech)/*dispach* **Bg** *dispa̱ch* M [U] 20c, +4a(3 tech)

dispatch *v.* +5 'distribute, expedite' **Fr** *dispatcher* [dispatʃe] 1970s (1 tech, ban) > *réguler, régulation, distribution dispatching* M **Cr** *dispećirati* mid20c (1 tech)

dispatcher *n.* +2 'a controller of the organization of public transport or of a production process', +5 'an organizer of labour in a planned economy'

This loanword is one of the few lexical items spread through Russian, as a term relating to the uniform organization of Communist economy. What seems to be the only Western exception is in fact a homonym whose meaning is independently derived. The 'Eastern' group of attestations has become obsolescent (notably in 'Eastern' German) through the reorganization of labour planning after the fall of Communism. **Ge** [dispe̱tʃa] M, pl. Ø, 1950s, via Rs, +5(1 reg/obs) **Fr** <=E>/*dispatcheur* [dispatʃœʀ] M, 1920s, +2(1 tech, ban) > *régulateur*/*régulatrice* **Rm** *dispecer* [dispe̱tʃer] M, mid20c, via Rs? (3)

(5) **Rs** *dispe̱tcher* M, pl. *-y*, beg20c, +2(2 tech) +5(2) → *-izatsiya* F; *-skiĭ* adj. **Po** *dyspeczer* M, beg20c, via Rs(1 arch) **Cr** *dispe̱ćer* M, pl. *-i*, mid20c, +5(1 tech) **Bg** *dispe̱cher* M, pl. *-i*, mid20c, via Rs, +2(3 tech) → *-ski* adj., *-izatsiya* F **Hu** *diszpécser*

[dispe:tʃer] pl. -ek, 20c, via Rs, +2(3) **Al** dispeçer [dispetʃer] M, pl. -ë, mid20c, +5(1 tech)

dispenser n. 2 'an automatic machine that dispenses an item or specific amount of something'

This word has the typical 'northwestern' distribution found with many post-war loanwords.

Ge [=E] M, pl. Ø, 1960s (1 tech) **Du** [=E] C, 1970s (1 tech) **Nw** [=E] M, pl. -e, mid20c (1 tech) **It** [dispenser] M, pl. Ø, 1960s (1 tech) = dosatore **Gr** dispenser N, mid20c, 2(1 tech)

displaced person n. '(post-1945) a refugee'

As a political term of 1945, this loanword was well-known in countries that had to deal with the associated social problems. Countries into which DPs were repatriated (unsurprisingly) tended to call these persons by other names.

Ge [=E] F, pl. -s, 1940s (1 arch) **Du** [=E] C, 1970s (1 jour) **Nw** [=E] M, pl. -s, 1940s (1 arch) **Fr** - < trsl personne déplacée **Sp** - < trsl despazado/a, persona desplacazada **Po** dipis/<=E> M, mid20c (1 tech, arch) **Cr** DP [depe] M/F, mid20c (3 tech) **Hu** [=E]/DP [de:pe:] pl. -k, mid20c (1 arch, rare)

display n. 1 'the act or an instance of displaying', 5a 'the presentation of signals or data on a visual display unit etc.', +5c 'a computer screen'

The currency of this anglicism was restricted to rare technical uses in Western Europe until the coming of the computer. The new meaning +5 has now boosted its use in the West and is often the only meaning elsewhere.

Ge [disple:] N, pl. -s, 1960s (1 tech) **Du** [=E] N, 1960s/70s (1 tech) **Nw** [=E] N, pl. -er, 1960s, 1(1 tech); 1970s, +5c(1 tech) **Fr** M, 1970s, 1(ban); +5c(1 tech, ban, obs) = carton (publicitaire); > +5c visuel, visu < écran, moni-

teur **Sp** [displei/displai] M, 1980s (1 tech) → displayar v. **It** [displei] M, pl. Ø/-s, 1970s, 5a(1 tech) **Rm** [=E] N, 1970s, +5c (1 tech) **Rs** displei M, pl. -i, end20c, +5c(1 tech) **Po** <=E> M, end20c, +5(1 tech) **Cr** [=E] M, pl. Ø, end20c, 1,+5c (1 tech) **Bg** displei M, pl. -eya/-ei, end20c, +5c (3 tech) **Fi** [=E] +5c(0) **Hu** [=E] pl. Ø, 1980s, +5c (1 tech) **Gr** <=E> N, end20c, 5a(1 tech)

dissenter n. 1 'a person who dissents (esp. politics)', 2 'a member of a non-established church'

Ge 2(Ø hist) **Du** [=E] C, beg20c (1) = 1: dissident **Nw** [=E] M, pl. -e, 20c (1 tech) **Sp** - < disidente **It** - < dissidente (5La) **Rs** dissenter M, pl. -y, 18/19c, 2(1 tech) **Bg** - < 1: disident **Hu** disszenter [dissenter] pl. -ek, 18c, 2(Ø)

Dixieland n. 2 'a kind of jazz or foxtrot'

Ge [diksilent] M [U] 1920s (1 obs) **Du** [diksilent] C [U] 1970s (1 tech) **Nw** [=E/-lan] M [U] beg20c (2) **Ic** [=E] N, freq. cp¹ [U] mid20c (2 tech) **Fr** <=E> M (1 tech) **Sp** <=E>/dixie [diksilan] M [U] mid20c (1 arch) **It** [diksilend] M [U] 1950s (1 tech) **Rm** [=E] N [U] mid20c (1 tech) **Rs** diksilend

dizzy adj. 1a 'giddy, unsteady'

Du [=E] 1990s (1 sla, mod) **Ic** [tɪs:i] end20c (1 sla)

DJ abbrev. 2 ↑'disc jockey'

This term is (still) slightly less frequent than the full form, although the acronym can be pronounced according to national conventions, and is thus easier to integrate.

Ge [di:dʒe:] M, pl. -s, 1970s (1 mod) < Discjockey **Du** d.j. [=E] C, 1970s (2); deejay [didʒej] M, 1970s (1 you) **Nw** [=E] M, pl. -er, 1980s (1 tech) **Ic** [=E] end20c (1 sla) < trsl PS **Fr** D.J. [déʒi/didʒe] mid20c (1 ban) > animateur **Sp** DJ/D.J./dj [dijei] pl. -s, 1970s (1 you) < disc-jockey, pinchadiscos **It** dee-jay/DJ/di gei [di dʒei] M, pl. Ø, 1960s (2 you) > disc jockey **Rm**

[=E] M, pl. Ø, end20c (1 you) **Rs** didzhei M, pl. -ei, end20c (1 you) **Cr** [di:dʒej] M, pl. -i, end20c (1) **Bg** <=E>/didzhei M, pl. -ei, 1990s (1 you/jour); <=E> (1 writ) **Fi** [=E] (2 you) **Hu** [=E/de:je:] pl. -k, mid20c (2) < trsl lemezlovas **Gr** [didzei] M/F, uninfl., 1980s (2 you, mod)

DNA abbrev. 'deoxyribonucleic acid'

This abbreviation is pronounced according to traditional conventions except in Greek, other languages (French, German, Romanian, Bulgarian) translate the term producing different acronyms.

Ge [de:ena] F [U] 1960s (3 tech) = trsl DNS **Du** [de:ɪn a:] N [U] 1970s (1 tech) **Nw** [de:ena:] N [U] 1950s (3 tech) **Ic** [tje:ɛn: a:] (freq. cp¹) mid20c (3 tech) = rend DKS **Fr** - < trsl ADN = acide désoxyribonucléique **Sp** [de-ene-a] M [U] mid20c (1 tech) = trsl ADN **It** [di-enne-a] M [U] 1950s (1 tech) **Rm** - < rend ADN **Rs** - < trsl DNK **Cr** (0) **Po** [de en a] end20c (2 tech) **Bg** - < trsl DNK > dezoksiribonukleinova kiselina **Fi** [de:ɛna:] (3) **Hu** < trsl dezoxiribonukleinsav/DNS (5) **Al** - < ADN **Gr** DNA [dienei] N [U] (1 tech)

dock n. 1 'an artificially enclosed body of water for the (un)loading and repair of ships', +6 'buildings around the dock', +7 'a cheap shop'

The etymology of this 'North Sea term' is opaque: it is attested for Dutch, Low German, and English in the fifteenth century and not all occurrences in other languages were necessarily borrowed from English (Semantic loans may also have played a part).

Ge [=E] N, pl. -s, 19c, 1(4) → andocken v.; docking N **Du** dok C, pl. -ken, 1(4) **Nw** dokk [=E] M/F, pl. -er, mid19c, 1(3) **Ic** dokk(a) [tohk(a)] F, pl. -ir (- ur) beg19c, 1(2 tech) = skipakví **Fr**

[dɔk] M, beg19c, 1,+6(2) +7(1 obs) **Sp** <=E> M, mid19c, 1(1 tech, rare) +6(1 tech, rare) = 1: *da̲rsena*; = +6: *almacén portuario* **It** [=E] M, pl. Ø/-*s*, 19c, 1(1) < *bacino, banchina* **Rm** *doc* [dok] N, beg19c, via Fr, 1,+6(3) **Rs** *dok* M, pl. -*i*, mid19c, 1,+6(3) **Po** *dok* M, mid19c, 1(3) → -*owanie* N **Cr** *dok* M, pl. -*ovi*, 19c (3) → -*ovanje* N **Bg** *dok* M, pl. -*a/-ove*, end19c, 1(2) → -*ov* adj.; -*uvane* N **Hu** *dokk* [=E] pl. -*ok*, 19c, 1(3) **Al** *dok* [dok] M, pl. -*e*, beg20c (3 tech) **Gr** *dok* N, 19c, 1(2)

dock *v.* 1 'bring or come into a dock', +4 'repair ships'
Ge *docken* (4) **Du** *dokken* [dɔkə(n)] 1(4) **Nw** *dokke* [dɔ̲ke] 19c (3 tech) **Rm** *andoca* [andoka̲] mid20c, 1(5Ge) **Po** (o) **Cr** *do̲kovati* (3 tech) **Bg** *doku̲vam* +4(3 tech) **Hu** *dokkol* [do̲kkol] 19c, 1(3 tech)

docker *n.* 'a man who (un-)loads or repairs ships in a dock'
This term obviously spread in connection with the more frequent *dock*, and together with a host of other shipping terms. However it has been frequently replaced by compounds ('dock worker') or translations.
Ge [do̲ka] M, pl. Ø, 19c (1 tech) **Du** *dokker* C (5) - < *dokwerker* **Fr** [dɔkɛʀ] M, end19c (2) < *débardeur* **Sp** [do̲ker] M, mid20c (1 tech, rare) < *estibador* **It** [dɔ̲ker] M, pl. Ø, 1900s (1 tech) < *scaricatore* M **Rm** *docher*

[doke̲r] M, 19c, via Fr (3) **Rs** *do̲ker* M, pl. -*y*, beg20c (2) **Po** *doker* [doker] M, mid19c (2) **Cr** *do̲ker* M, 19c (1 tech) **Bg** *do̲ker* M, pl. -*i*, beg20c (2) → -*ski* adj. **Hu** *dokker* [do̲kker] pl. -*ek*, 19c (1 tech, arch) < *dokkmunkás* **Al** *doker* [do̲ker] M, pl. -*ë*, beg20c (1 tech)

docking *n.* 'a manœuvre to join two space-ships'
Ge [=E] N [U] 1970s (1 tech) **Du** - < *koppelingsmanoeuvre* **Nw** [=E] M [U] 1970s (1 tech) **Fr** - < *arrimage* **It** [dɔking] M [U] 1970s (1 tech) < *agganciamento* **Po** (o) **Hu** *dokkol* [do̲kkol] 1970s (1 tech) → -*ás* n.

docksiders* *n pl.* 'shoes for sailing or leisure'
Nw [=E] 1980s (1 mod) **Fr** <=E> 20c (1 mod) **Fi** [=E]^TM; *dokkarit* (1 you, rare)

doeskin *n.* 2 'a kind of cloth'
Ge [do̲:skin] M/N [U] beg20c (1 tech, rare) **Hu** [do̲: skin] cp¹, end19c/beg20c (1 tech, arch)

dog *n.* +1c 'a large dog', +8 'a special breed of dog'
The Continental languages appear to have borrowed the English word to designate a specific, powerful mastiff, supplementing *Hund*, etc. Note that in English *hound* and *dog* changed places with *dog* becoming the generic term). A second wave of borrowing came when terms for canine breeds were borrowed from English *en masse* in the late nineteenth century.
Ge *Dogge* F, pl. -*n*, 17c, +8(3) **Du** [dɔx] C, pl. -*gen*, 17c, +8(3) **Nw** *dogg(e)* [=E/do̲ge] M, pl. -*er*, mid19c, +1c(1 arch) **Ic** *doggur* [tɔk:ʏr] M, pl. -*ar*, 17c, +1c(3 obs) **Fr** *dogue* [dɔg] M, 14c, +8(3) **Sp** *dogo* M, pl. -*s*, mid17c, +8(3 tech) **Rm** [=E] M, 19c,

via Fr, +8(3) **Rs** *dog* M, pl. -*i*, beg20c, +8(3) **Po** [dok] M, mid19c, +8(3) **Cr** *do̲ga* M, pl. -*e*, mid19c, +8(2) **Bg** *dog* M, pl. -*al-ove*, beg20c, via Fr, +8(3) **Hu** [dog] esp. as cp², pl. -*ok*, end19c/beg20c, +8(2>3) **Al** *dok* [dok] M [U] mid20c, +8(1 reg)

dog cart *n.* 'a two-wheeled horse-cart'
One of the many terms for fashionable horse-drawn vehicles which quickly became obsolete with the advent of the motorcar. The object and the name are no longer known, and certainly not used, outside museum contexts.
Ge [=E] M, pl. -*s*, end19c (1 arch) **Du** <=E>/*dogkar*/*dokkaart* [do̲kart] C, 1950s (1 tech) **Nw** [=E] M, pl. -*er*, 20c (1 tech) **Fr** [dɔgkaʀ(t)] M, mid19c (1 tech) **Sp** <=E> M, beg20c (1 tech, arch) **Rm**

docar [doka̲r] N, beg20c (1 arch/tech) **Hu** [=E] pl. -*ok*, end19c/beg20c (1 arch)

dogskin *n.* 'sheep leather'
Ge [=E] N [U] beg20c (1 tech) **Nw** *doggskinn* [=E/-ʃin] N [U] beg20c (1 tech)

do-it-yourself *phr./cp¹.* '(of work, esp. building, painting, decorating) done by amateurs at home'
This term – of complicated morphology for all receiver languages – has been popular in most of Europe since the 1950s. It has since – somewhat unexpectedly – been largely replaced by native terms, either calques or independent coinages.
Ge [=E] N [U] 1950s (1 obs) < *Heimwerker* **Du** - < trsl *doe-het-zelf* **Nw** - < trsl *gjør-det-selv* **Ic** [=E] end20c (0 coll) **Fr** - < trsl *faites-le vous-même*; < *bricolage* **Sp** - < *bricolage* **It** [=E] M [U] 1980s (2) < trsl *fai da te, bricolage* **Rs** - < trsl *sde̲laǐ sam* **Po** (0) **Cr** (0) **Bg** - < trsl *napravi si sa̲m* **Fi** - < trsl *tee-[se]-itse* **Hu** - < trsl *csináld magad* **Al** - < *ve̲t shër-bim* **Gr** - < trsl *kan' to monos su*

Dolby *n.* 'an electronic noise-reduction system' (named after the inventor R.M. Dolby)
Ge [=E] N [U] 1980s (1 tech) **Du** [dɔlbi] C [U] 1980s (2 tech) **Nw** [=E] M [U] 1970s (1 tech) **Ic** [=E] end20c (1 tech) **Fr** [dɔlbi] M, 1980s (1 tech) **Sp** <=E> M [U] 1980s (1 tech) **It** [dɔlbi] M [U] 1980s (1 tech) **Rm** [do̲lbi] N [U] 1980s (1 tech) **Rs** *siste̲ma Do̲lbi* F, uninfl. [U] end20c (1 tech) **Po** <=E> N, uninfl., 1980s (1 tech) **Cr** *dolbi siste̲m* M, end20c (1 tech) **Bg** *sistema Do̲lbi* F, end20c (5+1 tech) **Fi** [=E] (1 tech) **Hu** [=E] [U] end20c (1 tech); *Dolby-féle szűrő* (1 tech+5) **Gr** <=E>/*dolby* N [U] 1980s (1 tech)

doll *n.* 2a 'a pretty but silly young woman'
Nw *dolle* [ˈdo̲le] M/F, pl. -*r*, 20c (3 fac) → *dollete*

dollar *n.* 1 'a monetary unit in USA etc'
Although this word refers to the name of the US currency (and a few other less well-known units), it is

frequently used in a more generic sense, esp. in compounds (↑*Euro-*, *petro-*).
Ge [d<u>o</u>la(r)] M, pl. *-s*, 19c (Ø/2)   **Du** [d<u>ɔ</u>lar] C, 19c (Ø/2)   **Nw** [=E] M, pl. Ø/*-s*, mid19c (2)   **Ic** *dollar(i)* [tɔl:ar(ı)] M, pl. *-ar*, 1880s (Ø) > rend *dalur*   **Fr** [dɔlaʀ] M, mid18c (Ø/2)   **Sp** *dólar* pl. *-es*, end19c (3) → *dolarización*   **It** *d<u>o</u>llaro* M, pl. *-i*, beg19c (3)   **Rm** *dolar* [dolar] M, mid19c (3)   **Rs** *d<u>o</u>llar* M, pl. *-y*, mid19c (3) → *-ovyï* adj.   **Po** *dolar* [dolar] M, mid19c, via Ge (3) → *-ówka* F; *-owy* adj.   **Cr** *d<u>o</u>lar* M, pl. *-i*, end19c, via Ge (3) → *-ski* adj.   **Bg** *d<u>o</u>lar* M, pl. *-al-i*, end19c (2) → *-ov* adj.   **Fi** *dollari* 19c (Ø/2); *taala* (Ø fac)   **Hu** *dollár* [d<u>o</u>lla:r] also cp², pl. *-ok*, 17/18c (Ø,2)   **Al** <=E> [doll<u>a</u>r] M, pl. *-ë*, end19c (3)   **Gr** *dhollario*, N, 19c? (3/Ø)

doll up   *v.* 'dress up smartly'
Nw *dolle opp* ["d<u>o</u>le] end20c (3 coll) → *oppdolla* adj.

dolly   *n.* 2 'a movable platform for a cine-camera'
Sp <=E>/*doly* [d<u>o</u>li] F, 20c (1 tech)   **It** [d<u>ɔ</u>lli] M, pl. Ø, 1960s (1 tech) < *carrello*   **Rm** [=E] N, end20c (1 tech)   **Hu** [=E] pl. Ø, 20c (1 tech)

done   *adv.* +4 'utterly, completely'
Nw *dønn* [døn] 19c (3 coll)

donkey engine   *n./cp¹* 'a small auxiliary engine'
Du *donkey* [=E] C, beg20c (1 tech)   **Nw** *donkey* [=E/d<u>u</u>nke] cp¹ + *maskin*, beg20c (1 tech)

donor   *n.* 1 'a person who gives or donates something (for charity)', 2 'one who provides blood for transfusion, semen for insemination, or (esp.) an organ for transplantation', 4 'an impurity atom in a semiconductor which contributes a conducting electron to the material'
Du [do:nɔr] C, pl. *-s/donoren*, mid20c (3)   **Nw** [dun<u>u</u>:r] M, pl. *-er*, mid20c, 1(3 rare) 2(3 tech) < 2: *blodgiver*   **Sp** - < *donante*   **It** - < *donatore* (5La)   **Rm** [don<u>o</u>r] M, 1970s, 4(3 tech); mid20c?, via Fr, 2(3 rare) < *donator* 1(5Fr) 2(5)   **Rs** *d<u>o</u>nor* M, pl. *-y*, 2(3 tech) 4(1 tech) → *-skiĭ* adj.   **Po** *donator* (5La)   **Bg** *d<u>o</u>nor* M, pl. *-i*, mid20c, 2(2) → *-ski* adj.   **Hu** [=E] pl. *-ok*, 1950s, 2(5La)   **Al** *donator* [donat<u>a</u>r] M, pl. *-ë*, mid20c (5La)   **Gr** - < 1,2: mean *dhoritis*

doodle   *v.* 'scribble or draw absent-mindedly'
Du [=E] C, 1990s (1) = *droedelen*   **Nw** *drodle* ["dr<u>o</u>dle] 1970s? (3)

doomwriting*   *n.* 'a pessimistic view of the future, the prophesying of disasters'
It [d<u>u</u>mraitiŋ] M, pl. Ø, 20c (1 rare) = *rovinografia*

door-to-door   *cp¹/adv.* 'a type of mail-order'
Ge - < *Haus-zu-Haus-(Lieferung)*   **Du** - < trsl *huis aan huis*   **Nw** - < trsl *dør-til- dør*   **Fr** - < *porte-à-porte*   **Sp** - < trsl *de puerta, a puerta, a domicilio*   **It** [do:tudo:] adv. (o) < trsl *porta a porta*   **Fi** - < trsl *ovi ovelta*   **Hu** - < rend *háztólházig*   **Al** - < trsl *derë më derë*   **Gr** <=E>/*dor tu dor* adv., end20c (1 tech)

dope   *n.* 4a 'a narcotic', 4b 'a drug given to a horse, or taken by an athlete, to affect performance'
Ge [do:p] N/F [U] 1970s (1 you)   **Du** [do:p] C, 1950s (2)   **Nw** *dop* [du:p] N [U] 1960s (3)   **Ic** *dóp* [tou:p] N [U] 1970s, 4a(3 coll) → *dópisti* M; *dópismi* M; *dóperí*

N   **Fr** [dɔp] F, 1940s (2)   **Cr** - < *doping*   **Hu** - < *doppingszer*   **Al** - < *doping/narkotik* end20c (3)   **Gr** *dop/dopa* N/F [U] end20c, 4a(1 sla/3sla)

dope   *v.* 1 'administer dope to, drug', 4 'take addictive drugs' +5 'stimulate'
Ge [do:pən] 1970s, 1(3)   **Du** *dopen* [do:pən] 1960s, 1(2)   **Nw** ["du:pe] 1960s, 1,+5(3) → *dopa* adj.   **Ic** *dópa (sig)* 1970s, 4(2 coll) → *dópaður* adj.   **Fr** *doper* [dɔpe] beg20c, 1(3); mid20c, +5(3) → *dopeur* M   **Sp** *dopar* mid20c, via Fr, 1,+5(3) = *drogar* → *dopado, dopante*   **It** *dopare/doparsi* 1960s (3 rare) < *drogare, drogarsi* → *dopato* adj.   **Rm** *dopa* [dopa] (also refl.) mid20c, 1,+5(3)   **Cr** - < *dopingirati*   **Bg** - < *dopingiram* → *-iran* adj.   **Fi** *doupata* 1990s (1 sla, you)   **Hu** - < *doppingol*   **Gr** *dop<u>a</u>ro(-me)* end20c, 1(2), +5(2 coll, jour) → *dop<u>a</u>risma* N

Ic	Nw	Po	Rs
Du	Ge	Cr	Bg
Fr	It	Fi	Hu
Sp	Rm	Al	Gr

doping   *n.* 1 'the practice of taking/administering drugs to enhance athletic performance' +5 'a stimulant for support during sporting competitions'
This term has become universal through international sports events (mainly in athletics, cycling, and swimming) since the 1960s. The accompanying verb is less widespread, and its semantic overlap with the noun suggests it is backformed in many languages rather than borrowed. Less frequent is the use of ↑*dope n.* for drugs (where *doping* is preferred).
Ge [do:piŋ] N [U] 1960s, 1(2)   **Du** [=E] C [U] 1950s (2)   **Nw** [du:piŋ/"du:piŋ] M/F [U] 1950s (2)   **Fr** [dɔpiŋ] M, beg20c, 1(2 ban) > *dopage*   **Sp** <=E> M [U] mid20c, 1(2) < *dopage*   **It** [d<u>o</u>pinŋ] M [U] 1950s, 1(2)   **Rm** [doping] N [U] 1950s, 1(2 tech)   **Rs** *doping* M [U] beg20c (2) → *-ovyï* adj.   **Po** [dopink] M [U] beg20c (2) → *-owanie* N, v.; *z*-v.; *-ujcy* M/adj.; *-owy* adj.   **Cr** *doping* M [U] mid20c, 1(2)   **Bg** *doping* M [U] mid20c, via Fr, +5(3) → *-ov* adj.   **Fi** [=E] 1980s (2)   **Hu** *dopping* [d<u>o</u>ppiŋ] pl. Ø, 19c, +5(3); 1: ↑*dope* n.   **Al** <=E> [doping] M [U] mid20c (1 reg)   **Gr** *doping* N [U] end20c, 1(2) +5(2 coll, jour) → *dope* adj.

double   *n.* 3 'a game between two pairs of players' (tennis), +9 'two cards with the same suit or value' (cards)
Loanwords from Latin, French and English, all from the same source and all similar in form, compete; identification of an anglicism rests on <b>, the vowel, and the domain and time of acceptance. Romance languages often use the native term, Germanic languages the older Latin loan. The term for the film 'stand-in' is pronounced the French way in German (the meaning is in fact not recorded for English).
Ge (o arch) < *Doppel*   **Du** - < *dubbelspel*   **Nw** [=E] M [U] beg20c, 3(1 tech)   **Fr** [dubl] 1930s, 3(4)   **Sp** - < 3: mean *doble(s)*   **It** - < 3: *doppio*; +9: *coppia*   **Rm** - < 3: mean *dublu*; +9: mean *dublă*   **Rs** *dabl* M [U]

end20c, 3(1 tech)   **Po** *debel* [de-beli] M [U] beg20c (1 tech)   **Cr** *debl* M, beg20c, 3(1 tech)   **Bg** *dabŭls* M, end20c, 3(1 tech); *dubŭl* +9(5Fr) < 3: creat *igra po dvoĭki* **Fi** *tupla* beg20c, +9(5Sw)   **Hu** [=E] [U] 19c (51t) (1 tech) < 3: *kettős*   **Al** - < *dopio* +9 (1 tech); - < 3: trsl *dhiplo*

double-decker   *n.* 1 'a bus having an upper and a lower deck', +3 'an aircraft with a double pair of wings'
Ge - < trsl *Doppeldecker*   **Du** *dubbeldekker* [dybəl-dɛkər] C, 1960s (3)   **Nw** <=E> 20c (1) < trsl *dobbelt-dekker*   **Ic** - < +3 *tvípekja*   **Rs** (0)   **Bg** (0)

double-face* *n.* /cp¹ 'a kind of cloth'
Ge [dablfe:s] M/N [U] 1960s, via Fr (1 tech, rare)   **Du** [=E] 1990s (1 tech)   **Nw** [=E] M [U] 20c (1 tech)   **Fr** (5)   **It** [dublǝfas/dublefas] cp², 1900s (5Fr)   **Rm** [dubl fas] N [U] mid20c (5Fr)   **Rs** *dabl-feĭis* M [U] 1990s (1 tech, rare)   **Bg** - < *duble* (5Fr)   **Gr** *dubl fas/dubl(e) fas* N [U] (5Fr)

double-faced   *adj.* 2 '(of fabric or material) finished on both sides so that either may be used as the right side'
Ge [du:bəl fa:s] *n.* M/N [U] 1960s (1 tech, rare)   **Nw** [=E] 20c [U] (1 tech)   **Fr** (5)   **It** *double-face* (5Fr)   **Rm** - < rend *cu două feţe*   **Bg** - < rend *s dve litsa*   **Gr** *dubl fas/dubl(e) fas* adj., 20c (5Fr)

double-scull* *n.* 'a rowing-boat with two scullers'
Nw *dobbeltsculler* [dobeltskøler] M, pl. -e, 20c (5+1 tech)   **Fr** [dublǝskœl] M, 19c (1 tech)   **It** [d∧belsk∧l] M, pl. Ø, 1920s (1 tech)   **Bg** - < trsl *dvoĭka skul* (5+1 tech)

doubleton* *n.* 'two cards of the same suit' (cards)
Du [=E] C, 1970s (1 tech)   **Nw** [=E] M, pl. Ø, 20c (1 tech)   **It** [d∧blton] M, pl. Ø, 1960s (1 tech)   **Bg** - < *dubŭl* (5Fr)

doughnut (*US donut*)   *n.* 1 'a small fried cake'
This item has started to compete with similar cakes in West European countries, and the loanword has come to be preferred for its 'modern' appeal. It seems too early to say whether the special type of cake and the English name will establish itself – and in which spelling.
Ge *Donut* [dɔ:nat] M, pl. -s, 1990s (1 mod)   **Du** [dɔnʏt] M, 1990 (2)   **Nw** [=E] M, pl. -s, 1990s (1 mod, rare)   **Ic** *dónut* [=E] uninfl., mid/end20c (Ø>1 coll) < rend *kleinuhringur* **Sp** *donut* [donut] M, pl. -s, 1970s (2>3)   **Po** (0)   **Cr** (0)   **Fi** *donitsi* (2)   **Gr** *donat/* <donut> N, pl. Ø/-s, end20c (2)

Douglas fir   *n.* 'a variety of fir tree'
Ge *Douglasie/Douglastanne* [-u:-] F, mid20c (3 tech)   **Du** 20c (name+5)   **Nw** *Douglasgran* 20c (name +5)   **Fr** *douglas* M, mid19c (3 tech)   **It** *douglasia* [duglazia] M, pl. Ø, mid20c (1 tech) < *abete americano*;

also cp²: *legno douglas*   **Rm** *duglas/douglas* [duglas] M, 20c (1 tech)   **Po** *daglezja* [daglezia] F, mid20c (1 tech)   **Hu** *duglász (fenyő)* [dugla:s] pl. -ok, beg20c (3+5)

dowlas* *n.* 'a kind of cloth'
Ge *Dowlas/Daulas* [=E] N [U] beg20c (1 tech, rare)

down   *adj.* 4a 'depressed'
One of a set of predicative uninflected adjectives all of which are modern, but which have strikingly differ-ent distributions (cf. *high, in, out*). The homonymous command to dogs was used in the early twentieth century, but appears to be obsolete today (German).
Ge [daun] uninfl., 1960s (1 coll)   **Du** [daun] uninfl., beg20c (1 coll)   **Nw** [=E] end20c (1 coll, rare)   **Ic** *dán* [tau:n] uninfl., end20c (1 sla)   **It** - < *giù* adv.; *depresso, -a* adj.   **Cr** (0)   **Fi** [daun] uninfl., end20c (1 coll)   **Gr** *daun* 20c (1 coll)

downforce* *n.* 'downward force created to improve roadholding in cars'
Fi [=E] end20c (1 tech)

downhill   *n.* 1a 'a downhill race in mountain biking'
Ge [=E] M/N [U] 1990s (1 tech, mod) → -*er* M   **Du** [=E] C, 1990s (1 tech, mod)

down market   *adj.* 'towards or relating to the cheaper section of the market'
Du [daunma:kǝt] uninfl., 1980s (1 tech)   **Nw** [=E] end20c (1 tech)   **Fi** (0)

downsizing   *n.* 'a reduction of staff numbers'
Ge [=E] N [U] 1990s (1 tech, euph)   **Du** [=E] [U] 1990s (1 tech)   **Nw** [=E] M [U] 1990s (1 tech, euph)   **Fr** <=E> 1990s (1 ban) < *micromisation*   **It** [=E] M [U] 1990s (1 tech, euph)

Down's syndrome   *n.* 'a congenital disorder due to a chromosomal defect'
John Langdon-Down (1828–96) described the dis-ease otherwise popularly known as mongolism (now often avoided as descriptively inadequate and politic-ally incorrect); the term *D.S.* is, however, still re-stricted to specialists' uses.
Ge *Down Syndrom* [daunzyn-dro:m] N, pl. -e, 1980s (1 tech +5Gr)   < *Mongolismus* **Du** [daunsindro:m] N, pl. -*syndro-men*, 1980s (1 tech)   **Nw** *Downs syndrom* [=E+Nw] end20c (1 tech) = *mongolisme*   **Ic** *Downs-syndróm* N [U] 1970s (1 tech)   **Fr** - < *trisomie*   **Sp** *síndrome de Down* M (1 tech) < *mongolismo*   **It** *sin-drome di Down* (1 tech) < *mongolismo*   **Rm** *sindromul lui Down* N (5+1 tech) < *mongolism*   **Rs** *sindrom Dauna* (1 tech)   **Po** *Down* M [U] mid20c (1 coll)   **Cr** (0)   **Bg** *sindrom na Daun* (1 tech)   **Fi** *Downin syn-drooma* (1 tech)   **Hu** *Down-kór* [daun- ko:r] [U] 20c (1 tech+5) < *mongolizmus* → -*os* adj.   **Al** - < rend *mon-golizëm/mongolism por edle Dauni*   **Gr** *syndhromo Down* (1 tech)

downlights*   *n.* 'a small lamp that throws the light downwards'
Ge [=E] only pl., 1980s (1 tech, mod)   **Nw** [=E] N only pl., 1980s (1 tech, mod)

down period*   *n.* 'a period of depression, bad luck, poor results etc.' (esp. sport)
Nw *downperiode* [=E+Nw] 1950s (2)

downtown   *adj./n.* '(an area) in the lower or more central part of a town or city'
Ge [=E] 1960s (Ø >1 jour, mod)   **Nw** [=E] 1960s (1)   **Ic** [=E] (Ø)   **Sp** [daun taun] M [U] 1990s (Ø jour, rare)   **Cr** (o)   **Gr** <=E>/*daun taun* F/N, 1990s (o>1 jour, mod/Ø)

draft   *n.* 1a 'a preliminary written version', +8 'a chart, a map for navigation at sea', +9 'a drawing produced by a draftsman'
Du [=E] 1990s, 1a(1 jour)   **Nw** [=E] N, pl. Ø, 1970s, 1a(1 tech); [draft] 19c, +8(3)   **Cr** *draft* M, pl. *-ovi*, 1970s, 1a(1 tech) → *-irati* v.   **Hu** [=E] pl. *-ok*, mid20c, 1a(1 jour) +9(1 tech)

drag   *n.* 4 'an apparatus for recovering drowned people', 7a 'women's clothes worn by men', +13 'a dredge'
Du *dreg* 11c, 4,+13(5)   **Nw** [=E] [U] 1980s, 7a(1)   **Ic** *dragg* [trak:] N [U] end20c, 7a(2 sla)   **Fr** *drague* [dʀag] F, 16c, +13(3) → *draguer* v.   **Sp** [drag] end 20c, 7a (1 sla)   **It** - < *draga* (5Fr) → *dragare, dragaggio*   **Rm** *dragă* [dragə] F, end19c, 4,+13(5Fr)   **Rs** *draga* F, pl. *-i*, beg20c, 4,+13(1 tech) → *-irovat'* v.; *-er* M   **Po** *draga* [draga] F, beg20c, 4,+13(1 tech) → *dragowanie* N; *dragować* v.   **Bg** *draga* F, pl. *-gi*, beg20c, via Rs, +13(3 tech) → *-zhen* adj; *dragiram* v; *dragyor* M   **Al** *dragë* [dragë] F, pl. *-ve*, mid20c, 4(1 tech)

dragline   *n.* 'an excavator with a bucket pulled in by a wire rope'
Du [dreglajn] M, 1950s (1 tech)   **Fr** [dʀaglajn] F, 1950s (1 tech/ban) = *défonceuse tractée*   **Rm** *draglină* [draglinə] F, beg20c (3 tech)   **Rs** *draglaĭn* M, pl. *-y*, mid20c (1 tech)   **Bg** *draglaĭn* M, pl. *-al-i*, mid20c (1 tech)

drag queen   *n.* 'a male homosexual transvestite'
Du [=E] C, pl. *-s*, 1980s (1 tech)   **Nw** [=E] M, pl. *-s*, 1980s (Ø/1 rare)   **Ic** *drag(g)drottning* [=E] F, end20c (2+5)   **Fr** (o)   **Sp** [drag kwin] M, pl. *-s*, 1980s (1 tech)   **Fi** [=E] 1980s (Ø/1 tech)

drag (race)   *n.* 9b 'an acceleration race between cars'
Nw [=E] N, pl. Ø, end20c (1 tech)   **Ic** [=E] end20c (o tech)   **Fi** (o) = *kiihdytysajot*   **Gr** *aghones dragster* end20c (5+1 tech)

drag show   *n.* 'a show where male actors wear make-up and women's clothes and impersonate women'
Nw [=E] N, pl. Ø, *-s*, 1980s (1)   **Ic** [traksjou:] N, pl. Ø, end20c (1 coll)   **Fi** (o)   **Gr** <=E>/*drag sou* N, pl. Ø/*-s*, 1980s (1 sla)

dragster   *n.* 'a car built or modified to take part in drag races'
Ge (Ø)   **Du** [=E] 1990s (1 tech)   **Nw** [=E] M, pl. *-e*, 1960s (1 tech)   **Ic** [=E] end20c (o tech) < rend grind   **Fr** [dʀagstɛʀ] M, mid20c (1 tech)   **Sp** [draster]

M, pl. Ø/*-s*, end20c (1 tech)   **It** [dragster] M, pl. Ø. 1970s (1 tech)   **Rs** *dragstër* M, pl. *-y*, 1990s (1 tech, rare)   **Bg** *dragster* M, pl. *-al-i*, 1990s (1 jour, rare)   **Fi** *dragsteri* (1 tech)   **Gr** <=E>/*dragster* N, end20c (Ø)

drain   *n.* 1a 'a channel, conduit, or pipe carrying off liquid, esp. an artificial conduit for water or sewage', 1b 'a tube' (med.), 2 'a constant outflow' (cf. ↑*braindrain*)

Whereas ↑*drainage* and the underlying verb ↑*drain* were transmitted via French to almost all languages in the nineteenth century and often exhibit this transmission in their form, the noun *drain* often came in straight from English. The medical term and uses modelled on ↑*braindrain* have been adopted only on a limited scale.

Ge *Drain/Drän* [dre:n] M, pl. *-s*, end19c, via Fr, 1a(o arch) 1b(1 tech)   **Du** [dre:n] C, 1970s, 1a,b(1 tech)   **Nw** *dren* [drɛn] N, pl. Ø, 20c, 1a,b(3 tech)   **Ic** *dren* [trɛ:n] N, pl. Ø, mid/end20c, via Da, 1a(2 tech)   **Fr** [dʀɛ̃] M, mid19c (3)   **Sp** *dren* M, via Fr, 1a,b(2 tech); < 2: *drenaje*   **It** - < *drenaggio* (5Fr)   **Rm** *dren* [dren] N, mid19c, via Fr, 1a,b(3 tech)   **Rs** *drena* F/*dren* M, pl. *-y*, mid20c, 1a(3)   **Po** *dren* [dren] M, mid19c, 1a,b(3) → *-ik* M; *-arka* F; *-owanie* N; *-owy* adj.; *-owany* adj.; *-arski* adj.   **Cr** *dren*, end19c, 1b(1 tech) → *drenaža* F   **Bg** *dren* M, pl. *-al-ove*, 20c, via Fr, 1b(3 tech) → *drenche* N   **Hu** *drén* [dre:n] pl. *-ek*, mid19c, 1a,b(1 tech); *dréncső*, pl. *-vek*, 1a,b(1 tech+5)   **Al** *drenë* F, pl. *-a*, beg20c, 1a,b(1 tech)

drain   *v.* 1a 'make (land) dry', 1c 'drain a wound'
Ge *drainieren/-ä-*[dre:-] end19c, via Fr? (3)   **Du** *drainieren* [drɪne:rən] 19c, via Fr (2)   **Nw** *drene/drenere* ["dre:ne/dre:re] beg20c (3 tech)   **Fr** *drainer* [dʀene] mid19c (3)   **Sp** *drenar* 19/20c, via Fr (3/5Fr)   **It** *drenare*

mid20c, (3)   **Rm** *drena* [drena] mid19c, via Fr (3 tech)   **Rs** *drenirovat'* mid20c, via Fr (3 tech) → *-irovanie* v.   **Po** *drenować* [drenovatç] mid19c (2) → *wy-*v.   **Cr** *drenirati* end19c, 1c(2)   **Bg** *dreniram* 20c, via Fr (3 tech)   **Hu** *drénez* [dre:nez] end19/beg20c (3 tech) → *-és* n.   **Al** *drenoj* 20c (3 tech)

drainage   *n.* 1 'a process or means of draining'
Ge *Drainage/-ä-*[dre:na:ʒə] F, pl. *-n*, end19c, via Fr (3)   **Du** [drɪna:ʒe] C, 19c, via Fr(2)   **Nw** (o) < *drenering*   **Fr** [dʀena3] M, mid19c (3)   **Sp** *drenaje* M, 19/20c, via Fr (3)   **It** *drenaggio* (5Fr)   **Rm** *drenaj* [drena3] N, beg20c, via Fr (3 tech)   **Rs** *drenazh* M [U] mid20c, via Fr (2 tech) → *-nyĭ* adj.   **Po** *drenaż* [drena3] M [U] mid20c (2 tech) → v.; *wy-*v.; *-owy* adj.   **Cr** *drenaža* F, pl. *-e*, mid20c (1 tech)   **Bg** *drenazh* M, pl. *-al-i*, 20c, via Fr (3 tech)   **Hu** *drenázs*

[drena:ʒ] [U] end19/beg20c, via Fr (3 tech) **Al** *drenazh* [drenaʒ] M, pl. *-e*, mid20c (1 tech) **Gr** *drenaz* N, 20c, via Fr(3)

dram *n.* 1 'a small drink of spirits', 2 'a drachm'
Du C [U] 19c?, 1(1) **Nw** [dram] M, pl. *-mer*, 19c, 1(3) **Ic** *dramm* [tram:] N [U] mid19c, via Da 1(3) → *drammari* M **Bg** *dram* M, pl. *-a*, 19c, 2(5Gr)

draw *n.* 4 'a drawn game'
Du [=E] C, 1910s (2 tech/arch) **Rm** [draw/dro] N, mid20c (1 tech, rare) < *meci egal*

drawback *n.* 1 'a feature making something less satisfactory, a disadvantage', 3 'a return of import tax' **Ge** (0) < *Nachteil, Haken* **Du** [=E] C, beg20c (1) **Nw** [=E] N, pl. Ø, beg20c, 1(2) < *ulempe* **Fr** [drobak] M, mid/end18c, 3 (1 tech, ban) < *rembours* **It** [dro:bɛk] M, pl. Ø, 1940s, 3 (1 tech)

dreadlocks *n. pl.* 1 'a Rastafarian hairstyle'
Ge (Ø) **Du** [drɛdlɔks] 1980s (2) **Nw** [=E] pl./sg., M [U] 1970s (1 tech) **Ic** [=E] 1970s (Ø) **Gr** (Ø)

dreadnought *n.* 'a type of battleship greatly superior to its predecessors when first launched in 1906'
This term was universally known (and became generic) in the first decades of the twentieth century. Technological progress soon made this type of ship redundant and the word appears to be no longer current in any of the languages investigated. English pronunciation appears to have been the rule.
Ge [=E?] M, pl. *-s*, beg20c (1 arch) **Du** [drɪdno:t] C, beg20c (1 tech) **Nw** [=E] M, pl. *-er*, 20c (1 tech) **Fr** [=E] M, beg20c (1 arch) **Sp** - < *acorazado* **It** [drɛdno:t] F, pl. Ø, 1910s (1 tech) **Rm** [=E] N, beg20c (1 tech) **Rs** *drednout* M, pl. *-y*, beg20c (1 tech, arch) **Po** *drednot*/<=E> [-not] M, mid20c (1 tech) **Cr** *drednot* M, pl. *-ovi*, mid20c (1 tech) **Bg** *drednaut* M, pl. *-al-i*, beg20c, via Rs (3 tech, arch) **Hu** [drɛdno:t] pl. *-ok*, beg20c (1 tech) < *csatahajó* **Gr** *drednot*/*drɛtnot* N, beg20c (1 tech, obs)

dream team *n.* 1 (proper name) 'the US national basketball team', +1a 'any sports team with many star performers and an outstanding reputation'
Ge [=E] 1990s (0>1 tech) **Du** Ø **Nw** [=E] N, pl. Ø, end20c [=E] (1 mod) **Fr** Ø **Sp** [drimtim] M, end20c (1 tech) **It** [=E] F, pl. Ø, end20c (1 tech, jour) **Cr** [=E] M [U] 1990s, +1a(1 tech) **Hu** - < trsl *álomcsapat* **Gr** <=E>/*drim tim* N/F, 1980s, 1(Ø) +1a(1 tech)

dredge *n.* 'an apparatus used to scoop up objects or to clear mud etc.'
Ge *Dredsche* F, pl. *-n*, beg20c (3 tech) = *Schleppnetz*

dress *n.* 2 'clothing, esp. a whole outfit etc.', +5 'a training suit', +6 'tights', +7 'a swimming suit', +8 'a men's suit'
Apart from some fashionable uses of this word for formal and ceremonial costume around 1900, the loanword now appears to be confined to sports dress

and related items (except for Icelandic and Norwegian)
Ge [dres] M/N/F, pl. *-eslen*, beg20c, +5(1 coll) 1960s, 2(1 coll, jour) **Nw** [=E] M, pl. *-er*, beg20c, 2,+5,+8(3) **Ic** [trɛs:] N, pl. Ø, 1930s, 2(1 coll) **Rm** *dres* [dres] N, 1970s, +6(3); end20c, +8(1 techSPORT) **Po** *dres* M, mid20c, +5(3) **Cr** *dres* M, pl. *-ovi*, beg20c, +5(3) **Hu** *dressz* [=E] pl. *-ek*, end19/beg20c, +5(3) +6(3 tech) +7(3 obs) = +5: *mez* **Al** *dres* [dres] M, pl. *-e*, mid20c, +5(1 reg)

dressboy* *n.* 'a dummy for hanging clothes on'
Du [drɛsbɔj] M, 1980

dressing *n.* 2a 'a sauce for salad'
This word came to be widely known as a more specific term for sauces added to salad, no doubt because they were marketed under this name by mass food producers. The earlier meaning of 'shoe-polish' (1930s, in German) appears to be obsolete.
Ge [drɛsiŋ] N, pl. *-s*, 1970s (1 tech) **Du** [=E] C, 1970s (1 tech) **Nw** [=E] M, pl. *-er*, 1960s (3) **Ic** [trɛs:iŋ] N/F [U] mid/end20c (1 coll) **Rm** [=E] N, 1980s (1 mod) **Po** [-nk] M [U] end20c (1 tech) **Cr** *drɛsiŋ* M [U] end20c (1 tech) **Bg** - < *vinegret* **Hu** [=E] pl. Ø, mid20c (1 tech) < *öntet* **Gr** *drɛsiŋ* N, pl. Ø/*-s*, end20c (2 mod)

dressing room *n.* 'a room for changing one's clothes'
Nw (0) **Ic** *dressingherbergi* N, pl. Ø, 1960s (1+5) < trsl *búningsherbergi* **Fr** <=E>/*dressing* [drɛsiŋ rum] M, 19c (1 tech/ban) < *vestiaire* **Hu** [=E] [U] 19c (1 tech, arch) < *öltöző(szoba)* **Gr** *drɛsiŋ rum* N, via Fr (1 mod)

dressman* *n.* 'a male model'
One of the best-known German pseudo-loans, created to fill a gap for a *male* model, and exported to a few neighbouring languages. The term appears to be slightly obsolescent, implying that further exports to Eastern Europe are unlikely.
Ge [drɛsmɛn] M, pl. *-slmen*, 1960s (1 tech) **Du** [drɪsmɛn] C, pl. *-mannen/-men*, 1970s (1 tech) **It** [drɛsman] M, pl. Ø, end20c (1 tech) < *indossatore*

dress up *v.* 1 'dress (oneself) elaborately for a special occasion', +4 'buy clothes (for oneself)'
Nw *dresse (seg) opp* ["drɛse] 1960s(2) **Ic** *dressa (sig) upp* [trɛs:a vhp] mid20c 2 coll) → *(upp)dressaður* adj.

dribble *v.* 3 'move the ball forward with slight touches of the foot or hand' (ballgames)
One of the most popular (and apparently most needed) football terms adopted c.1900. Suggested calques (German *treiben*) have failed to replace the word – in contrast to many other football terms. The derivatives can, in many languages, be either loans or coinages based on national patterns.

Ge *dribbeln* beg20c (3 tech) → *-er* M **Du** *dribbelen* [drıbələn] beg20c (4/1 tech) **Nw** *drible* ["drible] beg20c (3) → *dribler* M **Ic** *dripla/dribla* [trı(h)pla] 1960s (3 tech) > rend *rekja* → *dripl* N **Fr** *dribbler* [dʀible] end19/beg20c (2) < *dribler* **Sp** *driblar* beg20c (3) < *regatear* **It** *dribblare* 1910s (3) **Rm** *dribla* [dribla] beg20c, via Fr (3) → *driblare* F **Po** *dryblować* [driblovatç] mid20c (1 tech) → *dryblowanie* N [U] **Cr** *driblati* beg20c (1 tech) → *driblanje* N **Bg** *dribliram* beg20c (3 tech) → *driblirane* N **Hu** *dribli* [dribli] end19/beg20c (1 tech/fac/4) → *-z* v.; *kidribliz* v. **Al** *dribloj* beg20c (1 tech) **Gr** *driblaro* beg20c (3 tech)

dribbler *n.* 'a player who dribbles the ball' (ball-games)

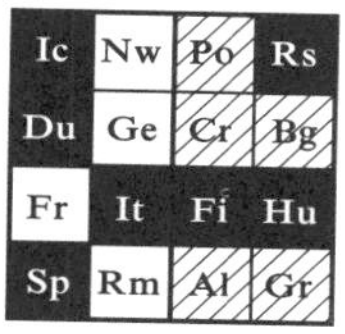

Ge [=E] M, pl. Ø, beg20c (3/5) (derivation is possibly Ge) **Nw** *dribler* [dribler] M, pl. *-e*, beg20c (3) (probably ← Nw *drible*) **Fr** *dribbleur* [dʀiblœʀ] M/F, beg20c (2) → *dribleuse* [dʀibløz] F **Sp** - < *driblador* **It** - < *dribblatore* M **Rm** *dribler* [dribler] M, via Fr (3) **Po** *drybler/* <=E> [-er] M, mid20c (1 tech) **Cr** *dribler* M, pl. *-i*, beg20c (1 tech) **Bg** *driblyor* M, pl. *-i*, beg20c, via Fr (3 tech) **Al** *driblues* M, pl. *-ë*, beg20c (1 tech) **Gr** *dribler* M, via Fr, beg20c (1 tech)

dribbling *n.* 'the action of dribbling'

Note that morpheme replacement is common even in languages in which loanwords ending in *-ing* are frequent.

Ge [driblıŋ] N [U] mid20c (2 tech) **Du** *dribbel* [=E] C [U] 1950s (1 tech) **Nw** *dribling* ["driblıŋ] M/F [U] (3) (probably ← Nw *drible*) **Fr** *dribble* [dʀibl] M, beg20c (2 ban) < *drible* (spelling change only) **Sp** *dribling* [driblin] M [U] beg20c (1 tech) < *regate, regateo* **It** [driblıŋ] M [U] 1910s (2 tech) > *dribblaggio* **Rm** *dribling* [dribliŋg] N, beg20c (3) **Rs** *dribling* M [U] mid20c (1 tech) **Po** *drybling*/<=E> [-nk] N [U] mid20c (1 tech) **Cr** *dribling* M, beg20c (1 tech) > *driblanje* **Bg** *dribŭl* M [U] beg20c (3 tech) **Hu** *dribli* [dribli] [U] end19/beg20c (1 tech, fac/4) → *-z* v. **Al** *driblim* M, pl. *-e*, beg20c (1 tech) **Gr** *dribla* F, beg20c (3 tech)

drift *n.* 1a 'a slow regular movement', +1c 'the movement of the continents', 5a,b 'deviation from a course', 8a 'material deposited by the wind or a current of water'

This word is shared, as a derivative of common verbal *drive*, by the North Sea Germanic languages; many meanings may be native in Dutch or Low German, which may in turn have been the source for loanwords in other languages. These complex interrelations would seem to require more detailed investigation.

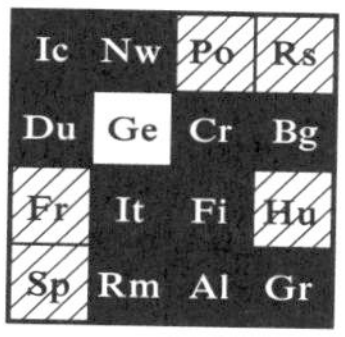

Ge [=E] F [U] 1a,5a,b(3) → *-en* v. **Nw** 1a,+1c,5a,b(4) **Fr** [dʀift] M, mid19c, 8a (1) **Sp** M, 20c, 8a(1 tech) **Rs** *drift* M [U] 20c, 8a(1 tech) < 5a,b: *dreif* **Po** *dryft* M [U] mid20c, 5a,b(1 tech) **Bg** - < *dreif* 5a,b (5Du) → *-ov* adj; *-uvam* v. **Hu** [=E] [U] mid20c, 1a,5a,b (1 tech$_{\text{PHYS}}$)

drifter *n.* 1 'an aimless person', 2 'a boat used for fishing with a drift-net'

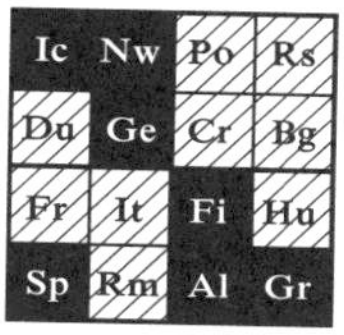

Du [driftər] C, beg20c, 2(1 tech) **Fr** [dʀiftœʀ] M, 1930s, 2(1 tech) **It** [drifter] M, pl. Ø, 1910s, 2(1 tech) < *motopeschereccio* **Rm** [drifter] N, mid20c, 2(1 tech) **Rs** *drifter* M, pl. *-y*, beg 20c, 2(1 tech) → *-nyĭ* adj. **Po** *dryfter* [-er] M, mid20c, 2(1 tech) **Cr** *drifter* M, pl. *-i*, beg20c, 2(1 tech) **Bg** *drifter* M, pl. *-al-i*, beg20c, 2(1 tech) → *-en* adj. **Hu** [=E] pl. *-ek*, 19c, 2(1 tech)

drill[1] (1) *n.* 2a 'rigorous military instruction', 2b 'other instruction', 2d 'an exercise, practice (esp. in language teaching)'

The verb ('to bore', 'to exercise') and the noun were probably first borrowed from Dutch/Low German into seventeenth-century English.; Dutch and German appear to have developed these words independently, and the few other languages represented could have borrowed the words from any of these – the military drill being associated, e.g., with German.

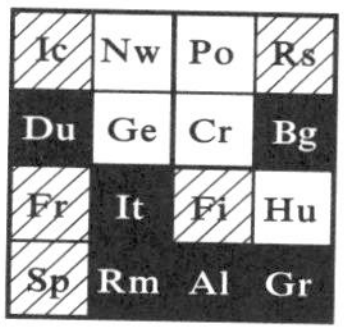

Ge [dril] M [U] 19c, 2a(3/5), 2b,d(1/5) **Du** M, pl. *-len* (5) **Nw** [=E] M, pl. *-er*, mid20c, 2a,d(2) **Ic** *drill* [trıl:] N, pl. Ø, mid20c, 2b,d(1 tech) **Fr** [dʀil] M, 1930s, 2a(1); 1970s, 2d(1 tech) **Sp** <=E> M, pl. *-s*, 1970s, 2d(1 tech) **Rs** *dril'* M [U] mid20c, 2d(1 tech) **Po** *dryl* M, mid20c, via Ge (2) **Cr** [=E] M, mid20c, via Ge, 2a,d(3) → *-ati* v. **Fi** [=E] 20c, 2d(1) **Hu** <=E> 20c, via Ge, 2a,b(3)

drill[2] (2) *n.* 2 'a small furrow for sowing seed in'

Ge *Drill(maschine)* F, pl. *-n*, mid20c (3+5) **Du** *dril(machine)* [=E] C, mid20c (1 tech) **Nw** [=E] M, pl. *-er*, 20c (1 tech) **Hu** [=E] pl. *-ek*, end19/beg20c (1 tech, obs)

drill[3] (4) *n.* 'coarse twilled cotton or linen fabric'

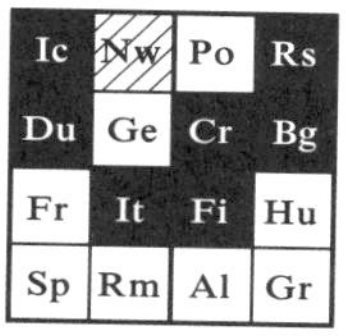

Ge [=E] M [U] 19c (3) < *Drillich* **Du** *dril* [=E] (5) **Nw** [=E] M [U] 19c (1 tech) **Fr** [dril] M, 19c (3) **Sp** *dril* [=E] M, 19c? (3) **Rm** *dril* [dril] N [U] via Ge (3) **Po** <=E> 20c, via Ge (3) **Hu** via Ge (3) **Al** *drill* M [U] 20c (3) **Gr** *drili* N [U] 19c, via Fr (3)

drill[1] (1) *v.* 2 'subject to or undergo discipline by drill', 3 'impart (knowledge) by a strict method'

Ge *drillen* 19c, 2(3/5) **Du** *drillen* [drılən] (5) **Nw** *drille* ["drile] 20c (3) **Ic** *drilla* [trıl:a] mid/end20c, 3(1 sla) **Po** *drylować* [drilovatç] mid20c, via Ge (2) **Cr** *drilati* mid20c (3)

drill[2] (2) *v.* 1 'sow (seed) with a drill', 2 'plant (the ground) in drills'

Ge *drillen* 19c (3/5) **Nw** *drille* ["drile] 20c (3)

driller   *n.* 'a (higher) oil rig worker'
 Nw [=E] M, pl. *-e*, 1970s (1 tech)
drink   *n.* 2a,b 'a portion of alcohol (or other drinks)'
 This word has had to compete with a host of native terms; its niche as a loanword is always in the colloquial fashionable register, often of 'good society', and designating weak (mixed) alcoholic beverages. Eastern and Southern Europe have notably fewer alternatives.
 Ge [=E] M, pl. *-s*, 1960s (1 coll) < *Getränk* **Du** [=E] C, 1970s (1 coll) < *drankje* **Nw** [=E] M, pl. *-er*, mid20c (2) **Ic** [triŋk] M, mid20c, 2b(o sla) < trsl *drykkur* **Fr** [=E] M, 19c (1 mod) **Sp** [=E] M, end20c (1 mod, rare) < *drinking* **It** [driŋk] M, pl. Ø, 1950s (2 coll) **Rm** (o) **Rs** *drink* M [U] 1990s (1 sla, you) → *-ovat'* v. **Po** M, mid20c (2 mod) → v. **Cr** *drink* M, mid20c (1) **Fi** *drinkki*, 20c (2 coll) **Hu** [=E] [U] mid20c (1 mod/jour) > *ital* **Gr** *drink* N, pl. *-s*, end20c (1 mod/you)

drink bar*   *n.* 'a place where drinks are bought and consumed'
 This seemingly pleonastic term arose because ↑*bar* had come to mean various eating places and shops where no drinks (or no hard drinks) could be had.
 Po [-ar] M, end20c (2) **Hu** *drinkbár* [drinkba:r] pl. *-ok*, mid20c (2 tech)
dripping   *n.* +3 'a style of painting'
 Du [=E] C [U] (1 tech, arch) **Sp** [dripin] M [U] 1970s (1 tech) **It** [dripiŋg] M, pl. Ø, 1940s (1 tech, rare)
drive   *n.* 2a 'motivation, energy', 4 'a driving stroke' (tennis, golf), 6a 'the transmission of power to machinery, the wheels of a motor vehicle, etc.', 6c '= disk drive' (comput.), +10 'rhythmical intensity' (jazz)
 Sense (2a) is typical of late twentieth-century youth language and colloquial usage; it is beginning to replace the more formal *elan*. Many of the uses of *drive* are still facetious, ironic or snobbish. (4), the tennis term (first adopted in German around 1900) has gained new popularity with the increased media representation of the sport since the 1980s.
 Ge [=E] M [U] 1960s, 2a(1 you) 4,+10(1 tech) < 2a: *Elan* **Du** [drajf] C, 1970s/1950s, 2a(1 you) 4(1 tech) **Nw** [=E] M, pl. *-r*, 20c, 2a,+10(1 coll) 4,6c(1 tech) < 2a,+10: *driv* **Ic** [=E] N [U] end20c, 2a,+10(1 sla); *drif* [trɪːf] N, pl. Ø, mid20c, 6a,c(4) **Fr** [dʁajv] M, end19c, 4(1 tech) < *coup droit* (tennis) < *coup de longue distance* (golf) **Sp** [draif] pl. *-s*, beg20c, 4,6a,c(1 tech); end20c, +10(1 tech) **It** [=E] M, pl. Ø, 1930s, 4(1 tech, obs); 1970s, 6c(1 tech) **Rm** <=E>/*draiv* [=E] N, mid20c?, 4,+10(1 tech); end20c, 6c(1 tech) **Rs** *draiv* M, pl. *-y*, end20c, 4,6c(1 tech); [U] +10(1 you) **Po** *drajw*/<=E> M [U] end20c, 2a,4(1 you) **Cr** *drajf* M, pl. *-ovi*, mid20c, 4(1 tech) **Bg** *draif*/*draiv* M [U]/pl. *-al-ove*, end20c, 4,6c(1 tech) **Fi** *draivi* 4(2_GOLF) **Hu** [=E] [U] end19c/beg20c, 6a(1 tech_NAUT) 4,6c(1 tech) **Gr** *draiv* N, end20c, 4(1 tech); 6c(1 tech) < *disk drive*

drive-in   *cp¹* 'allowing customers to use it without leaving their cars (e.g. cinema)'
 This term was exclusively adopted for cinemas in the 1960s and in Western Europe where these institutions were only marginally popular. It was later extended to include restaurants, banks, etc. accessible without leaving one's car, but the idea has not really caught on, and the term may in consequence be obsolescent.
 Ge [=E] 1950s (1 coll) **Du** [=E] 1960s (1 mod) **Nw** [=E] M, pl. *-s*, 1960s (1 mod) **Ic** [=E] end 20c (o coll) < rend *aktu-taktu;* *bílabió* **Fr** [dʁajvin] 1950s (1 ban) > *ciné-parc* **Sp** [draibin] M, pl. Ø/*-s*, 1970s (1 tech) **It** [draivin] M, pl. Ø, 1950s (2) **Rm** [=E] N, 1970s (Ø) **Rs** *draiv-in* 1990s (Ø) **Po** [=E] uninfl., end20c (1 mod) **Cr** [=E] M, end20c (1 coll) **Bg** - < creat *avto-kino* **Fi** [=E] 20c (1) **Hu** [=E] [U] 1970s (2) < *autósmozi* **Gr** *draiv in*/<=E> end20c (2) > *kinimatogh-rafos aftokiniton*

driver   *n.* 1 'a person who drives a vehicle', 2 'a club with a flat face and wooden head, used for driving from the tee' (golf), 3 'a device or part of a circuit providing power for output', 5 'software used to control peripherals' (comput.)
 Ge [=E] M, pl. Ø, 1980s, 2(1 tech, rare) **Nw** [=E] M, pl. *-e*, end20c, 2(1 tech); [drɪːver] 5(4) **Ic** [=E] M, pl. *-ar*, 1960s, 1(1 coll) 2,3(1 tech) < 1: *bílstjóri;* 2: *tré;* 3: rend *rekill* **Fr** <=E>/*driveur* [dʁajvœr/drivɛr] M, 19c, 2(1 tech, ban); 1980s, 5(1 tech, ban) < 2: *bois un, masse;* < 5: *pilote, gestionnaire de périphérique* **Sp** [draiber] M, pl. *-s*, 1950s, 2(1 tech); 1980s, 3,5(1 tech) **It** [draiver] M, pl. Ø, 1970s, 5(1 tech) **Rm** [=E] M, end20c, 1 (o > 1 tech) 2(1 tech); 1990s, 5(1 tech); [=E/driver] M, mid20c, via Fr, 1(1 rare) < 1,2: *crosă* **Rs** *draiver* M, pl. *-y*, end20c, 1(1 coll) 5(2 tech) **Po** [-er] M, end20c (1 mod) **Cr** [draiver] M, pl. *-i*, end20c, 5(1 tech) **Bg** *draiver*/*draivŭr* M, pl. *-al-i*, 1980s, 5(1 tech) **Hu** [=E] [U] mid20c, 5(1 tech) **Gr** <=E> [=E] M, pl. Ø/*-s*, end20c, 2(1 tech) 5(1 tech)

driving range   *n.* 'an area for practising drives' (golf)
 Ge [=E] F, pl. *-s*, 1990s (1 tech) **Du** [=E] C, pl. *-s*, 1990s (1 tech) **Nw** [=E] M, pl. *-r*, 1990s (1 tech)
drone   *n.* 6 'a remote-controlled pilotless aircraft or missile'
 Du [=E] C, 1980s (1 tech) **Nw** [drɪːne] M, pl. *-er*, 20c (1 tech) **Fr** [dron] M, 1950s (1 tech) **Sp** M, 1980s (1 tech, rare) **Hu** *dron* [=E] [U] mid20c, via Rs? (1 tech)
drop¹ (1)   *n.* 3c 'a sweet, a bonbon, a lollipop'
 This term originally referred to small round fruit-flavoured ('drop-shaped') sweets; the *-s* was not recognized as a plural morph (cf. ↑*cake,* ↑*coke*) in German, from which the word probably spread to neighbouring languages.
 Ge *Drops* M, pl. *-e*, mid19c (3) **Du** *drops* [drɔps] pl.,

19c (3) → *dropsje dim* **Nw** *drops* [=E] M [U]/N, pl. Ø, 19c (3) **It** [drɔp] M, pl. Ø, 1910s (1) **Rm** *drops* [=E] N, pl. *dropsuri*, mid20c, via Ge (3) **Po** *drops* M, mid20c (3) → *-ik* M **Cr** *drops* M, pl. *-i*, beg20c (2) **Bg** *drops* M, pl., mid20c, via Ge (3) **Hu** *dropsz* [=E] [U] beg20c, via Ge (3)

drop² (1)   *n.* +4d 'an act of dropping the ball or puck straight down between two competing players to decide who will get it' (sport)

Nw *dropp* [=E] M/N, pl. Ø, 20c (2) **Fr** - < ↑*dropping* **Sp** <=E> M, 1980s, +4d(1 tech) **It** [drop] M, pl. Ø, 1950s, +4d(1 tech) **Rm** [=E] N, end20c, +4d(1 rare) **Bg** *drop* M, pl. *-a*, mid20c, +4d(1 tech)

drop   *v.* 4b 'cease to associate with', 15 'deliver by parachute', +18 'take drugs, esp. LSD', +19 'let down'

Du *droppen* [drɔpən] 1970s, 4b,15(3) **Nw** *droppe* ["drɔpe] mid20c, 4b(3) 15(1) +18(1 tech) **Ic** *droppa* [trɔhpa] 1970s, 4b,+18(2 sla) **Fr** *dropper* [dʀɔpe] 20c, 15(1 tech) +19(1 coll) → *droppage* **Sp** *dropar* end20c (3 tech$_{GOLF}$)

drop-dead   *phr.* 1 'an exclamation of intense scorn' **Ic** [=E] excl. 1960s (1 you, obs)

drop goal   *n.* 1 'a goal scored from a drop kick' (rugby), +2 'a drop shot'

Fr [dʀɔpgol] M, end19c (1 tech) **Sp** <=E> M, end20c, 1(Ø/1 tech, rare) **Rm** *dropgoll/drop* [drɔpgol/dropgol] N, 20c, 1(1 tech) **Gr** *drop gol* N, 20c, 1(1 tech)

drop-in   *n./cp¹* 'a place where or arrangement whereby people may drop in without having made prior reservations or appointments'

Nw [=E] cp¹, 1980s (1 mod)

drop in   *v.* 'call casually as a visitor'

Nw *droppe inn* ["drɔpe] 1980s (1 coll) **Ic** *droppa inn* 1970s (2 coll)

drop-kick   *n.* 'a kick made by dropping the ball and kicking it on the bounce' (footb.)

Du *dropkick* [=E] C, 1980s (1 tech) **Fr** - < *coup tombé* **Sp** <=E> M, end20c (1 tech, rare) = *botepronto* **It** *drop* [=E] M, pl. Ø, 1950s (1 tech) < *calcio di rimbalzo* **Cr** [=E] mid20c (1 tech) **Bg** *drop/zhdrop* M, pl. *-a*, mid20c (1/3 tech) **Gr** *drop kik* N, 20c (1 tech)

drop-out   *n.* 1 'a person who has dropped out of conventional society', +3 'an interruption of data transmission'

The major sense, popularized by the hippie movement, is still confined to Northern and Central Europe, but is possibly on the increase.

Ge [=E] M, pl. *-s*, 1970s, 1(1 coll) +3(1 tech) < 1: *Aussteiger* **Du** *drop-out* [=E] C, 1980s, 1(1 mod) **Nw** [=E] M, pl. *-er/-s*, 1960s, 1 (1) **Ic** [=E] N, pl. Ø, 1970s, 1(1 sla) **Fr** 1970s (1 jour, obs) > *dropé* **Sp** [drɔpaut]

M, pl. *-s*, 1970s (1 ban, rare) **It** [drɔpaut] M/F, pl. Ø, 1970s (1) < *emarginato/-a* **Bg** *dropaut* M [U] 1990s, +3(1 tech) < trsl *uvisvane* **Fi** [=E] 1970s, 1(1 coll) **Hu** [=E] [U] 1980s, +3(1 tech)

drop out   *v.* 'cease to participate; cease to observe conventions of behaviour' etc.

Nw *droppe ut* ["drɔpe] end20c (1 coll) **Ic** *droppa út* 1970s (2 sla)

dropping*   *n.* 1 'an act of dropping parcels out of a plane', 2 'a game wherein a group of people is dropped at an unknown place and has to find the way back'

Du dr[ɔpɪŋ] F/M, 1980s (2) **Nw** [=E] C [U] 20c, 1(1 tech) **Fr** <=E> end 20c, 1 (1) < *droppage*

drop shot   *n.* 'a shot that drops abruptly after clearing the net' (tennis)

Ge [=E] M, pl. *-s*, 20c (0>1 tech) **Nw** [=E] N, pl. Ø, 20c (1 tech) **Fr** *drop/drop-shot* M, 20c (1 tech) **It** [drop ʃot] M, pl. Ø, 1940s (1 tech) < *colpo smorzato* **Rs** *dropshot* M, pl. *-y*, mid20c (1 tech) **Po** *dropszot* M, mid20c (1 tech) **Bg** *dropshot* M, pl. *-a*, mid20c (1 tech) **Gr** *drop sot* N, 20c (1 tech) < *plase*

drug   *n.* 2 'a narcotic, hallucinogen or stimulant, esp. one causing addiction'

Ge - < *Droge* **Du** [drʏg] M, 1960s (2) **Nw** [=E] M, pl. *-s*, 1980s (1 rare) < *narkotika, stoff, (droge)* **Ic** [=E] N [U] 1970s (1 sla) < *dóp, fíkniefni* **Fr** - < *drogue* **Sp** - < *droga* **It** - < *droga* **Rm** - < *drog* (5Fr) **Po** <=E> M, 1990s (1 jour) **Cr** *droga* **Bg** - < *droga* (5Fr) < *narkotik* **Hu** *drog* (5Du) **Al** - < *drogë* **Gr** *drugs* N, pl., end20c (1 sla); *droga* F (3 sla)

drug scene   *n.* 1 'a group of people known to use drugs'

Ge - < trsl *Drogenszene* **Du** [drʏksi:n] F/M, 1980s (2) **Nw** (0)

drugstore   *n.* 'a chemist's shop also selling light refreshments and other articles'

The term has not caught on, even for modern stores; the firm hold of French *droguerie* is apparently unchallenged.

Ge (0) **Du** [=E] C, 1980s (0) **Nw** (Ø) **Fr** <=E>/ *drug-store/drug* [dʀɛgstɔʀ] M, 1930s (2) **Sp** [drastor/drustor] M, pl. *-s*, 1970s (2) **Rm** 1970s (0) **Po** (0) **Cr** *dragstor* M, mid20c (1) **Hu** [=E] pl. *-ok*, mid20c (Ø) < *drogéria* **Gr** (0)

drum(s)   *n.* 1a 'a percussion instrument made of a hollow cylinder or hemisphere covered at one or both ends with stretched skin or parchment and sounded by striking', 1b (pl.) 'a drummer or a percussion section', 2a 'a cylindrical container'

Ge [dram] F, pl. *-s*, 1a,b(1 you) < 1a: *Trommel* < 1b: *Schlagzeug* **Du** [drʏm] 1a(2) 2a(1 tech) **Nw** 1a,2a(0) < 1a: *tromme*; 2a: *trommel* **Gr** *drams* N, pl., mid20c, 1a(1 tech)

drummer   *n.* 1 'a person who plays a drum or drums (mostly in jazz or rock bands)'

Ge [dr<u>a</u>ma] M, pl. Ø, 1970s (1 you) < *Schlagzeuger*
Du [drʏmər] C, mid20c (3)   **Nw** (0) < *tromme-slager*   **Ic** *trommari* M, pl. *-ar*, mid20c (3) = *trommu-leikari*   **Fr** [drœmœʀ] M, mid20c (1 tech)   **Rm** 1970s
(0)   **Bg** *dr<u>u</u>mŭr* M, pl. *-i*, 1990s (1 tech)   **Gr** *dr<u>a</u>mer* M/F, end20c (1 tech)

drumstick   *n.* 1 'a stick used for beating a drum' the
Du [drʏmstɪk] M, 1980s (2)   **Nw** (0) < *trommestikke*

dry   *adj.* 2 'not sweet' (of wine etc.), 5b 'abstaining
from alcohol or drugs' (of a person), +12 'pure, not
mixed' (usu. of alcoholic beverages)
   This loanword, itself a calque on French *sec*, is of
restricted distribution, with the French or native
equivalents being preferred, or at least coexisting.
(Extra) dry appears to be common mainly with English drinks (*sherry*).
Ge [drai] uninfl./postpos., 1870s,
2(2) < *trocken*   **Du** [=E] end19c,
2(2 tech) < *sec*   **Nw** [=E] 20c, 2(1
tech) < *tørr*   **Ic** [=E] uninfl.,
mid20c, 5b,+12(1 coll); *þurr* 2(4)
→ *dræjari* M   **Fr** [dʀaj] adj./M,
pl. *desdrys/desdry*, end19c, 2(1)
Sp [drai] beg20c, 2(1 tech) < *seco*   **It** [drai] uninfl.,
end19c, 2(2) < trsl *secco*   **Rm** [=E] uninfl., end20c,
2(1 mod) < *sec*   **Po** 2(0)   **Cr** 2(0)   **Bg** - < 5b: mean
sukh   **Fi** [=E] (1 tech) < mean *kuiva*   **Hu** [=E] 19c,
2(1 tech/writ, mod > 2) < *száraz* = *sec*   **Gr** [=E] adj.,
end20c, +12(2); - < 2: mean *xiros*

dual use*   *cp¹* 'for military and non-military use'
   This term has been used frequently in German
newspapers in the 1990s with reference to arms exports, relating to goods useful for both applications.
Ge [=E] 1990s (1 tech, jour)

dub   *v.* 1 'provide (a film etc.) with an alternative
soundtrack, esp. in a different language'
Ge - < *synchronisieren*   **Du** *dubben* [dʏbən] 1970s (1
tech) = *nasynchroniseren*   **Nw** *dubbe* ["d<u>u</u>be/"d<u>ø</u>be]
1960s (2) → *dubber* M; *dubbing* C   **Ic** *dubba/döbba*
[tʏp:a/tœp:a] 1970s (1 coll) = rend *talsetja*   **Sp** - <
doblar   **Fr** - < *doubler* (5)   **It** - < *doppiare, sincroniz-zare*   **Rm** - < *dubla*   **Cr** - < *sinkronizirati*   **Rs** *du-blirovat'* (5Fr)   **Po** (0)   **Bg** - < *dubl<u>i</u>ram* (5Fr)   **Fi**
dubata 20c (2)   **Al** - < *dubloj*   **Gr** - < *metaghlotizo*

dubbing   *n.* 1 'an alternative soundtrack for a film',
+2 'the process of transferring or making a copy of
recorded sound or images'
   The evidence is divided (as in the back-derived verb)
between borrowed items, possibly with suffix replacement, and renderings – for which the *doubl*-stem is
phonetically close to the English etymon.
Ge [=E] N [U] end20c, +2(1 tech); - < 1: *Synchronisa-tion*   **Du** [=E/drʏbiŋ] C [U] 1980s, 1(1 tech) +2(3 tech)
< 1: *nasynchroniseren* → *dubldubben* v.   **Nw** ["d<u>u</u>biŋ /
"d<u>ø</u>biŋ] C [U] 1960s (1 tech)   **Fr** - < *doublage*   **Sp** - <
doblaje   **It** - < *doppi<u>a</u>ggio, sincronizzazi<u>o</u>ne*   **Rm** - <
dublaj (5Fr)   **Rs** (5Fr)   **Po** [-nk] M [U] mid20c (2) →
v.; *z*-v.; *-owy* adj.   **Cr** - < *sinkronizacija*   **Bg** *d<u>u</u>biŋ* M
[U] end20c, +2(1 tech); - < 1: *dubl<u>a</u>zh*   **Fi** *dubbaus*

(2)   **Hu** *dabbing* [=E] [U] 20c (1 tech) < *szinkro-nizálás*   **Al** - < *dublim*   **Gr** - < *metaghlotismos*

duffel   *n.* 1 'coarse woollen cloth with a thick nap' (cf.
↑*duffel coat*)
Ge *Düffel* [dyfel] M [U] beg19c (3 arch, obs)   **Ic** *duffel*
[tʏf:el/=E] N, mid19c (2)   **Fi** *duffeli* (3)   **Hu** (5Fr)

duffel coat   *n.* 'a hooded overcoat'
   The word ↑*duffel* 'coarse woollen cloth' (probably
from Dutch) does not appear to have been widely
borrowed, but the compound became very popular
in Central and Northern Europe from the 1950s on
for a short overcoat fastened with toggles.
Ge [daflko:t] M, pl. *-s*, 1950s
(2)   **Nw** [d<u>ø</u>felkɔut /dyfel-] M,
pl. *-er*, *-s*, 1950s (2)   **Ic** [tœf:el-
kʰou:t] N/F [U] 1960s (1 mod)
Fr *duffel-coat/duffle-coat* [dœfœl-
kot] M, 1950s (1 arch) **Sp** - < *tren-ka* **It** - < *mongomeri* **Po**
duffel- coat/<=E> M, end20c (1 tech)
[U] end20c (1)   **Fi** *duffeli* 20c (3)

dull   *adj.* 1 'slow to understand; stupid', 2 'tedious,
boring', 4b (of colour, light) 'not bright, vivid, or keen'
Ic [=E] uninfl., 1970s (1 sla)

dumdum (bullet)   *n./cp¹* 'a soft-nosed bullet'
Ge *Dumdumgeschoß* [dumd<u>u</u>m-] 19c (3 tech+5)   **Du**
dumdumkogel [dʏmd<u>y</u>m-/dumd<u>u</u>m-] beg20c (1
tech+5)   **Nw** *dumdumkule* [d<u>u</u>mdum-] M, pl. *-er*,
beg20c (1 tech)   **Fr** *balle (de) dum- dum* [dumdum]
F, beg20c (1 tech)   **Sp** *(bala) dum-dum* [d<u>u</u>n d<u>u</u>n]
1930s (1 tech)   **It** [dum d<u>u</u>m] *cp²*, 1900s (1 tech) <
trsl *proiettili dum dum*   **Rm** *(glont) dum-dum* [d<u>u</u>m-d<u>u</u>m] N/cp², via Fr (3 tech)   **Rs** *dum-d<u>u</u>m* M, uninfl.,
beg20c (1 tech)   **Po** [dum dum] M, uninfl., beg20c
(2)   **Cr** *d<u>u</u>md<u>u</u>m* M, uninfl., beg20c (1 tech)   **Bg** *kur-shum d<u>u</u>m-d<u>u</u>m* M, mid20c (5+1 tech)   **Fi** *dumdum-luoti* (3 tech+5)   **Hu** [d<u>u</u>mdum] [U] end19/beg20c (1
tech, arch)   **Al** *dumdum* M, pl. *-ë*, mid20c (1 tech)

dummy   *n.* +1d 'a model of a human being used in
crash tests', 2b 'a prototype, esp. in publishing', 4 'a
stupid person', +10 'a grammatical element with a
formal but no semantic role' (linguist.), +11 'a math-
ematical variable'
Ge [dami] M, pl. *(-ie)s*, 1970s,
+1d(1 tech) < *Versuchspuppe*;
1980s, 2b(1 tech, rare) < *At-trappe*; +10(1 tech) **Du** [d<u>y</u>mi]
C, pl. *-'s*, 1970s/mid20c,
+1d,2b(1 tech) **Nw** [=E] M, pl.
-er, 20c, +1d,2b,+10(1 tech) **Ic**
[=E] N, pl. Ø, end20c, +1d,+10(1 tech) 4(1 sla) **Fr** -
< +10: tech *postiche* **Sp** [d<u>u</u>mi/d<u>a</u>mi] end20c,
+1d,2b,+11(1 tech) **It** - < +1d: *manich<u>i</u>no* **Al** - <
manikin **Gr** <=E>/d<u>a</u>mi F, pl. *-ies*, 1990s, +1d(1
tech) < *crash dummies*

dump   *v.* 2 'deposit or dispose of', 5 'send goods to a
foreign market for sale at a low price' (econ.)
Du *dumpen* [dʏmpə] 1960s (3)   **Nw** *dumpe* ["d<u>u</u>mpe/
"d<u>ø</u>mpe] beg20c (3)   **Po** (0)   **Fi** *dumpata* (2)

dumper *n.* 1b 'a truck that tilts or opens at the back for unloading'

This term competes with older native coinages; it usually refers to esp. big lorries.

Ge [da̱mpa/u̱] M, pl. Ø, 1960s (1 tech, rare) < *Kipper* **Du** [dʏmpər] C, 1960s (3) = *kip­kar* **Nw** [dømper/du̱mper] M, pl. -*e*, 20c (1 tech) **Fr** [dœmpœr] M, 1920s (1 tech, ban) > *tombereau* **Sp** [dumper] M, pl. -*s*, 1980s (1 tech) < *camión basculante* **It** [da̱mper] M, pl. Ø/-*s*, 1970s (1 tech) **Rm** [du̱mper] N, 1980s, via Fr (1 tech) **Rs** *du̱mper* M, pl. -*y*, mid20c (1 tech) **Cr** *damper* M, pl. -*i*, end20c (1 tech) **Hu** *dömper* [dømper] pl. -*ek*, 1940s (3)

dumping *n.* 'sale at a low price'

This word is one of the earliest and most widespread economic terms borrowed from English – but with very few accompanying verbs.

Ge [da̱mpiŋ] N [U] beg20c (2 tech) **Du** [dʏmpɪŋ] C, pl. -*s*, mid20s (1 tech) **Nw** [du̱mpiŋ/ dømpiŋ/"du̱mp-] C [U] 1920s (2) **Fr** [dœmpiŋ] M, beg20 (2 tech) **Sp** [dumpiŋ] M [U] beg20c (1 tech) **It** [dʌmpiŋ] M [U] 1910s (1 tech) **Rm** [da̱mpiŋ] N [U] mid20c (2 tech) **Rs** *de̱mping* M [U] beg20c (3 tech) → -*ovyĭ* adj. **Po** [-nk] M [U] beg20c (1 tech) → -*owy* adj. **Cr** *da̱mping* M [U] mid20c (1 tech) → -*ovati* v. **Bg** *du̱mping* M [U] beg20c (2 tech) **Fi** *dumppaus* (2) **Hu** *dömping* [dømpiŋ] pl. Ø, beg20c (1 tech>3 coll) **Al** <=E> [dumpiŋ] M [U] mid20c (1 tech) **Gr** *damping* [-mp-/-b-] N [U] beg/mid20c (1 tech)

dune-buggy *n.* 'a low wide-wheeled motor vehicle for recreational driving on sand' (↑*beach buggy*)

It [dju̱n ba̱ggi] F, pl. Ø, 1970s (1 tech, rare)

dungaree *n.* +3 'denim', +4 'clothes made of denim' +4a 'slacks made of denim'

Nw *dongeri* [dɔŋeri] M [U] beg20c, +3,+4(3) **Rm** *dangarizi* [dangarizj] M, pl., mid20c, +4a(1 coll, obs) **Rs** *dangeri* N [U] beg20c, 3(1 tech) **Bg** - < +4a: *du̱nki*

duty-free *cp¹* '(a -*shop* at an airport) at which duty free goods can be bought'

This loanword is an obvious consequence of international air travel; *shop* is frequently omitted from the compound – apparently because it does often not appear on the signs. This specialization probably makes the word different to native expressions/calques (like German *zollfrei*).

Ge [=E] 1970s (1 writ) < *zollfrei* **Du** [=E] 1980s (2) **Nw** [=E] 1980s (1) < *taxfree* **Ic** [=E] 1960s (0 coll) < rend *fríhöfn* **Fr** <=E> M, 1970s (1 ban) < (*boutique*) *hors taxes* **Sp** [diu̱ti fri] pl. Ø, 1970s (1 tech) = *duty free shop* **It** [diuti fri] M, pl. Ø, 1960s (2) = *duty free shop* **Rm** (0) **Rs** (0) **Po** <=E> N [U] 1970s (1 tech) **Cr** [djutifriʃop] M, mid20c (2) [=E] end20c (1 tech, writ/sla) < trsl *bezmiten; frishop* **Fi** - < *taxfree* **Hu** [=E] [U] mid20c (1 tech, writ) = *tax-free* **Gr** <=E> [=E] N, end20c (2) > *aforologhita*

d.w.t. *abbrev.* 'dead-weight tonnage' (cf. ↑*deadweight*)

Nw <=E>/*dwt* [de̱:ve:te̱:] 20c (1 tech) **Fr** (0) < *port en lourd* **Rm** *tdw* [te de ve] mid20c (1 tech) > *greutate moartă* **Rs** - < *de̱dveit* **Po** [de wu te] mid20c (1 tech) **Cr** [de vete] mid20c (1 tech) **Bg** - < *de̱dueĭt, de̱dveĭt* **Fi** - < trsl *kuollut paino* **Gr** (1 writ)

E

eagle *n.* 2 'a score of two strokes under par at any hole' (golf), 3 'a former gold coin worth ten dollars' **Ge** [=E] N, pl. *-s*, 1980s, 2(1 tech) **Du** [=E] C, pl. *-s*, end20c, 2(1 tech) **Nw** [=E] M, pl. *-r*, 1990s, 2(1 tech) **Fr** [=E] 2(1 tech, ban) > *aigle, moins deux* **Hu** [=E] [U] 3(Ø)

easy *adj.* 1 'not difficult; achieved without great effort', 3 'free from embarrassment, awkwardness, constraint, etc.; relaxed and pleasant' **Ge** [=E] uninfl., 1980s (1 you) < *leicht* **Du** [=E] uninfl., 1990s (1 you) < *makkelijk* **Nw** (0) **Ic** [=E] uninfl., end20c (1 sla) **Gr** (0)

easy *adv.* 'with ease; in an effortless or relaxed manner' (cf. ↑*take it easy*) **Ge** [=E] uninfl., 1980s (1 you) < *leicht* **Du** [=E] uninfl., 1990s (1 you) < *makkelijk* **Ic** [=E] end 20c (1 sla) → *ísa* v. **Fi** *iisisti* (3 sla) **Gr** (0)

easy *interj.* 'go carefully; move gently' **Du** [=E] 1990s (1 sla) **Ic** [=E] end20c (1 sla) **Rm** (0)

easy listening *n.* 'a style of music based on romantic melodies and love themes' **Ge** [=E] N [U] 1990s (1 you, mod) **Du** [=E] C [U] 1990s (1 tech, mod) **Nw** [=E] [U] 1990s (1 tech, mod) **It** [=E] M/F [U] 1980s (1 tech)

easy rider* *n.* 1 'a type of motor-bike' (made popular through the US film of the same name, 1969), 2 'a person riding this type of motor-bike' **Ge** [=E] M, pl. Ø, 1970s (1 you, obs) < 1: *chopper* **Du** Ø **Nw** [=E] M, pl. *-s*, 1970s (1 obs) **It** [izirai̯dɛr] M, pl. Ø, 1970s (1 you, obs) **Gr** <=E> [=E] M, 1970s, 2(Ø); - < 1: *tsoper*

ebonite *n.* 'a hard black vulcanized rubber' **Ge** *Ebonit* N [U] beg20c (3 tech, rare) **Du** *eboniet* [e:bonit] N [U] beg20c (1 tech) → *-en* adj. **Nw** *ebonitt* [ebunit̯] M [U] beg20c (3 tech) **Ic** *ebónít* N [U] 1920s, via Da (2 tech) **Fr** *ébonite* [ebonit] F, mid19c (1 tech) **Sp** *ebonita* F, end19c (3 tech, rare) **It** *ebanite* F [U] mid19c (3 tech) **Rm** *ebonită* [ebonit̯ə] F [U] *ebonit* N [U] beg20c, via Fr (3) **Rs** *ébonit* [ebonit] M [U] beg20c (2) → *-ovyĭ* adj. **Po** *ebonit* [ebonit] M [U] beg20c (2) → *-owy* adj. **Cr** *ebonit* M [U] beg20c (2) **Bg** *ebonit* M [U] mid20c, via Rs (1 tech) → *-ov* adj. **Fi** *eboniitti* (3) **Hu** *ebonit* [ebonit] [U] end19/beg20c (1 tech>3) **Al** *ebanit* [ebanit̯] M [U] beg20c (1 tech) **Gr** *evonítis* M, via Fr (3 tech)

economizer *n.* 1 'a person spending little money', 2 'an apparatus re-using steam'

Ge <=E>/*Ekonomiser* [=E] M, pl. Ø, 20c, 2(1 tech, rare) **It** - < *economizzatore* **Rm** *economizor* [ekonomizor] N, 1940s, 2(3 tech) **Rs** *ékonomaĭzer* M, pl. *-y*, mid20c, 2(1 tech) **Po** *ekonomajzer*/<=E> [ekonomaizer] M, mid20c, 2(1 tech) **Cr** *ekonomajzer* M, pl. *-i*, 20c, 2(1 tech) **Bg** *ekonomaĭzer*/*ikonomaĭzer* M, pl. *-al-i*, mid20c, 2(1 tech) **Hu** [=E] [U] 20c, 2(1 tech) **Al** - < *ekonomiqar*

economy *cp¹/adj.* 'a flight tariff' **Ge** *-klasse* [=E] 1950s (1 tech+5) < *Touristenklasse* **Du** *economy class* [=E] C, pl. *-es*, 1980s (1 tech) < *toeristenklasse* **Nw** (0) < *økonomiklasse* **Fr** - < *économique* adj. **Sp** - < *(clase) turista* **It** *economy class* [ɛkɔnomi klas] F, pl. Ø, mid20c (1 tech) < rend *classe turistica* **Rm** (0) **Po** - < trsl *klasa ekonomiczna* **Cr** - < trsl *ekonomska klasa* **Bg** *ikonǔmi (klas)* end20c (1 tech/sla) < rend *ikonomicheska/turisticheska klasa* **Hu** *economy-class* [=E] [U] mid20c (1 tech) < *túrista osztály* **Gr** *economy class* 20c (1 writ) < *turistikí thesi*

eco-pack* *n.* 'a refill' **Fi** - < *ekopakkaus* (3/5) **Gr** <=E> [eko pak] N [U] 1990s (1 mod)

Ecstasy *n.* 3 'a hallucinatory designer drug' **Ge** [=E] N [U] 1980s (1 you) **Du** [=E] N [U] 1980s (1 you) **Nw** <=E>/*E* [=E] M [U] 1980s (1 tech) **Ic** [=E] N [U] 1990s (1 you) = trsl *alsæla*; *E-pilla* **Fr** [ekstazi] M, 1980s (1 tech) **Sp** (0) < mean *éxstasis* **It** [ekstazi] F [U] end20c (1 jour, you, mod) **Rm** [ekstazi/=E] N [U] 1990s (1 tech) = *extaz* **Rs** *ékstazi* N [U] 1990s (1 tech) you) **Cr** (0) **Bg** *ekstŭsi* N [U] 1990s (1 tech) **Hu** [=E][U] end20c (1 tech) **Gr** *ekstasi* N [U] 1990s (1 you)

ECU *abbr.* 'Formerly planned European currency unit'

Although the words underlying this acronym are English, the form suggests an ancient French coin ('shield') – to tone down French concerns? – and is accordingly pronounced the French way in most languages. The term was in provisional use in the 1980s, and is now to be replaced by *Euro* when the common European currency is introduced.

Ge [e:ky̱:] M, pl. *-s*, 1980s (3, felt to be Fr) **Du** *E.C.U.* [e:ky:] C, pl. *-'s*, 1980s (2) **Nw** <=E>/*ecu* [eky̱:] M, pl. *-er*/Ø, 1980s (Ø) **Ic** [ɛ:kʰu] N, pl. Ø, 1990s (Ø); *eka* F, pl. *-ur*, 1990s (Ø) **Fr** *ecu* [eky̱:] C, pl. *-s*, 1980s (Ø) **Sp** [eku] M, pl. *-s*, 1980s (Ø) **It** [ẹku] M, pl. Ø, 1980s (2) **Rm** [eku/eky̱] M, pl. Ø, 1990s (3 tech) **Rs** *ékyu* N, uninfl., 1980s (1 tech) **Po** N [U] 1990s (1 jour, mod) **Cr** [eku] M, pl. *-ji*, end20c (2) **Bg** *ekyu* N, pl. Ø/-*ta*, end20c (3) **Fi** [=Fr] 1980s (3Fr) **Hu** [eky] [U] end20c (3Fr) **Al** *EKU* M [U] end20c (1 tech) **Gr** [ɛcu] N, 1980s (2, felt to be Fr)

editing *n.* 'the practice of preparing a text for printing or viewing by correcting mistakes, etc.'
It [ẹditin(g)] M [U] 1960s (1 tech) **Rm** - < *editare* **Fi** - < *editointi* ← *editoida* v.

editor *n.* 2 'a person who directs the preparation of a newspaper', 3 'a person who selects material for publication', 4 'a person who edits filmtracks', 5 'a computer program for modifying data'
Ge 2,3,4(5La); [=E] M, pl. Ø/-*s*, 1990s, 5(1 tech) **Du** [ɛdita] M, 1980s (2 tech) **Nw** [=E] M, pl. *-er*, 1990s, 4(1 tech, rare) **Ic** [ɛ:tɪtor] M, pl. *-ar*, 1980s, 5(2 tech, coll) > rend *ritill, ritþór* **Fr** *éditeur* 4(4) 2,3,5(5) **Sp** [editọr] M, 3,5(4); - < 2: *director* **It** [ẹditor] M, pl. Ø, 1980s (1 tech) < 2: *direttore*; - < 3: *curatore*; 4: - < *tecnico del montaggio* **Rm** [editọr] M, beg20c, 3(5Fr/La); mid20c, 2(5Fr/La); 1990s, 4,5(4 tech) **Po** *edytor* [editọr] M, 1980s, 5(1 tech) **Cr** *editor* M, pl. *-i*, 1990s, 5(1 tech) **Bg** - < 2,5: *redaktor* **Fi** *editoija* 3,4(3); *editointiohjelma* 5(3) **Hu** [=E] [U] end20c (5L) 5(1 tech) **Al** *editor* [editọr] M, pl. *-ë*, 2,3(1 reg) **Gr** <=E> [=E] M, pl. *-s*, end20c, 5(1 tech)

editorial *n.* 'a newspaper article written by or on behalf of an editor'
The status of this loanword is marginal as native and well-established terms are available, and the English term adds neither precision nor prestige. For Romance languages the word may be (considered) native.
Ge [editọ:riəl] N, pl. *-s*, 1970s (1 jour) < *Leitartikel* **Du** *editoriaal* N, pl. *editorialen*, 1970s (5Fr) < *hoofdartikel* **Nw** (o) < *leder* **Fr** *éditorial* [editɔʀjal] M, mid19c (3) **Sp** [editorial] M (4) **It** - < trsl *editoriale* **Rm** [editorjal] N, beg20c, via Fr (3) **Po** (o) **Cr** - < *uvodni članak* **Hu** - < creat *vezércikk* **Al** - < *artikull editorial* (5It) **Gr** <=E> [=E] N, 1990s (1 writ, jour, mod)

efficiency *n.* 1 'the state or quality of being efficient'
Ge *Effizienz* F (5La) **Du** [=E] C [U] 20c (2) **Hu** *efficiencia* (5La)

egghead *n.* 'an intellectual, an expert'
The evidence is neatly divided between loanwords, translations and absence (in the majority of languages) without exhibiting a regional pattern. All uses are

stylistically restricted (often facetious).
Ge [ekhet] M, pl. *-s*, 1960s (1 mod, rare) **Du** *egg-head* [ɪkhet] C, 1970s (1 mod) **Fr** - < trsl *tête d'œuf* **Sp** - < trsl *cabeza de huero* **It** - < trsl *testa d'uovo* **Rs** *égkhẹd* M, pl. *-y*, 1990s (1 jour) **Hu** - < trsl *tojásfejű*

ego-flip *n.* 'an activity devoted entirely to one's own interests and feelings'
Ic *egóflipp* [ɛ:kouflɪhp] N [U] end20c (1 sla)

ego-freak* *n.* 'a selfish and egocentric person'
Ic *egófrík* [ɛ:koufri:k] N, pl. Ø, end20c (1 sla)

ego trip *n.* 'an activity devoted entirely to one's own interests or satisfaction'
Ge [e̱:gotrip] M, pl. *-s*, 1970s (1 coll) **Du** *egotrip* [e̱:xotrɪp] C [U] 1970s (1 coll) **Nw** *egotripp* [e̱:gutrip] M, pl. *-er*, 1970s (3) → *egotripper* n. **Ic** *egótripp* [ɛ:koutrɪhp] N [U] end20c (1 sla) **Sp** M [U] 1980s (1 tech, rare)

elder statesman *n.* 'an influential, experienced politican (esp. retired)'
Ge [eldaste:tsmen] M, pl. *-men*, 1970s (1 jour) **Du** [=E] C, pl. *-men*, 1980s (1 jour)

electronic cash *phr.* 'payment by cheque card'
Ge [=E] N [U] 1990 (1 tech) **Nw** (o) **It** - < *pagamento con carta di credito* **Po** (o)

electrosmog* *n.* 'radiation from electrical appliances, which is considered unhealthy'
Ge *Elektrosmog* [=E] M [U] 1980s (5Gr+2)

elementary *adj.* 1a 'dealing with or arising from the simplest facts of the subject'
All languages have the Latin-derived adj., but only Icelandic adds the English loanword, significantly with a slang use.
Ic [=E] uninfl., end20c (0 sla)

elevator *n.* 1 'a hoisting machine', 3a '(US) a lift in buildings', 3b 'a place for lifting and storing grain', 4 'a muscle that raises a limb etc.'
The Latin base and the pronunciation as an internationalism in all the languages tested make the status as an anglicism very doubtful.
Ge 1(5La) **Du** [e:le:va:tər] 1,3b (5La) **Nw** [eleva:tur] M, pl. *-er*, beg20c (3 obs, rare) **Fr** - < *élévateur, rice, élévatoire* **Sp** - < mean *elevador* **It** - < 1: *elevatọre*; < 3a: *ascensore* M **Rm** [elevator] N, mid20c, via Fr/Ge, 1(3 tech) *lift, ascensor* → *elevatorist* **Rs** *élévator* M, pl. *-y*, mid20c, 3b(5La) **Po** 3a(0) **Cr** 3a(0) **Bg** *elevạtor* M, pl. *-al-i*, mid20c, 1,3b,4 (1 tech); - < 3a: *asansyọr* **Fi** *elevaattori* 3b(1 tech) **Hu** *elevátor* [eleva:tor] pl. *-ok*, end19c/beg20c, 3a(3 rare) < ↑*lift* **Al** *elevator* [elevatọr] M, pl. *-ë*, 3a(1 reg)

elf *n.* 1 'a mythological being', 2 'a sprite or little creature'
This word is one of the earliest loans in German, adopted with the immensely popular plays of Shakespeare during the eighteenth century and later spreading through German and French.
Ge *Elf*/*Elfe* M/F, pl. *-(e)n*, 18c (3) → *elfisch* adj. **Du**

elf (5) **Nw** *alf* (5) **Ic** *álfur* (5) **Fr** *elfe* [ɛlf] M, beg19c (3) **Sp** *elfo* M 19c (3) **It** *elfo* M, pl. -*i*, beg19c (3) **Rm** [=E] M, beg20c, via Fr/Ge, 1(3 rare) **Rs** *él'f* M, pl. -*y*, 20c(Ø) **Po** M, beg20c, via Ge (2) **Bg** *elf* M, pl. -*al-i*, 20c, 2(Ø)

e-mail/electronic mail *n.* 1 'messages distributed by electronic means, esp. from one computer system to one or more recipients', 2 'the electronic mail system'

This recent loan does not permit safe conclusions about how it will be treated; however, it is noteworthy that mainly Germanic languages have adopted the loanword whereas others have preferred to calque.
Ge [i̠:me:l] F [U] 1980s (1 tech) → *e-mailen* v. **Du** [=E] C, 1980s (1 tech) **Nw** [=E] M, pl. -*er*/[U] 1980s (1 tech) > trsl *e-post* → *maile* v. **Ic** [i:meil] N/[i:meitl] M [U] 1990s (1 tech, coll) < rend *tölvupóstur* **Fr** <=E> M, 1980s (1 tech/ban) > rend *messagerie (électronique)* < *courrier électronique* **Sp** [imei̠l] M [U] 1990s (1 tech, rare) < trsl *correo electrónico* **It** [=E] F [U] 1990s (1 tech) < trsl *posta elettronica* **Rm** *e-mail* [=E] N [U] 1990s (1 tech) > rend *poştă electronică* **Rs** *i-mei̠l* M, uninfl., 1990s (1 tech) < trsl *élektronnaya pochta* **Po** <=E> F, 1990s (1 tech) < trsl *poczta elektroniczna* **Cr** [imejl] F [U] 1990s (1 tech) < trsl *elektronska pošta* **Bg** *imei̠l* M[U] 1990s (1 tech) < trsl *elektronna poshta* **Fi** *meil/maili* [meili] (1 tech); - < 2: *sahköposti* → *mailata* v. **Hu** [=E] [U] 1980s (1>2 tech) → -*ez* v. **Gr** <=E> [imei̠l] N, pl. Ø/-s, 1990s (2)

emergency *n.* 1 'a sudden state of conflict requiring immediate action'
Du [=E] F/M, 1980s (1) **Nw** (0) **Ic** [=E] N [U] end20c (0 sla) < rend *neyðar-* **Sp** - < *emergencia* **It** - < trsl *emergenza* **Al** - < *emerjenzë* (5It)

emitter *n.* 'a region in a transistor producing carriers of current' (electr.)
Ge [emita] M, pl. Ø, 20c (1 tech) **Nw** [emi̠ter] M, pl. -*e*, 20c (1 tech) **Fr** *émetteur* M, beg20c (5) **Sp** - < *emisor* **Rm** *emitor* [emito̠r] N, mid20c **Rs** *émitter* M, pl. -*y*, mid20c (1 tech) **Po** *emiter* [emiter] M, mid20c (1 tech) **Bg** *emi̠ter* M, pl. -*al-i*, mid20c (1 tech) **Fi** *emitteri* (3 tech) **Hu** [emitter] [U] 20c (1 tech) **Al** *emiter* [emi̠ter] M, pl. -*ë*, beg20c (1 tech)

encounter *n.* 'a group-therapeutic meeting'
Ge [enka̠unta] N/M, pl. Ø, 1970s (1 tech, rare) **Du** *encounter groep* [ɪnka̠untər-] end20c (1 tech+5) **Bg** (0)

English Waltz* *n.* 'a slow waltz'
Ge [=E] M [U] beg20c (1 arch) < *langsamer Walzer* **Du** - < trsl *Eng wals* **Nw** - < trsl *sakte vals* **Bg** - < trsl *angliĭski vals* **Hu** - < trsl *angol keringő*

energy drink* *n.* 'an isotonic sports drink'
Ge [=E] M, pl. -*s*, 1990s (1 tech) **Ic** - < trsl *orkudrykkur* **Hu** - < trsl *energia ital*

engineer *n./cp[1]* 1 'a person qualified in a branch of

engineering', +7 'a specialist in the rationalization of work processes'

The French term is already widespread, having been well-established for more than a century. The marginal adoption of the English word is occurring in the field of economics, where it is used to refer to specialists working on the most effective production methods. The distribution of the word in -*ing*, which refers to the same domain, is better established.
Ge [=E] cp[2], M, pl. -*s*, 1960s, +7(1 tech, rare); 1(0) < *Ingenieur* (5Fr) **Du** [ɛnd3ini:r] M, 1980 (2) **Nw** (0) < *ingeniør* (5Fr) **Fr** - < *ingénieur* **Sp** - < *ingeniero* **It** - < *ingegnere* (5La) **Rm** - < *inginer* **Rs** (5Fr) **Po** (5Fr) **Cr** - < *inženjer* (5Fr) **Bg** - < *inzhener* (5Fr) **Fi** - < *insinööri* (5Fr) **Al** - < *inxhinier* (5Fr)

engineering *n.* 'used as an equivalent for industrial engineering, i.e. the application of technical and economic methods to improve work processes'
Ge [=E] N [U] 1960s (1 tech) **Du** [=E] N [U] 1970s (1 tech) **Nw** [=E] M [U] 1960s (1 tech) **Fr** [ɛn(d)3inirin/in-] M, 1950s (1 ban) < *ingénierie* **Sp** - < *ingeniería* **It** [=E] M [U] 1960s (1 tech) < *ingegneria* **Rm** [end3iniriŋ] N [U] end20c (1 tech) **Rs** *inzhiniring* M [U] end20c (1 tech) **Po** (0) **Cr** *inženjering* M [U] end20c (1 tech) **Bg** *inzhenering* M [U] 1980s (3 tech) → -*ov* adj. **Hu** [end3ini:ring] [U] mid20c (1 tech) **Al** *inxhiniering* [ind3injeriŋ] M, pl. -*ë*, 1980s (1 reg) **Gr** <=E> [endziniriŋ] N [U] end20c (1 tech)

enter *v.* **Ic** 'come in, come on stage', +11 'board a ship by force', +12 'a command used in operating in computers'
Ge *entern*, 19c, from Du?, +11(3); 1980s, +12(1 tech) **Du** *enteren* [ɛntərən] +11(5Sp) **Nw** *entre* ["ɛntrə] beg20c, 1c(3); +11(5Fr) **Fr** < trsl *entrée*, +12(1 tech) **Ic** [ɛŋter] end20c, +12(0 tech) **Sp** - < +12: mean *entrar* **It** [ɛnter] end20c, +12(1 tech) < rend *invio* **Rm** +12(0>1 tech) **Po** [-er] uninfl., 1980s, +12(1 tech) **Cr** *enter* 1980s, +12(1 tech) **Bg** *entŭr/*<=E> end20c, +12(1 writ) **Fi** [=E] +12(1 tech) **Hu** [enter] 1980s, +12(1 tech) **Gr** <=E> [=E] N, uninfl., +12(1 tech)

entertainer *n* 'a person who entertains, esp. professionally on stage, etc.'

The two words (-*er*, -*ment*) are almost exclusively found in Germanic where they compete with well-established native terms. The anglicisms are used exclusively for stage and TV comedians.
Ge [entate̠:na] M, pl. Ø, 1960s (1 jour) = *(Allein)unterhalter* → -*in* F **Du** [ɪntəte̠:nər] C, 1970s (2) **Nw** [=E] M, pl. -*e*, 1950s (2) > *underholdningsartist* **Ic** [ɛŋtert[h]ei:ner] M, mid/end20c (1 coll) < rend *skemmtikraftur* **Sp** [enterte̠iner] M, pl. -*s*, 1950s (1 tech) **It** [enterte̠iner]

M, pl. Ø, 1970s (1 tech) < trsl *intrattenitore* **Rm** (0) **Rs** *énteteiner* M, pl. -y, 1990s (1 tech)

entertainment *n.* 2 'a public performance'
Ge [entate:nment] N [U] 1970s (1 jour) < *Unterhaltung* **Du** [intəte:nmənt] N [U] 1970s (2) **Nw** [=E] N [U] 1960s (2) < *underholdning* **Sp** [entertinmen] M [U] end20c (1 tech, rare) **It** [enterteinment] M, pl. Ø, end20c (1 tech) < trsl *intrattenimento, spettacolo* **Rm** [=E] N [U] end20c (1 rare)

environment *n.* 1 'the physical conditions, surroundings, etc. in which a person lives', 4 'the overall structure within which a user, computer or program operates' (comput.), 5 'a structure designed to be experienced from inside as a work of art'

The currency of this term appears to be most frequent for the arts genre which grew (with *happening, performance* etc.) in the 1960s. For the much more general meaning of *e.*, native terms appear to be preferred.

Ge [=E] N, pl. -s, 1960s, 1(0) 4,5(1 tech) < 1: *Umwelt* **Du** [=E] N, 1970s, 4(1 tech) **Nw** (0) < *miljø* **Ic** - < trsl *umhverfi* **Fr** [=Fr] 1960s (4) **Sp** [=E] M, pl. -s, 1970s, 1(1 tech$_{ART}$) = *ambiente* **Rm** [=E] N, end20c, 1(1 tech) < *mediu* **Rs** - < *okruzhayushchaya sreda* **Po** <=E> M [U] end20c, 1,4(1 tech) **Cr** [=E] M [U] end20c (1 tech) → *environmentalist* M **Bg** - < rend *okolnata sreda* **Gr** - < 4: mean *perivalon*

Epsom salts *n.* 'a preparation of magnesium sulphate used as a purgative etc.' (medicine)
Du *epsomzout* [ɛpsɔm-] N [U] 1980s (1 tech+5) **Ic** *epsom-salt* end19c, N [U] (2 tech) **Fr** - < trsl *sel d'Epsom/epsomite* **Sp** - < trsl *sal de Epsom, epsomita* **It** *epsomite* F [U] 19c (3 tech) **Rm** - < *epsomit, epsomită*, rend *sare mază* **Rs** *épsomit* M [U] mid20c (1 tech) **Po** *epsomit* [epsomit] M, mid20c (1 tech) → *-owy* adj. **Cr** - < trsl *epsomska sol* **Bg** - < creat *angliiska sol* **Fi** *epsominsuola* (1 tech) **Hu** *epszomit* [epsomit] [U] 19c (1 tech) **Gr** *(alata) Epsom* N, pl., beg20c (5+1 tech)

equalizer *n.* +4 'a device raising or lowering sound frequencies'

This term exemplifies the pervasiveness of modern HiFi equipment (with notable exceptions in South-eastern Europe) and the inevitable replacement, by derivation, of related stems in Romance languages.

Ge [i:kvəlaiza] M, pl. Ø, 1980s (1 tech) **Du** *equaliser* [i:kwəlajzər] C, 1980s (1 tech) **Nw** [=E] M, pl. -e, end20c (1 tech) **Ic** [i:kulaiser] M, pl. -ar, end20c (1 tech) = rend *tónjafnari* **Fr** <=E> M, 1970 (1 tech, ban) < trsl *égaliseur* **Sp** - < trsl *ecualizador* **It** *equalizzatore* M, pl. -i, beg20c (3 tech) **Rm** [=E] N, 1990s (0) < trsl *egalizor* **Rs** *ékvalaizer* M, pl. -y, end20c (1 tech) **Po** [ekwalajzer] M, end20c (1 tech) **Cr** *ekvilajzer* M, pl. -i, end20c (1 tech) **Bg** *ekvalaizer* M, pl. -al-i, end20c (1 tech) **Fi** - < *ekvalisaattori* < *taajuuskorjain* **Gr** *ekualaizer* N, 1980s (1 tech)

equipment *n.* +1a 'technical articles necessary for certain functions'
Ge [ekvipment] N [U] 1980s (1 mod) < *Ausrüstung* **Du** [=E] N, 1990s (1 mod) **Nw** (0) < *utrustning, utstyr*

escalator *n.* 'a moving staircase'
As is the case with ↑*elevator*, the Latin-based word is felt to be an anglicism only in a few languages (as in French).
Ge - < *Rolltreppe* **Du** - < *roltrap* **Nw** (0) < *rulletrapp* **Ic** [ɛskalato:r] M, pl. -ar, 1960s (0 obs) < rend *rúllustigi* **Fr** [ɛskalatər] M, 1940s (1 ban) < *escalier mécanique* **Sp** - < *escalera mecánica* **It** - < creat *scala mobile* **Rm** [eskalator] N, mid20c, via Fr/Rs? (3 tech, obs) < *scară rulantă* **Rs** *éskalator* M, pl. -y, mid20c (3) **Po** *eskalator* [eskalator] M, mid20c, via Rs (1 tech) **Cr** *eskalator* M, pl. -i, end20c (1 tech) **Bg** *eskalator* M, pl. -al-i, mid20c, via Rs (2) **Al** *eskalator* [eskalator] M, pl. -ë, mid20c (1 tech) **Gr** - < *kiliomeni skala*

escapism *n.* 1 'the tendency to seek distraction and relief from reality, in politics or art'
Ge *Eskapismus* [-a:pis-] M [U] mid20c (3 tech) → *-istisch* adj. **Du** *escapisme* [ɪskɑpɪsmə] N, pl. -n, 1950s (3 tech) **Nw** *eskapisme* [eskapisme] M [U] 1950s (3 tech) **Sp** *escapismo* M, 20c (3 tech) **It** *escapismo* M [U]

Ic	Nw	Po	Rs
Du	Ge	Cr	Bg
Fr	It	Fi	Hu
Sp	Rm	Al	Gr

1980s (3 tech) **Rm** [eskapism] N [U] 1970s (3 tech) **Rs** *éskepizm* M [U] end20c (1 tech) **Po** *eskapizm* [eskapizm] M [U] mid20c (1 tech) → *eskapista* M; *eskapistyczny* adj. **Cr** *eskapizam* M [U] mid20c (1 tech) **Bg** *iskeipizüm* M [U] mid20c (1 tech, rare) **Hu** *eszképizmus* [eske:pizmuʃ] [U] mid20c (1 tech) **Gr** - < *tasis fighis*

escort *n.* 1 'one or more persons accompanying a person', 2 'a person accompanying a person of the opposite sex socially', +2a 'an act of accompanying a person socially'

The noun and verb are old loans from French, mainly with military reference (*escorte(r)*). Only Dutch appears to have adopted the English term referring to personal relations. This has prompted a series of new compounds, all unrecorded in English: *-boy, -girl, -lady* and *-service*.

Ge (5Fr) **Du** [ɛskɔ:t] F/M, 1980, 2,+2a(2/1 mod) **Nw** [=E/eskorte] M, pl. -er, 1980s, 2,+2a(1 rare) **Ic** [ɛskort] N [U] beg/mid20c, 1,2(5Da) **It** *scortare* (5Fr) **Rm** - < *escortă* **Rs** *éskort* (5Fr) **Po** (5Fr) **Cr** (5Fr) **Bg** *eskort* 1(5Fr) **Hu** 2,+2a(5Fr) **Al** (5Fr)

essay *n.* 1 'a composition, usu. short and in prose, on any subject', +1a 'a student paper'
A decision about whether this loanword is from English rather than from the French *essai* can be based on form and meaning. Since the English *essay* was a major form of literary influence in eighteenth/nineteenth-century Europe, the word can be consid-

ered to be an anglicism where recorded from such contexts. Cf. ↑*essayist.*
Ge [ese:] M/N, pl. -*s*, 19c, 1(2) +1a(1 tech) → -*istisch* adj.   **Du** [ɪse:] N, beg20c, 1(5Fr)   **Nw** [=E] N, pl. -*s*/ Ø/-*er*, beg20c, 1(2) +1a(1 tech) → *essayist* M   **Ic** *esseilessay* [ɛs:ei] N, pl. Ø; *esseyja* [ɛs:eija] F, pl. -*ur*, 1970s, 1(2 tech)   **Fr** *essai* [ese] (4)   **Sp** - < *mean ensayo*   **It** *essai* (5Fr)   **Rm** *eseu* [esew] N, 1940s, 1(5Fr)   **Rs** *ésse* N, uninfl., beg20c, via Fr, 1(3); +1a(1)   **Po** *esej* M, beg20c (2) → *eseistyka* F; *eseik* M; *eseistyczny* adj.   **Cr** *esej* M, pl. -*i*, beg20c, 1(3); +1a(1 tech)   **Bg** *ese* N, pl. -*ta*, beg20c, via Fr, 1(3); +1a(0) → -*istika* F; -*istichen* adj.   **Fi** *essee* 19c, 1,+1a(3)   **Hu** *esszé* [esse:] pl. -*k*, end19/beg20c, 1(3/ 5Fr?); +1a(1 tech)   **Al** *ese* [ese] F, pl. Ø, beg20c, 5Fr? (1 tech)

essayist   *n.* 'a writer of essays'
Ge [ese:ist] M, pl. -*en*, 19c (5Fr?)   **Du** [ɪse:ɪst] C, pl. -*en*, beg20c (2)   **Nw** [eseiist] M, pl. -*er*, beg20c (3) → *essayistikk* M; *essayistisk* adj.   **Ic** *essayisti* [ɛs:eijɪstɪ] M, pl. -*ar*, 1970s (2 tech)   **Fr** *essayiste* [esejist] M, 19c (3)   **Sp** *ensayista* (3)   **It** - < *saggista*   **Rm** *eseist* [eseist] M, 1940s, via Fr (3)   **Rs** *ésseist* M, pl. -*y*, beg20c, via Fr (3) → -*ka* F   **Po** *eseista* [eseista] M, beg20c (2) → *eseistka* F   **Cr** *esejist* M, pl. -*i*, beg20c (3)   **Bg** *eseist* M, pl. -*i*, beg20c, via Fr (3) → -*ka* F   **Fi** *esseisti* 19c (3)   **Hu** *esszéista* [esse:iʃta] pl. -*ók*, end19/ beg20c (3)   **Al** *eseist* [esejist] M, pl. -*ë*, beg20c (3)

essential(s)   *n.* 1 'basic/indispensable things'
As with ↑*elementary*, the Latin-derived word is common, but only German appears to have adopted also the English form (clearly marked by the pronunciation).
Ge [esenʃəl] N, mostly pl., 1960s (1 tech>mod)

establishment   *n.* 6a 'a group in a society that exercises authority or influence and is seen as resisting change'
This loanword was adopted as part of the political terminology of the student movement of the 1960s (also ↑*anti-e.*) regardless of the fact that the earlier French loan *établissement* was available for quite different senses. The word seems to have outlived most other slogans of the time.
Ge [isteblifment] N [U] 1960s (1 obs)   **Du** [=E] N [U] 1960s (2)   **Nw** [=E/es-] N, [U] 1960s (1)   **Fr** [establifment] M, 1960s (1 obs) → *établissement*   **Sp** *(e)st- ablishment* [establifmen(t)] M [U] 1970s (1 tech) > *establecimiento*   **It** [establifment] M [U] 1960s (1 jour/tech) < *classe dirigente*   **Rm** [=E], 1970s (Ø)   **Rs** *istablishment* M [U] end20c (1)   **Po** [-ment] M [U] end20c (1 jour)   **Cr** *establišment* M [U] end20c (1)   **Bg** *isteblishmŭnt* M [U] end20c (1 jour, rare)   **Hu** [=E/este:- blifment] [U] mid20c (1 rare/jour/tech_POLIT)   **Al** *establishment* [establifment] M [U] end20c (1 reg)   **Gr** - < *katestimeno*

ET   *n.* +2 'an extraterrestial being'

Ge (0)   **Sp** [ete] M, end20c (1)   **Hu** [=E/e:te:] [U] 20c (1_NAME)   **Gr** [iti] M [U] 20c (1_NAME)

eurocity*   *n.* 'a fast train travelling through European cities' (cf. ↑*intercity*)
Ge [ɔɪrositi] M, pl. -*s*, 1980s   **Du** [œrositi] M, pl. -*s*, 1980s   **Fr** [œrositi] M [U] end20c (1 tech)   **It** [eurositi] M, pl. Ø, 1980s (2)   **Rm** [eurositi] N, pl. Ø, end20c (1 rare)   **Rs** (0)   **Po** [eurosity] N [U] end20c (1 tech)   **Cr** (0)   **Hu** [eurositi] pl. Ø, end20c (2)

event   *n.* 1 'a spectacular thing taking place', 3 'an item in a sports programme, or the programme as a whole'
Ge [=E] M, pl. -*s*, 1980s, 1(1 you/jour)   **Du** [=E] N, 1990s (1 sla)   **Sp** - < *evento*   **It** - < *evento* (5La)   **Rm** [event, =E] N, 1960s, 3(1 tech, rare)   **Al** *ivent* M [U] 20c (1 reg)

evergreen   *n.* +3 'a song or film of enduring popularity'
This word appears to have been taken over only in its metaphorical sense of an everlasting song, film etc. (Used in relation to plants the term is sometimes calqued as in German *Immergrün*). The word has given rise to playful coinages such as German *nevergreen* and *everblues* (= 'jeans'), some of which are independent of English.
Ge [evagri:n] M, pl. -*s*, 1960s (2)   **Du** [=E] C, 1970s (2)   **Nw** [=E] M, pl. -*s*, mid20c (2)   **It** [evergri:n] M/adj., pl. Ø, 1980s (1 tech, mod)   **Rm** [=E] N, end20c (1 tech)   **Rs** *évegrin* M, pl. -*y*, 1990s (1 you, mod)   **Cr** *evergrin* M, pl. -*i*, end20c (2)   **Bg** *evŭrgrin* M, pl. -*al-i*, end20c (1 tech)   **Fi** - < *creat ikivihreä*   **Hu** [evergri:n] [U] mid20c (Ø) < *trsl örökzöld*   **Gr** *evergrin* N, 1960s (1 obs)

everybody's darling*   *n.* 'a person, esp. a politician (trying to be) popular with the public'
Ge [=E] M [U] 1970s (1 jour) = *trsl jedermanns Liebling*

exchange   *n.* 2a 'the giving of money for its equivalent in the money of the same or another country', +2c 'the place where such a transaction takes place', 4 'a place where merchants gather to transact business'
The English word appears to be slowly encroaching on native terms, mainly as a consequence of modern tourism, as conspicuous signs attract the foreigner's attention to the facility, always in Roman script.
Ge (0/1 writ)   **Du** [ɛkstʃendʒ] F/M, 1980s, +2c(0)   **Nw** (0) < 2a: *veksel, veksling*, < 4: *børs*   **Sp** - < 2a: *cambio*   **It** - < 2a: *cambio*, 4: *borsa*   **Rm** [=E] N [U] end20c, 2a,+2c(1 mod)   **Rs** (1 writ)   **Po** <=E> F, uninfl., end20c, 2a(2)   **Cr** - < 2a: *mjenjačnica*   **Bg** <=E> 1990s, 2a(1 tech, writ) < *change*; rend *obmen na valuta*; 4: *borsa*   **Hu** [=E] [U] mid20c, 2a(1 tech), 4(2 mod)   **Gr** 2a(1 writ)

executive   *adj./cp[1]* 1 'having managerial or admin-

istrative responsibility', +3 'characteristic of, or fit for, businessmen (-*jet*, -*briefcase* etc.)'
Ge [=E] cp[1], 1980s, 1(1 tech, jour) **Du** [=E] C, 1990s, 1(1 jour) **Nw** *eksekutiv* [ɛksekʉti̠:v] cp[1], 20c, 1(5) **Fr** - < *exécutif,-ve* **Sp** - < *ejecutivo* **It** [igzɛ̠kjutiv] cp[2]/n, 1960s (1 tech) **Rm** - < *executiv* **Al** *ekzekutiv* mid20c (3) **Gr** <=E> [egzɛ̠cutiv] adj./cp[1], 1990s (1 tech, jour, mod)

executive class* *n.* 'a class of air travel'
Du [ɛksəkju:tɪf kla:s] **Nw** - < *business class, business-klasse* **It** [ɛgzɛ̠kjutiv kla̠s] M, pl. Ø, end20c (1 tech) = *business class* **Rs** - < *biznes klass* **Cr** (0) **Bg** - < *biznes klasa* **Hu** - < *business class* **Al** - < *biznes klas* **Gr** (1 writ) < *business class*

exhaust *n.* 1a 'waste gases etc. expelled from an engine after combustion', 1b 'the pipe or system by which these are expelled', 1c 'the process of expulsion of these gases'
Du *exhauster, exhaustor* C, beg20c (1 tech) **Nw** *eksos* [ɛksu̠:s] M [U] beg20c (1 tech) **Hu** (5La)

exit poll *n.* 'a poll of people leaving a polling station'
It [ɛgzit po̠l] M, pl. Ø, 1970s (2 tech) **Rm** [=E] N [U] 1990s (0>1 tech) **Fi** [=E] 1990s (1 mod) > rend *ovensuukysely*

expander *n.* 1 'an apparatus used to strengthen muscles'

This word (and the apparatus) were spread as part of the 'fitness and bodybuilding culture', even, notably, to Slavic languages. The character of an anglicism is not always quite clear.

Ge [ɛkspa̠nda] M, pl. Ø, mid20c (3 tech) **Du** [ɪkspa̠ndər] C, beg20c (3) **It** - < *estensore* **Rm** - < *extensor* **Rs** *éspander* M, pl. -*y*, mid20c (1 tech) **Po** (5La) **Cr** *ekspander* M, pl. -*i*, end20c (1 tech) **Bg** *ekspa̠nder*

M, pl. -*al-i*, mid20c (1 tech) **Hu** [ɛkspander] pl. -*ek*, beg20c (1 tech) **Gr** <=E> [=E] M/N, 1990s (1 tech)

export *n.* 1 'the process of exporting', 2a 'an exported article or service'
Latin, French and English provenance or interpretations are all possible for the group of *export*-words, except where pronunciation and morphology determine the case (as in German *Exporteur* 5Fr). Although English impact is not in question, it can rarely be proved.
Ge [ɛksport] M, pl. -*e*, 19c (3/5) **Du** [ɛkspɔrt] M, pl. -*en*, beg20c (3) **Nw** *eksport* (5Fr) **Ic** [ɛkspɔrt] N [U] end19c < rend *útflutningur* **Sp** - < *exportación* **It** [ɛksport] M, pl. Ø, end19c < *esportazione* **Rm** [ɛksport] N, end19c, via Ge, 1(3) **Rs** *éksport* M [U] end19c, 1(3) → -*nyĭ*, adj. **Po** (5La) **Cr** *eksport* M, pl. -*i*, beg20c (3) < -*ni* adj. **Bg** *eksport* M [U] mid20c (2) → -*en* adj. **Hu** [ɛksport] pl. -*ok*, end19/beg20c, 1(3 tech), 2a(1 tech, rare) → -*ál* v. **Al** *eksport* [ɛksport] M, pl. -*ë*, end19c (3)

export *v.* 'send out goods for sale in another country'

Ge *exportieren* (3/5Fr) **Du** *exporteren* (5Fr) **Nw** *eksportere* (5Fr/Nw) **Fr** *exporter* [ɛkspɔʀte] mid18c (4) → *exportation* F **Sp** *exportar* (3/5La) **It** *esportare* (5La) **Rm** *exporta* [eksporta̠], end19c (5Fr) **Rs** *éksportírovat'* 19c (3 mod) **Po** (5La) **Cr** *eksportirati* (3) **Bg** *eksportiram* (3) **Hu** *exportál* [eksporta:l] end19/beg20c (3) → -*ás* n. **Al** *eksportoj* end19c (3)

exporter *n.* 'someone who exports'
Ge - < *Exporteur* (5Fr) **Du** - < *exporteur* (5Fr) **Nw** - < *eksportør* (5Fr) **Fr** - < *exportateur/-trice* (4) **Sp** - < *exportador* **It** - < *esportatore* **Rm** - < *exportator* **Rs** *éksportër* M, pl. -*y*, beg20c (2) **Po** *eksporter* [eksporter] M, mid20c (2) **Cr** *eksporter* M, pl. -*i*, mid20c (2) **Bg** *eksportyor* M, pl. -*i*, mid20c, via Rs/Ge (3 tech, obs) → -*ka* F; -*ski* adj. **Hu** *exportőr* (5Fr) **Al** - < *eksportues*

express *n./cp[1]* 1a 'an express train, bus or delivery service', +1b 'fast'
Ge (5Fr) **Du** *espres* C, pl. *expressen*, 19c (2) **Nw** *ekspress* (5La) **Fr** [ɛksprɛs] M, adj., mid19c (3) **Sp** [ɛksprɛs] 1880s, via Fr < *expreso* **It** [ɛksprɛ̠s] M, pl. Ø, end19c (2) < trsl *espresso* **Rm** *expres* [ɛksprɛs], N/cp[2], beg20c, via Fr (2) **Rs** *ékspress* M, pl. -*y*, end19c (3) → -*veĭ* M **Po** *ekspres/*<=E> M, beg20c (3) **Cr** *ekspres* M, end19c (3) → -*ni* adj. **Bg** *ɛ̠kspres* M, -*al-i*, mid20c, via Fr (2) → -*en* adj. **Fi** [=E] adj., end20c (2) **Hu** *expressz* [ɛkspress] pl. -*ek*, end19c (3) **Al** *ekspres* [ɛksprɛ̠s] M, pl. -*e*, mid20c (3) **Gr** *expres*, N, adv. (2)

eye-catcher* *n.* 'a striking, attention-getting device in advertising'
Ge [a̠iketʃa] M, pl. Ø, 1980s (1 mod) < *Blickfang* **Du** *eyecatcher* [=E] C, 1980s (1 mod) < *blikvanger* **Nw** (0) < *blikkfang*

eyeliner *n.* 'a cosmetic applied as a line round the eye'
The wide distribution of this word is unusual for a cosmetic term; calques do not appear to have been used extensively (cf. the much more restricted currency of the other two *eye*-words)
Ge [a̠ilaina] M, pl. Ø, 1960s (1 mod) **Du** *eyeliner* [=E] C, 1960s (1 tech) **Nw** [=E] M, pl. -*e*, 1960s (2) **Ic** [=E] M, pl. -*ar*, 1960s (1 coll) **Fr** [ajlajnœr] M, 1960s (1 tech) **Sp** [ejeliner/ajliner] M, 1980s (1 tech) > *(lápiz) perfilador de ojos*

It [a̠ilainer] M, pl. Ø, 1960s (2 tech) **Rm** [=E] N, 1970s (1 mod) **Po** [-er] M, end20c (1 mod) **Cr** [ajla̠jner] M, pl. -*i*, end20c (1 tech) **Bg** *a̠ilaĭnŭr* M, pl. -*al-i*, end20c (1 mod) **Fi** [=E] 20c (2) **Hu** [a̠:i-lainer] pl. Ø, mid20c (1 tech) < *szemceruza* **Gr** *ailainer* N, end20c (2)

eye-opener *n.* 1 'an enlightening experience, an unexpected revelation'
Du [a̠jopənər] F/M, 1980s (2) **Nw** (0) **Hu** - < rend *szemfelnyitó* adj.

F

---

face *n.* 1 'the front of the head'
Ge [=E] N, end20c (1 sla, rare) **Nw** *fjes* [fje:s] N, pl. Ø, 19c, via Da (3) **Ic** [=E] N, pl. Ø, end20c (1 sla); *fés* [fje:s] N, pl. Ø, mid20c, via Da (3 coll, pej); *fas* N, 17c, Middle English (4 obs) **Rs** *feĭs* M, pl. *-y*, 1990s (1 sla) **Bg** *feĭs* M, pl. *-al- ove*, 1990s (1 you, sla)
face *v.* 3a 'meet resolutely or defiantly; confront'
Nw ["feise] end20c (1 coll, sla) **Ic** [fei:sa] 1970s (1 sla)
facelift(ing) *n.* 1 'cosmetic surgery to remove wrinkles', 2 'a procedure to improve something's appearance' (cf. ↑*lifting*)
The rapid spread of this term is due mainly to the media coverage of plastic surgery undergone by film stars etc. *Lifting* is used by itself, but the metaphorical uses are based on the full form as the procedure is most commonly associated with facial cosmetic surgery.
Ge [=E] N, pl. *-s*, 1980s, 1(2 mod), 2(1 jour) = *Face-lift* **Du** *face-lift/facelift* [=E] C, 1960s (2) → *faceliften* v. **Nw** *facelift* [=E] M, pl. *-s*, 1980s, 1(1 rare) < 1,2: trsl *ansiktsløftning* **Ic** [=E] 1960s, 1(0 obs) < creat *andlitslyfting* **Fr** - < *lifting* **Sp** *(face) lifting* [feis liftin] M, 1980s, 1(1 tech), 2(1 tech) < 1: *estiramiento (facial)* **It** - < *lifting* < *plastica facciale* **Rm** 1(0) **Rs** *(feĭs)lifting* M [U] 1980s, 1(3 tech, mod) **Po** <=E> M [U] 1980s, 1(1 tech) **Cr** [fejslifting] M [U] 1990s (1 tech) **Bg** - < *lifting* **Hu** - < rend *arcfelvarrás* **Gr** - < *lifting* < *ritidhektomi*
fact *n.* 3 'an item of information, data, evidence'
Again, the Latinate word is commonly known all over Europe; only in German and Norwegian does the anglicism seem to have been added – for more informal contexts.
Ge [fɛkt(s)] M, freq. pl., 1960s (1 jour) < *Tatsache, Fakt, Faktum* (5La) **Du** *facta* (5La) **Nw** [=E] usu. pl., mid20c (2) < *faktum* (5La) **It** *fatti* (5La) **Rs** (5La) **Po** *fakt* M, pl. *-y*, beg20c (3) → *-icheskiĭ* adj. **Bg** *fakt* M, pl. *-al-i*, beg20c (5La) → *-icheski* adj. **Fi** *fakta* (5La) **Al** *fakt* M, pl. *-e*, end19c (3)
fact-finding *cp¹* '(a politician's) attempt to establish the truth about an issue'
Ge [=E] 1970s (1 jour)
faction *n.* 'a book, film, etc., using real events as the basis for a fictional narrative or dramatization' (a blend of *fact* and *fiction*)
Ge [=E] F? [U] 1980s (1 jour, rare) **Du** [fɛktʃən] M [U] 1980s (1 tech) **Nw** [=E] M [U] 1990s (1)
factoring *n.* 6 'the transfer of a manufacturer's in-voices to a company that takes the responsibility for collecting the payments due to them'
This recent economic term is as yet infrequent and restricted to specialist use in Western Europe.
Ge [=E] N [U] 1980s (1 tech) **Du** [=E] C [U] 1970s (1 tech) **Nw** <=E>/*faktoring* [=E,fakturiŋ] C [U] 1970s (1 tech) **Fr** [faktɔriŋ] M, 1970s/mid20c (1 tech/ban) < *affacturage* **Sp** [faktorin] M [U] 1970s (1 tech) > *facturación* **It** [fɛktoriŋ] M [U] 1970s (1 tech) **Rm** [faktoriŋ] N, 1990s (1 tech) **Rs** *faktoring* M [U] end20c (1 tech) → *-ovyĭ* adj. **Bg** *faktoring* M [U] end20c (1 tech) **Hu** - < *faktorálás* [faktora:-la:ʃ] [U] 1980s (3 tech)

factory *n.* 2 'a merchant company's foreign trading station' (hist.)
Du *factorij/faktorij* (5) **Nw** *faktori* [fakturi:] N, pl. Ø, 19c, 2(1 arch) **Ic** - < *verksmiðja* **Fr** - < *factorerie* **Sp** - < *factoría* **Rs** *faktoriya* F, pl. *-rii* (1 tech, arch) **Bg** *faktoriya* F, pl. *-rii*, 20c, via Rs (3 tech, hist)
fade *n.* 'the action or instance of fading in a picture or sound' (cinema.)
Du [=E] C [U] 1970s (1 tech) **Sp** [=E] M, end20c (1 tech) **It** [=E] M [U] mid20c (1 tech) **Fi** [=E] (1 tech)
fade *v.* 6a 'cause a picture to come gradually in or out of view' (cinema.), 6b 'make sound gradually more or less audible', +6c 'make the lights in a theatre etc. become more or less bright'
Nw <=E>/*fade ut* ["feide] mid20c (1) **Ic** [fei:ta] end20c (1 tech) **Fi** [=E] 6a,b(1)
fade-out *n.* 2 'the action or an instance of fading out a picture or a sound', +3 *cp¹* 'loss of colour'
Ge [=E] N [U] 1980s, 2(1 tech, rare); ~ *jeans* 1980s, +3(1 mod, rare) **Du** [=E] <=E>/*outfaden* [autfe:dən] 1990s, +2(1 tech) **Nw** → v. **Ic** [=E] N [U] 1970s (1 tech) **Fr** <=E> M (1 tech, ban) < *fondu, fondu au noir, fermeture en fondu*
fading *n.* 1 'loss of colour', 7 'varying intensity of a radio signal', 8 'reduced braking efficiency due to the heating up of brakes'
Ge [=E] N [U] beg20c, 7(1 tech); 1960s, 8(1 tech, rare) **Du** [fe:ding] C [U] beg20c, 7(1 tech) **Nw** [=E/feid-] C [U] mid20c, 7(1 tech) **Fr** [fadiŋ/fedin] M, beg20c, 7(1 tech, ban) < *évanouissement* **Sp** [=E/fadin] M [U] 1930s, 7(1 tech); 1980s, 8(1 tech) <

7: *desvanecimiento* **It** [f̱ɛ̱diŋ] M [U] 1920s, 7(1 tech) < *evanescenza* **Rm** <=E>/*feding* [f̱ɛ̱diŋ] N [U] 1930s, 1,7(1 tech) **Rs** *f̱ɛ̱ding* M [U] mid20c, 7(1 tech) **Po** [fadink/=E] M [U] mid20c, 7(1 tech) **Cr** *f̱ɛ̱ding* M [U] beg20c, 7(1 tech) **Bg** *f̱ɑ̱ding* M [U] mid20c, 7(1 tech) **Hu** [f̱ɛ̱:ding/f̱ɑ̱dding] [U] beg20c, 7(1 tech)

fair *adj.* 1 'just, in accordance with the rules' (mainly in sports and politics)

The spread of this term (together with ↑*fair play*, but much more restricted in ↑*fairness*) accompanied English influence in all sports disciplines in the late nineteenth century. Apparently, existing words for 'just, correct' were not felt to be precise enough for the new concept.

Ge [fe:r] mid19c (2) **Du** [fɛ:r] 19c (2) **Nw** [=E/fœ:r] beg20c (2) **Ic** [=E] uninfl., end20c (1 sla) **It** - < mean *corretto* **Rm** [fer] adj./adv., uninfl. (2) **Po** [fer] uninfl., mid20c (2) **Cr** *fer* uninfl., mid19c (2) **Hu** [fer] 19c (1 tech)

fairness *n.* 'justice'
Ge -*ss*/-*β* F [U] beg20c (2) **Nw** [=E] M [U] mid20c (1) **It** [=E] F, pl. ∅ (1) < *correttezza* **Po** (0) **Cr** *fernesa*/*fernes* F [U] 19c (2)

fair play *phr.* 'reasonable treatment or behaviour'
Ge [fe:r ple:] N [U] beg20c (1 tech) **Du** [=E] C [U] 19c (1 tech) **Nw** [=E] [U] beg20c (2) → *fair player* M **Ic** [=E] end20c (0 sla) **Fr** *fair-play* [fɛʀple] M [U] mid19c/1920s (2 ban, obs) < *franc-jeu* **Sp** [fer plei] M [U] 1920s (1 tech) = *juego limpio* **It** [=E] M [U] 1820s (2 tech) < *correttezza* **Rm** [f̱ɛ̱rplej] N [U] 1960s (2) **Rs** *fér pleĭ* M, uninfl., 1990s (1 tech) < rend *spravedli-vaya igra* **Po** [fer p̱lej] M [U] beg20c (1 tech) **Bg** *fe̱ŭrpleĭ* M [U] end20c (1 tech) < creat *sportsme̱nska igra* **Fi** [=E] beg20c (1 tech) < rend *reilu peli* **Hu** [fer ple:] [U] 19c (1 tech>2 coll) **Gr** *fer p̱lej* N [U] beg20c (1 tech)

fake *n.* 1 'a thing or person that is not genuine', +3 'bad or forged drugs'
Ge [=E] N/M?, pl. -*s*, 1990s, 1(1 jour) **Du** [fe:k] M [U] 1970, 1,+3(1 tech) **Nw** [=E] ["f̱ɛ̱ike-] cp[1], 1980s, 1(1 tech) **Ic** [=E] N, pl. ∅, 1970s (1 sla) **Fi** *feikki* 1990s, 1(1 sla)

fake *v.* 1 'make something that appears genuine but is not; forge, counterfeit,' +3 'deceive', +4 'sell bad drugs'
Du *faken* [feikən] 1970s, 1,+3(2) **Nw** ["f̱ɛ̱ike] 1970s (1 coll, sla) **Ic** *feika* [fei:ka] 1970s (1 sla)

fake *adj.* 1 'counterfeit, not genuine', +2 (of a feeling, illness) 'pretended'
Du [fe:k] 1970s (2) **Nw** [feik] 1980s (1 sla, rare)

fallout *n.* 1 'radioactive debris'

Acceptance of this term came with the increasing awareness of the consequences of nuclear waste in the 1960s, but was strengthened by the Chernobyl catastrophe in 1986. Native equivalents have proved to be too clumsy to compete with the concise *fallout* wherever it was adopted.

Ge [=E] M [U] 1960s (1 tech) **Du** *fall-out* [fɔ:laut] C [U] 1970s (1 tech) **Nw** (0) < *(radioaktivt) atomnedfall* **Fr** *fall-out* end20c (1 ban) < *retombées (radioacti-ves)* **Sp** [folaut] M [U] end20c (1 tech, rare) < creat *lluvia radiac-tiva* **It** *fall-out* [folaut] M [U] 1960s (1 tech) < rend *caduta di polveri radioattive* **Rm** [folawt/=E] N, 1970s (1 tech) < creat *cădere de pulberi radioactive* **Rs** 0 < trsl *radioaktivnye chastitsy* **Cr** [=E] M [U] end20c (1 tech) **Bg** - < creat *radioaktivni chastitsi* **Hu** [fal aut] [U] 1970s (1 tech)

false start *n.* 1 'a disallowed start in a race'
Ge - < trsl *Fehlstart* **Du** - < trsl *valse start* **Nw** - < *tjuvstart* **Fr** - < trsl *faux départ* **It** - < trsl *falsa partenza* **Sp** - < *salida en falso* **Rm** - < *start greşit* **Rs** *fal'start* M, pl. -*y*, mid20c (1 tech) **Po** *falstart* [falstart] M, mid20c (1 tech) **Bg** *falstart* M, pl. -*al-ove*, mid20c (3 tech)

family tennis* *n.* (orig.™) 'a version of tennis played with soft balls'
Ge [=E] N [U] 1970s (2)

fan *n.* 'a devotee of a particular activity, performer, etc.'

This word owes its remarkable spread to a number of factors: its popularity in youth culture, esp. music and sports; its ease of pronunciation; and its having more positive connotations than words like *freak*, *maniac* and combinations with -*nik*.

Ge [fen, fæn] M, pl. -*s*, 1950s (2) = *Anhänger* **Du** [fɛn] C, 1940s (2) **Nw** [=E] M [U]/pl. -*s*, 1950s (2) = *tilhenger, beundrer* **Ic** <=E> [=E] N, pl. *fön* M pl. *fönir*, 1960s (1 sla) < *aðdáandi, áhangandi* **Fr** [fan] M/F, 1950s (2) **Sp** M/F, pl. -*s*, mid20c (2) **It** [fan/fɛn] M, pl. ∅/-*s*, 1930s (2) **Rm** [fan/fen] M, end20c → *fană* [fanə] F (1 coll) **Rs** *fén/fan* M, pl. -*y*, end20c (1 you/coll) < *fanatik* → -*at* M, -*atka* F **Po** [fan] M, beg20c (2) → -*ka* F **Cr** *fan* M, pl. -*ovi*, mid20c (2) **Bg** *fen* M/cp[1], pl. -*ove*, 1990s (2 jour/you) = *pochitatel* → -*ka* F **Fi** *fani* end20c (3) **Hu** [=E] [U] 20c (2 coll/tech) < *rajongó* **Al** - < *fanatik* **Gr** *fan* M/F, pl. ∅/-*s*, end20c (2 coll, you) < *opadhos*

fan club *n.* 'an organized group of devotees'
Ge [f̱ɛ̱nklup] M, pl. -*s*, 1970s (2) **Du** [f̱ɛ̱nklʏb] M, 1970s (2) **Nw** *fanklubb* [fæ:nklʉb] M, pl. -*er*, 1960s (2) **Ic** *fanklúbbur* [fa:nkʰlup:ʏr] M, pl. -*ar*, 1960s (1

sla) < trsl *aðdáendaklúbbur* **Sp** - < trsl *club de fans*
It [fan klɛb/klab/klœb] M, pl. Ø, 1960s? (2) **Rm**
[fanklub] N, 1990s (1 you) **Rs** *fénklub* M, pl. -*y*,
end20c (1 you/coll) **Po** (0) **Cr** (0) **Bg** *fenklub* M,
pl. -*al-ove*, 1990s (2) **Fi** [=E]/*faniklubi* (1) **Gr** *fan
klab* N, pl. Ø/-*s*, end20c (2 coll, jour, you)

fancy *n.* 2 'a caprice or whim', 5a 'the faculty of using
one's imagination'
Du [fɛnsi] F/M, beg20c (2) **Nw** (0)

fancy *adj.* 1 'ornamental, not plain', 2 'capricious,
whimsical, extravagant'
Nw [=E] 1960 (2 coll) **Ic** [=E] uninfl., end20c, 2(1 sla)

fancy fair* *n.* 1 'a charity bazaar'
Du [fɛnsife:r] M, beg20c (2)

fan mail *n.* 'letters from fans'
Ge - < trsl *Fanpost* **Du** *fanmail* [fɛnme:l] F/M [U]
1970s (2) **Nw** [=E] M [U] 1970s (1) **Ic** - < trsl
aðdáendabréf **Fi** - < *faniposti*

fantasy *n.* 2 'a fanciful mental image', 4 'a fantastic
invention or composition; a fantasia', 5 'a literary
genre'
 The form of the loanwords does not make it clear
whether some are long-established items from Greek
or recent borrowings from English (most likely in the
literary sense).
 Ge [=E] F [U] 1980s, 5(1 tech) **Du** - < *fantastische
literatuur* **Nw** [=E] M [U] 1960s, 5(1 tech) **Ic** *fantasía* [fantasi:a] F, pl. -*ur*, beg20c (5Da) **Fr** 5(0) **Sp**
- < 2,4: *fantasía*; 5: - < *literatura fantástica* **It** [fan-
tazi] F/adj., pl. Ø, 1980s, 5(1 tech) **Rs** *fantaziya* F, pl.
-*zii*, beg20c, via Gr, 2(3); *fantastika* F [U] mid20c, 5(3);
fèntezi N [U] 1990s, 5(1 tech) **Po** (5Gr) **Cr** - <
fantazija **Bg** *fantaziya* F, pl. -*zii*, 20c, via Rs,
2,4(5Gr); *fentŭzi* N [U] end20c, 5(1 tech, mod) < *fantastika* **Fi** *fantasia* 5(3) **Hu** 5(5Gr) **Al** *fantazi*
[fantazi] F [U] beg20c, 5(1 tech) **Gr** *fadasia* F, 2(4)

farad *n.* 'the SI unit of capacitance' (electr.)
 Michael Faraday (1791–1867) was an assistant to
Sir Humphry Davy, professor of chemistry in London, from 1814, whom he succeeded in 1833; his name
survives in *farad, faraday* and *Faraday's cage*. The
status of an anglicism is questionable; the name
Farad has nothing English in its form, and since
the *Système internationale* is a standardized system,
local variants are taboo; and SI metric is French in
origin.
 Ge [fa:rat] N, pl. Ø, 19c (3 tech) **Du** [fa:rɑt] C [U]
beg20c (1 tech) **Nw** [fara:d] M, pl. Ø, beg20c (3
tech) **Ic** [fa:rat] N, pl. *faröd*, end20c (1 tech) **Fr**
[faʀad] M, end20c (1 tech) **Sp** [farad] M, pl.
-*s*, end19c (1 tech) = *faradio* **It** [farad] M, pl. Ø,
end19c (1 tech) **Rm** [farad] M, end19c/beg20c (1
tech) **Rs** *farada* F, pl. -*y*, beg20c (3 tech) → *mikro-
farada* F **Po** *farad* [farat] M, beg20c (1 tech) →
-*yzacja* F[U]; -*yzowanie* N; -*yzować* v.; -*yczny* adj.
Cr *farad* M, pl. -*i*, beg20c (1 tech) **Bg** *farad* M, pl.
-*a*, 20c (1 tech) **Fi** *faradi* **Hu** [fara:d] [U] end19/
beg20c (3 tech) → -*izál* v. **Al** *farad* [farad] M [U] (1
tech) **Gr** *farad* N, via Fr (1 tech)

far-fetched *adj.* (of an explanation etc.) 'strained,
unconvincing'
Nw [=E] uninfl., 1980s < *søkt*

farm *n.* 1 'an agricultural establishment', cp² 2 'a
place for breeding a particular type of animal etc.'
 This English word was originally borrowed from
French in the fourteenth century. Modern loanwords
have been taken from English or French and frequently designate (generally or exclusively) farms in
English-speaking countries – such as those owned by
Finnish immigrants in the USA. The same applies to
farmer. But note the more widespread use as cp² (2),
with native reference.
 Ge [farm] F, pl. -*en*, mid19c, 1(Ø/3); 2(2) < 1: *Bauern-
hof* **Du** [farm] C, 19c, 1(Ø) < *boerderij* **Nw** [farm]
M, pl. -*er*, end19c, 1(Ø) 2(2) → *farme* v. **Fr** <=E> 19c,
1(Ø/1 ban) < *exploitation agricole* **It** [farm] M, pl. Ø,
1900s, 1(1 obs) < *fattoria* **Rm** - < *fermă* (5Fr) **Rs**
ferma F, pl. -*y*, 19c, 1(3/5Fr) **Po** *farma* [farma] F,
beg20c, 1(2) **Cr** *farma* F, pl. -*e*, beg20c, 1(2) **Bg**
ferma F, pl. -*mi*, beg20c, via Rs, 1(5Fr) **Fi** *farmi*
1(Ø) **Hu** [farm] pl. -*ok*, beg19c, 1(2) **Al** *ferm* [ferm]
F, pl. -*ë*, beg20c, 1(5Fr) **Gr** *farma* F, 19/20c, 1(3/Ø)

farmer *n.* 1 'a person cultivating a farm', +3 'blue
jeans'
 Ge [farma] M, pl. Ø, 19c, 1(Ø/3)
< *Bauer, Landwirt* **Du** [farmər]
C, 19c, 1(Ø) < *boer, landbou-
wer* **Nw** ["farmer] M, pl. -*e*,
end19c (Ø/2) (← *farme* v.) < 1:
gardbruker, bonde **Fr** <=E>
19c, 1(Ø/1 ban) < *agriculteur/
agricultrice, exploitant(e) agricole* **Sp** [=E] M, pl.
-*s*, beg20c, 1(1) < *contadino* **Rm** - < *fermier* **Rs** *fermer*
M, pl. -*y*, mid19c, 1(3/5Fr) → -*stvo* N; -*skiĭ* adj. **Po**
[farmer] M, mid19c, 1(2); *farmerki* pl., +3(2 coll) →
-*ka* F; -*stwo* N [U]; -*ski* adj. **Cr** *farmer* M, pl.
-*i*, beg20c, 1(2) → -*ka* F; -*ski* adj. **Bg** *fermer* M,
pl. -*i*, beg20c, via Rs, 1(3/5Fr) → -*ka* F; -*ski* adj. **Fi**
farmari 1(Ø); *farmari*-cp¹ (3) **Hu** [farmer] pl. -*ek*, 17/
18c, 1(Ø/2); mid20c, +3(3) **Al** *fermer* [fermɐr] M, pl.
Ø, beg20c, 1(Ø/5Fr) **Gr** 1(Ø)

Ic	Nw	Po	Rs
Du	Ge	Cr	Bg
Fr	It	Fi	Hu
Sp	Rm	Al	Gr

far west *n.* +1a 'the wild west'
Du *Far-West* C/N [U] 19c? (2) **Nw** [=E] N (Ø) **Fr**
[farwɛst] M, mid19c (Ø) **Sp** [far wɛst] M, end19c (Ø)
= trsl *el (Lejano) Oeste* **It** [far wɛst] M, end19c
(2) **Rm** (Ø) **Po** - < *dziki Zachód* **Cr** - < *daleki
(divlji) Zapad* **Bg** - < creat *diviyat zapad* **Al** <
perëndimi i bargët **Gr** *far uɛst* N [U] end20c (Ø)

f.a.s. *abbrev.* 'free alongside ship'
Ge [efa:ɛs] 20c (1 tech, rare) **Du** [ɛf a ɛs] 1940s (1
tech) **Nw** <=E>/*fas* [efa:ɛs, fa:s] 20c (1 tech) **Ic**
[fa:s] freq. cp¹, mid20c (1 tech) = *frítt að skipshlið* **Fr**
FAS (1 tech) < *FLN* **It** *FAS*, 1930s (1 tech) < rend
franco banchina nave **Rm** *FAS* [fas] 20c (1 tech) **Rs**
fas, mid20c (1 tech) **Po** *fas* [fas] end20c (1 tech) **Cr**
fas, end20c (1 tech) **Bg** *fas*, mid20c (1 tech) **Fi** [=E]
(1 tech) **Hu** [ef a: es] 20c (1 tech) **Gr** (1 writ)

fashion *n.* 1 'the current popular custom or style' (dress, manners), +5 'the fashion industry'

This word has always been marginal, having to compete with well-established *mode*. It is interesting to see that *f.* is going out of use in some languages, but is a recent adoption on its way in, in others – a trend also reflected by the derivative ↑*fashionable*.

Ge [=E] F [U] 20c (0>1 mod) < *Mode* **Du** [fɛʃən] F/M [U] beg20c, 1(2) < *mode* **Nw** [=E] M [U] beg20c (1) **Fr** [faʃjɔn] F, 19c, 1(1 arch) **Sp** [=E] F, uninfl., mid19c, 1(0>1 mod) < *moda* **It** [fɛʃɔn] F [U] beg19c, 1(1 tech) < *moda* **Rm** [fɛʃn] N [U] end19c (1 arch) < *modă* **Rs** (0) **Po** (0) **Cr** [fɛʃn] F/M [U] beg20c, 1(2) < *moda* **Bg** - < *moda* **Hu** [=E] [U] 19c, 1(1 rare) **Al** - < *modë* **Gr** <=E> 20c (1 writ) < *modha*

fashionable *adj.* 'following, suited to, or influenced by the current fashion'

Ge *fesch* mid19c (1 reg); *fashionable* 19c/1960s (1 obs/rare, mod) **Du** [=E] 19c (1 arch) **Nw** *fasjonabel* [faʃunaːbel] beg20c (3) **Fr** [faʃjɔnabl?] 19c (1 arch) **Sp** [=E] mid19c (1 arch) **Rm** *faşionabil* [faʃionabil] end19c, via Fr (3 arch) **Rs** *feshenebel'nyĭ* 19c (1 arch) **Cr** (0) **Hu** [fɛʃøneːbl] 19c (1 tech/coll)

fashion victim *n.* 'a slavish follower of trends in fashion'

Gr <=E> [fasjon viktim] M/F, pl. -*s*, 1980s (1 mod, jour, you)

fastback *n.* 1 'a motor car with the rear sloping continuously down to the bumper', 2 'such a rear'

Ge [=E] M/N, pl. -*s*, 1960s (1 tech, obs) < 2: rend *Fließheck* **Du** [=E] C, 1960s (1 tech) **Nw** [=E] M, pl. -*er*, 1960s (1 tech) **Ic** [fastpahk] M, pl. -*ar*, 1970s, 1(0 tech) < rend *fleigbakur, sniðbakur, hlaðbakur* **Fr** (0) **It** [fastbɛk] M [U] 1990s (1 tech) **Rs** *fastbék* M, pl. -*i*, 1990s (1 tech) **Fi** (∅)

fast break* *n.* 'a sudden attack' (basketb.)

Ic [=E] N, pl. ∅, end20c (1 tech)

fast food *n./cp[1]* 1 'food that can be prepared quickly and easily, esp. in a snack bar or restaurant', +2 'a snack bar'

The currency of this widespread term is difficult to establish. It is known from eateries, but is not common as a generic term for such places. Its use for the type of food is even more restricted.

Ge [faːstfuːt] N/cp[1] [U] 1980s (1 mod) = 1: *Schnellgericht*; +2: *Schnellgaststätte* **Du** <=E>/ *fastfood* [faːstfuːt] N [U] 1980s (2) **Nw** [=E] 1980s, 1(2) = *gate-

kjøkkenmat; +2(1) < *gatekjøkken* **Ic** - < 1: creat *skyndibiti* **Fr** *fast-food* [fast fud] M, pl. *des fast-foods*, 1970s (1 ban, mod) > 1: *prêt à manger*; +2 *restauration rapide, fast-food restaurant* (1 ban) > *restovite* **Sp** [fasfud] F [U] 1980s, 1(1 tech) = 1: *comida rápida* **It** [fastfuːd] M [U] 1980s (2) **Rm** [=E] N [U] end20c (∅/1 mod) > *minuturi* **Rs** (0) **Po** [fastfut] M, uninfl., end20c (2 mod) → -*owy* adj. **Cr** [=E] M [U] end20c (2) **Bg** <=E> 1990s, +2(1 writ, mod_{NAME}) < creat *bŭrza zakuska* **Fi** [=E] end20c (1) = creat *roskaruoka* **Gr** <=E>/*fast fud/fastfud* N (2)

fathom *n.* 1 'a measure of six feet, esp. used in taking depth soundings'

Ge - < *Faden* (4) **Nw** - < *favn* (5) **Sp** M (∅) = *braza inglesa* **It** [=E/*fazom*] 19c (1 tech, rare) **Rm** [fatom] M, 1970s (1 tech) **Rs** *fatom* M, pl. -*y*, 18-19c (∅) **Cr** *fadom* M (∅) (1 tech) **Bg** *fadom* M (∅) **Hu** [fɛzɔm] [U] 19c (∅/1 tech_{NAUT})

fault *n.* 4a 'a service of the ball not in accordance with the rules' (tennis)

Ge (0 arch) < *Fehler* **Du** [=E] C, beg20c (2) **Nw** - < *feil* **Sp** [=E] M, pl. -*s*, beg20c (1 tech) **Rm** [fault/ =E] N, beg20c (3 tech_{FOOTB/TENNIS}) = 4a: *serviciu greşit* → *faulta* v.; *faultare* F **Cr** *folt* F [U] beg20c (1 tech) **Hu** [fault] [U] end19/beg20c (1 tech) → -*ol* v. **Gr** [=E] N [U] beg20c (1 tech) (only used by referees) < mean *lathos*

fax *n.* 1 'facsimile transmission', 2a 'a copy produced by this'

Ge [faks] N, pl. -*e*, 1980s (3 tech) **Du** [faks] M, pl. -*en*, 1970s, 1(3) **Nw** <=E> *faks* [faks] M, pl. -*er*, 1980s (2) **Ic** [faxs] N, pl. *fox*, 1980s (2) = rend 1: *bréfasími*, 2a: *simbréf* **Fr** <=E>/*fax* [faks] M, pl. ∅, 1980s (2) < *télécopie, télécopieur* **Sp** [=E/fas] M, pl. ∅/-*s*, 1980s (2) > *telefax* **It** [faks] M, pl. ∅, 1980s (2) > *telefax* **Rm** [faks] N, 1980s (2 tech) **Rs** *faks* M, pl. -*y*, 1980s (3) **Po** *faks*/<=E> M, 1980s (2) **Cr** [faks] M, pl. -*ovi*, end20c (3) **Bg** *faks* M, pl. -*a*/-*ove*, 1980s (2) **Fi** *fax* [faksi] (3) **Hu** [faks] pl. -*ok*, 1980s (2>3) **Al** *faks* M, pl. -*e*, end20c (3) **Gr** *fax* N, 1980s (2)

fax *v.* 'transmit a document by facsimile transmission'

Ge *faxen* 1980s (3 tech) **Du** *faxen* [faksən] 1970s (3) **Nw** *fakse*/*faxe* ["faksə] 1980s (2) **Ic** *faxa* [faxsa] 1980s (2) **Fr** *faxer*, end20c (2) > *télécopier* **Sp** *faxear* 1980s (3 tech) **It** *faxare* 1980s (3 tech) **Rm** *faxa* 1980s (3 tech) = *a da un fax* **Po** *faksować* [faksovatç] (2) **Cr** *faksirati* 1980s (3 tech) **Fi** *faksata* (3) **Hu** *faxol* [faksol] 1980s (2>3) **Al** *faksoj* end20c (3) **Gr** - < *stelno fax*

feasibility study *n.* 'a study of the practicability of a project'

Ge -*Studie* [=E+Ge] F, pl. -*n*, end20c (0>1 tech, jour) **Du** (0) **Nw** [=E] M, pl. -*ies*, end20c (1 tech, rare) **Fr** - < trsl *étude de faisabilité* **Sp** - < trsl *estudio de viabilidad* **It** - < trsl *studio di fattibilità* **Rm** - < rend *studiu de fezabilitate* **Po** <=E> N, uninfl., end20c (1 tech, mod)

feature *n.* +2a 'a striking appearance', 3 'a long

article on a special topic', 4a,b 'a broadcast or TV spot devoted to a particular topic, a documentary', +5 'a character, a sign'
Ge [=E] N, pl. *-s*, 1950s, 4a,b(1 tech) Du [=E] C, 1970s, 3,4a,b (1 jour) +2a(1 tech) Nw [=E] M, pl. *-s*, 1980s, 3,4a,b(1 tech) Fr (1 tech, jour, ban) > *varia* Rs (o) Cr (o) Hu [=E] [U] 1970s, 4a,b(1 tech) +5(1 tech$_{SCI}$)

feature *v.* 2 'be an important actor, participant or topic in a film', +2a 'present/promote a person (esp. a musician)'
Ge *featur(e)n* [=E] 1980s, +2a(1 you) Nw usu. → *featuring* [=E] 1980s, 2,+2a(1)

fed up *adj.* 'discontented or bored'
Nw [=E] mid20c (1 obs) Ic [=E] uninfl., end20c (o sla)

feedback *n.* 1 'information about the results of an experiment etc.; a response', 2a 'the return of a fraction of a signal to the input' (electr.), 2b 'a signal so returned'
This is considered a technical term when applied to electronics; by contrast the sense of 'response' has apparently spread into colloquial registers as a fashionable alternative to native expressions.
Ge [fi:tbek] N [U] 1960s, 1(1 tech, coll) 2a,b(1 tech) < 1: *Rückmeldung*; < 2a: *Rückkopplung* Du *feed-back* [fi:tbɛk] C [U] 1970s, 1(2 mod) Nw [=E] M [U] 1960s, 1(2 coll) 2a(1 tech) = 2a: rend *tilbakemelding* → *feedbacke* v. Ic [fi:tpahk] N [U] 1970s, 1(1 sla) 2a,b(1 tech) = rend *svörun* Fr *feed-back* [fidbak] M [U] 1950s, 1(2) Sp [fidbak] M [U] 1970s, 1(1 tech); 1930s, 2a(1 tech) = 1: creat *retroalimentación*; 2a: realimentación It [fi:dbɛk] M, pl. Ø, 1960s (1) < 2a,b: *contrareazione* Rm [fidbek] N [U] 1960s, 1(1 tech) Rs *fidbék* M [U] mid20c (1 tech) < creat *obratnaya svyaz'* Po [fidbek] M [U] end20c, 1(1 tech) Cr *fidbek* M [U] end20c, 1(1 tech) Bg *fidbek* M [U] end20c, 6a,b(1 jour) Cr *filing* M [U] mid20c (1 coll) Fi *fiilinkil(y)/fiilis*, 20c (3) Gr +6c(0)

feeder *n.* 7 'a main carrying electricity to a distribution point' (electr.)
Ge [fi:da] M, pl. Ø, 20c (1 tech, rare) Fr [fidœR] M, end19c (1 tech/ban) < *ligne de d'alimentation, coaxiol* Sp [fider] M, 1930s (1 tech) = *alimentador, línea de alimentación* It [fi:der] M, pl. Ø, 1900s (1 tech) Rm *fider/feeder* [fider, feder] N, 1940s (1>2 tech) Rs *fíder* M, pl. *-y*, 20c (1 tech) Po [fider] M, mid20c (1 tech) Cr *fider* M, pl. *-i*, mid20c (1 tech) Bg *fider* M, pl. *-ali*, mid20c, via Rs (1 tech) → *-en* adj.

feel *v.* +11 'like something'
Ic *fíla* [fi:la] 1960s (2 coll)
feeling *n.* 4b 'a vague awareness', 6a,b 'an emotional susceptibility and response', +6c 'an emotional response to circumstances, a mood'
The fashionable use of *feeling* is similar to that of ↑*touch* in many European languages; it is highly colloquial and imprecise, but of sufficient prestige to replace native equivalents, esp. in spoken use.
Ge [=E] N [U] 1960s, 6a,b(1 coll) Du [=E] N [U] 1940s, 6a,b(1 coll) Nw [=E] M [U] 1960s, 4b,6a,b(1 coll) < *følelse* Ic *filing/filingur* F/M [fi:liŋk(ʏr)] [U] 1960s, 6a,b,+6c(2 coll) Fr [filiŋ] M, 1950s (1 tech/mod) Sp [filin] M [U] 1970s (1 tech) It [fi:lin] M, pl. Ø, 1970s (1 coll) Rm [filiŋ] N [U] end20c (o) Po [-i-] M [U] end20c, 6a,b(1 jour) Cr *filing* M [U] mid20c (1 coll) Fi *fiilinkil(y)/fiilis*, 20c (3) Gr +6c(0)

fender *n.* 1 'a low frame bordering a fireplace', 2 'a bumper between a quay and a boat'
Ge [fɛnda] M, pl. Ø, beg20c, 2(3 tech) Du [fɛndər] C, 1970s (1 tech) Nw [=E] M, pl. *-el* *fendre*, beg20c, 2(1 tech) Bg *fender* M, pl. *-al-i*, 20c, via Ge, 2(1 tech) Fi *fendari*, 20c, 2(3)

ferry-boat *n.* 'a conveyance for people and goods'
The historical spread of this word (partly through French mediation) and the competition of native terms (partly calques) has left a unique distribution which requires closer investigation.
Ge - < *Fähre* Du *ferry(boat)* [fɛribo:t] C, 1940s (2 reg) < *veerboot* Nw (o) < *ferge, ferje* Ic - < *ferja* Fr [feribot/ferebot] M, 19c (2 ban) > *(navire) transbordeur*; ↑*(car) ferry* Sp <=E> M, end19c (1 arch); *ferry* M, pl. *-sl-ies*, beg20c (2>3) It [feri bo:t] M, pl. Ø, 1880s (1) < *traghetto* Rm *feribot* [feribot] N, 1940s, via Fr (3) Po (o) Cr *feribot* M, pl. *-ovi*, mid20c (3) *feribot* M, pl. *-al-i*, 1970s (2) → *-en* adj. Hu [=E] [U] 20c (Ø/1 tech) < trsl *komp(-hajó)* Gr *feribot/feril feribot* N, mid20c (2)

festival *n.* 2 'a concentrated series of concerts, plays etc. held regularly'
This loanword is widespread but not always felt to be from English, the vowels and stress being adapted to national conventions. *-ival* has been abstracted as a derivational morpheme of limited currency in German
Ge [=E] N, pl. *-s*, 1950s (2) = *Festspiele* Du [fistival] N, 19c? (3/5Fr?) Nw [festiva:l] M, pl. *-er*, 1950s (3) = *festspill* Ic [festiva:l] N, pl. *festivöl*, mid20c, via Da (2 coll) Fr [fɛstival] M, mid19c (3) Sp [festiba̱l] M, 19c (3) It [fɛstival] M, pl. Ø, mid19c (3) Rm

[festiv<u>a</u>l] N, 1910s, via Fr/It (3)   **Rs** *festival* M, pl. *-i*, 1950s, via Fr (3) → *-nyĭ* adj.   **Po** (5Fr)   **Cr** [f<u>e</u>stival] M, pl. *-i*, mid20c (3)   **Bg** *festival* M, pl. *-al-i*, 1950s, via Fr(2) → *-en* adj.   **Fi** (0) = *festivaali*   **Hu** *fesztivál* [f<u>e</u>stiva:l] pl. *-ok*, 1950s (3) → *fesztiváli* adj.   **Al** *festival* [festiv<u>a</u>l] M, pl. *-e*, mid20c (3)   **Gr** *festival* N, mid20c, via Fr (2)

fiction   *n.* 1 'an imaginary thing', 2 'literature' (cf. ↑*science fiction*)

Ge 1(5La)   **Du** [f<u>ɪ</u>ktʃən] F/M [U] 1980s (2) < *fictie*   **Nw** [=E] M [U] 20c (1 tech); *fiksjon* [fikʃ<u>u</u>:n] (3 tech)   **Ic** [fixsjoun] F [U] 1960s, 1(1 sla) 2(1 tech)   **Fr** 1(5) 2(4?)   **Sp** - < *ficción*   **It** [fik<u>ʃ</u>on/=E] F, 1980s, 2(1 tech)   **Rm** - < *ficţiune*   **Rs** (5La)   **Po** (5La)   **Cr** 2(0)   **Fi** *fiktio* (5La)   **Hu** 1(5La) (2)   **Al** *fiksion* [fiksj<u>o</u>n] M, pl. *-e*, end20c, 1(1 tech)

fifty-fifty   *n.* 'a boat powered equally by sail and motor'

Fr [=E] 1920s (1 tech)   **Sp** [=E] M, 1980s (1 tech, rare)

fifty-fifty   *adv./adj.* 1 'with equal shares'

The distribution of this term is almost universal and it appears always to occur in colloquial, spoken uses. There are various calques of similar style value.

Ge [=E] mid20c (2 coll) = *halbe-halbe*   **Du** [=E] 1940s (1 coll) < *half en half*   **Nw** [=E] mid20c (2 coll)   **Ic** [=E] uninfl., mid20c (1 coll)   **Fr** [=E] adv./M, 1920s (2 coll)   **Sp** [=E] 1970s (1 sla)   **It** [f<u>i</u>fti f<u>i</u>fti] 1950s (2 coll)   **Rm** [=E] end20c (1 coll)   **Rs** *fifti-fifti* end20c (1 coll)   **Po** <=E> end20c (2 coll)   **Cr** *fifti-fifti* end20c (2 coll)   **Bg** *fifti-fifti* mid20c (2 coll)   **Fi** [=E] 20c (1 coll)   **Hu** *fifti-fifti* [=E] mid20c (2 coll) = *fele-fele*   **Al** *fifti-fifti* end20c (1 you)   **Gr** *fifti fifti* end20c (1 tech, 2 coll) = *penida penida*

fight   *v.* 2 'contend with (an opponent)', +10 'contend aggressively with (an opponent)' (box.)

Ge [faitən] 1960s, +10(1 tech, coll)   **Nw** *fighte* [ˈf<u>ai</u>te] mid20c (1 coll)   **Ic** [fai:ta] end20c, 2(1 sla)   **Po** +10(0)   **Gr** - < mean *makhi*

fight   *n.* 1a 'a combat, esp. unpremeditated, between two or more persons, animals or parties', 1b 'a boxing-match'

Ge [=E] M, pl. *-s*, 1960s, 1a(1 jour); mid20c, 1b(1 tech, coll)   **Nw** [=E] M, pl. *-er*, mid20c, 1a,b(1 coll)   **Ic** [fai:t] M, end20c, 1a(1 sla) → *fætingur* M   **Rm** 1b(0)   **Po** 1b(0)

fighter   *n.* +3 'an aggressive boxer, (sometimes transferred to politicians etc)'

This term competes with native equivalents, having a more racy flavour. The related noun and verb are notably rarer. Extensions to include aggressive behaviour of, e.g., politicians are infrequent and often coined as nonce words.

Ge [f<u>ai</u>ta] M, pl. Ø, 1950s (1 coll)   **Nw** [=E/ˈf<u>ai</u>ter] M, pl. *-e* (1 coll)   **Ic** [=E] M, pl. *-ar*, 1970s (1 sla)   **It**

[f<u>ai</u>ter] M, pl. Ø, 1930s (1 tech)   **Rs** *f<u>ai</u>ter* M, pl. *-y*, end20c (1 tech)   **Po** *fajter/* <=E> M, mid20c (1 tech)   **Cr** *fajter* M, pl. *-i*, mid20c (1 coll)   **Bg** *f<u>ai</u>ter* M, pl. *-i*, mid20c (1 tech)

file   *n.* 1 'a folder, box, etc., for holding loose papers, esp. arranged for reference,' 2 'a set of papers kept in this', 3 'a collection of data stored under one name' (comput.)

Ge [=E] N/M, pl. *-s*, 1980s, 3(1 tech)   **Du** [fajl] M, 1970s, 3(1 tech)   **Nw** *fil* [fi:l] M/F, pl. *-er*, 1980s, 3(1 tech)   **Ic** *fæll* [faitl] M, pl. *-ar*, 1970s (3 coll) < *skrá*   **Fr** - < *fichier*   **Sp** - < trsl *archivo*   **It** [fail] M, pl. Ø, 1970s, 3(2 tech) > *archivio*   **Rm** 3(0 tech) < *fişier*   **Rs** *fail* M, pl. *-y*, end20c, 3(1 tech) → *-ovyĭ* adj.   **Po** <=E> M, end20c, 3(1 tech)   **Cr** [fajl] M, end20c, 3(1 tech)   **Bg** *fail* M, pl. *-al-ove*, 1980s, 3(1>2 tech)   **Fi** 3(0) < *tiedosto*   **Hu** <=E>/*fájl* [=E] pl. *-ok*, 1980s, 3(1 tech)   **Gr** <=E> [=E] N, pl. *-s*, end20c, 3(1 tech) = trsl *arkhio*

file   *v.* 1 'place (papers) in a file or among (esp. public) records'

Ic *fæla* [fai:la] 1970s (1 coll)   **Rm** (0 tech)

filibuster   *n.* 1a 'the obstruction of progress in a legislative assembly, esp. by prolonged speaking', 1b 'a person who engages in a filibuster', +2b 'a freebooter'

Ge 1a,b(Ø)   **Du** <=E> C, 1950s, 1a(1 tech)   **Nw** [filibuster] M, mid20c, 1a,b(1 tech)   **Sp** *filibustero* +2b(1 arch)   **Rm** [filibuster] N, 1970s, 1a(2 tech) → *filibusterism* N   **Rs** (5Fr)   **Cr** *filibaster* M, mid20c, 1a,b(1 tech) → *-ski* adj.   **Bg** *filib<u>ü</u>ster* M [U] 1990s, 1a(1 jour, rare)   **Fi** (Ø)   **Hu** [=E/-buster] pl. *-ek*, 19c, 1a,b(Ø)

film   *n./cp¹* 1 'a thin coating or covering layer', 2 'a strip covered with light-sensitive emulsion' (photogr.), 3b 'a filmed story'

The history of photography and films has left this loanword with no lexical competition (in either sense); it is generally no longer felt to be foreign (or of English provenance in particular). Various compounds and derivations attest to the universality of the term. Again, the related verb is (slightly) less widespread.

Ge [=E] M, pl. *-e*, mid20c, 1(3); end20c, 2,3b(3)   **Du** [film] C, end19c, 2,3b(3)   **Nw** [=E] M, pl. *-er*, 1(1 tech) 2,3b(3)   **Ic** *filma* [filma] F, pl. *-ur*, beg20c, via Da, 1,2(3) 3b(2 coll) < 3b: *kvikmynd*   **Fr** [film] M, 19c, 2(1) 3b(3) > *pellicule*; → *filmique* adj.; *filmer* v.; *filmage* n.   **Sp** M, 1(1 tech) 3b(2) < 1: *pelicula* = 3b: *pelicula* → *fílmico, filmina* etc.   **It** [film] M, pl. Ø, end19c, 1,2(2) 3b(3) < 1,2: *pellicola*   **Rm** [=E] N, 1930s, via Fr, 2,3b(3)   **Po** *fil'm* M, pl. *-y*, beg20c, 2(2) 3b(3)   **Po** M, beg20c, 2,3b(3) → *-iarz* M; *-owiec* M; *-owanie* N; *-owość* F, *-idło* N; *-ik* M; *-owy* adj.; *-owo* adv.   **Cr** *film* M, pl. *-ovi*, beg20c, 2,3b(3) → *-ski* adj.; *-aš* M   **Bg** *film* M, pl. *-al-i*, beg20c, 2,3b(2) → *-ov* adj. **Fi** *filmi*, beg20c 2,3b(2) **Hu** [=E] also as cp[1], pl. *-ek*, 19c/beg20c, 2(3 tech) 3b(3) → *-ez* v.; *-esít* v. **Al** *film* M, pl. *-a*, beg20c, 2,3b(1 tech) **Gr** *film* N, beg20c, 2,3b(2)

film *v.* 1a,b 'make a cinema or TV film'
  Ge *filmen* beg20c (3) **Du** *filmen/een film maken* beg20c (3) → *filmer* n. **Nw** *filme* ['filme] beg20c (3) **Ic** *filma* [filma] mid20c, 1b(2 tech, coll) < rend *kvikmynda* **Fr** *filmer* [filme] beg20c (2) > *tourner* **Sp** *filmar* (3) **It** *filmare* 20c (3) = *girare un film* → *filmato* adj./n.; *filmino* n. **Rm** *filma* beg20c, via Fr (3) **Po** *filmować* [filmovatç] beg20c (3) → *s-* v. **Cr** *filmovati* mid20c (3) → *filmovanje* N **Bg** *filmiram* mid20c (3) → *-iran* adj. **Fi** *filmata* (2) **Hu** *filmez* [filmez] 19/20c (3) **Al** *filmoj* **Gr** *filmaro* (3 tech) → *filmarisma* N

filmlet* *n.* 'a commercial spot on TV/cinema'
  Sp <=E> M, pl. *-s*, 1960s (1 arch, obs)

Filofax *n.* (orig.™) 'a portable loose-leaf filing system for personal or office use'
  Ge [=E] M, pl. Ø, 1990s (1 tech, rare) **Du** Ø **Nw** [fi:lufaks] M, pl. *-er*, 1980s (1 coll) **Ic** [fi:loufaxs] N, pl. *-föx*, 1980s (1 coll) **Gr** <=E>/*filofax* N, 1980s (1 tech)

fineliner* *n.* 'a pen with a very fine point'
  Du [fajnlajnər] M, 1980 (2 tech) > *fijnschrijver* **Rm** [=E] N, 1980s (1 tech)

finish *n.* 1b 'the point at which a race ends', +1d 'the quality of being able to finish well' (sport), 3 'what serves to give completeness' (cf. ↑*photo finish*)
  This word was first borrowed exclusively in the domain of sports (originally horse-racing) and then later, slightly less frequently, in the sense of technical perfection – the two borrowing processes and respective senses seem to be unrelated. The verb *finish* is much rarer in European languages.
  Ge [=E] N, pl. *-es*, beg20c, 1b(1 coll) 3(1 tech) **Du** [=E] C [U] 1940s, 1b(1 tech) 3(1 tech, reg) **Nw** [=E] M, mid20c, 1b,3(1) **Fr** [finiʃ] end19c, 1b,+1d(2) **Sp** - < 1d,3: trsl *acabado, terminación*

  It [finiʃ] M, pl. Ø, 1900s, 1b(1 tech) < *arrivo* **Rm** *finiş* [=E] N, 1960s, via Fr?, 1b,+1d(3) **Rs** *finish* M [U] beg20c, 1b,+1d(2 tech) 3(1 coll) → *-irovat'* v. **Po** *finisz* M [U] beg20c, 1b(3) 3(1 coll) → *-owanie* N [U] v.; *za-*v.; *-owy* adj. **Cr** *finiš* M [U] mid20c, 1b(3) **Bg** *finish* M [U] mid20c, 1b(2 tech) < *final* → *-iram* v. **Hu** *finis* [=E] [U] end19/beg20c, 1b(3 tech) → *-el* v. **Al** *finish* [finiʃ] M, pl. *-e*, mid20c, 1b,3(1 tech, you) **Gr** *finis* N [U] end20c, 1b,+1d,3(1 tech)

finishing touch *n.* 'the final details completing and enhancing a piece of work'
  Ge (0) **Du** [finɪʃɪŋ tatʃ] M [U] 1980s (2) **Nw** [=E] N [U] mid20c (1) **Sp** - < trsl *toque final* **It** - < rend *tocco finale*

Finn-dinghy see ↑*dinghy*

firmware *n.* 1 'a permanent kind of software programmed into ROM', +2 ' a computer component'
  Du [=E] C [U] 1970s (1 tech) **Fr** [firmwɛr] M, 1970s (1 tech, ban) < *microprogramme* **Sp** [firmwar/firwer] M, 1980s, 1(1 tech) **It** [farm wear] M, pl. Ø, 1980s (1 tech) **Rs** (0) **Po** - < rend *oprogramowanie firmowe* **Hu** [farmwer] pl. Ø, 1980s (1 tech) **Gr** (0 tech)

first-class *adj./cp[1]* 'of the best quality (e.g. accommodation in a hotel or degree of comfort in a train or plane)'; calques are notably frequent
  Ge [=E] uninfl., 1970s (1 coll) < *erste Klasse* **Du** [=E] 1980s (2) < *uitstekend* adv.; *eerste klasse* (cp[1]) **Nw** [=E] 20c (1) < *førsteklasse(s)* **Sp** [fers klas] F, end20c (1 tech, rare) < *primera clase* **It** [fərst klas/=E] F, uninfl., end20c (1 tech) **Rm** (0) < rend *clasa întâia* **Rs** *fërst klass* 1990s (1 jour) < trsl *pervyĭ klass, pervoklassnyĭ* **Po** (0) < trsl *pierwsza klasa* **Cr** - < trsl *prva klasa* **Bg** - < ?trsl *pŭrvoklasen* **Hu** [=E] beg20c (1 tech, coll, jour) < trsl *első osztályú* **Al** *fërst klas* 1990s (1 mod) **Gr** - < trsl *protis taxeos*

first lady *n.* 'the wife of a state president'
  This term exemplifies the gradual extension from status as a foreignism to its application to wives of presidents of states etc. in Europe. Calques are frequent (though the English model is often not unambiguous).
  Ge [först le:di] F, pl. *-(ie)s*, 1960s (1 jour) > trsl *Erste Dame* **Du** [=E] C, pl. *-'s*, 20c (Ø/2 jour) **Nw** (Ø) < *førstedame* **Fr** (Ø) < trsl *première dame* **Sp** [fers leidi] F (Ø/1 jour, rare) < *primera dama* **It** [fərst ledi] F, pl. Ø, 1950s (2) = trsl *prima donna* **Rm** (Ø/1 jour) < trsl *prima doamnă* **Rs** *fërst ledi* F, 1990s (1 jour) < trsl *pervaya ledi* **Po** [=E/fer-] F [U] end20c (1 jour) **Cr** - < trsl *prva dama* **Bg** < trsl *pŭrva dama* **Fi** [=E] (Ø) = trsl *ensimmäinen nainen* **Hu** [=E] pl. *-k*, 20c (Ø>1 jour) **Al** *fërst leidi* (0) **Gr** [ferst ledi] F, pl. *-ies*, end20c (0>1 jour) = trsl *proti kyria*

fish-eye (lens) *n./cp[1]* 'a wide-angle lens'
  The languages are neatly divided between those adopting loanwords, those creating calques, and those for which no term is recorded.
  Ge [=E] N, pl. *-s*, 1960s (1 tech, rare) < trsl *Fischauge* **Du** [=E] N, 1970s (1 tech) **Nw** *-objektiv* [=E] usu. cp[1], 1960s (1 tech) > trsl *fiskeøyelinse* **Ic** - < trsl *fiskaugalinsa* **Fr** [fiʃaj] M, pl. *-s*, 1960s (1 tech) **Sp** - < trsl *objetivo de ojo de pez* **It** [fiʃ ai] M, 1970s (1 tech) = *occhio di pesce, grandangolo* **Po** <=E> M [U] mid20c (1 tech) **Bg** *fishaĭ* M [U] mid20c (1 tech) < rend *obektiv ribeshko oko* **Fi** - < *kalansilmäobjektiivi* **Hu** *-objektív* [=E+Hu] cp[1], pl. *-ek*, 20c (1 tech+5)

fishy *adj.* 2 'arousing suspicion, questionable, mysterious'

Ic [fɪsːi] uninfl., end20c (1 sla)

fit *v.* 1 'be of the right size and shape for', 2a 'make suitable, adapt', 6 'be in harmony with, befit'
Du *fitten* [fɪtən] 1960s, 2a(2) **Ic** *fitta* [fɪhta] 1970s, 1,6(1 coll) **Cr** 2a(0)

fit *adj./cp¹* 2 'in good health or athletic condition'
This word was first borrowed as a sporting term (often for horses) in the late nineteenth century into German, Dutch, Polish, Hungarian, Romanian, its meaning being later extended to other contexts (German, Dutch). It is a late arrival in Norwegian, Icelandic, Croatian, Bulgarian, and is not (yet) recorded for the other languages. (The noun ↑*fitness* has an almost identical distribution, with the compound ↑*~ centre* trailing slightly behind). Note that the relationship between *fit* and *fitting* n., an older technical loan, is opaque even though the regional distribution is quite similar.

Ge [=E] end19c (3) **Du** [=E] beg20c (3) **Nw** [=E] 1990s (1 mod) **Ic** [fɪht] uninfl., 1970s (1 coll) **Rm** [=E] end19c (1 arch_HORSES) **Po** <=E> uninfl., beg20c (1 tech) **Cr** *fit* mid20c (1 tech) **Bg** *fit* uninfl., 1990s (1 mod) **Hu** *fitt* [=E] cp¹, end19/beg20c (3 tech>coll) → *-en* adv.

fitness *n./cp¹* 1 'good health or athletic condition', +2 'a type of fitness training usu. offered at a fitness centre'

Ge *-ß/-ss* F [U] 1960s, 1(3) **Du** [=E] C [U] 1980s, 1(2) > *fitheid* **Nw** [=E] M [U] 1990s, 1(1 mod) < *form* **Fr** 1(0/1 tech) **Sp** [fitness] M [U] 1980s, +2(1 tech) **It** [fitnes] F [U] 1980s, 1(1) **Rm** [=E] N [U] 1990s (1 mod/jour) **Rs** *fitnis* M [U] 1990s, +2(1 tech) **Po** <=E> F [U] 1990s, 1,+2(2 jour) **Cr** *fitnes* F [U] end20c (1 tech) **Bg** *fitnes* M [U] 1990s, +2(3 mod) **Hu** [=E] cp¹, end20c (2 mod) **Gr** (0)

fitness centre *n.* 'an establishment offering sports facilities'

Ge [=E] N, pl. ∅, 1960s (2) **Du** *fitnesscentrum* (2+5) **Nw** (0) < *helsestudio, treningssenter* **Ic** - < rend *likamsræktarstöð* **Fr** <=E> M, 1980s (1) **Sp** - < *centro de fitness* **It** [fitnes senter] M, pl. ∅, 1980s (1 mod) **Rm** [=E] N [U] end20c (0/1 mod) < rend *centru de fitness* **Rs** (0) **Po** (0) **Cr** *fitnes-centar* M, end20c (1 tech) **Bg** *fitnes tsentŭr* M, pl. *-ra/-trove*, 1990s (3+5 tech) **Hu** [=E+tsenter] pl. ∅, end20c (2 mod) **Gr** (0)

fitting *n.* 2b 'a linking element in apparatus', +2c 'a lamp-socket', +2d 'fixtures for pipes in a building' (plumbing)

Ge [=E] N, pl. *-s/-e*, beg20c, 2b,+2d(1 tech) < *Verbindung(sstück)* **Du** [=E] C, pl. *-s/-en*, beg20c, 2b,+2c(1 tech) **Nw** <=E>/*fittings* (sg.) [=E] M, pl. ∅/-s, beg20c, 2b(1 tech) **Ic** *fittings* [fɪhtiŋs] uninfl., mid20c, via Da, +2d(1 tech) **Rm** *fiting* [fiːtiŋg] N, 1940s, via Ge?, 2b,+2d(1 tech) **Rs** *fiting* M, pl. *-i*, +2d(1 tech) **Po** 2b(0) **Cr** *fiting* M, pl. *-zi*, mid20c, 2b(1 tech) **Bg** *fiting* M, mostly pl. *-i*, mid20c, 2b(1 tech) **Hu** <=E>/ *fiting* [=E] pl. ∅, beg20c, 2b(1 tech)

five-o'clock-tea* *phr.* 'afternoon tea'
This term and the social event it denotes are connected with late nineteenth-century anglophile high society on the Continent. The expression is now widely obsolescent, often replaced by translation, and the custom is no longer pursued.

Ge [=E] M, pl. *-s*, end19c (1 arch) < trsl *Fünfuhrtee* **Du** (∅) < *vijfuurthee* **Nw** [=E] end19c (1 arch) **Fr** *five o'clock* [=E] M [U] end19c (1 obs/fac) **Sp** <=E> M [U] end19c (1 obs) **It** - < trsl *tè delle cinque* **Rm** *five-o'clock* [=E] N [U] end19c (1 obs) **Rs** *faif-o-klok* M [U] mid20c (1 coll) **Po** <=E> M, uninfl., mid20c (1) **Cr** [=E] M [U] end19c (1 arch) **Bg** *faifoklok* M [U] beg20c (3 arch/mod) **Hu** [=E] [U] beg20c (1 arch) < trsl *ötórai tea* **Gr** (∅)

fix *n.* 3 'a dose of a narcotic drug to which one is addicted'

Nw <=E> *fiks* [=E] N, pl. ∅ (1 sla) **Ic** [=E] N, pl. ∅, end20c (1 sla) **Fr** *fix/fixe* M, 1970s (1 sla) → *fixette* n. **Sp** <=E>/*fise* [fiks] M, 1980s (1 tech) < *pinchazo, chute* **It** [=E] F, pl. ∅, 1980s (1 sla) **Cr** *fiks* M, pl. ∅, 1990s (1 sla) **Fi** *fiksi* (1 sla) **Gr** *fix* N, end20c (1 sla) → *fixaki* N

fix *v.* 2 'decide', 3 'mend, repair', 5a 'set (one's eyes, gaze, attention, affection)', 13b 'take an injection or a narcotic', +13c 'prepare narcotics for use', 14a 'make fast or permanent', +20 'speculate', +21 'obtain'

Older loans are clearly from Latin; the English influence is apparent in meaning, in certain forms (*fixing*) and in the group of expressions relating to drugs, now possibly the most common in the verb and the derived ↑*fixer* (which is of unexpectedly limited distribution).

Ge [fɪksən] 1970s, 13b(1 sla); 19c, +20(1 tech) **Du** *fiksen/fixen/*<=E> [fɪksən] 1970s, +13c(1 sla) 1980s, 3,13b(1 coll) > *spuiten* **Nw** *fikse* ["fɪkse] 3,13b (5Ge) **Ic** *fixa* [fɪksa] 1970s, 13b,+13c,+21(1 sla); mid20c, 3(5Da) **Fr** *fixer* [fikse] 14c → *fixette* n. **Rm** *fixa* [fiksa] beg20c, 2,5a(5Fr) **Rs** *fiksirovat'* beg20c, via Fr, 2,5a,14a(3 tech) **Po** *fiksować* [fikso-vatɕ] end20c, +21(2 sla) → *za*-v. **Cr** *fiksati* end20c, 13b(1 sla) **Bg** *fiksiram* beg20c, via Fr, 2,5a(3) 14a(3 tech) **Fi** *fiksata*, beg20c, 3(3 sla) **Hu** *fixál* 2,3,5a,14a(5La) **Al** *fiksoj* beg20c, 2,3,5,14a(3) **Gr** *fixaro* end20c, 14(3)

fixed focus *n.* 'a camera focus that cannot be adjusted' (photogr.)

It - < trsl *fuoco fisso* **Rs** (0) **Po** *fix-focus* [-fokus] M

[U] end20c (1 tech) **Bg** - < trsl *fiks(iran) fokus* **Hu** [=E] [U] end20c (1 tech)

fixer *n.* +4 'a drug addict', +5 'a speculator'
Ge [=E] M, pl. Ø, 1970s, +4(1 sla); 19c/end20c, +5(1 tech, rare) **Nw** ["fikser] M, pl. -e, end20c, +5(1 rare) **It** [=E] M, pl. Ø, end20c, +4(1) < +5: *speculatore* **Cr** *fikser* M, pl. -i, end20c, +4(1 sla) **Fi** *fiksari* +4(1 sla) **Hu**
[=E] pl. Ø, end20c, +4(1 tech/you, sla)

fixing *n.* +1a 'the fixing of gold prices, exchange rates or share values', +2 'a chemical stabilization process in developing photographic film'

This term is almost exclusively used in the financial domain; although *fix-* is used in the developing of photographs in other languages outside Finnish, *-ing* is not (and vice versa).
Ge [=E] N [U] 1970s, +1a(1 tech) **Du** [=E] N [U] 1980s, +1a(1 tech) **Nw** *fiksing* [fiksiŋ] C [U] 20c, +1a(3) (probably ← Nw *fikse*); *fiksering* +2(3 tech) **Fr** <=E> M, 1970s, +1a(1 tech, ban) > *fixage* **Sp** [fiksin] M, 1980s, +1a(1 tech) **It** [=E] M [U] 1980s, +1a(1 tech) **Rm** [=E] N [U] 1990s, +1a(1 tech) **Rs** -< *fiksatsiya* F **Bg** *fiksing* M [U] 1990s, +1a(2 tech) **Fi** - < *fiksaus* +2 **Hu** +1a(5La) **Gr** *fixing* N [U] end20c, +1a(1 tech)

fizz *n./cp²* 2 'an effervescent drink, esp. champagne'

This word rarely occurs by itself and is most common in the compound ↑*gin fizz* from which it is occasionally shortened.
Ge [=E] M [U] 1950s (1 tech) esp. in *gin-fizz* **Du** - < *gin fizz* **Nw** - < *gin-fizz* **Ic** - < *ginfizz* **Fr** - < *gin-fizz* **Sp** - < *gin-fizz* **It** - < *gin fizz* **Rm** [=E] N, end20c (1 rare) **Po** [-s] M, end20c (1 coll) **Cr** *fiz* M [U] end20c (1 tech) **Bg** - < *dzhin-fis* **Hu** [=E] [U] mid20c, mainly cp²: *gin-fizz* (1>2) **Gr** - < *gin fizz*

flag *n.* 1a 'a piece of cloth attached to a pole, bearing an emblem'

This word is of uncertain provenance in all Germanic languages but is first recorded in English – which *may* be the source of earlier loans. Other languages may have borrowed from or via Dutch or German.
Ge *Flagge* F, beg17c (3) < *Fahne* → *-en* v. **Du** *vlag* (5) **Nw** *flagg* via LowGe (3) **Ic** *flagg* [flak:] N, pl. *flögg*, end17c, via Da (3) **Rs** *flag* (5Du) **Bg** *flag* M, pl. *-al-ove*, beg20c, via Rs (2)

Flamaster* *n.* (orig.™) 'a marker'
Rs *flomaster* M, pl. *-y*, end20c (3) **Po** *flamaster* [flamaster] M, end20c (2 coll) **Cr** *flomaster* M, pl. *-i*, 1990s (3) **Bg** *fulmaster/flumaster* M, pl. *-al-stri*, end20c (3 coll/lit) **Al** *flamastër* M, pl. *-ëra* (1 tech)

flame out *n.* '(of a jet engine) lose power through the extinction of the flame in the combustion chamber'
Ge [fle:maut] N, pl. *-s*, 1980s (1 tech, rare) **Gr** *fleimaut* N, end20c (1 tech)

flange *n.* 'a projecting flat rim or collar for strengthening or attachment'
Ge - < *Flansch* (Fr?) **Du** *flens* [flɛns] C, pl. *flenzen*, 19c (3) **Nw** *flens* [flɛns] M, pl. *-er*, beg20c (3 tech) **It** *flangia* F, pl. *-e*, 19c (3 tech) **Rm** - < *flanşă* **Rs** *flanets* (5Ge) **Bg** - < *flanets* **Gr** *fladza* F (5It)

flannel *n.* 1a 'a woollen fabric (used in pyjamas, shirts etc.)', +1c 'a pullover', +1d 'a soft cotton fabric', +1e 'an underwear shirt'

The English provenance of this word is obscured by its very early adoption into French whence it spread on to other Continental languages.
Ge *Flanell* [fla:nɛl] M [U] 19c, via Fr, 1a(3) **Du** *flanel* [flanɛl] N [U] 17c, via Fr, 1a(3) **Nw** *flanell* [flanɛl] M [U] 19c, 1a(3) **Ic** *flannell/flón(n)ellflún(n)el* N [U] beg18c, via Da (but later also direct E. influence) 1a,+1d(2) **Fr** *flanelle* [flanɛl] F, 17c, 1a(3) **Sp** *flanela* < *franela* F [U] 1(3) → *franelata* **It** *flanella* F [U] mid18c, 1a(3) **Rm** *flanelă* [flanɛlə] F, mid19c, via Fr, 1a,+1c(3) **Rs** *flanel'* F [U] 19c, via Fr, 1a (3) → *-evyĭ* adj. **Po** *flanela* Fr, beg19c, via F, 1a(3) → *flanelka* F; *flanelowy* adj. **Cr** *flanel* M [U] beg20c, 1a(3) → *-ast* adj.; *-ski* adj. **Bg** *f(l)anela* F [U]/pl. *-li*, beg20c, via Fr/Rs, 1a(3 tech) +1c(3 reg) +1d(3 tech, arch) → *flanelka* F; *f(l)anelen* adj. **Fi** *flanelli* 1a(3) **Hu** *flanell* [flanɛl] pl. *-ek*, end17c, via Ge, 1a(3) → adj. **Al** *flanellatë* [flanɛllatë] F, a, beg20c, 1a(3) **Gr** *fanela* F, via It, 1a,+1d,+1e(3)

flare *n./cp¹* 2a 'a signal light used at sea', +3 'a flash' (photogr.)
Nw [=E] 20c, 2a(1 tech) < *signalrakett* **Fr** [=E] M, 1980s (1 tech, ban) > *fusée de signalisation, fusée éclairante* **Sp** <=E> end20c, +3(1 tech) **It** [=E] M, pl. Ø, 1980s (1 tech, rare) **Po** *flara* F, mid20c, 2a(1 tech) **Bg** *flaer* M, pl. *-al-i*, 20c (3 tech) **Hu** - *light* [fle:r] cp¹, end 20c, +3(1 tech)

flash *n.* +1a 'a sudden bright light' (cars), 3a 'a brief, sudden burst of feeling', +3c 'a strong unexpected and agreeable impression', 4 'a newsflash, a newsbrief', 5 'a flashgun' (photogr.), 10 'momentary exposure of a scene' (cinema), +12 'a drug experience'

The most common sense recorded is the photographic one, but the term was borrowed from the 1920s much later than ↑*film* itself. Other senses, including the drug slang, are more marginal.
Ge [fleʃ] M, pl. *-es*, 1980s, 5,+12(1 sla) < 5: *Blitz* **Du** [=E] C, pl. *-es*, 1970s, 5(2); 1980s, +12(1 sla) **Nw** [=E] M/N, pl. *-er/Ø*, 1960s, 5,10(1) < 5: *blits*, 10: < *glimt* **Ic** *flass* [flas:] N, pl. *flöss*, 1950s, 5(2) > rend *leifturljós* **Fr** [flaʃ] M, 20c, 5,10(2) +12(1 sla) → *flasher* v. **Sp** [flaʃ/flas] M, pl. *-es*, 1950s, +3c(1 sla) 5,10(2 tech); 1970s, +12(2 sla, you) > *pelotazo* → *flasazo, flashazo, flashear* v. **It** [flɛʃ] M, 1920s, 5,10(3) +12(1 sla) **Rm** [=E, flaʃ] N,

mid20c, 5,10(2 tech); end20c, 4(1 jour) < 5,10: *blitz* (Ge) **Po** *flesz* M, mid20c, 5(2) **Cr** *fleš* M, pl. -evi, mid20c, 5(2) **Bg** - < trsl? *svetkavitsa* **Hu** [=E] [U] mid20c, 5(2 tech) 10(1 tech) < 5: *vaku* **Al** *flesh* 3a,5,10 (1 tech) **Gr** *flas* N, mid20c, via Fr, +1a(2) 5(2); end20c, +12 (1 sla) → *flasaki* N

flash *v.* 4b 'move swiftly', 8 'indecently expose oneself'
Nw *flashe* ["flæʃe] 1970s, 4b(1 coll) **Ic** *flassa* [flas:a] 1970s, 8 (1 sla) **Po** (0)

flashback *n.* 1 'a scene set in a time earlier than the main action' (cinema.), +2 'a sudden flash of past memory appearing in one's mind', +3 'the reliving of a LSD high, often a long time after the original experience'

This term is restricted to specialist uses in cinema, literature and psychology. There are various calques, some of which are more current (and sound less affected) than the anglicism.

Ge [fleʃbek] M, pl. -s, 20c, 1(1 tech) +3(1 sla) < 1: rend *Rückblende* **Du** *flash-back* [fleʃbɛk] C, 1950s, 1(1 tech) **Nw** [=E] M/N, pl. Ø/-s, 20c, 1(1 tech) **Ic** *flassbakk* [flas:pahk] N, pl. -bökk, 1970s, 1(1 tech) +2,+3(1 sla) > 1: rend *endurlit* **Fr** *flash-back* [flaʃbak] M, mid20c, 1(2 ban) < rend *retour en arrière* **Sp** [=E] M, 1960s, pl. -s (1 tech) **It** [fleʃbɛk] M, mid20c, 1(1 tech) **Rm** [=E/flaʃbek] N, 1980s, 1,+2(2 tech) **Rs** *fleshbék* M, end20c, pl. -i, 1(1 tech); [U] +2(1 tech) < mean *retrospektsiya* **Cr** [fleʃbek] M [U] end20c, 1(1 tech) **Bg** *fleshbek* M [U] end20c, 1(1 tech) < mean *reminist-sentsiya* **Fi** (0) **Hu** [=E] [U] 20c, 1(1 tech) **Gr** *flas bak/flasbak* N, end20c, 1(1 tech) < mean *anaskopisi*; +2(1 coll) +3(1 sla)

flasher *n.* 1 'a man who indecently exposes himself' **Ic** *flassari* [flas:arı] M, pl. -ar, 1970s (1 sla)

flashing *n.* +2 'industrial processes such as burning, distilling, etc.' **It** [fleʃiŋg] M, pl. Ø, 1970s (1 tech)

flashy *adj.* 'showy, gaudy; cheaply attractive' **Du** [=E] 1970s (1 coll) **Nw** [=E] 1970s (1 coll) **Ic** [=E] uninfl., end20c (1 sla)

flask *n.* 2 'a hip flask, a flat-sided bottle' **Nw** (0) < *lommelerke* **Fr** [flask] M, 1920s (2)

flat *n.* 'a set of rooms used as a residence' **Du** [flɛt] M, beg20c (2) **Nw** (0) **Rs** (0)

fleece *cp¹* +2d 'made of synthetic, insulating material resembling a fleece, used mainly in outdoor clothes' **Ge** [=E] N [U] 1990s (1 tech) **Du** Ø **Nw** [=E] M [U] 1990s (2) **Ic** *flís* [=E] 1990s (2) **Fi** [=E] 1990s (2) **Gr** <=E>/*flis* N [U] 1990s (1 tech)

fletcher *v.* 'chew food very carefully'
This term is derived from the name of the American sociologist Horace Fletcher (1849-1919) whose advice appears to have had some popularity in the early twentieth century (is there a connection to the following noun?)

Ge *fletschern* beg20c (1 tech, obs) **Du** *fletcheren* beg20c (1 tech) **Hu** *fleccserez* [fletʃerez] end19/beg20c (1 arch)

Fletcher *n.* +2 'a dental filling'
Rm [fletʃer] N, mid20c (2 tech) < creat *dentină artificială* **Rs** *fletcher* M [U] beg20c (1 obs) **Po** *fleczer* [-er] M, mid20c (3) **Hu** *fleccser* [fletʃer] end19/beg20c (1 tech/arch)

flexible response* *n.* 'the military strategy practised by NATO in the 1960s–1980s'
Ge [=E] F [U] 1960s (1 tech, obs) **Du** [=E] C [U] 1960s (1 tech, obs)

flexi-disc* *n.* 1 'a gramophone record made of flexible material', 2 'a floppy disc'
Du [=E] C, 1980s (1 tech) **Nw** [=E] M, pl. -er, end20c (1 obs) **Hu** *flexible disk* [=E] M, pl. -ek, 1980s, 2(1 tech) < *floppi, floppy (disk)*

flexitime *n.* 2 'flexible working hours'
This term was variously translated from the German *Gleitende Arbeitszeit* in the early 1970s; calques in various languages may be from English or straight from German.
Nw - < trsl *fleksitid* **Fr** - < rend *horaire flexible* (5La) **Sp** - < trsl *horario flexible* **It** - < trsl *orario flessibile* **Po** *flexi time* M [U] end20c (1 jour) **Bg** - < creat *plavashto rabotno vreme* **Hu** - < trsl *rugalmas munkaidő*

flight *n.* 2b 'a timetabled journey made by an airline' **Nw** [=E] M, pl. -er/-s, 1950s (1 tech) **Hu** [=E] [U] mid20c (1 tech) < *járat*

flight recorder *n.* 'a device in an aircraft recording technical details during a flight'
Ge - < rend *Flugschreiber* **Du** [flajtriko:dər] M, 1980s (1 tech) < ↑*black box* **Nw** [=E] M, pl. -e, 20c (1 obs) < rend *ferdsskriver* **Ic** - < trsl *flugriti* **Fr** - < trsl *enregistreur de vol* **Sp** - < *caja negra* trsl (of ↑*black box*) **It** [flait rikɔrder/rekorder] M, pl. Ø, 1980s (1 tech) < *scatola nera, registratore di volo* **Rs** *flaït-rekorder* M, pl. -y, 1980s (1 tech) **Cr** *flajt rekorder* M, pl. -i, end20c (1 tech) **Bg** - < DFDR/*cherna kutiya* **Gr** *flait rekorder* N, end20c (1 tech)

flint *n.* 1a 'a hard stone', +3a 'a (flintlock) gun'
This word for the 'hard gray stone of nearly pure silica' was first borrowed in the seventeenth century. The stone formed the lock of a type of gun which came to be known as (German) *Flinte* – now the most common sense in German. The term has spread to a few neighbouring languages (although it is sometimes considered to be of Swedish provenance).

Ge [=E] M [U] end17c, 1a(1 tech); F, 17c, +3a(3) < la: creat *Feuerstein*; +3a: *Flinte* **Du** [=E] C, pl. -en, 19c (1 tech) < creat *vuursteen* **Nw** [=E] M [U] 19c, 1a(3) = *flintestein* **Rm** [=E] N [U] beg20c, 1a(1 tech); *flintă* [flintə] F, beg18c, via Ge, +3a(3) **Rs** (5Ge) **Po** *flinta* [flinta] F, 20c, via Ge (1 tech) **Cr** *flinta* F, pl.

-e, 19c, +3a(3) **Hu** [=E] [U] beg19c, via Ge, 1a(1 tech) +3a(3) < 1a: *tűzkő, kovakő; flinta*

flint glass *n.* 'a pure lustrous kind of glass orig. made with flint'

This term was exported together with the commodity during the period of British industrial dominance in the nineteenth century. It is widespread but highly technical, and in consequence infrequent.

Ge *Flintglas* N [U] beg19c (3 tech, rare) **Du** *flintglas* [=E] N [U] 19c (1 tech+5) **Fr** <=E>/*flint* [flint-glas] M [U] end18c (3 tech) **Sp** [=E] M, mid20c (1 tech) **It** *flint* [=E] M, pl. ∅, beg20c (1 tech) **Rm** [=E] N [U] 1930s, via Ge (3

tech, rare) < rend *sticlă flint* **Rs** *flint-glas* M [U] beg20c, via Ge (1 tech) **Po** <=E> 20c, via Ge (1 tech) **Bg** *flintglas* M [U] 20c, via Ge (1 tech) **Hu** *flint-üveg* [flint-yveg] pl. -ek, beg19c, via Ge (1 tech, obs+5) < trsl *ólomüveg* **Al** *flint* M [U] 20c (1 reg)

flip[1] (1) *n.* +4 'a trip, a hallucinatory experience caused by a drug', +5 'a joke, a jest', +6 'a passionate, but usu. not long-lasting, interest', +7 'a flippant action, out of control and without purpose'

Nw *flipp* [=E] M, pl. -er, 1970s (1 sla) **Ic** *flipp* [flɪhp] N [U] 1970s, +4(2 sla) +5,+6,+7(2 coll) → *flippari* M **Fr** [flip] M, 1980s, +4(1 you) **Sp** *flipe* M [U] 1970s, +4(2 coll) → *flipar*

flip[2] (2) *n.* 2 'a drink made from eggs, beer, brandy and sugar'

This word was borrowed, together with those for other popular drinks, in the late nineteenth century and is now obsolete. The totally unrelated sports term (below) is a recent acquisition.

Ge [=E] M, pl. -s, end19c (1 arch) **Du** [=E] C, pl. -pen, 18c (1 arch) **Fr** <=E> M, 19c (1 obs) **Sp** <=E> M 19c (1 obs) **Rm** [=E] N, end19c (1 arch) **Rs** *flip* M [U] beg20c (1 arch) **Po** M [U] mid19c (1

arch) **Cr** *flip* M [U] end20c (1 arch) **Bg** *flip* M, pl. -a, end20c (1 mod) **Hu** [=E] pl. ∅, beg19c (2)

flip[3] *n.* 'a special jump in figure-skating'

Ge [=E] M, pl. -s, 1970s (1 tech) **Nw** [=E] M, pl. -s, end20c (1 tech) **Rm** [=E] N, mid20c (1 tech) **Rs** *flip* M, pl. -y, mid20c (1 tech) **Cr** [=E] M, pl. -ovi, 20c (1 tech) **Bg** *flip* M, pl. -al-ove, end20c (1 tech) **Hu** [=E] pl. ∅, beg19c (1 tech)

flip *v.* 6 'become suddenly excited or enthusiastic', +7 'live life without purpose or control', +8 'be under the effects of drugs' (cf. ↑*flip out*)

Ge *herumflippen* 1970s, +7(1 coll, you) → *flippig* adj.; *Flippie* M **Du** *flippen* [flipən] 1970s (2) **Nw** *flippe (ut)* [ⁿflǐːpe] 1970s, 6,+7(1 coll, sla) → *utflippa* adj. **Ic** *flippa* [flɪhpa] 1970s, 6,+7(2 coll) → *flippaður* adj. **Fr** *flipper* [flipe] 1970s, +8(1 coll, sla) → *flippant, -e* adj. **Sp** *flipar* 1970s, 6,+8(3 coll, you) → *flipada, flipe, flipero, flipota* n.; *flipante, fliapdor* adj. **It** *flip-*

pare 6(1 sla) → *flippato* adj. **Gr** *flipáro* end20c, +8(3 sla)

flip album* *n.* 'a photo album with flip-over pockets for the pictures'

Ge [=E] N, pl. -en, 1980s (1+5) < rend *Steckalbum* **Nw** [flipalbum] N, pl. ∅, 1980s (1) **Fi** *flippialbumi* (1 coll)

flip chart *n.* 'a large pad bound on a stand so that one page can be turned over at the top to reveal the next', ↑*flip-over*

Ge [=E] N, pl. -s, 1970s (1 tech, rare) **Nw** - < *flipp-over* **Fr** - < *paperboard* M, 1980s **Fi** *flippitaulu* 1980s (2 tech)

flip-flop[1] (1) *n./cp*[1] +2a 'a backward jump in high jump; a Fosbury flop', 3 'a kind of electric switch'

Ge [=E] N, pl. -s, 1970s, 3(1 tech) **Du** [=E] C, 1970s, 3(1 tech) **Nw** <=E>/*flipp-flopp* [=E] M, pl. er, 20c, 3(1 tech) **Ic** [flɪhp flɔhp] N [U] 1970s, +2a(1 tech) **Fr** M, 1970s, 3(1 tech) > *bascule bistable* **Sp** *flip-flap* M, +2a(1 tech); <=E> 3(1 tech, rare) **It** [flip flɔp] M, pl. ∅, 1960s, 3(1 tech) **Rm** [=E] N [U] mid20c, +2a,3(1 tech) **Rs** *flip-flop* M [U] mid20c, 2a(1 tech) < *fosburi flop* **Bg** *flop* M [U]/pl. -a, 1970s, +2a(3 tech) **Hu** [=E] [U] 1970s, 3(1 tech) **Gr** *flip flop* N, end20c, 3(0 tech)

flip-flop[2] (1) *n.* 1 'a rubber sandal'

Nw [=E] usu. pl. -er, 1970s (1)

flip out* *v.* 'freak out (as a consequence of drugs or overexcitement) or be very depressed'

This slang term has been a popular expression of youth language particularly in the North-west of Europe, with cultural and political conditions limiting its spread. Its English provenance is no longer perceived by most users.

Ge *ausflippen* 1970s (2 coll) **Du** *flippen* 1960s (3 coll) **Nw** *flippe (ut)* [ⁿflǐːpe] 1970s (3 coll) → *utflippa* adj. **Ic** *flippa út* 1970s (2 coll) **Fr** *flipper* 1970s (1 sla) →

flippé, flippant adj. **Sp** *flipar* (3 coll) **Gr** *flipáro* end20c (3 coll, you) → *fliparismenos*

flip-over* *n.* 'a flip chart'

Du *flipover* [flipoːver] C, 1970s (1 tech) = *flapover (bord)* **Nw** <=E> *flippover* [=E] M, pl. -el-s, 1980s (1) **Fi** ↑*flip-chart*

flipper *n.* 2 'a rubber attachment worn on the foot for underwater swimming', +4 'a pinball machine', +5 'a mechanism used in such a machine'

This term came to be accepted together with the newly introduced pinball machines during the 1960s and in due course spread to (almost) all parts of the Continent. Since the term is *not* English (which has *pinball machine*) the term may be a German coinage based on English *to flip*.

Ge [=E] M, pl. ∅, 1960s, +4(1 you) → *flippern* v. **Du** *flipperkast* [=E] 1960s, +4(3+5) **Nw** usu. *flipperspill* [=E+Nw] M, pl. -e, 1970s, +4(3+5) **Fr** [flipœʀ] M, 1970s, +4(2) **Sp** [flipɛr] 1950s (1 tech, you)

It [flipper] M, pl. ∅, 1950s (3) **Rm** [=E] N, 1970s, +4(1 tech); end20c, 2(1 tech) **Rs** *flipper* M, pl. *-y*, end20c, +4(2 tech) **Po** *fliper* [-er] M, end20c (2 coll, mod) **Cr** *fliper* M, pl. *-i*, end20c, +4(3) **Bg** *fliper* M, pl. *-al-i*, end20c, +4(1 you) **Fi** *flipperi* 20c, +4(2) **Hu** [=E] pl. *-ek*, 1960s, +4(2>3 mod) **Gr** *fliper* N, end20c, +4(2) < *fliperaki*

flippie* *n.* 'a person who flips out'
Ge [=E] M, pl. *-s*, 1980s (1 you, obs)

flipping* *n.* 'changing between TV channels by remote control, zapping'
Ge [=E] N [U] 1980s (1 rare) < ↑*zapping*

flips* *n.pl.* 'salted snacks made from peanuts'
Ge [=E] pl, 1960s (1 rare)

flirt *n.* 1 'a person who indulges in flirting', +1a 'amorous play, flirtation', +3 'a superficial interest'
  This noun (for both the person and the activity) and the related verb are among the most common early loans in all European languages – the sociohistorical reasons for the adoption being largely unclear. The term was apparently used in a negative way, referring to the immoral nature of the activity.
Ge [flört/-i-] M, pl. *-s*, end19c, +1a(2),+3(1 jour) **Du** [flvrt] C, pl. *-en*, beg20c, 1(2); C [U] end19c, +1a(2) **Nw** *flort/flirt* [=E] M, pl. *-er*, beg20c, +1a(2) → *flørte* **Ic** *flört* [flœrt] N [U] mid20c, via Da, +1a(2 coll) < *daður* → *flörtari* M **Fr** [flœrt] M, end19c, 1,+1a(2) **Sp** <=E> M 1(1 obs); end19c, +1a(2) = *flirteo* **It** [flœrt] M, pl. ∅, 1900s, +1a(3) **Rm** [flœrt/flirt] N, end19c, via Fr, 1,+1a(2) **Rs** *flirt* M [U] beg20c, +1a(2) **Po** [flirt] M, beg20c, 1,+1a(3) → *flircik* M; *flirciarka* F; *flirciarz* M; *-owanie* N [U]; *-owicz* M; *-owy* adj.; *flirciarski* adj. **Cr** *flert* M [U] beg20c, via Ge, +1a(2) **Bg** *flirt* M, pl. *-al-ove*, beg20c, via Rs, +1a(3); mid20c, +3(3) → *-adzhiya* M; *-adzhiika* F; *-adzhiiski* adj. **Fi** *flirtti* 20c, 1(2 coll); *flirttailu* +1a(2 coll) **Hu** *flört* [=E] pl. *-ök*, end19/ beg20c, +1a(2>3) **Al** *flirt* M [U] mid20c, +1a (1 reg) **Gr** *flert* N, beg20c, 1,+1a(2)

flirt *v.* 1 'behave in an amorous or sexually enticing manner', 2a 'superficially interest oneself (in an idea)', 2b 'trifle (with danger etc.)'
Ge *flirten* [flœ:tən] end19c, 1(2); 1960s, 2a(1 jour) **Du** *flirten* [fly:tən] 1960s (2) **Nw** *flørte/flirte* ["flø:rte] beg20c (2) **Ic** *flörta* [flœrta] mid20c, 1,2a,b(2 coll) < *daðra* **Fr** *flirter* [flœrte] end19c, 1(3) → *flirteur, euse* **Sp** *flirtear* beg20c, 1,2a(3) **It** *flirtare* [flertare] end19c, 1(3) **Rm** *flirta* [flœrta/flirta] beg20c, via Fr (3) **Rs** *flirtovat* beg20c, 1(3) **Po** *flirtować* [flirto-vatç] beg20c, 1,2b(3) **Cr** *flertovati* beg20c, 1(3) **Bg** *flirtuvam* 1,2a(3) **Fi** *flirttailla* 20c (2 coll) **Hu** *flörtöl* [flørtəl] end19/beg20c, 1,2a(2>3) = *kacérkodik* → *-és* n. **Al** *flirtoj*, mid20c, 1(1) **Gr** *flertaro* beg20c, 1(2); end20c, 2a,b(1 coll)

float *v.* 6a 'allow the exchange rate to fluctuate' (econ.) (cf. ↑*floating*)

Ge [flo:tn] 1970s (1 tech) **Fr** - < mean *flotter* **Sp** - < mean *flotar* **Bg** - < mean *plavam* **Fi** - < mean *kellutta*

floatel *n.* 'a floating hotel'
Du [flo:tɪl] N, 1960s (1) **Nw** *flotell* [flutel] N, pl. *-er*, 1980s (1)

floater *n.* 5 'a government stock certificate with changing interest'
Ge [flo:ta] M, pl. *-s*, 1980s (1 tech, rare) **It** [flɔter] M, pl. ∅, end20c (1 tech)

floating* *n.* 1 'a fluctuating exchange rate', 2 'a method to concentrate ore' (cf. ↑*flotation*)
Ge [flo:tiŋ] N [U] 1970s, 1(1 tech) **Du** [=E] C, 1980s, 1(1 tech) **Nw** *float* [=E] M, 1980s, 1(1) = *flyt* **Ic** - < rend *fljótandi gengi* **Sp** - < 1: mean *flotación* **It** [flɔutiŋ] M [U] 1980s, 1(1 tech) < 1: mean *fluttuazione* **Rs** *floating* M [U] 1980s, 1(1 tech) **Bg** - < 1: mean *plavasht* **Hu** *flótálás* [flo:ta:la:ʃ] [U] 20c, 2(3 tech)

floodlight *n.* 1 'a large powerful light to illuminate a building', 2 'the illumination so provided'
Ge - < trsl *Flutlicht* **Du** [flu:dlajt] N, 1940s (2) **Nw** (0) < trsl *flomlys* **Ic** - < 1: trsl *flóðljós*; 2: *flóðlýsing* **Fr** *lampe floodlflood* F/M mid20c (1 tech)

floor show *n.* 'an entertainment presented on the floor as opposed to the stage'
Du *floorshow* C, 1980s (1) **Nw** [=E] N, pl. *-s*, 20c (1)

flop[1] (1) *n.* +1c 'a style in high jumping'
Ge [=E] M, pl. *-s*, 1970s (1 tech) = *floppen* v.; *Flopper* M **Du** [=E] C, pl. *-sl-en*, 1970s (1 tech) **Rm** [flop] N [U] 1970s (3 tech) **Rs** *flop* M [U] end20c (1 tech) < *flip-flop* **Bg** *flop* M [U]/pl. *-a*, 1970s (1 tech) **Fi** - < *floppaus* **Gr** *flop* N, end20c, +1c(1 tech)

flop[2] (1) *n.* 2 'a failure (of an action or person)'
  This term was adopted in highly colloquial youth language, esp. relating to pop music and entertainment, from the 1960s on, but has spread to various contexts in spoken, informal usage. The related verb (probably an independent derivation) is rarer.
Ge [=E] M, pl. *-s*, 1970s (1 coll) < *Mißerfolg, Versager* **Du** [flɔp] C, pl. *-sl-pen*, 1960s (3 coll) **Nw** *flopp* [=E] M, pl. *-er*, 1970s (2) **Ic** *flopp* [flohp] N, pl. ∅, 1970s (2 coll) **Fr** [flɔp] M, 1970s (1 jour, sla) **It** [flɔp] M, pl. ∅, 1980s (1 coll, jour) < *insuccesso, fiasco* **Gr** *flop* N [U] (1 mod/coll, you) < *fiasko*

flop *v.* 4 'fail, collapse (esp. of a play, film, book etc.)'
Ge *floppen* 1980s (1 coll, rare) **Du** *floppen* [flɔpən] 1970s (2 mod) **Nw** *floppe* ["flɔpe] 1970s (1) **Ic** *floppa* [flɔhpa] 1970s (2 coll) **Fi** *flopata* 20c (2 coll)

floppy disk *n.* 1 'a small (flexible) disk used in computers', +1a 'the disk drive for a floppy disk'
  Unsurprisingly, this term became widespread as a part of the computer culture of the 1980s in (almost) all of Europe – to be replaced with other terms as

technology progressed. Note various equivalents coined, often on the basis of *disk+ette*.

Ge [=E] F, pl. *-s*, 1980s, 1(1 tech) < *Diskette* **Du** [flɔpidisk] C, 1980s, 1(1 tech) = *schijfje, floppy* **Nw** [=E] M, pl. *-er*, 1980s, 1(1 obs) < *diskett* **Ic** *floppý-diskur* [flɔhpitɪskʏr] M, pl. *-ar*, 1980s, 1(1+4 tech) < *disketta, disklingur* **Fr** *floppy (disc)* M, 1980, 1(1 tech, ban) < *disquette* **Sp** <=E>/*(disco) floppy* M, 1980s, 1(1 tech/arch) = trsl *disco flexible* < *disquette* **It** [flɔppi disk] M, pl. Ø, 1970s, 1(2 tech) = *dischetto* **Rm** *floppy (disc/disk)* [=E] N, 1980s, 1(1 tech) **Rs** *floppi disk* M, pl. *-i*, 1980s, 1(1 tech) **Po** <=E> M, 1980s, 1(1 tech) **Cr** [=E] M, 1980s, 1(1 tech) **Bg** *flopi disk* M, pl. *-ka/-kove*, 1980s, 1(1 tech); *flopi* N, pl. *-ta*, +1a(3 tech) < 1: *disketa* **Hu** *floppy (disk)/floppi* [=E] pl. *-ek/-k*, end20c, 1(1 tech>2) **Gr** <=E> [=E] N, end20c (1 tech)

flotation *n.* 2 'the separation of the components of crushed ore' (cf. ↑*floating*)

In contrast to the equivalent ↑*floating* (2) there seems to be little in the form of this loanword to justify its classification as an anglicism.

Du *flotatie* [flo:tatsi] C, mid20c (1 tech) **Nw** *flotasjon* [flʉtaʃʉːn] M [U] (3 tech) **Fr** *flottation* 1923 (3 tech) **Rm** - < *flotaţie* [flotatsje] F, 1940s (5Fr) **Rs** *flotatsiya* F [U] 2(3 tech) **Po** *flotacja* [flotatsja] F [U] end20c (1 tech) → *flotownia* F; *flotownik* M **Cr** *flotacija* F [U] end20c (1 tech) **Bg** *flotatsiya* F [U] mid20c, via Rs (3 tech) → *flotator* M; *flotatsionen* adj. **Hu** *flotáció* [flota:tsio:] [U] 20c (1 tech) = *flótálás* **Al** *flotacion* M [U] mid20c (3 tech)

flotel see ↑*floatel*

flow chart *n.* 1 'a diagram of movement or action in a complex activity', 2 'a graphical representation of a computer program in relation to its sequence of functions'

Ge - < rend *Flußdiagramm* **Du** *flowchart/flow-chart* [=E] C, 1970s (1 tech) **Nw** [=E] N, pl. *-s*, 1970s (1 tech) = trsl *flytskjema* **Ic** - < creat *flæðirit*; rend *leiðarit, -mynd* **Fr** - < *organigramme* **Sp** - < 1: creat *organigrama*; 2: trsl *diagrama de flujo* **It** [flou tʃart] M, pl. Ø, 1980s (1 tech) < trsl *diagramma di flusso, schema a blocchi* **Rm** [=E] N, 1970s, 2(1 tech) **Hu** *flow process chart* [=E] [U] 1980s, 2(1 tech) **Gr** <=E> [=E] N, pl. *-s*, end20c (0 tech)

flower power *n.* 'the ideas of the hippies regarded as an instrument for changing the world'

This term, and the ideology it expresses, rapidly spread through Western Europe and became obsolete before it could affect other Continental countries; recently it has come back in connection with fashion.

Ge [=E] F [U] 1960s (1 you) **Du** [=E] C [U] 1960s (1 obs) **Nw** [=E] [U] 1960s (1) **Ic** [=E] 1970s (0 sla, obs) < trsl *blóma-* **Fr** [=E] M, 1970 (1 obs) **Sp** [flauer pauer] M [U] 1960s (1 you, obs) = trsl *poder de las flores/hipismo* **It** [flauer pauer] M [U] 1960s (1 you,

obs) **Rm** [=E] F, 1970s (1 obs) **Cr** [flauer pauer] M [U] mid20c (1 you, obs) **Gr** [=E] N [U] 1960s/1990s (1 you)

fluffy *adj.* 1 'of or like fluff', 2 'covered in fluff; downy' **Nw** [=E] mid20c, 1(1) **Ic** [=E] uninfl., 1960s, 2(1 coll, arch)

fluid *n/cp²* 1 'a gas or liquid', +3 'a fluid cosmetic'

The form is compatible with English, French or Latin provenance but this word appears to be perceived as an anglicism mainly in connection with cosmetics. Romance languages treat it as native, and others apparently regard it as French or Latin.

Ge [=E] cp², N, pl. *-s*, 1970s, +3(1 tech, mod) **Fr** *fluide* +3(5) **Sp** *fluido* (5La) **It** *fluido* M, pl. *-i* (3) **Rm** [fluid] N, mid19c, 1(5Fr/La); end20c, +3(5) = trsl *fluid cosmetic* **Rs** (5La) **Po** [-t] M, end20c, +3(2 mod) **Cr** [=E] M [U] end20c, +3(2 mod) **Bg** *fluid* M, pl. *-a/-i*, end20c, 1(5Fr) → *-en* adj. **Hu** 1(5La); [=E] [U] 1980s, +3(0>1 tech, writ) **Al** *fluid* [fluid] M, pl. *-e*, mid20c (1 tech)

flummery *n.* 2 'a sweet pudding'

This word (of alleged Welsh provenance) is a completely integrated loan in German (the product is slightly obsolescent). This pudding was apparently never introduced to other countries (cf. ↑*gully*.)

Ge *Flammeri* M, pl. *-s*, 19c (1 obs)

flush¹ *n.* 6c 'facial redness, esp. caused by fever etc.' **Sp** [=E] M, 1990s (1 tech)

flush² *n.* 'a hand of cards, all of one suit' (poker)

Ge (0) **Du** [=E] C, 1970s (1 tech) **Nw** [=E] M, pl. *-er*, 20c (1 tech) **Ic** [flœs:] N [U] 1960s (1 tech) = *röð* **Fr** [flœʃ/flɔʃ] M, beg20c (1 tech) **Cr** *fleš* M [U] beg20c (1 tech) **Bg** *flosh* M, pl. *-a*, beg20c, via Fr (3 tech) **Hu** *flös* [fløʃ] [U] end19/beg20c (1 tech) **Gr** *flos* N, beg20c, via Fr (1 tech)

flutter *n./cp¹* 4 'an abnormally rapid but regular heartbeat', 5 'an undesired oscillation in an aircraft', 6 'a rapid movement of the tongue in playing a wind instrument'

Ge - < *Flattern* **Du** [=E] C, 1970s, 5(1 tech) **Nw** [=E] N? [U] 20c, 4,5(1 tech) **Ic** [flœhter-] cp¹, end20c, 5,6(0 tech) **Fr** <=E> M, 1970s, 4(1 tech), 5(1 tech/ban) < *flottement* **Sp** <=E>/*fluter* M, 1990s, 4(1 tech) **It** [flatter/flutter] M, pl. Ø, 1950s, 4,5(1 tech) **Rm** [=E] N, 1960s, 4,5(1 tech) **Rs** *flatter* M [U] mid20c, 4(1 tech) **Po** *flatter* [-er] M [U] mid20c, 5(1 tech) **Bg** *flater* M [U] mid20c, via Ge/Rs, 5(1 tech) **Hu** [=E/*fluter*] [U] 20c, 4(1 tech)

fly-and-drive* *n.* 'a travel package including combined flight and car rental'

One of the many terms invented by the travel industry (cf. ↑ *rail and fly*, etc.) on the pattern of English ↑*park and ride*.

Ge [=E] 1970s (1 jour) **Nw** [=E] end20c (1) **Ic** - < trsl *flug og bíll* **It** [=E] M [U] 1970s (1 tech) **Hu** [=E] [U] end20c (1 jour)

fly-by *n.* 'a flight past a position, esp. the approach of a spacecraft to a planet'
It [fḷai bai] M, pl. Ø, 1980s (1 tech, rare)

flyer *n.* +3a 'a race-horse', +5a 'an advertisement (on a book cover or leaflet)', +8 'a kind of jacket worn by skin heads', +9 'a sprinter in a cycle race', +10 'a machine for weaving'

The data are very difficult to compare – different meanings were apparently borrowed at different times; +5a is likely to be expanding (but has not covered much ground so far), whereas other meanings appear to be obsolescent.

Ge *Flyer/Fleier* [=E] M, pl. Ø, beg20c, +5a(1 coll) +10(1 tech, arch) **Du** [=E] C, 1970s/1990s, +5a(1 coll) +9(1 tech) **Nw** [=E] M, pl. *-el-s*, 20c, +3a(1 tech) **Rm** *flaier* [flajer] N, 1940s, via Ge, +10(1 tech) **Rs** *flayer* M, pl. *-y*, mid20c, +3a(1 tech) **Po** *flyers* [-ers] M, end20c, +8(1 coll) **Cr** *flajer* M, pl. *-i*, 20c, +10(1 tech) **Bg** *flaer* M, pl. *-al-i*, 20c, +10(3 tech) **Hu** [flaːjer] [U] end19/beg20c, +3a,+9(1 tech, obs) +10(1 tech, obs)

Flying Dutchman *n.* 1 'a ghost ship', 2 'the captain of the ghost ship', +3 'a class in sailing contests'

The contrast here is clearly between languages using a calque for the ghost ship and the anglicism for the sailing class, and those using a calque for both.

Ge [=E] M [U] 1960s, 1(0) +3(1 tech) < trsl *Fliegender Hollän-der* **Du** C [U] 1980s, 1(1 writ) **Nw** [=E] M, mid20c, +3(1 tech); < 1: trsl *den flygende hollender* **Ic** - < 2: trsl *Hollend-ingurinn fljúgandi* **Fr** <=E> M, 1960s, +3(1 tech); 1: < rend *Vaisseau fantôme*; 2 < trsl *Hollandais volant* **Sp** [=E] 20c, 1(1 tech) **It** [flaijŋ datʃman] M, pl. Ø, 1960s, 1(1 tech); 1930s, +3(1 tech) < trsl *Olandese Volante* **Rm** - < rend *olandezul zburător* **Rs** (0) < *letuchiĭ gollandets* **Po** - < trsl *latający Holender* **Cr** - < trsl *leteći Holandez* **Bg** - < 1+3: trsl *letyasht kholandets* **Fi** - < trsl *lentävä hollantilainen* **Hu** - < trsl *bolygó hollandi* **Gr** <=E> [=E] N, end20c, 1,+3(1 tech)

flying junior* *n.* 'a racing boat (smaller than a Fly-ing Dutchman)'
It [flaijŋ dʒunior] M, pl. Ø, 1970s (1 tech)

flying saucer *n.* 'an unidentified flying object, popu-larly supposed to have come from outer space'

This term is unique because although it is widely known in its original English form, all languages pre-fer calques. (Compare the data for ↑*Flying Dutchman*, ↑*flying start* and ↑*UFO*.)

Ge - < trsl *Fliegende Untertasse* **Du** - < trsl *vliegende schotel* **Nw** - < trsl *flygende tallerken* **Ic** - < trsl *fljúgandi diskur* **Fr** - < trsl *soucoupe volante* **Sp** - < trsl *platillo volante* **It** - < rend *disco volante* **Rm** - < rend *farfurie zburătoare* **Rs** - < trsl *letayushchaya*

tarelka **Po** - < trsl *latający talerz* **Cr** - < trsl *leteći tanjur* **Bg** - < rend *letyashta chiniya, NLO* **Fi** - < trsl *lentävä lautanen* **Hu** - < trsl *repülő csészealj* **Al** - < trsl *disk fluturues* **Gr** - < rend *iptamenos dhiskos*

flying start *n.* 1 'a start of a race in which competi-tors pass the starting point at full speed'
Ge - < trsl *fliegender Start* **Du** - < trsl *vliegende start* **Nw** [=E] M, mid20c (2) **Bg** - < trsl *letyasht start* (5+2) **Hu** - < trsl *repülő rajt*

flyover *n.* 1 'a bridge carrying one road over another'
Du *fly-over* [flajovər] M, 1970s (2)

f.o.b. *abbrev.* 'free on board'
Ge [efoːbeː/fop] beg20c (1 tech, rare) **Du** [ɛf o be] beg20c (1 tech) **Nw** <=E>/*fob* [efubeː/fub] beg20c (1 tech) **Ic** *fob* [fɔːp] uninfl., freq. cp[1], beg20c, via Da (1 tech) = trsl *frítt um borð* **Fr** [ɛfobɛ] 1950s (1 tech, ban); *FOB* [fɔb] 1900s < *franco à bord, F.A.B.* **Sp** *FOB/fob* 1970s (1 tech) **It** [effe ɔ bi] end19c = trsl *franco a bordo* **Rm** *fob* end19c, via Fr (3 tech) **Rs** *fob* M [U] end20c (1 tech) **Po** *fob* [fop] beg20c (1 tech) **Cr** *fob* 20c (1 tech) **Bg** *fob* M [U] 20c (1 tech) **Fi** [=E] 20c (1 tech) **Hu** *fob* [fob] 20c? (1 tech) **Gr** [fob] 20c (1 tech)

fogging* *n.* 'an unhealthy evaporation of synthetic material'
Ge [=E] N, pl. *-s*, end20c (1 tech, jour)

foil *abbr.* 1 'a hydrofoil', +2 'the planes of a hydro-foil'
Nw [=E] M, pl. *-er*, mid20c (1)

folder *n.* 2 'a (folded) leaflet'

The limited currency of this term is noteworthy; the semantic feature 'folded' is neglected in the loan-words, and the term is used specifically in relation to certain types of advertising.

Du [fɔldər] C, beg20c (3) **Nw** [=E] M, pl. *-e*, 1920s (2); [fɔlər] (4) ← **Nw** *folde* **Fr** M, 1980s (1 tech, ban) < *porte-annonces* (ad-vertising only) **Rs** *folder* M, pl. *-y*, 1990s (1 tech) **Po** [-er] M, mid20c, 2(3) **Bg** - < trsl *di-plyanka*

folk *n./cp[1/2]* 4 'traditional or popular (music)'
Ge [=E] M [U] 1960s (1 tech) **Du** [=E] C [U] 1960s (2) < *folk-muziek* **Nw** [=E] M [U] 1980s (1 tech) **Ic** - < rend *þjóðlaga(tón-list)* **Fr** [fɔlk] M/cp[2], 1960s (1 tech) → *folkeux-leuse* n./adj. **Sp** [folk] M/adj., 1960s (1 tech) → *folkero* **It** *folk* (*music*) [fɔlk] M/cp[2] [U] 1960s (2) < *musica folk* **Rm** [folk] N/adj., uninfl., 1970s (2 tech/mod) **Rs** *folk/fol'k* cp[1] [U] end20c (2 jour, mod) **Po** M, uninfl., end20c (1 coll) → *-owy* adj. **Cr** *folk* M [U] 20c (1 tech) **Bg** *folk* cp[1]/M [U] end20c (2 mod/tech) **Fi** [fɔlk] 20c (1 tech) **Hu** [=E] cp[1], 20c (1 you) **Al** - < *muzikë popullore* **Gr** - < trsl *laiki musiki*

folklore *n.* 1 'the traditional beliefs and stories of a people; the study of these', +2 'traditional songs and music'

A loanword accepted into practically all European languages in the late nineteenth century/early twentieth century. The term was coined in 1846, obviously calqued on the German *Volkskunde* (cf. ↑*folksong*), in the puristic tradition of nineteenth-century English.
Ge [folklo:rə] F [U] end19c, +2(3) → *-istisch* adj. **Du** [fɔlklo:rə] C [U] 19c, +2(3) → *-istisch* adj.; *-ist* n. **Nw** [fɔlklɔ:re/-lu:re] M [U] beg20c (1) < *folkeminne* → *folklorisk* adj.; *folklorist* M **Ic** *fólklor* [foulklo:r] N [U] mid20c, 1(1 coll) < rend *þjóðfræði* **Fr** [fɔlklɔʀ] M [U] end19c, 1,+2(2) → *folklorique* adj.; *folkloriste* M; *folklorisation* n. **Sp** <=E>/*folclore* M, 1880s (2>3) → *folклórico*/*folclorico* adj.; *folclorista* n. **It** <=E>/*folclore* [fɔlklɔre] M [U] end19c (3) → *folclorico*/*folcloristico* adj. **Rm** *folclor* N [U] end19c, via Fr (3) **Rs** *fol'klor* M [U] beg20c, +2(2) → *-ist* M, *-istika* F; *-nyĭ* adj. **Po** *folklor* [folklor] M [U] beg20c (3) → *-ysta* M; *-ystka* F; *-ystyczny* F; *-ystyczny* adj. **Cr** *folklor* [folklor] M [U] beg20c, +2(2) → *-ist* M; *-an* adj. **Bg** *folklor* M [U] beg20c, via Rs, +2(3) → *-en* adj.; *-ist* M; *-istka* F; *-ristika* F **Fi** [fɔlklɔ:r] 20c (2) → *folkloristiikka* n. **Hu** *folklór* [folklo:r] [U] end19/beg20c (3) = *néprajz* → *-ista* n.; *-iszitikus* adj. **Al** *folklor* [folklor] M [U] beg20 (3) **Gr** *folklor* N [U] beg20c, via Fr (2) → *-ikos* adj., *-ismos* M

folkrock *n.* 'a style of music combining folk music and rock'
Ge [=E] [U] 1970s (1 tech) **Du** *folkrock* [=E] C, 1970s (1 tech) **Nw** [=E] M [U] 1980s (1) **Ic** - < rend *þjóðlagarokk* **Sp** [folk rɔk] M [U] 1970s (1 tech) **It** [fɔlk rɔk] M [U] 1960s (1) **Rm** [=E] N [U] 1970s (1 jour, mod) **Rs** *fol'krok* M [U] end20c (2 tech) **Cr** *folk- rock* [U] 1980s (1 tech) **Bg** *folkrok* M [U] end20c (2 tech) **Fi** [=E] (1) **Gr** <=E> [=E] N, end20c (1 tech)

folk song *n.* 'an American popular song'
This term, coined in 1847 and calqued on German *Volkslied* (itself an eighteenth-century calque of *popular song*), spread with American popular music after the 1960s; calques are frequent (the German or English source being disguised).
Ge [=E] M, pl. *-s*, 1960s (1 tech) **Du** C, 1970s (Ø) **Nw** (o) < *folkevise* **Ic** - < rend *þjóðlagasöngur* **Fr** *folk-song* M, 1950s (1 tech) < *chanson folk* **Sp** *folk song* M, 1960s (1 tech, rare/jour) < *canción folk*; trsl *canción popular* **It** *folk-song* [fɔlk sɔŋg] M, pl. Ø/-s, 1970s (1 tech) < *canzone popolare* **Rm** *folk-song* [=E] N [U] 1970s (1 jour, mod) **Po** (o) **Cr** [=E] M, pl. *-ovi*, mid20c (2) **Bg** (Ø) < *folkpesen* **Fi** - < trsl *kansanlaulu* **Hu** - < trsl *népdal* **Al** - < *kengë popullare*

follow-up *n.* 1 'an action, measure, etc., following or continuing an initial one', +2 'initial assistance given to new members of staff'
Ge [=E] N, pl. *-s*, 1970s, 1(1 tech, rare) **Du** [=E] C, 1970s, 1(1 mod) **Nw** [=E] M, pl. *-s*, mid20c, 1(1 tech, obs) < trsl *oppfølger, oppfølging* **It** [=E] M, pl. Ø, 1970 (1 tech) **Hu** [=E] [U] 1970s (1 tech_ECON)

font *n.* 'a set of type of one face or size' (printing)
Du [=E] N [U] 1980s (1 tech) **Nw** [=E] M, pl. *-er*, 1980s (1 tech) **Ic** *fontur* [fɔntʏr] M, pl. *-ar*, 1980s (2 coll) = rend *letur(gerð)* **Sp** [=E] M/F, pl. *-s*, 1980s (1 tech) **It** [=E] M, pl. Ø, 1980s (1 tech) **Rm** [=E] N, 1980s (1 tech) **Rs** *font* M [U] end20c (1 tech) **Po** [-o-] M [U] end20c (1 tech) **Cr** [=E] M, pl. *-i*, 1990s (1 tech) = *kirjasinlaji* **Hu** [=E] [U] end20c (1 tech) **Gr** <=E> [=E] N, end20c (1 tech) < *grammatosira*

food processor *n.* 'a machine for chopping and mixing food'
Du [fu:tprosɛsər] M, 1980s (2) < *keukenmachine* **Nw** [=E] M, pl. *-er*, 1980s (2) > rend *matmølle* **Rs** *protsessor* M, pl. *-y*, 1990s (3 tech)

fool *v.* +6 'deceive; trick' (sports), +7 'get on one's side with tricks'
Ic *fúla* [fu:la]/*fúlla* [ful:a] 1970s (1 coll) **Hu** [=E] *n.* +6(1 tech) < *skíz*

foolproof *adj.* 'simple' (of a mechanism that cannot be mis-used)
Ge - < trsl *idiotensicher* **Du** 1970s (0) **Nw** (0) < trsl *idiotsikker* **Rs** *fulpruf* 1990s (1 coll, mod) **Po** [ful pruf] end20c (1 mod) **Bg** - < trsl *durakoustoĭchiv* **Fi** - < trsl *idioottivarma*

football *n.* 1a 'soccer', 1b 'American football', 2 'a large inflated ball of a kind used in these'
This word for soccer was almost universally adopted into Continental languages from the late nineteenth century onwards, but was later replaced by calques in some. With the advent of the American game the distinction was made by accepting the loanword for the latter, or by using the related term ↑*rugby*, or adding 'American' (cf. ↑*American football*). Out of context, ambiguities remain, *soccer* (the normal unambiguous term used in Britain for the national variant) not having been adopted.
Ge only in: *American* - M [U] 20c, 1b(1 tech) < 1a: *Fußball* **Du** - but *American football* **Nw** [=E] M [U] 20c, 1b(Ø/1 tech) < 1a: trsl *fotball* **Ic** - < creat 1a,2:*fótbolti; knattspyrna*; 1b: *ameriskur fótbolti, ruðningur* **Fr** [futbol] M, end19c, 1a(2) → *footballeur*, *-euse* M/F; *footeux*, *-euse* n./adj.; *footballistique* adj. **Sp** *fútbol* M [U] end19c, 1a(2>3); *football* [futbol] end20c, 1b(1 tech, jour) > 1a: *balompié*; - < 1b: trsl *fútbol americano* → *-ero, -ista, -istico* **It** [=E/futbal] M [U] end19c, 1a(3) < 1a: *calcio*; 1b: *football americano*; 2: *pallone* **Rm** *futbol* [futbol] N [U] beg20c, via Fr, 1a(3 obs); *fotbal* [fɔtbal] N [U] 1a(3) < 1b: rend *fotbal american* → *-ist, -istă* M/F; *-istic* adj./adv. **Rs** *futbol* M [U] beg20c, 1a(2) → *-ist* M; *-ka* F; *-nyĭ* adj. **Po** *futbol*/<=E> [-bol] M [U] beg20c (2) = *piła nożna* → *-ista* M; *istka* F; *-ówka* F **Cr** *fudbal* M [U]

beg20c, 1a(1 tech) < 1a: *nogomet* → *-aš* M **Bg** *futbol* M [U] beg20c, 1a(2) → *-ist* M; *-istka* F; *-en* adj. **Fi** *futis* end20c < rend *jalkapallo* **Hu** *futball* [f<u>u</u>tbal] [U] end19/beg20c, 1a(3) 1b(2) > 1a: *labdarúgás*; - < trsl 1b: *amerikai futball* → *-ozik* v.; *-ista* n. **Al** *futboll* [fut-boll] M [U] end19c/beg20c, 1b(3); 2: *top futbolli* **Gr** *futbol* N [U] beg20c, 1a(2) < trsl *podhosfero*; end20c, 1b(∅)

footing *n.* 2 'position, status', +2a 'base, roots', +4 'jogging', +5 'using the legs' (box.)

This term is remarkable for the non-English senses developed outside the anglophone world, some apparently based on folk etymology, in a number of Continental languages.

Du [=E] N [U] end20c, +2a(1 jour) **Fr** [futin] M, end19c, +4(1 obs) **Sp** <=E>/*futin* [f<u>u</u>tin] M, beg20c, +4(1>2 tech); end19c, +5(1 tech) > +4: *jogging* → *futinero* **It** [fut<u>i</u>ng] M [U] 1930s, via Fr? +4,+5(2) **Rm** [=E] N [U] 1970s, +4(1 tech, jour) < +5: creat *joc de picioare* **Rs** *futing* M [U] 1990s, +4(1 tech) **Po** [-nk] M [U] end20c, +4(1 mod) **Cr** *futing* M [U] end20c, +4(1 tech) **Bg** *futing* M [U] end20c, +5(1 tech) **Gr** *futing* N [U] end20c, +5(1 tech)

f.o.p.* *abbrev.* 'free on plane' **Ge** [ef o: pe:/fop] uninfl., 20c (3 tech) **Du** [=E] uninfl., 1980s (1 tech) **Bg** ↑*fob* **Gr** [fop] 20c (1 tech)

f.o.r. *abbrev.* 'free on rail' **Du** [=E] uninfl., 1980s (1 tech) **Nw** [efu:ær] 20c (3 tech) **Sp** (1 tech) **Hu** [ef o: er] 20c (1 tech)

forcing* *n.* 1 'constraining (a person) by force or against his or her will', +2a (sport) 'continual attacking' **Du** [=E] C, 1970s, 1(1 tech) **Fr** [fɔrsiŋ] M, 1920s (2 ban) < *pression* It [fɔrsiŋ(g)] M [U] 1930s, 1(2 tech_{SPORT}) **Rm** [=E], 1970s (1 tech) **Rs** *forsing* M [U] mid20c, +2a(1 tech) **Bg** *forsing* M [U] mid20c, +2a(1 tech) **Hu** *forszing* via Fr, 1(3) **Al** - < *sforcoj*

forechecking* *n.* 'the interruption of an attack from the opposing team' **Ge** [=E] N, pl. *-s*, 1970s (1 tech, rare) **Nw** [=E] 1980s (1 tech) **It** [=E] M, pl. ∅, end20c (1 tech) **Rm** [=E] N, 1970s (1 tech)

forehand *n.* 1a 'a stroke played with the palm of the hand facing the opponent' (tennis)

The languages studied are divided between those favouring calques (replacing late nineteenth-century loans) and those using borrowings; the recent popularity of tennis appears to have revived the (limited) currency of loanwords in some languages.

Ge [fo:rhent] F/M, pl. *-s*, end19c (0 arch) < trsl *Vorhand* **Du** [fɔrhɛnt] C, 1970s (1 tech) > *voorhand* **Nw** [=E] M [U] 20c (1 tech) **Ic** *forhönd* (4) **Fr** - < rend *coup droit* **Sp** - < mean *derecha* **It** - < mean *diritto* **Rm** *forhend* [=E] N, 1960s (2 tech) **Rs** *forkhénd* M [U] mid20c (1 tech) **Po** *forhend/forhand* [forhent] M, mid20c (1 tech) **Cr** *forhend* M, pl. *-i*, beg20c (1 tech) **Bg** *forkhend* M, [U]/pl. *-a*, mid20c (1 tech) **Hu** [=E] [U] end19/beg20c (1 tech, arch) **Gr** *forkhad* N [U] beg20c (1 tech)

forepeak *n.* 'the end of the forehold in the angle of the bows' (naut.) **Rm** *forpic* [forpik] N, 1960s (2 tech) **Rs** *forpik* M, pl. *-i*, mid20c (1 tech) **Po** *forpik* M, mid20c (1 tech) **Cr** *forpik* [forpik] M, beg20c (1 tech) **Bg** *forpik* M, mid20c, via Rs (1 tech)

forsythia *n.* 'an ornamental shrub bearing bright yellow flowers'

The shrub was named after William Forsyth (1737–1804), botanist in charge of the Royal Gardens at St. James's and Kensington. The loanword was apparently transmitted through botanical literature; this fact and the word's neo-Latin form have allowed its pronunciation to be influenced by the phonetics of the individual receiver languages. The word has remained exotic, but has lost its English character.

Ge *Forsythie* [forzy:tsjə] F, pl. *-n*, beg20c (3) **Du** [fɔrsi:tja/fɔrsi:tsja] C, pl. - 's, beg20c (3) **Nw** *forsytia* [forsy:tia] M, pl. *-er*, 19c (3 tech) **Sp** <=E>/*forsitia* F beg20c (1<2 tech) **It** *forsizia* [forsittsja] F, pl. *-e*, 1930s (3) **Rm** *forsythia/forsitia* [forsitsja] F, beg20c (2<3) **Rs** *forzitsiya* F, pl. *-tsii*, mid20c (2) **Po** *forsycja* [forsitsja] F, mid20c (3) **Cr** *forsitija* F, 20c (3) **Bg** *forzitsiya* F, pl. *-tsii*, mid20c, via Rs (3 tech) **Hu** [forzi:tia/forzi:tsia] pl. *-ák*, beg20c (3) > *aranyfa, aranyvirág*

FORTRAN *n.* (name) 'a high-level programming language'

Ge [=E] N [U] 1970s (1 tech) **Du** *Fortran* [fortran] N, 1980s (1 tech) **Nw** [fɔ:rtran] M [U] 1970s (1 tech) **Ic** [fortran] N [U] 1980s (1 tech) **Fr** [fɔRtRã] M, 1960s (1 tech) **Sp** *FORTRAN/fortan* M [U] end20c (1 tech) **It** [fortran] M [U] 1970s (1 tech) **Rm** [fortran] N [U] 1960s, via Fr? (3 tech) **Rs** *fortran* M [U] 1970s (1 tech) **Po** [fortran] M [U] end20c (1 tech) **Cr** [=E] M [U] 1970s (1 tech) **Bg** *Fortran* M [U] end20c (1 tech) **Fi** (3 tech) **Hu** [=E] [U] 1970s (1 tech) **Gr** <=E> [fortran] F [U] 1970s (1 tech, obs)

forward *n.* 'an attacking player'

This loanword was introduced, together with other football terms, around 1900, but was later replaced by calques or other native terms in many languages (for German, regionally retained in Switzerland and Austria).

Ge [fo:rvart] M, pl. *-s*, end19c/beg20c (1 reg, obs) < *Stürmer* **Du** [=E] C, beg20c (1 tech) < *aanvaller, voorhoedespeler, spits* **Nw** [fɔ:(r)vard] M, pl. *-er/-s*, beg20c (1 obs) < *spiss* **Ic** - < rend *framherji* **Fr** - < *avant* **Sp** - < *delantero* **It** - < *attaccante/centravanti* **Rm** - < creat *ínaintaş* **Rs** *forvard* M, pl. *-y*, beg20c (1 tech) < trsl *napadayushchiĭ* **Po** [forwert] M [U]

beg20c (1 tech) **Cr** *forvard* M, beg20c (1 tech) **Bg** *foruard* M, pl. *-i*, beg20c (1 tech/arch) < *napadatel* **Hu** [forward] pl. *-ok*, end19/beg20c (1 tech, obs) < *csatár* **Al** - < *sulmues* **Gr** *forghuord* M, beg20c (1 tech) < *epithetikos (pekhtis)*

Fosbury flop* *n.* 'a style of high jump'

Richard Fosbury (*1947) invented a style of high jumping, with head first and face upwards, winning the gold medal at the 1968 Olympic Games. The term was widely current in the 1970s but is obsolescent in its full form, ↑*flop* being preferred.

Ge <=E>/*flop* [=E] M [U] 1970s (1 tech, obs) **Du** [=E] C, pl. *-s/-pen*, 1970s (1 tech) = *rolsprong* **Nw** [=E] M, pl. *-s*, 20c (1 tech) **Ic** *flopp* [flɔhp] N [U] 1970s (1 tech) = rend *Fosbury stökk/still* **Fr** *Fosbury (flop)* M, 1970s (1 tech) **Sp** *Fosbury (Flop)* [fosburi flop] M [U] end20c (1 tech) **It** *fosbury* [fozburi] M/adj., pl. ∅, 1960s (1 tech) = creat *(salto) dorsale* **Rm** - < ↑*flop* **Rs** *fosberi flop* M [U] mid20c (1 tech) **Bg** *(fozbŭri) flop* M, pl. *-pa*, 1970s (1 tech) **Hu** (0/1 tech) **Gr** <=E> [=E] N [U] 1970s (1 tech, obs)

foto finish see ↑*photo finish*

foul *n* 1 'an unfair stroke or piece of play (in various kinds of sports)'

As in *Macbeth*, the adj. *foul* is the opposite to ↑*fair* in twentieth-century football terminology, but *foul* is also a noun and a verb (the latter being more restricted). This loanword is widespread, but in Romance languages it is widely replaced by ↑*fault* – which is similar in form and meaning.

Ge [=E] N, pl. *-s*, end19c (2 tech) → *-en* v. **Du** [faul] N, mid20c (1 tech) **Nw** [=E] M, pl. *-s*, 1950s (1 tech) → *foule* v. **Ic** [=E] N, pl. ∅, mid/end20c (1 tech_BASKETB_) < *villa, brot* (football) **Sp** [faul] M, 1930s (1 tech) < *falta* **It** - < *fallo* **Rm** - < *fault* **Rs** *fol* M, pl. *-y*, mid20c (2 tech) → *sfolit'* v. **Po** *faul*/<=E> M [U] mid20c (2) → *s*-v.; *-ujący* M/adj. **Cr** *faul* M, pl. *-ovi*, beg20c (2) → *-irati* v. **Bg** *fal* M, pl. *-al-ove/faul* M [U] beg20c (3 coll/2 tech) → *fauliram* v. **Hu** [fu:l] [U] end19/beg20c (1 tech/obs) **Al** *faull* [faul] M, pl. *-e*, beg20c (1 tech) **Gr** *faul* N, beg20c (2 tech)

fouling *n.* 'dirtying, especially by sea creatures' (cf. ↑*anti-fouling*)

Ge [=E] N [U] end20c (1 tech, rare) **Fr** [fuliŋ] M, 1960s (1 tech)

foundation cream *n.* 'a cream used as a base for applying cosmetics'

Ge [=E] F, end20c (1 tech, rare) **Du** *foundation* [=E] C, 1970s (2) **Nw** *foundation* [=E] M, pl. *-s*, 1960s (1

tech) = trsl *underlagskrem* **Ic** - < trsl *grunnkrem* **Rm** [=E] N [U] end20c (0>1 tech) **Cr** (0) **Hu** - < trsl *alapozó krém* **Gr** <=E> [=E] F, end20c (1 writ, jour) < mean *vasi*

foxhound *n.* 'a hound bred and trained to hunt foxes'

Nw (∅) **Fr** *fox-hound* [fɔksaund] M, pl. *-s*, beg19c (1 tech) **Sp** [foks haund] M, pl. *-s*, beg20c (∅ jour/rare) < trsl *perro rapasero* **It** [fɔkʃaund] M, pl. ∅, beg20c (1 tech) **Rm** *rasa foxhound* [=E] N [U] beg20c (1

tech) **Rs** *fokskhaund* M, pl. *-y*, mid20c (1 tech) **Bg** *fokskhaund* M, pl. *-al-i*, mid20c (1 tech)

fox terrier *n.* 'a short-haired terrier'

This is one of the numerous adoptions of English names for breeds of dog; note the absence of calques.

Ge [=E] M, pl. ∅, 19c (3) = *Fox* **Du** [=E] C, 19c (3) **Nw** [=E] M, pl. *-e*, 19c (2) **Ic** [=E] mid/end20c (0 tech) **Fr** <=E>/*fox* [fɔksterje/fɔks] M, mid19c (2) **Sp** [fo(k)sterrier] M, pl. *-s*, beg20c (1 tech) **It** [fɔks terier/terie] M, pl. ∅, beg20c (2) **Rm** *foxterier* [foksterier] M, beg20c (2 tech) **Rs** *fokster'er* M, pl. *-y*, mid20c (2) **Po** *foksterier*/<=E> [-er] M, beg20c (2) **Cr** *foksterijer* M, pl. *-i*, beg20c (3) **Bg** *foksterier* M, pl. *-al-i*, mid20c (1 tech) **Fi** *foksterrieri* 20c (3) < trsl *kettuterrieri* **Hu** [=E] pl. *-ek* (1 tech); *foxi/fokszi* [foksi] pl. *-k*, end19/beg20c (3) **Gr** *foxterier/fox terie* M/N, 19c/20c, via Fr (2)

foxtrot *n.* 1 'a ballroom dance', 2 'the music for this'

The name of one of the most popular early twentieth-century dances, which originated c. 1910 in the USA, named after a horse's canter, and was adopted, without great changes, into all European languages. Nowadays the dance and the word are both slightly obsolescent.

Ge *Foxtrott/Fox* M [U] beg20c (1 obs) **Du** [fɔkstrɔt] C, beg20c (2) **Nw** [=E] M, pl. *-er*, beg20c (2) **Ic** [fɔxstʰroht] M [U] 1920s (2) **Fr** *fox-trott* [fɔkstrɔt] M, 1920s (1 obs) **Sp** M [U] beg20c (1 obs) **It** [fɔkstrɔt] M [U] 1910s (1 obs) **Rm** [=E] N [U] 1930s (2 obs) **Rs** *fokstrot* M [U] beg20c, 1(1 obs); [U] 2(1 tech, obs) **Po** *fokstrot* M [U] beg20c (1 obs) **Cr** *fokstrot* M [U] beg20c, (1 obs) **Bg** *fokstrot* M [U] 1930s (1 obs/tech) **Fi** [=E] 20c (2) **Hu** *foxtrott* [=E] [U] beg20c (2 tech/arch) **Al** *foks/fokstrot* [fokstrɔt] M, pl. *-e*, 1930s (2/3) **Gr** *foxtrot* N [U] beg20c (1 obs)

frame *n.* 1 'a case or border enclosing a picture', 2 'a basic rigid supporting structure', 8 'a single complete image or picture on a cinema film or transmitted in a series of lines by television', +13 'a sequence of information items' (comput.)

Du *frame/freem* [fre:m] N, beg20c, 1,2(2) 8(1 tech) **Nw**

(o) **Fr** [frɛ:m] M, 1980s, +13(1 tech, ban) > *cadre schéma* **Sp** [frẹim] M, pl. *-s*, end20c, 8(1 tech) **It** [freim] M, pl. Ø, 1980s, 8,+13(1 tech) **Rm** [=E] N [U] end20c, +13(1 tech) = *cadru* **Rs** *freim* M, pl. *-y*, end20c, 8,+13(1 tech) **Po** M, end20c, +13(1 tech) **Hu** *frém* [fre:m] [U] beg20c, 2(1 tech_{MECH})

franchising *n.* 3 'authorization granted to someone by a company to sell its goods or services'

This term is one of the more important innovations in international economic terminology. It spread all over Europe during the 1970s and 1980s, but is insufficiently understood by most and has thus not become part of the general vocabulary.

Ge [=E] N [U] 1970s (1 tech) = *Franchise* **Du** [=E] C [U] 1970s, via Fr (1 tech) **Nw** <=E>/*franchise* [=E] M [U] 1970s (1 tech) **Fr** - < *franchisage* → *franchisé, -ée* adj./n.; *franchiseur* M; *franchiser* v. **Sp** [franchaisin] M [U]

1980s (1 tech) > *franquicia* **It** [frentʃaizin(g)] M [U] 1970s (1 tech) **Rm** [=E] N, end20c, 3(1 tech) **Rs** *frantchaizing* M [U] 1980s (1 tech) **Po** [frantʃizink] M [U] 1980s (1 tech) **Cr** *fransising* M [U] 1980s (1 tech) **Bg** *franchaizing* M [U] 1990s (1 tech) **Fi** *fransiisi* 1980s (1 tech) **Hu** *franchize* [=E] [U] end20c (Ø>1 tech) → *-ol* v. **Gr** <=E> [frantsaiz] N [U] 1990s (1 tech)

freak *n.* 1 'a freak of nature', 3a 'an unconventional person', 3b 'an enthusiast for a specified activity etc', 3c 'a person who undergoes hallucinations; a drug addict', +3d 'a monster (metaph.), a person whose appearance and behaviour are abnormal', +3e 'a person abnormal in form'

Although this word is very popular in colloquial speech in Northern and Western Europe, it has not penetrated the East and South. Derivatives, such as the verb ↑*freak out*, are of even more restricted currency. The term appears to fill a semantic gap left between 'fan', 'maniac', and 'lunatic'.

Ge [=E] M, pl. *-s*, 1980s, 3a,b(1 coll) **Du** [=E] C, 1970s, 3b(1 coll) **Nw** <=E>/*frik(er)* [=E] M, pl. *-er/-s*, 1970s, 3a,b,c(2) → *frikete/freakete* adj. **Ic** *frík* [fri:k] N, pl. Ø, 1970s, 3a,c,+3d(2 sla); freq. cp², 3b(2 coll) **Fr** [frik] M, 1970s, 3b(1 sla) 3c(1 obs) **Sp** <=E>/*freaky/friqui* [frik(i)] M, pl. *-s*, 1970s, 1,3a,c,+3d(1>2 tech) **It** [fri:k] M [U] 1970s, 3a,b,c(1) < *fricchettone* **Cr** *frik* M [U] end20c, 3b(1) **Fi** *friikki* 20c, 3b(2) **Gr** *frik* M [U] 3b,+3e(1 coll, you) → *frikio* N, end20c, 1,3a(3 coll)

freak (out) *v.* 2 '(cause to) undergo hallucinations or a strong emotional experience', 3 'adopt a wildly unconventional lifestyle'

Ge *ausfreaken* 1970s (1 you, obs) **Du** *freaken* [fri:kən] 1980s, 3(1 coll, you) **Nw** *frike/freake ut* ["fri:ke] 1970s (2 coll) → *friker/freaker* M;

(ut)frika adj. **Ic** *fríka út* [fri:ka u:t] 1970s, 2,3(2 sla) **Sp** *freakear*, end20c (1 sla, you/rare) → *freakado/fricado* pp adj. **Gr** *frikaro*, end20c, 2(3 sla), 3(3coll)

free climbing* *n.* 'rock climbing without technical equipment'

Ge [=E] N [U] 1980s (1 tech, rare) = trsl *Freiklettern* **Du** [=E] C, 1980s (1 tech) **It** [fri klaimbin(g)] M, 1980s (1 tech) < trsl *arrampicata libera* **Rm** - < trsl *cățărare liberă* **Bg** *friklaiming* M [U] end20c (1 tech) < trsl *svobodno katerene*

free climber* *n.* 'a person who climbs mountains, climbing walls, etc. without any equipment'

Ge [=E] M, pl. Ø, 1980s (1 tech, rare) **Du** [=E] C, 1980s (1 tech) **It** [fri klaimber] M, pl. Ø, 1980s (1 tech) < *arrampicatore*

free flow* *n./cp¹* 'self-service' (econ.)

Ge cp¹ [=E] M [U] 1980s (1 tech, rare)

free jazz *n.* 'a style of jazz music'

Ge [=E] M [U] 1960s (1 tech) **Du** [=E] C [U] 1960s (1 tech) **Nw** [=E] M [U] 1960s (1 tech, obs) **Ic** [=E] M [U] 1960s (1 tech) **Fr** *free-jazz* [fʀidʒaz] 1960s (1 tech) **Sp** [friɣas] [U] 1990s (1 tech) **It** [fri dʒets/dʒez] M [U] 1960s (1>2) **Rm** [fridʒez/-dʒaz] N [U] 1970s (1 tech, rare) > trsl *jaz liber* **Rs** (o) **Po** [fri-e-] M [U] end20c (1 tech) **Cr** (o) **Bg** *frii dzhaz* M [U] 1970s (1 tech) < trsl *svoboden dzhaz* **Fi** [=E] M [U] 1960s (1 tech) **Hu** [=E] [U] 1960s (1 tech) **Gr** <=E> [=E] F [U] mid20c (1 tech)

freelance/freelancer *n.* 1 'a person offering services on a temporary basis', +1a cp¹ 'a freelance editor'

The concept reflects a tendency in Western economies, where the journalistic term has become increasingly used for all kinds of non-permanent jobs. West European languages have borrowed the term for the new situation, whereas the type of work was uncommon in the East before at least 1990 so that no word was obviously needed.

Ge *-er* [=E] M, pl. Ø, 1980s (1 mod) **Du** *free-lance* 1970s, +1a(2) → *freelancer* **Nw** *free-lance/frilans(er)* [fri:lans] 1950s (2/3) **Ic** *frílansari* [fri:lansarɪ] M, pl. *-ar*, 1970s, 1(1 coll) **Fr** *free-lance* [fʀilãs] M/adj., 1970s

(1 tech) **Sp** [frịlans/frilans] M, pl. Ø, 1970s (1 tech) **It** [frilans] M/F, pl. Ø, 1960s (1 jour) **Cr** [frilans/frilanser] M, pl. Ø, end20c (1 tech) **Fi** [=E] end20c (2)

freelance *v.* 'act as a freelance'

Du *free-lancen* 1980s (2) **Nw** <=E>/*frilanse* [fri:lanse] 1970s (2/3) **Sp** - < *trabajar freelance/por libre*

freelance *adj./adv.* (of workers) 'independent'

Du *free-lance* [=E] 1970s (2) **Nw** *freelans* [fri:lans] 1950s (2/3) **Ic** [fri:lans] 1970s (1 coll) **Fr** *free-lance* [frilãs] adj., 1980s (1 tech) < *pigiste, indépendant* **Sp** [frịlans/frilans] 1970s (1 tech) **It** [frilans] 1960s (1 tech) **Cr** *freelance* [=E] adj. 1980s (1 tech) **Bg** - < *creat na svobodna praktika*

Freemason *n.* 'a member of an international fraternity for mutual help and fellowship'

When Freemasonry spread to the Continent in the eighteenth century, the terms were translated into the various languages; there does not seem to be any use of the English word.

Ge - < trsl *Freimaurer* **Du** - < *vrijmetselaar; francmaçon* (5Fr) **Nw** - < trsl *frimurer* **Ic** - < trsl *frimúrari* **Fr** - < *franc-maçon* **Sp** - < *mason/francmason* **It** - < trsl *massone, franco muratore* **Rm** - < *francmason* **Rs** - < *mason → -skiĭ* N; *-stvo* N **Po** *mason* (5Fr) **Cr** - < trsl *slobodni zidar* **Bg** - < *(frank)mason* (5Fr) → *-ski* adj.; *-stvo* N **Fi** - < creat *vapaamuurari* **Hu** - < trsl *szabadkőműves* **Gr** *masonos* M/F, via Fr (5It) > *tekton(as)* M/F → *masonia* F, *masonismos* M; *framasonos* M/F, via Fr (5It) → *framasonia* F

freestyle *n./cp[1].* 'a sporting contest in which all styles are used', +3 'downhill skiing with jumps and acrobatic tricks and stunts', +4 'a contest, usu. for teenagers, where all styles are allowed' (dance)

Ge [=E] M [U] end20c, +3(1 tech) = 1: *Freistil → -er* M **Du** *free style* [=E] C [U] 1990s, +3(1 tech) < trsl *vrije stijl* **Nw** [=E] M [U] 1970s, +3(1 tech) = trsl *fristil → freestyler* M **Ic** <=E>/*frístæl* [=E] cp[1], end20c, +4(1 tech) **Fr**

- < *nage libre* **Sp** - < 1: trsl *estilo libre* **It** [=E] M [U] end20c, +3(1 tech) **Rm** [=E] N [U], 1970s, +3(1 tech) < trsl *(stiul) liber* **Rs** *fristaĭl* M [U] end20c, +3(2 tech) **Po** - < rend *styl wolny* **Bg** *fristaĭl* M [U] 1990s, +3(1 tech) < 1: trsl *svoboden stil* **Fi** - < *vapaa tyyli* **Hu** [=E] [U] end20c, +3(1 tech) **Al** - < *stil i berë* **Gr** <=E> [=E] 1990s, +3(1 tech); < 1 = mean *elefthero*

freethinker *n.* 'a person who rejects dogma or authority, esp. in religious belief'

The ideas of the "Free thinkers" spread to the Continent in the eighteenth century, the term being translated into the languages affected, as with ↑*Freemason* above.

Ge - < *Freidenker* **Du** - < *vrijdenker* **Nw** - < trsl *fritenker* **Ic** - < creat *frihyggjandi* **Fr** - < trsl *librepenseur* **Sp** - < trsl *libre pensador* **It** - < trsl *libero pensatore* **Rm** < *liber cugetător* **Rs** - < trsl *svobodomyslyashchiĭ* **Po** - < trsl *wolnomyś'liciel* **Cr** - < *slobodni mislilac* **Bg** - < rend? *svobodomislesht* adj. **Fi** - < *vapaa-ajattelija* **Hu** - < trsl *szabadgondolkodó* **Al** - < rend *mendimtar i lirë*

free trade *phr.* 'international trade left to its natural course without restriction on imports and exports'

In the nineteenth century this international concept was largely expressed by native terms in the countries affected, the English word apparently taken as the model for calquing.

Ge - < trsl *Freihandel* **Du** - < *vrihandel* **Nw** - < trsl *frihandel* **Ic** - < creat *friverslun, frjáls verslun* **Fr** - < trsl *libre-échange* **Sp** - < trsl *libre comercio* **It**

[=E] M [U] end19c (1 tech) < trsl *libero scambio/ mercato* **Rm** - < rend *comerț liber* **Rs** - < trsl *svobodnaya torgovlya → fritrederstvo* N, *fritreder* M **Po** [fri-] M [U] beg20c (1 tech) **Cr** [=E] M [U] mid20c (1 tech) **Bg** - < trsl *svobodna tŭrgoviya* **Fi** - < trsl *vapaa kauppa* **Hu** [=E] [U] 20c (1 tech) < trsl *szabad kereskedelem* **Al** - < rend *tregti e lirë* **Gr** - < trsl *elefthero eborio*

freeware* *n.* 'free software'

Nw [=E] F [U] 1990s (1 tech) **Fr** [friwɛr] M, 1990s (1 tech, ban) < *logiciel public* **Fi** [=E] end20c (1 tech) **Po** [friwer] N [U] end20c (1 tech) **Gr** <=E> [=E] end20c (1 tech)

freewheel *v.* 1 'ride a bike with the pedals at rest', +1b 'let a car slide downhill', 2 'move or act without constraint'

Du *freewheelen* [fri:wi:lən] 1930s (2) **Ic** - < *frihjóla*

freeze *v.* 6a 'make or become motionless or powerless through fear, surprise, etc.', +6c 'become motionless after smoking too much cannabis', 8 'make (credits, assets, etc.) temporarily or permanently unrealizable', 11 'arrest (a movement in a film) by repeating a frame or stopping the film at a frame', +12 'give up, stop doing'.

Nw *fryse* end20c, 6a,8,11 (1 mod) **Ic** *frisa* [fri:sa] 1970s, +12(1 sla); - < 6a,+6c: trsl *frjósa*; 6a,8,11: trsl *frysta* **It** - < 8: mean *congelare* **Bg** - < 8: mean *zamrazyavam* **Gr** - < mean *paghono*

freezer *n.* 'the coldest compartment in a refrigerator, or a separate apparatus for freezing food'

The languages studied are neatly divided between those using loanwords and those using calques.

Ge - < rend *Gefrierfach, Gefriertruhe* **Du** - < rend *diepvries, vriesvak* **Nw** - < trsl *(dyp)fryser* **Ic** - < creat *frystir* **Fr** [frizœr] M, 1960s (1 obs) **Sp** - < trsl *congelador; freezer* (SAm) **It** [fridʒer/frizer] M, pl. ∅, 1960s (3) = trsl *congelatore* **Rm** [=E] N, 1970s (1 tech, rare)

< *congelator* **Rs** *frizer* M, pl. *-y*, mid20c (1 tech) < creat *morozil'naya kamera* **Po** - < trsl *zamarazarka* **Cr** *frizer* M, pl. *-i*, mid20c (3) **Bg** *frizer* M, pl. *-al-i*, end20c (2) **Fi** - < rend *pakastin* **Hu** [fri:-zer] pl. ∅, end20c (1 tech) < *mélyhűtő*

French (jacket) *n.* +5 'a kind of military jacket with four patch pockets'

Rs *french* M, pl. *-i*, mid20c (1 arch) **Po** *frencz* M, mid20c (1 arch)

French knickers *n.* 'wide-legged knickers'

Ge [=E] M (mostly pl.) 1970s (1 tech, obs)

fresh *adj.* +7c 'cool, invigorating' (as a quality of deodorants, etc.)

Ge [=E] uninfl., 1980s (1 mod, rare) **Du** (∅) **Nw** [=E/fre:ʃ] 1980s (1 coll, sla) **It** cp[2] (1 tech_TM) **Rm** (0) **Hu** [=E] end20c (1 jour)

fret *n.* 'each of a sequence of bars or ridges on the fingerboard of some stringed instruments'

Du [frɛt] F/M, 1930s (1 tech)

friendly fire *n.* +1a 'criticism from one's own ranks, esp. in policy and business'
Ge [=E] N [U] 1990s (1 jour)

fringe benefit *n.* 'an employee's benefit supplementing a wage or salary'
Du *fringe benefits* [=E] pl., 1990s (1 jour/mod) < *bijkomende verdiensten, extraatjes* **Nw** [=E] pl. *-s*, 1980s (1 tech) < trsl *frynsegode* **Sp** - < *incentivo, complemento, extra* **It** *fringe benefits* [frĩndʒ benefits] M, pl., 1980s (1 tech) < creat *beneficio accessorio*

frisbee *n.* 1a 'a concave plastic disc for skimming through the air as an outdoor game', +1b 'the game'

The trademark of the Frisbie bakery in Bridgeport, Conn. was adopted as the name for the plastic disc invented in 1957. The sport became a worldwide success in the 1970s, and the term quickly became generic.

Ic	Nw	Po	Rs
Du	Ge	Cr	Bg
Fr	It	Fi	Hu
Sp	Rm	Al	Gr

Ge [=E] N, pl. *-s*, 1970s, +1b(1 tech, obs); cp¹ (*-scheibe*) 1a(1 tech) **Du** [frisbi:] C, pl. *-'s*, 1980s (1 tech) **Nw** [=E] M, pl. *-er*, 1970s (2) **Ic** *frisbí* [=E] N [U] 1970s, +1b(2); cp¹ *frisbídiskur* M, 1a(2+5) **Fr** [fʀizbi] M, 1980s (1 tech/obs) **Sp** [frisbi] M [U] 1990s (1 tech) **It** [frizbi] M, pl. Ø, 1970s (2) **Rm** [=E] N, 1980s (1 tech, mod) **Rs** *frizbi* N, uninfl., end20c (1 tech) **Po** N 1980s (1 mod) **Cr** [=E] M, 1980s (1 tech) **Bg** *frizbi* N, pl. *-ta*/[U], end20c (1 you) **Fi** [=E] 1970s (2) **Gr** *frisbi* N, mid20c (2)

frock *n.* 4a 'a frock-coat'

The phonological change to /a/ and the non-English meaning disguise the etymology of this word, which is also morphologically fully integrated into most languages (note German plural). The word survives in most languages, but not in French which helped to spread it.

Ge *Frack* M, pl. *Fräcke*, 18c (3) **Du** *frak, frac* [frak] C, pl. *frakken*, 19c (3) **Nw** *frakk* M, pl. *-er*, via Ge (3) **Ic** *frakki* [frahcɪ] M, pl. *-ar*, ca. 1800, via Da, +7(3) **Fr** *frac* M, 18c (3 arch) **Sp** *frac*/*fraque* [frak] M, 19c, via Fr (2) **It** *frac* [frak] M, pl. Ø, 18c (3) **Rm** *frac* [frak] beg19c, via Fr (3) **Rs** *frak* M, pl. *-i*, 19c, via Ge/Fr(3) **Po** *frak* [frak] M, beg 19c, via Fr(3) **Cr** *frak* M, pl. *-ovi*, 19c (3) **Bg** *frak* M, pl. *-al-ove*, 19c, via Ge/Fr (3) **Fi** *frakki* via Ge (3) **Hu** *frakk* [frak] pl. *-ok*, 17–19c, via Fr/Ge (3 obs) **Gr** *frako* N, via Fr (3)

frontman *n.* 3 'the leader of a group of musicians'
Ge *Frontmann* M, pl. *-männer*, 1980s (3 tech, you) **Nw** - < *frontfigur* **Ic** *frontmaður* M, pl. *-menn*, 1970s (3 tech) < *framlínuaður, frontur* **Sp** [frͻnman] M, end20c (1 tech, you, mod) **Rs** *frantmen* M, pl. *-y*, 1990s (1 tech, you, mod) **Po** [-en] M, end20c (1 tech) **Cr** (0) **Bg** *frontmen* M, pl. *-i*, 1990s (1 tech, mod) **Hu** [=E] pl. Ø, end20c (2 tech, mod) < rend *frontember* (3+5)

fuck *v.* 1 'have sexual intercourse', 2 'mess about, fool around', 3 'curse, confound'
Nw [=E] 1980s, 3(1 sla, you) **Ic** *fokka (upp)* [fͻhka] end20c, 2(2 sla) **Rm** [=E] 1980s, 3(1>0 you, mod) **Rs** - → *fakséishn* M **Po** (0) **Bg** <=E> end20c, 1(1 writ)

fuck *interj.* 1 'an expression of anger and annoyance'
Ge [=E] 1980s (1 sla, you) **Du** [fʏk] 1980s (1 coll) **Nw** [=E] 1980s (1 sla, you) **Ic** [fæhk] end20c (1 sla, you) **Rm** [=E], 1980s (0>1 you, mod) **Rs** (0) **Po** end20c (2 coll) **Bg** *fak*/*fŭk* 1990s (2 you, sla) **Gr** [=E] end20c (1 sla)

fuck-up *n.* 'a mess or muddle'
Ic [=E] N, pl. Ø, end20c (1 sla)

fucked (up) *adj.* 'run down'
Ge *abgefuckt*/*-a-* 1980s (1 sla, you) **Po** (0)

fuel oil *n.* 'oil used as fuel in an engine or furnace'
Du *fuel* [=E] C [U] 1970s (1 tech) < *stookolie* **Nw** [=E] M [U] mid20c (1 tech) < *brenselolje* **Ic** *fuelolía* [=E/fu:el-] F [U] mid20c (1 tech) < rend *brennsluolía* **Fr** *fuel*/*fioul* [fjul] M, 1950s (2) < *mazout* **Sp** *fuel (oil)* [fuel] M, 1920s (2>3 tech) = *fuelóleo* **Al** - < *mazut*

full *adj.* 1 'holding as much as its limits will allow'
Nw [ful] (4) **Po** uninfl., end20c (2 coll) **Hu** [=E] *n.* (1 tech_POKER) **Gr** *ful* (2) → *sto ful* phr.; *fularo* v.; *fularistos* adj.

full contact *n.* 1 'a kind of boxing with no restrictions to the rules', +1b 'a race where cars are allowed to crash into each other'
Ge - < 1: trsl *Vollkontaktboxen* **Fr** *full-contact* [fulkõtakt] M, 1970s (1 tech) **Sp** [fulkontak] M [U] 1980s (1 tech) **It** [ful kontakt] M [U] 1980s (1 tech) **Rm** [=E] N [U] 1990s (1 jour, mod) **Bg** - < 1: trsl *pŭlen contact*

full house *n.* 1 'a maximum attendance at a theatre etc.', 2 'a hand with three of a kind and a pair' (poker)
Ge [=E] N [U] 20c, 2(1 tech) **Du** [fulhaus] F/M, 1980s (2) **Nw** - < trsl *fullt hus* **Ic** - < trsl *fullt hús* **Fr** *full* [ful] M, end19c, 2(1 tech) < *main pleine* **Sp** *full* M, 2(1 tech) **It** *full* [ful] M, pl. Ø, 1940s, 2(3) **Rm** *ful* [ful] N, 1940s, 2(2 tech) **Po** *ful* M, mid20c (2 tech) **Cr** *ful* M [U] beg20c, 2(1 tech) **Bg** *ful* M, pl. *-a*, beg20c, 2(3 tech) **Hu** - < 1: trsl *teltház* **Gr** *ful* adj., 20c (1 tech)

full-rigger* *n.* 1 'a ship with three or more full-rigged masts', 2 'a large and impressive (female) person wearing conspicuous clothes'
Nw [fulriger] M, pl. *-e*, 19c (3)

full service *n.* 'comprehensive service covering advice, repair, etc. by various experts'
Ge [=E] M [U] 1970s (1 tech, rare) **Du** *full- service (-bureau)* N, 1980s (1 tech) **It** [=E] M [U] end20c (1 tech) < trsl *servizio completo*

full speed *adj.*/*cp¹* 'proceeding at maximum speed'
Ge [=E] 1970s (1 coll) **Du** [fulspi:d] beg20c (2) **Nw** [ful spi:d] 20c (5+2) **Ic** *fúllspítt* [ful:spiht] mid20c (1 coll) = *á fullu spítti* **Rm** (0 you,

mod) **Bg** - < creat *pŭlen napred* **Hu** - < trsl *teljes sebességgel* **Al** - < *me githë shpejtësinë*

(in) full-swing *n.* '(at) the height of activity'
Nw *full sving* [fʉl sviŋ] 20c (4)   **Ic** [ful:sviŋ] N [U] mid20c (1 coll)

full-time *adj./adv.* 'occupying or using the whole of the available working time'
Ge [=E] uninfl., 1980s (1 mod) < trsl *Vollzeit-* **Du** [=E] 1960s (2)   **Nw** (0) < *fulltids-, heltids-* **Ic** [=E] uninfl., 1970s (1 sla)   **Fr** - < (*à*) *temps complet* **Sp** [fʉl taim] 1970s (1 tech) < trsl *a tiempo completo/ journada completa = con dedicación exclusiva* **It** [=E] M [U] 1960s (2) = trsl *tempo pieno* **Rm** (0 you, mod)   **Cr** - < trsl *stalno zaposlen* **Bg** - < creat *pŭlna zaetost* **Gr** *ful taim* adj./adv., 1990s (2)

full-time job *n.* 'a job occupying all of someone's working-hours'
Ge [=E] M, pl. -*s*, 1960s (1 coll) < *Ganztagsarbeit, Vollzeitjob* **Du** [=E] C, 1960s (2) = *volledig betrekking, hele baan* **Nw** - < *fulltidsjobb* **Ic** [=E] N, pl. Ø, 1970s (1 sla) < trsl *full vinna* **Fr** - < trsl *emploi à temps complet* **Sp** - < trsl *trabajo a tiempo completo* **It** - < trsl *lavoro full-time/a tempo pieno* **Rm** (0 you, mod)   **Cr** - < *puno radno vrijeme* → *fultajmer* M, pl. -*i*, 1970s (1 tech)   **Hu** - < *teljes munkaidő*

fun *n.* 'amusement, esp. lively or playful'
Du Ø   **Nw** [=E] end20c (1 sla, rare)   **Ic** [=E] N [U] end20c (0 sla)   **Fr** [fœn] M, 1970s (1 you)   **Rm** 1990s (0)

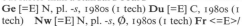

funboard *n.* 'a type of windsurfing board that is less stable but faster than a standard board'
Ge [=E] N, pl. -*s*, 1980s (1 tech) **Du** [=E] C, 1980s (1 tech)   **Nw** [=E] N, pl. -*s*, Ø, 1980s (1 tech) **Fr** <=E>/

fun [=E/fœn(bɔʀd)] M, 1980s (1 tech)   **Sp** <=E>/*fun* [fanbor/fan] M [U] 1980s (1 tech) → *funboarder/funboarder-o* **Cr** [fan bord] M, pl. -*ovi*, 1980s (1 tech)

fun-fur* *n.* 'a fur jacket or coat for young people'
Ge [=E] M, pl. -*s*, 1960s (1 tech, obs)

funk *n.* 1 'music with a heavy rhythmical beat'
As with other music terms, this word (and the derived adj.) though quite recent appears to be known in nearly all languages – but only to a limited group of enthusiasts.
Ge [=E] M [U] 1980s (1 tech)   **Du** [=E] C [U] 1970s (1 tech)   **Nw** [=E] M [U] 1980s (1 tech)   **Ic** *fönk* [fœ(y)ŋk] N [U] 1970s (2 tech)   **Fr** [fœnk] M/adj., 1980s (0?)   **Sp** [fank/funk] M [U] 1980s (1 tech, you) > *funky* **It** [faŋk] M [U] 1980s (1 tech, you)   **Rm** [=E] N [U] 1980s (1 tech) **Rs** *fank* M [U] 1980s (1 tech, you) **Po** *funk* M [U] 1980s (1 tech) **Cr** *fank* M [U] 1980s (1 tech)   **Bg** *fŭnk* M [U] 1980s (1 tech)   **Fi** [=E] 1980s, (1 tech)   **Hu** *funky* [=E] [U] 1980s (1>2 tech, you)   **Gr** *fank* F [U] 1980s (2)

funky *adj./n.* 1 'with a heavy rhythmical beat' (jazz)
Ge [=E] uninfl., 1970s (1 tech)   **Du** [fʏŋki] 1980s (1 you)   **Nw** [=E] 1970s (1 tech)   **Ic** [fœɲci] uninfl., 1970s (1 tech)   **Fr** [fœnki] adj./n., 1970s (1 tech)   **Sp** [fanki/funki] M [U] 1980s (1 tech, you)   **It** [faŋki] uninfl., 1980s (1 tech, you)   **Rm** [=E] N [U] 1980s (1 tech) **Rs** (0) **Po** uninfl., end20c(1 tech)   **Cr** *fanki* M, 1980s (1 tech)   **Bg** *fŭnki* uninfl., 1980s (1 tech) **Hu** *funky* [=E] [U] 1980s (1 tech, you)   **Gr** *fanki/* <=E> uninfl., 1980s (1 tech, jour)

furlong *n.* 'an eighth of a mile (particularly in horse-racing)'
Du [=E] C, 19c (0)   **Nw** (Ø)   **Fr** (Ø)   **Sp** M, 1930s (Ø/1 tech, arch/rare)   **Rs** *farlong* M, pl. -*i*, 19c (Ø) **Po** [furlonk] M, mid20c (Ø)   **Gr** *fɛrlon* N (Ø)

G

gadget *n.* 1 'an ingenious mechanical device', +2 'a gimmick'

The loanwords *gadget*, ↑*gag* and ↑*gimmick* are felt to be near-synonyms, and where a choice is to be made, *gag* – the best established item – is preferred in most languages; note that some languages have none of the three words.

Ge [getʃət] N, pl. -*s*, 1970s (1 mod) < *Gag* **Du** [=E] N 1970s (1 obs) **Nw** (0) **Fr** [gadʒet] 1950s, +2(2) → *gadgétiser* v.; *gadgetière* (*gadget shop*, rare) **Sp** [=E/gatʃet] M, pl. -*s*, 1960s, 1(1 tech) **It** [gadʒet] M, pl. Ø, 1970s (1>2) **Rm** [=E] N, 1970s (1 mod) **Po** *gadżet/<=E* [gadʒet] M, end20c (2 coll) **Gr** *gatzet* N, end20c (1 tech)

gag *n.* 5b 'a humorous action or situation'

This word appears to have become popular as a designation of clever tricks in films and the circus etc., but is used more freely now in most languages for anything that catches the eye. By contrast, the compound ↑*gagman* is recorded for fewer languages, and is also much more restricted in style and frequency.

Ge [gek] M, pl. -*s*, 1930s (2) → (*ver*)*gagen* v.; *gagig* adj. **Du** [=E] C, 1950s (1 coll, mod) **Nw** [=E] M/N, pl. -*er/-s*, 1960s (1) **Fr** [gag] M, 1920s (2) **Sp** [gag] M, pl. -*s*, 1970s (1 tech) **It** [geg] F, pl. Ø, 1930s (2) **Rm** [gag] N, mid20c, via Fr (2) **Rs** *gég*, pl. -*i*, end20c (1 rare, mod) → *gégster* M **Po** [gag] M, mid20c (3) **Cr** *geg* M, pl. -*ovi*, mid20c (2) **Bg** *geg* M, pl. -*al-ove*, end20c (1 jour) **Hu** <=E>/*geg* [=E] pl. -*ek*, 1930/60s (1 tech>2)

gag man *n.* 'a deviser or performer of gags'

Ge [gekmen] M, pl. -*men*, 1960s (1 mod, rare) **Fr** [gagman] M, 1920s (1 obs) **Sp** [gagman] M, pl. -*men*, 1970 (1 tech) **Rm** [gagman] M, pl. -*meni*, end20c (1 mod, rare) **Rs** - < *gégster* **Po** [gegmen] M, mid20c (1 jour) **Cr** *gegmen* M, pl. -*i*, mid20c (1) **Hu** *gagman* [=E] pl. Ø, beg20c (2)

gallon 1 *n.* 'a measure of capacity used for liquids'

This word is mostly used as a foreignism in countries that have used the metric system for generations. A limited use is also possible for goods still measured in gallons (such as crude oil).

Ge *Gallone* F, pl. -*n* (Ø/3 tech) **Du** [=E] [ɣalɔn] C/N, beg20c (1 tech) **Nw** [=E] M, pl. Ø/-*s*, mid19c (Ø) **Ic** <=E>/*gallón* [kal:o(u)n] N [U] beg20c (Ø/2 tech) **Fr** [galõ] M, 17c (0/3 tech) **Sp** *galón* M, end19c (Ø/3 tech) **It** *gallone* M, pl. -*i*, end18c (3 tech) **Rm** *galon* [galon] N, end19c, via Fr (3 tech) **Rs** *gallon* M, pl. -*y*, beg19c (Ø) **Po** *galon* [galon] M, beg19c (Ø) **Cr** *galon* M, pl. -*i*, beg20c (Ø/3 tech) **Bg** *galon* M, pl. -*al-i*, beg20c (Ø) **Fi** *gallona* (Ø) **Hu** [gallon] [U] 19c (Ø>1 tech) **Al** *gallon* M, pl. -*e*, beg20c (3 tech) **Gr** *ghaloni* N (5It)

Gallup poll *n.* 'an assessment of public opinion'

The founder of the American Institute of Public Opinion, George Horace Gallup (1901–84) devised a poll which is famous for predicting election results. The name has apparently become generic in many countries, which still leaves it open as to whether 'poll' is translated; in other languages it is a foreignism, or not sufficiently known.

Ge (Ø) **Du** *Gallup-Poll* [=E] C [U] 1980s (1 tech) **Nw** *gallup* [galʉp] M, pl. -*er*, 1940s (3) = *Gallup undersøkelse* **Ic** - < creat *Gallup-könnun* **Sp** - < *encuesta Gallup* **It** - < *opinion poll* **Rm** - < rend *sondaj Gallup* **Rs** *géllap* M [U] 1980s → *institut gellapa* **Po** - < rend *sondaż Gallupa* (Ø) **Cr** *galup* M [U] 20c (3) **Bg** - < rend *anketa na 'Galãp'/* <=E> **Fi** *gallup* [gal:upɪ] 1980s (3) **Hu** *Gallup* [galup] mid20c (2+5) **Gr** *gal(l)op* N, end20c (2) = *dhimoskopisi*

gamble *n.* 1 'a risky undertaking or attempt', 2 'a spell or an act of gambling'

Ic *gambl* [kampl] N [U] 1970s (2 coll) **Gr** *gabl* N [U] end20c, 2(1 rare)

gamble *v.* 1 'play games of chance for money', 3 'take great risks in the hope of substantial gain', 4 'act in the hope or expectation of'

Nw ["gæmble] 1960s, 1,3, 4(2) **Ic** *gambla* [kampla] 1970s, 1,3(2 coll)

gambler *n.* 1 'a person who plays games of chance for money', 2 'a person who likes to take great risks'

Nw ["gæmbler/=E] M, pl. -*e*, 1960s (2) **Ic** <=E>/ *gamblari* [=E/kamplarɪ] M, pl. -*ar*, 1970s (2 coll) < 1: *fjárhættuspilari*

game *n*. 2 'a single section of play forming a scoring unit', (tennis) +13 'a party, a festivity'

Although this word is used for all kinds of contests in English, its use appears to be restricted to a 'scoring unit in tennis' in the receiving languages. Alternatively, it may be replaced by a native term, most frequently created by the extension of the meaning of an existing word for 'play'.

Ge 2(0 arch) < *Spiel* **Du** [ge:m] C, 1940s, 2(1 tech) **Nw** [=E] N, pl. Ø, -*s*, 20c, 2(1 tech) **Ic** *geim* [=E/cei:m] N, pl. Ø, mid20c, 2(1 tech) +13(2 sla, arch) **Fr** <=E> M, beg20c, 2(1 tech/arch) **Sp** [geim] M, pl. -*s*, 1970s, 2(1 tech) **It** [geim] M, pl. Ø, 1930s, 2(1 tech) = *gioco* **Rm** *ghem/game* [gem/=E] N, beg20c, 2(2 tech) **Rs** *geĭm* M, pl. -*y*, mid20c, 2(1 tech) **Po** *gem* [gem] M, beg20c, 2(1 tech) **Cr** *gem* M, pl. -*ovi*, beg20c, 2(1 tech) **Bg** *geĭm* M, pl. -*al*-*ove*, mid20c, 2(2 tech) **Hu** <=E>/*gém* [ge:m] [U] end19/beg20c, 2(1 tech, arch) **Al** *gejm* [U] 20c(2) **Gr** [=E] N, beg20c, 2(1 tech)

game *adj* 1,2 'spirited, eager'
Nw <=E>/*gem* [ge:m] 1950s (3 coll, obs)

Game Boy™ *n. propr.* 'a hand-held electronic device with a small screen, used to play cartridge computer games'
Ge [=E] M, pl. -*s*, 1980s (1 tech) **Du** [=E] C, 1980s (1 tech) **Nw** [=E] M, pl. -*s*, end20c (1 tech) **Sp** [=E] M, 1990s (1 tech/mod) **It** [=E] M [U] 1990s (2) **Rm** (0 you) **Fi** [=E] 1980s (1 tech) **Gr** <=E> [=E] 1990s (1 tech, you, mod)

game show *n*. 'a TV programme in which people compete in a game or quiz for prizes'
Ge [ge:mʃo:] F, pl. -*s*, 1990s (1 mod) **Nw** [=E] N, pl. Ø, -*s*, 1980s (1) **Sp** - < *programa concurso*

gang *n*. 1a 'a band of persons acting or going about together, esp. a group of criminals', 2 'a set of workers'

This word competes with ↑*band* ~ German *Bande*, and the respective native equivalents in most of the other languages, which are usually much more common, so its distribution is more limited than the universally used ↑*gangster* (which is semantically differentiated from and slightly more common than ↑*bandit*).

Ge [geng] F, pl. -*s*, 1950s, 1a(1 coll) < *Bande* **Du** [=E] C, 1940s, 1a(2 coll) < *bende* **Nw** *gjeng* [jeŋ] M, pl. -*er*, beg20c (3) **Ic** [=E] 1a(1 sla); *gengi* [ceiɲcɪ] N, pl. Ø, 1960s, 1a(4 sla) 2(4 tech, coll) **Fr** [gãg] M, 19c, 1a(2) **Sp** [gang] M, pl. -*s*, 1970s, 1a(1 tech) < *banda, pandilla* **It** [geŋg] F, pl. Ø, 1940s, 1a(2) < *banda* **Rm** [=E] N, 1970s, 1a(Ø) < *bandă* **Rs** *gang* M, pl. -*i*, end20c, 1a(1c) < *banda* **Po** [gank] M, beg20c, 1a(3) **Cr** [-a-] M, pl. -*ovi*, beg20c, 1a(3) **Bg** - < *banda* **Fi** *jengi*, 20c, via Sw, 1a(2); *gängi*, 1a(1 you) **Hu** [=E] pl. Ø, 20c, 1a(1 jour/rare) < *rabló-*

banda **Al** *gangë* [gangë] F, pl. Ø, mid20c, 1a(2) 2(1 reg)

gang-leader* *n*. 'the boss of a criminal gang'
Ge [geŋgli:da] M, pl. -*s*, 1960s (1 jour) **Du** - < *bendeleider* **Nw** *gjengleder* [jeŋle:der] M, 20c (3+5)

gangster *n*. 1 'a member of a gang of violent criminals', +2 'someone acting like a gangster'
Ge [geŋsta] M, pl. Ø, 1940s, 1(2) **Du** [geŋgstər] C, 1940s, 1(2) **Nw** [=E] M, pl. -*e*, 1930s (2) **Ic** *gangster* [kaŋster] M, pl. -*ar*, mid20c (1 sla) **Fr** [gägstɛʀ] M, 1930s, 1(2) **Sp** <=E>/*gángster/gánster* [=E/ganster/gaster] M, pl. -*s/es*, 1930 (2>3) → -*il* adj.; -*ismo* n.; -*izar* v. **It** [geŋgster/gaŋster] M, pl. Ø, 1930s, 1(2) **Rm** [gaŋster] M, mid20c (2) → -*esc* adj. **Rs** *gangster* M, pl. -*y*, mid20c (2) → -*skii* adj. **Po** [gangster] M, mid20c (3) → -*stwo* N [U]; -*ski* adj. **Cr** *gangster* M, pl. -*i*, mid20c, 1(2) → -*ski* adj. **Bg** *gangster* M, pl. -*i*, mid20c, via Rs (2) → -*ski* adj.; -*stvo* N; -*ka* F **Fi** *gangsteri* 20c, 1(2) **Hu** *gengszter* [geŋgster] pl. -*ek*, beg20c (2>3) **Al** *gangster* [gangster] M, pl. -*ë* (3) mid20c **Gr** *gangster* M, pl. -Ø/-*s*, mid20c (2/Ø)

gangway *n*. 2b 'a bridge from ship to shore' +2c 'a bridge from an aeroplane to the ground'
Ge [gengwe:] F, pl. -*s*, 1950s (1 tech) **Nw** [=E] M, pl. -*er/-s*, mid20c (1 tech) **Hu** [=E] [U] mid20c (1 tech)

gap *n*. 3 'a wide divergence in views, sympathies, development etc.' (*generation gap*), +3a 'a wide divergence in technology (e.g. *missile gap*) and economy'.
Ge M/F/N, 20c, 1960s (0>1 jour) < mean *Lücke* **Du** [=E] 1990s, +3a(1 tech) **Nw** - < *kløft* **Fr** [gap] M, 1950s, +3a(1 obs) **Sp** [gap] M, 1980s, 3,+3a(1 tech) **It** [gεp] M, pl. Ø, 1960s (1 tech) **Hu** [=E] [U] 1970s, +3a(1 tech COMPUT) **Gr** - < mean *khasma*

gardenia *n*. 'a shrub with large white or yellow flowers and a fragrant scent'

As with ↑*forsythia*, the Englishness of this word has largely been lost as a consequence of its neo-Latin form and the consequent pronunciation according to national conventions.

Ge *Gardenie* [garde:njə] F, pl. -*n*, 19c (3 tech) **Du** *gardenia* [ɣarde:nija] C, pl. -'*s*, mid20c (3 tech) **Nw** *gardenia* [garde:nia] M, pl. -*er*, 19c (3) **Ic** *gardenia* [kartenija] F, pl. -*ur*, 1940s, via Danish (2) **Fr** *gardénia* [gaʀdenja] M, end18c, (3 tech) **Sp** [garde̱nia] F, 19c (3) **It** [garde̱nia] F, pl. -*e*, beg19c (3) **Rm** *gardenie* F, beg20c, via Fr (3) **Rs** *gardeniya* M, pl. -*ii*, beg20c (1 tech) **Po** *gardenia* [gardenia] F, beg20c (1 tech) **Cr** *gardenia* (1) **Bg** *gardeniya* F, pl. -*nii*, beg20c (3 tech) **Fi** *gardenia* (3) **Hu** *gardénia* [garde:nia] pl. -*ák*, end19c (3 tech) **Gr** *ghardhenia* F (3)

garden centre *n*. 'an outlet where plants and gardening equipment may be bought'
Ge *Gartencenter* [gartntsenta] N/M, pl. Ø, 1970s (5+2) **Du** - < *tuincentrum* **Nw** - < *hagesenter* **Fr** [gardεnsãteʀ] M, 1970s (1 ban) < *jardinerie* F **Sp** (0) < trsl *centro jardinería* **It** [=E] M, pl. Ø, 1970s (1>2)

garden party *n.* 'a social event held in a garden'

This compound indicates the adoption of a fashionable British term in the nineteenth century, the independent influence of 'American' lifestyle and the spread of a fashionable term for social events which are in themselves not new.

Ge *Gartenparty* [gartnpati] F, pl. *-(ie)s*, end20c (5+3) **Du** - < *tuinfeest, tuinpartij* **Nw** [=E] N, pl. *-er -ies*, mid20c (1) < *hageselskap* **Ic** [=E] N, pl. Ø, end20c (1 sla); *garðpartý* (5+2 coll) = trsl *garðveisla* **Fr** *garden-party* [gardenparti] F, end19c (2) **Sp** [garden parti] M/F, pl. *-s/-ies*, end19c (1 arch) **It** [garden parti] M, pl. Ø/ *-s*, end19c (1) **Rm** [=E] N, 1960s (0>1) **Rs** *garden party* F, uninfl., end20c (1) **Po** [garden parti] N, end20c (2 coll) **Cr** *garden parti* F, pl. *-ije*, 20c (2) **Bg** *garden parti* N, pl. *-ta*, 1990s (1 mod) < trsl *gradinsko parti* **Hu** [=E] pl. Ø, beg20c (2 obs) **Gr** *garden parti/-y* N, pl. Ø/-s, mid20c (1 mod)

gas oil *n.* 'diesel fuel'

Ic *gasolia* [ka:solija] F [U] end19c (2 tech) **Fr** *gasoil/ gas-oil* [gazwal/gazɔjl] M, 1930s (2 tech) > *gazole* M **Sp** *gasoil/gasóleo* M, 1920s (3 tech) **It** *gasolio* M [U] 1940s (3) **Rs** *gazoĭl'* M [U] beg20c (1 tech) **Bg** *gazyol* M [U] beg20c, via Ge (3 tech) **Hu** - < *gázolaj* **Al** *gazoil* M [U] mid20c (1 obs)

gate *n.* 4 'a numbered place of access to aircraft at an airport'

Ge [ge:t] N, pl. *-s*, 1970s (0>1 mod) **Du** [=E] 1990s (1 mod) **Nw** [=E] M, pl. *-er*, 1980s (2) **Ic** [=E] N, pl. Ø, end20c, 4(0 coll) < trsl *hlið* **Fr** - < *porte* **Sp** - < trsl *puerta (de embarque)* **It** [=E] F, pl. Ø, 1970s (1 tech) < *uscita* **Po** (0) **Cr** (0) **Hu** [=E] pl. Ø, mid20c (1 tech) < *kijárat* **Gr** (0, 1 writ) < *exodhos*

-gate *n.*, *cp[2]* 'after 'Watergate' in names for other scandals'

The second element was abstracted from *Watergate* (1973) and widely used in English to designate financial and other scandals; *-gate* has also been found as a loan-cp[2] in various other languages where it can form (mostly facetious) hybrid compounds.

Ge [ge:t] N [U] 1980s (1 jour, fac) **Du** [=E] 1980s (1 jour) **Nw** [=E] N [U] 1980s (Ø) **Fr** 1980s (1 tech, jour) **Sp** [=E] 1980s (1 jour, fac) **It** [=E] 1980s (1 jour) **Rm** [=E] cp[2], 1990s (1 jour, fac) **Rs** *-geĭt* cp[2] M [U] 1980s (2 jour) **Po** [=E] F, 1980s (2 jour) **Cr** [=E] M [U] 1980s (1) **Bg** *geĭt* M/cp[2], pl. *-al-ove*, 1980s (2 jour) **Gr** <=E>/*geĭt* N [U] 1980s (1 jour)

gatecrasher *n.* 'an uninvited guest at a party etc.'

Ge [=E] M, pl. Ø, 20c (1 mod, jour)

gay *adj./n.* 4a '(a) homosexual'

The spread of this term, which is still less frequent than any of the native equivalents, is probably due to a combined effect of 'modernity' and 'taboo'; it may

also owe something to the discussion of the AIDS problem. The *gay liberation* movement, spread from the USA, has probably been important too. It is not certain whether the distribution of *gay* is still on the increase, or is already declining.

Ge [gei, ge:] adj. (1 mod) < *schwul (er)* **Du** [ge:j] adj., 1980s (1 sla, mod) **Nw** [=E] 1970s (1 coll, mod) < *homo, homofil* **Ic** [=E] adj., uninfl., end20c (1 sla) mean *hýr* **Fr** *gay* [gɛ] adj. M, 1960s (1 mod) **Sp** <=E>/*gai* [gei/gai] M, pl. *-s*, 1970s (2) < *homosexual* **It** [gɛi] M, pl. Ø, 1970s (2) = *omosessuale* **Rm** <=E>/*ghei* [=E] M, 1990s (1 rare) < *homosexual* **Rs** *geĭ* M, pl. *-i*, end20c (1 coll) **Po** *gej* <=E> M, end20c (1 coll) → *-owski* adj. **Cr** [=E] M, pl. *-evi*, end20c (1 mod) **Bg** *geĭ* M/cp[1], pl. *geyove*, 1990s (1 jour, mod) < *khomoseksualist, pederast, pedi* **Gr** *geĭl* <=E> adj. (1 coll, jour, mod)

gear *n.* 1a,b 'a set of toothed wheels', 2 'a particular function or state of adjustment of engaged gears'

Du [=E] 1990s (1 mod) **Nw** *gir* [=E] N, pl. Ø, beg20c(3) **Ic** *gír* [ci:r] M, pl. *-ar*, beg20c, 1a,b,2(3)

gear *v.* 1 'adjust or adapt to suit a special purpose or need', 4 'put in gear; gear down (up)'

Nw *gire* (*inn mot, ned, opp*) ["gi:re] mid20c, 1,4(3) → *(opp)giret* adj. **Ic** *gíra (upp/niður)* [ci:ra] mid20c, 4(3) → *-giraður* adj., cp[2]

gearing *n.* 1 'a set of gears in a machine', +3 'a toothed wheel on the crank axis of a bike'

Du [gi:riŋ] M, beg20c (1 tech) **Nw** - < *gir* **Ic** - < *gírar*

gel *n.* 1 'a semi-solid colloidal solution or jelly of a solid dispersed in liquid', 2 'a jelly-like substance used for setting the hair'

Ge [ge:l] N [U] end20c (3) **Du** [ʃɛl] N+C, 1980s, 1(2) **Nw** [ge:l/gel] M [U] 1980s (1 tech, our) < *gelé* **Ic** [cɛ:l] N [U] 1980s, 2(2) **Fr** *gel* (5) **Sp** [xel] M pl. *-es*, mid20c (3/5Fr) **It** [=E] M [U] mid20c (3) **Rm** [=E] N, mid20c (5Fr/It) **Rs** *gel'* M [U] end20c, 1,2(3) **Po** (5Fr) **Cr** (5Fr) **Bg** *gel* M [U]/ pl. *-al-ove*, mid20c, via Ge (3) **Fi** *geeli*, 1(3) **Hu** via Ge (5Fr) **Al** *-gel, schel* 20c (2) **Gr** *tzel;zele, zel* N, 1980s, via Fr (2)

gentleman *n.* 2 'a man of refined behaviour', 3 'a man of good social position'

Although a very old loan and widespread all over Europe, this term has remained marginal for many languages as a foreignism or as a colloquial/facetious expression. Note the general absence of calques and scarcity of derivations.

Ge [=E] M, pl. *-men*, 18c, 2(1 coll) **Du** [=E] C, pl. *-men*, 20c, 2(2) **Nw** <=E>/*-mann* [=E/- man] M, pl. *-men(n)*, mid19c, 2(2) → *gentlemanaktig* adj. **Ic** *gentil-/gentlemaður* M, mid17c (1+5 arch); *séntilmaður* [sjɛntilma:ðʏr] M, pl. *-menn*, end19c, 2(2+5) **Fr** [ʒãtləman/dʒɛntləman] 17c, 2(1) **Sp** [jentelman] M, pl. *-s/-men*, mid19c, 2(2) **It** [dʒɛntlemen, -man] M, pl.

Ø, 18c, 2(2) < trsl *gentiluomo* M **Rm** [=E] M, pl. *-meni*, mid19c, 2(2) **Rs** *dzhentl'men* M, pl. *-y*, 18c, 2(2) → *-stvo* N; *-skii* adj. **Po** *dżentelmen*/<=E> [dʒentelmen] M, mid19c, 2(2) **Cr** [dʒentlmen] M, pl. *-i*, mid20c, 2(2) → *-ski* adj. **Bg** *dzhentlemen/dzhentülmen* M, pl. *-i*, end19c, 2(1 arch/2) → *-ski* adj., adv.; *-stvo* N **Fi** *gentlemanni* [g-] 20c, 2(1) = creat *herrasmies* **Hu** <=E>/*dzsentlemen* [=E] pl. *-ek*, end18/beg 19c, 2(2) **Al** *xhentëlmen* M, pl. *-ë*, mid20c, 2(2) **Gr** *tzedleman, tzedleman* M, 20c, 2(2 coll) = mean *kirios* M

gentleman-farmer *n.* 'a patrician landowner who actually farms his land'
Fr [ʒãtləman farmœr/ dʒɛntəlman farmœr] M, beg 19c (1 obs) **It** [=E] M, pl. Ø, 19c (1 tech)

gentlemanlike *adj.* 'gentlemanly'
Ge [=E] uninfl., 19c (1 coll, rare) **Du** [=E] 19c? (1 mod) **Nw** [=E] 19c (1) **Rm** end19c (Ø>1 arch) **Hu** [=E] beg19c (2 arch)

gentlemen's agreement *n.* 1 'an agreement binding in honour'
Ge [=E] N, pl. *-s*, 1940s (1 coll) **Du** [=E] C [U] 1940s (2) < trsl *herenakkoord* **Nw** [=E] N/M, pl. *-s*, 1960s (1) = trsl *gentleman(s)avtale* **Ic** [=E] N [U] end20c (0) < trsl *heiðursmannasamkomulag* **Fr** *gentleman's agreement/gentlemen's agreement* [=E] M, mid20c (1 jour) **Sp** <=E>/*gentleman's agreement* [=E] M, 1930s (1 tech, rare) < rend *acuerdo/pacto entre caballeros* **It** [=E] M, pl. Ø, 1930s (1 lit) **Rm** [=E] N [U] 1970s (0>1 jour) **Rs** (0) < trsl *dzhentl'menskoe soglashenie* **Po** [=E] M [U] mid20c (1 tech) **Cr** [=E] M [U] mid20c (1 tech) < trsl *dżentlemenski sporazum* **Bg** - < trsl *dzhentülmensko sporazumenie* **Fi** - < *herrasmiessopimus* **Hu** [=E] [U] mid20c (1 jour) **Gr** - < trsl *symfonia kyrion*

getter *n.* 'a substance that removes residual gas from an evacuated vessel' (physics)
Ge [geta] M, pl. Ø, mid20c (1 tech) → *gettern* v. **Nw** [=E] M, pl. *-e*, 20c (1 tech) **Fr** [getɛʀ] M, mid20c (1 tech) **Rm** [getər] N, 1940s (1 tech) **Rs** *getter* M [U] mid20c (1 tech) → *-nyĭ* adj. **Po** [-er] M, mid20c (1 tech) **Bg** *geter* M, [U] mid20c (1 tech) → *-en* adj. **Fi** *getteri* (1 tech) **Hu** [getter] [U] 20c (1 tech)

ghetto-blaster *n.* 'a large portable radio, esp used to play loud pop music'
Ge [=E] M, pl. Ø, 1980s (1 you, rare) **Du** *gettoblaster* [getoblastər] M, 1980s (1 you) **Nw** [=E] M, pl. *-e/-s*, 1980s (1 you, rare) **Ic** [=E] M, pl. *-ar*, 1980s (1 sla) **Fr** (Ø) **Gr** <=E> [=E] N, end20c (1 you)

ghost-writer *n.* 'a person who writes on behalf of another (esp. speeches for politicians)'
This word illustrates the typical 'northwestern' distribution of many loanwords, excluding much of Eastern and Southern Europe. Although it occurs

typically in journalese, the general absence of alternatives has secured the term a firm hold in political terminology.
Ge [goːstraita] M, pl. Ø/*-s*, 1960s (1 tech) > trsl *Geisterschreiber* **Du** *ghostwriter* [=E] C, 1970s (1 tech) **Nw** [=E] M, pl. *-e*, 1970s (1 tech) **Sp** - < *negro* **It** [gost raiter] M/F, pl. Ø/*-s*, 1960s (1 tech) **Rm** (0) **Rs** *gostraiter* M, pl. *-y*, end20c (1 tech) **Po** [-er] M, end20c (1 tech) **Cr** [=E] M, pl. *-i*, end20c (1 tech) **Fi** [=E] 20c (0) **Hu** - < *néger*

G.I. *n.* 'an American soldier'
Ge [=E] M, pl. *-s*, 1940s (Ø/1 coll) **Du** (Ø) **Fr** [dʒiaj] M, 1940s (1) **Sp** [=E] M [U] mid20c (Ø/1 tech, jour, rare) **It** [=E] M, pl. Ø, mid20c (1 rare) **Rs** *dzhi-aĭ/dzhiaĭ* uninfl., end20c (Ø) **Cr** (0) **Bg** *dzhi aĭ* M, Ø (Ø jour)

gig[1] (1) *n.* 1 'a one-horse carriage', 3 'a rowing-boat', +4 'part of a sailboard's rigging'
Of the three senses, the first is obsolete along with the designated vehicle (which used to be widespread at least in Western Europe). The term designating the boat is known to rowing specialists only – and, though widespread throughout Europe, little known.
Ge [=E] N, pl. *-s*, end19c, 1(1 arch); F/N, pl. *-s*, 3(1 tech) **Du** gik, [ɣix] C, beg20c, 1(1 tech, arch); *giek* [ɣik] C, pl. *-en*, mid19c, 3(1 tech) **Nw** *gigg* [=E] M, pl. *-er*, mid19c, 1(1 arch) **Fr** <=E> M, 1940s, 1,3(1 obs) **Rm** [dʒig] N, end19c, 1(2 tech/arch); 1940s, 3(2 tech) **Rs** *gig* M, pl. *-i*, beg20c, 3(1 tech) **Po** [-k], beg20c, 1(1 arch) 3(1 tech) **Cr** *gig* M, pl. *-ovi*, beg20c, 3(1 arch) **Bg** *gig* M, pl. *-a/-ove*, mid20c, +4(1 tech) **Hu** [gig] pl. *-ek?*, beg19c, 1(3 arch) 3(1 tech)

gig[2] (2) *n.* 'an engagement of an entertainer, esp. of musicians, usu. for a single appearance'
Ge [=E] M, pl. *-s*, 1970s (1 tech) **Du** [=E] 1990s (1 you) **Nw** [=E] M, pl. *-s*, 1980s (1 tech) **Ic** [cik:] N, pl. Ø, 1970s (1 sla) **Bg** *gig* M, pl. *-a/-ove*, 1980s (1 tech) **Fi** - < *keikka* **Gr** *gig* N, end20c (1 tech)

gimmick *n.* 'a device to attract attention' cf. ↑*gag*, ↑*gadget*
Ge [=E] M/N, pl. *-s*, 1970s (1 mod) **Du** 1990s (1 you) **Nw** [=E] M, pl. *-er/-s*, 1970s (2) **Ic** [=E] N [U] end20c (1 sla) **Fr** [gimik] M, 1970s (1 mod) **Sp** [=E] M, pl. *-s*, 1990s (1 tech, jour/rare)

gimp *n.* 'a twist of silk with cord'
Ge *Gimpe* F, pl. *-n*, 18c (3 tech, rare) **Du** [ɣimp] C [U] 17c, from Fr (1 arch) **Nw** [=E] M [U] beg20c (1 tech) → *gimpe* v. **Fr** *guimpé* (5) **Po** *gimpa* F, mid20c (1 tech)

gin   *n.* 'an alcoholic spirit flavoured with juniper berries'

This word was adopted from the Dutch *Jenever* into early eighteenth-century English, from where the shortened form spread to the Continent as the name of the cheapest and most popular alcoholic drink. Languages having both the English and Dutch loanword normally distinguish between two similar brands. **Ge** [=E] M [U] mid19c (2)   **Du** [=E] C, 1970s (2) < *jenever*   **Nw** [=E, ʃin] M [U] mid19c (2)   **Ic** *gin* [cɪːn] N [U] mid20c (3)   **Fr** [=E] M, end18c (2)   **Sp** [jin] M, end19c (1 tech, rare) < *ginebra*   **It** [=E] M [U] beg19c (3)   **Rm** [=E] N, end19c (2)   **Rs** *dzhin* M [U] 19c (2)   **Po** *džin* <=E> M, mid19c (2)   **Cr** *džin* [U] M, beg20c (2)   **Bg** *dzhin* M, [U]/pl. -*a*, beg20c (2)   **Fi** *gini* 20c (3)   **Hu** [=E] [U] beg19c (2)   **Al** *xhin* [xhin] M [U] (3)   **Gr** *tzin* N, 20c (2)

gin-fizz*   *n.* 'an alcoholic drink mixed from gin, mineral water, lemon, and sugar'
Ge [=E] M, pl. Ø/-*es*, 1940s (1 mod)   **Du** [=E] mid20c (2)   **Nw** [=E] M, pl. -*er*, mid20c (1 rare)   **Ic** [cɪnfɪsː] N [U] mid20c (0)   **Fr** [dʒin fiz] M, 1920s (1 obs)   **Sp** [jinfis] M, mid20c (1 tech, obs)   **It** [dʒin fits] M, pl. Ø, 1960s (1>2)   **Rm** (0/1 obs)   **Cr** [=E] M [U], mid20c (1)   **Bg** *dzhinfis* M [U]/pl. -*a*, mid20c (2)   **Hu** [=E] M pl. Ø, 20c (2)   **Gr** <=E>/*tzin fiz* N, mid20c (1 tech)

ginger   *n.* 'a hot spicy root usu. powdered for use in cooking'
The word comes from an Indic language and was transmitted to most European languages through Greek > Latin > Old French; English transmission is not recorded apart from Greek, in contrast to the compound ↑*ginger ale* which is more frequently attested as a loanword.
Ge - < *Ingwer*   **Nw** (0) < *ingefær*   **Ic** - < *engifer*   **Sp** - < *jéngibre*   **It** - < *zenzero*   **Bg** - < *dzhindzhifil*   **Al** - < *xhenxhefil*   **Gr** *tzíntzer* [dzindzɛr] N, 20c (1) = *piperoriza*

ginger ale   *n.* 'a drink'
Ge [=E] N [U] 20c (Ø) > trsl *Ingwerbier*   **Du** [=E] C end20c (1 tech)   **Nw** (0) < *ingefærøl*   **Ic** [=E] N [U] beg20c (1 coll) = trsl *engiferöl*   **Fr** M, mid20c (0)   **Sp** [jinjerel] M [U] 1940s (1 tech)   **Rm** [=E] N [U] 20c (0>1 tech)   **Cr** (0)   **Fi** [=E] 20c (Ø)   **Hu** [=E] [U] end20c (2/1 tech, mod) < trsl *gyömbér sör*   **Gr** <=E> [=E] N (1 tech) = *tzitzibira* F

gin-rummy   *n.* 'a card game'
Nw [=E] M [U] 20c (1 rare)   **Fr** <=E>/*gin-rami* [=E] M, 1960s (1 obs)   **Sp** M, 20c (1 obs)   **Rm** [=E] N [U] 1980s (1 writ)

gin-tonic*   *n.* 'a drink mixed from gin and tonic water'
Ge [=E] M, pl. -*s*, 1970s (1 tech, mod)   **Du** [=E] C, 20c (2)   **Nw** [=E] M, pl. Ø, 1970s (2)   **Ic** *gin og tónik* [cɪːn otʰ ouːnɪk] N+N mid20c (3)   **Fr** <=E> M, 1970s

(1 mod)   **Sp** [jintonik] M, 1960s (1 tech)   **It** [=E] M, pl. Ø, 1970s (2)   **Rm** [=E] N, pl. Ø, 1970s (1 mod) > *gin and tonic*   **Rs** *dzhintonik* M [U] end20c (1 tech, mod)   **Po** (0)   **Cr** *džin-tonik* M [U] mid20c (2)   **Bg** *dzhin s tonik*, mid20c (1 mod)   **Fi** [=E] 20c (0)   **Hu** <=E>/*gin & tonik* [=E] [U] end20c (1 tech, mod>2)   **Gr** <=E>/*tzin tonik* [dz-] N, mid20c (2)

girl   *n.* +5 a young (and easy) female, +5a 'a female working in a cabaret'

This term is well-known, but little used outside compounds, see ↑*call*~, ↑*play*~, relating to 'girls' only in a facetious or deprecatory way. The marginal uses make it difficult to predict whether the word will become established more widely.
Ge [görl] N, pl. -*s*, beg20c, +5(1 coll) +5a(1 tech)   **Nw** [=E] cp²/ M, pl. -*s*, 20c, +5(1)   **Fr** [gœrl] F, beg20c, +5a(1)   **Sp** [gel] F, pl. -*s*, 1920s, +5(1 tech)   **It** [gœrl/gɛrl] F pl. Ø/-*s*, 1910s, +5(2)   **Rm** +5a(0 coll, jour, euph, fac)   **Rs** *gerla/ gërl* F, pl. -*y*, mid20c (1 coll, fac)   **Po** *girlsa* [gerlsa] F, beg20c, +5a(2) → *gerlaska* F   **Cr** *gerla* F, pl. -*e*, beg20c, +5a (2)   **Bg** *gŭrla* F, pl. -*li*, beg20c, +5,+5a(3 pej)   **Hu** *görl* [gɛrl] pl. -*ök*, end19/beg20c, +5a(2 obs)

girlie   *n.* 'an attractive young woman of 20–24'
In German this term has become quite fashionable in journalese language and has been adopted by the group so named.
Ge [görliː] N, pl. -*s*, 1990s (1 mod)

glamour   *n.* 2 'alluring or exciting beauty or charm', +3 'showy decoration or ornament; gaudiness', +4 'showishness'

This word was firmly established through American films after 1945 – with the significant exclusion of Eastern Europe. The negative connotation, found in some English contexts, is more conspicuous in the loanwords.
Ge [=E] M [U] 1950s, +3(1 obs)   **Du** [=E] C [U] 1950s, +3(1 obs)   **Nw** [=E/glamuːr] M [U] 1950s, +3(1) → *glamorisere* v.   **Ic** *glamúr* [klaːmur] M [U] end20c, +3(1 coll)   **Fr** [glamur] M, 1970s, +3(1 mod)   **Sp** [glamur] M [U] 1960s, 2,+3(2) → *glamourizar* v.; *glamouroso* adj.   **It** [glɛmur/glamur] M [U] 1950s, 2(1) < *fascino, charme* M   **Cr** [glamur] M [U] mid20c, +3(1)   **Fi** [=E] 20c, +3(0)   **Hu** [glɛːmər] [U] mid20c, +3(1 tech)   **Gr** <=E>/*glamur* N, end20c, +3,+4(2 mod, jour)

glamour girl   *n.* 'an attractive woman, esp. a film star'
Ge [=E] N, pl. -*s*, 1950s (1 arch)   **Du** [=E] C, 1980s (1 obs)   **Nw** [=E] M, pl. -*s*, 20c (1 arch)   **Ic** *glamúrpía/*

-gella F, end20c (1+5 sla)   **Cr** *glamurgerla* F, pl. -e, mid20c (1 arch)

glamorous   *adj.* 'showy'
Ge *glamourös* 1960s, infl. by Fr (3)   **Nw** *glamorøs* [glamurø:s] 1960s (3)   **Ic** [=E] uninfl., end20c (1 sla)   **Sp** - < *glam(o)uroso*   **Cr** *glamurozan*, mid20c (1)   **Gr** *glamorus* 1990s (2 mod, jour)

glam rock   *n.* 'a type of rock music characteristic of the 1970s'
Ge [=E/glam-] M [U] 1970s (1 tech, obs)   **Nw** [glam-] M [U] 1970s (1 tech, obs)   **Ic** *glamrokk* [=E] N [U] 1970s (3 tech)   **Fr** [glam rɔk] M, 1970s (1 tech)   **Sp** [glam rok] M [U] 1980s (1 tech, you)   **It** [=E] M [U] 1990s (1 tech)   **Bg** *glemrok* M [U] 1970s (1 tech)   **Fi** [=E/glam-] M [U] 1970s (1 tech, obs)

**glencheck*   *n.* 'cloth with inconspicuous stripes'
Ge [=E] M, pl. -s, 1960s (1 tech)   **Nw** [=E] M [U] 1960s (1 tech)

glider   *n.* 1a 'an aircraft without an engine'
Du [=E] C, 1980s (1 tech) < *zeilvliegtuig*   **Nw** [=E] M, pl. -e, 20c (1 tech) < *glidefly, svevefly*   **Ic** - < rend *sviffluga*   **Rm** [=E] N, mid20c (1 tech)   **Rs** *glaider* M, pl. -y, mid20c (2 tech)   **Po** [-er] M, end20c (1 tech)   **Cr** (o)   **Bg** - < creat *bezmotoren samolet*   **Hu** - < *sárkányrepülő*

glitter-rock*   *n.* 'a type of rock music in the 1970s (esp. associated with Gary Glitter etc.)'
Du [=E] C [U] 1980s (1 tech)   **Nw** [=E] M [U] 1970s (1 tech) = *glamrock*   **Ic** *glitterrokk* [=E] N [U] 1970s (1 tech) = *glamrokk*   **Sp** [gliter rɔk] M, end20c (1 tech) < *glam rock*

globe-trotter   *n.* 'a person travelling widely'
This word was widely accepted in early twentieth-century Europe, and is fully integrated (cf. the German pronunciation and Slavic derivatives) but also has many calques coexisting with it.
Ge [glo:bətrota] M, pl. Ø, beg20c (2) = trsl *Weltenbummler* → v.   **Du** [xlo:bətrɔtər] C, beg20c (2) = *wereldreiziger*   **Nw** [=E, glu:-b(e)trɔter] M, pl. -e, beg20c (1 tech) → *globetrotterisk* adj.   **Ic** - < *heimshornaflakkari*   **Fr** *globe-trotter* [glɔbtrɔtœr/trɔtœr] M/F, end19c (1 obs)   **Sp** - < trsl *trotamundos*   **It** [globtrɔtter] M/F, pl. Ø/-s, 1900s (1) < rend *giramondo*   **Rm** [=E] M, mid20c? (o>1)   **Rs** *globtrotter* M, pl. -y, 1990s (1 jour)   **Po** *globtroter* [gloptroter] M, beg20c (2) → *-ka* F; *-stwo* N [U]; *-ski* adj.   **Cr** *globtroter* M, pl. -i, beg20c (2) → *-ka* F; *-ski* adj.   **Hu** [glo:btrotter] pl. -ek, beg20c (1 arch) < *világjáró*   **Gr** - < trsl *kosmoghyristis/-ismenos*

gloss   *n.* +3a 'a lipstick that gives a glossy finish' (cosmetics) (cf. ↑*lip-gloss*)
Ge [=E] N/M [U] 1970s (1 tech) = *lip-gloss*   **Du** Ø   **Nw** [=E] M [U] 1970s (1 tech) = *lipgloss*   **Ic** *gloss* [klɔs:] M [U] 1970s (2 coll)

glossy   *n.* 1 'a glossy magazine', 2 'a photograph with a glossy surface'
Du [=E] 1990s (1 mod)

glossy   *adj.* 2 '(of paper etc.) smooth and shiny', 3 'printed on such paper'
Du [=E] 1980s, 2(1 mod)   **Nw** [=E] 1980s, 2,3(1)   **Rm** [=E] uninfl., 20c, 2(1 tech)

G-man   *n.* 2 'a political detective'
It [=E] M, pl. -men, 1930s (1 tech)   **Rs** *dzhimen* M, pl. -y, end20c (1 tech)   **Cr** [=E] M, pl. -men, mid20c (1 tech)   **Hu** [=E] pl. Ø, 20c (Ø tech)

GMT   *abbr.* 'Greenwich Mean Time'
Du *G.M.T.* [=E] 1970s (1 tech)   **Nw** <=E>/*Gmt* [ge:emte:] mid20c (1 tech)   **Ic** *greenwich-tími* [=E+tʰi:mı] M [U] 20c (2+5 tech)   **Fr** (Ø)   **Sp** [xe eme té] 20c (Ø/1 tech)   **It** [dʒi emme ti] end19c (1 tech) < trsl *tempo medio di Greenwich*   **Rm** [=E] 20c (1 tech)   **Rs** - < creat *po Grinvichu*   **Po** - < rend *czas Greenwich*   **Cr** - < trsl *odreðenjó vrijeme po Greenwichu*   **Bg** - < creat *po Grinvich*   **Fi** [ge:em te]   **Hu** [ge:emte:] [U] 20c (1 tech)   **Gr** <=E> 20c (1 tech)

goal   *n.* 2a,b 'the place where the ball has to be sent to score' (ballgames), 2d 'a point won'
This word became well-established in early football terminology, and though competing with native equivalents in some languages, has survived very well – as have, in a more restricted way, the compounds ↑*goalgetter* and ↑*goalkeeper*.
Ge [go:l] N, pl. -s, mid20c (1 reg/obs) < *Tor*   **Du** [go:l] C, beg20c (2)   **Nw** [=E] M, pl. -er, beg20c (2) < *mål* N → *gålle* v.   **Ic** - < rend *mark*   **Fr** [gol] M, end19c (1 ban, obs) < *but*   **Sp** *gol*, M, pl. -es, beg20c (3 tech) < 2a,b: *metal/porteria* → *golear* v; *goleador* n.   **It** <=E>/*gol* [gɔl] M, pl. Ø, 1900s (3) = *rete* F   **Rm** *gol* [gol] N, beg20c, 2a,b,d(3)   **Rs** *gol* M, pl. -y, beg20c (3)   **Po** *gol* [gol] M, beg20c, 2a,b,d(3)   **Cr** *gol* M, pl. -ovi, beg20c (3)   **Bg** *gol* M, pl. -al-ove, beg20c, 2d(2) → *-ov* adj.   **Hu** *gól* [go:l] pl. -ok, end19/beg20c (3)   **Al** *gol* [gol] M, pl. -a, beg20c (1 tech)   **Gr** *gol* N, beg20c (2) → *goltzis* M

goal average   *n.* 'the ratio of the number of goals scored for and against a team in a series of matches' (footb.)
Nw *målaverage* [Nw+E] M, mid20c (1 tech, obs)   **Fr** [golaveraʒ] M, mid20c (1 tech, obs)   **Sp** <=E>/*gol average* M, 1930s (2 tech, obs)   **Rm** *golaveraj* [golaveraʒ] N, mid20c, via Fr (2 tech)   **Bg** - < creat *golova razlika*   **Al** *golaverask* M, 20c (1 tech)   **Gr** *goal-average* [gol avereidz] N [U] mid20c (1 tech) < trsl *dhiafora termaton*

goalgetter*   *n.* 'a successful scorer' (footb.)
Ge [go:lgeta] M, pl. Ø, 1960s (1 jour, reg)   **Du** [=E] C, mid20c (1 tech)   **Nw** [=E] M, pl. -e, 1960s (2)   **Rm** *golgheter* [golgetər] M, 1960s (2 tech)   **Cr** *golgeter* M, pl. -i, mid20c (2)   **Bg** - < rend *golmaĭstor*   **Al** - < *golshënes*

goalkeeper   *n.* 'a player stationed to protect the goal in various sports'
Ge [go:lki:pa] M, pl. Ø, beg20c (1 reg, obs) < rend *Torwart*   **Du** [go:lkipər] C, beg20c (2)   **Nw** *keeper*

[=E] M, pl. *-e*, beg20c (2) > trsl *málvakt* **Ic** - < rend *markvörður*, *markmaður* **Fr** *goal* (*keeper*) M, end19c (1 ban, obs) < rend *gardien de but* **Sp** - < trsl *guardameta* < *portero* **It** - < *portiere* **Rm** [golkiрər] M, 20c (1 tech) < *portar* **Rs** golkiper M, pl. *-y*, beg20c (1 tech, rare) < *vratar'* **Po** [-er] M, beg20c (1 tech) **Cr** - < *vratar* **Bg** golkiper M, pl. *-i*, beg20c (1 tech, arch) < *vratar* **Hu** - < *portier* **Al** - < *portier* **Gr** golkiper M, beg20c (1 tech) < trsl *termatofilakas* M

go-between *n.* 'an intermediary' (esp. in politics)

Ge [=E] M, pl. *-s*, 1960s (1 jour, obs) < *Vermittler* **Du** [=E] C, 1990s (1 mod) < *bemiddelaar, intermediair* **Nw** [=E] M, 1990s (1 mod) **Fr** (0) **Sp** - < *intermediario* **It** - < *intermediario* **Hu** - < *közvetítő*

go-cart *n.* 1 'a miniature motorcar used in contests', +2 'the sport'

The vehicle was invented in 1956 in the USA and quickly spread around the world – and with it, the term (often shortened to ↑*cart*, and the sport to ↑*carting*). Note the general absence of calques.

Ge *Go-Kart* [go:kart] M/N, pl. *-s*, 1960s (1 tech) **Du** [go:kart] C, 1970s (1 tech) **Nw** *(go)kart* [=E] M, pl. *-er*, 1960s (1 tech) **Ic** gókart [=E] M, pl. *-ar*, 1980s (1 coll) **Fr** *kart* [kaʀt] M, 1960s (1) → *karting* **Sp** *(go) kart* M, mid20c (1 tech) → *karting* **It** <=E>/*go-kart* [go kart] M, pl. Ø, 1960s (2) **Rm** - < 1: *cart*; +2: *carting* **Rs** gokart M, pl. *-y*, end20c (1 tech); [U] +2(1 tech) **Po** gokart [gokart] M, mid20c (2 tech) **Cr** go-kart M, mid20c (1 tech) **Bg** - < 1,+2: *karting* **Fi** *kartti* (3 sla) → *karting-ajot* **Hu** gokart [go:kart] pl. *-ok*, 1960s (2 tech) → *kartoz* v.; *kartozás* n. **Gr** [kart] N, usu. pl., 1990s (1 you, mod)

goggles *n.* 'spectacles'

Du [=E] C [U] 1970s (1 tech) **Nw** [=E] [U] 20c (1 tech) **Po** *gogle* [gogle] pl., mid20c (3)

go-go *n./cp*[1] +1b 'a dance-show performed by girls at a discothèque etc.', +3 'nightlife involving such entertainment'

Ge [go:go] cp[1], 1970s (1 col, obs) **Du** [=E] C 1970s (1) **Nw** [=E] usu. cp[1], 1960s, +1b(1 obs) **Ic** gógó [=E] N [U] 1970s (1 sla, arch) **It** (5Fr) **Fi** [=E] (2) **Hu** [=E] cp[1], 1980s, +1b(2 tech) **Gr** <=E> [=E] cp[1], 1970s, +3(1 coll, obs)

go-go-girl* *n.* 'a dancer in a night-club'

Ge [=E] N, pl. *-s*, 1960s (1 coll, obs) **Du** *gogo-girl* [E] C, 1970s (1 obs) **Nw** [=E] M, pl. *-s*, 1970s (1) **Ic** [=E] 1970s (0 arch) < trsl *gógópía, -stúlka* **Sp** *gogó-girl* F, pl. *-s*, 1970s (1 tech) < *(chica) gogó* **Cr** go-go *gerla* F, pl. *-e*, end20c (1) **Bg** *gou-gou gŭrla* F, pl. *-li*, 1990s (3 jour, mod) **Fi** *go-go-tyttö* 20c (2) **Hu** [=E] pl. *-ök*, 1980s (2 tech) **Gr** <=E> [=E] N, pl. *-s*, 1970s (1 coll, obs)

go-in* *n.* 'the break-up of a meeting'

One of the most popular coinages of the student movement of the 1960s, but apparently largely restricted to Germany. This term was modelled on ↑*sit-in*; cf. *love-in, teach-in* – all now obsolete.

Ge [=E] N, pl. *-s*, 1960s (1 obs) **Fr** (Ø) **Rs** gou-in M, uninfl. [U] 1970s (1 jour, obs)

gold *n.* 'the colour gold, esp. for leather'

Ge (4) **Fr** [gɔld] adj., N (1 mod) **Po** (0) **Bg** (0) **Hu** [=E] end20c, esp cp[2] (1 tech/mod)

golden delicious *n.* 'a variety of dessert apple'

The distribution of this common term is noteworthy for the presence of the shortened form *golden* in French, Spanish, Romanian, Hungarian and reduction to the second element in Croatian.

Ge [goldən deli:tsius] M [U] 20c (3) **Du** [=E] C [U] 20c (2) **Nw** <=E>/*golden* [=E] [U] end20c (1) **Ic** <=E>/*delisíos-epli* [=E] N, pl. Ø, 1960s (1 tech) **Fr** <=E> *golden* [gɔldɛn] F, 1960s (2) **Sp** *golden* [xolden] F, pl. Ø, 1970s (3) **It** [(gɔlden) dilisius/delitʃius] F [U] 1970s (1) > trsl *delizia* **Rm** *golden* [golden] N, 20c (3 tech) **Rs** golden *delishes* M [U] end20c (1 tech) **Po** [goldendelifes] M [U] end20c (1 coll) **Cr** *delišes* M [U] 20c (2) **Bg** goldelishes M [U] mid20c (1 tech, reg) < trsl *zlatna prevŭzkhodna* **Fi** [=E] **Hu** *golden delicsesz* [=E + deli:tʃes] [U] mid20c (1 tech) < *golden* (3) **Al** - < trsl *mollë gold* **Gr** <=E>/*golden delisius* N, pl., end20c (1 tech)

golden handshake *n.* 'payment given on redundancy or early retirement'

Ge [=E] M, pl. *-s*, 1980s (0>1 mod) < trsl *goldener Handschlag* **Du** - < *gouden handdruk* **Nw** [=E] N, pl. *-s*, 1980s (1) **Fi** - < creat *kultainen kädenpuristus*

golden retriever *n.* 'a breed of dog with a thick golden-coloured coat'

Ge [=E] M, pl. Ø, end20c (1 tech) **Du** [goldən ritri:vər] M, 1980s (2) **Nw** [golden retri:ver] M, pl. *-e*, 20c (2) **Ic** [=E] M, end20c (0 tech) **Fr** [=E] M, 20c (1 tech) **Sp** [golden retriber] M, end20c (1 tech) **Rs** golden retriver M, pl. *-y*, 1980s (1 tech) **Bg** goldŭn ritrivŭr M, pl. *-ral-ri*, end20c (1 tech) **Fi** - < creat *kultainen noutaja*

golden (twenties, etc.) *adj.* 'a period of memorable events'

Ge [=E] pl., 1950s (1 jour) < trsl *die goldenen zwanziger (Jahre)* **Du** *golden sixties* [goldən sɪksties] 1980 (2) **Nw** (0) **Sp** - < trsl *dorado, feliz* **Po** - < creat *złote lata dwudzieste* **Al** < *vitet e arta* **Gr** (0)

golden ten* *n.* 'a gambling game'

Du [goldən tɛn] M [U] (2)

gold-exchange (standard)* *n.* 'international currency regulation based on the gold standard'

It [gɔld ekstʃeindʒ standard] M, pl. Ø, mid20c (1 tech) **Sp** - < *patrón oro* **Rm** - < creat *schimb valutar pe baza etalonului aur* **Bg** - < rend *zlaten standart*

gold point *n.* 'the rate at which gold is preferable to currencies'

Fr [gɔldpɔjnt] M, end19c (1 tech) < *point d'or* **Rm** [=E] N [U] mid20c (1 tech)

golf *n.* 1 'a game played on a course set in open country in which a ball is struck into a series of holes', +2 'a golf course'

The term, together with the sport, became popular around the turn of the century; its currency is in conspicuous contrast to that of related compounds and other golfing terms which have remained restricted to (a small number of) golf enthusiasts; cf. ↑*birdie*, ↑*eagle*, ↑*putt*, etc. Note that the widespread homonym *golf* 'bay' (English *gulf*) is from French.

Ge N [U] 19c/1980s (3) → *-er* M **Du** [ɤɔlf/gɔlf] N [U] beg20c (2>3) **Nw** [=E] M [U] end19c (3) **Ic** *golf* [kɔlf] N [U] 1930s, 1(3) **Fr** [gɔlf] M, end19c (3) → *golfeur/euse*; → *golfique* **Sp** M [U] end19c, 1(3) → *golfista* n.; *golfístico* adj. **It** [gɔlf] M [U] 1820s (3) **Rm** [=E] N [U] beg20c, via Fr, 1(3) **Rs** *gol'f* M, uninfl., beg20c, 1(1 tech) **Po** M [U] beg20c (2) → *-ista* M; *-istka* F; *-owisko* N; *- owy* adj. **Cr** *golf* M [U] beg20c (3) → *-er* M; *-ski* adj. **Bg** *golf* M/cp[1] [U] beg20c, 1(2 tech) **Fi** [=E] (2) **Hu** [=E] [U] beg20c (2) → *ozik* v. **Al** *golf* M [U] mid20c (1 tech) **Gr** *golf* N [U] beg20c (2)

golf* 1 *cp[1]* 'knitted woollen (jacket, cardigan)', 2 *n.* 'a kind of woollen trousers'

Nw *golf(jakke)* [=E+Nw] beg20c, 1(3) **Ic** *golftreyja* [kɔl:tʰreija] F, pl. *-ur*, 1920s, via Da, 1(3+5) → *golla* F **Fr** [gɔlf] M, beg20c, 2(1 tech) **It** [gɔlf] M, pl. Ø, beg20c (3) = *maglione, pullover* → *golfino* n.; *golfetto* n. **Rs** *gol'f* M [U] mid20c, 1(1 obs) 2(2 arch) → *gol'fy* N, pl. **Po** via Fr, 1(3) **Cr** (0) **Bg** *golf* M, pl. *-a/-ove*, beg20c, via Fr, 2(3 arch) **Hu** - < 2: *golfnadrág*

golf *v.* 'play golf' (deficient v. in English, only in *-ing* form)

Ge *golfen* beg20c (3) **Du** [gɔlfən] beg20c (2) → *golfer* M **Nw** (0) **Sp** - < *jugar al golf* **Rm** - < *a juca golf* **Fi** *golf(f)ata* (2 sla) **Hu** *golfozik* mid20c (2)

golf-links *n* 1 'a golf-course'
Du [lɪŋks] 1950s (1 tech) **Nw** - < *golfbane* **Fr** *golf* **Bg** - < trsl *golf igrishte* **Hu** - < trsl *golfpálya*

golfstick* *n.* 'a golf club'
Du [gɔlfstɪk] M, 1980s (2) **Nw** - < *golfkølle* **Ic** - < *golfkylfa* **Bg** *stik* M, pl. *-al-ove*, mid20c (3 tech) **Hu** - < trsl *golf ütő*

gone *adj.* 2a 'tired, worn out'
Nw *gåen* ["gɔ:en] beg20c (3/4)

gong *n.* 1 'a metal disk with a turned rim, giving a resonant note when struck'
Ge [=E] M, pl. *-s*, 19c (3) **Du** [ɤɔŋ] (5Mal) **Nw** <=E>/*gonggong* [=E] M, pl. *-er*, mid19c (3) **Ic** <=E>/ *gong-gong* [=E] N, pl. Ø, beg20c (2 tech) **Fr** [gɔ(g)] M, end17c (5 Mal) **Sp** <=E>/*gongo*, pl. *-s/-as* M (2/ 5Mal) **It** [gɔŋg] M, pl. Ø, beg19c (3) **Rm** *gong* [goŋg] N, 19c, via Fr (3) **Rs** *gong* M, pl. *-i*, 19c (2) **Po** [-k] M, beg20c (5Mal) **Cr** *gong* M, pl. *-ovi*, 19c (3) **Bg** *gong* M, pl. *-a/-ove*, 19c, via Rs(2 lit) **Hu** [=E] pl. *-ok* end19/beg20c (3/5 Mal/ AmE) **Al** *gong* M, pl. *-e*, (3) **Gr** *go(n)g* [goŋ] N (1)

good-bye *phr.* 'farewell' (↑*bye-bye*)
Ge (0) **Du** (0) **Nw** [=E] end20c (1 coll, fac) **Ic** *gúddbæ* [=E] 1940s (1 sla) **Sp** [gudbai] end20c (1 mod/rare) **It** [gud bai] 1920s (2) < *arrivederci* **Rm** (0) = *bye-bye* **Rs** *gud-baĭ* mid 20c (1 coll) **Po** <=E> end20c (1 coll) **Cr** (0) **Bg** - < *baĭ-baĭ* (2 coll) **Hu** [=E] beg19c (1 arch, rare) **Al** *gudbaj*, end20c (1 sla) < *baj baj* **Gr** (0)

good old days *phr.* 'the past viewed nostalgically'
Ge - < *die gute alte Zeit* **Du** *good old days* [=E] pl., 1980s (1 mod) < rend *de goede oude tijd* **Nw** [=E] [U] usu. pl., end20c (1) < *gode gamle dager* **Ic** [=E] (0) < trsl *(þeir) góðu gömlu dagar* **It** - < rend *i bei vecchi tempi* **Po** - < rend *dobre stare czasy* **Cr** - < *dobra stara vremena* **Bg** - < rend *dobrite stari vremena* **Fi** - < creat *hyvät vanhat ajat* **Hu** - < *a régi szép idők* **Gr** (0) < *ton palio kalo kero*

Good Templar* *n.* 'a member of the I.O.G.T., an organization of total abstainers'
Ge *Guttempler* [guttempler] M, pl. Ø, end19c (3 tech, obs) **Nw** *godtemplar* [gutemplaː r] M, pl. *-er*, 19c (3) **Ic** <=E>/*gúddtemplari* [=E/kut:ɛmplarɪ/ku:tʰɛmplarɪ] M, pl. *-ar*, 1880s, via Nw (2 arch) = trsl *góðtemplar (i)* **It** - < *Templare* (5La) **Hu** - < [=E] [U] 19c (Ø)

goodwill *n.* 1 'kindly feeling', 2 'the established reputation of a business etc., as enhancing its value'
Ge [gutvɪl/=E] M [U] 1950s (1 tech) **Du** [=E] 1940s, 2(1) **Nw** [=E] M [U] 20c(2) **Ic** *gúddvill* [kut:vɪl:] N [U] mid20c, 2(1 coll) **Fr** <=E>20c, 2(1 tech, ban) > *fonds commercial* **It** [=E] M, pl. Ø, 20c (1 tech) < *avviamento* **Rm** [=E] N [U] end20c, 2(1 tech) **Fi** [=E] 20c, 2(1 tech) **Hu** [=E] [U] 1970s, 2(1 tech)

goodwill tour *n.* 'a trip undertaken to restore good relations'
Ge [=E] F, pl. *-s*, 1960s (1 tech, jour) = *Goodwill-Reise* **Du** *goodwillreis* [gudw[ɪ]l-] mid20c (1) **Nw** *goodwill-reise* [=E+Nw] mid20c (1) **Rs** - < rend *vizit dobroĭ voli* **Bg** - < rend *poseshtenie na dobra volya* **Gr** - < trsl *taxidhi kalis thelisis*

goody *adj.* +4 '(of a person) nice and easy-going'
Ic [ku:ti/kut:i] uninfl., end20c (1 coll)

Gordon (setter) *n.* 'a setter of a black and tan breed' (cf. ↑*setter*)
Ge - < *Setter* **Nw** *gordonsetter* [=E] M, pl. *-e*, 20c (1 tech) **Fr** *gordon* M (1 tech) **It** *gordon* [gɔrdon] M, pl. Ø, end19c (1 tech) **Rm** *setter Gordon* [setər gordon] M, 20c, (1 tech) **Rs** *gordon setter* M, pl. *-y*, beg20c (1 tech) **Po** *gordon* [gordon] M, beg20c (1 tech) **Bg** *gordūn seter* M, pl. *-ra/-ri*, mid20c (1 tech) **Fi** *gordoninsetteri* 20c (1 tech) **Hu** - < *ír szetter*

go-slow *n.* 'a form of industrial action in which employees deliberately work slowly'
Ge [=E] M [U] 1960s (1 jour) < creat *Bummelstreik* **Du** - < *stiptheidsactie* **Nw** (0) < rend *gasakte-aksjon* **Fr** - < creat *grève perlée* **Sp** - < creat *huelga de celo* **Hu** - < creat *lassító sztrájk*

gospel *n.* 5 'evangelical religious music (originating in the American South)'
This type of music is a development from ↑*blues* and the Negro ↑*spiritual*, and spread into Western Europe during the 1950s. The term started out as the compound *gospel song*, but is now common in the abbreviated form.
Ge [=E] N/M, pl. -*s*, 1960s (1 tech) → v. **Du** [=E] C, 1970s (1 tech) **Nw** [=E] M [U] 1960s (1) **Ic** [=E] N [U] 1970s, 5(1 tech) = *gospeltónlist* **Fr** [gɔspɛl] M, 1960s (1 tech) **Sp** [gospel] M [U] mid20c (Ø/1 tech) → *gospeliano* **It** [gospel] M, pl. Ø, 1930s (2 tech) **Rm** [=E] N, 1970s (1 tech) **Rs** *gospel*/-*s* M, pl. -*y*, 1980s, (1 tech) **Po** *gospels*, *gospel songs* pl., end20c (1 tech, coll) **Cr** *gospel* M [U] mid20c (1 tech) **Bg** *gospŭl* M, pl. -*al*-*i*, end20c (1 tech) **Fi** [=E] 20c (2) **Hu** [=E, *gaspel*] pl. Ø, mid20c (2); *gospel-song* **Gr** *gospel* N, pl. Ø/-*s*, mid20c (Ø)

gotcha* *n.* 'a game in which participants simulate military combat shooting capsules of paint at each other' (BrE ↑*paintball*)
Ge [=E] N? [U] 1980s (1 mod) **Du** - < *paintball* **Nw** - < *paintball*

grab *n.* +5 'a grab bucket, scoop of a dredger etc'
Nw *grabb* [grab] M, pl. -*er*, mid20c (3) **Bg** *grabs* M, pl. -*al*-*ove*, mid20c (3 tech)

grab *v.* 'take greedily or unfairly'
Nw *grabbe* ["grɑːbe] mid20c (3 coll) **Hu** *grabecsol* (5 sla)

graham bread *n.* 'a kind of wholemeal bread'
This term was coined in nineteenth-century American English, after the dietary reformer Sylvester Graham (1794–1851). Although popular with the health-conscious for a long time, this item did not spread to all European countries – hence the absence of the loanword in many languages.
Ge *Grahambrot* [grɑːham-] N, end19c (3+5) **Du** *grahambrood* [greːhəm-, ɤrɑːham-] beg20c (3) **Nw** *grahambrød* [grɑː(h)am-] 20c (3) **Ic** *grahamsbrauð* [krɑːhams-] N, pl. Ø, beg20c (2+5) **Rm** *graham* [graham] N, 20c, via Ge (3); *pâine graham* F (5+3) **Po** *graham* M, mid20c (3) → -*ka* F **Cr** *graham* M [U] mid20c (3) **Bg** *grakham* M [U] mid20c (3) **Fi** *grahamleipä* (3) **Hu** *graham kenyér* [=E/graham] pl. -*ek*, end19/beg20c (3+5)

Ic	Nw	Po	Rs
Du	Ge	Cr	Bg
Fr	It	Fi	Hu
Sp	Rm	Al	Gr

grand old man (/lady) *n.* 'an ageing person in a leading position'
Ge [=E] M, pl. -*men*/*ladies*, 1970s (1 jour) = trsl *großer alter Mann*/*große alte Dame* **Du** [=E] M, 1980s

(2) Nw [=E] M, pl. -*men*/-*ladies*, 20c (1) **Ic** [=E] end20c (0 coll) **Fi** [=E] (0)

grand slam *n.* 1 'the winning of the four major tennis contests', 2 'the winning of 13 tricks' (bridge)
Ge *Schlemm* 19c, via Fr?, 2(0); [grɛntslɛm] M, pl. -*s*, 1970s, 1(1 tech) **Du** [=E] C/N [U] 1980s (1 tech) **Nw** [=E] M [U] 20c (1 tech) < 2: trsl *storeslem* **Ic** - < 1: creat *stórslemma*, 2: *alslemm(a)* **Fr** *grand chelem* end18c, 2(3 tech); 20c, 1(1 tech) **Sp** *gram slam* [graneslam] M, end20c (Ø/1 tech) **It** *grande slam* [grande zlɛm] M, pl. Ø, 1940s (1 tech) **Rm** *marele şlem* [marele ʃlem] N [U] 1970s, via Fr (5+1 tech) **Rs** (0) < trsl *bol'shoĭ shlem* **Po** - < trsl *wielki szlem* **Cr** [grendslem] M [U] end20c, 1(1 tech) **Bg** - < trsl *golyam shlem* M [U] mid20c, via Ge (5+3 tech) **Fi** [=E] 20c (2) **Hu** <=E>/*G.S.* [grɛn slɛm] [U] 20c, 1(1 tech) **Gr** <=E>/*grand slam* N, 20c (1 tech)

granny smith *n.* 'an Australian green variety of apple'
Mary Ann Smith (died 1870) cultivated a type of apple in New South Wales which came to be named after her nickname. Despite a globalization of the fruit trade the term does not appear to be widespread internationally.
Ge [grenismis] M [U] 1960s (2 tech) **Nw** [=E] [U] 20c (1 tech) **Ic** [=E] (0) **Fr** [granismis] F, 1960s (1 tech) **Sp** [=E] F, end20c (1 tech, rare) **Po** [-s] N [U] 1990s (1 tech) **Fi** [=E] (2) **Hu** [=E] [U] 1980s (2 tech) **Gr** <=E>/*grani smith* N, pl., end20c (1 tech)

grant *n.* 2 'money given by the state for scientific projects'
Rm [grant] N, 1990s (2 tech) **Rs** *grant* M, pl. -*y*, 1990s (1 tech) **Po** [grant] M, 1980s (1 tech)

grapefruit *n.* 1 'a large round yellow citrus fruit'
This word is more widespread in Eastern Europe – apparently because the fruit was already known in the West by its Dutch-mediated term *pompelmoes*.
Ge [greːpfruːt] F [U] 20c (1 mod) < *Pampelmuse* **Du** [greːpfruːt] C, 1950s (2) < *pompelmoes* **Nw** *grapefrukt*/*grape* [=E+Nw/greːp] 20c (2+5) **Ic** [kreiːpfruht/-fruːt] mid20c (0 arch); *grape*/*greip* [kreiːp] N, pl. Ø 1970s (3) > creat *greipávöxtur*, *greipaldin* **Fr** <=E> *grape-fruit* [gʀɛpfʀyt] M, beg20c (1 reg) < *pamplemousse*, *pomélo* **It** - < *pompelmo* **Rm** <=E>/*grepfrut*/*grep*/*gref* [grɛpfrut/grep/gref] N, mid20c (2>3) **Rs** *greĭpfrut* M [U] mid20c (3) **Po** *grejpfrut* <=E> M, beg20c (2) → *grapefrucik* M; -*owy* adj. **Cr** *grejpfrut* M [U] 20c (2) **Bg** *greĭfrut*, *greĭfurt*, *greĭfrukt* M, pl. -*al*-*i*, mid20c (2,3) > *greĭpfrut* **Fi** *greippi* 20c (3) **Hu** [=E/greːpfruː/greːpfryi] pl. Ø, 1930-60s (2) → adj., *cp*[1] **Al** *greipfrutë* [grejpfrutë] F, pl. Ø 20c (1 coll) **Gr** *greĭpfrut* N, beg20c (2)

Ic	Nw	Po	Rs
Du	Ge	Cr	Bg
Fr	It	Fi	Hu
Sp	Rm	Al	Gr

graphics *n.pl./cp*[2] (usu. treated as sing.) 1c 'design and decoration involving or accompanying typographic work'
The modern anglicism is added to the universal

Greek term only in a few languages, for modern (and modish) senses.
Ge (5Gr) **Du** [=E] 1980s **Ic** *grafik* [kra:fik] F/cp² [U] end20c (2 tech) **Sp** - < *diséno gráfico* **It** *grafica* F [U] 1970s (5 tech) **Rm** - < *grafică* **Rs** (5Gr) **Po** (5Gr) **Bg** *grafika* (5Gr) **Fi** - < *grafiikka* (3) **Al** *grafikë* F, pl. *-a*, mid20c (5) **Gr** <=E> [=E] N pl., 1980s (1 tech) > *graphika* (4)

grass *n.* 5 'marijuana'
Ge *Gras* N [U] 1980s (4 sla) **Nw** (0) **Ic** *gras* [kra:s] N [U] 1970s (4 sla) **Fr** (0) < *herbe* **Sp** [gras] M, 1960s (1 sla/rare) < mean *hierba* **It** - < mean *erba* **Rs** - < trsl *travka* **Po** - < trsl *trawka* **Cr** - < mean *trava* **Bg** *gras* M [U] 1990s (1 tech/sla) = mean *treva* **Fi** - < mean *ruoho* **Hu** - < *fű* **Gr** *gras* N [U] end20c (1 sla) < mean *khorto*

grating *n.* 'parallel metal bars' (naut.)
Ge *Gräting* F, pl. *-el/-s*, beg20c (3 tech, rare) **Po** *greting, gretting* [gretink] M, mid20c (1 tech)

gravel *n.* 1a 'small pebbles used for paths and roads'
Du [grevəl] N [U] 1970s (1 tech) **Nw** (0) **Fr** *gravier* (5) **Sp** - < *gravilla* **Rs** (5Fr)

Gray *n.* 'the SI unit of the absorbed dose of ionizing radiation' (physics)
Ge [gre:] N, pl. *-s*, 1980s (1 tech, rare) **Du** [=E] C [U] 1980s (1 tech) **Ic** *grei* [=E] N, pl. Ø, 20c (1 tech) **Fr** [grɛ] M (1 tech) **It** [=E] M, pl. Ø, mid20c (1 tech) **Rm** [=E] M, pl. Ø, end20c (1 tech) **Rs** *gréĭ* M, pl. *-i*, end20c (1 tech) **Cr** *grej* M [U] end20c (1 tech) **Gr** <=E> [grɛi] N, end20c (1 tech)

grease *n.* 1 'oily or fatty matter'
Nw *gris* [=E] M [U] beg20c (3) **Fr** *graisse* (4) **Sp** *grasa* (4) **Bg** *gres* M [U] 20c (5 Fr)

greasy *adj.* 2b (of a person or manner) 'unpleasantly unctuous, smarmy'
Ic [=E] uninfl., 1970s (1 sla)

great *interj.* 'fine, very good'
Du (0) **Ic** [=E] uninfl., end20c (0 sla) **Gr** (0>1 jour)

green *n.* 3c (golf) 'a putting green'
Ge - < mean *Grün* **Du** [=E] C, 1980s (1 tech) **Nw** [=E] M [U] 1980s (1 tech) **Ic** [=E] N, pl. Ø, mid20c (1 tech) **Fr** [grin] beg20c (2 tech) = *putting green* **Sp** [grin] M, pl. Ø/-s, -es 1920s (2 tech) **It** [grin] M, pl. Ø, 1930s (1 tech) **Rm** [=E] 20c (1 tech) **Fi** *green, griini* 20c (2 tech)

greenager* *n.* 'a child younger than a teenager'
This word, modelled on ↑*teenager* and ↑*greenhorn*, had a limited popularity in the late 1960s, but appears now to be obsolete.
Ge [=E] M, pl. Ø, 1960s (1 coll, obs)

greenhorn *n.* 'an inexperienced person'
Ge [gri:nhorn] N, pl. *-s*, 19c (1 obs) < *Grünschnabel* **Nw** [=E] M, pl. *-s*, beg20c (1 rare, obs) **Fr** [=E] M, 20c (1 rare, ban) < *intendant de terrain* **Po** [grinhorn] M, beg20c (1 tech) **Cr** *grinhorn* M, pl. *-ovi*, 20c (1) **Bg** - < *zelen* **Hu** [=E] pl. Ø, 20c (1 obs) < rend *zöldfülü*

greenkeeper *n.* 'the keeper of a golf- course'
Du [=E] C, 1980s (1 tech) **Nw** [=E] M, pl. *-e*, 1980s (1 tech) **It** [=E] M, pl. Ø, 1980s (1 tech)

gremlin *n.* 1 'an imaginary creature responsible for mechanical faults', +3 'a figure from a movie of the same name', +4 'a small toy-figure'
Ge [=E] M, pl. *-s*, 1980s, +3,+4(1 tech) **Nw** [=E] M, pl. *-s*, 1980s, +3(1 you, obs) **Ic** [=E] M, pl. *-ar*, 1980s, +3,+4(1 you, obs) **Fr** 1(0) **Sp** [gremlin] M, 1980s, +3(Ø/1 tech, rare) **It** [=E] C, pl. *-s*, 1990s?, +3(1) **Rs** *griml* M, pl. *grimlyane*, 1990s, +3(1 you, coll) **Po** <=E> M, end20c, 1(1 coll) **Fi** [=E] +3(0) **Gr** *gremlins* N, end20c, +3,+4(1 coll, mod)

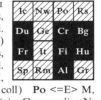

greyhound *n.* 1,2 'a breed of dog often used for racing', +3 'an overland bus'
Ge [grɛ:haunt] M, pl. *-s*, 20c, 1,2(1 tech, obs) +3(Ø) **Du** +3(Ø) **Nw** [=E] M, pl. *-er/-s*, 20c, 1,2(1 tech) +3(Ø) **Ic** [=E] end20c, 1,2(0 tech) +3(Ø) **Fr** <=E> M, 17c, 1,2(1 tech) +3(Ø) **It** [=E] M, pl. Ø, end20c, 1,2(1) < *levriere* **Rm** [=E] N [U], 1930s, 1(1 tech) **Rs** *greĭhaund* M, pl. *-y*, end20c, 1,2(1 tech) **Po** +3(0) **Cr** [=E] end20c, +3(Ø) **Bg** *greĭkhaund* M, pl. *-al-i*, end20c, 1,2(1 tech) **Hu** - < *agár*

grill *n.* 1a 'a device on a cooker radiating heat downwards', +1c 'a barbecue', 3 'a restaurant serving grilled food'
Ge [=E] M, pl. *-sl-e*, beg20c, 1a,+1c,3(2>3) **Du** [xril] C, 1970s (3) → *-en* v. **Nw** [=E] M, pl. *-er*, 1950s, 1a,+1c,3(3) **Ic** *grill* [kril:] N, pl. Ø, mid20c, 1a,+1c,3(3) **Fr** <=E>/*grille* [gril] M, mid20c, 1a,3(2) **Sp** [gril] M, pl. *-s*, 1960s, 1a(2); 1920s, 3(1 tech, rare) **It** [gril] M, pl. Ø, 1950s, 1a(3) +1c(3) = +1c: *griglia* **Rm** [=E] N, end20c, 1a(1 tech) < *grătar* **Rs** *gril'* M [U] end20c, 1a,3(2) → *-bar* M **Po** M, beg20c (2) **Cr** *gril* M [U] beg20c, 1a(2) **Bg** *gril* M [U] 1970s, 1a,+1c(2) **Fi** *grilli* 20c, 3(3) **Hu** [=E] pl. Ø, beg20c, 3(1 tech); *grillsütö* cp¹, 1a(2>3); *grillezés* 1960s, +1c(2>3) → *-ez* v. **Al** *grill* M, pl. *-e*, beg20c, 1a,+1c(3) **Gr** *gril* N, mid20c (2)

grill(e) *n.* 2 'a metal grid protecting the radiator of a motor vehicle'
The provenance of this term in this sense is uncertain: French and English have identical words, English often spelt with *-e* on the French pattern.
Ge [=E] M, pl. *-e*, beg20c (3) **Du** [=E] C, 1970s **Nw** *grill* [=E] M, pl. *-er*, 1950s (3) **Ic** *grill* N, pl. Ø, mid20c (3) **Rm** *grilă* (5Fr) **Al** *grilë* F, pl. *-a*, beg20c (3)

grill *v.* 1 'cook or be cooked under a grill or barbecue', 2 'subject or be subjected to extreme heat, esp. from the sun', +4 'cremate a dead body', +5 'handle roughly, defeat in a decisively physical manner'
Ge *grillen* 1930s, 1(3); *grillieren* (1 reg, obs) **Du**

grillen 1(3) **Nw** *grille* ["gri̯le]
1950s, 1(3) 2,+5(3 coll) +4(3 sla)
Ic *grilla* [kri̯l:a] mid20c, 1(3)
+4,+5(3 sla) = 1: *glóðarsteikja*
→ *grillaður* adj. **It** *grigliare*
1950s (3) **Cr** 1(0) **Fi** *grillata*
20c, 1(3) 2(1 coll) **Hu** *grillez*
[grillez] 1960s, 1(2>3)

grill-room *n.* 'a restaurant serving grilled food'

This word is a fashionable early twentieth-century adoption, but the full form is now obsolete in many languages, ↑*grill* being preferred (resulting in its becoming polysemous). The verb has, as is so often the case, a much more restricted distribution.

Ge [=E] M, pl. *-s*, beg20c (1 obs)
< *Grill* **Du** [grɪl̯ru:m] C, 1940s

(2) **Nw** *grill(rom)* [=E+Nw]
1960s (1+5 obs) **Ic** - < *grill* **Fr**
- < *grill* **Sp** [gril rum] M [U]
end19c (1 arch) < *grill* **It** [grill
rum] M, pl. Ø, mid20c (2>3)
Rm [=E] N [U] 1970s, via Fr? (1 rare) **Rs** - < *gril'*,
gril'-bar **Po** (0) **Cr** [=E] M [U] beg20c (1) **Hu**
[=E] pl. Ø, beg20c (1 tech, arch) < *grill-bár*, *grill-étterem* **Gr** *gril rum, gi̯lrum* N, pl. Ø-*s*, mid20c (2)

grind whale* *n.* 'a bottle-nose whale'

Whether the word was transmitted through English or adopted straight from a Nordic Language remains uncertain.

Ge *Grindwal* M, pl. *-e*, 19c? (3 tech) **Du** *grindewal*
(5Da) **Nw** *grindhval* (5 Faroese) **Ic** *grindl/grindhval-ur* F/M, 17c (5 Faroese) **Rs** (0) **Po** *grindwal*
[grindwal] M, mid20c (1 tech)

grizzly *n.* 'a variety of American bear'

Ge *Grizzlybär/Grislybär* M, pl.
-en, 19c? (3+5) **Du** [=E] C, pl.

-'s, 1980s (2); *grizzlybeer*, 1940s
(2+5) **Nw** *grizzlybjørn* [=E+
Nw] 20c (1+5) **Fr** <=E>/*-li*
[gri̯zli] M, 19c (2) **Sp** <=E>/*-li*
M, 20c (Ø/1 tech, rare) **It** [gri̯zli]
M, pl. Ø, mid20c (1>2) **Rs** *grizli* M, uninfl., mid20c (1
tech) **Po** <=E> M, uninfl., mid20c (2) **Cr** *grizli*
M, uninfl., beg20c (3) **Bg** *grizli* N/F, pl. Ø, 20c <
me̯chka grizli (5+Ø) **Hu** [=E] pl. *-k*, 20c (2)

grog *n.* 'a drink of rum and water'

The drink is named after Edward Vernon (1684–1757), whose nickname was 'Old Grog' from his characteristic grogram cloak. In 1740 he ordered that his sailors' official issue of rum should be diluted with water. The word *grog* spread quickly; it is an early loan from English and widespread throughout Europe. Its currency is decreasing because the drink is less fashionable now than it used to be.

Ge [grok] M, pl. *-s*, end18c (3) **Du** [ɤrɔk,ɤrɔx] C,
mid19c (2) **Nw** *grogg* [=E] M [U] mid19c (3
arch) **Ic** *grogg* [krok:] N [U] end19c, via Da (2
arch) **Fr** [gʁɔg] M, end18c (2) **Sp** <=E> M,

mid19c (1 arch) **It** [grɔg] M [U]

1820s (1) < *ponce* **Rm** [=E] N,
end19c (2<3 obs) **Rs** *grog* M
[U] mid19c (1 arch) **Po** [grok]
M, mid19c (1 arch) **Cr** *grog* M
[U] 19c (2) **Bg** *grog* M [U] end19c
(1 arch>2 mod) **Fi** *grogi* 19c
(2) **Hu** [=E] pl. Ø, 17/18c (3) **Gr** *grog* N 19c (1)

groggy *adj.* 1 'unsteady, dazed, semi-conscious', (esp. box.) +2 'very tired'

The etymological connection with ↑*grog* ('affected by too much grog') is lost in English and probably never existed in the loanwords. This term was adopted in the field of boxing and still is more or less restricted to this use in some languages, but was extended to all kinds of dizziness and exhaustion in others.

Ge [=E] pred., beg20c, 1(2>3)
+2(2 coll) → *-ness* n. (1) **Du**

[grɔgi] 1940s, 1(1 coll) **Nw**
[=E] 20s (2) **Fr** [gʁɔgi] adj.,
beg20c, 1(1 tech) +2(2) **Sp**
<=E>/*grogui* [grɔgi] 1920s (2<3)
It [grɔdʒi] uninfl., 1930s, 1(1 tech,
jour) **Rm** [=E] adj., uninfl., 1970s, 1(1 tech,
jour) **Rs** *groggi* uninfl., end20c, 1(1 coll) **Po**
uninfl., beg20c, 1(1 tech) **Cr** *grògi* mid20c, 1(1) →
-ran adj.; *-rati* v. **Bg** *grogi* pred., uninfl., mid20c, 1(1
tech) +2(3 coll) → *grogya̯sal* adj. **Hu** [=E] beg20c,
1(1 tech, arch)

groom *n.* 1 'a person employed to take care of horses', +4 'a bell-boy', +5 'an automatic door closer'

This word was borrowed together with a host of terms relating to horse-racing, but is now archaic in many languages. There are interesting extensions of meaning to valets and to a mechanical 'helper' (cf. the extensions of ↑*boy*).

Ge [=E] M, pl. *-s*, mid19c, 1(1
arch) **Du** [=E] C, beg20c, 1(1

arch) **Nw** [=E] M, pl. *-er*, 20c,
1(1 tech) **Fr** [gʁum] M, 19c, 1(1
arch) +4(1 obs) **Sp** [ʁrum/
grom] M, end19c (1 arch) **It**
[gru:m] M, pl. Ø, beg19c (1
arch?) < 1: *artiere*; +4,+5: *valletto* M **Rm** *grom*
[grom] M, mid20c, 1(3 arch); *groom* [=E] M, end19c,
+4(2 rare) **Rs** *grum* M, pl. *-y*, mid19c, 1(1 arch) **Po**
grum [grum] M, mid19c, 1(1 arch) **Cr** *grum* M,
beg20c, 1(3 arch) **Hu** [=E] pl. *-ok*, beg19c, 1,+4(1
arch) **Gr** *grum* M 19c

groove *n.* +3 'ecstasy (in pop concerts, etc.)', +4 'an engaging feeling or rhythm in jazz or pop music'

Ge [=E] M, pl. *-s*, 1970s (1 you) **Du** [=E] 1980s (1
sla) **Nw** [=E] M/N [U] 1970s, +3+4(1 tech) **Ic** [=E]
N [U] end20c, +4(1 sla) **It** [gru:v] M, pl. Ø, end20c,
+3(1) **Rm** [=E] end20c, +4(0>1 tech)

groove *v.* 2 'enjoy oneself', +3 'perform with engaging feeling and rhythm' (pop music or jazz)

Ge *sich eingrooven/grooven* 1980s, 2(1 sla, obs) **Nw**
["gru:ve] 1980s (1 sla) **Ic** [kru:va] end20c, +3(1 sla)

groovy *adj.* 1 'fashionable and exciting; enjoyable, excellent'
Ge [gru̱:vi] uninfl., 1970s (1 sla, obs?) **Du** [=E] uninfl., 1990s (1 you) **Nw** [=E] 1970s (1 coll) **Ic** [=E] uninfl., 1970s (1 sla) **Fr** (0) **Sp** <=E>/*groove* [gru̱bi/grub] end20c (1 jour, you, rare)

ground *n.* 5 'an area designated for sports'
It [graund] M, pl. Ø, 1930s (1 tech) < *campo* **Hu** - < *grund* (5Ge)

groupie *n.* 'an ardent follower of touring pop groups, esp. a young woman'
This term is a typical feature of American and Western European youth culture. It is unsurprisingly infrequent in Southern Europe and unknown in the East.
Ge [=E] M/N, pl. -*s*, 1970s (1 sla, obs) **Du** [=E] C, 1970s (1 sla) **Nw** [=E] M, pl. -*s*, 1960s (1 obs) **Ic** *grúp(p)í* [kru:pi/ kruhpi] N, pl. Ø, 1970s (1 sla); *grúppía* F, pl. -*ur* (2 sla) **Fr** [gʀupi] M/F, 1970s (1 obs) **Sp** <=E>/*groupy*/*grupi* [gru̱pi] C, pl. -*s*, 1970s (2 coll) **It** [gru̱pi] F/M, pl. Ø/-*s*, 1970s (1 sla, you) **Gr** <=E>/ *gru̱pi* F, pl. -*s*, 1980s (1 coll)

group sex *n.* 'sex performed by a group of people'
Ge - < trsl *Gruppensex* **Nw** - < trsl *gruppesex* **Ic** *grúppusex* [kruhpʏsɛxs] N [U] 1970s (1 sla) = creat *hópsex* **Sp** - < trsl *sexo en grupo* **It** - < rend *amore di gruppo* **Rm** - < rend *sex în grup*; creat *relaţii sexuale în grup* **Rs** - < trsl *gruppovoĭ seks* **Po** - < rend *seks grupowy* **Cr** - < trsl *grupni seks* **Bg** - < trsl *grupov seks* **Fi** - < trsl *ryhmäseksi* **Hu** (5Ge) **Gr** - < trsl *omadhiko sex*

grouse *n.* 'a game fowl'
Fr [gʀuz] F, 19c (1) > *coq de bruyère*

grubber *n.* 'an agricultural machine'
Ge [gru̱ba] M, pl. Ø, 20c (1 tech) = *Krümmer* **Rs** *grubber* M, pl. -*y*, beg20c (1 tech, obs) **Po** *gruber* [gruber] M, beg20c (1 tech) **Bg** *gruber* M, pl. -*al-i*, beg20c, via **Rs** (1 tech) **Hu** [gru̱bber] pl. -*ek*, 20c (1 tech)

grunge *n./cp*[1/2] 2 'a style of rock music characterized by a raucous guitar sound', 3 'the fashion associated with this music', +4 'a member of a grunge group'
The rapid spread of this recent term is typical of modern coinages connected with pop music. The term may well be obsolescent before it reaches all the potential languages.
Ge [grantʃ] M/N [U] 1991 (1 you) **Nw** <=E>/*grønsj* [=E/ grønʃ] M [U] 1990s (1 tech, you) **Ic** [=E] N [U] 1990s (1 sla, you) = rend *grensa* **Fr** <=E> M [U] 1990s (1 you) **Sp** [=E/grunx(e)] M, 1990s (1 you, mod) → *grungeriano; grungemania* **It** [=E] M/cp[2]

[U] 1990s (1 sla, you) **Rs** *granzh* M [U] 1990s (1 tech, mod) **Po** <=E> M [U] end20c (1 mod) **Bg** *gründzh* M/cp[1] [U] 1990s (2 tech, mod) → -*ar* M **Fi** [=E] 1990s (1 you) **Gr** <=E>/*grants* F [U] 1990s (1 you)

guard *n.* 2 'a person who protects', +3a 'a member of a guard or bodyguard', 10a 'a protective or defensive player', 10b 'a defensive posture or motion'
Du [=E] C, mid20c, +3a(1 tech) **Nw** [=E] M, end20c, 10a(1 tech) **Sp** - < *guardia* **Rs** *gvardeets* (5It) **Bg** *gard* M, pl. -*ove*, mid20c, via **Fr**, +3a(2) 10a(1 tech); [U] 10b(1 tech/2 coll) **Hu** [=E] pl. -*ok*, 1980s, esp. cp[2], 2,+3a(2) < *testőr* **Gr** *gard* M, beg20c, 10a,b(1 tech)

guernsey *n.* 2a 'a thick woollen sweater of a distinctive pattern'
Nw *genser* [ge̱nsər] M, pl. -*e*, 19c (3)

guest star *n.* 'an actor/actress invited to take part in a film or show'
Ge - < trsl *Gaststar* **Du** Ø **Nw** (0) **Fr** (0) **Sp** [=E] N, pl. -*s*, 1990s (1 writ, rare) < trsl *estrella invitada* **Hu** - < trsl *vendégművész* **Gr** *gest star* M/F, 1980s (2)

guide *n.* 1 'a person who leads or shows the way', 2 'a person who conducts travellers', 3 'a professional mountain climber in charge of a group', 6 'a book with essential information on a subject', +11 'a reference card in a filing system'
Ge (0) **Du** 1,6 (0); [=E] C, pl. -*en*, beg20c, 2(2) **Nw** [=E] M, pl. -*r*, beg20c, 1,2,3,6(2) +11(1 tech) **Ic** [=E] M, pl. -*ar*, 1970s, 2,6(1 coll) **Fr** (5) **Sp** - < *guía* **It** *guida* F, pl. -*e*, 20c (3/5Ge) **Rm** - < *ghid* (5Fr) **Rs** *gid* M, pl. -*y*, mid20c, via **Fr**, 1,2,3(2) **Po** M, end20c, 1,2,3(1 tech) **Bg** *gid* M, pl. -*ove*, mid20c, 1,2,3(5Fr) **Hu** [=E/gi:d] pl. -*ok*, mid20c, 1,2,6(1 jour, mod) **Al** - < 6: *guide* (5Fr)

guide *v.* 1a 'act as a guide; lead or direct'
Nw ["ga̱idə] 1960s (2) **Ic** [kai:ta] 1970s (1 coll) **Fr** *guider* (5) **Sp** - < *guiar* **It** - < *guidare* (5) **Po** (0)

gully *n.* 2 'a gutter, in streets'
This word is interesting for its unique occurrence in German (where it is the accepted term) and the change of meaning involved.
Ge [gu̱li] [U] M, pl. -*(ie)s*, end19c (3)

guppy *n.* 'a freshwater (aquarium) fish'
The fish is named after the Trinidad clergyman Robert John Lechmere Guppy (1836–1916) who sent a few specimens to the British Museum. They quickly spread in home aquarists' circles over most of Europe.
Ge [gupi] M, pl. -*(ie)s*, 20c (3 tech) **Du** [gupi] C, pl. -'*s*, 1960s (1 tech) = *gup* pl. -*pen* **Nw** [=E/gu̱pi] M, pl. -*er*, 1970s (1 tech) **Ic** *gúbbi(fiskur)*/*gúbbi* [kup:i-/kup:ɪ] M, pl. -*ar*, mid/ end20c (2 tech) **Fr** [gypi] M, 1950s (3 tech) **Sp** [gupi] M, pl. Ø, mid20c (3 tech) **Rm** *guppy, gupi* [gu̱pi] M, pl. Ø, mid20c (3 tech) **Rs** *gu̱ppi* uninfl., mid20c (1 tech) **Po** *gupik* [gupik] M,

mid20c (1 tech) **Cr** (o) **Bg** _gupa_ F, pl. _-pi_, mid20c (3 tech) **Hu** _guppi_ [guppi] pl. _-k_, 20c (3 tech)

guts _n._ 'courage, determination'
 Du [=E] C, 1990s (2) **Nw** [=E] sg. [U] 1980s (1 coll) **Ic** [=E] uninfl., end20c (1 sla)

gutta-percha _n._ 'a tough plastic substance obtained from latex'
 Ge [gutaperxa] F/N [U] 19c (3 tech) **Du** [=E] C/N [U] 19c (2) **Nw** _guttaperka_ [gutapærka] M [U] 19c (3 tech) **Ic** _gúttaperka/gúttaberg_ [guhtaphɛɾka/-pɛrk] N [U] end19c, via Danish (2 obs) **Fr** [gytapɛʀka] F, mid19c (1 tech) **Sp** _gutapercha_ F, 19c (1 tech) **It** _guttaperca_ [guttapɛrka] F [U] mid18c (1 tech) **Rm** _gutapercă_ [gutapɛrkə] F, end19c, via Fr/It (3

tech) **Rs** _guttapercha_ F [U] 19c (2 obs) → _-chevyĭ_ adj. **Cr** _guta-perka_ F [U] 19c (2 obs) **Bg** _gutapercha_ F, [U] end19c, via Rs (1 tech, arch) **Fi** _guttaperkka_ 19c (3) **Gr** _gutaperka_ N [U] (1 tech)

guy _n._ 1 'a man; a fellow', +5 'someone acting cool or dressing sharp'
 Du (Ø) **Ic** _gæi_ [kai:jɪ] M, pl. _-(j)ar_, mid20c (2 coll) **Gr** (o)

gypsy _n./cp¹_ 1 'a member of a nomadic people of Indian descent', 2 'a person resembling or living like a Gypsy'
 Nw [=E] usu. cp¹, 1980s, 1(1 jour, mod) < _sigøyner_ **Ic** [=E] (o) < _sigauni, ta(r)tari_ **Fr** 1(o) **Rm** 1(o) **Hu** [=E] pl. _-k_, 20c (o)

H

H *abbrev.* 3 'heroin'
  Ge *Äitsch* [eitʃ] N [U] 1980s (1 sla) **Fr** [aʃ] M, 1970s (4) **Gr** [eits] F [U] 1980s (Ø>1 sla)

hack *v.* 5b 'obtain unauthorized access to computer data'
  The verb and, much more extensively, the agent noun quickly spread along with other items of computer terminology. Semantic calques based on *pirat*, etc. form easy alternatives. The main vowel notably varies between *a* and *e*.
  Ge [hakən] 1980s (3 tech) **Du** [hɛka] 1980s (2) **Nw** *hacke* ["hæke] 1980s (1 tech) **Ic** *hakka* [hahka] end20c (2 tech) **Fi** *hakata* end20c (4 sla)

hacker *n.* 2 'a person who gets unauthorized access to computer data', +3 'a computer enthusiast'
  Ge [haka] M, pl. Ø, 1980s, 2(3 tech) **Du** [=E] C, 1980s, 2(2) → *hacken* v. **Nw** [=E] M, pl. -el/-s, 1980s (1 tech) > *datasnok (er)* **Ic** *hakkari* [=E/hahkarɪ] M, pl. -ar, end20c (1 sla) **Fr** 2(0) < *pirate* **Sp** [xaker] M, pl. -s, 1980s (1 sla, tech) < *pirata (informático)* **It** [ɛker] M, pl. Ø, 1990, 2(1 tech) < *khaker/khéker* M, pl. -y, end20c (1 tech) **Po** [heker] M, end20c, 2(1 coll) **Cr** [heker] M, pl. -i, end20c, 2(1 tech) → *hacking* n. **Bg** *khaker* M, pl. -i, 1990s, 2(1 tech) < *pirat* **Fi** *hakkeri* end20c (1 tech) **Hu** [heker] pl. Ø, 1980s (1 tech) **Gr** *khaker* M, pl. Ø/-s, 1990s, 2,+3(1 tech)

Ic	Nw	Po	Rs
Du	Ge	Cr	Bg
Fr	It	Fi	Hu
Sp	Rm	Al	Gr

haddock *n.* 'smoked fish'
  Nw (0) **Fr** [adɔk] M, beg18c (2)

hair extension *n.* 'the process of joining synthetic hair to natural hair to make it longer (and the hair thus added)'
  Ge [=E] F [U] 1980s (0 tech, rare) < *hair weaving* **Du** [=E] C [U] 1980s (1 tech, jour) **Nw** [=E] M [U] 1980s (1 tech)

hairspray *n.* 'a solution sprayed on to the hair to keep it in place'
  Ge *Haarspray* [-spre:] M/N, pl. -s, 1970s (5+2) **Du** [=E] M, 1970s (2) = *haarlak* **Nw** *hårspray* ["hoːɽsprai] M, pl. -er, 1960s (5+2) < *hårlakk* **Ic** *hársprey* [hauɽsprei] N [U] 1960s (5+2) < rend *hárlakk* **Fr** - < cf. ↑*spray* **Sp** - < *lacer, fijador* **It** *spray* [sprai] M, pl. Ø, 1920s (2) < *laccalfissatore* **Rm** - < *(spray) fixativ* **Rs** - < rend *lak dlya volos* **Hu** [=E/~ʃpre:] pl. Ø, 1980s (1 tech/mod) < *hajlakk* **Al** - < *blak*

hairstyling *n.* 'the act of choosing (and constructing) hair-styles for individual persons'
  Du (Ø) → *hairstylist; hairstylen* **It** [hɛrstailiŋ(g)] M [U] 1980s (1 tech, jour) **Hu** [=E] [U] end20c (1 tech, jour, mod) **Gr** <=E> [=E] N [U] 1990s (1 writ, you, mod)

half *n.* 2 '↑*half- back*' (in some types of sport)
  The football term was adopted along with the game in the late nineteenth century and was variously shortened to *half* – or translated in countries taking puristic measures. In German it was replaced by *Läufer*, but Switzerland and Austria were not affected and the original loanword survives as a regionalism.
  Ge [=E] M, pl. -s, beg20c (1 reg, obs) < *Läufer* **Nw** [=E] M, pl. -er, 20c (1 obs) **Ic** *haff* [haf:] M, pl. -ar, mid20c (1 tech) = *framvörður* **Rm** [half/halfie] M/F, mid20c (1 obs, rare) < *mijlocaş* **Po** [half] M, mid20c (1 tech) **Cr** *half* [half] M, pl. -ovi, beg20c (1 tech) **Bg** *khalf* M, pl. -ove, beg20c (1 tech) = rend *poluzashtitnik* **Hu** [half] pl. Ø, end19c/beg20c (1 tech/arch) < *fedezet* **Al** *half* M, pl. -ë, beg20c (1 reg) **Gr** *khaf* M, beg20c (1 tech)

Ic	Nw	Po	Rs
Du	Ge	Cr	Bg
Fr	It	Fi	Hu
Sp	Rm	Al	Gr

half-and-half *adv.* +1 'fifty-fifty'
  This adverb is much less frequent than the synonymous ↑*fifty-fifty*. Note that the earlier noun (c.1900, recorded for German) 'a mixture of porter and ale' has been obsolete for some time, as it has in Britain.
  Du *half en half* (5) **Nw** [=E] 20c (1) **Fr** [afenaf] beg20c (1 arch) → *afnaf* (1 sla, arch) **Rm** - < rend *juma-juma*

half-back *n.* 'a player between the forwards and the full-backs' (footb) cf. ↑*half*
  Ge [haːfbek] M, pl. -s, beg20c (1 reg/obs) **Du** *halfback* [=E] C, 1950s (2 tech) > *middenveldspeler* **Nw** [haːfbek] M, pl. -er, beg20c (1 arch) **Ic** [=E/hafpahk /hap:ahk] M, pl. -ar, mid20c (1 tech) < rend *framvörður* **Fr** - < *demi* **Rm** - < rend *mijlocaş* **Rs** *khavbek* M, pl. -i, beg20c (1 tech) **Po** [haf bek] M [U] beg20c (1 tech) **Bg** - < *khalf* **Hu** [halfbek] pl. Ø, end19c (1 tech/arch) **Gr** - < *khaf*

Ic	Nw	Po	Rs
Du	Ge	Cr	Bg
Fr	It	Fi	Hu
Sp	Rm	Al	Gr

half-pipe* *n.* 'a concrete structure for skateboarding'

This term is remarkably restricted, considering how popular skateboarding has been for some time; no calques appear to be recorded either.

Ge [haːfpaip] F, pl. *-s*, 1990 (1 you) **Du** [=E] C, 1980s (1 you) **Nw** [=E] M, pl. *-s*, 1980s (1 tech, you) **Bg** - < rend *trúba* **Fi** [=E] 1990s (1 you)

half-time *n.* 1 'the time at which half of the game is completed' (sports), 2 'a short interval occurring at this time'

The distribution of this term shows interesting similarities and contrasts with the structurally equivalent ↑*half-back* above, but calquing is much more widespread.

Ge [haːftaim] F [U] beg20c (1 reg/obs) < trsl *Halbzeit* **Du** [=E] C/N [U] beg20c (2 tech) **Nw** - < trsl *halvtid* **Ic** - < rend *hálfleikur* **Fr** - < trsl *mi-temps* **Sp** - < *descanso*; trsl *medio tiempo* **Rm** [half+=E] N, beg20c (1 rare) < *repriză* **Rs** *khavtaim* M, pl. *-y*, beg20c (1 tech) < trsl *poluvremya* **Po** [half-] M [U] mid20c (1 tech) **Cr** - < trsl *poluvrijeme* **Bg** *khalftaim* (0) < trsl *poluvreme* **Fi** - < creat *puoliaika* **Hu** - < trsl *félidő* **Al** - < trsl *pushim* **Gr** - < trsl *imikhrono*

half-track (vehicle) *n.* 2 'a vehicle with an endless driven belt used for traction'

Fr *half-track* [alftrak] M, 1950s (1 tech)

halibut *n.* 'a flatfish'

Ge *Heilbutt* (5) **Du** *heilbot* (5) **Nw** (0) < *hellefisk, kveite* **Fr** [alibyt] M < *flétan* **Sp** [ailbut] M, 20c (1 tech) **It** [alibut] M, pl. Ø, 1950s (1 tech) **Po** [halibut] M, mid20c (3)

hall *n.* 1a 'a space or passage into which the front entrance of a house etc. opens', 1b 'a corridor', +8 'a meeting/concert hall, a modern drawing-room'

The Germanic languages have variously extended the native terms on the basis of English, whereas others have adopted the word mainly for the meanings 'corridor', 'meeting/concert hall' and 'drawing-room'.

Ge (5) **Du** 1b(5) **Nw** [=E] M, pl. *-er*, beg20c, 1a(1) **Ic** *hol* [hɔːl] N, pl. Ø, 1940s, 1a(2 coll) **Fr** [ol] M, end19c, 1a(2) **Sp** [xol] M, pl. *-s*, 1980s, 1a(2) **It** [oːl] F, pl. Ø, 18c, 1a(2) **Rm** *hol* [hol] N, beg20c,

via Fr (3) **Rs** *kholl* M, pl. *-y*, beg20c, 1a,+8(3) **Po** *holl*<=E> M, beg20c, 1b(2) **Cr** *hal* M, pl. *-ovi*, beg20c, 1b(3) **Bg** *khol* M, pl. *-al-ove*, beg20c, via Fr, +8(2) → *-ov* adj. **Hu** [hal] pl. Ø, end17c/beg18c, +8(3) → *hallos* adj. **Al** *holl* M, pl. *-e*, beg20c (3) **Gr** *hol* N, beg20c, 1a,1b(2) +8(0>1 tech, mod)

hallo *interj.* 1a,b 'an expression of informal greeting, esp. used to begin a telephone conversation'

Ge (5) **Du** [haloː] 1940s (3) **Nw** (5Ge) **Ic** *halló* [hal:ou] (5Da) **Fr** *allô* [alo] beg20c (3) **It** [(h)ɛllo]

1960s (1) **Rm** *alo* [alo/alo] mid20c, via Fr (3) **Rs** *khellou* mid20c (1 coll/you) **Po** *halo* beg20c (3) **Bg** *khelou* end20c (1 sla, you) **Hu** [halo:] 1880s (3); *helló* [helo:] beg20c (3) **Al** *alo/halo* mid20c (1 tech) **Gr** (0)

halter-neck *adj./cp¹* '(a garment) held up by a strap around the neck'

Ge *Halterneck-Body* M, pl. *-(ie)s*, 20c (1 tech) **Nw** [=E] M, pl. *-s*, end20c (1 tech)

hamburger *n.* 1 'a beefburger, usu. served in a roll', +1a 'a burger with any filling' (**Bg** only)

This term, wrongly analysed as *ham+burger* in American English, and the source of other *-burger* compounds, has spread all over Europe. Note that many languages treat the word according to its ultimate German origin, but pronunciation shows it is an anglicism in German itself.

Ge [hɛmbörga/hamburga] M, pl. Ø, 1950s (2) **Du** [hɑmbʏrɣər] C, 1950s (3) **Nw** [hamburger] M, pl. *-e*, 1950s (2) **Ic** *hamborgari* [hamporkarɪ] M, pl. *-ar*, mid20c (3) **Fr** [ãburɡœʀ/ãbœʀɡœʀ] M, pl. *-s*, 1960s (2) **Sp** *hamburguesa* F (2) **It** [amburɡer] M, pl. Ø, 1960s (3) **Rm** [hamburɡər] M, 1970s (3 coll) **Rs** *gamburger* M, pl. *-y*, end20c (2) **Po** [hamberger/-burger] M, mid20c (2) **Cr** [hamburger] M, pl. *-i*, mid20c (2) **Bg** *khamburger* M, pl. *-al-i*, end20c, +1a(2) **Fi** - < rend *hampurilainen* **Hu** [hamburger] pl. *-ek*, 1980s (2>3) **Al** *hamburger* M, pl. *-el-a*, end20c (1 you) **Gr** *khaburger*/<=E> N, mid20c (2)

hammerless* *n.* 'a type of gun for hunting'

Fr [amɛrlɛs] M, end19c (1 tech, obs) **It** [(h)emerles] M, pl. Ø, 1930s (1 tech) **Rm** [hamerles] N, mid20c (1 tech, rare)

hammerlock *n.* 'a hold in which the arm is twisted and bent behind the back' (wrestling)

Nw - < *backhammer* **It** [hemerlok] M, pl. Ø, 1960s (1 tech) **Rs** *khammerlok* M, pl. *-i*, end20c (1 tech) **Po** *hamerlock* [hamerlok] M, end20c (1 tech)

hammock *n.* 1 'a bed of canvas or rope network, suspended by cords at the ends', +2 'a kind of garden swing-seat'

This word came from Arawakan, was transmitted to various European languages via Spanish and adapted according to English morphology in the seventeenth century. Evidence of English transmission is slight (in Norwegian?): most languages appear to have taken the word straight from Spanish, or through French/Dutch, partly affected by folk etymology (German, Dutch).

Ge *Hängematte* F, 18c (3) **Du** *hangmat* 18c (3) **Nw** [hamɔk] M, pl. *-er*, 1960s, +2(2); - < 1: *hengekøye* **Ic** - < 1: *hengirúm* **Fr** - < 1: *hamac* **Sp** - < 1: *hamaca* **It** - < 1: *amaca* (5Sp) **Rm** *hamac* [hamak] N, end19c, 1(5Fr) **Rs** (5Sp) **Po** *hamak* 1, +2(5Sp) **Bg** *khamak* M, pl. *-atsi*, beg20c, 1(5Sp)

hammond organ* *n.* 'a keyboard instrument'

Ge *Hammond(-Orgel)* [hɛmənd+5] 1960s (2+5 obs) **Du** *hammond orgel* N, 1950s (2 obs) **Nw** *hammondorgel* [hamun] mid20c (2+5) **Ic** *hammond* [ham:ont] M, pl. -ar; hammondorgel N, pl. Ø, 1960s (2 tech) Sp - < trsl órgano hammond

handball n. 1a 'a game similar to football in which the ball is thrown rather than kicked'

This word is derived from German in most languages, as is indeed natural, given the predominance of Germany in the discipline in the early twentieth century. The game is very marginal in English-speaking countries. The phonology of the loanword in Polish and Albanian points to English mediation.

Ge [hantbal] M, pl. -bälle (5) Du handbal (5) Nw håndball, hand- (5) Ic handbolti [hantpɔḷtɪ] M [U] 1920s (5Da/Ge) > trsl handknattleikur Fr (5Ge) Sp (5Ge) It - < trsl pallamano/palla a mano Rm handbal [handbal] N, 1930s (5Ge) Rs gandbol M [U] mid20c (1 tech) → -ist M; -istka, F; -nyĭ adj. Po [hendbol] M [U] mid20c (1 tech) < trsl piłka ręczna Cr - < trsl rukomet Bg khandbal M [U] mid20c (5Ge) → -ist M; -istka F; -en adj. Fi - < trsl käsipallo Hu - < trsl kézilabda Al hendboll M [U] mid20c (2 tech) Gr khadbol N [U] mid20c (1 tech) > trsl khirosferisi

handbrake n. 'a brake operated by hand'

Calques are almost universally preferred – if the English etymon can indeed be considered the source of various native compounds.

Ge - < Handbremse Du - < handrem Nw (hånd)-brekk [-brek] N, pl. Ø, beg20c (3) > håndbremse Ic - < trsl handbremsa Fr - < frein à main Sp - < freno de mano It - < trsl freno a mano Rm - < rend frână de mână Rs - < rend ruchnoĭ tormoz Po - < rend hamulec ręczny Bg - < trsl ručhna spirachka Hu - < trsl kézifék Gr - < trsl khirofreno

handicam* n. (™Sony) 'a small video camera'

Ge [=E] pl. -s, 1990s (1 tech) Du [=E] C, pl. -s, 1990s (1 tech) It [=E] F, pl. Ø, 1990s (1 tech) Rm [=E/handikam] N, 1990s (1 tech) Rs héndikam M, pl. -y, 1990s (1 tech) Gr <=E> [=E] F/N, 1990s (1 tech)

handicap n. 1a 'a disadvantage imposed on a superior competitor' (sports), 2 'the number of strokes by which a golfer exceeds par for the course', 3 'something that makes success difficult', 4 'a physical or mental disability', +5 'a privilege', +6 'an advantage' (sport)

This term spread as a late nineteenth-century horse-racing term for the weight added to eliminate the advantage of light-weight jockeys. It then developed into a more general 'impediment' or 'encumbrance' which is now the most prominent sense throughout Europe as well as English. Note that derivatives are much less frequent.

Ge <=E>/Handikap [hendikep] N, pl. -s, 19c, 1a,3(2) Du [=E] C, 1940s, 3(2); 1970s, 4(2e); beg20c, 1a(2 tech) Nw Handikap [=E/handikap] N, pl. Ø, beg20c, 1a,2,+5(1 tech); mid20c, 3,4(2) Ic [=E] N, mid20c, 1a(1 tech) 3,4(1 sla) < 1a: forgjöf forskot; 4: fötlun Fr

Ic	Nw	Po	Rs
Du	Ge	Cr	Bg
Fr	It	Fi	Hu
Sp	Rm	Al	Gr

[ãdikap/ãdikap] M, 19c/1930s, 1a,2,3,4(2) → handicaper v.; handicapé adj./n.; handicapant adj./p.p.; handicapeur M Sp [xándikap] M, 1880s, 1a(2 techHORSES); beg20c, 3(2) 4(2 techPSYCHOL); beg20c/1980s, +6(2 tech) → handicapado adj. It [endikap] M, pl. Ø, end19c, 1a,2(2 tech) 3,4(3) Rm [handikap] N, beg20c, via Fr, 1a(3 tech, obs) 3(3 tech); 1950s, 4(3) Po [hendikap] M, beg20c, 3(1 tech) +5(2) → v. Cr hendikep M, pl. -ovi, mid20c, 3(2) → -irati v. Bg hendikap M [U] mid20c, +6(3 tech) Hu hendikep [=E] [Ø] end19c, 1a,+5(1 tech/obs) 3(1) Al hendikep M [U] mid20c, 3(1 reg) Gr khadikap N, 1a(1 tech) 2(1 tech) 3(1 rare)

handicap v. 1 'impose a handicap on', 2 'place someone at a disadvantage'

Ge handicap(p)en/-k- [hendikepən] 1930s, 1(1 tech, obs); handicappieren 1(1 reg) Du [hendikɛpə] 1940s, 2(2) Nw handikappe [handikape/hændikæpe] beg20c (2) → handikappet Fr handicaper [ãdikape] 19c (2) Sp handicapar/handicapear [xandikapar/xandikapear] 1920s (1 tech) It (h)andicappare [endikappare/andikappare] 1900s (3) Rm handicapa [handikapa] beg20c, via Fr (3) → handicapat/-ă adj. Po hendikowai/handikapować 20c, 1,2(1 tech) Cr hendikepirati mid20c, 2(2) Hu hendikeppel [hendikeppe] end19c/beg20c, 1(1 tech/obs) 2(1 fig)

handicapped adj. 'suffering from a physical or mental disability'

Ge gehandikapt 1930s (2) Du gehandicapt [xəhɛndikɛpt] 1910s (2) Nw [handikapet/=E] mid 20c (2 obs) < funksjonshemmet Ic - < fatlaður Fr handicapé(e) [ãdikape] adj./n., 1910s/1950s (2) Sp handicapado [xandikapado] (1 tech) It (h)andicappato [endikappato/andikappato] 1930s (3) Rm handicapat (3) Cr hendikepiran mid20c (2) Hu <=E>/hendikepd [=E] mid20c (2 techPSYCHOL/euph/mod) Al handicapat 20c, via It (2)

handicapper n. 1 'someone who is given a disadvantage' (sport), 2 'an umpire deciding on handicaps'

Ge <=E>/Handikapper [hendikepa] M, pl. Ø, beg20c, 2(1 tech, rare) Du [=E] C, beg20c, 2(1 tech) Nw [hændikæper] M, pl. -e, 20c, 2(1 tech) Fr handicapeur [ãdikapœr] M, mid19c, 2(1 tech) Sp <=E> M, mid20c, 2(1 tech) Po hendikaper/handikaper M, end20c, 1(2) Cr (0) Hu hendikeper [hendikeper] pl. Ø, end19c, 2(1 obs) Al - < hendikapat M

handicap-race n. 'a race in which a disadvantage is imposed on a superior competitor'

Du [=E] C, 1980s (2) It - < trsl corsa and handicap Rm - < rend cursă/întrecere cu handicap

handle   *n.* 1 'a part by which something is held, carried or controlled'
Nw *hendel* [hɛndəl] M, pl. *hendler*, beg20c (3)
handle   *v.* 2 'manage a (difficult) situation'
Ge [hɛndəln] 1980s (1 mod)   **Nw** (0)
handling   *n.* 1 'management (of a difficulty)', 2 'ground handling in air transport'
     This term is not fully established in any of its senses; the verb is even less common, but has made some headway in colloquial use in German in spite of its morphological difficulties.
Ge [=E] N [U] 1970s, 1(1 mod)
Nw (0)   **Fr** 2(1 tech, ban) < *service d'escale*   **Sp** [=E/xanlin] M [U] 1980s, 2(1 tech)   **It** [(h)ɛndliŋ] M [U] 1960s (1 tech)   **Rm** [handling] N, 1970s, 2(1 tech)
Bg *khandling* M [U] end20c, 2(1 tech)   **Gr** *khandling* N [U] end20c, 2(1 tech)

handout   *n.* +3 'an information sheet for a lecture'
     This loanword has spread from academic teaching, possibly because no concise equivalent was available (in Germanic it is transparent, as in German *aushändigen* v., but calques were only rarely attempted).
Ge [hɛndaut] N/M, pl. -*s*, 1960s (1 tech)   **Du** *hand-out* [=E] C, 1980s (1 tech)   **Nw** [=E] M, pl. -*s*/-*er*, 1980s (1 tech) > *stotteark*   **Ic** [=E] N, pl. Ø, end20c (1 tech) = creat *úthenda*; *dreifiblað*   **Fr** (0) < *polycopié*, *exemplier*   **Rm** [=E] 1990s (0)   **Po** [hendaut] M, 1990s (1 tech)   **Cr** [=E] M, pl. -*i*, 1990s (1 tech) > *uručak*   **Bg** (0)   **Hu** [=E] pl. -*ok*, 1980s (1 tech)

hands   *n.* 'the foul of touching the ball with one's hands' (footb.)
     The tendency to translate, rather than adopt, this English term is even stronger than with other football expressions. The present-day distribution of the loanword is unique. (In German the English word is again restricted to Switzerland and Austria).
Ge [=E] N [U] 1960s (1 reg/obs) < *Hand(spiel)*   **Du** [hɑnts] N [U] 1950s (3 tech)   **Nw** [hens] M, pl. -*er*, mid20c (2) → *handse* v.   **Ic** - < trsl *hendi*   **Fr** - < *jeu à la main*   **Sp** - < *mano*   **It** - < trsl *mani, fallo di mano*   **Rm** *henţ* [hents] N, 1950s (3)   **Rs** *khénds* [U] mid20c (1 tech)   **Po** - < *ręka*   **Cr** *henc* M, pl. *hénčevi*, beg20c (1 tech)   **Bg** - < trsl *rŭka*   **Hu** [henc] [U] end19c (2 tech/arch) < *kezezés*   **Al** - < *me dorë*   **Gr** - < mean *kheri*

handshake   *n.* 'a gesture as a part of greeting or leaving' (cf. ↑*golden* ~, ↑*shakehands*)
Ge [=E] M, pl. -*s*, 1960s (1 coll, rare); *handshaking* N, pl. -*s*, beg20c (1 arch) < *Händeschütteln*   **Du** Ø < *handslag*   **Sp** - < *partidaro de la línea dura*   **Gr** (0)
hands free*   *phr.* 'a loudspeaker device on a car

phone that enables the driver to use the phone without holding the receiver' (cf. ↑*speakerphone*.)
Du [=E] 1990s (1 tech, jour)   **Nw** [=E] 1980s (1 tech) > trsl *håndfri*   **Fi** [=E] 1990s (1 tech)
hands up   *excl.* 'an instruction to raise one's hands (in westerns, robberies)'
Ge - < *Hände hoch*   **Du** 1940s (1 sla) < *handen omhoog*   **Nw** [hæ:nsøp] mid20c (2 coll)   **Ic** - < trsl *upp með hendur*   **Fr** - < *haut les mains*   **Sp** - < *manos arriba*   **It** - < trsl *mani in alto*   **Rm** - < *sus mâinile*   **Cr** - < trsl *ruke u vis*   **Bg** - < *gore rŭtsete*   **Hu** [=E] end19c/beg20c (2 obs) < *fel a kezekkel*   **Al** - < *duart lart*   **Gr** - < trsl *psila ta kheria*
handy*   *n.* 'a mobile telephone'
     Although this term is strikingly adequate (a *handy* carried in your *hands* being always *handy*) it has not spread to European countries outside Germany (nor indeed 'back' to Britain). In Germany it is the generic term, and much more frequent than the formal equivalent *Mobiltelefon*.
Ge [hɛndi] N, pl. -*s*, 1993 (3 mod) > *Mobiltelefon*
handy   *adj.* 1 'convenient to handle or use; useful'
Du - < *handig* (5)   **Nw** - < *hendig* (5)   **Ic** [=E] (uninfl.) end20c, 1(1 sla)   **Al** *hendi* M, 1995 (1 tech)
hang-glider   *n.* 1 'a frame with a fabric aerofoil stretched over it, from which the operator is suspended and controls flight by body movement', 2 'a person who practises hang-gliding'
Ge - < 1: trsl *Hängegleiter*; 2: rend *Drachenflieger*   **Du** *hangglider* [=E] C, 1970s (1 tech) < *deltavlieger*   **Nw** [=E] M, pl. -*e*, 1970s (2) > trsl *hengeglider*, *hengefly*   **Ic** - < rend *svifdreki*   **Fr** - < *déltaplane*   **It** - < creat *deltaplano*   **Rs** - < *del'taplan*   **Bg** - < *deltaplan*   **Hu** - < rend *sárkányrepülő*   **Gr** <=E> [=E] N, end20c (1 tech) < *anemoptero*
hang-gliding   *n.* 'the sport of flying with a hang-glider'
Ge - < rend *Drachenfliegen*   **Du** - < *deltavliegen*   **Nw** [=E] C, uninfl., 1970s (2) > *hengegliding*, *hengeflyging*   **Hu** - < rend *sárkányrepülés*   **Gr** <=E> [=E] N [U] end20c (1 tech)
hangover   *n.* 1 'a severe headache or other after-effects caused by drinking'
Nw [=E] M, pl. -*e* (1 rare) < *bakrus*   **Gr** <=E> [=E] N, 1990s (1 coll, mod)
happening   *n.* 2 'an improvised performance', +2a 'a multimedia art form'
     The wide distribution of this word is truly notable and although it has remained mainly a technical art term and thus an intellectual concept, it is striking to see that it has reached all the languages covered.
Ge [hɛpəniŋ] N, pl. -*s*, 1960s (1 tech)   **Du** [=E] C, 1960s, 2(1 tech) +2a(2)   **Nw** [=E] M, pl. -*er*/-*s*, 1960s (1 tech)   **Ic** [hahpening] N, pl. Ø, 1960s, 2(1 tech, arch) = creat *gjörningur*   **Fr** [ap(ə)niŋ] M, 1960s, 2,+2a(1 obs)   **Sp** [xapenin] M, pl. -*s*, 1960s, 2,+2a(1 tech>2)   **It** [(h)ɛppenin(g)] M, pl. Ø, 1960s, 2(1 tech>2); [U] +2a(1 tech)   **Rm** [hɛpəning] N, 1970s, 2(1 tech)   **Rs** *khéppening* M, pl. -*i*, 1980s (2 tech/o)

Po *heppening*/<=E> M, end20c (1 tech) → *-owy* adj.   **Cr** *hepening* M, end20c, +2a(1 tech)   **Bg** *khepüning* M, pl. *-al-i*, 1990s, 2(1 mod)   **Fi** [hæpnɪɲ/hæpnɪŋkɪ] 1980s (0)   **Hu** [=E] [U] 1960s, 2(1 tech/lit) +2a(1 mod/you)   **Al** *hepening* M, pl. *-e*, end20c, +2a(1 reg/mod)   **Gr** *khap(p)ening* N, pl. *-s*/Ø, 1990s, 2(2 mod) +2a(1 tech)

happy   *adj.* 1 'feeling or showing pleasure'
Although it can be argued that *happy-end* made the adoption of *happy* easy, the fact that it is borrowed remains striking. It clearly forms part of colloquial, informal youth language, with no specific semantic need for its adoption being apparent.

Ge [hepi] uninfl., 1970s (1 coll)   **Du** [=E] 1970s (1 coll)   **Nw** [=E] 1970s (1 coll)   **Ic** [=E] uninfl., mid20c (1 sla)   **Po** [hepi] uninfl., end20c (1 mod)   **Bg** *khepi* uninfl., end20c (1 you, sla)   **Hu** [=E] end20c (1 jour/coll/you)   **Gr** <=E>/*khapy*/-*i* end20c (1 coll, rare)

happy end*   *n.* 'a happy ending to a film, or to a potentially tragic or dangerous event'
This item has spread in its strikingly un-English form to almost all European languages (apparently a 'Hollywood' feature). Only Dutch and Norwegian have the common British English term as an alternative, obviously introduced as the 'more correct' expression.

Ge [hepi ent] N [U] mid20c (2) → *-en* v.   **Du** [=E] N, 1970s (2) > *happy ending*   **Nw** <=E>/*happy ending* [=E] M, mid20c (2)   **Ic** [=E] uninfl., mid20c (1 sla)   **Fr** [apiɛnd] M (1 fac, obs) 1940s (1)   **Sp** [xapi end] M [U] 1970s (1 tech) < *final feliz*   **It** [(h)eppi end] M, pl. Ø, 1960s (1 tech, jour>2) < *trsl lieto fine*   **Rm** [hepiend] N, 1970s (2)   **Rs** *khépiend* M [U] mid20c (2)   **Po** [hepient] M [U] mid20c (2)   **Cr** *hepiend* M [U] 20c (2)   **Bg** *khepiend* M [U] mid20c (2)   **Hu** <=E>/*hepiend* [=E] [U] beg20c (2)   **Al** *hepiend* M, pl. *-e*, 1960s (1 reg)   **Gr** *khapy*/-*i end* [ɛnd/end] N [U] mid20c, via Fr (2)

happy few   *n.pl.* 'a minority of lucky people'
Ge [=E] pl., 1960s (1 jour)   **Du** [=E] 1970s (2)   **Fr** [apifju] M, pl., beg19c (1 lit)   **Sp** [=E/xapifiu] M, pl., 1960s (1 jour)

happy hour   *n.* 'a period of the day when drinks are sold at reduced prices in bars, hotels, etc.'
Ge [=E] F, pl. *-s*, 1980s (1 mod)   **Du** [=E] N, 1980s (2)   **Nw** [=E] M, 1980s (1)   **Ic** [=E] uninfl., 1990s (0)   **Fr** (0)   **Sp** [=E/xapigu(a)r] M/F, end20c (1)   **Fi** [=E] 1990s (1)   **Gr** <=E> [xapi +E] uninfl., 1990s (1 writ, obs)

hard   *n.*/*cp*[1] +3 'a style of rock music'
Sp [xar(d)] M[U] 1980s (1 you)   **It** [=E] adj., uninfl., 1980s (1 tech) < *trsl rock duro, hard rock*   **Rm** [=E] N [U] end20c (1 you, mod)   **Rs** *khard* M [U] 1990s (1 you)   **Po** - < *hard rock*   **Cr** (0)   **Bg** *khard* M [U]

1990s (1 tech, you)   **Hu** [ha:rd] cp[1] [U] 1980s (2 tech, you) < *kemény (rock)*

hard   *adj.* 6 'harsh, unpleasant', 8b 'potent and addictive' (of drugs), 8d 'highly obscene and explicit' (of pornography)
Ge - < 8b: mean *hart*   **Du** <=E> [ha:t] 1970s, 8b(2)   **Nw** (5)   **Fr** [aʀd] adj./M, 1970s, 8b,d(1 sla)   **Sp** [=E] end20c, 8d(1 tech/jour)   **It** [(h)ard] 1970s, 8d(1 tech)   **Bg** *khard* uninfl., 1990s, 8d(1>2 sla)   **Gr** - < mean *skliros*

hard cash   *n.* 'negotiable coins and banknotes'
Nw [=E] uninfl., 1960s (1 tech)

hard copy   *n.* 'printed material produced by a computer'
Ge [=E] F, pl. *-(ie)s*, 1980s (1 tech)   **Fr** (1 tech, ban) > *tacsim, tirage*   **It** [(h)ardkopi] F, pl. Ø, 1980s (1 tech)   **Rm** rend *copie hard* 20c (1 tech)   **Bg** (0>1 tech, sla)   **Fi** [=E] 1990s (1 tech) < *printti*   **Hu** [=E/ha:rd-] pl. Ø, 1980s (1 tech)   **Al** [=E] pl. Ø, 1980s (1 tech)   **Gr** <=E> [=E] N, pl. *-ies*, 1990s (1 tech) > *ektypomeno adighrafo*

hard core   *n.* 1 'an irreducible nucleus', 4 'popular music, experimental in nature and usu. characterized by high volume and aggressive presentation', +5 'a type of hiphop dance music'
Du [=E] C, 1980s, 4(1 sla, you)   **Nw** [=E] M [U] 1980s, 4(1 tech)   **Ic** [=E] N [U] 1980s, 4(1 sla) +5(1 sla, you)   **Fr** [ardkoʀ] M, 1970s, 4(1 tech/you) → *hard* adj.   **Sp** [=E/xarkor] 1980s, 1,4 (1 tech/jour)   **It** [(h)ard kɔr] F [U] 1970s, 1(1 tech) 4(1 tech)   **Rs** *khardkor* M [U] 1990s 4(1 you/o)   **Po** [hardkor] [U] end20c (1 tech)   **Bg** *khardkor* uninfl., M [U] 1990s, 4(1 tech)   **Gr** *khard kor*/<=E> F, 1980s, 4(1 you)

hard-core   *adj.* (usu. *cp*[1]) 2 'blatant, uncompromising' (of music), 3 'explicit, obscene' (of pornography)
Ge [=E] cp[1], 1970s, 3(1 tech, rare)   **Nw** [=E] cp[1], 1980s, 2,3(1 tech)   **Ic** [=E] adj., uninfl., 1980s (1 sla)   **Fr** [ardkor] M, 1970s, 3(1 tech/you?) → *hard* adj.   **Sp** [=E/xarkor] 1980s, 3(1 tech, jour)   **It** [(h)ard kɔr] 1970s, 3(1)   **Po** [hardkor] uninfl., end20c (1 tech)   **Cr** *hardkor* 1990s, 3(1 tech)   **Bg** *khardkor*/*khard* end20c, 2(1 tech/you)   **Gr** <=E> [=E] 2(1 tech)

hardcover   *adj./n.* (esp. N. Amer.) '(a book) bound in stiff covers'
Ge [=E] N, pl. *-s*, 1960s (1 tech, rare)   **Nw** [=E] cp[1] M, end20c (1 tech)   **Sp** - < rend *libro de tapa dura*   **It** *hard-cover* [(h)ardkover] M, pl. Ø, 1980s (1 tech)   **Rm** - < *hardback* [=E] 1970s (1 tech, rare)   **Fi** - < *trsl kovakantinen*

hard discount*   *n.* 'a supermarket selling goods at less than normal retail price'
Fr [ardiskunt] M, 1980s (1 tech, ban) > *maxidiscompte*   **It** [=E] M, pl. Ø, 1990s (1)

hard disk   *n.* 'a rigid magnetic storage disk'
Ge [=E] F, pl. *-s*, 1980s (1 tech) < *Festplatte*   **Du** C,

1980s (1 tech) < *harde schijf* **Nw** *harddisk* [=E] M, pl. -*er*, 1980s (2 tech) **Ic** - < trsl *harður diskur* **Fr** - < trsl *disque dur* **Sp** - < trsl *disco duro* **It** [(h)a̱rdisk] M, pl. Ø, 1970s (1 tech) = rend *disco fisso, disco rigido* **Rm** <=E>/*hard disc* [=E] N, 1980s (1 tech) **Rs** - < *zhëstkii disk* **Po** - < *twardy dysk* **Cr** *hard di̱sk* M, pl. -*ovi*, end20c (1 tech) **Bg** *kha̱rd disk* M, pl. -*a*/- *ove*, end20c (1 tech) = trsl *tvŭrd disk* (5+4) **Fi** [=E] 1980s (1 tech) < trsl *kovalevy* **Hu** <=E>/*ha̱rd diszk* [=E] pl. -*ek*, 1970s (1 tech) **Gr** (0) < trsl *skliros dhiskos*

hard facts *n.* 'the naked truth'
Ge (0) **Du** 1990s (1 jour) < *harde feiten* **Nw** [=E] uninfl., end20c (1)

hardliner *n.* 'an uncompromising politician'
  This political term, in frequent use in American English from the 1970s, has had surprisingly little impact on European languages; the pattern of those in which it is attested is unique.
Ge [=E] M, pl. Ø, 1980s (1 jour) **Nw** [=E] M, pl. -*e*, 1980s (1 jour, rare) **Ic** - < *harðlínu-maður* **Rm** [=E] M, 1990s (1 jour) **Rs** *kha̱rdlaĭner* M, pl. -*y*, 1990s (1 tech, jour) **Cr** *hardlaj̱-ner* M, pl. -*i*, end20c (1 tech) **Bg** *kha̱rdlaĭner* M, pl. -*i*, 1990s (2 jour)

hard porno* *n.* 'explicit, brutal pornography'
  Whereas *porno* is an internationalism, *hard* identifies the expression as English. This element is often translated, but retained in many languages, apparently because the antonymic pair *hard* vs. *soft* is known from many other combinations.
Ge [=E] M, pl. -*s*, 1980s (1 mod) < trsl *harter Porno* **Du** [=E] C [U] 1980s (1 tech) **Nw** *hard-porno* (5Nw+5) **Fr** *hard porno* [aʀd pɔʀnɔ] adj., 1970s (1) **Sp** - < trsl *porno duro* **It** [(h)a̱rd po̱rno] F [U] 1970s (1) **Rm** [ha̱rd po̱rno] N, end20c (0) **Rs** *khard po̱rno* N, uninfl., end20c (1 mod) **Po** [hart porno] N, uninfl., end20c (2 coll) **Cr** *hard porno* M [U] end20c (2 coll) **Bg** *khard(porno)* N [U] end20c (2 coll) < trsl *tvŭrdo por-no* **Fi** [=E] 1980s (0) **Hu** - < trsl *keménypornó* **Gr** - < trsl *skliró porno*

hard rock *n.* 'a music style'
Ge [=E] M [U] 1970s (1 tech) **Du** *hardrock* [=E] C [U] 1970s (1 tech) **Nw** [=E] M [U] end20c (5+1) **Ic** <=E>/*ha̱rt rokk* [=E/ha̱rt rɔhk] N [U] end20c (1 tech)/ (5+3) **Fr** [aʀdʀɔk] M, 1970s (1) **Sp** [=E/xard rok] M [U] 1980s (1 tech) = trsl *rock duro* **It** [(h)a̱rd rɔk] M, 1970s (1 tech) = *rock duro* **Rm** [=E] N [U] 1970s (1 tech/you) **Rs** *kha̱rd ro̱k* M [U] end20c (1 tech) **Po** [hart-] M [U] end20c (1 coll) **Cr** *ha̱rdro̱k* [hardro:k] M [U] end20c (1 tech) **Bg** *kha̱rd ro̱k* M [U] end20c (1 tech) = trsl *tvŭrd rok* (5+2) **Fi** [=E] 1970s (1 tech) **Hu** [ha̱rdrokk] [U] 1970s (1 tech/you) = trsl *kemény rock* **Gr** *kha̱rd ro̱k* F/N [U] 1970s (1 tech)

hard-top *n.* 'a cabriolet with a rigid, detachable roof rather than a folding top'
  The distribution shows a neat contrast between the North-west and the South and East – with a few noteworthy exceptions. The difference is partly explained by the fact that in Eastern Europe (practically) *all* cars had hard tops. The word is occasionally also used for the entire sports car (German).
Ge [=E] M/N, pl. -*s*, 1950s (1 tech) **Du** [=E] (1 tech) **Nw** [=E] cp¹/M, 1950s (1 tech) **Ic** [=E] mid/end20c (1 tech) < trsl *harðtoppur* **Fr** (0) **It** [(h)a̱rd-tɔp] M, pl. Ø, 1960s (1 tech) **Rm** [ha̱rdtop] N, 1970s (1 tech, rare) **Gr** *kha̱rdtop* N, pl. -*s*, end20c (1 tech)

hardware *n.* 3 'the mechanical and electronic components of a computer'
  As with other computer terms, acceptance of this English term is not universal. There are many calques and paraphrases, and the French equivalent is indeed likely to push out *hardware* (as has practically happened in the case of *computer*).
Ge [ha̱rtveːr] F [U] 1960s (1 tech) **Du** [=E] C [U] 1970s (1 tech) **Nw** [=E] M [U] 1960s (1 tech) < rend *maskinvare* **Ic** [=E] N, 1980s (0 tech) < rend *vélbún-aður* **Fr** [ardwɛːʀ] M, 1960s (1 sla, ban, obs) < rend *matériel* **Sp** [xa̱rwer/xa̱rwar] M [U] 1980s (1 tech) > rend *material soporte fisico; equipo* **It** [(h)a̱rdwer] M [U] 1970s (2 tech) > *architettura* **Rm** [=E] N [U] 1970s (1 tech) = *hard* → *hardist* M **Rs** *khard-ver* M [U] end20c (1 tech) **Po** [hardwer] M [U] end20c (1 tech) → -*owy* adj. **Cr** *ha̱rdver* M [U] end20c (1 tech) → -*ski* adj. **Bg** *kha̱rduer* M [U] end20c (1 tech); *khard* (1 tech, sla) → -*en* adj. **Fi** [=E] (0) **Hu** *hardver* [hard-ver] pl. -*ek*, 1970s (1 tech > 2 tech) **Gr** <=E>/*kha̱rd-ghuer* N [U] end20c (1 tech)

harrier *n.* 1a 'a dog used for hunting hares'
Du [=E] M, 1970s (1 tech) **Fr** [aʀje] M, 16c (1 tech) **It** [(h)e̱rier] M, pl. Ø, 1950s (1 tech) **Bg** *khar-ier* M, pl. -*al-i*, 20c (1 tech)

Harris tweed *n.* 'a kind of tweed woven by hand on Harris'
Ge (Ø) **Du** (Ø) **Nw** [=E] M [U] 1980s (1 tech) **Ic** [=E] N [U] 20c (1 tech) **Sp** <=E>/*Harris* [=E] M, end20c (1 tech) **It** [(h)e̱rristuiːd] M [U] 1980s (1 tech)

has-been *n.* 'a formerly famous personality'
Du [=E] 1990s (1 jour, mod) **Fr** [azbin] M, 1930s (1 ban) < *fini* **Rs** *khés-bin* M [U] 1990s (1 jour, rare)

hash (2) *n.* 'hashish'
Ge *Hasch* (5Arab) **Du** *hasj* (5Arab) **Nw** *hasj* (5Arab) **Ic** *hass* [hasː] N [U] 1960s (2 tech) → *hassisti* N **Fr** *hasch* [aʃ] M [U] end20c (1) **Sp** <=E>/*has(s)*, *hasch* [xaʃ/xas] M [U] 1980s (1 you) **Po** [=E] M, end20c (1 sla) **Cr** (0) **Al** - < *hashish*

hatchback *n.* 'a car with a sloping back'

The limited currency of this term is remarkable considering the impact of English on modern car terminology. It remains uncertain how far the respective fashion, or the term, has managed to reach the individual communities.

Ge (o) < *Liftback* **Du** [=E] C, 1980s (1 tech) **Nw** (o) **Ic** [=E] 1980s (o tech) = rend *hlaðbakur* **Fr** [atʃbak] (1 tech, ban) < *bicorps* **Rs** *khetchbek*, pl. *-i*, end20c (1 tech, jour) **Po** [hetch-bek] M, end20c (1 jour) **Bg** *khechbek* M, pl. *-a*, 1990s (1 tech/rare) **Fi** [=E] (o) **Gr** <=E>/*khatsbak* N, end20c (1 tech)

hat-trick *n.* 2a 'the scoring of three goals in a single match' (mainly in football)
Ge [hetrik] M, pl. *-s*, 1960s (1 tech) **Du** *hattrick* [=E] C, 1970s (1 tech) **Nw** [=E/hatrik] N, pl. Ø, mid20c (2) **Ic** [hah-trıhk] N, pl. Ø, end20c (1 sla_FOOTB) < rend *prenna* **Fr** [atrik] (1 tech, ban) > *coup de chapeau* **Sp** [xatrik] M, end20c (1 tech) **It** [(h)etrik] M, pl. Ø, end20c (1 tech, jour) < *tripletta* **Rm** [hetrik] N, 1960s (2 tech_FOOTB) **Rs** *khettrik* M, pl. *-i*, end20c (1 tech) **Po** [hat-] M, mid20c (1 tech) **Cr** *het-trik* M, mid20c (1 tech) **Bg** *khettrik* M, pl. *-al-ove*, end20c (1 tech) **Hu** [=E] [U] 1970s (1 tech) **Gr** *khat trik* N, 20c (1 tech)

havelock* *n.* 'a sleeveless coat for men'
This term derives from the name of a nineteenth-century British major-general in India; it spread with other names of clothes to Central Europe, where it has long since been obsolete, as indeed in Britain (surviving mainly in the USA)

Ge [havəlok] M, pl. *-s*, mid19c (1 arch) **Du** [=E] C, beg20c (1 arch) **Nw** [=E] M, pl. *-er*, 19c (1 arch) **Ic** *havelock* [ha:velɔhk] M, pl. *-ar*, beg20c, via **Da** (1 arch) **Po** *hawelok* [havelɔk] M, beg20c (1 arch) **Hu** [hevlɔk] pl. Ø, end19c/beg20c, via **Ge** (1 arch)

head *n.* +24 'a cylinder head in a motor car'
Ge (o arch) **Ic** *hedd* [=E] N, pl. Ø, beg20c (2 tech) = *strokklok* **Sp** - < *cabecar* **Po** - < *główkować* **Bg** - < mean *glava*

head *v.* 5 'strike with the head' (footb.)
Ge - < mean *köpfen* **Du** - < *inkoppen* **Nw** *heade* ["hede] beg20c (2) → *heading* **Ic** - < *skalla* **Fr** - < *marquer de la tête* **It** - < creat *colpire di testa* **Rm** - < *lovi cu capul* **Hu** - < *fej* **Al** - < *gjuoj me kokë*

head-bang *v.* 'shake the body, esp. the head and torso, violently to hard rock music'
Ge *headbangen* [=E] 1980s (1 you) **Du** *headbangen* [=E] 1980s (1 sla) **Nw** *headbange* [hedbæŋe] 1980s (1 you, rare) **Ic** *heddbanka* [hɛt:pauŋka] 1980s (1 sla) = rend *flösupeyta*

headbanger *n.* 1 'a young person shaking violently to the rhythm of pop music'
Ge [=E] M, pl. Ø/-*s*, 1980s (1 you) **Du** [=E] C, pl. *-s*, 1980s (1 you) **Nw** [=E] M, pl. *-el- s*, 1980s (1 tech, you, obs)

headbanging *n.* 1 'violent shaking of the head, esp. by young music fans'
Ge [=E] [U] 1980s (1 you) **Du** [=E] N [U] 1980s (1 you) **Gr** *head-banging* 1980s (1 you)

header *n.* +5 'a reaping machine'
Rs *kheder* M, pl. *-y*, mid20c (1 tech) **Bg** *kheder* M, pl. *-al-i*, mid20c (1 tech)

headhunt *v.* 'fill a business position by approaching a suitable person employed elsewhere'
Nw *head-hunte* [hedhønte] 1980s (2) > trsl *hodejakte* **Po** (o)

headhunter *n.* 'a person who tries to find suitable persons for filling business positions'
The original, literal meaning of this term is commonly represented by calques (e.g. German *Kopfjäger*), while the modern metaphorical extension to personnel recruitment is still restricted to a few West European languages. The term for the activity (*-ing*) has a similar distribution, but the verb is notably rarer.

Ge [hethanta] M, pl. Ø, 1980s (1 mod) < trsl *Kopfjäger* **Du** [=E] C, 1970s (2) **Nw** [=E] M, pl. *-e*, 1980s (2) = trsl *hodejeger* **Fr** - < trsl *chasseur de têtes* **Sp** [xed xanter] M, pl. *-s*, 1980s (1 tech) = rend *cazatalentos* **It** - < trsl *cacciatore di teste* **Po** [headhanter] M, 1980s (1 mod) **Hu** - < trsl *fejvadász*

headhunting *n.* 2 'the practice of filling a business position by approaching a suitable person employed elsewhere'
Ge [hethantin] N [U] 1980s (1 mod) **Nw** [=E] M/F [U] 1980s (2) > trsl *hodejakt* **Sp** [=E] M [U] end20c (1 tech/jour) = rend *caza de talentos* **Po** [-nk] M, end20c (1 mod) **Hu** - < trsl *fejvadászat* **Gr** - < rend *kynighi teledon*

heading¹ (1) *n.* 1a 'a title at the head of a page etc.'
Du - < *kop* **Nw** [=E] M/F, pl. *-er*, 1960s (1) < *overskrift* **Sp** - < *encabezmiento* **It** - < creat *intestazione* **Al** - < *lajmet kryesore*

heading² *n.* 'a goal scored with the head' (footb.)
Nw ["hediŋ] M/F, pl. *-er*, beg20c (2) **Rm** [=E] N, 1970s (1 tech, rare) **Po** - < *giòwka*

headline *n.* 1 'a heading at the top of an article or page, esp. in a newspaper'
Ge [=E] F, pl. *-s*, 1960s (1 jour) < *Schlagzeile* **Du** 1940s (2) **Nw** (o) < *overskrift* **Ic** - < *fyrirsögn* **Fr** <=E> 20c (1 ban) < *titre* (advertisement) **It** [(h)edlain] M/F, pl. Ø, 1970s (1 tech) < creat *testata, titolo* **Rm** [=E] 1990s (o coll) **Rs** *khedlaĭn* M, pl. *-y*, 1995 (1 euph) < creat *broskiĭ zagolovok*

headliner *n.* (US) 'a star performer'
Bg *khedlaĭner* M, pl. *-i*, 1990s (1 jour, mod)

headphone *n.* 'a pair of earphones joined by a band placed over the head, for listening to audio equipment, etc.'
Du - < *koptelefoon* **Nw** - < *hodetelefoner, øretelefoner* **Ic** *heddfónn* [hɛt:foutn] M, pl. *-fónar*, 1970s (1 coll) = *heyrnartól*

headset *n.* 'a set of headphones'
Ge - < *Kopfhörer* **Du** - < *koptelefoon* **Nw** [=E] N, pl. Ø, 1980s (1) < *hodetelefoner, øretelefoner*

heal *v.* 2 'cause to heal or be healed (by prayer, touching, etc.)'
Nw *heale* ["hi̞:le] 1980s (2 coll) = *helbrede (ved håndspåleggelse)* **Ic** - < creat *heila*

healer *n.* +1a 'a doctor without academic training'
Nw [=E] M, pl. *-e*, 1980s (2) = *håndspålegger* **Ic** - < trsl *heilari* **Rs** *khi̞ler* M, pl. *-y*, 1980s (2 coll, mod) **Po** [hiler] M, end20c (2 coll, mod)

healing *n.* 'the act or activity of healing (by prayer, laying on hands, etc.)'
Du [=E] C, 1990s (1 mod) **Nw** [=E] M/F [U] 1980s (2) = *håndspåleggls* **Ic** - < trsl *heilun*

hearing *n.* 4 'the process of listening to evidence and pleadings in a law court'
The distribution of this term is restricted by the fact that Germanic languages easily produce calques, and that there was no need for such a term in Eastern European countries, the concept not existing in the form of parliamentary system used. It will be interesting to see whether political changes will cause an expansion of the concept and/or the loanword.
Ge [=E] N, pl. *-s*, 1960s (1 tech) < *Anhörung* **Du** [=E] C, 1960s (1 tech) **Nw** [=E] M, pl. *-er*, 1960s (1 obs) < trsl *høring* **Fr** [iʀiŋ] M, 1980s (1 tech, ban) < *audition publique* **It** [(h)i̞riŋg] M, pl. Ø, 1970s (1 tech, jour) < *udienza* **Po** - < *przesłuchanie* **Gr** - < *akroasi*

heat *n.* 6 'a round in a race or contest'
Ge (0 arch) **Du** [=E] C, 1970s (1 tech) **Nw** [=E] N, pl. Ø, mid20c (2 tech) **Rs** *git* M, pl. *-y*, mid20c (1 tech)

heave *v.* 1 'lift or haul (a heavy thing) with great effort' (naut.) 5 'haul by rope' (naut.)
Ge *hieven* [hi:vən/hi:fən] beg19c (3) **Nw** *hive* ["hi̞:ve] 19c, 5(4) **Ic** *hifa* [hi:va] beg20c, via Da(3) **Po** *hiw* M, mid20c, 1(1 tech)

heavy *n.* +6 'heavy metal music, heavy rock'
Nw [=E] M [U] 1980s (1 tech) **Sp** [=E/xe̞bi] M, pl. *-s*, 1980s (1 you) **Rm** [=E] N [U] 1990s (1 coll, you) **Rs** (0) **Po** N [U] end20c (1 tech) **Fi** [=E] (1 tech)

heavy *adj.* 4 'severe, intense, extensive, e.g. *heavy fighting*', 5 'doing something to excess, e.g. *heavy drinker*', 13a,b 'serious or sombre in tone or attitude; dull, tedious' (of a person, writing, music, etc.), 14b 'hard to read or understand' (of a literary work, etc.), 18 'hard to endure, oppressive', +20 'cool, groovy', +21 'bumptious', +22 'hard' (of liquor, drugs)

Ge [=E] 1980s, 18(1 you, rare) **Du** [=E] 1980s, 18(1 you) **Nw** [=E] end20c, 13a,b, 18,+20(1 sla) **Ic** [hɛ:vi/hɛv:i] 1970s, 4,5,13a,b, 14b,+20(1 sla) **Sp** [=E/xe̞bi] 1980s, 4,5,+20(1 sla) **Rs** (0) **Bg** *khe̞vi* uninfl., 1990s, +21, +22(1 sla, you)

heavy metal *n.* 3 'highly-amplified rock music with a strong beat'
The ubiquitousness of this term reflects the internationality of modern pop music which no longer has political boundaries to overcome; the modern appeal of the term does not permit calques either.
Ge [=E] M/N [U] 1980s (1 tech, you) **Du** [=E] C [U] 1980s (1 tech, you) **Nw** [=E] M [U] 1980s (1 tech) **Ic** [=E] N/*-metall* [me:tatl] M [U] 1970s (1 tech) < rend *þungarokk, bárujárnsrokk* **Fr** <=E> M, 1980s (1 tech, you) **Sp** [=E] M [U] 1980s (1 tech, you) → *heavy-metalero* **It** [(h)e̞vi me̞tal] M [U] 1980s (1 tech) **Rm** [=E] N [U] end20c (1 tech, you) **Rs** *khe̞vi me̞tal* M [U] end20c (1 coll) **Po** [- -al] M [U] end20c, 3(1 coll) → *-owy* adj. **Cr** [hevimetal] M [U] end20c, 3(1 tech) **Bg** *(khe̞vi)me̞tŭl* M [U] end20c (1 tech/you) **Fi** [=E] 1980s, 3(1 tech, you) **Hu** [=E] [U] 1960s, 3(1 tech>2 tech/you) **Gr** *khe̞vi me̞tal* F/N [U] 1980s (1 tech, you)

heavy rock* *n.* 'loud and highly-amplified rock music'
Ge [=E] M [U] 1970s (0>1 you) < *Hardrock* **Nw** [=E] M [U] end20c (1 tech) = trsl *tungrock, hardrock* → *heavy rocker* M **Ic** [=E] N [U] 1970s (1 tech) < creat *þungarokk* **Fr** [e̞vɪrɔk] M, 1980s (1 tech, you) **Sp** [=E] M [U] 1980s (1 tech, you) **It** [(h)e̞vi rɔk] M [U] end20c (1 tech) **Rm** [=E] N [U] 1980s (1 tech, you) **Rs** *khe̞vi rok* M [U] end20c (1 tech, you) **Po** M [U] end20c (1 tech) **Bg** *khe̞vi rok* M [U] end20c (1 tech) **Fi** [=E] 1980s (1 tech, you) **Hu** - < trsl *kemény rock* **Gr** <=E>/*khe̞vi rok* F/N [U] (1 tech)

heliport *n.* 'a place where helicopters take off and land'
This modern blend is more restricted as an anglicism than the data suggest; in Romance languages the second element is identified with native equivalents (the first part is Greek anyway), so that the status of the word as an anglicism is uncertain.
Ge [he̞liport] M, pl. *-s*, 1970s (1 mod, rare) **Du** [he̞li:po:rt] C, 1980s (1 tech, coll) = *helihaven* **Nw** [=E] M, pl. *-er*, 1950s (1 tech) **Fr** *héliport* [elipɔʀ] M, 1960s (2) **Sp** *helipuerto* M, 1960s (3) **It** *eliporto* M, pl. *-i*, 1950s (3 tech) **Rm** *(h)eliport* [(h)elipo̞rt] N, 1960s, via Fr (3 tech) **Cr** *he̞liport* M, end20c (1 tech) **Hu** [he̞liport] 1970s (1 tech, mod, rare)

hello *interj.* 1a 'an expression of informal greeting'
Ge - < *hallo* **Nw** - < *hallo* **Ic** - < *halló* **Fr** [ɛllo]

he-man

end19c (1 coll) < *allo* **It** [ell<u>o</u>] end20c (1 mod) **Rm** [=E/*helo*] [h<u>e</u>lo] 20c (3 coll, you) **Rs** *khel<u>o</u>u* mid20c (1 you, mod) **Po** - < *halo* **Hu** [=E] 20c (2<3 coll, you, mod)

he-man *n.* 1 'a virile man', +2 'the name of a cartoon character'

Although this term was adopted some forty years ago in the Germanic languages, its status has remained very marginal (note the absence in the East) – it may in fact be obsolescent today and this indicates that it is unlikely to spread.

Ge [hi̱:men] M, pl. *-men*, 1960s, +2(1 coll, rare) **Du** [=E] C, 1950s (2) **Nw** [=E] M, pl. *-men*, 1950s, 1(1) **Ic** [=E] M [U] 1980s, +2(1 you, obs) **It** [i̱men] M, 1990s, +2(1)

hemlock *n./cp¹* 2b 'timber of the hemlock fir'
Ge *Hemlock(tanne)* cp¹, beg20c (3 tech, rare) **Fr** [ɛml<u>ɔ</u>k] M, 19c (1 tech) < *pin canadien* **It** [(h)eml<u>ɔ</u>k] M, pl. Ø, 1950s (1 tech) **Rs** *geml<u>o</u>k* M [U] mid20c (1 tech)

henry *n.* 'a unit of inductance' (electr.)
The American meterologist Joseph Henry (1797–1878) discovered the method of producing induced current, so that the unit is aptly named after him.
Ge [=E] N, pl. Ø, 1940s (1 tech) **Du** [=E] C, pl. *-'s*, 1940s (1 tech) **Nw** [=E] M, pl. Ø, 20c (1 tech) **Ic** [=E] N, pl. Ø, 20c (1 tech) **Fr** [ãri] M, beg20c (3 tech) **Sp** <=E>/*henrio* [(h)<u>e</u>nri] M, pl. *-s*, 20c (1 tech) **It** [(h)<u>e</u>nri] M, pl. Ø, 1900s (1 tech) **Rm** <=E>/*henri* [=E] M, pl. Ø, beg20c, via Fr? (1 tech) **Rs** *g<u>e</u>nri* M, uninfl., mid20c (1 tech) **Po** *henri*<=E> M, mid20c (1 tech) **Cr** *h<u>e</u>nri* M, pl. Ø, mid20c (1 tech) **Bg** *kh<u>e</u>nri* M, pl. Ø, mid20c (1 tech) **Fi** (1 tech) **Hu** [=E] pl. Ø, end19c/beg20c (3 tech) **Al** *henri* M, pl. Ø, 1930s (1 tech) **Gr** [=E] N (1 tech)

herd book *n.* 'a book recording the pedigrees of cattle or pigs'
Ge - < trsl *Herdbuch* **Du** - < *herdboek* < *stamboek* **Fr** [ɛrdbuk] M, mid19c (1 tech) **Rm** [h<u>e</u>rd buk] N, 1930s (1 tech, rare)

hesitation *n.* +2 'a kind of slow waltz'
Fr *valse hésitation* (5) **It** [(h)eziteiʃon] M [U] 1920s (1 tech, obs)

hi *interj.* 'calling attention or as a greeting'
Ge [hai] end20c (1 coll) **Du** [=E] 1980s (2) **Nw** *hei* [hæɪ] (5) **Ic** *hæ* [=E] mid20c (3 coll) **Rm** (0) **Rs** *khaĭ* end20c (1 you, coll) **Po** end20c (1 coll) **Bg** *khaĭ* end20c (1 sla, you) **Al** *hej* end20c **Gr** (0)

hickory *n.* 1 'any North American tree of the genus Carya', 2a 'the wood of these trees', +3 'skis' (formerly made from hickory wood)
Ge [hi̱kori] M/F, pl. *-s*, 19c, 1(3 tech); N [U] 19c, 2a(3 tech) **Du** [=E] C, 1970s, 2a(1 tech) **Nw** [hi̱kuri:] M [U] beg20c, 2a(3) **Ic** *hikkorí(a)* [hhkori(ja)] N/F/(cp¹) pl. Ø/*-ur*, 19c, via Da, 1,2a(2 tech) **Fr** [ik<u>ɔ</u>ri] M, 18c, 2a(2 tech) **Sp** [i̱kori] M, 1(2<3 tech) = *mogal*

americano, caria **It** <=E>/*hickorá* [(h)i̱kori] M, pl. Ø, 1930s, 2a(1 tech) **Rm** *hickori* [=E] M, uninfl., 1940s, via Fr, 1,2a(3 tech) **Rs** *gik<u>o</u>ri* uninfl., beg20c (1 tech, arch) **Po** *hikora* F, beg20c, 2a(2); *hikory* beg20c, +3(1 arch) **Cr** *h<u>i</u>kori* M [U] beg20c, 2a(3) **Bg** *khi̱kori* N [U] mid20c, 2a(Ø) **Fi** *hickory/hikkori* beg20c, 2a(Ø) **Hu** *h<u>i</u>kory*/<hikori> [=E] [U] end19c/ beg20c, 1,2a(1 tech)

hi-fi *cp¹/²/n.* 'high-fidelity'
Although the abbreviated form is opaque, it has been much more widely adopted than ↑*high fidelity*, apparently because it is more economical. By contrast, the long form is a basis for calques in various (Romance) languages.
Ge [haifi] N [U] 1960s (1 tech) > *high fidelity* **Du** [haifai] 1960s (1 tech) **Nw** [=E] M, pl. *-er*, 1950s (1 tech) **Ic** [=E] mid/ end20c (1 tech) **Fr** *hi-fi* [ifi] F/ adj., uninfl., 1950s (1 tech) = trsl *haute-fidélité* **Sp** <=E>/*hifi Hi-Fi* [ifi] M/cp², uninfl., 1960s (2 tech) > trsl *alta fidelidad* **It** [(h)aifai] cp²/M, pl. Ø, 1960s (2 tech) > trsl *alta fedeltà* **Rm** [ha̱jfi/=E/hi̱fi] uninfl., 1970s (1 tech) > *high fidelity* **Rs** *khaĭ faĭ* N, uninfl., end20c (1 tech) **Po** [haifi] N, uninfl., mid20c (1 tech, coll) **Cr** *haifi* M [U] mid20c (1 tech) **Bg** *khaĭfi* uninfl., end20c, via Ge (3 tech, mod) **Fi** [hifi] 20c (2) **Hu** [hi̱fi] 1970s (3) **Gr** *khaĭ faĭ* N, mid20c (1 tech)

high *adj.* 8 'intoxicated by alcohol or drugs', +8a 'elated', +14 'in style'
This word shows the expected currency: distribution in North and West Europe as against the absence in the South and East. No calques appear to have been created (although words like the compound *Hochgefühl* exist in German).
Ge [=E] pred., 1970s, 8,+8a(1 coll) **Du** [=E] 1960s (1 coll) **Nw** [=E] 1970s, 8(1 sla, rare) < *høy* **Ic** [=E] 1970s, 8(1 sla) **Po** [=E] uninfl., end20c, 8,+8a(1 coll) **Cr** (0) **Bg** *khaĭ* pred., uninfl., 1990s, +14(1 sla, you) **Gr** *khaĭ* (uninfl.) 1990s, 8(1 sla) +8a(2 coll) +14(1 coll)

high *n.* 3 'a euphoric state, esp. drug- induced; +7 'high society'
Ge [=E] N, pl. *-s*, 1970s, 3(1 sla, rare) **Ic** [=E] N, pl. Ø, 1970s, 3(1 sla) **Sp** [xa̱j] M, 1980s, 3(1 sla, rare); F, 1980s, +7(1 sla) < +7: rend *subida/subidón* **Po** [=E] M [U] end20c, 3(1 coll)

highball *n.* 1 'a drink of spirits and soda'
Ge [=E] M, pl. *-s*, 1960s (0>1 rare) **Du** [=E] C, 1970s (2) **Fr** (0 obs) **Sp** [=E/xa̱ibol] M, pl. Ø, 1970s (1 tech, rare/obs) **It** [(h)a̱ibɔ:l] M, pl. Ø, 1960s (1 tech)

highbrow *cp¹* 'intellectual'
Ge [ha̱ibro:] M, pl. *-s*, 1960s (1 coll) **Du** *high brow* [=E] C, 1970s (1 coll) **Nw** [=E] 20c (1) **Sp** - < rend *(gente de) ceja alta* **Rs** *khaĭbrau* M, uninfl., end20c (1 coll, fac) **Po** (0)

high fidelity *n.* 'the reproduction of sound with little distortion' (cf. ↑*hifi*)

Ge [=E] F [U] 1960s (1 tech, obs) < *hifi* **Du** [=E] 1970s (1 tech, rare) < *hifi* **Nw** [=E] M [U] 1950s (1 tech, rare) < *hifi* **Fr** - < trsl *haute-fidélité* **Sp** - < trsl *alta fidelidad* **It** [(h)ai fidelíti] F [U] 1960s (1 tech) < trsl *alta fedeltà* **Rm** [=E] uninfl., 1970s (1 tech) < *hifi* **Po** [=E] N [U] end20c (1 tech) **Cr** [=E] M [U] mid20c (1 tech) **Hu** [hai fidelity] [U] 1970s (1 tech, rare) < *hifi* **Gr** - < trsl *ypsili pistotita*

high hat *n.* 2 'a pair of foot-operated cymbals' (mus.) **Ge** [=E] M, pl. *-s*, 20c (1 tech) **Nw** [=E] M, pl. *-er*, mid20c (1 tech) **Ic** <=E>+*hattur* [=E/hai:] M, pl. *-ar*, 1940s (1 tech(+5)) **It** [=E] M, pl. Ø, 20c (1 tech) **Rm** [=E] N, 20c, 2(1 tech) **Fi** *hi-hat* [=E/hihat] 20c (1 tech)

high life *n.* 1 'the glamorous life of the upper classes', +2 'high society', +2a 'a member of the high society', +3 'high jinks'

Of all the *high* compounds this is the earliest and most widespread loanword; it is so early that the *written* form was adopted in French. Note the 'confusion' with *high society*.

Ge [=E] N [U] 19c, 1(1 coll); 1970s, +3(1 you) **Du** [=E] N [U] beg20c 1,+2,+3(2) **Nw** [=E] [U] mid19c, 1(1 obs) **Fr** [iglif] beg19c, 1,+2,+3(1 obs) **Sp** [=E/xili] F [U] end19c, 1,+2, +3(1 obs) **It** [(h)ai laif] F [U]

end19c, 1,+2(1) < creat *bel mondo, alta società* **Rm** [=E] N [U] beg20c, 1,+2(1) **Rs** *khai laif* M, uninfl., end20c, 1,+2,+3(1 fac) → *-ist* M; *-istka* F **Po** <=E> M [U] beg20c, 1,+2(1 coll) **Cr** [=E] M [U] beg20c, 1(1 coll) **Bg** *khailaif* M [U] beg20c, +2(2); M, pl. *-i*, 1990s, +2a(1 mod) → *-en* adj.; *-adzhiya* M; *-adzhiiski* adj.; *laifka* F **Hu** [=E] [U] end19c, 1(writ, jour, arch) **Gr** *hai laif* F/N [U] end20c, 1(2 coll)

highlight *n.* 2 'an outstanding feature'

This word shows a typical northwestern distribution. All languages have a native equivalent, thus the adoption is determined by stylistic factors, mainly in colloquial/journalistic registers.

Ge [=E] N, pl. *-s*, 1970s (1 mod) < *Höhepunkt* **Du** [=E] C, 1980s (2) = *hoogtepunt* **Nw** [=E] 20c (1 tech) < *hoydepunkt* **Ic** [hai:lait(s)] N, pl. Ø, end20c (1 sla) **Fi** <=E>/*hailaits* [=E] (o) **Gr** <=E>/*khailait* N, pl. *-s*, 1990s (1 mod)

high-riser* *n.* 'a bicycle with high handlebars and a saddle with a high back'
Ge [=E] M, pl. Ø, 1970s (1 obs)

high society *n.* 'the upper crust'
Since this word is a post-1945 adoption, it is notably absent in Eastern Europe (contrast ↑*highlife*). The term partly replaced synonymous French terms, as it did in German. Note the frequency of calques.

Ge [=E] F [U] 1950s (1 mod) > *haute volée* **Du** [=E] C [U] 1980s (2) **Nw** [=E] M [U] 20c (1) **Ic** [=E] N [U] mid20c (1 sla) **Fr** - < *haute société* **Sp** [=E] F [U] 1960s (1>2) < trsl *alta sociedad* **It** [(h)ai sosaieti] F [U] 1960s (1) < trsl *alta società* **Rm** - < trsl *înalta societate* **Rs** (0) < trsl *vysshee obshchestvo* **Po** - < *wższe sfery* **Cr** [=E] M [U] mid20c (1) **Bg** - < trsl *visshe obshtestvo* **Al** - < *shoqëria e lártë* **Gr** <=E> [=E] [U] end20c (2 mod)

high-tech *cp¹/adj./n.* 1 'imitating styles more usual in industry etc., esp. using steel, glass, or plastic in a functional way', (of interior design etc.) 2 'employing, requiring, or involved in high technology'

This term, one of the buzzwords of the 1980s, significantly failed to spread to parts of Eastern Europe, although it is universal elsewhere. Note that the full form does not appear to have been borrowed.

Ge [=E] M/F/N [U] 1980s (2) = 2: rend/trsl *Spitzen-* /*Hochtechnologie* **Du** [=E] C [U] 1970s (2) **Nw** <=E>/*hi-tech* [=E] M [U] 20c (1 tech) > trsl *høytek*; = *høyteknologi* **Ic** [=E] uninfl., end20c, 1(1 tech); - < 2: trsl *hátækni-* **Fr** [ajtek] M, 1980s (1 mod) **Sp** <=E>/*hi-tech* [=E/xaitek] C/adj., 1980s (1 tech) < trsl (de) *alta tecnología* **It** [(h)aitek] F [U] end20c, 2(1 tech) < trsl *alta technologia* **Rm** [=E] N [U] end20c (o>1 tech) **Rs** *khai-tekh* M, uninfl., end20c (1 tech) **Po** <=E> adj. uninfl., end20c, 2(1 tech) **Cr** [=E] M [U] end20c, 1(1 tech) **Bg** *khai-tek* uninfl., 1990s (1 tech, mod) < rend *visoki/khaï tekhnologii* **Fi** <=E>/*hi-tech* [=E] end20c (2) **Hu** [=E] [U] end20c, 2(1 tech) < rend *csúcstechnológia* **Gr** <=E> [=E] adj. (2 tech, jour, mod)

highway *n.* +1c 'a main road, an autobahn'
Ge (Ø) **Du** (Ø) **Nw** (Ø) **Fr** (Ø) **Rs** *khaïveĭ/-véĭ* M, pl. *-i*, end20c (1 jour) **Po** M, end20c (1 coll) **Gr** (Ø)

hijacker *n.* 'a person who seizes control of an aeroplane'

This term is very widespread in German (less common: *-ing* n., *-en* v.) and has given rise to new adoptions like *skyjacking* – but is very rare in other European languages where calques are preferred.

Ge [haidzeka] M, pl. Ø, 1970s (1 mod) < *(Flugzeug-)Entführer* **Nw** (o) < *(fly)kaprer* **Ic** - < *flugræningi* **Fr** - < *pirate de l'air* **Sp** - < *pirata aéreo* **It** - < creat *dirottatore, pirata dell'aria* **Rs** *khaïdzheker* M, pl. *-y*, end20c (1 mod) **Po** - < *pirat powietrzny* **Cr** *hajdžeker* M, pl. *-i*, end20c (1) **Hu** - < *gépeltérítő* **Gr** - < *aeropiratis*

hike *v.* 1 'walk for a long distance, esp. across country', +4 'travel by hitchhiking'

Nw *haike* [ha̱i̱ke] 1950s, +4(3); 1980s, 1(1 tech, mod) **Ic** [hai:ka] 1970s, +4(1 coll) **Fi** *haikki* [=E] 1990s (1 sla)

hike *n.* 1 'a long country walk', +3 'a free ride (obtained by hitch-hiking)'
Du [=E] C, 1960s, 1(1 tech) → *hiken* v. **Nw** *haik* [=E] M, pl. *-er*, 20c, 1(1 tech); M [U] 1950s, +3(3) **Fi** <=E>/*haikki* [=E/Fi] 1990s, 1(1 tech)

hill-billy *n.* 2 (-music, -song) 'folk music of or like that of the southern USA'
Ge [=E] M [U] 1960s (Ø/1 tech) **Du** [=E] C [U] 1960s (1 tech) **Nw** [=E] M [U] mid20c (1 tech) **Ic** [=E] N [U] mid20c (1 tech) **Fr** (Ø) **Sp** *hillbilly* [=E/xibi̱li] end20c (1 tech, rare) **Rm** [=E] N [U] 1970s (Ø/1 tech) **Po** N [U] end20c (1 tech) **Gr** (Ø)

himself/herself *pron.* 1a 'in person' (used after proper names etc., to emphasise that this is indeed the person in question)
Du [=E] 1980s (2) **Nw** [=E] mid20c (2) **Fr** 1980s (1 mod)

hint *v.* 'suggest slightly'
Nw *hinte* [hi̱nte] mid20c (3) **Ic** *hinta* [hi̱nta] 1970s (2 coll)

hint *n.* 1 'a slight or indirect indication or suggestion'
Du [=E] M, beg20c (2) **Nw** [=E] N, pl. Ø, beg20c (3) → *hinte* v. **Ic** [hi̱nt] N, pl. Ø, 1970s, 1(2 coll) **Rm** (0)

hip *adj.* 1 'following the latest fashion; in, fashionable, stylish'
The adoption as a jazz term dates to the 1960s, with its more general application (partly replacing ↑*in*) still restricted to the Germanic North-west. It may be 'out' before it is adopted by the other languages.
Ge [=E] uninfl., 1980s (1 you) **Du** [=E] 1950s (1 coll) **Nw** *hipp*/*hypp*/<=E> 1970s (2 coll, sla) **Ic** [hɪhp] uninfl., end20c (1 sla) **Sp** [xip] end20c (1 jour, rare)

hiphiphurrah! *excl.* 'a cheer for a winner'
Ge *hip, hip, hurra!* [-a̱:] 19c? (3) **Du** *hiep, hiep, hiep!*/*hoera!*, beg19c, via Da? (3) **Nw** *hipp hipp hurra* [hi̱phiphhu̱ra:] mid19c (3) **Fr** *hiphiphip!*/*hourra!* [i̱p/hipura] 19c (3) from E? **Sp** *hip, hip, hurra!* 1920s (3) **It** *hip hip urrà* [i̱pip urra̱] 1930s (3 coll) **Rm** [hip hip ura̱] mid20c (3 coll) **Rs** *gip-gip ura̱* mid20c (1 coll) **Po** *hip hip hurra̱* mid20c (3) **Cr** *hiphiphura̱* beg20c (3) **Bg** *khip khip ura̱* 20c, via Fr (3) **Fi** *hip hip hurraa* (3) **Hu** *hip! hip! hurrá!* [hi̱p hip hu̱ra:] end19c (3 obs) **Al** *hip hip hurra* 20c (1)

hip hop *n.* 1 'a style of popular music of US black and Hispanic origin, featuring rap with an electronic backing', 2 'the subculture associated with this, including graffiti art, break-dancing, etc.'
Ge [=E] M [U] 1980s (1 tech, mod) **Du** [=E] M [U] 1980s (2) **Nw** <=E>/*hipphopp* [=E] M [U] 1980s (1 tech) **Ic** *hipp-hopp* [hɪhp hɔhp] N [U] 1980s (1 tech) **Fr** <=E> M [U] 1980s (1 mod) **Sp** [=E] M

[U] 1980s (1 tech, mod) **It** [=E] M [U] 1990s (1 tech, mod) **Rm** [=E] N [U] 1990s, 1(1 tech/you) **Rs** *khip-khop* M [U] end20c (1 mod) **Po** M [U] end20c, 1(1 tech) **Cr** [=E] M [U] 1980s (1 tech, mod) **Bg** *khi̱pkhop* M [U] end20c, 1(1 tech) **Fi** [=E] 1980s (1 tech) **Gr** *khipkhop* F/N [U] 1980s (1 tech)

hippie *n.* (esp. in the 1960s) 'a person of unconventional appearance, typically with long hair, jeans, beads etc., often associated with hallucinogenic drugs and a rejection of conventional values'
This word was a cult word for many in the younger generation of the late 1960s, connected with Western nonconformism; in the east, it was a term which had very pejorative overtones for the silent majority. The concept has long been obsolescent, developing into a term relating to an important era of modern social history. Note the extended sense in Bulgarian *khipar* 'youth of neglected appearance'.
Ge [=E] M, pl. *-s*, 1960s (2 obs) **Du** [=E] C, 1960s (2 obs) **Nw** [=E] M, pl. *-r*, 1960s (2) **Ic** *hippi(i)*/*hippi* [hɪhpi(ɪ)/hɪhpɪ], M, pl. *-ar*, 1960s (1/2 mod, arch) → *hippalegur* adj. **Fr** *hippy*/*hippie* [i̱pi] M/F, 1960s (1) **Sp** <=E>/*hippi*/*hipi* [xi̱pi] M/adj., pl. *-s*, 1960s (2) → *hipioso, hipismo* **It** [(h)i̱ppi] M, pl. Ø/-s, 1960s (2) **Rm** *hippy*/*hippi(e)* [=E] M, pl. Ø/-i̱și, 1970s (2) → *hipiot*/*hipioată* M/F **Rs** *khippi* M/F, uninfl., 1970s (1 you) → *-ovyĭ* adj.; *khipar'* M **Po** *hipis*/*hippis*/*hip* 1960s (1 arch) → *hippiska* F; *hippisowski* adj. **Cr** *hipi* M/F, pl. *-ci*, 1960s (2) → *-ca* F; *-jevski* adj. **Bg** *khipi* N, pl. *-ta*, 1970s (2) → *khipar* M; *khipa̱rski* adj. **Fi** *hippi* 1960s (3) **Hu** *hippi* [hi̱ppi] pl. *-k*, 1960s (2>3 pej, obs) → *-s* adj. **Al** *hipi* M, pl. *-të*, 1970s (1 obs) **Gr** *khipis* M/*khipissa* F, 1960s (3); <=E>/*khip(p)i* M/F, pl. *-s*, 1990s (1 jour, rare, mod)

hipster *n.* 1 'a person who is hip', +2 'a member of the beat generation'
Ge [=E] M, pl. Ø/-s, 1960s, +2(1 obs, rare) **Nw** [=E] M, pl. *-e*, 1960s, +2(1 obs) **Ic** [=E] M, pl. *-ar*, end20c, 1(1 sla) **Sp** [xipster] M, 1960s (1 tech) **Rs** *khipster* M, pl. *-y*, end20c, 1(1 you, obs) **Hu** *hipszter* [hi̱pster] pl. *-ek*/Ø, 20c, 1(1 coll, pej, obs)

hit *n.* 3a 'a popular success in entertainment', +8 'a commercial success', +9 'anything unusually popular or topical'
This word is almost universal; differences exist among the countries in particular with regard to its status as compared to native equivalents, and the degree to which its use has extended beyond the original meaning (in popular entertainment, esp. hit songs).
Ge [=E] M, pl. *-s*, 1960s (2) **Du** [=E] C, 1950s, 3a,+8(2) **Nw** [=E] M, pl. *-s*/*-er*, 1960s (1 coll) **Ic** *hitt* [hɪht] N, pl. Ø, 1970s, 3a,+9(1 coll) = rend *smellur* **Fr** [it] M, 1950s, 3a,+8(1) **Sp** [xit]

M, pl. *-s*, 1960s, 3a,+8(1 tech) **It** [=E] M, pl. Ø, 1970s, 3a(2 jour) +8(1 tech) < *successo* **Rm** [=E] M, 1970s, 3a(1 tech); 1990s, +8(3) **Rs** *khit* M, pl. *-y*, end20c, 3a(2) **Po** <=E> M, end20c (2) **Cr** [=E] M, pl. *-ovi*, mid20c, 3a,+8(2) → *-ovski* adj. **Bg** *khit* M, pl. *-al-ove*, end20c, +8,+9(2) **Fi** *hitti* 20c (3) **Hu** [=E] [U] 20c, 3a(1 tech_MUS) **Al** [=E] M, pl. *-e*, 1992, 3a(1 tech_MUS) **Gr** *khit* N, pl. Ø/*-s*, end20c, 3a(2 coll) < *suxe, epitykhia*

hitch-hike *v.* 'travel by seeking free lifts in passing vehicles'
Ge [hitʃhaikn] 1950s (1 obs) < *trampen* → *-r* M; *-ing* N **Du** - < *lift* **Nw** *haike* ["haike] 1950s (3) → *haiking* M/F; *haiker* M; *haik* M **Ic** [=E-a] 1970s (0 sla) = *fara á puttanum* **Sp** - < *hacer autostop* **It** - < *fare l'autostop* **Rs** -→ *khitchkhaiking* M **Po** - < *autóstop* **Cr** (0) **Bg** - < *na avtostop*

hitch-hiker *n.* 'a person travelling by seeking free lifts in passing vehicles'
Ge (0) < *Tramper* **Nw** *haiker* [haikər] M, pl. *-e*, 1950s (3) **Ic** - < *puttalingur, puttaferðalangur* **Fr** - < *autostoppeur* **Rs** *khitchkhaiker* M, pl. *-y*, 1990s (1 you, mod) **Cr** - < *autostoper* **Bg** - < *stopadzhiya*

hit list *n.* +2 'a list of the most popular records'
This term has been firmly established from the 1960s in Western Europe, and more recently taken up, with morphological adaptations, in Eastern Europe. Whether the synonymous and more recent ↑*chart(s)* will affect the currency of *h.* is impossible to predict.
Ge *Hitliste* F, pl. *-n*, 1960s (2+5) < *charts* **Du** *hitlijst* 1970s (3+5) **Nw** *hitliste* [=E+Nw] M/F, pl. *-r*, 1960s (1+5) **Ic** - < rend *vinsældalisti* **Rm** - < rend *lista hiturilor* **Po** - < *lista hitòw* **Bg** *khitlista* F, pl. *-sti*, 1990s (1 jour, mod) **Fi** *hittilista* 1980s (2) **Hu** - < *toplista* **Gr** *khit list*/<=E> N, end20c (1 tech)

hit parade *n.* 'a list of the most popular records'
As a compound, this is much less widespread than ↑*hit*; it is all the more remarkable that it is given a higher degree of acceptability in some languages (French, Spanish). As in the case of ↑*hit list* the word has been competing with, and losing some ground to ↑*chart(s)*.
Ge [hit para:də] F, pl. *-n*, 1960s (2 obs+5) = *charts* **Du** *hitparade* [hɪtpara:də] C, 1970s (3) **Nw** - < *hitliste* **Fr** *hit-parade* [itparad] M, 1950s/60s (2 ban) > *palmarès* **Sp** [xitpareid] M, pl. Ø/*-s*, 1970s (1 you) = rend *lista de exitos*/*charts* **It** [itpareid] F, pl. Ø, 1960s (2) **Rm** [=E] F, pl. Ø, 1990s (0>1 tech/jour) **Rs** *khit parad* M, pl. *-y*, end20c (1 you, mod) **Bg** *khitparad* M, pl. *-al-i*, end20c (1 jour, mod) **Fi** *hittiparaatti* 1970s (1) **Al** *hit pareid* 1980s (1 mod) **Gr** *khit pareid* N, end20c (1 tech, you)

hit single *n.* 'a short pop record with a very popular piece of music on it'
Ge [=E] F, pl. *-s*, 1980s (1 mod, rare) < ↑*Single* **Du**

[=E] M, 1980s (2) **Nw** *hitsingel* [-sinŋel] M, pl. *-singler*, 1980s (1) **Bg** - < ↑*single*

HIV *abbrev. cp¹* 'human immunodeficiency virus'
Ge [ha:i:fau] N [U] 1987 (3 tech) **Du** *H.I.V.* [ha: i: ve:] 1980s (2) **Nw** <=E>/*hiv* [hɔ:i:ve:/hi:v] 1980s (3) **Ic** [hau: : vaf:] cp¹, 1980s (2 tech) **Fr** [aʃive] M, 1980s (3 tech) < *V.I.H* **Sp** [atʃe i ube] M [U] 1980s (1 tech) = trsl *VIH* **It** [akka i vu] M [U] 1980s (1 tech) **Rm** [hiv] cp², 1990s (1 tech) **Rs** - < trsl *VICH* **Po** 1980s (2) → *-owiec* M **Cr** [hiv] M [U] 1980s (1 tech) **Bg** <=E>/*KHIV* M [U] 1980s (1 tech) **Fi** [hɔ:i:ve:] (3) **Hu** [hiv] 1980s (3 tech) **Gr** <=E> [=E] 1980s (1 tech)

hobby *n.* 1 'a person's favourite leisure-time activity'
This term was first adopted in its full form *hobby-horse* in the eighteenth century (the basis for the German calque *Steckenpferd*). Only the metaphorical sense is now current; the shortening *hobby* and its popularity are post-1945.
Ge [hɔbi:] N, pl. *-(ie)s*, mid20c (2) > *Steckenpferd* N **Du** [=E] C, pl. *'s*, 19c (2>3) **Nw** [=E] M, pl. *-erl-ies*, beg20c (2) **Ic** *hobbí* [=E]N, pl. Ø, mid20c (2 coll) **Fr** [ɔbi] M, pl. *-iesl-ys*, 19c/mid20c (1) **Sp** <=E>/*hobbie* [xɔbi] M, pl. *-(ie)s*, 1960s (2) **It** [ɔbbi] M, pl. Ø, 1950s (3) → *hobbista* n.; *hobbistica* n; *hobbistico* adj. **Rm** [hɔbi] N, 1970s (2) → *hobbyist* M **Rs** *khobbi* N, uninfl., mid20c (3) **Po** N, uninfl., mid20c (2) → *hobbista* M; *hobbistka* F; *hobbizm* M [U]; *hobbistowski* adj.; *hobbistyczny* adj. **Cr** *hobi* M, pl. *-ji*, mid20c (2) → *-ist* M; *-jaš* M **Bg** *khobi* N, pl. *-ta*, mid20c (2) **Hu** *hobbi* [hɔbbi] pl. *-k*, end19c/beg20c (3) **Al** *hobi* [hɔbi] M, pl. *-e*, end20c (1 obs) **Gr** *khɔbi* N, pl. Ø/*-s*, mid/end20c (2)

hobby-room* *n.* 'a cellar used for handicraft etc.'
Ge *Hobbyraum* (M) 1960s (2+5) **Du** *hobbykamer, -ruimte* 1960s (2>3+5) **Nw** *hobbyrom* 20c (2+5) **Ic** *hobbiherbergi* N, 1960s (2+5) **Hu** - < trsl *hobbiszoba* **Gr** *khɔbi rum* N, end20c (1 tech, rare)

hobo *n.* 'a wandering worker, a tramp'
Nw [=E/hu:bu] M, pl. *-erl-s*, 1970s (1 rare) **Ic** *hóbó* [=E] M, pl. *-ar*, end20c (1 sla) **Hu** [=E] pl. *-k*, 1960s (1 coll, obs)

hockey *n.* 1 'a game played on a field by two teams using curved sticks', 2 'ice hockey'
The early adoption of the sport made this term universal – particularly in the British English sense of 'field hockey' (cf. ↑*ice hockey*). Calques appear to have never been tried.
Ge [=E] N [U] end19c, 1(2) **Du** [=E] N [U] end19c, 1(2) **Nw** [=E] M [U] beg20c, 1(1 rare) 2(2) **Ic** *hokkí* [hɔhci] N [U] beg20c, 1(Ø), 2(2 coll) **Fr** [ɔkɛ] M, end19c, 1(2) → *hockeyeur, hockeyeuse* **Sp** [xɔkei] M, beg20c, 1(2) **It** [ɔkei] M [U] 1930s (2) → *hockeista* C; *hockeistico* adj. **Rm** *hochei*/*hockey* [=E] N [U] beg20c, 1,2(2>3); 1945, 2(3) → *hocheist* **Rs** *khokkei* M [U] beg20c, 1(3) → *-nyï* adj.; *-ist* M **Po** *hokej* [hokej] M [U] beg20c, 1(2) → *-ka* F; *-ówka* F; *-owy* adj. **Cr** *hokej* M [U] beg20c, 1(2) → *-aš* M; *-asica* F; *-ski* adj. **Bg** *khɔkei* M [U] mid20c, via Rs, 2(2 tech)

→ khokęen adj.; khokeįst M   Fi hockey/maahockey [hɔkeu] 20c (2)   Hu hoki [hǫki] [U] end19c (3) → -zik v./cp²   Al hokej [hokęj] M [U] mid20c, 1(2 you)   Gr khǫkei N [U] beg20c, 1(2/Ø)

holding¹ (1)   n/cp¹ 2 'stocks held by a company', +3 'the company'

This economic loanword appears to have no native equivalents. It spread quickly in Western Europe in the 1960s (as cp¹ from the 1940s) and, more recently, in the east.

Ge [hǫːldiŋ] F, pl. -s, 1960s, +3(2 tech)   **Du** [=E] C, beg20c (1 tech)   **Nw** [=E] cp¹, 20c (1 tech)   **Fr** [ɔldiŋ] M/F, 1930s, +3(1 tech)   **Sp** [xɔldin] M, 1970s (1 tech)   **It** [(h)ɔldiŋ(g)] F, pl. Ø, 1930s, +3(2 tech)   **Rm** [=E] N, 1970s, +3(1 tech); 1990s, +3(2)   **Rs** khǫlding M, pl. -i, end20c (1 tech) → -ovyĭ adj.   **Po** [-nk] M, mid20c, +3(1 jour) → -owanie N; -owy adj.   **Cr** hǫlding M, end20c, +3(1 tech)   **Bg** khǫlding M, pl. -a/-i, end20c, +3(3 tech) → -ov adj.   **Fi** [=E] cp¹, 20c, +3(2)   **Hu** [hǫlding] pl. -ok, mid20c (1 tech); end20c, +3(2 tech)   **Gr** <=E>/khǫlding F, pl. -s, end20c, +3(1 tech)

holding²   n. 'waiting in air traffic control'

Nw [=E] M [U] 20c (1 tech) = rend ventemønster   **Fr** <=E> 20c (1 tech, ban) < attente   **Gr** <=E> [=E] N [U] end20c (1 tech)

hold-up   n. 2 'an armed robbery'

The history of this term's adoption and its present-day distribution are unexplored and diverge significantly from what one might expect of anglicisms.

Nw [=E] N, pl. Ø/-s, 1950s (1 rare) < væpnet ran   **Fr** [ɔldœp] M, 1920s/50s (1) > vol à main armée   **Sp** - < attraco a mano armada   **Rm** [=E] N, 1970s (1 jour)   **Rs** kholdáp M, pl. -y, end20c (1 coll, rare) < creat voor-uzënnoe napadenie   **Cr** [=E] M [U] mid20c (1)   **Hu** [hǫld ap] [U] 20c (1)

hollywood (-swing)*   cp¹ 'a covered garden swing'

Ge Hollywoodschaukel F, pl. -n, 1970s (2+5)

holocaust   n. 1 'large-scale destruction', 2 'the mass murder of the Jews in 1941–45'

The earliest meaning of this word, 'a sacrifice wholly consumed by fire', is recorded in the technical lexis of archaeologists and religious historians. The prevailing modern sense relating to the mass murder of the Jews in the 1940s is taken from American English, where it was used in this specific sense from 1965. It became widespread esp. after the internationally distributed TV series in 1979. As a compound formed from Greek elements it is often treated as an internationalism.

Ge [hǫːlokaust] M [U] 1970s, 1,2(3)   **Du** [=E] C [U] 1970s, 2(3)   **Nw** [=E] M/N [U] 1980s (1 tech)   **Ic** [=E] end20c, 2(0) < rend Helförin   **Fr** holocauste [ɔlokost] M (4)   **Sp** - < mean holocạusto   **It** olo-

cạusto M, pl. -i, 14c, 1(5Gr); 1950s, 2(3)   **Rm** [holokaust] N, 1970s, 1,2(4)   **Rs** kholokǫst M [U] mid20c, 2(1 jour)   **Po** [holokaust] M [U] end20c, 2(2 mod)   **Cr** [holokost] M [U] end20c, 2(3)   **Bg** khǫlo-kǫst M [U] end20c, 2(1 jour)   **Hu** [holokaust] M [U] end20c (3)   **Al** holokaust M [U] 1990s, 2(3)   **Gr** olo-kạftoma N, mid20c(4)

holster   n. 'a leather case for a pistol or revolver'

The transmission of this term is disputed; in German it is also claimed to be derived from the Dutch/ Low German synonym of identical form.

Ge [hǫlsta] N, pl. Ø, 1980s (1 tech)   **Du** [=E] C, end19c (1 tech)   **Nw** - < hylster   **Fr** [ɔlstɛ] M, mid20c (1 tech)   **Po** (5Ge)

home   n. 1a 'the place one lives in', 4 'an institution for a person needing care, rest etc.'

The use of home itself is very limited (but it has increased the frequency and range of meanings of the German Heim since the nineteenth century); however, this term is frequently found as cp¹ in modern compounds (↑home-dress), many of which are unrecorded in English.

Du [=E] N, 1940s, 1a(1 coll, rare)   **Nw** (0) < -hjem/ -heim   **Fr** [ǫm] M, 19c, 1a(0) 4(1)   **It** (Ø)   **Hu** [hoːm] [U] 20c, 1a(0>1) 4(1 jour, mod)

home base   n. 'the point from where the ball is driven' (baseb.)

Du (Ø)   **Nw** [=E] M [U] end20c (Ø/1 tech, rare)   **It** [(h)oum/(h)ǫm beis] F, pl. Ø, 1970s (1 tech) < trsl casa base   **Fi** - < trsl kotipesä

home computer   n. 'a computer for personal use'

Ge [=E] M, pl. Ø, 1980s (2 tech) = trsl Heimcompu-ter   **Du** homecomputer [=E] C, 1980s (2 tech)   **Nw** [=E] M, pl. -e, 1980s (1 rare/o) < hjemmedatamaskin   **Ic** - < trsl heimilistölva   **Fr** (0) < ordinateur individuel   **It** [(h)ǫm/(h)oum kompjuter] M, pl. Ø, 1980s (1 tech) < personal computer   **Rm** (0)   **Po** - < komputer oso-bisty   **Hu** - < személyi számítógép   **Gr** <=E> [=E] M/N, pl. -s/Ø, 1980s (1 tech, rare) > trsl ikiakos ypo-loghistis

home-dress*   n. 'casual wear for women'

Ge [hǫːmdres] M, pl. -e, 1970s (1 obs)

home page   n. 'a page on the Internet representing a corporation, institution, etc., that provides links to other related subjects' (comput.)

Ge [=E] F, pl. -s, 1990s (1 tech, mod)   **Du** [=E] C, pl. -s, 1990s (1 tech, mod)   **Nw** [=E] M, pl. -er, 1990s (1 tech) < trsl hjemmesi-de   **Ic** - < trsl heimasiða   **Fr** [ompɛdʒ] F, 1990s (1 tech) < rend page d'accueil   **It** [=E] F, pl. Ø, 1990s (1 tech)   **Rm** [=E] N [U] 1990s (1 tech)   **Fi** [=E] (1 tech) < trsl kotisivu   **Hu** [=E] pl. Ø, end20c (1 tech)   **Gr** <=E> [=E] F, 1990s (1 tech)

home-party*   n. 'a meeting in a private home involving the demonstration and sale of goods (esp. cosmetics)'

Nw [=E] N, pl. -er/-ies, 1970s (2)

home run   *n.* 'a hit that allows the batter to make a complete circuit of the bases' (baseb).

Ge [E] M, pl. *-s*, end20c (Ø>1 tech)   **Du** [-rʏn] C, pl. *-s*, mid20c (Ø>1 tech)   **Nw** [=E] (Ø)   **Sp** [=E] M, end20c (1 tech) = *cuadrangular/hit de cuatro bases*

homespun   *adj./n.* 'a kind of cloth spun at home'

This term illustrates the late nineteenth-century dominance of the British cloth industry – and its concentration of exports to Central Europe; since then, the word has continuously lost currency and has become largely obsolete.

Ge [ho:mspan] N [U] end19c (1 tech, obs)   **Du** [ho:mspʏn] C [U] beg20c (2)   **Fr** [omspœn] M, end19c (1 tech)   **Sp** [=E] M, pl. *-s*, beg20c (1 arch)   **Rm** [homspun] N [U] beg20c (1 arch)   **Po** [-un] M, beg20c (1 arch)   **Cr** *homspun* [homspun] M [U] beg20c (1 tech)   **Hu** [ho:mspan] *n.* [U] end19c/beg20c (1 tech, arch)

hometrainer*   *n.* 'an apparatus for fitness training at home (exercise bicycle etc.)'

Ge [ho:mtre:na] M, pl. Ø, 1980s (1 mod) < trsl *Heimtrainer*   **Du** [=E] C, 1950s (2) > *kamerfiets*   **Fr** *home-trainer* [omtʀɛnœʀ] M, 1980s (1 mod)   **Gr** <=E> [=E] M, pl. Ø/-s, 1990s (1 writ/0 mod)

home video   *n.* 1 'a film or documentary recorded on tape and sold for home use', 2 'a branch of film production and marketing of videotapes', +3 'a video taken by a non-professional on a small video-recorder'

Du [=E] pl. -'s, 1990s, +3(1 tech)   **Nw** - < trsl *hjemmevideo*   **Ic** *heimavídeó* N, pl. Ø, 1990s, +3(5+2)   **It** [(h)ɔm/(h)oum video] M, pl. Ø, 1990s, 2(1 tech)   **Bg** - < trsl *domashno video*

home-wear*   *n.* 'casual dress'

Ge [ho:mve:r] F [U] 1970s (1 mod)

homing   *part.* 1 'trained to fly home' (of a pigeon), 2 '(a device) for guiding to a target'

Fr [ɔmiŋ] M, mid20c, 2(1 tech, ban) < *radioralliement*   **It** [(h)oming] M, pl. Ø, 1980s (1 tech)

hone   *v.* 'sharpen'

Ge [ho:nən] mid20c (3 tech, rare)   **Du** *honen* [ho:nə] 1950s (1 tech)   **Ic** *hóna* [hou:na] end20c (3 tech_{MECH}) → *hónari* M; *hónun* F

hone   *n.* +3 'a sharpening machine'

Ge - → *honen* v. (1 tech)   **Ic** - → *hóna* v. → *hónari* M; *hónun* F   **Rm** *hon* [hon] N, 1970s (1 tech) → *honui* v.   **Rs** *khon* M, pl. *-y*, end20c (1 tech)   **Po** → *honingowanie/honowanie* [honingovanie/honovanie] N, mid20c (1tech)   **Cr** (0)

honeymoon   *n.* 'a holiday spent together by a newly married couple'

This term (first recorded in the sixteenth century) has hardly been borrowed into other languages, native equivalents or calques being preferred everywhere.

Ge [=E] M, pl. *-s*, 1970s (0/1 mod) < *Flitterwochen*   **Du** (o) < *huwelijksreis*   **Nw** (o) < *bryllupsreise*, *hvetebrødsdager*   **Ic** [=E] mid20c (0c) < *brúðkaups-*

ferð, *hveitibrauðsdagar*   **Fr** - < trsl *lune de miel*   **Sp** - < trsl *luna de miel*   **It** - < trsl *luna di miele*   **Rm** - < rend *lună de miere*   **Rs** - < rend *medovyĭ mesyats*   **Po** - < trsl *miesiąc miodowy*   **Cr** - < trsl *medeni mjesec*   **Bg** - < trsl *meden mesets*   **Hu** - < rend *mézeshetek*   **Al** - < trsl *muaji i mjaltit*   **Gr** (o) < creat *minas tu melitos*

honky-tonk   *n./cp¹* 1 'ragtime piano music'

Du [=E] 1960s (1 tech)   **Nw** [=E] M [U] 1960s (1 tech)   **It** *honky-tonky* [(h)ɔŋki tɔŋki] M [U] 1960s (1 tech)   **Rm** [=E] N [U] 1970s (1 tech)   **Bg** *khonkitonk* M [U] end20c (1 tech)   **Fi** [=E] (1 tech)   **Gr** <=E> [=E] 1960s (1 tech)

hood   *n.* 3 'the bonnet of a motor vehicle'

Ic *húdd* [hut:] N, pl. Ø, 1930s (3 coll) > rend *vélarhlíf*

hook   *n.* 1b 'a fish-hook; a bent piece of wire, usu. barbed and baited, to catch fish', +1c 'the act of fishing with a hook', 4a 'a hooking stroke' (cricket/golf), 4b 'a short swinging blow with the elbow bent and rigid' (box.), +4c 'a swinging shot' (basketb.)

Du *hoek* [huk] C, 1950s, 1b(4) = *hoekstoot, hoekslag*   **Nw** *huk* [hʉ:k] M, pl. -er, 20c, 1b,+1c(4 tech); [hʉk] 1930s, 4a,b,+4c(1 tech) → *huke* v.   **Ic** *húkk* [huhk] N [U] mid20c +1c(3); pl. Ø, mid/end20c, 4b,+4c(3 tech); *húkkur* [huhkʏr] M, pl. -ar, mid20c, 1b(3) = +4c: *húkkskot*   **Fr** [uk] M, 19c, 4b(1 tech/arch) +4c(1 tech) < *crochet* → *hooker* v.   **Sp** [=E/xuk] M, pl. *-s*, end20c, 4a(1 tech); - < 4b: trsl *gancho*   **It** - < mean *gancio*   **Rm** - < 4b: *croșeu*

hook   *v.* 3 'catch with or as with a hook' (fishing)

Nw *huke* ["hʉ:ke] 19c(4)   **Ic** *húkka* [huhka] end19c, via Da (3 coll) → *húkkast (á)* v.; *húkktur*, *húkkaður* adj.; *húkkari* M

hooligan   *n.* 1 'a young ruffian, esp. a member of a gang', +2 'a rioting football fan'

This word was widely borrowed into European languages, where it competed with ↑*rowdy* (and still does). It gained special currency in Tzarist and Communist Russia as a general term for criminals and dissenters, which is likely to have influenced the frequency of use and range of meanings in Eastern Europe. In recent use, it is frequently employed for rioting football fans.

Ge [hu:ligən] M, pl. *-s*, beg20c/1980s, +2(2) < *Rowdy* → *Hooliganismus* M   **Du** [=E] C, 1980s, +2(2)   **Nw** [hu:ligan] M, pl. *-s*, 1980s, +2(1) < *fotballpøbel*   **Ic** [=E]/[hu:lɪka:nɪ] M, pl. -ar, 1980s, +2(1 sla) = rend *fótboltabulla*   **Fr** <=E>/*houligan* [uligan/uligã] M, 1920s/60s (1) → *hooliganisme, houliganisme* M   **Sp** [xuligan] M, pl. *-s*, 1970s, +2(2) → *hooliganismo; huliganear*   **It** [uligan] M, pl. Ø, 1950s (2)   **Rm** *huligan* [huligan] M, beg20c, via Rs (3) → *-ic* adj.; *-ism* N   **Rs** *khuligan* M, pl. *-y*, end20c (3) → *-ka* F; *-stvo* N, *-skiĭ* adj.; *-it'* v.   **Po** *chuligan* [huligan] M, beg20c, via Rs (3) → *chuligaństwo* N; *-eria* F; *-ka* F; *-ić* v.; *chuligański* adj.   **Cr** *huligan* M, pl. *-i*, beg20c (2) → *-ka* F; *-ski* adj.; *-stvo* N   **Bg** *khuligạn* M, pl. *-i*, beg20c (2) → *-ka* F; *-stvo* N; *-ski* adj.   **Fi** *huligaani* 20c (3)   **Hu** *huligán* [hụliga:n] pl. *- ok*, mid20c, 1(3 pej) → *-kodik* v.; *-izmus* n.   **Al** *huligan* M, pl. *-ë*, 1960s (1 you)   **Gr** *khụligan* M, pl. Ø/*-s*, end20c (2); → *khuligạnos* M (3 sla), *khuliganismos* M

hootenanny *n.* 'an informal gathering with folk music'
  Ge [=E] N/M/F, pl. *-s*, 1960s (1 reg, obs)   **Fr** (0)

hopeless *adj.* 2 'admitting no hope', 3 'inadequate, incompetent'
  Du - < *hopeloos*   **Nw** - < *håpløs*   **Ic** [=E] uninfl., 1960s (0 sla); *hóplaus* (2+5)

-hopping *cp²* 'the abrupt and seemingly unmotivated changing of partners, doctors, islands (on holiday), etc.'
  Ge [=E] N [U] 1990s (1 mod) → *-hopper* M   **Du** [=E] C [U] 1990s (1 mod)

hornpipe *n.* 1 'a lively dance', 2 'music produced by a wind instrument'
  Du [=E] C, end18c (1 tech)

horny *adj.* 3 'sexually excited'
  Du [=E] 1980s (1 you)   **Ic** [=E] end20c (1 coll) > trsl *hornóttur*

horror *n.* 3b 'a bad or mischievous person etc.'
  Ic [=E] M [U] mid20c (2 coll) = trsl *hryllingur* M   **Hu** (5La)

horror *cp¹* 'designed to arouse pleasurable feelings of horror' (of literature, films, etc.)
  Ge [=E] M [U] 1960s (3)   **Du** [=E] C [U] 1980s (3); *horreur* beg20c (5Fr); *horror* 1970s (5La)   **Nw** [họrour] M [U] 1960s (1); [họrur] M [U] 1980s (3) < *skrekk-*   **Ic** *horror-* [=E] mid20c (2 coll) < trsl *hryllings-*   **It** [(h)ọrror] M [U] 1970s (2 tech) = trsl *dell'orrore*   **Rm** [=E] N [U] end20c (1 mod) < *de groază*   **Po** (5La)   **Cr** [=E] M [U] mid20c (2)   **Hu** (5La)   **Gr** - < trsl *tromu*

horror show* *n.* 'a show which evokes fear'
  Ge (0)   **Du** (0)   **Nw** (0)   **Fr** (0)   **It** [ɔrror ʃoʊ] M, pl. Ø, 1970s (1)   **Po** M, uninfl., end20c (1 coll)   **Hu** [=E] [U] end20c (1 jour, mod)

horror trip* *n.* 1 'a trance after taking drugs, a bad trip, a bummer' 2 'an unpleasant experience'
  Ge [=E] M, pl. *-s*, 1970s (2)   **Du** (Ø)

horsepower *n.* 1 'a unit of power', 2 'the power of an engine' cf. ↑*hp*

The English term was more widely known in the nineteenth century, but was replaced by calques in all European languages. Although the concept is no longer used in technical terminology, these calques survive without any restriction in the common language.
  Ge - < trsl *PS (Pferdestärke)*   **Du** - < trsl *paardenkracht*   **Nw** - < trsl *hestekrefter*   **Ic** - < rende *hestafl* N   **Fr** - < *chevaux*   **Sp** - < trsl *caballo de vapor* = ↑*H.P.*   **It** *HP* < rend *cavallo vapore, potenza fiscale*   **Rm** - < trsl *cal putere*   **Rs** - < trsl *loshadinaya sila*   **Cr** <=E> 20c (1) < trsl *konjska snaga*   **Bg** - < trsl *konska sila*   **Fi** - < trsl *hevosvoima*   **Hu** *HP*

[ha:pe:] [U] 19c, 2(1 tech, arch) < *lóerő*   **Al** - < *kuaj fuqi*   **Gr** - < trsl *ippodhynami*

hospice *n.* 1 'a home for the (terminally) ill or destitute'
  Ge *Hospiz* (5La)   **Du** *hospies* [hɔspi:s] N, pl. *-en*, 1910s, via Fr (2 reg, rare)   **Nw** [=E] cp¹, 1980s (1 tech); *hospits* (5La)   **Fr** (5)   **Sp** *hospicio* (5La)   **It** *ospizio* (5La)   **Rm** *ospiciu* (5Fr)   **Rs** *khọspis* M, pl. *-y*, end20c (1 tech)   **Po** (5La)   **Hu** [hospis] [U] end20c (5Fr/1 tech)

hostel *n.* 2 'a cheap hotel for young people', +4 'a home for old and sick people'
  Du [=E] C, 1980s, 2(2)   **Nw** (0)   **Fr** 2(Ø)   **Sp** *hostal* M   **It** *ostello* (5Fr)   **Po** [- el] M, end20c (2 mod)   **Cr** [=E] M, mid20c, 2(2)   **Hu** [=E] pl. *-ek*, 1980s, 2(2)   **Gr** only in ↑*youth hostel*

hostess *n.* 1 'a guide (in exhibitions, hotels)', 3 'an air hostess', 4 'a prostitute'

This word is quite common for females of various occupations (some uses are euphemistic); its form possibly suggests non-English provenance in some languages.
  Ge [hostẹs] F, pl. *-en*, 1960s, 1(2 tech) 4(1 euph, rare)   **Du** [=E] C, pl. *-es*, 1980s, 1(2) 4(1 euph)   **Nw** [=E] M, pl. *-er/-es*, 20c, 1(1 arch)   **Fr** [ostes] F, 20c, 1(4)   **It** [ọstes] F, pl. Ø, 1950s, 1,3(3)   **Rs** *khostẹssa* F, pl. *-y*, end20c, 1,3(3)   **Po** *hostessa* F, end20c, 1(2)   **Cr** *hostẹsa* F, end20c, 1(2)   **Bg** - < 3: creat *bordna domakinya*   **Hu** [họstess] pl. *-ek*, 1960s, 1(2>3)

hot *adj.* 3 'pungent' (of pepper, spices, etc.), 6 'passionate, excited', 6c 'lustful', 6d 'exciting', 7 'fresh, recent' (of news), 10 'strongly rhythmical and emotional' (of music, esp. jazz), 11b 'wanted by the police' (of a person)

The major source of this loanword appears to have been the widespread adoption of ↑*hot jazz*; however, other more recent compounds have furthered the use of *hot*, extending both its frequency and its semantic range. Native equivalents are of course available and are freely used for senses borrowed from *hot*, so the loanword has remained largely restricted to colloquial or facetious uses among younger people.
  Ge [=E] *pred.*, 1950s, 10(1 you) → *hotten* v.   **Du** [=E] 1940s, 10(1 coll) 7(1 tech)   **Nw** [=E] pl. *-e*, mid20c, 3,6(1) 7(2 coll) 10(1 you) = mean *het*   **Ic** [=E] uninfl., end20c, 3(1 coll) 6c,d,7(1 sla) < 7,11b: mean *heitur*   **Fr** [ọt] adj./M, 1930s, 10(1 tech)   **Sp** [xot] 1980s, 6d,10(1 tech)   **Rm** [=E] 1970s, 10(0>1 tech)   **Po** <=E> uninfl., end20c, 10(1 you)   **Hu** [=E] 20c, 10(1 tech)   **Gr** <=E>/*khot* adj., 1980s, 6(1 coll) 7(1 coll, you, mod) 10(1 you)

hot dog *n.* 'a hot sausage sandwiched in a roll'

This item has spread with fast-food culture, the

term being unanalysed. It is remarkable that calques *have* been tried since they sound even funnier (or more disgusting) than the English loanword. Fanciful variants have been reported (*tofu dog*, noticed in Bonn 1997).

Ge [hotdok] M, pl. -*s*, 1960s (1 mod) **Du** [=E] C, 1970s (2) **Nw** [=E] M, pl. -*er*/-*s*, (1) < *varm pølse* **Fr** [ɔtdɔg] M, 1920s/60s (1) **Sp** [=E/xotdog] M, pl. -*s*, 1940s (1 tech) < trsl *perrito caliente* **It** [(h)ɔt dɔg] M, pl. Ø, 1950s (2>3) **Rm** [=E] M, pl. -*il*-*s*, 1970s (1>2) **Rs** *khot dog* M, pl. -*s*?, 1990s (2) **Po** [hod dok] M, 1980s (2) **Cr** [=E] M, pl. -*s*, end20c (1) **Bg** *khot-dog* M, pl. -*a*, end20c (2) **Fi** <=E> (2); *hodari* (3) **Hu** [hotdog] pl. Ø, 1970s (2) **Gr** <=E>/*khot dog* N (2)

hot jazz*   *n.* 'jazz of the 1920s/30s in contrast to the 'sweet' dancing music of that time'

Ge [hotdʒes] M [U] mid20c (1 tech, coll) **Du** [=E] C, 1940s (1 tech) **Nw** [=E] M [U] 1940s (1 tech) **Fr** <=E>/*jazz hot* [ɔt dʒaz] M [U] 1930s (1 tech) **Sp** <=E>/*jazz hot* M [U] (1 tech) **It** [(h)ɔt dʒez] M, pl. Ø, 1950s (1 tech) **Rm** [=E] N [U] 1970s (1 tech) **Rs** *khot dzhaz* M [U] end20c (1 tech, coll) **Po** [=E] M [U] end20c (1 coll) **Cr** *hot džez* M [U] end20c (1 tech, coll) **Bg** *khot dzhaz* M [U] end20c (1 tech) **Fi** [=E] M [U] mid20c (1 tech) **Hu** [=E] [U] 20c (1 tech) < *hot*; < trsl *forró dzessz* **Gr** <=E>/*khot tzaz* [=E] F [U] end20c (1 tech)

hotline   *n.* 1 'a direct exclusive line of communication, esp. for emergencies', +2 'a telephone line for exchanging erotic messages'

This recent term from the political register was normally translated – the two elements combine to make perfect sense as a calque in all the languages concerned; where the loanword is used it is mainly in journalese.

Ge [=E] F, pl. -*s*, 1980s, 1(2 mod) < rend *heißer Draht* **Du** [=E] M, 1980s, 1(2) **Nw** [=E] M, pl. -*r*/-*s*, 1980s (1) **Fr** [ɔtlajn] F, 1990s, 1(1 tech, ban) < *numéro d'urgence* **Sp** [=E] C, end20c, 1(1 tech) < *teléfono rojo* **It** [=E]

F, pl. Ø, 1960s (1) < 1: trsl *linea calda* **Rm** [=E] 1990s, 1(0 jour) < rend *linie fierbinte* **Rs** *khot-laĭn* M, uninfl., 1990s, 1(1 mod) < trsl *goryachaya liniya* **Po** - < trsl *gorąca linia* **Cr** [=E] F, end20c, 1(1 mod) **Bg** - < 1: trsl *goreshta liniya* **Hu** - < trsl *forró drót* **Al** - < *lidhur direkt* **Gr** <=E>/*khotlain* F, pl. Ø/-*s*, 1990s, +2(2 mod)

hot pants   *n.* +1a 'sexy shorts'

The short-lived fashion (regionally revived in the 1990s?) did not stay long enough to spark off many calques – which might have sounded too unexciting, provincial or strange to be useful in advertising, anyway. The term is still passively known but has not been used since c. 1980 and is thus unlikely to spread to languages hitherto unaffected.

Ge [hotpents] pl., 1970s (1 obs) > *heiße Höschen* **Du**

hotpants [=E] C [U] 1980s (1 tech, you) **Nw** [=E] M [U] 1970s (1 mod) **Fr** [ɔtpãnts] M, 1970s (1 obs) **Sp** [xotpan(t)s] M, pl., 1970s (1 mod, obs) < *minishorts* **It** [(h)ɔt pɛnts] M, pl., 1970s (1 tech, mod) **Po** *hot panty* [-panti] pl., end20c (1 tech), end20c (1) < *vruće hlačice* **Hu** - < trsl *forró nadrág* **Gr** *khot pants* N, mid20c (1 mod)

hotshot   *n.* 1 'an important or exceptionally able person'

Ge *Hot Shot* M, pl. -*s*, end20c (1 coll) **Du** [=E] C, pl. -*s*, mid20c (1 you) **Nw** [=E] M, pl. -*s*, end20c (1 coll, rare)

houseboat   *n.* 'a boat fitted up for living in'

Ge - < trsl *Hausboot* **Du** [=E] C, 1910s (1 rare) < *woonboot* **Nw** (0) < *husbåt* **Ic** - < trsl *húsbátur* **Fr** [ausbot] M, mid20c (1 tech, ban) > *coche (d'eau)* **It** [(h)aus bout/bot] F, pl. Ø, 1950s (1)

house (music)   *n.* 'a style of modern dance music'

Ge [=E] [U] 1980s (1 tech) **Du** [=E] C [U] 1980s (1 you) **Nw** [=E] M [U] 1980s (1 tech) **Ic** [=E] N [U] 1980s (1 tech, you) **Fr** [aus-] F, 1980s (1 you) **Sp** *house* [=E] M, 1980s (1 tech, you) < *música house* **It** [=E] F [U] 1980s (1 tech) **Rs** *khaus* M [U] end20c (1 tech) **Bg** *khaus (myuzik)* M [U] end20c (1 tech) **Fi** [=E] 1980s (1 tech, you) **Gr** *khauz*/<=E> F [U] 1980s (1 tech, you)

house party   *n.* +3 'a meeting (in a private home) of members of the Oxford Group', +4 (also ↑*warehouse party*) 'a large dance party for young people held in an empty warehouse etc.'

Ge [=E] F, 1980s, +4(1 you) **Du** [=E] C, 1930s, +3(1 obs); 1980s, +4(2) **Nw** [=E] N, pl. Ø/-*ies*, 1930s, +3(1 arch); 1980s, +4(1 you) **Sp** [=E] M, pl. -*s*, +4(1 you, rare)

house-warming party   *n.* 'a party in a newly built/ bought house'

Ge [=E] F, pl. -*(ie)s*, 1960s (1 coll) **Du** [=E] C, pl. -'*s*, 1980s (1 coll) = *inwijdingsfeest* **Nw** (0) < *innvielsesfest* **Ic** [=E] uninfl., end20c (0) = creat *húshitun* **Cr** (0)

hovercraft   *n.* 'a vehicle or craft that travels over land or water on a cushion of air provided by a downward blast'

The fact that this type of boat is esp. frequent in Channel ferries appears to have limited the currency of the word to Western Europe, but even here calques are frequent, the loanword being a stylistic choice.

Ge [=E] N, pl. -*s*, 1960s (Ø/1 tech) < *Luftkissen-* **Du** [hɔvərkra:ft] C, 1960s (2 tech) < *luchtkussenvaartuig, luchtkussentrein* **Nw** [=E] M, pl. -*er*/-*s*, 1960s (1 obs) < *luftputebåt* **Ic** [=E] 1960s (0 tech) < rend *svifnökkvi, loftpúðaskip* **Fr** [ovœrkraft] M, 1960s (1 tech, ban) < *aéroglisseur, hydroglisseur, naviplane* **Sp** [=E/oberkraf]

M, 1970s (1 tech) < *aerodestizador* **It** [(h)o̲verkraft]
M, pl. Ø, 1960s (1 tech) **Rm** [=E] N, 1970s (1 tech,
rare) **Po** - < *poduszkowiec* **Cr** [=E] M, mid20c (1
tech) < *lebdjelica* **Bg** - < creat *korab na vŭzdushna
vŭzglavnitsa* **Hu** - < *szárnyashajó* **Al** - < *anije me
jastëk ajri* **Gr** *kho̲verkraft* N, end20c (1 tech)

h.p.   *abbrev.* 1 ↑'horsepower'
   This English abbreviation was obviously widespread in the early days of British technological influence, but was widely replaced by calques (often
abbreviated). More recently, in technological descrip-
tions the measurement in ↑*kWh* is preferred.
   Ge [etʃpi] 19c (0 arch) < *PS* **Du**
- < *pk* **Nw** - < *h.k.* **Fr** < *CP*
Sp *HP* [at̲ʃepe] beg20c (0 arch)
trsl *cv* **It** *HP* [a̲kka pi] beg20c
(1 tech) < rend *cavallo vapore,
potenza fiscale* **Rm** *H.P.* [ha̲ʃpe]
beg20c (1 arch, rare) < trsl *c.p.
(cai putere)* **Rs** - < trsl *l.s.* **Po** *HP* [ha pe] beg20c
(1 tech) **Cr** *H.P.* [ha pe] beg20c (1 tech) **Bg** - < trsl
k.s. (*konska sila*) **Fi** - < trsl *hevosvoima* **Hu** *H.P.*
[ha̲:pe:] end19c/beg20c (1 tech, arch) < trsl *lóerő* **Al** -
< trsl *k.f. (kuaj fuqi)* **Gr** (1 writ)

hub   *n.* +3 'a major interchange airport'
   Du [=E] C, 1990s (1 tech) **Nw** [=E] M, pl. -*er*, 1980s
(1 tech) **Fr** ['œb] M, 1990s (1 tech, ban) > *pivot*

hula hoop   *n./cp¹* 1 'a large hoop for spinning round
the body with hula-like movements', +2 'the act of
doing this'
   Ge -*reifen* [hula:hu̲p] cp¹, 1950s (1 obs) **Du** *hoela-
hoep* [hu:lahu̲p] C, 1950s (1 obs) = *hoepel* → *hoelahoe-
pel* **Nw** - < *rockering* **Ic** *húlahopp* [hu:laho̲hp] N
[U] mid20c, +2(2 coll); *húla(hopp)hringur* M, 1(2+5
coll) **Fr** *hula-hoop* [ulaup] M, 1960s, 1(1 obs) **Sp**
<=E>/*hula-hop* [xulaxu̲p/xulaxo̲p] M, 1960s (1 obs) **It**
[ula̲:p] F, pl. Ø, mid20c (1>2) **Rm** [=E] N [U]
1960s, +2(1 obs) **Rs** *khulakhup* M, pl. -*y*, mid20c,
1(1 obs) **Po** [-hop] N [U] mid20c, 1(1 obs) **Cr** *hulahup* M [U] mid20c, 1(1 obs) **Bg** *khulakhup* M [U]
mid20c, +2(3 arch) **Hu** *hulahop* cp¹ [hu̲lahop] 20c
(3) **Al** *hulahup* [hulahu̲p] M [U] mid20c (1 reg) **Gr**
khu̲la khup N, mid20c (1 obs)

hulk   *n.* 1a 'a dismantled ship', 2 'an unwieldy vessel',
+4 'an old ship in poor condition'
   Ge *Hulk/Holk*, M/F, pl. -*e(n)*, 19c, 1a(1 arch) **Du**
[hʏlk] (4) **Nw** *holk* [hɔlk] M, pl. -*er*, 19c, 1a(3/5Du)
+4(1 tech/5Du) **Po** (5)

hully-gully   *n.* 'a dance similar to the samba from the
Southern USA' (of Caribbean derivation)
   Ge [=E] M [U] 1960s (1 obs) **It** [alli ga̲lli] M [U]
1960s (2 rare) **Rm** [=E] N [U] 1960s (1 obs) **Rs**
khali-gali N, uninfl., 1960s (2 obs) **Cr** *hali-gali*
1960s (1 obs) **Bg** *khali-gali* N [U] 1960s (2 obs)
Hu [=E] [U] 1960s (2)

human engineering   *n.* 'the management of industrial labour'
   Ge [=E] N [U] 1980s (1 tech, mod) **Rm** - < rend
inginerie umană

human relations   *phr.* 'relations between people'
(esp. as a term in economics)
   Ge [=E] pl., 1950s (1 tech) **Fr** - < trsl *relations hu-
maines* **Sp** - < trsl *relaciones humanas* **It** - < trsl
relazioni umane **Rm** - < trsl *relaţii umane* **Rs**
kh'yumen rile̲ishnz pl., 1980s (1 tech) **Po** <=E> pl.,
end20c (1 coll, mod) **Hu** [ju:men rile:ʃəns] end20c (1
tech) **Al** - < trsl *mardhëbië humane*

humbug   *n.* 1 'deceptive or false talk or behaviour', +4
'a cheap swindle', +5 'a cheap and useless thing', +6 'a
loose shirt-front with a tie and a collar fastened to it'
   This early loanword is so well integrated in North-
western Europe that it is no longer felt to be foreign;
borrowed from written sources, it spread via German
to neighbouring languages (Polish, Hungarian), but
then came to be largely disused in British English itself
and stopped expanding in Europe.
   Ge [humbuk] M [U] mid19c,
+4(3) **Du** [hʏmbʏx] C [U]
end19c, 1,+4(3) **Nw** [humbʉg]
M [U] mid19c, 1,+4,+5(3) **Ic**
húmbúg/húmbúkk [humpu(h)k]
N, pl. Ø, mid19c, via Da, 1,+5(3
coll) +6(3 mod, obs) **Fr**
[œmbœg] M, 1930s, 1(1 arch) **Po** [humbuk] M [U]
beg20c, 1,+4(1 tech) → -*ista* M; -*istka* F **Fi** *hum-
puuki* 20c (3) **Hu** [humbug] [U] mid19c, 1,+4(3)

humour   *n.* 1a 'the quality of being amusing or
comic'
   Since this word was available in the medical ter-
minologies of all European languages (but classified
as Latin), it is the meaning that has come to be borrowed.
   Ge [hu:mo̲:r] (5La) **Du** *humor* [hymor] (5La) **Nw**
(5La) **Ic** *húmor* M [U] beg20c (5Da) **Fr** [ymu̲r] M,
18c(3) **Sp** <=E> [=E] M, end19c (Ø/1 arch) < mean
humor → *humorismo; humorista, humorústico* **It**
[(h)ju̲mor] M, pl. Ø, mid18c, via Fr (2) = *umoris-
mo* **Rm** *umor/humor* [(h)umo̲r] N, mid19c, via Fr
(3) **Rs** *yumor* M [U] 19c, via La → -*ist* M; -*istka* F;
-*isticheskiĭ* adj. **Po** (5La) **Cr** *humor* M [U] 19c
(3) **Bg** *khumor* M [U] 20c, via Ge (3) → -*ist* M;
-*istichen* adj. **Hu** *humor* [hu̲mor] [U] 18c (5La) **Al**
humo̲r M, pl. Ø, mid19c (5/Ø) **Gr** *khiu̲mor* N [U]
19c? (2)

hunter   *n.* 1b 'a horse' (racing, hunting)
   This term was adopted together with various other
words relating to horse-racing. Many of these have
long since been obsolescent, as *hunter* has.
   Ge [-ö-/-a-] M, pl. Ø, end19c (1
obs) **Fr** [œntœr] M, mid19c (1
tech) **It** [(h)ʌntər/(h)anter] M,
pl. Ø, 1930s (1 tech) **Rm** [han-
ter] M, beg20c, via Fr (1 arch)
Po [-er] M, beg20c (1 tech) **Hu**
[hunter] pl. Ø, 19c (1 tech, arch)

hunting   *n.* +2 'a type of suede (for shoes)'
   Rm [=E] N [U] 1960s (1 obs) **Hu** [=E] [U] 20c (1
tech, obs)

hurricane *n.* 1 'a tropical storm', 2 'a wind of force' **Ge** *Hurrikan* [hȫrikən] M, pl. *-el-s*, 19c, 1(Ø/3) **Du** - < *orkaan* **Nw** [=E] M, pl. *-s*, mid20c, 2(Ø) < *orkan* **Fr** [ʏʀikan/œʀikan] M, 1950s (1 tech); *ouragan* via Sp (5 Carib.) **Sp** *huracán* (5Sp) **It** *uragano* (5Sp) **Rm** *uragan* [uraga̱n] N, beg19c, via Fr(3) **Rs** *uragan* M, pl. *-y*, via Sp(3) **Po** *huragan* M, via Fr, 2(3) **Cr** *hariken* M, pl. *-i*, 20c, 2(2) > *u̱ragan* **Bg** *uraga̱n* M, pl. *-al-i*, beg20c, via Fr, 1(5Sp) → *-en* adj. **Fi** *hurrikaani* 20c, 1(3) **Hu** *hurrikán* [hu̱rrika:n] pl. *-ok*, 20c (5Hindi/3) **Al** *uragan* M, pl. *-e*, 20c (5Fr/1 reg)

husky *n.* 1 'a dog used in the Arctic for pulling sledges' **Ge** [ha̱ski] M, pl. *-(ie)s*, 20c (1 tech/Ø) **Du** [hy̱ski] C, pl. *-'s*, 1950s (1 tech) **Nw** [=E] M, pl. *-ier/- ies*, 20c (1 tech) **Ic** - < *sleðahundur* **Fr** [œ̱ski] M, 1980s (1 tech) **Sp** [xa̱ski/xa̱nski] M, pl. *-s/-ies* (1 tech) **It** [(h)a̱ski] M, pl. Ø, 1970s (2) **Rm** [ha̱ski] M, pl. Ø, end20c (1 tech) **Rs** *khaski* M, uninfl., mid20c (1 tech) **Po** M, uninfl., mid20c (2) **Bg** *khu̱ski* N, pl. *-ta*, mid20c (1 tech) **Fi** [=E] (2) **Hu** [=E] pl. Ø/-*k*, 20c (1 tech/Ø) **Gr** <=E>/*kha̱ski* N, pl. *-ies*, 20c (1 tech/Ø)

hustle *v.* 6 '(try to) get a job from day to day' **Ic** *höstla* [hœstla] end20c (1 sla)

hydrofoil *n.* 1 'a boat equipped with a device consisting of planes for lifting its hull out of the water', 2 'the device' **Ge** - < creat *Tragflächenboot* **Du** - < *hydroplaan* **Nw** [hydrufo̱il] M, pl. *-er*, 1950s, 1,2(3) **Ic** - < creat *spaðabátur* **Fr** [idʀofɔjl] M, 1950s/80s (1 tech) = *hydroptère* **It** - < *idroplano* **Po** - < *hydroplan* **Cr** [hi̱drofojl] M, pl. *-i*, 20c, 1(1 tech) **Bg** - < creat *korab na podvodni krila*

hydroforming* *n.* 'the process of producing high quality petrol' **It** [(h)a̱idrofo̱rmiŋg] M [U] 1980s (1 tech) **Rm** - < trsl *hidroformare*

hype *v.* 1 'promote' **Nw** [ha̱ipe] 1990s (1 mod) **Ic** *hæpa (upp)* [hai:pa] 1980s (1 sla) **Fi** [=E] 1990s (1 you, sla)

hype *n.* 1 'extravagant or intensive publicity promotion' **Du** [=E] C, 1980s (1 jour, mod) **Nw** [=E] M [U] 1980s (1 mod) **Ic** [=E] N, pl. Ø, 1980s (1 sla) **Sp** [=E/xaip] M, 1990s (1 jour, rare) **Fi** [=E] (0)

I

IC* *abbrev.* 'a fast train' cf. ↑*Intercity*
Ge *IC* [i:tse:] 1980s (2) = *Intercity* **Du** [=E] C, 1980s (1 tech) **Nw** ["i̯:se:] 1980s (3 rare) **It** - < *intercity* **Rm** - < *intercity* **Po** (1 writ) **Bg** - < *intersiti* **Hu** [i:tse:] pl. Ø, 1990s (2>3)

-ical *suffix.* +3 'relating to (musical) performances of new types' (often facetious or pejorative)

The element was separated from ↑*musical* to form pseudo-anglicisms in the 1960s and 1970s, among which *grusical* ('gruesome horror show' 1 obs) was most common. All the other words were *ad hoc* formations attesting at best the relative productivity of the suffix.

Ge [=E] 1960s (1 fac, pej, obs)

iceberg *n.* 1 'a large floating mass of ice', +3 'an iceberg lettuce'

For German and Dutch it cannot be decided on formal principles whether the term is native or was borrowed; other languages could have borrowed the term from any of the three languages.

Ge *Eisberg* 1(5) < +3: *Eisberg-salat* (5) **Du** *ijsberg* 1(5) **Nw** 1(0) +3(1 rare) < 1: *isfjell*; +3: *issalat* **Ic** *iceberg* [=E] N [U] 1980s, +3(1 coll) = *ísberg* **Fr** [isbɛrg/ajsbɛrg] M, 19c, 1(2) **Sp** [=E/iΘebɛr] M, pl. -*s*, beg20c, 1(2); *lechuga iceberg* F, end20c, +3(1) **It** [aizsbɛrg] M, pl. Ø, end19c, via/from, 1(3/Du) **Rm** *aisberg/ iceberg* [=E] N, mid20c, 1(3/2) **Rs** a̱isberg M, pl. -*i*, beg20c, 1(3) **Po** [-erg] M [U] beg20c, 1(1 tech) **Bg** a̱isberg M, pl. -*al-i*, 20c, 1(5Ge) **Hu** - < trsl *jéghegy* **Al** *ajsberg* M, pl. -*e*, mid20c, 1(1 tech)

Ic	Nw	Po	Rs
Du	Ge	Cr	Bg
Fr	It	Fi	Hu
Sp	Rm	Al	Gr

icecream *n.* 'a sweet creamy frozen food'
Ge - < *Eis(krem)* **Du** - < *ijs* **Nw** - < trsl *is(krem)* **Ic** - < *is* **Fr** (0) **Sp** [=E] M, beg20c (1 obs) < *helado* **It** [a̱iskrem] F, pl. Ø, 1930s (1) < *gelato* **Cr** (0) **Bg** (0) **Hu** [=E] [U] 1970s (Ø>1 writ, mod) < trsl *jég-krém*

icefield *n.* 'an expanse of ice, esp. in polar regions'
Du - < *ijsveld* **Fr** *ice-field* [=E] pl. -*s*, mid19c (1 arch) **Sp** [aisfil(d)] M (1 tech) < trsl *banco de hielo, banquisa* **It** [a̱isfild] M, pl. Ø, 1930s (1 tech) < *banchisa* **Bg** - < rend *ledeni poleta* **Hu** - < trsl *jégmező*

ice hockey *n.* 'a form of hockey played on ice with a puck'
Ge *Eishockey* N [U] beg20c (5+2) **Du** *ijshockey*

[ɛiʃɔki] N [U] end19c (5+2) **Nw** *ishockey* [Nw+E] M [U] beg20c (5+2) **Ic** *íshokkí* [i:shɔhci] N [U] mid20c (2 coll) > rend *isknattleikur* **Fr** - < rend *hockey sur glace* **Sp** - < rend *hockey sobre hielo* **It** - < rend *hockey su ghiaccio* **Rm** - < rend *hochei pe gheaţă* **Rs** *khokke̱ĭ* M [U] mid20c (3 tech) < rend *khokeĭ na l'du* **Po** - < trsl *hokej na lodzie* **Cr** - < rend *hokej na ledu* **Bg** - < ↑*kho̱keĭ*; - < rend *khokeĭ na led* (2+5) **Hu** - < trsl *jéghoki* (5+2) **Al** - < *hokej në akull* **Gr** - < rend *khokei epi paghu*

icing *n.* 3a 'an act of shooting the puck from one end of the rink to the other without scoring a goal' (ice hockey)
Nw [=E] M [U] 1950s (1 tech) **Rs** a̱ising M [U] end20c (1 tech) **Gr** a̱ising N [U] end20c, 1(1 tech, rare/Ø)

ID *n./cp¹* 'identification, identity' (*ID card*)
Du *ID card* [=E] C, pl. -*s* (1 tech) **Nw** [i:de:] M/cp¹, pl. -*er*, end20c (3 rare) **It** - < *carta d'identità* **Rm** (0) **Rs** (0) **Cr** (0) **Bg** a̱idi N, pl. -*ta*, 1990s (1 coll) < a̱idi- karta **Hu** [=E/i:de:] [U] 20c (1 tech_COMPUT)

identikit *n.* 1 'a reconstructed picture of a person', +2 'the sum of the characteristics of a group'
Fr - < *portrait-robot* **Sp** [identikit] M [U] 20c (1 tech) < *retrato robot* **It** [identikit/ide̱ntikit] M, pl. Ø, 1960s (3) **Cr** - < *foto-robot* **Al** *identikit* M, pl. -*e*, end20c (1 tech/2)

igloo *n.* 'a dome-shaped Eskimo dwelling, esp. one built of snow'

The Eskimo word was transmitted through Canadian English (and French?) to European languages. It certainly looks foreign in all receiving languages, but it is uncertain how English it is in its form; its status as an anglicism is therefore uncertain.

Ge *Iglu* M/N, pl. -*s*, 19c (3) **Du** *iglo* [iχlo:] (5) **Nw** *iglo* [iglu] (5Eskimo) **Ic** <=E>/*ligló* [=E/ɪklou] mid20c (1 tech, rare) < *snjóhús* **Fr** <=E>/*iglou* [iglu] M, end19c (3) **Sp** <=E>/*iglú* M, pl. -*s*, 1950s (3) **It** [iglu̱] M, pl. Ø, 1940s (3) **Rm** *iglu* [iglu̱] N, mid20c, via Fr (3) **Rs** *iglu* N, uninfl., beg20c (Ø) **Po** [-lo] N, uninfl., mid20c (2) **Cr** *iglu̱* M [U] beg20c (2) **Bg** *iglu̱* N, pl. -*ta*/Ø, 20c (Ø) **Fi** *iglu* (3) **Hu** *iglu* (5Eskimo) **Al** *iglu* [iglu̱] F, pl. -*të*, end20c (1 reg) **Gr** *iglu* N, 20c (Ø)

image *n.* 2 'the character or reputation of a person or thing as generally perceived and promoted'

The fact that the written form of this word is both

French and English makes it difficult to decide about the status of the word – except where the pronunciation is clearly English. Otherwise the item could be (a) an early French loan, possibly with a recent English meaning added, (b) an English loan pronounced the French way, or (c) an anglicism transmitted via French.

Ge [imitʃ] N [U] 1960s, 2(1 coll) **Du** [=E] C/N, 1960s (2 coll) = *imago* **Nw** [=E] N/M, pl. Ø, 1960s (2 coll) **Ic** [=E] N [U] end20c (1 sla) < *imynd* **Fr** - < mean *image (de marque)* **Sp** - < mean *imagen* **It** - < mean *immagine* **Rm** - < mean *imagine* **Rs** imidzh M [U] mid20c (1 jour) **Po** M [U] end20c (1 jour) **Cr** imidž M [U] end20c (1) **Bg** imidzh M [U] 1990s (2 jour) **Fi** [=E]™ only, 20c **Hu** [=E/ima:ʒ] [U] 1970s (1 tech, jour, mod_ECON/5Fr) **Al** imazh (5Fr) **Gr** imatz N [U] end20c (2 mod, jour, you)

image-maker *n.* 'a person employed to create a public image for a politician, product, etc.'

Du (Ø) **It** [imedʒ meiker] M/F, pl. Ø, end20c (1) **Rs** imidzhmeiker M, pl. -y, 1990s (1 jour) **Bg** imidzhmeikŭr M, pl. -i, 1996 (1 jour) **Gr** <=E>/imatz meiker M, 1990s (1 jour, mod)

impact *n.* 2 'effect or influence'

Du [=E] M, 1970s (2) **Nw** (0) **Fr** [ɛ̃pakt] M, 1970s (4) **Sp** - < mean *impacto* **It** - < mean *impatto* **Rm** [impakt] N, 1970s (4) **Cr** impakt M, end20c (1)

impeachment *n.* 2 'charging (the holder of a public office) with misconduct', 3 'calling in question, disparaging'

Ge (Ø) **Du** (Ø) **Fr** [impitʃment] M, 18c (Ø) **Sp** <=E> [=E] M, pl. -s, 1970s (Ø/1 tech) **It** [impi:tʃ-ment] M, pl. Ø, 1970s (Ø) **Rs** impichment M [U] end20c (1 jour) **Po** [-pi-] M [U] end20c, 2(1 jour) **Cr** impičment, end20c (Ø/1 tech) **Bg** impichmŭnt M [U] 1990s, 2(1 tech, rare)

import *n.* 1 'the process of bringing foreign goods to a country'

The form and meanings may be both English and French, and the historical evidence is largely mixed; e.g. even though the derived ↑*importer* may be from English the word was adopted in the French form in much of nineteenth-century Europe. The derived verb is equally controversial.

Ge [import] M, pl. -e, 19c (3) → *importieren* v. **Du** [import] C, pl. -en, mid19c (3) **Nw** [impot] M [U] (5Ge) → *importere* v. **Ic** - < *innflutningur* **Fr** < *importation* **Sp** only in *import-export* M, 1970s (1 tech) **It** [import] M, pl. Ø, 1960s, via Fr (2) < *importazione* **Rm** [import] N, end19c, via Ge (3) **Rs** import M [U] beg20c (3) → -*irovat'* v.; -*nyi* adj. **Po** (5La) **Cr** import M [U] beg20c (3) → *importirati* v. **Bg** import M [U] beg20c (2 tech) < *vnos* → -*iram* v.; -*en* adj. **Hu** [import] pl. -ok, mid19c (3) → *importál* v. **Al** [import] M, pl. -e, beg20c (1 tech/3) → *importoj* [importoj] **Gr** (0 tech/1 writ)

importer *n.* 'someone who imports'

Ge - < *Importeur* (5Fr) **Du** - < *importeur* (5Fr) **Nw** (0) < *importør* (5Fr) **Ic** - < *innflytjandi* **Fr** - < *importateur* **Sp** - < *importador* **It** - < *importatore* (5Fr) **Rm** - < *importator* **Rs** importër M, pl. -y, mid20c (2) **Po** [-er] M, mid20c (2) **Cr** - < *uvoznik* **Bg** importyor M, pl. -i, beg20c, via Ge (3 tech) < *vnositel* **Hu** - < *importőr* (5Fr) **Al** *importues* [importues] M, pl. Ø, beg20c (1 tech)

in *adv./adj.* 6a 'in fashion, season, or office'

Although currently more widespread than ↑*hip* (which appears to be replacing *in* in youth language) this term is a West European item (particularly connected with the anti-establishment student protests of the 1960s) which stopped before the Iron Curtain and it is doubtful whether it will expand further in the 1990s. (Cf. the antonym ↑*out*)

Ge [=E] pred., 1960s (2 coll) **Du** [=E] 1960s (2) **Nw** [=E] 1960s (2) = *inn(e)* **Ic** [=E] 1970s (1 sla) = mean *inni* **Fr** [in] adj., 1960s (1 mod) **Sp** [=E] 1960s (1 coll, you, fac) **It** [=E] pred., 1960s (2 coll) **Cr** *(biti) in*, end20c (1) **Fi** [=E] 20c (0) **Gr** <=E> adj., end20c (1 coll, jour, you)

-in *cp²* 'a (protest) meeting involving a specified activity' (e.g. *go-in, love-in, sit-in, teach-in* etc.)

The distribution of these compounds, which were very popular during the student unrests of 1968–72, neatly illustrates the division of Europe as it was then, with the progressive North and West adopting the form. All the terms are now mainly of historical interest.

Ge [=E] N, pl. -s, 1960s (1 you, obs) **Du** [=E] C, 1960s (1 mod, obs) **Nw** [=E] M, pl. -s, 1960s (1 obs) **Fr** <=E> N, 1960s (1 you, obs) **Sp** [=E] N, 1960s (1 you, obs) **It** [=E] M, pl. Ø, 1960s (1)

inbreeding *n.* 'breeding from closely related animals or persons'

Nw (0) < *innavl* **It** [inbridiŋ(g)] M, pl. Ø, 1980s (1 tech) **Rs** inbriding M [U] beg20c (1 tech) **Po** inbred? M [U] beg20c (1 tech) → -*owanie* N; v. **Bg** inbriding M, [U]/pl. -i, mid20c (1 tech) → -*ov* adj.

incentive *n.* 2 'a payment or concession to stimulate greater output/raise the motivation of employees'

Ge [=E] N (often pl. -s) 1970s (1 tech, rare) **Du** [=E] C, 1980s (1 tech) **Nw** [=E/insenti:v] N, pl. -r/-s, mid20c (1 tech) **Fr** only *incentive tour* 1990s (1 tech, ban) > *voyage de stimulation* **Sp** - < mean *incentivo* **It** - < mean *incentivo* **Fi** *insentiivi* < *kannustin*

inch *n.* 1 'a unit of linear measure'

This English word appears to have had some impact on 'metric' Europe through goods imported during the nineteenth century (tools, bicycles etc. used to be measured in inches until recently, and jeans and diskettes still are); however, indigenous, pre-metric terms (like German *Zoll*) were also commonly used.

Ge (Ø) < *Zoll*   **Du** [=E] C/N, pl. *-es*, beg20c (Ø) = *duim*   **Nw** (Ø) < *tomme*   **Ic** - < *tomma*   **Fr** - < *pouce*   **Sp** - < *pulgada*   **It** - < *pollice*   **Rm** [=E] M, pl. Ø, 1950s (Ø) < *ţol*   **Rs** - < *dyuĭm*   **Po** - < *cal*   **Cr** *inč* M, pl. *-evi*, end20c (3)   **Bg** *inch* M, pl. *-al-ove*, 20c (Ø) < *tsol*   **Hu** [=E] pl. Ø, 20c (Ø) < *hüvelyk*   **Al** *inç* F, pl. *-e*, mid20c (1 tech)   **Gr** *i̱ntsa* F, 20c (3)

in concert   *adv.* 'live' (of a pop performance)
Ge [=E] 1980s (1 tech, rare) < ↑*live*   **Du** [=E] 1980s (1 jour)   **Nw** [=E] 1980s (1) < ↑*live*   **It** - < trsl *in concerto*   **Rm** - < trsl *în concert* < ↑*live*   **Gr** <=E> [=E] 1980s (1 tech, writ)

in crowd   *n.* 'a clique of trendy people'
Du [=E] M, 1970s (1 mod)

Indian summer   *n.* 1 'a period of unusually dry warm weather in late autumn', 2 'a late period of life characterized by comparative calm'
Ge - < 1: *Altweibersommer*   **Du** [=E] C, 1960s (2)   **Nw** [=E] M, 20c (1 tech)   **Ic** *Indiánasumar* N, 1920s, 1,2(Ø)   **Fr** - < trsl *été des Indiens, été indien* < *été de la Saint-Martin*   **Sp** - < *veranillo de San Martín/veranillo de San Juan*   **It** - < *estate di San Martino*   **Rm** 1(0) < rend *vară indiană* (Ø)   **Rs** - < *bab'e leto*   **Bg** - < *tsigansko lyato*   **Fi** - < trsl *intiaanikesä*   **Hu** - < 1: trsl *indián nyár*

indie   *n.* 1a,b 'an independent record or film company', +2 'a type of pop music (assoc. with New Wave), outside the mainstream and usu. released on independent record labels'
Ge 1980s, +2(1 tech, you)   **Du** - < +2: *independant music*   **Nw** [=E] cp¹/M, 1980s, +2(1 tech)   **Ic** [=E] N [U] 1980s, +2(1 sla)   **Sp** [i̱ndi] F/adj., pl. *-s*, 1980s (1 tech)

indoor(s)   *adj./cp*$^{1/2}$ 1 'situated, carried on, or used under cover, e.g. sports events, clothes', +1a 'an indoor game'

This term has seen a relative rise in popularity with the sports and the fashion industry since the 1960s, freq. used with syntactic restrictions (e.g. as cp¹ as in *indoor sports*)

Ge [=E] cp¹, 1980s (1 mod)   **Du** [=E] 1970s (1 tech)   **Nw** (o) < *innendørs*   **Ic** - < *innanhúss-*   **Fr** [indɔʀ] 1960s (1 ban) > rend *en salle*   **Sp** [indor/indur] M/adj., end20c (1 tech)   **It** [indɔr] cp², 1950s (2 tech)   **Rm** [=E]

uninfl., cp², 1960s (1 tech)   **Cr** [=E] end20c (1 tech)   **Bg** - < rend *v zala*   **Gr** <=E> [=E] adj./cp¹, 1980s (1 tech) < *klistos*

infight*   *n.* 'a hidden, often severe, conflict within an organization'
Ge [=E] M, pl. *-s*, 1960s (1 jour, rare)

infighting   *n.* 2 'boxing at closer quarters than arm's length'

Nw [=E] M [U] 1950s (1 tech)   **Sp** M [U] 1920s (1 arch) < *boxeo cuerpo, a cuerpo*   **Rs** *infaĭting* M [U] 1980s (1 tech) < rend *blizhniĭ boĭ*

information retrieval   *n.* 'the recovery of information stored in books etc.' (esp. comput.)
Ge (o>1 tech)   **Du** (o)   **Nw** [=E] [U] 1970s (1 tech, rare)   **Fr** - < rend *recherche d'information*   **It** [=E] M, pl. Ø, 1970s (1 tech) < rend *reperimento/recupero dei dati*   **Rm** - < rend *regăsirea informaţiei*   **Cr** (o)   **Bg** - < rend *izvlichane na informatsiya*

infotainment   *n.* 'broadcast material intended both to entertain and to inform'
Ge [=E] N [U] 1990s (1 tech, jour)   **Du** [=E] N, 1990s (1 tech, jour)   **Nw** [=E] [U] 1990s (1 jour)

ingot   *n.* 'an oblong piece of cast metal'
If the etymology is really from *in+got* 'poured in' (cf. German *Einguss*), then French derived the form with an agglutinated article, with which it was handed on to other Romance languages. Only forms without the *l*- can be considered to come straight from English.
Ge [=E] M, pl. *-s*, beg20c (1 tech, rare)   **Du** [=E] C, 1940s (1 tech) = *baar*   **Nw** [=E] M, pl. *-s*, 20c (1 tech)   **Fr** *lingot* (3)   **Sp** *lingote* via Fr (3)   **It** *lingotto* M, pl. *-i*, 17c, via Fr (3)   **Rm** *lingou* via Fr (3)   **Rs** - → *ingoti̱zm* M   **Po** <=E> M, mid20c (1 tech)   **Cr** <=E> M, pl. *-i*, mid20c (1 tech)   **Hu** [i̱ngot] pl. Ø, 20c (1 tech)

ingrain   *adj./cp*¹ 'dyed in the fibre before being woven'
Ge [i̱ngre:n] beg20c (1 tech, rare)

inlay   *n.* 3 'a type of dental filling'
Ge [i̱nle:] N, pl. *-s*, 20c (2)   **Du** [=E] C, 1980s (1 tech) = *rulling*   **Nw** - < trsl *innlegg*   **Fr** [inlɛ] M, end19c/1950s (1 tech) < *incrustation, obturation dentaire*   **Sp** [inlei̱] M, 20c (1 tech) < *incrustación*   **Rm** [=E] N, mid20c (1 tech)   **Rs** *inlei̱* M, pl. *-i*, 1980s (1 tech)   **Cr** *inlej* M, pl. *-i*, 20c (2)   **Bg** *inlei̱* M, pl. *-leya*, 20c (1 tech)   **Hu** [i̱nle:] pl. *-k/*Ø, 1960s/70s (1 tech)   **Gr** <=E>/*i̱nlei* [=E] N, pl. Ø/*-s*, 20c (1 tech) < trsl *entheto*

inlet   *n.* 2 'a piece inserted in dressmaking', +4 'a duvet'
The unexpected sense of 'duvet' is often explained as being a homonym from Low German which would make both the Finnish and Hungarian words Germanisms.
Ge *I̱nlett* 19c, +4(3)   **Rm** [inlet̲] N, mid20c, 2(1 tech, rare)   **Po** [=E] M, mid20c, via Ge (1 tech)   **Fi** *inletti* 20c, +4(1)   **Hu** (5Ge)

in-line-skating   *n.* 'skating with rollerblades'
Ge [=E] N [U] 1990s (1 mod)   **Du** [=E] C [U] 1990s (1 mod)   **Nw** [=E] M [U] 1990s (1 tech, mod)

in no time   *phr.* 'very quickly'
Du [=E] 1980s (1 coll)   **Nw** *på no time* [Nw+E] end20c (5+1)   **Ic** *á nótæm* [au nou:taim] 1970s (5+2) → *á nóinu*

input   *n.* 1 'what is put in or taken in, or operated on

by any process or system', 3 'the information fed into a computer', 5 'the contribution of information'
Ge [=E] M/N [U] 1960s, 3(1 tech) 5(1 coll) **Du** [=E] C, 1980s, 3(1 tech); 1960s, 5(1 tech) **Nw** [=E] M, pl. -er/-s, 1960s, 1,5(1) 3(1 tech) > trsl 1,5: *inputt*; = 3: rend *indata* **Ic** [=E] N [U] end20c, 1,3(1 tech) = rend *inntak*; *ilag*

Fr [input] M, 1950s, 3(1 tech, obs) > trsl *entreé* **Sp** <=E> imput M, 1970s, pl. -s, 1,3(1 tech) **It** [=E] M [U] 1960s, 1,3(2 tech) 5(1 coll) **Rm** [=E] N, 1970s, 1,3(1 tech) > rend *intrare* **Rs** (o) **Po** M [U] end20c, 3(1 tech) **Cr** input M [U] end20c, 3(1 tech) **Bg** input M [U] end20c, 3(1 tech) **Fi** [=E] 3(1 tech) **Hu** [=E] pl. Ø, 1960s, 3,5(1 tech) **Gr** <=E> [=E] N [U] end20c, 3(1 tech)

inrigger* *n.* 'a kind of boat'
Du [inrixǝr] C, 19c (5) **Nw** *innrigger* [=E] M, pl. -e, 20c (3 tech)

ins and outs *n.* 'all the details (of a procedure etc.)'
Du [=E] pl. (1 mod)

insert *n.* 1 'something inserted, e.g. a loose page in a magazine', +1a 'graphic information inserted in between TV spots'
Ge [=E] N, pl -s, 1970s, +1a(1 tech, rare) **Du** [=E] C, 1980s, 1(1 tech) **Fr** [ɛ̃sɛʀ] M, mid20c, 1(1 tech, ban) < *incrustation* **It** - < *inserto* (5La) **Rm** [insert] N, 1970s, via Fr/It?, 1(1 techCINEMA) **Cr** <=E> 20c (1 tech) **Hu** *inzert* [inzert] pl. -ek, 20c, +1a(1 tech)

inside *n./cp[1]* 4 'a position affording inside information'
Ge [=E] cp[1] 1970s (1 jour) **Du** [=E] C [U] 1970s (2) **Nw** [=E] cp[1], mid20c (1) **Ic** [=E] cp[1], end20c (o) **Gr** (o)

insider *n.* 1 'a person who is within a society, organization, etc.', 2 'a person privy to a secret'
The word has a typical 'Germanic' distribution: current in the Northwest it is practically unrecorded elsewhere. The (back-derived?) ↑*inside* is even more restricted.
Ge [=E] M, pl. Ø, 1960s (2) **Du** [=E] C, beg20c (2) **Nw** [=E] M, pl. -e, end20c (2) < trsl *innsider* **Fr** (o) **Sp** [insaider] M, end20c (1 tech, rare) **It** [=E] M/F, pl. Ø, end20c (1 tech) **Rm** (o) **Gr** [insaider] M/F pl. Ø/-s, end20c (1 coll, jour, mod)

insider dealing/trading *n.* 'the illegal practice of trading to one's own advantage through having access to confidential information'
Ge - < trsl *Insidergeschäft* **Nw** [=E] M [U] 1980s (1 tech) < trsl *innsidehandel* **Ic** - < rend *innherjaviðskipti* **Fr** - < *délit d'initié* **Sp** *insider trading* [=E] M [U] 1980s (1 tech) < *(uso de) información privilegiada* **It** *insider trading* [=E] M [U] end20c (1 tech)

instant *adj./cp[1]* 1 'occurring immediately', 2a 'pro-

cessed to allow quick preparation' (of food etc.), +2c 'coffee'
This borrowing originated with instant coffee, spread to other types of food needing little or no preparation, and has recently spread in to other contexts, sometimes facetiously (e.g. ~*sex*).
Ge [=E] cp[1], 1960s, 1(1 coll) **Du** [=E] cp[1], 1970s, 1(2); 1980s, 2a(2) **Nw** [=E] 1960s, 1,2a(1 obs) < *hurtig-* → *instantisere* v.; *instantisering* M/F **Ic** [instant] 1960s, 2a(1 coll) > trsl *skyndi-*

Fr - < trsl *instantané, -ée* **It** [=E] cp[1], uninfl., 1980s (1 jour) **Rm** [instant] uninfl., 1980s, 2a(1 rare) **Rs** (o) **Po** [-ant] end20c, 1,2a(1 mod) → *-yzacja* F **Cr** <=E> end20c, 2(1) **Bg** (o writ) **Hu** [=E] 1960s, 2a,+2c(2>3) **Gr** instant [-d, -nt] adj., +2c (1 writ, coll) < mean *stighmieos*

instrumental *n.* 'a piece of music performed by instruments without singing'
Ge [=E] N, pl. -s, 20c (o>1 tech) **Nw** [instrumenta:l] M, 20c (5La) **Po** (5La) **Bg** *instrumental* M, pl. -al-i, end20c (1 tech) → *-en* adj. **Hu** (5La) **Gr** *instrumental* [-d, -nt] adj., end20c (1 tech)

intelligence quotient *n.* 'a number denoting the ratio of a person's intelligence to the normal or average' (cf. ↑*IQ*)
Ge *Intelligenzquotient* (5La) **Du** *intelligentiequotiënt* (5) **Nw** ↑*IQ/intelligenskvotient* (5La) **Ic** - < trsl *greindarvísitala* **Fr** - < trsl *Quotient intellectuel*, *QI* **Sp** - < trsl *cociente/coeficiente intelectual*; *cociente de inteligencia* **It** - < rend *quoziente intellettivo*; trsl *quoziente d'intelligenza* **Rm** - < rend *coeficient de inteligenţă*, *CI* **Rs** - < rend *koefitsient umstvennogo razvitiya* **Po** - < trsl *iloraz inteligencji* **Cr** - < rend *kvoeijent inteligencije* **Bg** - < rend *koefitsient na inteligentnost* **Hu** - < *IQ* < trsl *intelligenciahányados* **Al** - < *koeficient i inteligjencës* **Gr** - < trsl *dhiktis noimosinis*

intensive care *n.* 1 'medical treatment with constant monitoring etc. of a dangerously ill patient', 2 'a part of a hospital devoted to this'
Du F/M [U] 1970s (2) **Ic** - < *gjörgæsla* **Fr** - < trsl *soins intensifs* < *réanimation* **Sp** - < trsl *cuidados intensivos* **It** - < trsl *terapia intensiva* **Rm** - < rend *terapie intensivă* **Cr** - < trsl *intenzivna njega* **Bg** - < trsl *intenzivna terapiya*; 2: creat *reanimatsiya* **Al** - < 1: *terapi intensive*; 2: *sttacioni i terapise intensive* **Gr** (1 writ)

intercity *n./cp[1]* 'a fast train' (cf. ↑*IC*)
The distribution of this term largely reflects whether such a service is available in the country; once established, it seems likely that the word will be taken over too (together with ↑*Eurocity*) to indicate the international appeal.
Ge [intasiti] M, pl. -s, 1970s (2) **Du** [=E] C, pl. -'s, 1980s (2) **Nw**

[=E] cp¹/(M), 1970s (2) **Sp** [interθiti] M, pl. Ø/-ies (2) **It** [=E] M, pl. Ø, 1980s (3) **Rm** [=E] N [U] 1990s (2 tech) **Po** [-er-] M, uninfl., end20c (2) **Cr** <=E> M [U] end20c (2) **Bg** _intersiti_ N [U] 1990s (1 tech) **Fi** <=E> 1990s (1) **Hu** [=E/iːtse] pl. -k, 1990s (2)

intercom _n._ 'a system of intercommunication between offices etc. by radio or telephone'
Du [=E] C, 1960s (2) **Nw** [=E] M [U] 1970s (1) = _calling_ **Fr** - < _interphone_ **Sp** [interkom] M [U] 1980s (1 tech) **It** [=E] F [U] 1960s (1 tech) **Rm** [interkom] N [U] 1980s (1 tech, rare) **Rs** _interkom_ M [U] end20c (1 tech) **Po** [interkom] M [U] end20c (1 tech) **Bg** _interkom_ M [U] end20c (1 tech) **Hu** [interkom] [U] (1 tech) 1980s **Gr** <=E> N, pl. -s, end20c, 3(1 tech)

interface _n._ 2 'the point where interaction occurs between two systems, processes, etc., 3 'an apparatus for connecting two pieces of equipment so that they can be operated jointly' (comput.)
Ge [=E] N, pl. -s, 1980s, 3(1 tech) = _Schnittstelle_ **Du** [=E] C, 1970s, 3(1 tech) **Nw** [=E] M [U] 1970s, 2,3(1 tech) < rend _grensesnitt_ **Ic** - < 3: _tengibúnaður, skil_ **Fr** [ētɛʀfas] F, 1960s/70s, 2,3(3) **Sp** _interfaz/interfase_ M, pl. -s, end20c (1>2 tech) **It** [=E] F [U] 1970s (1 tech) < trsl _interfaccia_ **Rm** - < trsl _interfață_ **Rs** _interfeis_ M [U] end20c (1 tech) **Po** <=E>/_interfejs_ M, end20c (1 tech) **Cr** <=E> M, end20c, 3(1 tech) **Bg** _interfeis_ M, pl. -al-i, end20c, 3(1 tech) **Hu** _interfész_ [interfeːs] [U] 1970s, 2,3(1 tech) **Gr** <=E> [interfeis, interfeis, iderfeis, iderfeis] N, pl. -s, end20c, 3(1 tech) > rend _syzefxi_

interlock _adj./cp¹_ 'knitted with closely interlocking stitches' (of a fabric)
Ge [=E] N [U] 20c (2 tech) **Nw** [=E] M [U] 1950s (1 tech) **Sp** [interlok] end20c (1 tech) **Hu** [interlok] [U] 20c (2 tech)

Internet _n._ 'an international computer network linking computers from educational institutions, government agencies, industry, etc.' (cf. ↑_WWW_ for _World Wide Web_)
Ge [=E] N [U] 1990s (1 tech) **Du** [=E] N, 1990s (1 tech, mod) **Nw** <=E>/_internett_ [=E] M [U] 1990s (2 tech) **Ic** _Internet(ið)_ [=E/ɱterneːt(ið)] N [U] 1990s (2 tech) < rend _alnet, lýðnet_ **Fr** [ētɛʀnɛt] N, 1990s (1 tech) **Sp** [internet] M [U] 1990s (2 tech) **It** [=E/internet] F [U] 1990s (1>2 tech) **Rm** [=E] 1990s (2 tech) **Rs** _Internet_ M [U] 1990s (1 tech) **Po** [-ter-] M [U] 1990s (1 tech, jour) **Cr** _internet_ M [U] 1990s (1 tech) **Bg** _Internet_ M [U] 1990s (1 tech > 2) **Fi** [=E] 1990s (1 tech) **Hu** [=E] [U] 1990s (1 tech) **Al** _Internet_ M [U] 1995 (1 tech) **Gr** <=E>/_Internet_, idernet, idernet] N [U] 1990s (2 tech) > trsl _dhiadhiktio_

Interrail _n./cp¹_ 'an arrangement by which young people purchase a special ticket which allows travel by train for one month in most European countries.'
Ge [intareːl] N? [U] 1970s (2) → _Interrailer_ n. **Du** [=E] 1980s (1 coll) **Nw** [=E/-ræil] 1970s (2) → _inter-railer_ M **Ic** [=E] uninfl., 1970s (Ø) **It** _inter-rail_ [=E]

M [U] 1970s (1) **Rm** [=E] N [U] 1980s (1 tech, rare) **Rs** _interreil_ M [U] end20c (1 tech) **Po** M [U] end20c (1 tech) **Cr** _inter-rejl_ M [U] 1980s (1 tech) **Bg** (0) **Fi** <=E> 1980s (2) **Fi** → _interreilata/reilata_ v. **Hu** [=E] [U] 1960s (2) **Gr** <=E>/_intereil_ N [U] 1980s (1 you)

intershop* _n._ 'a hard-currency shop (in the former GDR)'
This pseudo-English word was coined in spite of the anti-western attitudes of the East German government to denote the kind of shop where western goods could be bought for hard currency. (Similar shops went by other names, such as Russian _Beryozka_, Bulgarian _Korekom_ etc. in other East European countries)
Ge [intaʃop] M, pl. -s, 1960s (1 hist)

interview _n._ 1 'oral examination of an applicant for employment', 2 'a meeting/conversation between a reporter and a person of public interest'
This nineteenth-century loanword is almost universal and has not even been commonly replaced by re-Romanized forms. However, the meaning has remained largely restricted to public talk with celebrities and rarely extended to job interviews.
Ge [intərju:/-vju:] N, pl. -s, end19c, 2(2); → -en v.; → -er n. **Du** [=E] N, end19c (2) → -en v.; -er n. **Nw** _interview_ [inter(v)ju:] N, pl. Ø/-er, beg20c (3) → _intervjuer_ M; _intervjue_ v. **Ic** [=E] N, pl. Ø, mid/end20c, 1,2(1 sla) < _viðtal_ **Fr** [ētɛʀvju] F, end19c, 2(2) → _interviewer_ n.; _intervieweur/se_ M/F; _interviewer_ v.; **Sp** [intervju] M/F, end19c (1) > trsl _entrevista_ → _interviuar_ v.; trsl _intervista_ **Rm** _interviu_ [interviu] N, end19c, via Fr, 2(3); 1990s, 1(3 tech) → 2: _intervieva_ v. **Rs** _interv'yu_ N, uninfl., beg20c, 2(2) → -er M; _irovat'_ v. **Po** _interwiew_/<=E> [intervju/=E] N [U] end20c (1 tech) **Cr** _intervjū_ M, pl. -i, beg20c, 1(2) 2(3) → _intervjuirati_ v. **Bg** _intervyu_ N, pl. -ta, mid20c, 2(2) → -iram v.; -irasht M **Hu** _interjú_ [interju:] pl. -k, beg20c, 2(3 coll, jour); end20c, 1(3 tech) **Al** - < _intervistë_ **Gr** _interviu, intervju_ [interviu, idervju, idervju] N, pl. -s, end20c, 1(2 rare) 2(2) = _synedefxi_

investment _n._ 2 'money invested', 3 'property etc. in which money is invested'
Ge [=E] N, pl. -s, 1960s, 3(1 tech) **Du** _investering_ (5La) **Nw** (0) < _investering_ **Ic** - < _fjárfesting_ **Fr** - < _investissement_ **Sp** - < _inversión_ **It** _investimento_ (5La) **Rm** - < _investiție_ **Rs** - < _investitsiya_ **Po** (5La) < _inwestycja_ **Cr** - < _investicija_ **Bg** - < _investitsiya_ (5La) **Hu** (5La) → _investment company_ **Al** - < _investim_ [investim] M, pl. -e, end20c (1 tech) **Gr** (0)

investment funds* _n._ 'money invested by an investment trust'
Ge _Investmentfonds_ [=E+Fr] M, pl. Ø, 1960s (1 tech+5Fr) **Du** _investeringsfonds_ (5Fr) **Nw** _investeringfonds_ (5La/Fr) **Ic** - < _fjárfestingarsjóður_ **Fr** - < _fonds commun de placement_ **Sp** - < trsl _fondos de_

inversión **It** [investment fond] M, pl. Ø, 1930s (1) < rend *fondi comuni d'investimento* **Rm** - < *fond de investiţii* **Rs** (o) < trsl *investitsionnyĭ fond* **Cr** - < trsl *investicijski fondovi* **Bg** - < rend *investitsionen fond* **Al** - < rend *fond investími*

investment trust *n.* 'a trust that buys and sells shares'
Ge [=E] M, pl. -s, 1960s (1 tech) **Du** [=E] C, 20c (1 tech) **Nw** *investeringstrust* [Nw+E] M, pl. -er, 20c (5+1 tech) **It** [=E] M, pl. Ø, 1930s (1 tech) < rend *fondo comune di investimento mobiliare* **Rs** (o)

invoice *n.* 'a bill'
Du [invojs] C, 1980s (1 tech) **Nw** (o) **Rs** *invois* M, pl. -y, end20c (1 tech) **Po** M [U] end20c (1 tech) **Cr** (o) **Bg** *invois* M, pl. -al-i, 1990s (1 tech) **Gr** (o)

IQ *abbrev.* 'intelligence quotient' (cf. ↑*intelligence quotient*)
Ge [iku:] (5La) **Du** [iky:] **Nw** ["i: ku:] (5) **Ic** [=E] 1960s (1 tech) < rend *GV* **Fr** - < *QI* **Sp** *IQ* (1 tech, rare) < trsl *CI* **It** *QI* [ku i] M, pl. Ø, 1960s (1) **Rm** [=E] end20c (1 tech) **Rs** *aĭ-k'yu* N? [U]? 1990s (1 coll, mod) < rend *koéfitsient umstvennogo razvitiya* **Po** (1 tech) **Cr** *IQ* [=E] mid20c (3) < rend *kvocijent inteligencije* **Bg** *aĭ kyu* 1990s (1 mod) < rend *koefitsient na inteligentnost* **Fi** - < trsl *ÄO (älykkyysosamäärä)* **Hu** [i:ku:] pl. Ø, 20c (1 tech) **Gr** <=E> [aiku] N [U] end20c (1 tech)

Irish coffee *n.* 'coffee mixed with a dash of whiskey and served with cream on top'
Ge [=E] M, pl. -s, 1960s (Ø/1 tech) **Du** [=E] C, 1970s (2) **Nw** [=E] M [U] 20c (1 tech) **Ic** [=E] N [U] 1970s (1 coll) = trsl *írskt kaffi* **Fr** [ajʀiʃkɔfi] M, 1960s (o/1 tech) **Sp** [=E] M, 1970s (Ø) < trsl *café irlandés* **It** [=E] M, pl. Ø, mid20c (1>2) **Rs** - < trsl *Irlandskiĭ*

kofe **Po** [=E] F, uninfl., end20c (1 mod) **Bg** - < trsl *irish/irlandsko kafe* (1/5+5) **Fi** [=E] (o) **Hu** - < trsl *ír kávé* **Al** - < trsl *kafe irlandeze* **Gr** <=E> [=E] M end20c (1 tech) > trsl *irlandhikos kafes*

Irish stew *n.* 'a stew of mutton, potato, and onion'
Ge (Ø) **Du** [=E] C, 1980s (1 tech) **Fr** [ajʀiʃstju] M, 1930s (1 tech) **Rs** - < trsl *irlandskoe ragu* **Hu** [=E] [U] 1970s (1 tech)

iron man *n.* +2a 'a participant in a triathlon contest'
Ge [=E] M, pl. -men, 1990s (1 tech) **Du** [=E] C, pl. -men, end20c (1 tech)

ISBN *abbr.* 'international standard book number'
Ge [i:esbe:en] F [U] 1970s (5) **Du** [i:esbe:en] C [U] end20c (3) **Nw** [i:esbe:en] M [U] 1970s (3) **Fr** [i:esbe:en] **Sp** [isebeen] M [U] 1970s (1 tech) **Rm** [ísebene] end20c (1 tech) **Rs** <=E> end20c (1 tech) **Po** [iesbeen] M, end20c (1 tech) **Bg** <=E> end20c (1 tech, writ) **Fi** [i:esbe:en] 1970s **Hu** [i:eʃbe:en] pl. Ø, 20c(2>3) **Gr** (1 writ)

issue *n.* 3 'a point in question, an important subject in debate'
Du [=E] N, 1970s (2) **Nw** (o) **Sp** [=E] M, pl. -s, 1990s (o>1 jour, rare) **Gr** (o)

it *pron./n.* 9 'sexual intercourse; sex appeal'
Ge - < trsl *es* **Du** - < *het* **Nw** [=E] mid20c (1 obs) **Ic** - < trsl *það* **Sp** [it] M 1930s (1 jour/rare)

item *n.* 1a 'any of a number of enumerated or listed things', 2 'an article, esp. one for sale', 3 'a separate or distinct piece of news, information, etc.'
Du [=E] N, 1970s (2) **Nw** [=E] N, pl. -er/-s, 1960s, 1a(1 tech); cp² 1980s, 2(1 tech) **Ic** [=E] N, pl. Ø, end20c, 1a(1 sla) **Fr** [item] M, 1960s, 1a(2) **Sp** [=E] M, pl. -s, 1a(2) **It** [=E/item] M, pl. Ø, 1970s, 1a(1) **Rm** [=E/item] N, end20c, 1a,2(1 coll, mod)

J

jack *n.* I 'a device for lifting heavy objects, esp. the axle of a vehicle, off the ground while changing a wheel etc.', 2 'a court-card with a picture of a man, esp. a soldier, page, or knave', 3 'a ship's flag, esp. one flown from the bow and showing nationality', 4 'a socket designed to receive a jack plug'
Du [=E] C, 1980s, 4(1 tech) **Nw** *jekk* [jek] M, pl. -*er*, beg20c, 1(3) → *jekke* v. **Ic** *tjakkur* [tʰjahkʏr] M, pl. -*ar*, 1920s, 1(3) → *tjakka* v. **Fr** [(d)ʒak] M, end19c, 4(1 tech) **Sp** [dʒak/jak] M, pl. -*s*, beg20c, 4(1 tech) **It** [dʒɛk] M, pl. Ø, 1930s, 2,4(1 tech) **Rm** *geac*/<=E> [dʒeak] N, mid20c, 3(1/2 tech)

jacket *n.* Ia 'a sleeved short outer garment', +Ic 'a men's outer garment', +Id 'a women's outer garment', +Ie 'a black jacket with tails', 3 'a book jacket'

Nineteenth-century loans, whatever their provenance, look French – which may be a consequence of French transmission or origin.

Ge *Jackett* [ʒakɛt] N, pl. -*s*, 19c (5Fr) +Ic(3) **Du** *jack* [jɛk] N, 1950s, +Ic(2); *jacket* [=E] N, mid20c, (2 tech) = +Ic: *jek, jekker, jacquet* (5Fr) **Nw** (0) < *jakke* (5Ge), *sjakett* (5Fr) **Ic** *jakki* [jahcɪ] M, pl. -*ar*, end19c, via Da, Ia(5); *sjakket* [sjahket] M [U] beg20c, via Da, +Ie(5 mod, obs) **Fr** *jaquette* F, 1950s, 3(4) +Ic(5) **Sp** *chaqueta* (5Fr) **It** - < *giacca* (5Fr) **Rm** *jachetă* [ʒaketə] F, end19c, via Fr, +Ic,+Ie(3) **Rs** (5Fr) **Po** (5Fr) **Cr** *žaket* M, pl. -*i*, 19c, via Fr (3) +Ie(3) **Bg** *zhaket* M, pl. -*a*/-*i*, 20c, via Fr, +Id (3) **Fi** - < *jakku* **Hu** *dzseki* [dʒɛki] pl. -*k*, 19c/beg20c, Ia(2); end20c, via Fr, +Ic(3) + Ie(3) **Al** *xhaketë* [xhakɛt] F, pl. -*a*, beg20c, via Fr, Ia,+Ic,+Id(3) **Gr** *tzaket* N, pl. Ø/-*s*, mid/end20c, Ia,+Ic,d,e(1 jour, mod); *zaketa* F, via Fr, beg20c (3)

jacket crown* *n.* 'a dental fixture'

The pronunciation of this term in Germanic languages shows that the word is felt to be from English.
Ge *Jackettkrone* [dʒɛkət-] F, pl. -*n*, 1960s (2 tech+5) **Du** *jacket(kroon)* [=E] N, 1940s (1 tech) **Nw** *jacketkrone* [=E+Nw/ʃeket-] 1950s (1 tech) **Ic** - < *króna* **Fr** - < trsl *couronne jacket/jaquette* **It** - < *corona* (5La) **Rs** (0) **Po** - < *korona* **Bg** - < *koronka* **Hu** *jacket (korona)* [=E] [U] 1950s (1 tech+5)

jackpot *n.* 2 'a large prize or amount of winnings, esp. accumulated in a game or lottery'

This term became widely known in Europe with the introduction of TV lotteries; no calques appear to have been attempted.

Ge [ʒɛkpɔt] M, pl. -*s*, 1970s (2 tech, coll) **Du** [=E] C, 1970s (2) **Nw** <=E>/*jekkpott* [=E/ jɛkpɔt] M, pl. -*er*, 1950s (2) **Fr** [(d)ʒakpɔt] M, 1970s (1 tech) **It** [=E] M [U] 1970s (1) **Rm** [=E] N, 1980s (1 rare) **Rs**

Ic	Nw	Po	Rs
Du	Ge	Cr	Bg
Fr	It	Fi	Hu
Sp	Rm	Al	Gr

dzhek-pot M [U] 1980s (1 tech, you) **Cr** [dʒekpɔt] M [U] end20c (2) **Bg** *dzhakpot* M [U] end20c (2 mod) **Fi** [=E]/*potti* (3) = trsl *jättipotti* **Hu** [=E] 1980s (2 tech) **Gr** *tzakpot* N, 1990s (2)

jab *n.* I 'an abrupt blow with one's fist or a pointed implement' (box.)
Ge [=E] M, pl. -*s*, mid20c (1 tech, obs) **Nw** *jabb* [jab] M, pl. -*er*, (1 tech) **Fr** [ʒab] M, beg20c (1 tech) **Sp** [jab] M, 1970s (1 tech) = *(golpe) corto* **It** [=E] M, pl. Ø, beg20c? (1 tech) **Rm** [=E] N, 1960s (1 tech) **Rs** *dzheb* M, pl. -*y*, mid20c (1 tech) **Hu** [=E] [U] 20c (1 tech)

jail *n.* I 'a place to which persons are committed by a court for detention'
Nw (0) **Ic** [tjei:l] N, pl. Ø, 1970s (1 sla)

jail *v.* 'put in jail'
Nw (0) **Ic** [tjei:la] 1970s (1 sla)

jam *n.* I 'a conserve of fruit and sugar boiled to a thick consistency', 5 'improvised playing by a group of (jazz, rock) musicians', +6 'a party; partaking in (wild) night-life'

This word has an unusual East European distribution; in the west *jam* is recorded for the late nineteenth century, but did not catch on, words like *marmalade* or *confiture* being preferred for the generic senses. The modern senses relating to music are rare, or found in compounds only (↑*jam session*)

Ge I(0 arch) **Du** [=E] C [U] beg20c, 1(2/3) **Nw** [=E] M [U] mid20c, 1(1 obs); [=E/*jam*] M [U] 1950s, 5(2 tech) < *sylte-tøy* **Ic** *djamm* [tjam:] N [U] 1950s, 5(1 tech) +6(2 coll) **Fr** I(Ø) **Sp** [=E] F, 1980s, 5(1 tech)

Ic	Nw	Po	Rs
Du	Ge	Cr	Bg
Fr	It	Fi	
Sp	Rm	Al	Gr

Rm *gem* [=E] N, mid20c, 1(3) **Rs** *dzhem* M [U] beg20c, 1(3) **Po** *džem*/<=E> M, mid20c, 1(3) 5(1 tech) **Cr** *džem* M, pl. -*ovi*, beg20c, 1(3) **Bg** *dzhem* M [U] end20c, 1(1 mod) **Hu** *dzsem* [=E] pl. -*ek*, end19c/beg20c, 1(3) **Al** *xhem* [xhem] M [U] mid20c, 1(1 reg)

jam *v.* 8 'extemporize with other musicians' (in jazz, etc.), +9 'take part in (wild) night- life'

Ge *jammen* [jɛmən] 20c, 8(3 tech) **Du** *jammen* [dʒɛmə] 1970s, 8(2) **Nw** *jamme* ["jame] 1950s, 8(2 tech) **Ic** *djamma* [tjam:a] 1950s, 8(1 tech) +9(2 coll) → *djammari* M **Fi** *jammata* 20c, 8(3 tech) **Gr** *tzamaro* end20c, 8(3 tech)

jamboree *n.* 1 'a celebration or merrymaking', 2 'a large rally of scouts', +3 'a jazz meeting'

The wide range of applications, esp. to jazz and to organized youth meetings, has left an indistinct geographical pattern; the word is infrequent and marginal in most but not all languages tested.

Ge [ʒembori:] N, pl. -s, mid20c, 2(1 tech) +3(1 tech, mod) **Du** [=E] C, 1940s, 2(1 tech) **Nw** [=E/jam-/dʒam-] M, pl. -r, 20c, 2(1 tech) **Ic** [=E] N, pl. Ø, mid20c, 2(Ø) < *skátamót* **Fr** [ʒabɔʀe/ʒambɔri] M, 1910s, 2(1 tech) **Sp** [=E/jambori] M/F, beg20c, 2(Ø/1 tech, rare) **Rm** [ʒamboree] F, pl. Ø, mid20c, via Fr, 2(1 obs) **Rs** *dzhembori* M, uninfl., end20c, 2(1 tech, you) **Po** [dʒambori] N, uninfl., end20c, +3(1 tech) **Cr** *džembori*, M, uninfl., mid20c (1 tech) **Bg** *dzhambore* N, pl. -ta, mid20c, 1(2 coll, obs) 2(1 tech) **Fi** [=E/jambɔri:] 2(1 tech) **Hu** *dzsembori* [=E] pl. -k, beg20c, 2(2) **Gr** *tzabori* N, mid20c, 2(1 tech)

James Grieve *n.* 'a variety of apple'

Ge [ʒe:ms gri:f] M [U] 1960s (2 tech) **Du** [=E] C [U] 1960s (2)

jamming* *n.* 'interference in a radio or electronic signal which prevents it from being received or heard clearly'

Fr <=E> 1970s (1 ban) < *brouillage* **It** [=E] M [U] 1970s (1 tech)

jam session *n.* 'improvised playing by a group of jazz (or rock) musicians'

A popular term from pop music culture, this is well known in most of Europe, and occasionally shortened to ↑*jam* (compare the universal spread of ↑*jazz*).

Ge [=E] F, pl. -s, 1950s (1 tech, you) **Du** [=E] C, mid20c (1 tech) **Nw** <=E>/*jam* [=E/jam-] M, pl. -s, 1950s (1 tech) **Ic** *djammsessjón* [tjam:sɛs:joun] F, pl. -ir, mid20c (1 tech) **Fr** *jam-session*/*jam* [dʒamsesjõ] F, 1940s (1 tech) **Sp** [=E] F, 1980s (1 tech) **It** [dʒɛm seʃon] F, pl. Ø, 1950s (1 tech) **Rm** [=E/ʒeim sesn] N, 1970s (1 tech, rare) **Rs** *dzhem-seĭshn*/*séĭshn* M, pl. -y, end20c (1 tech, you) **Po** [=E] F, 1970s (1 tech) **Cr** [=E] M [U] end20c (1 tech) **Bg** *dzhemseshŭn* M, pl. -a/-i, end20c (1 tech, you) **Fi** [=E] mid20c (1 tech, you) **Hu** [=E] [U] 1970s (1 tech) **Gr** <=E> [dzam sesjon] F, end20c (1 tech, you)

jazz *n.* 1 'music of African-American origin characterized by improvisation, syncopation, and usu. a regular or forceful rhythm'

Ge [jats/dʒes] M [U] beg20c (2) → -*en* v.; *Jazzer* M **Du** [=E] C [U] 1940s (2) **Nw** [jas] M [U] beg20c (2) → *jazze* v.; *jazzete* adj. **Ic** *djass/jass* [(t)jas:] M [U] 1920s (2) → *djassisti* M **Fr** [dʒaz] M, 1920s (2) → *jazzifier* v.; *jazzique, jazzistique* adj. **Sp** [=E] M [U] 1920s (2) → *jazzístico, jazzy, jazzero* **It** [dʒɛts/dʒɛz] M [U] 1910s (3) → *jazzista* C; *jazzistico* adj. **Rm** *jaz*/<=E> [ʒaz/=E] N, 1920s, via Fr? (2<3) → *jazolog* M; *jazistic, -ă* adj. **Rs** *dzhaz* M [U] beg20c (2) → -*ovyĭ* adj. **Po** <=E>/*dżez*/*dżaz* M [U] beg20c (2) → -*owisko* N; -*owanie* N [U] v.; -*ujący* adj.; -*owy* adj. **Cr** *džez* M [U] beg20c (2) → -*er* M; -*irati* v. **Bg** *dzhaz* cp[1], M [U] mid20c (2) → -*iram* v.; -*ov* adj. **Fi** [jats/jatsɪ] 20c (2) **Hu** *dzsessz* [=E] [U] beg20c (2) **Al** *xhaz* M, pl. -e, mid20c (1 tech) **Gr** *tzaz* F [U] beg20c (2)

jazzband* *n.* 'a band of musicians playing jazz'

This compound is almost as frequent as the universally known elements ↑*jazz* and ↑*band* are: this indicates that the compound was borrowed as one item (unrecorded in most English dictionaries!)

Ge [dʒesbent] F, pl. -s, beg20c (2) **Du** [=E] C, 1940s (2) **Nw** [jas-ban] N, pl. Ø, 20c (2) **Ic** *(d)jassband* [(t)jas:pant] N, pl. -bönd, 1920s (2 coll) = *rend djasshljómsveit* **Fr** (o) **Sp** [=E/jas ban] M/F, beg20c (1 tech) **It** [dʒɛz bɛnd] F, pl. Ø, 1910s (2) < *rend orchestra di musica jazz* **Rm** *jazband* [ʒazband/=E] N, mid20c (1 tech) **Rs** *dzhaz band*/*bénd* M, pl. -i, beg20c (2 tech) **Po** [dʒezbent] M, beg20c (1 tech) **Cr** *džez-bend* M, pl. -ovi, beg20c (2) **Bg** *dzhazbend* M, pl. -al-ove, end20c (1 tech) **Fi** [jatsbændɪ] 20c (2) **Hu** [=E] pl. -ek, beg20c (2>3) **Al** *band xhazi*/*bande schezi* mid20c (1 tech) **Gr** *tzaz bad* F, beg20c (1 tech)

jazzman *n.* 1 'a male jazz-musician', +2 'a jazz enthusiast'

The geographical distribution of this word is quite exceptional, as it is not found in the Germanic languages; -*man*, which is frequent in French (even in pseudo-anglicisms, cf. ↑*tennisman*) and in Slavic languages, appears to have fitted the morphological pattern better than in Germanic languages which prefer equivalents of 'musician', 'player' etc.

Du - < *jazzmuzikant* **Ic** *djassmaður* M, pl. -*menn*, +2(2+5) **Fr** [dʒazman] M, pl. -*mans*/-*men*, 1930s (1 tech) **Sp** [jasman] M, pl. -*men*, 1980s, 1(1 jour) **It** [dʒɛzmɛn] M, pl. Ø, 1910s, 1(1) < *jazzista* **Rm** *jazman* [ʒazman/=E] M, pl. -*meni*, 1970s, 1(1 tech) **Rs** *dzhazmen* M, pl. -*y*, mid20c, 1(2) **Po** [dʒezmen] M, mid20c, 1(2) **Cr** *džezmen* M, pl. -i, mid20c, 1(1 tech) **Bg** *dzhazmen* M, pl. -i, mid20c, 1(2 tech) → -*ka* F

jazz up *v.* +2 'play or arrange (a melody, piece of music) with jazz rhythm and syncopation'

Ge - < trsl *aufjazzen*   **Nw** *jazze opp* ["ja̲se+Nw] 1960s (1 tech)   **Ic** *djassa upp* mid/end20c (2 tech)

jazzy *adj.* 1 'of or like jazz', +3 'modish'

   Ge *jazzig* [dʒɛsɪç/jatsik] 1970s, 1(3 tech)   **Du** [=E] 1970s, 1(1 tech) = *jazz-achtig*   **Nw** [=E] 20c, 1(1 rare) < *jazzig, jazza, jazzete*   **Ic** *djassi* uninfl., end20c, 1(1 sla)   **Fr** [dʒazi] uninfl., 1970s, 1(1 tech)   **Sp** [=E] pl. Ø/-*i(e)s*, 1980s, 1(1 jour)   **It** *jazzistico* [dʒɛttsi̲stiko/dʒa-] 1950s, 1(3)   **Po** *jazzowy* end20c, 1(2)   **Bg** *dzhazov* 1,+3(3 sla, you, mod)

jeans *n./cp¹* 1 'trousers made of denim', +2 'cords', +3 'denims'

   Nothing has stopped the spread of *jeans* (the term or the item) since the 1950s. Note the scarcity of calques and morphological problems which have led to 'incorrect' singular forms and 'double' plurals. (cf. ↑*blue jeans*)

   Ge [=E] pl. (used as sg.) 1960s (2) > *blue jeans* > *Nietenhose*   **Du** [=E] C [U] 1960s (2) = *spijkerbroek*   **Nw** [=E] M [U] 1960s (1 you, mod) < *olabukse, dongeribukse*   **Ic** - < *gallabuxur*   **Fr** *jean/jeans* [dʒin/-s] M, sg., 1960s (2); *blue-jean* [dʒin/-s] M, pl.; *jean* 1960s, 1,+3(2)   **It** [=E] M, pl., 1960s, 1,+2(3) → *jeanseria* n.   **Rm** *jeanşi/ginşi* [dʒi̲nʃi] M, pl., 1970s, 1(2 you) < *blugi*   **Rs** *dzhi̲nsy* pl., mid20c (3) → -*ovyĭ* adj.   **Po** *dżinsy/*<=E> pl., mid20c, 1(2) → *dżinsowiec* M, *dżinsówa* F, *dżinsowy* adj.   **Cr** *džins* M, pl., mid20c (3) < rend *traperice*   **Bg** *dzhins* M [U] (used as sg.) 1990s, 1,+3(3 mod); *dzhi̲nsi* pl., mid20c, 1(1 you) +2(3 obs) < : *dũnki* → -*ov* adj.   **Hu** [=E] [U] 1960s (2) < ↑*farmer*   **Al** *xhins* M, pl. -*e*, end20c (1 you/3)   **Gr** *tzin* N, pl. Ø, mid20c, 1,+3(2) > *blu tzin*

jeep *n.* 1 'a small sturdy esp. military motor vehicle with four-wheel drive'

   The car and its name (possibly from *G.P.* = *general purpose* [vehicle]) became proverbially popular after 1945 as ↑*jeans* did. The word is used universally and has not sparked off any native replacements.

   Ge [dʒ-/ʃ-] M, pl. -*s*, 1940s (2)   **Du** [=E] C, 1940s (2)   **Nw** [jiːp/jep/=E] M, pl. -*er*, 1940s (2)   **Ic** *jeppi* [jɛhpɪ] M, pl. -*ar*, 1940s (3)   **Fr** [(d)ʒip] F, 1940s (2)   **Sp** [=E/jip] M, pl. -*s*, 1940s (3)   **Rm** <=E>/*jep* [=E/ʒep] N, 1960s, via Fr (2/3)   **Rs** *dzhip* M, pl. -*y*, mid20c (3)   **Po** [dʒip] M, mid20c (2)   **Cr** *džip* M, pl. -*ovi*, mid20c (2)   **Bg** *dzhip* M, pl. -*a/-ove*, mid20c (2) → -*ka* F   **Fi** *jeeppi* mid20c (3)   **Hu** *dzsip* [dʒip] pl. -*ek*, mid20c (3)   **Al** *xhip* M, pl. -*e*, mid20c (3)   **Gr** *tzip* N, mid20c (2) → *tzipaki* N

jerrycan *n.* 'a kind of petrol- or water-can'

   Du [=E] M, 1950s (2)   **Nw** *jerrykanne* [jæri-] 1950s (3 tech)   **Fr** <=E>/*jerricane* [(d)ʒerikan] M, 1950s (1 tech) < *nourrice*

jersey *n.* 1a 'a knitted usu. woollen pullover or similar garment', 1b 'plain knitted (orig. woollen) fabric', +1c 'silk, nylon fabric', +4 'the identifying outfit worn by the members of a sports team while playing'

   As the fabric was successfully exported from England during the nineteenth century, so was the term to

all countries of the Continent. This was not the case for the homonymous breed of cows – note minor differences in the loanwords which serve to distinguish the two items.

   Ge [ʒörsi] M, pl. -*s*, beg20c, 1a,b(2); N, pl. -*s*, 1970s, +4(1 tech, jour) < *Trikot*   **Du** [=E] C, beg20c, 1a,b(2)   **Nw** [jø̲ːʃi] M, pl. -*er*, beg20c, 1a(1 obs); M [U] beg20c, 1b(2)   **Ic** *jersí/jersey* [jɛrs(e)i/jes:(e)i] N [U] end19c, via Da, 1b,+1c(2)   **Fr** [ʒɛrzɛ] M, end19c, 1a(1 obs) 1b(1 tech)   **Sp** [xersei̲] M, pl. -*s*/-*yes*, end19c, 1a(3)   **It** [ʒɛrsi] M, pl. Ø/[U] 18c, 1a,b(2)   **Rm** *jerseu/jerse* [ʒɛrsɛw/ʒɛrse] N, mid20c, via Fr, 1a,1b(3); 1970s, +1c(3)   **Rs** *dzhersi̲* N, uninfl., beg20c, 1b,+1c(2) → -*ovyĭ* adj.   **Po** [dʒersei] [U] beg20c, 1b(2); → -*owy* adj.   **Cr** *džersej* M [U] beg20c, 1b,+1c(2); → -*ski* adj.   **Bg** *zharse̲/zherse̲* N [U] beg20c, via Fr, +1c(3) → -*n* adj.   **Fi** [=E] 1b(1)   **Hu** *dzsörzé* [dʒøːrze:] pl. -*k*, end19c/beg20c, 1b(3) +1c(3) +4(2 tech, arch)   **Al** *zherse* [ʒɛrsɛ] M [U] mid20c, 1a,b,+1c(3)   **Gr** *tzersei* (1 obs), *ze̲rsei* N [U] beg20c, 1b,+1c(1 tech)

Jersey *n./cp¹ᐟ²*, adj. 'a light brown dairy cow from Jersey'

   Nw *jerseyfe* [jøːʃi+Nw] cp¹, 20c (1+5 tech)   **Ic** *Jersey-* cp¹, beg/mid20c (2 tech)   **Fr** *jersiais(e)* [ʒɛrzjɛ-jez] M/F/adj., 19c (4)   **Rm** [=E] cp², 1940s (1 tech)   **Rs** *dzhersi̲* F, uninfl., 20c (1 tech)   **Po** *dżerseje* [dʒerseie] pl., mid20c (1 tech)   **Bg** *dzhersei̲/zherze̲i̲* M [U]/pl. -*te*, 20c (1 tech) → -*ski* adj.   **Fi** (1)   **Al** 20c (1 tech) *lópë xherse̲j*

Jesus *interj.* 'an exclamation of surprise, dismay, etc.'

   Ic [=E] end20c (1 you)   **Sp** *Jesus* (4)   **Rm** [=E] end20c (1 you)   **Fi** [=E] end20c (1 you)

jet¹ *n./cp¹* 3a 'a jet engine', 3b 'an aircraft powered by one or more jet engines', +3c 'a jet ski'

   Ge [ʒet] M, pl. -*s*, 1960s, 3b(1 mod) < *Düsenflugzeug* → *jetten* v.   **Du** *jetmotor/jet* [=E] C, 1970s, 3a(2+5) 3b(2)   **Nw** *jetfly* [jet-] M/cp¹, mid20c, 3a,b(2)   **Ic** [=E] N/cp¹, 1960s, 3b(1 obs) < rend *þota*   **Fr** [dʒɛt] M, 1960s, 3b (1 ban, mod) < *avion à réaction*   **Sp** [=E] M, pl. Ø/-*s*, 1960s, 3a,b (1 tech)   **It** [=E] M, pl. Ø, 1960s, 3b(2)   **Rm** [=E] N, 1970s, 3b(1 tech) < *avion cu reacţie*   **Cr** *džet* M, pl. -*ovi*, mid20c, 3b(2)   **Bg** *dzhet* M, pl. -*a/-ove*, 1990s, +3c(3 mod)   **Hu** [=E] mid20c, 3b(2)   **Gr** *tzet* N, 1980s, 3b(2 mod) +3c(1 tech, rare)

jet² *n.* 1b 'jewellery made from polished coal'

   Ge *Jett* [jet] M/N [U] 19c (3 arch)   **Du** *git* (5)   **Nw** *jett* [jet] M [U] 20c (1 tech)   **Po** *dżet* M, beg20c (2 coll)

jet lag *n.* 'extreme tiredness and other symptoms felt after a long flight across time zones, jet fatigue'

   Ge [ʒetlɛk] M, pl. -*s*, 1980s (1 tech)   **Du** [=E/jet-] N [U] 1970s (1)   **Nw** [=E/jet-] N, pl. -*s*, 1970s (1 tech)   **Ic** [=E] end20c (0) = *flugþreyta; dægurvilla*   **Fr** (0)   **Sp** [=E] M [U] 1980s (1 tech)   **It** *jetlag* [dʒet lɛg] M [U] 1960s (1)   **Po** [=E] M [U] end20c (1 tech)   **Cr**

(o) **Fi** (o) **Hu** [=E] [U] 1980s (1) **Gr** *tzet lag* N [U] 1990s (1 tech)

jet liner* *n.* 'an aircraft'
Ge [ʒetlaina] M, pl. Ø, 1980s (1 mod, rare) **It** [=E] M, pl. Ø, 1960s (1) **Rm** (o>1 tech, mod) **Bg** ↑*liner*

jet set *n.* 1 'wealthy people frequently travelling by air, esp. for pleasure', +2 'much talked about and usu. wealthy people'
This compound is notably less frequent than the word ↑*jet*, but the distributions of the two items are quite complex when compared. Contrast the more or less synonymous ↑*jet society*.

Ge [ʒetset] M [U] 1980s (1 mod) **Du** [=E] C, 1970s (1 mod) **Nw** <=E>/*jettsett* [jetset] N, pl. Ø, 1960s (2) → *jet-sette* v. **Ic** [tjɛht sɛht] N [U] 1970s, +2(1 sla) = creat *þotuliđ* **Fr** *jet-set*/ *jet set* [dʒɛtsɛt] M/F, 1960s (1 mod) **Sp** <=E>/*jet* [=E] F [U] 1970s (1 fac) < *jet socíety* **It** *jet-set* [=E] M [U] 1960s (1 mod) < *jet-society* **Po** [=E] M [U] end20c (1 tech) **Cr** *džet-set* M [U] end20c (1 tech) **Bg** (o) **Fi** *jetsetti* (o) **Gr** *tzet set* N [U] 1980s, +2(1 jour/fac)

jet ski *n.* 'a jet-propelled vehicle like a motorbike, for riding across water', +2 'a downhill ski technique'
Du [=E] C [U] 1980s, 1 (1 tech) = *jetski* → *jetskiën* v. **Nw** [jetʃiː] M, pl. Ø, 1980s, 1 (1 tech+5) **Fr** [dʒɛtski] M, 1980s (1 tech) **Sp** [=E] M, 1980s, 1(1 tech) = *moto náutica* **Rs** (o) **Cr** [dʒetski] M [U] 1980s (1 tech) **Bg** *dzhet* M [U] end20c, +2(1 tech) **Gr** *tzet ski* N, 1990s, 1(2)

jet-society* *n.* 'rich international society people spending a considerable amount of time on business trips or on holiday'
Sp [=E] F, 1970s (1 tech) > *jet set* **It** [dʒet sosaieti] F, pl. Ø, 1960s (1) **Rm** [=E] N [U] 1970s (1 rare)

jet stream *n.* 'a narrow current of very strong winds encircling the globe several miles above the earth'
Ge [=E] M [U] 1980s (1 tech) **Du** [=E] C, 1970s (1 tech) > *straalstroom* **Nw** *jetstråle* [=E+Nw] 1960s (1+5 tech) **Ic** - < rend *skotvindur* **Fr** *jet-stream* [dʒɛtstrim] M, 1950s (1 tech, ban) < trsl *courant-jet* **Po** [-im] M [U] mid20c (1 tech) **Cr** *džetstrim* M [U] end20c (1 tech)

jig *n.* 1a 'a lively dance with leaping music', 1b 'the music for this'
Du [=E] C, 1960s (2) **Nw** [jig] M, pl. -*er*, 20c, 1a,b(1 tech) **Fr** *gigue* (4) **Sp** - < *giga* **It** - < *giga* **Rm** *gigă* [dʒigə] F, mid20c, via / from Fr (3 tech) **Rs** *dzhiga*/*zhiga* F [U] beg19c (3 tech, obs) **Po** <=E> M [U] mid20c (Ø) **Bg** *zhiga* F, pl. -*gi*, 20c, via Fr, 1a(3 tech) **Fi** - < *gigue* **Hu** *dzsigg* [dʒig] end19c, 1a(1 arch) **Gr** *zig* N, 20c, 1a(Ø)

jigger *n.* +7 'a machine used to dye textiles'
Ge [=E] M, pl. -*s*, 1940s (1 tech) **Du** [=E] C, 1970s (1 tech) **Fr** [(d)ʒigœʀ/(d)ʒigɛʀ] M, beg20c (1 tech) **It** [dʒiger] M, pl. Ø, 1930s (1 tech) **Rm** *jigher*/<=E> [ʒiger] N, mid 20c (1 tech) **Rs** *dzhigger*

jingle *n.* 2b 'a short verse used in advertising'
This word very clearly illustrates the typical distribution of an incoming media term: rare outside specialists' jargon and confined to Western Europe – so far.

Ge [(d)ʒɪŋəl] M, pl. -*s*, 1980s (1 tech, mod) **Du** [=E] C, 1970s (2) **Nw** [=E/jiŋel] M, pl. -*rl*-*s*, 1980s (1 tech) **Fr** [dʒiŋgœl] M, 1980s (1 tech, ban) > *sonal* **Sp** [=E/jiŋgvel] M, pl. -*s*, end20c (1 tech) **It** [dʒiŋgol] M, pl. Ø, 1980s (1 rare) **Rm** (o>1 jour) **Po** *džingiel* [dʒingiel] M, end20c (1 tech)

jitterbug *n.* 2a 'a fast dance, performed chiefly to swing music'
Together with ↑*charleston* this dance emerged in the USA in the 1920s ('the jazz-age') and became popular in Europe in the 1940s and 1950s when it appears to have been restricted mainly to Central Europe. Contemporary pronunciations cannot be fully reconstructed – some must have been based on the spelling.

Ge [ʒitabag] M [U] 1940s (1 arch) **Du** [dʒɪtərbyk] C [U] 1920s (1 obs) → *jitterbuggen* v. **Nw** [jitterbøg] M [U] mid20c (1 arch) **Ic** [(t)jɪhterbœg/tʰjuhter/tʰjuh-tibœg] N [U] mid20c (1 coll, arch); *tjútt* N, 1950s (2); → *tjútta* v.; *tjúttari* M **Rm** [=E] N, 1970s (1 arch, rare) **Po** [=E] M [U] beg20c (1 arch) **Cr** *džiterbag* M [U] mid20c (1 arch) **Fi** [=E] mid20c (1)

jive *n.* 1 'a jerky, lively style of dance, esp. popular in the 1950s, a kind of jitterbug', 2 'music for this dance'
The term seemed to be on its way out in Britain when it regained popular currency under the guise of *le jive*, a French dance style based on traditional jive.
Ge [=E] M [U] 1950s (1 obs) **Du** [=E] C, mid20c, 2(1 tech) → *jiven* v. **Nw** [=E] M [U] mid20c, 1(1 tech) 2 (1 arch) **Ic** [tjaiːf] N [U] 1950s (2) → *djæfa* v. **Fr** [dʒajv] 2(1 obs) **Rm** [=E] N, 1970s, 2(1 mod) **Rs** *dzhaiv* M [U] mid20c (1 tech, obs) **Cr** [=E] M [U] mid20c, 2(1) **Bg** *dzhaiv* M [U] mid20c (1 tech) **Fi** [=E] 2(1) **Hu** [=E] [U] 20c (1 tech) **Gr** *tzaiv* N [U] mid20c (1 obs)

job *n.* 1 'a piece of work, esp. one done for hire or profit', 2 'a paid position of employment', +2a '(temporary) work', 6 'an item of work regarded separately' (comput.)
For those accustomed to the ubiquity of *job* it comes as a surprise to find how restricted the currency is in Southern and Eastern Europe. Accordingly, the derived verb is found in even fewer languages (German, Norwegian, Icelandic), with compounds like ↑*job-hopping* and ↑*job-ticket* found in German only.
Ge [ʒop/ʃop] M, pl. -*s*, 1940s, 2, +2a(2) → *jobben* v.; -*er*

M **Du** [=E] C, 1940s (1 coll) = *baan* **Nw** *jobb* [jɔb] M, pl. -*er*, beg20c (3) → *jobbe* v. **Ic** *(d)jobb* [(t)jɔp:] N, pl. Ø, mid20c, 1(2 coll) 2(2 sla) → *djobba* v. **Fr** [dʒɔb] M, 1950s, +2a(2 coll) **Sp** [=E] end20c, 6(1 tech) **It** [=E] M, pl. Ø, 1970s (1 tech) **Rm** [=E] N, 1970s (2 coll) **Cr** *džob* M, pl. -*ovi*, end20c (1 coll) **Fi** *jobi* end20c (1 you) **Hu** [=E] [U] end20c (1 tech, mod) **Gr** <=E> end20c (1 writ)

job-hopping* n. 'a frequent change of jobs' (cf. ↑*hopping*)
Ge [=E] N [U] 1990s (1 mod)

job-killer* n. 'a thing (rarely: person) causing loss of jobs'
Ge [ʒɔpkila] M, pl. Ø, 1970s (1 mod) **Nw** [jobkiler] M, pl. -*s*, 1980s (1 rare)

job-sharing n. 'an arrangement whereby two people share a full-time job'
Ge [ʒɔpʃeːriŋ] N [U] 1980s (1 jour) **Fr** - < trsl *partage du travail* **It** [=E] M [U] end20c (1 tech)

job-ticket* n. 'a commuter rail ticket at reduced cost'
Ge [=E] N, pl. -*s*, 1990s (2 mod)

jockey n. 'a professional rider in horse-races'
Ge [ʒɔki/jɔkai] M, pl. -*s*, 19c (2) → *jockette* F **Du** [=E] C, end19c (2) **Nw** [jɔki/=E] M, pl. -*er*, end19c (2) **Ic** - < *knapi* **Fr** [ʒɔkɛ] M, end18c (2) **Sp** *joqvey* etc. [jɔkei/jɔki] M, pl. -*s*, mid19c (2) **It** [dʒɔkei] M, pl. Ø, end19c (1 tech) < mean *fantino* **Rm** <=E>/*jochei* [ʒɔkɛj] M, end19c, via Fr? (1 arch); *jocheu* [ʒɔkɛw] M, mid20c, via Fr (3) **Rs** *zhokei* M, pl. -*i*, mid19c (2) → -*skiĭ* adj. **Po** *żokej* M, mid19c (2) → -*stwo* N, -*ski* adj. **Cr** *džokej* M, pl. -*i*, end19c (2) **Bg** *zhokei* M, pl. -*kei*, end19c, via Fr (3) → -*ski* adj. **Fi** [jɔːkei] 20c (2) **Hu** *zsoké* [ʒɔkeː] pl. -*k*, 17c (3) **Al** *xhokej* [dʒɔkej] M, pl. Ø, beg20c (1 reg/3) **Gr** *tzokei* M, end19c (3)

jockey cap n. +1 'a cap originally worn by jockeys (recently a fashion item)'
Du - < *jockeypet* **It** [dʒɔkei kɛp] M, pl. Ø, beg20c (1 tech) **Rm** - < rend *cascheta de jocheu* **Rs** *zhokeĭka* F, 20c (2) **Po** *żokejka* [dʒɔkeika] F, beg20c (2) **Bg** *zhokeĭka* F, 20c (3) **Hu** - < trsl *zsoké sapka*

jodhpurs n. 'long breeches for riding etc.'
Ge *Jodhpur-Hose* F, end20c (1+5 obs, rare) **Du** [=E] pl., 1970s (1 tech) **Nw** [=E] end20c (1 rare) < *ridebukse(r)* **Fr** *jodhpur* [ʒɔdpyʀ] M, pl. -*s*, 1950s (1 tech) **It** [dʒɔdpurs] M, pl. Ø, 1970s (1 tech, rare, obs)

jog v. 1 'run at a slow pace, esp. for exercise'
Ge [ʒɔgən] 1980s (2) **Du** *joggen* [dʒɔɡə] 1970s (2) = *trimmen* **Nw** *jogge* ["jɔge] 1950s (3) **Ic** *jogga* [jɔkːa] 1960s (1 arch) < rend *skokka* → *jogg* N **Fr** *jogger* [dʒɔge] 1970s (1 tech) **Cr** *džogirati* end20c (1)

jogger n. 'a person who jogs'
Ge [ʒɔga] M, pl. Ø, 1980s (2) 1970s (2) **Nw** [jɔger] M, pl. -*e*, 1970s (3) **Fr** *joggeur/-euse/jogger* M/F, 1970s (1 mod) **It** [=E] M/F,

pl. Ø, 1970s (1) **Rm** [=E] M, 1990s (1 coll) **Rs** *dzhogger* M, pl. -*y*, 1980s (1 tech) **Cr** *džoger* M, pl. -*i*, 1980s (1)

jogging n. 1 'running as a form of exercise' (sport), 2 *cp*[1] 'used in jogging'
Ge *Jogging* [=E] N [U] 1980s, 1,+2(2) **Du** <=E> [=E] C [U] 1970s (2) **Nw** [jogin] M/F [U] (3) **Ic** [(t)jɔːiŋ-] cp[1], 1980s, 2(2 coll) **Fr** <=E> [dʒɔgiŋ] M, 1970s (2) < *footing* **Sp** [jogin] M [U] 1980s (2) < *footing* **It** [=E] M [U] 1970s (2) = *footing* (2 mod) **Rs** *dzhogging* M [U] 1980s (2 tech) **Po** [-nk] M [U] 1980s, 1(2 coll) **Cr** *džoging* M [U] 1980s (1) **Bg** *dzhoging* M [U] 1980s, 1(2) **Hu** *jogging* [=E] [U] 1980s, 1(2) < *kocogás* **Gr** <=E>/*tzokin(g)* N [U] 1980s (2)

John Bull n. 'a personification of England and the English'
The term was coined by John Arbuthnot in 1712. It was popular as a designation of Britain mainly in the nineteenth century.
Ge [ʒɔnbul] M [U] 19c (1 arch) **Du** (Ø) **Nw** [=E] 19c (Ø/1 arch) **Ic** - < trsl *Jón boli* **Sp** [=E] M [U] mid19c (1 rare) **Rm** [=E] M, end19c (1 arch/rare) **Rs** *dzhon Bul'* M [U] 18/19c (Ø) **Po** <=E> M [U] end19c (1 arch) **Bg** *Dzhon Bul* M [U] end19c (Ø) **Hu** [=E] [U] 18c (Ø)

joint n. 5 'a marijuana cigarette'
Ge [ʒɔint] M, pl. Ø, 1970s (1 you) **Du** [=E] C, 1970s (1 jour, sla, you) **Nw** [=E] M, pl. -*er*, 1970s (1 tech) **Ic** [=E] N, pl. Ø, *djöntur* [tjœntyr] M, -*ar*, 1970s (1 sla) > rend *jónta, jóna* F; *jonni* M **Fr** [ʒwɛ̃] M, pl. -*s*, 1970s (4) **Sp** <=E>/*joe/joi/yoe/yoin* [=E/dʒoin/join] 1970s (1 sla, you) < *porro* **It** [=E] M, pl. Ø, 1970s (1 sla) **Rs** (0) **Po** <=E> M 1980s (1 sla) **Cr** [dʒoint] M, pl. -*i*, end20c (1 sla) **Bg** *dzhoint* M, pl. -*al-ove*, 1990s (1 sla, you) **Gr** *tzoint* N, pl. Ø/-*s*, 1970s, 5(1 sla)

joint venture n. '(international) cooperation between two firms'
Ge [=E] N, pl. -*s*, 1970s (1 tech) **Du** [=E] C, 1970s (1 tech) **Nw** [=E] N, pl. -*s*, 1970s (1 tech) **Fr** *joint-venture/joint venture* [dʒɔ jnt vɛntʃœʀ] F, 1970s (1 tech, ban) > *coentreprise* **Sp** [=E] M/F, pl. -*s*, 1980s (1 tech) **It** [dʒɔint ventʃur] F, pl. Ø, 1980s (1 tech) **Rm** [=E] N [U] 1990s (1 tech, mod) **Rs** (0) < trsl *sovmestnoe predpriyatie* **Po** <=E> M [U] 1980s (1 mod) **Cr** [=E] M [U] end20c (1 tech) **Bg** *dzhoint venchŭr* M [U] end20c (1 tech) **Fi** [=E] end20c (1) **Hu** [=E] [U] end20c (1 tech) **Al** *xhointvençër* [=E] M [U] 1990s (1 tech) **Gr** <=E> [=E] N [U] 1990s (0> 1 tech, rare)

joke *n.* 1a 'a thing said or done to excite laughter', 1b 'a witticism or jest'

Ic *djók(ur)* [tjou:k(ʏr)] N/M [U] 1970s (2 coll) Fi [=E]/*djoukki* 1980s (1 sla, you)

joke *v.* 1 'make jokes', 2 'poke fun at; banter'

Ic *djóka* [tjou:ka] 1970s (2 coll) → *djókari* M

joker *n.* 1 'a person who jokes', 3 'a playing-card' (cf. ↑*wild card*)

Ge [jo:ka] M, pl. Ø, beg20c, 3(3) Du [dʒo:kər/jo:kər] C, 1940s, 3(2>3) Nw [ju:ker] M, pl. -*e*, beg20c, 3(3) Ic *djóker*/*djókari* [tjou:ker/-arı] M, pl. -*ar*, 1970s, 1(2 sla); *jóker* [jou:ker] M, pl. -*ar*, beg20c, 3(3) Fr [(d)ʒɔkɛʀ] M, beg20c, 3(2) Sp [joker] 1970s, 3(1 tech, rare) < *comodín* It [dʒɔker] M, pl. Ø, 1920s, 3(2) < *jolly* Rm <=E>/*jocher* [dʒokər] M, beg20c, 3(2) Rs *dzhoker* M, pl. -*y*, beg20c, 3(2) Po *dżoker*/<=E> M, beg20c, 3(2 coll) Cr *džoker* M, pl. -*i*, beg20c, 3(2) Bg *zhoker* M, pl. -*a*/-*i*, beg20c, via Fr, 3(3 tech) Fi *jokeri* 20c, 3(3) Hu *dzsóker* [dʒoker] pl. -*ek*, beg20c, 3(3) Gr *tzoker* M, beg20c, 3(1 tech)

jolly *n.*/*cp¹* +2 'a joker in card games', +3 'a factotum'

Whereas the distribution of ↑*joker* is almost universal, the shortening to *jolly (joker)* is much more restricted. (It is impossible to determine which languages originally had the two-word combination exclusively, or as an alternative to *joker*.)

It [dʒɔlli] M, pl. Ø, 1920s, +2(3); 1940s, +3(3) Rm *jolly jocker* [=E] N, 1920s (2 tech) Hu *dzsoli (dzsóker)* [=E] *cp¹*, beg20c, +2(3) < *dzsóker* Al *xhol* [dʒol] M, pl. -*e*, beg20c, +2,+3(3)

jolly *adj.* 1 'cheerful and good humoured'

Ic [tjol:i] uninfl., end20c (1 sla)

Jonathan (freckle) *n.* 'a variety of apple'

Ge [jo:nata:n] M [U] 20c (3) Du *jonathan* (5) Ic *Jónatanepli* N, end20c (3 tech+5) Fr *Jonathan* F, mid20c (1) Rm *ionatan* [jonatan] N, beg20c (3) Rs *dzhonatan* M [U] mid20c (3) Po *jonatan* [jonatan] M, mid20c (3) Cr *jonatan* M, mid20c (3) Bg *dzhonatan* M [U] mid20c (1 tech) Fi (3) Hu *jonatán* [jonata:n] pl. Ø, end19c/beg20c (3)

joule *n.* 'a unit of energy' (phys)

The British scientist James Prescott Joule (1818–89) is famous for determining the mechanical equivalent of heat and the conservation of energy; the pronunciation of *joule* appears to vary in English (/u:/ or /au/), an uncertainty reflected in the loanwords – where the term is occasionally thought to be of French provenance. As a technical term *joule* in German goes back to the beginning of the twentieth century. In 1978 it officially superseded *Kalorie* but seems not have been widely accepted by the speech community.

Ge [dʒu:l/dʒaul] N, pl. Ø/-*s*, 1970s (1 tech) Du [=E] C, beg20c, via Fr (3) Nw [jʉ:l] M [U] 20c (1 tech) Ic *joule*/*júl* [ju:l] N, pl. Ø, end20c (2 tech) Fr [ʒul] M, end19c (1 tech) Sp - < *julio* It [dʒaul] M, pl. Ø, 1920s (1 tech) → *joulometro* n. Rm [ʒul] M, beg20c,

via Fr (2 tech) Rs *dzhoul'* M, pl. -*i*, mid20c (1 tech) Po *dżull*/<=E> M, mid20c (1 tech) Cr *džul* M, pl. -*i*, mid20c (1 tech) Bg *dzhaul* M, pl. -*a*, mid20c (1 tech) Fi [joule] (3) Hu [=E] [U] end19c/beg20c (1 tech) Al *xhaul* M, pl. -*ë*, mid20c (1 tech/3) Gr *tzaul* N, mid/end20c (1 tech)

joyride *v.* 'ride for pleasure, esp. in a stolen motor-car'

Ge [=E] 1990s (1 you, rare) Du *joyriden* [dʒoirajdən] 1980s (2) → *joyrider* n.

joyride *n.* 'a ride for pleasure, esp. one in a stolen motor car'

Ge – → *Joyriding* N [U] 1990s (1 you, rare) Du [=E] C [U] 1990s (1 you, rare) Nw [=E] M, pl. -*s*, 1990s (1 rare) Gr (0)

joystick *n.* 2 'a lever that can be moved in several directions to control the movement of an image on a VDU screen'

Ge [=E] M, pl. -*s*, 1980s (1 tech) Du [=E] C, 1980s (1 tech, you) Nw [=E/joy-] M, pl. -*er*, 1970s (1 tech) Ic - < rend *stýripinni* Fr [(d)ʒɔjstik] M, 1980s (1 tech, ban) < *manche à balai* Sp M [joistik] M, 1980s (1 tech) =*mando* It [dʒɔistik] M, pl. Ø, 1980s (2) Rm [=E] N, 1990s (0>1 tech) Rs *dzhoistik* M, pl. -*i*, end20c (1 tech) Po *dżojstik*/<=E> M, end20c (2 tech) Cr [dʒojstik] M, pl. -*ovi*, end20c (1 tech) Bg *dzhoistik* M, pl. -*a*/-*ove*, end20c (1 tech) Fi [=E] 1980s (1) Hu [=E] pl. Ø, 1980s (1 tech, you, mod>2) Gr *tzoistik* N, pl. Ø/-*s*, end20c (1 tech) > *mokhlos elegghu*

judo *n.* 'a sport of unarmed combat derived from ju-jitsu'

This term is from Japanese and it is not clear whether English transmission is detectable in any of the 16 languages here investigated.

Ge [ju:do:] N [U] beg20c (3) → *Judoka* M/F Du [jydo:] [U] 20c Nw [jʉ:du] (5Jap) Ic *júdó* [ju:tou] N [U] 1950s (2) Fr [ʒydo] (5Jap) Sp [judo] M [U] 1950s (2) → *judoka*/*judoca* It (5Jap) Rm [dʒudo/judo] N [U] 1960s, via Fr.? Rs *dzyudo* N, uninfl. [U] mid20c (2) → -*ist* M Po *dżudo* [dʒudo] N, uninfl., mid20c (2) Cr *džudo* M [U] mid20c (2) Bg *dzhudo* N [U] mid20c (Ø) → *dist*/-*ka* M/F Fi [judɔ] 20c (3) Hu *dzsudó* [dʒudo] pl. Ø, beg20c (1 tech, rare); mid20c (5Jap) Al *xhudo* F [U] end20c (3) Gr *tzudo* N [U] mid20c (2)

juice *n.* +1b 'a drink made from fruits or vegetables', +5 'alcoholic beverages'

This word is restricted, but is still remarkably widespread considering the fact that it does not add any information to that of native terms; the attractiveness of the English word must, then, play a part in its adoption.

Ge [ju:s] M (F/N) pl. -*s*, 1960s, +1b(1 reg) < *Obstsaft* Du - < *vruchtesap* Nw [jʉ:s/=E] M [U] 1950s, +1b(2) Ic *djús* [tju:s] N/M [U] 1960s, +1b(2 coll) +5(2 sla) = +1b *safi* → *djúsa* v.; -*ari* M; -*erí*

N; -aður adj. **Fr** - < *jus* (4) **Rm** [dʒjus] N, 1970s, +1b(2 mod) < *suc* **Rs** *dzhus* M [U] 1990s (1 coll, mod) **Po** <=E> end20c,+1b(1 writ) **Cr** *džus* M, pl. -ovi, mid20c, +1b(2) **Bg** *dzhus* M, pl. -al-ove, end20c, +1b(1 mod) **Hu** *dzsúsz* [dʒuːs] pl. Ø, beg20c, +1b(2 mod>3) **Al** *xhus* M [U] 1990s, 1b(2)

juicy adj. 1 'full of juice', 2 'substantial or interesting; racy, scandalous'
   Nw [juːsi/=E] 1980s (1 coll, rare) **Ic** *djúsí* [tjuːsi] uninfl., 1970s (1 sla)

jukebox n. 'a coin-operated machine playing selected musical recordings'
   This term is obsolescent in some languages (where ↑*music box* is preferred), but remarkably vital in others. Its adoption during the 1950s is reflected in its limited currency in Eastern Europe.
   Ge [juːkboks] F, pl. -en/-es, 1950s (1 you, obs) < *Musikbox* **Du** [=E] C, 1960s (2 obs) > *muziek-automaat* **Nw** <=E>/*jukeboks* [juːkboks] M, pl. -er, 1950s (2 obs) **Ic** *djúkbox* [tjuːkpɔxs] N, pl. Ø, 1950s (2 coll, obs) **Fr** *juke-box* [ʒykbɔks/dʒukbɔks] M, pl. Ø, uninfl., 1960s (1 obs) **Sp** [=E/*jukeboks*] M, pl. -es, 1970s (1 obs) < *máquina de discos* **It** [dʒubɔks] M, pl. Ø, 1950s (3) **Rm** [=E] N, 1970s (1 rare) **Cr** *džuboks* M, pl. -i, mid20c (3) **Bg** *dzhuboks* M, pl. -al-ove, end20c (1 mod) < *muzikalen avtomat, muzikboks* **Fi** *juke-boxi* [jukebɔksi] 1970s (2) **Hu** [=E] pl. Ø, 1970s (1 tech, mod) < *zenedoboz* **Al** *xhuboks* [dʒu(k)boks] M, pl. -e, mid20c (1) **Gr** *tzuk box, tzukbox* N, mid20c (2)

jumbo n./cp¹ 1 'a large animal (esp. an elephant), person, or thing', +3 'a large vehicle for transporting ↑*drills* in ↑*mines*'
   Ge [jumbo:] cp¹, 1970s, 1(3) **Du** [dʒymbo:/jymbo:] cp¹, 1960s, 1(1 coll) **Nw** [jumbu] cp¹, 1960s, 1(3) **Sp** [jumbo] M/adj., pl. Ø, beg20c, 1(1 jour) **It** [dʒambo/dʒumbo] adj., 1960s, 1(2) **Rm** [=E] N, 1970s, +3(1 tech, rare) **Po** dʒambo N, uninfl., end20c, 1(1 tech) **Cr** *džambo* adj., end20c, 1(1 tech) **Bg** *dzhumbo* N [U] 1(1 mod, rare) **Gr** *tzabo* N/adj., end20c (1 coll, rare, mod)

jumbo-jet n. 'a large airliner (orig. mainly Boeing 747)'
   Ge [jumbo:dʒet] M, pl. -s, 1970s (3+2) **Du** [dʒym-bodʒ1t] C, 1970s (2) **Nw** [jumbujet] M, pl. -er, 1960s (2) **Ic** *júmbópota* [jumpou-] F, pl. -ur, end20c (2+5coll) = rend *breiðpota* **Fr** *jumbo* [(d)ʒæbo] M, 1970s (1 tech, ban) < *gros-porteur* **Sp** *jumbo* (-jet) M, pl. -s, 1970s (2) **It** [dʒambo dʒɛt/dʒumbo dʒɛt] M, pl. Ø, 1960s (2) [jumbojɛt] **Rm** <=E>/*jumbo* [=E] N [U] 1970s (1 tech) **Rs** *dzhambo-dzhet* M, pl. -y, 1990s (1 tech) **Po** [dʒambodʒet] M, end20c (1 tech) **Cr** *džambodžet* M, pl. -ovi, end20c (1 tech) **Bg** *dzhŭm-bodzhet*, pl. -al-i, end20c (1 tech) **Fi** *jumbojetti* (1) **Hu** [=E] pl. -ek, 1980s (2) **Gr** *tzabo tzet* N, end20c (1 tech)

jump v. 'leap'
   Ge [dʒampən] 1970s (1 coll) **Du** *jumpen* [dʒympə] 1970s (2) **Nw** *jumpe* ["jumpe] end19c (3) **Fr** - → *jumping* beg20c (1 tech_HORSES)

jumper n. 1 'a knitted pullover', +4 'a light two-piece woman's suit'
   This word was adopted from a sailor's term in the early twentieth century, but came to be superseded by ↑*sweater* (itself slightly obsolescent now) and ↑*pullover* from the 1930s onwards. The currency of *jumper* apparently never extended to Southern Europe.
   Ge [jumpa-/dʒampa-] M, pl. Ø, beg20c, 1(1 reg, obs) **Du** [jympər] C, 1940s, 1(1 obs) **Nw** [jumper] M, pl. -e, beg20c, 1(1 obs) **Rs** *dzhemper* M, pl. -y, mid20c, 1(1 obs) **Po** [-er] M, end20c, 1(1 arch) **Cr** *džem-per* M, pl. -i, mid20c, 1(1) **Bg** *dzhempŭr* M, pl. -al-i, beg20c, +4(3 obs) **Fi** *jumpperi* 20c (1) **Hu** *dzsöm-per* [dʒøːmper] pl. -ek, beg20c, 1(1 obs)

jumping n. 1 'in horse racing', 2 'bungee jumping'
   Du [dʒympiŋ] C [U] end 20c, 2(1 tech) **Fr** [dʒœmpiŋ] M, beg20c (1 tech) **Sp** [=E] M [U] end20c (1 tech) **Rm** [=E] N, 20c (3 coll, you) **Po** [-nk] M [U] mid20c (1 tech)

jungle n. 1 'a tropical forest', 3 'a place of bewildering complexity or confusion or of struggle for survival', 4 'a type of fast dance music'
   This word is one of the most widespread nineteenth-century anglicisms; it started out as a foreignism, but has since developed various metaphorical uses. Note that the pronunciation testifies to the adoption from books, e.g. travelogues on India.
   Ge *Dschungel* [dʒuŋgəl] M, pl. Ø, 19c, 1,3(2>3); [=E] cp¹, 1990s, 4(1 tech) **Du** [dʒyŋgəl] C, 1940s, 3(2) = *rimboe* **Nw** *jungel* [juŋel] M, pl. -gler, beg20c, 1,3(3); [=E] M [U] 1990s, 4(1 tech) **Ic** - < *frumskógur* **Fr** [ʒœ̃gl/ʒɔ̃gl] F, end18c/beg19c, 1(2>3) **Sp** *jungla* F, 1,3(3); *jungle* [=E] M, beg20c (1 tech) **It** *giungla/jungla* [dʒuŋgla] F, pl. -e, end19c, 1,3(3) **Rm** *jun-glă* [ʒuŋglə] F, 1870s, via Fr (3) **Rs** *dzhungli* pl., uninfl., beg20c, 1,3(3) **Po** *džungla* [dʒuŋgla] F, beg20c, 1,3(3) → *džunglowy* adj. **Cr** *džungla* F, pl. -e, beg20c, 1(3) **Bg** *dzhungla* F, pl. -gli, beg20c, via Rs, 1,3(3) **Hu** *dzsungel* [dʒuŋgel] pl. -ek, end19c/beg20c, 1(2) 3(3) **Al** *xhunglë* F, pl. -la, end19c, 1, 3(3) **Gr** *zugla* F, beg20c, via Fr, 1,3(3)

junk¹ (1) n. 2 'anything regarded as of little value', 3 'a narcotic drug, esp. heroin'
   Du [dʒyŋk] C, 1980s (1 tech) **Nw** [=E] M/N [U] 1970s, 2,3(1 sla) **Ic** *djönk* [tjœŋk] N [U] 1970s, 2(2 coll) 3(1 sla) **Rm** *joncă* (5Fr)

junk² (2) n. 'a flat-bottomed sailing vessel used in the China seas'
   As with ↑*jungle*, the word was adopted from nineteenth-century travelogues, and pronounced according to national conventions. However, the word is not

as widespread as ↑ *jungle* and was not transmitted through English in all languages.

Ge *Dschunke* F, pl. *-n,* 19c (3 tech)   **Du** *jonk* [tjɔnk] C, pl. *-en,* 19c (5 Mal)   **Nw** *djunke* [dju̯ŋke/dʒu-] M, pl. *-r,* 20c (3 tech)   **Ic** *djúnka* [tju̯ŋka] F, pl. *-ur,* mid20c (2 tech)   **Fr** *jonque* (5Port)   **Sp** - < *junco* (5Port)   **It** *giunca* via Port (5Mal)   **Rs** *dzhonka* F, pl. *-i* (3 tech/5Mal)   **Po** *dżonka* [dʒonka] F, beg20c (1 tech)   **Cr** *džu̯nka* F, pl. *-e,* beg20c (3 tech)   **Bg** *dzhonka* F, pl. *-ki,* 20c, via Rs (3 tech)   **Fi** *dzonkki* 19c (3)   **Hu** *dzsunka* 19c (5 Mal)

junk   *v.* +2 'inject (oneself) with heroin'

Nw *junke* [dʒøŋke] 1970s (1 sla)   **Ic** *djönka (sig)* [tjœɲ̊ka] 1970s, +2(1 sla) → *djönkari* M

junk food   *n.* 'food with low nutritional value'

Ge [=E] N [U] 1980s (0>1 mod)   **Du** *junkfood* [dʒʏŋkfu:d] N, 1980s (2)   **Nw** [=E] M [U] 1980s (1) < *gatekjøkkenmat*   **Ic** [=E] N [U] end20c (0 sla)   **Sp** [=E/jaɱ(k)fud] F, 1980s (1 jour/rare) < trsl *comida basura*

junkie   *n.* 'a drug addict'

The adoption of this slang term follows a well-established path, spreading from Germanic languages to neighbouring ones, but not (as yet) extending to Southern and Eastern Europe. Note that the basis of the derivation, ↑*junk* 'heroin', is rarely borrowed.

Ge [=E] M, pl. *-s,* 1960s (1 sla)   **Du** [dʒʏnki] C, 1970s (1 sla) = *junk*   **Nw** [=E] M, pl. *-er,* 1960s (1)   **Ic** *djönki/djönki* [tjœɲci/ɪ] M, pl. *-ar,* 1970s (1 sla)   **Fr** [dʒɔ̃ki] M/F/adj., 1970s (1 obs) → *junk*   **Sp** [=E/joŋki] M, pl. *-s,* 1970s (1 obs) < *yonqui*   **Cr** *džanki,* M, end20c (1 sla)   **Hu** (0 tech_{PSYCHOL})   **Gr** *tzanki* M/F, pl. *-s,* end20c (1 sla); *tzankis* M, end20c (3 sla)

juror   *n.* 1 'a member of a jury'

Hu [=E] pl. *-ok/*Ø?, 1970s? (1 tech)

jury   *n.* 1 'a body of persons sworn to render a verdict in a court of justice', 2 'persons selected to award prizes'

This word is from (Anglo-)French and Medieval Latin, but appears to have spread from England since the eighteenth century. Identification with the Romance stem was easy in French which has consequently led to its adoption, with French pronunciation, in Germanic languages, or identification with native morphemes in Romance languages.

Ge [ʒy:ri] F, pl. *-(ie)s,* 18c, via Fr, 2(3)   **Du** [ʒy:ri] C, pl. *-'s,* end19c, 1(3)   **Nw** [ju:ri] M, pl. *-er,* 19c (2) → *juryere* v.   **Fr** [ʒyʀi] M, pl. *-s,* 18c, 1,2(3)   **Sp** - < *jurado*   **It** *giuria* (5Fr)   **Rm** *juriu* [ʒurju] N, end19c, via Fr, 1(3 obs/Ø) 2(3)   **Rs** (5Fr)   **Po** 2(5Fr)   **Cr** *žiri* M, 18c, via Fr, 2(3)   **Bg** *zhuri* N, pl. *-ta,* beg20c, via Fr, 1(Ø) 2(3) → *-ram* v.   **Fi** [jury] 2(2)   **Hu** *zsüri* [ʒüri] pl. *-k,* 19c, via Fr, 2(5 Fr)   **Al** *juri* F, pl. Ø, mid20c (3/5Fr)

just-in-time*   *cp.¹* 'delivery at demand'

Ge [=E] 1980s (1 tech, mod) = *Jit*   **Nw** [=E] cp¹, 1980s (1 tech)   **Fr** - < trsl *juste à temps*   **Sp** [=E] M, uninfl., 1980s (1 tech)   **Al** - < trsl *taman ni̇̈ kohë*

jute   *n.* 1 'rough fibre made from the bark of a jute plant', 2 'the plant'

The term, borrowed into English from Bengali in the eighteenth century, quickly spread to all European countries in the nineteenth or early twentieth century, with other terms for fibres and cloths; the easy adoption is still widely evident from the pronunciations which are commonly based on the written form.

Ge [ju:tə] F [U] 19c, 1(3)   **Du** [jy:tə] C, pl. *-'s,* end19c, 1(3)   **Nw** ["ju:te] M [U] beg20c (1 tech)   **Ic** *júta* [ju:ta] F/N [U] mid20c, via Da, 1(3 tech)   **Fr** [ʒyt] M, mid19c (3)   **Sp** *yute* M [U] end19c (3)   **It** *juta/iuta* [juta] F [U] end19c (3)   **Rm** *iută* [jutə] F [U] end19c, via Ge/It/Fr (3)   **Rs** *dzhut* M [U] beg20c (1 tech) → *- ovyĭ* adj.   **Po** *juta* [juta] F [U] beg20c (1 tech) → *jutowy* adj.   **Cr** *juta* F [U] beg20c, 1(1 tech) → *juten* adj.   **Bg** *yuta* F [U] beg20c, via Ge (3 tech) → *yuten* adj.   **Fi** *juutti* (3)   **Hu** [juta] pl. *-ák,* end19c/beg20c, 2(3 tech)   **Al** *jutë* [jut] F [U] end19c (1>2)   **Gr** *ghiuta* [U] F, beg20c (3)

K

kangaroo *n.* 'a long-legged jumping marsupial'
This word is one of the earliest adoptions (*c.*1770) from an Australian language; the writings of Cook, Bankes, and Forster quickly spread it to European languages – first from written sources and later in close-to-English pronunciation as testified by the [a/ɛ] contrast.
Ge *Känguruh* [keŋgəru:] N, pl. *-s*, beg19c (3) **Du** *kangoeroe* [kaɲɣuru] C, end18c (3) **Nw** *kenguru* [keŋguru:] M, pl. *-er*, 19c (3) **Ic** *kengúra/kengúrú* [cʰeiŋkura] F/M, pl. *-ur*, beg19c, via Da (2) **Fr** *kangourou* [kãguʀu] M, beg19c (3) **Sp** *canguro* (3) **It** *canguro* M, pl. *-i*, 19c, via Fr (3) **Rm** *cangur* [kaŋgur] M, 1840s, via Fr (3) **Rs** *kenguru* M, uninfl., 19c (3) → *-ovyĭ* adj. **Po** *kangur* [kangur] M (3) → *-ek* M **Cr** *kengùrū* M, pl. *-i*, beg20c (1) **Bg** *kenguru* N, pl. *-ura*, beg20c, via Rs (3) **Fi** *kenguru* (3) **Hu** *kenguru* [=E] (5Ge) **Al** *kangur* M, pl. *-ë*, end19c (3) **Gr** *kaguro* N, via Fr (2)

KB *abbr.* 1 'kilobyte(s)'
This term is becoming infrequent; with the rapid advancement of technology *MB* = ↑*megabyte* is now mostly used.
Ge [kabe] 1980s (1 tech) **Du** *kb* [ka:be:] 1980s (1 tech) < *kilobyte* **Nw** [ˈkoːbeː] M, pl. Ø, 1980s (1 tech) **Ic** *k(b)* (1 tech) **Fr** *Ko(kilo-octet)* **Sp** *K/kbyte* M, pl. Ø, end20c (1 tech) **It** [kappa bi/kilobait] M, pl. Ø, end20c (1 tech) **Rm** *kb/KB* [kilobit/=E] M, 1980s (2 tech) **Rs** *kb* end20c (1 tech, writ) **Po** *kilobajt* M, end20c (1 tech, writ) **Cr** (0) **Bg** <=E> [kabaĭ] pl. *-ta*, end20c (1 tech, writ) **Fi** *kB* (1 tech) = trsl *kilotavu* **Hu** [ka:be:] (1 tech) < *kilobájt* **Gr** (1 writ)

keelson *n.* 'a timber fastening a ship's floor timbers to the keel'
Du *kolsem* (5) **Rs** *kil'son* M, pl. *-y*, 18-19c (1 tech) **Po** *kilson* [kilson] M, mid20c (1 tech) **Bg** *kil'son* M, pl. *-al-i*, beg20c, via Rs (1 tech)

keen *adj.* 2 'fond of, enthusiastic about'
Du [=E] C, end19c (2) **Nw** [=E] 1960s (1 coll, obs)

keeper *n.* 4b 'a goalkeeper'
This word appears to be rarer than ↑*goal-keeper*, from which it was shortened. Pushed out by purist tendencies in German, it is now making its way back as a modern stylistic alternative (almost exclusively used in footballing terminology).
Ge [kiːpa] M, pl. Ø, 1960s (1 reg, obs/mod) < *Torwart* **Du** [=E] C, 19c (2) = *doelmen* **Nw** [=E] M, pl. *-e*, beg20c (2) > rend *målvakt* **Ic** [cʰiːper] M, pl. *-ar*, 1970s (1 sla) < *markvörður* **Rs** - < *golkiper* **Po** - < *goalkeeper* **Gr** *kiper* M, beg20c (1 tech, rare)

keepsake *n.* 'a thing kept for the sake of or in remembrance of the giver or original owner'
Fr [kipsɛk] M, 1830s (1 arch) **Hu** [=E] [U] end19/beg20c (1 rare, arch)

keep-smiling* *n.* 'a relaxed life-style/attitude'
It is quite remarkable that this expression, which is in stable colloquial use in German and Dutch, has never spread any further.
Ge [=E] N [U] 1930s (1 coll) = *immer nur lächeln* **Du** [=E] phr., mid20c (1 coll) **Nw** (0) **Ic** [=E] excl., end20c (0) **Rm** (0) **Rs** *kip smaïling* end20c (1 coll, rare) **Po** (0) **Hu** [=E] [U] 1970s (0)

kelvin *n./cp¹* 'a unit of temperature'
The British physicist Sir William Thompson, first Baron Kelvin of Largs (1824–1907) was a prolific inventor and author of important scientific discoveries.
Ge [=E] N [U] mid20c (1 tech) **Du** [=E] C (1 tech) **Nw** [kelvin] M [U] 20c (1 tech) **Ic** [cʰɛlvɪn] cp¹, mid20c (2 tech) **Fr** [kɛlvin] M, mid20c (1 tech) **Sp** [=E] M, pl. *-s*, 20c (1 tech) **It** [=E] M, pl. Ø, 1950s (1 tech) **Rm** [=E] M [U] 1960s, via Fr? (2 tech) **Rs** *kel'vin* M, pl. *-y*, beg20c (1 tech) **Po** *kelwin*, M, mid20c (1 tech) **Cr** *kelvin* M, pl. *-i*, mid20c (1 tech) **Bg** *kelvin* M, pl. *-a*, 20c (1 tech) **Fi** [=E] (3) **Hu** [=E] [U] 20c (3 tech) **Al** *kelvin* M [U] 20c (1 tech) **Gr** *kelvin* N, mid20c (1 tech)

kennel *n.* 2 'a breeding or boarding establishment for dogs'
Ge *Kennel* [=E] M, pl. Ø, beg20c (1 tech) **Du** [kɛnəl] C, 1940s (3) **Nw** [=E] M, pl. *-er*, mid20c (3) **Po** *kenel* M [U] mid20c (1 tech) → *-ski* adj. **Fi** <=E>/*kenneli* (3) **Hu** [kennel] pl. *-ek*, end19c/beg20c (1 tech, arch)

Kerr's pink* *n.* 'a variety of potato'
Nw *kerrs pink* [kærs piŋk] M [U] mid20c (2)

ketch *n.* 'a two-masted sailing-boat'
The distribution of this rare and technical term illustrates the impact of nineteenth-century English shipbuilding. Since the word appears to have become more or less obsolete, together with the object, it is unlikely to spread any further.
Ge *Ketsch* F, pl. *-en*, end19c (3 tech) **Du** [=E] C, pl. *-en*, 1970s (1 tech) = *kits* **Nw** *ketsj* [=E] M, pl. *-er*, end19c (3) **Fr** [kɛtʃ] M, end18c (1 tech) **Sp** <=E>/

queche M, pl. *-s*, end19c, via Fr (1 tech) **It** [ketʃ] M, pl. Ø, 1930s (1 tech) **Rm** [ketʃj] N, 1970s (1 tech) **Rs** *kech* M, pl. *-y*, mid18c (1 tech) **Po** *kecz* M, mid18c (1 tech, arch) **Cr** *keč* M, pl. *-evi*, 19c (3) **Bg** *kech* M, pl. *-al-ove*, 20c (1 tech) **Fi** *ketsi* (1)

ketchup *n.* 'a spicy sauce'

This word was borrowed from Malay into English in the seventeenth/eighteenth century; the two English forms *catchup* and *ketchup* are reflected in the receiving languages where they cause some uncertainty as to their proper spelling – as in English. (The word is one of the few anglicisms to be respelt in the new German reform)

Ge *Ketch-up/Catchup* [ketʃap] M/N [U] beg20c (2) **Du** [kɛtʃʏp] C [U] 1940s (2) **Nw** [ketsʃʉp] M [U] 20c (2) **Ic** [=E] mid20c (0c) < rend *tómatsósa* **Fr** [ketʃœp] M, end19c (2) **Sp** <=E>/*catsup* [ketʃup/ketʃup] M, 1980s (2) **It** [ketʃap] M [U] beg18c (2) **Rm** [=E] N [U] 1970s (2) **Rs** *ketchup* M [U] mid20c (2) **Po** *keczup/*<=E> [ketʃup/=E] M, beg20c (2) **Cr** *kečap* M [U] mid20c (2) **Bg** *ketchup* M [U] mid20c (2); <=E> 1990s (1 writ) **Fi** [ketsu:pi] (3) **Hu** [=E/ketʃəp] pl. Ø, mid20c (2>3) **Al** *keçap* M [U] 1980s (1 you/3) **Gr** *ketsap* F/N, mid20c (2)

keyboard *n.* +1a 'a set of keys for entering data into a computer', 2 'an (electronic) musical instrument with a keyboard, e.g. a piano, organ, etc.'

Older meanings referring to typewriters and pianos etc. were apparently not borrowed; adoption started with the electronic musical device and the computer, fields in which the term has rapidly spread into various European languages. Note the infrequency of the derived agent noun (below).

Ge [=E] N, pl. *-s*, 1970s, 2(2); 1980s, +1a(1 tech) < *Tastatur* **Du** [ki:bɔrt] N, 1970s, 2(2 tech) < *toetsenbord* **Nw** [=E] N, pl. Ø/-s, 1970s, 2(2) +1a(0) > 2: *tangentinstrument*; +1a: *tastatur* → *keyboardist* **Ic** [=E] N,

end20c, 2(0) < creat 2: *hljómborð*; +1a: *lyklaborð* **Rm** [=E] N, 1970s, 2(1 tech); 1980s, +1a(1 tech) = *claviatură, tastatură* **Rs** (0) **Po** [-t] M, end20c, 2,+1a(1 mod) **Bg** *kiĭbord* M, pl. *-al-ove*, end20c, +1a(1 tech) → *-ist* M **Hu** [=E/ki:bord] [Ø] 1970s, +1a(1 tech COMPUT) **Gr** *kibord* N, pl. Ø/-s, end20c, 2(1 tech); +1a(1 tech, rare) < *pliktrologhio*

keyboarder *n.* 'a person who plays keyboards'

Ge [=E] M, pl. Ø, 1980s (1 tech) **Du** - < *toetsenist* **Nw** - < *keyboardist* **Bg** - < *kiĭbordist* **Gr** *kiborder* M, end20c (1 tech)

keyman* *n.* 'the most important person'

Ge - < rend *Schlüsselfigur* **Du** - < rend *sleutelfiguur* **Nw** - < *nøkkelperson* **Ic** - < creat *lykilmaður* **Fr** - < trsl *homme-clé* **Sp** - < trsl *hombre clave/persona clave* **Rm** - < rend *persoană cheie* **Po** [kimen] M, end20c (1

jour) **Fi** - < *avainhenkilö* **Hu** - < trsl *kulcsember* **Gr** - < trsl *anthropos klidhi*

keyword *n.* +2c 'a significant word used in indexing' **Ge** - < rend *Schlagwort* **Du** - < rend *slagwoord* **Nw** - < *nøkkelord* **Ic** - < *lykilorð* **Fr** - < trsl *motclé* **Sp** - < trsl *palabra clave* **It** [kiwərd] M, pl. Ø, 1970s (1 tech) < trsl *parola chiave* **Rm** - < rend *cuvânt cheie* **Fi** - < trsl *avainsana* **Hu** [=E/ki:word] pl. Ø, 1970s (1 tech) < *kulcsszó/password* **Gr** - < trsl *lexi klidhi*

khaki *n./adj.* 1 'cloth of a brownish-yellow colour', +1a 'a stout, tightly woven cotton fabric', 2 'a brownish-yellow colour',

This word was first used to designate the colour and cloth of the British cavalry in India in the mid-nineteenth century, but later became the standard colour for field uniforms in various armies – which explains the almost universal distribution.

Ge [ka:ki] N [U] beg20c, 1,2(3 tech) **Du** *kaki* [=E] N [U] beg20c (3) **Nw** *kaki* [ka:ki] M [U] beg20c(3) **Ic** *kaki* [kʰa:ci] N [U] mid20c, +1a(2) **Fr** *kaki* [kaki] M/adj., uninfl., 1910s, 1,2(2) **Sp** <=E>/*caqui* M/adj., uninfl., beg20c (3) **It** *cachi* [kaki] adj. uninfl., 1900s, 2(2) **Rm** *kaki* [kaki] adj., uninfl., 1930s, via Fr (3) **Rs** *khaki* M, uninfl., beg20c, 1,2(1 tech) **Po** [khaki/kaki] adj., uninfl., beg20c, 1,2(2) **Cr** *kaki* M [U] beg20c(2) **Bg** *kaki* adj., uninfl., mid20c, 2(1 tech MILIT) **Hu** [=E/kaki] [U] end19c/beg20c 2(3) 1(1 tech, arch MILIT) **Al** *kaki* adj./n., F, pl. Ø, mid20c, 1,2(3) **Gr** *khaki* adj./N, usu. pl., beg20c, from Fr, 1(2 tech MILIT) +1a,2(2)

kick *n.* +1c 'an unsuccessful stroke in which the player doesn't hit the ball', (footb.) 2a 'a sharp, stimulant effect, esp. of alcohol', 2b 'a pleasurable thrill', +2c 'anything that gives stimulant effects', 4 'a specified temporary interest or enthusiasm'

The football sense of this term is strikingly restricted (as in the derived ↑*kicker*). The modern slang/colloquial meaning, which is highly popular in Germanic languages, is not found outside this area, either.

Ge [=E] M, pl. *-s*; 1980s, 2a,2b,+2c(1 coll) **Du** [=E] C, 1960s, 2a,+2c(1 coll) → *kicken* v. **Nw** <=E>/*kikk* [=E] N/M, pl. Ø/-er, end20c, 2a,b,+2c,4(1 tech) → *kicke (på)* v. **Ic** *kikks/kings* [cʰɪxs/cʰiŋs] N, pl. Ø, mid/end20c, via Da, +1c(1 tech) → *kingsa* v.; *kikk* [cʰɪhk] N [U] 1970s, 2a,2b,+2c(1 sla) **Fr** *kick* M?, +1c(1 tech, ban, obs) < *tir* **Cr** *kik*, M, pl. *-ovi*, end20c, +1c(1 coll)

kick¹ (1) *v.* 2b 'express annoyance at or dislike for' **Nw** *kicke/kikke* [kike] mid20c (1)

kick² (1) *v.* +1a 'strike (a football) with the foot', +1b 'strike a football unsuccessfully'

This term is only thoroughly integrated and widely used in German where old names of football clubs (...*Kickers*) testify to its use for a hundred years now. Strangely enough, *kick-* is more widely attested in a number of compounds.

Ge [=E] beg20c, +1a(3 pej) → *-er* **M**   **Nw** +1a(0)   **Ic** *kingsa,* 20c, via Da, +1b(1 tech)   **Cr** (0)

kick-boxing   *n.* 'a form of boxing characterized by the use of blows with the feet as well as the hands'

This discipline appears to be a recent (re-?)invention which is not (yet) generally popular or recognized. It is therefore all the more remarkable that the word is so widely known throughout Europe. Thorough documentation might even record it in languages not included here.

Ge *Kickboxen* N [U] 1980s (3 tech, mod)   **Du** *kickboksen* [kikbɔksə] N [U] 1980s (2)   **Nw** *kick-boksing* [=E] M/F [U] 1980s (1 tech)   **Fr** [kikbɔksiŋ] M, 1980s (1 tech) < *boxe française, savate; boxe orientale*   **Sp** [=E]

M [U] 1990s (1 tech)   **It** [kikbɔksiŋg] M [U] 1980s (1 tech)   **Rs** *kikboksing/kikboks* M [U] 1990s (1 tech)   **Po** [-nk] N [U] end20c (2 tech)   **Cr** *kick-boks* M [U] 1990s (3 tech)   **Bg** *kikboks* M [U] 1990s (3 tech)   **Hu** *kick-box* [=E] [U] 1980s (1 tech); [=E] cp[1] [U] 1980s (1 tech)   **Gr** <=E> [=E] N [U] 1990s (1 tech, mod)

kick-down   *n.* 'a device for changing gear'
Ge [=E] M/N, 1960s (1 tech, rare)   **Fi** [=E] (1 tech, rare)

kicker   *n.* 'a footballer'
Ge [=E] M, pl. Ø, end19c (3 coll)

kick-off   *n.* 1 'the start of a football game'
Ge [=E] M, pl. *-s,* 1970s (1 reg) < *Anstoß*   **Du** [=E] C, 1990s (1 mod) < *aftrap*   **Nw** [=E] M, pl. *-s,* 20c (1 tech)   **Ic** [=E] N mid/end20c (1 tech) < *rend upphafsspyrna*   **Fr** - < *coup d'envoi*   **Sp** [=E] M, 1920s (1 arch) < *saque*   **It** - < *rend calcio d'inizio*   **Hu** [=E] [U] end19c/beg20c (1 tech/arch) < *kezdőrúgás*

kick-starter   *n.* 'a starter in a motorbike'
The currency of this word is restricted to motorcyclists, but it is noteworthy that it is regionally more widely known than the verb *kick.*

Ge [=E] M, pl. Ø, 1970s (1 tech)   **Du** [=E] C, 1970s (1 tech)   **Nw** <=E>/*kickstart/kick* [=E] M, pl. *-e,* 1970s (1 tech)   **Fr** <=E> *kick* [kik] M, 1920s (1 tech)   **Cr** *kik starter* M, pl. *-i,* end20c (1 tech)   **Gr** <=E> [=E] N, end20c (1 tech, rare) < *manivela*

kid   *n.* 2 'leather from a young goat', 3 'a child or young person'
The colloquial word *kids* (mainly in the pl.) is replacing the older loan ↑*teenager* in German. The currency of *kid(s)* in Europe makes it impossible to say whether this is a general trend (supported by the short and less complicated form).
Ge [kit] N [U] beg20c, 2(1 tech); *kids* pl., 1970s, 3(2

sla, mod)   **Du** [kɪt] C [U] 1970s, 2(1 tech); M, 3(1 coll); *kids* 3 (1 mod)   **Nw** *kidd* [=E] [U] 20c, 2(1 tech)   **Fr** *kid* [kid] sg./pl. M, 1930s, 2 (1 tech); 1980s, 3 (1 you)   **Rm** (0)   **Fi** - < *skidi*

kidnap   *v.* 'carry off a person (to obtain a ransom)'
The two nouns formed with *-er* and *-ing* appear to have been adopted first: both are of almost identical distribution and seem to have given rise to the less frequent verb in most languages (a back formation from the noun rather than an independent borrowing).

Ge *-ppen* [kitnɛpn] 1930s (2)   **Du** *kidnappen* [kɪtnɛpə] 1950s (2) < *ontvoeren*   **Nw** *kidnappe* [kidnape] beg20c (3) → *kidnapper* v.; *kidnapping* M/F   **Fr** *kidnapper* [kidnape] 1930s (2)   **Rm** *kidnapa* [kidnapa] 1970s (1 coll, fac)   **Cr** *kidnapirati* mid20c

(2)   **Al** *kidnapoj* mid20c (1 reg)

kidnapper   *n.* 'a person carrying out a kidnapping'
Ge [kitnepa] M, pl. Ø, 1930s (2)   **Du** [kɪtnɛpər] C, 1950s (2) = *ontvoerder*   **Nw** [kidnaper M, pl. *-e,* beg20c (3)   **Ic** - < *mannræningi*   **Fr** *kidnappeur/kidnappeuse* [kidnapœR/-øz] M/F, 1950s (2) > *ravisseur*?   **It** [kidnapper] M, pl.

Ø, 19c (1 jour) < *sequestratore*   **Rm** [kidnaper] M, 1970s (1 jour, rare)   **Po** *kidnaper* [-er] M, beg20c (2) → *-stwo* N; *-ka* F; *-ski* adj.   **Cr** *kidnaper* M, pl. *-i,* mid20c (1)   **Hu** [kidnepper] pl. *-ek,* 1970s (1 jour>2 jour, writ, mod) < *gyermekrabló (váltságdíjért)*   **Al** *kidnapues* M, pl. *-ë,* mid20c (1 reg)

kidnapping   *n.* 'the action/crime of a kidnapper'
Ge [kitnepiŋ] N, pl. *-s,* 1930s (2)   **Du** [kɪtnɛping] C, 1960s (2) < *ontvoering,* > *kidnap*   **Nw** [kidnapiŋ] M/F [U] beg20c (3)   **Ic** - < *mannrán*   **Fr** [kidnapiŋ] M, mid20c (2) > *kidnappage*   **It** [kidnapping] M [U] 1950s (1

jour) < *rapimento, sequestro di persona*   **Rm** [kidnapiŋ] N [U] 1970s (1 jour, rare)   **Rs** *kidnaping/kidnepping/kidnap* M [U] mid20c (1 jour)   **Po** *kidnaping* [-nepink] M [U] mid20c (2) → *-owy* adj.   **Cr** [=E] M [U] mid20c (1 jour)   **Hu** [=E] [U] 1970s/80s (1 tech, jour)   **Al** *kidnapim* M, pl. *-ë,* mid20c (1 reg)

kif   *n.* 'hashish (of bad quality)'
Ge *Kiff* [=E] M [U] 1970s (1 sla)   **Du** [=E] C/N [U] 1970s (1 sla)   **Fr** (5 Arab)   **Sp** (5 Arab)   **Bg** *kif* M [U] 1990s (1 tech, sla)

kif*   *v.* 'smoke hashish'
Ge *kiffen* 1970s (1 sla) → *-er* M

kill   *v.* 1 'put to death (brutally, by force)'
Ge *killen* 1940s (2 coll)   **Nw** *kille* [kile] end20c (1 coll, sla, you_COMPUT)   **Rm** (0)

killer *n.* 1a 'a person who kills (esp. for money, brutally)', 2a 'an impressive, formidable or excellent person or thing'

This word is widespread and always carries the pejorative connotations of brutality and ruthlessness. The much lower currency of the corresponding verb (probably backformed) is notable.

Ge [=E] M, pl. Ø, 1940s, 1a(2 coll) **Du** [=E] C, 1970s, 1a (1 coll) **Nw** [=E] M, pl. -e, mid20c, 1a(1 coll) **Ic** [cʰiːler] M, pl. -ar, end20c, 2a(1 sla) **Fr** *(serial) killer*, 1990s, 1a(1 jour) **Sp** [kiler] M, pl. -s, 1990s (1 jour) **It** [=E] M, pl. Ø, 1930s, 1a(3) **Rm** [=E] M, 1980s, 1a(1 jour/mod) **Rs** *kiler/killer* M, pl. -y, end20c, 1a(1 jour/you) **Po** [-er] M, end20c, 1a(1 coll) **Cr** *kiler* M, pl. -i, end20c, 1a(1 coll) **Bg** *kilŭr* M, pl. -i, 1990s, 1a(1 jour, mod) 2a(1 coll, mod) **Hu** [=E] pl. -ek, 1970s, 1a(1 you, writ, mod) **Al** *killer* M, pl. -a (1 reg) **Gr** *kiler* M, pl. Ø/-s, 1a(1 jour, mod)

kilobyte *n.* 'a measure of memory size' (comput.) (cf. ↑*KB*)

Ge (1 tech, obs) **Du** [=E] C, 1970s (1 tech) **Nw** [çiːlubait] M, pl. Ø, 1980s (1 tech) **Ic** *kilóbæt(i)* [çʰiːloupaiːt(ı)] N, pl. Ø, 1970s (2 tech) **Fr** - < *kilo-octet* **Sp** [=E] M, pl. -s, end20c (1 tech) = *kilooicteto* **It** [kilobait] M, pl. Ø, end20c (1 tech) **Rm** [=E] M, pl. -iţi, end20c (1 tech) **Rs** *kilobait* M, 1980s (1 tech) **Po** *kilobajt* M, end20c (1 tech) **Cr** *kilobajt*/<=E> M, pl. -ovi, end20c (1 tech) **Bg** *kilobait*/<=E> M, pl. -a, end20c (1 tech) **Fi** [=E] end20c (1 tech) = trsl *kilotavn* **Hu** *kilobájt* [=E] 20c (1 tech) **Gr** <=E>/*kilobait* N, pl. Ø/-s, end20c (1 tech) > *khiliopsifiolexi*

kilt *n.* 1,2 'a Scottish skirt'

This word has largely remained a foreignism designating part of the traditional Scottish costume; however, the garment has also formed part of modern women's wardrobes at various times all over Europe and this has established marginal (1 tech) uses in various languages.

Ge [=E] M, pl. -s, 19c (Ø) < *Schottenrock* **Du** (Ø) **Nw** [=E] M, pl. -er, beg20c (2 tech) **Ic** - < rend *skotapils* **Fr** [=E] M, end18c (3) **Sp** [=E] M, 20c (Ø) **It** [=E] M, pl. Ø, mid19c (3) **Rm** [=E] N, 1970s, via Fr? (Ø) **Rs** *kilt* M, pl. -y, mid20c (Ø) **Po** M, mid20c (Ø) **Cr** *kilt*, M, pl. -ovi, mid20c (3) **Bg** *kilt* M, pl. -a/-ove, mid20c(Ø) **Fi** *kiltti* (Ø) **Hu** [=E] pl. -ek, 20c (Ø)

king *n.* 2 'a person or thing pre-eminent in a specified field or class'

The distribution of this colloquial item in youth language is surprising.

Ge [=E] M, pl. -s, 1970s (1 you) **Du** (o) **Nw** (o) **It** [king] M, pl. Ø, 1960s (1) **Rm** [=E] M [U] 1980s (Ø/o mod, you_MUS) < trsl

rege **Rs** (o) **Bg** *king* M, pl. -ove, end20c (1 coll, you) **Fi** <=E> M, 1990s (1 you, mod) **Hu** [=E] pl. Ø, 1970s (1 tech, mod_CARDS) **Al** *king* M, pl. -ë, end20c (1 you) **Gr** < mean *vasilias*

kingbolt *n.* 'a main bolt in a central position'
Nw [=E+Nw] M, pl. -er, 20c (3 tech+5) **Fi** - < trsl *kuningaspultti*

king size *cp¹* 'large size' (in cigarettes, sweets, etc.)

Ge [=E] 1960s (1 obs) **Du** [kingsajs] 1980s (1 mod) **Nw** [=E] 1960s (1) **Ic** [=E] uninfl., end20c (1 coll) **Fr** (o) **Sp** [=E] adj., uninfl., end20c (1 mod) **It** [king saiz] 1960s (1 mod) **Rm** [=E] end20c (Ø mod) **Rs** *kingsaiz* cp¹, 1990s (1 mod) **Po** *king sajz*/<=E> adj., uninfl., end20c (1 mod) **Cr** [=E] adj., end20c (1) **Bg** <=E> [=E] M [U] end20c (2 tech) **Hu** [=E] 1960s (2 tech) **Gr** <=E>/*king saiz* [=E] adj., end20c (1 jour, mod)

kinky *adj.* 1a 'given to or involving abnormal sexual behaviour', 1b 'bizarre in a sexually provocative way' **Du** [=E] 1980s, 1a,b(1) **Nw** (o) **Ic** [cʰinci] uninfl., 1970s (1 sla)

kipper *n.* 1 'a smoked herring'

The borrowing of this word is complex since it appears to have happened independently at different times, no general pattern being detectable.

Du [=E] C, 1970s (3 tech) **Nw** *kippers* [kipers] M, sg. [U] beg20c (1) **Fr** [kipœr] M, pl. -s, end19c (1 tech) **Po** *kiper/kipers* M, end20c (1 tech) **Cr** (o) **Gr** *kiper* N? (1 tech)

kit *n./cp²* 1 'a set of articles, equipment, or clothing needed for a specific purpose', 3 'a set of all the parts needed to assemble an item', +5 'a package of fish for the market'

No clear pattern is visible from the distribution of the loanword. It would be interesting to know whether it designates the same sort of parts/sets in the individual languages.

Ge [=E] N/M/cp², pl. -s, 1970s, 1,3(1 tech) **Du** [=E] N, 1940s, 3(1 tech) **Nw** [=E] M, pl. -s, end20c, 1,3(1 tech) **Ic** [cʰıht] N, pl. Ø, 1930s, 1,3(2 coll) +5(2 tech, arch) **Fr** [=E] M, 1960s, 3(1 tech, ban) > *lot, prét à monter* **Sp** [=E] M, pl. Ø, 1980s, 1,3(2) **It** [=E] M, pl. Ø, 1970s, 1,3(2) **Rm** [=E] 1980s, 1(1 tech) **Hu** [=E] cp², pl. Ø, 1980s, 3(1) < *készlet*

kitchenette *n.* 'a small kitchen'

Ge [=E?] F, pl. -s 1970s (o>1 mod) **Du** [=E] C, 1970s (2) **Nw** (o) < *tekjøkken* **Fr** [kitʃənɛt] F, mid20c (1 tech, ban) > *cuisinette* **Sp** <=E>/*kichenete* [kiʃenɛt] F, end20c (o>1 mod) **It** - < rend? *cucinino, cucinetta* **Rm** *chicinetă* [kitʃinetə] F, 1950s (3) **Cr** (o)

klaxon *n.* 'a horn on a motor vehicle'
Du *claxon/klakson* [klɑksɔn] C, beg20c (1 tech) <
toeter **Nw** - < *horn* **Fr** [klaksɔn] M, 1910s (2 ban)
< *avertisseur* → *klaxonner* v. **Sp** *claxon* [klakson] M,
pl. *-es*, 1920s (2) **It** *clacson* [klakson] M, pl. Ø, 1910s
(3) **Rm** *claxon* [klakson] N, via Fr (3) → *claxona* v.;
-are F; *-at* N **Rs** *klakson*, M pl. *-y*, beg20c (1
obs) **Po** *klakson* [-on] M; mid20c (3) → *-ik* M **Cr**
klakson M, pl. *-i*, mid20c (2) **Bg** *klakson* M, pl. *-al-i*,
beg20c (2) **Hu** [klakson] pl. Ø, end20c (1 tech) **Gr**
klaxon N, beg20c (1 obs)

Kleenex *n.* (orig.^{TM}) 'a paper handkerchief'
This tradename has become generic in a number of
languages; in Spanish it has even developed a cp[1]/adj.
use to mean 'superficial, worthless' (1 fac, jour).
Ge (o^{TM}) **Nw** [=E] M, pl. Ø, 1990s (1 rare) **Ic** [=E]
N 1960s (1 obs) **Fr** [klinɛks] M, 1960s (o^{TM}) **Sp**
[=E] M, pl. Ø, 1970s (2) **It** [=E] M, pl. Ø, 1960s (2)
Rm (o) **Hu** [=E] [U] 1990s (1 writ, jour) **Gr** <=E>
20c (1 writ^{TM})

Klondike *n.* 'a source of valuable material'
Nw <=E>/*klondyke* [=E] N [U] 20c (1) **Rs** (Ø) **Bg**
Klondaïk M [U] 20c (1 jour)

knickerbockers *n.* 1 'breeches gathered at the calf'
The distribution of this word mirrors its early adoption. Based on a name invented by W. Irving, the word
came to be used as a nickname for New Yorkers of
Dutch ancestry, and from the 1880s on, for a specific
kind of trousers. This garment was quite popular from
1900 to the 1940s in Central Europe but has since
become old-fashioned, making the word obsolete as
well. The rare short form ↑*knickers* is attested in English but could also have been independently shortened
in Norwegian and Polish.
Ge [(k)nikaboka] pl., 19c (1 obs)
Du *knickerbocker* [nɪkərbɔkər]
C, 1940s (1 obs) **Nw** *nikkers/*
knickers [nikere] M, pl. *-er*,
beg20c (3) **Fr** [knikɛrbɔkɛrs
/nikɛrbɔkœr] M, pl., end19c (1
arch) → ↑*knickers* 1930s **Sp** [ni-
kerboker] M, pl., beg20c (1 arch) → ↑*knickers* **It**
[nikerbokerz] M, pl., mid19c (1) < *calzoni alla zua-*
va **Po** M, mid19c (1 obs) **Cr** *nikerboker* M, pl. *-i*,
19c (1) **Hu** [knikerboker] pl. Ø, end19c (1 arch) <
térdnadrág, → *knickerbockeres* adj.

knickers *n.* 2a 'knickerbockers'; +2c 'trousers for
sports'
Nw *nikkers/knickers* [nikers] M, sg., pl. *-er*, beg20c
(3) **Fr** [knikɛrs?] M, pl., 1930s, 2a(1 arch) **Sp**
<=E>/*niquers* M, pl. beg20c, 2a,+2c(1 arch) **Po**
knickersy pl., end20c, 2a(1 tech) **Cr** *knickers* pl.,
end20c (1 tech) < *knickers lilače*

knick-knack *n.* +3 'a small cake'
Ic *nikknakk* N, beg20c, via Da, +3 (1 coll, obs)

knockdown* *n.* 'the act of striking someone to the
ground with a blow' (cf. ↑*KO*)
Ge [=E] M, pl. *-s*, beg20c (1 tech, rare) < *k.o.* **Du**
[=E] 1970s (1 tech) **Fr** [(k)nɔkdɔn/ (k)nɔkdaun]

M, uninfl., beg20c (1 tech, ban)
= *au tapis, au sol* **Sp** [=E] M,
1920s (1 tech, arch) **It** [=E] M,
pl. Ø, 1930s (2 tech) **Rm** *cnoc-*
daun/<=E> [=E] N, beg20c (2
tech) **Rs** *nokdaun* M, pl. *-y*,
beg20c (2 tech) **Po** *nokdaun/*
<=E> M, beg20c (2 tech) **Cr** *nokdaun* M [U] beg20c
(2 tech) **Bg** *nokdaun* M, pl. *-a*, mid20c (1 tech) **Al**
nokdaun M, pl. Ø, mid20c (1 reg)

knockout *n.* 2 'a blow that knocks the opponent
out', (box.), 4 'an outstanding or irresistible person
or thing', +5 'a very strong drink'
Ge [=E] M, pl. *-s*, beg20c, 2(1 rare) < ↑*k.o.* **Du**
knock-out [=E] C, mid20c, 2(1 tech) **Nw** [=E] M,
pl. *-er*, beg20c, 2(2) 4(1 mod) → *knockoute* v.; *knocke*
ut v. **Ic** [nɔhkau:t] N [U] 1950s (1 coll) → *knokkáta*
v. **Fr** *knock-out* [(k)nɔkaut] M/adj., uninfl., beg20c,
2(1) > *K.-O.*, → *knock-outer* v. **Sp** <=E>/*nocaut* M
[U] 1920s, 2(1 tech, rare) < ↑*k.o.*; *cao* → *noquear* v. **It**
[=E] M, pl. Ø/adj./adv., 1910s, 2(3) = ↑*k.o.* **Rm**
cnocaut/<=E> [(k)nokawt] N, beg20c, 2(2 tech) →
cnocauta v.; *-are* F; *-at* adj. **Rs** *nokaut* M, pl. *-y*,
beg20c, 2(2) → *-irovat'* v. **Po** *nokaut/*<=E> M,
beg20c, 2(2) → *z-*v. **Cr** *nokaut* M, beg20c, 2(2) →
-irati v. **Bg** *nokaut* M, pl. *-al-i*, mid20c, 2(2) → *-iram*
v. **Hu** [kna:k/knokaut] [U] beg20c, 2(1 tech)
+5(2>3) **Al** *nokaut* M, pl. *-e*, mid20c (1 reg) **Gr**
nok aut N, mid20c, 2(1 tech)

know-how *n.* 1 'technique, expertise'
This word is attested in American English from
1838, but has spread only since the 1950s – most
recently to Eastern Europe which has made its currency almost universal. Note the infrequency of calques, which are not coined because its morphology
poses problems.
Ge [no:hau] N [U] 1960s (2) **Du**
[=E] C [U] 1960s (2) **Nw** [=E]
M [U] 1960s (1) < *ekspertise* **Fr**
[noao] M [U] 1970s (1 tech, ban) <
savoir-faire **Sp** [nouxau/noxau]
M [U] 1970s (1>2 tech) **It** [nou
au] M [U] 1950s (1 tech, jour)
Rm [=E] N [U] 1980s (1 tech, jour) **Rs** *nou-khau* N,
uninfl. [U] 1990s (1 tech) **Po** M [U] 1990s (1
tech) **Cr** [=E] M [U] end20c (2) **Bg** *nou-khau* N
[U] end20c (1>2 tech) **Fi** [=E] (1) > rend *tietotai-*
to **Hu** [=E] [U] 1970s (1 tech) **Gr** <=E>/*nou khau*
N [U] end20c (2)

KO *n.* 1 'knock-out' (in boxing etc.), +3 'a sudden
end' (metaph.) (cf. ↑*knockout*)
Ge *k.o.* [ka:oː] M pl. *-s*, beg20c (3) > ↑*knockout* **Du**
[ka:oː] 1940s (2) **Nw** *k.o./*<=E> ["koːu:] M, pl. Ø,
20c, 1(1 tech, rare) **Fr** *K.-O.* [kao] M/adj., uninfl.,
beg20c, 1,+3(2) **Sp** <=E>/*cao* [kao] M/adj., uninfl.,
1920s, 1,+3(2>3) → *noquear* v. **It** [kappa ɔ] M [U]
1910s, 1(3) **Rm** [kao] N [U] 20c, 1(1 tech/writ) <
cnocaut **Cr** *K.O.* M [U] beg20s, 1(2) **Hu** [ka:oː]
[U] 20c (2>3)

krill *n.* 'tiny planktonic crustaceans'

This item is clearly from Norwegian, but claimed to have been borrowed via English. It is here included to illustrate doubtful English transmission, and even erroneous ascriptions.

Ge (5Nw) **Du** (5Nw) **Nw** (5) **Fr** [kʀil] M, 1970s (1 tech/5Nw) **Sp** [kril] M, 20c (1 tech/5Nw) **It** [=E] M, pl. Ø, 1980s (1 tech) **Rs** via Du? (5Nw) **Po** (5Nw) **Fi** *krilli* (5Nw) **Hu** (5Nw)

K-way* *n.* (orig.^TM) 'a light rain jacket'

Ge [kɪwei] M, pl. -*s*, 1980s (1 obs) **Fr** [kawɛ] M, 1980s (1) **It** [=E] M, pl. Ø, 1980s (3)

kWh *abbr.* 'kilowatt-hours'

Ge [ka:ve:ha:] F, pl. -*s*, 19c (3) < *Kilowattstunde* **Du** [ka:ve:hai] N, 1940s < *kilowatt-uur* **Nw** [kɔ:vehɔ:] M, pl. Ø, 20c (3 tech) < *kilowattime* **Ic** *kWh* mid20c (read as: *kílóvattstund*) **Fr** [kadubləveaʃ] < trsl *kilowatt-heure* **Sp** <=E>/*kv*, etc, 20c = *kilovatios- hora* **It** [kilovattora] F, pl. Ø, 1910s (3) **Rm** *kWh* (2 writ) < *kilowatt- oră*, pl. *kilowaţi-oră* **Rs** - < trsl *kilovatt-chas, kvt/ch.* **Po** - < *kilowatgodzina* **Cr** (0) **Bg** - < trsl *kvch* = *kilovatchasa* **Fi** - < trsl *kilowattitunti* **Hu** [ka:ve:ha:] [U] 20c (1 tech) < trsl *kilowattóra* **Al** *kwh* [kilovat-orë] mid20c (1 tech) **Gr** (1 writ) < *kilovatora*

L

L¹ (2) *abbrev.* 2 'learner driver'
 Du [=E] (4) **Nw** [el] 1994 (4) **Sp** [ele] F, end20c (3)
It - < trsl *P* (= *principante*) **Rs** - < trsl *U* **Po** < L >
end20c (2) **Cr** *el* end20c (3) **Bg** - < trsl *U* **Gr** (1
writ, reg, rare)
L² *abbrev.* 'Large' (size, in shirts, etc.)
 This item occurs mainly in abbreviated form (but cf.
↑*large*) and printed uses only; the connection with the
English etymon is more or less opaque, and the pronunciation follows national conventions.
 Ge [el] 1960s (3) **Du** [=E] 1980s (2) **Nw** [el] 1960s
(4) **Ic** [larts] mid20c (0) **Fr** (0) **Sp** [ele] F, end20c
(1 tech) = *larga* **It** [elle] mid20c (3) **Rm** [el] end20c
(1 mod) **Rs** *él'* M [U] 1990s (1 writ, mod) **Po** *elka*
[elka] F, end20c (2 coll) **Cr** [el] N [U] end20c
(2) **Bg** <=E> [el] [U] end20c (2 mod) **Fi** [ɛllɛ]
(0) **Hu** [el] [U] 1970s (3) → *L-es* adj. **Gr** <=E>
[el/la͟rdz] N, end20c (2)
lab *n.* 1 'a laboratory', +2 'a photographic laboratory'
 Du 1(5) **Nw** [lab] M, pl. -er, 20c (3) **Ic** [=E] N, pl.
lǫbb, end20c, 1(1 coll) < rend *rannsóknastofa* **Po**
[lep] M, end20c, +2(2)
label *n.* +1a 'a piece of linen, etc. attached to a garment giving its name, washing instructions, etc.,' 3b 'a
piece of paper in the centre of a gramophone record,
etc.', 5 'a word placed before, after, or in the course of
a dictionary definition to give further information
about a word's provenance etc.'
 Ge [le͟:bəl] N, pl. -s, 1980s,
+1a,3b(1 mod) < 1a: *Eti-*
kett **Du** [le͟:bəl] C/N, beg20c
(2) < *etiket* → *-en* v. **Nw** [=E]
M, pl. -s, 1980s, +1a,3b(1 tech)
Fr [labɛl] M/F, beg20c, +1a(3);
1980s, 3b(3) **Sp** [=E/label] M,
end20c, 3b(1 tech) = *sello discográfico* **Rs** [le͟ɪbl/leɪ-
bla] M/F, end20c (1 mod, you) **Po** [-el] M, end20c,
+1a,3b(1 mod) **Cr** - < *etiketa* **Bg** - < *etiket* **Al** -
< *etiketë*

lac-dye* *n.* 'varnish'
 Po [-e-] M, uninfl., mid20c (1 tech) **Fi** *lakka* (3)
lace *n.* +4 'a sideman of a trawler' (naut.)
 Ic *leisi*[lei:sɪ] N, pl., mid20c (1 tech)
lace *v.* +3 'stitch a trawlnet together' (naut.)
 Ic *leisa* [lei:sa] mid20c (1 tech)
lacrosse *n.* 'a game like hockey'

Du [=E] 1950s (1 tech) **Nw** (Ø) **Ic** [=E] N [U] mid/
end20c (Ø) **Fr** (4 in Canada) **Sp** [lakro͟s] M, 1920s
(Ø/1 tech, arch) **Rm** (Ø) **Po** M [U] mid20c (1
tech) **Hu** (5Fr)
lad *n.* 4 (BrE) 'a stable worker'
 Fr [lad] M, 19c (1 tech) **It** [lad] M, pl. Ø, end19c (1
tech,obs)
ladies first *phr* 'permission to let women go first'
 Ge [=E] 20c (1 fac) **Nw** (0) **Sp** [=E] beg20c (0>1
fac, mod) **Rm** (0) **Rs** (0) **Gr** (0)
lady *n.* 1a 'a woman of superior social status and
having the refined manners associated with this', 1b
'the title', 5 'a form of address' (sg.)
 As with ↑*gentleman*, most senses of this term
have remained foreignisms, but it has variously
been adopted to refer to cultivated, upper-class
manners and dress etc. of members of the indigenous
high societies. The derivative ↑*ladylike* is more restricted.
 Ge [le:di] F, pl. -ies, 19c, 1a(1 coll)
1b(Ø) **Du** [=E] C, 19c,
1a,b(Ø) **Nw** [=E] M, pl. -er/
-ies, 19c, 1a(1) 1b(Ø) **Ic** [=E] F,
pl. -ar/-ur, beg20c, 1a(1 coll)
1b(Ø) = 1b: *lafði* **Fr** [lɛdi] F, pl.
-ies, 17c(Ø) **Sp** <=E>/*ladi*/*leidi*

[=E] F, pl. -ies, mid19c, 1a,b(1 fac) **It** [le͟di] F, pl. Ø/
-ies, 17c(Ø) **Rm** [le͟di/=E] F, uninfl., end19c, 1a,b(Ø)
5(1 fac) **Rs** *ledi*/*lédi*/*le͟ɪdi* F, uninfl., 1a,1b(2)/1b(Ø)
5(1 jour, fac) **Po** <=E> F, uninfl., mid19c, 1a(2)
Cr *ledi* F, beg20c, 1a,b(1) **Bg** *le͟di* F, end19c, 1b(Ø);
le͟ɪdi, mid20c, 1a(2) 5(1 you, fac) < 1a: *dama* **Fi**
<=E>/*leidi* [=E] 1a(0) **Hu** [le͟:di] pl. -k, 1a(2)
1b(Ø) **Al** *ledi* F, pl. Ø, mid20c, 1a, b(Ø) **Gr** *ledhi*/
ledi [=E] N [U] beg/end20c, pl. -ies, 1a (1 coll) 1b(Ø)
ladykiller *n.* 'a practised and habitual seducer'
 Ge [le͟:dikila] M, pl. Ø, 19c/1960s (1 coll) < *Frauen-*
held **Du** [le͟:dikilər] C, beg20c (1 coll) < *Don Juan*
ladylike *adj.* 'with the modesty, manners, etc. of a
lady'
 Ge [=E] mid19c (1 rare) < *damenhaft* **Du** [le͟:dilajk]
beg20c (2) **Nw** [=E] beg20c (1 arch) **Ic** [=E] (0)
Hu [=E] end19c (1 arch)
ladyshave* *n.* (orig.^TM) 'a woman's electric shaver'
 Ge [le͟:diʃe:f] M, pl. -s, 1970s (1 tech, rare/^TM) **Du**
[le͟:diʃe:f] C, 1970s (2) **Nw** (0) **Rm** (0) **Bg** *lei-*
disheif M, pl. -al-ove, end20c (1 tech, mod) **Fi** [=E]

(1 tech) **Hu** [=E] pl. Ø, end20c (1 tech, jour, mod) **Gr** <=E> [=E] N, end20c (0/1 writ/™)

lager *n.* 'a light beer'

Although this term is originally German, it is rare in present-day German (*Pils* or *Export* preferred instead); it is therefore likely that the currency of the word is indeed owing to English mediation. (First recorded in American English as *Lager beer* 1854, *lager* 1855)

Ge (Ø/5) **Du** [=E] 19c (5) **Nw** (5Ge) **Ic** *lageröl* [la:xer-] 1920s (2+5) < *pilsner* **Fr** [lagœr] F, 1950s (1) **Sp** [lager] end20c (Ø/1 tech, rare) = *cerveza rubia* **Rs** (0) **Po** [-er] M [U] end20c (1 tech) **Cr** (0) **Bg** (0) **Fi** (5Ge) **Hu** [la:ger] [U] 1970s (3 writ, mod/5 Ge) **Gr** lager F, end20c (1)

lambskin *n.* +2 'imitation lambskin made of plush'
Ge [lemskin] N [U] 20c (1 tech)

lambswool *n.* 'wool, or knitted fabric'

The relative absence of this term can be attributed to two reasons: Germanic languages may use a compound made up of cognate words (Dutch, Norwegian, Icelandic) and in other languages the word (and the item?) is unknown.

Ge [lemsvul] F [U] 1960s (1 tech) < *Lammwolle* **Du** - < *lamswol* **Nw** (0) < *lammeull* **Ic** - < *lambsull* **Fr** [lãbswul/lambswul] M, 1960s (1 tech) **Sp** [=E/*lansbul*] M, end20c (1 tech, rare) **It** [lemzwu:l] M [U] 1960s (1>2) **Rm** (0 writ, on export articles) **Rs** *lémzwul* M [U] end20c (1 writ) **Po** (0) **Cr** *lembsvul* M [U] mid20c (1 tech) **Bg** <=E> end20c (1 writ) **Gr** *lamsghul* N [U] end20c (1 tech)

land-art* *n.* 'an avant-garde art movement'
Ge [=E] F [U] 1970s (1 tech, rare) **Fr** [=E] M, 1970s (1 tech) **Sp** [=E] M [U] (1 tech, rare) **It** [lend art] F [U] 1970s (1 tech)

landlord *n.* +3 'the owner of a house, farm, etc.'
Nw (0) **Fr** (Ø) **Rm** [=E/landlord] M, 1960s, 2(Ø) **Rs** *lendlord* M, pl. -*y*, beg20c (Ø) **Po** [landlort] M, beg20c (1 tech) **Cr** *lendlord* M, pl. -*ovi*, mid20c (1 tech) **Hu** [lendlord] pl. Ø, mid20c (0)

landrover *n.* (orig.™) 'an off-road vehicle'

This term started out as the name of a car made by Rover (formerly British Leyland) and appears to have become generic on the Continent, used as a synonym for ↑*jeep* (which is still more widespread).

Ge [lentro:va] M, pl. Ø, 1960s (1 tech, mod) < *Jeep, Geländewagen* **Du** [=E] C, 1970s (1 tech) < *terreinauto* **Nw** [=E/landrɔvər] M, pl. -*e*, 1960s (2 obs) < *terrengbil* **Ic** *landróver* [lantrou:ver] M, pl. -*ar*,™ only, 1960s, 2(2 coll) **Fr** *land rover* [lãdrɔvœr] M/F, 1960s (1 tech) **Sp** [lanrober] M, 1970s (2 tech) **It** [lendrəver] F, pl. Ø, 1960s (2 tech) = *fuoristrada* **Rm** [=E] N, 1970s (1 tech, rare) **Rs** *léndrover* M, pl. -*y*,

1990s (1 tech) **Po** [-over] M, end20c (1 tech, mod) **Cr** *lendrover*, M, pl. -*i*, end20c (1 tech) **Bg** *lendrover/landrouvǔr* M, pl. -*al-i*, 1990s (1 mod™) < *dzhip* **Hu** [lendro:ver] pl. -*ek*, 1970s (2 tech/mod) < *terepjáró* **Gr** <=E>/*ladrover* N, end20c (1 tech, mod)

laptop *n.* 'a microcomputer that is portable and suitable for use while travelling'

The rapid spread of modern computer technology has left few regional gaps (and these are likely to be filled quite soon); note the use of calques in the most puristic languages Icelandic, French and Italian. This tendency may well spread and limit this word's currency.

Ge [leptop] M, pl. -*s*, 1980s (1 tech) **Du** [=E] C, 1980s (1 tech) **Nw** [=E] M, pl. -*er*, 1980s (1 tech) **Ic** [=E] end20c (0) < *rend ferðatölva, kjölturakki* **Fr** [=E] M, 1990s (1 tech/ban) > *ordinateur portatif* < *portable* **Sp** [=E] M, 1980s (1 tech/obs) < (*ordenador*) *portátil* **It** [leptop] M, pl. Ø, 1980s (1 tech) < *computer portatile* **Rm** [=E] N, 1990s (1 tech) **Rs** *léptop* M, pl. -*y*, 1990s (1 tech) < *komp'yuter-papka* **Po** [-e-] M, end20c (2 tech) **Cr** *leptop* M, pl. -*ovi*, end20c (1 tech) **Bg** *laptop* M, pl. -*al-ove*, end20c (1 tech) **Fi** [=E] (2 tech) **Hu** [=E] pl. -*ok*, 1980s (1 tech> 2 tech) **Gr** *laptop* N, 1990s (1 tech) > *ypologhistis tsadas*

lard *n.* 'the internal fat of the abdomen of pigs'
Du *larderen* [lardərə] 19c (5) **Rs** *lyard* M [U] end19c (1 tech) **Gr** *lardhi* N (5)

large *adj.* 'of great size' (in clothes) (cf. ↑*L*)
Ge - < *L* **Du** [=E] 1980s (1 tech, jour) **Nw** [=E] 1960s (2) **Ic** [=E] uninfl., mid20c (0 coll) **Fr** [laʀʒ(ə)] M/adv./adj.? **It** [la:rʒ] < *L* **Rm** (0 mod) **Cr** = *L* **Bg** - < *L* **Fi** - < *L* **Hu** - < *L* **Gr** <=E> [=E] end20c (2)

laser *n./cp²* 'a device that generates an intense beam of radiation'

This is an acronym standing for 'light amplification by stimulated emission of radiation'. It was coined in 1960 on the pattern of the earlier (but less well known) ↑*maser* and rapidly spread with modern technology.

Ge [le:za/-ei-] M, pl. Ø, 1960s (1 tech>3 tech) **Du** [le:zər] C, 1960s (1 tech) **Nw** [la:ser] M, pl. -*e*, 1960s (3) **Ic** [=E] cp¹, 1960s (1 tech) = creat *leysir* **Fr** [lazœr] M, 1960s (2) **Sp** <=E>/*láser* [láser] M, 1960s (3) **It** [lazer] M, pl. Ø, 1960s (1 tech) **Rm** [laser] N, 1960s, via Fr? (2 tech) **Rs** *lazer* M, pl. -*y*, mid20c (2) → -*nyi* adj. **Po** [laser] M, mid20c (1 tech) → v.; -*owy* adj. **Cr** *laser* M, pl. -*i*, mid20c (2) → -*ist* M; -*ski* adj. **Bg** *lazer* M [U] mid20c (2) → -*en* adj. **Fi** [la:ser] (3) **Hu** *lézer* [le:zer] pl. -*ek*, 1970s (2<3) → *lézeres* adj. **Al** *lazër* M [U] 1970s (1 tech) **Gr** *leizer* N, mid20c (2)

last but not least *phr.* 'in particular'

This item is one of the oldest and most widespread English loan phrases but it is most often quoted without *but*, in contrast to modern British English.

Although the phrase is common in Western Europe, it is absent, or considered highbrow, in the east.

Ge *last not least* [=E] 19c (2) **Du** [=E] 1940s (2) **Nw** *last not least* 19c (1 rare) < trsl *sist, men ikke minst* **Ic** - < trsl *síðast en ekki síst* **Fr** <=E> end19c (1) (with *but* certainly highbrow) **Sp** [=E] 1980s (1 lit/rare) **It** (0) **Rm** (0) **Po** (0) **Cr** [=E] end20c (1) **Hu** [=E]/*last not least* [=E] beg20c (1 rare) **Gr** (0)

lasting* *n.* 'durable cloth'
Ge [=E] M [U] 19c (1 tech, obs) **Nw** [=E] M [U] beg20c (1 tech, obs) **Ic** <=E>/*lastingur* [lastiŋkʏr] N/ M [U] end19c, via Da (2 arch) **Fr** [lastiŋ] M, mid19c (1 tech) **Rm** *lastic* [lastik] N, via Fr, mid19c (3 tech, arch)

last minute *cp¹* 'reduced prices for last-minute bookings' (in offers for package tours)
Ge [=E] 1980s (1 mod) **Du** *last-minute* 1980s (2) **Sp** [=E] M, pl. *-s*, end20c (1 tech) **Po** [last-] end20c (1 mod) **Gr** <=E> [=E] adj., 1980s (1 tech, mod)

latecomer *n.* 'a person who arrives late'
Ge [=E] M, pl. Ø, 20c (1 rare) **Hu** - < trsl *későn jövő*

latin lover *n.* 'a man from Latin countries whose manners and looks are particularly attractive to northern women'
Ge [=E] M, pl. *-s*, 1960s (1 rare) **Fr** [latinlɔvœr] M, 1980s (1 jour) **Sp** [latin laber/-lober] M, 1960s (1>2) **It** [latin lover] M, pl. Ø, 1960s (1 coll) > trsl *amante latino* **Rm** (0) **Gr** *latin laver* M, pl. Ø/*-s*, end20c (1 coll) = trsl *latinos erastis*

law and order *phr./cp¹* 'a conservative mentality'
Ge [=E] 1970s (1 mod) **Du** (0) **Nw** (0) **Fr** (Ø) **Bg** - < rend *red i zakonnost*

lawn tennis *n.* 'the usual form of tennis, played with a soft ball on an open grass or hard court'
The full form was adopted along with other tennis terms in the early twentieth century in many European languages, but is commonly shortened to *tennis*, or with the first element translated. The present-day distribution reflecting the retention of the full form is therefore somewhat irregular.
Ge [=E] N [U] 1890s (1 arch) < trsl *(Rasen-)Tennis* **Du** [=E] N, end19c (1 tech, arch) **Nw** [=E] M [U] beg20c (1 arch) < *tennis* **Fr** [lontenis] M, end19c (1 tech/ arch) **Sp** [=E] M [U] end19c (1 tech/arch) **It** - < *tennis* **Rm** - < rend *tenis de câmp* **Rs** *laun-tennis* M [U] beg20c (1 tech) **Po** [-o-] M [U] beg20c (1 arch) **Cr** *lontenis* M [U] beg20c (1 tech) **Bg** - < *tenis* **Hu** [=E] [U]

end19c/beg20c (1 tech/arch) < *tennis* **Gr** *lontenis* N [U] beg20c (1 obs) < trsl *tenis sto khorto*

layout *n.* 2 'the way in which printed matter is arranged'
This word is common in technical jargon and is increasingly found in everyday language. Note that in French it refers to rough layout only, otherwise the term used is *maquette*. The term has recently been adopted in the field of electronics, where the suggested replacement for French is *topographie*.

Ge [lɛːaut] N, pl. *-s*, 1950s (1 tech) → *-en* v.; *-er* M; *-erin* F **Du** *lay-out* [leːjaut] C, 1950s (1 tech) **Nw** [=E] M [U] 1950s (2) > *uttegning* **Ic** [=E] N [U] end20c (1 tech) = rend *umbrot* **Fr** [lɛaut] 1970s (1 tech, ban) < *topographie* **Sp** [lajaut] M, end20c (1 tech) **It** [leiaut] M, pl. Ø, 1950s (1 tech) **Rm** [=E] N, 1970s (1 tech) **Cr** *lejaut* M [U] end20c (1 tech) **Bg** *leiaut* M [U] 1990s (1 tech, sla) **Fi** [=E] end20c (1 tech) = *taitto* **Hu** [=E] pl. Ø, 1970s (1 tech) **Gr** <=E>/*leiaut* N, end20c (1 tech)

lead *n.* 6a 'the chief part in a play, music, etc.'
Ge [=E] N [U] 1960s (1 tech) **Sp** [=E] M, 1970s (1 jour)

leader *n./cp¹ʹ²* 1a 'person or thing that leads', +1c 'esp. in politics', +1d 'a horse or athlete that leads', +1e 'a firm leading in a certain field', 2a 'the principal player in a music group', 2b 'the first violin in an orchestra', 3 'a leading article', +9 'a signature tune on radio and TV'
This word has received a number of specifications, being applied to politics and sports in particular (native terms being available for more generic uses). Adoption of (*newspaper*) *leader* appears to be much less frequent.

Ge [liːda] often *cp²*, M, pl. Ø, 1980s, +1e,2a(1 mod) +1d(1 rare) **Du** [=E] C, beg20c, 3,+9 (1 jour/tech); *cp²*, 2a(1 tech, coll) **Nw** 1a,+1c,d,e,2a,3(0) < *leder* **Ic** [=E] M, pl. *-ar*, end20c, 1a(1 coll); - < 3: creat *leiðari, forystugrein* **Fr** [lidœr] M, mid19c, +1c(2) +1d(1 tech/ban) 3(1 obs): < +1c,3: cp *article leader* > +1d: *meneur/meneuse, premier(e), en tête* **Sp** <=E>/*lider* M/adj., uninfl., end19c, +1a,c,e,2a(3) → *liderato, liderazgo* **It** [lider] M, pl. Ø/*cp²*, beg19c, 1a,+1c,+1d,+1e,2a,3(3) **Rm** *lider*/<=E> [=E] M, mid19c, 1a,+1c,+1d(2); 20c, 2a,+1e(2 mod) **Rs** *lider* M, pl. *-y*, beg20c, +1d(1 tech) +1c,1a,2a(3) → *-sha* F; *-irovat'* v. **Po** *lider*/<=E> M, beg20c, 1a,+1c,+1d,+1e,2a(2) → *-ka* F **Cr** *lider* M, pl. *-i*, mid20c, 1,+1c(2) 2a(1) → *-ski* adj.; *-stvo* N **Bg** *lider* M, pl. *-i*, mid20c, +1c,+1d,+1e,2a(2); → *-ka* F; *-stvo* N; *-ski* adj.; *lidiram* v. **Hu** [liːder] pl. *-ek*, 19c, 3 +1c(1 jour/arch); 20c, 1a(1 mod/jour) < *vezető* **Al** *lider* M, pl. *-a*, mid20c (1 mod) **Gr** *lider* M, end20c, 2a(1 tech)

leadership *n.* 'the quality of being (suitable to be) a leader'
Ge [=E] F [U] 20c (0>1 jour) **Nw** (0) < *lederskap* **Fr** [lidœrʃip] M, end19c (1 jour) **Sp** - < *liderazgo* **It** [=E] F, pl. Ø, end19c (2 tech, jour) **Rs** - < *liderstvo* **Bg** - < *liderstvo* **Al** lidership M, pl. -*e*, end20c (1 mod)

lean production* *phr.* 'economic production achieved by reduction of workers and material'
Ge [=E] F [U] 1992 (1 tech, mod)

learning by doing *phr.* 'a pedagogical concept' (popularized by John Dewey)
Ge [=E] N [U] 1980s (1 tech, rare) **Du** [=E] 1980s (1 coll) **Nw** (0) **Rm** (0)

lease *v.* 'grant or take on lease'
Ge [liːzn] 1980s (2 tech) **Du** *leasen* [liːzə] 1970s (2) **Nw** ["liːse] 1970s (2) **Fi** *liisata*, end20c (2)

leasing* *n.* 'a scheme by which an object is acquired by rental'
This word became universal throughout Europe within the last few years – which happened to coincide with the major political developments in Eastern Europe.
Ge [liːziŋ] N [U] 1980s (1 tech) > *Mietkauf* **Du** [=E] C [U] 1960s (1 tech) > *lease* **Nw** [=E/"liːsiŋ] M/F [U] 1960s (1 tech) **Fr** [lizin] M, 1960s (1 tech, ban) > *location avec option d'achat (L.O.A.)* **Sp** [lísin] M [U] 1970s (1>2 tech) **It** [liːzin(g)] M [U] 1960s (1>2) **Rm** [=E] N, 1970s (1 tech) **Rs** *lizing* M [U] 1980s (1 tech) → -*ovyĭ* adj. **Po** [-nk] M [U] 1980s (1 tech) → *owy* adj. **Cr** lising M [U] end20c (1 tech) **Bg** *lizing* M [U] end20c (1 tech) → -*ov* adj.; -*ovam* v. **Fi** [=E] (1) = *liisaus* **Hu** *lizing* [=E] pl. -*ek* 1980s (1 tech>2) **Gr** *lizing* N [U] 1990s (1 tech)

legging(s) *n.* 1 'tight-fitting stretch trousers for women and children', 2 'a stout protective outer covering for the leg from the knee to the ankle'
The spread of this fashionable item (1) throughout Europe appears not to have been as universal as once thought; languages not affected are not likely to acquire the word because the object may become outdated soon. The historical source of the word (2) is a foreignism known to readers of eighteenth/nineteenth-century American travelogues.
Ge <=E>/*legging*/*leggin(s)* [=E/ legins/lɛgiŋs] pl., 19c, 2(Ø); 1990, 1(2) **Du** *legging* [=E] C, 1980s (2) **Nw** [=E] [U] beg20c, 1(1) **Ic** [lɛcːiŋs] F, uninfl. 1980s, 1(1 mod); - < 2: rend *legg-hlífar* **Fr** *leggins*/*leggings* [legins /legiŋs] M/F, pl., mid19c, 2(1 tech) **Sp** <=E>/*legui* [=E/legi] M, pl. -*s*, beg20c, 2(3 tech/obs) = 1: *polainas; leggings* M, pl.; 1980s, 1(2 tech) = *mallas* **Rm** [le-ginʃi] M, pl., 1990s (1 you) **Rs** *legginsy* pl., 1990s, 1(1 mod/you) **Po** *leggingsy* [-i] pl., end20c, 1,(2 you) **Hu** [=E] [U] 1980s, 1(2) **Al** *legins* M, pl. -*e*, 1990s (1 you)

leghorn *n.* 2b 'a breed of hen'
The name derives from the English form of the Italian port *Livorno*; since the form of the loanword was opaque it was subject to folk etymological reinterpretation (e.g. in German). German mediation is likely for Eastern European Languages. The breed (and the word) appears to be obsolescent.
Ge [leːghorn] N, pl. -*(s)*, 19c (3) **Du** [lɪghɔrn] C, 1940s (3 tech) **Fr** [legɔrn] F, end19c (1 tech) **Sp** <=E> N [U] 1930s (1 tech) **Rm** [leghorn] N [U] beg20c (1 tech) **Rs** *leggorn* M, pl. -*y*, mid20c (1 tech) **Po** [leg-horn] M, mid20c (1 tech) **Cr** [leghorn] M [U] mid20c (1) **Bg** *leghorn* M, pl. -*i*, 20c (1 tech) **Hu** [leghorn] pl. Ø, end19c/beg20c (1 tech/obs)

leg warmer *n.* 'either of a pair of knitted garments covering the leg from ankle to thigh (esp. used in aerobics)'
Ge [lɛkvorma] M, pl. Ø/-*s*, 1980s (1 mod, rare) **Du** - < trsl *beenwarmer* **Nw** - < trsl *leggvarmer* **Ic** - < *legghlíf* **It** - < rend *scaldamuscoli*

leisurewear* *n.* 'informal wear'
Ge *Leisurewear* F? [U] end20c (1 tech) **Du** [=E] C [U] end20c (1 tech)

lemming *n.* 1 'a small arctic rodent of the genus Lemmus'
This word is clearly from Norwegian and is thus classified in most languages. However, Italian labels it "English" – because it was transmitted through English or because the -*ing* makes it look English? Compare other 'pseudo- anglicisms' like ↑*krill*.
Ge (5Nw) **Du** [=E] C, pl. -*s*/-*en*, 19c (5) **Nw** *lemen* (5) **Ic** *læmingi* (5) **Fr** (5Nw) **Sp** [lemin] M (5Nw) **It** [lemiŋ] M, pl. Ø, 1900s (1 tech) **Rm** *leming* [lemiŋ] M, mid20c? via Fr (5) **Rs** *lemming* (5Nw) **Po** *leming* [lemink] M, beg20c (1 tech) **Hu** (5Nw) **Gr** *leming* N (1 tech)

lemon *n.* +1c 'an effervescent drink made from lemon juice'
Du (Ø) **Ic** [=E] N [U] end20c (1 coll) **It** *lemon soda* [lemon sɔda] F, pl. Ø, mid20c (3) **Rm** (0) **Po** (0) **Bg** - < trsl *limon*

lemon grass *n.* 'a fragrant tropical grass'
Du - < *citroengras* **Fr** *lemon-grass* [lemɔngʀas] M, 1920s (1 tech) **Po** - → *lemongrasowy* adj. **Hu** - < *citromfü*

letkiss* *n.* 'a dance from the 1960s with folkloristic character'
This word is interesting since the form suggests English provenance; this is, however, a Finnish word affected by popular etymology, and as such has very different connotations from the etymon.
Ge [=E] M [U] 1960s (1 obs) **Bg** *letkis* M [U] 1960s (2 arch) **Hu** [=E] [U] 1960s (2 arch)

level *n.* 2 'a height or value reached, a position on a certain scale', 3 'a social, moral, or intellectual standard'

Ge [=E] M/N, pl -s, 1970s (1 mod) < *Niveau, Ebene*
Du - < *niveau* Nw 2(0) < *nivå* Ic [=E/lɛ:vel] M [U]
end20c (1 sla) It - < *livello* Rm 2(0 tech)

lewisite *n.* 'a poisonous gas'
Ge *Lewisit* [le:vizi̯t] N [U] 20c (1 tech) Du *lewisiet*
[lewisi̯t] N [U] 1940s (3 tech) Fr [levizit] F, 20c (1
tech) It [luizi̯te] F, 1930s (1 tech) Rm *levizită*/lewi-
sită [levizi̯tə/-s-] F [U] mid20c, via Fr (1 tech) Rs
lyuizit M [U] beg20c (1 tech) Po *luizyt* [-zit] M [U]
mid20c (2) Cr *lujzit* M [U] 20c (1 tech) Bg *luizi̯t* M
[U] mid20c, via Rs (1 tech) Fi *levisiitti* 20c (3) Hu
[=E/lu̯izit] [U] 1970s (1 tech)

liberty *n.* +6 'a sort of glossy silk', +7 'a flowery style
in architecture, furniture and decorations'
   This term appears to derive from the trade-name
'designating materials, styles, colours, etc., characteristic of textile fabrics or articles sold by Messrs Liberty' (SOED). The word has long been obsolete in
most European languages; it is likely to have been
more widespread than is determinable today.

Ge [=E] F [U] end19c, +6(1
arch) Fr [libɛʀti] M/adj.,
uninfl., end19c, +6(1) Sp [lib-
erti̯] beg20c, +6(1 tech) It [lib-
erti̯] M [U]/adj., 1900s, +7(2)
Rm *liberti* [liberti] N/M [U]
1960s, +6(1 tech) Po M/N,
uninfl., beg20c, +6(1 tech) Hu [libərti] [U] 19c,
+6(1 arch)

life *n.* +13 'dolce vita'
Bg *laif* M [U] end20c (2 coll)

lifestyle *n.* 'the particular way of life of a person or
group (often used as a factor in advertising and promotion)'
Ge [=E] M, pl. -s, 1980 (1 mod) Du [=E] C [U] 1980s
(1 mod) Nw [=E] 1980s (1) < trsl *livsstil* Ic - < trsl
lifsstill Sp - < trsl *estilo de vida* It - < trsl *stile di
vita* Rm (0 jour) < trsl *stil de viaţă* Rs - < trsl *stil'
zhizni* Gr <=E> [=E] N [U] 1990s (1 jour, mod)

lift¹ (1) *n.* 2 'a free ride in a car', 3a 'an elevator', 3b 'a
ski-lift, a chairlift', +9 'plastic surgery to reduce wrinkles (esp. in the face)'
   This word is a rare instance of a term borrowed in
successive periods in a great range of senses (partly
transmitted through different languages). A full historical study of its complex history would be worth-
while.

Ge [=E] M/N, pl -el-s, 1900s,
3a(1 coll); mid20c, 2(1 coll)
3b(3); 1970s, +9(1 tech) < 3a:
Fahrstuhl; +9: ↑*Facelifting* Du
[=E] C, pl. -en, 1940s, 2(3);
end19c, 3a(3); *skilift* [=E] 1950s,
3b(3); *face-lift* [fe:slɪft] C, 1960s,
+9(1 tech) → *-en* v. Nw [=E] M, pl. -er, 1950s, 2(1
arch); 1970s, 3a,b(1 tech); +9(1 tech) < 2: *skyss, haik*;
< 3a,b: *heis, skiheis*; < +9: trsl *(ansikts-)løftning* Ic -
< 2: *far*; 3a,b: creat *lyfta* Fr [lift] M, 2(0), 3a(0 arch)
< +9: ↑*lifting* → *liftier/liftman* It [lift] M, pl. Ø,

1900s, 3a(1) Rm [=E] N, 1930s, 3a,b(2>3); 1980s,
+9(2 mod) → *liftier* M (5Fr) Rs *lift* M, pl. *-y*,
mid20c, 3a(3) → *-ër* M; *-ërsha* F Po (0) Cr *lift* M,
pl. *-ovi*, 19/20c, 3a(3) 3b(2) Bg *lift* M, pl. *-al-ove*,
mid20c, 3b(2); - < 3a: *asansyor* Hu [=E] pl. *-ek*,
19c, 3a(3); 3b: < rend *sifelvonó*; +9(1 tech, mod) →
liftes n.; *liftezik* v. Al *lift* M, pl. *-e*, 20c, 3a(1 rare)
Gr *lift* N, end20c, 3b(1 tech)

lift² *n.* 'a stroke in tennis'
Fr [=E] M, beg20c (1 tech) → *lifter* v., *balle liftée* Sp
[=E] (golpe) *liftado* M, 20c (1 tech) → *liftar* v.; *liftado*
adj. It [=E] M, pl. Ø, 1900s (1 tech) → *liftato* adj.,
liftare v. Rm [=E] N, 1930s (1 tech) Bg - < creat
liftiran udar (3+5) Hu [=E] 19c (1 tech/arch) < *áte-
melés*

lift *cp¹* 'remedial'
Ge *Lift(-kurs)* 1980s (2+5)

lift *v.* 1 'raise or remove to a higher position', +13a
'strike a ball' (tennis), 14 'perform cosmetic surgery
on', +15 'go uphill in a ski-lift', +16 'hitchhike'
Ge *liften* beg20c, 1(3); 1970s, 14(1 tech); mid20c,
+15(3) Du *faceliften* [fe:slɪftən] 1970s, 14(1
tech) Nw (0) Fr [lifte] beg20c, +13a(1 tech); *lifter*
14(1 tech) Sp *liftar* 20c (3 tech) Rm *lifta* [lifta̲]
mid20c, via Fr?, +13a,14(1 tech) Po (0) Fi *liftata*
+16(1 coll) → *liftari* n.

liftback* *n.* 'a car opening at back'
Ge [liftbek] M/N, pl. -s, 1970s (1 tech) =
↑*hatchback* Fr - < *à haïllon* Gr *liftbak* N, end20c
(1 tech)

liftboy *n.* 'a lift attendant (in uniform) in hotels and
department stores'
   The distribution of this term is remarkable because
around 1900 it was a fashionable modernism, the
compound being much more widespread than its components. Today the word appears to be obsolescent in
most languages.

Ge [=E] M, pl. -s, beg20c
(2) Du [=E] C, 1940s (2) Nw -
< *heisbetjent* Ic - < trsl *lyftu-
drengur, -strákur* Fr - < *liftier*
M Sp [=E] M, 1930s (0 arch)
It [=E] M, pl. Ø, 1900s (1
tech) Rm <=E>/*liftboi* [=E]
M, pl. Ø, mid20c (1) < *liftier* Po (0) Cr [=E] M,
pl. *-i*, beg20c (3) → *-ski* adj. Hu [=E] pl. *-ok*, 20c (3)
= *liftes fiú*

lifting *n.* 'tightening of skin' (med.) (cf. ↑*facelifting*)
   Whereas *lifting* and ↑*lift* appear to be largely inter-
changeable, the former is unambiguous; both are
often found as cp² in *faceliftling* etc.).
Ge *(face-)* N, pl. -s, 1960s (2)
< *Facelifting* Du - < ↑*face-
lifting* Nw- < trsl *(ansikts-)løft-
ning* Fr [liftin] M, 20c (2 ban)
> *lissage, remodelage, restylage*
(for car design) Sp *lifting* [liftin]
M, pl. -s, 1980s (2) It [liftiŋ(g)]
M, pl. Ø, 1980s (1 tech) Rm [=E] N, 1970s (1

tech) **Rs** *lifting* M [U] 1970s (2 tech) **Po** [-nk] M [U] end20c (1 mod) **Cr** - < ↑*facelifting* **Bg** *lifting* M [U] 1970s (1 tech) **Hu** - < ↑*facelifting* **Gr** *lifting* N, end20c, via Fr (2) > *ritidhektomi*

light *adj.* 4b 'low in fat, cholesterol, or sugar, etc.' (of food), 4c 'not heavy on the stomach or strongly alcoholic' (of drink), +4d 'low in tar' (of cigarettes)

The word was coined and promoted by the food industry, esp. to designate low-calorie slimming products; more recently it has been transferred to other contexts, often facetiously.

Ge [=E] uninfl., 1980s (2 mod) **Du** [=E] 1980s (1 mod/tech) **Nw** [=E] 1980s (2 mod) **Ic** [=E] uninfl., 1970s, +4d(0) **Fr** 1990s, 4c(1 mod) **Sp** [=E] 1980s (1>2) **It** [=E] uninfl., 1980s (2) **Rm** [=E] adj., uninfl., 1980s, 4c,+4d(1 mod) **Po** [=E] uninfl., 1980s (1 coll) **Fi** [=E] uninfl., 1980s (2 mod) **Hu** [=E] [U] 1980s (2 mod) **Gr** <=E>/*lait* adj., uninfl., 1980s(2)

lighter *n.* 'a device for lighting cigarettes' **Nw** [=E] M, pl. *-e*, 1950s (2)

light show *n.* 'a performance using lights (in discos)' **Ge** *lightshow* [laitʃo:] F, pl. *-s*, 1970s (1 you) **Nw** (0) < *lysshow* **Ic** *ljósasjó* [-sjou:] N, pl. Ø, 1970s (5+1 coll) **Fr** *light-show* M, 1970s(1) **Rs** (0) **Cr** *lajtšou* M [U] end20c (1 tech) **Hu** [=E] pl. Ø, 1980s (1 jour/mod/you) **Gr** *lait soul/laitsou* N, end20c (1 tech, rare, mod)

-like *cp²* 'used to form adj. from nouns indicating: similar to or typical of' **Ge** [=E] 1960s (1 jour, rare)

lilliputian *n./adj.* 'a diminutive person or thing' This word is an instance of an early loanword exclusively spread through literature. It came to be universally known (as an adj./name) through Swift's *Gulliver's Travels* from 1726. In English, this word is partly motivated through its similarity to *little*. The derivative *lilliputian* ('inhabitant of L.' etc.) was borrowed more rarely, native suffixes being preferred. **Ge** *Liliput* (cp.¹) 19c (3) → *-aner; -anisch* adj. **Du** *lilliputter* [lilipʏtər] C, beg19c (3) **Nw** *lilleputt* [lileput] M, pl. *-er*, beg20c (3/4) **Fr** *lilliputien/ne* [lilipysjẽ/-jɛn] C/adj., 18c (3) **Sp** *liliput* adj., uninfl., 19c (1 jour/rare) → *liliputiense* **It** - → *lillipuziano* [lilliputsiano] M, pl. *-i*, 19c (3) **Rm** *liliput* [liliput] adj., uninfl., end19c (3 rare) → *liliputan* M; *-ă* M,F/adj. **Rs** *liliput* M, pl. *-y*, mid19c (3) → *-ik* M; *-ka* F; *-skiĭ* adj. **Po** *liliput* [liliput] M, mid19c (3) → *-ek* M; *-ka* F; *lilipuci* adj. **Cr** - → *liliputanac* M, pl. *-ci*, end19c (3) **Bg** *liliput* M, pl. *-al-i*, beg20c, via Rs (3) → *-ski* adj. **Fi** *lilliputti* (Ø) **Hu** *liliputi* [liliputi] [U]/pl. Ø, 19c (2>3) → *liliputi* adj. **Al** *liliput* M, pl. *-ë*, mid20c (3) **Gr** - → *liliputios, -a, -o*, adj. (3)

lime *n.* 1a 'a rounded citrus fruit', 2 'the juice of limes as a drink', 3 'a pale green colour' **Du** - < *limoen* **Nw** [=E] M, end20c (1) **Ic** [=E] N, pl. Ø, end20c, 1a(1 coll) = *limóna* **Fr** [lim] F, 16c (1

tech)? **Sp** - < 1a: *lima*, 3: *verde lima* **It** [=E] M, pl. Ø, mid20c, 1a(1) **Rs** (0) **Po** (0) **Cr** (0) **Fi** *limetti* 1a; [=E] 2(0) **Hu** *lima* [lima] pl. Ø, end20c, 1a(2); [=E] [U] 1980s, 2(2)

lime-juice *n.* 'a drink' **Nw** [=E/-juːs] M [U] (1) **Ic** [=E] N [U] end20c (0) **Rs** (0) **Po** (0) **Cr** (0)

limerick *n.* 'a humorous five-line stanza' This word is of uncertain etymology, its connection with the city in Ireland being opaque. It is first found in Beardsley's *Letters* (1896). Its modern distribution appears to depend on whether the verse form has become popular in the national literatures. The term is commonly used for light verse in German. **Ge** [=E] M, pl. *-s*, 20c (2 tech) **Du** [=E] C, 1940s (2) **Nw** [=E] M, pl. *-er*, beg20c (2) **Ic** - < creat *limra* F **Fr** [limʀik] M, 20c (1) **It** [limerik] M, pl. Ø, 1980s (1 tech) **Rm** [=E] N, 20c (1 tech) **Rs** *liimerik* M, pl. *-i*, mid20c (1 tech) **Po** *limeryk* [-e-] M, mid20c (1 tech) **Cr** *limerik* M, pl. *-ci*, 20c (2) **Fi** *limerikki* 20c (2 tech) **Hu** [=E] pl. *-ek*, 20c (1 tech>2)

limit *n.* 1 'the level beyond which something may not extend', 3 'the greatest or smallest amount permissible or possible' (esp. in prices) **Ge** [=E] N, pl. *-s*, end19c/1970s (3) **Du** [=E] 1980s (1 coll) = *limiet* (via Fr) **Nw** (0) < *grense* **Sp** - < *limite* (5La) **It** [=E] M, pl. Ø, end20c, 1(1 mod) **Rm** - < *limită* **Rs** (5La) **Po** (5La) **Cr** *limit* M [U] pl. *-i*, mid20c (3) **Bg** *limit* M, pl. *-al-i*, mid20c, 1,3(2) → *-iram* v. **Fi** *limitti* end20c, 1(0) **Hu** (5Fr) **Al** *limit* M, pl. *-e* (1)

limited *adj.* 4 (after the name of a company) 'being a limited company' National terms, often calqued on English, are common for the legal term 'limited company' (*GmbH, S.R.L.* etc.) **Ge** (0) < *GmbH* **Du** [=E] beg20c (1 tech) **Nw** (Ø) **It** - < trsl *s.r.l.* **Rm** (Ø) < rend *S.R.L.* **Rs** (0) **Po** uninfl., beg20c (1 tech) **Cr** *limitid* uninfl., 20c (1 tech) **Bg** - < *Ltd* **Fi** [=E] (Ø) **Hu** [limitid] < *Ltd.* **Gr** <=E> [=E] mid20c (1 tech)

line up *v.* 1 'arrange or be arranged in a line or lines', +4 'set up equipment in a recording studio' **Nw** *line (opp)* ["laine] 1970s, +4(1 coll) **Ic** *læna (upp)* [lai:na] 1970s, +4(1 tech)

liner *n./cp²* 'a ship or aircraft carrying passengers on a regular line' **Ge** [=E] M/cp², pl. *-(s)*, mid20c (1 tech, rare) → *Luxus-* **Du** [=E] C, 1990s (1 tech) **Nw** [=E] M, pl. *-e*, beg20c (2) **Fr** [lajnœʀ] M, beg20c (1 tech) **Sp** [=E] M end20c (1 tech) **Rs** *lainer* M, pl. *-y*, beg20c (1 tech) **Cr** *lajner* M, pl. *-i*, mid20c (1) **Bg** *lainer* M, pl. *-al-i*, mid20c (2 tech) **Hu** [la:jner] pl. Ø, 20c (1 tech) **Al** *linjë* F, pl. *-a*, mid20c (1 tech)

link *n.* 2a 'a connecting part; one in a series', 3 'a means of contact by radio or telephone between two points'

The distribution of this word in its various technical uses is somewhat difficult to account for, esp. since the reasons for the adoption are not always clear.

Du [=E] C, 1970s, 2a(2) **Nw** [=E] M, pl. *-er*, 1950s, 3(2 tech) **Ic** [liŋk(ʏr)] M, pl. *-arl-ir*, end20c, 3(1 tech) **Sp** - → *linkaje* M; *linkar* v. **It** [=E] M, pl. Ø, 1970s (1 tech) **Cr** link M, pl. *-ovi*, end20c, 3(1 tech) **Fi** *linkki* 1970s, 2a(2 arch) 3(3) **Hu** [=E] pl. Ø, 1970s, 2(1 arch), 3(1 tech)

linkage *n.* 2b 'the tendency of genes on the same chromosome to be inherited together' (genetics)
Sp *linkaje* M, 1950s (1 tech) **It** [=E] M [U] 1930s (1 tech) **Rm** [=E] N [U] 1970s (1 tech) **Hu** [=E] [U] 20c (1 tech)

Linotype *n.* (orig.^TM) 'a composing machine producing lines of words as single strips of metal, used esp. for newspapers'
Ge [li:noty:pə] F, pl. *-s*, 19c (3 tech) **Du** [=E] C, 1910s (1 tech) **Nw** [=E/li̱:nu-] M pl. *-r*, 20c (1 tech) **Ic** [=E] mid/end20c (1 tech) = rend *linusetjari* **Fr** [linotip] F, end19c (1 tech) → *linotypie* F; *linotypiste* M/F **Sp** *linotipia* F, beg20c (3) → *linotipo; linotipista* **It** [linota̱ip] F, pl. Ø, end19c (2 tech) **Rm** *linotip* [linoti̱p] N, 1930s, via Fr (3 tech) → *linotipie* F; *linotipist* M, *-ă* F **Rs** *linotip* M, pl. *-y*, beg20c (1 tech) → *-ist* M; *-nyĭ* adj. **Po** *linotyp* [linoti̱p] M, beg20c (2 tech) **Cr** *linoti̱p* M [U] end19c (3 tech) **Bg** *linotip* M [U] beg20c (1 tech) → *-iya* F; *-en* adj. **Hu** [li̱notaip] pl. Ø, end19c (3 tech) **Al** *linotip* M, pl. *-e*, mid20c (1 tech) **Gr** *linotypiki mikhani* F, 20c (3 tech+5)

linter(s) *n.* 2 'short cotton fibres'
Ge *Linters* [li̱ntərs] pl., 1940s (1 tech, obs) **Du** *linters* [=E] pl., 1940s (1 tech) **Fr** *linter* [linter] M, 1940s (1 tech) **Sp** *línteres* pl., mid20c (3 tech) **Rm** *linters* [linters] N [U] mid20c, via Ge/Fr (3 tech) **Po** [-er-] M, mid20c (1 tech) **Hu** [=E] [U] 20c (1 tech)

lipgloss *n.* 'a cosmetic product that makes lips glossy'
Ge [=E] M/N [U] 1980s (1 tech, mod) **Du** [=E] C, 1990s (1 jour, mod) **Nw** [=E] M [U] 1970s (1/2) **Ic** - < *gloss*) **It** - < rend *lucidalabbra* **Gr** *lipglo̱s* N, end20c (1 tech)

lipstick *n.* 1 'a small stick of cosmetic for colouring the lips', +2 'a stick for protecting lips against the cold'
Ge - < 1: *Lippenstift* **Du** [=E] C, 1960s, 1(2) = *lippenstift* **Nw** 1(0) < *leppestift* **Ic** - < *varalitur* **Sp** - < trsl *barra de labios, lápiz de labios* **It** - < 1: *rossetto*; 2: rend *stick per le labbra, lucidalabbra in stick* **Cr** *lipstik* M, pl. *-ovi*, mid20c, 1(2) **Fi** *lipstikki* 1970s, +2(3) < 1: rend *huulipuna* **Hu** - < rend *ajakrúzs* **Gr** *lipstik* N, pl. *-s*/Ø, 1990s, 1(1 tech, jour, mod) < *kraghion*

listing *n.* +4 'a list, a computer print-out'

Ge [=E] N, pl. *-s*, 1980s (1 tech, rare) **Du** [=E] C, 1980s (1 tech) **Nw** [=E] M, pl. *-er*, 1980s (1 tech) **Fr** [=E] M, mid20c (2 ban) > *listage* **Rm** [=E] N, end20c (1 tech) > *listare* **Rs** *listing* M, pl. *-i*, 1990s (1 tech) **Po** [-nk] M [U] end20c (1 tech) **Cr** *listing* M, pl. *-zi*, end20c (1 tech) **Bg** *listing* M, pl. *-al-i*, end20c (3 tech) **Fi** - < *listaus*

live *adj./cp^{1/2}* 2a 'heard or seen at the time of its performance, not from a recording' (of a broadcast), +2c 'recorded directly, frequently at a concert'

Although translations, or semantic extensions of native words, would have offered easy solutions to avoid using this word, its connection with pop culture and modern media have made *live* almost universal.

Ge [-f/-v] uninfl., 1950s (2) > *Direkt-* **Du** [=E] 1970s (2) **Nw** [=E] 1960s (2) = *levende, direkte* **Ic** [=E] 1960s, +2c(1 tech) **Fr** [lajv] inv., 1980s (1>2) **Sp** [=E] (1 tech) < *en directo, en vivo* **It** [=E] adj., uninfl., 1970s (1) < trsl *dal vivo, in diretta* **Rm** [=E] adj./cp², uninfl., 1970s (1 tech/mod_MUS) = *în direct* **Rs** - < trsl *pryamoĭ* **Po** [-f] uninfl., end20c (1 mod) **Cr** [=E] end20c (1 tech) **Bg** *laĭf* M, pl. *-a*, 1990s, 2a(3 tech, mod) < rend *na zhivo* **Fi** [live] 1970s (2); often infl. *livenä* **Hu** [=E] 1980s/90s (1 tech) < *élő-* **Al** - < *direkt* **Gr** *laiv* adj., end20c (1 tech) < mean *zodanos, -i, -o*

living room *n.* 'a room for general day use'

This term appears to have been current as a fashionable alternative to native words in the early twentieth century, but is largely obsolete today. (It may have come to be felt as an affectation.) The short form *living* is at least partly due to French mediation.

Ge (0) < *Wohnzimmer* **Du** *living* [=E] C, 1970s (1 jour, rare) < *woonkamer, huiskamer* **Nw** (0) < *stue* **Fr** *living-roomlliving* [livin-rum] M, 1930s (2 ban) < *salle de séjour* **Sp** *living roomlliving* [li̱binrum/livin] M, 1920s (1 jour) **It** *living* [=E] M, pl. Ø, 1970s (1 mod) **Rm** *livingllivingrum* [=E] N, 20c (2/Ø) **Po** [-nk rum] M, end20c (1 mod) **Hu** [=E] pl. Ø, 1970s (1 rare) **Gr** *livingrum* N, beg20c (1 rare> obs) < *saloni*

loadsman* *n.* 'a guide on ships'

Borrowing of this term clearly took place at two different periods and of two different forms, an early one affecting the North Sea languages, and a later one affecting Russian and Bulgarian.
Ge *Lotse* M, pl. *-n*, 17c (3) → *lotsen* v. **Du** *loods* [lo:ts] C, pl. *loodsen*, 17c (3) **Nw** *los* [lu:s] M, pl. *-er*, 19c, via Ge (3) → *lose* v. **Ic** *lóðs(-)/lóss(maður)* [lou:ðs-/lous:-] M, pl. *-ar (-menn)*, 18c, via Da (3) → *lóðsa/lóssa* v. **Rs** *lo̱tsman* M, pl. *-y*, beg20c (3) **Bg** *lo̱tsman* M, pl. *-i*, beg20c, via Rs (3 tech)

loaf¹ (1) *n.* +1a 'white bread'
Nw *loff* [luf] M, pl. *-er*, 19c (3)

loaf² (2) *n.* 'the act or a spell of wasting time idly'

Nw usu. def. form *loffen* [lufen] M [U] 1930s (3)

loaf *v.* +4 'live as a tramp, seek adventure'
Nw *loffe* ["lufe] 1930s (3) → *loffer* n.

loafer *n.* 2 'a mocassin-type of shoe'
Du [=E] C, 1960s (1 tech) < *instapper* **Nw** [=E] M, pl. *-s*, 1970s (1 tech, mod)

lob *n.* 1 'a ball struck in a high arc'
Ge [lop] M, pl. *-s*, beg20c/1970s (1 tech, rare) → *lobben* v. **Du** [lɔp] C, 1950s (1 tech) **Nw** *lobb* [=E] M, pl. *-er*, beg20c (1 tech) → *lobbe* v. **Fr** [lɔb] M, beg20c (1 tech) → *lober* v. **Sp** [=E] M, 1980s (1 tech) = *globo* **It** [lob] M, pl. Ø, 1930s (1 tech) < *pallonetto* **Rm** [=E] N, 1960s (1 tech) **Po** [-p] M, mid20c (1 tech) **Cr** *lob* M, pl. *-ovi*, mid20c (1 tech) → *-ovati* v. **Bg** *lob* M, pl. *-al-ove*, mid20c (1 tech) **Fi** *lobbi* (1 tech) **Hu** [=E] pl. Ø, 1970s (1 tech) **Al** *lob* M, pl. *-ë*, mid20c (1 rare)

lobby *n/cp²* 1 'a porch, ante-room, entrance hall, or corridor (of hotels etc.)', 2 'an entrance-hall of parliament', 3 'a pressure-group'

The distribution of the meaning 'entrance hall (of parliament)' is widespread, but some languages went straight to the metonymic extension 'pressure group', which is more current in all languages affected. Note that derivatives with *-ing* and *-ist* are conspicuously rarer.

Ge [=E] F/cp², pl. *-ies*, mid20c, 1,2(1 tech) 3(2) → *-ismus* M **Du** [=E] C, mid20c, 1,3(2) → *-en* v. **Nw** [=E] M, pl. *-er*, mid20c, 1,3(2) → *lobbye* v. **Ic** *lobbý* [lɔpːi] N, pl. Ø, mid20c, 1(1 coll) = 1: *(gesta)móttaka*; 3: *þrýstihópur* **Fr** [lɔbi] M, 1950s, 2(1 tech/ban); 1950s, 3(1>2) < 2: *vestibule* **Sp** [lobi] M, pl. *-iesl-ys*, 1930s, 1(1); 1970s, 3(2) < 1: *vestíbulo*; = 3: *grupo de presión* **It** [lobbi] F, pl. Ø, 1920s, 1(1) 2(1 tech); 1970s, 3(2>3) → *lobbistico* adj. **Rm** [=E] N, 1970s, 2(1 tech) 3(2) **Rs** *lobbi* N, uninfl. [U] mid20c, 3(2) **Po** N, pl. *-ies*, end20c, 2,3(2) → *lobbistyczny* adj. **Cr** *lobi* M [U] end20c, 3(1) → *-st* M; *-stica* F; *-rati* v. **Bg** *lobi* N, pl. *-ta*, end20c, 3(2) → *-zŭm* M; *-ram* v. **Hu** [=E] pl. Ø, 1970s, 2(0) 3(2) **Al** *lobi* F, pl. *-tël-etllobe*, end20c (1 rare) **Gr** *lobi* N, mid20c, 3(2)

lobbying *n.* 'the activity of pressure groups'
Nw [=E] M [U] 1970s (1) < *lobbyvirksomhet* **Ic** - < *lobbýismi* **Fr** (1) < *influençage* **It** [lɔbbiːŋg] M [U] 1980s (1 tech) < *lobbismo* **Rm** [=E] N [U] end20c (1 tech POLIT) **Rs** - < *lobbirovanie* **Po** [-nk] M [U] end20c (2 mod) **Bg** - < *lobirane* **Fi** - < *lobbaus* **Hu** - < *lobbizás*

lobbyism* *n.* 'the act of trying to influence (exerted by a pressure group)' (cf. ↑*lobbying*)
Ge *Lobbyismus* M [U] 1950s (3) **Nw** *lobbyisme* M [U] 20c (3 rare) < *lobbyvirksomhet, lobbying* **Ic** *lobbýismi* M [U] end20c (2 coll) **Fr** [lɔbism] M, end20c (1 tech) > *influençage* **It** *lobbismo* [lɔbbizmo] M [U] 1950s (3) → *lobbista* n.; *lobbistico* adj. **Rm** [lobism] N [U] 1970s (2 tech) **Rs** *lobbizm* M [U] end20c (3 tech) **Cr** (0) **Bg** *lobizŭm* M [U] end20c (3 tech, jour) **Fi** - < *lobbaus* **Hu** *lobbizmus* [lobbismuʃ] [U] 20c (3/5La)

lobbyist *n.* 'a person trying to influence esp. members of parliament'
Ge [=E] M, pl. *-en*, mid20c (1 jour) **Du** [=E] C, 1960s (2) **Nw** [lɔbyist] M, pl. *-er*, 1960s (1) **Ic** *lobbýisti* [lɔpːiːstɪ] M, pl. *-ar*, end20c (1 coll) **Fr** *lobbyist* M, 20c (1) **Sp** *lobbystallobista* M, end20c (1>2 tech) **It** *lobbista* M/F, pl. *-il-e*, 1970s (3) **Rm** [lobist] M, end20c (1 tech POLIT) **Rs** *lobbist* M, pl. *-y*, mid20c (2) → *-ka* N; *-skiǐ* adj. **Po** *lobbista* [lobista] M, end20c (2) → *lobbistka* F **Cr** *lobist* M, pl. *-i*, end20c (1) **Bg** *lobist* M, pl. *-i*, end20c (1 jour) → *-ki* adj. **Fi** - < *lobbaaja* **Hu** - < *lobbizó*

locker *n.* 1 'a small lockable cupboard, esp. each of several for public use'
Ge (0) < *Schließfach* **Du** [=E] C, 1980s (2) **Nw** (0) < *oppbevaringsboks* **Ic** [=E] M, pl. *-ar*, 1970s, 1(Ø) < *skápur* **Fi** *lokero* 20c (3)

lockout *n.* 'the exclusion of employees from the workplace by their employer'

The companion term to ↑*strike*, this word is one of the most important stemming from nineteenth-century industrial practices. The word is still widespread (with few calques available).

Ge [=E] M, pl. *-s*, end19c (1 arch) < *Aussperrung* **Du** [=E] C, beg20c (2) **Nw** [=E] M, pl. *-er*, end19c (2) → *lockoute* v. **Ic** [=E] M < *verkbann* **Fr** *lock-outl<=E>* [lɔkawt] M [U] mid19c (1 tech) → *lock-outer* v. **Sp** [=E] M, pl. *-s*, 1920s (1 arch/obs) < *cierre patronal* **It** - < *serrata* **Rm** [=E] N, 1970s (1 jour) **Rs** *lokaut* M, pl. *-y*, beg20c (2) → *-irovat'* v. **Po** *lokaut* beg20c (2) → *-owy* adj. **Cr** [=E] M [U] mid20c (1 tech) **Bg** *lokaut* M, pl. *-al-i*, mid20c (1 tech) **Hu** [=E] [U] 20c (1 tech/arch) **Al** *lokaut* M, pl. *-ë*, mid20c (1 tech) **Gr** *lokaut* N [U] mid20c (1 tech) = *adaperghia*

loft *n.* +1a 'a large attic, used for living or as an artist's studio', 6 'a slant on a golf club'
Ge [=E] M, pl. *-s*, 1980s, +1a(1 mod) **Nw** +1a(5); [=E] M, 1980s, 6(1 tech) **Ic** *loft* 20c, +1a(5) **Fr** [lɔft] M, 1980s, +1a(1 mod); mid20c, 6(1 tech) **Sp** [=E] C, pl. *-s*, 1980s, +1a(1 jour, rare) **It** [=E] M, pl. Ø, 1980s (1)

log *n.* 2a 'a float attached to a line wound on a reel for gauging the speed of a ship' (naut.) 2b 'any apparatus measuring speed', 3 'a record of events occurring during and affecting the voyage of a ship or aircraft', 4 'any systematic record of things done, experienced, etc.', 5 'a logbook'

As an early and key nautical term *log* was borrowed into most North European languages. Its adoption further south has been more recent or non-existent.

Ge *Log/Logg(a)* [=E] N, pl. *-e*, 18c, 2a,b(3 tech) = *Logge* **Du** [lɔx] C, pl. *-gen*, mid19c, 2b(3 tech) **Nw** *logg* [=E] M, pl. *-er*, 1930s, 2b(1 tech) 3,4,5(3) → *logge* v. **Ic** *logg* [lɔk:] N (F) pl. Ø *(-ir)*, 18c, via Da, 2a,b(3 tech); *loggur* [lɔk:ʏr] M, pl. *-ar*, mid20c, 3(3 tech) **Fr** *loch* M, pl. *-es*, 19c, 2b(1 tech) **It** *loch* [lɔk] M, pl. Ø, mid19c, via Fr, 2a,b(1 tech) < *solcometro*; [=E] M, pl. Ø, mid20c, 3,4,5(1 tech) **Rm** *loch* [lok] N, beg20c, via Fr (1 tech) **Rs** *lag* M, pl. *-i*, beg20c, 2a(1 tech) **Po** [-k] M, beg20c, 2b(1 tech) **Cr** *log* M, pl. *-ovi*, beg20c, 2a(1 tech) **Bg** *lag* M, pl. *-al-ove*, beg20c, via Rs, 2b(3 tech) **Fi** *logi* 19c, 3(3) **Hu** [=E] pl. Ø, 20c, 2b(1 tech_NAUT)

log v. 1 'enter data in a ship's logbook', 2a 'enter data in a computer', +4 'measure or gauge by using a log (the apparatus)'

Ge *loggen* 18c, +4(3 tech) **Nw** *logge* ["lɔge] 19c, 1,+4(3 tech); 1980s, 2a(3 tech) **Ic** *logga* 18c, +4(3 tech) **Rm** *loga* [loga] end20c, 1,2a(1 tech, mod) **Bg** *logvam se* 1990s, 2a(3 tech, sla) **Fi** *logata* 1,2a(1 tech) **Hu** [=E] 1980s, 1,2a(1 tech)

loganberry n. 1 'a hybrid between a blackberry and a raspberry'

The Californian judge James Harvey Logan (1841–1928) produced the fruit (a blend of a blackberry and a raspberry) in his garden; the species does not seem to have caught on widely in Continental gardens and food stores.

Ge *Loganbeere* F, pl. *-en*, mid 20c (2+5) **Du** *loganbes* [lo:xanbɛs] C, pl. *-sen*, 1940s (3 tech+5) **Nw** *loganbær* [=E+ Nw] 20c (1 tech+5)

logbook n. 'a book containing a detailed record or log (of a ship's journey)'

As an early seafaring term, this word is, not unexpectedly, current mainly in the Northwest, with the second element quite naturally adapted to the form of the word 'book' in Germanic languages.

Ge *Logbuch* 18c (3+5) **Du** *logboek* [lɔx-] N, pl. *-en*, end18c (3+5) **Nw** *loggbok* [=E+Nw] end19c (3+5) < ↑*logg* **Ic** *loggbók* [lɔk:pou:k] F, pl. *-bækur*, beg19c, via Da (3+5 tech) **Fr** <=E> 19c (1 ban) < trsl *livre du loch*, *journal de bord* **It** - < ↑*log* **Po** [-k-] M, beg20c (1 tech) **Cr** *logbuk* M, beg20c (1 tech) < *brodski dnevnik* **Bg** *logbuk* M, pl. *-a*, end20c(1 tech, coll) < *vakhten zhurnal* **Fi** - < *logikirja*

log in/on, off v. 'go through the procedures to begin (or conclude) use of a computer system'

Ge - < trsl *ein-/ausloggen* **Du** *inloggen/uitloggen* [in-lɔxən/œytlɔxən] 1980s (1 tech) **Nw** *logge inn/ut* ["lɔge] 1980s (3 tech) **Ic** *logga (sig) inn/út* [lɔk:a] end20c (2 tech, coll) **Fr** *se loguer* 1990s (1 tech) **Sp** [=E] end20c (1 tech) **It** → [=E] M, pl. Ø, end20c (1 tech) **Rm** [=E] imperative/n., end20c (1 tech/

mod) **Po** *zalogowai się/wylogować się* end20c (1 tech, mod) **Bg** <=E>/*login* M [U] 1990s (1 tech, sla) **Fi** *logata sisään/ulos* **Hu** [=E] 1980s (1 tech) **Gr** <=E> [=E] N [U] end20c (1 tech) → *kano log in/on, off* v.

log-line n. 'a line to which a ship's log is attached' **Ic** *logglína* F, pl. *-ur*, beg19c, via Da (3 tech)

logo n. (abbrev. of '*logogram*' or '*logotype*') 'an emblem or device used as a badge of an organization in display material'

The two full forms were coined in English on the basis of neo-Greek morphology. The abbreviation is not English in form and is indeed pronounced according to national conventions in all receiving languages. Its status as an anglicism is therefore doubtful.

Ge [lo:go] N, pl. *-s*, 1980s (3 tech) **Du** [lo:xo:] 1970s (3) **Nw** [lu:gu] M, pl. *-er*, 1970s (2) **Ic** *lógó* [lou:kou] N, pl. Ø, end20c (1 tech) **Fr** [lɔgo] M, 1970s (3 tech) **Sp** [logo] M, end20c (3 tech) < *logotipo* **It** [=E] M, pl. Ø, 1980s < *logotipo* **Rm** [logo] N, end20c (1 tech) < *logotip/logogramă* **Po** [logo] N, uninfl., end20c (2 mod) **Cr** [=E] M [U] end20c (3 tech) < *logotip* **Bg** *logo* N, pl. Ø, 1990s (1 tech) **Fi** [lɔgɔ] 1980s (3) **Hu** (5 Gr) **Gr** *logo* N, pl. *-s*/Ø, end20c (1 tech) = *loghotypos* M/*loghotypo* N

lolly n. 1 'a flat rounded boiled sweet on a stick' **Ge** [=E] M, pl. *-(ie)s*, 1970s (1 coll) < *Lutscher* **Du** [=E] C, pl. *-'s* (4) **Nw** - < *kjærlighet-på-pinne* **Ic** - < *sleikibrjóstsykur*

long drink n. 'mixed drink with little alcohol, served in a tall glass'

A partial contrast is evident between Western and Eastern countries, but there is also one between open and purist societies, which results in an unusual distribution (much more limited than that of ↑*drink* by itself).

Ge [=E] M, pl. *-s*, 1960s (2) **Du** [=E] C, 1970s (2) **Nw** [=E] M, pl. *-er*, 1940s (1 obs) < *drink* **Ic** [=E] M [U] mid20c (1 coll) **Fr** [lɔŋdrɪŋk] M, 1960s (1 mod) **It** [lɔŋ drɪŋk] M, 1970s (2) **Rm** [=E] N [U] 1970s (1 rare) **Po** [-nk-] M, end20c (2 coll) **Cr** *long drink* M [U] end20c (2) **Fi** - < *lonkero* **Hu** - < rend *hosszúlépés* **Gr** *long drink* N, end20c (2)

long johns n. 1 'underpants with full-length legs', +2 '(woollen) tights' **Du** *long john* 1990s (1 jour, mod) **Nw** *longs* [lɔŋs] M, sg., pl. Ø, 1950s, 1(3); *stillongs* +2(3)

long-life cp'/adj. +2 'lasting' (e.g. for batteries) **Ge** [=E] 1960s (1 tech, mod) **Rm** [=E] adj., end20c (1 tech) **Gr** (1 writ)

longplay* n. 'a long-playing record' (cf. ↑*LP*) **Ge** [-e:/=E] F, pl. *-s*, 1970s (1 coll, rare) < *LP* **Du** - < trsl *langspeelplaat* < *LP/langspeler/elpee* **Sp** *long play* [=E] M, pl. *-s*, 1970s (1 obs) < *LP* **It** [lɔŋ(g)-plei/-o-] M/adj., pl. Ø, 1950s/60s (2/1 coll, rare) < *LP* **Rm** - < *LP* **Rs** *longplei* M, pl. *-i*, 1995 (1 coll, mod) **Po** [lonkplej] M, mid20c (2 obs) **Cr** [lo̱ngplej] F [U] mid20c (2 obs) **Bg** - < *LP* **Fi** - < *LP* **Hu** - < *LP*

long-playing *adj.* 'playing for about 20–30 minutes on each side' (of records) (cf. *LP*)

Nw [=E] 1950s (1 obs) < *LP, lp* **Ic** [=E] uninfl., 1960s (0 tech, arch) **It** [lo̱ŋ ple̱iŋ(g)] M, pl. Ø, 1950s (2) **Rm** - < *LP* **Cr** *long plej* mid20c (2) **Bg** - < trsl *dŭlgos-vireshta* **Fi** *LP/älppäri* (1 tech, you) **Hu** - < *LP* **Gr** *long ple̱i* adj., mid20c (1 rare) < *LP*

longseller* *n.* 'a product sold successfully over a long period'

Ge [=E] M, pl. Ø, 1960s (1 mod)

long shirt* *n.* 'a casual dress'

Ge [lo̱nʃört] N, pl. -s, 1990 (1 mod)

look *n./cp²* 2 'the appearance of a face; a person's expression or personal aspect', 3 'the appearance (of a thing)' (mainly in advertising)

The term which has been very popular in North-western and Central Europe has not much affected the East; not even calques appear to be used.

Ge cp² [=E] M [U] 1940s, 3(2) **Du** [=E] C, 1980s (1 coll) **Nw** [lʉk] M/N, pl. Ø, 1950s, 3(1 coll, mod) **Ic** [=E] N [U] end20c (1 sla) **Fr** [luk] M/cp, 1980s, 3(2 mod) **Sp** [=E] M [U] 1980s (1 tech) **It** [=E] M [U] 1970 (2 coll)

Rm [=E] N [U] end20c, 2,3(1 jour) **Cr** [=E] M [U] end20c, 3(1) **Fi** [=E] end20c (1) **Gr** *luk* N/cp², mid20c (2)

loop *n.* 1b 'a figure in which a curve crosses itself', 6 'a manoeuvre of an aeroplane', 7 'a manoeuvre in skating', 10 'a programmed sequence of instruction that is repeated' (comput.)

Du [=E] C, 1960s (1 tech) **Nw** [lʉːp] M, pl. -er, mid20c (1 tech) → *loope* v. **Ic** *lúppa* [luhpa] F, pl. -ur, end20c, 10(1 tech) **Sp** [=E] end20c, 10(1 tech) **It** [=E] M, pl. Ø, 1930s, 1b,6,7(1 tech); 1970s, 10(1 tech) = *iterazione, ciclo* **Rm** [lup] N [U] 1980s, 10(1 tech) **Po** (0) **Fi** *loopi/luuppi* 10(0) **Hu** [=E] [U] end20c, 6(1 tech) **Gr** *lup/<=E>* N [U] end20c, 7,10(1 tech); *luping* N, mid20c, 6(1 tech)

loop *v.* 5 'perform an aerobatic loop'

Nw *loope* ["lʉːpe] 1930s (1 tech)

looping* *n.* 'an aerobatic loop'

This term became well-known from the 1930s onwards, some languages preferring the shorter form ↑*loop* (Norwegian, Hungarian). It is sometimes extended to roller coasters, and metaphorically, to abrupt turns (of policy etc.).

Ge [=E] M/N, pl. -s, 1930s (2 tech) **Du** [=E] C, 1940s (2) **Nw** - < *loop* **Fr** [lupiŋ] M, beg20c (1 tech/ban) < *boucle* **Sp** [lupin/lupi̱n] M, pl. -s, 1930s (1 tech) **It** [lu̱ːpiŋ(g)] M [U] 1930s (1 tech) < *gran volta* **Rm** *luping* [lupiŋ] N, 1930s, via Fr (3 tech)

Rs *lu̱ping* M [U]

beg20c (1 tech) **Po** [-nk] M [U] beg20c (1 tech) **Cr** *luping* M, pl. *-zi*, mid20c (1 tech) **Bg** *lu̱ping* M, pl. *-al-i*, mid20c, via Rs (3 tech) **Hu** - < *loop* **Gr** *lu̱ping* N, mid20c (1 tech)

loran *abbrev.* 'a system of long-distance navigation which permits the navigator to determine the geographical position regardless of weather conditions'

The acronym, based on *long range navigation*, was coined in 1943 (earlier form: *LRN*).

Du [lo̱ːran] C [U] 1940s (3 tech) **Nw** [luran] M [U] 1950s (1 tech) **Ic** *lóran* [lou:ran] N/cp¹ [U] mid20c (2 tech) **Fr** [lɔʀã] M, 1960s (1 tech) **Sp** [lo̱ran] M, pl. Ø (1 tech) **It** [lo̱rãn] M [U] 1960s (1 tech) **Rm** [loran] N [U] 1960s (2 tech) **Rs** [lo̱ran] M [U] mid20c (1 tech) **Po** [loran] M [U] mid20c (1 tech) **Cr** *lo̱ran* M [U] mid20c (1 tech) **Bg** *Loran* M [U] mid20c (1 tech)

lord *n./cp²* 3 'the title', +7 'a press baron, a leading personality', +8 'a self-important person', +9 'an extravagantly dressed person'

As with ↑*lady*, the term was (and still is) mainly used as a foreignism, but various uses have been applied to outstanding males on the basis of status, behaviour, and dress; these uses are mainly metaphorical and generally do not seem to establish loanword status.

Ge [lort] M/cp², pl. -s, 19c, 3(Ø); 1960s, +7(1 jour) = +7: *-zar* **Du** (Ø) **Nw** [=E] M, pl. *-er*, 19c, 3(Ø) **Ic** [=E] M, pl. *-ar*, 17c, 3(Ø) = *lávarður* **Fr** [lɔʀ] M, 16c (Ø) > *lord-maire* **Sp** [lor] M, pl. *lores*, mid19c, 3(2>3) **It** [lord] M, pl. Ø, 17c, 3(Ø>1) +7(2) **Rm** [=E] M, mid19c, 3(3) **Rs** *lord* M, pl. *-y*, beg20c, 3(Ø) → *-stvo* N **Po** [lort] mid19c, 3(Ø) → *-ostwo* N; *-ówka* F; *-owski* adj. **Cr** *lord* M, pl. *-ovi*, mid20c, +7(1) **Bg** *lord* M, pl. *-ove*, 19c, 3(Ø) +8(2) +9(3 sla, you) **Fi** *lordi* 19c (Ø) **Hu** [lord] pl. *-ok*, 17c, 3(2); 20c, +7(2 coll) **Al** *lord* M, pl. *-ë*, mid19c, 3(3) **Gr** *lo̱rdhos* M, 19c, 3(Ø)

lorry *n.* 2 'an open goods wagon' (esp. in mining)

This term was borrowed long before it was used for modern motor trucks. A continental *lore* (earlier *lowry*, 0 arch) travels on rails, is drawn and can often be tipped. The limited distribution appears to be due mainly to German transmission.

Ge *Lore* F, pl. *-n*, 1870s (3) **Du** *lorrie* [=E] C, 1910s (3 tech) **Nw** (0) **Fr** [lɔri] M, pl. *-ies*, 19c (1 tech) **Po** *lora* [lora] F, beg20c, via Ge (1 tech) **Cr** (0) **Hu** *loré* [lo̱:re] pl. *-k*, end19c, via Ge (1 tech)

lose *v.* +14 'fail'

Ge *lo(o)sen* [lʉːzən] 1980s (1 coll/you) → *ab-* v.

loser *n.* 2 'a person who regularly fails'

The adoption of this colloquial term is reflected in its North-western distribution – even there it is doubtful whether it will last.

Ge *Loser* [lʉːza] M, pl. Ø, 1980s (1 coll/you) → *-in* F **Du** [=E] 1990s (1 coll, mod) **Nw** (0) < creat *taper* **Ic** [=E] M, pl. *-ar*, end20c (1 sla) = creat *tapari* **Fr**

[luzœr] M, 1980s (1 coll, mod)
Sp [l<u>u</u>ser] M, pl. Ø, 1980s (0/1
jour, rare)   **Rm** (0)   **Cr** [luzer]
M, pl. -i, end20c (1)   **Fi** *looseri/*
luuseri 1980s (1 you)   **Gr** *l<u>u</u>zer*
M, pl. Ø/-s, end20c (1 coll,
mod)

lotion   *n.* 'a cosmetic liquid'
    Since the root of this word is Romance, it is felt to
be from French or Latin in many languages; identification as an anglicism depends on close-to-English
pronunciation.
    Ge [lo:ʃn/lo:tio̯:n] F/often cp², pl. -s, 1960s (2)   **Du**
[=E] mid20c, via Fr (2)   **Nw** [=E] M, pl. -er, 1950s (1
jour) < *krem*   **Ic** [lou:sjon] N [U] mid20c (1 coll)   **Fr**
[lɔsjõ] F, mid20c (4)   **Sp** *loción* (5La)   **It** *lozione*
(5La)   **Rm** *loţiune* [lotsiu̯ne] F, 20c (5Fr)   **Rs** *los'o̯n*
(5Fr)   **Po** [locjon] M, beg20c (1 tech)   **Cr** (0)   **Bg**
losion M, pl. -al-i, mid20c, via Fr (3 tech)   **Hu** [=E/
lo:ʃion] pl. Ø, 1970s (1 tech/5Fr)   **Al** *locion/losion*
[locjo̯n] M, pl. -e, mid20c (1 rare)   **Gr** *losion* F, mid/
end20c (5Fr)

loudness   *n.* +4 'augmented bass sound on stereos
etc.'
    Du [=E] C, 1970s (1 tech)   **Nw** [=E] [U] 1970s (1
tech)   **Fi** (1 tech)   **Gr** (1 writ)

lounge   *n.* 1 'an ante-room in hotel and airport'
    Ge [launtʃ] F, pl. -s, 1970s (1 mod)   **Du** [=E] C,
1940s (2)   **Nw** [=E] M, pl. -r, 1950s (1 tech)   **Po**
(0)   **Cr** (0)

lounger   *n.* 2 'piece of furniture for relaxing on'
    Ge [=E] M, pl. Ø, 1970s (1 mod, obs)

lousy   *adj.* +4 'poor, worthless; corny'
    Ic *lási* [lau:si] 1960s (1 sla)

love   *n.* 4a 'a sweetheart' (often as a form of address),
8 'no score' (in some games)
    Du [=E] C [U] 1980s, 4a(1 coll) 8 (1 tech)   **Nw** (0)
Ic [=E] mid/end20c, 4a(1 coll)   **Rm** [=E] N [U] 1970s,
4a(0>1 you); 1980s, 8(0ᴛᴇɴɴɪs)   **Rs** *lav* 8(0)   **Po** M/
F [U] mid20c, 4a(2)   **Cr** (0)   **Bg** (0)   **Hu** [=E/ləf]
end19c, 4a(Ø>2); [=E] 8(1 tech/arch)

lover   *n.* 2 'a person with whom another is
having sexual relations' (the word is esp. frequent in
the combination ↑*Latin lover* in Spanish, Italian,
Greek).
    Ge [l<u>a</u>va] M, pl. -s, 1980s (1 mod)
< *Liebhaber*   **Du** [=E] C, 1990s
(1 mod) < *minnaar*   **Nw** (0)
< *elsker*   **Ic** [lɔv:er] M, end20c (1
sla) < *elskhugi*   **Sp** [l<u>o</u>ver] M,
1970s (1 sla)   **It** [l<u>ɔ</u>ver] M, pl.
Ø, 1960s (2>3)   **Rm** (0)   **Po**
(0)   **Cr** (0)   **Bg** (0)   **Gr** [l<u>a</u>ver] M, pl. -s, 1980s (0
coll/fac) < *erastis*

love story   *n.* 'an amorous relationship'
    Ge [=E] F, pl. -s/-(ie)s, 1970s (1 jour)   **Du** (Ø)   **Nw**
[l<u>o</u>vstori] M, pl. -er, 1970s (1)   **Fr** *love-story* [lɔvstɔri]
F, 1970 (1 jour)   **Sp** [lav/lob est<u>o</u>ri] F, 1970s (1 mod)
< *historia de amor*   **It** [lav/lov st<u>o</u>ri] F, pl. Ø, 1970s

(1>2)   **Rm** [=E] 1970s (0 coll)
Rs (0)   **Po** (0)   **Cr** (0)   **Bg** - <
trsl *lyubovna istoriya*   **Hu** [=E]
pl. Ø, 20c (2)   **Al** *llav stori* (1
mod)   **Gr** <=E>/*llav storil-y* F/
N, pl. -ies, 1990s (1 jour, mod)

low budget   *cp¹* 'produced with
little money' (cf. ↑*budget*)
    Ge [=E] (0>1 tech)   **Du** [loub<u>y</u>d3ət] 1980s (2)   **Nw**
(0) < *lavbudsjett-*   **Ic** [=E] end20c (0)

lower   *v.* 1 'let or haul down' (naut.)
    Nw *låre* ["l<u>o</u>:re] 19c (3 tech)

LP   *n.* 1 'a long-playing record'
    Of the various forms of this anglicism, *LP* is most
widespread, and often pronounced according to national conventions. Calques are also frequent. By contrast, ↑*long-play(ing)* is considerably rarer. However,
with the advent of CDs the word and the thing are
becoming obsolete.
    Ge [elpe:] F, pl. -s, 1970s (3) = *Langspielplatte*   **Du**
<=E>/*elpee* [ɪlpe:] C, pl. -'s, 1950s (2>3)   **Nw** <=E>/
lp [elpe:] M, pl. -er, 1950s (3) > *langspillplate*   **Ic** *LP-*
plata [ɛtl pʰjɛ:-] cp¹ 1960s (1 coll)   **Fr** [alpi] M, 1950s
(1 tech/obs, reg) < *microsillon*   **Sp** <=E>/*elepé* [elepé]
M, pl. -s, mid20c (3)   **It** [ellepi] M, pl. Ø, 1960s (2) =
33 giri > *longplaying*   **Rm** [=E] N, 1970s (2 tech)   **Rs**
- < trsl *dolgoigrayushchaya plastinka*   **Po** (0)   **Cr**
[=E] M, mid20c (2)   **Bg** <=E> [=E] M, pl. -ta,
end20c (1 coll, you) < trsl *dŭlgosvireshta plocha*   **Fi**
[elpe:]/*älppäri* (1 tech, you)   **Hu** [elpe:] pl. Ø, 1980s (2
tech)   **Gr** *elpi* N, mid 20c (2)

LSD   *abbrev./n.* 'a synthetic drug'
    This acronym is based on the German (!) chemical
term (*Lysergsäurediäthylamid*), but became popular
in the British drug scene during the 1960s (when it
was facetiously analysed as *£.s.d.*). Since it is always
found as an acronym form and mostly pronounced
according to national conventions, its status as an
anglicism is doubtful.
    Ge [elesde:] N [U] 1960s (1 tech, obs)   **Du** [=E] C [U]
1960s (2)   **Nw** <=E>/*lsd* [elesde:] M [U] 1960s (3)
Ic [ɛtl ɛs: tje:] N [U] 1960s (2)   **Fr** [ɛlesde] M, 1960s
(3)   **Sp** [elesede] M [U] 1960s (2 tech/5Ge)   **It** [elle
esse di̯] M [U] mid20c (1/2 tech, obs)   **Rm** [lesede] N
[U] 1970s (1 rare)   **Rs** *el̯esdé* M [U] mid20c (1
tech)   **Po** [=E/elesde] N [U] 1960s (1 tech)   **Cr** [=E]
M [U] 1960s (1)   **Bg** <=E> [elesede] N [U] 1970s (1
tech)   **Fi** [ɛlesde:] 1960s (3)   **Hu** [ele̯ʃde:] [U] 1970s
(1 you/tech)   **Gr** <=E> [el es di̯] N [U] 1960s (1 tech)

lugger   *n.* 'a small ship'
    The English provenance of this word is disputed, as
the Dutch -o- forms are possibly independent. It is
thus one of the numerous 'North Sea' nautical terms
shared by various Germanic languages, or borrowed
at such an early stage that provenance cannot be
established beyond doubt.
    Ge *Logger/Lugger* M, pl. Ø, end19c (1 tech, obs/
5Du)   **Nw** [l<u>u</u>ger] M, pl. -e, end19c (1 arch)   **Ic** *lug-*
gari [lyk:arɪ] M, pl. -ar, end19c, via Da (3 arch); *log-*

gorta [lɔkːɔrta] F, pl. *-ur*, end19c, via Da (2 arch) **Sp** *lugre* M, 19c (3 tech, arch) **It** [l<u>a</u>gger] M, pl. Ø, end19c (1 tech) **Rm** *lugher* [l<u>u</u>ger] N, mid20c (1 tech) **Rs** (5Du) **Po** *lugier* [lugier] M, 18c (1 tech, arch) **Hu** (5Du)

lumberjack *n.* 1 'one who fells, prepares or conveys lumber', +2 'a man's jacket with leather, cloth and knitted parts'

Ge [l<u>a</u>mbadʒek] M, pl. *-s*, 1950s, +2(1 tech); *Lumber*, M, pl. Ø, 1970s (1 tech) **Du** *lumberjacquet* [l<u>y</u>mbər-ʒaket] N, 1940s (1 tech+Fr) = *lumberjacket* **Nw** *lumberjacket* [=E] M, pl. *-er*, 1980s, +2(1 mod) **It** only^{TM} **Hu** *lemberdzsek* [l<u>e</u>mberdʒek] pl. *-ek*, end19c/beg20c, +2(3)

lunch *n.* 1 'a meal eaten in the middle of the day'

The status of this word is not easy to assess. As an early adoption around 1900 it became obsolete in most languages; however, it has remained known as a foreignism. More recently, it is coming to be re-adopted as a modish word, with [a] replacing the earlier [œ] pronunciation (in German).

Ge [lanʃ/lœnʃ] M, pl. *-el-s*, 19c/1960s (Ø/1 rare) → *-en* v. **Du** [lynʃ/lʏntʃ] C, pl. *-en*, *-es*, end19c (2) → *-en* v. **Nw** <=E>/*lunsj* [=E/l<u>u</u>nʃ] M, pl. *-er*, end19c (2) = *formiddagsmat* → *lunche*/*lunsje* v. **Ic** [lœns] M [U] end20c (1 coll) < *hádegisverður* M **Fr** [lœntʃ/~œʃ] M, pl. *-sl-es*, beg19c (2) → *luncher* v. **Sp** [luntʃ/lans, etc.] M, pl. *-s*, end19c (1 obs) **It** [l<u>a</u>ntʃ] M, pl. Ø, end19c (Ø>1) **Rm** [=E] N, end20c (o/1 coll) **Rs** *lentch/lantch* M, pl. *-i*, beg20c (Ø) **Po** M, beg20c (1 coll) → *-yk* M **Cr** *l<u>a</u>nč* M [U] mid20c (1) **Bg** *l<u>u</u>nch* M [U] end20c (1 mod) **Fi** - < *lounas* **Hu** *löncs* [lɔnts] pl. *-ök*, 17c (1 arch) **Gr** (Ø)

I<u>c</u>	Nw	P<u>o</u>	Rs
Du	Ge	Cr	Bg
Fr	It	Fi	Hu
Sp	Rm	Al	Gr

lunch room* *n.* 'a snack bar, a small restaurant'

Du [lvnʃ-] C, pl. *-s*, 20c (2) **Rm** (o) **Cr** (o)

lychee *n.* (also *litchi, lichee*) 'a sweet fleshy fruit with a thin spiny skin'

The fruit originates from China, but its name appears to have been widely transmitted through English.

Ge *Litschi* F, pl. *-s*, 20c (3 tech) **Du** *lychee* (5) **Nw** *lychee* [=E] 1980s (1 tech) **Fr** (5Chin) **Sp** [=E?] M, end20c (5) **It** <=E>/*leechee* [litʃi] M, pl. Ø, 18c? (5) **Rs** *l<u>i</u>chi* (o) **Po** *liczi(s)*/<=E> M, 1980s (1 tech) **Bg** *l<u>i</u>chi* (5Ch)

lynch* *n./cp¹* 'an execution (esp. a hanging) without a legal trial'

The term is derived from the name of William Lynch (1742–1820) who established a vigilance committee in 1780. The word was borrowed from American English mainly as a verb 'to inflict sentence of death without a lawful trial' into most European languages; some have it derived from the borrowed noun (which is generally rarer).

Ge cp¹ [lynç] beg20c (3) **Du** *lynchgerecht* cp¹, 20c (2+5) **Nw** *lynsj* [lynʃ] M [U] 20c (3) < *lynsjing* **Fr** - < *lynchage* 19c (2) **Sp** - < *linchamiento* **It** - < *linciaggio* **Rm** only *legea lui Lynch* end19c (1 rare) **Rs** *linch* M [U] beg20c (2 jour) → *linchevanie* N **Po** *lincz* M, beg20c (3) → *-owanie* N; *z–owanie* N; *-ować* v.; *z–ować* v. **Cr** *linč* M [U] beg20c (2 jour) → *lincovanje* N **Bg** *linch* M [U] beg20c (2 jour) → *-uvam* v. **Fi** - < *lynkkäys* **Hu** *lincs/lincselés* [lintʃ/lin-tʃele:ʃ] [U] end19/beg20c (3 obs) → *-el* v. **Al** - < *lin-çim* **Gr** - < *lyntsarima*

lynch *v.* 'put to death without a legal trial'

Ge *lynchen* [lynçən] mid19c (3) **Du** *lynchen* [lɪnʃən/lɪntʃən] beg20c (2) **Nw** *lynsje* ["l<u>y</u>nʃe] beg20c (2) **Fr** *lyncher* [lɛ̃ʃe] mid19c (2) → *lynchage* M; *lynch-eur/-se* M/F **Sp** *linchar* (3) → *linchamiento* M **It** *linciare* [lintʃ<u>a</u>re] mid19c (3) → *linciaggio* M; *linciatore* M **Rm** *linşa* [linʃ<u>a</u>] beg20c, via Fr (3) → *linşare* F; *linşaj* N **Rs** *linchevat'* beg20c (2 jour) → *-evanie* N **Po** *linczowac'* [lintʃovatç] beg20c (2) → *z-* v. **Cr** *linč<u>o</u>vati* beg20c (2) **Bg** *l<u>i</u>nchuvam* beg20c (3) **Al** *linç<u>oj</u>* beg20c (2) **Gr** *lyntsar<u>o</u>l/lintsaro* beg20c (3)

lyrics *n.* 3 'the words of a song'

Ge [=E] pl., 1980s (1 tech) **Nw** (o) **Ic** - < *texti* **Fr** *lyric* [lɪʀik] M, pl. *-s*, 1930s (1/o tech) **Rs** (5Gr) **Po** *liryk* (5Fr)

M

M *abbrev.* +4 'medium size' (in shirts, etc.) (cf. ↑*L*)
Ge [em] 1960s (3) **Du** 1980s (2) **Nw** [em/mɛːdiʉm]
1960s (2) **Ic** *M* [mɛːti.ʏm] mid2oc (o) **Sp** [ẹme] F,
end2oc (2 tech) (*talla*) *mediana* **It** [ẹmmɛ] mid2oc (3)
= (*taglia*) *media* **Rm** [em] end2oc (1 mod) **Rs**
(o) **Po** *emka* [emka] F, end2oc (2 coll) **Cr** *em*
end2oc (3) **Bg** <=E> [=E] [U] 1980s (1 writ,
mod) **Fi** [ɛm/ɛmːɛ] end2oc **Hu** [em] [U] 1970s (3)
→ *M-es* adj. **Gr** [em/mịdium] end2oc (2)

macadam   *n.* 2 'material used in road-making'
This term came to be almost universally known in
the nineteenth-century (coined after the Scottish inventor J.L. McAdam 1756–1836); it is certainly much
less used today outside specialist circles. Note that the
derived verb is much rarer.
Ge *Makadam* [makadạm] M/N,
pl. *-e*, 19c (1 tech, rare) **Du** [mɑ-
kadạm] C/N [U] mid19c (3
tech) **Nw** *makadam* [makadạm]
M [U] (1 tech) **Fr** [makadam]
M, mid19c (2) **Sp** <=E>/*maca-
dán* (3) M, pl. *macadams/maca-
danes* (3) mid19c (2<3) **It** [makadạm] M, pl. Ø,
beg19c (1 tech) **Rm** [makadạm] N, end19c, via Fr/
Ge (3 tech) **Rs** *makadam* M [U] mid2oc (1 tech) **Po**
makadam [makadam] M̄, mid2oc (1 tech) **Cr** *makadam* M [U] mid2oc (1 tech) **Bg** *makadạm* M [U]
mid2oc (1 tech) **Hu** *makadám* [mạkada:m] (cp¹) [U]
19c (2>3) **Al** *makadạm* M [U] mid2oc (1 reg)

macadamize   *v.* 'treat a road-surface with macadam'
Ge *makadamisieren* 19c (3 tech, arch) **Du** *macada-
miseren* [mạkadɑ mizẹːrə] mid19c (3 tech) **Nw**
makadamisere [mạkadamisẹːre] (1 tech) → *makada-
misering* M/F **Ic** *makadamisera* 19c, via Da (1 tech,
arch) → *makadamískur* adj. **Fr** *macadamiser* [maka-
damize] mid19c (1 tech) → *macadamisation* F; *maca-
damisage* M **Sp** *macadamizar* mid19c (3 tech) →
macadamizacion F, *macadamizado* adj. **It** *macada-
mizzạre* beg19c (1 tech) **Rm** *macadamiza* [makada-
mizạ] end19c, via Fr (3 tech) → *-are* F **Po** (o) **Cr**
makadamizịrati mid2oc (1 tech) **Hu** *makadamizál*
[mạkadamiza:l] 19c (1 tech/arch)

mackintosh¹   *n.* +3 'a variety of apple'
There are at least two people of the name of McIn-
tosh who gave their names to different products: the
inventor of a waterproofing process (1766–1843) to a
raincoat; an apple grower to a variety of apple; and the

computer firm for unknown reasons also chose the
name to refer to their system – the last is definitely
still a proper name, and therefore not included here
(but can be assumed to be known in all countries here
tested).
Du [=E] C, 1970s (1 tech) **Rs** *mẹkintosh* M [U]
end2oc (1 tech) **Po** *mekintosz/*<=E> M, end2oc (2)

mackintosh² (1)   *n.* 1,2 'a type of cloth, or a coat
made from it'
The earliest of the three senses of this word was
widespread in nineteenth-century Europe but has
long been obsolete in most countries (though still
listed in many dictionaries).
Ge [mẹkintoʃ] M, pl. *-e*, mid19c
(1 arch) **Du** [=E] C pl. *-en*,
beg2oc (1 arch/tech) **Fr** [makɪn-
toʃ] M, mid19c (1 arch) **Sp** [=E]
M, end19c (1 arch) **It** [mẹkin-
toʃ] M, pl. Ø/[U] end19c (1
tech) **Rs** *makintọsh* M, pl. *-i*,
beg2oc (1 arch) **Po** *mekintosz/makintosz/*<=E> M,
beg2oc (1 arch) **Cr** *mekịntoš* M, mid2oc (1 arch)
Bg *mạkintosh* M, pl. *-al-i*, beg2oc (1 arch) **Hu** [=E]
[U] 2oc (o)

made in...   *phr.* (followed by name of country) 'indicating the provenance of a product'
A label providing the origin of export articles is
required by international law (first coined as *Made in
Germany* as a protective measure by British industry
in 1887). This term is known to all users at least in
combination with their own country, but is of varying
currency outside such legal contexts.
Ge [mẹːdin] beg2oc (2) **Du** [=E] beg2oc (2) **Nw**
[=E] mid2oc (2) **Ic** [=E] mid2oc (o) **Fr** [mɛdin] 1930s
(2) **Sp** [=E/made in] mid2oc (2) **It** [=E] adj., 1900s
(2>3) **Rm** [mạde in/=E] mid2oc (2 coll>3) **Rs** *meí-
din* mid2oc (1 writ/you) **Po** beg2oc (2) **Cr** [mejdin]
beg2oc (2) **Bg** *meíd in/*<=E> [=E/made in] mid2oc (2
coll) **Fi** [made in] (2) **Hu** [=E/me:din] mid2oc (2)
Al *made in* mid2oc (2) **Gr** <=E> [=E] mid2oc (2)

madison*   *n.* 'a type of dance'
The distribution of this fashionable dance (1962,
similar to ↑*twist*) illustrates its rapid spread over
most of Europe – and its very fast obsolescence when
the craze was over.
Ge [=E] M [U] 1960s (1 arch) **Fr** [madisõ] M, 1960s
(1 obs) **Sp** [mạdison] M [U] 1960s (1 obs) **It** [mẹd-

izon] M [U] 1960s (1 obs) **Rm**
[=E] N, 1970s (1 rare) **Rs** *méd-*
ison M [U] mid20c (1 obs) **Po**
madison [madison] M, mid20c (1
obs) **Cr** *m̲e̲dison* M, mid20c (1
obs) **Bg** *m̲e̲dison* M [U] mid20c
(1 tech, obs) **Hu** [=E] [U] 1960s
(1 obs)

Mae West *n.* 'a life-jacket'
  The erratic distribution of this word is unexplained.
The frivolous comparison of the inflatable life-jacket
to the famous actress's bust made sense for the coinage in American English slang (1940), but not for its
adoption in Dutch, Polish, and Hungarian.
  Du *mae-west* [=E] C [U] 1940s (1 fac, obs) **Fr** (0 ban)
< *gilet de sauvetage* **Po** *maewestka* [maevestka] F,
end20c (1 tech) **Hu** [me:j west] pl. Ø mid20c (1 tech,
arch)

mahogany *n.* 1a 'a reddish-brown wood used for
furniture', 1b 'its colour'
  This word is from a Central American language and
was transmitted through Spanish. How much secondary influence there was from the English word is
doubtful, especially since the national forms are not
very close. Therefore, its status as an anglicism is very
uncertain.
  Ge *Mahagoni* [mahago:ni] N [U] 19c, 1a,b(3) **Du**
mahonie [maho:ni] C [U] mid19c (3) **Nw** *mahogni*
[maho̲ŋni] M [U] beg20c (3) **Ic** *mahóni* [ma:ho(u)ni]
N [U] beg19c, via Da, 1a(2) **Fr** [maɔgani] M, mid19c
(1 tech) < *acajou* **It** *mogano* M [U] mid18c (3) **Rm**
mahon [mahon] M [U] beg19c (5Turkish/Gr) **Rs**
(5) **Po** *mahoń* [mahon] M, pl. 'furniture', beg20c (3)
Cr *mahag̲o̲ni* M [U] beg20c, 1a(3) **Bg** *makhag̲o̲n* M
[U] beg20c, via Ge (3) **Fi** *mahonki* 20c, via Sw (3)
Hu *mahagóni* [m̲a̲hago:ni] [U] 17/19c (3) **Al** *m̲o̲gan*
M [U] beg20c, via It (3) **Gr** *mao̲ni* N, beg20c, 1a(3)

mail *v.* 1 'send (messages) by post', +2 'send (messages) by electronic mail'
  Ge *mailen* M [U], +2(1 tech) **Du** *mailen* beg20c, 1(2);
1990s, +2(1 tech) **Nw** *maile* ["m̲e̲ile/"m̲æ̲ile] 1990s,
+2(1 tech) **Ic** [mei:la] 1990s, +2(1 coll) **Po**
(0) **Fi** *mailata/meilata* 1990s, +2(2) → *meili* **Hu**
[=E] [U] 20c, 1(1 writ); end20c, +2(1 tech) **Gr**
<=E> [=E] N, end20c (1 tech)

mailbox *n.* +2 'an electronic device recording messages', +3 'a space on a disc where incoming e-mail
messages are kept'
  Ge [m̲e̲:lboks] F, pl. *-en*, 1980s, +2(1 tech) **Du** [=E]
C, pl. *-es*, 1990s, +2(1 tech) **Nw** +2,+3(0) < trsl
postkasse **Ic** [=E] end20c, +3(0) < trsl *pósthólf* **Fr**
<=E> 1980s, +2(1 ban) < trsl *boîte-aux-lettres,*
bal **It** [=E] M, pl. Ø, end20c, +3(1 tech) **Bg** *m̲e̲il-*
boks M, pl. *-al-ove*, 1990s, +3(1 tech) **Fi** 1990s, +2(1
tech) **Hu** [=E] pl. *-ok*, end20c, +2(1 tech) **Gr**
<=E> [=E] N, end20c, +2(1 tech)

mailing *n.* +3 'mail merging, i.e. the action of printing out identical letters to different addresses (via
computer)'

Du [=E] C, 1970s (1 tech) **Fr** [mɛliŋ] M, 1970s (2
tech/ban) > *publipostage* **Sp** [meiliŋ/mailiŋ] M, pl.
Ø, 1980s (2 tech) **It** [m̲e̲iliŋg] M, pl. Ø, 1980s (1 tech)

mailing list *n.* 'a list of people to whom advertising
matter etc. is to be posted'
  Du [=E] C, 1980s (1 tech) **Nw** *mailingliste* [=E+Nw]
1970s (1+5) **Ic** - < trsl *póstlisti* **It** [=E] F, pl. Ø,
end20c (1 tech)

mail order *n.* 'the ordering of goods by post'
  Ge [m̲e̲:lorda] F [U] 1960s (1 tech, mod) **Nw** (0) <
postordre **Ic** - < rend *póstverslun, póstpöntun* **It** - <
trsl *ordine postale* **Rm** - < rend *comandă prin poştă*

mainframe *n.* 1 'the central processing unit and pri-
mary memory of a computer'
  Ge [=E] M, pl. *-s*, 1980s (1 tech) **Du** [=E] N, 1980s (1
tech) **Nw** [=E] M [U] 1980s (1 tech) **Fr** <=E>
1960s (1 tech, ban) < *macroordinateur* **Sp** [=E] M,
pl. *-s/es*, 1980s (1 tech/obs) = *ordenador central* **It**
[=E] M, pl. Ø, 1970s (1 tech) **Rm** [=E] N, 1990s (1
tech) **Rs** *meînfreîm* M [U] 1990s (1 tech) **Po** M [U]
end20c (1 tech) **Cr** [=E] M, pl. *-ovi*, 1990s (1
tech) **Bg** *m̲e̲înfreîm* M [U] 1990s (1 tech, rare) **Hu**
mainframe computer [=E] pl. *-ek*, 1980s (1 tech) **Gr**
<=E> [=E] N, pl. *-s*, end20c (1 tech) > *meghalo sys-*
tima ypologhisti

mainstream *n./cp[1]* 1 'the prevailing trend in opinion, fashion etc.', 2 'a type of jazz based on swing'
  This term is internationally used by aficionados of
popular music. The more general sense of conformity
is a more recent adoption becoming fashionable
among intellectuals.
  Ge [m̲e̲:nstri:m] cp[1]/M [U] 1970s,
1(1 mod) 2(1 tech) **Du** [=E] C
[U] 1980s, 1(1 tech) **Nw** [=E]
1980s (1 coll) **Ic** [=E] cp[1], end
20c, 2(0 tech) **Fr** (0) **Sp** [=E]
1980s, 1(1 tech/rare) 2(1 tech) = 2:
jazz clásico **It** [=E] cp[1]/F [U]
1960s, 2(1 tech) **Rm** [=E] N 1970s, 2(1 tech) **Po**
M [U] end20c, 2(1 tech) **Cr** [mejnstrim] M [U]
end20c, 2(1 tech) **Bg** *m̲e̲instriîm* M [U] end20c, 2(1
tech) **Hu** [=E] [U] 1980s, 1(1 tech/jour) 2(1 tech, arch,
rare) **Gr** <=E> [=E] adj., end20c, 1(1 tech, mod)

maize *n.* 1 'a cereal plant', 2 'the cobs or grains of
this'
  The word, from sixteenth-century Arawakan, was
transmitted to most European languages through
Spanish. The contribution of English is difficult to
establish, but can only be marginal at best.
  Ge *Mais* M [U] 16c (5Sp) **Du** *maïs* (5Sp) **Nw** *mais*
[mais] M [U] 20c (5Sp) **Ic** *mais* [ma:is/maj:ɪs] M [U]
mid18c, via Da (3) **Fr** *maïs* (5Sp) **Sp** *maiz* (5) **It**
mais = *granoturco* **Rm** *mais* N [U] 19c, via Ge (1
arch) **Rs** *mais* (5Sp) **Po** (5Sp) **Fi** *maissi* (5Sw)
Al *m̲i̲sër* M, pl. *misra*, 20c **Gr** *mais̲* N, 19c (3)

maizena* *n./cp[1]* (orig.[TM]) 'cornstarch'
  Ge [maitse̲:na] (3 obs[TM]) **Du** [=E] C [U] beg20c
(3) **Nw** *maisenna* M [U] 20c (3) **Ic** *maísena* [ma:
isena/maj:ɪsena] N/cp[1] [U] beg/mid20c (2) **Fr**

maïzena [maizena] F, mid19c (3 tech)　Sp <=E>/*mai-cena* F, end19c (3)　It [maidzẹna] F [U] 1950s (3)　Rm *maizenă* [majzẹnə] F [U] mid20c, via Ge (3 tech)　Po *maizena* [maizena] F [U] beg20c (1 tech)

majorette *n.* (esp. US) 'a member of a female baton-twirling parading group'
Du [majorẹtə] C, pl. *-s*, 20c (3)　Fr [maʒɔʀɛt] F, mid20c (3)　Sp [majorẹt] F, pl. *-s*, 1970s (2)　It [ma-ʒorẹt] F, pl. Ø, 1940s (3)　Rm *majoretă* [maʒorẹtə] F, end20c, via Fr (Ø>3)　Rs *mazhorẹtki* F, pl., mid20c (3)　Cr *mazoretkinja* F, pl. *-e*, end20c (3)　Bg *mazhorẹtki* F, pl, mid 20c (3)　Hu [maʒoret] pl. *-ek*, 20c (3)　Gr *mazoret(t)a* f, end20c, via Fr (3)

make *v.* 7 'gain, acquire, produce (money, a profit, etc.)', 15 'accomplish (a distance, speed, score, etc.)', +25 'prepare (drugs for consumption)', +26 '(reflexive) apply make-up'
Ic *meika* [mei:ka] end19c, 7,15(1 coll) +25(1 sla) +26(2 coll)　Hu [=E] end20c, +25(1 tech, jour)

make *n.* 1 '(esp. of a product) a type, origin, brand, etc. of manufacture', +5 'make-up'
Ic *meik* [mei:k] N [U] 1960s, 1(1 sla) +5(2 coll)　Fi *meikki/maikkaus* mid20c, +5(3)

make it *v.* 1 'succeed in reaching a destination, a deadline, esp. in time', 2 'be successful'
Ic *meika það* [mei:kaða] 1970s (2 coll)

make-up *n.* 1 'cosmetics', 2 'the appearance of the face when cosmetics have been applied'
An obvious time-lag is evident in the spread of this popular term through Europe: where it was adopted in the East, it was some forty years later than in the West – and it has not reached some countries to date.
Ge [me:kạp] N [U] 1940s (2) = 1: *Schminke*　Du [meikỵp] C [U] 1940s, 1(2) > *opmaak*　Nw [=E] M [U] 1950s (1) < *sminke*　Ic *meiköpp* [=E] N [U] mid20c, 1(1 coll) < *meik*　Fr (0 arch) < *maquillage*　Sp [=E/makeạp] M, 1920s (1 arch) < *maquillaje*　It [meikạp] M [U] 1960s (2) < *trucco*　Rm [=E] N, 1980s, 1(1 you) < *makiyazh*　Po M [U] end20c (1 mod)　Cr [=E] M [U] end20c, 1(1 tech)　Fi *meikki* 20c (3)　Hu [=E] [U] mid20c (2 tech>3)　Al *mejkap* M, pl. Ø, 1(1 you)　Gr *meikạp* N, mid/end20c, 1(2); 2(1 rare) < *makighiạz*

malt *n.* 'barley or other grain that is steeped, germinated, and dried, esp. for brewing'
Ge *Malz* (4)　Du [malt] N [U] 19c (4) < *mout*　Nw (5)　Ic *malt* (4)　Fr [malt] M, 15c (3) → *malter* v.　Sp *malta* F (3)　It *malto* M, pl. *-i*, mid18c (3)　Rm *malṭ* [malts] N [U] end19c (5Ge)　Rs *mal'tọza* F [U] beg20c (3 tech)　Bg *malts* (5Ge)　Al *malt* M [U] mid20c (1 reg)

manage *v.* 1 'organize (work)', 'coach a musician, sportsman etc.'
The three related words exhibit striking contrasts: whereas ↑*manager* is universally and fully accepted, ↑*management* is much more restricted (but likely to be

expanding); the verb *manage* is by contrast found only in very few languages, and is mostly of limited currency in these.
Ge *managen* [mɛnedʒən] beg20c (2)　Du *managen* [mɛnedʒə] 1970s (1 coll/tech)　Nw (0)　Fr *manager* [mana(d)ʒe] 1920s (1 tech_ECON)　Hu *menedzsel* [mɛ-nedʒel] beg20c (2>3)　Gr *mana-tzạro* v., 1990s (1 tech, coll, rare)

management *n.* 2a 'professional administration of business concerns etc.', 2b 'the people engaged in running a business', +5 'management teaching'
Ge [mɛnetʃmənt] N [U] 1960s, 2a,b(2)　Du [=E] N [U] 1960s(2)　Nw [=E] N [U] 1970s (1 tech)　Fr [manaʒment] M, 1960s (2)　Sp [=E/manajemen] M [U] 1980s (1 tech)　It [mana-dʒment] M [U] 1930s (1 tech, jour)　Rm [menedʒment] N [U] 1970s (2)　Rs *mẹnedzhment* M [U] end20c (1 tech)　Po [menedʒ-ment] M [U] 1990s (1 tech)　Cr *mẹnedžment* M [U] end20c, 2a,+5(1 tech)　Bg *mẹnidzhmŭnt* M [U] end20c, 2a,+5(1 tech)　Hu [=E] [U] 1970s (2 tech>2 coll)　Al *menaxhim* [menadʒim] M, pl. *-e*, end20c, 2a,b(1 tech, reg)　Gr *mẹnatzment* [-nt, -d?] N [U] end20c, 2a,+5(2)

management buyout *n.* 'the purchase of at least a controlling share in a company by its directors'
Ge [=E] M/N, pl. *-s*, 1990s (1 tech) < *Buyout*　Du [=E] N, pl. *-s*, 1990s (1 tech)　Nw [=E] M, pl. *-s*, 1980s (1 tech)　It [=E] M, pl. Ø, end20c (1 tech) < *buyout*

manager *n.* 1 'a person controlling or administering a business', 2 'a person controlling or administering the affairs, training etc., of a person or a team in sports, entertainment'
Ge [mẹnedʒa] M, pl. Ø, beg20c (2) → *-in* F　Du [=E] C, beg20c (2)　Nw [=E] M, pl. *-e*, beg20c (2)　Ic [=E] M, end20c, 1(1 sla)　Fr [manadʒer] M, end19c (1); 1970s, 1(1 ban) < 1: *manageur, manageuse*　Sp [mana-dʒer/manaxer] M, pl. *-s*, beg20c (2 rare) = *gerente, apoderado*　It [manadʒer/menadʒer] M, pl. Ø, end19c (3) → *manageriale* adj.　Rm [manadʒer] M, mid20c, via Fr? (2 tech); [manadʒer] 1970s, 1(2>3_ECON)　Rs *mẹnedzher* M, pl. *-y*, end20c (2 tech)　Po *menedžer/<=E>* [mendʒer] M, end20c (2) → *-ski* adj.　Cr *mẹnedžer* M, pl. *-i*, end20c (2) → *-ka* F; *-ski* adj.　Bg *mẹnidzhŭr/mẹnadzher* M, pl. *-i*, end20c (2 tech); *mẹnazher*, mid20c, via Fr, 2(3 tech) → *-ka* F; *-ski* adj.　Fi [=E/managerı] end20c, 2(1)　Hu *menedzser* [mẹnedʒer] pl. *-ek*, end19c (2 tech>3)　Al *menaxher* M, pl. *-ë*, end20c (1 reg)　Gr *mạnatzer* M/F, pl. Ø/-s, 1980s (2)

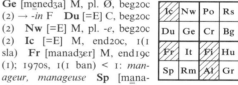

managerism *n.* 'the view that managers should rule in a country'

It *managerismo* [manadʒerizmo] M [U] end20c (3) **Po** *menedżeryzm/<=E>* [-ene-] M [U] end20c (2 tech)

manchester* *n.* 1 'strong corduroy', 2 'velvet trimming'

This term for a type of cord named after its main production site was the most popular word for the commodity in Germany until the 1960s. Whatever limited distribution it had or still has is likely to be owing to German mediation.

Ge *Man(s)chester* [manʃesta/ =E] M [U] end19c, 1(2 obs) **Du** [=E] N [U] beg20c, 1(1 obs) **Nw** - < *cord(fløyel)* **Rm** *mancister/<=E>* [mantʃister/=E] N [U] end18c, 2(1 reg, arch) **Po** *manczester* [-er] M [U] mid19c, 1(1 arch) → *manczestrowy* adj. **Cr** (0) **Hu** [mentsester] [U] 19c, 1(1 arch)

mandrill *n.* 'a large African baboon'

Ge [mandril] M, pl. -*e*, 19c (1 tech) **Du** *mandril* [mandril] C, 19c (5) **Nw** [mandril] (5) **Ic** *mandrill* [mantritl] M, pl. -*ar*, beg/mid20c (2) **Fr** [mɑ̃dril] M, 18c (1 tech) **Sp** *mandril* M, mid19c (3) **It** *mandrillo* M, pl. -*i*, mid19c (3/5Sp?) **Rm** *mandril* [mandril] M, end19c, via Fr (3 tech) **Rs** *mandril'* M, pl. -*i*, beg20c (1 tech) **Po** *mandryl* M, mid20c (1 tech) **Bg** *mandril* M, pl. -*al-i*, mid20c (∅) **Fi** *mandrilli* (3) **Al** *mandri(l)l* M, pl. -*ë*, mid20c (3)

mango *n.* 'a fleshy yellowish-red fruit'

The word is Tamil/Portuguese with uncertain English mediation.

Ge [mango:] F, pl. -*onen/-s*, 19c (3) **Du** <=E>/ *manga* (5) **Nw** [mangu] (5Port) **Ic** *mangó* [=E] N, pl. ∅, mid20c (2) **Fr** *mangue* [mɑ̃g] F (5Port) **Sp** *mango* M (5) **It** [mango] M, pl. -*ghi*, beg18c (5Port) **Rm** [mango] N, 20c (3 rare) **Rs** *mango* N, uninfl., beg20c (2) → -*ovyi* adj. **Po** [mango] N, uninfl., beg20c (2) → -*wy* adj. **Cr** *mango* M [U] mid20c (2) **Bg** *mango* N [U] mid20c (5Port) **Fi** [mangɔ] 20c (3) **Hu** (5Port) **Gr** *mango* N, mid/ end20c (2)

mangrove *n./cp¹* 'a tropical tree'

English transmission of this originally Carib-Arawakan word is said to have been supported by the folk-etymological adaptation to *grow*, and later to *grove*. However, the pronunciation of the loanword is normally according to national conventions disguising whatever English features there were.

Ge [maŋgro:və] F, pl. -*n*, end19c (3) **Du** [=E] C, pl. -*n*, beg20c (3 tech) ← *wortelboom* **Nw** [maŋgru:ve] M, pl. -*r*, beg20c (3 tech) **Ic** [=E] cp¹, end19c (0) < rend *fenjaviður, leiruviður* **Fr** [mɑ̃gʀɔv] F, beg20c (3) = *mangrove swamp* **It** *mangrovia/mangrova* [maŋgrɔvja/va] F, 1910s (3) **Rm** [mangrove] F, pl., beg20c, via Fr? (1 tech) **Rs** - → *mangrovyi* adj. **Po** *mangrowe* [mangrove] pl., uninfl., mid20c (1 tech) **Cr** *mangrove* F, pl., 20c (3) **Bg** *mangrov* adj., 20c, via Rs (3 tech) **Fi** [=E] (2) **Hu** [mangro:ve] pl. -*ék*, 20c (3)

maniac *n.* 1 'a person exhibiting extreme symptoms of wild behaviour; a madman', 2 'an obsessive enthusiast'

This word (originally from Greek/French) qualifies as an anglicism only where, as in its modern slang/ colloquial uses in Icelandic and German, its spelling or pronunciation betray English transmission.

Ge *Maniac/Maniak* [=E] M, pl. -*s*, 1970s, 2(1 jour, rare) **Du** *maniak* [ma:niak] C, pl. -*ken*, 1950s, via Fr (5) **Nw** (0) **Ic** *maniakk* [=E/ma:ni.ahk] M, pl. -*ar*, 1970s (1 sla) < *meinjaki* **Fr** *maniaque* (5) **Sp** - < *maniaco* (5) **It** *maniaco* (5Gr) **Rm** [maniak/manjak] M/adj., mid19c (5Fr) **Rs** (5Fr) **Po** (5Gr) **Cr** *manijak* M, pl. -*ci* (3) **Bg** *maniak* (5Fr) **Hu** (5Gr) **Al** *maniak* M, pl. -*ë*, end19c, 1,2(1 sla) **Gr** *maniakos, -i* (5)

manifold *n.* 2 'a pipe or chamber branching into several openings'

Du [=E] C, 1970s (1 tech) **Nw** [manifɔld] M, pl. -*er*, 20c (3 tech) **Fr** [manifɔld] M, 1930s (1 tech) **Rm** [manifold] N, 1950s, possibly via Fr (3 tech)

marble *n.* 3a 'a small ball of marble or glass used as a toy', 3b (in pl.) 'a game using marbles'

Ge *Marbel* F, pl. -*n*, 20c (3 reg) < *Murmel* **Du** *marbel* (5Fr)

marine *n.* 2a 'a member of a body of troops trained to serve on land or sea', 2b (US) 'a member of the marine corps'

Ge (∅) **Du** (∅) **Nw** (∅) **Fr** (∅) **Sp** *marines* M, pl. (3) **It** [marin] M, pl. -*s*, 1950s (2) **Po** [marines] pl., mid20c (2 coll) **Cr** - < trsl *marinci* **Al** *marins* 1990s (1 tech)

marker *n.* 3 'a felt-tipped pen (esp. of transparent colour)', +8 'a typical feature', +9 'a distinctive element' (science)

Ge [marka] M, pl. ∅, end20c, 3(2) +8,+9(1 tech) **Du** [=E] C, 1980s, 3,+8(3) +9(1 tech) **Nw** [=E] M, 20c, 3(0) < *markørpenn* **Ic** - < 3: rend *merkipenni* **Fr** *marqueur* 20c (3 mod) **Sp** - < trsl *marcador* **It** [marker] M,

pl. ∅, 1980s, 3,+9(1 tech) < 3: *evidenziatore*; +9: *marcatore* **Rm** [marker] N, end20c, 3(1 rare) **Rs** *marker/ markër* M, pl. -*y*, end20c, 3(1 tech); mid20c, +9(1 tech) **Po** [marker] M, 1980s, 3(1 coll) **Cr** *marker* M, pl. -*i*, end20c, 3(1) **Bg** *marker* M, pl. -*al-i*, 1980s, 3(2), +9(1 tech) **Fi** - < 3: mean *merkkaus (kynä)* **Hu** [ma:rker] pl. -*ek*, end20c, 3,+9(1 tech)

market *n./cp¹′²* +8 'a large self-service store', +9 'a shop'

Ge *Markt* (5) **Du** *markt* (5) **Nw** *marked* (5) **Ic** - < *markaður* **Fr** - < trsl *supermarché* **Sp** - < trsl *supermercado* **It** [market] M, pl. ∅, 1960s (2) < *supermarket* **Rs** *market* M, pl. -*y*, 1990s (2 tech) → *minimarket* **Po** [market] M, end20c (1) **Cr** *market* M, pl. -*i*, end20c (1) **Bg** *market/market* M, pl. -*al -i*, 1990s, +9(2 mod) < *minimarket* **Fi** [markɛt] 1980s (2) **Hu** [=E/ma:rket] cp¹′², pl. -*ek*, 1980s (2)

Al <=E>/*mark_atë* F, pl. *-a*, 1980s (3) **Gr** *m_arket* N, usu. cp,[1] end20c, +8,+9(1 writ, rare)

marketing *n.* 1 'the action or business of promoting and selling products, including market research and advertising'

This survey (in 1995) is likely to capture the moment when this term (rare and technical in some Western societies) is being pushed out by purist measures in a number of Western languages, while documenting the simultaneous, almost universal adoption in the East as a consequence of the new market economies.

Ge [=E] N [U] 1950s (2 tech) **Du** [=E] C [U] 1960s (2) **Nw** [=E] M [U] 1950s (1 obs) < rend *markedsføring* **Ic** - < rend *markaðssetning* **Fr** [maʀketiŋ] M [U] 1950s (2 tech, ban) < *mer-catique, marchéage, marchandis-age* **Sp** [m_arketin] M [U] 1970s (2 tech) > *mercadotecnia* **It** [m_arketiŋ] M [U] 1950s (2 tech) **Rm** [=E] N [U] 1970s (2 tech) **Rs** *m_arketing* M [U] end20c (2 tech) → *-ovyi* adj. **Po** M [U] 1990s (2) → *-owiec* M; *-owy* adj. **Cr** *m_arketing* M [U] end20c (1 tech) **Bg** *m_arketing/market_ing* M [U] 1990s (1 tech) → *-ov* adj. **Fi** - < trsl *markkinointi* **Hu** [m_arketing] pl. Ø, 1960s (2 tech>3 tech) Al *m_arketing* M, pl. *-ë* (1 reg?) **Gr** *m_arketing* N [U] 1980s (2)

marlin *n.* 'a large marine fish'

Du *marlijn* (5) **Fr** M, 1930s (1 tech) **Rm** [marl_in] M, 1960s (3 tech, rare) **Rs** *marl_in* M, pl. *-y*, end20c (1 tech) **Po** [-ar-] M, end20c (1 tech) **Bg** *marl_in* M, pl. *-a/-i*, 20c (1 tech)

marshmallow *n.* 'a soft sweet'

Du [=E] M, 1980s (2) **Nw** [=E] M, pl. *-s*, 20c (1) **Ic** [=E] N [U] mid20c (1 tech) > rend *sykurpúði* **Fr** (0) < *guimauve*

maser *abbrev.* 'microwave amplification by the stimulated emission of radiation'

Ge [m_e:za] M, pl. Ø, 1960s (1 tech) **Du** [=E] C, 1960s (1 tech) **Nw** [m_a:ser] M, pl. *-e*, 1950s (1 tech) **Ic** - < creat *meysir* **Fr** [mazɛR] M, 1950s (1/2 tech) **Sp** [m_aser] M [U] 1970s (2 tech) **It** [m_aser] M, pl. Ø, 1960s (1 tech) **Rm** [m_aser] N/M, 1960s, via Fr? (1 tech) **Rs** *m_azer* M, pl. *-y*, mid20c (1 tech) **Po** [maser] M, mid20c (1 tech) → *-owy* adj. **Bg** *m_azer* M [U] mid20c (1 tech) **Fi** [ma:sɛr] 1960s (1 tech) **Hu** *mézer* [m_e:zer] [U] 1970s (1 tech)

mash *n.* 'a soft mixture of fruit, vegetables etc.'

Fr <=E> M, 20c (1 tech) **Po** *mesz* M [U] mid20c (1 tech)

mass media *n.* 'the main means of mass communication'

Although this concept is largely English the form of the words is easily adapted to the individual languages in which, of course, the two parts were well established as lexical items long before the 1960s and the rise of mass media.

Ge - < trsl *Massenmedien* **Du** - < trsl *massa medium* **Nw** (0) < trsl *massemedia* **Ic** - < creat *fjölmiðlar* **Fr**

mass-média [masmedja] M, pl., 1960s (2) **Sp** <=E>/ *media* [masm_edja/] M, pl., 1960s (2) < trsl *medios de masas* < *medios de comunicación (social)* → *(mass)-mediático* **It** [m_edja/mas m_idja] M, pl., 1960s (3) > rend *mezzi di comunicazione di massa* **Rm** [masm_e-dia] F [U] 1970s (2) **Rs** *mass m_edia* F [U] mid20c (1 jour) < rend *sredstva massovoǐ informatsii* **Po** [-edia] pl., 1970s (2) → *-lny* adj. **Cr** *mas-medij* M, pl. *-i*, end20c (2) **Bg** *(m_as)m_edii* pl., end20c (3) > rend *sredstva za masova informatsiya* **Hu** [=E] [U] 1980s (1>2) > *tömegmédia* Al *mas media* F, pl. Ø (1 mod) **Gr** <=E>/*(mas)m_idia* N, pl., 1980s (2 coll, jour, mod) < rend *mesa mazikis epikinonias/enimerosis*

master *n.* +5c 'a clever student', +6 'a person holding a master's degree', 10 'the original version (of a film or gramophone record) from which a series of copies can be made', 11 cp[2] 'title', +15 'a master of ceremonies on a TV show', +16 'a hunting official', +17 'a form of address', +18 'a master key'

The distribution is difficult to describe, since many uses are foreignisms and others are found in compounds only.

Ge cp[2] (Ø); M, pl. Ø, 1960s, +15(2) **Du** (Ø); cp[2] [=E] +15(1 mod) **Nw** [=E] M, pl. *-e*, 20c, +6(Ø) 10(1 tech) **Ic** [master] M, pl. *-ar*, mid20c, +6(Ø) 10, +18(2 tech) **Fr** *mastère* M, 1980s, +6(1 tech) **Sp** [master] M, pl. *-s*, 1980s, +6(2 tech) 10(1 tech); beg20c, +16(1 arch) **It** [m_aster] M, pl. Ø, 1900s, +6,10(2) +16(1 tech) → *masterizzazione* **Rm** [m_aster] N, end20c, +6(1 tech) < *titlul de master* → *masterat* N **Rs** *m_aster* M, pl. *-a/-y*, beg20c, 11(3) **Po** [master] M, beg20c, 11(Ø) **Cr** *m_aster* M, pl. *-i*, mid20c, 10(2) **Bg** *m_astŭr* M, pl. *-i*, end20c, +5c(1 sla, you) 10(1 tech); [U] +17(1 coll, sla) **Fi** +6(Ø) **Hu** [ma_:ster] pl. Ø, 1970s, +6(Ø>1 tech_EDU) 10(1 tech) 11(Ø) +15(1 tech) **Gr** *m_aster* N, pl. Ø/-s, end20c, +6(2)

masterclass *n.* 'a class given by a person of distinguished skill, esp. in music'

Ge - < *Meisterklasse* **Du** - < *meesterklas* **Nw** - < *mesterklasse* **Ic** [=E] end20c (0 tech) **Fr** (0 tech) **Sp** - < *clase magistral* **It** [=E] F, pl. Ø, end20c (1) → *masterizzazione* **Rs** *m_aster-klass* M [U] end20c (1 jour) **Bg** - < trsl *maǐstorski klas*

master key *n.* 'a key that opens several locks, each of which also has its own key'

Du [=E] C, 1990s (1 tech) < *baassluitel* **Nw** - < *universalnøkkel* **Ic** *masterlykill* M, mid/end20c (2+5) **Sp** - < *llave maestra*

mastermind *n.* 1a 'a person with an outstanding intellect', 2 'the person directing an intricate operation'

Ge [=E] M, pl. *-s*, 1980s (0>1 mod) **It** *master-mind* [master maind] M, pl. Ø, 1980s (1 tech)

masters *n.* 'a sports competition' (golf, tennis, footb.)

Ge [m_a:stas] N, pl. Ø, 1980s (1 tech) **Du** [=E] end20c (1 tech) **Nw** [=E] [U] end20c (1 tech) **Ic** - < *meistarakeppni* **Fr** [=E] end20c M, 1980s (1 tech) **Sp**

[ma̱ster] M, pl. Ø/-s, 1980s (1 tech) **It** *master* [ma̱ster] M, pl. -s, end20c (1 tech) **Rm** (0>1 jour) **Po** (0) **Cr** *ma̱sters* M [U] end20c (1 tech) **Bg** *Ma̱sters* M, pl. -a, 1990s (1 tech_NAME) **Hu** - < trsl *mesterek tornája* **Gr** <=E>/*ma̱sters* N, 1980s (1 tech)

mastiff *n.* 1 'a dog of a large strong breed'

Du [mastif/=E] C, 1940s (2 tech>3 tech) **Nw** [ma̱stif] M, pl. -er, 20c (1 tech) **Fr** [mastif] M, 17c (1 tech) **Sp** - < *mastín* **It** - < *mastino* M **Rs** *mastif* M, pl. -y, mid20c (1 tech) **Po** *mastyf* M, mid20c (2) **Bg** *mastif* M, pl. -a/-i, mid20c (1 tech) **Fi** *mastiffi* 20c (3) **Hu** [ma̱s-tiff] 20c (1 tech) < *szelindek* **Gr** *ma̱stif* N, mid20c (1 tech) < *madroskylo*

match *n./cp^{1/2}* 1 'a contest between individuals or teams' (sport), 2a 'a person equal to another in some quality'

Ge [=E] M/N, pl. -es/-e, beg20c, 1(2) **Du** [=E] C, pl. -es/-en, beg20c, 1(2 tech) → -en v. **Nw** [=E] M, pl. -er, beg20c (2) = 1: *kamp* **Fr** [matʃ] M, mid19c, 1(2); cp^{1} *matchmaker* 1930s, 1(1 tech) **Sp** [matʃ] M, pl. -s/-es, Ø, end19c, 1(1 jour) < *encuentro, competición, combate (de boxeo)* **It** [metʃ] M, pl. Ø, 1900s, 1(2) = *incontro* **Rm** *meci* [me̱tʃj] N, beg20c, via Fr?, 1(3) **Rs** *match* M, pl. -i, beg20c, 1(3) → -turnir M **Po** *mecz* M, beg20c, 1(3) → *przed-* M; -*yk* M; -*owy* adj. **Cr** *meč* M, pl. -evi, beg20c, 1(3) **Bg** *mach* M, pl. -a/-ove, beg20c, 1(2) **Fi** *matsi* 1(3SPORTS) **Hu** *meccs* [=E] cp^{1/2}, pl. -ek, 19c, 1(3) **Gr** *mats* N, beg20c, 1(2)

match *v.* 1a 'correspond with, be harmonious with', 4 'find a person or thing suitable for another', 5 'prove to be a match for', +8 'participate in a match, (sports) play against'

Du *matchen* [me̱tʃən] beg20c, +8(1 tech) **Nw** *matche* ["mætʃe] 1960s (2) **Ic** [matsa] 1970s, 1a,5(1 coll) **Fr** *matcher* [matʃe] end19c, 1a(1) **Hu** - → *matching* 4(1 tech)

matchball* *n.* 'a matchpoint needed to win a game' (tennis)

The recently renewed interest in tennis has made this term, formerly known to specialists only, widely used (though incompletely understood) in sports reporting; even calques are poorly disguised paraphrases.

Ge [metʃbal] M, pl. -bälle, 1960s (1 tech+5) **Du** *matchbal* 1960s (2 tech+5) **Nw** [=E+Nw] mid20c (1 tech+5) **Fr** - < trsl *balle de match* **Sp** [=E/ma̱sbol] M, end20c (1 tech) < trsl *bola de match, pelota de match, pelota de partido* **It** [me̱tʃbol] M, pl. Ø, 1970s (1>2 tech) **Rm** *mecibol* [me̱tʃjbol] N, 1960s (1 tech) = rend *minge de meci* **Rs** *matchbol* M, pl. -y, mid20c (1 tech) **Po** *meczbol* [-bol] M, beg20c (1 tech) → -*owy* adj. **Cr** *me̱čbol* M, mid20c (1 tech) < trsl *meč lopta* **Bg** *ma̱chbol* M, pl. -a, mid20c (1 tech) **Hu** *meccslabda* [me̱ttslabda] pl. -ák (1 tech+5) **Gr** *matsbo̱l* N, 20c (1 tech)

matchbox *n./cp^{1}* +2 (orig.^{TM}) 'a toy motorcar'

Ge [metʃboks] cp^{1}, 1960s (2) **Du** *matchboxauto* [=E+Du] C, 1970s (1 tech) **Nw** [=E] cp^{1}, mid20c (2) **Ic** [matspoxs] cp^{1}, 1960s (2 you, obs) **Fr** (0) **Rm** [=E] N, end20c (2 coll, you) **Po** [metʃ-] M, end20c (2 coll) **Bg** *ma̱chboks* M [U] end20c (1^{TM}) **Hu** [=E] pl. -ok, 1960s (2>3) **Gr** <=E> [matsbo̱ks] N, end20c (1 you, mod)

matchplay *n.* 'play in which the score is reckoned by counting the holes won by each side' (golf)

Ic - < *holukeppni* **Fr** *match-play* [matʃ plɛ] M, 1960s (1 tech) **Sp** [=E] M, end20c (1 tech)

match point *n.* 1a 'the state of a game when one side needs only one more point to win the match' (tennis)

Du [=E] N, 1970s (2) **Sp** [=E] M, pl. -s, end20c (1 tech) < *punto de partido* **It** [metʃ point] M, pl. Ø, 1970s (1>2 tech) **Rm** (0) **Rs** (0) **Gr** *ma̱ts po̱int* N, pl. Ø/-s, end20c (1 tech)

matchwinner* *n.* 'a player in a team who contributes to the winning of a game'

Ge [me̱tʃvina] M, pl. Ø, 1980s (1 mod) **Du** [=E] C, 1980s (1 tech) **Nw** *matchvinner* [=E+Nw] end20c (2+5) **It** [me̱tʃwinner] M, pl. Ø, 1980s (1 tech)

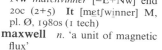

maxwell *n.* 'a unit of magnetic flux'

The Scottish scientist James Clerk Maxwell (1831–79) was professor of experimental physics at Cambridge where he made important contributions to the study of electricity and magnetism.

Ge [=E] N, pl. Ø, mid20c (1 tech, arch) **Du** [=E] C, 1950s (1 tech) **Fr** [makswel] M, beg20c (1 tech) **Sp** [=E]/*maxvelio* M, 20c (1 tech) **It** [ma̱kswel] M, pl. Ø, 1930s (1 tech) **Rm** [=E] M, beg20c, via Fr/Ge (1 tech) **Rs** *ma̱ksvell* M, pl. -y, mid20c (1 tech) **Po** *makswel* [-ue-] M, mid20c (1 tech) **Cr** *ma̱ksvel* M, mid20c (1 tech) **Bg** *ma̱ksuel* M, pl. -a, mid20c (1 tech) **Fi** (3) **Hu** [=E] [U] end19c/beg20c (1 tech) **Al** *maksue̱ll* M [U] mid20c (1 tech) **Gr** <=E>/*ma̱xghuel* N, mid20c (1 tech)

mayday *interj./n.* 'an international radio distress signal'

This term illustrates the shift from French to English in international sea-speak; the original (*venez*) *m'aider* was 'translated' into English pronunciation as the folk-etymological *Mayday* and was made a convention in 1927 (cf. ↑*SOS*).

Ge [=E] 20c (1 tech) **Du** [=E] interj., 1940s (1 tech) **Nw** [=E] 20c (1 tech) **Ic** [=E] N [U] mid20c (1 tech) **Sp** [=E] M [U] 20c (1 tech) **It** [=E] mid20c (1 tech) **Rm** [=E] mid20c (1 tech) **Rs** *me̱ĭdeĭ* mid20c (1 tech) **Po** (0) **Bg** <=E> [=E] mid20c (1 tech) **Fi** [=E] 20c (1 tech)

MC *abbrev.* +5 'a motor cycle'

Nw ["e̱mse:] cp^{1}, 1970s (3)

mean *adj.* 1 'niggardly, not generous or liberal', 5a 'malicious'

Du [=E] end20c, 5a(1 you) **Ic** [=E] end20c (1 sla)

media *n. pl.* 2 'the main means of mass communication', +2a 'one specific branch'

Ge - < 2: *Medien* **Du** [me̞:diə] pl., 1960s, 2(3) **Nw** [me̞:dia] 2(5La) **Fr** *média* [medja] M, 1960s, 2(2) **Sp** [media] M, pl., 1960s, 2(2) → *mediático* **It** [media/midja] M, pl., 1960s, 2(3) **Rm** [media] F, pl., end20c, 2(1 tech, mod) < *mass media* **Rs** *media* F [U] end20c, 2(3) **Po** [media] pl., end20c, 2(2) **Cr** *medija* pl. end20c, 2(2) < *masmedija, masovne komunikaije* **Bg** *media/mediya* cp¹/F, pl. -*dii*, end20c, +2a(3) → -*dien* adj. **Fi** *media* sg., 2(3) **Hu** *média* [me̞:dia] pl. -*ák* (2 tech, jour>3) **Al** *media* F, pl. Ø, 1990s, 2(2) **Gr** *midia* N, pl., end20c, 2(2 mod)

media man* *n.* 'a specialist responsible for advertising'

It [media men] M, pl. Ø, 1960s (1 tech)

medium *adj.* 1 'the middle quality, a degree between extremes', +3 'middle sized' (of clothes, etc.), +4 'fried fairly heavily' (of meat)

Ge [=E] 20c, 1,+4(1 tech); +3 - < ↑*M* **Du** [me̞:ciym] 1980s (2) **Nw** [me̞:dium/=E] end20c (5La/1) **Ic** [=E/me:ti.ym] uninfl., mid20c, +3,+4(1 coll) = trsl *meðal-* **Fr** *médium* [medjɔm] M, 19c (3) **It** [medium] uninfl., mid20c, +3(3) **Rm** - < *mediu, -ie* (5La) **Rs** +3(0) **Po** (0) **Fi** [medium] +3(2) **Hu** *médium* (5La) **Gr** <=E>/*midium* adj., +3(2) +4(1 tech)

medley *n.* 2 'a collection of musical items arranged as a whole', +3 'a medley relay' (swimming)

Ge [=E] N, pl. -*s*, 1970s, 2(1 tech) < *Potpourri* **Du** [=E] C, 1970s, 2(1 tech) < *potpourri* **Nw** [=E] M [U] 1970s, 2(1) +3(1 tech) < 2: *potpurri* **Fr** [=E] end20c, 2(0 tech) **Sp** [=E] M, end20c(1 tech) **It** [=E] M, pl. Ø, end20c (1) < *pot pourri* **Bg** - < 2: *potpuri*

meeting *n.* 2 'an assembly of people', +2a 'a political assembly of people' (cf. ↑*rally*), +3 'a sports contest',

The almost universal distribution of this term is based on sports and – partly supported by Russian transmission – political contexts.

Ge [=E] N, pl. -*s*, 1830s, +2a(1 reg, obs) +3(2 coll) < *Versammlung, Treffen* **Du** [=E] C, beg20(2) **Nw** (0) < 2,+2a: *møte*; +3: *stevne* **Ic** - < 2: *fundur*; +3: *mót* **Fr** [mitiŋ] M, 18c, +2a(2); 20c, +3(1 ban) > *réunion sportive* **Sp** <=E>/*mitin* [mitin] +2a(3); mid19c (3); *meeting*, M, pl. -*s*, end20c, +3(1 tech) < +3: *competición* → *mitinero* adj. **It** [mi:tiŋ(g)] M, pl. Ø, beg19c (2) **Rm** *miting* [mitiŋ] N, mid19c, via Fr, +2a(3); 1940s, +3(1 obs) **Rs** *miting* M, pl. -*i*, 19c, +2a(3) → -*ovat* v; -*ovyĭ* adj. **Po** *mityng/*<=E> [mitink] M, mid19c(2) **Cr** *miting* M, pl.; *mitinzi* beg20c, +3(3); mid20c, +2a(3) → -*ovati* v. **Bg** *miting/miting* M, pl. -*al-i* mid20c, via Rs, +2a(3) → -*uvam* v.; -*adzhiya* M; -*adzhiĭski* adj.; -*ov* adj. **Hu** *meeting/míting* [=E] pl. -*ek*, 19c, +2a,+3(1 tech, arch) < *találkozó* **Al** *miting* M, pl. *mitingje*, mid20c (3) **Gr** *miting* N, pl. Ø/-*s*, mid/end20c, +2a,+3(2)

megabit* *n.* 'c. one million bits, as a unit of data size or memory capacity' (comput.)

Ge [=E] N, pl. -*s*, 1960s (1 tech) **Nw** [me̞:gabit] M, pl. -*s*, 1970s (1 tech) **Fr** *megabit* M **Sp** *megabit* M, pl. -*s*, 1980s (1 tech) **It** [=E] M, pl. Ø, 1960s (1 tech) **Rm** [megabit] M, end20c (1 tech) **Rs** *megabit* M, pl. -*y*, end20c (1 tech) **Po** <=E> M, end20c (1 tech) **Cr** *megabit* M, pl. -*ovi*, end20c (1 tech) **Gr** <=E> [=E] N, pl. -*s*, end20c (1 tech)

megabyte *n.* 'c. 1,000,000 bytes as a measure of data capacity' (comput.)

Ge [=E] N, pl. -*s* (1 tech) = *MB* **Du** [me:xa:bait] C, 1980s (1 tech) **Nw** [=E] M, pl. Ø, 1980s (1 tech) **Ic** *megabæt(i)* [me:kapai:t(ı)] N, pl. Ø, 1970s (2 tech) **Fr** rend *mega-octet* M **Sp** [megabait] M, pl. -*s*, 1980s (1 tech) **It** [=E] M, pl. Ø, 1960s (1 tech) = *mega* **Rm** [=E] M, 1980s (1 tech) = rend *megaoctet* **Rs** *megabait* M, pl. -*y*, end20c (1 tech) **Po** *megabajt/*<=E>, M, end20c (1 tech) **Cr** *megabajt* M, pl. -*ovi*, end20c (1 tech) **Bg** *megabait* M, end20c (1 tech) **Fi** - < trsl *megatavu* **Hu** *megabájt* [=E] [U] end20c (1 tech) = *MB* **Gr** <=E>/*megabait* N, pl. Ø/-*s*, end20c (1 tech) > *meghapsifiolexi*

melting pot *n.* 2 'a place where races are mixed'

Ge (0) < trsl *Schmelztiegel* **Du** [=E] C (Ø) = *smeltkroes* **Nw** (0) < *smeltedigel* **Fr** *melting-pot* [mɛltiŋpɔt] M, mid20c (1 tech) < rend *creuset* **Sp** [=E] M [U] mid20c (Ø tech) < rend *crisol* **It** [=E] F, pl. Ø, mid20c (1) **Rm** (Ø) **Cr** [=E] M [U] mid20c (1) **Hu** - < trsl *olvasztótégely*

melton *n.* 1 'cloth used for overcoats', +2 'a tool for combing wool'

Du [mɛltɔn] N [U] 1970s, 1(3) **It** [mɛlton] M, pl. Ø, end18c (1 tech)

memory *n./cp¹* 4b 'the storage capacity of a computer etc.', +9 'the name of a popular game'

Ge [=E] N, pl. -*(ie)s*, 1980s, 4b(1 tech); 1960s, +9(3) **Du** - < *geheugen* **Nw** [=E] cp¹, 1980s, 4b(1 tech, rare); 1960s, +9(2) < 4b: *minne* **Ic** - < mean *minni* **Fr** - < mean *mémoire* **Sp** - < mean *memoria* **It** - < mean *memoria* **Rm** *memorie* F, end20c, 4b(4) **Rs** - < 4b: mean *pamyat'* **Po** N [U] end20c, 4b(1 tech) **Cr** [=E] F, end20c, 4b(1 tech) **Bg** - < 4b: mean *pamet* **Hu** 4b(5La) **Al** - < *memorie* **Gr** *memori* N [U] mid/end20c, +9(1 rare); <=E> [=E] F, pl. -*s*, end20c, 4b(1 tech); < mean *mnimi*

mercerize *v.* 1 'treat cotton to impart lustre', +2 'subject steel to a specific process'

Ge *merzerisieren* beg20c, 1(3 tech) → *Merzerisation* F, *Merzerisierung* F **Du** *merceriseren* 1940s (3 tech) **Nw** *mercerisere* [mærserise̞:re] beg20c, 1(1 tech) **Ic** *mercerísera* beg/mid20c, via Da, 1(1 tech) → *merceríserun* F **Fr** *merceriser* [mɛRsəRize] 1920s → *mercerisage* M; *merceriseuse* F **Sp** *mercerizar* 1(3 tech) → *mercerización* F, *mercerizado* adj. **It** - < *mercerizzare* **Rm** *merceriza* [mertʃeriza] beg20c, via Fr, 1(3 tech) → *mercerizare* F; *mercerizat, -ă* adj. **Rs** *merserizovat'* 20c (1 tech); *merserisatsiya* N **Po** *merceryzacja* [mercerizcja] F [U] mid20c, 1(1 tech) **Cr**

mercerizirati mid20c, I(I tech) → *mercerizacija* F
Bg *merseriziram* 20c, I(3 tech) **Fi** *merseroida* (I
tech) **Hu** *mercerez* [m̲e̲rtserez] end19c/beg20c, I(I
tech, rare) → -*és* n.

merchandiser *n.* 'a person who merchandises'
Du [=E] C, 1970s (I tech) **It** [=E/m̲e̲rtʃandaizer] M/
F, pl. Ø, 1960s (I tech) **Rs** *merchandaïzer* M, pl. -*y*,
1990s (I tech) **Gr** *mer(t)sandaizer* M, pl. -Ø/-*s*,
1990s (I tech, mod)

merchandising *n.* I 'a means to promote products',
2 'the re-use of titles etc. popularized by cinema/TV
ads'

Ge [=E] N [U] 1960s (I tech) < I:
Verkaufsförderung **Du** [=E] C
[U] 1970s (I tech) **Fr** [m̲e̲rʃā-
daiziŋ] M, 1960s, I(I tech/ban) >
marchandisage **Sp** [=E] M [U]
1970s, I(I tech) **It** [m̲e̲rtʃan-
daiziŋ(g)] M [U] 1960s (I tech)

Cr *merčendajzing* M [U] 1960s, I(I tech) **Bg** *mu̲r-
chandaïzing* M [U] 1990s, I(I tech) **Hu** [=E] [U] 20c
(I tech) **Gr** <=E>/*mer(t)sandaizing* N [U] 1990s,
I(2 tech) = *proothisi poliseon*

merchant bank *n.* 'a bank dealing in commercial
loans and finance'
Du [=E] C, pl. -*es*, 1980s, I(I rare) **Nw** [=E] M,
1980s (I tech) < *forretningsbank* **Sp** - < *banco mer-
cantil* **It** [m̲e̲rtʃant be̲nk] F, pl. Ø, 1970s (I tech)

merit *n.* 3a 'something that entitles one to a reward or
gratitude'
Nw [=E] M [U] 20c (I tech)

mess[1] *n.* 5b 'a place where a company of persons
takes meals together' (armed forces, and navy, esp.
senior personnel), +8 'an officers' club and eating-
place', +9 'a cook's assistant, usually a young boy'
(naut.)
Ge *Meß/Messe* F, pl. -*n*, 19c, 5b,+8(4) **Du** [=E] C,
pl. -*es*, 1950s (I tech); *messroom* 1940s **Nw** *messe*
["m̲e̲se] M, pl. -*r*, 19c, 5b(3) **Ic** *messi* M, pl. -*ar*,
beg20c, via Da, 5b,+9(2 coll) **Fr** [m̲e̲s] M, mid19c
(2) **Po** *mesa* [mesa] F, 19c, via Ge, 5b(2)

mess[2] (I) *n.* I 'a dirty or untidy state of things', 2 'a
state of confusion, embarrassment, or trouble'
Nw (o) **Ic** [=E] N [U] end20c (I sla)

message *n.* 2 'an inspired or significant communica-
tion'
Ge [m̲e̲sitʃ] F, pl. -*s*, 1980s (I coll) < *Aussage* **Nw** (o)
Fr (4) **Sp** - < mean *mensaje* **It** (5Fr) **Rm** (5Fr)

metal *n./cp*[1] +6 'heavy metal (music)', +7 'a fan of
heavy metal (music)'
Ge [=E] cp[1/2], 1980s, +6(I tech) **Du** [=E] C [U] 1980s
(I tech, you) **Nw** [=E] end20c, +6(I tech) **Ic** [=E]/
metall [m̲e̲:tatl] N/M [U] 1970s, +6(I sla) **Sp** [met̲a̲l]
M [U] end20c (I tech, you) **It** - < ↑*heavy metal* **Rm**
(o) < rend *rock metalic* +6(2+5) → *metalist* M, end20c,
+7(5) **Rs** *me̲tal* M [U] end20c, +6(I you) **Po**
[metal] M [U] end20c, +6(I coll) → -*owy* adj. **Bg**
me̲tŭl M [U] end20c, +6(3 coll, you); M, pl. -*al-i*,
+7(3 coll, you) → -*ist* M **Fi** *metalli* 1980s (I

you) **Hu** [=E] [U] 1980s, +6(2 coll, you) **Gr** *me̲tal*
N [U], 1980s, +6(I tech, you); *me̲talo* N, +7(4 sla)

metallic *adj.* 3 'having the shine or lustre of metals'
(of car paint)
Ge [met̲a̲lik] uninfl., 1960s (I tech) **Du** [=E] uninfl.,
1970s (I tech) < *metalliek* **Nw** [met̲a̲lik] 1960s (2)
Ic [=E] (uninfl.) end20c (I tech) = *sansérađur* **Fr** -
< mean *métallisé* **Sp** - < mean *metálico* **It** - < *me-
tallizzato* **Rm** - < *metalizat* **Po** *metalik* uninfl.,
end20c (I coll) **Bg** *metalik* adj., uninfl., mid20c (I
tech) **Hu** - < *metál* (5Gr) **Al** *metalik* 20c (5) **Gr**
metalliko̲s/-i̲l-o̲ (5)

Mickey Mouse *n.* I 'Walt Disney's cartoon char-
acter', 2 *cp*[1]/*adj.* 'ridiculous, trivial'
Ge *Mi̲ckymaus* F [U] 1960s, I(3+5); 1970s, 2(I coll, pej)
Du *Mickey muis* [m̲i̲ki-] C, mid20c (2+5) **Nw** *Mikke
Mus* [m̲i̲kemu̲:s] 1950s, I(3+5) **Ic** *Mikki mús* [m̲i̲hcɪ
mu:s] M, mid20c, via Da, I(3+5) **Fr** *Mickey*
[mik̲ɛ] **Sp** [=E] I(Øtech) **It** - < creat *Topolino* **Rm**
[=E] M, mid20c, I(2) **Rs** *Mikki Maus* M [U] mid20c,
I(2) **Po** <=E> F [U] mid20c, I(2) **Cr** [=E] M [U]
mid20c (2) → *mikima̲uzovski* adj. **Bg** *Miki Ma̲us* M
[U] mid20c, I(2) **Fi** *Mikki Hiiri* **Hu** [=E] [U] 1960s,
I(2>3) = *Miki Egér* **Al** *Miki Maus* 1960s, I(2) **Gr**
mi̲ki ma̲us M, mid20c, I(2)

microchip *n.* 'a small piece of semi-conductor used
to carry electronic circuits'
Ge [m̲i̲:kro:ʃip] M, pl. -*s*, 1970s (2
tech) **Du** [mikro:tʃip] C, 1970s
(2) < *chip* **Nw** <=E>/*mikrochip*
[m̲i̲:kruʃip] M, pl. -*s*, 1970s
(5La+I tech) **Fr** - < trsl *puce*
Sp [mikrotʃip] M, pl. -*s*, 1980s (2
tech) **It** [mikrotʃip] M, pl. Ø,

1970s (I tech) **Rm** [mikrotʃip/=E] N, end20c (I
tech) **Rs** *mikrochip* M, pl. -*y*, end20c (I tech) **Po**
[mikro-] M [U] end20c (I tech) **Cr** *mi̲kročip* M, pl.
-*ovi*, end20c (I tech) **Bg** *mikrochip* M, pl. -*al-ove*,
end20c (I tech) **Hu** [mikrotsip] [U] end20c (I tech)
Gr *mikrotsip* N, pl. Ø/-*s*, end20c (5+I tech)

microwave *n.* 2 'an oven that uses microwaves to
cook or heat food'
Ge - < trsl *Mikrowelle* **Du** [=E] 1980s (2) < *magne-
tron* **Nw** (o) < *mikrobølgeovn* **Ic** - < *örbylgjuofn,
örbylgja* **Fr** *(tour à)* micro-ondes M **Sp** - < trsl
(horno de) microondas **It** - < trsl *(forno a) microonde*
Rm - < rend *cuptor cu microunde* **Rs** - < rend *mik-
rovolno̲vaya pech'* **Po** - < trsl *kuchenka mikrofalowa*
Cr - < trsl *mikrovalna pećnica* **Bg** - < rend *mikrovŭl-
nova furna* **Fi** - < trsl *mikroaalto* **Hu** [=E/mikro-]
pl. Ø/-*ek*, end20c (2) < *mikro/mikrohullámú sütő* **Al**
mikrowiv F, pl. Ø (1) **Gr** (o) < rend *furnos mikroky-
maton*

midget *n./cp*[1] +1a 'a miniature racing car'
Nw [=E] M, pl. -*er*, 1960s (I tech, obs)

mid-life crisis *n.* 'an emotional crisis occurring in
middle age'
Ge [=E] F [U] 1970s (I mod) **Du** *midlife-crisis*
[m̲i̲tlajf krɪzɪs] C, pl. -*sen*, 1980s (2 coll) **Nw** (o) <

trsl *midtlivskrise* **Ic** [=E] mid20c (1 sla) **It** - < rend *crisi di mezz'età* **Gr** (o)

midrange* *n./cp¹* 'a loud-speaker for medium frequencies'
Du [=E] cp¹, end20c (1 tech) **It** [midrɛndʒ] M, pl. Ø, 1980s (1 tech)

midshipman *n.* 'a naval officer' (naut.)
The notable Eastern European distribution of this term is largely explained by Russian transmission; elsewhere, the term is very restricted.
Ge (Ø) **Nw** (o) **Fr** <=E>/ *midship* [mitʃipman/mitʃip] M, 18/19c (1 tech) **Rm** *miciman* [mitʃimạn] M, beg20c, via Rs (3 tech>arch) **Rs** *mịchman* M, pl. -y, beg20c (1 tech) **Po** *miczman* [mitʃman] M, beg20c, via Rs (1 tech) **Cr** *mịdšipmen* M, pl. -i, beg20c (1 tech) **Bg** *mịchman* M, pl. -i, beg20c, via Rs (3 tech)

mike *n.* 'a microphone'
Du [=E] C, 1960s (1 tech) **Nw** <=E>/*mikk* [=E/mik] M, pl. -er, end20c (1 coll, rare) **Ic** *mæk(ur)*/*mæki* [mai:k(ʏr)/mai:cɪ] M, pl. -ar, 1970s (1 coll) **Sp** [mai] M, 20c (1 tech) **Rm** [=E] N, 1970s (1 coll, rare) **Fi** *mikki* 1970s (1 tech)

milady *n.* 'a form used in speaking of or to an English noblewoman or great lady'
This term is even more of a foreignism than ↑*lady* is; also, its popularity has greatly declined since the nineteenth century (cf. ↑*milord*).
Ge *Mylady*/*Milady* (Ø arch) **Du** (Ø) **Nw** (Ø) **Fr** [milɛdi] F, mid19c (1 arch) **Sp** <=E>/*miladi* [mileɪdi] F, 19c (Ø) **It** [milẹdi] F, pl. Ø, 16c (Ø<1) **Rm** [milẹdi] F, uninfl., 19c, via Fr (Ø) **Rs** *milẹdi* F, uninfl., 19c (Ø) **Po** F, uninfl., beg20c (Ø) **Cr** *milẹdi* F [U] beg20c (Ø) **Bg** *milẹdi* F [U] end19c (Ø) **Hu** (o) **Al** *milẹdi* F, pl. Ø, beg20c (Ø) **Gr** *milẹdhi*/*milẹdi* F, 19/20c, via Fr (Ø arch)

mildew *n.* 1 'the name of several fungal diseases, especially of vines'
Whereas Germanic languages have a native term ('honey-dew' re-interpreted by folk-etymology as 'meal-dew'), others filled the gap from English (through French transmission?).
Ge - < *Mehltau* **Du** - < *meel-dauw* **Nw** - < *meldogg, mjøl-dogg* (5Ge) **Ic** - < *mjöldögg* **Fr** *mildiou* [mildju] M, end19c (3 tech) **Sp** *mildiu*/*mildiu* [mildịu] M, end19c (3 tech) **Rm** *mildiu* [mịldju] N [U] beg20c, via Fr (3 tech) = *mana viței de vie* **Rs** *mịld'yu* F, uninfl., end19c (1 tech)

miler *n.* 'a person or animal trained to run a mile'
It [maɪler] M, pl. Ø/-s, end19c (1 tech) **Rm** [=E] M, mid20c (Ø) **Po** [miler] M, mid20c (1 tech) **Fi** *maileri* 1950s (Ø)

military *n.* +2 'a triathlon in riding'
The restricted currency of this term is explained by

the fact that the discipline is called a *three-day event* in English (itself not borrowed into other languages, which have native expressions instead).
Ge [=E] F, pl. -s, 1960s (1 tech) **Du** [=E] C, pl. -'s, 1970s (1 tech) **Hu** [military] [U] 1920s (1 tech, arch)

milk *n.* 'a lotion' (cosmetics)
This English word may have given rise to various products being called 'milk' in the individual languages, but it has rarely been adopted as a loanword. It appears to be slightly more common as part of a product name.
Ge [milk] F [U] 1970s (1 tech) < mean *Milch* **Du** *melk* (5) **Nw** - < mean *melk* **Ic** - < mean *mjólk* **Fr** - < mean *lait* **Sp** - < mean *leche, crema* **It** - < mean *latte* (*detergente*) **Rm** - < rend *lapte demachiant* **Rs** - < mean *molochko* **Cr** - < mean *mlijeko* **Bg** (o) < rend *toalẹtno mlyạko* **Hu** [=E] 1980s (1 tech, writ) < (*testápoló*) *tej* **Gr** (1 writ) < rend *ghalaktoma*

milk bar *n.* 'a snack bar selling milk drinks and other refreshments'
Ge *Milchbar* F, pl. -s, 1950s (5+3) **Fr** *milk-bar* [milk-baʀ] M, 1950s (1) **Po** - < *bar mleczny* **Bg** - < trsl *mlechen bar*

milkshake *n.* 'a drink of milk and other ingredients mixed by shaking or whisking'
The drink and its English name were very popular in parts of Europe during the 1950s, but have since been found less appealing, the loanword being much less frequent now than it used to be. (It appears to be becoming fashionable again in parts of Eastern Europe?).
Ge [mɪlkʃeːk] M, pl. -s, 1950s (1 obs) = *Milchshake* **Du** [=E] C, 1970s (2 tech) **Nw** <=E>/*shake* [=E] M, pl. -r, 1950s (2) **Ic** [mɪlksjeiːk] M (freq. only *shake*) 1960s (1 coll) > trsl *mjólkurhristingur* **Fr** [milkʃɛk] M, mid20c (1) **Sp** - < trsl *batido (de leche)* **Rs** - < rend *molochnyĭ kokteil'* **Po** - < *koktajl* **Cr** [=E] M [U] end20c (1) **Bg** *mịlksheĭk* M, pl. -al-ove, 1990s (1 mod) < (*mlẹchen*) *sheĭk* **Fi** [=E] (1) **Hu** - < *turmix* **Gr** *milkseĭk* N, mid20c (2)

milord *n.* 'a title'
Ge *Mylord*/*Milord* (Ø arch) **Du** (Ø) **Nw** (Ø) **Fr** [milɔr] M, 14c (1 arch) **Sp** [milɔr] pl. *milores*, mid19c (2>1) **It** [milɔrd] M, pl. Ø, 16c (Ø<1) **Rm** [milɔrd] M, beg19c, via Fr (Ø) **Rs** *milọrd* M, pl. -y, beg20c (Ø) **Po** [-t] M [U] beg20c (Ø) **Cr** *mịlord* M [U] beg20c (Ø) **Bg** *milọrd* M [U] end19c (Ø) **Hu** [milord] pl. Ø, 17–19cc (o) **Al** *mịlord* M, pl. Ø, beg20c (Ø) **Gr** *milọrdhos* M, 19/20c, via Fr (1 arch)

mimicry *n.* 3 'close external resemblance of an animal to another animal or to a plant or inanimate object; similar resemblance in a plant' (biol.), +3a 'fig.', +4 'an unsuccessful copy' (arts)
This term is comparatively widespread in biology (in English recorded since the seventeenth century). It

was also somewhat rarely extended to figurative and other pejorative senses. The morphology of the exotic-looking word as *mimic+ry* is largely undetected by non-English speakers.

Ge *Mimikry* F [U] beg20c, 3, +3a(1 tech)   **Du** [mimikri] C [U] beg20c, 3,+4(1 tech)   **Nw** [=E] M [U] 20c, 3(1 tech)   **Fr** - < *mimétisme*   **It** - < *mimetismo*   **Sp** - < *mimetismo*   **Rm** - < *mimetism*

Rs *mimikriya* F [U] beg20c, 3,+3a(1 tech)   **Po** *mimikra* [-kra] F [U] beg20c, 3(1 tech)   **Cr** *mimikrija* F [U] beg20c, 3(1 tech)   **Bg** *mimikriya* F [U] 20c, via Rs, 3,+3a(3 tech)   **Hu** *mimikri* [=E] [U] end19/beg20c, 3(3 tech) +3a(3 pej)   **Al** *mimikri* M [U] 3(1 reg)   **Gr** - < 3: *mimitismos*

-minded *adj.* 1c 'interested in or enthusiastic about a specified thing'

Ge [=E] 1960s (1 jour, rare)   **Du** [majndɪd] 1980s (1 coll/you)   **Nw** [=E] 1960s (2 obs)

minibasket*   *n.* 1 'basketball played by children in a small court with lower baskets', 2 'a modification of basketball for use at home'

It [minibasket] M, pl. Ø, 1960s, 1(2 tech)   **Rm** *minibaschet* [minibasket] N [U] 1970s, via Fr, 1(2 tech)   **Po** [-basket] M [U] end20c, 2(1 tech$_{SPORT}$)   **Bg** *minibasket* M [U] 1990s, 2(2 tech)

minibus   *n.* 'a small bus for about twelve passengers'

Ge (5La)   **Nw** (5La)   **Ic** [mi:nipus:] M, pl. *-ar*, end20c (2)   **Fr** (5La)   **Sp** - < *microbús*   **It** [minibas/minibus/minibus] M, pl. Ø, 1960s (2>3) < *pulmino*   **Rm** *minibuz* [minibuz] N, 1970s, via Fr (3)   **Rs** - < trsl *miniavtobus*   **Po** [minibus] M, end20c (2 coll)   **Cr** *minibus* F, pl. *-ovi*, end20c (3)   **Bg** - < *mikrobus*   **Fi** *minibussi* < trsl *pikkubussi*   **Hu** [minibus] pl. *-ok*, 20c (3 mod)   **Al** - < *mikrobuz*   **Gr** *minibas* N, end20c (2)

minicomputer   *n.* 'a computer of medium power, more than a microcomputer but less than a mainframe' (comput.)

Ge [=E] M, pl. Ø, 1980s (2)   **Du** [=E] C, pl. *-s*, 1980s (2 tech)   **Fr** - < *mini-ordinateur*   **It** [minikompjuter] M, pl. Ø, 1980s (2 tech)   **Rm** [=E/minikompjuter] N, 1980s (2 tech)   **Rs** *minikomp'yuter* M, pl. *-y*, 1980s (2 tech)   **Bg** *minikompyutŭr* M, pl. *-a/-tri*, 1990s (2)   **Hu** [=E] pl. *-ek*, end20c (2)

minigolf   *n.* 'miniature golf'

A host of English compounds using *mini-* (esp. the ↑*miniskirt* of 1965) has certainly contributed to the frequency of its use (these compounds being often abbreviated to *mini*, as happened in the case of a type of car, skirts, etc.). However, the element *mini* itself is felt to be (5La); classification as a true anglicism then depends on the Englishness of the second element (cf. examples below).

Ge [minigolf] N [U] 1960s (3)   **Du** [minixolf] N, 1960s (3)   **Nw** [mi:ni-] M [U] 1970s (5+3)   **Ic** [mi:nikɔlf] N [U] mid20c (2)   **Fr** [minigɔlf] M, 1970s (2)   **Sp** [minigolf] M [U] 1970s (2)   **It** [minigɔlf] M, pl. Ø, 1960s (3)   **Rm** [minigolf] N [U] 1970s, via Fr? (3)

Rs *minigol'f* M [U] mid20c (1 tech)   **Po** M [U] end20c (2)   **Cr** *minigolf* M [U] mid20c (2)   **Bg** *minigolf* M [U] end20c (1 tech)   **Fi** [=E] mid20c (3)   **Hu** [=E] Ø, 1970s (2>3)   **Gr** *minigolf* N, mid20c [U] (2)

minimal art   *n.* 'art, esp. painting, characterized by simple forms'

Ge [=E] F [U] 1960s (1 tech)   **Du** [=E] C [U], 1970s (1 tech)   **Nw** - < *minimalistisk kunst*   **Ic** - < *minimalismi*   **Fr** <=E>/*minimal* [minimal] M, 1970s (1 tech)   **Sp** [=E] M [U] (1 tech) = trsl *arte minimal* = *minimalismo*   **It** *minimalismo* M [U] 1980s (3)   **Rm** - < rend *artă minimală*   **Po** - < *sztuka prymitywna*   **Hu** [minimal a:rt] [U] 1970s (1 tech)   **Gr** *minimal* N [U] 1990s (1 tech, mod) < *minimalismos*

minimarket*   *n.* 'a small shop based in a garage'

It [minimarket] M, pl. Ø, 1970s (3)   **Rm** [=E] N, 1990s (1 mod)   **Rs** *minimarket* M, pl. *-y*, 1995 (2)   **Po** [-market] M, end20c (2 mod)   **Bg** *minimarket*/*minimarket* M, pl. *-a/-i*, 1990s (3 mod)   **Hu** [minima:rket] pl. *-ek*, 1990s (2)   **Al** *minimarket* M, pl. *-e*, 1995 (2)

miniskirt   *n.* 'a very short skirt'

Ge - < trsl *Minirock*   **Du** - < trsl *miniskjørt*   **Nw** - < trsl *miniskjørt*   **Ic** *minipils* [mi:nipʰils] N, pl. Ø, 1960s (2+5) = trsl *pínupils*   **Fr** - < trsl *mini-jupe*   **Sp** - < trsl *minifalda*   **It** - < trsl *minigonna*   **Rm** - < *minijupă* (5Fr)   **Rs** *miniskёrt* F, pl. *-y*/uninfl.?, 1970s (1 mod) < trsl *mini-yubka*   **Po** < trsl *mini spódniczka*   **Cr** - < trsl *minisuknja*   **Bg** *mini* N, pl. *-ta*, 1960s (3 coll) = *minizhup* > trsl *minipola*   **Fi** - < trsl *minihame*   **Hu** - < trsl *mini szoknya* (5Fr+Hu)   **Gr** *mini* N, 1960s (2) > trsl *mini fusta*

minivan   *n.* 'a small van'

Du [=E] 1990s (1 tech, jour)   **Fr** [=E] 1990s (1 tech, ban) > *monospace*   **It** [=E] M, pl. Ø, 1980s (1 tech)   **Po** (0)

mink   *n.* 1 'an animal of the genus *Mustela*', 2 'the fur of these', 3 'a coat made of this fur'

Ge [=E] M, pl. *-e*, 1930s, 2(3 tech)   **Du** [=E] C, 1950s (5) < *nerts*   **Nw** [=E] M, pl. Ø/*-er*, 20c (3)   **Ic** *minkur* [miŋkʏr] M, pl. *-ar*, 1930s, via Da (3)   **Cr** [=E] M, pl. *-ovi*, mid20c, 3(3)   **Fi** *minkki* 20c (3 tech)

mint   *adj.* 'light green' (fashion)

This word is one of the many colour terms untiringly adopted by the fashion industry to indicate the novelty of its products; such terms are normally restricted to catalogues and fashion pages, and soon dropped, to make room for new loans. ('Mint flavour' is current exclusively in product names, German)

Ge adj. [=E] uninfl., 1980s (1 tech)   **Du** [=E] 1980s (2 tech)   **Nw** [=E] 1980s (1 tech)   **Ic** - < *myntugrænn*   **It** *menta* (5La)   **Al** *mente* mid20c (3)

mint   *n.* 1 'the plant', +3 'flavour'

Ge *Minze* (5La)   **Du** N [U] 1(1 tech), +3(2) < *munt*   **Nw** [=E] 1980s, +3(1 tech)   **Ic** [=E] end20c, +3(1 coll)   **Sp** *menta* (5La)   **Rm** *mentă* F (5La/Fr)   **Po** - < *mięta*   **Bg** *menta* (5La)   **Fi** *minttu* (3)   **Al** *mentja* (5)

miss¹ (1)   *n.* 1 'a failure to hit, reach, attain etc.'

Du - < *misser*   **Nw** [=E] M, pl. *-er*, end20c (1 coll)

miss² (2) *n.* 1 'a girl or unmarried woman', 2a 'the title of such a woman', 2b 'the title of a beauty queen', 4 'an elderly English teacher'

The currency of this word is difficult to assess: it is universally known as a foreignism and widespread as cp¹ in titles such as *Miss World*. The sense 'governess' was widely known around 1900 but has long been obsolete in most languages.

Ge *Miss/Miß* F, pl. *-es/-en*, 1950s, 2b(2); 19c, 4(Ø arch) **Du** [=E] C pl. *-ses/-sen*, 1950s, 2b(1 tech) 4(Ø) < *juffrouw* **Nw** [=E] M, pl. *-er*, 19c, 1,2a (Ø); 1950s, 2b(2); 19c, 4(Ø) **Ic** [=E] cp¹, mid20c, 2b(0) < *ungfrú* **Fr** [=E] F, 1930s, 2b(2) 4(0) **Sp** [mis] F, pl. *-es*, mid19c, 1,2a(Ø1>2); 1920s, 2b(2) **It** [=E] F, pl. Ø, 1920s, 2a(Ø) 2b(3) **Rm** [=E] F, pl. Ø, end19c, 1,2a,4(Ø); 1970s, 2b(1 mod) **Rs** *miss* F, uninfl., 19c, 1,2a(Ø); end20c, 2b(3) **Po** F [U] mid19c, 2b(2) → *-ka* F **Cr** [mis] F [U] mid20c, 2b(1) **Bg** *mis* F, pl. Ø/[U] end19c, 1,2a(Ø); mid20c, 2b(2) **Fi** *missi* 2b(3) **Hu** [=E] pl. Ø, 1920s, 2a,b(2) **Al** *mis* M, pl. *-ë*, mid20c, 1,2a,b(Ø) **Gr** *mis* F, mid20c, 2a(Ø) 2b(2)

miss *v.* 1 'fail to hit', 2 'fail to catch', 3 'fail to see', 4 'fail to meet a person', 5 'fail to seize an opportunity' **Du** - < *missen* **Nw** *misse* ["mise] (1 coll) **Fi** *missata* 1990s (2 sla, you)

missing link *n.* 2 'a hypothetical intermediate type, esp. between humans and apes', +3 'an item identified by reconstruction'

This biological term has been used as a loanword, or in translation, since the late nineteenth century; its adoption in other contexts has been less enthusiastic.

Ge [=E] N, pl. *-s*, 19c, 2(1 tech); 1960s, +3(1 coll) **Du** [=E] C, 1980s (1 tech) **Nw** [=E] M/N, pl. *-s*, mid20c, 2(1 tech) > trsl *manglende mellomledd* **Ic** [=E] 20c, 2(0) < trsl *týndi hlekkurinn* **Fr** [misiŋliŋk] M, 1900s, 2(1 tech, arch) > *chaînon manquant* **Sp** - < trsl *eslabón perdido* **Rm** (0) **Po** [-nk-] M, uninfl., mid20c, 2(1 tech) **Cr** [mising link] M, uninfl. 20c, 2(1 tech) **Bg** - < trsl *lipsvashto zveno* **Hu** [=E] [U] 1970s, 2(1 tech) < trsl *hiányzó láncszem*

mister *n.* 1 'a man without a title of nobility', 2 'a form of address to a man', +3 'the title of the winner in a beauty contest for men', +4 'a male person who is closely associated with a particular notion, thing etc. (e.g., a conjuror)', +5 'a term of address for a coach' (soccer)

The currency of this word is largely restricted to beauty contests where it is modelled on the female equivalent ↑*miss*; there does not seem to be a tendency to adopt this word beyond this limited context. (The word is of course well known as a foreignism.)

Ge [mista] M [U] 1960s, +3(2) +4(1 fac) **Du** [=E] C, 1940s, 1(2 coll, pej) +3(1 tech) **Nw** [=E] M, pl. *-e*, 19c, 2(Ø); mid20c, +3,+4(1/2) **Ic** [=E] mid20c, 2(1 coll) < +3: *herra* **Fr** - < +4: *Monsieur* **Sp** [mister] M, mid19c, 1(Ø/1 fac); beg20c, 2(2 coll); end20c, +3(1 tech); beg20c, +5(2) **It** [=E] M, pl. Ø, 1950s, 1,2(Ø) +3,+5(2) **Rm** [=E] M, pl. Ø, 19c, 1,2(1/Ø) +3(1 rare) **Rs** *mister* M [U] 19c, 2(Ø), 20c, +3(2) **Po** [-er] M, beg20c, +3(2) **Cr** *mister* M [U] beg20c, 1,+3(1) **Bg** *mistŭr* M [U] beg20c, 1(Ø), 2(Ø/2 coll, fac) +4(2); end20c, +3(2) **Hu** [=E] [U] 20c, 2,+3(2) +4(Ø) **Gr** *mister* M, end20c, +3(2) +4(1 jour)

mix *n./cp²* 1a 'an act or instance of mixing; a mixture', 1b 'the proportion of materials etc. in a mixture', 3 'ingredients prepared commercially for making a cake etc.', 4 'the merging of film pictures or sound', +4a 'a re-mixed version of a pop song' (music), +5 'a combination of various products or services' (advertising), +6 'a mixed drink', +7 'the making or repairing of something, esp. machinery, etc., from miscellaneous things', +8 'the producing of a combined recording' (music)

Ge [=E] M [U] 1970s (earlier as cp¹) 1a,+6(3) **Du** [=E] C, pl. *-en/-es*, 1970s, 1a,4,+5,+6(2 tech) **Nw** *miks* [=E] M, pl. *-er*, mid20c, 1a,b,3,4,+4a,+5(3) **Ic** [mıxs] N [U] beg/mid20c, partly via Da, 1a,3,+6(2 coll) 4,+4a,+7(2 tech) = 4: trsl *(hljóð)blöndun* **Fr** - < +4a: *mixage* **Sp** [=E] M/cp² [U] 1980s, 1,+4a,+5(1 tech) **It** [=E] M, pl. Ø, 1970s, 1a,b,3,+4a,+5,+6, +7(2) = +4a: re-mix; 4: *mixage* **Rm** [=E] N, end 20c, 1a,+5(1 jour, rare) < 4: *mixaj* **Rs** *miks* M, pl. *-y*, end20c, +4a(1 tech) **Po** (0) **Cr** (0) **Bg** *miks* M, pl. *-a/-ove* end20c, +4a (1 tech); M [U] +8(1 tech) **Hu** [=E] cp² [U] 1920s, 3,+6(2 > 3); mid20c, 4,+4a(2 tech>3 tech) **Al** *miks* M, pl. *-e*, mid20c, 3,4,+6,+7(3) **Gr** - < 4: *mixaz̧ N*

mix *v.* 1 'combine two or more substances', 2 'prepare (a cocktail etc.)', +2a 'shred and mix food', 7 'combine (two or more sound signals) into one', 8 'produce (a recording) by combining a number of separate soundtracks or recordings', +9 'make or repair something, using miscellaneous things (esp. in the absence of the appropriate spare parts)'

Ge *mixen* [=E] beg20c, 1,2,+2a(3) 7,8(1 tech) = *mischen* **Du** *mixen* [miksə] 20c (2) **Nw** *mikse* ["mikse] beg20c, 1,2,+2a(3); 1970s, 7,8(3 tech) → *mikser* M; *miksing* M/F **Ic** *mixa* [mıxsa] beg/mid20c, partly via Da, 1,2,+2a(2 coll) 8,+9(2 tech) = trsl *(hljóð)blanda* → *mixaður* adj. **Fr** *mixer* [mikse] 1930s/mid20c, 7(1 tech) > *mélanger* **Sp** - < *mezclar* **It** *mixare/missare* [miksare/missare] 1940s, 7,8(2 tech) **Rm** *mixa* [miksa] mid20c, via Fr, 1(3 rare) 7(3) → *mixat* adj.; *-are* F **Po** *miksować* [miksovatć] mid20c, 2(2) 7(1 tech) → *miksowanie* N [U]; z-v. **Cr** *miksati* 2(2) 7(1 tech) **Bg** *miksiram* end20c, 8(3 tech) **Fi** *miksata* end20c (3) **Hu** *mixel* [miksel] 1920s, 2,1,+2a (2>3); mid20c, 7(2 tech>3 tech) **Gr** *mixaro* end20c, 7,8(1+3 tech)

mixed *adj.* 3 'for or involving persons of both sexes' **Du** - < *gemengd* **Nw** [=E] mid20c (1 tech) **Sp** - < *mixto* **It** - < *misto* **Rm** *mixt* beg19c (5Fr/La) **Po** (0) **Bg** - < trsl *smesen* **Gr** - < mean *miktos, -i, -o*

mixed double(s), mixed *n.* 'a doubles game with a man and a woman as partners on each side' (tennis)

The distribution of this tennis term is restricted by the fact that Romance languages quite naturally use native equivalents, and that calquing is an obvious option elsewhere. Moreover, the concept is seen as singular (with the *-s* omitted) and frequently shortened to the first element. The recent popularity of tennis seems to favour the English term at least as a stylistic alternative.

Ge [=E] N [U] 20c (1 tech); *mixed* (1 coll) < *gemischtes Doppel* **Du** *mixed double* [=E] N, 1980s (1 tech)   **Nw** *mixed double* [=E] mid20c (1 tech)   **Fr** - < trsl *double mixte* (5)   **Sp** - < trsl *mixto* **It** - < trsl *doppio misto*   **Rm** - < trsl *dublu mixt*   **Rs** *mikst* M, pl. *-y*, end20c (1 tech, coll)   **Po** *mikst* M [U] mid20c → *miksista* M; *miksistka* F; *-owy* adj.   **Cr** *mikst dubl* M [U] mid20c (1 tech)   **Bg** *mikst dabŭls* [U] end20c (1 tech) < trsl *smeseni dvoĭki*   **Hu** - < trsl *vegyes páros*   **Gr** - < trsl *mikto*

mixed grill   *n.* 'a dish of various grilled meats'
Ge (0)   **Du** C, 1980s (1 tech)   **Nw** (0)   **Fr** [miksɛd gril] M [U] end20c (1 tech)   **It** - < rend *grigliata mista*   **Rm** (0)   **Cr** [mikstgril] M [U] mid20c (1 tech)   **Bg** - < trsl? *meshana skara*   **Hu** [=E] [U] 1970s (1 tech)   **Gr** *mixt gril* N, end20c (1 tech)

mixed media   *n./cp[1]* 'the use of a variety of media in an entertainment'
Ge [=E] 1960s (1 tech, obs)   **Hu** - < rend *médiamix* (1 tech, jour)

mixed pickles   *n.pl.* 'gherkins etc. in vinegar'
Ge *Mix(ed) Pickles* pl., 19c (2)   **Du** [=E] C [U] beg20c (2)   **Nw** (0)   **Hu** [=E] [U] end19/beg20c (Ø/ 1 arch)   **Gr** - < *pickles*

mixer[1] (1)   *n.* 1 'a device for shredding and mixing food', +5 'a person who mixes drinks', +5a 'a device for mixing cast iron', +6 'a person who likes to make or repair things (usu. from miscellaneous things); a mechanically minded person'

This word is almost universal as a term for a household gadget, but comparatively seldom used for the person mixing drinks at a bar etc. Some of the words could have been independently derived from the widespread v. *mix* (which is either partly native, or supported by similar loanwords from Latin). Contrast the more even distribution, but more limited frequency, of the modern technical term in relation to recording (next entry).

Ge M, pl. Ø, beg20c, +5(2); 1960s, 1(3)   **Du** [=E] C, 1950s, 1,+6(2)   **Nw** *mikser/miksmaster* ["mikser] M, pl. *-e*, 1950s, 1(3) +5(1 rare)   **Ic** [=E]/*mixari* [mɪxsarɪ] M, pl. *-ar*, mid/end20c, 1,+6(2 coll) = 1: trsl *blandari*   **Fr** <=E>/*mixeur* [miksœʀ] M, mid20c, 1(2)   **It** [=E] M, pl. Ø, 1970s, 1(2 tech) < *frullatore*   **Rm** [mikser] N, mid20c, via Fr?, 1(2 tech)   **Rs** *mikser* M, pl. *-y*,

mid20c, 1(2) +5a(1 tech)   **Po** *mikser* [-er] M, mid20c, 1(2) → *ek* M; *-ka* F; *-ski* adj.   **Cr** *mikser* M, pl. *-i*, mid20c, 1(1) +5(1 tech)   **Bg** *mikser* M, pl. *-al-i*, mid20c, 1(2)   **Hu** [mikser] pl. *-ek*, 1920s, +5(2>3); 1960s, 1(3)   **Al** *mikser* M, pl. *-ë*, mid20c, 1,+5(1 reg)   **Gr** *mixer* N, mid20c, 1(2)

mixer[2] (2)   *n.* 4a 'a device for merging input signals to produce a combined output in the form of sound', 4b 'a person in charge of this'

Ge [=E] M, pl. Ø, 1970s, 4b(1 tech)   **Du** [=E] C, 1950s (1 tech)   **Nw** *mikser* ["mikser] M, pl. *-e*, end20c, 4b(1 tech) ← Nw *mikse* v.   **Ic** [=E] M, pl. *-ar*, end20c, 4a(1 tech); - < 4b: *mixermaður*   **Fr** -trsl < *mélangeur* **Sp** [=E] M, 1930s, 4b(1 tech, arch)   **It** [=E] M, pl. Ø, 1970 (1 tech) < *miscelatore*   **Rm** [mikser] N, 1960s, 4a(2) < rend *pupitru/masă de mixaj*   **Po** *mikser* [-er] M, mid20c, 4a,b(1 tech)   **Cr** *mikser* M, pl. *-i*, end20c (1 tech)   **Bg** *mikser* M, pl. *-al-i*, end20c, 4a(1 tech)   **Fi** *mikseri* end20c (1 tech)   **Hu** [=E] pl. *-ek*, 1920s/1940s, 4a(2 tech>3 tech) 4b(2 tech)   **Gr** - < 4a: trsl *miktis*

mixing   *n.* 1 'the mixing of sounds' (music), 2 'other kinds of mixing (people, food etc.)'
Du (0)   **It** [=E] M, pl. Ø, 1970s, 1(1 tech) < *missaggio* **Rm** - < 1: *mixaj* **Po** - < 1,2: *miksowanie*   **Cr** (0) **Bg** - < +8: ↑*mix*   **Fi** - < *miksaus*   **Gr** - < 1,2 *mixarisma*; 1: *mixaz*

mob   *v.* +1d 'tease or bully a person collectively, esp. at school or working place' (cf. ↑*mobbing*)
Ge *mobben* 1990s (1 jour, mod)   **Nw** *mobbe* [mobe] beg20c (3)   **Ic** *mobba* [mop:a] end20c, via Da/ Nw (2 sla)

mob   *n.* 1 'a disorderly crowd'

This word is one of the earlier adoptions but it has remained restricted in Europe; the pejorative connotation, present in the English etymon, is probably strengthened when used as a loanword.
Ge [=E] M [U] mid19c (2 pej) **Nw** *mobb* [=E] M, pl. *-er*, end19c (3) → *mobbe* v.   **Hu** [=E] [U] 20c (2)

mobbing   *n.* 1 'psychological intimidation intended to push colleagues out of their jobs', +2 'crowding around a celebrity'

The origin of the recent sense 1 may be British English, but its currency is possibly more widespread in the Germanic languages.
Ge [=E] N [U] 1993, 1(1 mod) **Du** [=E] N [U] 1990s, 1 (1 mod) **Nw** ["mobin] M/F [U] 1970s, 1(3) ← *mobbe* v. **Ic** [=E] uninfl., end20c 1(1 sla)   **Fi** - < *mobbaus*

moccasin   *n.* 1 'a soft leather slipper of Native American origin', +1b 'a modern slipper, a loafer'
Ge *Mokassin* [mokasi:n] M, pl. *-s*, 19c, 1(Ø); 1960s,

+1b(3) **Du**[=E]C, 1940s, 1,+1b(3 tech) **Nw** *moka-sin* [m<u>o</u>kasi:n] M, pl. *-er*, beg20c, 1(Ø) +1b(3) **Ic** *mokkasí(n)a* [m<u>o</u>hkasi:(n)a] F, pl. *-ur*, mid20c, +1b(3) **Fr** *mocassin* [m<u>o</u>kas<u>e</u>] M, beg18c 1,+1b(3) **Sp** *mocasín* M, 19c, via Fr (3) **It** *mocassino* M, pl. *-i*, 19c, via Fr (3) **Rm** *mocasin* [mokas<u>i</u>n] M, 1960s, via Fr, 1,+1b(3) **Rs** *mokas<u>i</u>ny* pl., mid20c, 1(Ø) +1b(3) **Po** *mokasyn* M, mid20c (3) **Cr** *mokas<u>i</u>na* F, pl. *-e*, mid20c, +1b(2) **Bg** *mokas<u>i</u>na* F, usu. pl. *-<u>i</u>ni*, beg20c, 1(Ø) **Fi** *mokkasiini* (3) **Hu** *m<u>o</u>kaszin* [=E] pl. *-ek*, 17–19cc, 1(Ø); 20c, +1b(3) **Al** *mokasin* 1a(3) **Gr** *mokas<u>i</u>ni* N, via Fr (3)

mock turtle *n./cp¹* (soup) 'made from a calf's head to resemble turtle'
Ge *-suppe* [m<u>o</u>ckt<u>ö</u>rtl] beg20c (1+5 obs) **Nw** (0) < *forloren skilpadde* **Sp** *-soup* 1920s (1 arch)

mod *n.* 1 'a young person (esp. in the 1960s) belonging to a group aiming at sophistication and smart modern dress'
Ge [=E] M, pl. *-s*, (1 obs) **Nw** *mods*, sg. [=E] M [U] 1960s (1 obs) **Fr** (Ø) **Sp** [mod] M, pl. *-s/-er*, 1960s (Ø jour) **It** [=E] M/adj., pl. *-s*, 1960s (1 you, obs)

model *n./cp²* +1b 'a three-dimensional representation of a thing, esp. a ship, aircraft, etc., on a smaller scale, sold in kit form to be constructed and usu. made of plastic', 7a 'a person employed to pose for an artist, photographer, etc', 7b 'a person employed to display clothes etc. by wearing them' (cf. ↑*top model*), +9 *cp¹* 'a one-off garment etc.', +10 'vintage work, esp. cars'

The earlier French loanword (often characterized by end-stress) is widely available in European languages; it is not quite clear how far the anglicism supplements, competes with, or pushes out(?) the French-derived loanwords.
Ge [=E] N, pl. *-s*, 1970s, 7b(1 mod) < *Mannequin, Mod<u>e</u>ll* **Du** *model* 7b(5Fr) **Nw** *mod<u>e</u>ll* (5Fr/It) **Ic** *módel* [mou:tel] N, pl. Ø, mid20c, partly via Da, +1b,+10(2 coll) 7a,b(2 coll, mod) +9(2 arch, mod) = 7a: *fyrirsæta*; +10: *árgerð* **Fr** *cp²*, 1990s, 7b(1 mod) **Sp** *cp²*, 1990s, 7b(1 mod) **It** - < *modello* (5); ↑*top model* **Rm** [mod<u>e</u>l] N, end20c, 7a,7b(4) **Rs** *mod<u>e</u>l'* F, pl. *-i*, end20c, via Fr, +1,b,7a,b(2) < *manekenshchik-shchitsa* **Po** 7b(5La) **Bg** *mod<u>e</u>l* M/*cp²*, pl. *-al/-i*, 1990s, +1b,7a,b,+10(2 mod) → *-ka* F = *manekenka* **Hu** *modell* 7b(5It) **Al** *model* M, pl. *-e*, mid20c, 7b(3) **Gr** *mod<u>e</u>lo* N, from It, 1b,7a,b,+9(3); *m<u>o</u>d<u>e</u>l* N, pl. *-s*, 1980s, 7b(2) → *modeling* N

modem *abbrev.* 'modulator + demodulator'
Ge [m<u>o</u>:dɛm/mod<u>e</u>:m] M/N, pl. *-s*, 1980s (3 tech) **Du** [=E] N, 1980s (1 tech) **Nw** ["m<u>u</u>:dem/mud<u>e</u>:m] N, pl. Ø/-er, 1980s (3 tech) **Ic** [=E] N, pl. Ø, 1970s (2 tech) > creat *mótald* **Fr** [m<u>o</u>dɛm] M, 1970s (1 tech) **Sp** [=E/m<u>o</u>dem] M, 1980s (1 tech) **It** [m<u>o</u>dem] M, pl. Ø, 1960s (1 tech) **Rm** [mod<u>e</u>m] N, 1990s (1 tech) **Rs** *m<u>o</u>dem* M, pl. *-y*, end20c (1 tech) **Po** [modem] M, end20c (1 tech) **Cr** *m<u>o</u>dem* M, pl. *-i*, end20c (1 tech) **Bg** *mod<u>e</u>m* M, pl. *-al-i*, end20c (1 tech) **Fi** *modeemi* end20c (2 tech) **Hu** (5La) **Al** *modem* M,

pl. Ø, 1995 (1 tech) **Gr** <=E>/*m<u>o</u>dem* N, end20c (1 tech)

modern jazz* *n.* 'a jazz style that was developed after 1940, together with bebop'
Ge [=E] M [U] mid20c (1 tech) **Po** [modern] M [U] mid20c (1 tech) **Bg** - < trsl *moderen dzhaz* **Fi** [=E] M [U] mid20c (1 tech) **Hu** *modern dzsessz* [m<u>o</u>dern dz<u>e</u>ss] [U] 20c (5Fr+3) **Gr** - < trsl *moderna tzaz*

mohair *n./cp¹* 1 'the hair of the angora goat', 2 'yarn or fabric made of this'

This word is ultimately from Arabic, but is said to have been reinterpreted on the basis of English *hair*. If this is so, all *-h* forms must derive from English (possibly through French etc. transmission).
Ge *Mohär/Mohair* [moh<u>e</u>:r] M, pl. *-s/-e*, 19c (3) **Du** [=E] N [U] beg19c (3) → *mohairen* adj. **Nw** [muh<u>e</u>:r/-hæ:r] M/N [U] 19c (2 tech) **Ic** [mou:hɛr] N/*cp¹* [U] mid20c, 2(2) > creat *móhár* **Fr** [mɔɛʀ] M, end19c, 2(1 tech) **Sp** [mo<u>e</u>r/mo<u>a</u>ir] M [U] 1970s (1 tech) **It** [m<u>o</u>ɛr] M [U] mid19c (2 tech) **Rm** [moha<u>i</u>r] N [U] beg18c (5Turk/Fr) **Rs** *mokh<u>e</u>r* M [U] mid20c(3) **Po** *moher* [-er] M, end18c, 2(3) **Cr** *m<u>o</u>her* M [U] mid20c, 2(2) **Bg** *m<u>o</u>kher/mokh<u>e</u>r* M [U] 20c, 2(2) **Fi** [m<u>o</u>ha¹r] 19c (3) **Hu** *moher* [m<u>o</u>:her] mid20c, 1(1 tech) 2(3) **Gr** *mokh<u>e</u>r* N, via Fr [U] 2(2)

mokick* *n.* 'a small motorbike' (from: *moped* + *kick-starter*)
Ge [m<u>o</u>:kik] N, pl. *-s*, 1960s (1 obs)

moleskin *n.* +1a 'cotton velvet used esp. for lining', 2a 'a kind of cotton fustian with its surface shaved before dyeing'

This early fashion term was once widespread through much of Europe but has long been obsolescent, or restricted to highly technical uses.
Ge [m<u>o</u>:lskin] M/N, pl. *-s*, 19c (1 tech, rare) **Du** [m<u>o</u>:lskin/m<u>o</u>:lə-skin] N [U] 1940s (1 tech) **Ic** *molskinn* [m<u>o</u>lscɪn:] N [U] end19c, via Da, 2a(3) **Fr** *moleskine* [m<u>o</u>leskin] F, end19c (1 arch) **Sp** *molesquin/molesquina*

M/F, end19c? (2 tech) **It** *moleskine* [m<u>o</u>lskin] M [U] end19c, viaFr (3 tech) **Rm** *moleschin* [mole<u>s</u>k<u>i</u>n] N [U] beg20c, via Fr (3 tech, obs) **Po** [moleskin] M, beg20c, 2a(1 tech) **Cr** [m<u>o</u>lskin] M [U] beg20c (1 tech) **Hu** *moleszkin* [m<u>o</u>leskin] [U] via Fr (1 arch)

Molotov cocktail *n.* 'a homemade incendiary device'

This term is said to have been coined during the Finno-Russian war of 1939–40, to denote home-made hand grenades used against invading Russian tanks, at a time when Molotov was foreign minister. (Alternatively, it is said to have been used by Russians fighting against the Germans in late 1941.) The term has become widespread since the 1960s, in relation to various terrorist movements.
Ge [m<u>o</u>lotofk<u>o</u>kte:l] M, pl. *-s*, 1950s (Rs+2) **Du** *molotowcocktail* [=E] C, 1960s (name+2) **Nw** *molotov-* [=E] M, pl. *-er/-s*, 1950s (1 tech) **Ic** *mólotoffkok-*

teill [mou:lɔtofkʰɔxteil] M, pl. -*ar*, 1970s (2 coll)   **Fr** *cocktail Molotov* M, 1950s (1)   **Sp** *cóctel molotov* M, 1960s (2 tech)   **It** - < rend *(bottiglia) molotov* **Rm** *cocteil Molotov* N, 1960s (2+ name)   **Rs** *kokteĭl' Molotova* M,

pl. -*i*, mid20c (1 arch)   **Po** *koktajl Molotowa* M, mid20c (2)   **Cr** *molotov koktel* M, pl. -*i*, mid20c (1 tech)   **Bg** *kokteĭl Molotov* M, 1970s (3 obs)   **Fi** *molotovcocktail* (2)   **Hu** *Molotov-koktél* [=E] [U] 1950s (5Rs+3)   **Gr** *(kokteil) molotof* N 1950s (2+Rs)

money *n.* 1a 'a current medium of exchange in the form of coins and banknotes'

   Du [=E] C [U] 1940s (1 coll)   **Nw** (0)   **Ic** *monní* [mon:i] N [U] end19c (1 coll) → blend *monning-ur* M   **Sp** [mani/moni] M, end19c (1 fac, rare); *monil/monis* pl. *monises*, end19c (3 sla)   **Rm** (0)   **Rs** *mani* pl., end20c (2 coll)

   Po (0)   **Bg** *moni/muni* N [U] beg/mid20c (2 coll)   **Hu** [=E] [U] end20c (Ø>1 tech)   **Gr** <=E> [=E] N, 1990s (1 jour, fac, mod)

moneymaker *n.* 1 'a person who earns a lot of money'

   Ge [=E] M, pl. Ø, 1960s (1 coll, obs)   **Du** [=E] C, 1940s (1 coll)   **Nw** [=E] M, end20c (1 rare)   **Ic** [=E] (0)   **Rm** (0)   **Cr** *mani mejker* M, end20c (1 tech)

money-making *n.* +1a 'the excessive acquisition of wealth, of dubious legality'

   Ge [=E] N [U] 1980s (1 jour, rare)   **Hu** [=E] end20c (1 coll, pej, mod)

monitor *n.* 3a 'a television receiver used in a studio to select or verify the picture being broadcast', 3b 'a visual display unit', +3c 'a similar device used to control the sound in broadcasting and recording', 7 'a warship'

   Ge [mo:nito:r] M, pl. -*e*, beg20c, 3a,b(5La) 7(5 arch)   **Du** [mo:nitor] C, 1950s, 3a,b(5); beg20c, 7(5 obs)   **Nw** [mɔnitu:r] M, pl. -*er*, 1960s, 3a,b,7(1/2)   **Ic** *mónitor* [mou:nɪtor] M, pl. -*ar*, end19c, 3a,b,+3c (1 tech) 7(Ø arch) = *(eftirlits)skjár*; *vaktari*   **Fr** *moniteur* [mɔnitœr] M, mid19c/1970s, 3a,b(4) 7(1 tech)   **Sp** [monitor] M, pl. -*es*, 3a,b,7(3/5)   **It** [monitor] M, pl. Ø, 1960s, 3a,b(3) → *monitoraggio*   **Rm** [monitor] N, end19c, 7(5Fr); *monitor (de control)* mid20c, via Fr, 3a(3 tech); 1970s, 3b(2 tech)   **Rs** *monitor* M, pl. -*y* (1 tech)   **Po** (5La)   **Cr** *monitor* M, pl. -*i*, end20c, 3a,b(1)   **Bg** *monitor* M, pl. -*al-i*, mid20c, 3a,b(2 tech)   **Fi** *monitori* 1980s, 3a,b(3)   **Hu** [monitor] pl. -*ok*, beg20c, 7(1 tech, arch); mid20c, 3a(3); 1970s, 3b(3)   **Al** *monitor* [monitor] M, pl. -*e*, mid20c, 3a(3)   **Gr** <=E>/*monitor* N, pl. -*s*, end20c, 3a,b(1 tech) < *othoni*

monitoring *n.* 1 'a checking service in literature, data, etc. referring to a particular topic' (electronic), 2 'the systematic control or observation of situations/phenomena, using equipment or analytic techniques'

Du [=E] C [U] 1970s (1 tech)   **Nw** (0)   **Fr** [mɔnitɔriŋ] M, 1970s, 2(1 tech_MED/ban) < *monitorage*   **Sp** - < *monitorización*   **It** - < *monitoraggio* M   **Rm** - < trsl *monitorizare*   **Rs** *monitoring* M [U] end20c, 2(2) → -*ovyĭ* adj.

   Po [-nk] M [U] end20c, 2(2) → -*owy* adj.   **Cr** *monitoring* M [U] end20c, 2(1 tech)   **Bg** *monitoring* M [U] end20c, 2(1 tech, jour) < *monitorirane*   **Hu** [=E] [U] 1970s, (1 tech)

monkey business *n.* 'mischief'

   Nw [=E] M [U] end20c (1)   **Ic** [=E] M [U] end20c (1 sla)

monopoly *n.* +4 '(^{TM}) a game in which players use imitation money to engage in simulated financial dealings', +5 'transferred senses'

The game, invented in America in 1935, has been very popular in Europe since the 1950s.

   Ge [monopoli] N [U] 1950s, +4(3); 1980s, +5(1 fac, pej)   **Du** [monopoli] N [U] 1970s, +4(3) < *monopolie*   **Nw** - < *monopol* (5Gr)   **Ic** [mou:nopʰou:li] end20c, +4(1 you) < *matador* N   **Fr** [mɔnɔpoli] +4(^{TM})   **Sp** [monopoli/monopoli] M [U] end20c (1 mod)   **It** *Monopoli* [=E] M [U] 1960s, +4(3)   **Rm** [monopoli] N [U] 20c, +4(0>1)   **Rs** (5Fr)   **Po** [monopoli] N [U] end20c, +4(2 coll)   **Bg** *monopoli* N [U] 1990s, +4(1 mod)   **Fi** *Monopoli*^{TM} only   **Hu** [monopoli] [U] 1980s, +4(2>3)   **Gr** *monopoli* F/N [U] +4(5)

monorail *n.* 'a railway in which the track consists of a single rail'

   Du [=E] C, 1950s (2)   **Nw** [=E] M [U] 1960s (1 tech)   **Fr** [mɔnɔraj] M/adj., uninfl. (3 tech)   **Sp** <=E>/ *monorrail/monorriel* M (3 tech) = *monocarril*   **It** - < trsl *monorotaia*   **Rm** *monorai* [monoraj] N, 1970s, via Fr (3 tech, rare) = trsl *monoşină* F   **Rs** *monorel's* M, pl. -*y*, mid20c (1 tech) → *ovyĭ* adj.   **Po** - < *jednotorowy*   **Cr** [=E] M, end20c (1 tech)   **Bg** - < rend *monorelsova zheleznitsa*   **Fi** - > trsl *monorata*   **Hu** (0)   **Gr** <=E>/*monoreil* N, 20c (1 tech, rare)

monotype *n.* 1 'a typesetting machine'

   Ge [monoty:pə] F, pl. -*n*, beg20c (3 tech/5Gr)   **Du** [monotipə] C, beg20c (1 tech)   **Nw** [munutaip] M, pl. -*r*, mid20c (1 tech)   **Ic** [=E] mid/end20c (1 tech)   **Fr** [mɔnɔtip] F, beg20c (5/1 tech)   **Sp** *monotipo* 20c (3 tech/5)   **It** [monotaip] F, pl. Ø, 1910s (1 tech) < trsl *monotipo* → *monotipia* n.; *monotipista* n.   **Rm** *monotip* [monotip] N, 1930s, via Fr (3 tech) → *monotipist* M, -*ă* F   **Rs** *monotip* M, pl. -*y*, (3 tech/5Gr)   **Po** (5Gr)   **Cr** *monotip* M [U] mid20c (1 tech)   **Bg** *monotip* M, pl. -*al-i*, mid20c (1 tech) → -*en* adj.   **Fi** *monotyyppilatomakone* (3)   **Hu** [=E] [U] beg20c (1 tech)   **Al** *monotip* M, pl. -*e*, 20c (1 tech)   **Gr** *monotypia/ monotypiki mikhani* F, 20c (5 tech)

monsoon *n./cp*[1] 1 'a seasonal wind of the Indian Ocean', 2 'the rainy season accompanying a wet monsoon'

This word originates from Arabic and was transmitted through Italian, Dutch, and English; its complex history and the uncertain traces that English has left in the form of the loanwords cast doubt on its status as an anglicism.

Ge *Monsun* [mɔnsuːn] M, pl. *-e*, 19c (3)   **Du** *moesson* via Fr/via Port. (5Arab)   **Nw** *monsun* [mɔnsuːn] M, pl. *-er*, beg20c (3 tech)   **Ic** *monsún(n)* [=E/mɔnsutn] M/cp[1] [U] mid19c, via Da, 1,2(Ø)   **Fr** *mousson* (5Port)   **Sp** *monzón* M (5Port)   **It** *monsone* [monsone] M, pl. *-i*, 16c, via Sp (3/5Arab)   **Rm** *muson* [musɔn] M, end18c (5Fr)   **Rs** (5Arab)   **Po** (5Arab)   **Cr** *monsun* M, pl. *-i*, 19c (3)   **Bg** *muson* [musɔn] (3)   **Hu** *monsuuni* (3)   **Al** *musonlmonsun* M, pl. *-e*, (3)   **Gr** *monsun* M (1 tech, rare) < *musonas*

monster *n.* 1 'a frightening creature', 2 'an inhumanly cruel person', 4 'a large usu. ugly animal or thing', 5 *attrib.* 'huge; extremely large of its kind'

Since the etymon is Latin, it is not easy to distinguish any Englishness in the form and meaning; the modern distribution is, however, clearly influenced by English and often the word itself is from English. Note that to date it has affected only parts of Europe. Early attestations in German are the compounds *Monsterpetition* and *Monstermeeting* in mid nineteenth century.

Ge [mɔnsta] N, pl. Ø, 19c 1960s, 1,2(3); 4(3); adj/cp[1], 5(3) < 1,2: *Ungeheuer*; 4: > *Monstrum*; 5: = *Massen-/Riesen-*   **Du** (5+Fr)   **Nw** [mɔnster] N, pl. Ø/-stre, 20c, 1,2(2) = *uhyre*, > *monstrum*   **Ic** [=E] N, pl. Ø, mid/end20c, 1,2(2 coll) 4,5(2 sla); *monstur* N, 17c, 1(5Da) → *monstrólógía*   **Fr** *monstre* M, 20c, 5(4 mod)   **Sp** *monstruo* M (5La)   **It** *mostro* (5La)   **Rm** *monstru* [mɔnstru] M, beg18c, 1,2,4(5La/Fr)   **Rs** *monstr* M, pl. *-y*, mid20c (2)   **Po** (5Fr)   **Bg** *monstür* M, pl. *-i*, mid20c, 2(1 lit)   **Hu** (5La)   **Al** *monstër* M, pl. *-a* (1 sla)

monster show* *n.* 'a show that cost a lot to produce'

Ge [mɔnstaʃoː] F, pl. *-s*, 1960s (1 arch)   **Po** (0)   **Hu** *monstre-show* [mɔnstre ʃoː] Ø, 1970s (5+3)

montgomery* *n.* 'a short hooded overcoat'

Du (Ø)   **It** *montgomeri* M, Ø, 1940s (3)   **Gr** *modgomeri* [-d,-nt] N, mid20c (1 tech)

Moog *n./cp* (orig.™) 'a synthesizer'

Ge [=E] M/cp, pl. *-s*, 1970s (1 tech)   **Nw** [muːg] M, pl. *-er*, 1960s (1 tech)   **Ic** *múgg* [muk:] N, pl. Ø; *múggur/múggi* [muk:ʏr/muc:ɪ] M, pl. *-ar*, 1970s (2 tech)   **It** [muːg] M, pl. Ø, 1970s (1 tech)   **Rm** [=E] N [U] 1970s (1 tech)

moon boot(s) *n.* 1 'thickly padded boots for low temperatures', +2 'thick shoes'

The distribution of this term illustrates the limited impact of a short-lived fashion which reached only a few countries and became outdated before the term was really accepted.

Ge *moonboots* [=E] pl., 1980s, 1(1 obs)   **Du** *moonboots* [=E] pl., 1980s (2)   **Nw** - < trsl *månestøvler*   **Ic** [=E] uninfl., 1970, 1(1

mod)   **It** [muːnbuːts] M, pl. *-s*, 1970s (2>3)   **Po** (0)   **Fi** *moonbootsit* [muːnbuːtsɪt] 1980 (1)   **Hu** *mumbuc* [mumbuts] pl. Ø, 1970s, +2(2)

moon washed* *adj.* 'with a marble-like look' (of jeans material)

Ge *moon-washed* [=E] 1980s (1 tech)

moor *v.* 2 'make fast a boat etc.'

Ge *moren* 19c (3 tech) → *Muring* F   **Du** - < *meren*   **Nw** *more* ["muːre] 19c (3 tech) → *moring* M/F

mop *n.* 1 'a wad or bundle of cotton etc. fastened to the end of a stick, for cleaning floors, etc.'

This early loan is restricted to the North-west and a few neighbouring countries – possibly because the item is limited in a similar way. The word appears to be obsolescent in some languages.

Ge [=E] M, pl. *-s*, 1920s (1 obs)   **Du** C, 1970s (3) < *zwabber*   **Nw** *mopp* [=E] M, pl. *-er*, beg20c (3 obs) > *svaber* → *moppe* v.   **Ic** *moppa* [mɔhpa] F, pl. *-ur*; *moppur* M, pl. *-ar*, mid20c, via Da (3)   **Sp** *mopa* F, 1970s (3)   **Po** *mopal<=E>* [mopl/=E] F/M, 1990s (2 coll)   **Cr** (0)   **Hu** [=E] pl. Ø, 1970s (2)

mop *v.* 1 'wipe or clean with a mop'

Ge *moppen* beg20c (3 obs)   **Nw** *moppe* [mɔpe] beg20c (3)   **Ic** *moppa* [mɔhpa] mid20c (3) → *moppun* F

Mormon *n.* 1 'a member of the Church of Jesus Christ of Latter-Day Saints', +2 'a prophet'

The church was founded by Joseph Smith who published his *Book of Mormon* in 1830; although the church remained largely restricted to the USA, there are branches elsewhere for local reference.

Ge *Mormone* M, pl. *-n*, end19c, 1(3/Ø)   **Du** [mɔrmɔn] C [U] beg20c, +2(3 tech); *mormoon* [mɔrmoːn] C, pl. *mormonen*, beg20c, 1(3 tech)   **Nw** *mormoner* [murmuːner] M, pl. *-e*, 20c, 1(3) → *mormonsk* adj.; *mormonisme* M   **Ic** *mormón(i)* [mɔrmoun(ɪ)] M, *-ar*, mid19c, via Da, 1(2)   **Fr** *Mormon(e)* [mɔrmõ/on] M/F, 19c (Ø) → *mormonisme* M   **Sp** *mormón* M, 1(3 tech)   **It** *mormone* F/M, pl. *-i*, mid19c, 1(3)   **Rm** *mormon* [mɔrmɔn] M, beg20c, via Fr, 1(3)   **Rs** *mormony* M, pl. *-y*, beg20c, 1(Ø)   **Po** *mormon* [mɔrmon] M, beg20c (Ø) → *-izm* M [U]   **Cr** *mormon* M, pl. *-i*, mid20c, 1(3)   **Bg** *mormon* M, pl. *-i*, 20c, 1(2 tech)   **Fi** *mormoni* 20c (3)   **Hu** [mɔrmon] pl. *-ok*, 19c, 1(Ø)   **Gr** *Mormonos* M, 20c, 1(3) → *mormonismos* M

morning *interj.* 'good morning'

Du (Ø)   **Nw** *mornings* [=E] 20c (3 coll)

morning-after pill *n.* 'a contraceptive pill effective when taken some hours after intercourse'

Ge - < rend *die Pille danach*   **Du** *morning-afterpil* [mɔːnɪŋaftərpɪl] F/M, 1970s (2)   **Nw** - < *angrepille*   **It** - < trsl *pillola del giorno dopo*   **Gr** - < rend *khapi tis epomenis meras*

Morse (code) *n./cp*[1/2] 'an alphabet or code in which letters are represented by combinations of long and short light or sound signals'

The American painter Samuel Finley Breese Morse

(1791–1872) came to invent the code in the 1830s (the first successful transmission was in 1838). Whereas the use of the noun is universal (and not felt to be foreign in most languages), the verb is much more restricted: none of the Slavic languages saw the need to devise a verb, and neither did some other languages. The action is expressed in these languages by a verb + *Morse*. **Ge** [morzə] cp[1], end19c (3)   **Du** [mɔrsə] C [U] 1940s (3)   **Nw** ["mo͟rse] M [U] end19c (3)   **Ic** *mors* [mo͟rs] N [U] beg20c (3)   **Fr** [mɔʀs] M, mid19c (3)   **Sp** [mo͟rse] M [U] 19c (3)   **It** [mo͟rs] n./adj., pl. Ø, 1950s (3)   **Rm** [mo͟rse] M/cp[2] beg20c, via Fr (3)   **Rs** *mo͟rze* cp[1] [U] beg20c (3) → *-ist* M; *-yanka* F   **Po** *mors/alfabet Morse'a* [mors] M [U] beg20c (3)   **Cr** - < *morzeova abeceda*   **Bg** *morz* M [U] beg20c (2) = rend *morzova azbuka* → *-ov* adj.   **Fi** [mɔrsɛ] (3)   **Hu** *morze* [mo͟rze] [U] end19/beg20c (3) → *morzézik* v.   **Al** *mors* [mors] M [U] mid20c (3)   **Gr** *(ko͟dhikas) Mors* M, beg20c (5+2 tech); *morsikos ko͟dhikas* M (3+5)

morse   *v.* 'signal by morse code'
Ge *morsen* [morzən] end19c (3)   **Nw** ["mo͞rse] 20c (1 tech)   **Ic** *morsa* [mo͟rsa] beg20c (2) → *morsun* F   **Bg** < *predavam po morza*   **Fi** *morsata* (3)   **Hu** *morzézik* [mo͟rze:zik] end19c (3)

motel   *n.* 'a roadside hotel'
Although this blend was first coined in American English in 1925, most European languages appear to interpret the loanword as a modification of the French *hotel* (as shown by the stress); this interpretation is offset by the fact that the institution is still largely considered 'American', and the word interpreted as a foreignism.
Ge [mo:te͟l] N, pl. *-s*, 1950s (Ø/3)   **Du** [mo:te͟l] N, 1950s (3)   **Nw** *motell* [mute͟l] N, pl. Ø/*-er*, 1950s (Ø/3)   **Ic** [mou:tel] N, pl. Ø, 1960s (Ø > 2)   **Fr** [mɔte͟l] M, 1950s (2)   **Sp** <=E> M, pl. *-s*, mid20c (3)   **It** [mote͟l] M, pl. Ø, 1950s (3)   **Rm** [mote͟l] N, 1960s (3) → *-ier* adj.   **Rs** *mote͟l'* M, pl. *-i*, mid20c (2) → *-nyǐ* adj.   **Po** [mo-] M, mid20c (2) → *-owy* adj.   **Cr** *mo͟tel* M, pl. *-i*, mid20c (3) → *-ski* adj.   **Bg** *mo͟tel* M, pl. *-al-i*, mid20c (2)   **Fi** *motelli* 1970s (3)   **Hu** [=E] pl. *-ek*, 1950s (3)   **Al** *mo͟tel* M, pl. *-ë*, mid20c (1 reg)   **Gr** *mote͟l* N, mid20c (1 rare)

motocross   *n.* 'cross-country racing on motor-cycles'
This compound is first attested in French and may therefore have started out as a pseudo-anglicism. It has long been adopted by British and American English, and which more recent borrowings are likely to derive from it.
Ge [mo͟:to:krɔs] N [U] 1960s (2 tech)   **Du** [=E] C, pl. *-es*, 1950s (2 tech)   **Nw** [mu͟:tukrɔs] M [U] 1950s, via Fr (1 tech)   **Ic** [=E] N [U] 1980s (1 tech)   **Fr** *motocross* [mɔtɔkʀɔs] M, 1950s (2 tech)   **Sp** *motocros(s)* M, mid20c (2)   **It** [motokrɔ͟s] M [U] 1940s (3 tech)   **Rm** *motocros* [motokro͟s] N, 1960s, via Fr (3)   **Rs** *motokro͟ss* M, pl. *-y*, mid20c (1 tech) → *men* M   **Po** *motokros/*<=E> M [U] mid20c (1 tech) → *-owy* adj.   **Cr** *mo͟tokros* M [U] mid20c (1 tech) → *-ist* M   **Bg** *mo͟tokros* M [U] mid20c (2 tech)   **Fi**

[motɔkrɔs] (2)   **Hu** [=E] [U] mid20c (2 tech)   **Al** *motokros* M, pl. *-ë*, mid20c (1 reg)   **Gr** *motokro͟s* N [U] mid20c, via Fr (1 tech)

motorship* *n.* 'a motor-driven ship'
Du *motorschip* **Nw** - < *M/S* (abbrev.)   **Fr** [mɔtɔʀʃip] M, 20c, 1(1 tech)   **Po** - < *M/S* (abbrev.)   **Gr** <=E>/*mo͟torsip* N, 1990s (1 tech)

mountain bike   *n.* 'a bike originally designed for riding on mountainous terrain'
Ge [=E] N, pl. *-s*, 1980s (2) → *-er* M   **Du** [=E] C, 1980s (1 tech) < *ATB/allterrain bike*   **Nw** [=E] M, 1980s (1 tech) < *offroad(-sykkel)*   **Ic** - < trsl *fjallahjól*   **Fr** *mountain-bike* [muntɛnbajk] M, 1980s (1 mod, ban) > rend *vélo tout terrain*   **Sp** [mo͟ntanbaik] F, 1980s (2 mod) < trsl *bicicleta de montaña/MTB* → *-ing* n.   **It** [mu͟ntan ba͟ik/mau͟ntin ba͟ik] F, pl. Ø, end20c (2) < trsl *bicicletta da montagna*   **Rm** (0)   **Rs** *mau͟ntin ba͟ik*, pl. *-kal-kove*, 1995 (1 tech, mod)   **Po** [=E] 1990s (1 mod) = trsl *rower gòrski*   **Cr** (0)   **Bg** *mau͟ntin ba͟ik*, pl. *-kal-kove*, 1995 (1 tech, mod)   **Fi** [=E] (1) < trsl *maastopyörä*   **Hu** [=E] pl. *-ok*, 1990s (2)   **Gr** <=E>/*mau͟den ba͟ik* N, pl. Ø/*-s*, 1980s (2)

mouse   *n.* 3 'a small hand-held device which controls the cursor on a VDU screen' (comput.)
This expressive non-technical name for the computer device makes it an ideal candidate for calquing: the Germanic languages have words for the animal almost identical to the English word, and for others the native equivalent was obvious. Few languages, then, have opted for straightforward borrowing, or use both the loanword and the calque.
Ge *Maus* 1980s (4)   **Du** *muis* 1980s (4)   **Nw** *mus* 1980s (4)   **Ic** *mús* [mu:s] 1980s (4)   **Fr** - < mean *souris*   **Sp** [=E] C, 1980s (1 tech/rare) < mean *ratón*   **It** [=E] M, pl. Ø, 1980s (2 tech)   **Rm** [=E] N, 1980s (1 tech)   **Rs** - < mean *mysh'*, *myshka*   **Po** F, 1980s (1 tech) < mean *mysz*   **Cr** - < mean *miš*   **Bg** - < mean *mishka*   **Fi** - < mean *hiiri*   **Hu** [=E] [U] 1980s (1 tech) < mean *egér*   **Gr** <=E> [=E] N, end20c (1 tech) < mean *podiki*

move   *v.* 1 'change one's position or posture', 5 'take action, esp. promptly'
Du *moven* [mu:və] 1970s (1 coll)

Mr.   *n.* 1 'the title of a man without a higher title', 2 'a title prefixed to a designation of office etc.', +3 'an address to a male' (ironical; sometimes preceding fancy names)
Ge [mista] M [U] 1960s, +3(1 jour)   **Du** (Ø)   **Nw** [=E] M, 20c, 1,2(Ø) +3(2 writ)   **Sp** [=E] M, mid20c (1 fac)   **It** [=E] M, pl. Ø, 1950s, 1,2(Ø) +3(1 coll, fac)   **Rm** 1,2(Ø) +3(1 rare)   **Rs** - < ↑*mister*   **Po** (0)   **Cr** ↑*mi͟ster*   **Bg** <=E> end20c, 1(1 writ, rare); ↑*mi͟stŭr*   **Hu** [=E] [U] 20c, 1,+3(Ø>2)   **Gr** [mi͟ster] M, end20c, +3(1 jour, fac)

Mr. X *n.* 'a male person whose identity is or should be kept secret'
Du [=E] C [U] 1970s (1 tech)
Nw [=E] M, 20c (2) **Fr** - < trsl
M. X **It** [mɪster ɪks] M, pl. Ø,
mid20c (2) **Rm** (0) **Rs** *Mister
iks* M [U] 20c (1 coll) **Po** (0)
Cr (0) **Bg** - < trsl *G-n X* [-xiks]
Hu [mɪster ɪks] [U] 20c (1 fac,
rareTHEATR) **Gr** - < *khyrios H*

muffin *n.* 1 'a flat round spongy cake'
Du [=E] M?, pl. -s, 1990s (1 tech, mod) **Nw** *muffins*
[mʉfin(s)] M, pl. Ø, 20c (1) **Ic** [=E] mid20c (1
coll) **Fr** [myfin/mœfin] M, end18c (1 arch) **Fi**
muffins(s)i 20c (2)

mug *n.* +1c 'a pitcher, a jug'
Du - < *mok* **Nw** *mugge* ["mʉge] M, pl. -r, 19c (3)

mulch *n.* 'a mixture of straw, leaves, etc. spread over
soil or around a plant to enrich or insulate the soil'
(horticult.)
Ge *Mulch/Mulche* [mulçə] M/F
[U] 20c (3 tech) **Du** *muls* (1
tech) **Nw** *mulching* [=E] M [U]
20c (1 tech) **Rm** *mulci* [multʃj]
N [U] mid20c (1 tech); *mulcire*
[multʃire] F [U] 1960s (3
tech) **Rs** *mul'cha* F [U] mid20c
(1 tech) → *-chirovat'* **Bg** *mulch* M [U] mid20c (1 tech)
→ *-iram* v. **Hu** [=E] [U] 20c (1 tech)

mulch *v.* 'treat with mulch' (horticult.)
Ge *mulchen* [mulçən] 20c (3 tech) **Nw** *mulchere* [mʉl-
ʃɛːre] end20c (1 tech) **Fr** (0) **Rs** *mul'chirovat'*
mid20c (1 tech) → *-ovanie* N **Po** *mulczować* [multʃo-
vat'] mid 20c (1 tech) → *z-*v. **Cr** *malčirati* (3)

mull *n.* 'thin cotton, mainly used for medical purposes'
This word has remained a
North-western one despite having been borrowed more than a
hundred years ago. Native
equivalents exist, of course, in
all the other languages.
Ge [mul] M, pl. -e, end19c (3)
Du *mul* [=E] N [U] 1940s (3)
Nw [mʉl] N [U] beg20c (1 tech) **Hu** [mull] [U]
end19c/beg20c (1 tech)

multiple-choice *n./cp¹ᐟ²* 'accompanied by several
possible answers from which the correct one has to
be chosen'
This expression was adopted in schools and universities to denote easy-to-correct tests, some time after it
had already been used as a foreignism for procedures
employed in the USA. Calques have widely replaced
this unwieldy expression (but not in German, Dutch).
Ge [=E] cp¹, [U] 1980s (1 tech) **Du** [=E] C/cp¹, 1970s
(1 tech) **Nw** [=E] 1980s (1 tech) = trsl *flervalgsoppga-
ve* **Ic** - < creat *krossaprófl-spurning* **Fr** - < trsl *choix
multiple* **Sp** - < trsl *elección múltiple* **It** [=E/multip
tʃɔis] cp², end20c (1 tech) < trsl *a scelta multipla* **Rm**

(0) **Po** - < *test wyboru* **Cr** [=E]
M [U] end20c (1 tech) **Bg** (0) <
creat *vŭprosi s izbiraem otgo-
vor* **Fi** - < trsl *monivalinta* **Hu**
[=E] cp¹ [U] 1980s (1 tech) < trsl
többválasztós teszt **Gr** <=E>
[=E] N [U] 1980s (1 tech) > trsl
polaplon epiloghon

mumps *n.* 'a contagious viral disease'
The word, apparently a popular term related to
mump 'grimace' and taken as a singular also in English, was borrowed to complement various native
terms equally popular; the distribution of the loanword suggests German mediation.
Ge [mumps] M/F(reg) [U]
end19c (3) > *Ziegenpeter* **Po**
[mumps] M [U] mid19c (1 arch)
< *świnka* **Cr** *mums* M [U] 19c
(3) **Hu** <=E>/*mumsz* [=E/
mums] [U] end19/beg20c (3) →
mumszos adj.

mungo *n.* 'short fibres recovered from heavily felted
material'
Ge [mungo:] M, pl. -s, beg20c (3 tech, rare) **Du**
[myngo:] C [U] 1940s (1 tech) **Fr** [mɛ̃go] (1
tech) **Rm** [mungo] N [U] 1940s, via Fr? (3 tech) **Po**
[mungo] N, uninfl., mid20c (1 tech) **Cr** *mungo* M [U]
mid20c (1 tech) **Fi** [muŋgɔ] 19c (3)

Muppets* *n. pl.* 'puppets' (from the TV show)
The term is of course the name of a set of puppets of
'Sesame Street' but appears to become generic in a
number of languages (note morphological integration).
Ge [mapits] pl., 1970s (2) **Du** [=E] pl., 1970s (2)
Nw <=E>/*Muppetene* (def. form) [=E] 1970s (2)
Fr [mɔpɛts] pl., 1980s (1) **Sp** [=E] M, pl., 1980s (1
tech) **It** [mappets] M, pl., 1970s (2) **Rm** *muppet*
[=E] M < pl. *-ţi*, 1980s (1 mod) **Rs** *mappets* pl.,
end20c (2 coll) **Po** *mapety/muppety* [-ti] pl., end20c
(2) → *mapetka* F **Cr** *mapet* M, pl. -i, end20c (2) **Bg**
mŭpeti pl., 1980s (3 coll) **Fi** (Ø) **Hu** [=E] cp¹: *Muppets' show* (0) **Gr** <=E> [mapets] M, pl., 1970s (2)

musical *n.* 'a musical comedy'
This word is clearly the most popular of the ↑ *-ical*
terms; it is fully accepted throughout Europe, and
seems not to have sparked off many native replacements.
Ge [mjuːzikl] N, pl. -s, 1950s (2) **Du** [=E] C, 1960s
(2) **Nw** [=E] M, pl. -sl-er, 1950s (2); *musikal* [musi-
kaːl] M, pl. -er, 1980s (3) > *syngespill* **Ic** *músikal* [=E/
muːsikal] N, pl. -köl, 1960s (1 coll) < *söngleikur; dans-
og söngvamynd* **Fr** [myzikal] M, 1930 (2) > trsl *co-
médie musicale* **Sp** *musical* M, mid20c (3/4) **It**
[mjuːzikol] M, pl. Ø, 1960s (2) = rend *commedia musicale* **Rm** *muzical* [muzikal] N, 1960s (2) = *comedie
muzicală* **Rs** *myuzikl* M, pl. -y, mid20c (2) **Po** [mu-
zikal] M, mid20c (2) → *-owy* adj. **Cr** *mjuzikl* M, pl.
-i, mid20c (2) **Bg** *myuzikŭl* M, pl. -al-i, mid20c (2)
Fi *musikaali* mid20c (3) **Hu** [=E/muzikel] pl. -ek,

1970s (2>3)   **Al** - < *komedi̱ muziko̱re*   **Gr** *miu̱zikal*
N, pl. Ø/-s, mid20c (2)

music box   *n.* 'a juke box'

As with synonymous ↑*juke-box*, the distribution is quite limited, independent or translated expressions being preferred in the individual languages.
Ge *Musi̱kbox* F, pl. -*en*, 1950s (3) > *Jukebox*   **Du** - < *muziekauto-maat*   **Nw** - < *jukeboks*   **Ic** - < *djúkbox*   **It** - < ↑*juke-box*   **Rm** - < rend *cutie muzicală*   **Rs** - < trsl *muzyka̱l'nyĭ ya̱shchik*   **Po** M [U] end20c (2 mod)   **Cr** *mju̱zik-boks* M, pl. -*ovi*, mid20c (3)   **Bg** *mu̱zikboks* M, pl. -*al-ove*, mid20c (1 arch)   **Hu** - < rend *wurlitzer*

music hall   *n.* 1 'popular entertainment'

Ge (0 arch)   **Du** *music-hall* [=E] C, 1930s (1 obs) = *variété*   **Nw** [=E] M, pl. -*s*, mid20c (Ø/1 obs) < *varieté*   **Fr** *music-hall* [myzikol] M, mid19c (1 arch)   **Sp** [=E] M, end19c (1 arch)   **It** [mju̱zikho̱:l] M pl. Ø, end19c (1 tech)   **Rm** [=E] N, 20c, via Fr? (2)   **Rs** *my̱uzik-kho̱ll* M [U] mid20c (2)   **Po** *music-hall* [mju-zikhol] M, mid20c (2)   **Cr** *mju̱zik hol* M, pl. -*ovi*, mid20c (1 tech)   **Bg** *my̱uzikhol* M [U] mid20c (2)   **Fi** [=E] (Ø)   **Hu** [=E] [U] 1970s (1 tech/Ø)   **Gr** <=E>/*miuzik kho̱l* N, end20c (2)

must   *n.* 'a thing that cannot or should not be missed'

Whereas the word is a 'must' in Western Europe in advertising and in colloquial speech in general, it is totally absent from Eastern Europe. Since it is not a necessary word according to denotation, it will be interesting to see whether it will spread any further.
Ge [=E] N, pl. -*s*, 1980s (1 coll) < *Muß*   **Du** [mʏst] C, 1970s (2)   **Nw** [=E/møst] N [U] 1960s (1)   **Ic** [=E] N [U] 1970s (1 coll)   **Fr**

[mœst] M, 1980s (1 mod)   **Sp** [=E] M [U] 1980s (1 tech)   **It** [=E] M, pl. Ø, 1980s (1 mod)   **Gr** *mast* N/adj. [U] 1990s (2 coll, jour)

mustang   *n.* 1 'a wild horse'

Ge [mu̱staŋ] M, pl. -*s*, end19c (Ø)   **Du** (5Sp)   **Nw** [mu̱staŋ] M, pl. -*er* (5Sp)   **Fr** [mystãg] M, mid19c (1)   **Sp** [mu̱stang] (1 tech) > *caballo/mestenco/meste-ño*   **It** [mu̱stang] M, pl. Ø, 1910s (1)   **Rm** [mu̱stang] M, beg20c, via Fr, 1(Ø)   **Rs** *mustang* M, pl. -*i*, beg20c (2)   **Po** [mustank] M, beg20c (2)   **Cr** *mu̱stang* M, pl. -*i*, beg20c (3)   **Bg** *mustang* M, pl. -*al-i*, 20c (2)   **Fi** *mustangi* beg20c (Ø)   **Hu** *musztáng* [mu̱sta:ng] pl. -*ok*, 20c (1 tech)

mute   *n.* 2b 'a pad or cone for damping the sound of a wind instrument', +7 'a device on a stereo player for the same purpose'

Du [=E] 1990s, +7(1 tech)   **Nw** [=E] M, pl. -*r*, 20c (1 tech)   **Ic** - < *dempari*   **It** [=E] M, pl. Ø, 1990s (1 tech)   **Gr** +7(1 writ)

muting*   *n.* 'an amplification mechanism which lowers volume or eliminates background noise'

Nw [=E] M [U] end20c (1 tech)   **It** [mju̱tiŋ] M [U] 1990s (1 tech)   **Rm** [=E] N, 1990s (1 tech)   **Gr** (1 writ)

muzak   *n.* 1 'a system of music transmission for public places', 2 'recorded light background music'

Du [myza̱k] C [U] 1970s, 1(3)   **Nw** <=E>/*musak* M [U] 1970s (2).   **Ic** *músakk* [mu:sahk] N [U] end20c, 2(2 sla)   **Sp** [=E] M [U] 1970s, 1(1 tech)

mystery   *n./cp¹* 'a secret matter', 5 'a work of fiction dealing with a puzzling event'

Ge [=E] cp¹, 1950s, 1(1 tech)   **Nw** (0)   **Ic** *mysterí* N, pl. Ø; *mistería* F, pl. -*ur*, mid20c, 1,5(1 coll)   **Sp** - < *misterio*   **It** [=E] cp¹, mid20c, 5(1) < trsl *del mistero*   **Rm** 5(0)   **Rs** *misteriya* (5Gr)   **Bg** *misteriya* 1(5 La)   **Hu** (5La/Gr)   **Al** *miste̱r* M (5)   **Gr** *mystirio* N, 1(5); cp² *mystiriu* 5(4)

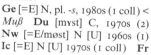

N

nainsook *n.* 'a fine soft cotton fabric, originally Indian'
Fr *nansouk/nanzouk* [nãzuk] M, mid19c (1 tech) **Sp** *nansouk/nansú* M, mid19c (1 tech) **Rm** *nansuc* [nansuk] N [U] beg20c, via Fr (1 rare) **Rs** (5Fr) **Po** *nansuk* [nansuk] M [U] mid20c (1 tech) → *-owy* adj. **Cr** (0) **Fi** [=E/nansok] 19c (1 tech)

name-dropping *n.* 'referring to famous people as being on familiar terms with one, as a form of boasting'
Ge [=E] N [U] 1970s (1 jour, rare) **Du** [=E] C [U] 1960s (1) **Nw** [=E] M/F [U] 1960s (1) **Ic** [=E] end20c (0)

napier* *n.* 'a unit for the attenuation of electrical and acoustical vibration' (phys.) (named after John Napier 1550–1617)
Ge *Neper* [ne:pa] N [U] 1960s (1 tech) **Rs** - → *neperovyĭ* adj. **Po** *neper* [neper] M, 20c (1 tech) **Hu** *neper* [neper] [U] 20c (1 tech) < *NP*

-napping see ↑*kidnapping*

nasty *adj.* 3 'ill-natured, spiteful', (of a person) 6b 'delighting in obscenity'
Du [=E] end20c (1 mod) **Nw** (0) **Ic** [nasti] uninfl., end20c (2 sla)

native speaker *n.* 'a person who has spoken a language from early childhood'
Although most languages have a native equivalent (many of these calqued), the predominance of English in (socio-)linguistics has led to wide acceptability of the English term in scholarly jargon.
Ge (0) < rend *Muttersprachler* **Du** [=E] C, 1980s (1 tech) **Nw** [=E] M, pl. *-s*, 20c (1 tech) **Ic** [=E] M, end20c (0 tech, sla) **Fr** (0) < trsl *locuteur natif* **Sp** - < trsl *hablante nativo* **It** - < trsl *parlante nativo* **Rm** (0) **Rs** - < creat *nositel' yazyka* **Po** [-iker] M, end20c (1 tech) **Cr** - < *izvorni govornik* **Fi** [=E] end20c (1 tech) < *äidinkielen puhuja* **Hu** - < trsl *anyanyelvi beszélő* **Gr** - < trsl *physikos omilitis*

navel (orange) *n.* 'a large seedless orange with a navel-like formation at the top'
Ge *Navelorange* [-a-/-ei-] F, pl. *-n/-s*, 1960s (2+5) **Du** *navel* [-a-] C, pl. *-s* (2) = *navel sinaasappel* **Nw** *navel-appelsin* [=E+Nw] 20c (1 tech) **Fr** [navel] F, 20c (2) **Sp** (*naranja*) *navel/nável* F,

pl. *-s*, 20c (2>3) **It** [navel] F, pl. Ø, end20c (1) < trsl *arancia navel*

necking *n.* +2 'a preliminary form of sexual contact (preceding petting)'
Ge [=E] N [U] 1970s (1 tech) < *Schmusen* **Nw** [=E] M [U] 1970s (1 tech, obs) < *klining* **Hu** [=E] [U] end20c (1 tech) < *szemezés*

Negro spiritual *n.* 'a religious song derived from the musical traditions of African Americans in the southern USA'
The full form appears to have been the first to be adopted in many European languages; now the short form (cf. ↑*spiritual*) is much more common. Whether this is due to general clipping tendencies or because of political correctness is difficult to say.
Ge [=E] N/M, pl. *-s*, 20c (1 tech) **Du** [=E] C, 1940s (2) **Nw** <=E>/*spiritual* [=E] M, pl. *-s*, 1950s (2) **Ic** *negraspiritúal* M, pl. *-ar*, mid20c (1 rare) < rend *negrasálmur* **Fr** (*negro-*)*spiritual* [negrospirityol] M, mid20c (1 tech) **Sp** (*negro*)/ *-spiritual* [=E] M, 1930s < trsl *espiritual (negro)* **It** *spiritual* [=E/spiritual] M, pl. Ø, 1930s (2 tech) **Rm** [=E] 1970s (2 tech) **Rs** (0) **Po** *spirituals* [=E] pl., end20c (1 tech) **Cr** [=E] M [U] mid20c (1 tech) **Bg** - < ↑*spirichuŭl* **Fi** (*negro*)*spiritual* [=E] mid20c (Ø) **Hu** *spirituálé* [ʃpiritua:le:] pl. *-k*, 20c (2 tech) **Gr** [spiritsual] N, pl. *-s*, 20c (1 tech)

nelson *n.* 'a wrestling hold in which one arm is passed under the opponent's arm from behind and the hand is applied to the neck or both arms and hands are applied'
Ge [=E] M, pl. *-s*, mid20c (2 tech) **Du** [=E] C, 1950s (1 tech) **Nw** [nelson] M, pl. Ø/-er, 20c (3 tech) **Ic** [=E] mid20c (Ø) **Fr** [nɛlsɔn] M (1 tech) > *double prise de tête à terre* **Rm** [nelson] M [U] 20c (1 tech) **Rs** *nel'son* M, pl. *-y*, 20c (1 tech) **Po** [-on] M, beg20c (2 tech) **Cr** [=E] M [U] 20c (1 tech) **Bg** *nelson* M, pl. *-a*, 20c (1 tech) **Fi** *nelsoni*, beg20c (3 tech) **Hu** [=E] [U] end19c (3 tech) **Gr** *lavi nelson* F, 20c (5+2 tech)

nerd (nurd) *n.* 'a foolish, feeble or uninteresting person'
Du [nʏrt] C, pl. *-s*, 1980s (1 you) **Nw** [=E/*nærd*] M, pl. *-er*, 1980s (1 sla, you) **Ic** *nörd* [nört] M, pl. *-ar*, end20c (2 sla) **Fi** *nörtti*, 1980s (2 sla, you)

net *v./interj.* 2 'hit (a ball) into the net, esp. of a goal' (sport)
Du *net* (5) **Nw** *nette* ["nɛte] (5) **Fr** [=E] end19c (1

arch) < *let, remettre* **Cr** *net* M, beg20c (1 tech) **Bg** *net* interj., mid20c (1 tech) < *mrezha* **Hu** [=E] [U] end20c (1 tech) < *háló*

net *n./cp²* 6 'a network'
Du (4) **Nw** *nett* [=E] N, pl. Ø, end20c (4) **Ic** [nɛːt] N, pl. Ø, end20c, 6(2) = *Netið* **It** [=E] M/cp², pl. Ø, end20c (1 tech) < mean *rete* **Rm** (0>1 tech) < cp²: *internet* **Cr** (0) **Hu** [=E] [U] end20c (1 tech)

net (ball)* *n.* 'a ball which hits the net' (tennis etc.)
Ge - < trsl *Netzball* **Du** *netbal* (5) **Nw** *nettball* (5) **Fr** *let/balle let* 1990s (1 tech) < *balle de filet* **Sp** *net* M, 1900s (1 tech) = *red* **It** *net* [=E] M, pl. Ø, 1900s (2 tech) < *rete* **Rm** [=E] N, end20c (1 tech) < *net* **Rs** *net-bol* M, pl. -*y* (1 tech) **Po** *net* M uninfl., pl. Ø, beg20c (1 tech) **Bg** *netbol* M, pl. -*a*, mid20c (1 tech) **Hu** [=E] [U] 20c (1 tech)

netting *n.* 1 'a netted fabric', 2 'a piece of this'
Nw [=E/ʺnetiŋ] M [U] 1,2(3)

network *n.* 1 'an arrangement of intersecting horizontal and vertical lines, like the structure of a net', 2 'a complex system of railways, roads, canals, etc.', 3 'a group of people who exchange information, contacts, and experience for professional or social purposes', 4 'a chain of interconnected computers, machines, or operations', 6 'a group of broadcasting stations connected for a simultaneous broadcast of a programme'
Ge [=E] N, pl. -*s*, 1980s, 4(1 tech) < trsl *Netzwerk* **Du** [=E] N [U] 1990s, 4,6(1 tech) < trsl *netwerk* **Nw** [=E] N, 1960s (1 obs) < 1,2,3: trsl *nettverk*; 4,6 *nett* **Ic** [=E] uninfl., end20c, 3,4(0 tech) < *net* N **Fr** (0) < mean *réseau* **Sp** [netwerk] M, pl. -*s*, 3,4(1 tech) = mean *red* **It** [=E] M, pl. Ø, 1980s, 3,4,6 (1 tech) < mean *rete* **Rm** [=E] N [U] 1990s, 4(1 tech) **Rs** *netverk* M [U] 1990s, 4(1 tech) **Po** *net* F [U] 1980s, 1(1 tech); *network* [=E] M [U] 1980s, 4(1 tech) **Cr** (0) **Bg** *netuŭrk* M [U] 1990s, 4(1 tech) > *mrezha* **Fi** - < *verkko/verkosto* **Hu** [netwərk] [U] end20c, 1,3 (1 tech) < 2,4,6: *hálózat* **Gr** <=E> [=E] N, pl. -*s*, end20c, 4(1 tech) < mean *diktio*

New Age *n./cp¹ᐟ²* 'a broad movement characterized by alternative approaches to traditional Western culture, with an interest in spiritual matters, mysticism, holistic ideas, environmentalism, etc.'
Ge [=E] cp¹, 1980s (1 tech, rare) **Du** [=E] C [U] 1980s (2 tech) **Nw** [=E] M [U] 1980s (1) → *New Ager* M **Ic** - < trsl *nýöld* F; *nýaldar-* **Fr** (0) **Sp** [=E] F, uninfl., 1980s (1 tech/mod) **It** [=E] F/cp²/ adj., 1980s (1 tech) **Rm** (0) **Po** <=E> M, uninfl., end20c (1 mod) **Fi** [=E] 1980s (1 tech) **Gr** <=E> [=E] N [U] 1980s (1 tech, jour)

newcomer *n.* +2a 'a (successful) beginner in some activity'
Ge [njuːkama] M, pl. Ø/-*s*, 1960s (1 mod) → -*in* F **Du** [=E] C, 1970s (1 coll/jour) < *nieuwko-*

mer **Nw** (0) **Bg** *nyukamer* M, pl. -*al-i*, 1990s (1 tech, mod_MUSIC) **Gr** *niukamer* M/F, end20c (1 jour)

new deal *n.* 'new arrangements or conditions, esp. when better than the earlier ones'
This term became well known esp. in connection with the policy of Roosevelt and the Democratic party in the USA in 1932; since then, the concept has been of historical relevance.
Ge (Ø) **Du** (Ø) **Nw** [=E] M [U] 1930s (1) → *new-dealer* M **Ic** (Ø) **Fr** (Ø) **Sp** [niu dil] M [U] 1980s (1 tech, jour) **It** [=E] M [U] 1930s (1 tech) **Cr** [=E] M [U] mid20c (1 tech) **Fi** (Ø) **Hu** (Ø) **Gr** - < rend *Neo Proghramma*

Newfoundland *n.* 1 'a dog of a very large breed with a thick coarse coat'
Ge - < trsl *Neufundländer* **Du** *newfoundlander* [=E] M, beg20c (3 tech) = trsl *nyfundlender* **Nw** *newfoundlender* [=E+lender] M, pl. -*e*, 20c (1 tech+5) = trsl *nyfundlender* **Ic** - < trsl *Nýfundnalandshundur* **Fr** - < rend *terre neuve* **Sp** - < rend *terranova* **It** - < rend *terranova* **Rm** - < *(câine) terra-nova* **Rs** *n'yufaundlend* M, pl. -*y*, mid20c (2 tech) **Po** *nowofundlandczyk* [novofuntlanttʃik] M, mid19c (3) **Cr** *njufaundlend* M, end20c (1 tech) → -*er* M **Bg** *nyufaundlend* M, pl. -*al-i*, 20c (1 tech) **Fi** *newfoundlandinkoira* [=E] (3) **Hu** *újfundlandi*, 20c (1 tech)

new look *n.* 1 'a new or revised appearance or presentation, esp. of something familiar', 2 'a style of women's clothing introduced after the second World War, featuring long full skirts and a generous use of material in contrast to wartime austerity'
This term became especially well known through Christian Dior's collection of 1947. Its more general uses, and its application to politics, concentrate on the 1960s, since when the expression appears to have receded – before there was time for it to spread to Eastern Europe.
Ge [=E] M [U] 1950s (1 jour) **Du** [=E] C [U] 1960s (1 tech) **Nw** [=E] M [U] mid20c, 1(1) 2(1 obs) **Ic** [=E] mid20c, 1,2(0) < trsl *nýtt look* **Fr** *new-look* [nju-luk] M/adj., uninfl., 1940s, 1,2(1 arch) **Sp** [njuluk] M [U] 1970s, 1(1 tech, jour); mid20c, 2(1 arch) **It** [=E] M [U] 1940s/70s (1 tech, jour) < trsl *nuovo look* **Rm** [=E] N, end20c, 1,2(0>1 tech) > trsl *nou(l) look* **Cr** [=E] M [U] mid20c (1 tech) **Fi** [=E] 1940s (1) **Hu** [=E] [U] 20c (1 tech, writ) **Gr** <=E>/*niu luk* N, mid20c, via Fr, 1(1 tech)

news *n./cp¹* 1 'information about important or interesting recent events, esp. when published or broadcast'
Ge [=E] F [U] 1960s (1 coll) < *Nachrichten* **Du** *nieuws* (5) **Nw** (0) < *nyheter* **Fr** [njuz] M (0); *news (magazine)* cp¹, 1970s (1 tech) **It** [=E] F, pl., end20c < *(ultime) notizie* **Po** *newsy* [njusi] pl., 1990s (2 coll) **Hu** [=E] [U] end20c (Ø mod) **Gr** *nius* N, pl., 1990s (0 mod/coll)

newsletter *n.* 'an informal printed report issued periodically to the members of a society, business, organization, etc.'
Ge (Ø) **Nw** [=E] N, pl. *-e*, end20c (1 tech, rare) **Ic** - < trsl *fréttabréf* **It** [=E] F, pl. Ø, end20c (1 tech) **Rm** (Ø) **Rs** (0) **Po** [-er] M, end20c (1 tech) **Cr** (0) **Bg** (0) **Hu** (0)

newton *n.* 'the SI unit of force that, acting on a mass of one kilogram, increases its velocity by one metre per second every second along the direction that it acts' (phys.)
Sir Isaac Newton (1642–1727), one of the greatest scientists of all time, president of the Royal Society, formulated the law of gravitation and thus had the unit appropriately named after him.
Ge [=E] N [U] 1950s (1 tech) **Du** [=E] C, 1940s (1 tech) **Nw** [=E] M, pl. Ø, 20c (1 tech) **Ic** *newton/ njúton* [=E] N, pl. Ø, mid20c (1 tech) **Fr** [njutɔn] M, 1950s (1 tech) → *newtoniano* adj. **It** [=E] M, pl. Ø, 1950s (1 tech) → *newtoniano* adj. **Rm** [=E] M, 20c (2 tech) **Rs** *n'yuton* M, pl. *-y*, mid20c (1 tech) **Po** *niuton* M, mid20c (2 tech) **Cr** *njutn* M, mid20c (1 tech) **Bg** *nyuton* M, pl. *-a*, 20c (2 tech) **Fi** [=E/nevton] mid20c (3 tech) **Hu** [=E] [U] 20c (2 tech) **Al** *njuton* M, pl. Ø, 1940s (1 tech) **Gr** <=E> [=E] N, mid20c (1 tech)

new wave *n.* +1a 'any movement in arts and culture promoting avant-garde ideas', 2 'a style of rock music popular in the 1970s', +3 'the hair style or dress of its fans'
Ge [=E] M/F [U] 1980s, 2,+3(1 tech, you) **Du** [=E] C [U] 1970s, 2(1 tech, you) **Nw** [=E] M [U] 1970s, +1a,2(1 tech) = 2: trsl *nyveiv* **Ic** [=E] N [U] 1970s, +1a,2(1 sla) < trsl *nýbylgja* **Fr** [njuwev] M, 1980s, +1a(1 you) **Sp** [=E] M [U] 1980s, 2(1 you) > trsl *nueva ola* **It** [=E] F [U] 1980s (1 tech) **Rm** [=E] N [U] 1990s, 2(1 tech) **Rs** - < trsl *novaya volna* **Po** [=E] F [U] end20c, +1a,2(1 tech) **Cr** [=E] M [U] end20c, 2,+3(1 tech) **Bg** *nyu ueiv* M [U] end20c, 2(1 tech/ you) +3(1 you) **Hu** [=E] [U] end20c (1 tech, you, mod) < trsl *újhullám* **Gr** <=E>/*niu ghueiv* N [U] end20c, 2,+3(1 tech)

nice *adj.* 1 'pleasant, agreeable, satisfactory', 2 'kind, good natured' (of a person)
Du [=E] 20c (1 you) **Ic** *næs* [=E] uninfl., mid20c, 1,2(2 coll) **Rm** 1,2(0)

nicol (prism) *n.* 'a device for producing plane-polarized light, consisting of two pieces of cut calcite cemented together with Canada balsam'
Ge *Nicol/Nikol* [=E] N, pl. *-s*, beg20c (1 tech) < rend *Nicolsches Prisma* **Du** *nicol (prisma)* [nikɔl (prisma)] N, 1940s (1 tech) **Fr** *nicol* [nikɔl]/*prisme de Nicol* M, mid19c (1/4 tech) **Sp** *nicol* M (1 tech) = trsl *prisma de nicol* **It** [nikol] M, pl. Ø, end19c (1 tech) = trsl *prisma di Nicol* **Rm** *prismă nicol* [nikɔl] mid20c (5+1 tech) **Rs** *nikol'* M, pl. *-i*, beg20c (1

tech) **Po** *nikol* [=E] M, beg20c (1 tech) **Cr** (0) **Bg** *nikol* M, pl. *-a*, 20c (1 tech) **Fi** *nicolin prisma* 19c (1,4 tech) **Hu** - < trsl *Nicol-prizma/nikol* **Gr** - < trsl *prisma Nikol*

nigger *n.* (offensive) 1 'a black person'
Ge [=E] M, pl. Ø, mid19c (1 arch) **Du** *nikker* (5) **Nw** [=E] M, pl. *-e*, beg20c (1 arch) **Ic** *niggari* [nɪk: arı] M, pl. *-ar*, end19c (2 coll, pej) **Fr** (Ø) **Rs** (Ø) **Cr** *niger* M, mid20c (1 arch) **Hu** [=E] pl. *-ek*, end19c/ beg20c (1 rare)

night *cp²* +5 'a performance, show, etc. that takes place at night'
Du [=E] C, 1990s, *cp²* (1 you) **Nw** [=E] M, pl. *-s*, 1980s (1) **Hu** *by night* [=E] *cp²* [U] end 20c (2 jour) **Gr** (0,1 writ)

nightclub *n.* 'a club that is open at night and provides refreshment and entertainment'
Most languages prefer calques or other native equivalents to the loanword; those which have the item form an unusual pattern. Note that the word has recently become marginally accepted, in advertising and trendy speech, even where a fully functional equivalent is available.
Ge [=E] M, pl. *-s*, 1960s (0>1 mod) < trsl *Nachtklub* **Du** - < trsl *nachtclub* **Nw** [=E] M, pl. *-s*, mid20c (0/1 obs) < trsl *nattklubb* **Ic** - < trsl *næturklúbbur* **Fr** *night-club* [najtklœb] M, 1960s (1 arch) < rend *boîte de nuit* **Sp** [nait klab] M, pl. *-s*, 1920s (2) **It** <=E>/ *night* [=E/-klœb/-klɛb/-klab] M, pl. Ø, 1910s (3) > rend *locale notturno* **Rm** (0) < rend *bar de noapte* **Rs** (0) < trsl *nochnoĭ klub* **Po** [- klup] M, end20c (2) **Cr** [=E] M, mid20c (2) **Bg** *nait klub* M, pl. *-al-ove*, end20c (1 mod) < trsl *noshten klub* **Fi** [=E] (1 mod) < trsl *yökerho* **Hu** [=E/-klub] pl. Ø/-ok, 1960s (2) **Al** - < trsl *klub nate* **Gr** *nait klab* N, pl. *-Ø/-s*, end20c (2)

nightlife *n.* 'entertainment available at night in a town'
Ge (0>1 mod) < trsl *Nachtleben* **Du** (0) **Nw** (0) < trsl *natteliv* **Ic** - < trsl *næturlíf* **It** - < trsl *vita notturna* **Rm** - < rend *viaţă de noapte* **Rs** - < trsl *nochnaya zhizn'* **Bg** - < trsl *noshten zhivot* **Al** - < trsl *jetë natë* **Gr** <=E>/*nait laif* N [U] 1980s (2 coll, jour) = *nykhterini zoi*

nipple *n.* 3 'a device like a nipple in function, e.g. the tip of a grease gun', 5 (US) 'a short section of pipe with a screw-thread at each end for coupling'
Ge *Nippel* M, pl. Ø, 20c, 5(3) **Du** *nippel* [=E] C, beg20c (3) **Nw** *nippel* [nipel] M, pl. *nipler*, beg 20c, 3,5(3 tech) **Ic** *nippill* [nɪhpɪtl] M,pl. *nipplar*, beg20c, via Da, 5(3 tech) **It** *nipplo* [nipplo] M, pl. *-i*, 20c, 5(3) **Rm** *niplu* [niplu] N, mid20c (3 tech) **Rs** *nippel'* M, pl. *-i*, beg20c (1 tech) **Bg** *nipel* M, pl. *-al-i*, 20c, via Rs, 5(1 tech) **Fi** *nippeli/nippa* 20c, 5(3 tech)

nit *n.* 'a unit of luminosity corresponding to 1 candle per m²' (cybernetics)

Fr *NIT* [nit] M (1 tech) **It** [=E] M, pl. Ø, 1950s (1 tech) **Rm** [=E] M, end20c (1 tech) **Rs** (5La) **Po** <=E> M, mid20c (1 tech)

nobody *n.* 'a person of no importance, authority, or position'

    The word is remarkable for its concentration in Germanic languages and Greek; it is recorded from Goethe in 1776, but appears to have been completely forgotten in German until mentioned again in 1909, and then in the 1970s – a rare case of repeated borrowing.

Ge [nọːbodi] M, pl. *-(ie)s*, 18c/ 1970s (1 mod) < mean *Niemand* **Du** [=E] C, pl. *-ies*, 1980s (2 coll) **Nw** [=E] M, end20c (1 mod) **Ic** *nóboddí* [nouːpɔtːi] N, pl. Ø, mid20c (1 coll) **Gr** <=E> [=E] M, pl. *-s* (1 mod)

no-claim(s) (bonus/discount) *n.* 'a reduction of the insurance premium when the insured has not made a claim within an agreed preceding period'

Du *no-claim (-korting)* [=E] F, pl. *-en*, 1980s (1 tech)

no comment(s) *phr.* 'an evasive reply' (esp. used by politicians)

    The phrase has become increasingly popular in political jargon – even in languages in which a calque is available.

Ge [noːkọment] 1970s (1 mod) < trsl *kein Kommentar* **Du** - < trsl *geen commentaar* **Nw** [=E] end20c (1 coll/fac) < trsl *ingen kommentar* **Ic** [nouːkʰomːɛnt] 1970s (0 sla) **Fr** (0) **Sp** [=E] 1970s (1 fac) = rend *sin comentarios* **It** [nọ kọmmɛnt] 1960s (2 coll, mod) > trsl *nessun commento* **Rm** - < rend *fără comentariu* **Po** - < trsl *bez komentrza* **Bg** - < rend *bez komentari* **Fi** [=E] 20c (1 mod) **Hu** [=E] end20c (1 fac, coll, mod) < trsl *kommentár nélkül* **Al** *no koment* end20c (1 mod) **Gr** [=E] (1 coll/fac/jour) < *udhẹn skholion*

no future* *phr./cp¹* 'an attitude expressing hopelessness (among young people)'

Ge [=E] 1980s (1 you) **Du** [=E] 1980s (1 jour, you, obs) **Fr** (0) **Gr** <=E> [=E] phr./cp², 1980s (1 coll, you)

no man's land *n.* 1 'a the space between two opposing armies' (mil.), 2 'an area not assigned to any owner', 3 'an area not clearly belonging to any one subject etc.'

Ge - < trsl *Niemandsland* **Du** - < trsl *niemandsland* **Nw** (0) < trsl 1,2,3: *ingenmannsland* **Ic** [=E] N [U] mid20c, 2(0) < trsl *einskismannsland* **Fr** [nomanslãd] M, 1910s (1) **Sp** [=E] M [U] 1960s (1 lit, rare) < trsl *tierra de nadie* **It** [=E] F [U] 1910s (1) < trsl *terra di nessuno* **Rm** - < 1,2: rend *ţara nimănui* **Po** - < trsl *ziemia*

niczyja **Cr** (0) **Bg** - < trsl *nichiya zemya* **Fi** - < trsl *ei-kenen-maa* **Hu** [=E] 20c (1) < trsl *senkiföldje*

no-name* *cp¹* 'a cheap product with no (or a fancy) name'

Ge [=E] cp¹, [U] 1980s (1 coll) > *weiße Ware* **Du** - < *wit artikel* **Nw** - < *merkeløs*

nonconformist *n./adj.* 1 'a person who does not conform to the doctrine or discipline of an established church, esp. a member of a (usu. Protestant) sect dissenting from the Anglican Church', 2 'a person who does not conform to a prevailing principle'

Ge *Nonkonformist* M, pl. *-en*, 20c, 1(Ø) 2(3) **Du** *nonconformist* 1(Ø) 2(5La) **Nw** *nonkonformist* [nɔnkɔnfɔrmist] M, pl. *-er*, beg20c (1 tech) → *nonkonformisme* M **Fr** *non-conformiste* adj./M/F, 17c, 1(0); mid19c, 2(3) → *non-conformisme* **Sp** - < 2: *inconformista* **It** *nonconformista* M/F, pl. *-ile*, 1930s, 1(3); *anticonformista* M/F, pl. *-ile*, 1950s, 2(3) **Rm** [nonkonformist] M, 2(5Fr) → *nonconformism* N **Rs** *nonkonformist* M, pl. *-y*, beg20c (1 tech) → *nonkonformizm* M **Po** *nonkonformista* M, mid20c, 2(2) → *nonkonformizm* M **Cr** *nonkomformist* M, beg20c, 1(1 tech) **Fi** *nonkonformisti* 19c (Ø) **Hu** 1,2(5La)

non-fiction *n.* 'literary works other than fiction, including biography and reference books'

Ge F [U] 1960s (1 coll) < *Sachbuch(literatur)* **Du** [=E] C [U] 1970s (1 tech) **Nw** [=E] M [U] 1980s (1 tech, rare) < *sakprosa* **Fr** (0) **It** [=E] F [U] 1980s (1 jour) **Rm** [=E] N [U] end20c (2 tech, rare) **Cr** [=E] M [U] end20c (1 tech) **Fi** [=E] end20c (1 tech)

non-food* *n./cp¹* 'goods other than food'

Ge [nonfut] N/cp¹ [U] 1970s (1 tech, mod) **Du** [nɔnfuːt] adj., 1980s (1 tech) **Nw** [=E] usu. cp¹, 1980s (1 tech) **Fr** (0) **Fi** [=E] 1970s (1 tech)

non-iron *cp¹/adj.* 'that needs no ironing' (of a fabric)

Ge *no iron* [=E] 1960s (1 obs) < *bügelfrei* **Du** - < *strijkvrij* **Nw** (0) < *strykefri* **Ic** - < rend *straufrír* **Fr** (0) < rend *sans repassage* **Rs** *non-ạiron* adj., end20c (1 mod) **Po** *nonajron/*<=E> [nonajron] adj., uninfl./M, mid20c (2) → *-owy* adj.; *-ka* F

non-profit *adj.* 'not involving or making a profit'

Du [nɔnprọfit] 1980s (1 tech) **Nw** [=E] 1960s (1 tech) **It** [=E] uninfl., end20c (1 tech) **Rm** [nonprofit] uninfl., end20c (1 jour) **Po** <=E> uninfl., end20c (1 jour) **Hu** *nonprofit szervezetek* [=E] cp¹, pl., end20c (1 tech)

nonsense *n.* 1a 'absurd or meaningless words or ideas; foolish or extravagant conduct'

    This word is one of the early loans (together with *humour*) from eighteenth-century English literary criticism, and the first of *non*-words borrowed (which as a category are often considered to be English). Its Romance derivation made it open for integration; it is difficult to ascertain how 'English' it is felt to be in the individual languages.

Ge *Nonsens* [nọnsens] M [U] 18c (2) < *Unsinn* **Du** *nonsens* [nɔnsens] C [U] mid18c (3) **Nw** *nonsens* [=E] N [U] mid19c (2) **Ic** *nonsens* [=E] N [U] mid20c (1 coll) **Fr** <=E> M, 1950s (1) < trsl *non-sens* **Sp** [nonsens] M [U] 1920s (Ø tech, rare) **It** <=E>/*nonsenso* M [U] 18c (3) **Rm** [nonsens] N, mid19c, via Fr (3) **Rs** *nonsens* M [U] beg20c (2) **Po** *nonsens* M (2) → *-owny* adj. **Cr** *nonsens* M, 20c (1) **Bg** *nonsens* M [U] beg20c (1 lit) **Fi** [=E] 20c (1) **Hu** *nonszensz* [=E] [U] end19/beg20c (3) → adj. **Al** *nonsens* M, pl. *-e*, 1970s (1)

non-stop *cp¹/²/adv.* 'without stopping or pausing'

This term was first adopted to refer to long-distance flights; its integration was certainly facilitated by the fact that both elements of the word were well known.

Ge [=E] cp¹, mid20c (2) < *Direkt(flug)* **Du** [nonstop] 1940s (2) **Nw** [nonstop] mid 20c (2) **Ic** [=E] end20c (1 sla) **Fr** [nonstop] adj./M, uninfl. [U] 1960s (2) **Sp** [=E] adj., uninfl., 20c (1 rare) **It** [=E] cp²/adv., 1960s (2) **Rm** [=E] adj. uninfl./adv., 1970s (1 mod) **Rs** *non-stop* cp¹/adv., end20c (1 you) **Po** uninfl., end20c (2) **Cr** *non-stop* adj., end20c (2) **Bg** *nonstop* adv., end20c (2) **Fi** [=E] cp¹, beg20c (2 coll) **Hu** [=E/-ʃtop] end20c (2) **Al** *non-stop* adv., 1995 (2 reg, coll) < *papushim* **Gr** *non stop, nonstop* adj./adv., end20c (2 tech)

no problem *phr.* 'something which can easily be dealt with'

The progress of this phrase illustrates the easy acceptance of tags in colloquial usage.

Ge [=E] 1980s (1 coll/you) < trsl *kein Problem* **Du** [=E] 1990s (1 coll, you) < trsl *geen probleem* **Nw** [=E] 1980s (1 coll, fac) **Ic** [=E] excl., end20c (1 sla) < rend *ekkert mál* **Sp** [=E] 1970s (1 coll, fac) < trsl *hay no problema* **It** [no problem] 1980s (1 coll, you) > trsl *nessun problema* **Rm** end20c (0) **Rs** (0) **Po** [-iem] end20c (1 coll) **Cr** (0) **Bg** (0) < rend *nyama problemi* **Fi** [=E] 1980s (1 coll/you) **Al** - < trsl *s'ka problem* **Gr** [=E] end20c (1 coll)

Norfolk* *n.* 'a man's loose belted jacket, with box pleats'

Du *norfolkpakje* [=E] N, 1950s (1 tech) **Fr** [nɔʀfɔlk] M, 1920s (1 obs) **Sp** <=E> M, beg20c (1 obs) **Po** *norfolk* [norfolk] M, end20c (1 tech)

not done *adj.* 'not socially accepted'
Du [=E] (1 mod)

notebook *n.* 2 'a portable computer smaller than a laptop'
Ge [no:tbuk] N, pl. *-s*, 1990 (1 tech) **Du** [=E] N, 1990s (1 tech) **Nw** [=E] M, pl. *-s*, 1990s (1 tech) > trsl *notablokk-(PC)* **Fr** <=E> 1990s (1 tech, ban) < *ordinateur bloc-notes* **Sp** [notbuk] M 1990s (1 tech) <

ordenador portátil **It** [noutbuk] M, pl. Ø, 1990 (1 tech) < *computer portatile* **Rm** [=E] N, 1990s (1 tech) **Rs** *noutbuk* M, pl. *-i*, 1990s (1 tech) **Po** [=E] M, 1990s (1 tech) **Cr** *notbuk* M, pl. *-ovi*, 1990s (1 tech) **Bg** *noutbuk* M, pl. *-a/-butsi*, 1990s (1 tech) **Fi** [=E] 1990s (1 tech) **Hu** [=E] pl. Ø/*-ok*, end20c (1 tech) **Gr** <=E> [=E] N, pl. Ø/*-s*, end20c (1 tech)

notepad *n.* +2 'a computer', +3 'a computer program'
Ge - < *Notebook* **Nw** - < *notebook* **Fr** <=E> 1990s, +2(1 tech, ban) > *ardoise électronique* **It** [=E] M, pl. Ø, end20c (1 tech) **Rs** +2(0) **Po** [- pet] M, 1990s, +2(1 tech) **Cr** (0) **Bg** *noutpad* M pl. *-a/-i/* [U] 1990s (1 tech)

notice *n.* 1 'attention, observation', +2a 'news' (naut.), +3c 'a formal announcement of a ship's readiness to get unloaded or loaded' (naut.)
Ic *nótis* [nou:tis] M [U] mid20c, 1(1 coll) **Fr** (4) **Rs** *notis* M, pl. *-y*, 19c, +3c(1 tech) **Po** *notis* M, mid20c, +3c(1 tech) **Cr** (0) **Bg** *notis* M, pl. *-a/-i*, mid20c, via Rs, +2a,+3c(1 tech) **Fi** *notiisi* 19c, +2a,+3c(5Sw)

novel food* *n.* '(esp.) gene-manipulated food'
One of the most recent arrivals, whose currency is likely to increase with the growing concern about genetic manipulations.
Ge [=E] N [U] 1990s (1 tech, jour) **Nw** - < *genmat*

nugget *n.* 1a 'a lump of gold, platinum, etc., as found in the earth'
Ge [nagət] N/M, pl. *-s*, 19c (Ø/1 obs) **Nw** (0) **Hu** [=E/*nuget*] pl. *-ek*, 19c? (1 tech)

number one *phr.* 'the best, most important'
As with other phrases, the usual way of adoption is by calquing. (Synonyms not related to the English item are here omitted). A recent wave of influence appears to have affected Eastern European countries in particular, or is adding the English phrase to the native equivalent to create a 'modern' synonym.
Ge [nambavan] F [U] 1970s (1 mod, rare) < trsl *Nummer eins* **Du** [=E] C [U] 1990s (1 coll) < trsl *nummeréén* **Nw** (0) < trsl *nummer en* **Ic** [=E] N [U] end20c (0 sla) < trsl *númer eitt* **Fr** - < trsl *numéro un* **Sp** [=E/nambergwan] F, pl. Ø, end20c (1 jour) < trsl *número uno* **It** [=E] M/F, pl. Ø, mid20c (1 mod) < trsl *numero uno* **Rm** [=E] end20c (0) **Rs** *namber uan* M, end20c (1 jour) < trsl *nomer odin* **Po** [-er-] M, uninfl., end20c (1 jour) **Cr** (0) **Bg** *nambǔr uan* M [U] end20c (1 mod) < trsl *nomer edno* **Hu** [=E] mid20c (1) **Hu** [=E] end20c (1 you, fac, mod) < *első számú* **Al** - < *num(u)ri një* **Gr** [namber ʏuan] N [U] end20c (1 jour, mod) < trsl *numero ena*

nurse *n.* +2a 'a woman caring for children'
Distribution reflects the early adoption of the term in the 'high society' in Continental countries at the turn of the century (cf. ↑*miss*).
Ge (0 arch) **Du** [=E] C, 1940s (1 arch) **Nw** (0) **Fr** [nœRs(ə)] F, end19c (1 arch) **Sp** [nurse] F, pl. *-s*,

beg20c (2>3 obs)　**It** [=E] F, pl.
Ø, beg20c (1 tech, arch) < *bambi-
naia*　**Rm** *nursă* [n<u>u</u>rsə/nœrsə] F,
beg20c, via Fr (3 rare)　**Po**
nersal/<=E> [nersa] F, beg20c (1
arch)　**Hu** *nörsz* [nərs] pl. *-ök*,
beg20c (2>3 obs)

nursery　*n.* 1a 'a room or place equipped for young
children'
　Fr [nœrsəri] F, 18c/beg19c (1)　**Sp** <=E> M, end19c
(0>1 jour, rare)　**It** [=E] F, pl. Ø, 1930s (2)　**Rm**
nurserie [nurs<u>e</u>rie] F, 20c, via Fr (2 rare)

nursing　*n.* 1 'the practice or profession of caring for
the sick as a nurse'
　Nw (0)　**Fr** [nœʀsiŋ] M, 1960s (1 tech, ban) > *nursa-
ge*　**It** [=E] M [U] 1970s (1 tech)　**Rm** (0)

nut(s)/nutcase　*n.* 5a 'a crazy or eccentric person'
　Ic *nött* [nœht] N, pl. Ø, mid20c/end20c (1 sla); *nutcase*
[=E] N, pl. Ø, 1970s (1 sla); *nuts* [=E] uninfl., 1970s (1
sla)

nutshell, in a　*phr.* 'in a few words'
　Du *in a/een nutshell* [n<u>y</u>tʃɛl] 1970s (2)　**Nw** (0) < trsl *i
et nøtteskall*　**Ic** - < trsl *í hnotskurn*　**Fi** - < trsl *päh-
kinäkuoressa*

nylon　*n.* 1 'any of various synthetic polyamide fibres
having a protein-like structure, with tough light-
weight, elastic properties, used in industry and for
textiles etc.', 2 'a nylon fabric', +4 'fishing-line made
of nylon'
　Though nylon (and the similar perlon) were in-

vented in 1939, they became well known only after
1945, with reference to ladies' stockings. The material,
and the word, spread regardless of political boundaries, the only variation being whether the loanword is
based on the spoken or the written form.
　Ge [=E] N [U] 1940s, 1(2 obs)　**Du** [najlɔn] C/N [U]
1940s, 1(2); C, 1960s, +4(1 tech)　**Nw** [n<u>ai</u>lon/ny:lɔn]
N/M [U] 1940s (3)　**Ic** *nælon/<=E>* [nai:lon] (freq.
cp[1]) N [U] mid20c, 1,2(2)　**Fr** [niˡɔ] M, 1940s,
1(2)　**Sp** *nilón/nailon* [náilon] M [U] 1940s, 1(2)　**It**
<=E>/*nailon* [n<u>ai</u>lon] M [U] 1940s, 1(3)　**Rm** *nailon*
[najlon] N [U] mid20c, via Fr, 1,2(3)　**Rs** *neilon* M [U]
mid20c, 1,2(3) → *-ovyï* adj.　**Po** [nilon] M [U] mid20c,
1(3) → *-owy* adj.　**Cr** *n<u>a</u>jlon* M [U] mid20c, 1,2(3) →
-ski adj.; *-ke* n.　**Bg** *naïl<u>o</u>n/n<u>a</u>ilon* M [U]/pl. *-al-i*,
mid20c, 1,2(2) → *-ov* adj; *-che* N　**Fi** *nailon* mid20c
(3)　**Hu** <=E>/*nejlon* [=E/n<u>e</u>jlon] pl. *-ok*, mid20c,
1,2(3) +4(1 tech) → adj.　**Al** *najlon* M [U] 1940s,
1(3)　**Gr** *n<u>a</u>ilon* N, mid20c, 2(2); [U] 1(3)

nylons　*n. pl.* 'stockings made of nylon'
　Ge [n<u>ai</u>lons] 1940s (2 arch)　**Du** [n<u>a</u>jlɔns] pl., 1940s
(2) = *nylonkousen/nylonpanty*　**Nw** [=E] 1940s (1
arch) < *(nylon)strømper, strømpebukse*　**Ic** - < *nælon-
sokkar*　**Fr** - < *bas nylon*　**Sp** - < *medias de nylon*　**It**
- < *calze di nylon*　**Rm** - < rend *ciorapi de nailon*　**Rs** -
< rend *neïl<u>o</u>novye chulki*　**Po** *nylony* [niloni] pl.,
mid20c (3)　**Cr** - < *najlonke*　**Bg** - < *nail<u>o</u>novi chor-
<u>a</u>pi*　**Fi** *nailonit* mid20c (3)　**Hu** - < *nylon/nejlonhar-
isnya*　**Al** - < *çorape najloni*

O

obo *abbrev./cp¹* +2 'oil-bulk-ore'
 Du *O.B.O.* [=E] 1980s (1 tech) **Nw** [u̲bu] cp¹, 20c (1 tech) **Fr** [obeo] 1980s (1 tech, ban) < *pétrolier-vraquier-minéralier*

odds *n.* 1 'the ratio between the amounts staked by the parties to a bet, based on the expected probability either way', 2 'the chances or balance of probability in favour of or against some result', 3 'the balance of advantage'
 Nw [=E] M, pl. Ø (3) **Hu** [=E] sg., end19c/beg20c, 1,2(1 tech_HORSE, ³_CARDS)

off *n/cp.* +3 'background (voice etc. in radio/TV productions)'
 Ge [=E] N [U] 1970s (1 tech) **Fr** [ɔf] adj./adv./M, uninfl., mid20c (1 tech, ban) > *hors champ* **Sp** *(voz)en off* [=E] 1960s (2 tech) **It** [=E] M [U] 1970s (1 tech) **Rm** [=E] adv./adj., 1970s (1 tech) **Fi** *voice-off* [=E] mid20c (1 tech)

offbeat *adj.* 1 'not coinciding with the beat' (mus), 2 'eccentric, unconventional'
 Ic [=E] adj., uninfl., end20c, 1(1 tech) 2(1 sla) **Fr** - < 1: *contretemps* **It** [=E] uninfl., 1960s (1 tech) **Gr** <=E> [=E] N [U] end20c, 2(1 tech)

offbeat *n.* 1 'any of the unaccented beats in a bar', +2 'a particular rhythm in jazz and rock'
 Ge [=E] N [U] 1960s, +2(1 tech) **Du** [=E] C [U] 20c (1 tech) **Nw** [=E] N/M [U] end20c (1 tech) **Ic** [=E] N [U] mid/end20c (1 tech) **Rm** [=E] N [U] 1970s, +2(1 tech, rare) < *contratimp* **Rs** *ofbi̲t* M [U] end20c (1 tech, mod) **Po** [-i-] M [U] end20c (1 mod) **Cr** [=E] M [U] mid20c (1 tech) **Bg** *o̲fbii̲t* M [U] end20c, +2(1 tech) **Hu** [=E] [U] 20c(1 tech)

off-Broadway *cp¹/cp²* 'alternative' (theatre etc.)
 Ge [ofbrɔ̲tve:] 1970s (1 tech) **Du** [=E] adj., 1980s (1 tech) **Nw** [=E] 1980s (1) **Ic** (Ø) **Fr** (Ø) 1970s = *festival off* **Sp** cp², 1980s (Ø tech) **It** *off* [=E] cp², 1950s (1 tech) **Po** (0)

office *n.* 1 'a room or building used as a place of business', 3 'the local centre of a large business', +12a 'a storage room'
 Du [=E] N, 1990s, 1(1 tech) < *kantoor* **Fr** +12a(5) **Sp** <=E>/*ofis* [o̲fis] M, pl. Ø, 1930s, +12a(2) **It** [=E] M, pl. Ø, end20c, +12a(1 tech) **Rm** [=E] N, end20c, 1(1 rare) **Rs** *o̲fis* M, pl. -y, mid20c, 1(2) **Bg** *o̲fis* M,

pl. *-al-i*, mid20c, +12a(3); 1990s, 1,3(2) **Hu** [=E] pl. Ø, 20c, via Fr? 1,3(1 tech) +12a(1 tech)

off-line *adj./cp¹* 1 'not directly controlled by or connected to a central processor' (comput.), +2 'referring to breakdowns in an ↑*on-line* system'
 Ge [=E] cp¹/adj., 1970s (1 tech) **Du** [=E] C, 1970s (1 tech) **Nw** [=E] 1970s, 1(1 tech) **Ic** [=E] end20c (1 tech) = rend *sambandslaus* **Fr** [ɔflajn] 1970s, 1(tech, ban) = *autonome* **Sp** [=E] end20c (1 tech) **It** [=E] 1970s (1 tech) **Rm** [=E] end20c, 1(0>2 tech) **Rs** *ofla̲in* M, uninfl., 1990s (1 tech) **Po** [=E] end20c, 1(1 tech) **Bg** *ofla̲in* uninfl., 1990s, 1(1 tech) **Fi** [=E] 1980s (1 tech) **Hu** [=E] [U] end20c (1 tech) **Gr** <=E> [=E] end20c (1 tech) = *ektos liturghias*

off-off* *cp²* 'alternative style' (mainly theatre, music)
 Ge [=E] 1970s (1 tech, rare) **Nw** [=E] 1980s (1) **Fr** <=E> cp¹, M, 1970s (1 tech, obs) **Sp** [=E] 1980s (1 jour, rare) **It** [=E] cp², end20c (1 tech)

off-road *cp¹/²* 2 '(a vehicle) designed for rough terrain or for cross-country driving'
 Ge [ofrɔ̲:t] 1980s (1 mod) < *Gelände-* **Du** *off the road* [=E] 1990s (1 tech) < *terrein-* **Nw** <=E>/*off-roader* M, pl. -e, 1980s (2 mod) → *offroade* v. **Ic** - < *torfæru-* **Fr** - < *4x4 (tous-terrains)* **Sp** [ofrou̲d] M/adj., end20c (1 tech) **It** - < trsl *fuoristrada* **Fi** [=E] 1980s (1) **Al** - < *fuoristrada* (5It) **Gr** <=E> [=E] cp², 1980s (1 tech) < trsl *ektos dhromu*

offset *n./cp¹* 7 'a method of printing in which ink is transferred from a plate or stone to a uniform rubber surface and from there to paper etc.'
 Ge [o̲fset] M [U] beg20c (2 tech) **Du** [ɔfset] C [U] 1940s (1 tech); cp², beg20c (1 tech) **Nw** [=E] M [U] 20c (2 tech) **Ic** [ɔfsɛ:t] cp¹, mid20c (2 tech) **Fr** [ɔfset] M, beg20c (2) → *offsettisti* M/F **Sp** [=E] M [U] 1930s (2 tech) → *offsetista* M **It** [o̲fset] M/adj. [U] 1930s (1 tech) **Rm** <=E>/*ofset* [=E] N, 1940s, via Fr? (2>3 tech) **Rs** *ofse̲t* M [U] mid20c (1 tech) → *-nyï* adj. **Po** [=E] M [U] mid20c (1 tech) → *-owy* adj. **Cr** *o̲fset* M [U] mid20c (1 tech) → *-ni* adj. **Bg** *ofse̲t* M [U] mid20c (2 tech) → *-ov* adj. **Fi** [=E] mid20c (2 tech) **Hu** *ofszet* [=E] [U] beg20c (2>3 tech) **Al** *ofse̲t* M [U] 1960s (1 tech) **Gr** *ofset* N [U] mid20c (1 tech)

offshore *cp¹* +1a '(oil drilling) in coastal waters', +3a 'operating from tax havens', +4 'a speed boat'

The meaning most often found is that relating to oil drilling in coastal waters; note the rarity of calques – as in much of the oil industry. The unrelated (and less transparent) meaning relating to tax havens is much less common.

Ge [=E] 1970s, +1a,+3a(1 tech) **Du** [=E] adj., 1970s, +1a,+3a(1 tech) **Nw** [=E] 1970s, +1a(2) > trsl *utaskjærs* **Fr** [ɔfʃɔʀ] adj./M, uninfl., 1950s, +1a(1 tech, ban); 1980s, +3a(1 tech, ban); 1980s, +4(1 tech) > +1a: *marine*; +3a *extraterritorial* **Sp** [=E] adj., 1970s, +1a(1 tech); 1980s, +3a(1 tech) **It** *off-shore* [=E] M/cp², pl. Ø, 1950s, +1a,+3a(1 tech) +4(2 tech) **Rm** [=E] adj., end20c, +1a(1 tech) **Rs** *off-shor* M, pl. -y, mid20c, +1a,+3a(1 tech_ECON) → *-nyi* adj. **Cr** [=E] adj., end20c, +1a(1 tech) **Bg** *ofshoren* adj., 1990s, +1a,+3a(3 tech) **Fi** [=E] 1980s, +1a,+4(1 tech) **Hu** [=E] 20c, +1a,+3a(1 tech)

offside *adj./n.* 1 '(of a player) in a position, usu. ahead of the ball, that is not allowed if it affects the play' (sport), +2 'dangerous, difficult'

As with other football terms, this word was adopted in most languages around 1900, but replaced by calques in some. The spread to some Eastern languages is a more recent phenomenon.

Ge [=E] N, 1990s, 1(0 arch) < trsl *Abseits* **Du** [=E] 1910s, 1(2) < *buitenspel* **Nw** [=E] mid20c, 1(2) **Ic** [=E] adj., uninfl., mid20c (1 tech) < rend *rangstæður* **Fr** [ɔfsajd] beg20c, 1(1 arch, ban) < *hors jeu* **Sp** <=E>/*orsa/orsai/orsay* [=E] M [U] 1920s, 1(2 tech) < *fuera de juego; en orsay* **It** [=E] M/adj./adv., pl. Ø, 1910s, 1(2 tech) < rend *fuorigioco* **Rm** *ofsaid* [=E] N, mid20c, 1(3) **Rs** *ofsaïd* [U] mid20c, 1(1 tech) **Po** *ofsajd/*<=E> [-t] M, mid20c, 1(2) **Cr** *ofsajd* M [U] mid20c, 1(2) **Bg** *ofsaïd/ opsaïd* M [U] mid20c, 1(1 tech); adj., uninfl., +2(3 tech) **Fi** - < creat *paitsio* **Hu** <=E>/*ofszájd* [=E] end19/beg20c, 1(1 tech, arch) < *lesállás* **Al** *ofsajd* M [U] 1940s, 1(2) **Gr** *ofsaïd* N, beg20c, 1(2)

off the record *phr.* 'as an unofficial or confidential statement etc.'

Ge [=E] 1980s (1 jour, rare) **Du** [=E] 1980s (1 coll, jour, you) **Nw** [=E] 1980s (1) **Sp** [ofderekor] 1970s (1 coll, jour) **Rm** (0) **Rs** (0) **Gr** <=E> [=E] 1990s (1 jour)

off-white *adj.* 'of a white colour with a grey or yellowish tinge'

Ge [=E] 1980s (1 tech, rare) **Du** [=E] 1980s (1 tech) **Nw** [=E] 1980s (1 mod) **Ic** [=E] uninfl., mid/end20c (1 coll) **Gr** *of ghuaït*, 1980s (1 tech, rare)

oh boy *interj.* 'expressing surprise, excitement, etc.'

Du [=E] 1960s (1 coll, obs) **Nw** <=E>/*åboy* [=E/ ɔbɔi] mid20c (2) **Ic** [ou: poj:] mid/end20c (1 sla, you)

OK *adv./adj./interj.* 1 'all right; satisfactory', +2 *adj.* 'in good condition'

This term is certainly among the most widespread anglicisms worldwide. Its provenance from spoken English is clearly testified by the absence of 'native' pronunciations (apart from Norwegian) which are otherwise normal with abbreviations.

Ge [oke:] beg20c, 1,+2(3) → *O.K./Okay* N **Du** <=E>/*oké/okay* [oke:] 1940s (2>3 coll) **Nw** <=E>/ *åkei* [=E/u:kɔ:] beg20c (2/3) **Ic** *ókei* [=E/ou:chei] mid20c, 1(2 coll) = *allt í lagi* **Fr** *O.K.* [ɔke] adj./ adv., uninfl., 1940s (2>3 coll) **Sp** <=E>/*okay/okey* [oke/okei] 1930s, 1(1 coll, fac) → M **It** ok/*okay* [okei] 1930s (3) **Rm** [okej] 1970s, 1(2 coll) **Rs** *okeï* mid20c (1 coll) **Po** [okej] beg20c (1 coll) **Cr** *okej* mid20c (1 coll) **Bg** *o'kei* end20c, 1(2 coll) **Fi** [okei] 1(2); [o:ko:] 1950s, +2(3) **Hu** <=E>/*oké* [o:ke:] mid20c (3) → *-s* adj.; *-z* v. **Al** *okej* 1970s (1 you) **Gr** *okei* adj./interj./N, 1(2 coll) +2(1 coll)

old boy *n.* 1 'a former male pupil of a school', +1c 'an old sportsman', +3 'a competition class for sportsmen over the age of the ordinary competition classes'

Ge (Ø) **Du** (Ø) **Nw** *old boys* [=E] 20c, 1,+3(2) **Ic** *old boys* [=E] cp¹, beg/mid20c, +3(1 tech) = trsl *öldunga-* **Rm** [old boj] 1960s, 1(1 rare) +3(2 tech) **Po** *oldboj/old boj/*<=E> [olt boi] M, beg20c, +3(2) **Cr** *old boj* M, mid20c, 1(2) **Hu** [=E] end19/beg20c, +1c(1 tech/arch) < trsl *öreg fiú*

old girl *n.* +3 'a competition class for sportswomen over the age of the ordinary competition classes'

Nw *old girls* [=E] 20c (1)

oldie *n.* +2 'an old film or song', +3 'a veteran' (in a profession, ironic), +4 'an old car'

This term of affectionate nostalgia seems to be continuing to spread from the colloquial language from the domain of hit songs to other fields, registers, and countries.

Ge [o:ldi] M, pl. -s, 1970s (2 coll) < +4: *Oldtimer* **Du** *golden oldie* [=E] phr., 20c, +2(1 coll) = *gouwe ouwe, ouwetje* **Nw** [=E] M, pl. -s, end20c (1 mod) **Ic** [=E] N, pl. Ø, mid/end20c, +2(1 sla) **Fr** +2(0) **Sp** [=E] M, pl. -s, 1980s, +2(1 tech) **Rm** +2(0) **Gr** *oldi* N, pl. -s, 20c, +2(1 tech)

old-timer *n.* 1 'a person with long experience or standing', +2 'a veteran car'

The distribution of the term is very patchy and somewhat irregular; more conspicuous is the apparent Continental extension to refer to veteran/vintage cars.

Ge [=E] M, pl. Ø, 1960s, 1(1 mod) +2(2) **Du** [=E] C, 1970s (2) **Nw** [=E] M, pl. -e/-s,

1930s, 1(1) **Ic** [=E] M, mid/end20c, +2(0 sla) < *forn-bill* **Cr** *oldtajmer* M, 20c, +2(2) **Hu** [=E] pl. *-ek*, 20c, +2(2) **Gr** *oldtaimer* N, mid20c, +2(2 tech)

on call *phr.* 'available to be called any time' (of a prostitute)
  Po [on kol] end20c (1 jour)

on demand *phr.* 'available at request' (comput.)
  Ge [=E] 1990s (1 tech, mod) **Nw** [=E] 1990s (1 tech) **It** [=E] end20c (1 tech) **Rm** (0) **Rs** (0) **Bg** (0) **Fi** [=E] 1990s (1 tech)

one-man-show *n.* 1 'an entertainment by a single person', 2 'used of businesses etc. run by a single person'
  Ge [=E] F, pl. *-s*, 1970s (1 coll) **Du** [=E] C, 1970s (2 tech) **Ic** [=E] N [U] end20c (1 sla) **Fr** *one man show* [wanmanʃo] M, mid20c, 1(1 coll, ban) > *spectacle solo* **It** [wan mɛnʃou] M, pl. Ø, 1970s, 1(1 tech) **Rm** [=E] N, 1990s, 1(1 jour, mod) **Cr** [=E] M [U] 1970s, 1(1) **Fi** - < trsl *yhden-miehen-show* **Hu** - < rend *egyszemélyes show*

one-night stand *n.* 2 'a sexual liaison lasting only one night'
  Ge [=E] M, pl. *-s*, 1980s (1 you, mod) **Du** [=E] 1980s (2) **Nw** [=E] M, pl. *-s*, 1980s (1 jour, rare) **Fi** - < trsl *yhden illan pysäkki* **Gr** [=E] N, pl. *-s*, 1980s (1 coll, you)

one size *phr.* 'that come in just one size, intended to fit all' (of clothes etc.)
  Ge [=E] end20c (0) < *Einheitsgröße* **Du** [=E] 1980s (1 tech, jour) **Nw** [=E] end20c (1) **Ic** [=E] end20c (0) **Fr** - < rend *taille unique* **It** - < rend *taglia unica* **Rm** - < *măsură unică* **Po** - < trsl *jeden rozmiar* **Bg** (0) **Fi** - < trsl *yhdenkoon* **Hu** [=E] end20c (1 tech/jour, writ) < trsl *egy-méret* **Gr** <=E> [=E] end20c (2)

one-step *n.* 'a vigorous kind of foxtrot in duple time'
  The distribution of this term was widespread in the 1920s (cf. ↑*two-step*), but the dance has long ceased to be popular, and with it the word.
  Ge [vanstep] M [U] beg20c (1 arch) **Du** *one-step* [=E] C, 1940s (1 obs) **Nw** [=E] M [U] beg20c (1 arch) **Ic** [=E] beg20c (1 mod, obs) > trsl *einskref* **Fr** [wanstɛp] M, uninfl., beg20c (1 arch) **Sp** [=E] M, beg20c (1 arch) **It** [wan stɛp] M, pl. Ø, 1920s (1 arch) **Rm** (Ø) **Rs** *uan step* M [U] beg20c (1 tech, arch) **Po** <=E> M [U] mid20c (1 arch) **Cr** [=E] M [U] beg20c (1 arch) **Bg** *uanstep* M [U] beg20c (1 tech) **Fi** [=E] beg20c (1) **Hu** [=E] [U] end19/beg20c (1 arch)

on-line *cp¹/²/adj.* 'directly controlled by or connected to a central processor' (comput.)
  Ge [=E] cp¹/adj., 1970s (1 tech) **Du** [=E] adv., 1970s (1 tech) **Nw** [=E] 1970s (1 tech) **Ic** [=E] end20c (1 tech) = *sambands-* **Fr** [ɔnlajn] adj., 1970s (1 tech, ban) < *en ligne* **Sp** [=E] 1980s (1 tech) **It** [=E] cp²/

adj., 1970s (2 tech) = *in linea* **Rm** [=E] end20c (0>2 tech) **Rs** (0) **Po** [=E] adj., end20c (1 tech) **Cr** [=E] end20c (1 tech) **Bg** *onlaĭn* adj., uninfl., 1990s (1 tech) **Fi** [=E] 1980s (2 tech) **Hu** [=E] end20c (1 tech) **Al** - < *në linjë* **Gr** <=E>/*on lain* adv., 1990s (1 tech) > *se liturghia*

on record *phr.* 'officially; in public'
  Nw [=E] end20c (1)

onshore *adj.* +3 'on the land, as opposed to at sea' (of extraction of oil/gas)
  Du <=E> [=E] 1980s (1 tech) **Nw** [=E] 1980s (1 tech) **Rm** [=E] 1980s (1 tech)

on speaking terms *phr.* 'on friendly terms'
  Du [=E] 1980s (1 mod) **Nw** (0) **Fi** - < trsl *puhevälissä*

on the road *phr.* 'travelling, esp. as a firm's representative, itinerant performer, or vagrant'
  Du [=E] end20c (1 mod) **Ic** [=E] (0) **It** [=E] 1960s (1 tech, jour)

on the rocks *phr.* 'with ice' (of a drink)
  Ge [onzərɔks] 1960s (1 mod) **Du** [=E] 1980s (2) **Nw** [=E] 20c (1) **Ic** [=E] mid20c (0) **Fr** [ɔnzərɔks] 1960s (1 mod) **Sp** [onderɔks] 1970s (1 jour) **It** [=E] 1960s (1 jour) **Rm** (0) **Po** (0) **Cr** (0) **Fi** [=E] 1960s (1 tech) **Gr** <=E> [=E] mid20c (2)

op art *n.* 'optical art; a form of abstract art that gives the illusion of movement by the precise use of pattern and colour'
  Ge [=E] F [U] 1960s (1 tech, obs) **Du** *op-art* [=E] C [U] 1970s (1 tech) **Nw** [=E/upa:rt] M [U] 1960s (1 tech) **Ic** *op(p)list* [ɔ:p-/ɔhp-] 1970s (2 tech+5) **Fr** *op-art/op'art/*<=E>/*op* [ɔpaʀ] M, 1960s (1 tech) **Sp** *op-art* M, 1960s (1 tech) **It** *op-art* [opart] F [U] 1960s (1 tech) **Rm** [=E] [U] 1970s (1 tech) **Rs** *op-art* M [U] mid20c (1 tech) → *-izm* M **Po** [opart] M [U] mid20c (1 arch/tech) → *-owski* adj. **Cr** [=E] M [U] mid20c (1 tech) → *-ist* M **Bg** *opart* M [U] mid20c (1 tech) **Fi** [=E] 1960s (1 tech) **Hu** [=E] [U] mid20c (3) **Gr** <=E> [=E] F [U] mid20c (1 tech)

open *adj./n.* 10 'unrestricted as to who may compete' (of a contest, mainly in tennis or golf), 17 'not restricted as to day of travel' (of a return ticket)
  Of the many English senses, only the tennis term is evidently well known in European languages where it has spread recently with the increasing popularity of the sport.
  Ge [o:pn] F/N, pl. Ø, 1970s, 10(1 tech) **Du** *open* 10(5) **Nw** [=E] M [U] 1980s, 10(1 tech) **Ic** - < mean *opinn* **Fr** [ɔpɛn] adj., 1930s, 10, 17(1 tech, ban) < *(tournoi) ouvert, billet open, billet ouvert* **Sp** [open] adj./M, 1970s, 10(1 tech) = mean *abierto* **It** [open] adj./M, pl. Ø, 1950s, 10(2 tech) 17(1 tech) **Rm** [=E/opən] adj/N,

1960s (1 tech) **Rs** *opén* adj., 1990s (1 tech) **Po** [open] adj., uninfl., end20c, 10,17(1 tech) **Cr** [=E] M [U] end20c, 10(1 tech) **Bg** - < 10: trsl *otkrito* **Fi** [=E] (1 tech) = creat *avoimet* **Hu** [=E] mid20c (2 tech) **Gr** *open*/<=E> N, 10(1 tech); < 17: trsl *anikhtos, -i, -o*

open air *cp¹/adj.* 'out of doors'
Ge [o:pəne:r] 1960s (1 mod) > *Freiluft-* **Du** - < *open-lucht* **Nw** (0) < *frilufts-* **Ic** - < trsl *úti-* **Gr** *open er* N/adj., end20c (1 coll)

open-end* *cp¹* 'having no determined limit' (of discussions, concerts)
Ge [o:pənent] 1970s (1 mod) **Du** - < *open*

operations research *n.* 'the application of scientific principles to business management, providing a quantative basis for complex decisions'
Ge [=E] F [U] 1960s (1 tech, rare) < rend *Unternehmensforschung* **Du** [=E] C, 1990s (1 tech)

orange juice *n.* '(fresh) unsugared juice from oranges'
Nw [=E] M [U] 1960s (1 obs) < *(appelsin)juice* **Ic** [ou:ranstju:s] N [U] mid20c, via Da (2 coll, arch); *appelsínudjús* N/M [U] mid20c (5+2 coll) > *appelsínusafi* **Rm** (0) **Rs** (0) **Po** (0) < *sok poaran'czowy* **Cr** [=E] M, pl. -*a*, (2) < *sok od naranie* **Bg** (0) **Hu** [=E/oranʒ-] pl. Ø, mid20c (2 jour/tech ON LABELS)

orbit *n.* 1a 'the curved, usu. closed course of a planet, satellite, etc.'
Ge [=E] M, pl. -*s*, 1970s (1 mod) < *Umlaufbahn* **Du** [=E] C, 1970s (1 tech) **Nw** (0) < *(omløps)bane* **Fr** *orbite* [ɔʀbit] F (5La) **Sp** *órbita* F (5La) **It** *orbita* (5La) **Rm** *orbită* [orbitə] F, 1960s (5Fr/La) **Rs** (5La) **Po** (5Fr) **Cr** [=E] M [U] end20c (1 tech) **Bg** *orbita* (5La) **Fi** *orbitti* (3) < *kiertorata* **Hu** (5La) **Al** *orbitë* [orbit] F, pl. -*a*, 1960s (1 tech)

organizer *n.* 1b 'a loose-leaf notebook with sections for various kinds of information including a diary, etc.', +1c 'a hand-held microcomputer'
Ge [=E] M [U] 1980s, 1b, +1c(1 mod) **Du** Ø **It** [=E] M, pl. Ø, end20c, 1b(1 mod) **Rs** *organaizer* M, pl. -*y*, 1990s, 1b(2 tech, mod) **Po** *orgenajzer* [orgenajzer] M, end20c, 1b(1 coll) **Cr** (0) **Bg** *organaizer* M, pl. -*al-i*,

1990s, 1b,+1c(1>2 tech, mod) **Hu** [=E/organa:izer] pl. Ø, end20c, 1b(1 tech, jour, mod) **Gr** <=E>/*organaizer* N, pl. Ø/-*s*, 1980s (2)

orienteering *n.* 'a competitive sport in which runners cross open country using a map, compass, etc.'
Nw *orientering* (5Fr.+*ing*) **It** [orjentiriŋ(g)] M [U] 1980s (1 tech) **Po** [-nk] M [U] end20c (1 jour) **Rm** - < rend *orientare turistică* **Bg** - < trsl *orientirane* **Gr** (0) - < mean *prosantolismos*

otter-trawl* *n.* 'a fishing-net specifically for catching otters'
Du [=E] C, mid20c (1 tech) **Rs** *ottertral* M, pl. -*y*,

20c (1 tech) **Bg** *otertral* M, pl. -*al-ove*, mid20c (1 tech)

out¹ *adj./adv.* +1a 'played away' (of a match), 7 'unconscious', 16 'unfashionable', 17a 'no longer taking part', +27 'expelled, no longer a member of a circle or group', +28 'under the strong influence of drugs'
The distribution is complex, as a consequence of the quite divergent meanings of the term. While the distribution of (16) 'unfashionable' is identical to that of its antonym *in*, the earlier sports term *out²* was variously replaced by calques.
Ge [=E] uninfl., 1970s, 16(2 coll) **Du** [=E] 1970s, 16(1 coll); 1970s, +28(1 sla); 1990s, 7(1); - < 1: *uit-wedstrijd* **Nw** [=E] 1970s, 16(1 coll) **Ic** [=E] adv., end20c, 16(1 sla) = trsl *úti* **Fr** [awt] adj./adv., 1970s, 16(1 mod) **Sp** [=E]

1970s, 16,+27(1 mod) **It** [=E] 1900s, 7,16,17a,+27(1 coll) < 7: *fuori di testa*; 16: *fuori moda* **Po** *aut* [=E] uninfl., beg20c, +27(2) **Cr** *aut/biti aut* adv., end20c, 16(1) **Bg** *aut* uninfl., mid20c, 17a(2 tech) +27(2 coll) **Fi** [=E] end20c, 16(1 coll) +27(2) **Hu** [=E] end19c/beg20c, +1a(1 tech) **Al** *aut*, uninfl., end20c, +1a(3) +27(1 mod) < *jashtë* **Gr** *aut* adv., end20c, +1a(1 tech) 16(2 coll)

out² *adv./n.* 17b 'outside the boundary of the playing area' (footb., tennis etc.)
Ge [aut] N, pl. -*s*, beg20c (1 reg, arch) < mean *aus* **Du** [=E] beg20c (2 tech) > *buitenspel* **Nw** (0) < *ute* **Fr** [=E] adj./adv., uninfl., beg20c (1 tech TENNIS, ban) < *dehors* **Sp** [=E] mid20c (1 tech TENNIS) **It** [=E] adj./adv., 1900s (2 tech) = *fuori* **Rm** *aut* [=E] N/adv., beg20c (3 tech) **Rs** *aut* M/adv., pl. -*y*, beg20c (3 tech) **Po** [=E] M [U] beg20c (2) **Cr** *aut* M, beg20c (1 tech) **Bg** *aut* adv./n., mid20c (2 tech) **Hu** [=E] end19/beg20c (1 tech TENNIS) **Al** *aut* M, pl. -*e*, 1980s (3) **Gr** *aut* adv./N (1 tech)

out *v.* 4 'reveal the homosexuality of (a prominent person)'
The verb has been popular in German, Dutch and Norwegian in journalistic and colloquial uses from 1990 onwards, but has apparently not spread any further (cf. the related word ↑*outing*).
Ge [autən] 1990 (1 mod) **Du** - → *outing* **Nw** *oute* ["aute] 1990s (1)

outboard *n./cp¹* 1 '(of a motor) portable and attachable to the outside of the stern of a boat', 2 '(of a boat) having an outboard motor', +3 'a racing sport for boats with outboard engines'
Ge - < 1: rend *Außenborder* **Nw** [=E] M, pl. -*er*, 1930s (1) = *utenbord(s-motor)* **Ic** - < 1: rend *utanborð(smótor)* **Fr** - < 2: trsl *hors-bord* **Sp** [=E] M, pl. -*s*, 1930s < *(motor)fuerborda* **It** - < trsl *fuori bordo*

outcast *n.* 1 'a person cast out from or rejected by his or her home, country, society, etc.'
Ge [=E] M, pl. -*s*, 1960s (1 jour) < *Außenseiter* **Du** [=E] C, beg20c (1 coll) **Nw** [=E] M, pl. -*s*, 1960s (1) < *utstøtt* **Hu** [=E] pl. -*ok*, 20c (1 arch) < *kitaszitott*

outdoor   *cp¹ᐟ²/adj.* +3 'appropriate for out-of-doors activities' (esp. of clothes)
Ge [au̱tdo:r] 1970s (1 mod) **Du** [=E] 1990s (1 coll_SPORT) **Nw** (0) < trsl *frilufts-, utendørs-* **Ic** - < *útivistar-/útilifs-* **Sp** [=E] cp², 1990s (1 tech_SPORT) **It** [autdɔ:r] cp², 1970s (1 tech_SPORT) **Gr** <=E> [=E] adj., end20c (1 tech_SPORT)

outfit   *n.* 1 'a set of clothes worn or esp. designed to be worn together', 2 'a complete set of equipment etc. for a specific purpose'
Ge [=E] N/M, pl. *-s*, 1970s (2 mod); N [U] 1980s, 1(1 jour) < 1,2: *Ausrüstung* **Du** [=E] C, 1970s, 1(1 tech) **Nw** [=E] M/N, pl. *-s*, 1960s, 1(1) **Ic** [au:tfiht] N, pl. Ø, end20c, 1(1 sla) **Rs** *a̱utfit* M [U] 1990s, 1(1 mod) **Cr** [=E] M, end20c, 2(1 tech)

outfitter   *n.* 'a supplier of equipment'
Ge [=E] M, pl. Ø, 1970s (2 mod)

outing   *n.* 4 'the practice or policy of revealing the homosexuality of a prominent person'
Ge [=E] N, pl. *-s*, 1990 (1 mod) **Du** [=E] C [U] 1980s (1 mod) **Nw** [=E] M/F, pl. *-er*, 1990s (1) **Fr** (0) **Sp** [au̱tin] M [U] 1990s (1 tech)

outlaw   *n.* 1 'a fugitive from the law'
Ge (0) **Du** (0) **Nw** (0) **Ic** - < *útlagi* **Fr** [awtlo] M, end18c (1 arch) < trsl *hors-la-loi* **It** - < trsl *fuorilegge* **Cr** - < *izvan zakona* **Hu** [=E] [U] 20c (0>1 tech) < *törvényen kívüli személy* **Al** - < trsl *i jashtligjshëm*

outplacement   *n.* 'the act or process of finding new employment esp. for executive workers who have been dismissed or made redundant'
     This term is a striking instance of the euphemistic use of an anglicism: as the positive action of commerce and management is expressed in English, so is the word for one of the negative consequences.
Ge [=E] N [U] 1980s (1 tech) **Du** [=E] N [U] 1980s (1 tech) > *uitplaatsing* **Nw** [=E] N [U] 1980s (1 tech) **Fr** <=E> M, 1980s (1 tech, ban) > *replacement* **Sp** [=E] M [U] 1980s (1 tech) **Po** <=E> M, 1990s (1 tech)

output   *n.* 2 'the quantity or amount of the product of a process', 3 'the printout, results, etc. supplied by a computer', 5 'a place where energy, information, etc. leaves a system', +6 'efficiency'
Ge [=E] M/N, pl. *-s*, 1970s, 2,+6(1 tech) **Du** [a̱utput] C [U] 1960s, 3(1 tech); +6(1 tech) = 3: *uitvoer, uitdraai*; < +6 *opbrengst* **Nw** [=E] M [U] 1970s, 2,3(1 tech) > trsl *utputt* **Ic** [au:tp(ʰ)uht] N, pl. Ø, 1970s, 3,5(1 tech) = rend *úttak, frálag* **Fr** [awtput] M, 1960s, 2(1 tech, ban) < *produit de sortie, sortie* **Sp** [=E] M, pl. *-s*, 1970s, 2,3(1 tech) **It** [=E] M [U] 1900s, 2(1 tech); 1960s, 3(1 tech) **Rm** [=E] N, 1980s, 3,5(1 tech) **Rs** 3(0) **Po** <=E> M [U] 1980s, 2,3(1 tech) **Cr** [=E] M [U] end20c, 2(1 tech) **Bg** *a̱utput* M [U] 1990s, 3(1

tech) **Fi** [=E] end20c, 2,+6(1 tech) **Hu** [=E] [U] end20c, 3,+6(1 tech) **Gr** <=E> [=E] N, end20c, 3(1 tech) > *exodhos*

outrigger   *n.* +3a 'a boat fitted with spats projecting over a ship's side'
Ge [=E] M, pl. Ø, beg20c (1 arch) **Du** [=E] C, 1980s (1 tech) **Nw** *utrigger* [Nw+E] M, pl. *-e*, beg20c (5+1 tech) **Fr** [awtʀigœr] M, end19c (1 tech) **Sp** <=E> M, pl. *-s*, 1920s (1 tech) **It** [=E] M, pl. Ø, end19c (1 tech) **Rs** *autriger* M, pl. *-y*, beg20c (1 tech)

outside   *adv.* 1 'on or to the outside (of a playing field)'
Ge [au̱tsait] beg20c (1 reg) < *Aus* **Nw** (0) < *ute* **Rm** - < *aut* **Rs** (0) **Po** (0) **Cr** (0) **Fi** [=E] 20c (1)

outside   *n.* 7 'an outside player in football, etc.'
Ge [=E] M, pl. *-s*, beg20c (1 reg) < *Außenstürmer* **Du** - < *buitenspeler* **Fr** - < *ailier* **It** - < *ala* **Rs** (0) **Po** (0) **Bg** - < creat *vŭnshen igrach*

outsider   *n.* 1a 'a non-member of some circle, party, profession, etc.', 2 'a person not fit to mix with good society', 3 'a competitor, applicant, etc. thought to have little chance of success'
     This term was first adopted in the context of horse-racing in the late nineteenth century but has since spread to many other domains; note that fewer calques are available than might have been expected.
Ge [=E] M, pl. Ø, end19c, 1a,3(1) < *Außenseiter* **Du** [=E] C, beg20c, 1a(2 coll) 3(2 tech) < 1a: *buitenstaander* **Nw** [=E] M, pl. *-e*, beg20c, 1a,3(2) **Ic** [=E] M, pl. *-ar*, end20c, 1a,2(1 sla) **Fr** [awtsajdœr/utsidɛr] M, 19c, 1a(2 tech, mod) 3(2 tech) **Sp** [autsa̱ider] M, pl. *-s*, 1920s, 1a,3(1 tech) **It** [autsa̱ider] M, pl. Ø, end19c (2) **Rm** [=E/autsi̱der] M, mid20c, 1a,3(2) **Rs** *autsa̱ider* M, pl. *-y*, beg20c, 1a,3(1 tech) **Po** *autsajder*/<=E> [-er] M, mid20c, 1a,2(1 tech) **Cr** *autsa̱jder* M, pl. *-i*, mid20c, 1a(1) 3(1 tech) **Bg** *a̱utsa̱ider* M, pl. *-i*, mid20c, 1a(2) 3(2 tech) **Hu** [=E] M, pl. *-ek*, end19/beg20c, 3(1 tech); 20c, 1a(1) < *kívülálló* **Al** *autsajder* M, pl. *-ë*, 1990s (1 tech) **Gr** *autsa̱ider* M/N, pl. Ø/*-s*, mid20c (2)

outsourcing   *n.* 'the action of contracting (work) out'
Ge [=E] N [U] 1990s (1 mod) **Du** [=E] C [U] 1990s (1 mod) **Nw** [=E] M [U] 1990s (1 tech) → *outsource* v.

over   *adv.* 11 'said to indicate that it is the other person's turn to speak' (in radio conversations etc.)
Ge [o̱:va] end20c (1 tech) **Nw** (4) **Po** [-er] end20c (1 tech) **Gr** [o̱ver] 20c (1 tech)

overall   *n.* 1 'an outer garment worn to keep out dirt, wet, etc.', 2 (in pl.) 'protective trousers, dungarees, or a combination suit worn by workmen, etc.', +4 'a sports ski garment'
     The spread from the early twentieth century onwards has made this term practically universal – with the exception of Romance and a few peripheral languages. The meaning was variously extended to

include dresses of similar patterns - even cocktail dresses and ski garments.

Ge [o̲:vəral] M, pl. *-s*, 1930s, 2(2) **Du** [=E] C, 1940s, 2(2) **Nw** <=E>/*overalls* [ɔ̲]:veral(s)/-ɔl(s)] M, pl. *-er*, beg20c, 2(2) **Ic** *óverols* [=E] M, pl. *-ar*, beg/mid20c, 2(1 coll, arch) < rend *samfestingur* **Sp** <=E>/*overoles*

beg20c, 2(1 rare) < *mono* **Rs** *overol* M, pl. *-y*, 1990s, +4(1 tech) **Po** *owerol/overol/overoll* [overol] M, pl. *owerole*, beg20c, 2,+4(2) **Cr** *overal* M, pl. *-i*, mid20c, 2(1) **Bg** *overal̲l/overo̲l* M, pl. *-al/-i*, end20c, +4(1 tech, rare) **Hu** <=E>/*overál* [o̲vera:l] pl. *-ok*, beg20c, 2(3); mid20c, +4(3)

overarm *n./cp¹* 2 'applied to a swimming stroke in which one or both arms are lifted out of the water.'
Fr *over (arm stroke)* [ɔvɛʀ aʀmstʀok] M, 19c (1 tech, arch) **It** *over* [ɔ̲ver] M, pl. Ø, 1930s (1 tech) = *nuoto/ stile alla marinara* **Rs** *overarm* M [U] beg20c (1 tech) **Po** *ower* [over] M [U] mid20c (1 tech)

overbooking *n.* 'the act of making too many bookings for an aircraft, hotel, etc in relation to the space available'
Du [=E] C [U] (1 tech) **Nw** [=E] C [U] 1960s (2) **Ic** - < trsl *yfirbókun* **Fr** - < *surbooking* **Sp** [oberbu̲kin] M [U] 1970s (1 tech, ban) > *surréservation* **It** [=E] M [U] end20c (1 tech) **Cr** - < trsl *prebuki̲ranje*

overdone *adj.* 1 'carried to excess, taken too far'
Du [ovərdy̲n] uninfl., 1970s (1 coll) **Nw** (o)

overdose *n.* 'an excessive dose (of drugs etc.)'
Ge - < trsl *Überdosis* **Du** - < trsl *overdosis* **Nw** - < trsl *overdose* **Ic** *óverdós* [=E] N/F [U] 1970s (1 sla) **Fr** [ɔvœʀdoz] F, 1970s (1 sla) > *surdose* **Sp** [oberdo̲se] F [U] end20c (1 sla) < trsl *sobredosis* **It** [overdo̲se] F, pl. Ø, 1970s (1>2 tech) **Rm** *overdoză* [overdo̲zə] F [U] end20c (1 sla) **Cr** (o) **Bg** - < trsl *svrŭkhdoza* **Hu** [o̲:verdo̲z] [U] end20c (1 tech) **Al** - < *mbidozë* **Gr** [=E] F, end20c (1 sla) < rend *ypervoliki dhosi*

overdose *v.* 'give or take an excessive dose (of a drug etc.)'
Ic [ou:verdou:sa] 1970s (1 sla)

overdraft *n.* 1 'a deficit in a bank account caused by drawing more money than is credited to it', 2 'the amount of this'
Ic - < *yfirdráttur* **It** [=E] M, pl. Ø, 1970s (1 tech) **Rm** [=E] N, 1990s (o>1 tech) **Rs** *overdraft* M, pl. *-y*, 1990s (1 tech_ECON) **Bg** *ovŭrdraft* M [U] pl. *-al/-ove*, end20c (1 tech) **Hu** [=E] [U] end20c (1 tech)

overdressed *adj.* 'dressed with too much display or formality'
Ge [=E] uninfl., 1960s (1 jour, fac) **Du** [=E] 1985 (1 jour, you)

overdrive *n.* 1b 'an additional speed-increasing (or energy-saving) gear'

Ge [o̲:vadraif] M, pl. *-s*, 1960s (1 tech) **Du** [=E] C, 1970s (1 tech) **Nw** [=E] M [U] 1970s (1 tech) **Fr** M, 1960s (1 tech) **Sp** N [U] 1980s (1 tech) **It** [o̲verdra̲iv] M, pl. Ø, 1960s (1 tech) **Rm** [ovərdrajv] N, end20c (1 tech) **Po** [-er-] M [U] end20c (1 tech) **Cr** *overdrajv* M [U] end20c (1 tech) **Fi** [=E] 1960s (1 tech) **Hu** [=E] [U] 20c (1 tech) **Gr** <=E>/*overdra̲iv* N [U] end20c (1 tech)

overfishing *n.* 'the act of depleting (a stream, stock of fish, etc.) by too much fishing'
It [=E] M [U] end20c (1 tech)

overhaul *v.* 1b 'examine the condition of (and repair if necessary)'
Ge - < trsl *überholen* **Nw** *overhale* ["o̲:verha:le] 19c (3) → *overhaling* M/F **Ic** - < *yfirhala*

overhead *n.* 'overhead expenses'
Du [=E] C [U] 1970s (1 tech) = *overhead-kosten* **Nw** [=E] M [U] 1970s (1 tech) **Po** [=E] M, end20c (1 tech)

overhead (projector) *n.* 'a device that projects an enlarged image of a transparency on to a surface above and behind the user'

The device became widely available as an aid to teaching in West European countries in the 1960s; the distribution of the term is therefore restricted by economic reasons in the east and by the use of calques mainly in Romance languages. The much more restricted distribution as an economic term (above) is interesting.

Ge [o̲:vahet] M, pl. *-s*, 1970s (1 tech+3) **Du** *overheadprojector* [=E+- pro:jɛktor] C, 1970s (1 tech) **Nw** *-prosjektør/-projektor* [=E+Nw] M, pl. *-er*, 1960s (2/3) **Ic** - < creat *myndvarpil-varpa* **Fr** - < *rétroprojecteur* **Sp** - < *retroproyector* **It** - < *lavagna luminosa* **Rm** - < *retroproiector* **Po** - < *grafoskop* **Bg** - < *shra̲ibproektor* **Fi** [=E] 1970s (1 tech) < mean *piirtoheitin*

overkill *n.* 1 'the amount by which destruction or the capacity for destruction exceeds what is necessary for victory or annihilation', +1a 'used metaphorically in other contexts'

Ge [o̲:vakil] M [U] 1960s, 1(1 tech); 1970s, +1a(1 jour) **Du** [=E] C, 1970s, +1a(1 jour) **Nw** [=E] M [U] 1970s (1 tech) **Po** [over-] M [U] end20c, 1(1 tech) **Fi** [=E] 1970s, 1(1 tech) **Hu** [=E] [U] end20c, 1(1 tech)

overknees* *n.* 'stockings extending over the knee'
Ge [=E] pl., 1970s (1 tech, obs)

overlap *v.* 3 '(of two things) partly coincide; not be completely separate'
Ge - < trsl *überlappen* **Du** *overlappen* 1980s (1 mod) **Nw** *overlappe* ["o̲:verlape] 20c (3) → *overlapping* M/F

overlap *n.* 1 'an instance of overlapping', 2 'the extent of this'
Du [=E] C, 1980s (1 mod) < *overlapping* **Nw** *overlapp* ["o̲:verlap] M/N [U] 1960s (3) < *overlapping* **Ic** - < *skörun* **It** [=E] M [U] 1970s (1 tech)

overlay *n./cp¹* +3c 'a particular structure given to a program in order to save it in an otherwise insufficient memory space' (comput.), +5 'modern telecommunication (-network)'
Ge [=E] N? [U] 1980s (1 tech, rare) **Du** (o) **It** [=E] M [U] 1970s, +3c(1 tech)

overlock* *n.* 1 'a kind of sewing', 2 'a kind of sewing machine'
Nw [=E] M [U] 20c, 1(1 tech) **Ic** [=E] N [U] (freq. cp¹) end20c, 1(1 tech) **Fr** - < 2: *surjeteuse* **Rm** [=E] N [U] mid20c, 2(1 tech) **Rs** *overlok* M, pl. *-i*, end20c (3 tech) **Po** *owerlok*/<=E> [overlok] M [U] mid20c (2) **Bg** *overlog* M [U]/pl. *-a*, mid20c (3)

oversexed *adj.* 'having unusually strong sexual desires'
Du *oversekst* [ovərsɛkst] uninfl., 1970s (3 coll) **Nw** (o) **Bg** *overseks* uninfl., 1990s (3 sla)

oversized *adj.* 'of more than the usual size' (of dresses)
Ge [o:vasaist] uninfl., 1980s (1 mod) **Du** [=E] uninfl., 1980s (2) **Nw** [=E] 1980s (1 mod) **Ic** [=E] uninfl., end20c (o) < trsl (i) *yfirstærð* **It** *oversize* [=E] uninfl., 1980s (1 tech, mod)

over there *phr.* 'in the USA'
Nw [=E] mid20c (1)

overtime *n.* 3 'extra time in a sporting contest' (sport)
Nw (o) < *overtid* **Ic** - < rend *framlenging* **It** [=E] M [U] 1960s (1 tech) < rend *tempi supplementari* **Rm** - < creat *prelungiri* **Rs** *overtaïm* M [U] end20c (1 tech) **Bg** (o) **Fi** - < trsl *aikalisä* **Hu** - < rend *túlmunka, túlóra*

oxer *n.* 2 'an obstacle similar to an ox-fence used in showjumping'
For an early term of horse racing (and a formally easy one, too) one might have expected a wider distribution: apparently it remained restricted to a 'Central European' culture.
Ge [oksa] M, pl. Ø, beg20c (3 tech) **Du** [=E] C, 1970s (1 tech) **Fr** [ɔksɛʀ] M, 1920s (1 tech) **Sp** [okser] M, 1970s (1 tech, rare) **It** [ɔkser] M, pl. Ø, 1960s (1 tech) **Hu** *okszer* [okser] pl. Ø, 20c (1 tech)

oxford* *n.* 'a cotton cloth for shirts'
Ic [=E] N [U] end19c (2 obs) **Sp** [oksford] M, 20c (1 tech, rare) **It** [ɔksford] M, pl. Ø, 19c (1 tech) **Rm** [=E] N [U] mid20c (2 tech) **Cr** *oxford* M, pl. Ø, beg20c (1 tech) **Bg** *oksford* M [U] beg20c (1 tech, arch)

P

pace *n.* 2 'a speed in walking or running', +6 '(having) somebody who increases or keeps up the speed' (sport)
Ge [=E] F [U] 1890s, 2(1 tech)　**Du** [=E] C, 1910s, 2(1 tech)　**Nw** [=E/pe:s] M [U] mid20c (2)　**Rs** *peïs* M, mid20c, +6(1 tech)

pace *v.* 3 'set the pace for (a rider or runner etc.)' (sport), +5 intr. 'rush'
Ge *pesen* [pe:zn] 19c, +5(1 coll, reg)　**Du** *pacen* [pɛisə(n)] 19c (1 tech) < *pezen*　**Nw** ["pe:se/"peise] beg20c, 3(1)

paceclock* *n.* 'a device that measures the speed of a runner' (sports/races)
Bg *peïsklok* M, pl. *-al-ove*, end20c (3 tech)

pacemaker *n.* 1 'a competitor who sets the pace in a race', 2 'a natural or artificial device for stimulating the heart muscle and regulating its contractions' (med.)

The distribution is clearly divided between the homonymous sports and medical terms: although the use of the term in cycle races must be widespread, there is little linguistic evidence. By contrast, the term for the heart implant has spread to most European countries as a loanword or a calque from the 1960s.

Ge [pe:sme:ka] M, pl. Ø, beg 20c, 1(0 arch); 1970s, 2(0) < 1: trsl *Schrittmacher*, 2: trsl *(Herz-) Schrittmacher*　**Du** [=E] C, beg20c, 1(1 tech); 1960s, 2(1 tech)　**Nw** [=E] M, pl. *-e*, beg20c, 1(2); 1960s, 2(1) < 2: rend *hjertestimulator*　**Ic** [=E] M, pl. *-ar*, 1960s, 2(1 tech, obs) < 2: rend *(hjarta)gangráður*　**Fr** [pɛsmɛkɛʀ] M, 1960s, 2(1 tech, ban) < 2: *stimulateur (cardiaque)*　**Sp** - < trsl *marcapasos*　**It** [=E/pɛsmeɪker] M, pl. Ø, 1960s (2 tech)　**Rm** [=E] M, 1960s, 2(1 tech) 1(0)　**Po** [-er] M, end20c, 1(1 tech)　**Cr** *pejsmejker* M, pl. *-i*, end20c, 2(2)　**Bg** *peïsmeïkŭr* M, pl. *-al-i*, end20c, 2(1 tech)　**Fi** - < 2: *tahdistin*　**Hu** [pe:sme:ker] pl. *-ek*, end19/beg20c, 1(1 tech, arch); mid20c, 2(2) < 1: *lépésjelző*　**Gr** - < trsl *vimatodhotis*

pacer* *n.* 'a pacemaker' (sport)
Nw [=E] M, pl. *-e*, 20c (1)

pack *n./cp²* 1a 'a collection of things wrapped up or tied together for carrying', 9 'an area of pack ice'
Ge *Pack* [a] N/M, cp², pl. *-s*, 1970s, 1a(4)　**Du** [=E] N, 1990s, 1a(1 tech_COMPUT_)　**Nw** <=E>/-*pakk* [=E/pak] cp²/M, 1980s, 1a(2) < *pakning, pakke*　**Ic** *pakki* 17c, 1a(5)　**Fr** [pak] M, 1980s, 1a(2)　**Sp** [pak] M, pl. *-s*, 1970s, 1a(1 tech)　**It** [pak] M [U] end19c, 9(1 tech)　**Hu** (5Ge)　**Al** *pako* F, pl. Ø, 1950s, 1a(1 tech)　**Gr** *pako* N, 19c/20c, 1a(3 tech 5It)

package *n.* 2 'a set of proposals or items offered or agreed to as a whole', 3 'a piece of software suitable for various applications rather than one which is custom-built' (comput.), 4 'a package holiday', +5 'a set of documents'
Ge (0)　**Du** [=E] N, 1980s, 3,+5(1 tech)　**Nw** (0) < 2,3,4: *pakke(-)*　**Ic** - < 2,3,4: *pakki*　**Fr** [pakɛdʒ] M, 1970s, 3(1 tech/ban); 4(1 tech, ban); +5(1 tech) < 3: *progiciel*; < 4: *forfait*　**It** [=E] M, pl. Ø, 1970s, 2,3(1 tech) < trsl *pacchetto*　**Rm** - < trsl *pachet* 3(5 tech)　**Po** - < *pakiet* (5Fr)　**Bg** - < 3: trsl *paket*　**Hu** [=E] cp¹ [U] end20c, 4(2 jour, mod); end20c, 3(1 tech)　**Al** - < *paketë*　**Gr** <=E> [=E] N, end20c, 3(0 tech)

package deal *n.* 2 'a set of proposals or items offered or agreed to as a whole'
Ge [=E] M/N, pl. *-s*, 1960s, 2(1 jour, tech)　**Fr** *package* [pakɛdʒ] M, 1970s (1 tech, ban) < *forfait*　**Sp** - < rend *paquete (vacacional)*　**Cr** (0)　**Bg** - < rend *paket uslugi*

package tour *n.* 1 'a tour with all arrangements made at an inclusive price'
Ge [=E] F, pl. *-en*, 1980s (1 mod) < *Pauschalreise*　**Nw** - < trsl *pakketur*　**Ic** - < trsl *pakkaferð*　**Sp** - < *paquete (vacacional)*　**It** - < mean *pacchetto*　**Rs** (0)　**Cr** (0)　**Bg** - < rend *paket*　**Fi** - < *pakettimatka*　**Hu** [=E] [U] 1980s (1 tech, jour)

packaging *n.* 2 'the process of packing goods'
Fr [pakɛdʒiŋ] M, 1970s (1 tech, ban) > *emballage, conditionnement*　**Sp** <=E> [pakaxin] M [U] end20c (1 tech, rare) < *embalaje*　**It** [=E] M [U] 1970s (1 tech) < *imballaggio*

packet-boat *n.* 'a mailboat or passenger ship'
Ge - < trsl *Paketboot*　**Fr** *paquebot* [pakbo] M, 18c (3)　**Sp** *paquebot/paquebote* M, via Fr (3) = *paquete*　**Rm** *pachebot* [pakebot] N, beg19c, via Fr (3)　**Rs** *paketbot* M, pl. *-y*, 19c (1 arch)　**Po** *paketbot* [paketbot]

M, mid19c (1 arch) **Bg** *pak*<u>*e*</u>*tbot* M, pl. *-al-i*, beg20c (1 tech, arch) **Hu** [=E] [U] pl. Ø, 18c (1 tech, arch)

pack ice   *n.* 'an area of large crowded pieces of floating ice in the sea'

The distribution is characterized by the native look of the word in Germanic languages (which makes its status as an anglicism difficult or impossible to determine) and widespread clipping, which was at least partly mediated through French (cf. ↑*pack*).

Ge - < trsl *Packeis* **Du** *pakijs* (5) **Nw** (0) < *pakkis* (4) **Ic** - < *íshella* **Fr** *pack* M, 19c (1 tech) **It** *pack* [pak] M, pl. Ø, end19c (1 tech) **Rm** *pack* [=E] N, pl. *-uri*, 1960s, via Fr (2 tech) **Rs** *pak* M [U] end19c (1 tech) < trsl *p*<u>*a*</u>*kovyĭ lëd* **Po** *pak*/*pakajs* [pak/pakais] M, beg20c (1 tech) **Bg** - < trsl *pakov led*

paddle   *n.* 1 'a short broad-bladed oar used without a rowlock', 2 'a paddle-shaped instrument'

Ge *Paddel* N, pl. Ø, 19c, 1(3); end20c, 2(1 tech) **Du** *paddel* [=E] C, 19c (3) = *peddel* **Nw** *paddel* [p<u>a</u>del] M, pl. *padler*, beg20c (3) **Rm** *padelă* [pad<u>e</u>lə] F, mid20c, via Ge (3 tech) **Bg** *p*<u>*e*</u>*dŭls* M, pl. *-al-i*, mid20c, 2(1 tech) **Hu** [=E] [U] 20c, 1(1 tech) < *kajakevező*

paddle   *v.* 1 'move on water or propel a boat by means of paddles'

Ge *paddeln* 19c (3) → *Paddler* M **Du** *paddelen* [p<u>ɛ</u>dələ(n)] 19c (3) = *peddelen* **Nw** *padle* ["p<u>a</u>dle] 19c (3) → *padler* M; *padling* M/F **Rm** *padela* [pad<u>e</u>la] 1960s, via Ge (3 tech) **Hu** *paddliz* [p<u>a</u>dliz] 20c, via Ge (3)

paddle boat   *n.* +1a 'a rowing boat'

Ge *Paddelboot* N, pl. *-e*, 19c (3) **Du** *paddelboot* (3+5) = *peddelboot* **Fr** (Ø)

paddock   *n.* 1 'a small field, esp. for keeping horses in', 2 'a turf enclosure adjoining a racecourse where horses or cars are assembled before a race', +4 'a bed'

This word was adopted in connection with horse racing at an early date but has never spread beyond the domain and has never reached many languages, particularly in the east.

Ge [=E] M, pl. *-s*, end19c, 1(1 tech, rare) < *Koppel* **Du** [=E] C, beg20c (1 tech) **Nw** [=E] M, pl. *-er*, beg20c, 1(1 tech) **Fr** [pad<u>ɔ</u>k] M, 19c, 1(1 tech) +4(1 sla, arch) **Sp** [pad<u>o</u>k] M, beg20c, 1,2(1 tech) **It** [p<u>e</u>dok] M, pl. Ø, 18c, 1,2(1 tech) **Rm** *padoc* [pad<u>o</u>k] N, beg20c, via Fr (3 tech) **Po** *padok*/<=E> [pad<u>o</u>k] M, beg20c, 1(1 tech) **Fi** [=E] 19c, 1(1 tech)

paddy   *n.* 2 'rice before threshing or in the husk'

Ge [=E] M [U] beg20c (1 tech) **Du** *padie* (5) **Nw** *paddy* [p<u>æ</u>di-] cp[1], 1970s (1 tech) **Fr** [padi] M, uninfl. [U] 18c (1 tech) **Sp** [=E] M (1 tech, rare) **Hu** [=E] [U] 20c (1 tech)

pads*   *n. pl.* 'a piece of soft material for cleaning the skin' (cosmetics)

Ge [pets/pats] pl., 1960s (1 tech) **Du** [=E] 1980s (1

tech, jour) **Nw** [=E] M/cp[2], pl. Ø, 1980s (1 tech) **Hu** [=E] [U] end20c (0/1 writ, jour)

pager   *n.* 'a radio device with a bleeper, activated from a central point to alert the person wearing it'

The spread of this term apparently continues, but it is restricted to specialists; elsewhere the more colloquial ↑*beeper* (or native equivalents) seem to be more widely accepted.

Nw (0) < *personsøker* **Fr** *pager* M, 1980s (1 mod) → *paging* **Rm** [=E] N, 1990s (1 tech, mod) **Rs** *p*<u>*e*</u>*ĭdzher* M, pl. *-y*, 1995 (1 tech) → *-nyĭ* adj.; *-ing* N; *-ovyĭ* adj. **Po** [-er] M, end20c (1 mod) **Cr** *pejdžer* [=E] M, pl. *-i*, end20c (1 tech) **Bg** *p*<u>*e*</u>*ĭdzhŭr* M, pl. *-al-i*, 1990s (1>2 tech, mod) **Hu** - → *paging* < *személyi hívórendszer*

pageturner   *n.* 'a book that is so exciting that one has to keep on reading (and therefore turns the pages)'

Nw [=E] M, pl. *-s*, 1980s (1)

painkiller   *n.* +2 'a-jack-of-all-trades'

This word illustrates a unique development in Bulgarian. Once used as a tradename for a medicine (and likely to have been more widespread at the time; cf. the German product named *pain expeller* which was widely known around 1900), it became extended to be used as a generic term for 'problem-solver', the only sense that survives in common, mainly ironic use.

Bg *p*<u>*e*</u>*nkiler*/*p*<u>*e*</u>*nkeler* n./adj., uninfl., beg20c (3 coll)

paintball   *n.* 'a game in which participants simulate military combat using airguns to shoot capsules of paint at each other' (cf. ↑*gotcha*)

Du [=E] N [U] 1990s (1 tech) **Nw** [=E] M [U] 1980s (1) **Rs** *p*<u>*e*</u>*ĭntbol* M [U] 1990s (1 tech) **Gr** <=E> [=E] N [U] 1990s (1 mod)

paintbox   *n.* +2 'a selection of processes available in computer graphics' (comput.)

Du [=E] C [U] 1990s (1 tech) **Nw** [=E] M [U] 1980s (1 tech) **Nw** [=E] M [U] 1980s (1 tech) **Fr** (0) **It** [=E] M [U] 1990s (1 tech) **Rm** [=E] N [U] 1990s (1 tech) **Rs** (0) **Bg** (0)

pal   *n.* 'a friend, a mate'

Nw (0) **Ic** *palli* [p[h]al:i] M, pl. *-ar*; *palla* F, pl. *pöllur*, end20c (4s) **Hu** [pa:l] [U] 1990s, cp[2] (1 writ, jour)

palaver   *n.* 2 'profuse or idle talk', 3 'cajolery'

Although certainly from Portuguese, the word was probably spread largely through English sailor's slang, esp. as a verb; however, the form has little English about it, so its status as an anglicism is doubtful.

Ge [=E] N, 19c, via Port., 2(3) **Du** [pal<u>a</u>vər] N, 19c, via Port? (5) **Nw** [pala:ver] M, pl. *-e*, 19c, via Port (3 arch) **Rm** *palavră* [pal<u>a</u>vrə] F, beg19c (5Turk/Gr) **Bg** (5Gr/Turk) **Fi** *palaveri* 19c (3) **Hu** *paláver* [pala:ver] [U] beg20c, 2(5Port) **Al** *pallavër* F, pl. *-a*, 1950s, 2(3)

pallet   *n.* 'a transportable platform for transporting and storing loads'
Ge *Palette* (5Fr)   **Du** [=E] C, pl. *-s* (1 tech)   **Nw** *pall* (5)   **Ic** *pallet(t)* [pʰal:e(h)t] N, pl. Ø, mid20c (5Da); *palletta* [-ehta] F, pl. *-ur*, mid20c (5Da)   **It** [pallet] M, pl. Ø, 20c (1 tech)   **Rm** *paleta* (5Fr)   **Bg** *palet* (5Fr)   **Fi** *palli* (4)   **Hu** (5It)   **Gr** *palet(t)a* F, 20c, via Fr (3)

pampers*   *n.* 'babies' nappies'
This term started as a tradename (and has so remained in many countries). In others it has become generic as the best-known product of its kind.
Ge *Pampers*™ [pɛmpas] pl., 1970s (2 coll) > *Wegwerfwindel*   **Du** [pɛmpər] M, 1980s (2 coll)   **Nw**™ < *papirbleier*   **Ic**™ [pʰampe(r)s] end20c (0)   **Fr**™ (0)   **Rm** [=E] M, pl. Ø, end20c (1 mod, coll); [pɛmpərʃį/=E] M, pl., end20c (1 mod, coll); *pampersuri* [pɛmpersurį] N, pl., end20c (1 mod, coll)   **Rs** *pampersy* pl., 1990s (2)   **Po** [-ers] M, 1980s (2)   **Cr** *pamperice* pl., end20c (2)   **Bg** *pampers* M, sg., pl. *-al-i*, 1990s (3 mod)   **Fi** (0™) **Hu** [=E] [U] 1990s (2 jour, mod)   **Al** <=E> M, pl. *-a*, end20c (1 reg)   **Gr** *pampers* N, sg./pl., 1970s (2)

pamphlet   *n.* +1a 'a short text on a political subject'
Ge (5Fr)   **Du** *pamflet* N, 19c (5)   **Nw** *pamflett* [pamflɛt] M, pl. *-er*, 19c (3 obs)   **Fr** [pãflɛ] M, 18c (3)   **Sp** *panfleto* M, 19c (3) → *panfletista; panfletario*   **It** [pamflé/pamflet] M, pl. Ø, 18c (2 obs)/(5Fr) < *libello satirico*   **Rm** *pamflet* [pamflɛt] N, 19c, via Fr (3)   **Rs** *pamflet* M, pl. *-y*, 18–19c (3)   **Po** *pamflet* [pamflet] M, beg20c (3)   **Cr** *pamflet* M, pl. *-i*, beg20c (3)   **Bg** *pamflet* M, pl. *-al-i*, 19–20c (3 lit)   **Fi** *pamfletti* 19c, via Sw (3)   **Hu** *pamflet* [pamflet] pl. *-ek*, before 19c, via Ge (3)   **Al** *pamflet* M, pl. *-e*, 1900s (3)

pancake   *n.* 2 'a flat cake of make-up etc.'
Du [=E] C [U] 1980s (2)   **Fr** *pannequet* [pankɛ] M, 19c (3); [=E] 20c (Ø)   **Sp** *panqueque* M, pl. *-s*, 20c (1 tech, rare, reg)

panel   *n.* 1c 'an instrument board', 3 'a group of people forming a team (of experts) in a broadcast game, discussion, etc.', +6 'a statistical sample'
Ge [pɛnəl] N, pl. *-s*, 1960s, 3(1 mod)   **Du** [=E] N, 1960s, 3(2); *paneel*, 1c(5)   **Nw** [pane:l] N, pl. *-er/Ø*, mid20c, 1c,3(4)   **Ic** *panell/panill* [pʰa:nɪtl] M [U] (frequ. cp¹: *panelumræður*) end20c, 3(4) < *pallborðsumræður*   **Fr** [panel] M, 1960s, 3(3) → *panélisé,e* adj.; *panéliste* M   **Sp** [panel] M, 1960s, 3(3)   **It** [=E] M, pl. Ø, mid20c (1 tech) < 1c: *pannello*   **Rm** 3(0)   **Rs** *panel'* F, pl. *-i*, beg20c, via Ge/Fr, 1c(1 tech) → *-nyĭ* adj.   **Po** [panel] M, 1980s, 1c,3(2) → *-owy* adj.   **Cr** *panel* M, pl. *-al-i*, end20c, 1c(4 tech, rare)   **Bg** *panel* M, pl. *-al-i*, end20c, 1c(4 tech, rare)   **Fi** *panelli/paneeli* end20c, 3(3)   **Hu** [panel] pl. *-ek*, mid20c, via Rs, 1c(3); [pɛnəl] [U] end20c, 3(1 tech)   **Al** *panel* M, pl. *-ë*, 1970s, 1c(1 tech), 3(1 reg)   **Gr** *panel* N, pl. Ø/-s, end20c, 3(1)

pantie-girdle   *n.* 'a woman's girdle with a crotch shaped like pants'
Nw *panty* [=E] M, pl. *-ies*, end20c (1)

panties   *n.* 1 'short-legged or legless underpants worn by women and girls', +1a 'a child's undergarment', +2 'tights'
Ge *Panty* [=E] F/M/N, pl. *-(ie)s*, 1960s, 1,+2(1 rare) < +2: *Strumpfhose*   **Du** *panty* [pɛnti] C, 1970s, 1,+2(2) > *pantykous*   **Nw** [=E] end20c, 1,2(1 rare)   **Sp** [pantis] M, 1960s, +2(1 tech, rare)   **Rs** (0)   **Gr** *pady* N, 20c, +1a(2)

pantihose   *n.* 'women's usu. sheer tights'
Du *pantykous* (2+5)   **Nw** (0) < *strømpebukse*   **Ic** - < *sokkabuxur*   **Fr** *panty* [pãti] M, 1960s (2)   **Bg** - < rend *chorapogashtnik*

pantry   *n.* 1 'a small room or cupboard in which crockery, cutlery, table linen, etc., are kept', +2a 'a room for food on a ship, aeroplane, or camper'
Ge [pɛntri:] F, pl. *-(ie)s*, end19c, +2a(1 tech)   **Du** [=E] C, pl. *-'s*, 1940s, +2a(2)   **Nw** <=E>/ *pent(e)ri* [=E/pantri/pentri] N, pl. *-er*, beg20c (2 tech)   **Fr** [pãtri] M, 1970s (1 tech, ban) < *office*   **Po** *pentra* [pentra] F, mid20c, +2(1 tech)   **Cr** *pentri* M, mid20c, +2a(1 tech)   **Fi** *pentteri* 19c, via Sw, +2a(3 tech)

Ic	Nw	Po	Rs
Du	Ge	Cr	Bg
Fr	It	Fi	Hu
Sp	Rm	Al	Gr

panty*   *n.* 'women's tights'
Ge *panty* [=E] M/N, pl. *-(ie)s*, 1960s (1 tech); F, pl. *-(ie)s*, 1970s (1 tech) < *Strumpfhose*   **Du** [pɛnti] C, pl. *-'s*, 1970s (2)   **Fr** [pãti] M, 1960s (1 tech)   **Sp** [panti] M, pl. *-sl-ies*, 1960s (1)   **Rm** [=E] M/N, pl. *-sl-iesl-uri*, end20c (1 you)

paper   *n.* 8 'an essay or dissertation, esp. one read to a learned society or published in a learned journal'
Ge [pe:pa] N, pl. *-s*, 1970s (1 tech)   **Du** [=E] C, 1970s (1 tech)   **Nw** [=E] N pl. *-s*, 1970s (1 tech)   **Ic** *pappír* M, pl. *-ar*, end20c (4 tech)   **Fr** (0) < mean *papier*   **Po** [=E] end20c (1 tech)   **Fi** [=E] 1980s (1 tech) = *esitelmä*   **Gr** (0)

paperback   *n.* 'a book bound in stiff paper'
This term has gained only a marginal position; although the equivalents preferred in most languages do not mean the same, they appear to have delayed the adoption. (Note that ↑*hardback* is even rarer.)
Ge [=E] N/M, pl. *-s*, 1960s (1 rare, mod) < *Taschenbuch*   **Du** [=E] C, 1960s (2) < *pocket(boek)*   **Nw** [=E] M, pl. *-s*, mid20c (2) > *pocketbok*   **Ic** [=E] mid20c (0) < *creat (pappírs)kilja*   **Fr** M, mid20c (1 obs) < *livre de poche*   **Sp** [=E] M, pl. *-s*, 1970s (1 tech, rare) < *libro en rústica*   **It** [=E] M, pl. Ø, 1960s (2) < *edizione economica, tascabile*   **Rm** [=E] N, end20c (1 tech)   **Rs** *peĭper-bek* M, uninfl., 1990s (1 tech)   **Po** [-bek] M, end20c (2)   **Bg** (0)   **Fi** [=E] end20c (1 obs)   **Hu** [=E] pl. Ø, end20c (1 tech>2)   **Al** - < *kapak letre*   **Gr** (0) < *khartodheto vivlio*

Ic	Nw	Po	Rs
Du	Ge	Cr	Bg
Fr	It	Fi	Hu
Sp	Rm	Al	Gr

paper clip   *n.* 'a clip of bent wire or of plastic for holding several sheets of paper together'

Du [=E] C, 1940s (2) > *papierklem*   **Nw** (0) < *binders* **Ic** - < *bréfaklemma*   **It** *clip* [=E] F, pl. *-s*, 1930s (2)

paraglider   *n.* 1 'a hang glider with a parachute', 2 'a person who practises paragliding'
Ge [paːraglaida] M, pl. Ø, 1980s (1 mod, rare)   **Du** [=E] C, 1980s (1 tech)   **Nw** [para-+E] M, pl. *-e*, 1980s, 2(1)   **Fr** - < *parapendio*   **It** - < 2: rend *parapendio*   **Rm** - < *parapantă*   **Rs** (0)   **Po** (0)   **Cr** (0)   **Bg** *paraglaider* M, pl. *-a/-i*, 1990s, 1(1 tech, mod) < *paraplan*

paragliding   *n.* 'a sport resembling hang-gliding, using a parachute-like canopy attached to the body by a harness, allowing a person to glide after jumping from or being hauled to a height'
Ge [paːraglaidiŋ] N [U] 1980s (1 tech/mod) < *Gleitschirmfliegen*   **Du** [=E] C, 1980s (1 tech)   **Nw** [para-+E] M/F [U] 1980s (1)   **Fr** - < *parapente*   **Sp** [=E] M [U] 1990s (1 tech, rare) < *parapente*   **It** - < rend *parapendio*   **Rs** (0)   **Po** [-nk] M, end20c (1 tech)   **Cr** (0)   **Bg** *paraglaiding* M [U] 1990s (1 tech, mod) < *paraplanerizŭm*   **Gr** <=E>/*paraglaiding* N [U] 1990s (1 mod)

parboiled   *adj.* 'partly cooked by boiling'
Ge (0)   **Nw** [=E] 1980s (1/2)   **It** [=E] M, uninfl., 1980s? (1>2)   **Gr** <=E>/*parboild* 1980s (1 writ)

park   *n.* 1 'a large public garden in a town, for recreation', 3a 'a large area of land kept in its natural state for public recreational use', +4a 'a fleet of buses, taxis, etc.', 5 'the gear position or function in automatic transmission in which the gears are locked, preventing the vehicle's movement', 6 'an area devoted to a specified purpose', +8 'the parking lights of a car'
The English term (which is ultimately from French) was adopted with the idea of landscape gardening and has since been nativized in many European countries. Stimulated by English *amusement park* and *technology park*, the word was variously extended, as it was by the French innovation of calling a fleet of lorries etc. a 'park'.
Ge [park] M, pl. *-s*, mid18c, 1(3); 20c, +4a(3); end20c, 6(2 mod)   **Du** (5Fr)   **Nw** [park] M, pl. *-er*, 19c, 1,3a(5Fr); 20c, +4a,6,+8(4)   **Ic** *parkur* [pʰarkʏr] M, pl. *-ar*, 1920s, 1(Ø); <=E> [pʰark] uninfl., mid20c, 5,+8(2 coll)   **Fr** *parc* M, 1,3a,6(4) +4a(5)   **Sp** *parque* (5Fr)   **It** *parco* [parco] M, end19c, 1,3a,+4a,6(3); <=E> cp², 6(1)   **Rm** *parc* [park] N, beg19c, 1,6(5Fr); 20c, 3a,+4a(5Fr)   **Rs** *park* M, pl. *-i*, 19c, 1,3a; mid20c, +4a(3) → *-ovyĭ* adj.   **Po** [park] M, 19c, 1(3)   **Cr** *park* M, pl. *-ovi*, 19c, 1(3)   **Bg** *park* M, pl. *-al-ove*, beg20c, 1,3a(3) +4a(5Fr) → *-ov* adj.   **Fi** *parkkivalot/parkit* pl., mid20c, 5(2 coll) +8(3 coll)   **Hu** [park] pl. *-ok*, 17–19c, 1,3a(3); 20c, +4a,6(3) → *-ol* v.   **Al** *park* M, pl. *parqe*, beg19c, 1,+4a(3)   **Gr** *parko* N, 1,3a,6(3,5It)

park   *v.* 1 'leave (a vehicle) usu. temporarily, in a car park, by the side of the road, etc.', 2 'deposit and leave (esp. money), usu. temporarily'
Ge *parken* beg20c, 1(3); *-ier-* (1 reg); end20c, 2(3 mod)   **Du** *parkeren* 1940s, 1(5Fr)   **Nw** *parkere* [par-

keːre] 20c, 1(5Fr)   **Ic** *parkera* [pʰarkera] mid20c, 1(5Da) = *leggja*   **Fr** *parquer* beg20c 1(3)   **Sp** *aparcar* beg20c 1(3)   **It** *parcheggiare* 1930s, 1(3)   **Rm** *parca* [parka] mid20c, 1(5Fr) → *parcare* F; *parcat* adj.   **Rs** *parkovat'* mid20c, 1(3) → *-ovanie* N; *-ovka* F   **Po** *parkować* [parkovatɕ] mid20c (3) → *parkowanie* N; *za-* v.   **Cr** *parkirati* 20c (3) → *parkiralište* N; *parkiranje* N   **Bg** *parkiram* mid20c, 1(3) → *parkirane* N   **Fi** *parkeerata* mid20c, 1(3 coll) < *pysäköidä*   **Hu** *parkol* [parkol] via Ge, 1(3) → *-íroz* v.   **Al** *parkoj* 1990s, 1(1 reg)   **Gr** *parkaro* 1(3)

parking*   *n.* 'a parking site'
Since the compound *parking-lot* cannot be shortened to the modifying element in Germanic, but is likely to be in French, *parking* is as natural as *dancing* etc. are; languages having this 'French' form are likely to have got it through French mediation – as with the best-known nineteenth-century example *smoking*.
Ge - < *Parkplatz*   **Du** [=E] C, 1970s (2 reg) < *parkeerterrein*   **Nw** (0) < *parkering(-s/plass)*   **Fr** [parkiŋ] M, mid20c (2) > *parc (de stationnement)*   **Sp** [parkin] M, pl. *-s*, mid20c, via Fr (2) = *aparcamiento*   **It** [=E] M, pl. Ø,

1930s (1) < rend *parcheggio*   **Rm** <=E>/*parching* [=E] N, 1970s (2>3)   **Rs** *parking* M, pl. *-i*, 1990s (1 tech) < *parkovka*   **Po** [par-] M, mid20c, via Fr (3) → *-owy* adj./M   **Cr** [parking] M, pl. *-zi*, mid20c (3)   **Bg** *parking* M, pl. *-al-i*, mid20c, via Fr (3) → *-ov* adj.   **Fi** - < *parkkipaikka*   **Hu** <=E>/*P* [parking] [U] 20c (1 rare) *parkoló (hely)*   **Al** *parking* M, pl. *-ë*, 1950s (1 reg); *parkim* M, pl. *-e*, 1990s   **Gr** *parkin(g)* N, mid20c, via Fr (2)

parking meter   *n.* 'a coin-operated meter which receives fees for vehicles parked in the street and indicates the time for which they may remain'
Ge - < *Parkuhr*   **Du** - < *parkeermeter*   **Nw** *parkometer/-metre* [parkumeːter] N, pl. Ø, 20c (3)   **Ic** - < creat *stöðumælir*   **Fr** *parcmètre/parco-* [parkmɛtr(ə)/parkɔ-] M, 1960s (3)   **Sp** *parquímetro* M, 20c (3)   **It** *parchimetro* [parkimetro] M, pl. *-i*, 1940s (3)   **Rm** *parcometru* [parkometru] N, 1970s (5Fr)   **Po** (0)   **Cr** (0)   **Bg** - < ↑*timer*   **Fi** *parkkimittari* mid20c(3)   **Hu** - < trsl *parkolóóra*   **Al** *parkometer* M, pl. *-tra*, 1990s (3)   **Gr** - < trsl *parkometro*

Parkinson's disease   *n.* 'a progressive disease of the nervous system with tremor, muscular rigidity, and emaciation'
The British surgeon James Parkinson (1775–1824) first identified the disease, but this term has become more widely known only in the twentieth century. All languages translate 'disease' or replace it with a derivation on *-ism*.
Ge *Parkinsonsche Krankheit* 20c (2+5)   **Du** *ziekte van Parkinson* 20c (5+2) → *Parkinson* n.   **Nw** *Parkinsons sykdom/parkinsonisme* [paːrkinsɔns+Nw/ parkinsɔnism] M [U] 20c (3+5/3)   **Ic** *Parkinson (sveiki)* [pʰarcɪnson(sveiːcɪ)] F [U] mid20c (2+5)

Fr *maladie de Parkinson/parkinson* [paʀkinsɔn] F/M, 20c (3 coll) → *parkinsonien/ne* adj./N **Sp** - < trsl *enfermedad de Parkinson, Parkinson* → *parkinsonis- mo* **It** - < rend *morbo di Parkinson* → *parkinsoniano* adj. **Rm** *(boala) Parkinson/parchinsonism* N (2+5) **Rs** *bolezn' Parkinsona* **Po** *choroba Parkinsona* F, 20c (2) **Cr** *Parkinsonova bolest* F [U] 20c (3) **Bg** *parkinsonova bolest* (3+5), *parkinson(izŭm)* (3) **Fi** *Parkinsonin tauti* (2) **Hu** *Parkinson-kór* (2+5) **Al** *Parkinson* M [U] **Gr** *(nosos) parkinson* F [U] 20c (5+2)

park & ride *phr.* 'a system whereby drivers park their cars outside cities and use public transportation'
    This term became necessary when the crowding of inner cities made an alternative for motorists desirable (first in the 1960s, but popular from the 1980s only); it is therefore restricted to countries with such traffic problems. Note that calques must contain *P(&)R* to match the abbreviation. The phrase has sparked off a list of English combinations in German railway ad- vertisements (*Fly & Drive, Rail & Road*).
    Ge [paʀkenrait] cp¹, 1980s (1 mod) > *Parken & Reisen* **Du** [=E] 1990s (1 tech) = *P+R; Park- eer en Reis* **Nw** [=E] 1970s (1) **Fr** [parkanrajd] 1980s (1 tech, ban) > *parc relais* **Po** <=E> 1990s (1 tech) **Fi** [=E] 1990s (0) **Hu** <=E>/*P+R* [=E] end20c (1 tech, jour, mod)

parkway *n.* 'an open landscaped highway'
Po [par-] M, end20c (1 tech)

partner *n.* 1 'a person who shares or takes part with another or others, esp. in a business firm with shared risks and profits', 4 'either member of a married couple or of an established unmarried couple'
    The closeness of the English and the French term make it difficult to establish the source in many lan- guages (or to determine whether the word was bor- rowed *via* French).
    Ge [paʀtna] M, pl. Ø, beg19c, 1(3); 1970s, 4(3) → *-schaft* F **Du** [=E] C, 19c, 1(3) **Nw** [=E] M, pl. *-e*, mid19c (3) → *partnerskap* **Ic** [pʰaʀtner] M, pl. *-ar*, end20c, 1(1 coll) < rend *meðeigandi* **Fr** - < *partenaire* **Sp** [paʀner] M, 1970s (1 tech) = *partenaire* **It** [paʀtner] M, pl. Ø, mid19c (3) **Rm** *partener* [par- tener] M, beg19c (5Fr) **Rs** *partnër* M, pl. *-y*, mid19c, 1(3) → *-sha* F **Po** [partner] M, mid19c (3) → *-ka* F; *-stwo* N; *-owanie* N **Cr** *partner* M, pl. *-i*, 19c, 1(3) → *-ica* F; *-ski* adj.; *-stvo* N **Bg** *partnyor* M, pl. *-i*, beg20c, via Rs (5Fr) → *-ka* F; *-stvo* N **Fi** *partneri* 19c, 1(2) **Hu** [partner] pl. *-ek*, 20c, 1(3) **Al** *partner* M, pl. *-ë*, beg20c, 1(3) **Gr** *partener* M/F, beg20c, via Fr, 4(2)

partner look* *n.* 'a partner- or relationship of two persons expressed by dressing in the same way'
Ge [=E] M [U] 1970s (2) **Du** (0)

partnership *n.* 1 'the state of being a partner or partners', 2 'a joint business'

Ge - < *Partnerschaft* **Du** [=E] N, 1910s, 2(2) = *part- nerschap* **Nw** [=E] N [U] mid20c (1 obs) < *partner- skap* **Ic** [pʰartnersjihp] N [U] end20c, 1(0 sla) **Fr** - < trsl *partenariat* **It** [=E] F, pl. Ø, end19c (1 tech, jour) **Rm** - < trsl *parteneriat* **Rs** - < trsl *partnër- stvo* **Po** - < trsl *partnerstwo* **Cr** - < trsl *partnerstvo* **Bg** - < trsl *partnyorstvo* **Hu** [partnerʃip] [U] end20c, 2(1 tech)

part-time *adj.* 'occupying or using only part of the usual working week'
Ge - < trsl *Teilzeit* **Du** [pa:tajm] 1970s (2) < *deeltijds* → *parttimer* **Nw** (0) < *deltids-* **Ic** [=E] uninfl., end20c (0 rare) < *hluta-* **Fr** - < rend *à temps par- tiel* **Sp** [partaim-] 1970s (1 rare) < rend *a tiempo parcial* **It** [=E] adj./adv., uninfl. **Rm** [=E] 1990s (0/1 mod) < *(cu) jumătate de normă* **Cr** - < trsl *skraćeno radno vrijeme* **Fi** - < trsl *osa-aika (inen)* cp¹ (adj.) mid20c (3) **Gr** *part taim* 1990s (2)

party *n.* 1 'a social gathering, usu. of invited (young) guests'
    Although this term fulfilled no denotational need, it was accepted as a badge of modernity, competing with native equivalents (or French *fête*). The earlier use to mean 'political party' has apparently not survived in any of the European languages.
    Ge [parti:] F, pl. *-(ie)s*, 1940s (2) < *Fete* **Du** [=E] C, pl. *-'s*, 1970s (2) = *partij(tje), feest(je)* **Nw** [=E] N, pl. *-ies/-er*, 1960s (1 you, coll) = *fest* **Ic** *partí* [pʰartí] N, pl. Ø, mid20c (2>3 coll) **Fr** - < ↑*surprise-party, surprise-partie* **Sp** [parti] M, pl. *-ies/-ys*, 1930s (1>2) < *fiesta* **It** [parti] M, pl. Ø, 1930s (2) < *ricevimento, festa* **Rm** [=E] F/N, pl. Ø, 1970s (2) **Rs** *parti* N, uninfl., end20c (1 mod) **Po** [parti] N, uninfl., beg20c (2) < *przyję- cie* **Cr** *parti* M/F, mid20c (3) **Bg** *parti/parti* N, pl. *-ta*, end20c (2 coll, mod) < *kupon* **Fi** [=E] 1970s (1 coll) **Hu** <=E>/*parti* [parti] pl. *-k*, 19c (1 reg); 1960s [=E] (3) **Al** *parti* end20c (1 you) **Gr** *parti* N, mid20c (2)

party line *n.* +2b 'a commercial phone service where callers are able to talk to each other'
Ge [=E] F, pl. *-s*, 1990s (0>1 mod) **Nw** - < *pratelin- je* **Sp** [=E] F, 1990s (1 jour) **It** [=E] F, pl. Ø, 1990s (1 tech, mod) **Po** [party-] F, end20c (1 mod) **Hu** [parti lain] [U] end20c (1 writ, mod)

pass boat* *n.* 'a small and fast open boat with an outboard engine'
Nw *passbåt* [pas-] 1950s (3+5)

passing shot *n.* 'a shot aiming the ball beyond and out of reach of the other player' (tennis)
Ge - < *Passierschlag* **Du** [=E] N, 1980s (1 tech) < *passeerslag* **Fr** *passing-shot* [pasiŋ ʃɔt] M, 1930s (1 tech, ban) > *coup passant* **Sp** [=E] < *passing* **It** - < rend? *passante* **Rm** [=E] N, 1970s (1 tech) **Bg** - < trsl *prekhvŭrlyasht udar* **Hu** - < *elütés*

password *n.* 1 'a selected word or phrase, or a string of characters securing recognition, admission, etc.',

+1a 'the same securing admission to data or programs' (comput.)
Ge [=E] pl. -s, 1980s, +1a(1 tech) < trsl *Paßwort, Kennwort* **Du** [=E] N, 1980s, +1a(1 tech) **Nw** (0) < trsl *passord* **Ic** [=E] N, pl. Ø, end20c, +1a(1 sla) < rend *lykilorð, aðgangsorð* **Fr** 1(5) < +1a: trsl *mot de passe* **Sp** [=E] M, end20c, +1a(1 tech) < creat *contráseña* **It** [pạsswɔrd/-wœrd] M, pl. Ø, 1970s (1 tech) < *parola d'ordine* **Rm** [=E] N, 1990s, +1a(0 tech) **Rs** (0) **Po** [pasuord] M, end20c, +1a(1 tech) **Cr** - < *lozink, zaporka* **Bg** pạsuữrd M, pl. -al-i, 1990s, +1a(1 tech) < *parola* **Hu** [=E] pl. Ø, end20c, +1a(1 tech) **Al** [=E] 1995, +1a(1 tech) **Gr** <=E> [=E] N, pl. Ø/-s, end20c, +1a(1 tech)

paste-up *n.* 1 'a document prepared for copying, combining various sections' (advertising), +2 'a person in an advertising agency responsible for making paste-ups'
Nw [=E] M, pl. -s, 1960s (1 tech) **Ic** [=E] N, mid/end20c, 1(tech, arch) = rend *upplímingur*

patchwork *n.* 1 'needlework in which small pieces of cloth in different designs are sewn together to form one article', 2 'something composed of small pieces'
This word was adopted in the restricted context of the artistic discipline (or hobby); the composite character of the word has, however, given rise to various applications to objects composed of small bits, sometimes with negative connotations.
Ge [=E] N [U] 1970s, 1(1 tech) 2(1 coll) **Du** [=E] N [U] 1960s, 1(1 tech) **Nw** [=E] M/N, 1970s, 1(1 tech) 2(1) < 1: *lappeteknikk*; < 2: *lappeteppe* **Ic** [=E] uninfl., end20c, 1(0 tech) < rend *bútasaumur* **Fr** [patʃwœrk] M,

1960s (1) **Sp** [patʃwerk] M [U] 1980s, 2(1 tech) **It** [patʃwœrk] M [U] 1970s (1>2 tech) **Rm** [=E] N, 1990s, 2(1 rare) **Rs** (0) **Po** [-uork] M, end20c (1 tech) → *-owy* adj. **Cr** pạčvork M [U] end20c (1 tech) **Bg** pạchuữrk M [U] 1990s, 1(1 tech) **Hu** [petʃwərk] [U] end20c (2 tech) **Gr** pạtsghuork N, mid20c (1 tech)

pattern *n.* 2 'fixed or regular behaviour' (psychol, sociol), +9 'a rule, a simplified model for a complicated system'
Ge [pẹtərn] N, pl. -s, 20c, 2(1 tech) < *Muster* **Du** *patroon* [patro:n] +9(5) **Nw** - < *mønster* **Ic** - < *munstur* **Fr** [patɛrn] M, 20c, 2(1 tech/ban) > *forme, motif, modèle, schéma, type*? **Sp** [=E] M, 20c, 2(1 tech, rare) **It** [patɛrn] M, pl. Ø, 1960s (1 tech) **Rm** [=E] N, 1970s, 2(2 tech, rare) **Po** [patern] M, end20c, +9(1 tech) **Bg** pạtern M [U] mid20c, 2(1 tech) **Hu** [=E] pl. Ø, 20c, +9(1 techSCI)

pattern drill *n.* 'an exercise for practising linguistic structures, used in teaching'
Ge [pẹtərndril] M, pl. -s, 1960s (1 tech) **Du**

(Ø) **Nw** - < trsl *mønster-drill* **Ic** - < trsl *munsturæfing* **Fr** - < *exercise structural*

pay per view *n.* 'a TV system where one pays only for those programmes one actually watches'
Ge [=E] 1990s (1 tech) **Du** [=E] 1990s (1 tech) **Nw** [=E] 1990s (1 tech) **Sp** [=E] M [U] 1990s (1 tech)

pay-TV* *n.* 'a television channel available for extra payment'
Ge [=E] N [U] 1980s (1 mod) **Du** [=E] C, 1980s (1 tech, obs) < *betaaltelevisie, betaal-tv* **Nw** (0) < trsl *betal-tv* **Fr** <=E> 1980s (1 ban) > *télévision à péage, télévision payante* **Sp** - < trsl *televisión de pago* **It** [peịtivụ/-vi] F, pl. Ø, 1990s (2 tech) **Rm** [=E] N, pl. Ø, 1990s (2 tech) **Al** - < *television me pagesë*

PC *abbrev.* 3 'personal computer', 4 'political correctness'
This term is now universally accepted in sense 3 (nearly always preferred as an abbreviation, cf. ↑*personal computer*). This may have contributed to the fact that *PC* 4 = 'political correctness' has not gained ground.
Ge [pe:tsẹ:] M, pl. -s, 1980s, 3(3 tech) **Du** *p.c.* [pe:sẹ:] C, pl. -'s, 1980s, 3(2) **Nw** ["pẹ:se:] M, pl. -er, 1980s, 3(3) > trsl *PD* **Ic** <=E>/*pési* [pʰjɛ:sjɛ:/ pʰjɛsɪ] M, pl. -ar, 1980s, 3(2) **Fr** [pese] M, 1980s, 3(1 tech) < *ordinateur individuel* **Sp** [pesẹ] M, pl. -s, 1990s, 3(2 tech) **It** [pitʃi/pisị/ pẹrsonal compjụter] M, pl. Ø, 1980s, 3(2) **Rm** [=E] N, 1990s, 3(2 tech) **Rs** [pisị] end20c, 3(2 tech) **Po** [pe ce/pe cet] end20c, 3(2 mod) **Cr** [=E] M, pl. -ovi, end20c, 3(2) **Bg** <=E> [pisị] N, pl. -ta, 1990s, 3(2 tech, coll) **Fi** [pe:se:] 1980, 3(2) **Hu** [pẹ:tse:] pl. -k, end20c, 3(2) **Al** *PC* [pëcë] end20c, 3(0 tech) **Gr** <=E> [=E] N, end20c, 3(1 writ)

Peach Melba *n.* 'a dish of ice cream and peaches with liqueur'
Ge - < trsl *Pfirsich Melba* **Du** *pêche melba* (5Fr) **Nw** (0) < *pære melba* **Fr** - < trsl *pêche Melba* **It** - < trsl *pesca melba* **Rm** *melba* [mẹlba] F [U] 20c (3 rare) **Po** *melba* [melba] F, mid20c (3) **Cr** (0) **Bg** mẹlba F, pl. -i, mid20c (3) **Gr** <=E> [melbạ] N, 20c, via Fr (1 tech)

pea-jacket *n.* 'a sailor's short double-breasted overcoat of coarse woollen cloth'
This term represents an early nautical term which spread along the coast to Poland and Russia; it appears to have been much more popular around 1900, when it could refer to a type of children's dress.
Ge *Pyjeck/Pijacke* F, pl. -n, 19c (3 tech, arch) **Du** *pijjecker* (5) **Rs** *pidzhạk* M, pl. -i, beg20c (3) **Po** *pidżak* [pidʒak] M, beg20c, via Rs (1 tech)

peak *n.* 1e 'the narrow part of a ship's hold at the bow or stern' (naut.), 1f 'the upper outer corner of a sail extended by a gaff', +1g 'the lowest room in a ship'
Ge *Piek* F, pl. -en, mid20c, +1g(3 tech) **Du** *piek* (5Fr) **Rm** *pic* [pik] N, beg20c, via Ge?, 1e,f(3

tech) **Po** (5Du) **Cr** [=E] M, beg20c, 1e(3 tech) **Bg** *pik* M, pl. *-al-ove*, beg20c, +1g(1 tech) **Fi** *piikki* 19c, via Sw?, 1e(3 tech)

peanut(s) *n.* 1 'a leguminous plant (Arachis hypogaea)', 2 'the seed of this plant', 3 (pl.) 'a trivial thing or amount of money'

The term for the fruit is largely native (possibly calqued). The non-literary use in German is a nice illustration of how an anglicism can become common: it was used by a leading banker on TV with regard to losses of hundreds of millions of DM in a building scandal, and the public outcry popularized the word.

Ge [=E] pl., 1980s, 3(1 mod); - < 1,2: = *Erdnuß* **Du** [pi:nʏts] 1980s, 3(1 coll) **Nw** *peanøtt* [pi:(a)-] mid20c, 1,2(2); *peanuts/peanøtter* [=E] 1970s, 3(1) < 1,2: *jordnøtt*; < 3: *blåbær* **Ic** [=E] mid20c, 2(1 coll) 3(1 sla) > 2: *jarð-hneta* **Rs** 1(0) **Po** (0) **Cr** (0) **Fi** [=E] end20c, 3(1coll)

peeling* *n.* +2 'a treatment for removing impurities in the skin' (cosmetics)

The remarkable spread of this word contrasts with the very limited knowledge outside groups interested in cosmetics.

Ge [=E] N [U] 1970s (1 tech, mod) **Du** [=E] C, 1980s (1 tech) **Nw** [=E] M [U] 1980s (1 tech) **Fr** [piliŋ] M, 1960s (1 tech) **Sp** [pilin] M, 1980s (1 tech) **It** [pi:liŋ(g)] M [U] 1970s (1 tech) **Rm** (0) **Rs** *piling* M [U] 1980s (1 tech) **Po** [pi-] M, end20c (1 mod) **Cr** *piling* M [U] end20c (1 tech) **Bg** *piling* M [U] end20c (1 tech) **Fi** [=E] 1980s (1 tech) **Hu** [=E] [U] end20c (2 tech) **Gr** *piling* N, pl. Ø/-s, 1980s (1 tech)

peep-show *n.* +1a 'a sex show viewed through a hole'

The distribution may well reflect cultural boundaries rather than linguistic ones, with various Eastern and Southern countries becoming affected only in the 1990s. The euphemistic use of this loanword has stopped calques from being suggested.

Ge [pi:pʃo:] F, pl. *-s*, 1970s (2) **Du** [=E] C, 1970s (2) **Nw** [=E] N, pl. Ø, 1980s (1) **Ic** [pʰi:p-sjou:] N [U] mid/end20c (1 sla) **Fr** [pipʃo] M, 1980s (1) **Sp** <=E>/*peeping-show* [pipʃou] M, 1980s (1 tech) **It** [=E] M, pl. Ø, 1980s (1) **Rs** (0) **Po** <=E> M, uninfl., 1990s (1 mod) **Cr** [=E] M [U] end20c (1) **Bg** *pi(i)pshou* N, pl. *-ta*, 1990s (1 mod) **Fi** [=E] 1980s (1) **Hu** [=E] pl. Ø, end20c (2) **Gr** <=E>/*pip sou* N, end20c (1 rare)

peer group *n.* 'a group of people having the same age, status, interests, etc.'

Ge [=E] F, pl. *-s*, 1980s (1 tech) **Du** *peergroup* [=E] C, 1980s (1 tech) **Fr** (0) < rend *groupe affinitaire,*

groupe de pairs **Sp** - < trsl *grupe de pares* **It** - < trsl *gruppo di pari*

pemmican *n.* 1 'a cake of dried pounded meat mixed with melted fat', 2 'beef so treated, for use by Arctic travellers etc.'

Borrowed from Algonquian in American English, the word became widely known through travel literature, but has remained a foreignism.

Ge *Pemmikan* [pɛmika:n] M [U] 19c (Ø) **Du** *pemmikan/pemmikaan* [pɛmikɑn]/*pɛmɪka:n] N [U] 1940s (1 tech) **Nw** *pemmikan* [pemikan] M, pl. *-er*, beg20c, 1(3 tech) **Ic** *pemmikan* N [U] end19c, via Da, 2(1 tech) **Fr** [pemikã/pe-] M, 19c (Ø) **It** [pemikan] M [U] end19c (1 rare, obs) **Po** *pemmikan* [pemikan] M, beg20c (1 tech) **Hu** *pemmikán* [=E] [U] via E, 20c (0)

penalty area *n.* 'the ground in front of the goal in which a foul involves the award of a penalty kick'

Ge - < trsl *Strafraum* **Du** - < trsl *strafschopgebied* **Nw** - < trsl *straffefelt* **Ic** - < rend *vítateigur* **Fr** - < rend *surface de réparation* **It** - < trsl *area di rigore* **Rm** - < rend *spaţiu de penalizare* **Bg** *penal(t)* M, pl. *-a*, 20c (1 tech) **Fi** - < trsl *rangaistusalue* **Al** - < *zona e panalltisë*

penalty (kick) *n.* 3b '(a disadvantage) awarded against a side incurring a penalty'

Ge [penalti/penalti] M, pl. *-s*, 1960s (1 tech ICE-HOCKEY); 1900s (1 reg FOOTB) < trsl *Strafstoß* **Du** [=E] C, beg20c (1 tech) < *strafschop* **Nw** (0) < trsl *straffe(spark)* **Ic** - < rend *vítaspyrna, víti* **Fr** [penalti] M, pl. *-ies*, end19c (2 tech, ban) > *tir de réparation* **Sp** <=E>/*penalti* [penalti] pl. *-s*, beg20c (2<3 tech) = *castigo, pena máxima* **It** [penalti] M, pl. Ø, 1900s (1>2 tech) < rend *calcio di rigore, rigore* **Rm** <=E>/*penalti* [penalti] N, 1930s (2>3 tech) **Rs** *penal'ti* M/N, uninfl., 19c (3 tech) **Po** - < trsl *rzut karny* **Cr** *penaltik* M, mid20c (1 tech) **Bg** - < trsl *nakazatelen udar, duzpa* **Hu** [=E] [U] end19/beg20c (1 tech, arch) < trsl *büntető(rúgás)* **Al** *penallti* F, pl. Ø, beg20c (1 sla) **Gr** *penalti* N, beg20c (1 tech)

penfriend *n.* 'a friend communicated with by letter only'

Ge (Ø) **Nw** - < trsl *pennevenn* **Ic** - < trsl *pennavinur* **It** [=E] M/F, pl. Ø, mid20c? (1) < rend *amico/-a di penna* **Rm** (0)

penny *n.* 1 'a British monetary unit', +1a 'a small coin'

This word has largely remained a foreignism referring to the British unit exclusively. Note that the English plural *pence* was sometimes taken over as a non-count word, or even as a singular (rare in Finnish, but current in Polish).

Ge [=E] M, pl.-*(ie)s* (*pence* not used) 19c, 1(Ø) +1a(1 coll) **Du** 1(Ø) **Nw** [=E] M, pl. *pence*, mid19c, 1(Ø) **Ic** *penni* [=E] N, pl. Ø, end19c, 1(Ø) **Fr** [peni] M, pl. *-ies*, 18c, 1(Ø) **Sp** *penique* M, 1(Ø/3) **It** [penni] M, pl. Ø, 18c, 1(Ø) **Rm** <=E>/*peni* [=E] M, pl. Ø, beg20c, 1(Ø) **Rs** p*e*nni N, uninfl. [U] mid19c, 1(Ø) **Po** *pens* [pens] M, mid19c, 1(Ø) **Cr** p*e*ni M, 20c, 1(Ø) **Bg** p*e*ni N, pl. -*ta*, end19c, 1(Ø) **Fi** *penni* [=E] 1(Ø) +1a(3) **Hu** [=E] pl. -*k*, 20c (1 coll, fac) **Al** p*e*ni F, pl. Ø, beg20c (3) **Gr** p*e*nna F, 1(3/Ø); *penny* N, 1(1/Ø)

penthouse *n.* 'a house or flat on the roof or the top floor of a tall building'
Ge *Penthaus*/-*house* N, pl. -*häuser*, 1970s (2+3) **Du** [=E] N, 1970s (2) **Nw** (Ø/1) **Ic** [pʰɛnthaus] N, pl. Ø, end20c (1 coll) > rend *þakíbúð* **Fr** (Ø) **Sp** [=E] M, 1970s (1 tech, jour, rare) **Rs** *pentkh*a*us* M, pl. -*y*, 1990s (Ø) **Po** (0) **Gr** (0)

pep *n.* 'vigour, go'
Ge [pep] M [U] 1960s (1 coll) < *Schwung* → *peppig* adj.; *aufpeppen* v. **Du** [=E] C [U] 1960s (3) **Nw** *pepp* [=E] M [U] 1950s (3) → *peppe (opp)* v. **Ic** [pʰɛhp] N [U] mid/end20c (2 coll) ← *peppa (upp)* v. **Fr** <=E>/*pep's* [pɛp(s)] M [U] 20c (1 mod)

peppermint liqueur *n.* 'an alcoholic drink'
Ge - < trsl *Pfefferminzlikör* **Du** - < *pepermuntlikeur* (5) **Nw** - < *peppermyntelikør* **Ic** *piparmyntulík (j)ör* M [U] end19c (5Da) **Fr** *peppermint* [pepǝrmint/pepɛRmᾶt] M, end19c (1) **Sp** *peppermint*/*pippermint* M (1 tech) → *pipermín* **Rm** *piperment* <=E> [piperm*e*nt/peperm*i*nt] N, beg20c, via Fr (3 tech) **Po** *peperment* [peperment] M, beg20c (2) **Cr** *pepermint* 20c (2) **Bg** - < *menta* **Al** - < *liker mente*

pep talk *n.* 'a short talk intended to enthuse, encourage, etc.'
Du [=E] C [U] 1970s (2) **Nw** [=E] M, pl. -*er*, 1960s (1)

pep (up) *v.* 'fill with vigour'
Ge *aufpeppen* 1970s (1 coll) **Du** *oppeppen* end20c (3 coll) **Nw** *peppe opp* [pɛpǝ] mid20c (2) **Ic** *peppa upp* [pʰɛhpa wvhp] mid/end20c (2 coll)

perfect *adj.* 3 'very satisfactory'
The Latin-based word is available in nearly all languages, but only a few add the English equivalent as a modern slang term.
Ic [pʰœrfext] uninfl., end20c, 3(1 sla) **Bg** p*u*rfekt uninfl., 1990s (1 sla/mod) **Al** *perfekt* uninfl., 1960s (3)

performance *n.* 2 'a staging or production (of a play, piece of music, etc.)', 3 'a person's achievement under test conditions', +7 'an art form' (an unconventional presentation of art, mixing music, dance, and audio-visual elements), +8 'a sporting achievement'
In the Germanic languages, English pronunciation shows the word to be an anglicism, a fact largely disguised by adaptation of pronunciation and suffix replacement elsewhere.
Ge [=E] F [U] 1980s, +7(1 tech) **Du** [=E] C, 1970s, 2,+8(1 tech), +7(1 tech, euph) **Nw** [=E] M, pl. -*s*, 1960s, +7(1 tech) **Ic** [pʰɛrfɔrmans] M, pl. -*ar*, 1960s, 3(1 sla) +7(1 tech) = +7: *gerningur*/*gjörningur* **Fr** [pɛRfɔRmᾶs] F, mid19c, +8(3) **Sp** [performans] M, 1920s, 2,+7,+8(1 tech) **It** [performans/perfor-

mans/performãs] F, end19c, 2,+7,+8(2) **Rm** *performanţă* [performantsǝ] F, beg20c, via Fr, 3,+8(3); [=E] N, 1990s, +7(1 tech, mod) **Rs** *perf*o*rmans* M, pl. -*y*, end20c, 2,+7(1 tech) **Po** *perf*o*rmancje* [performencie] pl., N [U] end20c, 2,+7(1 tech) **Cr** *perf*o*rmans* M [U] end20c, 2(1 tech) **Bg** p*u*rf*o*rm*a*ns M, pl. -*al*-*i*, 1990s, +7(1 mod) **Fi** *performanssi* 1980s, +7(1 tech) **Al** - < +7,+8: *shfaqje artistike, sportive*

permalloy *n.* 'an alloy of nickel and iron'
Du *permalloy* (0) **Fr** *permalloy* [pɛRmalwa/pɛRmelɔj] M, 20c (1 tech) **Sp** <=E>/*permaloy* M, 20c (1 tech) = *permaleación* **It** [=E] M [U] 1940s (1 tech) **Rm** *permaloi* [permal*o*j] N [U] mid20c, via Fr/ Rs (2>3 tech) **Rs** *permall*o*i* M [U] mid20c (1 tech) **Po** *permaloj* [permaloj] M [U] mid20c (1 tech) **Cr** (0) **Bg** *permal*o*i* M [U] mid20c (1 tech) **Hu** *permalloy*/*permalloj* [permalloi] [U] mid20c (1 tech)

pershing* *n.*/*cp²* (name) 'an American nuclear cruise missile'
In the political discussion of the 1970s, this term appears to have been on its way to becoming generic for a 'cruise missile'; it has now become obsolete.
Ge [pörʃin] F, pl. -*s*, 1970s (1 tech, obs) **Du** [=E] C, 1970s (2) = *pershing-raket* **Nw** [=E] (1NAME) **Ic** [=E] (0NAME) **Fr** *fusée Pershing* 1970s (1 tech, obs) **Sp** <=E>/*misil Pershing* [perʃin] 1970s(Ø/1 tech) **It** *missile Pershing* [=E] M, pl. Ø, 1970s (1 techNAME) **Rm** *rachetă pershing* [perʃiŋ] cp², 1970s (1 tech, rare) **Rs** p*e*rshing M, pl. -*i*, 1970s (2 tech) **Po** [perʃink] M, end20c (2 tech) **Cr** *peršing* M, pl. -*zi*, end20c (1 tech) **Bg** (*raketa*) P*u*rshing M, pl. -*al*-*i*, 1970s (5+2 tech) **Hu** *Pershing* [pərʃiŋ] pl. -*ek*, 1970s (2 tech) **Gr** p*y*ravlos p*e*rsing 1970s (5+1 tech)

personal computer *n.* 'a computer designed for use by a single individual' (cf. ↑*PC*)
Ge [=E/=Ge] M, pl. -*s*, 1980s (2 tech) < *PC* **Du** [=E] C, 1980s (2) < *p.c.* **Nw** (0) < trsl *personlig datamaskin, PC* **Ic** - < rend *einkatölva* * < trsl *ordinateur individuel* **Sp** <=E> M, pl. -*s*, 1990s (1 tech, rare) < trsl *computador personal* < *PC* **It** <=E>/*personal* [=E] M, pl. Ø, 1980s (2) **Rm** (0/1 tech) - < *PC* **Rs** - < *personal'nyï komp'yuter* **Po** - < trsl *komputer osobisty* **Cr** *personal kompj*u*tor* M, end20c (2 tech) *PC* **Bg** - < trsl *personalen kompyut*u*r* (3+2) **Fi** - < trsl *henkilökohtainen tietokone* **Hu** [=E] pl. -*ek*, end20c (1 tech) *PC* **Al** *kompjut*ë*r perso-nel* end20c (0) **Gr** <=E> [=E] M/N, pl. Ø/-*s*, end20c (1 tech, writ) < *computer*

personality *n.* 2 'a famous person', 3 'a person who stands out from others by virtue of his or her character', +6 'a positive, assertive, etc. personality'
Only the Germanic languages, in which the English word supplements earlier Latin-based loans, have the anglicism defined by its English form; in other languages there is an extension of meaning at best.
Ge [=E] F, pl. -*(ie)s*, 1970s, 2,3(1 jour) < *Persönlich-keit* **Du** [=E] C, pl. -*ies*/'*s*, 1970s, 2(1 jour, rare) 3(Ø)

< *persoonlijkheid* **Nw** [=E] M [U] 1950s, 3(1 rare) < *personlighet* **Ic** - < 3: *persónuleiki* **Fr** - < *personalité* **Sp** - < *personalidad* **It** - < *personalità* (5La) **Rm** - < *personalitate* **Po** - < *osobowość* **Fi** - < *personallisuus* **Al** - < *personalitet* **Gr** - < *prosopikotita*

personnel manager   *n.* 'a person in charge of appointment, training, and welfare of employees'
Ge - < *Personalchef* **Du** (Ø) < *personeel(s) chef* **Nw** [=E] M, pl. -e, 1980s (1) < *personalsjef* **Ic** - < trsl *starfsmannastjóri* **Fr** - < *directeur du personnel* **It** - < *direttore del personale* **Hu** - < trsl *személyzeti vezető*

petrodollar   *n.* 'a notional unit of currency earned by a country exporting petroleum'
Ge [pe:tro:dolar] M, pl. -*s*, 1970s (2 tech) **Du** [=E] C, 1980s (1 tech) > *oliedollar* **Nw** - < *oljepenger* **Fr** *pétrodollar* [petʀodɔlaʀ] M, 1970s (1 tech) **Sp** *petrodólar* M, 1970s (1 tech) **It** *petrodollaro* M, pl. -*i*, 1970s (3) **Rm** *petrodolar* [petrodolar] M, 1970s (1 tech/jour) **Rs** *petrodollar* M, pl. -*y*, 1990s (1 tech) < trsl *neftedollar* **Po** *petrodolar* [petrodolar] M, 1970s (2 coll) **Cr** *petrodolar* M, end20c (2 tech) **Bg** *petrodolar* M, pl. -*al-i*, end20c (2 tech) **Hu** [petrodolla:r] pl. Ø, 1970s (1 tech) **Gr** *petrodholario* N, mid20c (3/Ø)

petticoat   *n.* 1 'a woman's or girl's undergarment in the form of a skirt or a skirt and bodice'
The garment was so central to teenager fashion in the 1950s in Germany and The Netherlands that the term's restriction comes as a surprise since the *thing* must have been much more widespread.

Ge [peti:ko:t] M, pl. -*s*, 1950s (2>1 obs) **Du** *pettycoat*/<=E> [=E] C, 1950s (2>1 obs) **Ic** [=E] N, 1960s, 1(1 mod, obs)

petting   *n.* 'sexual fondling, without coitus'
Ge [=E] N [U] 1960s (2) **Du** [=E] 1960s (2 coll) = *vrijpartij* **Nw** [=E] M [U] 1950s (1) **Fr** (0) **Sp** [petin] M [U] 1980s (1 tech) < *magreo* **It** [pettiŋ(g)] M [U] 1950s (1 you) **Rm** (0) **Rs** *petting* M [U] end20c (1 you) **Po** [petink] M [U] end20c (1 mod) **Cr** *peting* M [U] end20c (1) **Bg** *peting* M [U] end20c (1 tech) **Fi** [=E] 1960s (2) **Hu** [petting] [U] 20c (2>3)

photo finish   *n.* 1 'a close finish of a race', +1a 'the finish as recorded on a film'
Ge [=E] N, pl. -*es*, 1980s (1 tech) **Du** *foto-finish* [=E] C, pl. -*es*, 1980s (1 tech) **Nw** *fotofinish* [fu:tu-+E] M [U] 1960s, +1a(2) **Fr** *photo-finish* [fɔtɔfiniʃ] F, mid20c (1 tech, ban) < *photo d'arrivée* **Sp** [fotofini/fotofiniʃ] M, mid20c (1 tech) **It** <=E>/f-[fɔto finiʃ] M, pl. Ø, 1960s (2 tech) **Rm** *fotofiniʃ/-finish* [fotofiniʃ] N, 1960s (1 tech, jour) < rend *la fotografie* **Rs** *fotofinish* M [U] end20c (1 tech) **Po** (0) **Cr** *fotofiniš*

M, end20c (1 tech) **Bg** *fotofinish* M, pl. -*al-i*, 1980s, +1a(1 tech) **Hu** <=E>/*fotofinis* [=E] [U] 20c (1 tech) < *célfotó* **Gr** *foto finis* N, mid20c, +1a(1 tech)

pickle(s)   *n.* 1a 'food preserved in vinegar' (cf. ↑*mixed pickles*), 2 'a plight'
The history and present-day distribution of this term should be compared with those of ↑*mixed pickles*, of which it is an accepted clipping.
Ge *Pickles/Pickels* [=E] pl., 19c (1 arch) **Du** *pickles* [=E] pl., 19c, 1a(1 tech) > *pekelzuur* **Nw** *pickles/ pikkels* [pikels] M [U] mid19c, 1a(2) **Ic** *pikkles* [pʰɪhkles] N/M [=E] end19c, via Da, 1a(2 coll) 2(2 sla) **Fr** *pickles* [pikœls] M, pl., 19c, 1a(1 tech) **Sp** [=E] pl., end19c, 1a(1 tech, rare) **Rm** *pickles* [=E] N, pl., 1980s, 1a(1 rare) **Rs** *pikuli* pl., 19c, 1a(2) **Po** *pikle* [pikle] pl., mid19c, 1a(3) **Fi** *pikkelsi* 19c, 1a(3) **Gr** *pikles* F, pl., end20c, 1a(1 rare)

pick up   *v.* 3b 'stop for and take along with one, esp. in a vehicle', 4 'make the acquaintance of (a person) casually, esp. as a sexual overture'
Du *oppicken* end20c, 3b(1 tech) **Nw** *pickelpikke opp* [pikə] mid20c, 3b(1 coll, rare) **Ic** *pikka upp* [pʰɪhka ʏhp] mid/end20c (4 coll)

pick-up   *n.* 1 'a small open motor truck', 2a 'the part of a record-player carrying the stylus', 2b 'a device on a musical instrument which converts sound vibrations into electrical signals for amplification', +8 'a record player'
Ge [=E] M, pl. -*s*, 1980s, 1(1 tech), 2a,b(1 tech, rare) **Du** [pɪkʏp] C, 1950s (2) **Nw** [=E] M, pl. -*er*, 1950s, 1(1); 1930s, 2a(2) **Ic** *pikköpp* [pʰɪhkœhp] M, pl. -*ar*, mid20c, 1(1 coll); N, pl. Ø, mid/end20c, 2a,b(1 tech) **Fr** [pikœp] M, uninfl., beg20c, 2a(o); 1930s, +8(1 obs) **Sp** [pikap] M, pl. -*s*, end20c, 1(1 tech); <=E>/*picú* [piku] 1920s, 2a,+8(3 tech) **It** [pikap] M, pl. Ø, 1930s (1>2 tech, mod) **Rm** <=E>/*picup* [=E/pikup] N, mid20c, 2a,+8(2>3) **Rs** *pikap* M, pl. -*y*, mid20c (2 tech) **Po** *pikap*/<=E> M, mid20c, 1(1 tech) **Cr** *pikap* M, mid20c, 2a(1 tech) **Bg** *pikap* M, pl. -*al-i*, mid20c, 1(2) **Fi** [=E] mid20c (2) **Hu** *pick-up/piköp* [=E/pikəp] pl. Ø, beg20c, 2a(3) **Gr** *pikap* N, beg20c, via Fr, +8(2)

pick-up line   *n.* 'a phrase used to break the ice when flirting, esp. for sexual purposes'
Ic [=E] N/*pikköpplína* F, pl. -*ur*, end20c (1+5 sla, you) **Hu** [=E] [U] end20c (1 writ, jour)

picnic   *n.* 1 'an excursion including an outdoor meal'
The history of this item is complex. The originally French term *pique-nique* was borrowed into various European languages (including English), in the seventeenth/eighteenth centuries, meaning 'a meal in a restaurant or private house for which expenses are shared'. The modern meaning is English; this has pushed out the older sense even in French.
Ge *Picknick*, N, pl. -*s*, beg20c (3) → *picknicken* v. **Du** *picknick/piknik* [pɪknɪk] C, mid19c (3) → -*en* v.; -*er* n. **Nw** <=E>/*piknik* [=E] M, pl. -*er*, beg20c (2) → *picknikke* v. **Ic** *pikknikk* [pʰɪhknɪhk] N/M/F [U] end19c, via Da (2 coll) = *lautarferð*

Fr *pique-nique* (4)   **Sp** [pi̱knik] M, pl. Ø, beg20c
(2)   **It** [pikni̱k] M, pl. Ø, end19c (3)   **Rm** [=E/pik-
ni̱k] N, end19c, via Fr (3)   **Rs** *pikni̱k* M, pl. -*i*, beg20c
(3)   **Po** *piknik* M, beg19c (3)   **Cr** *pi̱knik* M, pl. -*ci*,
beg20c (3)   **Bg** *pi̱knik* M, pl. -*al-nitsi*, mid20c (2) →
-*ov* adj.   **Fi** *piknikki* 19c; *picnic* 20c (2)   **Hu** *piknik*
[=E] pl. -*ek*, 20c, via E (5Fr)   **Al** *pikni̱k* M, pl. *pikniqe*,
end19c (5Fr)   **Gr** *pikni̱k* N, beg20c (5Fr)

picture, in the   *phr.* 'fully informed or noticed'
  Ge - < trsl *im Bilde sein*   **Du** *in de picture komen*
[pɪktʃə] 1970s (1 you)   **Ic** - < trsl *(vera) inni i myn-
dinni*

pidgin   *n./cp¹* 'a simplified language containing vocabulary from two or more languages, used for communication between people not having a common
language'
  Ge [=E] N, pl. -*s*, beg20c (Ø>1 tech>2 mod)   **Du**
[=E] N, 1940s (1 tech)   **Nw** [=E] M, pl. -*er*, beg20c
(1 tech)   **Ic** [=E] end20c, 1(1 tech)   **Fr** [=E] M, 19c (1
tech)   **Sp** [=E] M, mid20c (1 tech)   **It** [pidʒin] M, pl.
Ø, 1920s (1 tech)   **Rm** [=E] N, mid20c (1 tech)   **Rs**
pi̱dzhin M, pl. -*y*, mid20c (1 tech)   **Po** M, uninfl.,
beg20c (1 tech)   **Cr** [=E] M [U] beg20c (1 tech)   **Bg**
pidzhin M [U] mid20c (1 tech_LING)   **Fi** [=E/pidgin]
mid20c (Ø<2tech_LING)   **Hu** -*English* [=E] cp¹ [U] 20c
(1 tech)   **Al** *pixhin-inglish* M/cp¹ [U] 1980s (1
tech)   **Gr** *(ghlossa) pi̱tzin* F, 20c (5+1 tech)

pie   *n./cp²* 1 'a baked dish with a top and base of
pastry', +3 'a girl'
  Ge (Ø)   **Du** - < *taart*   **Nw** *pai* [=E] M, pl. -*er*,
beg20c, 1(3)   **Ic** *pælpie* [=E] N, pl. Ø/*pæi* M, pl.
-*(j)ar*, 1920s, 1(2); *pæja* [pʰai:ja] F, pl. -*ur*, mid20c,
+3(3 coll) = 1: *baka*   **Bg** *pai* M, pl. *payal-yove*,
end20c, 1(2 tech)   **Hu** [=E] cp² [U] end20c, 1
(0>1)   **Gr** *pai̱* cp², N, end20c, 1(1 rare)

piece   *n.* +3c 'the completed picture of a graffiti artist',
+6a 'a quantity of hash'
  Ge [=E] N, pl. -*s*, end20c, +3c(1 tech, you) +6a(1
sla)   **Nw** [=E] M, pl. -*r*, 1990s, +3c(1 tech, you)

piece of cake, a   *phr.* 'something easily achieved'
  Du [=E] mid20c (1 you)   **Ic** [=E] end20c (1 sla)

pier   *n.* +4 'a landing site in a port'
  Ge [pi:r] F/M, pl. -*e/-s*, 19c
(3)   **Du** [pi:r] C, pl. -*en*, 19c (3)
Nw *pir* [pi:r] M, pl. -*er*, mid19c
(3)   **Rs** *pirs* M, pl. -*y*, beg20c (3)
Po *pirs* [pirs] M, mid20c (1
tech)   **Cr** *pir* M, pl. -*ovi*, 20c (2)
Bg *pirs* M, pl. -*al-ove*, beg20c, via
Rs (3 tech)

piercing*   *n.* 'perforation of the skin to fasten orna-
ments'
  Ge [=E] N [U] 1994 (2 mod) →
gepierced adj.; *piercen* v.   **Du**
[=E] N [U] 1990 (1 mod)   **Nw**
[=E] M, pl. -*er*, 1990 (1 you,
mod) → *pierce* v.   **Fr** (0)   **Sp**
[pirsin] M [U] 1990s (1 you,
mod)   **Rm** [pirsiŋ] N [U] 1990s

(1 you)   **Rs** *pi̱rsing* M [U] 1995 (1 mod/jour)   **Gr**
<=E>/*pi̱rsing* N [U] 1990s (1 mod/jour)

piggyback   *n.* +2 'a system for transporting trucks
on trains'
  Ge - < rend *Huckepack(verkehr)*   **Nw** [=E] 20c (1
tech)   **Fr** <=E> 20c (1 tech, ban) < *ferroutage*

pilling   *n.* 'the formation of knots on the surface of
cloths'
  Ge [=E] N [U] 1970s (1 tech)   **Fr** - < *pilochage*   **Sp**
[pi̱lin] M, end20c (1 tech, rare)   **It** [=E] M [U] 1970s (1
tech)   **Rm** *piling* [pi̱ling] N [U] 1960s, via Ge? (1 tech,
rare)

pimp   *n.* 'a man who lives off the earnings of a pros-
titute'
  Du [=E] C, pl. -*s*, mid20c (1 you)   **Nw** (0)   **Ic** [=E]
M, pl. -*ar*, end20c (1 sla) < *(mellu)dólgur*

PIN   *abbrev./cp¹* 'personal identification number'
  Ge [=E] F [U] 1980s (0>1 tech, mod)   **Du** *pin-code*
[=E] C, 1990s (3) → *pinnen* v.   **Nw** *pin-*[=E] cp¹,
1990s (1)   **Ic** *pin-* [=E] cp¹, end20c (1 tech) < *leyni-
númer* N   **Rm** [=E] N, 1990s (1 tech)   **Hu** *PIN* [pin]
end20c (1 tech_COMPUT)

pin¹ (1)   *n.* 1a 'a piece of steel wire', 1d 'a badge
fastened with a pin', +1e 'a particular kind of slim nail'
  Ge [=E] M/N, pl. -*s*, 1980s, 1d(1
rare, mod)   **Du** [=E] C, 1980s,
1a(5) < *speld*   **Nw** *pins* [pins]
M, pl. Ø, 1990s, 1d(3)   **Ic** *pinni*
[pʰɪn:ɪ] M, pl. -*ar*, 18c, +1e(4) →
pinna v.   **Fr** *pin's* [pins] F, 1990s,
1d(1 mod, ban) < *épinglette*   **Sp**
[=E] M, pl. -*s/- es*, 1990s, 1a,d(1 tech)   **It** [=E] F, pl.
Ø, 1990s (1)   **Fi** *pinssi* 1990s, 1d(2)   **Al** - < *pineskë* F

pin² (1)   *n.* 2 'a wooden skittle used in bowling', +2a 'a
score in bowling'
  Ge [=E] M, pl. -*s*, 1970s (1 tech, rare)   **Nw** (0) < 2:
kjegle   **Bg** *pin* M, pl. -*al-ove*, 1990s (1 tech)

pin   *v.* 1a 'fasten with a pin or pins'
  Ge *(an-)pinnen* (3 coll)   **Du** *pinnen* (5)

pinboard   *n.* 'a board, usu. made from cork, on
which notices are pinned'
  Ge [=E] N, pl. -*s*, end20c (2) < *Pinnwand*

pincher*   *n.* 1 'a dog with a cropped tail', 2 'a pip
squeak'
  The distribution of this term is more restricted
than that of names for other breeds; this may be
because it is one of the older quasi-English words,
coined on an English basis in German, and spread
from there.
  Ge *Pinscher* [pi̱nʃa] M, pl. Ø,
end19c, 1(3) 2(3 coll)   **Du**
pincher [=E] C, beg20c (2
tech)   **Nw** *pinsjer* [pi̱nʃer] M,
pl. -*e*, beg20c, via Ge (1 tech)   **Fr**
pincher M, 20c, via Ge (1 tech)
Rm [=E] M, 20c (1 tech)   **Rs**
pi̱ncher M, pl. -*y*, beg20c (2)   **Po** *pinczer* [-er] M,
20c, via Ge (3)   **Cr** (0) < *pinč*   **Bg** *pi̱ncher* M, pl.
-*al-i*, mid20c, via Rs, 1(3)   **Fi** *pinseri* beg20c (3)

ping-pong *n./cp[1]* 1 'table tennis' (non-contest), +2 'the ball'
Ge [=E] N [U] beg20c, 1(3 obs) < *Tischtennis* **Du** [=E] N [U] beg20c, 1(3) **Nw** [=E] M [U] beg20c, 1(3) < *bordtennis* **Ic** *pingpong* [=E] N [U] mid20c, 1(1 coll) < *borðtennis* **Fr** [piŋpɔŋ] M [U] beg20c, 1(3) → *pongiste* **Sp** <=E>/*pimpón* M [U] beg20c, 1(2) < *tenis de mesa* **It** [piŋ pɔŋ/pim-] M [U] 1900s, 1(3) > *tennis da tavolo* **Rm** [=E] N [U] beg20c, via Fr, 1(3 obs) < *tenis de masă* → *pingpongist, - ă* M/F **Rs** *ping-pong* M [U] beg20c, 1(1 obs) < *nastol'nyĭ tennis* **Po** <=E> M [U] beg20c, 1(3) → *-ista* M; *-istka* F; *-owy* adj. **Cr** *ping-pong* M [U] beg20c, 1(3) → *-aš* M **Bg** *ping-pong* M [U] mid20c, 1(2 obs); pl. *-a*, +2(3) → *-ov* adj. **Fi** - < *pingis* **Hu** [piŋpoŋg] [U] 19c, 1(3) = *asztali tenisz*; cp[1] + *labda* +2(3+5) **Al** *ping pong* M [U] 1970s (3) **Gr** *ping-pong*/*pingpong* N [U] 1(2) > *epitrapezia antisferisi* F

pink *adj.* 'a pale red colour'
pink was adopted into various languages exclusively for ladies' fashion and has remained restricted to this function, the 'normal' uses being covered by *rosa* (German) or other alternatives (which can now contrast with *pink* in the terminology of fashion).
Ge [=E] uninfl., 1960s (1 mod) < *rosa* **Du** [=E] 1980s (1 mod) **Nw** [=E] 1980s (1 mod) < *rosa, lyserød* **Fr** (0) **It** [piŋk] uninfl., 1980s (1 mod) **Po** (0) **Cr** (0) **Fi** *pinkki* (1 mod) < *vaaleanpunainen* **Hu** [=E] end20c (0>1 writ, mod) **Gr** *pink* end20c (1 mod)

pint *n.* 1 'a unit of liquid or dry capacity equal to one-eighth of a gallon', 2a 'a pint of beer'
Ge 2a(Ø) **Du** 1(5 arch) **Nw** [=E] M, pl. *-s*, mid19c, 1,2a(Ø) **Ic** [=E] mid20c (Ø) **Fr** *pinte* [pɛ̃t] 1(5) **Sp** *pinta* (5Fr) **It** *pinta* (5Fr) **Rm** [=E] N, 1970s, 1(Ø) **Rs** *pinta* F, pl. *-y*, 19c, 1(Ø) **Po** M, mid20c, 1(Ø) **Cr** *pinta* F, pl. *-e*, mid20c, 1(Ø) **Bg** *pinta* F, pl. *-nti*, 20c, via Rs, 1(Ø) **Fi** [=E] 19c, 2a(Ø) **Hu** 1(5Fr) **Al** *pinë* F, pl. *-a*, end20c (3) **Gr** *pída* F, 20c, 1(3/Ø)

pin-up (girl) *n.* 1 'a photograph of a popular or sexually attractive person, designed to be hung on the wall', 2 'a person shown in such a photograph'
What would seem to have become a universal expression, spread by the US Army and more general American influence, was in fact adopted only in Central Europe at first and has spread to various mainly Eastern countries more recently, not affecting other, peripheral, languages at all. Note that the loanword appears to invariably refer to females. Since the term has long become obsolete, a further spread is unlikely.
Ge *Pin-up girl* N, pl. *-s*, 1940s (1 obs) **Du** *pin up* [pɪn ʏp/=E] C, 1970s (2) **Nw** [=E/pinʉp/(joc.) pinʉpe] M, pl. *-er/-s*, 1950s (1 obs) **Fr** *pin up* [pinœp] M, pl. Ø, 1940s (1 obs) **Sp** [pinap gel] F, pl. *-s*, 1960s (1) < *pin-up* **It** [pin∧p (gœr)] F, pl. Ø, 1950s (2) **Rm**

[pinapgərl] F, pl. Ø, 1970s (0) **Rs** *pinap(gërl)* F, pl. *-y*, 1990s (1 mod) **Po** F, uninfl., end20c, 1(1 you) **Cr** [=E] adj., end20c; *pin-ap gèrla* F, end20c (1) **Fi** [=E] end20c (1) **Hu** [=E] pl. Ø, end20c, 1(0>1 jour, you) **Gr** <=E>/*pinap gerl* N, pl. *-s*, end20c (1 you/jour)

pipeline *n.* 1 'a pipe for conveying oil', 2 'a channel supplying information', +3 'procedure'
Whereas the word is commonly known in Germanic and Romance languages, it has to compete with native equivalents which tend to be more common, leaving technical and journalistic uses to the anglicism. Eastern languages are generally not affected.
Ge [=E] F, pl. *-s*, mid20c, 1(1 tech) = *Ölleitung* **Du** *pijpleiding*/*pijplijn* 1(5); [=E] C, 1990s, 2,+3(1 coll) **Nw** [=E] M, pl. *-s*, 1960s, 1(1 obs) < trsl *rørledning* **Fr** <=E>/*pipe-line* [piplin/pajplajn] M, end19c, 1(1 tech, ban) < *gazoduc, oléoduc* **Sp** <=E> M, pl. Ø, mid20c, 1(1 tech, arch, obs) < *oleoducto* **It** [paiplain] F, pl. Ø, 1930s, 1(1 tech) < creat *oleodotto* **Rm** [=E] N, pl. ?, 1970s (1 tech, rare) **Cr** *pajplajn* M, mid20c, 1(1 tech) **Hu** [=E] pl. Ø, end20c, 1(1 tech)

pit bull terrier *n.* 'a dog of an American variety of bull terrier, noted for its ferocity'
The distribution is complex, because two different abbreviations, *pitbull* and *bullterrier*, are current alongside the full form. In contrast to the names of other breeds, the adoption of the word is often recent, certainly 'popularized' by news reports about accidents caused by the aggressive dogs.
Ge [=E] M, pl. Ø, 20c (1 tech) **Du** *pitbullterriër* [pɪtbɪltɛriər] C, 1980s (2) = *pitbull* **Nw** [=E] M, pl. *-e*, 1980s (2) < *pitbull* **Fr** *pitbull*/*pit* [pitbul/pitbyl/pit] M, 1990s (1 tech) **Sp** *pitbull* [=E] M, 1990s (1 tech) **It** [=E] M, pl. Ø, 1900s (1 tech) **Rm** [pitbul terier] M, 1990s (2 rare) **Rs** *pit bul'ter'er* M, pl. *-y*, 1980s (1 tech) **Po** [-er] M, end20c (1 tech) **Cr** *pitbul* 20c (1 tech) **Bg** *pitbul/bul terier* M, pl. *-al-i*, 20c (2 tech) **Fi** *pitbull* [=E] 1980s (2) **Hu** [=E] pl. *-ek*, 1990s (1) < *pitbull* **Gr** *pitbul terie* N, end20c, via Fr (1 tech)

pitcher *n.* 'a player who delivers the ball to the batter, esp. in baseball'
Du [=E] C, pl. *-s*, end20c (1 tech) **Nw** [=E] M, pl. *-e*, end20c (1 tech, rare) **Sp** [pitʃer] M, end20c (1 tech) **It** [=E] M, pl. Ø, end20c, 1(1 tech) **Rs** *pitcher* M, pl. *-y*, mid20c (1 tech) **Cr** (0) **Bg** *pičŭr* M, pl. *-i*, end20c (1 tech)

pitch pine *n.* 'any of various pine trees with very resinous wood'
Ge [=E] F, pl. *-s*, 1910s (1 tech, rare) **Du** [=E] C, 1910s (1 tech) **Nw** [=E] M [U] 20c (1 tech) **Fr** *pitchpin* [pitʃpɛ̃] M, end19c (3 tech) **It** [=E] M [U] 1910s (1 tech) **Rm** *pitchpin* [=E/piʃpin̩] M, 1970s (1 tech); [pitʃpin̩] M (1+5)

pit prop *n.* 'a balk of wood used to support the roof of a coal mine'
Nw *pitprops* [=E] M, sg. [U] beg20c (3 tech)

pitting* *n.* 'corrosion'
Ge [=E] N [U] 20c (1 tech) **Nw** *pitting* [=E] M [U] 20c (1 tech) **Po** [-nk] M [U] mid20c (1 tech) **Hu** [=E] [U] 20c (1 tech)

pivot *n.*+2a 'a position player in basketball, playing near the goal in handball'
Du - → *pivoteren* v. **Fr** *pivot* (4) **Sp** [pibo] M, 1980s (1 tech/5Fr) **It** [pivo/pivot] M, pl. Ø, 1950s (2 tech/5Fr) **Rm** (5Fr) **Bg** *pivot* M, pl. *-i*, mid20c (1 tech) → *-iram* **Gr** *pivot* M, 1980s (1 tech)

place *n.* 2 'a city, town, village, etc. +4c 'a lodging, salon, club etc.'
Ic *pleis* [=E] N, pl. Ø, 1960s (2 sla)

place mat *n.* 1 'a small mat on a table underneath a person's plate'
Du *placemat/place-mat* [ple:smet] M, pl. *-s*, 1970s (2) **Nw** (0)

plaid *n.* +1a 'a (chequered) blanket for travelling', 2 'a long piece of plaid worn over the shoulder as part of Scottish Highland dress', +3 'light summer cloth'
This term was very common in many nineteenth-century languages but has since become obsolete outside technical or historical contexts in some. Mediated partly through French (and German?) it did not reach some of the peripheral languages then, and there was little reason for it to be adopted later.
Ge [ple:t] M/N, pl. *-s*, mid19c, +1a,2(1 obs) **Du** [ple:t] C, end19c, +1a(2) **Nw** *pledd* [pled] N, pl. Ø, mid19c, +1a(3) **Ic** <=E> N, beg20c, 2(Ø) **Fr** [plɛd] M, 18c, +1a(1 obs) 2(1 arch) **Sp** <=E> M, 1880s, +1a,2(Ø tech, arch) **It** [plɛd] M, pl. Ø, 18c, +1a,2(2) **Rm** *pled* [pled] N, end19c, via Fr, +1a(3) **Rs** *pled* M, pl. *-y*, mid19c, +1a,2(2) **Po** *pled* [-t] M, mid19c, +1a(2) → *-zik* M **Cr** *pled* M, pl. *-ovi*, beg20c, 2(1) **Fi** *pleedi* 19c, +1a,2(3 tech) **Hu** *pléd* [ple:d] M, *-ek*, 19c, +1a,2(3) **Gr** *pled* N, beg20c, +1a(1 obs)

plain *adj.* 3a 'uncomplicated; not elaborate', 6 'unsophisticated'
Ic [=E] uninfl., mid/end20c (2 coll)

planning *n.* 1 'design(ing)', 2 'work planning', 3 'a schedule'
Du [=E] C [U] 1940s (1 tech) **Fr** [planiŋ] M, 1940s, 2,3(2 ban) > *planification, planigramme* **Sp** [planin] M, 1970, 2(1<2 tech) **It** [plɛniŋ (g)] M, pl. Ø, 1950s (1 tech) < *pianificazione* **Rm** (0) **Rs** - < trsl *planiro-*

vanie (n'e) N **Po** (0) **Bg** - < trsl *planirane* **Al** - < *planifikim*

plate *n./cp²* 5b 'objects of plated metal'
Du - < *plaat/pleet* **Nw** *plett* [plet] M [U] beg20c, 5b(3) **Ic** *plett* [pʰleht] N/cp² [U] end19c, via Da (3) **Rs** (5Fr) **Po** - < *plater*

platform *n.* 1 'a raised level surface; a natural or artificial terrace', 6 'the declared policy of a political party'
Ge *Plattform* 6(4) **Du** [platfo:rm] N, 1970s, 6(1 tech, jour) < *programma* **Nw** *plattform* 6(4) **Fr** *plate-forme* F, mid20c, 1(5) 6(4) **Sp** *plataforma* (5Fr) **It** *piattaforma* (5Fr) **Rm** *platformă* [platformə] F, beg20c (5Fr) **Rs** *platforma* F, pl. *-y*, beg20c, 6(3) **Cr** *platforma* F, pl. *-e*, beg20c, 6(3) **Bg** *platforma* F, pl. *-mi*, beg20c, via Rs, 1(5Fr) 6(4) **Hu** [platform] pl. *-ok*, beg20c, 6(3/5Fr) **Al** *platformë* F, pl. *-a*, 1940s, 6(3 tech) **Gr** *platforma* F, via Fr, 1(3) 6(3 tech)

play! *interj.* 1 'begin!' (sport), 2 'the start button on tape recorders, CD-players, etc.'
Nw [=E] 1970s, 2(1 tech) **Ic** [=E] uninfl., 1970s, 2(1 coll) **Fr** [plɛ] end19c (1 arch) **Sp** [=E] M, end20c (1 tech) **It** [=E] 1940s (1 tech) < *inizio* **Rm** [=E] beg20c (0>1 tech) **Rs** *pleǐ* mid20c (1 tech) **Po** beg20c (1 tech) **Bg** *pleǐ* mid20c, 2(1 tech) **Hu** end19c (1 tech) **Gr** <=E>/*plei̯* N, beg20c, 2(2)

playback *n.* 1 'the playing back of a sound or sounds', +2 'synchronization of sound and film', +3 'miming (by a singer/actor pretending to sing while a recording is played)'
This term is virtually universal, applied to both films and music-record production; differences therefore concern mainly the degree of frequency/acceptability and the date of adoption.
Ge [ple:bek] N, pl. *-s*, 1960s, +2,+3(1 tech) **Du** [=E] N, 1970s (2) → adv.; *-en* v. **Nw** [=E] M, pl. *-s*, 1960s, +3(1 tech) **Ic** [=E] N [U] end20c (1 tech) **Fr** *playback* [plɛbak] M, mid20c, +3(1 tech/ban) > *présonorisation* **Sp** [pleibak] M, 1960s, 1,+2(1>2 tech) > *sonido pregrabado, previo* **It** [=E/pleibɛk] M [U] 1940s (2) **Rm** [=E] N, 1970s, +2,+3(1 tech) **Rs** *pleǐbek* M [U] 1960s, +3(1 tech) **Po** [pleibek] M [U] mid20c (2 tech) **Cr** *plejbek* [=E] M [U] mid20c (1 tech) **Bg** *pleǐbek* M, pl. *-al-betsi*, end20c, 1(1 tech) +3(3 tech) **Fi** [=E] 1960s (2) **Hu** [ple:bek] pl. *-ek*, mid20c, +2(1 tech); 1960s, +3(2 tech) **Al** *pleibek* M [U] 1970s (3) **Gr** *pleibak* N [U] end20c, +3(1 tech)

playboy *n.* 1 'an irresponsible pleasure-seeking man, esp. a wealthy one'
This term became immediately popular after 1945 when it replaced earlier synonyms (like French *belami* or *bonvivant*); it became known even more widely after the magazine of this name was started in 1954. Note the much smaller acceptability of ↑*playgirl*.
Ge [ple:boi] M, pl. *-s*, 1960s (2) **Du** [=E] C, 1960s

(2) **Nw** [=E] M, pl. *-er/-s*, mid20c (2) **Ic** [=E] M, pl. *-ar*, 1960s (1 coll) **Fr** *play-boy* [plɛbɔj] M, 1960s (2) **Sp** [pleiboi] M, pl. *-s*, mid20c (2) **It** [pleiboi] M, pl. Ø, 1950s (3) **Rm** [=E] M, pl. Ø, 1970s (2 coll) **Rs** *pleiboi* M, pl. *-boi*, end20c (1 jour, you) **Po** <=E> M, end20c (2) **Cr** *plejboj* M, pl. *-i*, mid20c (2) **Bg** *pleiboi* M, pl. *-boyove*, mid20c (2) → *-ski* adj.; *-ka* F **Fi** [=E] (2) **Hu** [plɛːboj] pl. *-ok*, 1960s (2) **Gr** <=E>/*pleiboi* M, mid20c (2)

player *n./cp²* 4 'any device for playing records, compact discs, cassettes, etc.'
Ge [plɛːa] M, pl. Ø, 1980s (1 tech, mod) = *-spieler* **Du** [=E] C, 1980s (1 tech) < *cd-speler, cassettespeler* **Nw** (0) < *-spiller* **Ic** - < trsl *-spilari* **It** [=E] M, pl. Ø, 1980s (1 tech) **Rm** [=E] N, 1980s (1 tech>2) **Rs** *pleier* M, pl. *-y*, 1980s (1 tech, mod) **Po** (0) **Cr** (0) **Bg** *pleur* M, pl. *-al-i*, 1990s (1 tech, mod) **Gr** [=E] N, end20c (1 tech, mod)

playgirl* *n.* 'the female counterpart of a playboy'
Ge [plɛːgøːl] N, pl. *-s*, 1960s (1 mod/euph) **Nw** [=E] M, pl. *-s*, 1960s (1) **Sp** [=E] F, pl. *-s*, 1990s (1 rare) **It** [=E] F, pl. Ø, 1960s (1) **Rs** (0) **Po** (0) **Cr** *plejgerl* [=E] F, end20c (1) **Gr** <=E>/*pleigerl, pleigerl* N, pl. *-s* (1 mod)

playmaker *n.* 'a player in a team game who leads attacks or brings players in the same side into a position to score' (sport)
Ge - < *Spielmacher* **Du** (Ø) < *spelmaker* **Nw** [=E] M, pl. *-e*, end20c (1 tech) **Sp** [=E] M, 1990s (1 tech, rare) **It** [=E] M/F, pl. Ø, 1960s (1>2 tech) **Rs** *pleimeiker* M, pl. *-y*, 1990s (1 tech) **Cr** *plejmejker* end20c (1 tech) **Bg** *pleimeikŭr* M, pl. *-i*, 1990s (1 tech) **Gr** *pleimeiker* M, end20c (2 tech)

playmate *n.* 1 'a child's companion in play', +3 'a nude girl in men's magazines'
Ge [plɛːmeːt] N, pl. *-s*, 1970s, +3(1 jour, rare) **Du** [=E] N, 1970s, +3(1 jour, rare) **Ic** - < +3: rend *leikfang* **Fr** [plɛmɛt] F, 1970s, +3(1 rare) **Sp** [=E] F, pl. *-s*, 1990s, +3(1 tech) **Po** <=E> F, uninfl., end20c, +3(1 jour) **Fi** [=E] end20c (1) **Gr** *pleimeit* F, pl. *-s*, end20c, +3(1 jour, mod)

play-off *n.* +1a 'the method of selecting finalists in a sports contest by play-off matches'
   The term was evidently first adopted for ice hockey in the 1970s, but has spread to other contests organized as tournaments, such as football. No calques or other native equivalents appear to have been tried.
Ge [plɛːof] N, pl. *-s*, 1980s (1 tech) **Du** [=E] C, 1970s (1 tech) **Nw** [=E] N, end20c (1 tech) **Fr** [plɛɔf] M, 1990s (1

tech/ban) > *départage, tour final* **Sp** [plejof/plajof] M, pl. 1980s (1 tech) **It** [pleiof] M, pl. Ø, 1980s (1>2 tech) **Rm** [=E] N [U] 1980s (1 tech) **Rs** *pleioff* M, uninfl., 1990 (1 tech) **Po** <=E> M, end20c (1 tech) **Cr** *plej-of* M [U] end20c (1 tech) → *-ski* adj. **Bg** *pleiof* M, pl. *-al-i*, end20c (1 tech) → *-en* adj. **Fi** [=E] 1980s (1 tech) **Gr** *pleiof* N, usu. pl., 1980s (1 tech)

playroom *n.* +2 'a partyroom'
Gr <=E> [=E] N, pl. *-s*, 1990s (1 mod)

please *interj.* 5 'a tag used in polite requests'
Du interj. [=E] 1980s (1 coll, rare) **Nw** [=E] mid20c (1 coll) **Ic** [=E] interj., mid20c (1 sla) **Sp** [=E] mid20c (0>1 mod, rare) **It** [pliːs] end20c (1 coll, mod) **Rm** (0) **Rs** (0) **Po** (0) **Cr** (0) **Bg** (0) **Fi** <=E>/*pliis* [=E] 1980s (0 coll) **Hu** [=E] 20c, interj. (0) **Gr** (0 coll)

plenty *adj.* 'existing in an ample quantity'
Du [=E] beg20c (1 coll) **Nw** [=E] end19c (1 coll) **Ic** [pʰlɛnti] uninfl., 1940s (1 sla)

plot *n.* 2 'the interrelationship of the main events in a play, novel, film, etc.', 3 'a conspiracy or secret plan, esp. to achieve an unlawful end', 4 'a diagram, chart, or map', +6 'the marking of the position of a ship, aircraft, etc. on a chart'
Ge [=E] M/N, pl. *-s*, 1970s, 2(1 tech, mod) **Du** [=E] C, 1960s, 2(2) **Nw** <=E>/*plott* [=E] N, pl. Ø, 20c, 2(1) 3,+6(1 tech) **Ic** *plott* [pʰlɔht] N, pl. Ø, mid/end20c, 2,3(3 coll) 4,+6(3 tech) **It** [=E] M, pl. Ø, 1970s, 2(1) **Cr** (0)

plot (in) *v.* 1 'make a plan or map of (an existing object, a place, or a thing to be laid out, constructed, etc)', 2 'plan or contrive secretly (a crime, conspiracy, etc.), 3 'mark (a point or course etc.) on a chart or diagram', 4a 'mark out or allocate (points) on a graph'
Ge *plotten* [plɔtən] 1980s, 1(1 tech) **Du** *plotten* [plɔtən] 1960s (1 tech) **Nw** *plotte (inn)* ["plɔte] 20c, 3,4a(3 tech) → *innplotte* v.; *innplotting* C; *plotter* M **Ic** *plotta* [pʰlɔhta] mid/end20c, 2(3 coll) 3,4a(3 tech) **Cr** *plotirati* 20c, 3(3 tech)

plotter *n.* +2 'a device to convert computer calculations', +3 'a person who is apt to plot'
Ge [plɔta] M, pl. Ø, 1980s, +2(1 tech) **Du** [=E] C, 1960s, +2(1 tech) **Nw** [=E] [plɔter] M, pl. *-e*, 20c, +2(1 tech) **Ic** [=E] M, pl. *-ar*, mid/end20c, +2(1 tech); [pʰlɔhtari] *plottari* M, pl. *-ar*, mid/end20c, +3(3 coll) **Fr** [plɔtœʀ] M, 1980s, +2(1 tech) < *traceur, table traçante* **Sp** [ploter] M, 1980s (1 tech) = *trazador (de gráficos)* → *ploteo, plotear* **It** [plɔter] M, pl. Ø, 1980s, +2(1 tech) **Rm** [plɔter] N, 1980s, +2(1 tech) **Rs** *plotter* M, pl. *-y*, 1960s, +2(1 tech) **Po** [-er] M, 1980s, +2(1 tech) **Cr** [ploter] M, pl. *-i*, end20c, +2(1 tech) **Bg** *ploter* M, pl. *-al-i*, end20c, +2(1 tech) **Hu** [plɔtter] pl. Ø, end20c, +2(1 tech) **Gr** <=E> [=E] N, end20c, +2(1 tech) = *skhedhioghrafos*

plug *v.* 3 'seek to popularize (an idea, product etc.) by constant recommendation', +5 'connect electrically by inserting a plug in a socket'

Du *pluggen* [plʏxən] 1960s, 3(2)   Nw *plugge* ["plʉge]
+5(4)   Ic *plögga* [pʰlœk:a] end20c, 3(2 sla) +5(2
tech)

plug   *n.* 2a 'a device of metal pins in an insulated
casing fitting into holes in a socket for making an
electric connection', 2b 'an electric socket', 4 'a piece
of (often free) publicity'
   Nw *plugg* 2a(5LowGe)   Ic *plögg* [=E] N, pl. Ø; *plögg-
ur/plöggi* [pʰlœk:ʏr/pʰlœc:ɪ] M, pl. *-ar*, end20c, 2a,b(1
tech) 4(1 sla)

plum cake   *n.* 'a cake containing raisins, currants,
etc.
   Nw *plumkake* [plʉmka:ke] M, pl. *-r*, 19c (1+5)   Sp
[plʉmkei] M, 1930s (1)   It [plumkeik/plamkeik/
plʉŋke] M, pl. Ø, beg19c (3)   Rm *plumchecl-cheic*
[plʉmke(j)k] N, 20c (2)

plunger   *n.* 1 'a part of a mechanism that works with a
plunging or thrusting movement'
   The word illustrates the limited distribution of a
loan from British nineteenth-century technology;
some of the spread is possibly due to German mediation (notice consistent [u] pronunciation). The word
remained technical and may be obsolescent in some
languages.
   Ge *Plunger/Plunscher* M, pl. Ø,
end19c (1 tech) < *Tauchkol-
ben*   Du *plunjer* [plʏnjər] C,
mid19c (3 tech)   Rm [plʉndʒer/
=E] N, mid20c (2>3 tech) =
piston plonjor   Rs *plʉnzher* M,
pl. *-y*, end19c (1 tech)   Cr *plʉnd-
žer* M, pl. *-i*, beg20c (1 tech)   Bg *plʉnzher* M, pl. *-al-i*,
beg20c, via Rs (3 tech)   Hu [=E] pl. Ø, 1910s (1 arch)
< *hazárdőr*   Al *plunzher* [pluńdʒer] M, pl. *-ë*, beg20c
(3 tech)

Plymouth Rock*   *n.* 'a breed of large domestic fowl
of American origin, having grey plumage with black-
ish stripes'
   The breed and its name appear to have been more
popular in the nineteenth century (cf. ↑*leghorn*)
   Ge [=E] pl., 19c (1 tech, rare)
Du (Ø)   Fr *Plymouth-Rock* F
(1 tech)   Rm *plymouth* [=E] N,
pl. Ø, 20c (1 tech)   Rs *plimutrok* M, pl. *-i*, mid20c (1 tech)   Po
plimutroki [plimutroki]   pl.,
mid20c (1 tech)   Cr *Plymouth*
F, mid20c (1 tech)   Bg *plimutrok* [U]/M, pl. *-ka/-rotsi*
mid20c (1 tech)   Hu *plymouth* [plimut] pl. Ø, beg20c
(2>3 tech, obs)

P.O. Box   *abbrev.* 'post office box'
   Native terms (many of them calques) still predominate, even though *P.O. box* is very widely known; it is
significant that the French equivalent has no international currency although French used to be the international language of postal services.
   Ge (o) < *Postfach*   Du (o) - < *postbus*   Nw (Ø) <
postboks   Ic *(P.O.) Box* beg20c (o) < *pósthólf*   Fr -
< *boîte postale*   It - < *casella postale*   Rm - < *căsuţă*

poştală   Po [pe o-] M, end20c (1 tech)   Bg (o) < *p.k.*
Fi - < trsl? *postilokero; PL*   Gr (o) < *T. Th.*

pocket-   *n./cp¹* 8b 'smaller than the usual size', +9 'a
small camera'
   Ge [=E] cp¹, 1970s, +9(1 tech) < *Pocket-Kamera*
Du [=E] cp¹, 1950s (2 tech)   Nw [=E] mid19c, 8b(1)
< *lomme-*   Ic - < trsl *vasa-*   Fr - < mean *de po-
che*   Sp - < mean *de bolsillo*   It [pɔket-] 1920s,
8b(2)   Rm - < rend *de buzunar*   Rs *pɔket-cp¹*,
end20c, 8b(1 tech, jour, mod)   Po M, end20c, 8b(1
mod)   Cr (o)   Bg *pɔket* M [U] end20c, 8b(1 tech) <
dzhoben format   Hu [=E] end20c (1 tech, jour, mod)
< *zseb-*   Gr [=E] (o) < trsl *tsepis*

pocketbook   *n.* 1 'a notebook', 4 'a paperback or
other small book'
   Ge [=E] N, pl. *-s*, 1950s, 4(1 obs) < trsl *Taschenbuch*   Du *pocketboek/pocket* 4(2 tech+5)   Nw *pocketbok* [=E+N] 1950s, 4(2+5)   Ic [pʰɔhket-] *-bók* F,
mid20c, 4(1 coll+5) = 4: *vasabrotsbók*   Fr *pocketbook* [pɔketbuk] M, end19c, 4(1 arch) < trsl *livre de
poche*   Sp 4(o) < trsl *libro de bolsillo*   It [pɔket buk]
M, pl. Ø, 1960s, 4(1>2) < rend *libro tascabile*   Rm - <
rend *carte de buzunar*   Rs *pɔketbuk* M, pl. *-y*, end20c,
4(1 jour)   Po *pocket (book)* [-et-] M, end20c, 4(1
mod)   Fi - < *pokkari*   Hu - < *zsebkönyv*   Al - < 4:
trsl *libër schepi*   Gr - < trsl *vivlio tsepis*

point(s)   *n.* 12a 'a unit of scoring in games or of
measuring value, etc.', 13a 'the significant or essential
thing; what is actually intended or under discussion',
13b 'sense or purpose; advantage or value', 17 'a
junction of two railway lines'
   Du *punt* 12a,17(5) 13a(1 tech)   Nw [=E] N, pl. *-s*,
1960s, 12a(1 tech) 13a(1 coll, fac); *pens* [pens] M, pl.
-er, 19c, 17(3)   Ic [=E] N [U] end20c, 13a(1 sla)   It
punto (5La)   Bg - < 12a: mean *tochka*   Fi *pointi*
13a(1 sla)   Hu 12a (5Fr)   Gr - < 12a: mean *podos*

point, to the   *phr.* 'relevant or relevantly'
   Du [=E] uninfl., 1980s (2)   Nw [=E] end20c (1)

pointer   *n.* 4 'a dog trained to point at game, i.e. that
on scenting game stands rigid looking towards it'
   Ge [=E] M, pl. Ø, end19c (1 tech, obs)   Du [=E] C,
end19c (2 tech)   Nw [=E] M, pl. *-e*, 20c (1 tech)   Fr
pointer, pointeur [pwɛtœR] M, mid19c (1 tech/ban) <
pointeur   Sp *póinter* [pɔinter] M, pl. *-s*, 1930s (2 tech)
It [pɔinter] M, pl. Ø, mid19c (2 tech)   Rm *poanter/
<=E>* [pɔanter/=E] M, beg20c, via Fr (2>3 tech)   Rs
pɔinter M, pl. *-y*, beg20c (2 tech)   Po [-er] M, beg20c
(1 tech) → *-ek* M   Cr *poenter* M, pl. *-i*, beg20 (1
tech)   Bg *pɔinter* M, pl. *-al-i*, 20c (1 tech)   Fi *point-
teri* beg20c (3)   Hu [pɔinter] pl. *-ek*, 19c (2 tech)   Gr
pɔider [-d-,-nt-] N, 20c (1 tech)

poker   *n.* 1 'a card-game in which bluff is used as
players bet on the value of their hands', +2 'any venture at high risk', +3 'a combination of four cards of
the same value'
   The card-game was invented in America in 1834 (of
uncertain etymology); the word was a foreignism at
first, but the game was quickly taken over into all
European societies together with its name.

Ge [po̯:ka] M/N [U] beg20c, 1(3 coll); 1970s, +2(3) →
-*n* v.   Du [po̯:kər] N [U] 1940s, 1,+2(3) → -*en* v.
Nw [pu:ker] M [U] beg20c, 1,+2(3)   Ic *póker*
[pʰou:ker] M [U] beg20c, via Da, 1,+2(2)   Fr
[pɔkɛʀ] M, mid19c, 1(3) = 2: *partie de poker* > *poker
d'as*   Sp <=E>/*póquer* M, beg20c, 1(3)   It [po̯ker] M
[U] mid19c, 1,+3(3) +2(1) → -*ista* M; -*ismo* M; -*ino* M
Rm *pocher* [po̯ker] N, beg20c, via Fr, 1(3) → -*aş* dim.;
-*ist*/-*istă* M/F   Rs *poker* M [U] beg20c, 1,+2(3)   Po
[poker] M, beg20c, 1,+2(3) → -*ek* M; -*zysta* M; -*owy*
adj.   Cr *poker* M [U] beg20c, 1,+2(3) → -*aš* M; -*ski*
adj.   Bg *poker* M [U]/pl. -*a*, beg20c, 1(2) → -*dzhiya* M
Fi *pokeri* 19c, 1(3)   Hu *póker* [po̯:ker] pl. Ø, end19/
beg20c, 1(3) → -*ez* v.   Al *poker* M [U] beg20c, 1(1
reg)   Gr *poker* N [U] 1(2); *poka* F [U] beg20c, 1(3)

poker-face   *n*. 1 'the impassive countenance appropriate to a poker player'
    Ge [po̯:kafe:s] N [U] 1960s (1 coll) > *Pokerge-
sicht*   Du [=E] N, 1960s (2 coll) > *pokergezicht*   Nw
(0) < *pokeransiktl-fjes*   Ic [=E] N, pl. Ø, end20c (1);
pókerfés N, pl. Ø, mid/end20c (2); *pókerandit* N, beg/
mid20c (2+5)   Sp - < trsl *cara de poker*/*cara de póquer*   Fi - < trsl *pokerinaama*, *pokkanaama*   Cr
(0)   Hu - < trsl *pókerarc*

pole position   *n*. 'the most favourable position at the
start of a motor race'
    The term is apparently spreading with the increas-
ing TV reports on motor racing. Note frequent
English pronunciation in loanwords where a native
one would have been available for an internationalism.
    Ge [=E] F [U] 1980s (1
tech)   Nw [=E] M [U] 1980s (1
tech)   Fr [polpozisjɔ] F, 1980s (1
tech)   Sp <=E>/*pole* [=E] F,
1980s (1 tech)   It [=E/po̯l pozi-
ʃon] F [U] 1970s (2 tech)   Rm
[polpoziʃon] F/N, 1990s (1
tech)   Fi - < trsl *paalupaikka*

policy   *n*. 1 'a course or principle of action adopted or
proposed by a government, party, business, or individual, etc.'
    Du [=E] C, 1990s (1 coll, jour) < *beleid*   Nw [=E] M,
pl. -*ies*, 1960s (1 jour)   Sp - < mean *política*   It - <
mean *politica*

polish   *n*. 1 'a substance used for polishing', 2
'smoothness or glossiness produced by friction', 4
'refinement or elegance of manner'
    Nw [=E] M, pl. -*er*, 1960s (2)   Rm [=E] N [U] end20c
(1 coll)   Hu [=E] [U] end20c, 1(0>1 tech, jour)

poll   *n*./*cp²* 2 'an assessment of public opinion by
questioning a representative sample, esp. as the basis
for forecasting the results of voting', +5 'a poll to
select candidates for an election' (cf. ↑*exit-poll*)
    Ge [=E] M/*cp²*, pl. -*s*, 1960s, 2(1 jour, rare) < (*Mei-
nungs-*) *Umfrage*   Du [=E] C, 1960s (1 tech) < *opinie
peiling*, *enquête*   Nw (0) < *meningsmåling*   Ic - < 2:
skoðanakönnun; +5: *prófkjör*   Rm [=E] N, 1970s (1
tech, rare)   Bg (0)

polo   *n*./*cp*¹/² 1 'a game of Eastern origin resembling
hockey, played on horseback with a long-handled
mallet', +2 'a short-sleeved casual shirt, with a collar
and two or three buttons'
    Although the name of the game (from Indian Eng-
lish) was mediated through British English, and the
name of the shirt comes from early twentieth-century
American English, there is nothing English in the form
of the loanword. Its status as an anglicism is therefore
doubtful.
    Ge [po̯:lo] N [U] end19c, 1(3); *Polohemd* 1950s,
+2(3)   Du [=E] C [U] 1940s, 1(1 reg); *polohemd* N,
1940s, +2(3+5)   Nw [pu:lu] M [U] beg20c, 1(2);
<=E>/*pologenser* M, pl. -*er*, 1970s, +2(2)   Ic *póló*
[=E] N [U] beg20c, 1(ø); *póló-cp*¹, +2(2)   Fr [pɔlo]
M, end19c, 1(3); beg20c, 2(3)   Sp [polo] M, end19c,
1(3); mid20c, +2(3)   It [po̯lo] M [U] end19c, 1(3); pl.
Ø, +2(3) → *polista* M   Rm [po̯lo] N [U] 1930s, via Fr,
1(3 obs)   Rs *polo* N, uninfl., beg20c, 1(1 tech)   Po
polo [polo] N, uninfl., beg20c, 1(1 tech); beg20c,
+2(2)   Cr *polo* M [U] beg20c, 1(1 tech)   Bg *polo* N,
pl. -*la*, mid20c, 1(Ø) +2(3)   Fi [polo] beg20c, 1(3);
polopaita mid20c, +2(3)   Hu *póló* [po̯lo] usu. *cp*² [U]
end19/beg20c, 1(3); +2: pl. -*k*, end19c/beg20c (3)   Gr
polo N, 20c, 1(1 tech); +2(2)

pond   *n*. +3 'a small pool aboard a fishing vessel, filled
with water in which to wash the fish'
    Ic *pond* [=E]/*pont* [pʰont] N, pl. Ø, mid20c, +3(3 tech)
→ *pontari* M

pony¹ (1)   *n*. 1 'a horse of any small breed'
    Ge [poni] N, pl. -*(ie)s*, 19c (3)   Du [=E] C, pl. -'*s*,
end19c (3)   Nw *ponni* [po̯ni] M, pl. -*er*, mid19c
(3)   Ic *póní(-)* [=E] N/M, pl. Ø/-*ar*, (freq. *cp*¹)
mid20c (2 coll)   Fr *poney* [po̯nɛ] M, mid19c (3) →
ponette F   Sp *poney*/*poni* etc. [poni] M, pl. -*s*, beg20c
(2); *poney* end19c, via Fr (3)   It [po̯ni] M, pl. Ø,
mid19c (3)   Rm *ponei* [ponej/po̯nej] M, pl. Ø,
beg19c, via Fr (3)   Rs *poni* M, uninfl., 19c (2)   Po
[poni] M, uninfl., beg20c (1 tech)   Cr *poni* M, pl. -*ji*,
beg20c (3)   Bg *poni* N, pl. -*ta*, beg20c (2)   Fi *poni*
19c (3)   Hu *póni* [po̯:ni] pl. -*k*, 19c (3)   Al *poni* M [U]
mid20c (1 reg)   Gr *poneil*/*poni*/*pony* N, 20c (2)

pony² (1)   *n*. +5 'a fringe' (hairstyle)
    Whereas this word is used for 'fringe' in a non-
English way in German and Dutch only, the compound *ponytail* is more widespread, though normally
represented by (semi-)calques, as in German *Pfer-
deschwanz* or Finnish *ponihänta* (sla *ponnari*). Note
that the 'fringe' sense predates English *ponytail*
which is said to date to 1952.
    Ge [poni] M, pl. -*(ie)s*, end19c (3)   Du [=E] C/N [U]
end19c (3)   Rm - < rend *coadă de cal*   Po (0)

pool¹ (1)   *n*. 3 'a swimming pool'
    The slow acceptance of this term (only in modish/
facetious use, though preferred to the full ↑*swimming-
pool*) is explained by the existence of native words;
contrast ↑*pool²* and ↑*pool³* which appear to fill lexical
gaps.
    Ge [=E] M, pl. -*s*, 1970s (1 mod) < *Schwimmbecken*

Du - < *zwembad* **Nw** [=E] 1980s (1 mod, rare) < *svømmebasseng* **Fr** (Ø) **Rs** *pul* M [U] end20c (1 tech)

pool² *n.* 1 'a common supply of persons, vehicles, commodities, etc., for sharing by a group of people', 2a 'the collective amount of players' stakes in gambling', 2b 'a group of persons sharing duties etc.', 3a 'a joint commercial venture, esp. an arrangement between competing parties to fix prices and share business to eliminate competition'

Ge [=E] M [U] beg20c, 1(1 mod) 2a(1 tech, obs) **Du** [=E] C, 1980s, 1(2); 1950s, 2a(1 tech) **Nw** [=E] M, pl. *-er*, 1970s, 1(2); 1930s, 3a(2 tech) **Fr** [pul] M, beg20c, 1(1 ban) *underwriting pool* < *syndicat de prise ferme* **Sp** [pul] M, 1930s, 1,3a(1 tech) **It** [pu:l] M [U] 1930, 1(1 tech, jour) 2a,2b,3a(1 tech) **Rm** [=E] N, 1970s, 3a(1 tech) **Rs** (0) **Po** *pul* [pul] M, mid20c, 3a(1 tech) **Bg** *pul* M [U] 1990s, 1(1 jour); pl. *-al-ove*, mid20c, 3a(1 tech) **Fi** *pooli* 1980s, 1(1); *pooli* beg20c, 3a(2) **Hu** [=E] [U] end19/beg20c, 2a(1 arch); mid20c, 3a(1 arch)

pool³ (2) *n.* 4a 'an American game played on a billiard table with 16 balls', 4b 'a British game played on a billiard table with one coloured ball per player'

Ge [=E] N, pl. Ø, 1980s, 4a(1 tech) < *Poolbilliard* **Du** *poolbiljart* N, pl. *-en*, 1980s, 4a(1 tech) **Nw** [=E] M [U] mid20c, 4a(Ø/1) **Sp** [pul] M, end20c, 4a(1 tech) **It** [pu:l] M [U] 1930s, 4a(1 tech) **Rs** 4a(Ø) **Po** [pul] M [U] end20c, 4a(1 mod) **Cr** (0) **Fi** *pool* [=E] 1980s, 4a(1) **Hu** [=E] cp¹ [U] mid20c, 4a(2 tech) = *pool billiard* **Gr** *pull*/<=E> N [U] end20c, 4a(1 tech)

pool (2) *v.* 'put (resources etc.) in a common fund'

Ge [pu:lən] 1960s (1 tech) **Du** *poolen* [pu:lən] 1960s (1 tech) **Nw** (0) **Po** (0)

poop *n.* 'the stern of a ship'

Nw [=E] M, pl. *-er*, end19c (1 tech) **Fr** *poupe* (4) **It** *poppa* (5Fr) **Rm** *pupă* (5Fr) **Al** *pupë* (Fr)

pop *v.* 1 'make or cause to make a pop', 2 'go, move, come, or put unexpectedly or in a quick or hasty manner', 3b 'heat (popcorn etc.) until it pops', 6 'take or inject (a drug etc.)', +8 'arrange (a tune, etc.) in a pop-like style'

Ge *auf-/verpoppen* 1980s, +8(1 obs) **Du** [=E] 1990s, 2(1 tech) **Nw** *poppe (opp)* [pɔpe] end20c, 1,2,3b(3 coll) **Ic** *poppa* [pʰɔhpa] 1960s, 3b(3) 6(3 sla); *poppa upp* 1970s, +8(3) → *poppaður* adj.

pop *n./cp¹/²* 1 'commercial popular music (and art), esp. that produced since the 1950s', +3 'popcorn'

Ge [pop] M [U] 1950s, 1(2) → *poppig* adj.; *verpopt* adj. **Du** [=E] C [U] 1960s, 1(2>3) **Nw** [=E] M [U] 1950s, 1(3) → *popete* adj.; *poppe (opp)* v. **Ic** *popp* [pʰɔhp] N [U] 1960s, 1,+3(3) → *poppari* M **Fr** [pɔp]

adj., uninfl., mid20c 1(2) = *musique pop* **Sp** [pop] adj., uninfl., 1960s, 1(2) → *popero* 1(2) **It** [pɔp] adj./cp², uninfl., 1960s, 1(3) **Rm** *muzică pop* [pop] 1960s, 1(3) **Rs** *pop(-muzyka)* M [U] mid20c, 1(2) **Po** *muzyka pop* adj., uninfl., mid20c, 1(2) **Cr** *pop (musika)* adj./cp¹, mid20c, 1(2) **Bg** *pop* M/cp¹ [U] (in *popmuzika*, etc.) mid20c, 1(2 tech) **Fi** [=E] 1960s, 1(2) **Hu** [=E] [U] 1960s, 1(3) → *-zene, -song, -fesztivál* n. **Al** *pop-muzikë* F [U] 1980s, 1(1 reg) **Gr** *pop* adj./F [U] mid20c, 1(2)

pop art *n.* 1 'art based on modern popular culture and the mass media, esp. as a critical comment on traditional fine art values'

This term is one of the earliest and most widespread of the *-art* compounds in European languages, and may have served as a model for later borrowings or coinages (cf. ↑*minimal art*, ↑*op art*).

Ge [pɔpart] F [U] 1960s (1 tech) **Du** [=E] C [U] 1970s (1 tech) **Nw** [=E] M [U] 1960s (1 tech) **Ic** - < *popplist* **Fr** *pop'art* [pɔpaʀ(t)] M, mid20c (1 tech) **Sp** [pop art] M [U] 1960s (1 tech) **It** [pɔp art] F [U] 1960s (1 tech) **Rm** [=E] N [U] 1970s (1 tech) **Rs** *pop-art* M [U] mid20c (1 tech) **Po** [-art] M [U] mid20c (1 tech) → *-ysta* M; *-ystka* F; *-owski* adj.; *-owy* adj. **Cr** *pop-art* M [U] mid20c (1 tech) → *-ist* M; *-istički* adj. **Bg** *popart* M [U] end20c (1 tech) **Fi** [=E] 1960s (1) **Hu** [=E] [U] 1960s (1 tech) **Al** *popart* M [U] 1980s (0/1 tech) **Gr** <=E>/*pop art* F [U] mid20c (1 tech)

popcorn *n.* 2 'popped maize, as a cereal'

It may have to do with the combined novelty of the food and expressive form of the word that this term became as widespread as it did. Though the term was coined in American English in the mid-nineteenth century, and there are a few attestations in European languages in the early twentieth, the great popularity came at the time of pop art and pop music.

Ge [=E] N [U] 1960s (2 coll) > *Puffmais* **Du** [=E] N [U] 1970s (2) **Nw** <=E>/*popkorn* [pɔpku:rn] N [U] 1950s (3+5) **Ic** *poppkorn* [pʰɔhpkʰɔ(r)tn] N [U] mid20c, 2(3) → *popp* N **Fr** *pop-corn* [pɔpkɔʀn] M, uninfl. [U]

mid20c (2) **It** [pɔpkɔrn] M, pl. Ø, 1950s (3) **Rm** [=E] N [U] 1970s (1 you) > *floricele (de porumb)* **Rs** *popkorn* M [U] end20c (1 coll) **Po** [-korn] M, end20c (1 coll) **Cr** *popkorn* M, end20c (1 coll) **Bg** <=E> M [U] 1990s (1 mod) < *pukanki* **Fi** [=E] 1950s (3) **Hu** [=E] [U] 1980s (2>3) < rend *pattogatott kukorica* **Gr** *popkorn* N, mid20c (2)

popper *n.* +4 'an exquisitely dressed conformist youth'

Ge [pɔpa] M, pl. Ø, 1980s (1 you, obs) **Hu** [popper] pl. *-ek*, 1980s (1 you, obs)

popper(s) *n.pl.* 3 'a small vial of amyl nitrate used (as drug) for inhalation'

Ge [pɔpas] N [U] 1980s (1 sla, obs?) **Du** [pɔpərs] C [U] 1970s (1 tech) **Nw** [=E] [U] 1980s (1 tech)

Ic [=E/pʰɔhp(e)is]; *popp* N [U] end2oc, 3(1 sla)   **Fr** (0)   **Sp** [p̯opers] M, 1980s (1 tech); also in sing. → *popero*   **Hu** (0)

pop song   *n.* 'a popular song'

Although ↑*pop* is widely current, the compound is less so, various languages preferring semi-calques.

Ge [=E] M, pl. *-s*, 1960s (1 mod)   **Du** *popsong* [=E] C, 1960s (1 mod)   **Nw** *pop-sang* (3+5)   **Ic** *popplag* [pʰɔhplax] N, pl. *-lög*, 1960s (3+5)   **Fr** - < trsl *chanson pop*   **Sp** - < trsl *canción pop*   **It** [=E] F, pl. Ø, 1960s (1) < trsl *canzone pop*   **Rm** [=E] N, 1970s (0) = trsl *cântec pop*   **Rs** (0)   **Po** *pop-song* [-nk] M, end2oc (1 mod)   **Cr** *popsong* M, pl. *-ovi*, end2oc (1)   **Bg** - < trsl *pop-pesen*   **Fi** - < trsl *poplaulu*   **Hu** [=E] [U] 1960s (2 you, mod) > *táncdal*

port   *n.* 3 'a socket or aperture in an electronic circuit, esp. in a computer network'

Ge [=E] M, pl. *-s*, 1980s (1 tech)   **Du** [=E] C, 1990s (1 tech)   **Nw** (4 tech)   **Rm** [port] N, 1980s (1 tech)   **Rs** *port* M, pl. *-y*, 1990s (1 tech)   **Po** [port] M, end2oc (1 tech)   **Cr** *port* M, pl. *-al-ove*, 1990s (1 tech)   **Gr** <=E> [=E] pl. *-s*, end2oc (1 tech) = *pyli*

portable   *n./cp¹* 'a portable object, e.g. a radio, computer, etc.'

In contrast to the adjective (which is always treated as an internationalism or translated), the noun has a limited currency designating equipment which can be moved around.

Ge [=E] M/N, pl. *-s*, 1960s (1 mod)   **Du** [=E] C, 1980s (2) < *draagbaar* (+object)   **Nw** [=E] mid2oc (1 arch) < *reise-*; *bærbar*   **Ic** - < rend *ferða-*   **Fr** (4) = *portatif*   **Sp** - < *portátil*   **It** - < *portatile*   **Hu** [=E] cp¹, 1920s (1 arch) < *hordozható*   **Al** - < *portabël*

porter   *n.* 1a 'a person employed to carry luggage etc., esp. a railway, airport, or hotel employee', 2 'a dark brown bitter beer brewed from charred or browned malt'

Ge [=E] M [U] 19c, 2(Ø)   **Du** 2(Ø)   **Nw** [=E] M [U] beg2oc, 2(Ø)   **Ic** [=E] M, pl. *-ar*, end19c, via Da, 1a(1 coll) 2(Ø)   **Fr** [p̯ɔʀtɛʀ] M, 18c, 2(1)   **Rm** [=E] N [U] mid19c, 2(Ø)   **Rs** *porter* M [U] mid19c, 2(1 tech) → *-nyĭ* adj.   **Po** [porter] M, mid19c, 2(3)   **Cr** (0)   **Bg** *porter* M [U] 2oc, 2(1 tech)   **Fi** <=E>/*portteri* [=E] 19c, 2(Ø)   **Hu** [p̯orter] [U] before 19c, 2(1 arch)

Portland cement   *n.* 'a cement manufactured from chalk and clay which when hard resembles Portland stone in colour'

Ge *Portlandzement* [p̯ɔrtlanttsement] M [U] beg2oc (3+5)   **Du** *portlandcement* [p̯ɔrtlantsement] C/N [U] end19c (name+5)   **Nw** [=E/p̯urtlan-] M [U] beg2oc (1 obs)   **Ic** *Portlandsement* N [U] beg2oc, via Da (2)   **Fr** *portland/ciment Portland (artificiel)* [p̯ɔrtlãd] M, 1920s (1 tech)   **Sp** *(cemento) Portland* [p̯orlan] M, uninfl., end19c (1 tech)   **It** *cemento Portland*, beg2oc (1 tech)   **Rm** *(ciment) portland* [(tʃiment) p̯ortland] N [U] mid2oc, via Fr (3 tech)   **Rs**

portland-tsement M [U] beg2oc (1 tech)   **Po** *portlandzki cement* [cement portlantski] adj., beg2oc (2)   **Cr** *portland cement* M [U] beg2oc (3)   **Bg** *portland tsiment* M [U] mid2oc (1+5)   **Fi** *portlandsementti* beg2oc (1 tech)   **Hu** *portland (cement)* [portland (tsement)] [U] before 19c (2 tech+5La/Ge)   **Gr** *tsimedo Portland* N [U] 2oc (1 tech+5)

port wine   *n.* 'a strong, sweet, dark-red fortified wine of Portugal'

North-western countries appear to have taken the word from English, with German handing it on to Eastern languages; by contrast, Romance languages got the commodity and its designation straight from Portugal (cf. ↑*sherry*).

Ge *Portwein* M, pl. *-e*, 19c (3+5) = *Port*   **Du** *portwijn* [p̯ɔrtwɛjn] M, beg2oc (3) < *port*   **Nw** (0) < *portvin*   **Ic** *port-/púrtvín* [pʰɔrt- /pʰurtvin] N [U] 18c, via Da (3/5Da) → *púrtari/portari* M   **Fr** - < *porto*   **Sp** - < *vino de Oporto; Oporto; Porto* (5Port)   **It** - < *vino porto*   **Rm** - < *vin de Porto*   **Rs** *portvеin* M beg2oc, via Ge(3)   **Po** via Ge (3)   **Cr** *portvajn* M [U] beg2oc (3 tech)   **Bg** *portvain* M [U] 2oc, via Ge (3 tech)   **Fi** *portviini* (Ø)   **Hu** - < trsl *portói (bor)*   **Al** - < *porto*   **Gr** - < *Porto*

pose   *v.* 1 'assume a certain physical attitude (e.g. in body-building, photography, etc.)'

Ge [p̯o:zən] 1960s (1 tech, rare) < *posieren*   **Du** *poseren* (5Fr)   **Nw** - < *posere*   **Ic** *pósa* [pʰou:sa] end2oc (1 tech)   **Sp** *posar* end2oc (4)   **It** *posare* (4)   **Rm** *poza* [poza] end2oc (4)   **Rs** *pozirovat'* (5Fr)   **Po** (5Fr)   **Cr** *pozirati* (5Fr)   **Bg** - < *poziram* (3 tech)   **Hu** *pózol* (5Fr)   **Al** *pozoj* mid2oc (3)   **Gr** *pozaro* (5It)

pose   *n.* +1b 'an attitude of the body assumed by body-builders to expose certain muscle groups'

Ge (5La) → *posen* v.   **Du** - → *posieren* (5Fr)   **Ic** *pósa* [pʰou:sa] F, pl. *-ur*, end2oc (2 tech)   **Sp** - < mean *pose*   **It** *posa* (5La)   **Rm** *poză* [poza] F, end2oc (4)   **Rs** (5Fr)   **Cr** (0) < *poza*   **Bg** *poza* (5Fr)   **Hu** (5Fr/La)   **Al** *pozë* F, pl. *-a*   **Gr** - < mean *poza*

posing*   *n.* 'a body-building contest in which certain attitudes are required'

Ge [p̯o:siŋ] N [U] 1980s (1 tech, rare)   **Du** [=E] C, 1980s (1 tech)   **Rm** - < *pozare*   **Rs** (0)   **Cr** (0) < *poziranje*   **Bg** - < *pozirane*   **Hu** - < *pózolás*   **Al** - < *pozim*

post   *v.* 1 'put (a letter etc.) in the post'

Du *posten* [p̯ɔstə(n)] end19c (5)   **Nw** *poste* ["p̯ɔste] 2oc (3) > *postlegge*   **Ic** *pósta* [pʰousta] beg2oc (3 rare) < *póstleggja*   **Fr** *poster* [p̯ɔste] end19c (4 obs)   **It** *impostare* (4)   **Fi** - < *postittaa* ← *posti* n.   **Al** *postoj* beg2oc (3)

post   *n.* +3 'the outer limits of the V- shaped area next to the basket on basketball courts'

Ic [pʰoustʏr] M, pl. *-ar*, end2oc (4 tech) → *póstari* M   **It** [p̯ost] M, pl. Ø, end2oc (1 tech)

poster   *n.* 1 'a placard in a public place', 2 'a large printed picture or photograph', +4 'a concise display reporting on scientific work'

This term has encroached on the domain of *placard/plakat* in many European languages, originally as an informal, trendy equivalent, but quickly losing such stylistic restrictions. Note Finnish and Icelandic which have adopted only the rare sense derived from (*conference*) *poster presentation*.

Ge [poːsta] N/M, pl. Ø, 1960s, 1,2(3) = *Plakat* **Du** [=E] C, 1960s (2) **Nw** [=E] M/N, pl. -*el-s*, 1970s, 2(1 obs) < *plakat* **Ic** [=E] M, pl. -*ar*, end20c, +4(1 tech) = *veggspjald* **Fr** [pɔstɛʀ] M, 1960s, 2(2) +4(1 tech) **Sp** [pɔster] M, 1960s, 2(3) **It** [pɔster] M, pl. Ø, 1970s, 1,2(3) **Rm** [pɔster] N, 1970s, 1,2(1 mod) M, pl. -*y*, 1990s, 1,2(1 mod) **Po** [poster] M, end20c (1 tech) **Cr** *poster* M, pl. -*i*, end20c, 1,+4(1) **Bg** *poster* M, pl. -*al-i*, end20c, 2(1 mod) +4(3 tech) < 2: *plakat* **Fi** <=E>/*posteri* [=E] 1980s, +4(1 tech) < 1,2: *juliste* **Hu** *poszter* [poster] pl. -*ek*, 1970s, 1,2(3) **Gr** *poster* N, pl. Ø/-*s*, end20c, 1,2(3) < *afisa*

pot *n.* 'marijuana'
Ge [=E] N/M [U] 1960s (1 sla) < *Marihuan*a **Du** [=E] C [U] 1970s (1 sla) **Nw** [=E] M [U] 1970s (1 sla, rare) **Ic** *pott(ur)* [pʰɔht(ʏr)] N/(M) [U] end20c (1 sla) **Sp** [=E] M [U] 1990s (1 sla, rare) **Po** M [U] end20c (1 sla)

potato *n.* 1 'a starchy plant tuber that is cooked and used for (staple) food', 2 'the plant bearing this'
Nw *potet* [puteːt] M, pl. -*er*, 18c (3) **Ic** *poteta* F, pl. -*ur*, end18c, 1(1 obs) < *kartafla* **Fr** *patate* (5Sp) **Sp** *patata* (5Sp) **It** *patata* (5Sp) **Al** *patate* (5Sp)

power *n.* 8 'vigour, energy' (cf. ↑*black ~*, ↑*flower ~*), 15 'the rate of energy output' (phys.)
This highly colloquial word has gained a firm hold in the North-west, with a corresponding verb and a number of compounds (German *Powerfrau*) now being quite common. However, it is rarely attested in these general uses in other languages.
Ge [=E] F [U] 1980s, 8(1 coll) < *Energie* **Du** [=E] C [U] 1990s, 8(1 coll) **Nw** [=E] cp¹, 1990s, 8(1) **Ic** [pʰauːer] N [U] end20c, 8(1 sla) 15(1 tech) **Fi** [pɔveri] 1990s, 8(2 coll) **Gr** <=E>/ *pauer* F/N [U] 1990s, 8(1 coll, you, mod)

power *v.* +3 'follow up with great intensity'
Ge [pauan] 1980s (1 coll, jour)

powerlifting* *n.* 'an athletic discipline' (cf. ↑*body-building*)
Ge [=E] N [U] 1980s (1 tech, rare) → *Powerlifter* M **Du** [=E] C, 1980s (1 tech) < *powerliften* → *power-lifter* **Ic** - < trsl *kraftlyftingar* **It** - < rend *solleva-mento pesi* **Rs** *pauer-lifting* M [U] end20c (1 tech) **Bg** *pauerlifting* M [U] 1990s (1 tech, rare)

power pack *n.* 1 'a unit for supplying power', +3 'a combination of stereo recorders etc.'

Ge [=E] N, pl. -*s*, 1980s, 1,+3(1 tech, rare) **Du** [=E] 1980s (1 tech, jour) **Bg** *pauŭrpak* M, pl. -*al-ove*, 1990s, +3(1 tech, rare) **Fi** [=E/*pɔverpak*] 1980s, 1(1 tech) **Hu** - < trsl *energiacsomag*

power play *n.* 2a 'tactics involving a concentration of resources and effort in business, politics, etc.', +2b 'the intensive playing of a piece of music on the radio to promote its popularity', 3 'play involving a formation of players adopted when the opponents are one or more players down' (icehockey, footb.)
The fact that icehockey terminology tends to be derived from English has gained this term a wider distribution than *power* by itself; the use has now been extended to other sports, but only rarely metaphorically to human behaviour in general.

Ge [=E] N [U] 1960s, 3(1 tech); 1970s, 2a(2 jour) **Du** [=E] N, 1970s, 3(1 tech) **Nw** [=E] N [U] 1980s, 3(1 tech) **Rm** [=E] N, 1990s, +2b(1 rare) **Po** [pawer-] M [U] end20c (1 tech) **Cr** (o) **Bg** *pauŭrplei* M [U] end20c, 3(1 tech) **Fi** [=E] 1980s, +2b(1 tech), 3(1 tech) < trsl *ylivoimapeli* **Gr** *pauer plei* N [U] end20c, 3(1 tech)

powersteering* *n.* 'servo-assisted steering'
Du [=E] C [U] 1980s (1 tech) < *stuurbekrachtiging* **Nw** - < *servostyring* **Ic** *powerstýri* [pʰauːersti:rɪ] N, pl. mid/end20c (1+5 tech) > trsl *aflstýri* **Fr** - < *direction assistée* **It** - < rend *servo sterzo* **Hu** - < *szervokormányzás* **Gr** - < *servo-steering*

PR *abbrev.* 1 'public relations'
Ge [peːɛr] F [U] 1960s (1 jour) **Du** [peːɛr] C, 1960s (2) **Nw** [peːær] M [U] 1960s (3) **Ic** *PR* [pʰjeːɛːr:] end20c (2 tech) **It** [piɛrre] 1960s (2) < trsl *pubbliche relazioni* **Bg** (o) **Fi** [peːer] 1970s (2) **Hu** [=E/peːeːr] [U] 1960s < *kapcsolatszervezés* **Gr** (o)

practical joke *n.* 'a humorous trick played on a person'
Du [=E] C, 1970s (2) → *practical joker* C **Nw** [=E] M, pl. -*s*, 20c (2) **Ic** [=E] N/M, end20c (0 sla)

prairie *n.* 'a large area of usu. treeless grassland, esp. in North America'
Ge *Prärie* [preːriː] F, pl. -*n*, 19c, via Fr (Ø/3) **Du** [=E] C, pl. -*ën/-s*, beg20c (Ø) **Nw** *prærie* [prærie/preː-] M, pl. -*r*, 19c (Ø/3) **Fr** (4) **It** *prateria* (5La) **Rm** *prerie* [prerie] F, 1930s, via Fr (Ø/3) **Rs** *preriya* pl. -*ii*, beg20c (1 tech/5Fr) **Po** (5Fr) **Cr** *prerija* F, pl. -*e*, beg20c (5Fr) **Bg** *preriya* (5Fr) **Fi** *preeri* 19c (Ø) **Hu** *préri* [preːri] pl. -*k*, 19c (3) **Al** *preri* F, pl. Ø, mid20c (3)

pre-print *n.* 'a printed document issued in advance of general publication'
Ge - < *Vorabdruck* **Du** [=E] C, 1950s (1 tech) **Ic** [=E] N, pl. Ø, end20c (1 tech) **Fr** (o) **It** [=E] F, pl. Ø, 1970s (1 tech) **Rm** [=E/preprint] N, 1970s (1 tech) **Rs** (o) **Hu** [=E] (pl. -*ek*) end20c (1 tech_SCI)

Presbyterian *adj.* 'governed by elders all of equal

rank' (of a Church, esp. with reference to the national Church of Scotland)

Ge (Ø)   **Du** (Ø)   **Nw** (Ø)   **Fr** *presbytérien/ne* M/F, 17c (Ø/3)   **Sp** *presbiteriano/-a* M/F (Ø/3)   **It** *presbiteriano* [prezbiteri̯ano] M/F, pl. *-il-e*, 17c (3)   **Rm** [prezbiteri̯an] M/F, beg19c, via Fr (3)   **Rs** *presviterianskiĭ* 17c (Ø)   **Po** (5Gr)   **Bg** *prezviterianski* 20c (3)   **Hu** (5Gr/La)   **Al** *prezbiterian* adj., mid20c (3)   **Gr** *presviterianos/-i*, M/F (Ø/3)

Presbyterianism   *n.* 'the religion of the Presbyterian Church'

Ge *Presbyterianismus* [presby:te:riani̯smus] M [U] (Ø/3)   **Du** *presbiterianisme* [prɪsbiteriani̯mə] N [U] 17c (3)   **Nw** *presbyterianisme* [presbyteriani̯sme] M [U] 20c (Ø/3)   **Ic** *presbyter(i)a(n)-* cp[1], end19c (Ø) = *öldungakirkja*   **Fr** *presbytérianisme* [pʀɛsbiterjanism(ə)] M, 17c (Ø/3)   **Sp** *presbiterianismo* M (Ø/3)   **It** *presbiterianesimo* M [U] 1920 (3)   **Rm** *prezbiterianism* [prezbiteriani̯sm] N [U] beg19c, via Fr (3Ø)   **Rs** - < trsl *presviterianstvo*   **Po** *prezbiterianizm* [presbiterienizm] M [U] mid19c (Ø)   **Cr** *presbiterijanizam* M [U] beg20c (Ø/3)   **Bg** - < trsl *prezviteriạnstvo* N   **Fi** *presbyterianismi* (Ø)   **Hu** *presbiterianizmus* (5La/Gr)   **Al** *presbiterianizëm* M [U] mid20c (3)   **Gr** *Presvyterianismọs* M [U] 20c (3/Ø)

presence   *n.* 3b 'a person's force of personality'
Ic [pʰre:sens] M [U] end20c (1 coll)

preshave (lotion)*   *n.* 'a cosmetic used before electric shaving'
Ge [pri:ʃe:f lo:ʃn] F, pl. *-s*, 1970s (1 jour) < *Rasierwasser*   **Du** [=E] C, 1960s (1 jour)   **Ic** [=E] M [U] 1960s (1 coll)   **It** [=E] M [U] 1960s (1 jour) < rend *prebarba*   **Rm** - < rend *(loțiune) preras/înainte de ras*   **Rs** (0)   **Po** (0)   **Hu** [=E] [U] end20c (1 tech, jour) < rend *borotválkozás előtti*   **Gr** [=E] end20c (1 writ)

pressbook*   *n.* 'a book presenting an artist'
Fr <=E>/*press-book/book* [prɛzbuk] M, 1960s (1 tech)   **Sp** [=E] M, pl. *-s*, 1970s (1 tech)   **It** [=E] M, pl. Ø, 1960 (1 tech)

pressing   *n.* 1 'steam ironing', +4 'laundry', +5 'offensive tactics' (footb.) +6 'the application of (moral) pressure to somebody'

The French use for 'steam ironing' and 'laundry' (nowadays rather 'cleaner's') has apparently not spread beyond the French realm, apart from neighbouring Flanders; by contrast, the more widespread (but also non-English) use in football, with metaphoric extensions, is not found in French.

Ge [=E] N [U] 1980s, +5(1 tech)   **Du** [=E] C, 1970s, +6 (1 reg)   **Nw** [presiŋ] +6(5)   **Fr** [presiŋ] M, mid20c, 1(2); 1920s, +4(2)   **Sp** [presin] M [U] 1970s, +5, +6(2 tech)   **It** [pressin(g)] M, pl. Ø, 1950s, +5(2 tech)   **Rm**

presing [=E] N [U] 1970s, 1+5(2>3 tech) **Rs** *pressing* M [U] mid20c, +5,+6(2)   **Po** (0)   **Cr** [=E] M [U]

end20c, +5(2 tech)   **Bg** - < +5: trsl *presa*   **Gr** *presiŋg* N [U] beg20c, +4(1 tech) → *presạro* v., *presarisma* N

pressure group   *n.* 'a group or association formed to promote a particular interest or cause by influencing public policy'
Ge [=E] F, pl. *-s*, 1960s (1 mod) < ↑*Lobby*   **Du** [=E] C, 1960s (1 tech) < *pressiegroep*   **Nw** (0) < *pressgruppe*   **Ic** - < *þrýstihópur*   **Fr** - < trsl *groupe de pression*   **Sp** - < trsl *grupo de presión*   **It** - < trsl *gruppo di pressione*   **Rm** - < trsl *grup de presiune*   **Rs** (0)   **Po** - < trsl *grupa naciskn* (0)   **Cr** (0)   **Bg** - < *lobi*   **Hu** [=E] pl. Ø, end20c (1 tech)

pretest*   *n.* 'the preliminary screening of a TV show to test audience reaction'
Ge *Pretest* [=E] M, pl. *-s*, 1990s (1 tech, rare)   **Po** (0)

preview   *n.* 2a 'the showing of a film, play, exhibition, etc., before the official opening', +3 'a mode that allows a person to see the final layout of a page on the screen' (comput.)
Ge [=E] M, pl. *-s*, 1980s, 2a(1 tech, mod)   **Du** [=E] C, 1970s, 2a(2)   **Nw** 2a(0) < *forhåndsvisning*   **Ic** [=E] N, pl. Ø, end20c, 2a(1 sla) +3(1 tech) < 2a: rend *forsýning*   **Sp** <=E> F, pl. *-s*, 1930s, 2a(0>1 tech, obs, rare) < *preestreno*   **It** - < *anteprima*   **Rm** - < *vizionare*   **Bg** +3 (0)   **Gr** - < 2a: *avant première*

price list   *n.* 'a list of current prices of items on sale'
Ic *príslisti* [pʰri:slɪstɪ] M, pl. *-ar*, mid20c (3)   **Rs** *praĭs list* M, pl. *-y*, 1990s (1 tech)

pricing   *n.* 'fixing the price for a thing for sale'
Fr [=E] 20c (1 ban) < *prisée*

primaries*   *n.* 2 'a preliminary election'
Fr *primaires* (4)   **Sp** - < mean *primarias*   **It** - < mean *primarie*   **Rs** *praĭmariz* pl., 1996 (1 jour, mod)   **Bg** *praĭmŭriz* M, pl. *-al-i*, 1996 (1 jour, mod)

primer   *n.* 1 'a substance used to prime wood etc.', 2 'a cap, cylinder, etc., used to ignite the powder of a cartridge etc.'
Du [=E] C, 1970s, 1(2) < *grondverf*   **Nw** [=E] M, pl. *-e*, 20c(1 tech)   **Rm** [primer] M [U] mid20c, 1(1 tech, rare) < *ulei brut/ulei bule*   **Cr** *prạjmer* M [U] 1(1 tech)

prime rate   *n.* 'the lowest rate at which money can be borrowed commercially'
Ge [=E] F [U] 1980s (1 tech, rare)   **Du** [=E] C [U] 1980s (1 tech)   **Fr** [prajm rɛt] M, 1970s (Ø)   **It** [=E] M, pl. Ø, 1980s (1 tech)   **Rs** *praĭm-reĭt* M [U] 1990s (1 tech)   **Bg** *prạĭm reĭt* M [U] 1990s (1 tech)   **Fi** *prime-* [=E] cp[1], 1990s (1 tech)

prime time   *n.* 'the time at which a radio or television audience is expected to be at its highest'

This term is marginally accepted in fashionable journalism and media language. It has made little headway against native expressions, or perhaps the need to express the concept has not been felt to be urgent.

Ge [=E] F [U] 1980s (1 tech, rare) < *beste Sendezeit*   **Du** [=E] C [U] 1980s (1 tech, jour)   **Nw** [=E] M [U] 1980s (1 tech) <

beste sendetid **Fr** [prajm tajm] M, 1980s (1) > *heure de grande écoute* **Sp** [=E] M [U] 1980s (1 tech) **It** [=E] M [U] 1980s (1 tech) **Rm** *orǎ/ore prime time* [orə+E] 1990s (1 tech) **Rs** *praĭm-taĭm* M [U] 1990s (1 tech) **Hu** - < rend *főműsoridő*

print *n./cp¹* +2f 'texts in printed form'
Ge *Print-*[=E] cp¹, 1980s (1 tech) **Du** [=E] C, 1970s (1 tech_COMPUT) < *computeruitdraai* **Nw** (o) **Rm** [=E] N, end20c (1 tech) **Rs** (o) **Po** (o) **Hu** [=E] [U] end20c (2 tech_COMPUT); cp² (2>3)

printer *n.* 3 'a device that prints, esp. as part of a computer system'
   The recent adoption of computer terminology has made this word more widely current in Eastern Europe than in the rest of the Continent; apparently, these printers are linguistically set off from traditional printing machines. Contrast the data for ↑*printout n.* and ↑*print out* v.
Ge [=E] M, pl. Ø, 1980s (1 mod) < *Drucker* **Du** [prɪntər] C, 1960s (3 tech) **Nw** [=E] M, pl. *-e*, 1980s (2) < *skriver* **Ic** *prent-ari* [pʰrɛntarɪ] M, pl. *-ar*, end20c (4) **Fr** - < rend *imprimante* **Sp** - < trsl *impresora* **It** - < trsl *stampante* **Rm** [prɪnter] N, 1980s (1 tech) < *imprimantǎ* **Rs** *printer* M, pl. *-y*, 1980s (2 tech) **Po** [-er] M, 1980s (1 tech) < trsl *drukarka* **Cr** *printer* M, pl. *-i*, end20c (3 tech) **Bg** *printer* M, pl. *-a/-i*, end20c (2 tech) **Fi** *printteri* 1980s (3) = creat *kirjoitin* **Hu** [printer] pl. *-ek*, end20c (2 tech) **Al** *printer* M, pl. *printera*, 1990 (1 tech) **Gr** *prider* [-d-,-nt-] M, pl. Ø/*-s*, end20c (1 tech) < trsl *ektypotis*

print (out) *v.* 6 'produce output in printed form' (comput.)
Ge - < *ausdrucken* **Du** *(uit) printen* [œytprintə(n)] 1980s (1 tech) **Nw** *printe (ut)* [printe] 1980s (2) < *skrive ut* **Ic** *prenta (út)* end20c (4) **Fr** - < *imprimer* **Sp** - < trsl *imprimir* **Rm** *printa* [printa] 1980s (2 tech) = *a face/da un print* **Cr** *isprintati* end20c (2) **Bg** *printiram/printvam* = trsl *pechatam* **Fi** *printata* (3) **Hu** *printel* 20c (2) **Al** - < *shtyp (me printer)* **Gr** - < trsl *ektypono*

printout *n.* 'output in printed form' (comput.)
Ge - < *Ausdruck* **Du** [=E] C, 1980s (1 tech, obs) < *uitdraai (print)* **Nw** [=E] M, pl. *-er*, 1980s (1 obs) < *utskrift* **Ic** [=E] N, pl. Ø, end20c (o) < *útprent* **Fr** - < *sortie papier, listing* **Rm** *print* [print] N, 1980s (1 tech) **Rs** - < trsl *raspechatka* **Po** - < *wydruk (komputerowy)* **Cr** *printout* M [U] end20c (2) **Bg** - < rend *razpechatka* **Fi** *printti* (3) **Hu** [=E] [U] end20c (1 tech) **Gr** <=E> [=E] N, pl. *-s*, end20c (2 tech)

privacy *n.* 1a 'the state of being private and undisturbed', 2 'freedom from intrusion or public attention'
Du [=E] C [U] 1940s (2) **Nw** (o) **Ic** [=E] N [U] end20c, 1a(1 sla) **Sp** - < *privacidad* **It** [praivəsi] F [U] 1950s (2) > *privatezza* **Rm** [=E] N [U] 1990s (1 tech) **Hu** (5La)

pro *adj.* 1 'professional'
Ge - < *Profi* **Nw** - < *proff* **Ic** [=E] uninfl., end20c (1 sla) → *próari* M **Fr** [pro] M/F, 20c (1 sla) **Sp** (o) **It** [pro] uninfl., end20c (1 tech) **Bg** - < *profi-*

processor *n.* +1a 'the principal operating part of a computer'
   The status of this loanword as an anglicism is uncertain; the word is Latinate and is apparently treated as such by most languages.
Ge *Prozessor* [pro:tsesor] M, pl. *-en*, 1980s (3 tech) **Du** [=E] C, 1980s (1 tech) **Nw** *prosessor* [prusesu:r] M, pl. *-er*, 1980s (3 tech) **Ic** [=E] M, pl. *-ar*, end20c (1 tech) = creat *gjörvi* **Fr** *processeur* M, 1960s (4) **Sp** *procesador* M (4) **It** *processore* [protfessore] M, pl. *-i*, 1970s (3 tech) **Rm** *procesor* [protfesor] N, 1980s (3 tech) **Rs** *protsessor* M, pl. *-y*, 1990s (2 tech) → *-nyĭ* adj. **Po** [procesor] M, 1980s (1 tech) **Cr** *procesor* M, pl. *-i*, end20c (1 tech) **Bg** *protsesor* M, pl. *-al-i*, end20c (3 tech) → *-en* adj. **Fi** *prosessori* 1980s (3) **Hu** *processzor* [protsessor] pl. *-ok*, end20c (2 tech) **Al** *proçesor* M, 1990s (1 tech) **Gr** <=E> [=E] M, pl. *-s*, end20c (1 tech); *prosesoras* M (3 tech)

producer *n.* 2 'a person generally responsible for the production, esp. of films, records etc.'
Ge [=E] M, pl. Ø, 1960s (1 jour, rare) < *Produzent* **Du** [=E] C, 1960s (2) **Nw** [=E] M, pl. *-e*, 1980s (2) **Ic** - < *pródúsent* (5Da); rend *framleiðandi* **Fr** - < *producteur* **Sp** [=E] M, 1920s (o>1 tech, obs) < mean *productor* **It** [=E] M, pl. Ø, 1930s (1 tech) < trsl *produttore* **Rm** - < *producǎtor* **Rs** *prodyuser* M, pl. *-y*, mid20c (2) **Po** - < *producent* (5La) **Bg** - < *produtsent* **Hu** [produtser] pl. *-ek*, beg/mid20c (3) **Al** - < *prodhues/producent* **Gr** <=E> [=E] M, 1990s (o>1 jour, mod) < *paraghoghos*

product manager *n.* 'a manager in charge of promotion and sales for a certain product range'
Ge [=E] M, pl. Ø, 1960s (1 tech) = trsl *Produkt-Manager* **Du** [-y-/a-+E] C, pl. *-s*, mid20c (1 tech) **Sp** [=E] M, pl. *-s*, 1980s (1 tech) **It** [prɔdakt menadʒer] M, pl. Ø, 1980s (1 tech) **Hu** - < trsl *termékigazgató*

professional *n.* 3 'a person engaged in a specific activity as their main paid occupation (esp. in sports)'
Ge [pro:fi] M, pl. *-s*, end19c (3) = *Berufs-, Profi* **Du** <=E>/*prof* [=E] C, end19c (1 tech_SPORT) **Nw** *proff* [pruf] M, 20c, pl. *-er* (3) **Nw** *profesjonell* adj.? **Ic** - < *atvinnumaður* **Fr** *professionnelle* M/F (4) **Sp** *profesional* M/F (4) **It** - < *professionista* (5La) **Rm** - < *profesional, -ǎ* (5It) **Rs** *profesional* M, pl. *-y*, mid20c (3) → *-nyĭ* adj.; *-ka* F; *-izm* M **Po** - < *profesjonalista* → *profesjonalizm* M [U]; *profesjonalizacja* F [U]; *profesja* F; *profesjonalny* adj. **Cr** *profesionalac* M, pl. *-ci*, beg20c (3) **Bg** *profesional (ist)* M, pl. *-al-i*, mid/end20c (1 rare/3) → *-lizǔm* M; *-len* adj. **Fi** [=E] mid20c (2) < *pro* **Hu** (5La) **Al** - < *profesionist* **Gr** - < trsl *epagelmatias* M/F

professional *adj.* 1 'of or belonging to or connected with a profession', 2a 'having the skill of a professional, competent', 2b 'worthy of a professional',

Ic	Nw	Po	Rs
Du	Ge	Cr	Bg
Fr	It	Fi	Hu
Sp	Rm	Al	Gr

3 'engaged in a specified activity as one's main paid occupation (esp. in sport)'

Du [=E] C, pl. *-s* (2) **Nw** (0) **Ic** [=E] end20c, 1,2a,b(1 coll) < 3: rend *atvinnu-* **Fr** *professionnel* (4/5) **Sp** *profesional* (4) **It** - < *professionista* (5La) **Rm** *profesional* 1,2a,b(4/5Fr) **Rs** *professional'nyĭ* beg20c (3) → *-nost'* F **Po** (5La) **Cr** (0) **Bg** *profesionalen* (3) **Hu** (5La) **Al** *profesionale* 1,2a, 2b(5It)

profit *n.* 2 'financial gain; excess of returns over out-lay'

The status as an anglicism is uncertain; the word is Latinate and is apparently treated as such by most languages.

Ge (5La) **Du** - < *profit/winst* **Nw** *profitt* (5La) **Fr** (4) **It** *profitto* (5La) **Rm** [profit] N, beg19c (5Fr) **Rs** *profit* (5Fr) **Po** (5Fr) **Cr** (5Fr) **Hu** (5Fr via Ge) **Al** *profit* M, pl. *-ë*, end20c (3)

program(me) *n.* 'a series of coded instructions to control the operation of a computer or other machine'

The status as an anglicism is uncertain; the word is Latinate and is apparently treated as such by most languages.

Ge (5La) → *-ieren* v.; *Programmierer/in* M/F **Du** *programma* N, 1960s (5) → *-eren* v. **Nw** (5La) → *programmere* v.; *programmerer* M **Ic** [=E] N, pl. *-grömm*, end20c (4 tech, coll) = rend *forrit* N → *prógrammera* v. **Fr** *programme* M, mid20c (4) → *programmeur* M; *programmer* v. **Sp** *programa* M, end20c (4) → *programador* **It** *programma* (5La) → *-are* v.; *-atore* n.; *-azione* n. **Rm** *program* [program] N, 1960s (4) **Rs** *programma* F, pl. *-y*, end20c (5Gr) **Po** *program* M, end20c (3) **Cr** *program* M, pl. *-i*, end20c (3 tech) → *programer* M **Bg** *programa* F, pl. *-mi*, end20c (4) → *-en* adj. **Hu** (5Gr) **Al** *program* M, pl. *-e*, end20c (3) → *programoj* v. **Gr** *proghramma* N, end20c (4)

progressive jazz* *n.* 1 'a kind of jazz', 2 'modern jazz (at any moment)'

Ge [=E] M [U] 1980s, 1(1 tech) **Nw** *progressiv -* [prugresi:v jas] M [U] end20c, 1(5La+2) **Ic** [=E] 2(0) < *framsækinn djass* **Fr** 1(0) **Sp** - < trsl *jazz progresivo* **It** [=E] M [U] 1980s (1 tech) **Rm** - < trsl *jaz(z) progresiv* **Rs** (0) **Po** M, uninfl., end20c, 1(1 tech) **Cr** *progresiv džez* M [U] end20c, 1(1 tech) **Bg** *progresiven dzhaz* M, 1(3+2 tech) **Hu** *progressziv dzsessz* 1(5La+3) **Gr** <=E> [=E] F [U] end20c (1 tech)

project manager *n.* 'a person responsible for the execution of a project'

Du [=E/projekt+E] C, pl. *-s*, end20c (1 tech) **It** [prɔdʒekt manadʒer] M, pl. Ø, 1980s (1 tech) **Hu** [=E/projekt-menedzser] pl. *-ek*, end20c (1 tech)

promote *v.* 3 'publicize and sell (a product)', +3a 'enhance the progress of (an entertainer, group, etc.) by publicizing'

Ge *promoten* [promo:tn] 1970s, 3(1 jour, rare) **Du** *promoten* [promo:tə(n)] 1980s, 3(2) **Nw** *promotere*

[prumute:re] 1970s, 3,+3a(3 tech) **Ic** *prómótera* [pʰrou:moutera] end20c, 3,+3a(1 tech) **Sp** < *pro-mover* **It** - < *promuovere* (5La) **Rm** - < *promova* **Po** 3(5La) **Cr** *promotirati* (0) **Al** - < *promovoj*

promoter *n.* 2 'a person who finances, organizes, etc. a sporting event, theatrical production, etc.', +5 'a specialist in sales promotion'

The status as an anglicism is uncertain; the word is Latinate and is apparently treated as such by most languages.

Ge [pro:mo:ta] M, pl. Ø, 1940s, 2(1 mod); 1960s, +5(1 jour) **Nw** <=E>/*promotor* [prumu:ter/-tor] M, pl. *-e(r)*, mid20c, 2(1 tech) **Ic** [=E] M, pl. *-ar*, end20c (1 tech) **Fr** - < *promoteur* **Sp** - < *promotor* **It** [pro-mo:ter] M, pl. Ø, 1980s (1 tech) < *promotore* **Rm** *promotor* [promotor] M, end20c, +5(4 rare) **Rs** *promouter* M, pl. *-y*, 1990s, +5(1 tech) **Po** (5La) **Cr** *promoter* M, pl. *-i*, mid20c, 2(1) **Fi** - < *promoottori* **Al** *promotor* M, pl. *-ë*, mid20c, 2(1 reg)

promotion *n.* 1 'advertising support for a band', 2 'marketing of a product'

As with other Latin-based words borrowed from English the anglicism can be added (in certain English-dominated fields) to existing Latinisms, retaining English pronunciation – or lead to a semantic extension (mainly in Romance languages).

Ge [pro:mo:ʃn] F [U] 1970s (1 mod) = *Verkaufsförderung* **Du** [=E] C, 1980s (1 mod/tech) = *promotie* **Nw** <=E>/*promosjon* [=E/prumuʃu:n] M [U] 1970s (1 tech) **Ic** [pʰrou:mousjou:n] F [U] end20c (1 tech) **Fr** (5) **Sp** - < *promoción* (1 tech) **It** [promɔʃon] F, pl. Ø, 1960s (1 tech) < *promozione* → *-onale* adj.; *promo* **Rm** (0) < *promovare* **Rs** *promoushen* M [U] 1990s (1 tech) **Po** (5La) **Cr** *promocija* (0) **Bg** *promotsiya* F, pl. *-ii*, 1990s, 1(4) **Fi** *promootio* end20c (3) **Al** *promocion* M, pl. *-ë*, end20c, 2(3) **Gr** <=E> [=E] F/N [U] 1990s (1 tech, you) < mean *proothisi, proaghoghi*

proof *n.* 5 'the standard or strength of distilled alcoholic liquors'

Ge (Ø) **Du** Ø **Fr** (Ø) **Po** [-u-] M, uninfl., end20c (1 tech) **Gr** (1 writ)

prop¹ *n.* 1 'a rigid support, esp. one not an integral part of the thing supported'

Nw *props* [prɔps] M, pl. *-er*/Ø, 1930s (3 tech)

prop² *n.* 'property (used on stage)' (theatre, film), 2 'a property man or mistress'

Ic *props* [pʰrofs] N, sg. [U] mid20c (2 tech) = *leikmunir* → *propsari* M

propeller *n.* 2 'a revolving shaft with blades, esp. for propelling a ship or aircraft', +3 'a type of steam ship'

Ge [pro:pela] M, pl. Ø, end19c, 2(3) **Du** [=E] C, beg20c, 2(3 tech) **Nw** *propell* [prupel] M, pl. *-er*, beg20c, 2(3) **It** - < *propulsore* (5Fr) **Rm** *propelă/probelă* [propelə/probelə] F, mid19c, via Ge, +3(3 obs) **Rs** *propeller* M, pl. *-y*, beg20c, 2(2) **Po** [-er] M, beg20c, 2(1 tech) **Cr** *propeler* M, pl. *-i*, beg20c, 2(1 tech) **Bg** *propeler* M, pl. *-al-i*, mid20c, 2(1 tech) **Fi** *propelli* 19c, 2(5Sw) **Hu** [propeller] pl. *-ek*, end19/

beg20c, 2(3)+3(2 tech) **Al** *propeler* M, pl. *-ë* mid20c, 2(1 reg) **Gr** *propẹla* F, mid20c, 2(3)

prospector *n.* +2 'a person who explores a region for gold', +3 'someone who looks for new clients'

The status as an anglicism is uncertain; the word is Latinate and is apparently treated as such by most languages.

Ge *Prospẹktor* M, pl. *-en*, 19c, +2(5La) **Du** [=E] C, 19c (2) **Nw** *prospekter* [pruspẹkter] M, pl. *-e*, 1930s, +2(2) **Fr** *prospecteur/-trice* M/F, end19c (3) **It** *prospettore* M, pl. *-i*, 1930s, +2(1 tech) **Rm** *prospector* M, 1930s, via Fr, +2(3) **Fi** *prospektori* 19c, +2(1) < mean *malminetsijä*

prosperity *n.* 'a state of being prosperous; wealth or success'

Du *prosperiteit* (5Fr) **Nw** (o) **Fr** *prospérité* (4) **Sp** *prosperidad* (5La) **It** *prosperità* (5La) **Rm** - < *prosperitate* **Rs** *prospẹriti* N, uninfl., end20c (1 jour) **Po** <=E> N, uninfl., beg20c (1 tech) **Cr** *prọsperitet* (5Fr) **Bg** - < *prosperitet* **Hu** <=E>/*prosperitás* [=E/prọʃperita:ʃ] (5La/1 techECON) **Al** *prosperitet* M [U] end20c (o)

provider *n.* +1a 'a person who provides someone with drugs'

Ge [=E] M, pl. Ø, end20c (1 sla) **Hu** - < ↑*dealer*

psychedelic *adj.* 1a 'expanding the mind's awareness, esp. through the use of hallucinogenic drugs', 2a 'producing an effect resembling that of a psychedelic drug (esp. music); having vivid colours or designs etc.', 2b 'bright, bold, and often abstract' (of colours, patterns, etc.)

English pronunciation is obviously a minority choice; most languages treat the item as an internationalism in spite of its British origin.

Ge [=E/psy:xodẹ:liʃ] 1960s, 2a,b(3 obs) **Du** *psychedelisch* [psixədẹ:lis] 1960s, 2b(3 obs) **Nw** *psykedelisk* [(p)sykedẹ:lisk] 1960s, 2a,b(1) **Ic** [sai:katẹ:liskʏr] 1970s, 1a,2a(1 sla) = rend *sýrður* **Fr** *psychédélique* [psikedelik] 1960s, 2a,b(3 obs) **Sp** *psiquedélico/psicodélico* 1960s, 2a(3 obs) **It** *psichedelico* [psikedẹliko] 1960s (3) **Rm** *psihedelic* [psihedẹlik] 1970s, via Fr, 1a,2a,b,(3 tech) **Po** *psychodeliczny* [psixodelitschni] 1960s, 2a,b(2) **Cr** *psihodeličan* adj., end20c, 2a,b(1) **Bg** *psikhedelichna* 2a(3 tech) **Fi** *psykedeelinen* 1960s, 2a,b(3) **Hu** *pszichedélikus* [psihedẹ:likuʃ] 20c, 2a,b(1 techMED) **Gr** *psykhedhelikos-i,-o*, 1960s (5 tech) pl. → *psykhedhelia* F; *psykhedhelismos* M

psycho *n.* 'a psychopath'

Du [=E] C, pl. *-s*, end20c (1 sla) **Ic** [=E] N, pl. Ø, end20c (1 sla)

psychopath *n.* 1 'a person suffering from chronic mental disorder, esp. with abnormal or violent social behaviour', 2 'a mentally or emotionally unstable person'

Ge (5Gr) **Du** (5Gr) **Nw** (5Gr) **Ic** [=E] M, pl. *-ar*, end20c (1 sla) **Fr** *psychopathe* (5Gr) **Sp** *psicópata* (5Gr) **It** *psicopạtico* (5Gr) **Rm** *psihopat* [psihopạt] M, 1,2(5Fr) **Rs** (5Gr) **Po** (5Gr) **Cr** (5Gr) **Bg** *psikhopat* (5Gr) **Fi** *psykopaatti*

(5Gr) **Hu** (5Gr) **Al** *psikopat* M, pl. *-ë* (5Gr) **Gr** *psykhopathịs* (4)

pub *n.* 1 'a public house'

This term has been well-known as a foreignism referring to British drinking-places for some time, but in recent years appears to have become marginally accepted (at least in names) for places aspiring to the atmosphere of a British pub on the Continent. It is too early to say whether this trend is going to continue (which could lead to a status like that of ↑*bar*).

Ge [pab] N/M, pl. *-s*, 1960s (Ø>1 mod) < *Kneipe* **Du** [pap/pʏp] C, 1980s (2) **Nw** [=E] M, pl. *-er*, 1960s (2) **Ic** *pöbb/pöbbur/-i* [pʰœp:(-ʏr/- 1)] M, pl. *-ar*, mid20c, 1(Ø>2 coll) = *(bjór)krá* **Fr** [pœb] M, 1930s (o); 1960s (1 mod) **Sp** [pab/paf] M, pl. *-(e)s*, 1960s (2) **It** [pab] M [U] 1950s (Ø>1) **Rm** (Ø/1) **Rs** *pab* M, pl. *-y*, end20c (Ø) **Po** M, 1990s (2) **Cr** *pab* M, pl. *-ovi*, end20c (1) **Bg** *pŭb* M, pl. *-al-ove*, end20c (1 mod) < ↑*bar* **Fi** *pub/pubi* [=E] end20c (Ø>3) **Hu** [=E] pl. *-ok*, end20c (1 jour, you, mod) **Al** - < ↑*bar/birrare* **Gr** <=E>/*pab* F/N, pl. Ø/*-s*, mid/end20c (2) < ↑*bar*

publicity *n.* 1a 'the professional exploitation of a product, company, or person by advertising or popularizing', 2 'public exposure; notoriety'

Ge [=E] F [U] 1960s (1 jour>2) = *Publizität* **Du** *publiciteit* 1a(5Fr) **Nw** [=E] M [U] mid20c (1) < ↑*PR* **Ic** [=E] N [U] end20c (o sla) **Fr** *publicité* 1a(4) **Sp** *publicidad* (5) **It** *pubblicità* (5Fr) **Rm** - < *publicitate* **Rs** *pablisiti* N, uninfl., 1990s (1 jour) **Po** N, uninfl., 1990s, 1a(1 jour) **Cr** *pabliṣiti* M [U] end20c, 1a(1 tech) **Bg** (o) **Hu** [=E] [U] end20c, 1a(1 tech) 2(1 jour) **Al** *publicitẹt* (5Fr)

public relations *n. pl.* 1 'the professional maintenance of a favourable public image, esp. by a famous person or company', cf. ↑*PR*

Ge [=E] pl., 1960s (1 tech) = *Öffentlichkeitsarbeit*, ↑*PR* **Du** <=E>/*p.r.* [pʏblɪk rilẹ:ʃəns/pe ɛr] 1980s (1 tech) **Nw** [=E] M [U] 1960s (1 rare) < ↑*PR* **Ic** [=E] end20c (o) = trsl *almannatengsl* **Fr** *public-relations* [pœblikrilɛʃəns] F, pl., 1950s (1 obs) > trsl *relations publiques* **Sp** [=E] M/F, 1970s (1 tech) < trsl *relaciones públicas* **It** [pạblik relẹiʃons] F, pl., 1960s (1 tech, jour) < trsl *pubbliche relazioni* **Rm** [=E] pl., 1990s (1 jour) **Rs** *pablik rilẹiʃhnz* M [U] 1990s (1 jour) **Po** pl., 1990s (1 jour) **Cr** [=E] M, sg., end20c (1 tech) **Bg** *pŭblik rilẹiʃhŭns* M [U] 1990 (1 tech) **Hu** *public relations/P.R.* [=E/pẹ:er] [U] 1960s (1 tech, mod) < trsl *dhimosies skhesis* **Al** - < *mardhënie ndër kombëtare* **Gr** (o>1

public service *n./attrib.* 'serving a broad section of the public' (usu. about TV)

Du - < *publieksomroep* **Nw** [=E] cp¹, 1980s (1) **Fr** *service public* (5) **It** - < *servizio pubblico* (5) **Po** (0)

puck¹ (1) *n.* 1 'a rubber disc used as a ball in ice hockey'

Ge [puk] M, pl. -*s*, 1960s (3 tech) **Du** [pʏk] C, 1950s (1 tech) **Nw** [=E] M, pl. -*er*, mid20c (2 tech) **Ic** *pökkur* [pʰœhkʏr] M, pl. -*ar*, mid20c (3 tech) **Fr** (0) < *palet* **It** [puk] M, pl. Ø, mid20c (1 tech) < *disco* **Rm** *puc* [puk] N, mid20c (3 tech) **Po** [puk] M, mid20c (1 tech) **Cr** *pak* M, pl. -*i*, 20c (1 tech) **Fi** - < *iekko* → *pukata* v. **Hu** *pakk* [pakk] pl. Ø, 1940s (1 tech) < *korong* **Gr** *pak* N, end20c (1 tech)

puck² (2) *n.* 1 'a mischievous or evil sprite' (from Shakespeare)

This word is one of the earliest loanwords from a literary source; it was adopted from Shakespeare whose works became very popular in eighteenth-century Germany.

Ge [puk] M, pl. -*s*, 18c (1 arch) **Du** - < *kabouter* **Nw** (0) < *puke* **Bg** *pŭk* (Ø)

pudding *n.* 1a 'any of various sweet cooked dishes'

The very early adoption of this word made it possible in principle for it to spread to all European languages, often via French or German. Note that a Continental pudding is normally sweet.

Ge [pudiŋ] M, pl. -*el*-*s*, end17c (3) **Du** [pʏdɪŋg] C, pl. -*s*/-*en*, mid19c (3) **Nw** [pudiŋ] M, pl. -*er*, mid19c (3) **Ic** *búðingur* [puːðiŋkʏr] M, pl. -*(ar)*, 1800s, via Da (3) **Fr** *pudding/pouding* [pudiŋ] M, 17c (2) **Sp** <=E>/ *pudín/budín* M, end19c (3) **It** *budino* M, 19c (3) [puding] M, pl. Ø, 19c (1) **Rm** *budincă* [budiŋkə] F, end19c, via Fr (3); *puding* [puding] N, beg20c (3) **Rs** *puding* M, pl. -*i*, mid19c (2) **Po** [-nk] M, mid19c (1 tech) < *budyń* **Cr** *puding* M, 19c (3) **Bg** *puding* M, pl. -*al*-*i*, beg20c (Ø/1 tech) **Hu** *puding* [=E] pl. -*ok*, 18c (3) **Al** *puding* M, pl. -*e*, mid20c (3) **Gr** *putiga* F, beg20c, via Fr/It (3)

puddling* *n./v.* 'the heating of molten iron, so as to oxidize and remove the carbon and produce wrought iron'

This technical term was adopted with nineteenth-century British dominance in steel making, as both a verb and a verbal noun in most European languages. Note the frequency of suffix replacement.

Ge *Puddeln* N [U] 19c (3 tech, arch) **Nw** [pudliŋ] M [U] beg20c (1 tech) → *pudle* v. **Fr** *puddlage* [pydlaʒ] M, mid19c (1 tech) → *puddler* v.; *puddleur* M **Sp** *pudelaje* 19c (3 tech) **It** *puddellaggio* M [U] end19c (3 tech); *puddellare* v. (1940s) → *puddellatura, pudellazione* (1960s) **Rm** *pudlaj* [pudlaʒ] N [U] end19c, via Fr (3 tech) → *pudla* v.; *pudlare* F; *pudlat/-ă* adj. **Rs**

---

pudlingovanie N [U] mid19c (1 tech) **Po** *pudlingowanie* [pudlingovanie] N [U] mid19c (1 tech) **Cr** *pudlovanje* N [U] 20c (1 tech) **Bg** *pudlingovane* N [U] beg20c, via Rs (3 tech) **Fi** *putlaus* 19c (3 tech)

puff *n.* +9 'hemp, hashish, marijuana'

Ic [=E] N [U] 1970s (1 sla)

puff *v.* +13b 'smoke hemp, hashish, or marijuana'

Ic *pöffa* [pʰœf:a] 1970s (1 sla)

puffed rice *n.* 'rice puffed up by heating, eaten as a breakfast cereal'

Ge *Puffreis* (3+5) **Du** - < *gepofte rijst* **Nw** *puffet ris/puff* [pufet/puf] M [U] 20c (3+5) **It** - < *trsl riso soffiato* **Hu** - < *trsl puffasztott rizs*

pull *v.* 6a 'move (a boat) by pulling on the oars', 9a 'check the speed of a horse', 15a,b 'strike the ball' (cricket, golf)

Ge [pulən] beg20c, 6a,9a(1 tech) **Po** imp., beg20c (1 tech) **Hu** *pullol* [pullol] end19/beg20c, 9a(1 tech)

pull *n.* 8 'a spell of rowing', 10 'a pulling stroke' (cricket, golf)

Hu [=E] end20c, 10(1 tech); end19/beg20c, 8(1 tech) → -*oz* v.

puller *n.* 'a person who strikes a ball etc.'

Po [-er] M, mid20c (1 tech)

pulli* *n.* see ↑*pullover*

Pullman *n./cp*¹ 1 'a comfortable railway carriage or motor coach', 2 'a sleeping car'

This term was taken from the name of the American constructor G.M. Pullman (1831–97) and coined for the first type of a comfortable railway coach; it was transferred to buses etc. but became widely obsolescent by 1950.

Ge [=E] M/cp¹ [U] end19c, 1(1 obs) **Du** [=E] C, beg20c (1 obs) **Nw** [pulman] M, 20c, 1(1 arch) **Fr** [pulman] M, end19c, 1(1 arch) **Sp** [pulman] M, pl. Ø, 1920s, 1(1 tech, arch) = *autopullman* **It** [pulman] M, pl. Ø, mid19c, 1(3) → *pulmino* n. **Rm** *pulman* [pulman] N [U] mid20c, 1(1 tech, obs) **Rs** *pul'man* M, pl. -*y*, end19c (1 tech, obs) **Po** *pulman* [-men] M, beg20c, 1(1 tech) → -*owski* adj. **Cr** *pulman* M, beg20c (1 obs) **Bg** *pulmanov vagon* M, beg20c, 1(Ø) **Fi** *pullman (vaunu)* 19c (Ø) **Hu** [=E] [U] end19c, 1(2 obs) < cp¹ -*kocsi* (2/3+5Hu) **Gr** *pulman* N, mid20c, 1(2)

pullover *n.* 'a knitted garment put on over the head'

The distribution of this word is almost universal, the pronunciation largely following national conventions. A number of morphological adaptations include *Pulli* (German), *Pull* (Dutch, French, Italian), *pulczi* (Hungarian) and new coinages like *minipull* (Spanish) and *Pullunder* 'light sleeveless pullover worn over a shirt' (German).

Ge [pulɔːva] M, pl. Ø, 1920s (2); *Pulli* M, pl. -*s*, 1960s (3) **Du** <=E>/*pull* [pʏlɔːvər] C, 1950s (3) = *trui, sweater* **Nw** [pulɔːver] M, pl. -*el*-*s*, beg20c (1 obs) < *genser* **Fr** *pull-over/pull* [pylɔvɛʀ/pulɔvœʀ] M,

1920s (2) **Sp** [pulóber/puj̲o̲ber] M, 1920s (1 arch, obs) → *mini-pull* **It** [pul̲o̲ver] M, pl. Ø, 1920s (3); *pull* [pull] M, pl. Ø, 1970s (1) **Rm** pulover [pul̲o̲vər] N, 1940s, via Fr (3) **Rs** pul̲o̲ver M, pl. -*y*, beg20c (2) **Po** *pulower* [-over] M, beg20c (3) → -*ek* M **Cr** pul̲o̲ver M, pl. -*i*, beg20c (3) **Bg** pul̲o̲ver M, pl. -*al-i*, beg20c (2) **Fi** [=E] beg20c (2 obs) **Hu** *pulóver* [pul̲o:ver] pl. -*ek*, beg20c (3) → *pulcsi* **Al** pul̲o̲vër M, pl. *pulovra*, mid20c (3) **Gr** pul̲o̲ver N, beg20c (2)

pulp *n.* 1 'the soft fleshy part of fruit etc.', 3 'a soft shapeless mass derived from rags, wood, etc., used in papermaking', 4 'popular or sensational writing, often regarded as of poor quality'

Ge 1,3(5La/Fr) **Du** *pulp* 1(5Fr) **Nw** [pʉlp/=E] M [U] 20c, 3(1 tech) **Sp** *pulpa* 1,3(5La); *pulp* 1990s, 4(1 tech) → *pulpero* **It** [=E] M [U] 1990s, 4(1 tech, mod) < *pulp fiction*; 1: *polpa* (5La) **Rm** *pulpă* [pul̲pə] F [U] 1,3(5Fr) **Rs** pul'pa F [U] beg20c, 1,3(1 tech) **Po** 1(5Fr) **Bg** *pulp* M [U] beg20c, 1(1 tech) **Hu** [pulp] [U] 1950s, 1(1 tech)

pumps *n. pl.* 'a light (lady's) shoe for dancing etc.'

The word, always adopted with final -*s* and partly transmitted through German, is an early and permanent loanword in the field of ladies' fashion.

Ge [pömps] M, pl. Ø, 1940s (2) **Du** [pʏmp] C, 1940s (2) = *pumpschoen* **Nw** [=E] M, pl. Ø, mid20c (3) **Po** (0) **Fi** *pumpsit* beg20c (2 obs) **Hu** *pömpsz* [pəmps] pl. Ø, 20c (2>3 obs)

punch *v.* 3b 'pierce a hole by punching' (e.g. transfer data to computer-readable cards)

Ge [panʃən] beg20c (1 obs) **Nw** *punche* ["pønʃe] 1950s (1 obs)

punch[1] (1) *n.* 1 'a blow with a fist', 2 'the ability to deliver this', 3 'vigour, momentum; effective force', +4 'a punch-card machine'

Ge [=E] M, pl. -*s*, mid20c, 1,2(1 tech); beg20c, +4(1 tech, obs) → -*en* v.; -*er* M **Du** [pynʃ] C, pl. -*es*, 19c, via Fr, 1,3(1 tech) 2 (1 reg) < +4: *pons(kaarten)machine* **Nw** [=E] M, pl. -*er*, mid20c, 1,2,3(2 tech) **Ic** [pʰæns] N [U] end20c, 3(0 sla) **Fr** [pœnʃ] M, beg20c, 2(3 tech); mid20c, 3(2) **Sp** [puntʃ/pantʃ] M, 1920, 1,2,3(1 tech > 2) = *pegada* **It** [pantʃ] M, pl. Ø, 1950s, 1(1 tech) **Rm** *punci* [=E/puntʃj] N, 1930s, via Fr?, 1(2 tech) **Bg** pʉnch M, pl. -*al-ove*, mid20c, 1(1 tech) **Hu** [pəntʃ] [U] end19/beg20c, 1(1 tech, arch) < *lefogás-*

punch[2] (3) *n.* 'a drink of wine and spirits mixed with water, fruit juices, spices, etc., and usu. served hot.'

The name of this drink is certainly by far the best preserved among the many drinks imported from Britain in the nineteenth century. The word was widely transmitted through German and appears to

have lost its Englishness in all but etymology in all European languages (supposed to be derived from an Indian language, referring to the 'five' ingredients).

Ge *Punsch* [punʃ] M [U] beg18c (3) **Du** [pʏn(t)ʃ] C [U] 17c (2) **Nw** [<=E>/*punsj* [pʉnʃ/=E] M [U] mid19c (2) **Ic** *púns* [pʰuns] N/M [U] end18c, via Da (3) **Fr** [põʃ] M, 17c (2) **Sp** *ponche* M, 18c (3) **It** *punch/ponce* [pʌntʃ/pɔntʃ] M [U] 18c (3) → *poncino* n. **Rm** *punci* [puntʃj] N, beg19c, via Fr (3) **Rs** *punsh* M [U] 18/19c, via Ge (2) → -*evyĭ* adj. **Po** *poncz* [pontsch] M [U] 18/19c (2) → -*owy* adj. **Cr** pu̲nč M [U] 19c (3) **Bg** *punsh* M [U]/pl. -*a*, beg20c, via Ge (Ø>3) **Fi** *punssi* 19c (3) **Hu** *puncs* [puntʃ] [U] before 19c (3) **Gr** *pan(t)s* N, mid/end20c (2)

punch-drunk *adj.* 'stupefied from or as though from a series of heavy blows'

Du [=E] 1980s (2) **Nw** [=E] mid20c (1 tech)

puncher* *n.* 'a boxer'

Ge (0) **Du** - < *bokser* **Nw** (0) **Fr** *puncheur* [pœnʃœʁ] M, 1940s (1 tech) **Rm** *puncer/puncheur* [puntʃer/puntʃœr] M, 1960s, via Fr (2>3 tech) **Po** *punczer* [-er] M, mid20c (1 tech) **Cr** *pančer* 20c (1 tech)

punching bag *n.* 'a stuffed bag suspended at a height for boxers etc. to practise punching'

Nw [=E] M, pl. -*er*, mid20c (1 tech) **Sp** [=E/punʃin-bag] M, 20c (1 tech, rare) **It** [=E/puntʃing beg] M, pl. Ø, 1930s (1 tech) **Rm** - < cf. ↑*punching ball* **Po** - < cf. ↑*punching ball* **Bg** - < cf. ↑*punching ball*

punching ball* *n.* 'a leather bag used in training' (box.)

This technical boxing term had a much better chance of adoption than the n./v. ↑*punch* by itself, but has not spread beyond the very limited range of reference.

Ge [panʃinbal] M, pl. -*bälle*, 1930s (1 tech) **Du** - < *boks-bal* **Nw** [=E+-bal] M, pl. -*er*, 20c (1 tech+5) **Fr** *punching-ball* [pœnʃinbol] M, beg20c (1 tech) **Sp** [=E/puntʃinbol] M, 1930s (1 tech) **It** [pantʃing bɔ:l/ pundʒibol] M, pl. Ø, beg20c (2 tech) **Rm** [puntʃingbol] N, 1960s, via Fr? (1 tech) **Rs** *penchingbol* M, pl. -*y*, beg20c (1 tech) **Po** [-bol] M, beg20c (1 tech) **Cr** *pančing bol* M, beg20c (1 tech) **Bg** pu̲nchingbol M, pl. -*al-ove*, mid20c (1 tech) < *boksova krusha*

punchline *n.* 'words giving the point of a joke or story'

Du - < *clou* **Nw** [=E] M, pl. -*s*, end20c (1) < *poeng* **Ic** [=E] N [U] end20c (1 sla)

punk *n./cp¹* 2a 'a loud fast-moving form of music', +2c 'an anti-fashion life style'

The term for the music style, created in Britain in the late 1970s as a new type of rock, became popular within a few years in most of Europe. The aggressive nature of the music found its expression, too, in dress, life-style, and anti-establishment protest, receding again from the mid-1980s.

Ge [=E] M [U] 1970s (1 you, obs) → *-ig* adj. **Du** [pʏnk] C, 1970s (2) **Nw** <=E>/*pønk* [=E] M [U] 1970s, 2a(2) → *punkete* adj. **Ic** *pönk* [pʰœ(y)ŋk] N [U] 1970s (2 coll, you) > 2a: rend *ræflarokk* **Fr** [pɛ̃k] M/F/adj., uninfl., 1970s (2) → *punkette* F **Sp** [punk/pank] M [U] 1970s (2 tech, you) → *punkismo, punkitud* **It** [=E] M/F/adj., pl. Ø, 1970s (2 mod) **Rm** [=E] N/adj., uninfl., 1970s (1 tech) → *punkist/ă* M/F **Rs** *pank* M [U] 1980s (1 you, mod) **Po** M, end20c, 2a(1 tech) **Cr** *pank* M [U] end20c (1 tech) **Bg** *pŭnk* M/cp¹ [U] 1980s (2) **Fi** [=E] 1970s (1 tech) **Hu** [=E] [U] end20c, 1970s/1980s, 2a(2 obs) +2c(2 pej, obs) **Gr** *pank* F/N [U] 1970/80s (1 you)

punk *adj./cp¹* 2 'denoting punk rock and its associations'

Fr [pɛ̃k] adj./M/F, 1970s (2) → *punkette* F **Sp** [=E/punk] adj., uninfl., 1970s (2) **It** [=E] uninfl., 1970s (2) **Rm** [=E] uninfl., 1970s (2) **Po** (0) **Bg** *punk* M [U] 1980s (2 tech, you) **Hu** [=E] 1970s (2) **Gr** *pank* adj, cp¹, 1970s (2)

punk(er) *n./cp¹* 2b 'a devotee of punk music', 3 'a hoodlum, a ruffian', +7 'a member of a juvenile protest group'

The English *punk* refers to a worthless person in general; thence *punk rock* and *punk rocker*. The Continental languages appear to have developed the 'music' sense to include attitudes and life styles, and this formed the basis for *punker*, which developed towards a general term of abuse, but is now starting to become obsolescent.

Ge *Punker* [paŋka] M, pl. Ø, 1980s, 2b,+7(2 pej, obs) **Du** *punker* [pʏŋkər] C, 1970s (2) **Nw** <=E>/*pønker* ["pønker] M, pl. *-e*, 1970s, 2b,+7(2) **Ic** *pönkari* [pʰœ(y)ŋkarɪ] M, pl. *-ar*, 1970s, 2b,+7(2 coll, you) > 2b: rend *ræflarokkari* **Fr** [pɛ̃k] M, 1970s, 2b,+7(1 obs) **Sp** *punky/punkie/punqui* M/F, pl. *-s*, 1970s (2) < *punk, punkero* **It** [pank] M, pl. Ø, 1970s, 2b,+7(2) **Rm** *punker* [=E] M, 1970s (1 rare) > *punkist/-ă* M/F **Rs** *pank* M, pl. *-i*, 1980s, 2b(1 you, mod) +7(1 obs, you) **Po** *punk* M, 1980s, +7(2) → *-owski* adj. **Cr** *panker* M, pl. *-i*, end20c, 2b,+7(1) → *-ica* F, *-ski* adj. **Bg** *pŭnk* cp¹, M, pl. *-ove*, 1980s, 2b(2); adj., uninfl.; *pŭnkar* M, pl. *-i*, 2b(3) → *-ski* adj. **Fi** *punkkari* 1970s, 2b,+7(3) **Hu** *punk* [=E] pl. *-ok*, 1970s/80s, 2b,+7(2 pej, obs) **Gr** *pank* M/F 1980s, 3,+7(1); *pankio* N (3 sla)

pup *n.* 1 'a young dog'

Du [pʏp] M/N, 1910s (3)

puppy *n.* 1 'a young dog'

Du [pʏpi] M/N, 1910s (2) **Nw** (0)

pure nonsense *phr.* 'absurdity'

Du *pure nonsens* (5+3) **Nw** (0) **Po** *purnonsens*/<=E> [pur-] M, mid20c (1 tech)

purser *n.* 1 'the head steward on a ship or aeroplane', +2 'a bank official'

Ge [=E] M, pl. Ø, 1970s, 1(1 tech, rare) → *-ette* F **Du** [=E] C, beg20c (2) **Nw** [=E] M, pl. *-e*, mid20c (2) **Ic** [=E] M, mid20c, 1(1 sla) **Bg** *pŭrser* M, pl. *-i*, 1990s, +2(1 tech) **Fi** *purseri* beg20c (3 obs)

push *v.* 1 'exert a force on (a thing) to move it', 5 'move forward by force', 11 'promote sales', 13 'deal with drugs'

Ge *puschen* 1970s, 1(1 you) 11 (1 mod) 13 (1 sla) **Du** *pushen* [pʉʃən] 1970s (1 sla) **Nw** *pushe* ["pʉʃe] 1970s (1 sla) → *pusher* M **Ic** [pʰus:a] 1970s, 13(1 sla) → *púss(j)erí* N

push *n.* 3 'a vigorous effort', 5 'enterprise, determination to succeed', 6 'the use of influence to advance a person'

Ge [=E] M [U] 1970s (1 coll) **Du** [=E] C, 1940s, 3(2) **Nw** ["pʉʃ] N, pl. Ø, 1930s, 3(1)

pusher *n.* 1 'an illegal seller of drugs'

Ge [pʉʃa] M, pl. Ø, 1960s (1 sla, obs) < *Dealer* **Du** [=E] C, 1970s (2) **Nw** ["pʉʃer] M, pl. *-e*, 1970s (3) **Ic** [pʰus:(j)er] M, pl. *-ar*, 1970s (1 sla) **Sp** <=E>/*púcher* M, 1970s (1 tech) **It** [=E] M, pl. Ø, 1970s (1 sla) **Rm** [=E] 1970s (0>1 jour) **Rs** *pusher* M, pl. *-y*, 1990s (1 jour/you) **Hu** [pʉʃər] pl. Ø, end20c (0>1 tech) < *közvetítő*

push-pull *n./cd.* 2 '(a device) consisting of two valves etc. operated alternately' (electr.)

Fr [pʉʃpul] M, uninfl. [U] beg20c (1 tech/ban) < *à moteurs en tandem, symétrique* **Sp** [pʉʃpul] M, 1930s (1 tech) **It** [=E] M, pl. Ø, 1930s (1 tech) **Rm** [=E] N [U] 1970s (1 tech) **Rs** → *push-pul'nyĭ* adj. **Po** M, uninfl., end20c (1 tech) **Cr** (0) **Bg** *pushpul* M, pl. *-a*, mid20c (1 tech) → *-en* adj. **Hu** [=E] [U] 20c, cp¹ (1 tech) **Gr** *pus pul* adj., mid20c (1 tech, arch)

push-up *n.* 'a press-up'

Du [=E] C, 1990s (1 tech) < *opdrukoefening* **Nw** [=E] M, pl. *-s*, 1970s (1) < *armheving* **Ic** [pʰus:œhps] end20c (1 sla) < *armbeygjur* F **Gr** *pusap* N, pl. *-s*, mid/end20c (2)

put *v.* 1 'move sth. to a specified position', 4a 'cause (a person) to go or be, habitually or temporarily'

Nw *putte* ["pʉte] 19c, 1(3) **Ic** *pútta* [pʰuhta] end18c, 1(4/5Da)

putt *v.* 'strike' (golf)

Ge *putten* [u/a] 1970s (1 tech) **Du** *putten* (5) **Nw** *putte* ["pøte] 20c (1 tech) **Ic** *pútta* [pʰuhta] mid20c

(2 tech) **Fr** [pœte] (1) **Sp** *patear* end20c (1 tech, fac) **Fi** *putata* 20c (3) **Hu** [putt] end20c (1 tech) < *lyukba igazít*

putt *n.* 'a putting stroke' (golf)

The (slowly) increasing popularity of golf has introduced terms into the individual languages which are becoming better known to non-specialists, *putt* n./v. being one of the first to spread.

Ge [u/a] M, pl. -s, 1970s (1 tech) **Nw** [=E] M, pl. -er, 20c (1 tech) → *putte* v. **Ic** *pútt* [pʰuht] N, pl. Ø, mid20c (2 tech) **Fr** [pœt] M, beg20c (1 tech) **Sp** [put/pat] M, pl. -s, end20c (1 tech) **It** [pat] M, pl.

Ø, mid20c (1 tech) **Rs** (o) **Bg** (o) **Fi** *putti* 20c (3) **Hu** [putt] pl. Ø, end20c (1 tech) < *lyukbaigazítás*

puttee *n.* 1 'a long strip of cloth wound spirally round the leg from ankle to knee for protection'

Du [=E] C, 1910s (1 tech, arch) **Nw** *puttis* [pу̱tis] M, pl. -er, beg20c (3 arch)

putter *n.* 'a golf club used for putting'

Ge [pу̱ta] M, pl. Ø, 1970s (1 tech) **Du** [pytər] C, 1950s (4) **Nw** [=E] M, pl. -er, 20c (1 tech) **Ic** <=E>/*púttari* [=E/pʰuhtarı] M, pl. -ar, mid20c (2 tech) **Fr** [pœtœʀ] M, beg20c (1 tech) **Sp** [pу̱ter] M, end20c (1 tech) **It** [=E] M, pl. Ø, mid20c (1 tech) **Rs** (o/1 tech) **Fi** *putteri* 20c Hu [pу̱tter] pl. Ø, end20c (1 tech) < *begurító ütő*

puzzle *n./cp¹* 1 'an enigma', +3 'a toy consisting of cardboard pieces to be put together, a jigsaw puzzle', (also used figuratively)

The early borrowing appears to be a shortening of *(jigsaw) puzzle*, a sense which still greatly dominates in most languages; the meaning 'enigma' is, by contrast, rare, concentrating surprisingly on Eastern Europe.

Ge [puzl/pazl] N [U] end19c, +3(2) **Du** *puzzel*/<=E>

[pу̱zəl] C, end19c (2>3) → *puzzelen* v. **Nw** *puslespill* [pу̱sle-] cp¹/ N, end19c, +3(3) **Ic** *púsl/púsluspil* [pʰustl] N, pl. Ø, mid20c, via Da, +3(3) **Fr** [pœzl(ə)] M, beg20c, +3(2) **Sp** [puƟle] 1,+3(2>3) **It** [pazəl/pу̱ttsle] M,

pl. Ø, 1920s (3) **Rm** [=E] N, 1970s (2) **Po** [puzle] pl., 1980s, +3(2 coll/jour) **Cr** *pazl* M [U] end20c (1) **Bg** *pу̱zel* M, pl. -a/-i, 1990s, +3(1 mod) **Fi** [=E/putsle] 1980s (1) **Hu** [=E] [U] end20c, +3(2) **Al** [pazel] +3(3) < *gjëagjerë* **Gr** *pazl* N, end20c, +3(2)

puzzle *v.* +5 'put together a jigsaw puzzle'

Ge *puzzlen* [a/u] 1970s (2) **Du** *puzzelen* [pyzələn] 19c (3) **Nw** *pusle* [ˈpу̱sle] 20c (3) **Ic** *púsla* [pʰustla] mid20c (3) **Po** (o)

pyjamas *n. pl.* 1 'a suit of loose trousers and jacket for sleeping in', 2 'loose trousers worn in Asia'

The Hindi word was transmitted through British English to almost all European languages, where 'singular' uses are common; the American English spelling is not found – but occurs in American Spanish.

Ge *Pyjama* [pyd3a̱:ma] M, pl. -s, beg20c, 1(2) **Du** *pyjama/piama* [pija:ma:] C, pl. -'s, end19c (2>3) **Nw** <=E>/*pysj* [pyja:mas/pyʃ(a̱:mas)] M, pl. -er, beg20c, 1(3) > *nattdrakt* **Fr** *pyjama* [pi3ama] M, beg20c, 1(3); beg19c, 2(3) **Sp** *pijama* M, beg20c, 1(3) **It** *pigiama* [pid3ama] M, pl. -i, beg20c, 1(3) **Rm** *pijama* [pi3ama̱] F, beg20c, via Fr, 1(3) **Rs** *pizhama̱* F, pl. -y, mid20c, 1(3) → *-amnyĭ* adj. **Po** *piżama/pidżama* mid20c, 1(3) 2(1 tech) **Cr** *pidžama* M, pl. -e, beg20c, 1(3) **Bg** *pizha̱ma* F, pl. -mi, beg20c, via Rs, 1(3) → -*a̱men* adj. **Hu** *pizsama* [pi3ama] pl. -ák, via Ge, 1(3) **Al** *pixhame/ pizhame* F, pl., mid20c (3) **Gr** *pi(t)za̱ma* F, beg20c, via It, 1(3)

Q

Q *abbrev.* +4 'quality'
Rm [=E] (1 tech, writ)   **Po** [ku] end20c (2)
Quaker *n.* 1 'a member of the Society of Friends, a Christian movement'

Early attestations are foreignisms relating to the religious community especially in the USA. However, the term became widely known in compounds such as *quaker-oats* (nineteenth century) and *Quäker-Speisung* 'free school meal' (twentieth century in Germany), acquiring more generic meanings which are now largely obsolete.

Ge *Quäker* [kwɛ̱:ka] M, pl. Ø, 19c (Ø/3)   **Du** *quaker* [kwɛ̱:kər] C, 17c (2) > *kwaker*   **Nw** *kveker* [kvḛ:ker] M, pl. *-e*, mid19c (3)   **Ic** *kvekari* [kʰvɛ̱:karɪ] M, pl. *-ar*, beg19c, via Da (3)   **Fr** [kwɛkœʀ] M, 17c (Ø/3)? → *quakeresse* F; *quakerisme* M   **Sp** *cuáquero* M, 18c (Ø/3)   **It** *quacchero* [kwa̱kkero] M, pl. *-i*, 18c (Ø/3)   **Rm** *quaker* [kwa̱ker/=E] M, beg20c, via Fr (2/Ø)   **Rs** *kva̱ker* M, pl. *-y*, 18/19c (Ø)   **Po** *kwakier* [kvakier] M, 18/19c → *-ka* F; *-stwo* N; *kwakryzm* M; *-ski* adj.   **Cr** *kve̱ker* M, pl. *-i*, 19c (Ø/3) → *-ski* adj.   **Bg** *kva̱ker* M, pl. *-i*, end19c, via Rs (Ø)   **Fi** *kveekari* 19c (Ø)   **Hu** *kvéker* [kvḛ:ker] pl. *-ek*, 19c (Ø/2 arch)   **Gr** *Kuakeros* M (Ø/3)

quark *n.* 'any of a class of unobserved subatomic particles with a fractional electric charge, of which protons, neutrons, and other hadrons are thought to be composed' (The term was suggested in 1964 by the American physicist Murray Gell-Mann, who took the word from Joyce's *Finnegans Wake*.)

Ge [kvork] N, pl. *-s*, 1960s (1 tech)   **Du** [=E] C, 1960s (1 tech)   **Nw** *kvark* [kvark] M, pl. *-er*, 20c (3 tech)   **Ic** *kvarkur/-i* [kʰva̱rkʏr/kʰva̱rcɪ] M, pl. *-ar*, end20c (3 tech)   **Fr** [kwark] M, 1960s (1 tech)   **Sp** [kwark] M, end20c (1 tech)   **It** [kwark] M, pl. Ø, 1960s (1 tech)   **Rm** *quarc* [kwark] M/N, 20c (2 tech)   **Rs** *kvark* M, pl. *-i*, 20c (1 tech)   **Po** *kwark* [kvark] M, end20c (1 tech)   **Cr** (0)   **Bg** *kva̱rka* F, pl. *-ki*, end20c, via Rs (1 tech)   **Fi** *kvarkki* 1960s (3 tech)   **Hu** *kvark* [kvark] [U] 1970s (1 tech)

quarter *n.* +13d 'a liquid measure, a quarter of a gallon'

Ge (Ø)   **Du** *kwart* [kwart] N (Ø)   **Nw** [=E] mid19c (1 tech, arch)   **It** *quarto* M (5La)   **Rs** *kvarta* F, pl. *-y*, 19c (Ø)   **Po** *kwarta* [kvarta] F, beg19c (Ø)   **Cr** *kvarter* (0)   **Bg** *kva̱rta* F, pl. *-ti*, end19c (Ø)   **Hu** [=E] [U] 20c (Ø)   **Al** *kuart* M, pl. *-e*, beg20c (3)

quarterback *n.* 'a player in American football who directs attacking play'

Ge (Ø)   **Du** (Ø)   **Nw** [=E] M, pl. *-er*, 1980s (Ø/1 tech)   **Ic** [=E] M, pl. *-ar*, end20c (Ø)   **Sp** [=E] M, pl. Ø, end20c (Ø tech)   **It** [=E] M, pl. Ø, 1980s (1 tech)   **Rs** (0)

quarterdeck *n.* 1 'part of a ship's upper deck'

Ge [kva̱rtadek] N, pl. *-s*, end19c (3+5)   **Du** - < *halfdek*   **Nw** - < *akterdekk*   **Rm** *cuarterdec* [kwarterdek] N, 20c (1 tech)   **Rs** *kvarterdek* M, pl. *-i*, 19c (1 tech)   **Bg** *kvarterdek* M, pl. *-al-ove*, beg20c, via Rs (1 tech) → *-dechen* adj.

quarter-pounder *n.* 'a kind of large hamburger'

Du [=E] C, 1980s (1 jour)   **Nw** [=E] M, pl. *-e*, 1980s (1 NAME)   **Ic** *kvartpundari* [kʰva̱rtpʰʏntarɪ] M, pl. *-ar*, end20c (2)

queen *n./cp²* +9a 'a woman pre-eminent in a specified area'

Ge [kvi:n] F/cp², pl. *-s*, 1980s (1 mod, rare)   **Du** (0) < *koningin*   **Nw** [=E] M/cp², 1980s (1 mod, rare)   **Hu** (Ø) < *királynő*   **Gr** <=E> [=E] F, 1980s (1 rare) < mean *vasilissa*

quick *adj./cp¹* +8 'fast to handle'

Ge [kvik] 1960s (1 jour)   **Du** - < *kwik, kwiek*   **Nw** *kvikk* (5)   **Fr** <=E> cp¹, end 20c (1 mod)   **Gr** <=E> [=E] end20c (0>1 mod/jour)

quickie *n.* 3 'a brief act of sexual intercourse', +4 'a quickly made film', +5 'a prefabricated cigarette'

This term is remarkable for its proliferation of independent meanings in a single language, German. How many of these will prove shortlived it is too early to say but apparently the form has a particular expressiveness that makes it immediately acceptable (cf. ↑*handy*).

Ge <=E>/*quicky* [kvi̱ki:] M, pl. *-s*, 1980s, 3,+4(1 mod); F, pl. *-s*, 1990s, +5(1 jour)

quickstep *n.* 'a fast foxtrot'

The dance style was very popular in the 1930s; whether the restricted distribution of the word is due to the fact that it did not spread any further at the time, or is a consequence of obsolescence, is difficult to determine; all its uses now appear to be historical.

Ge [kvi̱kstep] M [U] 1930s (1 obs)   **Du** *quick- step* [=E] C, 1950s (2)   **Nw** [kvi̱kstep] M [U]

Ic	Nw	Po	Rs
Du	Ge	Cr	Bg
Fr	It	Fi	Hu
Sp	Rm	Al	Gr

mid20c (1 obs) **Ic** [kʰvɪhkstɛhp] N [U] mid20c (2) **Rm** (0) **Rs** (0) **Po** (0) **Cr** [kvi̯kstep] M [U] mid20c (1 obs) **Bg** *kui̯kstep* M [U] 20c (1 tech) **Fi** [kvikstep] mid20c (1 obs) **Hu** [=E] [U] 1950s (2 arch)

quilt *n.* 1 'a padded bed-covering', +1b 'the act of quilting'
Ge [kvilt] M, pl. -*s*, 1980s, 1(1 tech) **Du** [kwilt] C, 1960s, 1(1 tech) **Nw** <=E>/*kvilt* [kvilt] M, pl. -*er*, 1980s, 1(1) **Ic** [=E] N [U] end20c, +1b(1 tech); 1: < *vattteppi*

quilt *v.* 1 'cover or line with padded material', 2 'make or join together after the manner of a quilt'
Ge [kviltən] 1980s (1 tech) **Du** - < *watteren* **Nw** *quilte/kvilte* [ⁿkvi̯lte] 1980s (1) < *vattere* → *quilting* M/F **Ic** [kʰvɪta] end20c (1 tech) = 1: *vattera*

quiz (1) *n.* 1 'a test of knowledge as a form of entertainment'

This term became immensely popular with contests on the radio and public entertainment, and later on TV; note that there are few calques, which are probably felt to be clumsy compared to the brief and 'enigmatic' English form. The compound ↑*quizmaster* in German and Dutch is one of the most conspicuous quasi-anglicisms.

Ge [kvis] N, pl. Ø/-*ze*, 1940s (2) **Du** [kwɪs] C, pl. -*zen*, 1940s (2>3) = *kwis* **Nw** [kvis] M, pl. -*er*, mid20c (1) < *spørrekonkurranse* **Ic** - < *spurningakeppni* **Fr** [kwiz] M, 1960s (1 obs) **Sp** [kwis] M, 1960s (1>2) **It** [kwits] M, pl. Ø, 1940s (3) **Rs** *kviz* M, pl. -*y*, mid20c (1 tech) **Po** *kwiz*/<=E> [kvis/=E] M, mid20c (2) → -*owy* adj. **Cr** *kviz* M, pl. -*ovi*, mid20c (2) → -*ovac* M; -*ovka* F; -*ovski* adj. **Bg** - < *viktorina* **Hu** *kvíz* [=E] [U] 1960s (1>2 writ, jour, mod) < *vetélkedő* **Al** *kuiz* M, pl. -*e*, mid20c (1 reg) **Gr** *kui̯z* mid20c N (2)

quiz (1) *v.* +3 'act as a quizmaster'
Ge *quizzen* 1980s (1 coll, rare) **Du** *quizen/kwissen* 1980s (1 tech) **Nw** (0) **Po** (0)

quizmaster* *n.* 'a person who presides over a quiz'
Ge [kvisma:sta] M, pl. Ø, 1950s (2) **Du** [=E] C, 1950s (2) **Po** (0)

quizzer *n.* 'a person in charge of a quiz contest, or being questioned'
Ge [kvi̯sa] M, pl. Ø, 1970s (1 coll, rare) **Du** - < *quizmaster* **Po** (0)

R

---

race *n.* 1 'a contest of speed between runners, horses, etc.', 3 'a contest between persons to be first to achieve something'

Ge (0 arch) **Du** [re:s] C, beg20c, 1(2) **Nw** [re:s] N, pl. Ø, beg20c, 1,3(2)

race *v.* 1 'take part in a race'

Du *racen* 19c (2) **Nw** ["rɛ:se/"rɛise] 20c (1 rare)

racer *n.* 1 'a horse, yacht, bicycle, toboggan, car, etc. of a kind used for racing', +3a 'a person who is the best in a specific field'

Du [=E] C, 19c, 1(2 rare) **Nw** [rɛ:ser] M/cp¹, pl. *-e*, beg20c (2) **Fr** [RESŒR] M, beg20c, 1(1 tech) **Sp** <=E> M, pl. *-s*, end19c (1 tech) **It** [=E] M, pl. Ø, 1930s, 1(1 tech) **Po** [-er] M, end20c (1 coll) **Bg** *rɛ̄iser* M, pl. *-al/-i*, 1990s, 1(1 tech)

Racing Club* *n.* 'a French sporting association'

Du (Ø) **Fr** [rasiŋ klœb] M, end19c (2) **Hu** *racing club* [=E/-klub] 'sportsclub', 20c (Ø/1 tech) < *verseny-klub*

racingman* *n.* 'a member or player of the Racing Club'

Fr [rasiŋ man] M, 20c (1)

rack *n.* 1a 'a framework for holding things', +1b 'a framework for storing video equipment'

Ge [=E] N, pl. *-s*, 1980s, +1b(1 tech) **Du** [=E] N, 1980s, +1b(1 tech) **Nw** [=E] M, pl. *-s/Ø*, 1980s, +1b(1 tech) **Fr** [rak] M, 1980s, 1b(1 tech, ban) < *baie* **Sp** [rak] M, 1980s (1 tech) **It** [=E] M, pl. Ø, 1980s, +1b(1) **Rm** [rak] M, 1980s, 1a(2 tech) **Hu** [=E] pl. Ø, end20c, +1b(1 tech)

racket¹ (1) *n.* 1 'a bat with a round or oval frame used in tennis, squash, etc. to hit the ball'

The distribution is complex; the earlier layer is represented by the tennis term, which could have been borrowed straight from English, or from French (*raquet*) or via French. The unrelated homonym was borrowed in the context of illegal doings much later and is experiencing a new popularity in Eastern Europe.

Ge N, pl. *-s*, end19c (3 arch/5Fr); [=E] N, pl. *-s*, 1980s (1 mod) < *(Tennis)schläger* **Du** [=E] N, 19c, via Fr

(2) **Nw** [rɛket/=E] M, pl. *-er*, end19c (3) **Ic** - < rend *spaði* **Fr** *raquette* (5) **Sp** *raqueta* F (5Fr) **It** *racchetta* (5Fr) **Rm** *rachetă* [rakɛ̄tə] F, beg20c (5Fr) **Rs** *raketka* F, pl. *-i*, beg20c (5Fr) **Po** (5Fr) **Cr** *rɛket*, M, pl. *-i*, beg20c (3) **Bg** *raketa* F (5Fr) pl. *-ek*, 19c (5Fr?) < *teniszütő* **Al** *rakɛtë* F, pl. *-a*, mid20c (5Fr?) **Gr** *raketa* F, beg20c, via It (5Fr?) **Hu** *rakett* [rakett]

racket² (2) *n.* 2a 'a scheme for obtaining money or attaining other things by fraudulent and often violent means', +4 'a criminal gang'

Ge [=E] N, pl. *-s*, 1960s, +4(1 coll, rare) **Du** [=E] C, 1940s, +4(2 rare) **Fr** [rakɛt] M, 1930s, 2a(2) → *racketteur/racketter* M **Sp** [rakɛt] M, 1930s (Ø/1 tech, rare) **It** [rakɛt] M, pl. Ø, 1930s (2) **Rm** [rakɛt] N, 1970s, 2a(1 rare); *rachɛti* [rakɛtsj] M, pl., 1990s, +4(2 jour) **Rs** *rɛ́ket* M [U] 1990s (3) **Po** *rekieter* [rekieter] M, 1990s, +4(2 mod) **Cr** *rɛket* M [U] end20c, 2a(1 rare) **Bg** *rɛket* M [U] 1990s, 2a(2) → *-iram* v.

racketeer *n.* 'a person who operates a dishonest business'

Du [=E] C, 1940s (2 rare) **Fr** *racketteur* **It** [=E] M, pl. Ø, 1930s (1 rare, obs) **Rm** [=E] M, 1970s (1rare) **Rs** *rɛ́ketir/-tɛr* M, pl. *-y*, end20c (2) **Po** (0) **Cr** *rɛ́ketir* M, pl. *-i*, end20c (1 rare) **Bg** *reketyor* M, pl. *-i*, 1990s (3) → *-ski* adj.; *-stvo* N

radar *n.* 2 'a system for detecting the direction, range, or presence of aircraft etc.'

The system was developed in 1941 in America and named in the form of an acronym of *radio detection and ranging*; the etymology is now widely opaque in English and certainly in the loans which are treated as 'normal' words.

Ge [rada:r] M/N [U] 1940s (3 tech) **Du** [ra:dɑr] C [U] 1940s (3 tech) **Nw** [ra:dar] M, pl. *-er*, mid20c (3) **Ic** *radar* [ra:tar] M, pl. *-ar*, 1940s (2) > creat *ratsjá* **Fr** [radar] M, 1940s (3) → *radariste* **Sp** [radar/radar] M, mid20c (3) **It** [radar] M/cp², pl. Ø, [U] 1940s (3 tech) **Rm** [radar/radar] N, mid20c, via Fr/Ge? (3) **Rs** *radar* M, pl. *-y*, mid20c (1 tech) → *-nyǐ* adj. **Po** [radar] M, mid20c (2 tech) → *-owy* adj. **Cr** *radar* M, pl. *-i*, mid20c (3 tech) → *-ist* M; *-ski* adj.

Bg *radar* M, pl. *-al-i*, mid20c (2) → *-en* adj.   **Fi** [radar] mid20c (0) < creat *tutka*   **Hu** [radar] pl. *-ok*, 1940s (3)   **Al** *radar* M, pl. *-ë*, 1940s (3)   **Gr** *radar* N, mid20c (2)

raft   *v.* +2a 'go down (rapid) rivers on inflatable rafts as a sport'
Du *raften* 1985 (1 tech, coll)   **Nw** *rafte* ["rafte] 1980s (2 tech) → *rafter* M

rafting   *n.* 'canoeing'
The newly invented (or rather, renamed) sport is still spreading through Europe, the adoption again being led by the north and west.
Ge [=E] N [U] 1980s (1 tech, mod)   **Du** [ra:ftiŋ] N [U] 1980s (1 tech)   **Nw** [=E/"raftiŋ] M/F [U] 1980s (2 tech)   **Fr** [raftiŋ] M, 1980s (1 tech, mod) → *rafteur* M   **Sp** [raftin] M [U] 1980s (1 tech)   **It** [=E] M [U] 1980s/90s (1 tech)   **Cr** [=E] M [U] 1980s (1 tech, mod)   **Gr** *rafting* N [U] 1990s (1 tech, mod)

rag   *n.* 'a ragtime composition or tune' (cf. ↑*ragtime*)
Ge [rek] M, pl. *-s*, 1970s (1 tech)   **Du** [reg] C [U] 1970s (2 tech)   **Nw** [=E] M, pl. *-s*, 1970s (1 tech)   **Ic** *ragg* N [U] 1970s (1 tech)   **Sp** [rag] M [U] 1980s (1 tech)   **It** [reg] M, pl. Ø, 1930s (1>2)   **Rm** [reg] N [U] 1970s (1 tech)   **Rs** *rég* M [U] 1980s (1 tech)   **Po** (0)   **Cr** (0)   **Hu** - < *ragtime*

raglan   *n./cp¹* 'a style of coat, blazer, etc. where the sleeves run up to the neck'
The overcoat was named after Fitzroy James Herbert Somerset, first Baron Raglan (1788–1855), the commander-in-chief of the British forces in the Crimean War, who died at Sebastopol (cf. ↑*cardigan*).
Ge [raglan] cp¹, beg20c (1 tech)   **Du** [=E] C, beg20c (1 tech)   **Nw** [raglan] cp¹, beg20c (3 tech)   **Ic** [raklan-] cp¹, 1940s, via Da (2 tech)   **Fr** [raglã] M, 19c (1 arch)   **Sp** <=E>/*ranglán* [raglan] M, beg20c (3 tech)   **It** [raglan] M [U] mid19c (1>2)   **Rm** [raglan] N, 1920s, via Fr (3)   **Rs** *reglan* M [U] beg20c (3)   **Po** [raglan] M, beg20c (3)   **Cr** [raglan] M [U] beg20c (1 tech/3)   **Bg** *reglan* M [U] beg20c, via Rs (2 tech)   **Fi** [raglan] 19c (3)   **Hu** *raglán* [ragla:n] end19/beg20c (3)   **Gr** *reglan, raglán* N, beg20c, via Fr (1 tech)

ragtime   *n.* 'music characterized by a syncopated melodic line and regular accented accompaniment'
This early type of jazz was particularly popularized by Scott Joplin (1868–1917); it spread to Europe after the 1920s, since when the term is sporadically attested in Western languages; the real breakthrough came in the 1950s/60s. The word is slightly more common in its full form than abbreviated to ↑*rag*.
Ge [rektaim] M [U] 1950s (2 tech)   **Du** [=E] C [U] 1940s (2 tech)   **Nw** [=E] M [U] 20c (2 tech) → *ragtimer* M   **Ic** [=E] N [U] 1930s (1 tech)   **Fr** *rag-time* [ragtajm] M, 1920s (1 tech)   **Sp** [ragtaim] M, pl. *-s*,

1930s (1 tech)   **It** [regtaim] M, pl. Ø, 1930s (2 tech)   **Rm** [regtaim] N [U] 1970s (1 tech)   **Rs** *régtaim* M [U] end20c (1 tech)   **Po** [rektaim] M [U] end20c (1 tech)   **Cr** *regtajm* M [U] beg20c (1 tech)   **Bg** *ragtaim* M [U] end20c (1 tech)   **Fi** [=E] 1920s (2 tech)   **Hu** [=E] [U] 1970s (2 tech>3)

raid   *n.* 1a 'a rapid surprise attack in warfare', 1b 'an act of committing a crime or doing harm', +1c 'a surprise attack in soccer and other team sports', +1d 'an unexpected check-up on social organizations', 3 'an attempt to lower prices by the concerted selling of shares', +5 'an excursion', +6 'a rally'
This word came to be popular in Romance and Slavic languages, with quite a few new meanings and applications, all this contrasting somewhat with the general trend of adoption; note its practical absence from German.
Ge [=E] M, pl. *-s*, 1930s, 1a(0 tech, arch)   **Du** [=E] C, beg20c (2)   **Nw** [raid/=E] N, pl. Ø/*-s*, 1930s, 1a,1b(2); 1960s, +1c(1 tech); 1980s, 3(1 tech)   **Fr** [red] M, end19c, 1a,+6(2)   **Sp** [raid] M, pl. *-s*, beg20c, 1a(1 tech); end20c, +6(1 tech)   **It** [raid] M, pl. Ø, end19c, 1a,b(2 tech) +6(2 arch, rare)   **Rm** [rajd] N, beg20c, via Fr, 1a(3); mid20c, +1d(3) +5(3 coll)   **Rs** *reíd* M, pl. *-y*, beg20c, 1a(2); mid20c, +1d(1 obs)   **Po** *rajd/* <=E> [rait] M, beg20c, 1a,+1d,+5(3) → *-owiec* M; *-owicz* M; *-owy* adj.   **Cr** (0)   **Bg** *reíd* M, pl. *-al-ove*, mid20c, via Rs, +1d(3 jour)   **Hu** [re:d] [U] 20c, 1a(1 tech)

raid   *v.* 1 'make a raid on', 2 'plunder, deplete'
Nw *raide* ["raide] mid20c (1) → *raider* M   **It** - < 1: *fare un raid*   **Rm** - < 1: *face un raid*

raider   *n.* (esp. US) 'a person who mounts an unwelcome takeover bid by buying up a company's shares on the stock market'
Du [=E] C, 1980s (1 tech)   **Nw** ["raider/=E] M, pl. *-e*, 1980s (1 tech)   **Fr** <=E> M, 1980s (1 tech, ban) = *corporate raider* > *attaquant*   **Sp** [reider] M, 1980s (1 tech) < *tiburón*

rail   *n.* 1c 'a level or sloping bar or series of bars forming part of a fence or barrier (esp. on a racing track)', 2 'a continuous line of steel bars forming a railway track'
Ge *Reling* F, pl. *-s?*, 1c(3 tech)   **Du** *reling* [re:liŋ] C, pl. *-en*, 1940s, 1c(3)   **Nw** [=E/ræil] M, pl. *-er*, 1970s, 1c(1 tech)   **Fr** [raj] M, 19c, 2(3)   **It** *guardrail* [=E/ gardreil] M, pl. Ø, 1960s (2 tech)   **Rs** *rel'sa* F, pl. *-y*, 19c, 2(3)   **Bg** *relsa* F, pl. *-si*, end19c, via Rs, 2(3)

rail & fly*   *n.* 'a system whereby a flight passenger is transported directly to the airport by train'
Ge [=E] [U] 1990s (1 mod)

railroute*   *n.* 'a railway'
Fr *rail-route* [ʀajʀut] M, 1940s (1)

railway *n.* 1 'a track or set of tracks made of steel rails along which trains run', +5 'a person who makes his living by (travelling around and) building railways' **Nw** *rallar* [ra̲lar] M, pl. *-er*, beg20c, via Sw (3 arch) **Fr** [rɛlwɛ] N, beg19c (1 arch) < *chemin de fer* **Sp** [=E] M, end19c, 1(o)>1 tech, obs) < *ferrocarril* **Bg** - < creat *zheleznitsa* **Fi** *rallari* beg20c, +5(5Sw) **Hu** [=E] pl. Ø, 20c, 1(1 tech, writ, mod)

rally *n.* 3 'a mass meeting of supporters or persons having a common interest', +3a 'a common effort by a number of trawlers and a research institution to investigate the amount of fish in the fishing banks', 4 'a competition for motor vehicles, usu. over public roads or rough terrain'

Of the various meanings, the one relating to motor sports is most popular; this was borrowed into French and reborrowed by English so that the anglicism may, or may not, be via French (the quality of the vowel may indicate this). For 'mass demonstration' (esp. political) the term used to be more typical of Eastern Europe.

Ge *Rallye* [re̲li/rali] F, pl. *-(ie)s*, 1950s, 4(2) **Du** *rally* [=E] C, pl. *-'s*, 1940s, 3(2); 1960s, 4(2) **Nw** [ra̲li/=E] N, pl. Ø/*-er*, mid20c, 4(2) **Ic** *rallý* [ral:i] N, pl. Ø; *rall* [ral:] N, pl. *röll*, 1970s, +3a(2) **Fr** *rallye* [rali] M, 20c, 3(1) 4(2) → *rallyeman* **Sp** <=E>/*rallye* [ra̲li] M, pl. *-ys/-yes/-ies*, 1930s, 4(2) **It** [re̲lli] M, pl. Ø, 1930s, 4(3) → *rallistico* adj. **Rm** *raliu* [ra̲liw] N, 1960s, via Fr, 4(3) **Rs** *ralli* N, uninfl., mid20c, 4(1 tech) → *-ist* **Po** <=E>/*rallye* [rali] N, uninfl., via Fr, mid20c, 4(1 tech) **Cr** *reli* M, pl. *-ji*, mid20c, 4(1 tech) **Bg** *rali* N, pl. *-ta*, mid20c, 4(2) **Fi** *ralli*/<=E> [ral:i] mid20c, 4(3) **Hu** *rali* [ra̲li] pl. *-k*, beg20c, 4(3) **Al** *reli* M, pl. *-e*, 1960s, 3,4(1 reg) **Gr** *ra̲li* N, mid20c, 4(2)

rallycross *n.* 'a form of motor racing over roads and cross-country' **Ge** [=E] N [U] 1970s (1 tech, rare) **Du** [=E] C, 1980s (2 tech) = ↑*cross-country* **Nw** [ra̲likros] M [U] 1960s (1 tech) **Ic** [=E] N [U] end20c (1 tech) **It** [re̲llikrɔs] M [U] 1980s (1 tech) **Rs** (o) **Po** (o) **Cr** (o) **Hu** *ralikrossz* [ra̲likross] [U] end20c (1 tech)

RAM *abbrev.* 1 'random-access memory' (cf. ↑*random access*) **Ge** [ram] N, pl. *-s*, 1980s (1 tech) **Du** [=E] C, 1980s (1 tech) = *werkgeheugen* **Nw** <=E>/*ram* [ram] M, pl. Ø, 1980s (1 tech) **Ic** [ra:m] end20c (1 tech) < rend (*rit-/innra*) *minni* **Fr** [ram] M, 1980s (1 tech) < rend *mémoire vive* **Sp** [ram] N, pl. Ø, 1980s (1 tech) < *memoria de acceso directo* **It** [ram] F [U] 1970s (1 tech) **Rm** [ram] M, 1980s (1 tech>2 tech) **Rs** *RAM* M [U] 1990s (1 tech) **Po** [ram] M, 1980s (1 tech) **Cr** [ram] M, end20c (1 tech) **Bg** *RAM* M [U] 1990s (1 tech) **Fi** [ram] 1980s (2 tech) > mean *työmuisti* **Hu** [ram] [U] end20c (1 tech) **Gr** <=E> [ram] sg. F/pl. N, end20c (1 tech)

ramp *n.* 1 'a slope or inclined plane, esp. for joining two levels of ground, floor, etc.', +1a 'a sloping U-shaped construction for skateboarding' (cf. ↑*halfpipe*) **Ge** *Rampe* (5Fr) **Du** [=E] C, 1980s, +1a(1 tech) **Nw** [=E] M, pl. *-s*, 1980s, +1a(1 tech) > *rampe* **Ic** *rampur/rampi* [ra̲mpʏr/-ɪ] M, pl. *-ar*, 1970s, 1,+1a(3) > *skábraut* **Fr** *rampe* (4) **It** *rampa* (5Fr) **Rm** *rampă* (5Fr) **Bg** *rampa* (5Fr) **Fi** *ramppi* 1980s, +1a(3) **Hu** *rámpa* (5Ge) **Gr** *raba* (5Fr)

ranch *n.* 1 'a cattle-breeding establishment, esp. in the western USA and Canada', +1a 'a small private farm'

This word provides two problems: in how many languages does it really refer to farms in the country/outside the South-western US context; and can the Spanish word be assumed in all to have come via English and is this determinable from its form, as in Italian [æ/ɛ]? **Ge** [rɛn(t)ʃ], F, pl. *-es*, 1(Ø) → *-er* M **Du** 1(Ø) **Nw** [=E/ranʃ] M, pl. *-er*, beg20c, M, 1(Ø/1 fac) → *-er* M **Fr** <=E>/*rancho* [rãtʃ/ʀãtʃo] M, end19c, 1(Ø) **Sp** *rancho* (5Sp) **It** [rentʃ] M, pl. Ø, 1900s, 1(2) **Rm** [rantʃj] N, 1970s, 1(Ø/1 coll, jour) → *mega-ranch* **Rs** (5Sp) **Po** *rancho* (5Sp) **Cr** *ranč* M, pl. *-evi*, mid20c, 1(Ø) → *-er* M, **Bg** *ra̲ncho* N, pl. *-cha*, beg20c, via Rs, 1(5Sp/Ø) +1a(3) **Fi** [=E] beg20c (Ø) **Hu** <=E>/*ranch* [rantʃ/=E] pl. *-ek/-ok*, end20c (Ø) **Gr** *ra̲dso* N, beg20c, 1(3, Ø)

random-access *cp* 'having all parts directly accessible' (comput.) (cf. ↑*RAM*) **Ge** [=E] M [U] 1980s (1 tech, rare) < ↑*RAM* **Du** [=E] C, 1980s (1 tech) **Nw** [=E] 1980s (1 tech, rare) **Ic** [=E] uninfl., end20c (1 tech) **Fr** - < *aléatoire* **It** [=E] M [U] 1970s (1 tech) < trsl *accesso random/accesso casuale* **Rm** - < rend *acces aleator* **Po** M [U] end20c (1 tech) **Fi** [=E] 1980s (1 tech) **Hu** *ram*

randomize* *v.* 'set up a sample etc. in a random way, for statistical validity' **Ge** *randomisieren* 1980s (3 tech) **Du** *randomiseren* 1980s (1 tech) **Nw** *randomisere* [ra̲ndomise̲:re] 1970s (1 tech) → *randomisering* M/F **Fr** *randomiser* [ʀãdɔmize] 1970s **Sp** *randomizar* (3 tech) **It** *randomizzare* [randomiddza̲re] 1980s (3 tech) **Rm** *randomiza* [randomiza̲] 1980s (1 tech, rare) → *-are* F; *randomizat* adj. **Po** (o) **Fi** *randomisoida* end20c (1 tech) = *satunnaistaa* **Hu** *randomizál* [ra̲ndomiza̲l] end20c (1 tech)

randomization* *n.* 'a method of setting up a sample in a random way' **Du** *randomisatie* [ra̲ndomisa̲:tsi] C, 1980s (1 tech) **Nw** (o) < *randomisering* **Fr** *randomisation* [rãdɔmizasjɔ̃] F, 1970s (3 tech) **Sp** *randomización* F (3 tech) **It** *randomizzazione* [randomiddzatsjo̲ne] F [U] 1980s (3 tech) **Rm** *randomizare* [randomiza̲re] F, 1980s (3 tech) **Po** *randomizacja* [randomizacie] F [U] mid20c (1 tech) **Cr** (o) **Hu** *randomizálás* [ra̲ndomiza:la:ʃ] [U] 20c (1 tech)

random sample *n.* 'a sample set up in a random way' (statistics)

Ic	Nw	Po	Rs
Du	Ge	Cr	Bg
Fr	It	Fi	Hu
Sp	Rm	Al	Gr

Ge [rɛndəm sempl] N [U] 1980s (1 tech, rare) > *Randomverfahren* **Du** (o) **Nw** (o) < = *tilfeldig utvalg* **Ic** - < *slembiúrtak* **Fr** - < *échantillon prélevé au hasard* **Sp** - < trsl *muestra aleatoria* **It** [=E] M, pl. Ø, 1980s (1 tech) < trsl *campione random, campione casuale* **Rm** - < rend *eşantion aleatoriu* **Po** (o) **Cr** (o) **Bg** - < rend *sluchaĭna izvadka*

ranger *n.* 1 'a keeper of a royal or national park, or of a forest', 2a 'a mounted soldier', 2b 'a commando', 3 'a senior guide', +5 'a short boot'

Ge 1,2a(Ø) **Du** 2a(Ø) **Nw** [=E] M, pl. -*e*, 1(Ø) 3(2) **Fr** [rɑ̃dʒɛʀ] M, 1960s, 1(1); 1950s, 2a(o); 1940s, +5(2) **Sp** [randʒer] M, 1980s, 2a(1 tech) 3(1 tech) **It** [rɛndʒer] M, pl. Ø, 1940s, 1,2a,2b,3(2 tech) **Rm** [=E] N, 1970s, 2a(Ø) **Rs** *reĭndzher* M, pl. -*y*, 1990s, 2a(1 jour) **Cr** *rendžer* 20c, 1(1 tech) **Bg** *reĭndzhŭr* M, pl. -*i*, 1990s, 2b(1 tech, mod) → -*ski* adj.; -*ka* F **Fi** - < 3: trsl *vaeltaja* **Hu** [rɛːndʒer] pl. -*ek*, 20c, 2a,2b(1 tech)

rank *v.* 2 'classify, give a certain rank to (esp. in sports)'

Du - < *rangschikken* **Nw** *ranke* ["ʀæŋke] mid20c (1) **Po** (o)

ranking *n.* 1 'ordering by rank; classification (esp. of universities)' (cf. ↑*rating*)

Although the terms *ranking* and *rating* are not strictly synonymous, they cover so much common ground that the adoption of one might well be considered sufficient for filling a lexical gap; in fact, there are only few languages in which both are attested (German and Norwegian).

Ge [rɛŋkiŋ] N [U] 1980s (1 mod) **Du** - < *rangschikking, classificatie* **Nw** [raŋkiŋ/ʀæŋkiŋ/ʀækiŋ] M/F [U] mid20c (2) → *ranke* v. **Sp** [rankin] M, 1970s (1 tech > 2 tech) **It** [reŋkiŋ] M [U] 1980s (1 tech) **Po** [rankiŋk] M, 1980s → -*owy* **Fi** [=E] 1980s (1 tech)

ranking list* 'a list where (sports) competitors are classified according to their assumed abilities'

Ge - < *Rangliste* **Du** - < *ranglijst* **Nw** *rankingliste* [=E+Nw] 1950s (2+5) **It** *ranking* [reŋkiŋ] M [U] 1980s (1 tech) **Po** (o) **Cr** <=E> (o) **Bg** - < rend *ranglista* **Fi** *rankinglista* end20c (1 tech)

rap *n./cp[1]* 5b 'a style of black popular music with a pronounced beat to which words are recited rather than sung'

While the adoption of the noun is almost universal, as a consequence of the (commercialized) public interest of the 1980s, often in combination with ↑*breakdance*, the distribution of the corresponding verb, as might be expected, is more limited (even though western languages tend to have both). The fact that ↑ *rapper* is again more frequent shows that the item was borrowed rather than individually derived in the languages concerned.

Ge [rep] M [U] 1980s (1 you) **Du** [=E] C, 1980s (1 tech, you) **Nw** <=E>/*ræpp* [=E] M [U] 1980s (1 tech, you) **Ic** *rapp* [rahp] N [U] 1980s (2 tech, you)

Fr [rap] M, 1980s (1 you) **Sp** [rap] M [U] 1980s (1 you) → *rapero* **It** [rɛp] M [U] 1980s (2) **Rm** [rep] N [U] end20c (1 you) **Rs** *rép* M [U] end20c (1 you, mod) **Po** [-e-] M [U] end20c (2) → -*owy* adj.; -*owski* adj. **Cr** *rep* M [U] end20c (2) → -*er* M; -*erki* adj. **Bg** *rap* M/cp[1] [U] 1980s (2 tech, you) → -*adzhiya* M **Fi** [=E] 1980s (1 tech) **Hu** [=E/rap] [U] end20c (2 you) **Al** *rep* M [U] (1 you) **Gr** *rap* F/N [U] 1980s (1 you)

rap *v.* 5 'perform rap music'

Ge [repən] 1980s (1 tech, you) **Du** *rappen* [rɛpən] 1980s (1 tech, you) **Nw** *rappe/rap'e/ræppe* [ræpe] 1980s (1 tech, you) → *rapping* M/F; *rapper* M **Ic** *rappa* [rahpa] 1980s (2 tech, you) **Fr** *raper*, 1990s (1 you) **Sp** *rapear* 1990s (3 tech, you) → *rapeado* n. **It** [rɛp] 1980s (2 you, mod) < *fare il rap* → *rappare* v.; *rappato* adj. **Po** *rapować* [rapovatɕ] end20c (2 coll) **Cr** *repati* end20c (1 you) **Fi** *räpätä* 1980s (2 tech) **Al** < *kërcej rep*

rapper *n.* 'a person who plays or sings rap'

Ge [repa] M, pl. Ø, 1980s, (1 tech) **Du** [=E] C, 1980s (1 tech, you) **Nw** <=E>/*ræpper* [ræper] M, pl. -*e*, 1980s (1 tech, you) **Ic** *rappari* [rahparɪ] M, pl. -*ar*, 1980s (1 tech, you) **Fr** [rapœʀ] 1990s (1 you) **Sp** [raper] M, pl. -*s*, 1980s (1 you, tech) < *rapero* **It** [rapper] M, pl. Ø, 1980s (1 you, mod) **Rm** [repər] M, 1990s (1 you) **Rs** *répper* M, pl. -*y*, 1990s (1 mod) **Po** *raper* [-er] M, end20c (2 coll) **Cr** *reper* (o) **Bg** *rapŭr* M, pl. -*i*, 1980s (2 tech, you) → -*ski* adj. **Fi** *räppäri* 1980s (2 tech) **Hu** [repper/rapper] pl. -*ek*, end20c (2 you) **Gr** *raper* M, pl. -*s*, 1980s (1 you)

rating *n.* 1 '(a method to establish) the act or instance of placing into a class or rank or assigning a value to', 2 'the estimated standing of a person as regards credit', 6 'any of the classes into which racing yachts are distributed by tonnage' (cf. ↑*ranking*)

Ge [reːtiŋ] N, pl. -*s*, 1980s, 2(1 tech, mod) **Du** [reːting] C, 1970s (1 tech) **Nw** [=E] M/F, pl. -*er*, 1960s, 1,2(1 tech) **Fr** [ʀat(e)iŋ] M, 1960s, 6(1 tech) 1980s, 1(1 tech, ban_ECON) < 1: *notation* **Sp** [reitin] M, 1980s, 1,2(1 tech) **It** [=E] M [U] 1980s (1 tech) **Rm** [rating/=E] N[U] 1990s, 1,2(1 tech) **Rs** *reĭting* M, pl. -*i*, end20c, 1,2(2) **Cr** *rejting* M [U] mid20c, 1(1 tech) **Bg** *reĭting* M/[U] pl. -*al-i*, mid20c, 1(1 tech); 1990s, 2(2)

rat race *n.* 'a fiercely competitive struggle for position, power, etc.'

Du [=E] C, 1980s (1 jour, mod) **Nw** [=E] N, pl. Ø, 1970s (1) = trsl *rotterace* **Ic** - < trsl *rottukapphlaup*

rave *v.* +6b 'participate in a rave- party', +7 'dance to hip-hop music'

Ge *raven* [=E] pl. *-s*, 1990s, +7(1 you)   **Du** *raven* [=E] 1990s, +6b,+7(1 you)   **Nw** [re͡ive] 1990s, +6b,+7(1 you)   **Ic** *reifa* [rei:va] 1990s, +6b,+7(1 sla, you)

rave *n.* 3b 'a large often illicit party or event with dancing to loud fast pop music', +3c 'a culture connected with hip-hop music', +3d 'a style of pop music'

Ge [=E] M, pl. *-s*, 1990s, 3b(1 you)   **Du** [=E] C, pl. *-s*, 1990s, 3b,+3c,d(1 you)   **Nw** [=E] pl. *-s*, 1990s, 3b(1 you)   **Ic** *reif* [=E] N [U] 1990s, 3b(1 sla, you)   **Fr** [rav] M, 3b(1 you)   **Sp** [=E] M, pl. *-s*, 1990s (1 jour, you)   **It** [=E] M/adj., pl. Ø, 1990s (1 sla, you)   **Rm** [=E] N/adj. [U] 1990s, +3c(1 you)   **Rs** *reĭv* M [U] 1990s, +3c(1 you, mod)   **Cr** *rejv* (o)   **Bg** *reĭv* M [U] 1990s, +3d(1 tech, you)   **Gr** *r̲e̲iv* F/N [U] 1990s, +3c,d(1 mod, you)

raver *n.* +3 'a person who goes to rave parties'
Ge [=E] M, pl. Ø, 1990s (1 you)   **Du** [=E] C, pl. *-s*, 1990s (1 you)   **Nw** [re͡iver] M, pl. *-e*, 1990s (1 you)   **It** [=E] M/F, pl. Ø, 1990s, (1 sla, you) < *ravista*   **Rm** (o)   **Rs** *reĭver* M, pl. *-y*, 1990s (1 you, mod)   **Cr** *rejver* (o)   **Gr** *r̲e̲iver* M/F, pl. *-s*, 1990s (1 you)

ray-grass see ↑*ryegrass*

re-break* *n.* 'a game won after the opponent has won a service game' (tennis)
Ge [=E] N, pl. *-s*, end20c (1 tech)   **Fr** [=E] M, pl. *-s*, end20c (1 tech)   **Hu** [=E] pl. Ø, 20c (1 tech)

reader *n.* 2 'a book of extracts', 4 'a university lecturer'
Ge [r̲i:da] M, pl. Ø, 1970s, 2(1 tech)   **Du** [=E] C, 1970s, 2(1 tech) 4(Ø) < *docent, lector*   **Nw** (o)   **Ic** [=E] M, pl. *-ar*, end20c, 2(o sla)   **Rm** [=E] M, end20c, 4(Ø) < *lector*   **Po** (o)

reading *n.* 4 'an entertainment at which a play, poems, etc. are read' (*poetry~*), +10 'a reader, an anthology'
Ge - < *Lesung*   **Du** [=E] C, 1980s, 4(1 tech, mod)   **Nw** [=E] M, pl. *-er/-s*, 1960s, 4(1 tech)   **Sp** [r̲iding] M, pl. *-s*, end20c, +10(1 tech, rare)   **It** [=E] M [U] 1980s, 4(1 tech, rare)

ready *adj./interj.* 1 'with preparations complete', 2 'in an appropriate state', 3 'willing, inclined, or resolved', +10 'begin the game' (tennis)
Ge [=E] beg20c, +10(1 tech, arch) < *fertig*   **Du** [=E] beg20c (1 tech, arch)   **Nw** [=E] 20c, +10(1)   **Ic** [rɛt:i] uninfl., mid20c, 1,2,3(1 sla)   **Fr** [redi] end19c, +10(1 arch)   **It** [r̲e̲di] adj., 1900s, +10(1 tech)   **Rm** [=E] beg20c, +10(o>1 tech)   **Rs** *r̲e̲di* interj., mid20c, +10(1 tech)   **Po** adj., uninfl., beg20c, +10(1 tech)   **Cr** [=E] beg20c, +10(1 tech)   **Bg** *r̲e̲di* interj., mid20c, +10(1 tech)   **Hu** [=E] end19c, +10(1 tech)   **Gr** [=E] 20c, +10(1 tech)

ready-made *adj./n.* 1 'made in a standard size, not to measure', (esp. of clothes), +2 'an industrial object reinterpreted as a work of art'

This word has spread among specialists of modern art through most countries of Europe but has not so far been applied to other domains.

Ge [=E] N pl. *-s*, 1960s (1 tech)   **Du** <=E/*ready made*> [=E] C, 1970s (1 tech)   **Nw** [=E] N, pl. *-s*, 1960s (1 tech)   **Ic** [=E] adj., uninfl., end20c, 1(1 sla) < *tilbúinn*   **Fr** [redimɛd] beg20c (1 tech)   **Sp** [=E] M, pl. *-s/Ø*, 1980s (1 tech)   **It** [=E] M, pl. Ø, 1970s (1 tech)   **Rs** (o)   **Po** *ready mades* pl., end20c (1 tech)   **Cr** (o)   **Hu** [=E/-me:d] pl. Ø, end20c (1 tech)

ready-to-wear *cp¹* 'made in a standard size, not to measure' (of clothes)

This phrase was coined in American English, borrowed into various languages and translated as French *prêt-à-porter* which stopped the adoption of the synonymous anglicism – except in German.

Ge [r̲e̲dituvɛ:r] 1960s (1 tech, rare) < *prêt-à-porter*   **Nw** - < *prêt-à-porter*   **Fr** - < *prêt- à-porter*   **It** - < *prêt-à-porter*   **Rm** - < *prêt-à-porter*; *de-a gata*   **Po** - < *gotowc (ubranie)*   **Bg** - < *prêt-à-porter*   **Gr** - < *prêt-à-porter*

realignment *n.* 'the fixing of currency rates after floating'
Ge [=E] N, pl. *-s*, 1970s (1 tech)   **Sp** - < mean *realineamiento*   **It** - < *riallineamento*   **Rm** *realiniere* (4)

reality TV show* *n.* 'TV in documentary style, often with gruesome detail'
Ge [=E] N [U] 1990s (1 mod)   **Du** [=E] C [U] 1990s (1 tech)   **Nw** [=E+te̲:ve] [U] 1990s (1 tech)   **Fr** *reality show* [realiti ʃo] M, 1990s (1 mod)   **Sp** *reality show/reality* M, pl. *-s*, 1990s (1 tech)   **Po** (o)   **Cr** <=E> (o)   **Gr** *r̲ialiti so̲u* N, pl. *-s*, 1990s (2 mod)

real time *n./cp¹* 1 'the actual time during which a process or event occurs' (comput.)
Ge [=E] F [U] 1970s (1 tech, rare) = *Echtzeit*   **Du** [=E] C [U] 1980s (1 tech)   **Nw** [=E] 1980s (1 tech) > *sanntid*   **Ic** [=E] cp¹, end20c (o tech) < *trsl rauntíma-*   **Fr** - < *trsl temps réel*   **It** - < *trsl tempo reale*   **Rm** - < *rend timp real*   **Rs** - < *trsl real'noe vremya*   **Bg** - < *trsl realno vreme*   **Fi** [=E] 1980s (1 tech)   **Hu** [=E] [U] end20c (1 tech)   **Gr** (o) < *trsl praghmatikos khronos*

rebound *n.* 1 'the act or an instance of rebounding', (basketb.) +3 'taking an examination for the second time'
Ge [=E] M, pl. *-s*, 1970s, 1(1 tech)   **Du** [r̲i:baunt] M, 1980s, 1(Ø) +3(1 you)   **Nw** [=E] M, pl. *-s*, 1980s, 1(1 tech)   **Ic** - < 1: rend *frákast*   **Gr** *rib̲aud* [-d,-nd] N, pl. *-s*, 1980s, 1(2 tech)

receiver *n.* 4 'a radio or television receiving apparatus'
Ge [=E] M, pl. Ø, 1970s (1 tech) < *Empfänger*   **Du** [=E] C, 1970s (1 tech) = *ontvanger*   **Nw** [=E] M, pl. *-e*, 1970s (1 tech) < *mottaker(apparat)*   **Sp** - < *receptor*

It [risi:ver] M, pl. Ø, 1970s (1 tech) = *radio ricevitore*
Rm [=E] N, end20c (1 tech) < *radioreceptor/receptor radio* **Rs** *resiver* M, pl. -*y*, end20c (1 tech) **Cr** *risiver* 20c (1 tech) < trsl *prijemnik* **Bg** - < trsl *priemnik* **Hu** [=E] pl. Ø, end20c (1 tech) < *vevő (készülék)*

receptionist *n.* 'a person employed in an office or a hotel to receive clients, guests, etc.'
Du [=E/resepʃonist] C, pl. -*s/-en* **Cr** (5La) (1 tech) **Sp** - < *recepionista* **It** [resepʃonist] M, pl. Ø, 1950s (1 tech) **Po** (5La)

recital *n.* 2 'a performance by a soloist', +2a 'a poetry reading'
This term is remarkably widespread, but has not been extended beyond the technical uses in films, records, and poetry readings – and it is not quite clear which items are straight from English or transmitted through French (or even independent Latin-based coinages?).
Ge [=E] N, pl. -*s*, beg20c/1970s, 2(1 tech) **Du** [=E] N, 1940s (2 tech) **Nw** [=E] M, 1980s, 2(1 tech) **Fr** *récital* [resital] M, pl. -*s*, end19c (3) **Sp** [reθital] M, end19c (3/5La) **It** [retʃital/resital] M, pl. Ø, end19c, 2(2) +2a(1 tech) **Rm** [retʃital] N, mid20c, via Fr, 2,+2a(3) **Rs** *retsital* M, pl. -*y*, beg20c, 2(1 tech) **Po** [retchital] M, beg20c, 2(2) **Cr** [recital] M, pl. -*i*, beg20c (3) **Bg** *retsital* M, pl. -*al-i*, beg20c, via Fr, +2a(3); end20c, 2(4) **Hu** (5La) **Al** *recital* M, pl. -*e*, mid20c (3) **Gr** *resital* N, beg20c, via Fr, 2(2)

record *n.* 7 'the best performance on record', 9 'interrelated data handled as a unit' (comput.), +10 'the knob on a tape recorder which is pushed to start or stop recording'
Ge *Rekord* [rekort] M, pl. -*e*, end19c, 7(3); 1960s, +10(1 tech, writ) **Du** [rəkor] N, beg19c, via Fr, 7(3); [=E] C, 1980s, 9(1 tech) **Nw** *rekord* [rekord] M, pl. -*er*, beg20c, 7(3); [=E] M, pl. -*s*, end20c, 9,+10(0/1 tech) < 9: *post* **Ic** [=E] uninfl., end20c, +10(1 tech) **Fr** [r(ə)kɔR] M/adj., uninfl., end19c (3) → *recordman*; *recordwoman* **Sp** [rekor] M, pl. -*s*, end19c, 7(2) → *recordman, recordwoman* **It** [rekord] M, pl. Ø, end19c (3) > *primato* → *recordman, recordwoman* **Rm** [rekord] N, beg20c, via Fr, 7(3) **Rs** *rekord* M, pl. -*y*, beg20c, (3) → -*ist* M; -*istka* F; -*nyĭ* adj. **Po** *rekord* M, beg20c (3) → -*zista* M; *zistka* F; -*owy* adj.; -*owo* adv. **Cr** *rekord* M, pl. -*i*, beg20c, 7(3) → -*er* M; -*erka* F; -*an* adj. **Bg** *rekord* M, pl. -*al-i*, beg20c, via Rs, 7(2) → -*yor* M; -*yorka* F; -*en* adj. **Hu** *rekord* [rekord] pl. -*ok*, 1920s, 7(3); [=E/-e-] [U] end20c, 9(1 tech); 20c, +10(1 tech, writ) **Al** *rekord* M, pl. -*e*, 1930s (3) **Gr** *rekor* N, end19c/beg20c, via Fr, 7(2); <=E> [=E] N, pl. -*s*, end20c, 9(1 tech) +10(1 writ)

recorder *n./cp²* 1 'an apparatus for recording', +5 'a person achieving records (sports)'
Although this word might seem to be truly international (for recording sounds and, more recently, films), it is in fact available in only some languages.
Ge [rekɔrda] M pl. Ø, 1960s, 1(2) **Du** [=E] C, 1940s (2) **Nw** [=E] M, end20c, 1(1 tech) < -*spiller* **It** [rekorder] M/cp², pl. Ø, 1940s, 1(1 tech) < *registratore, magnetofono* **Rm** [rekorder] N/cp², 1980s (1 tech>mod) **Rs** (0) **Cr** *rekorder* M, pl. -*i*, beg20c, +5(3) **Bg** *rekorder* M, pl. -*al-i*, end20c, 1(1 tech) **Hu** *rekorder* [rekorder] pl. -*ek*, beg20c, +5(3); cp², end20c 1(2) < *felvevő*

record(s)man* *n.* 'a sportsman who has achieved a record'
Pseudo-English formations on -*man* are most frequent in French, but not restricted to it. Items in other languages may therefore be borrowed via French or independent coinages.
Ge - < *Rekordler* **Du** - < *recordbreker* **Fr** *recordman/-woman* M/F, end19c (1 tech, ban) > *détentuer/-trice d'un record* **Sp** *recordman/-woman* [rekorman/rekorbuman] M/F, end19c (1 tech) = *plusmarquista* **It** *recordman/-woman* [=E] M/F, pl. Ø, 1900s (1 tech) < creat *primatista* **Rm** *recordman, -ă* [rekordmen, -ə] M/F, 1960s, via Fr (1 tech) **Rs** *rekordsmen* M, pl. -*y*, mid20c (1 tech/jour) **Bg** - < *rekordyor* **Hu** - < *rekorder* **Al** *rekordmen* M, pl. -*ë*; *rekordmene* F, pl. Ø, mid20c (3) **Gr** *rekordman/-ghuman* M/F (1 tech)

recycle *v.* 'convert (waste) to reusable material'
Ge *recyceln* [risaikln] 1980s (2) > *rezyklieren* **Du** *recyclen* 1960s (2); *recycleren* 1960s (1 obs) < *hergebruiken* **Nw** *resyklere* [resykle:re] 1970s (1 tech, obs) < rend *gjenvinne*; trsl *resirkulere* **Ic** - < rend *endurvinna* **Fr** *recycler* (4) **Sp** *reciclar* (4) **It** *riciclare* (4) **Rm** *recicla* [retʃikla] 1980s (4) **Po** (0) **Cr** *reciklirati*, end20c (3) **Bg** *retsikliram* (3) **Hu** *reciklál* [retsikla:l] end20c (1 tech) **Al** *ricikloj* end20c (1 tech) **Gr** - < trsl *anakyklono*

recycling *n.* 'the conversion of waste to reusable material'
The neo-Classical basis of this new derivative has permitted most languages to pronounce the word in an un-English way and to replace the suffix so that the English provenance is now apparent only in a few languages (mostly Germanic). Compare similar adaptations of the verb.
Ge [=E] N [U] 1970s (2) = *Wiederverwertung* **Du** [=E] C [U] 1970s (1 tech) = *hergebruik* **Nw** [=E] M [U] 1970s (1 tech, obs) < rend *gjenvinning* **Ic** - < rend *endurvinnsla* **Fr** - < *recyclage* **Sp** - < *reciclaje* **It** - < *riciclaggio* **Rm** - < *riciclare* **Rs** *risaĭkling* M [U] end20c (1 tech) **Po** *recykl/recykling/<=E>* [recykl(ink)/=E] M, end20c → *recyklizacja* F **Cr** - < *reciklaža* **Bg** - < *retsiklirane* **Hu** - < *reciklálás* **Al** - < *riciklim* **Gr** (0) < trsl *anakyklosi*

redingote see ↑*riding-coat*

redline* *n.* 'a red centre line on an ice-hockey rink' **Nw** [=E] M [U] 1960s (1 tech)

redneck *n.* 1 'a working-class white in the southern USA', +2 'a stiff-necked person'

Du [=E] C, 1940s, 1(1 tech); 1990s, +2(1 mod)   **Nw** (Ø)

redwood   *n.* 1 'a sequoia, esp. the very tall specimens in the western USA'

Du Ø   **Nw** [=E] M, pl. *-er*, 20c (Ø/1 tech)   **Ic** - < trsl *rauðviður*   **Cr** [=E] M < *sekvoja*

reef   *n.* 1 'a ridge of rock or coral'

Ge *Riff* (4)   **Du** *rif* (4)   **Nw** *rev* (4)   **Ic** *rif* (4)   **Rs** *rif* M, pl. *-y*, 20c (2 tech/5Ge)   **Cr** (0)   **Bg** *rif* M, pl. *-al- ove*, 20c (5Ge)   **Hu** *riff* [riff] pl. Ø, 20c (2 tech)

reefer   *n.* 1 'a marijuana cigarette'

Du [=E] 1970s (1 sla, you, obs)   **Nw** [=E] M, pl. *-e*, 1960s (1 sla, obs) = *rev*   **Hu** [riːfer] [U] end20c (1 tech)

reel   *n.* 1 'a cylindrical device on which thread, yarn, etc. are wound', 4 'a revolving part in various machines', 5a 'a lively folk or Scottish dance, for two or more couples facing each other'

Ge 5a(0)   **Du** 5a(Ø)   **Nw** [=E] M, pl. *-er*, mid19c, 5a(1 tech)   **Ic** *rill* [ritl] M, pl. *-(l)ar*, beg19c, via Da, 1,4(3 tech) 5a(3 obs); *ræll* [raitl] M, pl. *-(l)ar*, beg20c, 5a(3)   **Fr** 5a(Ø)   **Bg** *ril* M [U] 20c, 5a(Ø)   **Fi** [=E] 19c, 5a(Ø)   **Hu** [=E] [U] 20c, 5a(0)

referee   *n.* 1 'an umpire' (sports), +2a 'a scholar who assesses the quality of articles submitted to a journal'

As applied to sports, the term competes with ↑*umpire* and with native terms which existed before the impact of English sports terminology or which were coined for the purpose; the preference for one term or another can vary with the individual discipline.

Ge [=E] M, pl. *-s*, beg20c/1970s, 1(1 obs/mod) < *Schiedsrichter* **Du** [=E] C, beg20c, 1(1 tech); [=E] C, 1980s, +2a (1 tech) < 1: *scheidsrechter* **Nw** (0) < *dommer* **Fr** 1(0) **Sp** [referi] M, pl. *-s*, beg20c (1 arch); [referi] +2a(1 tech) **It** - < 1: *arbitro* **Rm** [referi] M, end20c, 1(1 tech, rare) **Rs** *referi* M, uninfl., beg20c, 1(2 tech) **Po** - < *sędzia (sportowy)* **Bg** *refer* M, pl. *-i*, mid20c, via Rs, 1(3 tech) < *sŭdiya* **Gr** *referi* M, beg20c, 1(1 tech) < *dhietitis*

refill   *n.* 1 'a new filling', 2 'the material for this'

Ge [=E] M, pl. *-s*, 1980s (0>1 mod)   **Nw** [refil] M, pl. *-er*, mid20c, 2(1/2) < *påfyll*   **Ic** [=E] (0) < *(á)fylling/ ábót*   **It** [refil] M, pl. Ø, 1970s (1>2) < trsl *ricarica*   **Rs** (0)   **Cr** *refil* M, pl. *-i*, mid20c, 1(3)

reforming*   *n.* 'the act of converting (a straight chain hydrocarbon) by catalytic reaction to a branched molecular form for use as petrol'

Du - → *reformen* v.   **Fr** - < *reformage*   **Sp** [reformin] M, 20c (1 tech) = *reformaje*   **It** [=E] M [U] 1950s (1 tech)   **Rm** - < *reformare*   **Po** [re-] M [U] end20c (1 tech)   **Hu** (5La)

reggae   *n./cp¹/adj.* 'a Caribbean style of music with a strongly accented subsidiary beat'

This term (of uncertain etymology) is internationally attested from 1968 since when it has spread as a hallmark of Caribbean folk culture. Note that the form has little English about it.

Ge [reːge:] M [U] 1970s (1 tech)   **Du** [=E] C [U] 1970s (2 tech)   **Nw** [=E] M [U] 1970s (1 tech)   **Ic** *reggi/ raggi* [rɛciː/raciː] N cp¹ [U] 1970s (2 tech)   **Fr** [rege] M, 1970s (1) → *reggaeman*   **Sp** [rege/rigi] M, 1970s (1 tech, you)   **It** [regge] M [U] 1970s (2 tech)   **Rm** [rege] N/adj. 1970s (1 tech, you)   **Rs** *reggi* N, uninfl., end20c (1 tech)   **Po** [rege] N, uninfl., end20c (1 tech)   **Cr** [rege] M [U] end20c (1 tech)   **Bg** *rege* N [U] mid20c (3 tech)   **Fi** [=E] 1970s (1 tech)   **Hu** [regi] [U] 20c (2)   **Gr** *rege* F [U] 1970s (2)

relax   *v./interj.* +1a 'become less tense' (of muscles), 5 'be at ease, be unperturbed'

Ge *relaxen* [rilɛksən] 1980s, 5(1 you)   **Du** *relaxen* [rilɛksən] 1970s, 5(2); *relaxeren*, via Fr, 5(2 reg)   **Nw** *relaxe* [relækse] mid20c, 5(1 rare, obs)   **Ic** [=E] interj., end20c, 5(1 sla)   **Fr** *se relaxer* [r(ə)lakse] mid20c, 5(1)   **Sp** *relajarse* 4   **It** *rilassarsi* (4)   **Rm** *relaxa* [relaksa] refl., 19c, via Fr, +1a,5(3); [=E] interj., end20c (0)   **Po** *relaksować* [relaksovatɕ] mid20c, +1a,5(3) → *z-, wy-*   **Cr** *relaksirati* mid20c, 5(3)   **Bg** *relaksiram* 5,+1a(3)   **Fi** *relaksoida* (v.tr.) end20c, 5(1 tech)   **Hu** (5La)   **Al** - < *shplodhem*   **Gr** *rilaxaro* (3 sla, mod)

relax*   *n./cp¹* 1 'physical and mental rest', 2 'sexual contact with a prostitute', 3 'a baby's chair'

Ge *Relax-*[rilɛks] cp¹, 1970s, 1(1 tech)   **Du** [rəlɑks] [=E] C [U] 1970s, 1(1 tech)   **Fr** *relax(e)* [rəlaks] M, adj./adv., interj., mid20c, 1(1 coll)   **Sp** [relaks] M [U] mid20c, 1,3(2) 2(2 euph)   **It** [relaks] M [U] 1950s, 1(3)   **Rm** - < *relaxare*   **Rs** (0)   **Po** *relaks* [relaks] M [U] mid20c, 1(3) → *-owy* adj.   **Hu** (5La)   **Gr** *rilax* N [U] 1990s, 1(1 coll, mod); mid20c, 3(2)

relaxed   *adj.* 'at ease, informal'

Ge <=E>/*relaxt* [rilɛkst] 1960s (1 coll)   **Du** [=E] 1970s (1 coll)   **Nw** [=E] 1960s (1 coll)   **Ic** [=E] uninfl., end20c (1 sla)   **Fr** *relaxé, relax* (4)   **Sp** *relajado* 4   **It** *rilassato* (4)   **Rm** *relaxat, -ă* [relaksat, -ə] 19c (4)   **Po** *zrelaksowany* [zrelaksovani] mid20c (3)   **Cr** *relaksiran* (3)   **Bg** *relaksiran* (3)

release   *n.* 4b 'the act or an instance of releasing a film or a record'

Du [=E] C, 1980s (1 tech) → *releasen* v.   **Nw** [=E] M, 1970s (1 tech) → *release* v.

REM   *abbrev.* 'rapid eye movement'

Ge *REM-Phase* [rem] cp¹, 1970s (1 tech+5)   **Du** *R.E.M./rem* [rɛm] C [U] 1970s (1 tech)   **Nw** [rem] cp¹, 20c (1 tech)   **Fr** [ʀɛm] M, mid20c (1 tech)   **Sp** *fase REM* [rem] end20c (1 tech)   **It** [rem] M/cp², pl. Ø, 1950s (1 tech) < *fase rem*   **Cr** *-REM* M [U] end20c (1 tech)   **Bg** (0)   **Fi** [er eː em/rem] cp¹, mid20c (1 tech)

remainder   *n.* 4 'the copies of a book left unsold when demand has fallen'

It [rimeinder/remainder] M, pl. Ø/-s, 1960s (2 tech)

remake   *n.* 1 'a thing' (film, record, song) that has been remade'

This term is remarkably widespread, but has not been extended beyond the technical uses referring to films and records.

Ge [r̲i̲me:k] N, pl. -s, 1950s (1 tech) **Du** [=E] C, 1960s (1 tech) **Nw** [=E] M, pl. -s, 1980s (1 tech) **Ic** [=E] N, pl. Ø, end2oc (o) < trsl *endurgerð* **Fr** [rimɛk] M, mid2oc (1 tech, jour) **Sp** [re-m̲e̲ik] M, pl. -s, 1970s (1 tech) **It** [rim̲e̲ik] M, pl. Ø, 1960s (1>2 tech) **Rm** [=E/rim̲e̲jk] N, 1970s (1 tech>jour) **Rs** *rim̲e̲ik/rem̲e̲ĭk* M, pl. -i, end2oc (1 tech/jour) **Po** [rimeik] M, end2oc (1 tech) **Cr** [=E] M [U] end2oc (1 tech) **Bg** *rim̲e̲ĭk* M, pl. -a/-ove, 1990s (1 tech, mod) **Hu** [=E] [U] end2oc (1 tech) < *felújítás* **Gr** *rim̲e̲ik* N, end2oc, 1(1 tech)

reminder *n.* 1a 'something that reminds one of something'

Du [=E] C, 1980s (1 tech, mod) = *geheugensteuntje* **Nw** [=E] M, pl. -e, 1970s (1 rare)

Remington* *n.* (orig.ᵀᴹ) 1 'a type of shotgun', 2 'a kind of typewriter'

The tradename (for both products) was on its way to becoming generic, but since the items are less well known today the words are obsolescent, too.

Ge *Remingtongewehr* cp¹, end19c (1 arch) **Nw** [=E] M, pl. -er, end19c, 1,2(1 tech) **Ic** [=E] cp¹ mid2oc (1 tech) **Sp** [r̲e̲minton] end19c (1 tech) **It** [r̲e̲mington] F, pl. Ø, beg2oc (2 arch) **Rm** [r̲e̲mington] N, beg2oc (3 tech) **Rs** *remingt̲o̲n* M, pl. -y, beg2oc (1 tech) **Po** M, beg2oc, 2(1) **Cr** M, pl. -i, beg2oc (1 tech, arch) **Bg** *r̲e̲mington* M, pl. -a/-i, beg2oc, 2(1 tech, arch) **Hu** [=E] pl. -ok, end19c, 1(1 arch); 2(3 arch) **Gr** *r̲e̲mington* N, 2oc, 1(1 tech)

remix *v.* 'mix (a sound recording) again' (music)

Ge *remixen* [=E] 1990s (1 tech) **Du** *remixen* [=E] 1990s (1 tech) **Nw** *remixe* [r̲e̲:miksə] 1980s (1 tech) **Ic** [ri:mixsa] end2oc (1 tech) > trsl *endurhljóðblanda* **Fr** <=E> M [U] 2oc (1 tech) **Rm** *remixa* [remiks̲a̲] end2oc (1 tech) **Po** *remiksować* [remiksovatɕ] end2oc (1 tech) **Fi** *remiksi* 1980s (1 tech)

remix *n.* 'a sound recording of a song that has been mixed again to produce a new or different version'

Ge [=E] M, pl. -e/-es, 1990s (1 tech) **Du** [=E] M, pl. -en/-es, 1990s (1 tech) **Nw** <=E>/*remiks* [r̲e̲:-] M, end2oc (1 tech) → *re-mixe* v; -mikse v. **Ic** [=E] N, pl. Ø, end2oc (1 tech) > trsl *endurhljóðblöndun* **Fr** (o) **Sp** [rem̲i̲ks] M, pl. -es, end2oc (1 tech) = *remezcla* **It** [=E] M, pl. Ø, 1990s (1 tech) **Rm** [rem̲i̲ks] N, end2oc (2 tech) **Rs** *rem̲i̲ks* M, pl. -y, 1990s (1 mod/tech) **Po** [re-] M [U] end2oc (1 tech) **Cr** *remiks* M, pl. -i, 1990s (1 tech) **Bg** *rem̲i̲ks* M, pl. -a/-ove, 1990s (1 tech) **Fi** [=E] 1980s (1 tech) **Gr** *rimix*/<=E> N, 1990s (1 tech)

remote control *n.* 'control from a distance by means of signals'

Ge [=E] F [U] 1980s (1 tech, rare) < *Fernbedienung* **Du** [=E] C, 1990s (1 tech, mod) < *afstandsbe-*

diening **Nw** (o) < trsl *fjernkontroll* **Ic** - < creat *fjarstýring* **Fr** - < *télécommande* **Sp** - < trsl *control remoto*; rend *mando a distancia* **It** - < rend *comando a distanza, telecomando* **Rm** - < *telecomandă* **Rs** - < trsl *distantsionnoe upravlenie* **Po** - < rend *kontrola na odległość* **Cr** - < trsl *daljinsko ufmavljanje* **Bg** *rim-o̲ut* M [U] 1990s (1 tech, mod) < trsl *distantsionno upravlenie* **Hu** [=E] [U] 1980s (1 tech, writ, jour) < *távirányítás* **Al** - < *telekomandë* **Gr** - < trsl *tilekontrol*

rent-a- *cp¹* 'denoting availability for hire'

This item was first adopted in the set phrase *rent-a-car* in all languages, but *car* is now increasingly replaced by other elements thus making *rent-a* available for new coinages.

Ge [r̲e̲nta] 1980s (1 mod) **Du** [=E] 1990s (1 tech) **Nw** (o) < *leie-* **Ic** *rent-a-* [r̲e̲nta-] end2oc (o) **Fr** (Ø) **Sp** *rent-a-car* M [U] end2oc (1 tech) **Rm** *-car* [=E] end2oc (1 jour>mod) **Rs** (o) **Po** *rent a car* [- kar] end2oc (1 mod) **Cr** *rent-a-* M [U] end2oc (1 tech) **Bg** *r̲e̲nt-a-k̲a̲r*/<=E> M [U] end2oc (1 tech/writ) **Hu** *rentacar* [r̲e̲nt-a-ka:r] 1980s (1) **Gr** <=E> [=E] end2oc (1 writ)

repeat *n./cp¹ᐟ²* +6 'a device on a recording machine that makes the machine go (back) to the start and may repeat the playing'

Ge [=E] cp¹, 1980s (1 tech, writ) **Du** [=E] C, 1980s (1 tech, coll, mod) → *repeaten* v. **Nw** [=E] M, 1980s (1 tech) **Ic** [=E] uninfl., end2oc (o) **Fr** (o) **Po** [-pit] end2oc (1 mod) **Bg** *ripi̲i̲t* M [U] end2oc (1 tech/mod) **Fi** [=E] cp², end2oc (o) **Hu** [=E] mid2oc (1 tech, writ) **Gr** <=E> [=E] N, end2oc (1 tech/writ)

repeater *n.* 1 'a person who repeats' (esp. in the 'socio-medical' sense)

Nw [=E] M, pl. -e, 1970s (1 tech) < *gjenganger*

replay *n.* 1 'the act or instance of replaying (a match, recording)'

Since both elements are well known from other loans, the adoption was not difficult and need not have been stimulated by the highly contextualized labels on recorders etc. *record, replay* (which are here not listed as not forming part of language X).

Ge [r̲i̲:ple:] N, pl. -s, 1970s (1 mod) **Du** [=E] C, 1970s (1 tech) **Nw** [=E] M, pl. -s, 1970s (1 tech) < *repetisjon* **Ic** [=E] uninfl., end2oc (o) **Fr** - < trsl *match rejoué* **Sp** - < *repetitión* **It** [repl̲e̲i] M, pl. Ø, 1980s (2) **Rm** [=E] N [U] 1980s (1 mod) **Po** <=E> M, end2oc (1 mod) **Cr** <=E> (o) **Bg** (o) **Gr** *repl̲e̲i* N, end2oc, 1(2) < mean *epanalipsi*

report *n.* 'a survey, esp. of the results of polls etc.'

Ge [re:p̲o̲rt] M, pl. -e, beg19c (3) < *Bericht* **Du** *rapport* (5Fr) **Nw** *rapport* (5Fr) **It** [rep̲o̲rt] M, pl. Ø, end19c (1 tech) < *rapporto* **Po** (5Fr) **Cr** [r̲e̲port] M,

beg2oc (3)   **Fi** *rapportti* (5Fr)   **Hu** *riport* [riport] pl.
-ok, 19c (3)   **Al** *raport* (5Fr)   **Gr** - < *reportaz*

reporter   *n.* 1 'a journalist in all news media, esp. radio and TV'
Ge [re:porta] M, pl. Ø, beg19c (3)   **Du** [rəpɔrtər] C, beg19c (3) = *verslaggeuer*   **Nw** [repɔ:rter] M, pl. *-e*, end19c (3)   **Ic** - < *fréttaritari*   **Fr** [r(ə)pɔRtɛR] M, beg19c (2) > *reporteur (d'images)*   **Sp** [reporter] M, mid19c (1 arch) < *reportero*   **It** [reporter] M, pl. Ø, end19c (3)   **Rm** [reporter] M, 19c, via Fr/Ge (3) → *reporteră* F; *reporteraş* dim.; *-icesc* adj.   **Rs** *reportër* M, pl. *-y*, beg2oc (3)   **Po** [reporter] M, beg2oc, (3) → *-ia* F; *-ka* F; *-skość* M; *-stwo* N; *-zyna* M; *-owanie* N; *-ski* adj.   **Cr** [reporter] M, pl. *-i*, beg2oc (3) → *-ka* F; *-ski* adj.   **Bg** *reporter/reportyor* M, pl. *-i*, beg2oc, via Rs (2/3 arch) → *-ka* F; *-ski* adj.   **Fi** *reportteri* 19c (3)   **Hu** *riporter* [riporter] pl. *-ek*, 19c (3)   **Al** *reportēr* M, pl. *-ë*, 1930s (3)   **Gr** *reporter* M/F, pl. Ø/*-s*, end2oc (2)

reprint   *n.* 2 'a reprinted book etc.'
Although native words have been available (and still are), the English word has made headway as a catchy expression of modern publishing.
Ge [=E] M, pl. *-s*, 1970s (1 tech) < *Nachdruck*   **Du** [=E] C, 1970s (1 tech) = *herdruk*   **Nw** (o) < *opptrykk, særtrykk*   **Ic** - < *rend endurprentun*   **Fr** [rəprint] M, 1960s (1 tech)   **Sp** - < *trsl reimpresión*   **It** [reprint] M, pl. Ø,

1970s (1 tech) < *trsl ristampa*   **Rm** [=E] N, 1970s (1 tech)   **Rs** *reprint* M, pl. *-y*, end2oc (1 tech) → *-nyĭ* adj.   **Po** [reprint] M, end2oc (2 tech) → *-owy* adj.   **Cr** *reprint* M, pl. *-i*, mid2oc (1 tech)   **Fi** - < *creat uusintapainos*   **Hu** [reprint] pl. *-ek*, 1970s (2 tech)

research   *n.* 1a 'the systematic investigation into and study of materials in order to establish facts'
Ge [=E] N [U] 1960s (1 tech, rare)   **Du** [risɣ:tʃ] C [U] 1940s (1 tech) → *researchen* v.   **Nw** [=E] M [U] 1970s (1 tech)

researcher   *n.* 'a person who systematically studies sources, attitudes etc.'
Ge [=E] M, pl. Ø, 1980s (1 tech, rare)   **Du** [=E] C, 1980s (1 tech, jour, rare)   **Nw** [=E] M, pl. *-e*, 1980s (1 tech)

reset   *v.* 'set (a broken bone, gems, a mechanical device, etc.) again or differently'
Du *resetten* end2oc (1 tech)   **Fr** [rizɛte] end2oc (1 tech)   **It** *resettare* 1990s (1 tech COMPUT)   **Rm** *reseta* [reseta] end2oc (o>1 tech)   **Po** *resetować* [resetovatç] end2oc (1 tech)   **Cr** *resetirati* end2oc (1 tech)   **Hu** [=E] 2oc (1 tech COMPUT)

reset*   *n./cp[1]* 'a mechanism that resets or brings something back to start or zero'
Ge [=E] cp[1], 1980s (1 tech, writ)   **Du** [=E] C, 1980s (1 tech) → *resetten* v.   **Nw** [=E] M/usu. cp[1], 1970s (1 tech)   **Ic** [=E] uninfl., end2oc (o)   **Fr** [rizet] end2oc (1

tech)   **It** [rɛsɛt] M, pl. Ø, 1960s (1 tech)   **Rm** [=E] N, 1980s (1 tech) → *reseta* v.   **Rs** (o)   **Fi** [=E] cp[1] (1 tech)   **Hu** [=E] [U] end2oc (1 tech, writ)   **Gr** <=E> [risɛt] N, end2oc (1 tech, writ) > *epanafora*

response   *n.* +2a 'a reaction' (psychol.)
Ge [=E] F, pl. *-s*, 1970s (1 tech)   **Du** [rɪspɔns] C [U] 1960s (1 tech) < *respons*   **Nw** *respons* [respɔns] M [U] mid2oc (3)   **Sp** - < *respuesta*   **Rm** - < *răspuns*   **Bg** *rispɔns* M, pl. *-al-i*, mid2oc (1 tech)   **Hu** [=E] [U] 2oc (1 tech)   **Gr** (o) < *adidhrasi*

restyling*   *n.* 'redoing in new style'
Du [=E] N, 1990s (1 mod) → *restylen* v.   **Fr** [ristajliŋ] M, 1980s (1 tech, ban) > *restylage, remodelage*   **Sp** [restailiŋ] M [U] end2oc (1 tech, jour)   **It** [ristailiŋ(g)] M [U] 1990s (1 tech)   **Po** [-nk] M [U] end2oc (1 jour)

retrieval   *n.* 'the recovery of information' (comput.)
Ge [=E] N [U] 1980s (1 tech, rare)   **Du** [=E] C [U] 1980s (1 tech)   **Nw** (o)   **Fr** - < *récupération*   **Sp** - < *recuperación*   **Rm** - < *regăsire, recuperare*   **Rs** (o)   **Fi** [=E] 1980s (1 tech)   **Gr** <=E> [=E] N [U] end2oc (o/tech) = *anaktisi*

retrieve   *v.* 2b 'obtain (information stored in a computer etc)'
Fr *retriever* [RɛtRivɛR] M, mid19c (1 tech)   **Hu** [=E] end2oc, 2b(1 tech)

return   *n.* +2a 'the act of hitting or sending back the ball' (sport), 6 'a second match between the same opponents', 11b 'a key or button on a computer keyboard that enters input into the computer's memory and/or leads the cursor to the beginning of a new line'
The distribution of this term is mainly restricted to tennis, where the popularity of the game has led to a new adoption, or reintroduction, of the word.
Ge [ritörn] M, pl. *-s*, 1970s, +2a(1 tech)   **Du** [=E] C, 1970s, +2a(1 tech) 6(1 tech)   **Nw** (o) < *retur(-)*

Ic [=E] uninfl., 11b(o)   **Fr** - < +2a: *retour*; 6: *match retour*   **Sp** - < +2a: *devolución*; 6: *(partido) de vuelta*; 11b: *retorno*   **It** - < +2a: *ribattuta*; 6: *ritorno*; 11b: *invio*   **Rm** - < 6: *(meci) retur*   **Rs** (o)   **Po** [return] M, end2oc, +2a,11b(1 tech)   **Cr** *retern* M, pl. *-i*, end2oc (1 tech) → *-irati* v.   **Bg** *ritŭrn* M, pl. *-a*, 1990s, 11b(1 tech, sla)   **Gr** <=E> [=E] N, end2oc, 11b(1 tech)

reverser*   *n.* 'something that reverses gear or motion'
Nw - < *revers*   **Rm** *reversor* [reversor] N, mid2oc (3 tech)   **Rs** *revers* M, pl. *-y*, mid2oc (2 tech)   **Po** *rewerser/rewersor* M, mid2oc (1 tech)   **Cr** (o)   **Bg** *reverser* M, pl. *-al-i*, mid2oc (1 tech) → *reversiven* adj.   **Hu** (5La)

review   *n.* 3 'a revision or reconsideration', 5 'a published account or criticism of a book, play, etc.', +8a 'a facility for playing a video tape recording during a fast rewind'

Ge [=E]/[rɪvju:] M/F, pl. -*s*, end20c, 5(1 tech_SCI) +8a(1 tech) **Hu** [=E] pl. Ø, end19c/beg20c, 3(1 arch); 20c, +8a(1 tech) **Gr** 5(0/1 writ)

revival *n.* 1 'the act of reviving', 2 'a new production of an old play, etc.', 3 'a revived use of an old practice, custom etc.', 4a 'a reawakening of religious fervour'
Ge [=E] N, pl. -*s*, 1960s, 2(1 jour) 4a (Ø) **Du** [=E] C, 1950s (2) **Nw** [=E] M, pl. -*s*, end20c, 1,3,4a(1) < *renessanse* **Sp** [=E/rebibal] M, pl. -*(e)s*, end20c (1 jour) **It** [=E/revaival] M, pl. Ø, 1920s (3) → *revivalista* n.; -*ismo* n.; -*istico* adj. **Rm** [=E] N [U] end20c, 2(1 jour) **Cr** [=E] M [U] mid20c, 2(1)

revolver *n./cp¹* 1 'a pistol with revolving chambers enabling several shots to be fired without reloading'
Ge [revolva] M, pl. Ø, end19c (3) **Du** [rəvolvər] C, mid19c (3) **Nw** [revolver] M, pl. -*e*, end19c (3) **Ic** <=E> M/cp¹, pl. -*ar*, beg20c (Ø) **Fr** [revolveʀ] M, mid19c (3) **Sp** *revólver* [rebolber] M, pl. -*es*, mid19c (3) **It** [revolver] M, pl. Ø, mid19c (3) < creat *rivoltella* → *revolverata* n. **Rm** [revolver] N, mid19c, via Fr/ Ge (3) **Rs** *revol'ver* M, pl. -*y*, mid19c (3) → -*owiec* adj. **Po** *rewolwer* [revolver] M, mid19c (3) → -*owiec* M; -*ówka* F; -*owy* adj. **Cr** *revolver* M, pl. -*i*, 19c (3) → -*aš* M; -*ski* adj. **Bg** *revolver* M, pl. -*al-i*, end19c, via Rs (2 tech) → -*en* adj. **Fi** *revolveri* 19c (3) **Hu** [revolver] pl. -*ek*, end19c/beg20c (3) → -*ez* v. **Al** *revolver* M, pl. -*ë*, 19c (3) **Gr** *revolver* N, end19c/ beg20c (1 tech) < trsl *peristrofo*

revolving credit *n./adj.* 'credit that is automatically renewed as debts are paid off'
Du *revolverkrediet* N, 1940s (3+5) **Fr** *crédit révolving* [kredi revolviŋ] M, mid20c (1 tech/ban) > *crédit permanent* **Sp** *crédito revolving* M, end20c (1 tech) **Rm** *credit revolving* [kredit revolviŋ] N, end20c, via Fr? (5+1 tech) **Po** *rewolwingowy* [revolvingovi] adj., end20c (1 tech) **Cr** *rivolving kredit* M, end20c (1 tech) **Bg** - < trsl *revolvirasht kredit* **Fi** [=E] end20c (1 tech) **Hu** [=E] [U] end20c (1 tech) < *rulírozó hitel*

rewrite *v.* 'write again or differently' (esp. of a professional writer)
Du - < *herschrijven* **Fr** *rewriter* [rirajte/ʀəʀajte] 1960s (1 tech, ban) < *réécrire, remodeler*

rewriter* *n.* 'a reviser' (journalism)
Nw [=E] M, pl. -*e*, 1970s (1 tech) **Fr** *rewriter* [ʀi-ʀajtœʀ/ʀəʀajtœʀ] M, 1960s (1 tech)

rewriting *n.* 'revision' (journalism)
Nw [=E] M [U] 1960s (1 tech) **Fr** *rewriting* [ʀiʀajtiŋ/ ʀəʀajtiŋ] M, mid20c (1 tech)

Rhode Island Red *n.* 'an originally American breed of reddish-black domestic fowl'
   This word is remarkable for its degree of integration in most languages, which has left few traces of its English provenance in its 'Eastern' distribution in German, Russian, Polish, etc.
Ge *Rhodeländer* N, pl. Ø, beg20c (3 tech) **Fr** *Rhode-Island* F, 20c(1 tech) **Sp** *(gallina) Rhode Island* 20c (1 tech) **Rm** *(găină) Rhode Island* F, mid20c (1 tech)

tech) **Rs** *rodaïland* M, pl. -*y*, mid20c (1 tech) **Po** *rodajlendy* [rodailendi] pl., end20c (1 tech) **Cr** *rodajlend* M, pl. -*i*, mid20c (1 tech) **Bg** *rodailand* M, pl. -*al-i*, mid20c (3 tech) **Hu** *Rhode Island* [ro:d ailend] pl. Ø, beg20c (1 tech)

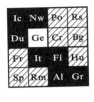

rhythm and blues *n.* 'popular music with a blues theme and a strong rhythm'
Ge [=E] M [U] mid20c (1 tech, rare) **Du** [=E] C [U] 1970s (1 tech) **Nw** [=E] M [U] mid20c (1 tech) > *R&B* **Ic** [=E] (o) **Fr** [ritmənbluz] M, 1970s (1 tech) **Sp** [=E/rimamblus] M [U] 1970s (1 tech, you) **It** [=E/ ritmen blu:z] M [U] 1970s (2 tech) **Rm** <=E>/*R'n'B* [=E] N [U] 1970s (1 tech) **Rs** *ritm-énd-blyuz* M [U] 1980s (1 tech) **Po** [ritm-] M [U] end20c (1 tech) **Cr** <=E> (o) **Bg** *ritŭmendblus* M [U] end20c (1 tech) **Fi** [=E] mid20c (1 tech, rare) < *R&B* **Gr** <=E> [=E] N [U] mid20c (1 tech)

ribs* *n./cp¹* 'a textile fabric with a corded surface'
   This term is one of the many loans of nineteenth-century British names for types of cloth; its form, however, is disguised by devoiced [ps] and the invariable *s* interpreted as part of the stem. This points to German mediation in many European languages (cf. ↑*cakes, cokes, drops, slips*, etc.)
Ge *Ribs/Rips* [rips] M, pl. -*e*, 19c (3) **Du** *rips* (4) **Nw** *rips* [rips] M [U] beg20c, via Ge (1 tech) **Ic** *repp* [rɛhp] N/cp¹ [U] end19c (1 obs); *rips/rifs* [rɪfs] N [U] 1930s, via Da (2) **Fr** *reps* [ʀɛps] M, 19c (1 tech) **It** *reps* via Fr (1 tech) **Rm** *rips* [rips] N [U] 19c, via Ge (3 tech) → *ripsat* adj., 20c **Rs** *reps* [reps] M [U] 20c, via Fr (1 tech) **Po** *ryps* [rips] M [U] beg20c, via Ge (3) **Cr** [rips] M [U] beg20c (1 tech) **Bg** *rips* M [U] beg20c, via Ge (3) → -*en* adj. **Fi** *ripsi* 19c (3) **Hu** *ripsz* [=E] [U] 20c (3)

riding coat* *n.* 'a long coat'
   This word is here listed under its English etymon although all instances of the modern loanword are via French, including even the term ↑*redingote* which was reborrowed into English in 1793 at the time when the item spread to a few other European languages. Since the garment seems to be rediscovered by the fashion industry at intervals, it is difficult to say whether the term is really archaic or obsolescent, and to what degrees, and in which languages.
Ge *Redingote* M/F, pl. -*sl-n*, beg19c/1960s, via Fr (1 obs) **Nw** *redingot* [rediŋɔt] M, pl. -*er*, via Fr/Ge (1 obs) **Fr** *redingote* [ʀədɛ̃gɔt] F, 18c (3 arch) **Sp** *redingote* M, beg18c, via Fr (3 arch) **It** *redingote* [redingɔt] F, pl. Ø, 18c, viaFr (3 obs) **Rm** *redingotă* [redingotə] F, mid19c, via Fr (3 arch) **Rs** *redingot*

M, pl. -*y*, beg20c, via Fr (3 arch)
Po *redingot/redingote* [redingot] M, beg20c, via Fr (1 obs) **Cr** *redingot* M, pl. -*i*, 19c/beg20c, via Fr (1 arch/1 obs) **Bg** *redingot* M [U]/pl. -*al-i*, beg20c, via Fr (3) **Hu** *redingot* [redingot] pl. -*ok*, 19c, via Fr (3 arch) **Gr** *redi(n)gota* F, 19c, via Fr (3 arch/mod)

riff   *n.* 'a short repeated phrase in jazz and rock'
Ge [=E] M [U] 1970s (1 tech) **Du** [rɪf] C, 1980s (1 tech) = *loopje* **Nw** [=E] N, pl. Ø/-*s*, 1950s (1 tech) **Ic** *riff* [rɪf:] N, pl. Ø, mid/end20c (1 tech, sla) **Fr** [rif] M, 1960s (1 tech) **Sp** [rif] M, pl. -*s*, end20c (1 tech) **It** [=E] M, pl. Ø, 1950s (1 tech) **Rm** [=E] N [U] 1970s (1 tech) **Rs** (0) **Po** M [U] end20c (1 tech) **Cr** *rif* M [U] end20c (1 tech) **Bg** *rif* M, pl. -*al-ove*, mid20c (1 tech) **Fi** *riffi* mid20c (1 tech) **Hu** [=E] [U] end20c (1 tech) **Gr** *rif* N, end20c (1 tech) → *rifaki*

rifle   *n.* 1 'a gun with a long rifled barrel, esp. one fired from shoulder level'
Ge (0) **Du** (0) **Nw** ["rifle] from Ge **Ic** *riffill* (5Da) **Fr** *rifle* [rifl(ə)] M, beg19c (1 tech) **Sp** [rifle] M, pl. -*s*, mid19c (3)

rig[1] (1)   *v.* 1a 'provide a sailing ship with sails, rigging, etc.', 1b 'prepare ready for sailing', 2 'fit with clothes or other equipment', 3 'set up hastily or as a make-shift'
Ge *riggen* 19c (3 tech) **Du** - < *optuigen* **Nw** *rigge* ["rige] mid19c (3) → *rigg* N; *rigging* M/F **Ic** *rigga* [rɪk:a] beg20c, via Da, 1a,1b(3 arch) → *riggaður* adj.; *riggari* M

rig[2] (2)   *v.* 'manage or conduct fraudulently'
Nw *rigge* ["rige] 1980s (1) < *fikse*

rig (1)   *n.* 1 'the arrangement of masts, sails, rigging, etc., of a sailing ship', 3 'an oil rig'
Ge *Rigg* N, pl. -*s*, 19c, 1(3) → *riggen* v. **Du** [=E] C, 1990s, 3(1 tech) = *boortoren*; < 1:*tuigage* **Nw** *rigg* [=E] M, pl. -*er*, mid19c, 1(3); 1970s, 3(3) → *rigge* v. **Po** *ryg* [rik] M, mid20c, 3(1 tech)

ring   *n.* 6c 'a roped enclosure for boxing or wrestling'
Ge [ring] M, pl. -*e*, end19c (4) **Du** [rɪng] C, pl. -*en*, beg20c (4) = *boksring* **Nw** [rin] M (4) **Ic** - < trsl *hringur* **Fr** [rin] M, beg19c (2) **Sp** *ring* M, pl. -*s*, beg20c (2) = *cuadrilátero* **It** [ring] M, pl. Ø, end19c (3) **Rm** [ring] N, beg20c, via Fr (3) **Rs** *ring* M, pl. -*i*, beg20c (3) **Po** [- nk] M, beg20c (3) **Cr** *ring* M, pl. -*ovi*, beg20c (3) **Bg** *ring* M, pl. -*al-ove*, beg20c (2) → -*ov* adj. **Hu** [=E] pl. Ø, end19/beg20c, via Ge (3) **Al** *ring* M, pl. -*je*, mid20c (3) **Gr** *ri(n)g* N, 20c (1 tech)

ringside   *adv.* +1a 'very close to something happening, with a good view'
Nw [=E] mid20c (2)

ripple mark   *n.* 'a ridge or ridged surface left on sand, mud, or rock by the action of water or wind'
Ge - < trsl? *Rippelmarken* **Du** *ribbel* (5) **Fr** *ripple-mark* [ripəlmark] F, beg20c (1 tech) **Rm** [=E] N [U] 1970s (1 rare) **Po** *ripplemarki* [riplemarki] pl., mid20c (1 tech)

risk   *n.* 1 'a chance or possibility of danger, loss, injury, or other adverse consequences'
Ge - < *Risiko* **Du** - < *risico* **Nw** [=E] M, pl. -*er*, beg20c (3) **Ic** [rɪsk] N/M [U] end20c (1 sla) **Rm** *risc* [=E] N, 19c (5Fr) → *risca* v. **Rs** (5Fr) **Po** (5It) **Bg** *risk* M, pl. -*al-ove*, beg20c (5Fr) → *uvam* v; -*ov* adj. **Fi** *riski* 18c? (5Sw) **Al** - < *rrezik* **Gr** *risko* N, 20c (2 coll) → *riskaro* v.

risky   *adj.* 1 'involving risk'
Nw [=E] mid20c (1 coll) **Ic** [rɪsci] uninfl., end20c (1 sla) **Rs** - < trsl *riskovyi* **Po** (5It) **Bg** - < *riskov(an)*

riverboat shuffle*   *n.* 'a jazz party on a boat'
Ge [=E] F, pl. -*s*, 1960s (1 you, obs) **Du** [=E] C, 1960s (1 obs)

RNA   *abbrev.* 'ribonucleic acid'
Ge - < *RNS* **Du** [ɪr ɪn ɑ] N [U] 1980s (1 tech) **Nw** [ærena:] [U] 20c (3 tech) **Ic** [ɛr: ɛn: a:] freq. cp[1], mid20c (3 tech) = rend *RKS* (*ríbósakjarnsýra*) **Fr** - < trsl *ARN* **Sp** [erre-ene-a] M, 20c (1 tech) = *ARN* **It** [ɛrre-ɛnne-a] M [U] 1960s (1 tech) < trsl *acido ribonucleico* **Rm** - < rend *ARN (acid ribonucleic)* **Rs** - < trsl *RNK* **Po** [er en a] mid20c (1 tech) **Cr** (0) **Bg** - < trsl *RNK* **Fi** [er en a:] mid20c (1 tech) **Hu** - < *RNS* **Al** - < *ARN (acidi ribonukleik)* **Gr** <=E> [=E] N, 20c < trsl *rivonukleiko oxy* N

roadie   *n.* 'an assistant employed by a touring band of musicians to erect and maintain equipment'
Ge [ro:di] M, pl. -*s*, 1970s (1 you, obs) **Du** [ro:di] C, 1970s (1 tech) **Nw** [=E] M, pl. -*r/-s*, 1970s (1 tech) **Ic** *rótari* [rou:tarɪ] M, pl. -*ar*, 1960s (3 coll) → *róta* v. **Fr** (0) **Sp** [roudi] M, pl. -*s*, 1980s (1 tech) **Fi** *roudari* 1970s (1 you)

road manager   *n.* 1 'the organizer and supervisor of a musicians' tour', +2 'a roadie'
Ge [=E] M, pl. Ø, 1970s (1 tech, rare) **Du** [ro:d+=E] C, 1970s, 1(1 tech, rare), +2(1 tech, euph) < 1: *tourmanager* **Nw** [=E] M, pl. -*e*, 1970s (1 tech) **Sp** [roud manager] M, pl. -*s*, 1980s (1 tech) **It** [=E/manadʒer] M, pl. Ø, end20c (1 tech) **Bg** - < 1: *menidzhŭr* **Fi** [=E] 1970s (1 coll)

road-movie   *n.* 'a film featuring life on the road' (as in *Easy Rider*)
Ge [=E] N, pl. -*s*, 1980s (1 tech) **Nw** [=E] M, pl. -*s*, 1980s (1 tech) **Ic** [=E] end20c (0 tech) **Fr** (0) **Sp** [roud mubi] N, pl. -*s*, 1980s (1 tech) **It** [rɔd muvi] M, pl. Ø, 1980s (1 tech) **Rs** (0) **Fi** [=E] 1980s (1 tech)

road-racing*   *n.* 'car (or motor bike) racing'
Nw [=E] M [U] 1970s (1 tech)

roadster   *n.* 1 'an open two-seater motor car'
   This term was first adopted in the 1930s, but became more widespread only from the 1950s onwards, so that it had already become archaic in some languages before it reached others. It does not seem to have become really widespread outside enthusiasts' circles anywhere.

Ge [ro:tsta] M, pl. Ø, 1950s (1 tech) Du [=E] C, 1970s (1 tech) Nw [=E] M, pl. -e, 1950s (1 tech) Ic [=E] M, pl. -ar, end20c (0 tech) Fr [rodstɛr] M, 1930s (1 arch) Sp [rodster/roster] M, pl. -s, 1920s (1 tech) It [rodster] M, pl. Ø, end20c (1 tech) Rm [rodster] N, 1970s (1 tech) Rs rodster M, pl. -y, end20c (1 tech) Po [-er] M, end20c (1 tech) Cr rodster M, pl. -i, mid20c (1 tech) Hu [ro:dster] pl. -ek, 20c (1 tech>2) Gr roudster N, mid20c (1 tech)

roastbeef* n. 1 'a piece of meat', 2 'the English'
This word is one of the classic eighteenth-century loans (cf. ↑beefsteak, rumpsteak) which spread via French (and German) to most European languages; increased competence in English has since brought the word closer to English in spelling and pronunciation. The use as a nickname (2) is significantly restricted to French whence it was borrowed into Romanian.

Ge [rostbeef/-i-] N, pl. -s, via Fr?, end18c, 1(2) Du [ro:stbi:f] C [U] 17c (2) < rosbief Nw roastbiff [roustbif/ro:st] M, pl. -er, 19c, 1(2) Ic [rou(:)stbi:f] N [U] mid20c, 1(2) Fr rosbif/roastbeef [rozbif] M, 18c, 1(3) 2(1 sla, arch) Sp <=E>/rosbif [rosbif] M, mid19c, via Fr, 1(2) It roast beef/rosbif/rosbiffe [rozbif/rostbif] M [U] beg19c, 1(3) Rm rosbif [rosbif] N, 19c, via Fr Rs rostbif M, pl. -y, mid19c, 1(1 tech/2) Po rostbef [rostbef] M, mid19c, via Ge, 1(1 arch) Cr rostbif M [U] 19c, 1(3) Bg rostbif M [U]/pl. -al-i, end19c, via Fr, 1(3 tech) Hu [ro:sbi:f] [U] 19c, 1(2) Gr rosbif N, via Fr, 1(2)

Robinson* n. 1 'a ship-wrecked person', 2 'a secluded person'
Defoe's Robinson Crusoe (1719) became the prototype of the shipwrecked hermit for Western Europe immediately after the novel was published, and his name thereby became generic, as did ↑robinsonade (1) (possibly a German coinage).

Ge [ro:binzon] M, pl. -s, 18c (3) Nw (0) Fr (0) Sp [robinson] M, pl. -es, end19c (Ø/1 lit) → robinsonismo Rm Robinson [robinson] M, beg20c (3) Rs robinzon M, pl. -y, 19c, 1 (Ø) 2(3) Po [-on] M, beg20c (3) Cr Robinzon M, pl. -i, 19c (3) → -ada F; -ski adj. Bg Robinzon M, end19c, 1(Ø) 2(3) Gr Rovinsonas M, 1(3) 2(3 rare)

robinsonade*1 n. 'a story similar to the story of Robinson Crusoe'

Ge Robinsonade F, pl. -n, 18c (3) Du [robinsonədə] 19c (3) Nw [robinsona:de] M, pl. -r, 19c (3 rare) Fr robinsonnade F, 1930s

(3 tech) Rm robinsonadă [robinsonadə] F, mid20c, via Fr/Ge (3) Rs robinzonada F, pl. -y, 19c (3) Po robinsonada [robinsonada] F, beg20c (2) Cr robinzonada F, pl. -e, 19c (3) Bg robinzonada F, pl. -di, 20c (1 tech, lit) Hu robinzonád [robinzona:d] 19c (3)

robinsonade*2 n. 'a spectacular dive by a goalkeeper' (after John Robinson, 1878–1949)

Ge [robinzona:də] F, pl. -n, 1930s (3 tech, obs) Rm robinsonadă [robinsonadə] F, beg20c (1 arch) Po robinsonada [robinsonada] F, beg20c (1 tech) → robinsonować Hu robinzonád [robinzona:d] 1930s (3 tech)

rock v. 5 'dance to or play rock music'
Ge rocken 1950s (3 obs) Du rocken 1950s (3 obs) Nw rocke [rokə] 1950s (3) → rocker Ic rokka [rohka] 1950s (3 coll) → rokkari M Sp - < rockanrolear Fi rokata 1950s (3) Hu rockizik [rokizik] 1960s/70s (3 obs)

rock n./cp1 3a 'rock and roll', 3b 'any of a variety of types of modern popular music with a rocking or swinging beat, derived from rock and roll'
Ge [=E] M [U] 1960s, 3b(2) → rocken v.; rockig adj. Du [=E] C [U] 1960s, 3b(2) → -en v. Nw [=E] M [U] 1960s, 3a,b(2) → rokka v.; rocka adj.; rockete adj. Ic rokk [rohk] N [U] 1950s(3) → rokka v.; rokkari M Fr [rok] M [U] adj., 1950s, 3b(2) Sp [rok] M [U] adj., uninfl., 1970s (2) → rockero; roquero It [rok] M [U] 1960s, 3b(3) Rm [=E] N [U] mid20c, 3b(2) Rs rok M [U] end20c (2) → -ovyĭ adj. Po M [U] end20c, 3b(2) → -owy adj. Cr rok M [U] mid20c, 3b(2) Bg rok n./cp1, M [U]/pl. -a, mid20c (2) → -adzhiya M; -adzhiĭski adj. Fi [=E]/ rokki 1960s, 3b(2) Hu [=E] [U] 1950s, 3b(3) Al rok M [U] 1980s, 3b(1 you) Gr rok F/N [U] mid20c (2)

rockabilly n. 'a kind of popular music combining rock and roll and hill-billy'
Ge [=E] M [U] 1970s (1 tech, rare) Du [=E] C [U] 1970s (1 tech, coll, rare) Nw [=E] M [U] 1980s (1 tech) Ic [=E] N [U] 1960 (1 arch) Fr [rokabili] M, 1970s (1 tech) Sp [rokabili] M [U] 1980s (1 tech, you) It [=E] M [U] 1960s (1 rare) Rm [=E] N [U] end20c (1 tech) Rs rokabilli N, uninfl. [U] end20c (1 tech) Po [=E] N [U] end20c (1 tech) Cr [=E] M [U] end20c (1 tech) Gr <=E>/rokabili F [U] 1970s (1 tech) → rokabilas M, rokabili N

rock and roll n. 1 'a type of popular dance music originating in the 1950s, characterized by a heavy beat and simple melodies, often with a blues element', +2 'a dance'
Ge [rokentrol] M [U] 1950s (2) Du rock en roll/rock 'n roll [=E] C [U] 1950s (2) Nw [rokenrol] M [U] 1950s (2) Ic <=E>/rokk og ról [=E/rohk o: rou:l] N [U] 1950s (1 coll, arch/3 arch) Fr [rokənrol] M, 1950s (1) Sp [rokanrol] M [U] 1950s (1 sla, you) It [roken(d) rol] M [U] 1960s (3) Rm [rokənrol] N [U] mid20c (2) Rs rok-n-roll M [U] mid20c (2) Po [rokentrol] M [U] mid20c (2) Cr rokenrol M [U] mid20c (2) Bg roken(d)rol M [U]/pl. -al-i, 1950s (2) Fi [=E] 1950s (Ø>2) Hu [=E] [U] 1950s,

1,+2(3)　**Al** *rokenrol* M [U] 20c (1 you)　**Gr** *rok ed r̲o̲l* N [U] mid20c (2)

rocker　*n.* 4a 'a devotee of rock music, characteristically associated with leather clothing and motorcycles', 4b 'a rock musician', +8 'a rock and roll record, rock and roll music'

Ge [r̲o̲ka] M, pl. Ø, 1960s, 4a(2 you, obs)　**Du** ["r̲ɔ̲kər] C, 1960s, 4a(2) > *nozem*　**Nw** ["r̲ɔ̲ker] M, pl. -*e*, 1950s, 4a(2) +8(1 rare)　**Ic** *rokkari* [r̲ɔ̲hkarı] M, pl. -*ar*, 1970s, 4b(3); end20c, via Da, 4a(Ø)　**Fr** *rockeur/euse/rocker* [r̲ɔkœr] M, 1970s, 4a(1)　**Sp** [r̲o̲ker] M, pl. -*s*, 1970s, 4a(1 you)　**It** [r̲ɔ̲ker] M, pl. Ø, 1960s, 4a(2) = *rockettaro/rocchettaro*　**Rm** [=E] M, end20c, 4a(2 you) → -*iță* F　**Rs** *r̲o̲ker* M, pl. -*y*, end20c, 4a(1 you)　**Po** [-er] M, end20c, 4a(1 you)　**Cr** *r̲o̲ker* M, pl. -*i*, end20c, 4a(1)　**Bg** *r̲o̲ker* M, pl. -*i*, end20c, 4a(2) → -*ski* adj.　**Fi** *rokkari* 1960s (2)　**Hu** [r̲o̲kker] pl. -*ek*, 1950/60s, 4a(3 obs)　**Gr** *rok̲a̲s* M, 4a(3); *r̲o̲ker* M, end20c, 4a(1 rare)

rocking chair　*n.* 'a chair mounted on rockers or springs for gently rocking in'

Ge - < trsl *Schaukelstuhl*　**Du** - < *schommelstoel*　**Nw** (0) < *gyngestol*　**Fr** *rocking-chair* [r̲ɔkiŋ(t)ʃɛr] M, mid19c(1) > *chaise/fauteuil à bascule*　**Sp** - < *mecedora*　**It** - < *sedia a dondolo*　**Bg** - < trsl *lyuleesht se stol*

rock-wool　*n.* 'inorganic material made into matted fibre, esp. for insulation or soundproofing'

Du - < trsl *steenwol*　**Nw** [=E] M [U] mid20c (1 tech) < trsl *steinull*　**Ic** - < *steinull*

roger　*interj.* 1 'your message has been received and understood' (in radio communications)

Ge [=E]/[-g-] 20c (1 tech)　**Du** [=E] 20c (1 tech)　**Sp** [r̲o̲je] 20c (1 tech)　**Cr** *r̲o̲džer* 20c (1 tech)　**Bg** *r̲o̲dzhŭr* mid20c (1 tech)

roll　*n.* 4 'a complete revolution of an aircraft about its longitudinal axis'

Nw [=E] M, pl. -*er*, 1930s (2) → *rolle* v.

rollback　*n.* +2 'revisionist policies, a counter offensive' (milit., polit.)

Ge [=E] N, pl. -*s*, 1950s (1 tech, obs)　**Fr** [r̲ɔlbak] M, 1970s (0 obs)

roll bar　*n.* 'an overhead metal bar strengthening the frame of a vehicle (esp. in racing)'

Du [=E] C, pl. -*s*, 1980s (1 tech)　**It** [=E/r̲ɔl bar] M, pl. Ø, 1980s (1 tech)　**Rm** [=E] N, 1990s (1 tech)

Rollerblade　*n.* 'each of a pair of boots fitted with small wheels, one behind the other, for roller skating in a manner resembling ice-skating'

Ge [=E/r̲o̲lable:t] M, pl. -*s*, 1990s (1 tech/mod) < *Inline Skates*　**Du** - < *skeelers*　**Nw** [=E] pl. -*s*, 1990s (1 mod) > *in-line-skøyter*　**Ic** - < *linuskautar*　**It** [=E] M, pl., end20c (1 mod)　**Rm** *roller/role* [r̲o̲ler/r̲o̲le] N/F, pl., 1990s (1 tech, mod)　**Bg** - < *bleĭder* M

roller skate　*n.* 'each of a pair of metal frames with small wheels, fitted to shoes for gliding across a hard surface'

Ge [r̲o̲laske:t] M, pl. -*s*, 1980s (1 you/obs) → -*ing* N; -*er* M　**Du** [=E] C, 1980s (1 you) < *rolschaats*　**Nw** (0) < *rulleskøyte*　**Ic** *rúlluskautar* [rul:y-] M, pl.,

mid20c, via Da (2 you, arch) < rend *hjólaskautar*　**Fr** *roller* [r̲ɔlœr] M, 1980s (1 you)　**It** - < *pattini a rotelle*　**Rm** - < *role, (patine cu) rotile*　**Rs** - < trsl *rolikovye kon'ki*　**Po** - < *łyżwo-rolki*　**Bg** *r̲o̲ler* M, pl. -*al-i*, end20c (1 tech, mod/2you) < trsl *rolkovi kŭnki*　**Hu** - < trsl *görkorcsolya*　**Al** - < *patine me rrota*　**Gr** <=E>/*ro̲ler(ske̲it)* N, usu. pl. *rollers*, 1980s (1 you)

rolley*　*n.* 'a hair curler'
Gr *r̲o̲lei* N, beg20c (2)

roll-on　*n./cp¹* 1 'a light elastic corset', +2 'a deodorant stick, etc.'

Ge [ro:l̲o̲n] cp¹, 1960s, +2(1 tech, rare)　**Du** [=E] C, 1980s, +2(1 tech, jour, rare) = *roller*　**Nw** [=E] M, pl. -*er*, 1940s, 1(1 arch); 1960s, +2(2)　**Ic** [r̲ɔl:on] N, pl. Ø, mid20c, +2(1 coll)　**Sp** [rol̲o̲n] M, end20c, +2(1 tech)　**Rm** +2(0)　**Rs** (0)　**Po** [rolon] M, end20c, +2 (1 coll)　**Bg** - < +2: creat *rolkov dezodorant*　**Fi** [=E] 1960s, +2(2)　**Hu** [=E] cp¹, 1970s, +2(1 tech, writ, jour)　**Gr** <=E> [=E] N, end20c, +2(1 writ)

roll-on roll-off　*cp¹* 'in which vehicles are driven directly on at the start of a voyage and off at the end of it' (of a ferry)

Ge [=E] 1960s (1 tech) = ↑*Roro*　**Du** -*boot*, -*ship*, *systeem* cp¹ (1 tech+5) = *roroboot*, *rij-op-rij-af-schip*, *rij-op-rij-af-systeem*　**Nw** [=E] 1960s (1 tech) = *roro*　**Fr** [r̲ɔlɔnr̲ɔlɔf] M, 1980s (1 tech, ban) < *roulier; roulage*　**Sp** <=E>/*roll-on* 20c (1 tech)　**It** [rol on rol of] cp², 1970s (1 tech) < ↑*ro-ró*　**Po** (o)　**Cr** [=E] *brod* M, end20c (1 tech)　**Bg** *r̲o̲l- on- r̲o̲l-of* end20c (1 tech) = ↑*Ro-Ro*　**Fi** 1960s (1 rare)　**Hu** *ro-ro* [r̲o̲:ro:] 20c (1 tech)

ROM　see ↑*CD-Rom*

roof garden　*n.* 'a garden on the flat roof of a building'

It [=E] M, pl. Ø, 1910s (1 tech); *roof* [ru:f] M, pl. Ø, 1980s (1 tech)　**Hu** - < rend *tetőterasz*　**Gr** *ruf garden* N, beg20c (2)

rooming-in*　*n./cp¹* 'a mother's stay with a hospitalized or newborn child'

Ge [=E] N [U] 1980s (1 mod)　**Du** [=E] C [U] 1980s (1 tech)　**Nw** [=E] cp¹, 1970s (1 rare)　**Po** *rooming* [-nk] M [U] end20c (1 tech)

room service　*n.* 'service whereby food or drink is taken to a guest's room' (in a hotel etc.)

Du (Ø)　**Nw** <=E>/*romservice* [=E/Nw+=E] M [U] end20c (1)　**Ic** - < *herbergisþjónusta*　**It** - < *servizio in camera*　**Rm** [=E] N [U] end20c (1 tech)　**Rs** (o)　**Cr** *rumserviz* (o)　**Bg** *r̲u̲msŭrvis* M [U] 1990s (1 tech, mod)　**Hu** [=E] [U] end20c (Ø>1 tech) < *szobaszolgálat, szobaszerviz*

roots　*n.* (usu. *cp*) 1 'social, ethnic, or cultural origins, esp. as the reasons for one's longstanding emotional attachment to a place, community, etc.' +2 'a style of

folk music'   **Du** [=E] C [U] 1980s, 1(2)   **Nw** cp¹ [=E]
1980s,+2 (tech, mod)   **Sp** [ruts] M [U] end20c, +2(1
tech, you, rare)

rope   *n*. 1a 'a stout cord made by twisting together
strands of hemp, sisal, flax, etc. or similar material',
+5 'a measure of 6.096m'
   Nw 1a(0)   **Ic** *rópur* [rou:pʏr] M, pl. *-ar*, mid20c,
1a(2ₙₐᵤₜ)   **Rs** *rop* M, pl. *-y*, +5(1 tech)   **Po** *rop*
[rop] M, end20c, 1a(1 tech)

ro-ro   *cp¹/adj., abbrev.* 'roll-on roll-off'
   Ge [roro:] 1970s (1 tech)   **Du** [roro:] 1960s (1 tech,
rare)   **Nw** [ru̱:ru] 1970s (1 tech)   **Fr** [rɔro] M, 1970s
(1 tech, ban) < *roulier, roulage*   **Sp** 20c (1 tech)   **It**
ro-ró [rɔrɔ̱] cp², 1970s (1 tech)   **Cr** *ro-ro* (brod), M,
mid20c (1 tech)   **Bg** *ro̱-ro̱* cp¹, adj., uninfl., end20c (1
tech)   **Fi** [ro:ro:] 1970s (2)   **Hu** *ro-ro* [ro̱:ro:] end20c
(1 tech)

rotaprint*   *n.* (orig.™) 'a type of printing machine'
   Ge [ro̱:taprint] F [U] mid20c (3 tech)   **Rm** [rotaprint]
N, mid20c (1 tech)   **Rs** *rotaprint* M, pl. *-y*, end20c (1
tech)   **Po** [rota-] M [U] mid20c (1 tech)   **Hu** [=E] pl.
-ek, mid20c (1 tech)

rotary   *n./cp¹* 1 'a rotary switchboard/machine', 3
'(*Rotary (International)*) a worldwide charitable society of businessmen and professional men (founded
in Chicago in 1905)'
   Ge *Rotary(Club)* [ro:ta̱:ri klup] M, pl. *-s*, 1970s, 3(2
techₙₐₘₑ) → *Rotarier* M   **Du** *Rotary* [=E] C, 1940s,
3(2)   **Nw** *Rotary- klubb* [ro̱tariklu̱b] M, pl. *-er*, 20c,
3(2) → *rotarianer* M   **Ic** *rótarý* [rou:tariʰ] N/cp¹,
1930s, 3(2)   **Fr** 1(1 tech, arch); [rɔtaʀi] M, end20c,
3(1) → *rotarien* M   **Sp** [ro̱tariklub/klab] 20c, 3(1
tech) = *Club Rotario*   **It** [ro̱tari klab/klɛb] M, pl. Ø,
1920s, 3(3ₙₐₘₑ) → *rotariano*   **Rm** 3 [ro̱tari] N [U]
mid20c, 1(1 tech); *(Clubul) Rotary* 1990s, 3(1 rare)
   Po [roteri-klup] M [U] end20c, 3(1 tech)   **Cr** *Rotari-*
klub M [U] mid20c, 3(1 tech)   **Bg** *Ro̱tari klu̱b* M [U]
1990s, 3(1+3)   **Fi** [=E] cp¹, mid20c, 3(2)   **Hu** *Rotary*
Club [ro̱:ta:ri klub] [U] end20c, 3(1)   **Al** *Rotari Klub*
M [U] 1990s, 3(3)   **Gr** *Rotarianos O̱milos* M, end20c,
3(3+5) → *Rotarianos* M/*Rotariani* F

rough   *adj.* 4a 'not mild or gentle' (of a person or
behaviour), 7 'harsh, insensitive, unpleasant', +8
'cool, modern, fashionable in an informal, unpreten-
tious, rugged sort of way' (of clothes, also used to
characterize persons), 11a 'preliminary'
   Nw *røff* [røf] beg20c, 4a,7,+8(3) → *røffhet* M   **Ic**
röff [ræf:] end20c, 4a,7(1 coll) → *röffaður* adj.   **Fr**
[ʀæf] 1980s, 11a(1 tech, ban) > *crayonné, esquesse* →
roughman

rough   *n.* 4 'rough ground of the fairway between tee
and green' (golf)
   Du [=E] C [U] 1980s (1 tech)   **Nw** [=E] M [U] 1980s
(1 tech)   **Sp** [=E] M, 1980s (1 tech)   **It** [=E] M, pl. Ø,
1930s (1 tech)

roughly   *adv.* 2 'approximately'
   Nw <=E>/*røflig* [=E/rø̱fli] 1930s (1)

roughneck   *n.* 2 'a worker on an oil rig'
   Nw [=E] M, pl. *-er*, 1970s (1 obs)

round   *n.* 2c 'a recurring succession or series of meetings for discussion etc.', 6b 'one stage in a competition
(e.g. boxing)', +6c 'such a stage in chess'
   Ge *Runde* 2c,6b(4)   **Du** *ronde* 2c,6b(4)   **Nw** *runde*
2c,6b(4)   **Fr** [rawnd/ʀund] M/cp², beg19c, 2c(1); 19c,
6b(2) < *reprise*   **Sp** [ra̱und] M, pl. *-s*, 1980s, 2c (1
tech); 1920s, 6b(2) < 2c: *ronda* < 6b *casalto*   **It** [=E]
M, pl. Ø, 19c, 2c(1 tech) 6b(2 tech) < 6b: *ripresa*   **Rm**
rundă/rund [ru̱ndə/rund] F/N, mid20c, via Ge,
6b,+6c(3); 1980s, 2c(3)   **Rs** *ra̱und* M, pl. *-y*, mid20c,
2c,6b(3)   **Po** *runda* [runda] F, mid20c, 2c,6b,+6c(3)
   Cr *ru̱nda* F, pl. *-e*, beg20c, 6b(3)   **Bg** *rund* M, pl. *-a*,
20c, 6b(5Ge); < 2c: mean *krúg*   **Hu** [=E] pl. Ø, 19c,
6b(1 tech, arch) < *menet*   **Al** *rund* M, pl. *-e*, mid20c
(3)   **Gr** - < *ghyros*

round table   *n.* 2 'an assembly for discussion, esp. at
a conference'
   Ge (0) < trsl *runder Tisch*   **Du** - < trsl *ronde ta-*
fel   **Nw** (0) < trsl *rundebord(s-)*   **Ic** - < trsl *hring-*
borð(-s)   **Fr** - < trsl *table-ronde*   **Sp** - < trsl *mesa*
redonda   **It** - < trsl *tavola rotonda*   **Rm** - < trsl *masă*
rotundă   **Rs** (0) < trsl *kruglyĭstol*   **Po** - < trsl *okrągly*
stół   **Cr** (0) < trsl *okrugli stol*   **Bg** - < trsl *krúgla*
masa   **Fi** (0) < trsl *pyöreä pöytä*   **Hu** - < trsl *kerek-*
asztal   **Al** - < *tryezë e rrumbullaktë*   **Gr** - < trsl
strogyli trapeza

rout   *n.* 4 'a large evening party or reception'
    The survival of this early loanword is significant –
now obsolete or used facetiously, or retained in more
marginal languages, similar to the 'bicycle' sense of
the next item.
   Ge [=E?] M, pl. *-s*, 1870s (0
arch)   **Du** *raout* [=E] C, beg20c,
via Fr (1 arch)   **Nw** (0 arch)   **Fr**
raout [raut] M, beg19c (1 arch/
fac)   **Rs** *ra̱ut* M, pl. *-y*, mid19c
(2 arch)   **Po** *raut* M, mid19c
(3)   **Cr** *raut* M, beg20c (3)   **Bg**
raut M, pl. *-al-i*, end19c (1 arch)   **Hu** [=E/rut] pl. Ø,
19c (0 arch)

rover   *n.* 5 'a senior scout', +6 'a bicycle'
   Ge [ro̱:va] M, pl. Ø/-*s*, 19c, 5(Ø/3
tech) +6(0 arch)   **Nw** [=E] M,
pl. *-e*, 20c, 5(1 tech)   **Sp** [ro̱ber]
M, pl. *-s*, 20c, 5(1 tech, obs) <
ruta   **It** [ro̱ver] M, pl. Ø, 1950s,
5(1)   **Rs** *ro̱ver* [rover] M, pl. *-y*,
beg20c, +6(1 arch)   **Po** *rower*
M, beg20c, +6(3) → *-ek* M; -*owy* adj.   **Cr** *rover* 20c
(1)   **Bg** 5(0)

rowdy   *n.* 'a rowdy person'
    It comes as a surprise that this word is as restricted as
it is in contrast to the much more
widespread ↑ *hooligan* (which is,
however, much less frequent in
German).
   Ge [=E] M, pl. *-ies*, mid19c (3) →
-tum N   **Du** [=E] C, pl. *-ies*,
1970s (2 rare)

royalty *n.* 3 'a sum paid (to an author, patentee, etc.)', 4b 'a payment made by a producer of minerals, oil, or natural gas to the owner of the site or of the mineral rights over it'

Du [=E] C, pl. -'s, beg20c, 3(1 tech) **Nw** [rɔialti] M, pl. -ies, beg20c, 3(2) 4b(1 tech) **Fr** *royalties* [rwajalti] F, pl., 20c, 3(1 tech/ban) > *redevance* **Sp** [rojalti] M, pl. -s/ies, end19c (2 tech) **It** [rɔialti] F, pl. -ies, 1950s (1 tech) < 3: *diritti (d'autore)* **Rm** *roialitate* [rojalitate] F, end20c, 4b(3 tech, rare) < *redeventă* **Fi** [=E] 19c, 3(2)

rubber[1] (1) *n.* 1 'a tough elastic polymeric substance', 3 'a condom'

Ge [=E] M [U] beg20c, 1(o>1 tech) **Du** [rvbər] M/N, 20c, 1(3) 3(3 coll) **Nw** - < *gummi* **Hu** [rabber] [U] beg20c, 1(1 arch) < *gumi*

rubber[2] (2) *n.* 1 'a match of three or five successive games between the same sides or persons at whist, bridge, cricket, tennis, etc.'

Ge *Rubber/Robber* M, pl. Ø, 19c (1 obs) **Du** *robber* (F) **Nw** *robber* [rɔber] M, pl. -e, 19c (1 tech) **Ic** *rúberta* [ru:pertͅa] F, pl. -ur, 20c, via Da (2 tech) **Fr** *rob/robre* [rɔbr(ə)] M, 19c (3 tech) **It** [rΛbber/raͅbber] M, pl. Ø, 1900s (1 tech) **Rm** *rober* [rober] N, mid20c (1 tech) **Rs** *rober* M [U] mid19c, via Fr (2) **Po** *rober* M, mid19c, via Fr (2) → -*ek* M **Bg** *rober* M, pl. -al-i, beg20c, via Fr (3 tech) **Fi** *robbertti* 19c, via Sw (3 tech) **Hu** *robber* [robber] M, pl. Ø, end19/beg20c, via Ge (1 tech)

rugby *n.* 'a team game played with an oval ball that may be kicked, carried, and passed from hand to hand'

Ge [raͅgbi] N [U] beg20c (O>2) **Du** [rvɣbi] [=E] N [U] beg20c (2) **Nw** [=E] M [U] beg20c (Ø/1 tech) **Ic** [rukpi] N [U] beg20c, via Da (Ø) **Fr** [rygbi] M [U] beg20c (3) → *rugbyman* M **Sp** [rugbi] M, beg20c (2) → *rugbistico* adj. **It** [ragbi/regbi] M [U] 1920s (3) → *rugbista* **Rm** <=E>/*rugbi* [rugbi/rujbi/=E] N [U] 1930s, via Fr? (2>3) → *rugbist* M; *rugbistic* adj. **Rs** *regbi* N, uninfl., beg20c (1 tech) → *regbist* M **Po** N, uninfl., beg20c (1 mod) **Cr** *ragbi* M [U] mid20c (1 tech) **Bg** *rũgbi* N [U] mid20c (Ø/2 tech) → -*ist* M **Fi** [=E] beg20c (Ø) **Hu** *rögbi* [raͅgbi] [U] beg20c (2) → -*z* v. **Al** *regbi* N [U] end20c (3) **Gr** *ragbi* N [U] mid20c (2/Ø)

rum *n.* 1 'a spirit distilled from sugar cane residues or molasses'

Ge [rum] M [U] beg17c (3) **Du** [rvm] C [U] 18c (3) **Nw** *rom* [rum] M [U] mid19c (3) **Ic** *romm* [rɔm:] N [U] end18c, via Da (3) **Fr** *rhum* [rɔm] M [U] 17c (3) **Sp** *ron* M, 18c (3) **It** [rum] M [U] 18c (3) **Rm** *rom* [rom] N, end18c, via Fr (3); *rum* [rum] via Ge (3 reg) **Rs** *rom* M [U] 18/19c (2) → -*ovyi* adj. **Po** [rum] M [U] 18/19c (3) → -*owy* adj. **Cr** *rum* M [U] 19c (3) **Bg** *rom* M [U]/pl. -a, mid19c, via Rs (3) → -*ov* adj. **Fi** *rommi* 18c(3) **Hu** [rum] [U] before 19c (3) → -*os* adj. **Al** *rum* M [U] end19c (3) **Gr** *rumi* N, 19c (3)

Rumford-* *n./cp*[1] 'soup made from cheap ingredients'

Ge *Rumford-Suppe* [rumfort] F, pl. -n, 19c (3 obs) **Po** *zupa rumfordzka* F, beg20c (2)

rummy *n.* 'a card game played with two packs in which the players try to form sets'

The card game was invented c. 1900 in America (etymology uncertain); it was very popular until recently in Germany, but always under its French name *Rommé*.

Ge *Rummy* [=E?] N [U] 1900s (1 reg, arch); *Rommé* [rome:] N [U] 1900s, via Fr (3) **Nw** [=E] M [U] 20c (1 tech) **Ic** *rommí* [rɔm:i] N [U] 20c, via Da (2) **Fr** *rami* [rami] M, beg20c (3) **Sp** [=E] M [U] 20c (1 tech) **Rm** [rœmi] N [U] mid20c (2) **Cr** *remi* M [U] 20c (3) **Hu** *römi* [raͅmi] 1920s, via Ge (3) **Gr** *rami* N [U] beg20c (1 obs)

rump steak *n.* 1 'a cut of beef from the rump'

This early loan was largely distributed via French and German, leaving gaps mainly in the South of Europe.

Ge [rumste:k] N, pl. -s, end19c (2) > trsl *Rump(f)stück* **Du** - < *lendebiefstuk* **Nw** [=E] M, pl. -er/-s, 20c (1 obs) **Ic** *rump-/rúmpsteik* [rvmp-/rumpstei:k] F, pl. -ur, end20c (2) **Fr** *romsteck/rumsteck* [ʀɔmstɛk] M, end19c (2) **Sp** (0) **Rm** *ramstec* [ramstek] N, 20c, via Fr? (3 obs) **Rs** *romshteks* M, pl. -y, beg20c, via Ge (3) **Po** *rumsztyk* [rumʃtik] M, beg20c, via Ge (3) → -*czek* M **Cr** *ramstek* M, pl. -i, end19c (3) **Bg** *ramstek* M, pl. -a, beg20c, via Fr (3 tech) **Hu** *ramsztek* [ramstek] [U] end19/beg20c (3 arch) < *hátszin* **Al** *ramstek* M, pl. -ë, mid20c (3)

run *v.* 19 'direct or manage (a business, etc.)'

Du *runnen* [rvnən] 1960s (3) **Nw** (0)

run *n.* 8a 'a high general demand (for a commodity, currency, etc.)'

This word, taken over for occasions of people storming a bank after a financial crash, remained more or less confined to the North-west; its use is receding and is largely obsolescent.

Ge [ran] M, pl. -s, end19c/1970s (1 tech, coll) **Du** [rvn] C [U] beg20c (1 tech) **Nw** [røn] N, beg20c (1 obs) **It** [=E] M, pl. Ø, 1900s (1 obs) **Po** [run] M, beg20c (3) **Hu** [ran/=E] [U] end19/beg20c, via Ge (1 tech, arch)

runner *n.* 5 'a messenger, a scout'

Nw [=E] M, pl. -e, 1930s (1 obs)

runner-up *n.* 'the competitor or team taking second place in a contest'

Du [=E] C, 1970s (1 jour) **Nw** [=E] M [U] 1950s (1 tech)

runway *n.* 1 'a specially prepared surface along which aircraft take off and land'
Ge (o) < *Start-, Landebahn* **Nw** [=E] M, pl. *-er*, mid20c (1 tech) **Fr** [rœnwe] F (1 tech) **Po** M, mid20c (1 tech)

rush *v.* 4/5 'perform or deal with hurriedly, force to act hastily', 6 'attack or capture by sudden assault' (team sports)
Nw *rushe* ["rø∫e] 1970s, 4/5(1 coll) 6(1 tech)

rush *n.* 1a 'an act of rushing; a violent advance or attack', 2 'a period of great activity', 7a 'a combined dash by one or several players with the ball' (footb.), +8 'a sudden influx', +9 'a sprint'
Ge [=E] M, pl. *-(e)s*, end19c, 7a,+9(1 tech, rare) **Du** [=E] C, end19c, +8(2); 1980s, 7a(1 tech); end19c, +9(1 tech); 1990s, 2(1 tech) **Nw** [rø∫] N, pl. Ø, 1930s, 2(2) 7a(1 tech) **Fr** [rœ∫] M, 19c, +8(1 obs); 19c, +9(1

tech); 1960s, 7a(1 tech, ban) > *épreuve de tournage* **It** [ra∫] M, pl. Ø, end19c, 1a,7a,+9(1>2 tech) **Rm** [=E] 1970s, +9(1 tech_HORSE, rare) **Hu** *rössz* [rəs] [U] end19/beg20c, 2,7a(1 tech, arch) → *-öl* v.

rush hour *n.* 'the time(s) each day when traffic is at its heaviest'
Ge [=E] F, pl. *-s*, 1960s (1 coll) **Nw** *rushtid* [rø∫-] 1930s (2+5) = *rush* **Gr** (o)

rye *n.* 2 'whisky distilled from fermented rye'
Fr <=E> [raj] M, beg20c (1 tech) **Gr** (1 writ)

ryegrass *n.* 'any forage or lawn grass of the genus Lolium' [obs. ↑*ray-grass*]
Ge *Raigras/Raygras* N [U] 19c (1 tech) **Fr** *ray-grass* [rɛgras] M, 18c (1 tech) **Rm** *raigras* [rajgras] N [U] beg20c (1 tech) **Rs** *raigras* [-as] M [U] beg20c (1 tech) **Po** *rajgras* M, beg20c (1 tech) **Cr** (o) **Bg** *raigras* M [U] mid20c (2 tech)

S

S *abbrev.* +3a 'a size, in shirts etc.' (cf. ↑*small*)

Ge [es] 1960s (3)　**Du** 1980s (2)　**Nw** [=E] 1960s (3) **Ic** *S* [smɔ:l] mid20c (0)　**Fr** (0)　**Sp** (0)　**It** [ɛsse] mid20c (3)　**Rm** [es] end20c (1 mod)　**Rs** (0)　**Po** *eska* [eska] F, end20c (2)　**Cr** *es* N, end20c (3)　**Bg** <=E> [=E] end20c (1>2)　**Fi** [ɛs:ɛ/smɔ:l] 1970s (2)　**Hu** [eʃ] 1970s (3) → *-es* adj.　**Gr** [es] end20c (2)

sabbatical *n.* 2 'leave granted at intervals to a university teacher for study or travel'

Ge [=E] N, pl. *-s*, 1980s (1 tech, mod)　**Du** [=E] C, 1980s (1 tech)　**Nw** (0) < *forskningsfri*　**Fr** - < trsl *année sabbatique, congé sabbatique*　**Sp** - < trsl *(año) sabático*　**It** - < trsl *anno sa(b)batico, congedo*　**Rm** - < rend *an sabatic*　**Po** - < *urlop naukowy*　**Fi** *sabatti-vuosi/-vapaa* end20c (∅>3)

saddleback *n.* 3 'a black pig with a white stripe across the back'

Nw [=E] M, pl. *-er*, 20c (1 tech)　**Bg** *sedŭlbek* M [U]/ pl. *-a*, mid20c (1 tech)

safe *adj.* 1a 'free from danger or injury', 2 'affording security or not involving danger or risk'

Du [=E] 1910s (1 coll)　**Nw** [=E] 1960s (1 coll) → *safe* v.; *(kjøre) safe* adv.　**Ic** [sei:f] uninfl., 1970s, 2(1 sla)

safe *n.* 1 'a strong lockable cabinet etc. for valuables'

This word, adopted from the late nineteenth century on, is widespread and well known; native equivalents have normally proved too clumsy or too vague.

Ge [se:f] M/N, pl. *-s*, end19c (2)　**Du** [=E] C, beg20c (2) < *kluis*　**Nw** <=E>/*seif* [=E] M, pl. *-(e)r*, beg20c (2)　**Rm** *seif* [sejf/seif] N, end19c (3); *sef/safe/ safeu* [sef/safe/safew] (1 rare, obs)　**Rs** *seif* M, pl. *-y*, mid20c

(2)　**Po** *sejf* M, mid20c (3)　**Cr** *sef* M, pl. *-ovi*, mid20c (3)　**Bg** *seif* M, pl. *-al/-ove*, mid20c (2) < *kasa*　**Fi** [=E] beg20c (1 obs) < *kassakaappi*　**Hu** *széf* [se:f] pl. *-ek*, beg20c (3)　**Gr** *seif* N, mid20c (2)

safe sex *n.* 'sexual activity in which precautions are taken to reduce the risk of spreading sexually transmitted diseases, esp. Aids'

The concept arose as a reaction to Aids infections. The origin of the (un-English) *-r* is debatable: it could be a comparative form, or (in German) an inflexion.

Ge *safer sex* [se:fa seks] M [U] 1980s (2)　**Du** [=E] C, 1980s (2)　**Nw** (0) < *sikker sex*　**Ic** [=E] N, 1980s (0) <

trsl *öruggt kynlíf*　**Fr** *safe(r) sex* [sef seks] M, 1980s (1) > *SSR* < *sexe sans risque*　**Sp** - < trsl *sexo seguro*　**It** - < trsl *sesso sicuro*　**Rs** - < trsl *bezopasnyĭ seks*　**Po** - < trsl *bezpieczny seks*　**Cr** *safer seks* 1980s (1) < trsl *bezopasan seks*　**Bg** - < trsl *bezopasen seks*　**Fi** [=E] 1980s (2) = trsl *turvaseksi*　**Hu** - < rend *biztonságos szex*

safety first *phr.* (popular slogan)

Ge [=E] 1970s (1 coll)　**Du** [=E] 1980s (1)　**Nw** (0)

sales director *n.* 'the director of the section of a firm which is concerned with selling as opposed to manufacturing etc.'

Ge (0)　**Du** [=E] M, 1980s (1 tech)　**Nw** [=E] M, pl. *-s*, 1980s (1 tech)　**It** [seilz di-/dairektor] M/F, pl. ∅, 1960s (1 tech) < rend *direttore commerciale*　**Rm** [=E] 1990s (0)　**Po** (0)　**Gr** (0)

salesman *n.* 'a person employed to sell goods'

Du <=E> 20c (1 writ)　**Ic** - < trsl *sölumaður*　**It** [=E] M, pl. ∅/-*men*, 1960s (1 tech) < rend *agente di vendita*　**Rm** [=E] N, pl. *-i*, end20c (1 tech, jour)

sales manager *n.* 'a person in charge of sales in an enterprise'

Ge [=E] M, pl. ∅, 1960s (1 tech)　**Du** [=E] C, 1980s (1 tech, jour)　**Nw** [=E] M, pl. *-e*, 1980s, end20c (1 tech)　**It** [=E] M/F, pl. ∅, 1960s (1 tech)　**Gr** <=E> [=E] M/F, pl. ∅/-*s*, 1990s (1 tech)

sales promotion *n.* 'a strategy to increase sales'

Ge [=E] F [U] 1960s (1 tech)　**Du** [=E] F [U] 1970s (1 tech) → *sales promoter*　**Nw** [=E] M [U] 1960s (1 tech)　**It** [=E] F, pl. ∅, 1960s (1 tech) < trsl *promozione vendite*　**Rm** (0)　**Gr** <=E> [=E] N, 1990s (1 tech, rare)

salmonella *n.* 1 'any bacterium causing food poisoning'

The American veterinary surgeon Daniel Elmer Salmon (1850–1914) identified the genus of bacteria; although the word is thus of American English provenance, it is not always identified as an anglicism.

Ge *-nelle* F, pl. *-n*, 20c (3)　**Du** [salmo:n̩la] C, pl. *-s*, 1970s (3)　**Nw** [salmun̩la] M [U] end20c (3)　**Ic** [salmonel:a] F [U] end20c (2)　**Fr** <=E>/*salmonelle* [salmɔnɛl] F, beg20c (3 tech)　**Sp** <=E>/*salmonella* [salmon̩ela] F, pl. *-s*, 20c (2 tech) → *salmonelosis*　**It** *salmonella* [salmon̩ela] F [U] 1950s (3 tech$_{MED}$)　**Rm** *salmonelă* [salmon̩elə] F, mid20c (5Fr/tech)　**Rs**

salmonella F, pl. *-y*, end20c (2)   **Po** [salmonella] F, end20c (3)   **Cr** *salmonela* F, pl. *-e*, end20c (3)   **Bg** *salmonela* F, pl. *-li*, mid20c (2 tech) → *-len* adj.   **Fi** *salmonella* mid20c (3)   **Hu** *szalmonella* [salmonella] [U] mid20c (3)   **Al** *salmonelë* F, pl. *-a*, end20c (3); *salmonela* [U] 1970s (3)   **Gr** *salmonela* F, mid/ end20c (3)

saloon   *n.* +4a 'a bar in the Wild West'
   Ge (Ø)   **Du** [=E] C, 1970s (2)   **Nw** [=E] M, pl. *-er/-s*, mid20c (Ø)   **Ic** *salon/salón* [sa:lo(u)n] M, pl. *-ar*, end19c (Ø)   **Fr** [salun] M, end19c (Ø)   **Sp** [=E] M, pl. *-s*, 1930s (Ø/1 tech)   **It** [=E] M, pl. Ø, 1920 (Ø/2)   **Rm** [=E] 1970s (Ø)   **Rs** *salun* M, pl. *-y*, 19c (Ø)   **Po** (Ø)   **Cr** *salun* [=E] M   **Fi** *saluuna* 19c (Ø)   **Hu** (Ø)   **Gr** (Ø)

salvationist* *n.* 'a member of the Salvation Army'
   Nw *salvasjonist* [salvaʃunist] M, pl. *-er*, 1930s (3 jour) < *frelesarmésoldat*   **It** *salvazionista* [salvatsjonista] M/F, pl. *-il-e*, end19c (3)

sample   *n.* 1 'a small part or quantity intended to show what the whole is like', 3 'a specimen, esp. one taken for scientific testing or analysis', +4a 'a representative selection', +5a 'a digital recording of sounds which can be played back by means of a sample keyboard'
   Ge [sa:mpl] N, pl. *-s*, 1960s, 1(1 tech); 1980s, +5a (1 tech, rare) < 1: *Stichprobe*   **Du** [=E] N, 1980s (1 tech)   **Nw** <=E>/*sampel* N, pl. Ø/*-pler*, 1960s (1 tech) < *stikkprøve* (1 tech)   **Ic** [sampl] N, pl. *sömpl*, +5a(1 tech) < 1: rend *sýnishorn*; 3: *sýni*   **Bg** (0)   **Gr** <=E> [seimpl] N, pl. *-s*, 1990s, +5a(1 tech)

sample   *v.* 3 'get a representative selection/experience of' (statistics), +4 'record digitally for sample keyboard use'
   Ge *sampeln* [sa:mpəln] 1980s, +4(1 tech)   **Nw** [sæmple/sample] 1970s (1 tech) → *sampling* M/F   **Ic** [sampla] end20c, +4(1 tech)   **Sp** *samplear* 1980s, +4(3 tech) → *sampleo*   **Fi** *samplata* 1980s (1 tech, coll)

sampler   *n.* 1 'a person who samples', 2 'an electronic device for sampling music and sound', +3a 'a collection of popular songs'
   Ge [=E] M, pl. Ø, 1987, 2(1 tech); 1970s, +3a(1 coll)   **Du** [=E] C, 1980s, 1,2(1 tech) < +3a: *compilatie*   **Nw** [=E/sampler] M, pl. *-e*, 1970s, 2(1 tech); 1980s, +3a(1 tech)   **Ic** [=E/sampları] M, pl. *-ar*, end20c, 2(1 tech)   **Fr** <=E> M, pl. *-s*, 1980s, 2(1 tech) > *échantillonneur*   **Sp** [sampler] M, 1980s, 2(1 tech)   **Fi** *sampleri/sämpläri* 1970s (1 tech, coll)   **Gr** <=E> [-ei-/-a-] N, end20c, 2(1 tech)

sampling   *n.* 1 'the taking of a sample e.g. for a statistical survey', 2 'computer storage of short musical pieces'
   Ge [sa:mpliŋ] N [U] 1980s, 2(1 tech, rare)   **Du** [=E] C [U] 1980s (1 tech)   **Nw** [=E/sampliŋ] M/F [U] 1970s, 1(1 tech); 1980s, 2(1 tech)   **Fr** <=E> M, end20c, 1(1 tech)   **Sp** [sampliŋ] M, pl. *-s*, 1980s (1 tech)   **It** [sampliŋ(g)] M, pl. Ø, 1930s, 1(1 tech)   **Bg** *sempling* M [U] 1990s, 2(1 tech, mod)   **Gr** <=E> [=E] N [U] 1990s, 2(1 tech)

sandwich   *n./cp[1]* 1 'two or more slices of usu. buttered bread with a filling of meat, cheese, etc., between them', +3 'something that is composed of several layers'
   This term is derived from the name of John Montague, fourth Earl of Sandwich (1718–92) who is claimed to have invented the snack so as not to be forced to interrupt his gambling. (He also gave his name to the 'Sandwich Islands', which were later renamed 'Hawaiian Islands'). The word was first recorded in travelogues from the eighteenth century and remained a foreignism for a long time; even in the twentieth century some languages prefer native equivalents. By contrast, there has been a proliferation of technical terms based on metaphoric uses, often containing *s.* as cp[1].
   Ge [sɛntwitʃ] N, pl. *-es*, end19c, 1(2); 1970s, +3(1 tech)   **Du** [=E] C, pl. *-es*, beg20c, 1(2)   **Nw** [=E] M, pl. *-er*, beg20c, 1(1 rare) < *smørbrød*; cp[1], 1960s, +3(1 tech)   **Ic** - < *samloka*   **Fr** [sãdwitʃ/sãdwiʃ] M, pl. *-s*, beg19c, 1(2) →

sandwicher (2 coll)   **Sp** [sanwitʃ/sanwiʃ] M, pl. *-s/-es*, mid19c, 1(2); end20c, +3(1 tech) → *sandwicherie*   **It** [sɛndwitʃ] M, pl. Ø, end19c, 1(2) < *panino*   **Rm** *sandviş/sandvici/sen-/sanviş* [sandviʃ/sandvitʃ/sanviʃ] N, end19c, via Fr (3)   **Rs** *sandvich* M, pl. *-i*, mid20c, 1(3)   **Po** *sandwicz* [sandvitʃ] M, beg20c, 1(3)   **Cr** *sendvič* M, pl. *-i*, beg20c, 1(2)   **Bg** *sandvich* M, pl. *-al-i*, mid20c, 1(3)   **Fi** [=E] beg20c, 1(Ø)   **Hu** *szendvics* [sɛndvitʃ] pl. *-ek*, beg20c, 1(3); cp[1], +3(3+5)   **Al** *sanduiç* M, pl. *-e*, mid20c, 1(1 you)   **Gr** *saduits* N, beg20c (2) → *saduitsadhiko* N

sandwich-man   *n.* 'a man who walks the streets with sandwich-boards hanging on his back and chest'
   Ge *-man/-mann* M, pl. *-men/-männer*, mid20c (1 obs)   **Du** [=E+man] C, pl. *-nen*?, beg20c (2 arch)   **Fr** - < trsl *homme-sandwich*   **It** - < trsl *uomo-sandwich*   **Rm** - < rend *om sandviş* M, 1970s (1 rare)   **Rs** (Ø)   **Po** [sandwitʃmen] M, end20c (1 tech)   **Cr** *sendvič čovjek* M, mid20c (1 tech)   **Bg** - < rend *chovek sandvich*   **Hu** - < trsl *szendvicsember*   **Gr** - < *saduitsas* M

scab   *n.* 2 'a person who refuses to strike or join a trade union'
   Rs *skéb* M, pl. *-y*, beg20c (Ø)   **Po** [skep] M, beg20c (1 tech)   **Cr** (0)

scale   *v.* 2 'represent in proportional dimensions'
   Nw *skalere (opp. ned)* [skale:re] 1970s (3 tech)   **Po** (5La)   **Fi** *skeilata* 1970s (1 tech, sla)   **Hu** (5La)

scalp   *v.* 'take the scalp of (an enemy)'
   Ge *skalpieren* 19c (3)   **Du** *scalperen* (3)   **Nw** *skalpere* 19c(3)   **Fr** *scalper* [skalpe] 18c (3)   **It** *scalpare* 1930s (3)   **Rm** *scalpa* [skalpa] end19c, via Fr (3)   **Rs** *skal'pirovat'* 20c (3)   **Po** *skalpować* [skalpovatç] beg20c (2 coll)   **Cr** *skalpirati* 20c (3)   **Bg** *skalpiram* 20c (3)   **Fi** *skalpeerata* 20c (3)   **Hu** *skalpol* 20c (3)   **Al** - < *i keq skalpin*

scalp   *n.* 1 'the skin covering the top of the head', 2a 'the scalp of an enemy cut or torn away as a trophy by an American Indian', 2b 'any trophy'

This term became widely known through nineteenth-century travelogues and James Fenimore Cooper's novels; it has developed various metaphorical senses.

Ge *Skalp* M, pl. *-e*, 19c, 2a(2) → *-ieren* v. **Du** [skɑlp] C, pl. *-en*, beg20c, 2a,b(2>3) → *-eren* v. **Nw** *skalp* [skalp] M, pl. *-er*, mid19c, 2a(3) → *skalpere* v. **Fr** [skalp] M, beg19c, 2a,b(2) → *scalper* v. **It** *scalpo* M, 1930s, 1,2a(3) **Rm** [skalp] N, end19c, via Fr, 1(3 tech) 2a,b(3 lit) → *scalpa* v.; *-are* N, *-atlă* adj. **Rs** *skal'p* M, pl. *-y*, beg20c, 1,2a(1 tech) → *-irovanie* N; *-irovat'* v. **Po** *skalp* M, beg20c, 2a,b(2) → *-owanie* N; *-ować* v. **Cr** *skalp* M, pl. *-ovi*, beg20c, 2a,b(2) → *-irati* v.; *-iranje* N; *-iran* adj. **Bg** *skalp* M, pl. *-al-ove*, beg20c, 1,2a(2) → *-iram* v.; *-irane* N; *-iran* adj. **Fi** *skalppi* 19c, 2a(2) → *skalpeerata* v. **Hu** *skalp* [ʃkalp] pl. *-ok*, end19/beg20c, 1,2a(2/o) 2b(3) → *-ol* v. **Al** *skalp* M, pl. *-e*, mid20c, 1,2a(3)

Ic	Nw	Po	Rs
Du	Ge	Cr	Bg
Fr	It	Fi	Hu
Sp	Rm	Al	Gr

scan v. +3c 'read into a computer by means of a scanner', 4 'resolve (a picture) into its elements of light and shade for the purposes esp. of television transmission', 6a 'make a scan of (the body or part of it)', 6b 'examine (a patient etc.) with a scanner'

Ge *scannen* 1980s, +3c,6b(1 tech) **Du** *scannen* [skɛnə] 1980s (1 tech) **Nw** *scanne/skanne* [skæne/skɑne] 1960s (1 tech) → *skanning* M/F **Ic** *skanna* [skan:a] end20c (3 tech) < 6a,b: rend *skim, skönnun* F **Fr** *scanner/scanneriser* **Sp** *escanear* 1980s (3 tech) **It** *scannerizzare* [skanneridzɑre] 1970s (3) **Rm** *scana* [skanɑ] 1970s, via Fr, 4,6a,b(1 tech); 1990s, +3c(1 tech) → *scanare* F; *-at* adj. **Rs** *skannirovat'* end20c (1 tech) → *skannirovanie* N **Po** *skanować* end20c (1 tech) **Cr** *skanirati* end20c, 6a,b(1 tech) **Bg** *skaniram/skeniram* 20c (3) **Fi** *skannata* 1980s (3) **Gr** *skanáro* end20c (3 tech)

scan n. 1 'the act or an instance of scanning'

Du [=E] C, end20c (1 tech) **Nw** <=E>/*skann* [skæ(:)n/skan] N, pl. Ø, 1960s (1 tech) **It** *scanning* [=E] M, pl. Ø, 1970s (1 tech) < *scansione* **Rm** → *scanare* Rs → *skannirovanje* N **Po** (o) **Cr** (o) **Bg** - → *skanirane* **Fi** - → *skannaus* **Gr** <=E>/*skan* N, end20c (1 tech) = *sarosi*

scanner n. 1 'a device for scanning, systematically examining, reading, or monitoring something', 2 'a machine for measuring the intensity of radiation, ultrasound reflections, etc., from the body as a diagnostic aid', 3 'a person who scans or examines something critically'

Ge [skɛna] M, pl. Ø, 1970s, 1,2(1 tech) → *scannen* v. **Du** [=E] C, 1950s (1 tech) → *scannen* v.; *scan* n. **Nw** <=E>/*skanner* [=E/skaner] M, pl. *-e*, 1970s, 1(2) → *scanne* v. **Ic** <=E>/*skanni* [=E/skan:ı] M, pl. *-ar*, end20c, 1,2(2 tech) < 2: rend *skimari* **Fr** [skanɛr]

M, 1960s, 1,2(1 tech, ban) > *scanneur, scanographe* → *scanner* v.; *scannage* M, Ø **Sp** <=E>/*escáner* [eskaner] M, pl. *-s*, 1970s, 1,2(1 tech) **It** [skanner] M, pl. Ø, 1960s, 1,2(2 tech) **Rm** *scaner/scanner* [skaner/=E] N, 1970s, 2(1 tech); 1990s, 1(1 tech) **Rs** *skanner* M, pl. *-y*, end20c, 1,2(1 tech) **Po** *skaner* [skaner] M, end20c, 1,2(1 tech) → v. **Cr** *skener* M, pl. *-i*, end20c, 1,2(2 tech); *skanyor* M, 3(3 tech) **Bg** *skener* M, pl. *-al-i*, end20c, 1,2(2 tech) **Fi** *skanneri* 1980s (3) **Hu** *szkenner* [skɛnner/=E] pl. Ø, end20c, 1,2(1 tech) **Al** *skanner* M, pl. *skanera*, end20c (2) **Gr** <=E>/*skaner* M/N, end20c, 1(1 tech) = *sarotis*

scat v. 'sing scat'

Nw *scatte* [skæte] mid20c (1 tech, rare) **Ic** [skahta] mid20c (1 tech) **Hu** [=E] 20c (1 tech)

scat n./cp¹ 'improvised jazz singing using sounds imitating instruments instead of words'

The distribution shows the expected decline towards the east, as explained by the topic and the peak of its popularity in the 1960s and 1970s.

Ge [=E] M, pl. *-s*, 1960s (1 tech, rare) **Du** [=E] C [U] 1980s (1 tech) **Nw** *scatsang* [=E] cp¹, 1950s (1 tech) **Ic** [=E] N [U] mid/end20c (1 tech) → *skatta* v. **Fr** [skat] M, mid20c (1 tech) **It** [=E] M [U] 1950s (1 tech) **Rm** [=E] N [U] 1970s (1 tech, rare) **Po** [sket] M [U] end20c (1 tech) **Cr** (o) **Bg** *skat* M [U] mid20c (1 tech) **Hu** [=E] 20c (1 tech >2)

scenic railway n. +3 'a railway at a fair etc.'

Fr [senikrɛlwɛ] M, beg20c (1 obs) < *montagnes russes*

schooner n. 1 'a fore-and-aft rigged ship with two or four masts, the foremast being smaller than the other masts'

First recorded in eighteenth-century American English, where the quasi-Dutch spelling was added, this word spread to nearly all European languages together with other shipping terms.

Ge *Schoner* [ʃoːna] M, pl. Ø, 19c (3) **Du** *schoener* [sxunər] C, beg18c (3) **Nw** *skonnert* [skɔnet] M, pl. *-er*, 19c (3) **Ic** *skonnorta* [skɔn:orta] F, pl. *-ur*, beg19c, via Da (2 tech, arch) **Fr** [skunœr/ʃunœr] M, beg19c (1 tech, obs) **Sp** [eskuner] M, pl. *-s*, mid19c (1 arch) < *goleta* **It** [skuːner] M, pl. Ø, 1800s (1 tech) < *goletta* **Rm** *scună* [skunə] F, beg20c, via It? *scuner* [skuner] N, mid20c (3 tech) **Rs** *shkhuna* F, pl. *-y*, mid19c (2) **Po** *szkuner/skuner* [ʃkuner/skuner] M, mid19c, via Ge (2) **Cr** *škuner* M, pl. *-i*, 19c (3) **Bg** *shkhuna* F, pl. *-ni*, beg20c, via Rs (3) **Fi** *kuunari* 18c, via Sw (3) **Hu** *szkúner* [skuːner] pl. *-ek*, 19c (1 tech, arch) **Al** *skunë* F, pl. *-a* (3); *skuna* F, pl. *-ë*, 20c, via It (1 reg) **Gr** *skuna* F, beg20c (3)

science fiction n. 'the genre of fiction based on imagined future advances in science and technology'

Although similar genres existed before the adoption of *s.f.* in the 1960s, the term has been widely borrowed, both to refer to the specifically American genre and to stress the modernity; however, several languages have preferred to use calques or abbreviated the foreign-looking term.

Ge [=E] F [U] 1960s (2 tech) > *SF* **Du** [=E] C [U] 1970s (2 tech) **Nw** [=E] M [U] 1950s (2 tech) > *sci-fi*, *SF* **Ic** [=E] F [U] mid20c (1 tech) = trsl *vísindaskáldskapur* **Fr** *science-fiction* [sjãsfiksjõ] F, 1950s (3) **Sp** - < trsl *ciencia ficción* **It** [saiəns fikʃion] F [U] 1950s (2) < rend *fantascienza* **Rm** [=E] N [U] 1970s (2) = *SF* > rend *literatură ştiinţifico-fantastică* **Rs** (0) < rend *nauchnaya fantastika* **Po** [=E] F, uninfl., mid20c (2) **Cr** [=E] M [U] mid20c (1 tech) **Bg** - < rend *nauchna fantastika* **Fi** <=E>/*scifi* [=E/skifi] 1960s (1 tech) **Hu** <=E>/*sci-fi* [=E/stsi-fi] pl. *-k*, 1960s (2) > rend *tudományos-fantasztikus* **Al** - < rend *fantastiko shkencor* **Gr** (0) < rend *epistimoniki fantasia* F

Scientology *n.* 'a religious system based on self-improvement and promotion through grades of self-knowledge'

This word is used as a name for the so-called group only, but various uses appear to become generic.

Ge [=E] F [U] 1990s (1 tech) **Du** [=E] C [U] 1980s (1 tech) **Nw** *scientologi* [sientulugi:/saien-] M [U] 1970s (1 tech) **Fr** *scientology* F, 1980s (1 tech) **Sp** - < trsl *cienciología* **It** *scientologia* [ʃjentɔlɔdʒia] 1980s (3) **Rm** (0) **Po** *scjentologia* [scientologia] F [U] end20c (1 tech) **Cr** (0) **Bg** *stsientologiya* F [U] 1990s (3 tech) → *stsientolog* M **Fi** *skientologia* 1980s (1 tech) **Al** *sintelogji* 1990s (1) **Gr** *Saientolotzi* F [U] end20c (1 mod)

scone *n.* 'a small sweet or savoury cake of flour, fat, and milk, baked for a short time in an oven'
Du Ø **Nw** <=E>/*scones* sg. [=E] M, pl. *-s*, 20c (Ø/1 jour) **Ic** *skonsa* [skɔnsa] F, pl. *-ur*, beg20c (3) **Rm** (0) **Fi** *scones/skonssi* [skons:1] sg., mid20c (Ø>1 tech)

scoop *v.* 3 'forestall (a rival newspaper, reporter, etc.) with a scoop'
Ic *skúbba* [skup:a] 1970s (1 tech) **Fi** *skuupata* (2 tech)

scoop *n.* 4 'a piece of news published by a newspaper etc. in advance of its rivals', +8 'a kind of game where a plastic ball is thrown and caught using a scoop-like object'
Ge [=E] M, pl. *-s*, 1960s, 4(1 jour, rare) **Du** [=E] C, 1970s, 4(1 tech, jour) = *primeur* **Nw** [=E/skʉ:p] N, pl. Ø, 1960s, 4(1 jour); 1970s, +8(1 obs) → *scoope* v. **Ic** *skúbb* [skup:] N, pl. Ø, 1970s, 4(1 tech, sla) → *skúbba* v. **Fr** [skup] M, 1970s, 4(1 ban, mod) < *exclusivité* **Sp** [eskup] M, 1970s, 4(1 tech) < *primicia (periodística)/pisotón* **It** [=E] M, pl. Ø, 1960s, 4(2) **Rm** [=E] N, 1990s, 4(1 tech, jour) **Fi** [=E] 1960s, 4(1 jour, rare)

scooter *n.* 2 (*motor-*) 'a light two-wheeled open motor vehicle with a shieldlike protective

---

front', 3 'a powerboat', +4 (*auto-*) 'a bumper car', +5 'a railcar'

The proliferation of meanings in the field of vehicles in English ('plow', 'child's toy', 'motor-scooter' and 'motor-boat') went still further abroad where 'bumper car' and 'rail car' were added.

Ge [=E] M, pl. Ø, 1940s, 2(0) +4(1 tech) < +4: *Auto-skooter* **Du** [=E] C, 1940s, +5(1 tech); 1950s, 2(2) → *-en* v. **Nw** <=E>/*skuter* [=E/skʉ:ter] M, pl. *-e*, 1950s, 2(2) **Ic** - < 2: *vespa* **Fr** [skutɐʀ/skutɐʀ] M, mid20c, 2(2) < +4: *auto-tamponneuse* → *scootériste* M **Sp** <=E>/*escúter* [eskuter] M, mid20c, 2(2) **It** [skuter/motoskuter] M, pl. Ø, 1940s/50s, 2(3/2 tech) **Rm** *scuter* [skuter] N, mid20c, 2(3); *motoscuter* [motoskuter] N, 1960s, via Fr, 2(3 tech) **Rs** *skuter* M, pl. *-y*, mid20c, 2,3(2) **Po** *skuter* [skuter] M, mid20c, 2,3(3) **Cr** *skuter* M, pl. *-i*, mid20c, 2(2) **Bg** *skuter* M, pl. *-a/-i*, mid20c, 3(2) **Hu** [skʉ:ter] pl. *-ek*, 1960s, 2(2) > *robogó* **Al** *skuter* M, pl. *-e*, mid20c, 2(1 reg) **Gr** *skuter* N, mid20c, via Fr, 2(2)

score *n.* 1a, b 'the number of points, goals, runs, etc., made by a player, side, etc., in some games', +11 'a test result'

Du [sko:rə] C, 1910s, 1a,b(2) +11(1 tech) **Nw** <=E>/*skåre* [=E/skɔ:re] M, pl. *-r/-s*, 1960s, 1a,b(1 rare) < *poengsum*; +11(1 tech) **Fr** [skɔʀ] M, end19c, 1a,b(2 ban) > *marque* **Sp** [eskor] M, 1920s (1 tech, rare) **It** [skɔr/=E] M, pl. Ø, 1920s, 1a,b(1 tech) < *punteggio, risultato* **Rm** *scor* [skor] N, 1930s, via Fr, 1a,b(3) **Cr** *skor* M, beg20c, +11(2) **Gr** *skor* N, beg20c (1 tech)

score *v.* 1a 'score a goal' (sport), 2a 'make a score in a game or on a test etc.', 7a 'use/obtain drugs illegally', +10 'impress through one's success'
Du *scoren* [sko:rən] beg20c, 1a(1 tech) 7a(1 sla) +10(2 tech) → *score* n.; *scorer* n.; *scoring* n. **Nw** <=E>/*skåre* [skɔ:re] beg20c, 1a,2a(2) → *(stor)scorende* adj.; *scorer* M; *scoring* M/F **Ic** *skora* [skɔ:ra] beg/mid20c, 1a, 2a(4) **Gr** *skoraro* 1a(1 tech) 2a(1 coll)

Scotch *n.* 2 'Scotch whisky'
Ge [=E] M [U] mid20c (1 mod) **Du** *scotch* [=E] C [U] 1970s (1 tech) **Nw** [=E] M [U] mid20c (1 tech) **Ic** - < mean *skoti* **Fr** [skɔtʃ] M, mid20c (1) **Sp** [eskotʃ] M, pl. Ø, 1930s (1) > *(whisky) escocés* **It** [skɔtʃ] M, pl. Ø, 1930s (2) **Rm** [=E] N, 1970s (2 mod) **Rs** *skotch* M [U] mid20c (1 jour) **Po** (0) **Cr** *skoč* M [U] mid20c (1 tech) **Bg** *skoch* M [U] mid20c (2 coll) **Fi** [=E] 19c (Ø) = trsl *skottiviski* **Hu** [=E] [U] end20c (1>2) < *skót whisky* **Al** *skoç uiski* 20c (1) **Gr** <=E> [=E] N [U] end20c (1 tech)

Scotch (tape) *n.* (orig.™) 'adhesive transparent tape'

Originally a tradename, the term came to be generic in France and seems to have spread from there to the south and east; many countries were entirely unaffected by the spread of the product and its name (names of native products often having become generic).

Fr *scotch* [skɔtʃ] M, mid20c (2) → *scotcher* v. **Sp** *scotch* (o) < *cello, celo* **It** *scotch* [skɔtʃ] M [U] 1960s (3) = *nastro adesivo* **Rm** *scotch* [=E] N [U] mid20c (2) > *scoci, bandă scotch* **Rs** *skotch* M [U] end20c (2) **Po** *skocz/ scotch* M, end20c (2 tech) **Cr** (o) **Bg** *skoch* M [U] mid20c (3) < *tikso* **Gr**™

scout *n.* 3 'a talent-scout', 4 'a member of the Scout Association (an international youth organization, originally for boys), +8 'a spacecraft designed for reconnoitring' (cf. ↑*Boy Scout*)

This word is known worldwide, but has remained a foreignism in many languages, in which calques are preferred. There is a limited distribution in Eastern Europe where the movement has traditionally held some prestige.

Ge [=E] M, pl. *-s*, beg20c, 4(0 arch); 1970s, 3(1 jour) < 4: *Pfadfinder* **Du** [=E] C, beg20c (2) → *scouten* v. **Nw** (o) < trsl *speider* **Ic** *skáti* [skau:tɪ] M, pl. *-ar*, beg20c, 4(3) **Fr** <=E>/ *scoute* [skut] M, 1920s, 3,4(2) > *boy-scout* **Sp** <=E>/*boyscout* [eskaut] M, pl. *-s*, beg20c, 3,4(2) > *explorador* **It** [skaut] M, pl. Ø, 1950 (3) < *boy-scout* → *scoutismo/-au-* M.; *scoutista/ -au-* n.; *scoutistico/- au-* adj. **Rm** *scout/boy-scout* [=E] M, beg20c, 4(0/1 tech) < *cercetaş* **Rs** *skaut* M, pl. *-y*, beg20c, 4(1 you) → *skiĭ* adj. **Po** *skaut* M, beg20c, 4(1 obs); *scout* [=E] [U] 20c, +8 (1 tech) → *-ka* F; *-owski* adj. **Cr** *skaut* M, pl. *-i*, beg20c, 4(3) **Bg** *skaut* M, pl. *-i*, 1930s, 4(2) → *-ka* F; *-ski* adj. **Al** *skaut* M, pl. *-ë*, mid20c, 4(1 reg)

scout* *adj.* 1 'referring to boy-scouts' **It** [=E] uninfl., 1950s (3) **Po** *skautowski* [skawtovski] beg20c (1 obs) **Bg** *skautski* (3)

scouting *n.* 1 'the scout movement'; 2 'a search for talent' (music) **Du** [=E] C [U] 1960s (1 tech) **Nw** (o) < *speiderbevegelse; speiding* **Fr** *scoutisme* [skutism(ə)] M, 1920s, 1(2) **Rm** - < rend *cercetăşie* **Rs** - < creat *skautskoe dvizhenie* **Po** *skauting* [-nk] M [U] beg20c, 1(1 arch) **Cr** (o) **Bg** - < 1: creat *skautsko dvizhenie*

Scrabble *n.* 2 (orig.™) 'a game in which players build up words from letter-blocks on a board'

The tradename is likely to have become, or to be about to become, generic in a few languages which borrowed the word.

Ge [skrɛbəl] N [U] 1970s (2 tech) **Du** [skrɛbəl] C [U] 1970s (2) **Nw** [=E] [U] 1950s (2) **Ic** [skrapl] N [U] 1980s (2) → *skrabla* v. **Fr** [skrabəl] M, 1970s (2 tech) → *scrabbler* v.; *scrabbleur, -euse* n. **Sp** [eskra-

bel] M [U] end20c (1 tech) **It** - < *scarabeo* **Rm** *scrabble* [=E] N [U] 1980s (2) **Po** [skrable] end20c (2 mod) **Cr** *skrabel* 20c(1) **Bg** (o) **Gr** *skrabl* N, end20c (2)

scramble *v.* 6 'change the speech frequency of a broadcast transmission or telephone conversation so as to make it unintelligible', 8 'take off quickly in an emergency or for action' (of fighter aircraft)

Du *scrambelen* [skrɛmbələ] 1980s, 6(1 tech); *scramble* [=E] 1980s, 8(1 tech) **Nw** [skrɛmble] 20c (1 tech)

scrambler *n.* 1 'a device for scrambling telephone conversations', +2a 'a small motorcycle', +4 'a decoding device'

Du [=E] C, 1970s, 1,+4(1 tech) **Nw** [=E] M, pl. *-e*, 1970s, 1(1 tech) **It** [skrambler] M, pl. Ø, 1970s, +2a,+4(1 tech) **Rs** *skrémbler* M, pl. *-y*, 1995 (1 tech) **Cr** (o) **Bg** *skrambler* M, pl. *-al-i*, end20c, +4(1 tech)

scrap *n./cp¹* 4 'discarded metal for reprocessing' **Nw** *skrapjem(metall)* [skra:p] cp¹ (4) **Rs** *skrap* M [U] mid20c (1 tech) **Bg** *skrap* M [U] mid20c (1 tech) → *-ov* adj.

scrapbook *n.* 'a book of blank spaces for sticking cuttings, drawings, etc. in' **Nw** <=E>/*scrapbok* [=E/E+Nw] 1960s (1+5) **Ic** - < *úrklippubók* **Fr** [skrapbuk] M, 20c (1 lit)

scraper *n.* 1 'a device used for scraping, esp. for removing dirt or paint from a surface', +2 'a device used for loading ore onto mine carts'

This term may be a survival of Britain's early leading position in mining terminology; some of the distribution in Eastern Europe may well be secondary, transmitted via Russian.

Du [=E] C, 1960s, 1(1 tech) = *schraapwagen/schraper* **Fr** [skrepœr] M, 1940s, 1(1 tech, ban) > *scrapeur* **Sp** [=E] M, 20c, 1(1 tech) **It** [skreiper] M, pl. Ø, 1930s, 1(1 tech) **Rm** *screper* [skreper] N, mid20c, via **Rs** (3 tech) **Rs** *skreĭper* M, pl. *-y*, mid20c, 1,+2(2 tech) → *-nyĭ?* **Po** *skreper* [skreper] M, mid20c, 1(1 tech) **Cr** (o) **Bg** *skreper* M, pl. *-al-i*, mid20c, via Rs, +2(3 tech) **Hu** *szkréper* [skrɛ:per] pl. Ø, mid20c, 1(1 tech) → *-es* n. **Al** *skreper* M, pl. *-e(r)*, mid20c (1 tech)

scratch *v.* 8 'withdraw (a competitor, candidate, etc.) from a race or competition', +10 'scrape a record' **Ge** [skretʃən] 1980s, +10(1 tech, you) **Du** *scratchen* [skrɛtʃən] 1980s, +10(1 tech/you) **Nw** *scratche* [skrɛtʃe] 1980s, +10(1 tech, you) **Ic** [skratsa] 1980s, +10(1 tech, you) **Fr** *scratcher* [skratʃe] 1920s, 8(1 tech); 1980s?, +10(1 tech, you) **Sp** - < *hacer scratch*

scratch *n./cp¹* +5c 'a race with no handicap imposed on the best competitor' (sport), +8a 'music produced by moving a record on a player', +9 'the best time' (racing), +10 'a victory in a sports competition due to retirement of an opponent', +11 'a scratch, a fault on a film' **Ge** [=E] cp¹ [U] 1980s, +8a(1 tech, you) **Nw** [=E] [U]

20c, +5c(1 tech) **Ic** [=E] N [U] 1980s, +8a(1 tech,
you) **Fr** [skʀatʃ] M, end19c, +5c, +9(1 tech); 20c,
+11(1 tech, ban) < *accroc* → *scratchman* **Sp** [eskʀatʃ]
M, pl. -*s*, 1980s, +5c, +8a(1 tech) **It** [skretʃ] M, pl.
Ø, 1900s, +5c, +10(1 tech) **Rm** [=E] N [U] end20c,
+10(1 tech) **Po** *skrecz*/<=E> [-e-] M [U] beg20c,
+9(1 tech) **Cr** (o) **Bg** *skrech* M [U] end20c, +8a(1
tech/you) **Gr** *skrats* N, 1980s, +8a(1 tech, you)

scratch, from *phr.* 1 '(from) the beginning'
Nw *(starte fra, på) scratch* [=E] 1930s (2)

scratching *n.* 'the technique of stopping a record by
hand and moving it back and forth'
Ge [=E] N [U] 1980s (1 tech, you) **Du** [=E] C, 1980s
(1 tech, you) **Nw** *scratching* [=E] M [U] 1980s (1
tech, you) **Cr** (o) **Bg** *skręching* M [U] 1990s (1 tech)

screen *v.* 5 'test for the presence or absence of a
disease'
Du *screenen* [skriːnən] 1970s (1 tech) **Nw** *screene*
[skriːne] 1970s (1 tech) **Gr** - < *kano (to) skrin*
1980s

screening *n.* 12 'a system of checking for presence or
absence of a disease, ability, attribute, etc.'
  The English word has remained marginal even as a
medical term, native equivalents being easily available.
Ge [=E] N, pl. -*s*, 1970s (1 tech)
Du [=E] C, 1970s (1 tech) **Nw**
[=E] M/F [U] 1960s (1 tech) **Fr**
<=E>/*screenage* M, 1980s (1
tech, ban) > *criblage* **Sp** [eskri-
nin] M, end20c (1 tech) **It**
[skriːniŋ(g)] M, pl. Ø, 1970s (1
tech) **Rm** [=E] N [U] end20c (0>1 tech) < *rend
ecranare* **Po** [skrinink] M [U] end20c (1 tech) **Cr**
(o) **Bg** *skrining* M [U] end20c (1 tech) → -*ov* adj.

scribble *v.* 1 'write carelessly', 3 'draw carelessly'
Nw *skrible* [skrible] (3) → *scribler* M; *skribleri* N **Hu**
skribál (3)

scrip *n.* 'a provisional certificate of money subscribed
to a bank or company etc., entitling the holder to a
formal certificate and dividends' (econ.)
Ge <c/k> [=E] M, pl. -*s*, 1900s (1 tech, rare) **Hu**
<=E/-s> [=E] 20c (1 tech)

script *n.* 4 'the text of a play, film, or broadcast', +7 'a
handout for a lecture'
Ge *Skript* [=E] N, pl. -*en*/-*s*, 1970s (3/5La) **Du** [=E]
C/N, 1950s, 4(2) **Nw** [=E] N, pl. Ø, 1970s, 4(1 rare)
< *manuskript*/*manus* **Ic** - < 4: mean *handrit* **Fr**
[skript] M, mid20c, 4(3) **Sp** [eskript] M, 1960s, 4(1
tech) **It** [=E] M, pl. Ø, 1940s, 4(1 tech) < *copione,
sceneggiatura* **Rm** [=E] N, 1990s, +7(1 tech) **Cr**
skript M, pl. -*ovi*, mid20c, 4(2) **Al** *scriptë* F, pl. -*e*,
end20, +7(3)

script-girl* *n.* 'a secretary in a film studio'
Ge [=E] N, pl. -*s*, mid20c (1 tech) **Du** [=E] C, 1960s
(1 tech) **Nw** <=E>/*script* [=E] M, pl. -*er*, mid20c (1
tech) **Ic** - < rend *skrifta* **Fr** <=E>/*script* [skript
(gœrl)] F, 1930s (1 tech, ban) < *scripte* **Sp** <=E>/
script F, pl. -*s*, 1950s (1 tech, rare) = *anotadora, secre-*

taria de rodaje **It** [skript görl] F,
pl. Ø, 1940s (1 tech) < *segretaria
di produzione* **Rm** [=E] F,
uninfl., end20c (1 tech) **Cr**
skript gerla F, mid20c (1
tech) **Bg** *skripterka* F, pl. -*ki*,
1990s (3 mod) **Fi** *skripta*

mid20c (2 tech) **Hu** [=E] pl. Ø, end20c (1 tech)

scriptwriter *n.* 'a person who writes a script for a
film, broadcast, etc.'
Nw [=E] M, pl. -*e*, 1980s (1 tech) **It** [=E] M, pl. Ø,
1960s (1 tech) < *sceneggiatore* **Cr** *skript vrajter* 20c
(1 tech)

scroll *n.* +4 'a cone-shaped wafer baked in a special
oven'
Nw *skrull* [skrul] M, pl. -*er* (1 reg) < *krumkake*

scrolling *n.* 'the moving of computer information on
the screen'
Ge [=E] N [U] end20c (1 tech) **Du** [skrolin] C [U]
end20c (1 tech) **Nw** [=E/skrolin] C [U] end20c (1
tech) **Bg** *skroll*/*skrul* M [U] end20c (3 tech) **Fi**
skrollata N [U] end20c (1 tech) **Hu** - < trsl *gördí-
tés* **Gr** <=E> [=E] N [U] end20c (1 tech)

scrub *n.* 1a 'brushwood', 1b 'land covered with
scrub', +5 'tobacco of inferior quality', +6 'a hard
brush'
Ge *Skrubs* [skraps] pl., beg20c, +5(1 tech) **Du**
+1a(Ø); [skrvp] C, usu. pl., 1980s, +6(1) **Fr** [skrœb]
M, mid20c, 1a,b(Ø) **It** [=E] M [U] end19c, 1a(1 tech,
rare) **Rm** [=E] N [U] 1970s, 1a(1 tech) **Po** *skrub*/
<=E> [skrub] M [U] beg20c, 1b,+5(1 tech) **Hu** [=E]
[U] 20c, 1b(Ø>1 tech)

scrubber *n.* 1 'an apparatus for purifying gases'
Ge *Skrubber* M [U]/pl. Ø, beg20c
(1 tech) **Nw** *skrubber* [skruber]
M, pl. -*e*, 20c (1 tech) **Fr**
[skrœbœr] M, end19c (1 tech,
arch) **Rm** [skruber/=E] N,
mid20c (2 tech) **Rs** *skrubber*
M, pl. -*y*, mid20c (1 tech) **Po**

skruber/ <=E> [skruber] M, mid20c (1 tech) **Cr**
(o) **Bg** *skruber* M, pl. -*al-i*, mid20c, via Rs (3
tech) **Hu** [skrabber] pl. Ø, 20c (1 tech)

scull *n.* 1 'either of a pair of small oars used by a single
rower', 3 'a rowing boat propelled with a scull or pair
of sculls for each rower', +5 'the specific discipline of
rowing a scull'
Ge [=E] N, pl. -*s*, 1980s, 1(1 tech) **Du** [skvl] C, 1980s,
1,3(1 tech) **Fr** <=E> [skyl/skœl] M, 1920s, 1(1
tech) **Sp** [eskal/eskul] M, end20c, 3(1 tech) **It** [=E]
M, pl. Ø, end19c, 3(1 obs) **Po** *skul*/*skull*/ <=E>
/*skuling* [skul/-nk] M, mid20c, 1,3(1 tech) **Cr** *skul*
M, mid20c, 3(1 tech) **Bg** *skul* M, pl. -*al-ove*,
mid20c, 3(1 tech) +5(3 tech) → -*ov* adj. **Hu** [=E] pl.
Ø, end19/beg20c, 1,3(1 tech)

scull *v.* 'propel a boat with sculls'
Ge *skullen* mid20c (1 tech)

sculler *n.* 1 'a user of sculls', 2 'a boat intended for
sculling'

Ge *Sku̱ller* M, pl. Ø, end19c, 2(1 tech)   Du [sky̱lər] C, beg20c (1 tech)   Nw [=E] M, pl. -e, mid20c, 2(1 tech)   Fr *scull* [skyl/skœl] M, 1920s (1 tech)   It [=E] M, pl. Ø, end19c (1 obs)   Hu *scullboat* [=E] pl. Ø, 20c, 2(1 tech)

scullery   *n.* 'a small room at the back of the house for washing dishes'

Du [=E] C, 1950s (1 tech, rare)   Nw [=E] N, pl. Ø/-er, mid20c (1 rare) < *vaskerom*

SDI   *abbrev.* 'strategic defence initiative'

Ge [=E] 1980s (1 tech, obs) < *Krieg der Sterne*   Du [=E] 1980s (1 tech, obs)   Nw (0) < *Starwars* (fac)   Ic - < rend *stjörnustríðsáætlun*   Sp [esedei̱] F, 1980s (1 tech, obs) > *IDE*; < rend *guerra de las galaxias*   It [ɛssediai̱] 1980s (1 tech) < trsl *difesa strategica*   Rs - < trsl *SOI*   Bg - < rend *ISO* = *i̱nitsiativa za stra̱tegicheska o̱tbrana*   Fi - < *tähtisota*   Hu [=E] end20c (1 tech) < trsl *stratégiai védelmi kezdeménye-zés*   Gr <=E> [=E] N, 1985 (1 tech, obs/Ø)

sealskin   *n.* 1 'the skin of a seal, or imitation fur'

   The evidence is divided between the 'real' product and imitation plush, the word being applicable to both indiscriminately in some languages. Norwegian and Icelandic have native equivalents almost identical with the English word in written form.

Ge [=E] M/N [U] mid20c (1 tech) = *Seal*   Du [=E] N [U] 1940s (1 tech/not for imitations)   Nw *selskinn* (5)   Ic *selskinn* (5)   Fr [silskin] M, mid19c (1 tech, arch)   It [=E] M [U] mid19c (1 arch)   Po *selskiny* [selskini] pl., mid20c (3)   Cr *si̱lskin* M [U] mid20c (1 tech/3)   Hu *szilszkin* [=E] [U] beg20c (3) → *seal-* cp[1]

search   *n.* +1a 'the process of retrieving data' (comput.)

Du [=E] C, pl. -es (1 tech) → *searchen* v.   Ic [=E] end20c (0 tech)   Rm (0 tech)   Bg *su̱rch* M [U] end20c (1 tech, coll)   Hu [=E] [U] end20c (1 tech)

second   *n.* +1a 'abbrev. for second engineer' (naut.)

Nw *sekken* [se̱ken] [U] 20c (1 tech)

second-hand   *cp[1]*, *adj* 1a 'having had a previous owner; not new' (of goods)

   Although a great number of native equivalents exist, this loanword (and various calques) have made some inroads; however, there is unlikely to be a further expansion in Western Europe – although this could happen in the east.

Ge [sekənthent] 1960s (2)   Du [=E] 1990s (1 rare) < *tweedehands*   Nw [=E] mid20c (1 mod) < *brukt-*   Ic [=E] uninfl., end20c (0)   Fr - < trsl *seconde main/d'occasion*   Sp - < trsl *de segunda mano*   It - < *di seconda mano*   Rm [=E] 1990s (2 mod)   Rs *seko̱ndkhénd* 1990s (1 jour/mod) < creat *byvshii̱ v upotreblenii*   Po - < trsl *z drugiej reki*   Cr [=E] end20c (1)   Bg *seku̱ndkhend* adj., uninfl., 1990s (1>2 mod) < trsl *vtora*

upotreba   Hu [=E] end20c (1 tech > 2) < *használt cikk*   Gr (0)

secret service   *n.* 1 (esp. in Britain) 'a government department concerned with espionage'

Ge (0) < trsl *Geheimdienst*   Du (Ø)   Nw [=E] 20c (Ø) < trsl *de hemmelige tjenester*   Ic - < trsl *leyniþjón-usta*   Fr - < *service secret*   Sp - < trsl *servicio secreto*   It - < trsl *servizi segreti*   Rm (0) < trsl *servicii(le) secrete*   Rs - < trsl *sekretnaya sluzhba*   Po - < trsl *tajna służba*   Cr (0)   Bg (0) < trsl *tai̱ni sluzhbi*   Hu (0)   Al - < trsl *shërbimi sekret*   Gr - < trsl *mystiki ypiresia*

security   *n.* 3a 'the safety of a state, company, etc., against espionage, theft, or other danger', 3b 'an organization for ensuring this'

Ge (0)   Du [=E] C [U] 1980s (1 tech)   Nw [=E] M [U] 1950s (1) < *sikkerhet*   Ic - < rend *öryggisgæsla*   Sp - < mean *seguridad*   It - < *sicurezza*   Rm - < mean *securitate* (5Fr/5La)   Rs *sek'yuriti* N, uninfl. [U] 1990s (1 jour)   Po N [U] end20c, 3b(1 tech)   Cr (0)   Bg *Seku̱riti* 1995, 3a(1 mod_NAME) < 3b: rend *Du̱rzhavna Sigurnost*   Hu (5La)   Al - < mean *sigurim*   Gr *sekiu̱riti* F, 1990s, 3b(2 coll) → *sekiuritas* M

sedan   *n.* 2 'an enclosed motor car for four or more people'

Du [=E] C, 1950s (1 tech) = *vierdeurs-auto*   Nw [seda̱:n] M, pl. -er, 20c (3 tech)   Ic [=E/sɛ:tan] uninfl., mid/end20c (1 tech, rare)   Sp [=E] M, mid20c (1 tech, rare) < *berlina*   Rm [sedan̲] N, 1970s (1 rare) < *berlină*   Rs *sedan̲* M, pl. -y, end20c, via Fr (1 tech)   Po [sedan] M, end20c (1 tech)   Cr *sedan* M, pl. -i, end20c (1 tech)   Bg *sedan̲* M, pl. -al-i, 1990s (1 tech, mod)   Fi [=E] beg20c (1 tech)   Hu *szedán* (5Fr)   Gr *sedan̲* N, mid/end20c (1 tech)

see?   *interj.* 'You see? You understand?'

Du *you see?* [=E] 1990s (1 rare) < *snap je?*   Nw [=E] 1980s (1 coll, sla)

seed   *v.* 6a 'assign to a position in an ordered list so that strong competitors do not meet each other in early rounds' (sport), 6b 'arrange (the order of the play) in this way'

Nw *seede* [si̱:de] 1950s (2) → *seedet* adj.

seeding   *n.* 'ranking of (the best) players or participants' (sport)

Nw [=E/si̱:diŋ] M/F [U] 1950s (1 tech)

see you!   *interj.* 1 'an expression on parting', +2 'an expression on meeting'

Du [=E] 1990s, 1(1 coll)   Ic [=E] end20c, 1 (1 sla) < trsl *sjáumst*   Gr (0)

seiner   *n.* 1 'a small fisherman', +1a 'a boat provided with seine-nets'

Rm [sejne̱r] N, 1970s, +1a(1 tech)   Rs *se̱jner* M, pl. -y, mid20c, 1(1 tech) → -*nyĭ*   Po *sejner* [-er] M, mid20c, 1(1 tech)   Bg *se̱iner* M, pl. -al-i, mid20c, via Rs, 1(1 tech) → -*en* adj.

seizing   *n.* 'cord(s) used for fastening' (naut.)

Du *seizing* via Fr (3)   Nw *seising* [sæisiŋ] M/F [U] beg20c (1 tech)   Po *sejzing* [seizink] M, mid20c (1 tech)   Fi *seisinki* 19c, via Sw (3)

self- *cp¹.* 1 'of or directed towards oneself', 2 'by oneself or itself, esp. without external agency', 3 'on, in, for, or relating to oneself or itself'

This morpheme has, apart from the items listed below, become very productive in French (Picone 1996: 291–6 lists various combinations including many hybrids like: *-achèvement, -allumeur, -centré, -entretien, -filtrage* etc.; there is also *-banking*). This has sparked off purist replacements with *auto-*. The international aspects of *self*-compounds deserve further investigation.

self-actor/-ing* *n.* (tech) 'automatic' (esp. in spinning machines)

This word, in both possible forms, is of especial historical interest since it represents the forerunner of modern *automation* and *automatic*; the international words have all but replaced the earlier anglicisms.

Ge *Selfaktor* [selfaktor] M, pl. *-s*, end19c (1 arch) Nw *selfaktor* [selfaktur] M, pl. *-er*, 19c (1 arch) Fr *self-acting* M, 19c (1 tech) It *self-acting* [selfektiŋ(g)] M, pl. Ø, 1930s (1 arch) Rm *selfactor* [selfaktor] N, 1930s, via

Ge (3 tech) Po *selfaktor* [selfaktor] M, beg20c (1 tech) Bg *selfaktor* M, pl. *-al-i*, mid20c (3 tech, obs) Hu *szelfaktor* [selfaktor] pl. Ø, beg20c (1 tech)

self-control *n.* 'the power of controlling one's external reactions, emotions, etc'.

Du [=E] C [U] (1 tech) Nw - < *selvkontroll* Ic - < trsl *sjálfstórn* Fr [selfkõtʀol] M, end19c Sp [=E] M [U] 1970s (1 tech, rare) < trsl *autocontrol* It [self kɔntrɔl] M [U] 1940s (2) = trsl *autocontrollo* Rm [=E] N [U] 1970s (1 tech) < trsl *autocontrol* Rs - < trsl *samokontrol* Cr (0) Bg - < *samoobladanie* Hu - < trsl *önkontroll* Al - < trsl *vetkoñtroll*

self-fulfilling prophecy *phr.* 'a prediction bound to come true as a result of actions brought about by its being made'

Ge [=E] F [U] 1980s (1 coll) Du [=E] 1970s (1 coll, pej) Nw (0) < trsl *selvoppfyllende profeti*

self-government *n.* 1 'government by its own people' (of a former colony, etc.), 2 'self-control'

Ge (Ø) Ic - < *sjólfstjóm* Fr [selfgɔvεʀnment] M, beg19c, 1(1 tech) Sp (0) < trsl *autogobierno* It - < trsl *autogoverno* Bg - < trsl *samoupravlenie* Hu [selfgavement] [U] 19c (1 obs)

self-inductance *n.* 'the property of an electric circuit that causes an electromotive force to be generated in it by a change in the current flowing through it' (electr.)

Fr [self ēdyktãs] F, 1930s (1 tech) = *autoinductance* Sp - < trsl *autoinducción* It - < trsl *autoinduttanza* Rm - < rend *inductanță proprie* Hu - < trsl *öngerjesztés*

self-induction *n.* 'the production of an electromotive force in a circuit when the current in that circuit is varied' (electr.)

Du *zelfinductie* via Fr, 20c (3 tech) Fr *self-induction*

[selfēdyksjō] F, end19c (1 tech) = *autoinduction* Sp - < trsl *autoinducción* It - < trsl *autoinduzione* Rm *self inducție* [self induktsie] F, 1970s, via Fr? (1+5/3 tech) < *inducție proprie* Rs - < trsl *samoinduktsiya* Cr - < trsl *samoindukcija* Bg - < trsl *samoinduktsiya* Hu - < trsl *önindukció* Al - < trsl *autoinduksion*

self-made (man) *n.* 1 'someone who has become successful or rich by his own effort', cf. *COD* **self-made** adj. 1

This term first spread in the late nineteenth century to Western Europe where it has now become at least slightly obsolescent; by contrast, a restricted expansion to Eastern Europe seems under way.

Ge [=E] M, pl. *-men*, mid19c (1 obs) Du [=E] C, pl. *-men*, beg20c (2) Nw [=E] M, pl. *-men(n)*, mid19c (1 obs) / also *-woman/-women* Ic [=E] mid/end20c (0) Fr *self-made man* [selfmεdman] M, pl. *-mans/-men*, end19c (1 obs) Sp [=E] M, pl. *-men*, end19c (1 obs) < trsl *hombre hecho a sí mismo* It [self meid mεn] M, pl. Ø, end19c (1>2) Rm [=E] M, 1970s (1 jour) Po [-men] M, beg20c (1 tech) Cr [=E] M, mid20c (1 tech) Fi [=E] 19c (1 obs) Hu [=E] pl. Ø, end19/beg20c (1 arch)

self-service *n.* 1 'shops, restaurants, etc. where customers serve themselves and pay at a checkout counter etc.'

The evidence points to marginal acceptance in most languages, but quick replacement by calques, which are now dominant in almost all languages.

Ge [=E] N [U] 1950s (1 obs) < *Selbstbedienung, SB* Du [=E] C [U] 1980s (0) = *zelfbediening* Nw (0) < trsl *selvbetjening* Ic [=E] uninfl., mid/end20c (0) < trsl *sjálfsafgreiðsla* Fr *selfl* <=E> [selfsεrvis] M, 1950s (= restaurant); *self-service station* (1 ban) < *station libre service* Sp [selfsεrbis] M [U] 1970s (1 rare) < trsl *autoservicio* It [self sεrvis] M, pl. Ø, 1960s (3) Rm [=E] N [U] 1970s (2 rare) < rend *autoservire* Rs (0) < trsl *samoobsluzhivanie* Po [-servis] end20c (1 coll) Cr [=E] M [U] mid20c (1) = trsl *samoposlužiranje* Bg - < trsl *na samoobsluzhvane* Fi - < trsl *itsepalvelu* Hu [=E-servis] pl. Ø, 1980s (2) Al - < *vetëshërbim* Gr *self servis* N, end20c (2)

seller *cp²/n.* 2 'a commodity that sells well' (modelled on ↑*best-seller*)

Ge [=E] M, pl. Ø, 1970s (1 jour) Du [=E] C, mid20c (2) = *best seller* Nw [=E] M, pl. *-e*, 1980s (1 jour)

semi-trailer *n.* 'a trailer having wheels at the back but supported at the front by a towing vehicle'

Nw [se:mitrailer/-treiler] M, pl. *-e*, 1950s (2) Fr - < *semi-remorque* Rm- < *remorcă trailer*

sense *n.* 5 'practical wisdom or judgement, common sense', 6b 'intelligibility or coherence or possession of meaning' (cf. ↑*common sense*)

Nw [=E] M [U] 1970s (1 coll)   **Ic** [sɛns] M/N [U] 1970s, 6b(1 coll: esp. in: *meika sens*)

sense   *v.* 2 'be vaguely aware of'
Nw [sɛnse] 1980s (1 coll, mod)

septic tank   *n.* 'a tank, usu. underground, in which the organic matter in sewage is decomposed through bacterial activity'
Du [=E] C, 1950s (1 tech)   **Nw** *septiktank* [septik-taŋk] M, pl. *-er*, mid20c (3)   **Ic** - < creat *rotþró*   **Sp** - < *pozo negro/pozo séptico*   **Bg** - < rend *septichna yama*

sequel   *n.* 2 'a novel, film, etc. that continues the story of an earlier one'
Ge [=E] N, 1990s (1 mod)   **Du** [=E] C, 1990s (1 tech)   **Nw** [=E] M, pl. *-s*, 1980s (1 tech, mod) = *oppfølger*

serial   *n./cp²* 1 'a story, play, or film which is published, broadcast, or shown in regular instalments'
The status of this word is not quite clear; where pronunciation is as in English (German, Croatian, Greek), there is no doubt – but it may be interpreted as Romance elsewhere.
Ge [=E] N, pl. *-s*, 1970s (1 tech, mod) < mean *Serie*   **Du** - < mean *serie*   **Nw** (o) < mean *serie*   **Ic** - < *seria; framhalds-*   **Fr** <=E> M, pl. *-s*, 1960s (1 tech, ban) < *série, feuilleton*   **Sp** <=E> [serjal] M, end20c (4)   **It**

[sirial/serjal] M/cp¹, pl. Ø/-s, 1960s (2)   **Rm** [serjal] N, 1970s, via Fr (3)   **Rs** *serial* M, pl. *-y*, end20c (3)   **Po** [serial] M, end20c (3)   **Cr** *serijal* M, pl. *-i*, end20c (3)   **Bg** *serial* M, pl. *-al-i*, end20c (2)   **Fi** - < mean *sarja*   **Hu** - < mean *széria* (5La)   **Al** *serial* M, pl. *-e*, end20c (1)   **Gr** *sirial* N, end20c (2)

serve   *v.* 12 'deliver a ball etc. to begin or resume play' (sport)
Ge - < mean *servieren* = *aufschlagen*   **Du** *serven* [sʏrvən] 1940s (1 tech) = *opslann, serveren*   **Nw** [sørve] beg20c (1/2)   **Fr** - < mean *servir*   **Sp** - < mean *servir*   **It** - < mean *servire*   **Rm** - < mean *servi*   **Po** *serwować* [servovatɕ] M [U] mid20c (1 tech)   **Cr** - < mean *servirati*   **Bg** - < mean *serviram*   **Hu** *szervál* [serva:l] beg20c (2 tech)   **Gr** - < mean *serviro*

serve   *n.* 1 'the act of serving' (cf. ↑*service*) (tennis, volleyball)
Du [=E] C, 1940s (1 tech)   **Nw** [sørv] M, pl. *-r*, 1930s (1 tech)   **Ic** - < *uppgjöf*   **Sp** - < mean *servicio*   **It** - < mean *servizio*   **Rs** (o)   **Po** *serw* [serv] M, mid20c (1 tech)   **Cr** *serva* M [U] beg20c (1 tech)   **Hu** *szerva* [serva] pl. *-ák*, beg20c (2 tech)   **Al** *servis* M [U] mid20c (3)

server   *n.* 2 'a person who serves the ball' (sport), 4b 'a computer that manages shared access to a central resource or service in a network' (comput.)
Ge [=E] M, pl. Ø, 1970s, 2(1 obs); 1990s, 4b(1 tech)   **Du** [=E] C, 1950s (1 tech)   **Nw** [sørver] M, pl. *-e*, 20c, 2(2); [=E] M, pl. *-e*, 1980s (1 tech)   **Ic** [=E] M, pl. *-ar*,

1990s, 4b (1 tech) < creat *netþjónn*   **Fr** - < mean *serveur/-euse*   **Sp** - < 4b: *servidor*   **It** [server] M, pl. Ø, 1970s (1 tech)   **Rm** [server] N, end20c, 4b(1 tech)   **Rs** *server* M, pl. *-y*, end20c (1 tech)   **Po** *serwer/* <=E> [server] M, end20c, 4b(1 tech)   **Cr** *server* M, pl. *-i*, beg20c, 2(1 tech)   **Bg** *sърvър* M, pl. *-al-i*, 1990s, 4b(1 tech) < 2: trsl *servirasht igrach*   **Fi** *serveri* 1980s, 4b(2) = mean *palvelin*   **Hu** *szerváló* [serva:lo:] pl. Ø, beg20c, 2(2 tech); *szerver* [server] pl. Ø, end20c, 4b(1 tech)   **Gr** <=E> [=E] M, end20c, 4b(1 tech)

service   *n.* 3 'assistance or benefit given to someone', 11b 'periodic routine maintenance (of a car, TV set, etc.)', 12 'assistance or advice given to customers after the sale of goods', 13b 'a tip, extra money given to a waiter etc.', 15a 'the act of serving' (tennis, volleyball), +16 'a sailor who takes odd jobs; an unreliable fellow'
The evidence is complex due to a homograph pair from English [sɜ:vɪs] and French [servi:s] – both words coexist in many languages, with 'table service' being mostly French, but the tennis and car repair ones being English, and 'tip' possibly divided. Romance languages employ their cognate forms anyway.
Ge [sörvis] M [U] 19c, 15a(2) < *Aufschlag*; 1940s, 11b,12(2) < *Kundendienst*   **Du** [=E] C [U] 1940s, 15a(1 tech); 12(2); beg20c, 11b(2)   **Nw** [=E] M [U] 15a(0) < *serve*; 1930s, 11b,12(2); 13b(1 obs?); *servis* [særvis] M, pl. *-er*, end19c, +16(1 arch)   **Ic** *sörvis* [=E] M [U] mid20c, 3,12(2 coll) 11b(2 tech) < *þjónusta*   **Fr** (5)   **Sp** - < 15a: mean *servicio*   **It** - < 15a: mean *servizio*   **Rm** *service* [servis] N, 20c, 11b(3); N [U] end20c, 12(2 mod); < 3,15a: *serviciu*   **Rs** *servis* [U] mid20c, 11b,12(3) → *-nyĭ* adj.   **Po** *serwis/serw* M [U] mid20c, 15a(1 tech), 11b(3) → *serwowanie* N; *serwować* v.; *za-* v.   **Cr** *servis* M, pl. *-i*, mid20c, 15a(1 tech) → *-ni* adj.; *-er* M   **Bg** *servis* M, pl. *-al-i*, mid20c, 15a(1 tech); *serviz* M, pl. *-al-i*, mid20c, 11b(3) = 15a: *nachalen udar* → *-en* adj.   **Hu** *szerva* [serva] pl. *-ák*, beg20c, 15a(2 tech); *szerviz* [serviz] end19c/beg20c, 11b,12(3/5Fr) = 15a: *adogatás*   **Al** *servis* M [U] mid20c, 11b,15a(3)   **Gr** *servis* N, beg20c, via Fr, 15a(1 tech); *servis* N, mid20c, 11b,12(2)

session   *n./cp¹ᐟ²* +2b 'a single meeting at a conference, symposium etc.', 5a 'a period devoted to an activity', +5c 'a period of drug-taking', +7 'a spontaneous meeting of musicians used for playing together, improvising, trying out new ideas, etc.' (cf. ↑*jam session*)
Ge [=E] F, pl. *-s*, 1970s, +7(1 tech)   **Du** [=E] C, 1990s, +7(1 mod) > *sessie*   **Nw** *-session* [=E] M/cp², pl. *-s*, 1980s, 5a(1); 1960s, +7(1) < *jam, jam session*   **Ic** *sessjón* [sɛs:joun] F, pl. *-ir*, mid/end20c, +2b,5a,+7(1 tech, coll)   **Fr** [sesjõ] F, 18c, +2b(4)   **Sp** - < +7: *jam session*   **It** *sessione* +2b,5a(5La); +7: ↑*jam session*   **Rm** *sesiune* +2b(5Fr/La); +7: ↑*jam session*   **Rs** *seshn/seĭshn* M, pl. -y, 1990s, +7(1 sla)   **Po** *sesja* (5La)   **Cr** - < +2b: mean *sesija*   **Bg** *seshŭn* M, pl. *-al- i*, 1990s, +5c(1 tech)   **Hu** (5La)   **Al** *sesion* M, pl. *-e*, end20c, 5a(1 tech)   **Gr** <=E> [=E] F/cp¹/cp², +7(1 tech)

set   *n.* 4 'a collection of tools, china, etc.', +4a 'two pieces matching in colour and shape', 6 'a group of games' (tennis), 18 'a setting, including stage furniture etc., for a play or film', 19 'a sequence of songs or pieces performed in jazz or pop music', +25 'a tablemat'

The great number of senses of the English item is basically reduced to three (4, 6, +25; whether these were individually borrowed, or how they were transmitted from one language to another, is uncertain.

Ge [=E] N/M, pl. -s, 1960s, 4, +4a(2) 6(1 arch); 1980s, 18(1 tech); +25(2) < 4,+4a,6: *Satz*   **Du** [=E] C, 1950s, 4, +4a(2); 1930s, 6(1 tech)   **Nw** *sett* [=E] N, pl. Ø, 19c, 4, +4a,6,18(4)   **Ic** *sett* [seht] N, pl. Ø, end18c, 4,+4a(5Da); mid/end20c, 6,18,19(4 tech)   **Fr** [set] M, end19c, 6(1 tech), +25(2)   **Sp** [set] M, pl. -s, beg20c, 6(2 tech); end20c, 4(1 tech); 1930s, 18(1 tech) > 6: *serie/manga* = 4: *conjunto, juego*   **It** [set] M, pl. Ø, 1900s, 4, +4a,6(3)   **Rm** [=E] N, beg20c, via Fr, 4,+4a,6,+25(3)   **Rs** *set* M, pl. -y, beg20c, 6(1 tech)   **Po** [=E] M, beg20c, 6(1 tech)   **Cr** *set* M, pl. -ovi, beg20c, 6(1 tech)   **Bg** *set* M, pl. -a/-ove, mid20c, 6(1 tech)   **Fi** *setti* 19c, 4(3 coll) 6(0) < 6: *erä*   **Hu** *szett* [sett] pl. -ek, end19/beg20c, +4a,6,+25(3); mid20c, 4(3)   **Al** *set* M, pl. -e, beg20c, 6(3)   **Gr** *set* N, mid20c, 4,+4a(2) 6(1 tech)

setter *n.* 1 'a dog of a large long-haired breed trained to stand rigid when scenting game'

This term exhibits the almost universal spread of an early word related to dog breeding (cf. ↑*pointer*, ↑*terrier* etc.).
Ge [zẹta] M, pl. Ø, 19c (2)   **Du** [=E] C, beg20c (2)   **Nw** [=E] M, pl. -e, beg20c (2)   **Ic** [=E] M, pl. -ar, mid/end20c (0)   **Fr** [setɛʀ] M, pl. -s, end19c (2) **Sp** [sẹter] M, pl. -s, end19c (1 tech)   **It** [sẹtter] M, pl. Ø, mid19c (3)   **Rm** *setter/seter* [sẹter] M, beg20c, via Fr? (2>3) → -iţă F   **Rs** *sẹtter* M, pl. -y, beg20c (2) **Po** *seter* [-er] M, beg20c (2) → -ek M; -ka F   **Cr** *sẹter* M, pl. -i, beg20c (2)   **Bg** *sẹter* M, pl. -a/-i, mid20c (2 tech)   **Fi** *setteri* 19c (3)   **Hu** *szetter* [sẹtter] pl. -ek, end19/beg20c (3)   **Gr** *sẹter* N, 20c (1 tech)

setting *n.* 4 'the place and time of a story, drama, etc.'
Du [=E] C, 1970s (2)   **Nw** [=E] M/F, pl. -er, end20c (1)

settle *v.* 6 'resolve (a dispute etc)', 12a (with reference to the USA) 'colonize'
Ge *setteln* [setəln] 1980s, 6(1 coll, rare)   **Du** *settelen* [setələn] 1980s, 6(1 coll, rare); 1970s, 12a(2 rare)   **Nw** [sẹtle] 20c, 12a(Ø)   **Ic** *settla* [sẹhtla] mid20c, 6(2 sla) → *settlast (á)* v.

settled *adj.* 'well-situated'
Ge *gesettelt* 1980s (1 coll, rare)   **Du** *gesetteld* [ɣǝsẹtəlt] 1980s (2)

settlement *n.* 2b 'a place or area occupied by settlers (esp. with reference to the USA)', +2d 'an establishment in poorer parts of a city where educated people live in close contact with lower classes for the purpose of social reform', 3a 'a political or financial agreement', 3b 'an arrangement ending a dispute'
Ge 2b(0)   **Du** [=E] C, 1980s, 3a,b(1 mod)   **Nw** [=E] N, pl. Ø/-er, end19c, 2b,+2d(=Ø)   **Rs** *sẹttl'ment* M,

beg20c, 2b(Ø)   **Fi** *setlementti* beg20c, +2d(1 tech) **Hu** 2b(Ø arch)

settler *n.* (esp. with reference to the USA) 'a person who goes to settle in a new country or place'
Ge (0)   **Du** [=E] C, beg20c (2)   **Nw** [=E] M, pl. -e, end19c (Ø)

set-up *n.* +3 'preparations that are necessary to start a piece of machinery, esp. a computer'

Ge [=E] N [U] 1980s (1 tech, rare)   **Du** [setvp] C, pl. -s, end20c (1 tech)   **Ic** [=E] N, end20c (1 tech)   **It** [set ạp] M, pl. Ø, 20c (1 tech)   **Cr** (0)   **Bg** <=E>/ *setüp* M [U] 1990s (1 tech)   **Hu** [=E] pl. Ø, end20c (1 tech)   **Gr** <=E> [=E] N [U] end20c (1 tech)

sex *n./cp¹* 4 'sexual instincts, desires, etc.', 5 'sexual intercourse'

The modern meanings (4/5) almost universally borrowed are first recorded from early twentieth-century English but spread only after 1945; euphemistic functions and the short form have certainly played a role in the quick adoption – apart from the word's expressing a new life-style.
Ge [s-/z-] M [U] 1950s (2)   **Du** [=E] C [U] 1960s (2>3) < *seks*   **Nw** [=E] M [U] mid20c (2) → *sexig* adj.   **Ic** [=E] N [U] 1970s (1 sla)   **Fr** *sexe* (5)   **Sp** *sexo* (5) < *relaciones sexuales*   **It** [=E] M/cp¹ [U] 1920s (2)   **Rm** [=E] N [U] end20c, 5(4)   **Rs** *seks* M [U] mid20c (3)   **Po** (5La)   **Cr** *seks* M [U] mid20c, 4(2)   **Bg** *seks* M/ cp¹ [U] mid20c, 5(2) → -ualen adj.   **Fi** *seksi* 1960s (3)   **Hu** *szex* [=E] pl. Ø, 1960s (3)   **Al** *seks* M [U] mid20c, 4(3)   **Gr** *sex* N [U] mid20c (2)

sex and crime* *phr.* 'as characteristics of cheap fiction and film'
Ge [=E] 1960s (1 coll)   **Nw** [=E] 1960s (1)   **Gr** - < *sex ke via*

sex-appeal *n.* 'sexual attractiveness'

This compound is first recorded for 1924 in American English; it appears to have spread very quickly with American films – perhaps even before the simplex ↑*sex* became widely known.
Ge [=E] M [U] 1920s (1 coll)   **Du** [=E] C/N [U] 1930s (2)   **Nw** <=E>/*sex-appell* [=E(+Nw)] M [U] mid20c (1 obs)   **Ic** [=E] N/*sexap(p)ill* [sɛxsa(h)pitl] M [U] mid20c (2 sla) < *kynþokki*   **Fr** [sɛksapil] M, 1930s (1 coll)   **Sp** [sɛksapil] M [U] 1930s (1 coll) = *atractivo sexual*   **It** [sɛks api:l] M [U] 1930s (2) < *fascino*   **Rm** [=E] N [U] mid20c, via Fr (1 coll, rare)   **Rs** *seksapil* M [U] mid20c (1 you) → -nyi adj.   **Po** *seksa-pill*/<=E> M [U] mid20c (1 you)   **Cr** *sẹksepil* M [U] mid20c (2)   **Bg** *seksapil* M [U] mid20c (2) → -en adj.   **Fi** [=E] end20c (0)   **Hu** *szexepil* [sẹksepi:l] [U] beg20c (3a) → -es adj.   **Gr** *sexapil*/<=E> N [U] mid20c, via Fr (2)

sex-shop *n.* 'a shop selling pornography etc.'

This compound illustrates the spread of a life style better than other words of the group, with Eastern Europe still lagging behind conspicuously.

Ge [=E] M, pl. -s, 1970s (2) Du [=E] C, 1970s (2) Nw - < *pornosjappe* Ic [=E] 1970s (0) Fr [sɛksəʃɔp] M/F, 1970s (1) Sp [=E] M/F, pl. -s, 1970s (1) It [=E] M, pl. Ø, 1970s (2) Rm [=E] N, end20c (1 rare) Rs *seks-shop* M, pl. -y, end20c (2) Po [=E] M, end20c (2) Cr *sekssop* (0) Bg *seksshop/<=E>* M, pl. -*al-ove*, 1990s (1 mod) < trsl *seks magazin* Fi [=E] 1970s (1) Hu [=E] pl. -*ok*, end20c (1 jour, you, mod) Gr <=E>/*sex sop* N, end20c (2)

sex symbol   *n.* 'a person widely noted for his or her sex appeal'

Ge [=E+symbo:l] N, pl. -*e*, 1970s (3+5) Du [=E+symbo:l] C, pl. -*e*, 1970s (3+5) Nw [=E+Nw] M, pl. -*er*, 1970s (3+5) Ic [sɛxsɪmpoul] N, pl. Ø, mid/end20c (0) < trsl *kyntákn* Fr *sex-symbol/sexe- symbole* [sɛksɛbɔl] M, 1980s (1 jour) Sp [=E] M, pl. -*s*, 1970s (1) It [sɛks simbol] M, pl. Ø, 1980s (1>2) Rm *sex simbol* [seks simbol] N, 1990s (1 mod) Rs - < trsl *sekssimvol* Cr (0) Bg - < trsl *sekssimvol* Fi - < trsl *seksisymboli* mid20c (3) Hu - < trsl *szexszimbólum* Al - < trsl *simbol seksi/seks simbol* Gr - < trsl *symvolo tu sex*

sexy   *adj.* 1 'sexually attractive or stimulating'

This word is added to congeners of *sexual* which exist in all languages with a neutral biological meaning (as ↑*sex* is added to existing biological terms in the receiving languages).

Ge [s-/z-] 1950s (2) Du [=E] 1960s (2) Nw [=E] 1950s (2) > *sexig* Ic *sexí* [sɛxsi] uninfl., mid20c (2 coll) = *kynþokkafullur* Fr [sɛksi] uninfl., 1950s (1 coll) Sp [sɛksi] 1960s (2) It [sɛksi] uninfl., 1960s (2>3) Rm [=E] uninfl., 1970s (2 coll) Po uninfl., end20c (1 coll) Cr *seksi* end20c (2 coll) Bg *seksi* uninfl., end20c (2 coll) Fi *seksikäs* end20c (3) Hu *szexi/szekszi* [=E] 1960s (3 coll) → -*s* adj. Al *seks* adj., end20c (2) Gr *sexi/<=E>* uninfl., mid20c (2)

shabby   *adj.* 1 'in bad repair or condition', 2 'dressed in old or worn clothes'

Ge - < *schäbig* (4) Du [=E] 1950s (1 coll) Nw [=E] beg20c (2) Ic [sjap:i] uninfl., mid20c (2 coll) Hu (5Ge)

shackle   *n.* 1 'a metal loop closed by a bolt used to connect chains' (naut.)

Various terms of related or identical meanings in Germanic languages are genetically related rather than borrowed; loanwords in other languages need not be from English, either.

Ge - < *Schekel* (4) Du - < *schakel* (4) Nw *sjakkel* [ʃakel] M, pl. -*kler*, beg20c (1 tech) Po *szakla* [ʃakla] F, mid20c (1 tech) Bg *shegel* M, pl. -*al-i*, beg20c (1 tech), via /from Ge (3 tech) Fi *sakkeli* 19c (3)

shackle   *v.* 'connect by means of a shackle' (naut.)

Nw *sjakle* [ʃakle] 20c (1 tech) Po *szaklować* [ʃklovatç] mid20c (1 tech)

shag   *n.* 2 'a coarse kind of cut tobacco'

The early borrowing into nineteenth-century Ger-

manic languages was continued in other parts of Europe; in modern use forms close to English spelling and pronunciation appear to be preferred.

Ge [ʃek/ʃæg] M [U] 19c (1 tech) → *Scheckpfeife* Du [ʃɛk] C [U] 1930s (1 tech) < *shagje/sjekkie* Nw [=E] M [U] 19c (1 tech)

shake   *v.* +1a 'dance with shaking movements'

Ge *shaken* [e:] 1960s (1 arch) Du *shaken* [ʃe:kə(n)] 1970s (1 tech, obs) Nw [ʃeike] 1960s (1 obs) Ic *sjeika* [sjei:ka] 19c (1 you, obs) Rm - < rend *a dousa shake* Hu *shakel* [ʃe:kel] 1960s (2 arch)

shake   *n./cp²* 5 'a milk shake', +5a 'a mixed drink made from various components', +6 'a dance style'

The evidence is clear for Western Europe, where the word (together with the compound ↑*milk shake*) became common from the 1950s onwards. However, Eastern Europe is divided in a unique way. Contrast the much more widespread ↑*shaker* for the instrument.

Ge [ʃe:k] M, pl. -*s*, 1960s, 5,+5a(1 coll) +6(1 arch) Du [=E] C, 1960s, 5(2) Nw [=E] M [U] 1960s, 5(2) +6(1 obs) Ic <=E>/*sjeik* [sjei:k] M, pl. -*ar*, mid20c, 5(2 coll); N [U] 1960s, +6(1 you, obs) > 5: creat *(mjólkur) hristingur* It [=E/ʃe:k] M [U] 1960s, +5a(1) +6(2 obs) Rm [=E] N, 1960s, +6(1 you, obs) Rs *sheĭk* M [U] mid20c, +6(1 obs) Cr (0) Bg *sheik* M, pl. -*al-ove*, mid20c (2) Hu [ʃe:k] [U] 1960s, +6(2 arch); pl. Ø, end20c, +5a(2 tech) Gr *seik* N, 1960s, +6(1 obs)

shakehands*   *n.* 'a greeting', 'cf. ↑*handshake*'

Ge [ʃekhents] N [U] end19c (1 coll) Fr *shake-hand* M, mid19c (1 arch) Sp *shake-hand* M, end19c (1 arch) < *apretón de manos* Po *shakehand/shake hand* [-ent] M [U] beg20c (1 coll) Cr (0) Hu [=E] [U] end19/beg20c (1 coll, arch)

shake hands   *v.* 'salute or greet'

Du [=E] 1980s (1 coll, rare) Nw [ʃeike hæ:ns] 1960s (1 coll, fac)

shaker   *n.* 2 'a container for shaking together the ingredients of cocktails etc.'

Ge [=E] M, pl. Ø, mid20c (2) → -*en* v. Du [ʃe:kər] C, 1950s (1 tech) → *shaken* v. Nw [=E/ʃeiker] M, pl. -*e*, 20c (1 tech) Ic - < trsl *(kokteil)hristari* Fr [ʃekœR] M, end19c (1 tech) It [ʃeker] M, pl. Ø, end19c (2 tech) → *shakerato* adj.; *shakerare* v. Rm [ʃakər/=E] N, 1970s (1 tech) Rs *sheĭker* M, pl. -*y*, end20c (1 tech) Po [-er] M, end20c (1 coll) Cr *šejker* M, pl. -*i*, end20c (1 tech) Bg *sheĭkŭr* M, pl. -*al-i*, mid20c (2 tech) Fi [=E] mid20c (0) Hu [=E] pl. Ø, beg20c (1 tech) Gr *seiker* N, mid/end20c (2)

shaky   *adj.* 1 'unsteady, trembling', +4 'nervous'

Du [=E] 1980s (1 coll, rare) Nw [=E] 1960s (1 coll) Ic [sjei:ci] uninfl., end20c (1 sla)

shampoo   *n.* I 'liquid for hair washing', 2 'a similar substance for washing a car or carpet, etc.'

This Hindi term was transmitted through nine-teenth-century Indian English. The sense relating to the cleansing of hair is first recorded in 1866; it is the one dominant in loanwords. The spellings of the loan-word vary, some clearly indicating English prove-nance (note orthographic integration in recent reform proposals in Norwegian and German).
Ge *Shampoo(n)/Schampon/Schampun* [ʃampu:] N, pl. *-s*, end19c, 1(2); 1980s, 2(1 tech) → *schamponieren/ schampunieren* v.   **Du** [ʃampo/=E] C, 1930s (2) → *shampooing* n.   **Nw** <=E>/*sjampo* [ʃampu] M, pl. *-er*, beg20c (2) → *sjamponere* v.   **Ic** *sjampó* [sjampou] N [U] mid20c, 1(2)   **Fr** *shampoing/shampooing* [ʃapuɛ̃] M, 1870s (3) → *shampouiner/shampooiner* v.; *shampouineur* M; *shampouineuse* F   **Sp** <=E>/ *champú* [ʃampu/tʃampu] 1930s (3)   **It** [ʃampo] M, pl. Ø/-*i*, 1930 (3)   **Rm** *şampon* [ʃampon] N, 1930s, via Fr/Ge (3) → *şampona* v.; *-are* F, *-a* adj.   **Rs** *shampun'* M [U] mid20c (3)   **Po** *szampon* [ʃampon] M, mid20c, 1,2(3) → *-ik* M   **Cr** *šampon* M, pl. *-i*, mid20c (3) → *-irati* v.   **Bg** *shampoan* M, pl. *-al-i*, mid20c, via Fr (3)   **Fi** *shampoo/sampoo* [=E/sampo:] beg20c (3)   **Hu** *sampon* [ʃampon] pl. *-ok*, end19/beg20c (3)   **Al** *shampo* M [U]/F, pl. Ø, 1(3); mid20c (3)   **Gr** *sabouan* N, beg20c (5Fr)

shanghai   *v.* I 'force a person to be a sailor by using drugs and tricks', 2 'put into an awkward situation by trickery'

(I) is recorded from American English sailor's slang from 1871; the loanwords have retained the register specification.
Ge *schanghaien* 20c, 1(1 tech, obs)   **Du** *shangaaien* [ʃangha:jen] 1960s (1 tech, obs) < *ronselen*   **Nw** *shanghaie* [ʃaŋhaie] beg20c, 1(1 arch) 2(1) → *shanghai-ing* M/F   **Ic** *sjanghæja* [sjaŋhai:ja] beg20c, 1(1 sla)

shanty   *n.* 'a song sung by sailors'

This word is thought to be a variant of *chant(e)y*, but loanwords tend to have *sh*-(unless respelt), the relation to the original connection with French *chan-ter* being lost.
Ge [ʃenti] N, pl. *-(ie)s*, 19c (1 tech/obs)   **Du** [=E] C, pl. *-s*, 1960s (1 tech)   **Nw** <=E>/*sjanti* [=E/ʃanti] M, pl. *-er/-ies*, beg20c (1 tech)   **Ic** [=E] (0)   **Fr** (0)   **Po** *szanta* [ʃanta] F, end20c (1 mod) → *szantowy* adj.

shanty town   *n.* 'a depressed area of a town; consist-ing of shanties'

Various terms of similar meaning are in use, differ-entiated according to the regions referred to, but all are foreignisms in principle: *shanty town, bidonville, slums, favela* etc.
Du (Ø)   **Ic** [=E] N, mid/end20c (Ø)   **Fr** [=E] 20c (1 ban) < *bidonville*   **It** - < *bidonville*   **Po** (0)   **Bg** - < *bidonvil*

shaping*   *n./cp¹* I 'a planing machine for metal', 2 'the process done by a machine called a *shaper*'
Ge *Shaping-Maschine* cp¹/F, mid20c, 1(0 tech)   **Rm** *şeping* [=E] N, 1970s, 1(1 tech)   **Rs** *sheping* M, pl. *-i*,

mid20c, 1(1 tech)   **Bg** *sheping (-mashina)* M/F, pl. *-al-i*, mid20c, via Ge, 1(3 tech)   **Hu** *séping* [=E] [U] beg20c, 2(1 tech)

share   *n.* 3 'part-proprietorship of parts into which a company's capital is divided entitling the owner to a proportion of profits', +4 'the size of the audience attracted by a TV programme'   **Sp** [=E] M [U] end20c, +4(1 tech, jour) = *cuota de partalla*   **It** [ʃer] M, pl. Ø/[U] 1980s (1 tech)

shareware   *n.* 'software that is available free of charge and often distributed informally for evalua-tion' (comput.)
Ge [E] F [U] 1990s (1 tech)   **Du** [=E] C [U] 1980s (1 tech)   **Nw** [=E] 1990s (1 tech)   **Ic** [=E] end20c (0) < trsl *deilihugbúnaður*   **Fr** [ʃɛRWER] M, 1990s (1 tech, ban) < *logiciel contributif, logiciel à contribution volontaire*   **Sp** [=E] M [U] 1990s (1 tech, rare)   **It** [=E] M [U] 1990s (1 tech)   **Po** N [U] 1990s (1 tech)   **Cr** M [U] 1990s (1 tech)   **Bg** *she(ŭ)ruer* M [U] 1990s (1 tech)   **Fi** [=E] 1990s (1 tech)   **Hu** [ʃer-ver] pl. *-ek?*, end20c (1 tech)   **Gr** <=E> [=E] F, end20c (1 tech)

shark   *n.* +3 'a kind of fishing boat'
Nw *sjark* [ʃark] M, pl. *-er*, via Rs? (3)

sharper   *n.* 'a swindler, esp. at cards'
Nw [=E] M, pl. *-e*, 19c (1 arch)

shawl   *n.* I 'a piece of fabric, usu. rectangular and often folded into a triangle, worn over the shoulders or head or wrapped round a baby'

This word is from Persian and was transmitted through either English, French (mainly western lan-guages), or Turkish. Its form was clearly English in early German, before it became adapted in spelling and pronunciation.
Ge *Schal* [a:] M, pl. *-el-s*, beg19c (3); *shawl* (1 arch)   **Du** *sjaal* [ʃa:l] C, mid19c (3)   **Nw** *sjal* [ʃa:l] N, pl. Ø, mid19c (3)   **Ic** *sjal* [sja:l] N, pl. *sjöl*, mid19c, via Da (3)   **Fr** *châle* [ʃal] M, pl. *-s*, 17c (3)   **Sp** *chal* (5Fr)   **It** *scialle* (5Fr)   **Rm** *şal* [ʃal] N, 18c (5Tur-kish)   **Rs** *shal'* F, pl. *-i*, beg20c (5)   **Po** *szal* [ʃal] M, beg20c, via Ge (3) → *-ik* M   **Cr** *šal* M, pl. *-ovi*, 19c (3)   **Bg** *shal* M, pl. *-al-ove*, beg20c, via Turk (5)   **Fi** *saali* 19c, via Ge (3)   **Hu** *sál* [ʃa:l] pl. *-ak*, 18c, via Ge/ Fr (3)   **Al** *shall* M, pl. *-e*, beg19c (5)   **Gr** *sali* N, beg20c, viaFr (3)

shearling   *n.* I 'a sheep that has been shorn once', 2 'wool from a shearling'
It [ʃiːrlin(g)] M, pl. Ø/[U] mid20c (1>2)

shed   *n.* I 'a one-storeyed structure for storage or shelter for animals etc., or as a workshop'
It [=E] M, pl. Ø, 1900s (1 tech) < *capannone*   **Rm** [=E] N, 1970s (1 tech)

shed roof*   *n.* 'a roof with only one slope'
Ge *Sheddach* N, beg20c (2 tech+5)   **Du** *sheddak* [ʃedak] N, beg20c (2)   **Fr** *shed* [ʃɛd] M, mid20c (1 tech)   **It** *shed* [=E] M, pl. Ø, 1960s (1 tech) < *tettoia,*

Ic	Nw	Po	Rs
Du	Ge	Cr	Bg
▨	It	Fi	▨
Sp	Rm	Al	Gr

copertura a shed **Rm** *shed* [=E] N, mid20c (1 tech) **Cr** (0) **Hu** *shed* [=E] [U] 20c (1 tech)

shelf *n.* 2c 'an area of relatively shallow seabed between the shore of a continent and the deeper ocean'

This word (in full: *Continental shelf*) started as a specialized geographical term, but has, in a time of offshore oil drilling, become quite common; native equivalents tend to be cumbrose.

Ge *Schelf* N/M, pl. *-s/-e*, beg20c (3) = *Festlandssockel* **Du** - < *vastelandsplat* **Nw** [=E] M, pl. *-er*, 20c (1 tech) = trsl *(kontinental)hylle* **Fr** - < *plateforme continentale* **Rm** *şelf* [=E] N, mid20c, via Ge (1 tech, rare) < *platformă continentală* **Rs** *shel'f* M, pl. *-y*, mid20c (1 tech) **Po** *szelf* M, mid20c (1 tech) → *-owy* adj. **Cr** *šelf* M, mid20c (1 tech) **Bg** *shelf* M, pl. *-al-ove*, mid20c (2 tech, jour) **Fi** [=E] 20c (1 tech) **Hu** *self* [ʃelf] pl. *-ek*, 20c (1 tech)

shelterdecker* *n.* 'a kind of boat'

Du *shelterdekschip* [ʃɛltərdɛkʃxip] N, 1940s (2 tech) **Nw** *shelterdekker* [=E] M, pl. *-e*, beg20c (1 tech) **Ic** - < rend *hlífðarþilfarsskip* **Fr** *shelterdeck* [ʃɛltœrdɛk] M, beg20c (1 tech) **Rm** *shelterdeck* [=E] N, beg20c (1 tech) **Rs** *shel'terdek* M, pl. *-i*, end19c (1 tech) **Cr** (0) **Bg** *sheltŭrdek* M, pl. *-al-ove*, 20c (1 tech) → *-dechen* adj.

sherardize *v.* 'coat (iron or steel) with zinc' (from the name of Sherard Cowper-Coles, English inventor, d. 1936)

Fr *shéradiser* beg20c (1 tech) → *shéradisation* (1 tech) **Rm** *sherardizal şerardiza* [ʃerardiza] mid20c (1 tech) → *-re* F; *-at* adj. **Po** *szerardyzacja* [serardizacia] F [U] end20c (1 tech) **Cr** (0) **Bg** *sherardiziram* 20c (1 tech) **Fi** *sherardisoida* 20c (1 tech)

sheriff *n.* 1 (Brit.) 'the chief law-enforcing officer in a county', 2 (US) 'an elected officer in a county, responsible for keeping the peace'

While the US use of this word is universally known through westerns, it does not appear to have been widely applied to European conditions and metaphoric uses.

Ge [=E] M, pl. *-s*, 17c, 1(Ø/1 arch); 19c, 2(Ø/1 fac) **Du** [=E] C, 19c (2) **Nw** [ʃærif] M. pl. *-er*, 20c (Ø/1 fac)) **Ic** [=E] mid20c, 2(Ø) **Fr** *shérif* [ʃerif] M, 19c (Ø) **Sp** [(t)ʃerif/serif] M, pl. *-s*, 1930s, 2(Ø/2) **It** *sceriffo* M, pl. *-i*, 15c, 1(Ø/3 tech); 18c, 2(3) **Rm** *şerif* [ʃerif] M, mid19c, via Fr (Ø) **Rs** *sherif* M, pl. *-y*, 19c (Ø) **Po** *szeryf* M, beg20c, 2(Ø) **Cr** *šerif* M, pl. *-i*, 19c (Ø) **Fi** *sheriffi* 19c (Ø) **Hu** *seriff* [=E] pl. *-ek*, beg20c (Ø) **Al** *sherif* M, pl. *-ë*, mid20c (2) **Gr** *serifis* M, mid20c, 2(3/Ø)

sherry *n.* 1 'a fortified wine originally from Jerez in southern Spain'

Ge [=E] M [U] 19c (2) **Du** [=E] C, pl. *-s*, beg20c (2) **Nw** [ʃæri] M [U] mid19c (2) **Ic** *sérrí/* <=E> [sjɛr:i] N [U] mid19c, via Da (2) **Fr** [ʃeʀi] M, 19c (1 tech) < *Xérès, Jerez* **Sp** [=E] M, pl. *-s*, 1970s (1 rare)

< *Jerez* **It** [ʃɛrri] M, pl. Ø, beg19c (3) **Rm** [=E] N [U] end19c (1 rare) < *(vin de) Xeres* **Rs** *sherri* N, uninfl., beg20c (2) **Po** [=E] N, uninfl., beg20c (1 tech) **Cr** *šeri* M [U] beg20c (2) **Bg** *sheri* N [U] 20c (2) **Fi** [ʃer:y] 19c (2) **Hu** [=E] [U] end19/beg20c (2) **Al** *verë sherri* 20c (2) **Gr** *seryl-i* N, beg20c (2)

shetland* *n./cp¹* 1 'a kind of wool sweater etc.', 2 'wool'

The use of *s.* to refer to wool/pullovers appears to be most widespread, followed by ~ *pony* (which is always used as a compound); the ~ *sheepdog* appears not to have been borrowed. Note the confusion of *Shetland* and *Scotland* in Russian and Bulgarian.

Ge [ʃetlent] cp¹, 20c (1 tech) = 1: *-pullover*, 2: *-wolle* **Nw** [=E(+Nw)] cp¹, 20c (1 tech+5) = 1: *-genser* 2: *-ull* **Ic** *shetlands-* [=E] cp¹, end19c, 2(2) **Fr** [ʃetlãd] M [U] end19c (1 tech) **Sp** [=E/setland] M [U] mid20c (1 tech) **It** [ʃetland] M [U] 1960s (1 tech) → *shetland* adj. **Rm** [=E] N, mid20c (2 tech) **Rs** *shotlandka* F [U] mid20c, 2(3) **Po** *szetland* [-ant] M, end20c → *zki* adj. **Cr** *šetland* M [U] mid20c, 2(2) **Bg** (0) < 1: rend *shotlandski pulover* **Fi** [=E] 20c, 2(1) **Hu** [=E] [U] beg20c, 2(3) → *-szövet* **Gr** *(malli) setlad* N [U] end20c, 2(5+1 tech)

shift *n.* 4a 'a woman's straight unwaisted dress', 7 'a key on a keyboard used to switch between lower and upper case'

Ge [=E] N, pl. *-s*, 1960s, 4a(1 tech, obs); end20c, 7(1 techCOMPUT) < 4a: *Shiftkleid* **Nw** [=E] [U] 20c, 7(1 tech) **Ic** [sjift] uninfl., end20c, 7(1 tech) **It** [=E] M, pl. Ø, 1960s, 7(1 tech) → *shiftare* **Rm** [=E] uninfl., end20c, 7(1 tech) **Po** M, end20c (1 tech) **Cr** (0)

shilling *n.* 1 'a former British coin and monetary unit equal to one-twentieth of a pound or twelve pence', +1a 'of small value'

This word is a foreignism in all languages; modern spellings are often replacing earlier adoptions. Note that the Austrian *Schilling* becomes homonymous in transliterating languages.

Ge *Sh-/Sch-* [=E] M, pl. Ø/-s/-e, 19c, 1(Ø) **Du** 1(Ø) **Nw** [=E] M, pl. Ø, mid19c, 1(Ø) **Ic** *shilling(ur)* [sjıl:iŋk(ʏr)] M, pl. *-ar*, mid19c, 1(Ø) = trsl *(enskur) skildingur* **Fr** *chelin* M, 17c, 1(Ø arch) **Sp** *chelin* mid19c, 1(Ø/3) **It** *scellino* M, pl. *-i*, 17c, 1(Ø) **Rm** *şiling/shil(l)ing* [=E] M, mid19c, via Fr (Ø) **Rs** *shilling* M, pl *-i*, end19c, 1(Ø) **Po** *szyling* [-nk] M, mid19c, 1(Ø) **Cr** *šiling* M, pl. *-zi*, 19c, 1(Ø) **Bg** *shiling* M, pl. *-al-i*, beg20c, 1(Ø) **Fi** *shillinki* 18c, 1(Ø); *killinki* 18c, via Sw, +1a(3) **Hu** [=E] pl. Ø/-ek, 20c, 1(Ø) **Al** *shilingë* [ʃiliŋ] F, pl. *-a*, mid19c (3/Ø) **Gr** *selini* N, beg20c, via Fr, 1(3/Ø)

shimmy *n.* 1 'a kind of ragtime dance in which the whole body is shaken, popular in the USA in the 1920s', 3 'an abnormal vibration of esp. the front wheels of a motor vehicle'

Ge [ʃimi:] M [U] 1920s, 1(1 tech, obs) **Du** [=E] C [U] 1940s, 1(1 obs/tech); N [U] 1940s, 3(2 tech) → *shimiën* v. **Nw** [=E] M [U] 1920s, 1(1 obs) **Fr** [ʃimi] M, 1920s, 1(1 tech, obs) **Sp** [ʃimi/tʃimi] M, pl. *-s*,

1920s, 1(1 tech, obs) **It** [=E/ʃimmi] M [U] 1920s, 1(1 obs) 3(1 tech) **Rm** shim(m)y/șimi [=E] N [U] mid20c, 1(1 tech, rare/obs) **Rs** shịmmi M, uninfl., mid20c, 1(1 tech) **Po** N, uninfl., mid20c, 1(1 tech) **Cr** șịmi M [U] 1920s, 1(1 tech, obs) **Bg** shịmi N [U] beg20c, 1(Ø/1 tech) **Hu** [=E] [U] 1920s, 1(2)

shingle *n.* 1 'a rectangular wooden tile used to cover esp. roofs', +4 'shingled hair'
  Du [=E] C, 1960s, 1(1 tech) **Nw** shingel [ʃiŋel] M [U] 1920s, 1(2) +4(1 tech) → sjingle v. **Fr** [ʃiŋɡœl] M, 1970s, 1(1 tech, ban) < bardeau **Gr** - < +4: à-la-garçon

ship chandler *n.* 'a vendor of ship supplies'
  Du [=E] C, 1980s (1 tech) **Fr** [ʃipʃãdlœʀ] M, end19c (1) **Rm** <=E>/șipșandru [=E/ʃipʃạndru] M, mid20c (1 tech/3 tech)

shipping *n.* +1a 'the seafaring industry as a whole'
  Nw [=E] M [U] 1930s (2) < skipsfart **Bg** shiping M [U] end20c (1 tech) → -ov adj.

shirt *n./cp²* +1a 'an upper-body garment with a collar, a (short-sleeved) garment' (cf. ↑T-Shirt)
  Although *s.* is more frequent in the compound ↑T-shirt it is also used by the fashion industry by itself and to form new compounds (↑long-shirt).
  Ge [ʃört] N/cp², pl. -s, 1970s (1 mod) **Du** [=E] N, 1940s (2) **Nw** [=E] cp²/M, pl. -s/Ø/-er, 1970s (1 jour, mod) < -skjorte **It** - < T-shirt, tee-shirt **Rm** - < T-shirt **Rs** (0) **Po** (0) **Cr** širt end20c (1 mod) **Bg** - < T-shirt **Gr** sert N, pl. Ø/-s, end20c (1 mod)

shirting* *n.* 'a fabric orig. used in making men's shirts'
  Ge Schirting [ʃörtiŋ] M, pl. -e/-s, 19c (1 tech, obs) **Du** [=E] N [U] end19c (1 tech, obs) **Nw** <=E>/sjirting [ʃirtiŋ/ʃærtiŋ] M/F [U] mid19c (1 tech) **Ic** sértingur [sjɛr̥tiŋkʏr] M/shirting(ur) [ʃịr̥tiŋkʏr)] N/M [U] mid19c (2/1 tech) **Fr** [ʃœʀtiŋ] M, end19c (1 tech, arch) **It** [ʃɛːrtiŋ(g)] M [U] 19c (1 obs) **Rm** [ʃịrtiŋ] N [U] end19c (1 tech, arch) **Po** szerting [ʃertiŋk] M, beg20c (1 tech) **Cr** (0) **Hu** [ʃịrtiŋ] [U] end19/beg20c (1 tech, arch)

shit *n.* 3 'a contemptible or worthless person or thing', +4a 'useless stuff, dirt', 5 'an intoxicating drug', +6 'pejorative interjection'
  Ge [=E] M [U] 1970s, 5(1 sla) +6(1 sla, you) < 5: Hasch(isch), +6: Schiet **Du** [=E] C [U] 1970s, 5(1 sla); cp¹, 3(1 sla) +6(1 sla/5) **Nw** [=E] M [U] 1980s, 3(1 coll, sla) = 3: skitt; 1960s, 5(1 sla); 1980s, +6(1 coll, you) **Ic** [sjı̣ht] interj., end20c, +6(1 sla); skitur M [U] 1970s, 5(4 sla) **Fr** [ʃit] M, 1970s, 5(1 sla) **Rm** [=E] end20c, 3,+6(0) **Rs** +6(0) **Po** [=E] M/N, uninfl., mid20c (1 sla) **Cr** šit (0) **Bg** shet 1990s, +6(1 sla, mod) → shịtvam v. **Fi** [=E] 1980s, +6(0) **Hu** sitt [ʃit] [U] mid20c, +4a(5Ge) **Gr** [=E] +6(0>1 sla)

shiver *v* +3 'flap in the wind' (naut.)
  Nw sjevre [ʃevre] end19c (1 tech)

shock *n.* 2 'a sudden effect on the emotions or physical state', 3 'an acute state of prostration following a wound, pain, etc.', 5 'a disturbance causing instability in an organization'
  The history of this word is complex. It was first borrowed from French *choc* (the source of the English word, too) in many languages, with the English meanings added later. As a consequence, 'via' French and 'from' French cannot always be distinguished.
  Ge Schock M, pl. -s, end19c, 2(2) → -ier- v.; -en v. **Du** [=E] C, beg20c, 2,3(1 tech) < schok **Nw** sjokk via Fr, 2(3) **Ic** sjokk [sjɔhk] N [U] beg/mid20c, via Da, 2,3(3 coll) > 3: lost **Fr** choc (4) < 2,3: choc opératoire, état de choc **Sp** [=E] M, pl. -s, 1930s, 2,5(2) **It** [=E] M, pl. Ø, end19c, 2,3(3) **Rm** șoc [ʃok] N, beg20c, 2,3(5Fr) **Rs** shok (5Fr) **Po** szok M [U] beg20c (3) → -ujący adj.; -ujạco adv. **Cr** šọk M, pl. -ovi, 20c (3) **Bg** shok M, pl. -al-ove, beg20c, 2,3(3) → -iran adj.; -ov adj. **Fi** shokki/sokki 19c, 2,3(3) **Hu** sokk [=E] [U] 20c, 2,3(3/5Fr) → -ol v. **Al** shok M [U] 1930s (3) **Gr** sok N, beg/mid20c, via Fr, 2,3(2)

shock *v.* 1a 'affect with shock', 2 'treat with an electric shock'
  Ge schocken 1960s (3); schockieren 19c, 1a(5Fr) **Du** shockeren [ʃɔkeran] 1940s, 1a(2); shocken [ʃɔkan] 1950s, 2(2) = 1a: choqueren **Nw** sjokkere [ʃɔkẹːre] 1a(5Fr); sjokke [ʃɔke] 1930s, 1a(1 coll) 2(1 tech) **Ic** sjokkera [sjɔhkɛra] mid20c, 1a(5Da) **It** shoccare/scioccare/shockare [ʃɔkkạre] 1950s, 1a(3) **Rm** șoca [ʃokạ] beg20c, 1a(5Fr) → -at adj. **Rs** shokirovat' beg20c (5 Fr?) **Po** szokować beg20c, 1a(3) → za- v. **Cr** šokịrati mid20c, 1a(3) **Bg** shokiram 1a(3) **Fi** shokeerata/sokeerata 19c, 1a(2) **Hu** sokkol [ʃokkol] 1a,2(3/5Fr) → -ó adj. **Al** shokoj mid20c (3) **Gr** sokạro beg/mid20c, via Fr, 1a(3)

shocker *n.* 1 'a shocking, horrifying, unacceptable, etc. person or thing'
  Ge Schocker M, pl. Ø, 1970s (1 coll) **Rs** shọker M, pl. -y, 1990s (1 tech) **Po** (0) **Cr** (0)

shocking *adj.* 1 'causing indignation', +3 *cp¹* 'glaring' (an intensifier used in names of colours in fashion)
  This word was one of the trendy words of nineteenth-century society, got lost in various languages and is being rediscovered in a more modest way, e.g. as a qualifier in fashion colours.
  Ge [=E] uninfl., 19c, 1(1 arch); 1960s, +3(1 tech, jour) **Du** [=E] beg20c (1 coll) **Nw** (0) < sjokkerende **Ic** [=E] end20c, 1(0) **Fr** [ʃɔkiŋ] uninfl., mid19c (1 fac, obs) **Sp** [=E] uninfl., 19c, 1(1 arch) **It** [ʃɔkiŋ(g)] 19c, +3(1>2) < scioccante **Rm** [=E] uninfl., end19c (1 rare) < șocant **Po** szoking [-nk] M, uninfl., end20c (1 coll) **Cr** šọking end20c, 1(1) **Bg** shọking uninfl., beg20c, 1(1 arch) **Fi** - < shokeeraava/sokeeraava

Hu - < *sokkoló* **Al** - < *shokues* **Gr** s<u>o</u>kin uninfl., beg/mid20c, 1(1 coll)

shoddy *n.* 1b 'a fibre made of old woollen cloth'

The commodity was one of the common products of nineteenth-century industry, so much so that an industrialist nouveau riche was called a *shoddy baron* in German. However, the word has long been lost from the common core, now serving technical functions at best.

Ge [=E] N/M [U] mid19c (1 tech) **Nw** *sjoddi* [=E] M [U] beg20c (1 tech) **Fr** [ʃɔdi] M (1 tech) **Rm** [=E] N [U] 20c (1 tech) **Rs** sh<u>o</u>ddi N, uninfl., mid20c (1 tech) **Po** *szody* pl., mid20c (1 tech) **Cr** (o) **Fi** <=E> 19c (2)

shoot *v.* 9a 'take a shot at (the goal)', (footb.), 9b 'score (a goal)' (footb.), 15 'inject oneself with (a drug)'

Du - < 9a,b: *schieten*; 15: *spinten* **Nw** (o) < trsl *skyte* **Ic** - < trsl *skjóta* **Fr** *shooter* [ʃute] end19c, 9a,b(1 obs); 1970s, 15(1) → *shoot* M **Sp** *chutar* beg20c, 9a(3); *chutarse* 1970s, 15(3 tech) **Rm** *şuta* [ʃuta] 1930s, via Fr?, 9a(3) **Cr** *šutirati* beg20c, 9a,b(3) **Bg** *shutiram* 20c(3) → *shut* M **Hu** *suttol* [ʃuttol] end19/beg20c, 9a,b(3+5 tech, arch) < 15: *belövi (magát)* **Al** *shutoj* beg20c, 9a,b(1 tech) **Gr** *sutaro* beg20c, 9a,b(1 tech) 15(1 sla, obs)

shooting-star *n.* +2 'a person with a rapidly progressing career'

Ge [=E] M, pl. -s, 1980s (1 mod)

shop *n., cp$^{1/2}$* 1 'a place for selling and buying goods', +1a 'a candy store; a kiosk', 5 'an institution, establishment, place of business, etc.'

Two things are especially remarkable about the distribution of *shop*: (*a*) it illustrates the dominance of British English, *store* being very rare; and (*b*) the peculiar restriction to the second position in compounds: while it is near-universal in German combinations, it hardly ever occurs by itself (cf. Dutch, French, Italian, Hungarian, Greek: a pan-European phenomenon).

Ge [=E] cp^2, M, pl. -s, beg19c (1 arch); cp^2, 1960s, 1(1 mod) < *Laden* **Du** [ʃɔpə(n)] C, cp^2, 1970s, 1(1 tech) → *shoppen* v. **Nw** *sjapp(e)* [ʃap(e)] M, pl. -er, end19c, 1(3); *shop* [=E] cp^1, M, pl. -(p)er, 1930s, 1(2) → *shoppe* v. **Ic** *sjoppa* [sjɔhpa] F, pl. -ur, 1930s, +1a(2 coll) 5(2 sla, pej) → *sjoppulegur* adj. **Fr** <=E> cp^2, 20c, 1(1 mod) **Sp** <=E> cp^2, 1(1 mod) **It** [ʃɔp] cp^2, M, pl. Ø, 1960s, 1(2) **Rm** [=E] N, 1970s, 1(2 mod) **Rs** *shop* M, pl. -y, 1990s, 1(1 mod) **Po** <=E> M, beg20c, 1(2) **Cr** *šop* M, pl. -ovi, end20c, 1(1) **Bg** <=E> cp$^{1/2}$, M, pl. -al-ove, 1990s, 1(1 mod) **Fi** *shoppi/soppi* 19c, 1(1) **Hu** [=E] cp^2, pl. Ø >-ok, beg20c, 1(2) **Gr** <=E> [=E] cp^2, N, end20c, 1(2 mod)

shop *v.* 1a 'go to a shop or shops'

Ge *shoppen/shoppieren* end19c (1 mod/o arch) **Du** *shoppen* [=E] 1980s (1 coll) < *winkelen* **Nw** *shoppe* [ʃɔpe] mid20c (1 coll) < *handle*; → *shopper* M, *shopping* M/F **It** - < *fare shopping* **Po** (o) **Cr** (o) **Hu** *shoppingol/soppingol* [ʃɔpingol] beg20c (1); end20c (2 jour, mod) **Gr** - < *kano soping* (o > 1 mod, coll)

shopper *n.* 1 'a person shopping', 2 'a shopping bag or trolley'

Ge [=E] M, pl. Ø, 1970s, 1,2(1 jour) **Du** [=E] 1970s, 2(1 jour) **Nw** [ʃɔper] M, pl. -e, 20c, 1(1) ← *shoppe* v. **It** [ʃɔppɛr] M, pl. Ø, 1980s, 2(1 tech)

shopping *n./cp^1* 1 'the purchase of goods', +3 'the consultation of various doctors', +4 'trading'

As one of the frequent *-ing* words denoting activities this word is clearly marked as English and is well established, in fact, even slightly more so than ↑*shopping-centre* (even though the frequency of this as used as a *name* might have led one to expect otherwise). In general, there is a certain 'Eastern' lag, unsurprisingly.

Ge [=E] N [U] 1970s, 1(1 mod) **Du** [=E] C [U] 1,+3(1 coll) **Nw** [=E] M/F [U] mid20c, 1(1) **Fr** *shopping/shoping* [ʃɔpiŋ] M, beg20c, 1(1 mod) **Sp** [ʃopin] M [U] 1960s, 1(1 mod) **It** [ʃɔppiŋ(g)] M [U] 1930s, 1(3) **Rm** [=E] N [U] end20c, 1(o>1 mod) **Rs** sh<u>o</u>pping M [U] 1990s, 1(2 mod) **Po** (o) **Cr** *šoping* M [U] end20c, 1(1 tech) **Bg** sh<u>o</u>ping M/cp^1 [U] 1990s, 1(1 jour, mod) +4(3 mod) **Fi** - < *shoppailu/soppailu* → *sopata, soppailla* v. **Hu** [=E] cp^1 [U] beg20c, 1(1 arch); *sopping* end20c, 1,+4(2 jour, mod) **Al** *shoping* M [U] mid20c (1 reg) **Gr** <=E>/*soping* N, end20c, 1(o>1 mod, coll)

shopping centre *n.* 'an area or complex of shops'

Ge [=E] N, pl. -s, 1960s (1 coll) < *Einkaufszentrum* **Du** - < *winkelcentrum* **Nw** *shopping-senter* [=E] N, pl. -tre/-tra, mid20c (1) < *kjøpesenter* **Ic** [=E] end20c (o) < *verslunarmiðstöð* **Fr** <=E> mid20c (1 ban) < *centre commercial/galerie marchande* **Sp** [ʃopinsenter] M, end20c (1 writ, jour) < *centro comercial* **It** [ʃɔppiŋ(g) senter] M, pl. Ø, 1950s (2) < *rend centro commerciale* **Rm** [=E] 1990s (o) **Rs** - < trsl *torgovyi tsentr* **Po** - < *centrum handlowe* **Cr** *šoping centar* M [U] end20c (1 tech) **Bg** - < trsl *tŭrgovski tsentŭr* **Fi** - < trsl *ostoskeskus* **Hu** [=E] pl. Ø, end20c (1 > 2 writ, jour) < trsl *bevásárló központ* **Gr** <=E> end20c (1 writ) < rend *eboriko kentro*

short cut *n.* 1 'a route shortening the distance travelled', 2 'a quick way of accomplishing something'

Ge *Shortcut* M, pl. -s, 20c (o>1 mod) **Nw** [=E] M, pl. -s, 1980s (1 mod) < *snarvei* **Ic** [=E] uninfl., end20c, 1(o) **Rm** [=E] N, end20c, 2(1 tech$_{COMPUT}$)

shorthorn *n.* 2 'a breed of cattle with short horns'

Ge [=E] N [U] end19c (1 tech) **Nw** - < trsl *korthornfe* **Ic** - < trsl *stutthyrningur* **Fr** <=E> M 20c (1 tech) **Rm** [=E] 20c (1 tech, rare) < *(rasa) Durham* **Rs** *shortgorn* M [U] beg20c (1 tech) **Po** *szorthorny*/<=E> [ʃorthorni] M, pl., beg20c (1 tech) **Bg** *shortkhorn*/*shortgorn* M [U]/pl. *-al-i*, mid20c (1 tech) → *-ski* adj.

shortlist   *n.* 'a list of selected candidates from which a final choice is made'
Ge (0)   **Du** [=E] C, 1990s (1 tech)   **Nw** *shortliste* [=E+Nw] 1980s (1 tech, mod+5)

shorts   *n.* 1 'trousers reaching only to the knees or higher'
   The distribution of this word has been almost universal from the 1950s on. The morphology of the loanword is complex: it is occasionally used as a sg. despite its *-s*; it is often used in the non-English singular form *short* (French, Spanish, Romanian, Hungarian), and, as an alternative, in Dutch (and German); it has a native plural form replacing *-s* (Russian, Polish, Bulgarian); it can have a double plural (Finnish, Norwegian).
   Ge [ʃorts] pl., beg20c (2)   **Du** [=E] C [U] 1940s (2) = *short* [=E] C, 1970s (2)   **Nw** [ʃɔːrts/=E] M, pl. Ø/-er, beg20c (2) > *kortbukse(r)* **Ic** [=E] (0) < *stuttbuxur* **Fr** *short* [ʃɔʀt] M, beg20c (2)   **Sp** *short(s)* [ʃort(s)/ sor(t)] M, pl. *-s*, 1930s (2)   **It** [ʃɔrts] M, pl., 1930s (2)   **Rm** *şort* [ʃort] N, mid20c, via Fr? (3); *short* (2 rare)   **Rs** *shorty* pl., mid20c (3)   **Po** *szorty* [ʃorti] pl., beg20c (3) = *krótnie spodnie* **Cr** *šorts* pl., mid20c (2)   **Bg** *shorti* pl., beg20c, via Rs (3)   **Fi** *shortsit* pl., beg20c (3)   **Hu** *sort* [ʃort] pl. *-ok*, beg20c (3)   **Al** *shorte* F, pl., beg20c (3)   **Gr** *sorts* sg., mid20c; *sort* N, pl. *-s*, end20c (2)

short story   *n.* 'a short literary prose genre'
   This term came to be adopted in critical literary diction because it is different from native 'equivalents' such as *Kurzgeschichte* or *novelle*.
   Ge [=E] F, pl. *-(ie)s*, 1920s (1 tech) = trsl *Kurzgeschichte* **Du** [=E] C, pl. *-ies*, 1940s (1 tech)   **Nw** [=E] M, pl. *-er*, beg20c (1 tech) < *novelle* **Ic** - < trsl *smásaga* **Fr** (0)   **Rm** (0)   **Po** [ʃor-] N, uninfl., end20c (1 tech)   **Hu** [=E] pl. *-k*, 20c (0>1 tech) < *novella*

short track*   *n.* 1 'a track of only 111 metres', 2 'the sport' (ice-skating)
   Ge *Short-Track* [=E] M, pl. *-s*, end20c, 1(1 tech)   **Du** [=E] C, pl. *-s*, end20c (1 tech)   **Nw** - < trsl *kortbane* **Po** [ʃort trek] M [U] end20c, 1(1 tech)   **Bg** *shorttrek* M [U] 1990s, 1(1 tech) 2(3 tech)

shorty   *n.* 2 'a short garment, esp. a woman's nightdress'
   Ge [ʃorti:] N, pl. *-(ie)s*, 1960s (1 mod)

shot   *n.* 4a 'a photograph', 4b 'a film sequence photographed continuously by one camera', +13 'an injection of drugs'
   Ge [=E] M, pl. *-s*, 20c, 4b(0 tech)   **Du** [=E] C, 1940s,

4a(2 rare)   **Nw** [=E] N, pl. *-s*, 1950s, 4a(1 obs) < trsl *(blink)skudd* **Ic** - < 4b: trsl *skot* **Po** [=E] M, end20c, +13(1 sla)

shovel   *n.* 2 'a machine having a form or function like a shovel, a shoveldozer'
   Du [=E] C, 1980s (1 tech)   **Nw** [=E] M, pl. *-er*, 1960s (1 tech) = *shoveldozer* **Ic** - < mean *skófla*

show   *n./cp[1]* 2a 'a spectacle', 2b 'a collection of things shown for public entertainment or in a competition', 3a 'a play, esp. a musical', 3b 'a light entertainment programme on TV etc.', 4 'an outward appearance', +8 'a lot of fun'
   The distribution of this item is universal (and has been for some time), both as a word and as an element in compounds (including hybrids). In Germanic languages the genetically related word may have helped its integration – and the transfer to it of the meaning of the English etymon.
   Ge [ʃoː/ʃou] F, pl. *-s*, end19c/mid20c, 2a,b,3a,b(2) 4(1 you) > *Schau* **Du** [ʃoː/=E] C, beg20c (2) → *showen* v. **Nw** [ʃɔv/=E] N, pl. Ø, mid20c, 2a,3a,b,+8(2) →*showe* v.; *show* adj. **Ic** *sjól*/<=E> [sjou:] N, pl. Ø, 1960s, 2a,3a(2 coll) → *sjóa* v. **Fr** [ʃo] M/cp[1/2], 1930s, 2a(2)   **Sp** [ʃou/tʃou] M, pl. *-s*, 1930s, 2a(2) = *espectáculo* **It** [ʃou] M, pl. Ø, 1950s, 4(1) 2a,b,3a,b, +8(2) = *spettacolo* **Rm** [ʃow] N, 1970s, 2a,3a,b(2)   **Rs** *shou* N, uninfl., beg20c, 2a,b,3a,b(2)   **Po** [ʃow] M, uninfl., beg20c, 2a,b,3b,4(2)   **Cr** *šou* M, mid20c (2)   **Bg** *shou* N/cp[1], pl. *-ta*, 1970s, 3b(2) +8(3)   **Fi** [=E] mid20c (2 mod)   **Hu** [=E] pl. *-k*, mid20c, 2a,b,3b, +8(2>3)   **Al** *shou* M, pl. Ø, mid20c, 2b,3a,+8(1 coll)   **Gr** *sou* N, pl. Ø/-s, end20c, 2a,3a,b(2)

show business   *n.* 1 'the theatrical profession', +2 'the business of musicals and other light entertainment'
   Ge <=E>/*Showbiz* [=E] N [U] 1960s (1 mod) < *Schaugeschäft* **Du** [=E] N [U] 1970s (2); *showbizz* [ʃoː:bis/ =E]   **Nw** <=E>/*showbiz* [=E] M [U] mid20c, +2(2)   **Ic** *sjó-*/*showbisness* [sjou:pɪsnes] M [U] mid/end20c, +2(1 coll)   **Fr** *show-business* [ʃobiznes] M [U] 1950s (1); *showbiz* (1 coll)   **Sp** <=E>/*showbiz* [=E] M [U] 1970s (1)   **It** [ʃou biznes] M [U] 1960s (1>2) = *industria dello spettacolo* **Rm** [=E] N [U] 1970s (2); *showbiz* [ʃowbiz] N [U] end20c (2 coll)   **Rs** *shou-biznes* M [U] end20c (2)   **Po** *showbiznes*/*szołbyznes* M, end20c, +2(2)   **Cr** *šoubiznis* M [U] end20c (1)   **Bg** *shoubiznes* M [U] end20c, +2(2)   **Fi** [=E] beg20c (0)   **Hu** [=E] [U] end20c (1 tech > 2 coll)   **Gr** *sou biznes* N [U] end20c, +2 (2)

showdance*   *n.* 'a type of Latin-American competition dancing' (sport)
   Nw *showdans* [=E+Nw] 1980s (1 tech+5)   **Po** (0)   **Bg** (0)

showdown   *n.* 1 'a final test or confrontation, a decisive situation'
   Ge [=E] M [U] 1960s (1 mod)   **Du** (Ø)   **Nw** [=E] M/ F, pl. *-s*, 1950/60s (1 jour)   **It** [ʃoudaun] M, pl. Ø, 1950s (1 rare)

showman   *n.* 2 'a person skilled in self-advertisement', +3 'an entertainer'

Ge [=E] M, pl. *-men*, 1960s (0>1)
Du [=E] C, pl. *-men*, 1970s, 2(2
coll+5) **Nw** <=E>/*-mann* [=E/
E+Nw] M, pl. *-men(n)*; mid20c,
+3(1(+5)) < *entertainer* **Ic** *sjó-
maður* [sjou:maðʏr] M, pl.
-menn, 1970s, +3(4 sla) **Fr**
+3(0) **Sp** [ʃouman/tʃouman] M, pl. Ø, 1980s, +3(1)
It [ʃoumɛn] M, pl. Ø/*-men*, 1950s (2) **Rm** [=E/ʃow-
man] M, pl. *-meni*, 1970s, +3(2 rare) **Rs** *shoumen* M,
pl. *-y*, 1980s, +3(1 you, mod) **Po** [ʃowmen] M,
end20c, +3(1 jour) → *-ić* v. **Cr** *šoumen* M, pl. *-i*,
end20c, +3(2) **Bg** *shoumen* M, pl. *-a/- i*, end20c,
+3(3 mod) **Hu** [=E] pl. Ø, end20c, 2(1 coll, fac)
+3(2 coll, mod) **Gr** *souman* M, 1990s, +3(1 mod)

showmaster* *n.* 'an entertainer'
Ge [ʃo:ma:sta] M, pl. Ø, 1960s (2) > *Conféren-
cier* **Du** [=E] C, 1970s (2) **Po** (0)

show-off *n.* +2 'the act of showing off'
Nw [=E] M, 1980s (1 rare) **Ic** [E=] N [U] end20c
(1 sla)

showroom *n.* 'a room used to display goods for sale'
The distribution is quite uneven, possibly because
the English word is felt to be too trendy, no real need
being seen to employ it. The well-established use of
show-words may however, support its further integration.
Ge [=E] M, pl. *-s*, 1980s (0>1
mod) < *Ausstellungsraum* **Du**
[=E] C, 1940s (2) **Nw** <=E>/
-rom [=E/E+Nw)] N, pl. Ø,
1960s (1 tech) **Fr** <=E> M,
1970s (1 tech, ban) > *salle d'expo-
sition* **Sp** [ʃourum] M, pl. *-s*,
1980s (1 tech, jour, rare) **It** [ʃouru:m] F, pl. Ø,
1970s (1>2) **Rm** [=E] N, pl. Ø, end20c (1 rare) **Po**
<=E> M, end20c (1 jour) **Cr** (0) **Bg** *shourum* M,
pl. *-a*, 1990s (1 mod, rare) **Gr** *sourum*, N, pl. Ø/*-s*,
1990s (2 tech)

shrapnel *n.* 2 'a shell containing bullets or pieces of
metal timed to burst short of impact'
The British army officer Henry Shrapnell (1761–
1842) invented the shell which was filled with explosive and ball-shot in 1784; its devastating effect is said
to have been decisive at the battle of Waterloo.
Ge *Schrapnell* N, pl. *-e*, 19c, via Fr (3 tech) **Du**
<=E>/*schrapnel* [=E/sxrɑpnəl] C, beg20c (1
tech) **Nw** [=E] M, mid20c (1) **Fr** *shrapnel/shrap-
nell* [ʃrapnɛl] M, 19c (1 tech) **Sp** *shrapnell* M, 1930s,
viaFr/Ge (1 tech, rare) **It** [ʃrɛpnɛl] M, pl. Ø, 1870s (1
tech) **Rm** *şrapnel* [ʃrapnɛl] N, end19c, via Fr/Ge (3);
şrapnea [ʃrapnea] F (5) **Rs** *shrapnel'* F [U] 19c (2
tech) **Po** *szrapnel* [-el] M, mid20c, via Ge (2 tech)
→ *-owy* adj. **Cr** *šrapnel* M, pl. *-i*, beg20c (3 tech) → *-a*
F **Bg** *shrapnel* M, pl. *-al-i*, beg20c, via Fr/Ge (2
tech) **Hu** *srapnel* [ʃrapnel] [U] 19c (1 tech, arch) **Al**
shrapnel M, pl. *-a*, beg20c (1 tech) **Gr** *srapnel* N,
beg20c (1 tech)

shredder *n.* 1 'a machine used to reduce documents

to shreds', 2 'any device used for shredding', +3 'a
maize harvester'
Ge *Sh-/Sch-* [=E] M, pl. Ø, 1970s,
1,2(2 tech) → *-n* v. **Du** [=E] C,
1980s, 2(2 tech) **Rs** *shreder* M,
pl. *-y*, mid20c (1 tech) **Cr** (0)
Bg *shreder* M, pl. *-al-i*, mid20c,
via Rs, +3(1 tech)

shrink *v.* 1 'make or become smaller; contract esp. by
the action of moisture, heat, or cold' (of cloth)
Ge *sh-/sch-* 20c (1 tech) **Nw** (0) < *krympebehandle*

shunt *v.* 2 'provide (a current) with a shunt' (electr.),
+3c 'sidetrack'
Du *shunten* [=E] 1940s (1 tech) **Nw** *shunte* [ʃɵnte]
20c, 2(1 tech) **Fr** *shunter* 20c, 2(1 tech) **Sp** *shuntar*
1930 (1 tech) → *shuntado* n. **It** *shuntare/sciuntare*
end19c (3) **Rm** *şunta* [ʃunta̱] mid20c, via Fr? (3)
Rs *shuntirovat'* 20c (1 tech) → *-irovanie* N **Bg** *shun-
tiram/shúntiram* (3) **Hu** *söntöl* [ʃøtøl] 20c, 2(1 tech)

shunt *n./cp¹* 2 'a conductor joining two points of a
circuit' (electr.), 3a 'an alternative path for the circulation of blood' (med), +5 'electric derivation', +6 'a
smoke extractor', +7 'tape-splicing'
Ge [=E] M [U] beg20c, 2(1 tech); 1980s, 3a(1 tech)
Du [ʃʏnt] C/*cp¹*, beg20c (1 tech) → *shunten* v. **Nw**
[=E] M, pl. *-er*, beg20c, 2(1 tech) **Fr** [ʃœt] M, end19c,
2,3a(1 tech); 19c, +5(3 tech); +6,+7(1 tech, ban) < +6:
conduit collectif < +7: *fondu* → *shuntage* **Sp** [ʃun(t)]
M, 1930s, 2,3a,+5(1 tech) → *shuntar* **It** [=E/ʃant] M,
pl. Ø, 1890s, 2,3a,+5(1 tech) → *sciuntaggio, shuntag-
gio* M **Rm** *şunt* [ʃunt] N, mid20c, 2,+5(1 tech) **Rs**
<=E> M, pl. *-y*, mid20c, 2,3a,+5(1 tech) → *-ovyĭ*
adj. **Po** *szunt* [ʃunt] M, mid20c, 2(1 tech) **Cr**
(0) **Bg** *shŭnt* M, pl. *-al-ove*, mid20c, 2,3a(1 tech) **Fi**
shuntti beg20c, 2(1 tech) **Hu** *sönt* [ʃønt] pl. Ø,
beg20c, 2,3a(1 tech) → *-öl* v.

shuttle *n.* 2 'a train, bus, etc. going to and fro continuously over a short route', +2a 'the Channel train
connection', 3 'a cork with a ring of feathers used in
badminton', 4 'a space shuttle', +5 'a device on a VCR
remote control'
Formerly known as an item in weaving (but without
any documentation on whether this sense was ever
borrowed), this English word became known from
the 1970s as the term for a type of spacecraft and
regular train/bus services serving airports, trade fairs
etc.
Ge [=E] M/F/N, pl. *-s*, 1980s, 2(1
mod) 4(1 tech) **Du** [=E] C,
1960s, 2(1 mod) +2a(1 tech)
3(2) **Nw** [=E] M, pl. *-r*, 1980s,
+5(1 tech); *skyttel-2*, +2a(4) < 4:
romferje **Ic** < < 2,4: *trsl skula*
Fr [ʃœtœl] M, 1980s, 2(1 tech,
ban); *Le Shuttle* 1990s, +2a(1) < 2,4: *navette* **Sp**
[=E] M, pl. *-s*, 1980s, 4(Ø/1 tech, rare); 1990s, +5(1
tech, rare) **It** [ʃatəl] M, pl. Ø, 1980s, 2,4(2) < mean
navetta; 4: *navetta spaziale* **Rm** [=E] 1970s, 4(0) <
navetă **Rs** *shattl* M, pl. *-y*, end20c, 4(Ø) **Po** (0)

Cr [=E] M, end20c, 4(2) **Bg** - < 4: mean *sovalka*
Hu [=E] [U] end20c, 2,4(1 jour, mod) +5(1 tech) **Gr**
satl N, end20c, 3(1 tech) 4(Ø)

shuttletanker* *n.* 'a kind of ship'
Nw [=E+ -tanker] M, pl. *-e*, 1980s (1 tech)

sideback* *n.* '(a position for) a player on a soccer team' (sport)
Nw [Nw+bek] M, pl. *-er*, mid20c (5+3) **Rm** - < rend
fundaş lateral **Gr** *saidbak* M/N, beg20c (1 tech)

sideboard *n.* 1 'a flat-topped cupboard at the side of a dining room'
Ge [saitbort] N, pl. *-s*, 1960s (2) < *Anrichte* **Nw** [=E]
N, pl. Ø, 20c (1 rare) < *anretningsbord, skjenk*

sidecar *n.* 1 'a small cabin for a passenger attached to the side of a motor-cycle', +1a 'a sports motor-cycle with a sidecar', 2 'a cocktail of orange liqueur, lemon juice, and brandy'
Ge [=E] M?, 1970s, 2(1 tech)
Du [=E] C, beg20c, 1(1 tech) <
zijspanwagentje **Nw** (0) < *side-vogn* **Ic** - < trsl *hliðarvagn* **Fr**
side-car [sidkar/sajdkaʀ] M,
beg20c (1 tech) **Sp** [sidekar] M,
pl. *-(e)s*, beg20c, 1,2(1 tech) **It**
[saidkar/saidekar] M, pl. Ø, 20c (1 tech) **Rm** [=E]
N, 20c, 1(1 tech) < *ataş* **Bg** *saidkar* M, pl. *-al-i*, 1990s,
+1a(1 tech) **Hu** [=E] pl. Ø, beg20c, 1(1 arch) **Gr**
saidkar N, pl. *-s*, mid20c, 1(1 tech) = *kalathi* N

sidekick *n.* 'a close associate, an assistant'
Nw [=E] M, pl. *-s*, 1980s (1 tech)

sigh *n.* 'the act or an instance of sighing'
It [sig] M, pl. Ø, 1970s (1 tech)

sightseeing *n.* 'visiting places of interest as a tourist'
The present situation is difficult to determine; the word is not fully established in many languages, but is universally known (often in the compound *~tour*), and with the increase in tourism (and no native term being really equivalent) there is a likelihood that *sightseeing* will establish itself (more so than *sightseer*, for which *tourist* will do).
Ge [=E] N [U] 1960s (1 mod) <
Besichtigung **Du** [=E] C, 1940s
(2) → *sightseeën* v. **Nw** [=E] M/
F [U] 1930s (2) → *sightseer* M **Ic**
[=E] uninfl., 1960s (1 coll) =
skoðunarferð **Fr** (0) **Rm** [=E]
end20c (0) **Po** *sight-seeing* [=E]
M, end20c (1 tech) **Cr** *sightseeing* M [U] 1970s
(2) **Fi** [=E] 1970s (0 writ) **Hu** [=E] 1970s (2) **Gr**
<=E> [=E] N [U] end20c (0>1 mod/writ)

sign *v.* 3 'engage or be engaged by signing a contract' (esp. of pop/rock bands)
Nw *signe* [saine] 1980s (1 tech)

silent partner *n.* 'a sleeping partner' (cf. ↑*sleeping partner*)
Ge - < trsl *stiller Teilhaber* **Nw** [=E] M, pl. *-e*, 1970s
(1 tech) **Hu** - < trsl *csendestárs*

sill *n.* +1a 'a shelf or plate of metal beneath the doors of a car', 3 'a tabular sheet of igneous rock' (geol.)

Ic *síls* [sils] M, pl. *-ar*, mid20c, +1a(2 tech) **Fr** <=E>
M, 20c, 3(1 tech) **Rm** *sil(l)* [=E] N [U] mid20c, 3(2 tech>3 tech) **Rs** *sil'* M [U] mid20c, 3(1 tech) **Po** M, mid20c, 3(1 tech) **Cr** (0) **Bg** *sil* M [U] mid20c, 3(1 tech)

silt *n.* 'sediment deposited by water in a channel, harbour, etc.'
Nw [=E] M [U] 20c (1 tech) **It** [=E] M, pl. Ø, 1980s (1 tech) → *siltite* F **Bg** *silt* M [U] 20c (1 tech) **Fi** *siltti* 20c (2 tech)

silver plate *n.* 'vessels, spoons, etc., of copper etc. plated with silver'
Nw *sølvplett* [Nw+E] M [U] 19c (5+3) **Ic** *silfurplett* [silvʏrpʰleht] N [U] end19c, via Da (5+3) **It** [=E] M [U] mid20c (2) **Gr** (0/1 writ)

simpleton *n.* 'a foolish person'
Nw [=E] M, pl. *-er*, mid20c (1 rare)

singback* *n.* 'a performance where an artist sings to a prerecorded accompaniment'
Nw [=E] M [U] 1980s (1 tech)

single *adj.* 1 'one only, not double' (in card games)
Ge [=E] **Nw** <=E>/*singel* [siŋel] beg20c (1 tech) **Rm** [=E] N, 20c (1 tech) **Po** *singel* [-gel] M, mid20c (1 tech)

single¹ *n.* 3 'a record with one piece of music on each side'
The distribution of the 'record' and the tennis term is similar: though both concepts can generally be expressed by native equivalents, a certain modernity and the fact that pop music and tennis are fields especially prone to anglicisms have secured the terms a wide acceptance. By contrast, the concept of 'unmarried person' with modern connotations appears to be an element of western life style which has not yet penetrated to Southern and Eastern Europe. The concept 'single room' is even less frequent.
Ge [=E] F, pl. *-s*, 1960s (2) **Du**
[=E] C, 1950s (2) **Nw** <=E>/
singel [siŋel] M, pl. *-(e)r*, 1960s
(3) **Ic** *singull* [siŋkʏtl] M, pl. *-glar*, 1980s (1 tech) < rend *smá-skífa* **Fr** [siŋɟœl] M, end19c (1 you) **Sp** [siŋel] M, pl. *-s*,
1970s (1 you) **It** [siŋol] M/F, pl. Ø, 1980s (1>2) <
mean *singolo* **Rm** [=E] N, 1970s (2 mod) **Rs** *singl*
M, pl. *-y*, end20c (1 you) **Po** *singel* [-gel] M, mid20c
(1 obs) **Cr** *singl* M, pl. *-i*, mid20c (2) **Bg** *singŭl* M,
pl. *-gŭlal-gli*, end20c (1 tech) **Fi** [siŋgle] 1960s (2
you) **Gr** *si(n)gl* N, end20c (2) → *siglaki* N

single(s)² *n./cp¹* 5 'a game with one player on each side' (tennis)
Ge [=E] N, pl. *-s*, 19c (1 tech, obs)
< *Einzel* **Du** [=E] C, 1940s (1
tech) **Nw** <=E>/*singel* [siŋel]
cp¹, mid20c (1 tech) **Ic** - < *ein-liðaleikur* **Fr** <=E> M, end19c
(1 tech) < *simple* **Sp** *singles* [singels] M, pl., 1920s (1 tech, obs) >
individuales **It** - < mean *singolo* **Rm** [=E] N [U]

beg20c (1 tech) < mean *simplu, individual* **Rs** *singl* M, pl. *-y*, end20c (1 tech) **Po** *singel* [-gel] M, beg20c (1 tech) → *singlowy* adj. **Cr** *singl* M, pl. *-i*, beg20c (1 tech) **Bg** *singŭl* M, mid20c (1 tech, sla) < trsl *poedinichno* **Hu** *szingli* [singli] [U] end19/beg20c (1 tech, arch) **Gr** - < mean *mono*

single³ *n. /adj./cp¹* 6 'an unmarried person'
Ge [=E] M, 1970s (1 mod) **Du** [=E] C, 1990s (2 coll) **Nw** <=E>/*singel* [sinel] cp¹, mid20c (1 coll) **Ic** [=E] adj., uninfl., end20c (0) < *einhleypur* **It** [singel] M/F, 1980s (2) < mean *singolo* **Fi** *sinkku* 1980s (2 coll) **Gr** (0)

single⁴ *n.* +8 'a single compartment in a sleeping car', +9 'a room occupied by one person'
Fr M, end19c (1 ban) > *simple* **Rm** [=E] N, end20c, +9(1)

single out *v.* 'select from a group as worthy of special attention, praise, etc.'
Nw *single ut* [sinle] 1930s (1 coll)

singlet *n.* 1 'a vest'
Du [=E] C, 1950s (1 jour) < *hemd* **Nw** [=E] M, pl. *-er/-s*, 1930s (1)

singleton *n.* 1 'one card only of a suit', 2a 'a single person or thing', +4 'a real character' (cf. ↑*doubleton*)
Ge [=E] M, pl. *-s*, end19c, 1(1 arch) **Du** [=E] C [U] beg20c, 1(1 tech); 1990s, 2a(1 coll) **Nw** [sinelton] M, pl. Ø, beg20c, 1(1 tech) **Fr** [sēglətō] M, 18c, 1(3 tech) **It** [singleton] M, pl. Ø, 1960s, 1(1 tech) **Rm** [singəlton] N, mid20c, 1(2 tech) **Po** *singelton* [singelton] M, beg20c, 1(1 coll) **Cr** (0)

sinker *n.* +4 'a type of small surfboard'
Ge [=E] M, pl. Ø, 1980s (1 tech, rare) **Du** [=E] C, 1980s (1 tech)

sir *n.* 1 'a respectful form of address to a man', 2 (GB) 'a titular prefix to the forename of a knight or baronet'
Ge [=E] M, 2(Ø) **Du** Ø **Nw** [=E] M, 19c, 1(Ø/1 fac) 2(Ø) **Ic** [=E] beg20c, 2(Ø); excl.: *yes/o.k. sir* [=E] 1(1 coll, fac) **Fr** (Ø) **Sp** [sir/ser] M [U] 19c (Ø) **It** [=E/sœr] M, pl. Ø, end19c, 2(Ø) **Rm** [=E] M, uninfl., beg19c, 1(2); beg20c, 2(Ø) **Rs** *sér* M, pl. *-y*, end19c (Ø) **Po** [ser] M, uninfl., beg20c (Ø) **Cr** [ser] M [U] beg20c (2) **Bg** *sŭr* M [U] beg20c, 1(Ø/2) 2(Ø) **Fi** (Ø) **Hu** [=E][U] 20c, 1(o>2 coll, fac) 2(Ø) **Al** *sër* M [U] mid20c (2) **Gr** *ser* M, 19c, 1(2) 2(Ø)

sitcom *abbrev.* 'situation comedy'
Ge [=E] F [U] 1980s (1 mod) **Du** [=E] C, 1980s (1 tech) **Nw** <=E>/*sit-kom* [sitkum/-kom] M [U] 1980s (1 mod) **Fr** (0) **Sp** [=E] M/F, end20c (1 tech) < trsl *comedia de situación* **It** [=E] F, pl. Ø, 1980s (1 mod) **Rm** <=E>/*sitcomedy* [=E] N, pl. *-ies*, 1990s (1 tech) **Fi** [=E] 1970s (1 tech)

sit-down(-strike)* *n.* 'applied to a protest etc. in which demonstrators occupy their workplace or sit down on the ground in a public place'
Ge - < trsl *Sitzstreik* **Du** *sit-downstaking* [=E+sta:kiŋ] 1940s (2) **Nw** [=E] M, mid20c (1) > *sittnedstreik* **Ic** - < trsl *setuverkfall* **Rs** - < rend *sidyachaya zabastovka* **Hu** - < trsl *ülősztrájk*

sit-in *n.* 1 'occupying a place as a protest'
Sit-in was the most frequently used *-in* word of 1968–1972 during the student demonstrations; although its use is now mainly historical (or facetious), the geographical distribution still clearly reflects political realities around 1970 – that is, largely indicates the regions in which such protests took place, and where they did not.
Ge [=E] N, pl. *-s*, 1960s (1 obs) **Du** [=E] C, 1960s (2) **Nw** [=E] M, pl. *-s*, 1960s (1 obs) **Fr** [sitin] M, uninfl. [U] 1970s (1 jour, coll) **Sp** [sitin] M, pl. *-s*, 1970s (0>1 jour, rare) < *sentada* **It** [sitin] M, pl. Ø, 1960s (2) **Rm** [=E] N [U] 1970s (0>1 jour, rare) **Rs** *sit-in* M, uninfl., 1970s (1 jour) **Po** [=E] M, uninfl., end20c (1 tech) **Cr** [=E] M [U] end20c (1 tech)

sitting duck *n.* 'a vulnerable person or thing'
Nw [=E] M, pl. *-s*, 1970s (1 rare)

sit-up *n.* 'a physical exercise in which a person sits up from a supine position without using the arms for leverage'
Ge [=E] M/N, pl. *-s*, 1980s (1 tech, rare) **Du** [=E] C, 1980s (1 tech) **Nw** [=E] M, pl. *-s*, 1980s (1 tech) **Gr** <=E> [=E] N, end20c (1 tech) < *kiliaki*

six-days* *n.* 'a bicycle race'
Ge - < rend *Sechstagerennen* **Du** - < trsl *zesdaagse* **It** - < trsl *sei giorni* **Po** *six-day* M, uninfl., end20c (1 tech)

sixpence *n.* +3 'a cloth cap with a narrow brim'
Nw *sikspens* [=E] M, pl. *-r*, beg20c (2/3) **Ic** *six-/sexpensari* [sixs- /sɛxspɛnsarı] M, pl. *-ar*, beg20c, via Da (2 coll)

size *n./cp²* 2 'a class into which things are divided according to size'
Nw [=E] M, pl. *-r*, 1980s (1 fac) **Sp** cp², 1990s (1 mod, rare) **Rs** *saiz* M, pl. *-y*, 1990s (1 tech) **Hu** [=E] [U] end20c (1 tech)

size *v.* 'glaze or stiffen or treat with size'
Nw *seise* [sæise] 20c (1 tech)

skate *n.* 1 'each of a pair of steel blades for gliding on ice', +4 'a skateboard'
Du - < *schaats* (4) **Nw** - < *skøyte* (4) **Ic** *skauti* [skœy:tı] M, pl. *-ar*, beg19c, via Da (3) → *skauta* v. **Sp** [eskeit] M, pl. *-s*, end20c (you, rare) **It** *schettino/* <=E> [skɛttino/=E] M, end19c (1) < rend *patti-no* **Bg** *skeït* M, pl. *-al-ove*, 1980s, +4(3)

skate *v.* +1c 'ride on or perform tricks on a skateboard'
Ge *skaten* [=E/sketən] 1980s (1 tech, you) → *Skater* M **Du** *skaten* [=E] 1980s (1 tech, you) < *skateboarden* **Nw** [skeite] 1980s (1 you, coll) → *skater* M; *skating*

M/F **Ic** [skei:ta, sc-] end20c (1 you) **Fi** *skeitailla*
1980s (2 you)

skateboard *n.* 1 'a short narrow board on roller-skate wheels', +2 'the sport of skateboarding'

The sport has become immensely popular since the 1970s. Although various calques and other native equivalents have been tried, these have been only moderately successful.

Ge [ske:tbort] N, pl. -*s*, 1970s (2)
> *Roll(er)brett* **Du** [=E] N,
1970s (2) → -*en*, *skaten* v. **Nw**
[=E] N, pl. -*s*, 1970s (2) > *rulle-
brett* → *skateboarding* M/F **Ic**

- < rend *hjólabretti* **Fr** *skate-
board/skate* [skɛtbɔʀd] M, 1970s
(1 you) > trsl *planche à roulettes* **Sp** [eskei(ɛ)bo(a)r]
M, pl. Ø, 1970s (1 tech) < *monopatín* **It** [=E] M, pl.
Ø, 1970s (2) **Rm** [=E] N, end20c (1 you) **Rs** *skeitbord* M, pl. -*y*, 1980s (1 tech) **Po** [-bort] F, 1980s (1
jour) < trsl *deskorolka* **Cr** *skejtbord* M, mid20c (1)
Bg *skeitbord* M, pl. -*al-ove*, 1980s, 1(2) +2(3 tech) →
-*ist* M **Fi** - < *skeittilauta* **Hu** [=E] pl. Ø, end20c (1)
< *gördeszka* **Al** *skeitbord* M, pl. Ø, 1995 (1 you)
Gr *skeitbord* N, end20c (2 you)

skater *n.* 1 'a youth who practises skateboarding', +2 'a roller skater'

Ge [=E/skɛta] M, pl. Ø, 1980s, 1(1 you) **Du** - <
skateboarder **Nw** [skeiter/=E] M, pl. -*e*, 1980s 1(0)
Sp [eskeiter] M, pl. -*s*, end20c, 1(1 you) **Rs** 1(0)
Cr *skejter* end20c (1 mod) **Bg** *skeitŭr* M, pl. -*al-i*,
1980s, 1(3 you); 1990s, +2(3 tech) **Gr** *skeiter* M,
end20c (1 you)

skating *n.* 1 'a technique in skiing imitated from ice-skating', 2 'roller-skating', 3 'a skating rink'

Ge [ske:tiŋ] N [U] 1980s, 1(1 tech, rare) <
Schlittschuhschritt **Du** [=E] C [U] 1980s (1 tech,
rare) **Nw** (0) < 1: *skøyting, skøyteteknikk* **Fr**
[sketiŋ] M, mid19c, 2,3(1 tech, obs?) **Sp** [eskeitin]
M [U] end19c, 2(1 tech, rare) **It** [=E] M
[U] beg20c (1 tech) < *pattinaggio* **Rm** [skejting] N
[U] 1930s?, 2(1 arch) < *patinaj cu rotile* **Gr** *skeiting/
<=E>* N [U] end20c (1 tech)

skeet *n.* 'a shooting sport in which a clay target is thrown from a trap'

The distribution of this word is restricted not so much by purist or other linguistic reasons as by the fact that the sport is probably not very widely known (native equivalents can be assumed to exist in most languages).

Ge [=E] N [U] 1970s (1 tech) <
Tontaubenschießen **Du** [=E] N

[U] 1980s (1 tech) = *skeetschieten*
Nw [=E] M [U] 20c (1 tech) **Fr**
[skit] M, 1970s (1 tech) **Sp**
[eskit] M [U] end20c (1 tech,
rare) **It** [ski:t] M, pl. Ø, 1960s
(1 tech) **Rm** [sket/=E] N [U] mid20c (1 tech) →
skeetist M **Po** [-i-] M [U] mid20c (1 tech) **Cr** (0)
Bg - < creat *strelba po letyashta mishena* **Fi** [=E]

mid20c (1 tech) **Hu** [=E] [U] mid20c (1 tech) →
cp¹; adj.

skeg *n.* 2 'the after part of a vessel's keel'
Du [skej] (3 tech) **It** [=E] M, pl. Ø, 1980s (1 tech)

skeleton *n.* +7 'a kind of low bobsleigh for sport competition'

Ge [=E] M, pl. -*s*, 1930s (1 tech, obs) **It** [=E] M, pl.
Ø, 1930s (1 tech) **Rm** *scheleton* [skeletọn] N, 1970s
(1 tech) **Hu** *szkeleton* 20c (3/5Gr)

sketch *n./cp²* 2 'a brief account; a rough draft or general outline', 3 'a short humorous story on stage' (often in cabaret)

This word is derived via Dutch from the Italian *schizzo*; most languages borrowed this for various forms of draft (literature, painting, music, etc.), so that there was no need for the anglicism in these senses: not unexpectedly sense 3 predominates. German *kitsch* is also believed to derive from the English *sketch*; the word was reborrowed into many languages (including English), but is considered a Germanism.

Ge *Sketch/Sketsch* [=E] M, pl. -*e*, beg20c, 3(2) **Du**
[=E] C, pl. -*es*, 1960s, 3(2) **Nw** *sketsj* [=E] M, pl. -*er*,
beg20c, 3(3) → *sketsje* v. **Ic** [scɛts/skɛts] N/M, pl.
Ø/-*ar*, end20c (1 sla) **Fr** [skɛtʃ] M, end19c,
3(2) **Sp** [eskeʃ] M, pl. -*s/-es*, 1920s (2>1) **It** [sketʃ]
M, pl. Ø, 1910s, 3(2) **Rm** *scheci* [sketʃi] N, beg20c,
via Fr, 3(2) **Rs** *sketch* M, pl. -*i*, beg20c, 3(2) **Po**
skecz M, beg20c, 3(3) → -*yk* M; -*owy* adj. **Cr** *skeč* M,
pl. -*evi*, 20c, 3(3) **Bg** *skech* M, pl. -*al-ove*, beg20c,
3(2) **Fi** *sketsi* beg20c, 3(3) **Hu** *szkeccs* [=E] *n./cp²*,
pl. -*ek*?, end19/beg20c, 3(3 jour, arch) **Al** *skeç* M, pl.
-*e*, mid20c, 3(3) **Gr** *skets* N, beg20c, 3(2)

ski-bob *n.* 'a machine like a bicycle with skis instead of wheels'

Ge [=E] M, pl. -*s*, 1970s (2 tech) **Sp** [=E] M, 20c (1
tech) **It** [=E] M, pl. Ø, mid20c (2) **Rm** *schi-bob*
[=E] N, 1970s (1 tech) **Rs** (0) **Po** *skiboby* [-i] pl.,
end20c (2 coll) **Cr** *ski-bob* M, pl. -*ovi*, end20c (2
tech) **Bg** *skibob* M, pl. -*al-ove*, end20c (1 tech)

skiff *n.* 1 'a light rowing boat'

This loanword has established itself as a technical term for a light rowing boat, but has not been extended beyond this specialized context.

Ge [=E] N, pl. -*s/-e*, end19c (1
tech) **Du** [=E] C, 1940s (1
tech) **Nw** [=E] M, 20c (1 tech,
rare) **Fr** *skif/skiff* [skif] M,
mid19c (1 tech) → *skif(f)eur*;
skif(f)euse **Sp** [eskif] M,
end20c (1 tech, rare) **It** <=E>/

schifo [skif/skifo] M, pl. Ø/-*i*, 1900s (1 tech/3) **Rm**
schif [=E] N, mid20c, via Fr? (1 tech); *skif(f)* (1 obs)
→ *schifist/-ă* M/F **Rs** *skif* M, pl. -*y*, beg20c (1 tech)
Po <=E> M, mid20c (1 tech) → -*ista* M; -*istka* F **Cr**
skif M, pl. -*ovi*, beg20c (1 tech) → -*ist* M; -*istica* F
Bg *skif* M, pl. -*al-ove*, mid20c (1 tech) → -*yor* M **Hu**
szkiff [skiff] pl. -*ek*, beg20c (1 tech, arch) **Gr** *skif* N,
20c (1 tech)

skiffle *n./cp¹* 'jazz deriving from blues, ragtime, and folk music, and using improvised as well as conventional instruments'

The music style was developed in the 1920s in the USA and became very popular in Britain in the 1950s–1960s. The term is now historical (or obsolescent); its geographical limits are easily explained by the state of European society in the 1950s.

Ge [=E] M/N [U] mid20c (1 tech, obs)   **Du** [=E] C [U] mid20c (1 tech)   **Nw** cp¹ [=E] M [U] mid20c (1 tech)   **Fr** (0)   **Sp** [eskifel] M [U] 1970s (1 tech, rare)   **Rm** [=E] N [U] mid20c (1 tech)   **Rs** (0)   **Po** - → *skifflowy* adj.   **Cr** (0)   **Bg** *skifül* M [U] mid20c (1 tech)   **Fi** [=E] cp¹, mid20c (1 tech, obs)

skimmer   *n.* 1 'a device for skimming liquids', +1a 'an instrument for skimming oil (after a tanker collision, etc.)'

Ge [=E] M, pl. Ø, 1980s (1 tech, rare)   **Nw** [=E] M, pl. *-e*, 1970s, +1a(1 tech)   **Sp** [eskimer] M, end20c (1 tech)   **It** [skimmer] M, pl. Ø, 1980s, 1(1 tech)

skin diving   *n.* 'swimming with an aqualung and flippers'

Nw [=E] M/F [U] 20c (1 rare)

skin effect   *n.* 'the tendency of a high-frequency alternating current to flow through the outer layer only of a conductor' (electr.)

Ge *Skineffekt* M, pl. *-e*, 20c (1 tech+5)   **Nw** *skinneffekt* (4+5)   **Ic** - < trsl *húðhrif*   **Fr** [skin efɛkt], 20c (1 tech) < trsl *effect pelliculaire*   **Rm** *efect skin* N, mid20c (5+1 tech)   **Rs** *skin éffekt* M, pl. *-y*, beg20c (1 tech)   **Po** [-ef-] M, beg20c (1 tech)   **Bg** *skin efekt* M [U] mid20c (1+2 tech) = trsl *povŭnosten efekt*   **Hu** *skin-effektus/-jelenség* [skin-effektuʃ/-jelenʃe:g] pl. *-ok/-ek*, 20c (1 tech+5)

skinhead/skin   *n.* 1 'a youth with close-cropped hair (a member of an aggressive gang, often right-wing and brutal)'

The explosive spread of this word was occasioned by obvious political and social reasons; there are only slight degrees of differences in frequency in the individual parts of Europe. The shortened form *skin* is an alternative for most languages, though generally more restricted.

Ge [skinhet/skin] M, pl. *-s*, 1980s (2)   **Du** [=E] C, 1970s (2)   **Nw** [=E] M, pl. *-s*, 1970s (2) < rend *snauskalle*   **Ic** [=E] N, pl. Ø, end20c (Ø) < rend *snoðinkollur, skalli*   **Fr** [skinɛd/skin] M, 1980s (2)   **Sp** [eskinxed/eskin] M, pl. *-s*, 1970s (2)   **It** [skined/skin] M, pl. Ø, 1980s (2)   **Rm** *Skinhead* [=E] M, pl. *-s*, end20c (1 jour) > rend *capete rase*   **Rs** *skinkhéd* M, pl. *-y*, end20c (1 jour) < rend *britogolovyi*   **Po** [-het] M, end20c (2) → *skinówa* F; *skinowski* adj.; *skin-headzki* adj.   **Cr** *skinhed* M, pl. *-si*, end20c (1)   **Bg** *skinheds* pl. Ø/-*dove*, end20c (1 jour, mod); *skin* M, pl. *-ove* = rend *brŭsnati glavi* → *-ar*

M   **Fi** *skini/*<=E> 1980s (3)   **Hu** [=E] pl. *-ek*, 1980s (2)   **Gr** *skinkhed* M, pl. Ø/-*s*, end20c (2); *skinas* M (3 sla, you)

skip¹ (2)   *n./cp¹* 1 'a large container for builders' refuse etc.', 2 'a cage, bucket, etc., in which men or materials are lowered and raised in mines and quarries'

Ge - < *Container*   **Du** [=E] C, 1950s (1 tech)   **Nw** - < *container*   **Fr** [skip] M, 1930s, 2(1 tech)   **Sp** [eskip] M, pl. *-s*, 1920s, 2(0/1 tech, rare)   **It** [=E] M, pl. Ø, 1940s (1 tech)   **Rm** <=E>/*schip* [=E] N, mid20c, via Fr?, 2(3)   **Rs** *skip* M, pl. *-y*, beg20c (1 tech)   **Po** M, mid20c, 2(1 tech) → *-owy* adj.   **Cr** (0)   **Bg** *skip* cp¹/M, beg20c, 2(1 tech) < *skipokletka, kosh*   **Hu** *szkip* [=E] [U] 20c, 2(3 tech, arch)

skip² (3)   *n.* 'the leader of a side at bowls or curling'

Ge [=E] M, pl. *-s*, 1980s (1 tech, rare)   **Nw** [=E] M, pl. *-(p)er*, 20c (1 tech)

ski-pass   *n.* 'a ticket or document allowing access to skiing facilities'

Ge (5)   **Du** *skipas* (4)   **It** [skipas] M, pl. Ø, 1970s (2 tech)   **Po** <=E> M, end20c (1 tech)

skipper   *n.* 1 'a sea captain', +3a 'a captain in sailing sports'

Ge [=E] M, pl. Ø, 1970s, +3a(5/1 tech, coll)   **Du** [=E] C, 1970s, 1(5) +3a(1 tech); *schipper* 1(5)   **Nw** [ʃiper] (5MLowGe)   **Ic** <=E>/*skippari* [scɪhper/-arɪ] M, pl. *-ar*, beg/mid20c, 1(2 coll) = *skipstjóri*   **Fr** [skipær] M, 18c(1)   **Sp** [eskiper] M, 20c, +3a(1 tech)   **It** [skipper] M, pl. Ø, 1930s (2 tech)   **Rm** *schiper* [skiper] M, 1970s, 1(1 tech)   **Rs** *skipper* M, pl. *-y*, beg20c (1 tech)   **Po** [-er] M, end20c, 1(1 tech)   **Cr** *skiper* M, pl. *-i*, beg20c (1 tech)   **Bg** *shkiper* M, pl. *-i*, beg20c, via Rs (3)   **Fi** *kippari* (5MLowGe)

skip it   *v.* 1 'abandon a topic'

Du *skippen* (2 coll)   **Ic** [scɪhpa] end20c (2 coll)

ski stopper*   *n.* 'a device for stopping skis when becoming detached'

Ge (5)   **Du** [=E] C, pl. *-s*, mid20c (1 tech)   **It** [ski stopper] M, pl. Ø, 1980s (1 tech)   **Po** [-er] M, end20c (1 tech)   **Bg** *(ski) stoper* M, pl. *-a/-i*, end20c (1 tech)

skunk   *n.* 1a 'a cat-sized mammal having a distinctive black and white striped fur and able to emit a powerful stench', 2 'a thoroughly contemptible person'

The name of this animal was replaced by various transparent designations; the distribution of the loanword differs slightly as to whether the animal or the fur (cf. ↑*skunks*) is concerned (combined in the grid).

Ge 1a(0) < *Stinktier*   **Du** 1a(Ø) < *stinkdier*   **Nw** [=E/skunk] M, pl. *-er*, beg20c, 1a(3) > *stinkdyr*   **Ic** *skunkur* [skuŋkɪr] M, pl. *-ar*, 1920s, 1a(3) 2(3 coll)   **Sp** <=E> M, pl. *-s*, beg20c, 1a(1 arch) < 1a: *mofeta*   **It** [skaŋk] M, pl. Ø, end19c, 1a(1) < *moffetta*   **Rm** *sconcs* [skɔnks] M, mid20c, via Fr, 1a(3)   **Rs** *skuns* M, pl. *-y*, mid20c, 1a(3) → *-ovyĭ* adj.   **Po** *skunks* [skunks] M, mid20c, 1a(3) → *-owy* adj.   **Cr** *skunk* M, mid20c, 1a(3)   **Bg** *skunks* M, pl. *-a/-ove*, 20c, 1a(1 tech)

skunks*   *n.* 'the fur of a skunk'

Ge *Skunk* [=E] beg20c (0> 1 tech)   **Du** *skunk* [skʏnk] N [U] beg20c (1 tech)   **Nw** *skunk* [skuŋk] M, pl. *-er*, beg20c (3)   **Fr** [skõs] M, 19c (1) < *sconse* **Sp** <=E>/ *skunk* M, 20c (1 tech) < *piel de mofeta*   **It** *skunk* [skaŋk] M [U] end19c (1)   **Rm** *skunk* 20c (1)   **Rs** *skuns* M [U] beg20c (3)   **Po** *skunksy* pl., beg20c (3) → *skunksowy* adj.   **Cr** *skunks* M [U] beg20c (3)   **Bg** *skunks* M [U] 20c (1 tech, rare)   **Hu** *szkunksz* [sku̲nks] [U] beg20c (2 tech, obs)

Skye terrier   *n.* 'a small long-haired variety of Scottish terrier'

Ge [=E] M, pl. Ø, end19c (1 arch)   **Du** (Ø)   **Nw** [=E] M, pl. *-e*, 20c (1 tech)   **Fr** *skye-terrier* [skajtɛrje] M, end19c (1)   **Sp** [eskaiterije̱r] M, beg20c (0>1 tech, arch)   **Rm** [=E] N, 20c (1 tech)   **Rs** *skaï-ter'e̱r* M, pl. *-y*, end19c (1 arch)   **Po** [-er] M, mid20c (1 tech)   **Bg** (Ø)   **Fi** Ø   **Hu** [=E] pl. *-ek*, 20c (2)   **Gr** (Ø)

skylab*   *n.* 'an American spacecraft'

Although a name in English, the word appears to have become generic in many receiving languages, an impression which cannot strictly be proved.

Ge [=E] N [U] 1970s (1 tech, obs)   **Sp** [eskai̱lab] M [U] 1970s (1 tech, obs)   **It** [=E] M, pl. Ø, 1970s (1 tech)   **Rm** [=E] N [U] 1970s (1 tech)   **Rs** *ska̱ĭlab* M [U] 1970s (1 tech)   **Cr** (0)   **Bg** *ska̱ĭlab* M, 1970s (2_NAME)   **Hu** [=E] pl. Ø, 1970s (1 tech) < trsl *űrlaboratórium*

skylight   *n.* 1 'a window set in the plane of a roof or ceiling', +1a 'a small window on the deck of a ship', +2 'a photographic filter'

Ge *Skylightfilter* M, pl. Ø, 1970s, +2(1 tech+5) < 1: *Oberlicht* **Du** - < 1: *dakraam* **Nw** <=E>/*skeileit* [=E/ʃæilet] N, pl. Ø, mid19c, +1a(1 tech) < 1: *takvindu, overlysvindu*   **Ic** *skælæt/skælett(i)/skelett(i)* N, pl. Ø, beg/mid20c, +1a(1 coll_NAUT)   **It** [ska̱ilait] adj./M, pl. Ø, 1970s, +2(1 tech)   **Po** *skajlajt* M, mid20c, 1(1 tech)

skyline   *n.* 'the outline of hills, buildings, etc., defined against the sky'

Ge [=E] F, pl. *-s*, 1960s (1 mod) < *Silhouette* **Du** [=E] C, 1940s (2)   **Nw** [=E] M, pl. *-s*, mid20c (1)   **Sp** [eskai̱lain] M [U] 1980s (1 tech)   **Hu** [=E] [U] end20c (0 > 1 mod) < *horizont*

skyscraper   *n.* 'a very tall building of many storeys'

This word was very rarely adopted as a loanword (although it is widely known as a foreignism with regard to America); rather, languages consistently preferred to calque and thus produce expressive native equivalents.

Ge - < rend *Wolkenkratzer* **Du** (Ø) < rend *wolkenkrabber* **Nw** (0) < trsl *skyskraper* **Ic** < rend *ský́jakljúfur* **Fr** - < trsl *gratte-ciel* **Sp** - < trsl *rascacielos* **It** - < trsl *grattacielo* **Rm** - < rend *zgârie-nori* **Rs** - < trsl *neboskrëb* **Po** - < trsl *drapacz chmur* **Cr** - < trsl *neboder* **Bg** - < trsl *nebostŭr-*

gach **Fi** - < *pilvenpiirtäjä* **Hu** - < rend *felhőkarcoló* **Al** - < rend *qiellgërvishtës, gradaçel* **Gr** - < trsl *uranoxystis*

slab   *n.* 1 'a flat broad fairly thick usu. square or rectangular piece of solid material', +5 'an inferior type of rubber'

Fr [slab] M, +5(1 tech)   **Sp** [esla̱b] M, 1980s, 1(0/1 tech, rare)   **Rs** *slyab* M, pl. *-y*, mid20c (1 tech)   **Cr** (0)   **Bg** *slyab* M, pl. *-a/-ove*, mid20c, via Rs, 1(3 tech)

slabbing*   *n.* 'a steel process'

Fr <=E> M, mid20c (1 tech)   **Rs** *slya̱bing* M [U] mid20c (1 tech)   **Po** *slabing* [-nk] M, mid20c (1 tech)   **Cr** (0)   **Bg** *slyabing* M [U] mid20c, via Rs (3 tech)

slack   *n.* 1 'a slack part of a rope', 2 'a slack time in trade'

Nw *slakk* [slak] M [U] 19c, 1(1 tech, obs); <=E> [=E] M [U] 1970s, 2(1 tech, mod)

slam   *v.* +2a 'drink tequila by mixing it in a glass with soda and slamming it down onto the table prior to drinking', +8 'dance a ↑*slamdance*'

Du *slammen* [=E] end20c, +2a(1 sla)   **Ic** *slamma* [stlam:a] end20c (1 sla)

slam   *n.* 1 'the winning of every trick in a game' (whist and bridge), +2a 'a big circuit of important competitions' (skiing, tennis)

This term was widely adopted in whist and bridge in nineteenth-century Europe, but the knowledge of it has become somewhat rare with the decline of these games. Recently the tennis term ↑ *grand slam* has made the word popular in a different context, the different forms failing to identify the two as deriving from the same etymon.

Ge *Schlemm* M, pl. *-s/-e*, 19c, 1(3 tech, arch)   **Du** *slem*, mid19c, 1(1 tech)   **Nw** *slem* [slem] M, pl. *-mer*, mid19c, 1(3 tech); *(grand)-slam* [=E] 20c, +2a(1 rare)   **Ic** *slemm* [stlɛm:] N, pl. -Ø, beg/mid20c, 1(2 tech); *slemma* [stlɛm:a] F, pl. *-ur*, beg/mid20c, 1(2 tech)   **Fr** *chelem/schelem* [ʃlɛm] M, 18c, 1(1 tech)   **Sp** [esla̱m] M, end20c (1 tech)   **It** [zlɛm] M, pl. Ø, 1940s, 1(2 tech); *grande slam* +2a(1 tech)   **Rm** *şlem* [ʃlem] N, mid19c, via Fr/Ge, 1(3 tech); *grand slam* end20c, +2(1 tech) < trsl *marele şlem* **Rs** *shlem* M, pl. *-y*, 20c, +2a(1 tech) **Po** *szlem* [ʃlem] M, beg20c, via Ge (1 tech) → *-ik* M   **Cr** (0)   **Bg** *shlem* M, pl. *-a/-ove*, beg20c, via Fr/Ge (3 tech)   **Hu** *szlem* [slem] [U] end19/beg20c, 1(1 tech)   **Gr** - < only in *grand slam*

slamdance*   *n.* 'a dance, usu. associated with hard rock or punk, where participators bump each other violently'

Ic [stlam:tans] M [U] end20c (1 sla) → *slamm* N; *slammdansa* v.

slang   *n.* 1 'informal language restricted to a particular group, context, etc.', +2 ' "the sport" practised esp. by young people of stealing fruit etc. from someone's garden'

This term started as a foreignism but quickly became applied to native conditions. In non-technical colloquial use the word has become quite vague and is often used interchangeably with similar terms (*jargon, argot* etc.)

Ge [slɛŋ] M [U] end19c, 1(1 tech) **Du** [=E] N [U] beg20c, 1(1 tech) **Nw** [=E/slaŋ] M [U] beg20c, 1(2); [slaŋ] M, pl. -*er*, beg20c, +2(3) **Ic** <=E>/*slangur* [=E/stlauŋkʏr] N [U] 1930s, via Da, 1(1/4) **Fr** 1(Ø) **Sp** [=E/*eslan̪*] M [U] beg20c (1 tech) **It** [zlɛŋ(g)] M [U] 1920s, 1(1 tech) < *gergo* **Rm** [=E/slang] N, mid20c, via Fr?, 1(1 tech) **Rs** *sléng* M [U] mid20c, 1(1 tech) **Po** [slank/slenk] M, mid20c, 1(1 tech) → -*owy* **Cr** *sleng* M [U] mid20c, 1(1 tech) **Bg** *slengl* <=E> M, pl. -*al-ove*, mid20c, 1(1 tech) < *zhargon* → -*ov* adj. **Fi** *slangi* 19c, 1(3) **Hu** *szleng* [sleng] pl. Ø, 1960s, 1(2>3) **Gr** *slang* F [U] end20c, 1(tech)

slapdash* *n.* 'a fool; a hasty and careless person'
   Nw *slabbedask* [slabedask] M, pl. -*er*, 19c (3)

slapstick *n.* 1 '(a trick in a) boisterous knockabout comedy'
   Ge [slɛpstik] M [U] 1960s (1 tech) **Du** [=E] C, 1960s (1 tech) **Nw** [=E] M, pl. -*s*, mid20c (1 tech) **Ic** [=E] N, 1(0) **Fr** (Ø) **It** [=E] M, pl. Ø, 1960s (1 tech) **Rm** [slɛpstik] N, 1970s (1 tech, rare) **Po** [slep-] M, end20c (1 tech) → -*owy* adj.

sleazy *adj.* 1 'squalid, tawdry'
   Ic [=E] uninfl., end20c (1 sla)

sled dog *n.* 'a dog used in polar expeditions'
   Ge - < trsl *Schlittenhund* **It** [sled dɔg] M, pl. Ø, 1990s (1 tech)

sleeper *n.* 2 'a beam laid horizontally to support rails'
   This word is recorded for nineteenth-century German (but has long been obsolete), which makes it plausible to interpret the remaining attestations as survivors of a previously more widespread English railway terminology, variously replaced in individual languages.
   Ge [=E] M, pl. -*s*, 19c (0 arch) **Nw** <=E>/*slipers* [sli:-per(s)] sg., M, pl. Ø, 19c (2/3 tech) **Cr** *šliper* M, pl. -*i*, beg20c (3) **Hu** *slipper* [ʃlipper] pl. -*ek*, 20c (1 tech)

sleep-in* *n.* 'a cheap hostel'
   Du [=E] C, 1970s (2)

sleeping bag *n.* 'a lined or padded bag for sleeping in, esp. out of doors'
   Ge - < *Schlafsack* **Nw** (0) < *sovepose* **Du** - < *slaapzak* **Fr** - < *sac de couchage* **Sp** - < trsl *saco de dormir* **It** - < rend *sacco a pelo* **Rm** - < rend *sac de dormir* **Rs** - < trsl *spal'nyĭ meshok* **Po** - < rend *śpiwór* **Cr** - < *vreča za spavanje* **Bg** - < trsl *spalen chuval* **Hu** - < rend *hálózsák* **Gr** *sliping bag* N, mid/end20c (2) = trsl *ypnosakos*

sleeping car *n.* 'a carriage in a train provided with beds or berths'

Ge (0 arch) < *Schlafwagen* **Nw** (0) < *sovevogn* **Ic** - < *svefn-vagn* **Fr** *sleeping (car)* [slipiŋ] M, end19c (1 arch) < *wagon-lit, voiture-, lits* **Sp** <=E>/*sleeping* [eslipin̪] M, end19c (0/1 arch) < rend *coche cama*/*wagon-lit* **It** [=E] M, pl. Ø, 19c (1 tech) < *vagone letto* **Rm** [=E] N, beg20c (1 arch) < *vagon de dormit* **Rs** - < trsl *spal'nyĭ vagon* **Po** *slipling/sleeping* M, beg20c (2) **Cr** - < *spavaća kola* **Hu** [=E] pl. Ø, end19/beg20c (1 arch) < trsl *hálókocsi*

sleeping partner *n.* 'a partner not sharing in the actual work of a firm' (cf. ↑*silent partner*)
   Du [=E] C, 1980s (1 tech, mod) < *stille vennoot* **Nw** [=E] M, pl. -*el-s*, mid20c (1 tech) **Cr** - < *tihi kompanjon* **Fi** - < trsl *nukkuva partneri*

sleep timer* *n.* 'an electronic device in a radio alarm clock which makes the radio switch off at a given time'
   Ge *Sleeptimer* [=E] M, end20c (1 tech, rare) **Du** *sleeptimer* [=E] C, pl. -*s*, end20c (1 tech) **Bg** *slip (taĭmer)* M, pl. -*i*, end20c (1 tech)

slice *n.* 4 'a slicing stroke' (sport, esp. golf, tennis)
   The distribution of this highly specialized word neatly illustrates the impact that English terms have on present-day tennis language
   Ge [=E] M, pl. -*s*, 1980s (1 tech, rare) **Du** [=E] C, 1980s (1 tech) → *slicen* v. **Nw** [=E] M, pl. -*r*, end20c (1 tech) → *slice* v. **Fr** [slajs] M, 1920s (1 tech) → *slicer* v. **Sp** [eslais] M, end20c (1 tech) **It** [zlais] M, pl. Ø, end20c (1 tech) = *colpo tagliato* **Rm** [=E] N, 1980s (1 tech) **Rs** *slaís* M, pl. -*y*, end20c (1 tech) **Po** *slajs* M, end20c (1 tech) **Cr** (0) **Bg** *slaís* M, pl. -*al-ove*, mid20c (1 tech)

(fire) slice* *n.* +3 'an implement for scraping the furnace of a steam ship'
   Nw *sleis* [slæis] M, pl. -*er*, 19c (1 tech, arch)

slide *v.* +8 'glide from one note to another by sliding the string to the side or using a bottleneck' (in playing guitar)
   Nw [saide] end20c (1 tech) **Ic** [stlai:ta] end20c (1 tech)

slide¹ *n./cp^{1/2}* +2a 'an inclined plane for evacuating passengers from an aeroplane', 4 'a sliding part of a machine or instrument', +8 'a kind of guitar', +9 'a device for playing a slide guitar', +10 'a plastic mat used in aerobics to slide on'
   Ge [=E] N, pl. -*s*, 1990s +10(1 tech, rare) **Du** [=E] C, 1950s, +8(1 tech); 1960s, +9(1 tech) **Nw** [=E] M, pl. -*r*, 1970s, +2a(1 tech); *sleid(e)* [slæid(e)] M, pl. -*er*, 20c, 4(1 tech); [=E] cp¹, 1970s, +8,+9(1 tech) < 2: *rutsje-bane* **Ic** [=E] N [U] end20c, +8(1 tech) **Sp** [eslaid] M, end20c, 4,+9,+10(1 tech); cp², +8(1 tech)

Rm <=E>/*slide guitar* [=E] end20c, +8(1 tech, rare)   **Rs** *slaĭd* M, pl. -*y*, mid20c, +8, +9(1 tech)   **Cr** (o)   **Bg** *slaĭd* M, pl. -*al-ove*, end20c, +9(1 tech) < +8: trsl *slaĭd-kitara*

slide²   5b 'a mounted transparency'
Nw [=E] M, pl. -*s*, 1960s (1) < *lysbilde*; > *dia(s)*   **Ic** [stlai:ts] (frequ. cp¹ *slædsmynd*) mid20c, 5b(2 coll) = creat *(lit)skyggna*   **It** [zlaid] M, pl. Ø, 1970s (1 tech) < *diapositiva*   **Rs** *slaĭd* M, pl. -*y*, mid20c (1 tech)   **Po** *slajd*/<=E> [-t] M, mid20c (2)   **Cr** *slajd* M, pl. -*ovi*, mid20c (2)   **Bg** *slaĭd* M, pl. -*al-ove*, end20c (1 mod) < *diapozitiv*   **Gr** *slạids* sg., N; *slạid* N, pl. -*s*, mid20c (2)

slim   *adj.* 1a 'narrow, of small girth' (of the size and cut of shirts)
Nw [=E] 1960s (1 obs)

slim   *n./cp¹* +1a 'of or associated with slimming'
Ge 1970s (1 mod)   **Nw** [=E] 1970s (1 rare) < *slanke-* **Ic** - < *megrunar-*   **It** [zlim] 1980s (1 mod)   **Po** (o) **Hu** [=E] end20c (2)   **Gr** *slim* cp, 1990s (1 mod)

slimming   *n./cp¹* 'the reduction of weight through diet and exercise'

This term has been a catchword for north-western well-to-do health-conscious middle classes but less so in societies in which *food* is the problem.

Ge [=E] N [U] 1980s (2)   **Du** [=E] N [U] 1980s (1 tech, jour, mod) < *afslanken*   **Nw** (o) < *slanking*   **Ic** - < *megrun*   **It** [zlimmiŋ(g)] M [U] 1980s (1 mod)   **Rs** (o)   **Po** (o)   **Bg** *slĭming* cp¹, 1990s (1 mod)   **Hu** [=E] [U] end20c (2)

sling   *n.* 1 'a strap, belt, etc., used to support or raise a hanging weight', +6 'a sling-back, a shoe held in place by a strap above the heel'
Ge [=E] M, pl. -*s*, 1960s, +6(1 tech, rare) = *Sling-Pumps*   **Rm** [=E] N, 1980s, 1(1 tech)

sling-back   *n.* 1 'a shoe held in place by a strap above the heel'
Nw [=E] M, pl. -*s*, 1960s (1 tech)

slip   *v.* 1 'slide unintentionally; lose one's footing or balance', +11 'take fingerprints'
Du *slippen* [slɪpən] 19c (3)   **Nw** (o)

slip¹   *n.* 1 'the act of slipping'
Du [=E] C [U] 19c (2)

slip² (1)   *n.* 4b 'a reduction in the distance travelled by a ship or aircraft arising from the nature of the medium in which its propeller revolves', 5b 'an inclined structure on which ships are built or repaired', +8 'a slide that takes a boat into the water'
Ge *Schlipp* M, pl. -*e*; *Schlippe* F, pl. -*en*, end19c, +8(1 tech) → *Slip-Anlage*   **Du** [=E] C [U] end19c, 4b(1 tech)   **Nw** *slipp* [=E] M, pl. -*er*, beg20c, +8(3/4 tech)   **Ic** *slippur* [stlɪhpʏr] M, pl. -*ar*, beg20c, 5b, +8(3)   **Fr** [slip] M, beg20c, +8(1 tech)   **Rm** [=E] N, mid20c, 5b, +8(1 tech)   **Rs** M, pl. -*y*, beg20c, 5b, +8(1

tech)   **Po** M, mid20c, +8(1 tech)   **Hu** *szlip* [=E] [U] 20c, 4b, +8(1 tech)

slip³   *n.* 'an item of underwear'

This word serves euphemistic functions and also sounds modern and trendy – these reasons combined apparently spread the term (first recorded in French in 1913) quickly throughout Europe, and placed it in the central vocabulary, in contrast to various shortlived fashion terms.

Ge [=E] M, pl. -*s*, 1940s, via Fr (2)   **Du** [=E] C, 1950s (2)   **Fr** [slip] M, beg20c (3)   **Sp** [eslip] M, pl. -*s*, mid20c (2)   **It** [zlip] M, pl. Ø, 1930s (3) → *slippino*   **Rm** [=E] N, mid20c, via Fr (3)   **Po** *slipy* [-i] pl., mid20c (3) → *slipki* pl.   **Cr** *slip* M, pl. -*ovi*, mid20c (2)   **Bg** *slip* M, pl. -*al-ove*, mid20c, via Fr (3, mainly men's)   **Hu** *szlip* [=E] pl. Ø, end20c (1 tech>2)   **Gr** *slip* [sl-/zl-] N, mid20c (2) → *slipaki*, N

slip⁴   *n.* 'a necktie'

This term is recorded as the North German word for the necktie worn round the collar and tied in a knot. Since the word can be interpreted as a native variant of a word for 'scarf', and *slip* is not clearly documented for 'necktie' in English, the status of the word as an anglicism is doubtful.

Ge *Schlips* M, pl. -*e*, end19c (3)   **Nw** *slips* [slips] N, pl. Ø, 19c (3)   **Ic** *slifsi/slipsi* [stlɪfs(ɪ)] N, pl. Ø, end19c, via Da (3)   **Fi** *slipsi* via Ge (3)

slip-on   *n.* +1a 'a sports coat'
Ge *Slipon* M, pl. -*s*, 1940s (1 tech, obs)   **Du** [=E] C, 1940s (1 tech, obs)

slipover   *n.* 'a pullover, usu. without sleeves'
Du [=E] C, 1940s (1 tech, obs)   **Nw** <=E>/*slippover* [=E] M, pl. -*e*, beg20c (1 obs)   **Fi** [=E] beg20c (1 obs)

slipper   *n.* 1 'a light indoor shoe', 2 'a light shoe for dancing, without shoe laces'
Ge [=E] M, pl. Ø, 1970s, 2(2)   **Du** [=E] C, 1970s (2)   **Nw** (o) < *tøffel*   **Fr** - → *slipperette* (1 tech, obs)

slogan   *n.* 1 'a catchy phrase, esp. in advertising or politics'

By the time this word was borrowed into European languages it had totally lost its Celtic provenance and bellicose connotations (first used in English in 1513 meaning 'war-cry'); rather, it became a favourite term of advertising and, unsurprisingly, politics (note the Bulgarian equivalent *lozung* from German).

Ge [slo:gən] M, pl. -*s*, 1930s (2) < *Schlagwort*   **Du** [slo:gən/slo:xən] C, 1940s (2)   **Nw** [=E] N, pl. Ø/-*s*, mid20c (1 tech) < *slagord*   **Ic** [stlou:kan] N, pl. -*gön*, 20c (1) < *slagorð*   **Fr** [slɔgã] M, 20c (3)   **Sp** <=E>/*eslogan* M, pl. -*sl-es*, mid20c (2>3)   **It** [zlɔgan] M, pl. Ø, 1930s

(3) **Rm** [slog<u>a</u>n] N, beg20c, via Fr (3)   **Rs** *slogan* M, pl. -*y*, end20c (1 jour)   **Po** [slogan] M, mid20c (3) → -*owość* F; -*eria* F; -*owy* adj.; -*owo* adv.   **Cr** *slogan* M, pl. -*i*, mid20c (2)   **Bg** - < *lozung* (5Ge)   **Fi** [=E] 1990s (1 tech, coll) < *iskulause*   **Hu** *szlogen* [sl<u>o</u>gen] pl. -*ek*, beg20c (2 obs) < *jelszó*   **Al** *slogan* M, pl. -*e*, end20c (3)   **Gr** *slogan* N, mid20c (2)

sloop   *n.* 1 'a small one-masted boat'

As in other words for early ships the etymological connections are not clear. The word may be French borrowed into Dutch (*sloep*) and Low German, and ultimately into English whence it was (re-)borrowed into various languages.

Ge *Sloop/Slup/Schlup* [sl<u>u</u>:p] F, pl. -*s*/(-*en*), 19c (1 tech) = *Schaluppe* (5Fr)   **Du** *sloep* (5Fr)   **Nw** [=E] M, mid19c (1 tech) = *slupp* (5MLowGe)   **Ic** *slúp* (*pa*)/*slup*(*p*)*ur* F/M, 17c, via Da (5 arch)   **Fr** [slup] M, 18c (1 tech)   **Sp** [esl<u>u</u>p] M (1 tech, rare)   **It** [zlu:p] M, pl. Ø, end18c (1 tech); *scialuppa* (5Fr)   **Rm** *slup* [slup] N, mid20c (1 tech)   **Rs** *shlyup/shlyupka* (5Du)   **Po** *slup* [slup] M, mid18c (1 arch)   **Cr** *slup* M, mid20c (1 tech)   **Bg** *shlyup* M, pl. -*a*/-*ove*, end19c, via Rs (5Du) → -*ka* F   **Fi** *sluuppi* 18c (5Fr)   **Hu** [=E] pl. Ø, 20c? (1 tech)   **Gr** *slup* N, 19/20c (1 tech)

slop   *n.* 'a quantity of liquid spilled or splashed'

It [zlap] M, pl. Ø, 1980s (1 tech)

slop-chest*   *n.* 'a box containing clothes etc. that the crew onboard a ship may purchase during voyages' (naut)

Nw *slappkiste* [slap-+Nw] 19c (1 arch+5)

slot   *n.* +3a 'a scheduled time for landing or take-off'

Ge [=E] M, pl. -*s*, 1980s (1 tech, mod)   **Sp** [eslot] M, pl. -*s*, end20c (1 tech)

slotting machine*   *n.* 'a planing machine where the steel moves vertically'

Nw *slottingmaskin* [=E+Nw] 20c (1 tech+4)

slow   *adj.* 1a 'taking a relatively long time to do a thing or cover a distance', 5 'not understanding readily' (of a person)

Ic [=E] uninfl., end20c (1 sla)

slowfox*   *n.* 'a slow foxtrot'

The dance was very popular in the 1920s which explains why the word was so widespread and is now obsolescent, the fashion having long been set by music of different kinds.

Ge [sl<u>o</u>:foks] M [U] 1920s (1 obs)   **Du** [=E] C [U] 1920s (2)   **Nw** [=E] M [U] mid20c (1 tech)   **Fr** <=E> *slow* [slo] M, 1920s (1 obs)   **Sp** <=E>/*slow* [=E] M [U] 1920s (1 obs)   **It** [slouf<u>o</u>ks] M [U] 1930s (1 obs)

Rm <=E>/*slow* [slawfoks/=E/slaw/=E] N [U] mid20c (1 obs)   **Rs** *sloufoks* M [U] 1920s (1 obs)   **Po** M [U] mid20c (1 arch)   **Cr** *sloufoks* M [U] mid20c (1 arch)   **Bg** *sloufoks* M [U] 20c (1 tech)   **Hu** [=E] [U] beg20c (2 arch)   **Gr** *slou* N [U] mid20c, via Fr (1 obs)

slow motion   *n.* 1 'a speed of a film using slower projection', 2 'the simulation of this in real action'

Ge (0)   **Du** [=E] C, 1970s (2)   **Nw** <=E>/*slow* [=E] M [U] 1960s (2) = *langsom/sakte kino*   **Ic** [=E] uninfl., end20c, 1(1 tech) 2(1 sla) → *slómó* adj.   **Sp** - < rend *cámara lenta*   **Bg** - < trsl *zabaven kadans*   **Gr** [=E] end20c, 1(0>1 tech) < trsl *arghi kinisi*

slugger*   *n.* 'a hard, brutal boxer' (also used metaphorically)

Nw [sl<u>u</u>ger] M, pl. -*e*, mid20c (2)

slump   *n.* 2 'a sharp or sudden decline in trade or business, usu. bringing widespread unemployment'

Ge (0)   **It** [=E/zlamp] M, pl. Ø, 1960s (1 tech)

slum(s)   *n.* 1 'a squalid district'

This word started off as a foreignism relating to squalid industrial workers' quarters in Britain (in nineteenth-century German these were also referred to as *rookeries*); significantly enough, many languages still have the term only with reference to foreign conditions: the ↑*shanty towns, favelas* and *bidonvilles* are always other societies' problems.

Ge [slam] M, pl. -*s*, end19c (2) → *verslumt* adj. (2); *Verslumung* F   **Du** [slʏm] C, 1950s (2) < *slop*   **Nw** [slʊm] M [U] beg20c (3) → *forslummet* adj.   **Ic** *slömm* [stlœm:] N/(F), pl. Ø, 1960s (2 coll)   **Fr** (Ø) < *bidonville*   **It** [zlam] M [U] pl. Ø/-*s*, 1930s (1) < *bidonville*   **Rm** *slum(s)* [=E] 1970s (Ø)   **Po** *slums* [=E] M, mid20c (2)   **Cr** *slam* M [U] mid20c (3)   **Hu** <=E/szlam> [slam] pl. -*ok*, mid20c (2>3 obs)   **Gr** *slam* N, pl. -*s*, 20c (1/Ø)

Ic	Nw	Po	Rs
Du	Ge	Cr	Bg
Fr	It	Fi	Hu
Sp	Rm	Al	Gr

slurry   *n.* 1 'thin mud', +5 'viscous explosive material'

Nw [=E] M [U] 20c, 1(1 tech)   **Fr** [slœri] M, 20c, +5(1 tech, ban) > *bouillie explosive*   **Fi** *slurri* beg20c, 1(1 tech)

small   *adj.* +1a 'small in size' (of clothes) (cf. ↑*S*)

Ge 1980s (1 tech, writ)   **Du** [=E] 1980s (2)   **Nw** [=E] 1960s (2 tech)   **Ic** [smɔ:l] uninfl., mid20c (0)   **It** [zmɔl/=E] mid20c (2) < *(taglia) piccola*   **Rs** (0)   **Bg** (0)   **Fi** [=E] end20c (1)   **Hu** - < ↑*S*   **Gr** <=E> [smol/zmol] end20c (2)

small business   *n.* 'a small enterprise'

Du (0)   **Nw** (0)   **Rm** - < rend *întreprindere mică*   **Rs** - < trsl *malyĭ biznes*   **Po** [-0-] M, end20c (1 jour)   **Cr** - < *malo poduzeće*   **Bg** - < *drebniya biznes*   **Fi** - < trsl *pienyritys*

small talk   *n.* 'light social conversation'

Ge [=E] M/N, pl. -*s*, 1960s (1 coll)   **Du** *small-talk* [=E] C [U] 1980s (1 coll)   **Nw** (0)   **Ic** [=E] end20c (0)   **Rs** *smol tok* M, uninfl., 1990s (1 coll)   **Fi** [=E] 1960s (Ø>0)

smart   *adj.* 1a 'quick-witted', 1b 'keen in bargaining', 1c 'unscrupulous to the point of dishonesty', 4 'stylish, fashionable'

Considering the time it has been available this word has spread remarkably little; whether it will now spread, as an epithet of businessmen and a shibboleth of modern life style, in Eastern Europe, remains to be seen. It is difficult to say whether the term is predominantly negative or used with a certain admiration.

Ge [smart] end19c (2 pej)   **Du** [=E] 1980s (1 coll, jour) < *slim*   **Nw** [=E] end19c, 1a,4(3) → *smarting* M; *smarthet* M   **Ic** *smart(ur)* [smart(ʏr)] frequ. uninfl., end19c, 1a,c(2 rare) 4(2 coll) → *smartheit* N   **Fr** [=E] uninfl., end19c, 4(1 arch)   **Sp** [=E] beg20c, 4(0<1 arch)   **It** [zmart] M, pl. Ø, 1960s, 4(1 mod)   **Hu** [=E] end20c, 1a,b,4(1 tech, mod) 2(1 fac, pej)

smart card   *n.* +2 'a card that unites the functions of various cards, such as ID card, credit card, debit card, copy card, etc.'

Ge [=E] F, pl. *-s*, 1980s (0>1 tech)   **Du** [=E] C, 1980s (1 tech)   **Nw** *smartkort* [=E+Nw] 1990s (1+5)   **Ic** *smartkort* N, pl. Ø, 1990s (1 tech)   **Fr** - < *carte à puce*   **Rs** *smart kard* M, pl. *-y*, end20c (1 tech)   **Bg** *smart karta* end20c (1 tech +5)   **Fi** - < trsl *älykortti*

smartness   *n.* 'cleverness'

Ge [smartness] F [U] 20c (1 rare)   **Nw** [=E] M [U] beg20c (1)

smash   *v.* 1a 'break into pieces', 4 'hit (a ball, etc.) with great force, esp. downwards'

Du *smashen* [smɛʃə(n)] 1940s (2)   **Nw** *smashe* [smæʃe] mid20c, 1a(1 coll) 4(1 tech) → *smasher* M   **Ic** *smassa* [smas:a] mid/end20c, 4(1 tech) → *smassari* M   **Fr** *smasher* [sma(t)ʃe] beg20c, 4(1 tech)   **Sp** *esmashar/esmasar* end20c, 4(1 tech)   **It** *smecciare* [zmetʃare] 1930s, 4(3) < *schiacciare*   **Rm** *smecia* [smetʃja] 1960s, 4(3 tech)   **Po** *smeczować* [smetʃovatç] mid20c, 4(1 tech)   **Cr** *smečirati* mid20c, 4(3)   **Bg** *smachiram* (3)

smash   *n.* 4 'a stroke in which the ball is hit esp. downwards with great force' (tennis, squash)

This word is widely popular throughout Europe but restricted to sports contexts (of various disciplines, like tennis, volleyball, etc.).

Du [=E] C, pl. *-es*, 1940s (1 tech) → *-en* v.   **Nw** [=E] M, pl. *-er*, mid20c (2) → *smashe* v.   **Ic** *smass* [smas:] N, pl. *smöss*, mid/end20c (1 tech)   **Fr** [sma(t)ʃ] M, end19c (1 tech) → *smasher* v.; *smasheur* n.   **Sp** [esmaʃ/esmas] M, end20c (1 tech, rare) → *esmashar*; *esmesar*   **It** [zmɛʃ] M, pl. Ø, 1930s (2 tech) < *mean schiacciata* → *smecciare* v.   **Rm** *smeci* [smetʃi] N, mid20c, via Fr? (2 tech); <=E> [smaʃ] (1 obs)   **Rs** *smésh* M, pl. *-y*, mid20c (1 tech)   **Po** *smecz/<=E>* [smetʃ] mid20c (1 tech) → *-ować* v.   **Cr** *smeč* M, pl. *-evi*, mid20c (1 tech) → *-irati* v.   **Bg** *smach* M, pl. *-al-ove*, mid20c (3 tech) → *-iram* v.   **Hu** [=E] [U] end19/beg20c (1 tech) < *leütés*   **Gr** *smas* N, end20c (1 tech)

smiley*   *n.* 'a motif of a smiling round yellow face; since the 1990s, the sign of the acid movement'

Ge [=E] M, pl. *-(ie)s*, 1970s (2 you, mod)   **Du** [=E] C, pl. *-'s* (1 you)   **Nw** [=E] M, pl. *-ies*, 1970s (1)   **Sp** [=E] M (1 you, mod)   **Fi** [=E] (1 mod) = creat *hymiö*

smog   *n.* 1 'fog intensified by smoke'

This word was coined with reference to London fog in 1905 and exported mainly from the 1950s when London was still the unchallenged capital of smog. Note that Norwegian and Finnish have not developed generic uses, still using the word only for English conditions.

Ge [smok] M [U] 1950s (2)   **Du** [=E] C [U] 1960s (2)   **Nw** [=E] M [U] mid20c (Ø/1)   **Ic** - < creat *preykur*   **Fr** [smɔg] M, uninfl. beg20c (1)   **Sp** [esmog] M, 1980s (Ø/1 tech) > *neblumo/niebla tóxica*   **It** [zmɔg] M (1)   **Nw** [=E] M [U] 1950s (3)   **Rm** [=E] N [U] 1970s (2)   **Rs** *smog* M [U] mid20c (2)   **Po** [-k] M [U] mid20c (2)   **Cr** *smog* M [U] mid20c (2)   **Bg** *smog* M [U] mid20c (2)   **Fi** [=E] 1950s (Ø)   **Hu** [=E] [U] mid20c (2>3)   **Al** *smog* M [U] 1970s (3)

smoke   *n.* 2 'an act or period of smoking tobacco'

Ic *smók(ur)* [smou:k(ʏr)] M, pl. *-ar*, mid20c (2 coll)   **Po** uninfl., end20c (2 coll)

smoking*   *n.* 'a dinner-jacket'

This term is a classical instance of a false friend: the *smoking jacket* is now normally a *dinner jacket* in Britain and a *tuxedo* in the USA, and the 'French' shortening of the compound left no morphological classification. As a fossilized loanword, mainly transmitted via French, the word has enjoyed an unbroken popularity.

Ge [smo:kiŋ] M, pl. *-s*, end19c (2)   **Du** [=E] C, beg20c (2)   **Nw** [smo:kiŋ] M, pl. *-er*, beg20c (3)   **Ic** *smóking* [smou:ciŋ] M, pl. *-ar*, beg20c (2)   **Fr** *smoking* (*-jacket*) [smɔkiŋ] M, beg20c (2)   **Sp** *smoking/esmoquin* M, pl. *-sl-es*, end19c, via Fr (2<3)   **It** [zmɔkiŋ(g)] M, pl. Ø, end19c (3)   **Rm** *smoching* [smɔkiŋ] N, beg20c (3)   **Rs** *smoking* M, pl. *-i*, beg20c (2)   **Po** [smokink] M, beg20c (2) → *-owy* adj.   **Cr** *smoking* M, pl. *-zi*, end19c (3)   **Bg** *smoking* M, pl. *-al-i*, beg20c (2)   **Fi** *smokki* beg20c (3)   **Hu** *szmoking* [smɔking] pl. *-ok*, end19/beg20c (3)   **Al** *smoking* M [U] end19c (1 reg)   **Gr** *smokin* [sm-/zm-] N, beg20c (2)

smolt   *n.* 'a young salmon'

Nw [=E] M [U] 1980s (3 tech) → *smoltifisere* v.   **Fr** [smɔlt] M, end19c (1 tech)   **Po** [-o-] M, mid20c (1 tech)

snack   *n.* 1 'a light, casual, or hurried meal', 2 'a small amount of food eaten between meals (esp. crisps etc.)'

Ge [snek] M, pl. *-s*, 1970s (0 > 1 mod)   **Du** [=E] M,

1970s, 1(2) **Nw** *snacks* sg. [=E]
M [U] 1960s, 2(2) → *snackse* v.;
snacksy adj. **Ic** *snakk* [stnahk]
N [U] 1970s, 2(2 coll) < 1: *snarl*
Fr *snack* M, 1950s (2) **Sp**
[esn̪ak] M, pl. *-s*, 1960s, 1(1
mod/writ, jour) **It** [znek] M, pl.
Ø, 1950s (2>3) **Rm** [snek] N, end20c, 1(1>2
mod) **Rs** 1(0) **Po** (0) **Cr** *snek* end20c (1 mod)
Bg *snek* M, pl. *-al-ove*, end20c, 1(1 coll, you) **Hu**
[=E] pl. Ø, end20c, 1(1 writ, jour, mod) **Gr** *snak* N,
pl. Ø/-s, end20c, 1(1 mod)

snack bar *n.* 1 'a place where snacks are sold'
   This term has been widely accepted as a 'modern'
word for a place for fast and light meals, even in
France; note that ↑*snack* is slightly less widespread:
it is likely that the distribution of *snack* largely relies
on the previous adoption of the compound.
Ge [sn̪ekba:r] F, pl. *-s*, 1960s (1
mod) < *Imbiß* **Du** *snackbar*
[=E] C, 1940s (2) **Nw** [=E] M,
pl. *-er*, 1950s (1 obs) < *gatekjøkken* **Fr** *snack-bar/snack* [snak-
bar] M, 1930s/1950s (2) **Sp**
<=E>/*snack/snak-bar* [esnak bar]

M, pl. *-s*, 1960s (1 arch, obs) **It** [znak bar/zn ek bar]
M, pl. Ø, 1950s (3) **Rm** [sn̪ekbar] N, 1970s (0); 1990s
(2 mod) **Rs** *snék-bar* M, pl. *-y*, end20c (1 mod) **Po**
[snekbar] M, 1980s (2 mod) **Cr** *sn̪ek-bar* M, pl. *-ovi*,
end20c (2) **Bg** *sn̪ek bar* M, pl. *-al-ove*, 1980s (2) **Fi**
[=E] end20c (1) **Hu** [=E] pl. *-ok*, end20c (2) **Gr**
<=E> 20c (1 writ)
snapshot *n.* 'a casual photograph taken quickly'
Ge (0) < trsl *Schnappschuß* **Du** [=E] N, 1940s (1) =
momentopname **Nw** [=E] N, pl. Ø/-s, 1930s (1 obs,
writ) → *snapshotte* v.
sniff *v.* 2 'inhale drugs'
Ge *sniffen* 1980s (1 sla) → *sniffer*
M **Du** - < *snuiven* (4) **Nw**
sniffe [snife] 1960s (3) **Ic** *sniffa*
[stnɪf:a] 1970s (2 coll) → *sniff* N;
sniffari M **Fr** *sniffer* [snife]

1980s (1 sla) → *snif/sniffe* interj.;
sniffeur; *sniffing* **Sp** *esnifar*
1970s (3 sla) **It** *sniffare* [zniffare] 1970s (3 sla) **Cr**
snifati end20c (1) **Gr** *snifaro* 1980s, +3a(3 sla) →
snif, *snifarisma*; *snifaki* N
sniper *n.* 1 'a person who fires from hiding, usu. at
long range', 2 'an optical device on a firearm', +2b 'a
rifle with such a device'
   The gruesome facts of the recent wars on the Balkans have made us aware how much *sniper* has become a 'regional' anglicism, other languages tending
to calque or using earlier equivalents.
Ge - < 1: *Heckenschütze* **Du** [=E] C, 1980s, 1(1 tech,
jour) < *shipschutter* **Nw** (0) < *snikskytter* **Fr**
[snajpœr] M, 1990s, 1(1 jour, ban) < *franc tireur* **Sp**
- < *francotirador* **It** [znaiper] M, pl. Ø, 1960, 1(1) <
tiratore scelto **Rs** *snaiper* M, pl. *-y*, mid20c, 1(2) →

-skiĭ adj. **Po** *snajper* [-er] M,
mid20c, via Rs, 1(2) → *-ski* adj.
Cr *snajper* M, pl. *-i*, mid20c, 1(2)
→ *-ist* M; *-ski* adj. **Bg** *snaiper*
M, pl. *-al-i*, mid20c, 2,+2b(2
tech) → *-ist* M; *-istki* adj. **Al**
snajper M, pl. *-ë*, end20c (2)

snob *n.* 1a 'a person with an exaggerated respect for
social position', +1d 'an exaggerated respect for social
position' (**Ic** only)
Ge [snop] M, pl. *-s*, end19c (2) → *-istisch* adj.; *-ismus*
M; *versnobt* adj. **Du** [=E] C, beg20c (3) → *-istisch*
adj.; *-bish* adj.; *-isme* n. **Nw** *snobb* [=E] M, pl. *-er*,
beg20c (3) → *snobbe* v.; *snobbete* adj.; *snobbethet* M;
snobberi N; *snobbisme* M **Ic** *snobb* [stnɔp:] N [U]
end19c (3) → *snobba* v.; *snobbaður* adj. **Fr** [snɔb]
M/F/adj., end19c (2) → *snobisme* M; *snobinard* adj.;
snober v. **Sp** <=E>/*esnob* M, pl. *-s*, end19c M, *esno-
bistico* adj. (2) → *esnobismo*, *esnobista*. **It** [znɔb] adj./
M/F, pl. Ø, end19c (3) → *snobbismo* M; *snobbare*
v. **Rm** [=E] M, beg20c, via Fr (3) → *snobism* N
[U]; *snoabă* F **Rs** *snob* M, pl. *-y*, beg20c (2) → *-izm*
M **Po** [-p] M, beg20c (2) → *-izm* M; *-ka* F; *-stwo* N;
-owanie N; *-izowanie* N; *-izować się* v.; *-istyczny*
adj. **Cr** *snob* M, pl. *-ovi*, beg20c (2) → *-izam* N;
-ovski adj. **Bg** *snob* M, pl. *-i*, beg20c (2) → *-izŭm*
M; *-ski* adj.; *-eya* v.; *-ar* M; *-ka* F **Fi** *snobi* 19c
(2) **Hu** *sznob* [snob] pl. *-ok*, end19/beg20c (3) **Al**
snob M, pl. *-ë*, mid20c (2) **Gr** *snob* M/F/adj., beg20c
(2) → *snobaria* F; *snobismos* M; *snobaro* v.
snooker *n./cp¹* 1 'a game played with cues on a rectangular table', 2 'a position in this game in which a
direct shot at a permitted ball is impossible'
Ge [=E] M/N [U] 1980s, 1(Ø >1 mod) **Du** [=E] N/
cp¹, 1980s (1 tech) → *-en* v. **Nw** [=E] M [U] 1980s,
1(Ø) **Ic** *snóker* [stnou:ker] M [U] mid20c, 1(2) **Sp**
M, end20c, 1(0) **It** [znu:ker] M [U] 1980s, 1(1
tech) **Rs** *snuker* M [U] end20c, 1(1 mod) **Po** [snu-
ker] M [U] end20c, 1(1 mod) **Cr** (0) **Bg** *snukŭr* M
[U] 1990s, 1(1 mod) < *bilyard* **Fi** [=E] 1980s,
1(Ø) **Hu** [snu:ker] [U] end20c, 1(1 tech) **Gr** *snuker*
N [U] end20c, 1(1 mod)
snow *n.* 5 'cocaine'
Ge - < mean *Schnee* **Du** - < mean *sneeuw* **Sp** *esno*
end20c (1 sla) **Fi** - < mean *lumi*
snowboard *n.* 1 'a wide single ski used for sliding
downhill', +2 'the winter sport using a snowboard'
   The new discipline became immediately popular
straight after its invention in the early 1980s. The
word may have been supported by ↑ *skateboard* and
↑ *surfboard*, adopted at roughly the same time. Various derivations (*-ing*, *-er*, *-Ø* vb.) are recorded in the
individual languages.
Ge [sno:bort] N, pl. *-s*, 1980s, 1(1 tech) → *-en* v.; *-er*
M **Du** [=E] N, 1990s (1 tech) → *-en* v. **Nw** [=E] N/
M, pl. Ø/-s, 1980s, 1(1 mod) > trsl *snøbrett* → *snow-
boarder* M **Ic** - < 1: trsl *snjóbretti* **Fr** [snobord] M,
1990s (1 tech) **Sp** [esnoubor(d)] M, 1990s, +2(1
tech) **It** [znoubord] M [U] 1980s, +2(2) **Rm** [snow-

bord] N, end20c (1 tech) **Rs**
snoubord M, pl. *-y*, 1980s (1
tech); [U] 1980s (1 tech) **Po**
[-bort] M, end20c (1 mod) →
-zista M; *-zistka* F **Cr** [sn<u>o</u>u
bord] M, pl. *-ovi*, end20c, 1(1
tech) **Bg** *snoubord* M, pl.
-al-ove, end20c (1 tech) → *-ist* M
Hu [=E] pl. Ø, end20c (1 tech, mod) **Gr** *snoubord*
N, 1980s, 1(2 tech) +2(2 mod)

snowboarding *n.* 'a winter sport using a snowboard'
Ge [sn<u>o:</u>bordiŋ] N [U] 1980s (1 tech, rare) **Du** [=E] C
[U] 1990s (1 tech) **Nw** [=E] M/F [U] 1980s (1
tech) **Rm** [snowboarding] N [U] end20c (1 tech,
rare) **Po** (o) **Hu** - < *snowboardozás* **Gr** <=E>
[=E] N [U] end20c (1 jour)

snow boot *n.* 'an overboot of rubber and cloth'
Du [=E] C, pl. *-s*, 20c (1 tech) **Fr** *snow-boot* [snobut]
M, end19c (1 arch)

snowmobile *n.* 'a motor vehicle with caterpillar
tracks for travelling over snow'
Ge *Snowmobil* [sn<u>o:</u>mobi:l] N, pl. *-e*, 1980s (1
tech) **Nw** *snowmobil* [sn<u>o</u>umubi:l] M, pl. *-er*, 1940s
(1 tech) **Ic** - < rend *snjóbíll* **Sp** - < rend *gato de nieve*
It - < rend *gatto delle nevei*; **snowcat*) **Hu** [sn<u>o</u>:-
mobil] pl. *-ok*, end20c (1 tech)

soap (opera) *n.* 'a sentimental broadcast drama,
serialized in many episodes, dealing with domestic
themes'
The spread of this term, mainly from the 1980s,
documents the impact of international media culture.
Although calques are frequent, and generally preferred where available, the English term has been expanding continually.
Ge <=E>/*soap* F, pl. *-s*, 1980s
(o>1 mod) < trsl *Seifenoper* **Du**
<=E>/*soap* [=E] C, pl. *-'s*, 1970s
(1 tech, rare) < *soap (serie)* **Nw**
<=E>/*soap* [=E] M, pl. *-s*, 1980s
(1) < trsl *såpeopera* **Ic** - < trsl
sápuópera; mean *sápa* **Fr** *soap-
opera/soap* [sop opeʀa] M, 1980s (1) **Sp** (o) < creat
telenovela **It** [s<u>o</u>p opera] F, pl. Ø, 1980s (1 > 2 tech) <
telenovela **Rm** [s<u>o</u>p opera] F, end20c (1 rare) **Rs** -
< trsl *myl'naya opera* **Po** [-opera] F, end20c (1
coll) **Cr** [soup <u>o</u>pera] F, pl. *-e*, end20c (1) < trsl
sapunska opera, sapunica **Bg** - < trsl *sapunena opera*
Fi [=E] end20c (1 coll) = trsl *saippuaooppera* **Hu** (o)
< trsl *szappanopera* **Gr** (o) < trsl *sapunopera*

socializing *n.* 'social activity'
Gr <=E> [=E] N [U] 1990s (1 mod)

soda (water) *n.* 2 'gassy water'
Ge - < trsl *Sodawasser* **Du** [s<u>o</u>:da w<u>a</u>:tər] N [U]
mid19c (5 arch) **Nw** (o) < *soda(vann)* **Ic** - < trsl
sódavatn **Fr** *soda* [sɔda] M, mid19c (3) > *eau de
Seltz* **Sp** [s<u>o</u>da] F, beg20c (3a) **It** [sɔda] F [U]
1960s (5La/3) **Rs** - < trsl *sodovaya voda/gazvo-
da* **Po** - < trsl *woda sodowa* **Cr** s<u>o</u>da F [U] end19c

(3) **Bg** s<u>o</u>da F, pl. *-di*, mid20c (4) < *gazirana vo-
da* **Fi** - < trsl *soodavesi* **Hu** *szódavíz* [s<u>o</u>:davi:z]
[U] 19c (3+5) **Gr** s<u>o</u>dha F, mid20c, via It (3)

soft *adj.* 2 'having a smooth texture', 6 'gentle' (of
sounds), 11 'feeble, lenient', +11a 'gentle' (of character)
Ge [=E] 1970s, 2,6,11(1 tech/you)
→ *softig* adj. **Du** [=E] 1970s,
+11a(2 pej) → *soften* v. **Nw**
[=E] mid20c, 2,6,11(1) < *myk*
Ic [=E] end20c, 6,11,+11a(1) **It**
[=E/soft] 1970s, 6(1) +11a(1) **Rm**
[=E] end20c, 6(1 rare) **Cr** [=E]
mid20c, 2(1 tech) **Bg** *soft* uninfl., 1990s, 6,11(1 sla,
you) **Hu** *szoft* [=E] 20c, 2(only in ping-pong) (1
tech) **Gr** [=E] uninfl., end20c, 6(1 you)

softball *n.* 1 'a ball like a baseball but softer', 2 'a
modified form of baseball'
Ge [s<u>o</u>ftbal] M [U] 1980s, 2(2+5)
Du [s<u>o</u>ftbal] N [U] 1960s (2) **Nw**
[softbal] M [U] 1980s,
2(1+5) **Sp** [=E] M, end20c (1
tech) **It** [=E] M [U] 1950s, 2(1
tech) **Rs** *softbol* M [U] 1990s (1
tech) **Cr** (o) **Bg** *softbol* M [U]
1990s, 2(Ø/1 tech) **Hu** *szoftball* [softball] [U] end20c,
2(1 tech)

soft-core* *n.* 'a pornographic film or magazine'
Du [=E] **Sp** [sofkor] adj./M, end20c (1 tech) = *porno
blando* **It** [s<u>o</u>ft kor] 1980s (1 tech) **Gr** - < *soft*

soft drink *n.* 'a non-alcoholic drink'
Ge [=E] M, pl. *-s*, 1970s (1 mod)
Du [=E] C, 1970s (2 rare) < *fris-
drank* **Nw** [=E] M, pl. *-er*,
1970s (1) **It** [=E] F, pl. Ø,
1970s (1) < *analcolico* **Rm**
[=E] end20c (o) **Fi** [=E] 1970s
(1) **Gr** [=E] N, pl. *-s*, end20c (1
mod)

soft drug *n.* 'a mild drug not likely to cause addiction'
Ge [=E] (1 sla) < *weiche Drogen* **Du** C, 1960s
(2) **Fr** - < *drogue douce* **Sp** - < trsl *droga blanda* **It**
- < *droga leggera* **Po** - < trsl *miękkir narkotyki* **Gr**
- < trsl *malako narkotiko*

soft-ice(cream)* *n.* 'a special kind of ice cream sold
in a soft, i.e. semifluid, form'
Ge *Softeis* N [U] 1960s (2+5) **Du** *softijs* [softeis] C/N
[U] 1970s (2+5) **Nw** *softis* [=E+Nw] M, 1950s
(2+5) **Fr** (o) **Cr** - < trsl *soft sladoled* **Fi** *soft ice*
[=E] 1960s (o) < rend *pehmis* **Hu** (o)

soft porno* *n./adj.* 'suggestive porn'
Ge [softporno:] M, pl. *-s*, 1980s (1 mod) **Du** [=E] C,
pl. *-'s*, 1970s (1 tech>2) **Nw** (o) < trsl *mykporno* **Fr**
[=E] *soft* 1980s (1 sla) **Sp** [soft] M, end20c (o sla) <
trsl *porno blando, porno light* **It** [s<u>o</u>ft porno] M/adj.
[U] end20c (1 mod) = *soft core* adj. **Rm** [softporno]
N [U] end20c (1 jour, rare) **Rs** *soft porno* N [U] 1990s
(1 mod) **Po** [-porno] N, uninfl., end20c (1 coll)

Cr [s<u>o</u>ft p<u>o</u>rno] M [U] end20c (1 coll) **Bg** *soft porno* N [U] end20c (1 coll, mod) **Fi** [=E] 1980s (1) **Al** - < trsl *puha pornó* **Gr** <=E> [=E] N, end20c (1 coll)

soft power*   *n.* 'a concept according to which opponents cooperate in finding solutions for a problem' (psychol.)
    Ge *Softpower* F [U] end20c (1 tech, mod)

software   *n.* 1 'the programs used by a computer' (comput.)
    Ge [s<u>o</u>ftwe:r/z-] F [U] 1970s (1 tech) **Du** [=E] C [U] 1970s (1 tech>2) **Nw** [=E] M [U] 1960s (1 tech) < *programvare* **Ic** - < creat *hugbúnaður* **Fr** <=E>/ *soft* [software/-wEr] M (1 tech, ban) < creat *logiciel* **Sp** [softwer/softbar/softwea] M [U] (1 tech) **It** [s<u>o</u>ftwEr] M [U] 1970 (2 tech) → *softwarista* M **Rm** [s<u>o</u>ftwer] N [U] 1970s (1 tech); *soft* (1 tech, coll) → *softist*, *-ă* M/F **Rs** *soft-ver* M [U] 1980s (1 tech) **Po** M [U] end20c (1 tech) → *softwarowy* adj. **Cr** *s<u>o</u>ftver* M [U] end20c (1 tech) **Bg** *s<u>o</u>ftuer* M [U] end20c (2 tech) → *-en* adj.; *-ist* M **Fi** <=E>/ *softa* [=E] 1970s (1 tech) **Hu** *szoftver* [=E] pl. *-ek*, 1980s (2 tech) **Gr** <=E>/*softghuer* N [U] end20c (1 tech) < *loghismiko*

software house*   *n.* 'a company creating or marketing computer software'
    Du [=E] C, pl. *-s*, end20c (1 tech) **It** [s<u>o</u>ftwer h<u>a</u>us] F, pl. Ø (1 tech)

soft white*   *n.* 'a fluorescent lamp'
    It [=E] F, pl. Ø, 1960s (1 tech)

softy   *n.* +1a 'an effeminate man'
    Ge *Softie/Softy* [=E] M, pl. *-(ie)s*, 1980s (1 coll, pej) **Du** *softie* [=E] C, 1970s (1 coll, fac > 2 pej) **Fi** - < trsl *pehmo*

sonar   *n./cp¹* 1 'a system for the underwater detection of objects by reflected or emitted sound', 2 'a medical apparatus (used esp. for analysing the development of a foetus)'
    This acronym (formed from *sound, navigation, ranging* on the basis of ↑*radar* in 1946) is probably not felt to be an anglicism, having nothing English in its form. **Ge** [son<u>a</u>:r] N [U] 1960s (3 tech) **Du** [=E] C/cp¹, 1960s, 1(2>3 tech) **Nw** [sun<u>a</u>:r] M, pl. *-er*, 1960s, 1(3 tech) **Ic** *sónar* [sou:nar] M, pl. *-ar*, 1960s (2) **Fr** [s<u>ɔ</u>naʀ] M, 1950s, 1(1 tech) **Sp** [sonar] M, mid20c, 1(1 tech) **It** [s<u>o</u>nar] M, pl. Ø, 1950, 1(3 tech) **Rm** [sonar] N, 1960s, via Fr? (1 tech) **Rs** *son<u>a</u>r* M, pl. *-y*, mid20c, 1(1 tech) **Po** [sonar] M, mid20c (1 tech) **Cr** [s<u>o</u>nar] M [U] mid20c, 1(1 tech) **Bg** *son<u>a</u>r* M [U] mid20c, 1(1 tech) = *ekholokator* **Fi** [=E] 1950s (1 tech) **Hu** *szonár* [son<u>a</u>:r] pl. *-ok*, 20c, 1(1 tech) **Al** *sonar* M, pl. Ø, 1(1 tech)

song   *n.* 1 'a poem meant to be sung (esp. in modern pop music)'
    Native terms being available, the adoption can only be used to add a specific type of song to the set (cf. the borrowing of *lied, chanson*, etc.); the pattern visible is again dominated by north-western and central languages.

Ge [=E] M, pl. *-s*, 1930s (2) **Du** [=E] C, 1960s (2) **Nw** (0) **Fr** - < only ↑*folk-song, protest-song* **Sp** (0) **Rm** [song] N, 1970s (1 rare) **Rs** *song* M, pl. *-i*, mid20c (1 tech) **Po** [-nk] M, mid20c (2) → *-owy* adj. **Cr** *song* M, pl. *-ovi*, mid20c (2) **Bg** *song* M, pl. *-al-ove*, end20c (1 tech) **Hu** [=E] pl. *-ok*, beg20c (2)

songbook   *n.* +1a 'a collection of pop songs'
    Ge [=E] N, pl. *-s*, 1980s (1 tech, rare) **Du** [=E] C, 1960s (2) **Nw** (0)

songwriter   *n.* 'a composer of songs (in pop music)'
    Ge [=E] M, pl. Ø, 1970s (1 tech) **Du** [=E] C, 1970s (2) **Nw** [=E] M, pl. *-e*, 1970s (1 tech)

sonnyboy*   *n.* 'a successful good- looking man'
    The combination *s.b.* was the title of a 1928 song, which became popular in Germany and led to the adoption of the item; this was later influenced by folk etymology so that *sunny boy* is probably more frequent in German (Busse 1996).
    Ge *Son-/Sun-*[sonib<u>ɔ</u>i/=E] M, pl. *-s*, 1970s (1 coll) **It** [s<u>ɔ</u>nnib<u>o</u>i] M, pl. Ø/*-s*, 1980s (1 mod)

sophisticated   *adj.* 1a 'educated and refined', 2 'highly developed' (of a thing, idea, etc.), +3 'modish'
    Ge [=E] 1970s, 1a, +3(1 jour, rare) **Du** [=E] 1970s, 1a,+3(1 mod); *gesofistikeerd* 2(3 reg) **Nw** [=E] mid20c, 1a,+3(1 obs) < *sofistikert* **Ic** *sófistikeraður* [sou:fɪstɪkeraðʏr] end20c, via Da, 1a,2(1 coll); [=E] 1,2(0) **Fr** *sophistiqué,e* mid20c, 2,+3(4) **Sp** - < mean *sofisticado* **It** *sofisticato* [sofistik<u>a</u>to] M/F, pl. *-i/-e*, 1930s **Rm** *sofisticat/-ă* [sofistik<u>a</u>t/-ə] M/F, 1960s, 2,+3(4) **Po** <=E> end20c, 1a(1 jour) **Cr** *sofistic<u>i</u>ran* end20c, 1a(1) **Fi** - < *sofistikoitunut* **Hu** (5La/Gr) **Al** - < *i sofistikuar* mid20c (2) **Gr** - < *sofistik<u>e</u>* (2/5Fr)

sorry   *adj.* 1 'pained or regretful', 4 'wretched; in a poor state'
    Nw [=E] end20c, 1(1 coll) **Ic** *sorrí* [=E] uninfl., 1970s (1 sla) **Rs** (0) **Cr** (0) **Bg** *s<u>o</u>ri* uninfl., end20c, 1(2 coll) **Hu** [=E] end20c, 1(2 sla, fac) **Al** *sori* end20c (1 you) **Gr** *s<u>o</u>ri* end20c, 1(1 coll)

sorry!   *interj.* 3 'an expression of apology'
    Ge [s<u>o</u>ri:] 1970s (1 coll, rare) **Du** [=E] 1940s (1 coll) **Nw** [=E] 1970s (1 coll) **Ic** *sorrí* [=E] mid20c (1 sla) **Sp** [=E/sorri] 1970s (0>1 writ, fac) **It** [s<u>ɔ</u>rri] end20c (1 coll, jour) **Rm** [=E] end20c (0) **Rs** (0) **Po** [=E] 1980s (1 coll) **Cr** *sori* (0) **Bg** *s<u>o</u>ri* end20c (1 you, coll) **Fi** *sori* end20c (2 coll) **Hu** [=E] end20c (1 coll) **Al** *s<u>o</u>ri* end20c (1 you) **Gr** (0>1 coll, mod)

sorter   *n.* 'a machine for sorting copies'
    Ge [=E] M, pl. Ø, 1980s (1 tech) **Rm** [=E/sorter] N, end20c (0>1 tech) < rend *sortator* **Rs** *s<u>o</u>rter* M, pl. *-y*, end20c (1 tech)

SOS   *n.* 1 'an international code-signal of extreme distress', 2 'an urgent appeal for help'

Ge [eso:es] N [U] beg20c (3)　Du [es o: es] beg20c (3);
[=E] (2)　Nw [esu:es] N, pl. Ø, beg20c (3)　Ic *S.O.S.*
[ɛs: o: ɛs:] beg20c (3)　Fr *S.O.S.* [ɛsoes] M, beg20c (3)
Sp [sos/ese o ese] M [U] beg20c (2)　It [esse ɔ esse] M,
pl. Ø, 1920s (3)　Rm [esoes] N, beg20c, via Fr?
(3)　Rs *sos* M [U] beg20c (2)　Po [esoes] M [U]
beg20c (2)　Cr [=E] M [U] beg20c (3)　Bg <=E>
[es o es] N [U] beg20c (2)　Fi [es o: ɛs] beg20c (3)
Hu [eʃo:eʃ] [U] beg20c (3)　Al *SOS* uninfl., mid20c (1
reg)　Gr *sos* [sos, esoes] N, beg20c (2)

soul *n./cp[1]* 8 'a kind of music incorporating elements
of rhythm and blues and gospel music, popularized by
African-Americans'

Ge [so:l] M [U] 1960s (1 tech)　Du [=E] C [U] 1960s
(2 tech)　Nw [=E] M [U] 1960s (1 tech)　Ic [sou:l]
1960s (1 tech)　Fr [sul] adj./M, uninfl., 1960s (1
tech)　Sp [soul] M [U] 1970s (1 you) → *soulero*
adj.　It [so:l] M [U] 1960s (1 tech)　Rm [sowl] N
[U] 1970s (1 tech)　Rs *soul* M [U] end20c (1 tech)
Po M, uninfl., end20c (1 tech)　Cr *soul* M [U]
end20c (1 tech)　Bg *soul* M/cp[1] [U] end20c (1 tech)
Fi [=E] 1960s (2)　Hu [so:l] [U] 1960s (2 tech)　Gr
soul F [U] 1960s (2)

sound *v.* +7 '(of music, instruments, amplifiers etc.)
produce a sound of a certain quality'
Ic *sánda* [saunta] end20c (1 tech)

sound *n.* +10 'the tonal quality of music, of an instrument, or of an amplifier'
　This word has been widely accepted in the youth
and music culture (although many equivalents are
available in all the languages); the term is obviously
penetrating into Eastern Europe. Although the use of
↑*soundtrack* is much more technical, its distribution is
very largely the same.

Ge [zaunt/s-] M, pl. -*s*, 1960s (1
tech)　Du [=E] C, 1970s (1 mod/
tech >2)　Nw [=E] M [U] 1960s
(1 tech)　Ic *sánd* [=E] N [U]
1960s (1 tech, sla)　Fr (0)　It
[saund] M [U] 1960s (1
tech)　Rm [=E] N [U] 1970s (1
tech)　Rs *saund* M [U] 1990s (1 tech, mod)　Po [-t] M
[U] end20c (1 tech)　Cr [saund] M, end20c (1
tech)　Bg *saund* M [U] end20c (1 tech)　Fi *sound(i)*
[saundi] 1970s (1 you)　Hu [=E] [U] 1970s (1 tech,
writ)　Gr <=E> [=E] N [U] end20c (1 tech, mod)

sound card *n.* 'a device which can be slotted into a
computer to allow the use of audio components for
multimedia applications' (comput.)
Ge [=E] F, 1980s (1 tech) < trsl *Soundkarte*　Du [=E]
C, 1980s (1 tech)　Nw - < trsl *lydkort*　Ic - < trsl
hljóðkort　Fr - < trsl *carte son*　It - < rend *scheda
audio*　Rm - < rend *placă de sunet*　Rs *saund kard* M,
pl. -*y*, 1990s (1 tech)　Po - < *karta dźwiękowa*　Bg - <
trsl *saund karta*　Fi - < *äänikortti*　Gr <=E> [=E] F,
end20c (1 tech) < trsl *karta ikhu*

soundcheck *n.* 'a test of sound equipment before a
rock or jazz concert'
Ge [=E] M, pl. -*s*, 1970s (1 you/tech)　Du [=E] C, pl.

-*s*, end20c (1 tech)　Nw - < *lydsjekk*　Ic *sándtékk*
[=E] N, pl. Ø, end20c (1 tech)　Rm (0) > rend *probă
de sunet*　Bg *saundchek* M [U] (1 tech, mod)

soundtrack *n.* 1 'the recorded music of a motion
picture or a television series'
Ge [=E] M, pl. -*s*, 1960s (1
tech)　Du [=E] C, 1970s (1
tech)　Nw [=E] N, pl. Ø/-*s*,
1980s (1 tech)　Ic [=E] N [U]
end20c (1)　Fr - < *bande sonore*
Sp M, end20c (0) < rend *banda
sonora*　It - < creat *colonna
sonora*　Rm [=E] N [U] end20c (0) < *coloană sonoră*
Rs *saundtrék* M, pl. -*i*, 1990s (1 tech)　Po [=E] M [U]
end20c (1 tech)　Cr *sandtrek* M, pl. -*ovi*, end20c (1
tech)　Bg *saundtrak* M, pl. -*al-ove*, end20c (1
tech)　Gr *saund(t)rak* N, end20c (2)

sour cream *n.* 'cream deliberately fermented by adding bacteria'
Ge [=E] F [U] 1990s (1 mod) < *Sauerrahm/saure Sah-
ne*　Du <=E> [=E] M/F [U] 1990s (1 mod)　Ic - <
rend *sýrður rjómi*　Sp [=E] M/F [U] end20c (1 mod,
rare) < trsl *crema agria*

space *n.* 1c 'an empty area; room'
Ic [spei:s] N [U] end20c (1 coll)

space cake* *n.* 'a cake filled with hashish'
Ge [=E] M, 1990s (1 tech, rare)　Du [spe:s ke:k] C,
1980s (1 tech)

spaced *adj.* 1 'in a state of euphoria, esp. from taking
drugs', +2 'weird, far out'
Nw *speisa* [spæisa] 1970s (1 coll)　Ic *speisaður* [spei:-
saðyr] 1970s (2 sla)　Hu [=E] end20c, 1(1 tech, sla)

space lab *n.* 'a manned space station' (cf. ↑*skylab*)
Ge [spe:slep] N, pl. -*s*, 1980s (1 tech)　Du [spe:slep/
=E] N, 1980s (1 tech) < *ruimtelaboratorium*　Nw (0)
< *romlaboratorium*　Fr - < trsl? *laboratoire spa-
tial*　Sp - < trsl *laboratorio espacial*　It [=E] M, pl.
Ø, 1970s (1 tech) < trsl *laboratorio spaziale*　Rm [=E]
N [U] 1970s (0<1 tech) < trsl *laborator spaţial*　Rs - <
trsl *kosmicheskaya laboratoriya*　Cr *spejslab* [=E] M,
pl. -*ovi*, end20c (1 tech)　Bg - < trsl *kosmicheska
laboratoriya*　Hu [spe:sleb] [U] end20c (1 tech) < trsl
űrlaboratórium

space shuttle *n.* 'a rocket for repeated use'
　The evidence is clearly divided between loanwords,
calques and the coexistence of the two, with no regional pattern being clearly visible.
Ge [spe:sʃatl] M/F/N, pl. -*s*,
1970s (1 tech) < *Raumfähre*　Du
[=E/-ʃᵊtəl] C, 1980s (1 tech) >
ruimteveer, *ruimtependel*　Nw
(0) < trsl *romferje*　Ic - < trsl
geimskutla　Fr - < trsl *navette
spatiale*　Sp [=E] M, pl. -*s*,
1980s (1 tech, rare) < rend *transbordador espacial*　It
[speisʃatəl] M, pl. Ø, 1970s (2 tech) < rend *navetta
spaziale*　Rm - < rend *navetă spaţială*　Rs *speis-
shatl* M, pl. -*y*, end20c (1 tech)　Po - < *prom
kosmiczny*　Cr *spejs šatl* M, pl. -*ovi*, end20c

(1 tech)   **Bg** - < trsl *kosmicheska sovalka*   **Fi** - < trsl *avaruussukkula*   **Hu** [=E] pl. Ø, end20c (1 tech) < *ŭrkomp*

spaniel   *n.* 1a 'a dog of any of various breeds with a long silky coat and drooping ears'

One of the most widespread adoptions of English terms related to dog breeding; the word is an old borrowing from French but the English form dominates throughout.

Ge [ʃpaːniel] M, pl. *-s*, 19c (3)   **Du** *spaniël* [=E/spaːnjəl] C, 1930s (2 tech > 3 tech)   **Nw** [spaːnjel] M, pl. *-er*, 20c (2)   **Ic** [=E] M, end20c (0)   **Fr** - < *épagneul* (4)   **Sp** [ispanjel] M, beg20c (2 tech)   **It** [spaniel] M, pl. Ø, 1900s (3)   **Rm** [spanjel] M, mid20c (1 tech)   **Rs** *spaniel'* M, pl. *-i*, mid20c (3)   **Po** [spaniel] M, mid20c (3) → *-ek* M   **Cr** *španijel* M, pl. *-i*, 20c, via Ge? (3)   **Bg** *shpanyol* M, pl. *-al/-i*, 20c, via Ge (3 tech)   **Fi** *spanieli* 19c (3)   **Hu** [ʃpaːniel] pl. *-ek*, 20c, via Ge (3)   **Gr** *spaniel* N, 20c (2)

sparring   *n./cp¹* 'a boxing match (for training)'

Ge [ʃpariŋ] N [U] 1960s (1 tech, rare)   **Nw** [spariŋ] M/F [U] 20c ← *sparre* v. (3)   **Rs** *sparring* M, pl. *-i*, mid20c (1 tech)   **Po** *sparing* [-nk] M, mid20c (1 tech) → *owy* adj.   **Cr** [=E] M, end20c (1 tech)   **Bg** *sparing* M/cp¹ [U] mid20c (1 tech)   **Fi** - < *sparraus*   **Hu** [=E] [U] 19c (1 tech, arch) → *-ol* v.; *-ás* n.

sparring partner   *n.* 1 'a boxer sparring with another for training'

Ge *Sparringspartner* [ʃpariŋspartna] M, pl. Ø, mid20c (1 tech)   **Du** [=E] C, 1950s (1 tech) → *sparren* v. (3 tech)   **Nw** [=E] M, pl. *-e*, mid20c (1 tech)   **Fr** *sparring-partner* [spariŋ partnɛr] M, 1930s (1 tech, ban) > *partenaire d'entraînement*   **Sp** *sparring* [esparrin] M, pl. *-s*, 1930s (1 tech) = *pareja de entrenamiento*   **It** [sparriŋ partner] M, pl. Ø, 1940s (1 tech)   **Rm** <=E>/ *sparing partener* [sparing partener] M, mid20c (1 tech) < *partener de antrenament*   **Rs** *sparring partnër* M, pl. *-y*, end20c (1 tech)   **Po** *sparing partner* [-nk partner] M, end20c (1 tech) < *partner sparingowy*   **Cr** *sparing partner* M, pl. *-i*, end20c (1 tech)   **Bg** *sparing partnyor* M, pl. *-ra/-ri*, mid20c (1+5)   **Fi** <E>/*sparrauspartneri* [E] beg20c (1 tech)   **Hu** [=E] pl. *-ek*, 20c (1 tech)

speaker   *n.* 3 'the presiding officer in a legislative assembly e.g. in parliament', 4 'a loudspeaker', +5 'a radio announcer', +6 'a sports reporter' (radio/TV), +7 'an announcer in a sports stadium', +8 'an announcer', +9 'voice-over parts in audiovisual media'

This term is surprisingly widespread in the sense 'radio announcer' (where native words are likely to be available). As a parliamentary term, the word is mainly a foreignism, the institution not being existent in continental democracies.

Du [=E] C, 1970s, +7(2); mid19c, 3(Ø); 1960s, 4(2); 1970s, +6(2 tech) < 4: *luidspreker (box)*, *box*   **Nw** [=E] M, pl. *-e*, beg20c, 3(Ø) +5(1 obs) +7(2) < +7:

(radio/TV-)kommentator   **Ic** [=E] M, pl. *-ar*, end20c, 4(1 tech) < 4: *hátalari*; +5: *þulur*   **Fr** [spikœr] M, 20c, +5(1 obs) > *annonceur, -euse (officiel)* < *présentateur, -trice* → *speakerine*   **Sp** [espiker] M, pl. *-s*, end19c, 3(Ø tech); beg20c, +5(1 arch); end20c, +8(1 tech, rare) < +5: *locutor*   **It** [spiker] M, pl. Ø, 1920s, 3(Ø) 4,+5,+6,+7(2) = 4: *altoparlante* < *annunciatore* → *speakeraggio/spikeraggio* n.   **Rm** *spicher/spicher* [spiker/ʃpi-] M, 1930s, via Fr, +5(3); 1970s (3(Ø); *speaker* [=E] 3(Ø), +5(1 obs) → *spicheriță* F   **Rs** *spiker* M, pl. *-y*, 1980s, 3(1)   **Po** *spiker* [spiker] M, beg20c, +5(2) → *-ka* F; *-ski* adj.   **Cr** *spiker* M, pl. *-i*, beg20c, +5(2)   **Bg** *shpiker* M, pl. *-i*, beg20c, +5, +6(3 arch); *spiker* mid20c, 3(Ø)   **Fi** *spiikkeri* mid20c, +5(2) +9(1 tech) → *spiikkaus* n.   **Hu** [=E] pl. *-ek*, beg20c, 3(2/0); *szpiker* [spiːker] pl. *-ek*, beg20c, +5(3 arch) < *bemondó*   **Al** *spiker* M, pl. Ø, beg20c, +5,+6,+7(2)   **Gr** *spiker* M, 1960s, via Fr, +5,+6,+7(2)

speakerphone   *n.* 'a telephone which does not need to be held in the hand' (cf. ↑ *hands free*)

Du - < *handsfree*   **Nw** - < *handsfree*   **It** - < *vivavoce*   **Rm** [=E] N, 20c (1 tech)   **Rs** *spikerfon* M, pl. *-y*, 1990s (1 mod)

special   *n./adj.* 1 'a special person or thing, e.g. a special edition of a newspaper', +2 'a radio or television programme or a series of programmes on a special topic'

Ge [speʃəl] N, pl. *-s*, 1970s, +2(1 jour/mod)   **Du** [=E] C, 1970s (2)   **Nw** [=E] M, pl. *-s*, 1990s, +2(1 jour, rare)   **It** [spetʃal] M, pl. Ø, 1960s, +2(2 jour)   **Po** *specjalny* (5La)   **Bg** *spechŭl* adj., uninfl., 1990s, 1(1 you, sla)   **Fi** [spesial] 1970s (2)   **Hu** (5La)   **Gr** *spesial* adj., end20c, 1(2)

speech   *n.* 2 'a (short) formal address delivered to an assembly'

Ge [=E] M, pl. *-e(s)*, 19c (0 arch)   **Du** [=E] C, pl. *-es/-en*, mid19c (2) → *-en* v.   **Nw** [=E] M, beg20c (1 rare)   **Fr** [spitʃ] M, 19c (2 jour)   **Sp** <=E>/*espiche* [espitʃ/ espitʃe] M, pl. *-s*, 1940s (1 coll/pej)   **Rm** [=E] N, 1970s (1 mod); *spici* (1 rare)   **Rs** *spich* M, pl. *-i*, beg20c (1 rare)   **Po** [-i-] M, mid20c (2 coll)   **Cr** [spiːtʃ] M, mid20c (2 coll)   **Hu** *szpícs* [=E] pl. *-ek*, 19c (2 fac, obs) → *-el* v.

speed   *v.* 1 'go fast (esp. in a vehicle)', +2d 'increase the speed of an engine', +5 'use stimulant drugs, esp. amphetamine'

Nw *speede* [spiːde] end20c, 1,+2d(1 coll)   **Ic** *spít(t)a* [spiːta/spihta] mid20c, 1,+2d(2 coll) +5(2 sla) → *spítt-aður* adj.   **Hu** [=E] end20c, +5(1 tech)   **Gr** *spidaro* end20c, +2d,+5(1 sla)

speed   *n.* 1 'rapidity of movement', 5 'an amphetamine drug', +7 'velocity'

Ge [=E] N [U] 1980s, 5(1 sla); M, pl. *-s*, beg20c,

+7(1 jour) **Du** [=E] C [U] 1960s (1 tech >2); beg20c, +7(2) → -*y* adj. **Nw** [=E] M [U] 1960s, 5(1 tech) **Ic** *spit(t)* [=E/spiht] N [U] mid20c, 1(2 coll) 5(1/2 sla) → *spíttari* M; *spit(t)frik* N **Fr** [spid] M/adj., 1970s, 5(1 sla) → *speedél-eé* adj. **Sp** [espid] M, 1970s, 5(1 sla) → *espídico/espitoso* adj.; *espitar* v. **Rm** [=E] N [U] end20c, 5(1 tech) **Gr** spid N [U] end20c, 5(1 sla) → *spidaki* N

speedball *n.* +1a 'a mixture of cocaine with hashish' **Ge** [=E] M, pl. -*s*, 1980s (1 sla) **Sp** [espidbol] M, 1980s (1 sla)

speedboat *n.* 'a motor boat designed for high speed' **Ge** <=E>/*Speedboot* [=E/-bo:t] N, end20c (1 tech) **Du** *speedboot* [=E] C, pl. -*boten* (2 tech) **Nw** *speedbåt* [=E+Nw] mid20c (1 tech)

speedway *n./cp¹* 1a 'motorcycle racing', 1b 'a stadium or track used for this'
The racing term is remarkably evenly spread over Europe; note that it seldom refers to the race course (as it does in Britain).
Ge [spi:dve:] N, pl. -*s*, 1960s, 1a(1 tech) **Du** [=E] C/N [U] 1950s (1 tech) **Nw** [=E] M [U] mid20c, 1a(1 tech) **Sp** [=E] M, end20c, 1b(0>1 rare) < *dirt track* **It** [spi:dwei] M, pl. Ø, 1970s (1 tech) **Rs** *spidveĭ* M [U] mid20c (1 tech) **Po** [-i-] M [U] end20c (1 tech) **Cr** *spidvej* M [U] end20c (1 tech) **Bg** *spidueĭ* M [U] end20c (1 tech) **Fi** [=E] 1960s (1 tech)

spencer *n.* 1 'a short close-fitting jacket', 2 'a woman's woollen under-bodice'
This nineteenth-century word (derived from the British politician John Spencer, 1758–1834, but referring mainly to a lady's dress) was adopted fairly widely; changes of fashions have reduced it to archaic or regional functions, despite occasional revivals by the fashion industry.
Ge -*c*-/-*z*-/-*s*- M, pl. Ø, beg19c, 1(1 reg/arch); 1960s, 2(1 tech) **Du** [=E] C, beg19c, 1(1 arch) 2(1 tech) **Nw** <=E>/*spenser* [=E] M, pl. -*e*, mid19c, 1(1) **Fr** [spɛnsœr/spɛnsɛr] M, end18c, 1(1 tech, arch) **Sp** [espɛnθer] M, 20c, via Fr, 1(1 tech) **It** [spɛnser] M, pl. Ø, beg19c, 1(1 obs) **Rm** *spenţer/spenţur* [spɛntser, -tsur] N; *spenţeră* [spɛntserə] F, beg19c, via Ge (1 reg, arch) **Rs** *spenser* M, pl. -*y*, mid19c, 1(1 arch) **Po** [-er] M, mid19c, 1(1 arch) → -*ek* M **Cr** *špencer* M, pl. -*i*, 19c, 1(1 arch) **Hu** <=E/szpenszer> [=E] pl. Ø, 18c, 1(1 obs) **Gr** <=E> [=E] N [U] end20c (1 tech, mod)

spider *n.* +4 'an open, two-seated sports car', +5 'a dicky seat', +6 'a place for luggage in a sports car'
Ge [=E] M, pl. Ø, 1960s, +4(1 tech) **Du** [=E] C,

1980s (1 tech) **Fr** [spidɛr] M, end19c, +4,+5(1 tech) **It** [spaider] F/M, pl. Ø, 1910s, +4(3) → *spiderino* n. **Rm** [spider] N, mid20c, +4(1 tech) +6(1 obs) **Rs** (0) **Gr** *spaider* F, mid20c, +4(1 tech)

spikes *n.* 2a 'metal points set into the sole of a running shoe to prevent slipping', 2b 'running shoes with spikes', +2c 'studs in tyres', +2d 'tyres'
This term is still current for athletics, but less so for motorcars, ever since studded tyres were declared illegal in Germany because of their effects on the road surface.
Ge [ʃpaiks] pl., 1960s (2) **Du** [=E] C, 1980s, 2a(2 tech); 1940s, 2b(2 tech); 1970s, +2c(1 tech) **Nw** (0) < 2a,+2c *pigger* **Cr** *spajks* M, pl., mid20c, +2c(1 tech) **Bg** *shpaikove* pl., mid20c, via Ge, 2b(3 tech) **Gr** *spaiks* N, pl., mid20c, 2a,b,+2c(1 tech)

spin *n.* 3a 'a revolving motion through the air, esp. in a rifle bullet or in a billiard or tennis ball struck aslant', 5 'the intrinsic angular momentum of a subatomic particle' (phys.)
Ge [=E] M [U] 1940s, 5(1 tech) **Du** [=E] C, 1950s, 5(1 tech) **Nw** *spinn* [=E] N, pl. Ø, 20c, 5(4) **Fr** [spin] M, 1930s, 5(1 tech) **Sp** <=E>/*espín* [espin] M, pl. -*(e)s*, 20c, 5(1 tech) **It** [spin] M, pl. Ø, 1920s (1 tech) < 3a: *effetto* **Rm** [=E] M, mid20c, 5(1 tech) **Rs** *spin* M [U] mid20c, 5(1 tech) **Po** <=E> M [U] mid20c, 5(1 tech) **Cr** (0) **Bg** *spin* M [U] mid20c, 5(1 tech) **Fi** [=E] mid20c, 5(2) **Hu** [=E] [U] 20c, 5(1 tech) **Al** *spin* M [U] mid20c, 5(1 tech)

spinnaker *n.* 'a triangular sail carried opposite the main sail'
Ge [=E] M, pl. Ø, beg20c (1 tech) **Du** [spina:kər] C, mid20c (1 tech<3) **Nw** [spinaker] M, pl. -*e*, end19c (1 tech) **Ic** [=E] 20c (1 tech) = *belgsegl* **Fr** [spinakɛr/spinɛkœr] M, 19c (1 tech) **Sp** [espinaker] M, mid20c (1 tech) **It** [spinnaker] M, pl. Ø, 1930s (1 tech) **Rm** *spinacher/spinaker* [spinaker] N, mid20c (1 tech) **Rs** *spinaker* M, pl. -*y*, 19c (1 tech) **Po** *spinaker* [spinaker] M, mid20c (1 tech) **Cr** *spinaker* M, pl. -*i*, 19c (1 tech) **Bg** *spinaker* M, pl. -*al/-i*, beg20c (1 tech) **Fi** *spinaakkeri* 19c (2) **Hu** *spinakker* [spinakker] pl. -*ek*, beg20c, via Ge (1 tech)

spinning *n.* +2 'fishing with a spinner', +3 'a revolving mechanism in a spinner'
The distribution of this item is remarkable for its concentration on Eastern Europe (mediated through Russian?)

It [spinniŋ(g)] M [U] mid20c,

+2(1 tech)   **Rm** *spining* [spiniŋ] N [U] 1970s, +2(1 tech)   **Rs** *spinning* M [U] mid20c, +2(1 tech); pl. *-i*, +3(3)   **Po** [-nk] M, mid20c, +2(1 tech) → *-ista* M; *-owiec* M; *-ówka* F; *-owy* adj.   **Cr** (0)   **Bg** *spining* M [U] 1970s, +3(3 tech) → *-ov* adj.

spin-off   *n.* 1 'an incidental result, esp. as a side benefit from industrial technology', +2 'the forming of a new business by employees displaced from an existing business'
Ge [=E] M, pl. *-s*, 1980s, 1(1 tech, mod)   **Du** [=E] C, 1980s, 1(1 tech, jour)   **Nw** [=E] M, pl. *-s*, 1970s, 1(1 mod)   **Fr** [spin ɔf] M, 1980s, +2(1 tech, ban) > *essai-mage*   **It** [=E] M, pl. Ø, 1980s, 1(1 tech)   **Fi** [=E] 1980s, 1(1 tech, mod)

spiritual   *n.* 'a religious folksong, esp. of African Americans' (cf. ↑*Negro spiritual*)
Ge [=E] N/M, pl. *-s*, 1950s (1 tech)   **Du** [=E] C, 1940s (2)   **Nw** [=E] M, pl. *-s*, 1950s (1 tech)   **Sp** [=E] M, 1930s (1 tech) < mean *espiritual*   **It** [spiritual] M, pl. Ø, 1930s (2)   **Rm** [=E] N, pl. *-s*, 1970s (1 tech)   **Rs** *spirichuél* M, pl. *-y*, end20c (1 tech)   **Po** *spirituals* [=E] pl., end20c (1 tech)   **Cr** *spiritual* M, pl. *-i*, mid20c (1 tech)   **Bg** *spirichual* M, pl. *-al/-i*, end20c (1 tech)   **Hu** *spirituálé* [ʃpirituaːleː] pl. *-k*, 20c (2 tech)   **Gr** <=E> [=E] N, pl. *-s*, mid20c (1/Ø)

splash   *v.* 1 'spatter or cause (liquid) to spatter in small drops'
Nw *splashe* [splæʃe] end20c (1 coll)   **It** [=E/splaʃ] 1950s (1 coll, sla)

splatter   *n./cp²* +3 'a fan of excessive brutality (esp. in films)', +4 'film or fiction characterized by scenes of bloodshed'
Ge [=E] M, pl. Ø, 1980s (1 tech, mod)   **Nw** [=E] M, pl. *-e/-s*, 1980s, +4(1)   **Ic** [=E] M/cp¹, pl. *-ar*, end20c, +4(1 sla)   **It** [splatter] M/cp², pl. Ø, 1990s, +4(1 tech)

spleen   *n.* 2 'lowness of spirits', +3 'an eccentricity, a quirk'
This word was adopted as a quasi-medical term (for 'melancholy' as a consequence of an inflammation of the spleen) in the eighteenth century. It has since become obsolescent in most European languages but is very much alive in German for 'whim, eccentricity'.
Ge *Spleen* [ʃpliːn] M [U] end18c, +3(3) → *-ig* adj.   **Du** [=E/spleːn] N [U] beg20c, 2(2 rare)   **Nw** [=E] M [U] mid19c, 2(1 arch)   **Fr** [splin] M [U] 18c, 2(1 arch) → *spleenétique* adj.   **Sp** *esplín* [esplín] M [U] mid19c, 2(1 arch/

obs)   **It** [spliːn] M [U] mid18c, 2(1 obs) < *malinconia, noia*   **Rm** [splin] N [U] 1840s, via Fr, 2(2); *splenă* [splenə] F, 2(1 arch); *splin* [splin] N, 2(1 obs)   **Rs** *splin* M [U] 19c, 2 (1 arch)   **Po** *splin* [-i-] M [U] mid19c, 2(1 arch)   **Cr** *splin* M [U] beg20c, 2(1 arch)   **Bg** *splin* M [U] beg20c, via Rs, 2(1 lit, arch)   **Hu** [=E] [U] 19c, 2(1 arch)

splice   *v.* 1 'join the ends of (ropes) by interweaving strands', 2 'join (magnetic tape, film, etc.) in an overlapping position', +4 'treat someone to something; spend money'
Ge *spleißen* (4)   **Nw** *spleise* [splæise] end19c, 1,2(3 tech)   **Ic** *splæsa* [splai:sa] beg20c, via Da, 1,2(3 tech) +4(3 coll)

splice   *n.* 1 'a joint of two ropes', (naut.), +2 'the act of spending money as in a Dutch treat'
Ge *Spleiß* M, pl. *-e*, 1(4)   **Du** - < *splitsing* (4)   **Nw** *spleis* [splæis] M, pl. *-er*, beg20c (3) → *spleise* v.   **Ic** *splæs* [splai:s] M, beg20c, via Da, 1(2 tech) +2(2 sla)   **It** [spleis] M, pl. Ø, beg20c (1 tech)   **Rm** - < ↑*splicing, matisare*   **Po** *splis* [splis] M, mid20c, 1(1 tech)   **Cr** (0)   **Fi** *pleissi* 18c (5Sw) → *pleissata* v.

splicing   *n.* +2 'the act of joining the ends of (ropes) by interweaving strands'
Ge *Spleißen* (4)   **Nw** *spleising* [splæisiŋ] C [U] 19c (3 tech)   **It** [=E] M, pl. Ø, 1980s (1 tech)   **Rm** *splicing* 20c (1 tech)

splint   *n.* 1a 'a flat piece of board for holding a damaged bone immobile', +5 'a cotter pin'
Ge [ʃplint] M, pl. *-e*, 19c, +5(3/4)   **Nw** (5)   **Rm** [=E]/ *splint* [ʃplint] N, 1920s, +5(3 tech); *splintur* [splintur] N, +5 > *cui spintecat* N   **Fi** *splintti* 19c, 1a, +5(3)

split   *v.* 1b 'divide into parts', +1d 'give first and second vote to different parties'
Ge *splitten* [splitən] 1970s, 1b,+1d(2)   **Du** *splitten* [splitə] 19c, 1b(3) < *splijten, splitsen*   **Nw** *splitte* [splite] 1b(5LowGe)   **Ic** *splitta* [splihta] 1970s, 1b(2 coll)

split-level   *cp¹* 'a flat etc. having some rooms somewhat higher than others'
Ge [=E] 1970s (1 tech, rare)   **Du** [=E] 1970s (1 tech, rare)

splitting   *n.* 'a form of taxation by which the income of husband and wife are added and then split in two'
Ge [ʃplitiŋ/sp-] N [U] 1970s (1 tech)   **It** [splittiŋ(g)] M [U] 1990s? (1 tech)

spoiler   *n.* 2a 'a device on an aircraft to retard its speed by interrupting the airflow', 2b 'a similar device on a motorcar to improve road-holding'
This term was adopted for planes and cars/ trucks from the 1970s on and has become reasonably established, precise and easy equivalents not being available.
Ge [ʃpoila] M, pl. Ø, 1970s (1 tech)   **Du** [=E] C, 1970s (1 tech>2)   **Nw** [=E] M, pl. *-e*, 1970s (1 tech)   **Ic** [=E] M, pl. *-ar*, 1980s (0) < rend *vindskeið, vindkljúfur*   **Fr** <=E> M, 1970s, 2b (1 tech, ban) > *déflecteur, déporteur*   **Sp** [espoiler] M, pl. *-s*, end20c (1 tech) = *alerón*   **It** [spɔiler] M, pl. Ø, 1970s (1>2 tech) < *alettone*   **Rm** [spɔjler] N, 1970s (1 tech)   **Rs** *spoiler* M, pl. *-y*, 1980s (1 tech)   **Po** [-er] M, end20c (1 tech)   **Cr** *spojler* M, end20c (1 tech)   **Bg** *spoiler* M, pl. *-al/-i*, end20c (1 tech)   **Fi** *spoileri* 1970s (2)

sponsor *n.* 2a 'a person/organization that promotes or supports an artistic or sporting activity', 2b 'a business organization that promotes a broadcast programme in return for advertising time'
Ge (3/5La) **Du** [=E] C, 1960s (3) **Nw** [spɔnsu:r] M, pl. -er, mid20c (3/5La) **Ic** [spɔnsor] M, pl. -ar (1 coll) **Fr** [spõsɔʀ] M, 1970s (2 ban) > *parrain, mécène* **Sp** <=E>/*esponsor* [espɔnsor] M, pl. -s, 1980s, 2a(1 tech) < *patrocinador* **It** [spɔnsor] M, pl. Ø, 1960s (3) → *sponsorizzatore* **Rm** [spɔnsor] M, 1970s (3 mod) → *sponsoriza* v. → *sponsorizare* F → *sponsorizat, -ă* adj. **Rs** *spɔnsor* M, pl. -y, end20c (2) **Po** [-or] M, end20 (2 mod) → *-owany* adj. **Cr** *spɔnzor* M, pl. -i, end20c (3) **Bg** *spɔnsor* M, pl. -i, end20c (2) → *-ski* adj.; *-stvo* N **Fi** *sponsori* 1980s (2) **Hu** *szponzor* [spɔnzor] pl. -ok, end20c (2 mod) → *-ál* v. **Al** *sponsor* M, pl. -a, 1990s, 2a(3 mod) **Gr** *spɔnsor* M, end20c (2); *spɔnsoras* M (3)

sponsor *v.* 'support financially'
Ge *sponsern* 20c (1 mod) **Du** *sponsoren* [spɔnsərə] 1950s (3) **Nw** *spons(r)e* [spɔns(r)e]/*sponsorere* [sponsure:re] 1980s (3/5) → *sponsing* M/F **Ic** *sponsor(er)a* [spɔnsor(er)a] end20c (1 coll) = trsl *kosta* **Fr** *sponsoriser* 1970s (1 tech) > *parrainer* **Sp** *esponsorizar* 1980s (3 tech) < *patrocinar* **It** *sponsorizzare* [spɔnsoriddzare] 1970s (3) **Rm** *sponsoriza* 20c(1 mod) **Rs** *sponsirovat'* 20c (1 mod) **Po** *sponsorować* [sponsorovatç] end20c (2 mod) **Cr** *sponzorirati* end20c (3) **Bg** *sponsoriram* 20c (3) **Fi** *sponsoroida* 1980s (2) **Hu** *szponzorál* [sponzora:l] (2+5) → *-ás* n. **Al** *sponsporizoj* 20c (1 mod) **Gr** *sponsoraro* end20c (3 coll, jour)

sponsoring *n.* 'paying for a programme or a sportsperson'
Whereas *sponsor* n./v. are largely internationalisms, the *-ing* makes the word a clear anglicism; note, however, widespread morphological integration by the replacement of the derivational morpheme.
Ge [ʃpɔnsəriŋ/sp-] N [U] 1980s (1 tech) **Du** [=E] C, 1960s (2) **Nw** *sponsing* [spɔnsiŋ] M/F [U] 1980s *sponse* v. (3) ← **Fr** [spõsɔʀiŋ] M, 1970s (2 ban) > *parrainage, mécénat* **Sp** [=E] M, end20c (1 mod, rare) < *esponsorización* **It** - < *sponsorizzazione* **Rm** - < *sponsorizare* **Rs** - < *spɔnsorstvo* **Po** [-nk] M [U] end20c (2 mod) **Cr** - < *sponzoriranje* **Bg** - < *sponsorstvo* **Fi** - < *sponsorointi* **Hu** - < *szponzorálás* **Al** - < *sponsorizim* **Gr** <=E> [=E] N [U] end20c (1 mod)

sport *n* 1a 'a game or competitive activity, esp. an outdoor one involving physical exertion', 1b 'such activities collectively', 3 'amusement, fun', +7 *cp¹* 'referring to casual clothes'
Ge [ʃport] M [U] 1820s, 1a,b(3) → *-ler* M; *-lich* adj. **Du** [=E] C, pl. -en, mid19c (1a(3>5) → *-en* v.; *-er* n.; *-ief* adj. **Nw** [=E] M [U] 19c, 1a,b(3) < *idrett* → *sporte* v.; *sport(s)lig* adj. **Ic** [spɔrt] N [U] end19c, via Da, 1a,b(3 coll) = *íþrótt(ir)* **Fr** [spɔʀ] M,

mid19c, 1a,b(3) → *sportif* M/F *sportive* adj.; *sportivité* F **Sp** <=E> [espɔr(t)] M/adj., uninfl., end19c, +7(2) **It** [spɔrt] M, pl. Ø, 1820s (3) → *sportivo* adj.; *sportività* F.; *sportivamente*, adv. **Rm** [sport] N, end19c, 1a,b(3); *haine sport* +7(5+3) **Rs** *sport* M [U] beg20c, 1a,3(3) → *-ivnyĭ* adj. **Po** [sport] M, beg20c (3) → *-owiec* M; *ówka* F; *-ować się* v.; *-owy* adj.; *wy- -owany* adj.; *poza–owy* adj.; *-owo* adv. **Cr** *šport* M, pl. -ovi, beg20c, 1a(3) → *-aš* M; *-ašica* F; *-ski* adj. **Bg** *sport* M, pl. -al-ove, beg20c, 1a,b(2) → *-en* adj.; *-ist* M; *-istka* F **Hu** [ʃport] pl. -ok, 19c, 1a(3); mid20c, 3(3) **Al** *sport* M, pl. -e, end19c, 1a,3(3) **Gr** *spor* N, usu. pl., end20c, via Fr, 1a,b,+7(2) < *athlima, athlitikos*

sportsman *n.* 1 'a person engaged in sport', 2 'a person who behaves fairly'
This word is almost as widespread as *sport* is (but *sportswoman* is much rarer). Note morpheme replacement by *-ist* in Icelandic, Bulgarian and Albanian.
Ge *Sportsmann* M, pl. -männer, 19c, 1(3+5) < *Sportler* **Du** [=E] C, pl. -men, 1940s (1 mod) < *sportman* **Nw** *sportsmann* [=E+Nw] mid19c, 1(3+5) < *idrettsmann* **Ic** - < *sportisti, íþróttamaður* **Fr** - < *sportif* **Sp** [=E] M, mid19c, 1(0>1 arch) **It** [spɔrtmɛn/-man] M, pl. Ø/-men, mid19c, 1(1) **Rm** <=E>/*sportsmen* [sportsman/-mɛn] M, pl. *sportsmeni*, end19c (3 rare) < *sportiv* → *sportsmană* F **Rs** *sportsmɛn* M, pl. -y, beg20c, 1(2) → *-ka* F **Po** *sportsmen* [sportsmɛn] M, beg20c, 1(2) → *-ka* F; *sportsmeński* adj. **Cr** *sportsmen* M, pl. -i, beg20c, 1(3) **Bg** *sportsmɛn* M, pl. -i, mid20c, via Rs, 1(1 rare) 2(2 jour); *sportist* M, pl. -i, 1(3) → *sportsmɛnski* adj.; *-mɛnstvo* N **Hu** [=E] pl. -ek, 19c, 1(2) < *sportoló* **Al** - < *sportist* **Gr** *sportsman/sportsghuman* M/F, pl. -en/-Ø, end20c, 1(2) 2(1)

sportswear *n.* 'clothing for leisure'
Ge [ʃportsve:a/sp-] M/N [U] 1970s (2 mod) **Du** [=E] C, 1980s (1 tech, jour) **Nw** (0) **Ic** - < trsl *sportfatnaður* **Fr** <=E>/*sportwear* [spɔʀt(s)wɛʀ] M, 1960s (1 tech) **Sp** [=E] M [U] 1990s (1 tech, you) **It** [spɔrtswɛr] M [U] 1980s (1 tech) **Cr** *športsver* (0) **Al** - < *veshje sportive* **Gr** <=E> [=E] end20c (0 > 1 tech)

spot *v.* 1d 'catch sight of'
Du *spotten* [=E] end20c (1 you) **Ic** *spotta* [spohta] end20c (2 coll)

spot¹ *n.* +4c 'a short radio or TV commercial'
Ge [spot/ʃp-] M, pl. -s, 1970s (1 tech) **Du** [=E] C, 1960s (2>3 tech) **Nw** [=E] M, pl. -s, 1980s (1 tech) **Fr** [spɔt] M/adj., uninfl. (2 ban) < *message publicitaire*; *spot (credit)* end19c/1970s (1 tech, ban) > *message publicitaire, finance* < *crédit ponctuel* **Sp** [espɔt] M, pl. -s, 1970s (2 tech) < *anuncio (publicitario)* **It** [spɔt] M, pl. Ø, 1970

(3) **Rm** [=E] N, 1970s (3 mod) **Po** <=E> M, end20c (2 mod) **Cr** *spot* M, pl. *-ovi*, end20c (2 tech) **Bg** *spot* M, pl. *-al-ove*, 1990s (1 mod, rare) **Fi** *spotti* 1970s (1 tech) **Gr** *spot* N, end20c (2) → *spotaki* N

spot² *n.* +6a 'a beam of light directed on a small area, esp. on a particular part of a theatre stage or of the road in front of a vehicle', +6b 'a lamp projecting a spotlight'

Ge [=E] M, pl. *-s*, 1970s, +6b(1 mod) **Du** [=E] C, 1960s, +6b(2) **Nw** <=E>/*spott* [=E] M, pl. *-er*, *-s*, 1960s, +6b(2) > *punktbelysning* **Ic** [spɔht] N, pl. Ø, 1970s (1 tech) **Fr** [=E] M, end19c, +6b(2) **Sp** [espɔt] M, 1980s, +6a,b(1 tech) **It** [spɔt] M, pl. Ø, 1940s (2>3) **Rm** [=E] N, mid20c, +6a(1 tech THEATRE,PHYS) **Fi** *spotti* 1970s, +6b(2) **Hu** +*lámpa* [spotla:mpa] pl. *-ák*, 20c, +6b(1 tech) **Gr** *spot* N, end20c, +6b(2)

spotlight *n.* 1 'a lamp projecting a beam of light directed on a small area'

The word for the lamp is frequently shortened to ↑*spot*.

Ge [=E] N, pl. *-s*, 1980s (1 tech) = *Punktstrahler* **Du** [=E] N, 1940s (1 tech > 2) **Nw** [=E] N/M, pl. Ø/*-s*, mid20c (1 tech) = *spottlys*, *(lys)prosjektør* **Ic** [=E] (o); *spottljós* N, pl. Ø, 1970s (1+5 tech) **It** - < ↑*spot²* **Po** <=E> M, mid20c (1 tech) **Fi** - < trsl *kohdevalaisin*

spray *n.* 2 'a liquid preparation to be applied with an atomizer etc., esp. for medical purposes', 3 'an instrument or apparatus for such application'

Ge [ʃpreː] N/M, pl. *-s*, beg20c, 2(2) 3(1 arch); = 3: *Sprühdose* **Du** [=E/spreː] C, 1960s, 2(2) 3(1 tech, jour, rare); < 3: *spuitbus* **Nw** [=E/sprai/spræi] M, pl. *-er*, 1950s, 2,3(2) → *spraye* v. **Ic** *sprey/spreil spray* [=E] N [U] mid20c (2 coll); *spreybrúsi* M, 3(2+5 coll) = 3: trsl *úðabrúsi* **Fr** [sprɛ] M, 1960s, 2,3(1); < 2: *pulvérisation*; < 3: *atomiseur, vaporisateur* **Sp** [esprai] M, pl. *-s*, 1960s (2) **It** [sprai/sprei] M, pl. Ø, 1920s (3) < *nebulizzatore, vaporizzatore* **Rm** [sprej/ʃprej/spraj/ʃpraj] N, 1970s (2 mod) **Rs** *spreĭ* M, pl. *-i*, end20c (1 tech) **Po** *sprej/*<=E> M, beg20c (2) → *-owiec* M **Cr** *sprej* M, pl. *-evi*, mid20c, 2(2) → *-ati* v. **Bg** *shpreĭ/spreĭ* M, pl. *-eyal-eyove*, mid/end20c, 3(3/2) = *aerozol* **Fi** [=E] mid20c (2) **Hu** [=E/ʃpreː] pl. *-k*, beg20c, 2(3) **Al** *sprej* M, pl. *-e*, mid20c, 2(3) **Gr** *sprei* N, mid20c (2)

spray *v.* 1 'throw (liquid) in the form of spray', 2 'sprinkle with small drops or particles'

Ge *sprayen* [ʃpreː ən] 1980s (2>3) → *-er* M **Du** *sprayen* [spreː ən] 1960s (1 rare) < *spuiten* **Nw** *spraye* [spræ ie/sprai e] 1960s (2) **Ic** *spreyja/spreia* [sprei:ja] mid20c, 2(2 coll) = rend *úða* **Rm** *spreia* [spreia] 1970s (2) **Po** (o) **Cr** *sprejati* end20c (2 tech) **Fi** *sprayata* [spreijata] end20c (1 tech, coll) **Hu** *bespréz* [beʃpreːz] end20c (3)

spread *n.* 9 'a sweet or savoury paste for spreading on bread'

Du [spreːd] C, 1980s (1 mod)

spreadsheet *n.* 'a computer program allowing manipulation and flexible retrieval of esp. tabulated numerical data' (comput.)

Ge (o > 1 tech) **Du** [=E] C, 1980s (1 tech) **Nw** (o) < rend *regneark* **Ic** [=E] N, end20c (o tech) < rend *töflureiknir, reiknivangur* **Fr** - < *tableur* **It** [spredʃiːt] M, pl. Ø, 1980s (1 tech) < rend *foglio elettronico* **Rm** - < *tabel* **Rs** (o) **Bg** *spredshit* M, pl. *-a*, 1990s (1 tech) **Fi** 1980s (1 tech) < rend *taulukkolaskenta* **Hu** [=E] [U] end20c (1 tech) **Gr** <=E> [=E] N, pl. Ø/*-s*, end20c (1 tech)

spring *n.* 4 'a resilient device usu. of bent or coiled metal used esp. to drive clockwork or for cushioning in furniture or vehicles'

It [=E] M, pl. Ø, 1960s (1 tech)

spring roll *n.* 'a Chinese pancake filled with vegetables, and fried'

Ge - < trsl *Frühlingsrolle* **Nw** - < trsl *vårrull* **Ic** - < trsl *vorrúlla* **Fr** - < trsl? *rouleau du printemps* **Sp** - < trsl *rollo de primavera* **It** - < trsl *involtino primavera* **Fi** - < trsl *kevätrulla* **Gr** <=E> /*spring ro(u)l* N, pl. Ø/*-s*, 1980s (1 tech) = trsl *anixiatiko rolo*

sprinkler *n.* 'a device for sprinkling water to extinguish fires'

Ge [ʃprɪŋkla] M, pl. Ø, beg20c (3) < trsl *Sprinkleranlage* **Du** [sprɪŋklər/=E] C, 1970s (2 tech) = *sprinklerinstallatie* **Nw** [=E] M, pl. *-e*, 20c (3 tech) **Ic** - < rend *úðari* **Fr** [=E] M, mid20c (1 tech, ban) < *gicleur d'incendie* **Sp** [esprɪŋkler] M, pl. *-s*, end20c (1 tech) **It** [sprɪŋkler] M, pl. Ø, 1930s (1 tech) **Rm** [sprɪŋkler] N, 1960s, via Fr (2 tech) **Cr** *šprinkler* M, pl. *-i*, 20c (1 tech) **Bg** *sprinkler* M, pl. *-al-i*, mid20c (1 tech) **Fi** *sprinkleri* mid20c (2)

sprint *v.* 1 'run a short distance at full speed'

Ge [ʃprɪntn] 1930s (3) **Du** *sprinten* [sprɪntə] 1940s (5) **Nw** *sprinte* [sprɪntə] beg20c (3) → *sprinter* M **Fr** *sprinter* [sprɛ̃te] end19c (2) **Sp** *esprintar* mid20c (3) **It** *sprintare* [sprɪntare] mid20c (3 tech) **Rm** *sprinta* [sprɪnta] mid20c, via Fr? (3) **Po** (o) **Cr** *šprintati* mid20c (3) **Bg** *sprintiram* (3) **Fi** *sprintata* beg20c (3) **Hu** *sprintel* [ʃprɪntel] beg20c (3) → *-és* n. **Al** *sprintoj* mid20c (1 tech) **Gr** *spridaro* mid20c (3)

sprint *n.* 1a 'a short run at full speed', 2 'a similar short effort in cycling, etc.'

Ge [ʃprɪnt] M, pl. *-s*, 1930s (3) **Du** [sprɪnt/=E] C, pl. *-enl-s*, beg20c (2 tech > 5) **Nw** [=E] M, pl. *-er*, 1930s (3) **Fr** [=E] M, end19c (2) **Sp** *esprint/esprin* M, pl. *-(e)s*, 1920s (3) **It** [sprint] M/adj., pl. Ø, beg20c (3) **Rm** [=E] N, mid20c (3) **Rs** *sprint* M [U] mid20c (2) **Po** M, mid20c, 1a,2(3) **Cr** *sprint* M, pl. *-ovi*, mid20c (3) **Bg** *sprint* M, pl. *-al-ove*, mid20c (2) → *-ov* adj. **Fi** *sprintti* beg20c (3) **Hu** [ʃprint] [U] beg20c, 1a(3) **Al** *sprint* M, pl. *-e*, mid20c (1 tech) **Gr** *sprid* N, mid20c (2)

sprinter   *n.* 1 'a person who runs, cycles, etc. a short distance at full speed'

    Ge [ʃprinta] M, pl. Ø, 1930s (3)   **Du** [sprɪntər/=E] C, beg20c (2 tech>5) **Nw** [=E/sprinter] M/F, pl. *-e*, 1930s (2) → *sprinterske* C **Ic** - < rend *spretthlaupari* **Fr** *sprinteur/sprinter* [spʀintœʀ] M, end19c (2) **Sp** [esprinter] M, pl. *-s*, beg20c (2) = *velocista* **It** [sprinter] M, pl. Ø, beg20c (2) = *velocista* **Rm** [sprinter] M, mid20c (3) → *-ă* F **Rs** *sprinter* M, pl. *-y*, mid20c (2) **Po** [- er] M, mid20c (2) → *-ka* F; *-ski* adj. **Cr** *sprinter* M, pl. *-i*, mid20c (2 tech) **Bg** *sprintyor* M, pl. *-i*, mid20c, via Fr (3) → *-ka* F; *-ski* adj. **Fi** *sprintteri* beg20c (3) **Hu** [ʃprinter] pl. *-ek*, beg20c (3 tech) **Al** *sprinter* M, pl. *-ë*, mid20c (1 tech) **Gr** *sprider* [-nt-/-d-] M/F, mid20c (2)

spurt   *n.* 2 'a short sudden effort or increase of pace, etc. in racing'

    This word (and the related verb) are conspicuously rarer than the similar ↑*sprint* (with derivatives), although *spurt* was adopted much earlier. It is uncertain why this is so – it may be that to *sprint* is to go for a fixed short distance, whereas to *spurt* is an option in any athletic race, at any point.

    Ge [ʃpurt] M, pl. *-s/-e*, end19c (3) → v. **Du** [spʏrt] C [U] end19c (3 tech) → *-en* v. **Nw** [spurt] M, pl. *-er*, end19c (3) → *spurte* v. **Rs** *spurt* M [U] beg20c (1 tech) → *-ovat'* v. **Po** [spurt] M, beg20c (1 tech) **Cr** (o) **Fi** *spurtti* beg20c (2) **Hu** [spз:t/ʃpurt] [U] end19/beg20c (1 tech, arch) → *-ol* v.

squall   *n.* 1 'a sudden or violent gust or storm of wind, esp. with rain or snow or sleet'

    Rs *shkval* M, pl. *-y*, 19c (3) → *-istyĭ* adj.; *-nyĭ* adj. **Po** *szkwał* [ʃkvaw] M, mid20c, via Ge? (1 tech) → *-owy* adj. **Bg** *shkval* M, pl. *-a/-ove*, beg20c, via Rs (3 tech)

square   *v.* +11 'prepare, make (a ship or trawler) ready' (naut.), +12 'get (oneself) ready', +13 'finish in a hurry'

    Nw *skvare* [skvæ:re] 19c, +11(1 tech, arch) **Ic** *skvera* [skvɛ:ra] beg/mid20c, +11(2 tech) +12,+13(2 coll)

square   *n.* +2e 'the middle piece of a trawl-net' (naut.), 3a 'an open four-sided area between buildings', +11 'a small public garden surrounded by a fence'

    Du (Ø) **Nw** (o) **Ic** *skver* [skvɛ:r] M/(N), pl. *-ar/Ø*, beg/mid20c, +2e(2 tech) **Fr** [skwar] M, 18c, 3a(Ø); 19c, +11(2) **It** [skwɛr] F, pl. Ø, 18c (Ø) **Rm** *scuar* [skwar] N, mid20c, via Fr, 3a, +11(3) **Rs** *skver* M, pl. *-y*, 19c, +11(3) → *-ik* M **Po** *skwer* [skver] M, mid19c, 3a, +11(2) → *-ek* M; *-owy* adj. **Cr** (o) **Hu** [=E] [U] 20c, 3a(1 tech)

square   *adj.* 12. 'conventional or old-fashioned, unsophisticated, conservative'

    Ic [=E] 1970s (1 sla) = trsl *ferkantaður*

square dance   *n.* 'a dance for four couples facing inwards'

    Ge (Ø) **Du** [=E] C, 1960s (1 tech) **Nw** [=E] M [U] 20c (Ø) **Ic** *skverdans* [skvɛr:tans] M [U] 20c (Ø > 2 tech) = *ferdans* **Fr** (Ø) **It** [skwer dɛns] F [U] 1960s (1 tech) **Po** (o) **Cr** (o) **Fi** [=E] (Ø)

squash   *v.* +5 'play squash'

    Du *squashen* [skwɔʃən] 1980s (2) **Po** (o) **Cr** (o)

squash   *n.* 4 'an indoor game played with rackets and a small fairly soft ball against the walls of a closed court'

    Ge [skvoʃ] N [U] 1970s (1 tech) → *-er* M **Du** [=E] N/cp¹ [U] 1960s (2 tech) → *-en* v. **Nw** [=E] M [U] 1970s (1 tech) **Ic** [=E]/*skvass* [skvas:] N [U] end20c (1 coll) = rend *veggjatennis* **Fr** [skwaʃ] M, 1930s (1 tech) **Sp** [eskwoʃ/-aʃ/as] M [U] 1980s (1 tech) **It** [skuɔʃ] M [U] 1950s (2 tech) **Rm** [=E] N [U] end20c (0 <1 tech, rare) **Rs** *skvosh* M [U] 1980s (1 tech) **Po** [=E] M [U] end20c (1 tech) **Cr** *skvoš* M [U] end20c (1 tech) **Bg** *skuosh* M [U] end20c (1 tech, mod) **Fi** [=E] 1980s (1) **Hu** [skvaʃ] [U] end20c (2) **Gr** *skuos* N [U] end20c (2)

squatter   *n.* 1 'a person who occupies a house/premises illegally', 3 'a person who settles on new public land without title'

    Ge (0) < *Hausbesetzer* **Du** [=E] C, 19c, 1(Ø) < *kraker* **Nw** [=E] M, pl. *-e*, mid19c, 1(1 arch) < *husokkupant* **Fr** [skwate] M, 1940s, 1(2 ban) = *squatteur* **Sp** [eskwoter] M, pl. *-s*, 1970s (Ø/1 tech) < *okupa* **It** [skwɔtter] M/F, pl. Ø, 19c (Ø/1) **Rm** [=E] N, end20c, 1(1) **Rs** *skvatter* M, pl. *-y*, 19c, 3(Ø); 20c, 1(1) → *-skiĭ* adj. **Po** *skwater/<=E>* [skvater] M, pl. *-si*, end20c, 1(1 mod) **Cr** *skvoter* M, pl. *-i*, end20c, 1(1)

squaw   *n.* 'a North American Indian woman or wife'

    Ge (Ø) **Du** (Ø) **Fr** [skwo] F, end18c (1 tech) **It** [=E] F, pl. Ø, 19c (2) **Po** [-o] F, uninfl. (Ø) **Hu** (Ø)

squeeze   *v.* 3a 'force into or through a small or narrow space'

    Nw *skvise* [skvi:se] 1970s (2 sla) **Ic** *skvísa* [skvi:sa] mid/end20c (2 sla) **Fr** [skwize] 1960s (1)

squeeze   *n.* +2b 'a girl'

    Ic *skvísa* F, pl. *-ur*, mid20c (3 coll)

SS   *abbrev.* 2 'steamship'

    Du [=E] attrib., beg20c (3) **Nw** (o) < *DS, D/S* **It** *S/S, s/s* (Ø) **Po** *s/s* mid20c (1 tech) **Cr** *S/S* 20c (1 tech) **Fi** [ɛs:ɛs] 19c (3)

staff   *n.* 2a 'a body of persons employed in business etc.'

    Ge (Ø) **Ic** [=E] N [U] mid/end20c (2 coll) **Sp** [estaf] M, pl. *-s*, 1970s (1 tech, jour) **It** [=E] M [U] 1960s (1>2) **Rm** [=E] N, 1990s (1 jour, mod) **Cr** (0) **Bg** (o) **Hu** (o) **Al** *staf* M, pl. *-e*, 1990s

(at) stake   *phr.* +1b 'going badly (after having been risked)'

    Ic *(i) steik* [(i) stei:k] mid20c (3 coll)

stand   *n.* 4 'a rack, set of shelves, table, etc., on or in which things may be placed', 5a 'a place where one shows and sells goods', 5b 'a structure occupied by a participating organization at an exhibition', +10 'a place for testing machinery'

The situation is complex because German *Stand* is largely identical in form and meaning to the English item; it is therefore impossible to determine which senses were added from English, or whether German was the source or transmitter of the item in languages such as Hungarian or Romanian.

Ge [ʃtant] M, pl. *Stände*, 5a(4) **Du** [=E/stant] C, beg20c, +10(2<3) **Nw** [=E] M, pl. *-s*, 20c, 5a,b(2) **Ic** *standur* [stantvr] M, pl. *-ar*, mid20c, 4(4) **Fr** [stãd] M, end19c, 5a(2) **Sp** [estand] M, pl. *-s*, end19c, 5a,b(2) **It** [stɛnd] M, pl. Ø, 1905, 5a,b(3) → *standista* M; *standistico*, adj. **Rm** [stand] N, 1920s, via Fr/Ge, 5a,5b,+10(3); *ştand* [ʃtand] (3 rare) **Rs** *stend* M, pl. *-y*, beg20c, 5a,b,+10(3 tech) **Po** [stent] M, beg20c, 5a(1 tech) **Cr** *štand* M, pl. *-ovi*, beg20c, 5a(5Ge?) **Bg** *stend* M, pl. *-a*/*-ove*, mid20c, via Rs, +10(3 tech) **Hu** (5Ge) **Gr** *stad* N, pl. Ø/*-s*, end20c, 5a(1 tech) < *periptero*

standard *n.* 1 'an object or quality or measure serving as a basis or example', 2a 'a degree of excellence', 2b 'average quality', 9 'a tune or song of established popularity', +13 'a switchboard', +14 'a standard of living'

Ge [ʃtandart] M, pl. *-s*, end18c, 2b(2) → *-isieren* v. **Du** *standaard* [stãnda:rt] C, pl. *-en*/*-s*, end18c, 2b(4<5) **Nw** [stãndar(d)] M, pl. *-er*, 19c, 2a,b(3) → *-isere* v. **Ic** [stantart] M, pl. *-ar*, 1920s, via Da, 1(2 tech, arch) 2b,9,+14(2 coll) < 1: creat *staðall* → *-isera* v; *-isering* F **Fr** [stãdar] M/adj., uninfl., mid19c, 2b(2); end19c, +13(2) → *-iser* n.; *-isation*; *-iste* M/F **Sp** <=E>/*estándar* pl. *-es*; *standard* M, pl. Ø/*-s*, beg20c, 1,2b(2>3) → *estandarizar* v.; *estandarización* F **It** [stãndard] M, pl. Ø, mid18c, 1,2a,b,+14(3) → *-izzare* v.; *-izzazione* F **Rm** [stãndard] N, end19c, via Fr/Ge, 2a,2b(3); mid20c, 1(3); adj. uninfl., 2a,b,4(3); *ştandard* [ʃta-] (3 rare) **Rs** *standart* M, pl. *-y*, beg20c, 2b(3) → *-nyĭ* adj.; *-izatsiya* F; *-no* adv. **Po** [standart] M, beg20c, 1,2a,b,+14(2) → *-owość* F; *standaryzacja* F; *standaryzowanie* N; *standaryzować* v.; *-owy* adj.; *standaryzacyjny* adj.; *-owo* adv. **Cr** *standard* M, pl. *-i*, beg20c, 2b(3) → *-an* adj.; *izacija* F; *-izirati* v. **Bg** *standart* M, pl. *-a*/*-i*, beg20c, via Rs, 1,2b,+14(3) → *-en* adj.; *-iziram* v.; *-izatsiya* F **Fi** *standardi* 19c, 2b(3) → *standardisoida* v. **Hu** *sztenderd* pl. *-ek*, end19/beg20c, 2b(3) → *-izál* v.; *-izáció* n. **Al** *standard* M, pl. *-e*, 1930s, 2b(3) → *-izoj* v. **Gr** *stãdar(d)* N, pl. *-s*, end20c, 1,2b(2)

standby¹ *cp¹./adj.* 1 'ready for immediate use, action (e.g. television, hifi)', +4 'an electric device making a TV set etc. ready for immediate use'

Ge [=E] 1980s (1 tech) **Du** [=E] 1980s, +4(1 tech) **Nw** [=e] 1960s (1 tech) **Ic** *standbœ* [stantpai] uninfl., frequ. cp¹, 1970s, 1(1 coll) **Sp** *en stan by* [estanbai] adv., end20c, 1(1 tech) **It** [stɛndbai] uninfl., 1980s (1 tech) **Cr** [stendbaj] 1980s (1

tech) **Hu** [=E] end20c, 1(1 tech_ECON) **Gr** <=E> [stadbai] 1980s (1 tech)

standby² *cp¹/²* 2 'not booked in advance but allocated on the basis of earliest availability' (air travel), *n.* +3 'a person waiting for a flight seat'

Ge [=E] cp¹, 1980s, 2(1 tech) **Du** [=E] 1970s, (2) **Nw** [=E] cp¹, 20c, 2(2) **Ic** [=E] end20c, 2(1 tech) **Fr** [stãdbaj] M/adj., uninfl., 1970s (1 tech, ban) > *en attente* **Sp** [estanbai] M, end20c, 2(1 tech) **It** [stendbai] M [U] 1980s (2) **Rm** [stendbai] cp², end20c (1 tech, mod) **Po** [-e-] M, uninfl., 1980s (1 tech) **Cr** [=E] M [U] end20c (1 tech) **Bg** *stendbaĭ* uninfl., 1990s, 2(1 tech_ECON) **Fi** [=E] 1980s, 2(1 tech) **Hu** [=E] [U] end20c (1 tech) < *várólistás* **Gr** [stadbai] cp², +3 (1 tech)

standing *n.* 1 'status, position'

The distribution is remarkable for the word's popularity among Romance languages; it is much less well accepted elsewhere and almost totally absent from Eastern Europe.

Ge [-e-] N [U] 1960s (1 jour, rare) < *Stellung* **Du** [=E] C [U] 1980s (1 coll, mod, rare) < *stand* **Nw** (0) **Fr** [stãdiŋ] M, 1930s (2 ban) < *classe* **Sp** [estandin] [U] 1970s (2>1) **It** [stendiŋ(g)] M [U] 1940s (1 tech) **Rm** [stending] N [U] end20c (1 jour) **Po** [-e-] M [U] end20c (1 mod) **Cr** (0)

standing ovation *n.* 'a period of prolonged applause during which the crowd or audience rise to their feet'

Ge [=E] F, pl. *-s*, 1980s (1 mod) < trsl *stehender Beifall* **Du** - < trsl *staande ovatie* (5) **Nw** (0) < trsl *stående ovasjon* **Ic** [=E] 20c (0) **Fr** (0) **Po** - < *owacja na stojąco* **Gr** (0>1 mod, jour)

star *n.* 8a 'a famous or brilliant person', +8c 'a famous actress', +8d 'an actor'

The distribution of this seemingly universal loanword is in fact restricted by calques which may coexist with, or have replaced, the English term; compare the similar situation for ↑*starlet*.

Ge [ʃta:r/st-] M, pl. *-s*, end19c (2) **Du** [=E] C, 1970s (1<2 mod, rare) < *ster* → *-dom* n. **Nw** (0) < trsl *stjerne* **Ic** - < 8a: trsl/ *stjarna* **Fr** [=E] F, 1920s, +8c,d(2) → *-iser* v. **Sp** [estar] M/F, 1920s, +8c,d(1 jour) < mean *estrella* **It** [star] F, pl. Ø, 1920s, +8c,d(3) > mean *stella* **Rm** [star] N, mid20c, via Fr?, 8a(3 coll) +8c,d(3) > *stea* F **Rs** (0) < mean *zvezda* **Po** [star] M, uninfl., beg20c, +8d(1 tech) < *gwiazda* **Cr** *star* M, pl. *-ovi*, mid20c, +8c,d(2) **Bg** *star* F/cp¹, 1990s (1 you, mod) < mean *zvezda* **Hu** *sztár* [sta:r] pl. *-ok*, end19/beg20c (3) **Al** *star* M, pl. *-ë*, mid20c (1 you) **Gr** *star* M/F, beg20c, +8c,d(2); < 8a: mean *asteri, asteras*

stark delicious* *n.* 'a type of apple'

It [=E]/(stark) dilịtʃius/de-] M, pl. Ø, 1980s (2/3) **Hu** - < *starking*

starlet *n.* 1 'a (promising) young performer, esp. a woman'
Ge [ʃtạ:rlet/st-] N, pl. -*s*, 1960s (2 pej) > trsl *(Film)sternchen* **Du** [=E] C, 1970s (1 tech, rare) **Nw** [=E] M, pl. -*s*, 20c (1 obs) **Ic** - < rend *smástirni* **Fr** *starlette* [starlet] F, 1920s (1 obs) **Sp** [estarlet] F, pl. -*s*, 1970s (1 tech) < *starlette* **It** [starlet] F, pl. Ø, 1950s (1) < trsl *stellina* **Rm** *starletă* [starlẹtə] F, mid20c, via Fr (1 pej) > *stelụță* **Rs** (0) **Po** *starletka* [starletka] F, end20c (1 coll) **Cr** *starlẹta* F, pl. -*e*, end20c (2) **Bg** *starletka* F, pl. -*ki*, end20c (3 you) **Gr** *stạrlet* F, mid20c (1 obs)

star system* *n.* 'using star performers to make a film or play attractive'
Sp [=E] M [U] 1970s (1) **It** [=E] M [U] mid20c (1) **Rm** [=E] N [U] end20c (1) **Cr** (0) **Gr** *stạr system/<=E>* N [U] mid/end20c (1 jour)

start *v.* 1 'begin', 2 'set in motion', 6a 'begin operating', 6b 'cause a machine etc. to begin operating', 8 'originate', 10 'give a signal to start a race', +19 'take off'
Ge [ʃtartn] beg20c, 1,2,6a,10,+19(3) **Du** *starten* [startə] mid20c, 1,2,6a,+19(5) **Nw** *starte* [stạ:rte] beg20c, 1,2,6a,b,10,+19(3) → *starter* M **Ic** *starta* [starta] mid20c, 1,2(2 coll) 6a,b(2 tech, coll) 10(2 tech) = 6b: *gangsetja, ræsa* **Rs** *startovạt* 20c (3) **Po** *startować* [startovatç] beg20c (3) → *wy-, za-* v. **Cr** *stạrtati* beg20c, 1,2,6a,10(3) **Bg** *startiram* 20c,1,2(3) **Fi** *startata* beg20c (3) **Hu** [ʃtạrtol] end19/beg20c,1,6a(3 coll) 10, +19(3) **Al** *startoj* mid20c, 1,2,6a(3)

start *n.* 1 'the beginning of an event', 2 'the place from which a race etc. begins', 4 'an advantageous initial position in life', +8 'the take-off of an air- or spacecraft'
Ge [ʃtart] M, pl. -*s*, 1870s, 1,2,4(3); 1920s, +8(3) **Du** [=E] C, beg20c (3<5) **Nw** [=E] M, pl. -*er*, beg20c, 1,2(3) → *starte* v. **Ic** [start] N [U] mid20c, via Da, 1,2,4(2 coll) **It** [start] M, pl. Ø, 1920s, 2(1 tech) < *partenza* **Rm** [start] N, 1940s, 1,2,4(3); *ştart* [ʃtart] via Ge (3 rare) **Rs** *start* M, pl. -*y*, beg20c, 1,2,4(3) → *-ovyĭ* adj. **Po** [start] M, beg20c (3) → *-owanie* N; -*owy* adj.; -*ujący* adj. **Cr** *start* M, pl. -*ovi*, beg20c (3) → *-ni* adj.; -*ati* v. **Bg** *start* M, pl. -*a/-ove*, beg20c, 2,4,+8(2) → *-ov* adj. **Fi** *startti* beg20c, 1,2,4(3) **Hu** [ʃtart] pl. -*ok*, end19/beg20c, 1(3 coll) 2(3) → -*ol* v. **Al** *start* M, pl. -*e*, beg20c, 1,2,4(3)

starter *n./cp[1]* 2 'an esp. automatic device for starting the engine of a motor vehicle etc.', +2a 'a similar device in fluorescent lamps', 3 'a person giving the signal for the start of a race', 5 'the first course of a meal'
Ge [ʃtạrta] M, pl. Ø, beg20c, 2(1 arch); 1870s, 3(2); 5(0) < 2: *Anlasser* **Du** [=E] C, beg20c, 2,3(3) **Nw** [stạ:rter] M, pl. -*e*, 20c, 2(1 tech) 3(2) 5(1) **Ic** *startari* [startarı] M, pl. -*ar*, mid20c, 2(3 tech, coll) **Fr**

[starter] M, end19c, 2(1 tech); *self-starter* (1 obs) > 2: *départeur*, *démarreur* **Sp** <=E>/*estárter* [estarter] M, beg20c, 2(2); end20c, 3(1 tech) < 2: *arranque/ aire* **It** [starter] M, pl. Ø, end19c, 3(2); 1950s, 2(2) **Rm** [starter] M, beg20c, via Fr?, 3(1 tech); mid20c, 2(1 tech); 1960s, +2a(3) **Rs** *stạrter/startër*, M, pl. -*y*, beg20c, 2(1 tech); *startër*, M, pl. -*y*, beg20c, 3(1 tech) **Po** [starter] M, beg20c, 2,3(2) **Cr** *stạrter* M, pl. -*i*, beg20c, 3(1 tech) **Bg** *stạrter* M, pl. -*al-i*, mid20c, 2(2 tech); pl. -*i*, 3(1 tech) **Fi** *startti-* cp[1], mid 20c, 2(3) **Hu** [ʃtạ:rter] [U] end19/beg20c, 3(1 tech) **Gr** *stạrter* N, 20c, via Fr, 2(2 tech) < *miza*

starting block *n.* 'a shaped rigid block for bracing the feet of a runner at the start of a race'
Ge *Startblock* M, pl. -*blöcke*, mid20c (3+5) **Du** *startblok* 20c (3+5) **Nw** *startblokk* 20c (3+5) **Ic** - < rend *viðbragðsstoðir* **Fr** *starting-block* [startiŋ blɔk] M, 1930s (1 ban) > *bloc de départ, cale de départ* **It** - < trsl *blocco di partenza* **Rm** *startbloc* [startblok] N, mid20c, via Ge (1 tech) < rend *blockstart* N **Po** - < trsl *blok (startowy)* **Cr** *starting blok* 20c (1 tech) **Bg** - < trsl *stạrtovo blọkche*

starting gate *n.* 'a movable barrier for securing a fair start in horse races'
Fr *starting-gate* [startiŋgɛt] M, beg20c (1 tech)

statement *n.* 2 'a thing stated, a declaration', +2a 'a public declaration'
Ge [stẹ:tment] N, pl. -*s*, 1960s (1 mod) < *Erklärung* **Du** [=E] N, 1970s (1 jour, you) **Nw** [=E] N, pl. -*s*, 1980s (1 mod) **Ic** [=E] end20c, 2(0) < rend *yfirlýsing* **Fr** (0) **It** [stɛtment] M, pl. Ø, end20c (1 jour, mod) **Cr** (0)

stationcar* *n.* 'an estate car'
Du [stẹʃənka:] M, 1970s (2) = *kombi* **Ic** [=E] /-*bíll* M, mid20c (2+5 coll) > rend *skutbíll*

station-wagon *n.* 'an estate car'
Nw - < trsl *stasjonsvogn* **Ic** *station(vagn/- bíll)* [steisjo(u)n(vakn/-pitl)] M, pl. -*ar*, mid20c (2+5 coll) = rend *skutbíll, langbakur* **Sp** [esteiʃon bagon] M, pl. Ø, 1990s (tech, obs) **It** [stɛʃon vɛgon/wegon] F/adj., pl. Ø, 1980s (2) **Gr** *steison vạgon* N, end20c (2)

status symbol *n.* 'a possession etc. taken to indicate a person's high status'
Ge *Statussymbol* [ʃtạ:tus symbọ:l] N, pl. -*e*, 1960s (5) **Du** *statussymbool* [stạtysymbo:l] N, pl. -*en*, mid/end20c (5) **Nw** *statussymbol* (5) **Ic** [sta:tvs sımpo(u)l] N [U] mid/end20c (1 coll) **It** [status sımbol] M, pl. Ø, 1970s (2) **Cr** (5La) **Fi** *statussymboli* 1960s (3) **Hu** *státusszimbólum* [ʃtạ:tussimbo:lum] pl. Ø/-*ok*, 1960s (3 fac, pej)

stayer *n.* 1 'a person or horse specialized in long-distance races', 2 'a medium distance cyclist, runner', +3 'a person who has been successful for quite a while'
Ge *stayer* [=E] M, pl. Ø, end19c, 1(0 arch); *Steher* M, pl. Ø, 20c, 2(3 tech) **Du** [=E] C, pl. -*s*, 1,+3(2) **Nw** [=E] M, pl. -*e*, beg20c (1 tech) **It** [stɛier] M, pl. Ø,

end19c (1 tech) < 2: *mezzofondista* **Bg** *stær* M, pl. -*al*-*i*, 20c, via Rs, 1(1 tech)

steady *adj.* 4 'serious and dependable in behaviour; safe; cautious' (of a person), 5 'regular, established' **Du** [=E] end20c, 4(1 sla) **Ic** [stɛt:i] uninfl., 1970s (1 sla)

steak *n.* 1 'a thick slice of meat' (cf. ↑*beefsteak, rumpsteak*)
  While this word is widespread, and has been from the nineteenth century, its distribution differs from those of the compounds ↑*beefsteak* and ↑*rumpsteak*.
  Ge [ʃte:k] N, pl. -*s*, beg19c (2) → -*let* N **Du** [=E] C, 1960s (2) < *biefstuk* **Nw** [=E] M, pl. -*s*, end20c (1) < *biff* **Ic** *steik* [stei:k] F, pl. -*ur* (4) **Fr** [stɛk] M, end19c (2) **Sp** [esteik/estik]

M, 20c (1 mod) **It** - < *bistecca* **Rm** *stek* [stek] N, 1970s (2 rare) **Po** *stek* [stek] M, beg20c (3) **Cr** *stek* M, pl. -*ovi*, mid20c (2) **Bg** *stek*/*steïk* M, pl. -*al-ove*, mid/end20c (3 tech/1 mod) **Hu** *steak*/*szték* [=E] pl. Ø, end19/beg20c (2) **Al** *stek* M, pl. -*ë*, mid20c (2) **Gr** *steïk* N (2) < *fileto*

steam *n.* +4 'the fast progress of an engine-powered ship'
  Nw <=E>/*stim* [=E] M [U] 20c (2) **Ic** *stím* [=E] N [U] beg20c (3 tech)

steam *v.* 3b 'proceed or travel fast or with vigour' (esp. of a ship)
  Nw *stime*/*steame* [sti̧:me] 20c (2) **Ic** *stíma* [sti:ma] beg20c (3 tech/coll)

steamer *n.* 2 'a ship propelled by a steam engine'
  This word was adopted in the nineteenth century, but was normally replaced by national equivalents, so that present-day uses tend to be archaic or facetious.
  Ge [=E] M, pl. Ø, beg19c (1 arch) < *Dampfer* **Nw** [=E] M, pl. -*e*, 19c (1 rare) < *damper* **Fr** [stimœr] M, 19c (1 arch) **Sp** [=E]

M, end19c (1 tech, arch) < *rend barco, buque de vapor* **It** [sti̧:-mer] M, pl. Ø, end19c (1 arch) < *nave, battello a vapore* **Rm** <=E>/*steam* [stim] N, 1860s (2 tech) **Cr** [=E/-r] M, 19c (1 tech) **Bg** - < *rend parakhod* **Hu** [=E] pl. -*ek*, 19c (1 tech) < *rend gőzös*

steamship *n.* 'a ship propelled by a steam engine' (↑*SS*)
  Nw (0) < *dampskip* **Ic** - < trsl *gufuskip* **Rs** - < *rend parokhod* **Cr** < *rend parabrod* **Bg** - < *rend parakhod* **Hu** - < trsl *gőzhajó* **Gr** - < trsl *atmoplio*

steel band *n.* 'a group of usually West Indian musicians with percussion instruments'
  Ge (Ø) **Du** [=E] C, 1950s (1 tech) **Nw** [=E/-ban] N, pl. Ø, 20c (1 tech) **Fr** [=E] M, end20c (1 tech) **Sp** [=E] F, pl. -*s*, end20c (1 tech) **Fi** [=E] 1970s (Ø)

steel drum *n.* 'a drum made of an empty barrel'
  Du [sti̧:ldrʌm] C, 1980s (1 tech) **Fi** [=E] 1970s (Ø)

steelon* *n.* 'a fibre'

Rm [stilon/stelon] N [U] mid20c (1 tech) **Po** *stylong* -*i*- M [U]/pl. -*y*, mid20c (3) → -*owy* adj.

steeple *n.* '3000m hurdles' (athletics)
  Fr [stipl] M, end19c (1 tech) **Bg** - < cf. ↑*steeplechase* **Gr** *stipl* N [U] beg20c, via Fr (1 tech)

steeplechase *n.* 1 'a cross country horse race'
  This racing term was widely adopted in nineteenth-century Europe, but has remained a technical term and is now generally archaic.
  Ge [sti:pltʃe:s] F, pl. -*en*, 19c (Ø/1 arch) **Du** [=E] C, 1940s (1 tech)

steeplechaser N **Nw** [=E] M [U] 19c (1 arch) **Fr** *steeple* (*-chase*) [stipœl (ʃez)] M, 19c (1 arch) **Sp** [=E] M, 19c (1 arch) **It** [=E/sti̧:pltʃez] F/M, pl. Ø, mid19c (1 tech) < trsl *corsa al campanile* **Rm** [=E] N [U] 20c (1 tech) **Rs** *stipl'-chez* M, pl. -*y*, 19c (1 tech) **Po** [sti-] M, uninfl., beg20c (1 tech) **Cr** *stipl-čez* M [U] beg20c (1 tech) **Bg** *stipúlcheïz* M [U] mid20c (Ø/1 tech) **Hu** [=E] [U] end19/beg20c (1 tech, arch)

steepler* *n.* 'a horse specially prepared for a cross country horse race'
  Ge [=E] M, pl. Ø, end19c (1 arch) **Du** [=E] C, end19c (1 tech, rare) **Rs** *stipler* M, pl. -*y*, 19c (1 tech) **Cr** (0)

stencil *n.* 1 'a thin sheet of plastic etc. in which a pattern is cut, used to produce a corresponding pattern on the surface beneath it', 3 'a waxed sheet from which a stencil is made'
  Du [=E] C, 1940s (1 tech) **Nw** *stensil* [stensi̧:l] M, pl. -*er*, 20c (3) → *stensilere* v. **Ic** *stensill* [stɛnstl] M, pl. *stenslar*, 1950s, via Da (3) **Fr** [stensil] M, beg20c (1 tech, arch) **Sp** [estensil/esten] M, end20c (1 tech, rare) **Hu** [ʃtentsil] pl. -*ek*, beg20c (3 obs) → -*ez* v.

stencil *v.* 1 'produce (a pattern) with a stencil'
  Du *stencilen* [stɛnsilə(n)] 1940s (1 tech) **Nw** *stensilere* [stensilẹ:re] 20c (3) **It** - < *ciclostilare* **Hu** [ʃtentsilez] (3+5) → -*és* n.

Sten gun *n.* 'a type of lightweight sub-machine gun'
  Du *stengun* [stɛngyn/stɛnɣyn/=E] C, 1940s (1 tech <2) **Nw** *stengun* [=E] M, beg20c (1 tech) **Fr** - < *mitraillette Sten* **Sp** - < rend *metralleta tipo Sten* **It** *sten* M, pl. Ø, 1940s (1 tech) **Po** *sten* M, mid20c (1 tech)

step *n.* 2 'a unit of movement in dancing', +12 'a stepdance or tapdance', +13 'step aerobics'
  Ge [ʃtep] M [U] mid20c, +12(1 tech); *step-aerobic* N [U] 1990s, +13(1 tech) < +12 = *Steptanz* **Du** [=E] C, 1940s, 2(1 tech) **Nw** *stepp* [=E] N, pl. Ø, 20c, 2(3); M [U] 20c, +12, +13(3 tech) < *stepping* **Ic** *stepp* N [U] beg20c, +12(3) < 2: *skref* **Sp** [estẹp] M, end20c, +13(1 tech) **Rm** [=E] N, 1970s, +12(2) **Rs** *stép* M [U] mid20c, +12(1 tech) **Po** *stepowanie* [stepovanie] M [U] mid20c, 2,+12(3) **Cr** [=E] M [U] mid20c, +12(1 tech) **Bg** *step* M [U]/pl. -*a*. mid20c, +12(3 tech) **Fi** *steppi* mid20c, 2(3); *steppaus* beg20c, +12(2) **Hu** *sztepp* [stepp] [U] 20c,

+12(2) → -el v. **Gr** step N, mid20c, +12(1 tech); N [U] 1990s, +13(1 tech, mod) → steper M/F

step v. +5a 'tapdance', +7 'trot lifting the front hooves high' (of a horse) +8 'dance a one- or twostep' **Ge** [ʃtɛpən] 1930s, +5a(3) **Du** tapdansen +5a(3+5); steppen [stɛpə(n)] 1940s, +7,+8(1 tech) **Nw** steppe [stɛpe] 1930s, +5a,+7(3) → stepper M **Ic** steppa [stɛhpa] beg20c, +5a(3) → steppari M **It** steppare [steppare] 1970s, +7(1 tech) **Rm** - < rend bate step **Po** stepować [stepovatɕ] mid20c (3) **Cr** stepati mid20c (3) **Fi** steppata beg20c (2) **Hu** szteppel [steppel] 5a(2) → -és n.

stepper* n. 1 'a step- dancer', 2 'a horse that trots lifting its front hooves high'
Ge [ʃtɛpa] M, pl. Ø, 20c, 1(1 tech) **Du** [=E] C, 1950s (1 tech) < 1: tapdanser **Nw** [stepper] M, pl. -e, 1930s (3) → stepperske M/F **Ic** steppari [stɛhpari] M, pl. -ar, beg20c, 1(3) **Fr** <=E>/steppeur [stepœr] M, 19c, 2(1 tech) → steppage **Fi** steppari beg20c, 1(2) **Hu** - < rend sztepptáncos

stetson n. 'a slouch hat with a very wide brim and a high crown'
The American Walter John Batterson Stetson (1830–1906) opened a factory in Philadelphia in 1865; his name was connected with the wide-brimmed felt hat favoured by cattle-men.
Ge (Ø) **Du** (Ø) **Nw** [=E] M, 20c (Ø/1 tech) **Ic** [=E]/stetsonhattur M, mid20c (1 arch, mod+5) **Fr** (Ø) **Sp** <=E>/sombrero Stetson M, 1990s (Ø/1 rare) **Po** [-son] M, end20c (1 tech) **Cr** [stetson] M, end20c (1 tech) **Fi** [=E] (Ø) **Hu** [=E] cp¹ -kalap, 20c (1 tech+5) **Gr** (Ø)

stevedore n. 'a person employed in loading and unloading ships'
The term was borrowed into American English in the nineteenth century and was partly handed on to other languages, but straight borrowing from Spanish cannot be excluded.
Du stuwadoor [stʏwadoːr] C (1 tech) **Sp** estibador (4) **Rm** stivador [stivador] M, 20c (1 tech) < stivator **Rs** stividor M, pl. -y, mid20c (1 tech) **Bg** stivador/stifador M, pl. -i, mid20c (1/3 tech) → -ski adj. **Gr** stivadhoros M, 20c (5)

steward n. 1 'an attendant on a ship or aircraft' +7 'a cook on a ship'
The steward is not strictly the male equivalent of a ↑stewardess, but it is none the less noteworthy that the distribution of the two terms is not strictly the same in all languages; where stewardess is used, it appears to be better known than steward.
Ge [stuːart] M, pl. -s, mid19c, 1(1 tech) **Du** [=E] C, beg20c, 1(2 tech) **Nw** stuert [stuːert] M, pl. -er, mid19c, +7(3); steward [=E] M, pl. -er, beg20c, 1(1 tech) **Ic** stjúart [stju:art] M, pl. -ar, mid20c, 1(1 sla_NAUT) < bryti, flugþjónn **Fr** [stiwar] M, mid19c, 1(2) **Sp** <=E> M, 1930s, 1(0>1 tech) < camarero,

auxiliar (de vuelo) **It** [stjuard] M, pl. Ø, 1930s, 1(2) = cameriere di bordo, assistente di volo **Rm** [stjuard] M, mid20c (2) **Rs** styuard M, pl. -y, beg20c, 1(2) **Po** [stjuwart] M, beg20c, 1(2) **Cr** stjuard M, pl. -i, mid20c (1 tech) **Bg** styuard M, pl. -i, mid20c, 1(2) **Fi** stuertti 19c, 1(3) **Hu** [=E] pl. -ok, 19c, 1(2) **Al** stjuard M, pl. -ë, mid20c, 1(3)

stewardess n. 'a female attendant on a ship or aircraft'
Ge [ʃtuardes/stj-] F, pl. -en, beg20c (2) **Du** [=E] C, pl. -en, 1940s (2 tech) **Nw** [=E] M, pl. -er, beg20c (1) < flyvertinne **Ic** - < (skips)þerna, flugfreyja **Sp** <=E> F, beg20c (0 tech) < azafata **It** [stjuardes] F, pl. Ø, mid20c (1) < hostess, assistente di volo **Rm** stewardesă [stjuardesə] F, mid20c (2) **Rs** styuardessa F, pl. -y, mid20c (3) **Po** stewardesa [stjuwardesa] F, mid20c (2) **Cr** stjuardesa F, pl. -e, mid20c (2) < domnćia **Bg** styuardesa F, pl. -si, mid20c (3) **Hu** [=E] pl. -ek, end19/beg20c (2) **Al** stjuardesë F, pl. -a, mid20c (3)

stick n. 3a 'an implement used to propel the ball in hockey, polo, etc.', +3c 'a golf club', 6a 'cosmetics in a slender form, e.g. a deodorant', +14 'a walking stick', +15 'a salty biscuit in the form of a stick'
Various stick-like instruments or commodities have been termed 'stick' in preference to native words, for apparent connotations of modernity, but the objects so named are not always the same across cultures.
Ge [=E] M, pl. -s, 1970s, 6a(1 mod); 1980s, +15(1 mod) < 6a: Stift +15: Salzstange **Du** [=E] C, 1940s, 3a(2) = stok **Nw** [=E] M, pl. -s, 1980s, 6a(1 tech) **Fr** [stik] M, end19c, 3a(1 tech); end18c, +14(1 arch), 1960s, +15(1) **Sp** <=E>/estic(k) [estik] M, pl. -s, 1960s, 3a(1 tech); beg20c, +3c(1 tech); end20c, 6a(1 tech) **It** [=E] M, pl. Ø, 1940s, 6a(3) **Rm** sticksuri [stiksurj] N, pl., 1970s, +15(2); [=E] N, end20c, 6a(1) **Rs** stek M, pl. -i, 19c, +14(Ø) **Cr** [=E] M, pl. -ovi, mid20c, +15(1) **Bg** stik M, pl. -al-ove, mid20c, 3a,+3c(1 tech) **Gr** stik N, end20c, 6a,+15(2)

sticker n. 1 'an adhesive label or notice'
There is a limited currency of this word, for which native terms exist and are often (still) more common.
Ge [=E] M, pl. Ø, 1970s (1 mod, rare) < Aufkleber **Du** [=E] C, 1970s (2) **Nw** [=E] M, pl. -e, end20c (1 mod) < klistremerke **Ic** - < rend límmiði **Fr** (0) **Rs** stiker M, pl. -y, 1990s (1 mod) **Cr** stiker 20c (1 mod) **Bg** stiker M, pl. -al-i, 1990s (1>2 mod) **Hu** [=E] pl. -ek,

end20c (o>1 mod, writ)   **Gr** *stiker* N, pl. -*s*, end20c (1 mod)

stikkie*   *n.* 'a self-made cigarette with hashish'
   Du [=E] N, 1970s (1 coll)

Stilton   *n.* 'a kind of strong rich cheese'
   Ge (Ø)   **Du** [=E] C [U] 1970s (1 tech)   **Nw** (Ø)   **Fr** [stilton] M, end19c (1 tech)   **Rs** (o)   **Po** *stilton* [-on] M, end20c (1 tech)   **Cr** *stilton* M [U] 20c (1 tech)   **Fi** (Ø)   **Gr** *stilton* N, end20c (1 tech)

stock   *n.* 1 'a store of goods ready for sale'
   This economic term was important a hundred years ago, and still is in French (note the derived verb and widespread *stockist*).
   Du [=E] C, beg20c (2 rare)   **Nw** (o)   **Fr** [stɔk] M, end19c (2) → *stocker* v.; *stockage, stockeur, stockist* M   **Sp** [estók] M, pl. -*s*, end19c, via Fr (2)   **It** [=E] M, pl. Ø, 18c (3) → *stoccaggio* n.; *stoccare* v.; *stoccabile* adj.; *stocchista* n.   **Rm** *stoc* [=E] N, 1870s, via Fr (3) → *stoca* v.; *stocaj* N; *stocare* F   **Cr** [=E] M, beg20c (2)   **Hu** [=E] [U] end20c (1 tech)   **Al** *stok/stoge* M, pl. -*e*, 20c (2)   **Gr** *stok* N, beg20c, via Fr (2)

stock car   *n.* 1 'a strengthened production car for use in racing in which collision occurs', +3 'a stock-car race'
   Ge [=E] M/N?, pl. -*s*, 1970s, 1(1 tech, rare)   **Du** [=E] C, 1970s, 1(1 tech)   **Fr** [stɔkaʀ] M, 1950s, 1 (1)   **It** [=E] M, pl. Ø, 1960s, 1 (1 tech)   **Rm** [=E] N, 1970s, 1, +3(1 tech)   **Gr** (Ø)

stockhouse*   *n.* 'a shop selling at retail prices'
   It [stokauz] M, pl. Ø, 1990s (1 reg)

stock-shot*   *n.* 'frames of film kept for further use'
   Nw [=E] N, pl. -*s*, 1950s (1 tech)   **Fr** [stɔkʃɔt] M, 1950s (1 tech, ban) < *image d'archive*

stoker   *n.* 1 'a person who tends to the furnace on a steamship' (naut.), +2 'an installation for the automatic supply of coal on steam engines'
   Du [=E] C, 19c, 1(5)   **Fr** <=E>/*stocker* [stɔkœr] M, 19c, 1(1 tech, arch)   **Rm** *stoker/stocher* [=E/stoker] N [U] mid20c, +2(1 tech)   **Rs** *stoker* M, pl. -*y*, mid20c (1 tech)   **Po** [stoker] M, mid20c (1 tech)   **Cr** (o)

stokes   *n.* 'the cgs unit of kinematic viscosity' (phys.)
   Ge [sto:ks] N [U] beg20c (1 tech)   **Fr** [stɔks] M, 1950s (1 tech)   **Rm** [=E] M, mid20c, via Fr? (2 tech)   **Rs** *stoks* M, pl. -*y*, mid20c (1 tech)   **Hu** [=E] [U] 20c (1 tech)

stomp   *n.* 1 'a lively jazz dance with heavy stamping'
   Du (Ø)   **Nw** (o/Ø)   **Fr** (o)   **Rs** (o)   **Po** M [U] end20c (1 tech)   **Cr** (o)   **Bg** *stomp* M [U]/pl. -*a*, mid20c (1 tech)   **Hu** [=E] [U] 20c (1 tech)   **Gr** <=E> [-mp] N [U] 20c (1 tech)

stoned   *adj.* 'under the influence of alcohol or drugs'
   Ge [=E] uninfl., 1970s (1 you, rare)   **Du** [=E] 1970s (1 coll) = *high, stomdronken*   **Nw** (o) < trsl *stein*   **Ic** [=E] uninfl., 1970s (1 sla) = creat *steindur, steinaður*

stonewashed   *adj.* 'washed with abrasives to produce a worn appearance'

Ge [sto:nvoʃt] 1980s (1 tech)   **Du** [sto:nwɑʃt] 1980s (1 tech)   **Nw** [=E] 1980s (1 tech) > trsl *steinvasket*   **Ic** - < trsl *steinþveginn*   **It** [=E] uninfl., 1980s (1 tech)   **Po** (o)   **Cr** [=E] end20c (1 tech)   **Fi** [=E] 1980s (1 tech)   **Hu** [=E] 1980s (1 tech, writ)   **Gr** [=E] (1 tech) 1980s < trsl *petroplymeno*

stop   *v.* 1a 'put an end to', 'cause (an opponent's action) to cease, defeat' (sport), +20 'take the time' (in races), +21 'hitchhike'
   Ge [ʃtopən] 1870s (3/4?)   **Du** *stoppen* [stɔpə] 19c, 1a(5)   **Nw** *stoppe* [stɔpe] 1a(4/5MLowGe) → -*per* M   **Ic** *stoppa* 19c, via Da, 1a(5MLowGe)   **Fr** *stopper* [stɔpe] mid19c, 1a(2/3?)   **It** [=E] 19c, 1a(3) → -*pare* v.   **Rm** *stopa* [stopa] beg20c, via Fr, 1a(3 tech) → -*are* F, -*at* adj./N   **Rs** *stop* interj., beg20c, 1a(2)   **Po** *stopować* beg20c, (3) → *za-* -*ować* v.   **Cr** *stopirati* mid20c, 1a(2)   **Bg** *stopiram* mid20c, +21(3 you); end20c, 1a(3 jour)   **Hu** *stoppol* v. [ʃtoppol] 20c, +20,+21(3)   **Al** *stopoj* mid20c, 1a,+20(3)   **Gr** *stoparo* beg20c, 1a(1 tech) → *stoparisma* N

stop   *n./interj.* 1 'the act or instance of stopping', 11 'a full stop' (in telegrams etc.), +14 'halt!' (on traffic signs), +15 'an autostop', +16 'a stop-lamp'
   Ge [ʃtop] M, pl. -*s*, 1870s, 1(3/4); 1970s, +14(3)   **Du** [=E] C, 19c, 1(4); 1970s, +14(4)   **Nw** *stopp* [=E] M, pl. -*er*, 1(4/5) +14(3)   **Ic** *stopp* [stɔhp] mid20c, +14(2); *stopp* [stɔhp] N [U] end19c, 1,11(4)   **Fr** [stɔp] M, end18c, 11, +14(3) +15(2); interj. +14(3)   **Sp** [estóp] M, pl. -*s*, 20c, 1,11(2); mid20c, +14(2)   **It** [stɔp] M, pl. Ø, mid19c, 1(3); 1960s, +14(3); 1970s, +16(3)   **Rm** [=E] N/interj., beg20c, via Fr? (3)   **Rs** *stop* M, mid20c, 1, +14(3)   **Po** M [U] mid20c (3) → -*owy* adj.   **Cr** *stop* M, mid20c, 1(2) +14(3)   **Bg** <=E> M [U] mid20c, +14(2); *na stop* adv., +15(3 coll); *stop* M, pl. -*a/-ove*, +16(3 tech) → -*adzhiya* M   **Fi** *stop* 20c, +14(3)   **Hu** [ʃtop] [U] beg20c, 1,11,+14,+15(3)   **Al** *stop* interj., 19c (3)   **Gr** *stop* N, beg20c, 1,11,+14(2)

stop-and-go*   *phr.* 1 'stop-go, alternate stopping and restarting' (in traffic, economy), 1a 'a penalty in car races'
   Ge [ʃtopentgo:/-st-] N [U] 1970s, 1(1 jour, rare)   **Sp** [=E] 1980s, 1(o>1 tech)   **It** [=E] 1980s, 1a(1 tech)

stopover   *n./cp¹* 1 'a break in one's journey', +2 'a break in an air trip'
   Ge [=E] M, pl. -*s*, 1980s, +2(1 mod) < *Zwischenlandung*   **Du** *stop-over* [=E] C, 1980s, 1(1 tech, rare) < *tussenlanding, overstap, tussenstop*   **Nw** [=E/-over] M, pl. -*s*, 1980s (1 mod)   **Ic** [=E] N/cp¹, end20c, +2(1 tech) = rend *viðdvöl*   **Fr** *stop-over* [stɔpovœr] M, uninfl., 1970s, +2(tech, rare)   **Fi** [=E] 1980s (1 tech)

stopper   *n.* 2 'a person or thing that stops something', +2a 'a rubber plug for doors, etc.', 3 'a clamp for checking a rope' (naut.), +4 'a centre half' (footb.), +5a 'a timekeeper', +5b 'a device to measure time', +6 'a hitchhiker'
   Various derivatives from ↑*stop* (persons or instruments) are recorded (although the football term

clearly predominates), some of which may come straight from English, whereas others are more likely to be nationally derived.

Ge [ʃtɔpa] M, 1980s, 2(1 tech, rare); beg18c, 3(1 tech); 1940s, +4(2 obs) < +4: *Mittelläufer* **Du** [=E] C, beg18c, 3(1 tech); 1940s, +4(1 tech) **Nw** [stɔper]

M, pl. -*e*, 20c, +2a,+4(3) 3(3 tech); < +5a: *tidtaker* +5b: *stoppeklokke* **Ic** *stoppari* [stohparı] M, -*ar*, end19c, 2(3) 3, +5b(3 tech) **Fr** *stoppeur* [stɔpœR] M, 1940s, +4(1 tech) +6(2) **Sp** [estɔper] M, pl. -*s*, 1970s, +4(0>1 jour) **It** [stɔpper] M, pl. Ø, 1960s, 3,+4(3) < +4: *centromediano* **Rm** *stopă* [stopə] F, beg20c, 3(2 tech); *stoper* [stɔper] M, mid20c, +4(2 tech); N, +4, +5a,b(3 tech) **Rs** *stɔpper* M, pl. -*y*, mid20c, +4(1 tech) **Po** [-er] M, beg20c, via Ge, 2,+2a,3,+4,+5b(1 tech) **Cr** *stɔper* M, pl. -*i*, mid20c, 3(1 tech) +4(1) **Bg** *stɔper* M, pl. -*i*, mid20c, +4(1 tech) < +6: *stɔpadzhiya* **Fi** *stoppari/toppari* 19c, +2a(3) **Hu** [ʃtɔpper] n./cp[1], pl. Ø, 20c, +5b(3) = +6 *stoppos/stoppoló* **Gr** *stɔper* M, beg20c, +4(1 tech)

stopping *n.* +2 'the ceasing of action' (sport)
 Po *stoping* [-nk] M [U] beg20c (1 tech)

stopwatch *n.* 'a watch with a mechanism for recording elapsed time, used to time races etc.'
 Ge - < trsl *Stoppuhr* **Du** [=E] C, pl. -*es* (1 tech) **Nw** - < trsl *stoppeklokke* **Hu** - < trsl *stopperóra*

store manager *n.* 'the manager of a department store'
 Gr <=E> [=E] M/F, 1990s (1 tech)

story *n./cp[1]* 3 'the narrative or plot of a novel or film', 5 'a fib, lie, or piece of sensational news'

In a field adequately covered by native terms in all languages, the adoption of this loanword is almost exclusively restricted to journalistic uses, often with pejorative connotations.

 Ge [ʃtɔ:ri/st-] F, pl. -*(ie)s*, 1950s, 3(1 tech, mod) 5(2 pej) **Du** [=E] C, 1970s (2) **Nw** [=E] M, pl. -*er*, 1950s, 3(1 tech) **Fr** [stɔri] cp/F, 1970s (1 jour) **Sp** [estɔri] F, pl. -*s*, end20c, 3(1 jour) **It** [=E] cp[2]/F, pl. Ø/-*ies*, 1970s, 5(1 mod) **Rm** [=E] N/F 1970s, 3(1 jour) **Po** F, uninfl., end20c (1 jour) **Hu** *sztori* [stɔri] pl. -*k*, beg20c, 3(3); mid20c, 5(3) **Gr** *stɔri* N, pl. -*s*, end20c (1 jour, mod)

storyboard *n.* 'a displayed sequence of pictures etc. outlining the plan of a film, television, advertisement, etc.'
 Ge [=E] N, pl. -*s*, 1970s (1 tech, rare) **Nw** [=E] M, pl. -*s*, 1980s (1 tech) **Fr** *story-board* [stɔribɔrd] M, 1980s (1 tech) **It** [=E] M, pl. Ø, 1980s (1 tech) **Fi** [=E] 20c (1 tech)

straddle *n.* 2 'an option giving the holder the right of either calling for or delivering stock at a fixed price' (econ.), +3 'a style of high jump'
 Ge [-a-] M [U] 1970s, +3(1 tech, obs) > *Wälzsprung* →

-*n* v. **Du** [=E] C, 1980s, 2(1 tech) **Fr** [stradl] M, 1980s, 2(1 tech, ban) < *ordre lié, double option, stellage* **Rs** *strédl* M, pl. -*y*, 1990s, 2(1 tech) **Bg** - < rend *s razkrachka*

straight *adj.* 7a 'unmodified', 8a 'conventional or respectable' (of a person), 8b 'heterosexual', +8c 'in a period of not drinking or using drugs'
 Ge [=E] 1980s, 8a,b(1 sla) **Nw** *streit/*<=E> [stræit/ =E] 1970s, 7a,8a,b(2c) **Ic** [=E] uninfl., end20c, 8a, +8c(1 sla) → *streitari* M **Gr** *streit* 1980s, 7a(1 tech) 8a(1 coll) 8b(1 sla)

strapless *adj.* 'without straps' (of a garment)
 Du [strɛpləs] 1950s (1 tech) **Gr** *straples* N, mid20c (2)

strap* *n.* 'a suspender'
 Ge [ʃtraps] M, pl. -*e*, 19c/1960s (3)

streaker *n.* 1 'a naked runner', 2 'a runner'

Although this word is not very common, its distribution is noteworthy for the strong presence of countries normally not among the avid borrowers (also cf. next item).

 Ge 1(0) < *Blitzer, Flitzer* **Du** [=E] C, 1970s, 1(2 obs) → *streaken* v. **Nw** (0) **Fr** 1(0) **Sp** [estrıker] M, pl. -*s*, 1970s, 2(1 tech, jour) **It** [stri:ker] M, pl. Ø, 1980s, 1(1 tech) **Rs** *striker*

M, pl. -*y*, end20c, 1(1 jour) **Po** *striker/*<=E> [striker] M, end20c (1 jour) **Cr** *striker* M, pl. -*i*, end20c, 1(1) **Bg** (0) **Gr** *striker* M, 20c, 1(1 rare)

streaking *n.* 1 'running', 2 'the act of running naked in a public place as a stunt'
 Sp [estrıkin] M [U] 1970s, 2(1 tech, jour) **It** [stri:k-ıŋ(g)] M [U] 1980s, 2(1 tech) **Rs** *striking* M [U] end20c, 2(1 jour) **Po** [strikink] M [U] end20c, 2(1 jour) **Gr** *strikin* N [U] 1(1)

streamer *n.* 4 'the aurora borealis or australis', +5 'a device for copying large amounts of data' (comput.)
 Ge [=E] M, pl. Ø, 1980s, +5(1 tech) **Du** [=E] C, 1980s, +5(1 tech) **Nw** [=E] M, 1980s, +5(1 tech) **Fr** [strimœR] M, 1980s, +5(1 tech, ban) > *dévideur* **It** [stri:mer] M, pl. Ø, 1980s, +5(1 tech) **Rm** *strimer* [strimer] N, 1980s, +5(1 tech) **Rs** *strimer* M, pl. -*y*, end20c, +5(1 tech) **Po** [strimer] M, end20c, +5(1 tech) **Cr** (0) **Bg** *strimer* M, pl. -*al-i*, mid20c, 4(1 tech) **Hu** [stri:mer] pl. Ø, end20c, +5(1 tech) **Gr** <=E> [=E] N, end20c, +5(1 tech)

streamline *v.* 2 'make simple or more efficient'
 Ge [stri:mlainən] 1970s (1 coll) **Du** - < *stroomlijnen* **Nw** (0) < trsl *strømlinjeforme*

streetball* *n.* 'a kind of basketball with one basket'
 Ge [=E] M/N [U] 1990s (1 tech, mod) **Du** [=E] C, 1990s (Ø/1 tech) **Ic** - < trsl *götubolti* **Fr** <=E> [stritbɔl] M, 1990s (1 mod) **Sp** [estrıtbol] M [U] 1990s (1 tech, rare) **Rm** [=E]

N, end20c (1 tech, jour) **Rs** *stritbol* M [U] 1990s (1 tech) **Po** [stritbol] M [U] 1990s (1 mod) **Cr** (o) **Bg** *striitbol* M [U] 1990s (1 tech, mod) **Gr** *strit bol* N [U] 1990s (1 tech, mod)

streetfighter   *n.* 'a member of a youth gang provoking the police etc.'
Ge [=E] M, pl. Ø, 1980s (1 mod) **Du** - < trsl *straatvechter*

streetworker*   *n.* 'a social worker walking the streets'
Ge [stri:tvørka] M, pl. Ø, 1980s (1 tech) → *-in* F **Du** - < *streetcornerworker*

stress   *n.* 2a 'demand on physical or mental energy', 2b 'distress caused by this'
Ge *Streß* [ʃtres] M [U] 1960s, 2a,b(3) → *stressig* adj.   **Du** [=E] C [U] 1950s (2 > 3) → *-er* n.; *-erend* adj.   **Nw** [=E] M [U] 1960s, 2a,b(3) → *-e* v.   **Ic** *stress* [strɛs:] N [U] 1960s (3 coll) > rend *streita*   **Fr** [strɛs] M, 1950s, 2a,b(3) → *-er* v.; *-ant* adj.   **Sp** <=E>/*estrés* estrɛs] mid20c, 2a(3) → *stresar* v.   **It** [strɛs] M [U] 1950s (3)   **Rm** *stres* [stres] N, 1970s, 2a,2b(3)   **Rs** *stress* M [U] beg20c(3) → *-ovyĭ* adj.   **Po** *stres* M, beg20c(2) → *-ik* M, *-owy* adj.; *bez-...-owy* adj.; *-ujący* adj.   **Cr** *stres* M, pl. *ovi*, mid20c (3) → *-ni* adj.   **Bg** *stres* M [U] 1970s (2) → *-ov* adj.   **Fi** *stressi* mid20c, 2b(2)   **Hu** *stressz* [ʃtress] [U] mid20c (3) → *-el* v.; *-es* adj.   **Al** *stres* M [U] end20c, 2a(3)   **Gr** *stres* N [U] mid/end20c (2)

stress   *v.* 2 'subject to physical or mental stress'
Ge *stressen* [ʃtresn] 1970s (1 tech) → *gestreßt* adj.; *-ig* adj.   **Du** *stressen* [strɛsə(n)] 1980s (3 coll)   **Nw** *stresse* [strɛse] 1970s (3) → *-ing* M/F; *-et/-a* adj.; *-ende* adj.   **Ic** *stressa* [strɛs:a] 1960s (3 coll) → *-aður* adj.   **Fr** *stresser* 1970s (2)   **Sp** *estresar* 1970s (3)   **It** *stressare* 1950s → *stressato* adj.   **Rm** *stresa* [stresa] 1970s (3) → *stresare* F; *stresat* adj.   **Po** *stresować* [stresovatç] beg20c (2) → *ze-*   **Cr** (o)   **Bg** *stresiram* (3 coll) → *-an* adj.   **Fi** *stressata* mid20c (2)   **Gr** *stresaro/-me*, end20c (3) → *stresarisma, stresarismenos* pt./adj.

stretch   *n./cp¹* 3 'an elastic fabric'
Ge [=E] M [U] 1960s (1 mod)   **Du** [=E] adj./cp¹, 1970s (2 tech)   **Nw** [=E] M [U] 20c (1 tech)   **Ic** [strɛts] N/cp¹ [U] 1960s (2)   **Fr** [strɛtʃ] M, 1960s (1 tech)   **Sp** [estrɛtʃ] M [U] end20c (1 tech)   **It** [stretʃ] M/adj. [U] 1980s (1 tech)   **Rm** *stretch/streci* [=E] N [U] 1960s (2 tech)   **Rs** *stréch* M [U] end20c (1 mod)   **Po** *strecz* attrib., uninfl., end20c (1 tech)   **Cr** *streč* M [U] mid20c (1 tech)   **Bg** *strech* M [U]/pl. *-ove*, 1990s (1 mod)   **Fi** [=E/strets] 1970s (1 tech)   **Hu** *sztrecs* [=E] [U] end20c (1 tech)   **Gr** *strets* N [U] end20c (1 tech)

stretcher   *n.* +1a 'a garden chair'
Du [=E] C, 1970s (2)

stretching   *n.* 'a kind of gymnastics'
A modern insiders' term, clearly widespread but unknown outside devotees' circles.
Ge [=E] N [U] 1980s (1 tech, mod)   **Du** [=E] C [U] 1990s (1 tech, mod)   **Nw** [=E] M/F [U] 1980s (1 tech)   **Ic** - < rend *teygjuæfing*   **Fr** [strɛtʃiŋ] M,

1980s (1 tech, mod)   **Sp** [estretʃin] M [U] 1980s (1 tech, rare)   **It** [stretʃin(g)] M [U] 1980s (1 > 2)   **Rm** *strecing* [=E] N [U] end20c (1 tech, mod)   **Rs** (o)   **Po** *streczing/*<=E> [-nk] M [U] end20c (1 coll)   **Cr** *strecing* M [U] end20c (1 tech, mod)   **Bg** *streching* M [U] end20c (1 tech, mod)   **Fi** [=E] end20c (1 tech)   **Gr** *stretsing* N [U] 1980s (1 tech, mod)

strike   *v.* 17a 'cease work as a protest', +17c 'cease to function' (of instruments etc.), +17d 'refuse to do something'
Ge *streiken* [ʃt-] 1860s, 17a(3); 1950s, +17c,d(3)   **Du** - < *staken*   **Nw** *streike* [strǽike] end19c, 17a(3); 20c, +17c,d(3)   **Ic** *stræka* [strai:ka] mid20c, 17a(2 rare) +17d(3 coll)   **Po** *strajkować* [strajkovatç], 17a(3) → *za-*   **Cr** *štrajkati* 19c, 17a(3)   **Hu** *sztrájkol* [straikol] end19/beg20c, 17a(3); mid20c, +17c(3 coll, fac)

strike¹   *n.* 2a 'the organized refusal to work', 2b 'a refusal to participate in some activity'
The currency of this term is restricted by native equivalents in Dutch, Spanish, etc., and by the adoption of French *grève* in others. The distribution of the corresponding verb is identical with that of the noun.
Ge *Streik* [ʃtraik] pl. *-s*, 1860s (3)   **Du** - < *staking*   **Nw** *streik* [strǽik] M, pl. *-er*, end19c, 2a(3); 20c, 2b(3) → *streike* v.   **Ic** *strækur/stræk* [strai:k(ʏr)] M/N [U] end19c (2 coll) < rend *verkfall*   **Sp** [estraik] M, pl. *-s* (1 arch, obs) < *huelga*   **It** - < *sciopero*   **Po** *strajk* M, beg20c (3) → *-owanie* N; *-owicz* M; *-ujący* M; *-owy* adj.   **Cr** *štrajk* M, pl. *-ovi*, beg20c, 2a(3) → *-ati* v.; *-aš* M   **Hu** *sztrájk* [=E] pl. *-ok*, end19/beg20c (3)   **Al** - < *grevë* (Fr)

strike²   *n.* 5 'a batter's unsuccessful attempt to hit a pitched ball, or another event counting equivalently against a batter' (baseb.), 6 'the act of knocking down all the pins with the first ball in bowling'
Du [=E] C, pl. *-s*, end20c (1 tech)   **Nw** [=E] M, pl. *-s*, end20c, 6(1 tech)   **It** [=E] M, pl. Ø, 1970s (1 tech)

striker   *n.* 4 'an attacking player positioned well forward in order to score goals' (footb.)
Rs *straiker* M, pl. *-y*, mid20c (1 tech, arch)   **Po** [-er] M, end20c (1 tech)   **Bg** *straiker* M, pl. *-i*, mid20c (1 tech) → *-ski* adj.

string   *n.* 12 'a linear sequence of characters, records, or data' (comput.), *cp¹* +13 *Stringregal* 'wallshelves connected by strings', +14 'a string-bikini', +15 'string theory'
Ge [ʃtriŋ-] 1970s, +13(2 obs) +14(1 tech)   **Du** [=E] C, 1980s, 12(1 tech) +15(1 tech+5)   **Nw** (o)   **Fr** [striŋ] 1970s, +14(1)   **It** *stringa* [striŋga] F, pl. *-ghe*, 1970s, 12(3)   **Gr** <=E> [=E] N, end20c, 12(1 tech), +14 (1 mod)

strip   *v.* +2a 'practise striptease', +4a 'lay bare' (fig.)

+16, 'take metal bars out of a mould with the help of a special device'

Although the term ↑*striptease* is almost universal, the backderived verb is much more infrequent, practically restricted to the North-west of Europe.

Ge *strippen* [ʃtrɪpən] 1960s, +2a(3) **Du** *strippen* [strɪpə(n)] 1960s, +2a,+4a(2>3) **Nw** *strippe* [stripə] 20c (3) → *stripper* M; *stripping* C **Ic** *strippa* [strɪhpa] mid/end20c, +2a(2 coll) **Fr** *stripper* [stripe] mid20c, +16(1 tech) **Rm** *stripa* [stripa̱] mid20c, +16(1 tech) < +2a: *face striptease* → *stripare* F; *stripaj* N **Po** - < *robić striptiz/striptease* **Fi** *stripata* 1960s (3)

Ic	Nw	Po	Rs
Du	Ge	Cr	Bg
Fr	It	Fi	Hu
Sp	Rm	Al	Gr

strip[I] *n.* 1 'an act of stripping, esp. in striptease' **Ge** [=E] M, pl. *-s*, 1960s (2 coll) **Nw** *stripp* [=E] M, pl. *-er*, 1970s (2) < *stripping* **Ic** *stripp* [strɪhp] N [U] mid/end20c (2 coll) **Sp** [estrip] M, 1970s (1 tech, rare) **It** [=E] M, pl. Ø, 1960s (2) < *spogliarello* **Fi** *strippi* cp[1], 1960s (2)

strip[2] *n.* +1a 'a narrow piece of sticking plaster', 3 'a strip cartoon' **Ge** [ʃtrip] M, pl. *-s*, 1960s, +1a(1 tech, rare) 3(1 mod, rare) < 3: *Comic Strip* **Du** [=E] C, 1960s, 3(5) **Nw** - < 3: *stripe* **Fr** [strip] M, 1960s, 3(1 tech) **It** [=E] M/F, pl. Ø, 1970s, 3(1>2) < *trsl striscia* **Cr** [=E] M, pl. *-ovi*, mid20c, 3(3) **Al** *strip* M, pl. *-e*, 1980s, 3(3)

strip mining *n.* 'open-cast mining' **Du** (Ø) < *dagbouw* **Nw** (o) **Rm** - < rend *stripare* **Po** [-nk] N, uninfl., end20c (1 tech)

stripper *n.* 1 'a person or thing that strips something', 3 'a striptease performer', +4 'a device to take metal bars out of a mould', +5 'an instrument for removing varicose veins' **Ge** [ʃtripa] M, pl. Ø, 1960s, 3(2 coll) → *-in* F **Du** [=E] C, 1960s, 3(3) **Nw** [striper] M, pl. *-e*, 1960s, 3(3) → *stripperske* **Ic** *strippari* [strɪhparɪ] M, pl. *-ar*, mid/end20c, 3(2 coll) < *fatafella* **Fr** [strɪpœr] M, 1960s, +5(1 tech) > *tire veine* **Sp** [estripe̱r] M, pl. *-s*, 1970s, 3(1 tech) **Rm** *striper* [striper] N, 1960s, via Ge?, +4(2 tech) **Rs** *stripper* M, pl. *-y*, mid20c, 1(1 tech) (o) **Cr** [=E/-r] M, pl. *-i*, mid20c, 3(2) **Bg** *striper* M, pl. *-al-i*, mid20c, +4(1 tech) **Fi** *strippari* 1960s, 3(2)

Ic	Nw	Po	Rs
Du	Ge	Cr	Bg
Fr	It	Fi	Hu
Sp	Rm	Al	Gr

stripping *n.* 1 'the purification of petrol', 2 'the removal of varicose veins', 3 'a nuclear reaction' **Fr** [stripiɲ] M, 1960s (1 tech); - < 2: *stripage* **It** [strippin(g)] M [U] 1970, 1,2(1 tech) < *strippaggio* **Rm** [=E] N [U] 1970s, 2(1 tech)

strip poker *n.* 'a card game in which the loser has to take off his clothes' **Ge** [=E] M/N, pl. Ø, 1960s (1 tech, rare) **Du** [=E] N, 1980s (2) **Nw** - < *klespoker* **Ic** - < rend *fatapóker* **Fr** (o) **Sp** [=E] M, 1990s (1 tech) **It** [=E] M, pl. Ø, mid20c (1) = *poker strip* **Fi** *strippipokari* mid20c (2) **Gr** *strip po̱ker* N [U] 1980s (1 you)

striptease *n.* 1 'gradual undressing before an audience', +2 'giving away feelings and secrets' **Ge** [=E] M [U] 1950s, 1(2); cp[2], 1970s, +2(1 jour) → *-erin* F (1 rare) **Du** [=E] C, 1950s (2) **Nw** [=E] M [U] mid20c, 1(2) < *stripping* **Ic** *strip(p)tis* [=E] M/N [U] mid20c (1 coll) **Fr** *strip-tease/strip(tease)* [striptiz] M, 1950 (2) **Sp** <=E>/*striptis* [estriptis/estriptis] M, mid20c (2) **It** [striptíːz] M, pl. Ø, 1950s (2) < *creat spogliarello* **Rm** *striptis*/[=E] 1960s, via Fr? (2<3) **Rs** *striptiz* M [U] mid20c (2) **Po** *striptiz*/<=E> M [U] mid20c (2) → *-owy* adj. **Cr** *striptiz* M [U] mid20c(2) **Bg** *striptiiz/striptiz* M [U] mid20c(2) **Fi** [=E] mid20c (2) **Hu** *sztriptiz* [stripti:z] mid20c (3) **Al** *striptizëm* M [U] end20c (1 you) **Gr** *striptiz* N, mid20c, via Fr (2)

stripteaser* *n.* 1 'someone performing a striptease' (↑*stripper*), 2 'someone who lays things bare' **Du** [=E] C, 1950s (2) < *stripper, stripteasedanser* **Fr** *stripteaseur*/<=E> [striptizœr] M, 1950s, 1(2) → *stripteaseuse* F, *stripteasereuse* F **Sp** <=E> 1990s (1 mod) **It** - < *stripteaseuse* (5Fr) **Rs** *striptizër* M, pl. *-y*, end20c, 1(2) → *-sha* F **Po** *striptizer* [-er] M, end20c, 1(2) → *-ka* F **Cr** *striptizer* M, pl. *-i*, mid20c, 1(2) → *striptizeta* F **Bg** *striptizyor* M, pl. *-i*, via Fr, 1(3) → *-ka* F **Hu** - < rend *sztriptiztáncos* **Gr** *striptizer*/*-ez* M/F, mid20c, via Fr (2)

stroke (oar) *n.* 'the oar nearest the stem' **Du** - < *slagroeier* **Po** *strok* [-o-] M, mid20c (1 tech) **Hu** *stroke* [=E] [U] end19/beg20c (1 tech) < *vezérevezős*

stuck *adj.* 'unable to get rid of or escape from something, permanently involved with something or someone' **Nw** [støk] 1980s (1 coll) **Ic** [stœhk] uninfl., 1970s (1 sla)

stud book *n.* 'a book containing the genealogy of pure-bred horses' **Ge** - < trsl *Stutbuch* **Fr** [stœdbuk] M, 19c (1 tech) **Sp** <=E> M, 20c (1 tech) **It** [=E] M, pl. Ø, 19c (1 tech) **Rm** [=E] N, 20c (1 tech)

stuff *v.* +11 'use drugs (esp. cannabis)' **Ic** [stœf:a] 1970s (1 sla)

stuff *n.* 2 'a substance or things of an indeterminate kind or a quality not needing to be specified', +6a 'drugs' **Ge** - < +6a: mean *Stoff* **Du** [stʏf] C [U] 1970s, +6a(1 coll, sla) **Nw** - < mean *stoff* **Ic** *stöff* [stæf:] N [U] 1970s (1 sla) **Bg** *staf* M [U] 1970s, +6a(3 you, sla) **Gr** *staf* N [U] end20c, +6a(1 sla)

stunt *n.* 1 'something unusual done to attract attention', 2 'a daring manoeuvre in a film' **Ge** [stant] M, pl. *-s*, 1970s, 2(1 tech) **Du** [stʏnt] C, 1940s, 2(3); cp[1] (1 tech) → *-en* v. **Nw** [=E] N, pl. Ø/-*s*, 1960s, 2(1 tech); 1980s, 1(2) → *-e* v. **Ic** [stœnt] N [U] end20c (1 tech) **Fi** *stuntti* 1980s, 2(1 tech)

Ic	Nw	Po	Rs
Du	Ge	Cr	Bg
Fr	It	Fi	Hu
Sp	Rm	Al	Gr

stunt girl* n. 'a female employed to take an actor's place in performing dangerous stunts'
Ge [stʌntgøl] N, pl. -s, 1970s (1 tech) > *Stunt-frau* **Nw** (0) < *stuntkvinne* **Sp** end20c (0) < *stunt* **It** [stʌntgœrl] F, pl. Ø, 1970s (1 tech) **Po** - < *kaska-derka* **Cr** *stantgerl* (0) **Fi** [=E] end20c (1 tech) **Gr** <=E>/*stad gerl* N, pl. -s, end20c (1 tech)

stuntman n. 'a man employed to take an actor's place in performing dangerous stunts'
Even though this term is more widespread than ↑*stunt* by itself, there is (still) a clear West: East cline.
Ge [=E] M, pl. -*men*, 1960s (1 tech) **Du** *stuntman* [stʏntman] C, pl. -*men*/-*en*, 1960s (3+5) **Nw** *stuntmann* [=E+Nw] M, pl. -*menn*, mid20c (2+5) **Ic** *stönt-maður* M, pl. -*menn*, end20c (1+5 tech) = rend *áhættuleikari* **Fr** - < *cascadeur* **Sp** <=E>/*stunt* [estʌnman] M, end20c (1 tech, rare) **It** [stʌntmɛn] M, pl. Ø, 1950s (1 tech) = *cascatore* **Rm** [=E] M, end20c (1 tech) < *cascador* **Po** [-men] M, end20c (1 tech) < *kaskader* **Cr** [=E] M, pl. -i, end20c (1 tech) **Bg** - < *kaskadyor* **Fi** [=E] end20c (1 tech) **Gr** *stadman* M, end20c (1 tech)

style n./cp² 5a 'a superior quality' (fashion)
With *style* and *stylist* the provenance of loanwords is difficult or even impossible to establish English, French, or classical origin being alternatives. More detailed research is obviously needed.
Ge [stail] M [U] 1960s (1 jour) < *Stil* **Nw** [=E] M [U] 1980s (1 coll, fac) < *stil* **Ic** *stæll* [staitl] M [U] mid20c (3 coll) **Fr** (5) **Sp** (0) **It** [=E] M, pl. Ø, 1970s (1 mod) **Rm** - < *stil* N (5Fr) **Rs** *stil'* (5Fr) → -*nyï* adj. **Po** (0) **Bg** *stil* (5Fr) **Fi** [=E] 1960s (1 mod) **Hu** [=E] cp² end20c (1 jour, writ) **Al** *stil* 5a (5Fr) **Gr** <=E>/*stail* N, end20c [U] (0 > 1 coll, mod jour) < *stil*

style v. 1 'design or make in a fashionable way'
Ge [stailən] 1970s (2) **Du** *stylen* [stajlə] 1990s (2 mod) **Nw** [staile] 1980s (1 tech, mod) **Rm** - < *stila* (5Fr) **Po** (0) **Gr** - < *stilizaro*

styling n. 1 'a design for an industrial product', 2 'styling elements'
Ge [=E] N [U] 1960s, 1(1 tech, mod) **Du** [=E] C [U] 1970s (1 tech) **Nw** [=E] M/F [U] 1960s, 1(1 tech, mod) **Fr** <=E> 20c, 2(1 tech, ban) > *stylisme* **It** [stailiŋ(g)] M [U] 1980s (1 tech, mod) **Rs** *stailing* M [U] 1990s (1 tech, mod) **Cr** *stajling* end20c (1 mod) **Hu** [=E] [U] end20c, 2(1 writ, jour, mod) **Gr** <=E>/*stailing* N [U] end20c (2 mod)

stylist n. 1a 'a designer', 1b 'a hairdresser', 2a 'a writer noted for or aspiring to good literary style'
Ge [=E] M, pl. -en, 1960s, 1a(1 tech, mod); 2a (5La/Fr) **Du** [=E] C, pl. -en, 1970s, 1a,b(1 tech); *stilist* 19c, via Fr, 2a(3) **Nw** [=E/stailist] M, pl. -er, 1980s, 1b(1 tech, mod); *stilist*, 2a(5) **Ic** *stílisti* [sti:lɪstɪ] M, pl. -ar, end20c, 1a(4); 18c, 2a(5Da) **Fr** *styliste* 1a(4) **Sp** *estilista* 1a,2a(4) **It** *stilista* 1970s, 1a,b(3) **Rm** < *stilist, -ă* M/F, 1a,2a(5Fr) **Rs** *stilist* M, pl. -y, 1990 (1 mod/tech) **Po** *stylista* [stilista] M, end20c, 1a,2a(1 tech) → *stylistka* **Cr** *stilist* M, pl. -i, end20c, 2a(1 tech) **Bg** *stilist* M, pl. -i, end20c, via Fr, 1b(2 mod); mid20c, 2a(2 lit) **Fi** *stilisti* end20c, 2a(2 tech) **Hu** (5La) **Al** *stilist* M, pl. -ë, end20c (1 tech) **Gr** *stilis-tas* M, end20c (5Fr)

subway n. 2 (US) 'an underground railway'
Ge (Ø) < rend *U-Bahn* **Du** (Ø) < *metro* **Nw** (0) < trsl/rend *undergrunn/tunnelbane/T-bane* **Ic** [=E] mid/end20c (Ø) **Fr** (Ø) **Po** <=E> M, beg20c (Ø) **Cr** - < *podzemna zěljeznica* **Hu** [=E] (0) **Gr** (Ø)

sudden death phr. 'the winning of an ice-hockey or football match by the first goal scored in the extension'
Ge [=E] M [U] 1980s (1 tech, rare) **Du** [=E] C, 1990s (1 tech) **Nw** [=E] M [U] 20c (1 tech) **Ic** - < rend *bráðabani* M **Fr** - < trsl *mort subite* **It** [=E] M, pl. Ø, 1990s (1 tech) **Fi** [=E] 1980s (1 tech) **Gr** <=E> [=E] N [U] 1990s (1 tech) < trsl *xafnikos thanatos*

sulky n. 1 'a light two-wheeled horse-driven vehicle (in harness racing)'
Ge [zulki:] M, pl. -s, 1930s (3 tech) > *Traberwagen* **Du** [sʏlki] C, pl. -'s, beg20c (1 tech) **Nw** [=E] M, pl. -er, 20c (1 tech) **Fr** [sylki] M, mid19c (1 tech) **It** [sʊlki] M, pl. Ø, 1890s (1 tech) = *sediolo* **Rm** [=E] N, 20c (1 tech) **Po** [sulki] pl., mid20c (1 arch) **Hu** [=E] pl. Ø, end19/beg20c (1 tech, arch)

summit n. 3 'a discussion between heads of government'
Ge (0) < mean *Gipfel* **Nw** (0) < *toppmøte* **Ic** [=E] end20c, 3(0) < *leiðtogafundur* **Fr** *(au) sommet* M, end20c (4) **It** [sammit/summit] M, pl. Ø, 1960s (2 jour, mod) < rend *incontro al vertice* M **Rm** [=E] N, end20c (1>2 jour) **Rs** *sammit* M, pl. -y, end20c (1 jour) **Po** <=E> M [U] end20c (1 jour) < *szczyt* **Cr** *samit* M [U] end20c (1 tech) < *sastamak na vrhu* **Bg** (0) < creat *na visoko ravnishte* **Al** *samit* M, pl. -e, 1990s (1 jour, mod) **Gr** - < mean *(synadisi) koryfis*

super-G* n. 'a skiing race, a blend of downhill and slalom'
Ge [=E] M, pl. -s, 1980s (1 tech) < *Superriesensla-lom* **Nw** [su:perge:] M [U] 1980s? (3 tech) **Fr** [sypɛʀʒe] M, 1980s (1 tech) **It** [super dʒi] M, pl. Ø, 1980s (3 tech) = *supergigante* **Rs** (0) **Po** (0) **Cr** (0) **Gr** (Ø)

superman n. 2 'a man of exceptional strength or ability'
Ge - < trsl *Supermann* **Du** [=E/syparman] C [U] 1980s (1 tech) **Nw** - < trsl *supermann* **Ic** - < trsl

súpermaður **Fr** [sypɛrman] M, 1950s (1 obs) < *sur-homme* **Sp** <=E>/*supermán* [superman] M, pl. *-esl-men* mid20c (2) **It** [supermen] M, pl. Ø, mid20c (3) < trsl *superuomo* **Rm** [=E] M, 1980s (1 coll) **Rs** *supermen* M, pl. *-y*, mid20c (2 mod) **Po** [supermen] M, mid20c (2) **Cr** *supermen* M, pl. *-i*, beg20c (2) **Bg** *supermen* M, pl. *-i*, mid20c (2) **Hu** [=E] pl. Ø, 1990s (2) **Gr** *superman* M, end20c (2)

supermarket *n.* 'a large self-service store' **Ge** - < trsl *Supermarkt* **Du** [=E] C, 1960s (3) **Nw** (0) < trsl *supermarked* **Ic** - < trsl *súpermarkaður*, pl. rend *stórmarkaður* **Fr** - < trsl *supermarché* **Sp** - < trsl *supermercado* **It** [supermarket] M, pl. Ø, 1960s (3) < trsl *supermercato* **Rm** [=E] M, 1970s (2 mod) > trsl *supermagazin* **Rs** *supermarket* M, pl. *-y*, mid20c (2) **Po** [supermarket] M, mid20c (2 coll) **Cr** [=E] M, pl. *-i*, mid20c (3) **Bg** *supermarket/super* M, pl. *-al-i*, 1970s (2/3 coll) **Fi** [supermarket] 1960s (2) **Hu** *supermarket/szupermarket* [superma:rket] pl. *-ek*, mid20c (2) **Al** *supermarket* M, pl. *-ë* (1 reg) < trsl *supermarkatë* **Gr** *supermarket* N, mid20c (2)

superstar *n.* 'an extremely famous or renowned actor, film star, musician, etc.' (cf. ↑*star*) **Ge** [=E] M, 1970s (1 you, mod) **Du** [=E] C, 1970s (2) < *superster* **Nw** [=E] M, pl. *-s*, 1970s (1) > trsl *super-stjerne* **Ic** [=E] end20c (0) < *súperstjarna* **Fr** [sypɛr-staʀ] F, 1970s (1 mod) **Sp** [superestar] C, pl. *-s*, end20c (1) **It** [superstar] F, pl. Ø, 1970s (3) **Rm** [superstar] N, 1980s (3) **Rs** *superstar* M, pl. *-y*, end20c (1 mod) **Po** [superstar] M/F, end20c (1 coll) **Cr** *superstar* M, pl. *-ovi*, end20c (2) **Bg** *super-star* M, pl. *-i*, end20c (1 jour, you) **Hu** *szupersztár* [supersta:r] pl. *-ok*, end20c (2) **Gr** *superstar* M/F, mid20c (2)

supporter *n.* 1 'a person or thing that supports; esp. a person supporting a team' **Du** [sɪ-] C, pl. *-s* (2>3) **Nw** [supɔ:rter] M, pl. *-e*, mid20c (2) **Fr** [sypɔʀtœr] M, beg20c (2) **Sp** [=E] M, pl. *-s*, 1970s (1 jour)

surf *v.* 1 'go surf-riding (without a sail)', +3 'go wind-surfing (with a sail)', +4 'explore the Internet' This term was generally adopted for ↑*windsurfing* (probably because there was little opportunity for surfing in the breakers in Europe). More recently the verb came to be applied to various kinds of 'bravery' such as riding outside underground trains etc. (German *U-Bahn-Surfen*). **Ge** [sörfən] 1960s, 1, +3(2); 1990s, +4(1 tech) = 1: *Wellenreiten* → *er* M **Du** *surfen* [sœrfən] 1960s, 1(2) +3(2) < +3: *plankzeilen* **Nw** *surfe* [søRfe/suRfe] mid20c (1 tech) → *surfer* M, *surfing* M/F **Ic** [sörva/surva] end20c (1 tech) **Fr** *surfer* [sœrfe] 1960s, 1(2) → *surfeurle* **Sp** *surfer* end20c, +4(3 sla/tech) < *practicar el surf(-ing)*; +4: *navegar* **It** - < 1, +3: *fare surf*; +4: trsl *navigare* **Rm** - < rend *naviga* **Po** M [U] end20c (1 coll) **Cr** *surfati* mid20c (1) → *surfer* M **Bg** *sŭrfiram* 20c, +3(1 tech, coll) → *-rane* N **Fi** *surfatalsurfailla* 1960s, 1,+3(2); 1990s, +4(3) **Hu** *szörf* [=E] 1970/80s, 1,+3(2>3) **Gr** - < *kano serf*

surfboard *n.* 'a long narrow board used in surfing' **Ge** - < trsl *Surfbrett* **Du** [syrf-] N, pl. *-s* (1) < trsl *surfplank* **Nw** - < trsl *surfebrett* **Ic** - < creat *brim-bretti* **Fr** *surf* [sœrf] M, 1960s (1) < trsl *planche de surf* **Sp** - < trsl *tabla de surf* **It** *surf* [sœrf] M, pl. Ø, 1960s (2) **Rs** (0) **Bg** *sŭrf* M, pl. *-al-ove*, 1970s (3) **Fi** - < *surffilauta* **Hu** *szörf* [sø:rf] pl. *-ök*, 1980s (3) < trsl *szörfdeszka*

surfer *n.* 'a windsurfer' **Ge** [=E (2)] M, pl. Ø, 1960s (2) **Du** [syrfə] C, pl. *-s* (2) **Fr** [sœrfœʀ] M, pl. *-s*, end20c (2) **Sp** [surfer] M, end20c (1 tech) < *surfista* **It** [surfer] M, pl. Ø, 1960s (1 tech) < *surfista* **Rs** - < *serfingist* **Bg** - < *sŭrfist* (3) **Hu** *szörföző* [sørføzø:] pl. *-k*, 1980s (2>3) **Gr** *serfer* M, end20c (2) = *serfistas*

surfing *n.* 1 'surf-riding either with or without a sail' (cf. ↑*windsurfing*), 2 'using a sailboard', 3 'on the Internet' **Ge** - < 1,3: *Surfen* **Du** [syrfing/=E] C [U] 1970s, 1(2 jour) **Nw** [=E/sørfiŋ/ surfiŋ] M/F, mid20c, 1,3(1 tech) **Fr** <=E>/*surf* [sœrf] M, 1960s, 1(2) **Sp** *surf* M [U] 1960s, 1(2) → *surfer/surfero* v.; *surfista* **It** [sörfiŋ(g)] M [U] 1960s, 1(2) **Rm** [=E] N, 1970s, 1,2(1 tech) **Rs** *sërfing* M [U] end20c, 1(1 tech) **Po** *surfl*<=E> [serfink] M [U] end20c, 1,2(1 coll) → *-owy* adj. **Cr** *surfing* M [U] end20c, 1(1 tech) **Bg** *sŭrfing* M [U] end20c, 1(3 tech, mod); *sŭrf* M, pl. *-al-ove*, 2(3) < 1: *sŭrf* → *-ist* **Fi** - < *surffaus* **Hu** - < *szörfözés* **Gr** *serf(ing)* N [U] end20c, 1(1) → *serfarisma*

surf-riding* *n.* 'the sport of being carried over the surf to the shore on a surfboard' **Ge** (0) **Du** [sɪ:frajding/=E] N [U] 1940s (1 tech, obs) → *surfrider* n. **Nw** [=E] M/F [U] 1930s (1 tech, obs) **Po** (0)

surprise *n.* 1 'an unexpected or astonishing event or circumstance' **Du** [=E/syrprizə] C [U] (1 you/5Fr) **Ic** [=E] N [U] mid20c (1 sla) **Rm** *surpriză* (5Fr) **Rs** (5Fr) **Cr** (0) **Bg** *syurpriz* (5Fr) **Al** *surprizë* (5Fr) **Gr** [=E] F [U] end20c (1 coll)

surprise party *n.* 'an informal party' **Du** [=E] C, pl. *-s*, 1980s (1 mod) **Nw** [=E] N, pl. Ø/*-ies*, 1980s (1 mod, rare) **Ic** [=E] N, pl. Ø, mid20c (1 sla) **Fr** *surprise-partie/surprise-party* [syr-prizparti] F, 19/20c (1 obs) **Gr** [=E] N, end20c (1 you)

survey *n.* 1 'a poll, a critical analysis' **Ge** [E] M, pl. *-s*, 1980s, 1(1 tech, mod) **Du** [=E] C, 1950s, 1(1 tech, jour) **Fr** (0) **Sp** (0)

survival *n./cp* 2 'a person, thing, or practice that has remained from a former time', 3 'the practice of coping with harsh or warlike conditions, as a leisure activity or training exercise' **Ge** [=E] N/*cp*[1] [U] 1980s, 3(1 jour, mod) **Du** [=E] C, 1950s, 2(2); [syr-] C/*cp*[1] [U] 1980s, 3(1 mod) **Nw** [=E] cp,[1] 1980s, 3(1 tech) = *overlevelses-* **It** [sərvai-val] M [U] 1980s, 3(1 tech) **Po** [ser-] M [U] end20c, 3(1 tech) **Cr** (0) **Fi** [=E] 1980s, 3(1 tech)

swagger *n.* +5 'a loose coat'

Nw [sv‿æger] M, pl. *-e*, mid20c (1 tech, obs)   **Ic** *svagger* [svak:er] M, pl. *-ar*, 1930s (2 arch, mod)

swap   *n./cp[1]* +3a 'the financial swapping (of foreign currency to stabilize exchange rates)'
Ge [=E] cp,[1] 1960s (1 tech, mod)   **Du** <=E>/*swapping* [=E] 1970s (1 tech)   **Fr** [swap] M, 1960s (1 tech, ban) > *crédit croisé, échange financier* → *swapper* **Sp** [swop] M, pl. *-s*, end20c (1 tech)   **It** [swap] M, pl. Ø, 1970s (1 tech, mod)   **Rs** *svop* M [U] 1990s (1 tech)   **Bg** *suap* M [U] end20c (1 tech) → *-ov* adj; *-iram* v.   **Hu** [=E/svap] cp,[1] end20c (1 tech)

sweater   *n.* 1 'a pullover'
Ge [sv‿e(:)ta] M, pl. Ø, end19c (2 obs) < *Pullover* **Du** [=E/swi:tər] C, beg20c (2)   **Nw** [=E] M, pl. *-e*, beg20c (1 arch) < *genser* **Fr** [swit‿œr/swet‿œr] M, beg20c (0 arch)   **Sp** <=E>/*suéter* M, pl. *-es*, 1920s (3)   **It** [sw‿eter] M, pl. Ø, 1920s (1 obs) < *maglione, pullover pesante* **Rm** *sveter* [sv‿eter] N, beg20c, via Fr (3)   **Rs** *sviter* M, pl. *-y*, beg20c (3) → *-ok* M   **Po** *sweter* [sveter] M, beg20c (3) → *-ek* M   **Cr** *sviter* M, pl. *-i*, beg20c (3)   **Hu** *szvetter* [sv‿etter] pl. *-ek*, end19/beg20c (3)

sweating system*   *n.* 'a system of exploiting workers'
Ge [=E] N, end19c (0 arch) = *Schwitzsystem* **Du** *sweating(-systeem)* [=E+ siste:m] N [U] beg20c (1 tech+5)   **Fr** (0)   **It** [=E] M [U] 1900s (1 tech, obs)   **Rs** - < trsl *potogonnaya sistema* **Po** [-tem] M, beg20c (1 tech)   **Bg** - < rend *potosmukacheska sistema*

sweatshirt   *n.* 'a cotton sweater'
Ge [sv‿etʃœrt] N, pl. *-s*, 1970s (2 mod)   **Du** [=E] N, 1980s (2) = *sweater* **Nw** [=E] M, pl. *-s*, 1980s (1 mod)   **Fr** *sweat(-shirt)* [swit/swɛt(ʃœrt)] M, mid20c (1 mod)   **Po** [swetʃert] M, mid20c (1 coll)   **Cr** *svetshirt* end20c (1 mod)   **Bg** *suichŭrt* M, pl. *-a/-i*, 1990s (1 you, mod)   **Fi** *swetari* 1970s (2)

sweep   *v.* +16 'increase the volume of a certain frequency'
Ic [svi:pa] 1970s (1 tech)

sweeper   *n.* 3 'a defensive player usu. positioned close to the goalkeeper' (footb.)
Ge - < trsl *Ausputzer* **Nw** [svi:per] M, pl. *-e*, 1960s (1 tech)   **Ic** [svi:per] M, pl. *-ar*, 1970s (1 tech)   **Bg** - < trsl *metach* **Hu** - < trsl *söprögető*

sweepstake   *n.* 1 'a form of gambling on horse races etc.', 2 'a horse race with betting', +4 'a lottery in which numbers and prizes are previously arranged'
Ge [svi:pste:k] N/M, pl. *-s*, 19c, 1,2(Ø/1 arch); 1970s, +4(1 tech, rare)   **Du** [=E] C, 1940s, 1(1 tech)   **Nw** [=E] M, pl. *-s*, beg20c, 1(Ø)   **Fr** [swipstɛk] M, 1930s,

1,2(1 obs)   **It** [=E] M, pl. *-s*, end19c, 1,2(1 tech, obs)   **Gr** *suipsteik* N, mid20c, 1(2)

sweet   *adj.* 3 'melodious or harmonious' (music), 7 'amiable, pleasant'
Ge [svi:t] 1960s, 3(1 tech, rare)   **Du** [=E] 1980s (1 mod)   **Nw** [=E] 20c, 3(1)   **Rm** [=E] 1970s, 3(1 tech) 7(1 rare)   **Rs** 3(0)   **Po** [-i-] M, uninfl., end20c, 3(1 tech)   **Cr** (0)   **Bg** *suit-myuzik* cp,[1] mid20c, 3(1 tech)

swimming pool   *n.* +1a 'a (private or luxury) artificial pool for swimming'
Ge [sv-] M, pl. *-s*, 1960s (1 mod)   **Nw** [=E] M, mid20c (1 rare)   **Cr** *svíming pul* (0)   **Gr** [=E] N, 1990s (0 > 1 mod)

swing   *v.* 9a 'play music/dance with swing', 9b 'play (a tune) with swing'
Ge [svin‿ən] 1970s, 9a(1 you, rare)   **Du** *swingen* 1940s, 9a(2)   **Nw** *swinge/svinge* [sv‿ine] 1930, 9a(3/5)   **Ic** *svina* mid20c (1 tech)   **Fr** *swinguer* [swinge] 1950s, 9a(1 tech)   **Po** *swingować* [swingovatç] mid20c, 9a(2)   **Cr** - < *svirati; plesati sving*

swing   *n.* 1 'an act of swinging', 2 'the motion of swinging', 7a 'jazz or dance music', 7b 'a rhythmic feel or drive of this music', +9 'a bracket for international credits', +10 'an extravagant loafer', +11 'a blow' (box.)
Ge [svin‿] M [U] 1930s, 7a(1 obs); 1950s, +9(1 tech)   **Du** [=E] C [U] 1940s, 7a(2); 1940s, +9(1 tech)   **Nw** [=E] M [U] 1930s, 7a(2) → *swinge/svinge* v.   **Ic** *sving* [svin‿] N [U] mid20c, 7a, b(1 tech) = trsl *sveifla* **Fr** [swin‿] M, end19c, 1,2 (1 tech_GOLF) 7a(1 tech) +11(1 tech) > *balancé* → *swinguer* v.   **Sp** [=E] M, end20c, 1,2,7a,+9(1 tech)   **It** [swin‿] M [U] 1920s, 7a,b(2) +9(1 tech)   **Rm** [=E] N, 1970s, 7a(2 tech) +11(1 tech)   **Rs** *sving* M [U] mid20c, 7a(1 obs)   **Po** [-nk] M, mid20c, 7a,b,+11(2) → *-owanie* N; *-owy* adj.; *-ujacy* adj.   **Cr** *sving* M [U] mid20c, 7a(2)   **Bg** *suing* M [U] mid20c, 7a(1 tech); 7a,*-al-i*,+10(3 arch); *sving* M [U]/pl. *-a*, beg20c, via Rs, +11(3 tech)   **Fi** [=E] 1930s, 7a(2)   **Hu** *szving* [=E] [U] 1930/40s, 7a,b(2)   **Gr** *suing* N [U] mid20c, 7a(1 obs)

swinger   *n.* 'a loose ladies' jacket'
Ge [svin‿a] M, pl. Ø, 1980s (1 tech, rare)   **Rs** *svinger* M, pl. *-y*, end20c (2)   **Po** [-er] M, end20c (1 mod)

switch   *n./cp[1]* 1a 'a device for turning on/off an electrical appliance', +1b 'a starter switch in a car', +8 'an export arranged via a third country, switch dealing'
Ge [svitʃ] M [U] 1970s, +8(1 tech, rare) < *Switchgeschäft* **Nw** *svitsj* [svitʃ] M, pl. *-er*, 20c, 1a(1/2 tech)   **Ic** *sviss* [svis:] M, pl. *-ar*, mid20c, +1b(3 tech)   **Fr** [switʃ] M, 1980s, 1a(1 tech, ban) < *interrupteur, commutateur* **Rm** [=E] N [U] end20c, +8(1 tech)   **Rs** *svitch* M [U] 1980s, +8(1 tech)   **Bg** *suich* M [U] 1990s, +8(1 tech)   **Hu** [=E] cp,[1] end20c, +8(1 tech)

switch   *v.* +1b 'turn on a car's ignition', 2 'change or transfer position'
Du *switchen* [sw‿itʃə] 1960s, 2(1 coll)   **Nw** *switche/*

svitsje [svi̯tʃe] end20c, 2(1 tech, mod)　**Ic** *svissa* [svɪsːa] mid20c, +1b(3 tech) 2(3 coll)

synthesizer　*n.* 'an electronic keyboard which generates synthetic sounds'

　　Since this word is phonetically very difficult, one might have expected simplified, shortened forms of it – or calques; this has largely not happened, although there are some adaptations bringing it closer to an 'international' form.

Ge [zʏntesai̯za] M, pl. *-s*, 1970s (1 tech)　**Du** [=E] C, 1970s (1 tech<2)　**Nw** [=E] M, pl. *-e*, 1970s (2 tech)　**Ic** [=E] or *synti* [sɪntɪ] M, pl. *-ar*, 1970s (1/2 tech) = creat *hljóðgerfill*　**Fr** *synthétiseur* M, 1960s (3/4); *synthé* M, 1970s (3/4)　**Sp** *sintetizador* M, end20c (5)　**It** *sintetizzatore* 1970s (3)　**Rm** *sintetizator* [sintetizator] N, 1970s (3)　**Rs** *sintezator* M, pl. *-y*, 1970s (2 tech)　**Po** *syntetajzer* [sintetajzer] M, 1980s (1 coll)　**Cr** *sintesajzer* M, pl. *-i*, end20c (1 tech)　**Bg** *sintesai̯zŭr* M, pl. *-a/-i*, end20c (1 tech); *sinti* N, pl. *-ta* (3 tech, coll) < *sintezator*　**Fi** *syntesisaattori* (5La)　**Hu** (5La)　**Gr** *synthesaizer* N, end20c (4 tech)

tacker*   *n.* 'an instrument for fixing tacks into wood etc.'

Ge [ta̲ka] M, pl. Ø, 1980s (1 tech, rare)   **Du** [=E] C, 1980s (1 tech) < *nietpistool*

tackle   *v.* 1 'try to deal with (a problem or difficulty)', 4 'obstruct, intercept, or seize and stop (a player running with the ball)'

Du *tacklen* [=E] mid20c, 1(1 you) 4(1 tech)   **Nw** *takle* [takle] 1960s, 1(3); 1930s, 4(3 tech)   **Ic** *takla/tækla* [tʰa(i)hkla] mid20c, 1(2 coll) 4(2 tech)   **Fi** *taklata* beg20c, 4(3)

tackler*   *n.* 'a (footb.) player who tackles'

Nw [takler] M, pl. -e, 1960s (3 tech)   **Ic** *taklari* [tʰahklarɪ] M, pl. -ar, mid20c (2 tech)

tackling   *n.* 4 'an act of tackling in football etc.'

The evidence is neatly devided between the nouns *tackling* and *the tackle* – and absence of the term. There is no doubt, however, that the verb is less frequent and likely to be backderived in most cases.

Ge [ta̲klɪŋ] N, pl. -s, 1980s (1 tech) **Du** *tackle* [tɛkəl] C, 1970s (2) → *tackelen/tekkelen* v.   **Nw** *takling* [ta̲klɪŋ] M/F, pl. -er, beg20c (3) **Ic** *takling/tækling* [tʰa(i)hklɪŋk] F [U] mid20c (2 tech) = *tæklun, töklun*   **Fr** *tackle/tacle* /<=E> [takl/ taklɪŋ] M, beg20c (2) → *tacler* v.; *tackling* **Sp** *tackle* [takle] M [U] 1930s (1 tech) **It** *tackle* [tɛkl/teikl] M, pl. Ø, 1950s (2 tech)   **Rm** [=E] N, 1970s (1 tech, rare); *tackle* [=E] N (1 tech)   **Fi** - < *taklaus* → *taklata* v.   **Gr** *taklin* N, beg20c (1 tech)

Ic	Nw	Po	Rs
Du	Ge	Cr	Bg
Fr	It	Fi	Hu
Sp	Rm	Al	Gt

tag   *n.* +12 'the individual label of a tagger'

Nw <=E>/*tagg* [=E] M, pl. -s/-er, 1990s (1 sla, mod) → *tagge* v.   **Fr** [tag] M, 1990s (1 mod) → *taguer* v.

tagger*   *n.* 'a person who sprays graffiti on to walls, fences etc.'

Du [=E] C, 1980s (1 mod/you) → *tag* n.   **Nw** [=E] tager] M, pl. -e, 1990s (2)   **Fr** *tagueur/tagger* [tagœR] M, 1990 (1 mod) → *tagueuse* F   **Sp** *tager/tagueur* [tager] M, pl. -s, 1980s (1 you, mod)   **Rs** *tegger* M, pl. -y, 1990s (1 mod/you)

take   *v.* +5a 'grab a (moving) car's bumper and let oneself be pulled along on icy roads'

Ic *teika* [tʰei̲ka] mid20c (3 you)

take   *n.* 2 'a scene or sequence of film photographed continuously at one time'

Ge [te:k] M/N, pl. -s, 1980s (1 tech)   **Du** <=E>/*teek*

[te:k] M, 1970s (1 tech)   **Nw** [=E] M, pl. -s, 1980s (1 tech)   **Ic** [=E] N, pl. Ø, 1960s (1 tech) < mean *taka*

take-off   *n.* 1 'the act of becoming airborne' (of an aeroplane or rocket)

Ge [=E] M/N, pl. -s, 1970s (1 mod) < *Start, Abflug* **Du** *take off* [=E] N, 1970s (1 tech)   **Nw** [=E] M, pl. -er, 1950s (1 tech)   **Ic** [=E] N, mid/end20c (1 tech) < *flugtak*   **Fr** (0 ban) < *décollage*   **It** [teik ɔf] M, pl. Ø, 1970s (1 tech) < *decollo*   **Rm** (0) < *decolare*   **Rs** - < creat *vzlët, otryv ot zemli*   **Po** - < *odlot*   **Bg** *te̲ikof* M, pl. -al-i, end20c (1 tech)

take-over   *n.* 'the assumption of control of a business'

Ge [=E] M, pl. Ø/-s, 1990s (1 tech, rare)   **Du** [=E] C, pl. -s, end20c (1 tech)   **Nw** [=E] 1980s (1 tech)   **Fr** [te:kovœR] M, pl. Ø, 1990s (1 tech, jour)   **It** [=E] M, pl. Ø, end20c (1 tech)   **Rm** - < rend *preluare*

talent scout   *n.* 'a person looking for talented performers, esp. in sport and entertainment'

Nw - < trsl *talentspeider*   **It** [=E] M, pl. Ø, 1950s (2 tech)

talk   *n.* 1 'conversation or talking', +7 'a talk-show'

Ge [=E] M, pl. -s, 1970s (1 jour) → -en v.; -er M   **Du** [=E] C, 1980s, 1(1 you, mod) < *praatje*   **Rm** (0)   **Po** [tok] M [U] end20c, +7(1 coll, mod)

talkmaster*   *n.* 'the host of a talk show'

Ge [=E] M, pl. Ø, 1970s (1 tech, coll) → -in F   **Du** [=E] C 1980s (1 tech)   **Rs** (0)

talk show   *n.* 'a chat show on TV'

As a regular form of TV entertainment, *talk shows* have greatly increased since the 1970s in most European countries; the discussion of trivia with prominent interviewees apparently meets a popular demand. Note the absence of calques, and the proliferation of *talk* words all originating from this compound.

Ge [ta̲:kʃo:] F, pl -s, 1970s (2) **Du** [=E] C, 1970s (2)   **Nw** [=E] N, pl. Ø/-s, 1970s (1)   **Ic** [=E] N, pl. Ø, end20c (0) < *rabbþáttur* **Fr** <=E> M, 1980s (1)   **Sp** [=E] M, pl. -s, end20c (1 jour)   **It** [tɔ(l)kʃɔu] M, pl. Ø, 1980s (2)   **Rm** [=E] N, 1990s (1 mod)   **Rs** *tokshou* N, uninfl., 1990s (1 jour)   **Po** [to-] M [U] uninfl., end20c (1 coll, mod)   **Cr** [=E] M [U] end20c (1 tech)   **Bg** *to̲kshou* N, pl. -ta, 1990s (1 jour)   **Fi** [=E]

Ic	Nw	Po	Rs
Du	Ge	Cr	Bg
Fr	It	Fi	Hu
Sp	Rm	Al	Gt

1980s (1)   **Hu** [=E] pl. *-k*/Ø, end20c (2 mod)   **Gr** *tok sou*, N, pl. *-s*, 1990s (1 jour, mod)

tallyman   *n.* +3 'a controller'
   Ge *Tally-(mann)* [talı-] M, pl. *-leute*, beg20c (1 tech, rare)   **Du** [talıman] C, pl. *-men*, 20c (1 tech)   **Cr** *taliman* 20c (1 tech)   **Bg** *taliman* M, pl. *-i*, mid20c (1 tech_{NAUT}) → *-ka* F.; *-ski* adj.; *-ya* v.

tandem   *n.* 1 'a bicycle or tricycle with two or more seats one behind another', 2 'a group of two persons or machines etc. with one behind or following the other', 3 'a carriage driven tandem', +4 'a duo, two people/ partners'
   This term was borrowed together with other bicycle terms around 1900 into various European languages (the pun on Latin *tandem* 'at length' being opaque in English and the receiving languages). Other meanings, some of which give up the idea of 'behind-each-other', appear to be later, and often independent of English.
   Ge [tandem] N, pl. *-s*, end19c, 1(3)   **Du** [tandəm] C, end19c, 1(2); 1970s, 3, +4(2)   **Nw** [tandem] M, pl. *-er*, beg20c, 1(3)   **Fr** M, end19c, 1(3) 3(3) +4(2 coll)   **Sp** [tandem] M, end19c, 1,2,+4(2)   **It** [tandem] M, pl. Ø, end19c, 1,2,+4(3)   **Rm** [tandem] N, end19c, via Fr, 1,2,+4(3)   **Rs** *tandem* M, pl. *-y*, beg20c, 1,+4(2)   **Po** [tandem] M, beg20c, 1,2,+4(3) → *-owy* adj.   **Cr** *tandem* M, pl. *-i*, beg20c, 1(2) 3(1) +4(2 euph)   **Bg** *tandem* M, pl. *-al-i*, beg20c, 1(1 arch); mid20c, +4(2) → *-no* adv.   **Hu** [tandem] [Ø] end19c/beg20c, 1(3 obs) 3(3 arch)   **Al** *tandem* M, pl. *-ë*, 20c, 1,3(1 reg)

tank¹ (1)   *n.* 1 'a large receptacle or storage chamber usu. for liquid or gas', 1a 'such a receptacle for petrol'
   This word is an old loan (originally from an Indian language?) transmitted through English sailors' language for 'water reservoir' from the eighteenth century on. This was later extended to include reservoirs for gas, petrol, etc. (whence German *tanken* 'to fill in petrol'). It is noteworthy that the early loan is virtually restricted to Western Europe.

Ic	Nw	Po	Rs
Du	Ge	Cr	Bg
Fr	It	Fi	Hu
Sp	Rm	Al	Gr

   Ge [taŋk] M, pl. *-s*, end18c, 1(3); beg20c, 1a(3)   **Du** [=E] C, end19c, 1,1a(2>3)   **Nw** [taŋk] M, pl. *-er*, beg20c, 1(3) 1a(3)   **Ic** *tankur* [tʰauŋkɪr] M, pl. *-ar*, beg/mid20c, via Da (3) = creat *geymir*   **Fr** *tank* M, end19c, 1,1a(2 ban) < *réservoir*   **Sp** *tanque* M, beg20c, 1,1a(3)   **It** [teŋk] M, pl. Ø, 1910s, 1(1 obs); *tanica* [tanica] F, pl. *-che*, 1940s, 1a(3)   **Rm** *tanc* [tank] N, mid20c, via Fr/Ge (3 tech) < *rezervor*   **Rs** *tank* M, pl. *-i*, end19c (1 tech)   **Cr** *tank* M, pl. *-ovi*, mid20c (2)   **Fi** *tankki* beg20c (3)   **Hu** [tank] pl. *-ok*, end19c/beg20c, 1,1a(3) → *-ol* v.   **Al** *tank* M, pl. Ø (3 tech) < *rezervuar*

tank² (1)   *n.* 2 'a heavy armoured fighting vehicle carrying guns and moving on a tracked carriage', +6 'platform shoes' (Bg only)
   The new meaning 'armoured vehicle' was used as a secret designation by the British Army in 1915. It quickly spread through Europe during the First

World War, but has become obsolete in some languages.

Ic	Nw	Po	Rs
Du	Ge	Cr	Bg
Fr	It	Fi	Hu
Sp	Rm	Al	Gr

   Ge [taŋk] M, pl. *-s*, beg20c, 2(1 arch) < *Panzer*   **Du** [=E] C, 1910s, 2(2>3)   **Nw** *tank/tanks* [tæŋk(s)] M, pl. *-sl-er*, mid20c, 2(2)   **Ic** - < 2: *skriðdreki*   **Fr** <=E> M, 1910s, 2(1 obs, ban) < *char* → *tankiste*   **Sp** *tanque* M, beg20c, 2(3) < *carro de combate*   **It** [teŋk/tɛnk] M, pl. Ø, 1910s, 2(1 tech, obs) < *carro armato*   **Rm** *tanc* [tank] N, mid20c, via Fr/Ge, 2(3)   **Rs** *tank* M, pl. *-i*, beg20c, 2(3) → *-ist* n.; *-ovyǐ* adj.   **Po** [tank] M, mid20c, 2(1 arch) < *czołg* → *-ietka*   **Cr** *tenk* M, pl. *-ovi*, mid20c, 2(2) → *-ist* M; *-ovski* adj.   **Bg** *tank* M, pl. *-al-ove*, beg20c, 2(2); usu. pl., mid20c, +6(3) < +6: *-etki* pl. → *-ov* adj.; *-ist* M   **Fi** *tankki* mid20c, 2(2) < *panssarivaunu*   **Hu** [tank] pl. *-ok*, beg20c, 2(3) = *harckocsi*   **Al** *tank* M, pl. *tanqe*, beg20c, 2(3)   **Gr** *tank(s)* N, pl. *-s*, beg20c, 2(2)

tank   *v.* 1 'fill the tank (of a vehicle etc.) with fuel', 2 'drink heavily, become drunk'
   Ge *tanken* beg20c, 1(3); 1960s, 2(3 coll) → *Tankstelle* F   **Du** *tanken* [tɛngkə(n)] 1940s (2>3)   **Nw** *tanke* [taŋke] 20c, 1(3)   **Rm** *tanca* [tanka] 20c, via Ge?, 1(3 rare)   **Po** *tankować* [tankovatç] mid20c, 1,2(3) → *za-* v.   **Cr** *tankirati* mid20c, 1(3)   **Fi** *tankata* beg20c, 1(3)   **Hu** *tankol* [tankol] end19c/beg20c, 1(3); 20c, 2(3 fac)

tanker   *n.* 'a ship, aircraft, or road vehicle for carrying liquids, esp. mineral oils, in bulk'
   This word is generally known, as a consequence of the importance of oil, and the media coverage of disasters. It is remarkable that the distribution has nothing to do with ↑*tank* n./v., the word for the ship not being seen as connected.

Ic	Nw	Po	Rs
Du	Ge	Cr	Bg
Fr	It	Fi	Hu
Sp	Rm	Al	Gr

   Ge [taŋka] M, pl. Ø, 1930s (3)   **Du** [=E] C, 1940s (2>3)   **Nw** [taŋker] M, pl. *-e*, beg20c (3) = *tankskip*   **Ic** - < *tankskip* N, *-bíll* M   **Fr** <=E> M, 1930s (1 ban) < *navire-citerne*   **Sp** (0) < *buque (avión,* etc.*) cisterna*   **It** [=E] M, pl. Ø, 1940s (1 obs) < *nave cisterna*   **Rm** - < *tanc petrolier*   **Rs** *tanker* M, pl. *-y*, mid20c (3)   **Po** - < *tankowiec*   **Cr** *tanker* M, pl. *-i*, mid20c (3)   **Bg** *tanker* M, pl. *-al-i*, mid20c (2) → *-en* adj.   **Fi** *tankkeri* mid20c (3) = *säiliölaiva*   **Hu** [tanker] pl. Ø, 20c (1 tech) < *tankhajó*   **Al** *tanker* M, pl. *-ë*, mid20c (1 tech)   **Gr** *tanker* N, mid20c (2)

tape   *n.* 3 'a strip of opaque or transparent paper or plastic etc. coated with adhesive for fastening, sticking, etc.', 4a 'a long narrow flexible material with magnetic properties used for recording sound or pictures or data', 4b 'a length, reel, or cassette of this'; cf. ↑*cellotape*.
   Ge [te:p] M/N, pl. *-s*, 1970s, 4b(1 tech, obs) < *Tonband*   **Du** [=E] M, 1960s, 3,4a(2)   **Nw** <=E>/*teip* [tæip] M, pl. *-er*, mid20c, 3(2); 1970s, 4a,b(1 tech) =

3: *limbånd* < 4a,b: *kassett, lydbånd* **Ic** [=E] N, pl. Ø, mid20c, 3(1 coll) 4a,b(1 tech) < 3: *limband*; 4a,b: *(segul)band* **It** [=E] M, pl. Ø, 1970s (1 tech) < trsl *nastro* **Rm** - < *bandă* **Fi** *teippi* mid20c, 3(3) **Gr** (1 writ)

tape *v.* 1a 'tie up or join with a tape', 3 'record on magnetic tape'
Du *tapen* [tẹːpən] 1980s (2) **Nw** <=E>/*teipe* [tæipe] mid20c, 1a(2); 1980s, 3(1 tech) **Ic** [tʰei:pa] mid20c, 1a(1 coll) 3(1 tech) **Fi** *teipata* mid20c, 1a(3)

tape deck *n.* 'a piece of equipment for playing audio-tapes, esp. as part of a stereo system'
Ge [=E] N, pl. -s, 1980s (1 mod) < *Kassettendeck* **Du** *tapedeck* [=E] C, 1970s (1 tech) **Nw** [=E] N, pl. Ø, 1970s (1 rare) < *kassettdeck* **Fr** - < *platine* **Rm** [=E] N, 1980s (1 tech) < *deck* **Hu** [=E] pl. Ø, 20c (1 tech)

target *n.* +3a 'a group of potential customers targeted by advertising'
Du [=E] C, pl. -s, end20c (1 tech) **Nw** - < *målgruppe* **Fr** - < trsl *cible* **Sp** [tárget] M, end20c (1 tech) **It** [tárget] M, pl. Ø, 1970s (1 tech_ECON)

tarpaulin *n.* 1 'heavy-duty waterproof cloth, originally of tarred canvas'
Du [=E] N [U] 1940s (1 tech) **Po** *tarpolina* [tarpolina] F, mid20c (1 tech)

tartan[1] (1) *n.* 1 'a pattern of coloured stripes crossing at right angles, esp. the distinctive plaid worn by Scottish Highlanders to denote their clan', 2 'woollen cloth in this pattern'
Ge [tạrta:n] M, pl. -s, 19c (Ø) **Du** 1,2(Ø) **Nw** [tạrtan] M/N [U] mid19c, 1(Ø) 2(1 tech) < 1: *skotskrutet* **Fr** M, end19c (o) **Sp** *tartán* M, 1(3); via Fr, 2(3) < *tela escocesa* **It** [tartan] M [U] end18c, 2(1 tech) **Rm** [tartạn] N, via Fr, mid19c (3 tech) **Rs** *tartạn* M [U] beg20c, 2(Ø) **Po** [tartan] M, beg20c, 1,2(1 tech) **Cr** [tạrtan] M [U] beg20c (1 tech) **Bg** *tartạn* M [U] 20c, 2(Ø) → -*ov* adj. **Fi** *tartaani* 19c (Ø) > *skottiruutu* **Hu** *tartán* [tạrta:n] [U] 17c, 1(Ø) 2(1 rare, obs) **Al** *tarton* M, pl. -*ë*, beg20c, 2(1 reg)

tartan[2] *n./cp*[1] +3 'the elastic surface of an athletic racecourse'
Ge [tạrta:n] M [U] end20c (1 tech) **Du** [=E/tạrtan] N [U] 1970s (1 tech) **Nw** [tarta:n] M [U] 20c (t tech) **Sp** <=E> M (1 tech) **It** [tạrtan] M [U] 1970 (2 tech) **Rm** [tartạn] N, 1970s, via Fr (3 tech) **Rs** *tartạn* [U] M, end20c (1 tech) **Po** [tartan] M [U] (1 tech) **Cr** *tạrtan* M[U] end20c (1 tech) **Bg** *tartạn* M [U] mid20c (3 tech) → -*ov* adj. **Hu** *tartán* [tạrta:n] [U] 1960s (1 tech) **Gr** *tartạn* N, end20c (1 tech)

task force *n.* 2 'a unit specially organized for a task'
Ge (o) **Du** [=E] C, 1980s (1 tech, jour, rare) < *gerechtsgroep* **Fr** [taskfɔrs] F, 1980s (1 ban) < *groupe de projet* **It** [tạsk fɔrs] F, pl. Ø, 1940s (1 tech, jour) **Rm** (o>1 tech, rare) < *unitate specială*

taste *v.* 1 'sample or test the flavour of (food etc.) by taking it into the mouth', 2 'perceive the flavour of'
Ic [tʰei:sta] 1970s (1 sla)

tattoo[1] (1) *n.* 1 'an evening drum or bugle signal recalling soldiers to their quarters', 2 'an elaboration of this with music and marching presented as an entertainment'
Ge [=E] N, pl. -s, 20c (1 tech, rare) < *Zapfenstreich* **Du** *taptoe* (5) **Nw** [=E] M, pl. -er, 20c, 2(1 tech) **Fi** *tattoo* [=E] end20c, 2(1)

tattoo[2] (2) *n.* 'an indelible design marked on the skin by puncturing it and inserting pigment'
This word first came to be well known as a term for South Sea practices through the accounts of James Cook's journal, the early adoption being reflected in formal differences and widespread morphological adaptation. French and German appear to have played a vital role in the dissemination of the term.
Ge *Tatau(ierung)* 19c (0 arch); [=E] N, pl. -s, 1980s (1 you, rare) < *Tätowierung* **Du** [=E] C, 1980s (2 jour, mod) < *tatoeage* **Nw** - < *tatovering* **Ic** [tʰahtu] N, pl. Ø, end20c (1 sla) < *tattóvering, tattúering, húðflúr* **Fr** - < *tatouage* → *tatoueur/-se* M/F; *tatouer* v. **Sp** *tatuaje* via Fr (3) **It** [tẹtu:] M, pl. Ø, end20c (1 tech) < *tatuaggio* **Rm** *tatuaj* N, 20c, via Fr (3) **Rs** - < *tatuiŗovka* F, pl. -*i*, mid20c (3) **Po** - < *tatuaz* via Fr **Cr** - < *tetoviranje n.* → *tetovirati* v. **Bg** - < *tatuirovka* F **Fi** - < *tatuointi* 19c, 2(3) **Hu** *tattoo* [=E] [U] end20c (1 writ, jour) < *tetoválás* ← *tetovál* v.; *tátoviroz* 18c **Al** - < *tatuazh* M, pl. -*e*, mid20c (2) **Gr** - < *tatuạz*

tax-free *adj* 'exempt from being taxed'
Du [tɛks friː] 1980s (1 mod) = *belastingsvrij* **Nw** [=E] 1960s (2) **Ic** [=E] end20c (o) < *tollfrjáls* **It** - < *duty-free* **Rm** (o) **Rs** (o) **Cr** <=E> (o) **Hu** [=E] 20c (1 jour) < *vámmentes* **Fi** [=E] cp[1], 1960s (1) **Gr** <=E> 20c (1 writ)

tax-free shop* *n.* 'a duty-free shop'
Ge (o) < *duty-free shop* **Du** [tɛks friːʃɔp] C, 1970s (2) **Nw** <=E>/*taxfree* [=E] M, 1960s (2) **Fr** *tax free shop*, 20c (2 ban) > *boutique hors taxes* **It** - < *duty free shop* **Rm** end20c (o) **Rs** (o) **Po** - < *duty-free shop* **Cr** [=E] M, end20c (2) **Bg** *frishop* M, pl. -*al-ove*, mid20c (3) **Fi** [=E] 1960s (1) **Hu** [=E] [Ø] mid20c (2) > *vámmentes bolt*

taxi-girl* *n.* 1 'a dancer in a cabaret', 2 'a female paid for dancing with customers'
Ge [taksigøl] N, pl. -s, 1940s, 2(1 obs) **Fr** [taksigœrl] F, 1960s, 1(1) **Sp** [=E] F, pl. -s, 1930s (0/1 jour, arch) **It** [tạksi gœrl] F, pl. Ø, 1930s, 2(1 tech) **Rm** [tạksigərl] F, pl. Ø, end20c, 2(1 rare)

taylorism*/Taylor system* *n.* 'a system of scientific management and work efficiency' propounded by F.W. Taylor (US engineer, 1856–1915)
Ge *Taylorsystem* N [U] 1920s (2+5 tech) **Du** *taylorsysteem* N [U] 20c (1 tech +5) **Nw** *Taylorsysstem* N [U] 20c (1 +5 tech) **Ic** - < *Taylorsstefna* **Fr** *taylorisme* [telɔrizm] M, 1920s (3 tech) → *tayloriser* **Sp** *taylorismo* M, mid20c (2 tech) **It** *taylorismo* [teilorịzmo] M [U] 1920s (3) → *tayloristico* adj. **Rm** *tailorism/-ay-* [tejlorịsm/tail-] N [U] mid20c, via Fr (2 tech) **Rs** *téilorịzm/te-* M [U], beg20c (1 tech) **Po** *tayloryzm* [tajlorizm] M [U] beg20c (2 tech) **Cr** *tejlorizam* M [U] beg20c (2 tech) **Bg** *teĭlǔrịzǔm* M [U]

beg20c (1 tech) **Hu** *Taylor-rendszer* [U] 20c (2+5 tech_{MECH}) **Al** *tejlorizëm* M [U] mid20c (3) **Gr** *systima teilor* N, beg20c (5+1 tech)

teach-in *n.* 1 'an informal lecture and discussion on a subject of public interest'

This word was adopted from America as a typical expression for a characteristic form of protest of the student unrest of the late 1960s, but seems to have remained restricted to the Germanic countries. It sparked off similar formations (cf. ↑ *-in*). With the changes of political and social culture, the phenomenon and the word have now become obsolete, useful only for historical reference.

Ge [=E] N, pl. *-s*, 1960s (1 obs) **Du** [=E] C, 1960s (1 obs) **Nw** [=E] M/N, pl. Ø/-*s*, 1960s (1 obs) **Fr** (0) **It** [=E] M, pl. Ø, 1960s (1 obs) **Rs** *tich-in* M, uninfl., 1970s (1 obs) **Hu** [=E] [U] 20c (Ø)

teak *n.* 2 'the hard durable timber of the deciduous teak tree'

The word for the wood, which is very popular in furniture, was transmitted partly through Portuguese and partly through English or taken straight from Oriental languages. Only forms containing /i/ are definitely derived via English.

Ge *Teak/Tick* [=E] N [U] end19c (2) **Du** [=E] 1920s (3) **Nw** [=E] M [U] beg20c (2) **Ic** *tekk* [tɛhk] N [U] beg20c, via Da (3) **Fr** *teck/tek* [tɛk] M, end18c (2) **Sp** - < *teca* **It** <=E>/*tek/teack* [tɛk] M [U] end19c (2 tech) **Rm** *tec/teck* [tek] M[U] end20c, via Fr (3 tech) **Rs** *tik* M [U] beg20c (2 tech) **Po** *tek* (5Malay) **Cr** *tik* M[U] beg20c (1 tech) → *tikovina* F **Bg** *tik* M[U] beg20c, via Rs (Ø tech) → *-ov* adj. **Fi** *tiikki* 19c (3) **Hu** *tikfa* (5Port) **Gr** *tik* N [U] 20c (1 tech)

team *n.* 1 'a set of players forming one side in a game', 2 'people working together'

Although first spread with various sports disciplines like football, this term is now widely used especially with the connotation of friendly cooperativeness; it competes with ↑*crew* and has largely replaced earlier *équipe* from French, which is retained in some languages for teams in specific sports (for riding contests in German). The compound ↑*teamwork* (which is exclusively based on the 'friendly' connotation) is much rarer.

Ge [=E] N, pl. *-s*, beg20c, 1(1 tech); 1960s, 2(2) < *Mannschaft* **Du** [=E] N, beg20c (2) = 1: *ploeg* **Nw** [=E] N, pl. *-er*, mid20c (2) < *lag* **Ic** [=E] N, pl. Ø, end20c, 1(0) 2(1 sla) < 1: *lið*; 2: *teymi* **Fr** [=E] M, 20c (1 ban) < *équipe* **Sp** [tim] M, pl. *-s*, end20c (1 tech, mod) < *equipo* **It** [ti:m] M, pl. Ø, 1900s, 1(1 tech); 1960s, 2(1 tech) > mean *squadra, équipe* **Rm** [=E] N, mid20c, 1(1 tech, rare); end20c, 2(1 mod, jour) < *echipă* **Rs** (0) **Po** [tim] M, beg20c (1 tech) **Cr** *tim* M, pl. *-ovi*, beg20c (2) **Bg** *tim* M, pl. *-a/-ove*, beg20c, 1(2) 2(1 mod) < 1: *otbor*; 2: *ekip* **Fi** <=E>/*tiimi* [=E] end20c (3) < *joukkue* **Hu** [=E] pl. *-ek*, end19/beg20c, 1(3

tech, arch); 1960s, 2(2) **Al** *tim* M, pl. *-e*, end20c (1 reg) **Gr** *tim* N, pl. Ø/-*s*, end20c, 1(2) 2(2 mod, jour)

teamer* *n.* 'a person instructing a team'

Ge [=E] M, pl. Ø, 1970s (1 tech, rare) **Du** - < *teamleider*

teamwork *n.* 'the combined action of a team, group, etc., esp. when effective and efficient'

Considering the widespread use of ↑*team*, the restriction of this term largely to Germanic languages – where it has been a very popular concept for many years – comes as a surprise.

Ge [ti:mvørk] N [U] 1960s (1 coll) < *Teamarbeit* → *-er* M **Du** [=E] N [U] 1970s (2) < *teamwerk* **Nw** [=E] N [U] 1960s (1) **Ic** - < *hópvinna*, rend *teymisvinna* **It** [=E] M [U] 1960s (1 tech) **Fi** [=E] end20c (1) **Hu** [ti:mvørk] [U] 1960s (2) < *csoportmunka*

tearoom *n.* 'a small restaurant or café where tea is served'

Ge [=E] M, pl. *-s*, end19c (Ø/1 arch) **Du** [=E] C, 1940s (1 arch) **Fr** (0) **It** [=E] M, pl. Ø, end19c (1 arch) **Rm** (0) **Gr** (0)

techno *n./cp.*[1/2] 'a style of popular music making extensive use of electronic instruments and synthesized sound'

Ge [tɛkno(ʊ)] M [U] 1990s (1 tech, mod) **Du** [=E]/tɛχno:] C [U] 1990s (1 tech) **Nw** [tɛknu] M [U] 1990s (1 tech) **Ic** [=E] N [U] 1990s (1 tech, you) **Fr** [tɛkno] M, 1990s (1 mod) **Sp** <=E>/*tecno* [tɛkno] M [U] 1990s (1 you, mod) **It** [tɛkno] M [U] 1990s (1 tech, mod) **Rm** <=E>/*techno* [tɛkno] N/cp[2] [U] 1990s (1 tech, mod) **Rs** *tekhno* M [U] 1990s (1 tech, mod) **Po** [texno] N, uninfl., 1990s (1 tech, mod, you) **Cr** (0) **Bg** *tɛkhno* N/cp[1] [U] 1990s (1 tech) **Fi** <=E>/*tekno* [=E] 1990s (1 tech, mod) **Hu** [tɛkno(:)] [U] 1990s (1 tech, you) **Al** *tekno* F [U] end20c (1 tech, mod) **Gr** *tɛkno* F [U] 1990s (1 tech, mod, you)

teddy *n.* 2 'a woman's undergarment combining vest and panties', *cp.*[1] +3 'furry cloth'

Ge [=E] M, pl. *-s*, 1980s, 2(1 tech, rare); 1960s, +3(3) **Du** [=E] 1960s (3 tech) **Nw** *cp.*[1] [=E] mid20c, +3(1 tech); M, pl. *-er*, 1980s, 2(1 tech, rare) **Fr** [tedi] +3(1 tech, obs) **Fi** *cp.*[1] [=E] 1960s, +3(2)

teddy bear *n.* 'a soft toy bear'

The toys were produced from c. 1900 onwards, the word being based on the short form of Theodor Roosevelt's first name. The limited distribution in Europe at least partly reflects the restricted range of the toy (produced from 1903 by the Steiff Company in Germany).

Ge *Teddy(bär)* M, pl. *-en*, beg20c (3+5) **Du** *teddybeer* [tɛdi-] C, pl. *-beren*, 1940s (2+5) **Nw** *teddybjørn* [=E+

Nw] 1920s (3) < *bamse* **Ic** *teddybjörn* M, 20c (1+5 rare, obs) < *bangsi* **Fr** *teddy* M, 1960s (1 obs) **Rm** [tediber] M, mid20c, via Ge (1 obs) **Rs** (0) **Hu** *teddi(ber)/teddy(bear)* [=E] [U] beg20c, +3(3) < *játék-/plüssmackó*

Teddy boy *n.* 'a youth, esp. of the 1950s, affecting an Edwardian style of dress and manner, usu. a long jacket and drainpipe trousers'

The fashion spread to Western Europe in the 1950s and 1960s, but was short-lived, so that the word is now obsolete, the type of youth it referred to is no longer known, and the word is likely to be misunderstood. (cf. the more recent ↑*Popper*).

Ge [=E] M, pl. -s, 1950s (1 coll, obs) **Du** [=E] C, 1950s (1 obs) **Nw** [=E] M, pl. -s, 1950s (1 obs) **Sp** [=E] M, pl. -s, mid20c (1 obs) **It** [=E] M, pl. Ø/-s, 1950s (1 obs) **Rs** (0) **Cr** *tediboj* [=E] M, mid20c (1) **Bg** *tedibois* M, pl., end20c (1 you, rare) **Fi** (Ø) **Gr** *tedyboisl - boissa* M/F, 1950s (3 obs) → *tedyboismos* M

teen *n.* 'a youth aged 13 to 19'

Ge [=E] M, pl. -s, 1960s (2 coll, obs) < *Teenager* **Du** - < *tiener* **Nw** - < *tenåring* **Sp** [tin] n./adj., pl. Ø, 1990s (1 jour, mod) **Rs** (0) **Fi** *teini* 19c (5Sw) **Hu** - < *tini* **Gr** *teens* M/F, pl. (1 mod)

teenager *n.* 'a person (esp. a girl) from 13 to 19 years of age'

This word became very fashionable in the 1950s/ 60s, when it was predominantly used for girls; it has receded slightly from the 1980s onwards (in German ↑*Kids* is now preferred). It has been variously shortened (↑*Teen*, ↑*Teenie*) and occasionally used for facetious coinages (German *greenager**). The non-English term ↑*twen** was coined to contrast with it.

Ge [ti:neidʒa/ti:ne:tʃa] M, pl. Ø, 1950s (2 obs) > *Teen, Teenie* **Du** [=E] C, 1950s (2 obs) < *tiener* **Nw** [=E] M, pl. -e, mid20c (1 obs) < *rend* *tenåring* **Ic** - < *creat* *táningur* **Fr** *teen-ager* M/F, 1950s (1 mod) **Sp** [=E] M, pl. -s, 1970s (1 jour) **It** [tinedʒer] M/F, pl. Ø, 1950s (2) **Rm** (0) **Rs** *tineidzher/tinéïdzer* M, pl. -y, end20c (1 tech, jour, mod) **Po** [tineidʒer] M, end20c (1 tech) < *trsl* *nastolatek* **Cr** *tinejdžer* M, pl. -i, mid20c (2) **Bg** *tïïneidzhür* M, pl. -i, end20c (2) → *-ka* F; *-ski* adj. **Hu** *tinédzser* [tine:dzer] pl. -ek, 1960s (3) = *tizenéves* **Gr** *tineitzer* M/F, pl. -s, end20c (1 mod, jour)

teenie* *n.* 'a female teenage pop fan'

Ge [=E] M, pl. -s, 1970s (1 coll, pej) **Du** [=E] C, 1970s (1 pej, obs) **Hu** *tini* [tini] pl. -k, 1960s (3)

teeny-bopper *n.* 'a young teenager, usu. a girl, who keenly follows the latest fashion in clothes, pop music, etc.'

Ge [=E] M, pl. Ø/-s, 1970s (1 you, pej, obs) **Du** *teeny bopper* [=E] C, 1990s (1 you) **Fi** [=E] 1970s (1 you, obs)

Teflon *n./cp'* 'non-stick coating' (orig.™)

Ge [te:flon] N [U] 1970s (2 tech) **Du** *teflon* [tɛflɔn] N [U] 1970s (3 tech) **Nw** [tɛflu:n] M [U] 1960s (3) **Ic** [=E] N/cp' [U] 1960s (2 tech) **Fr** [tefal] M, 1960s (1 tech) **Sp** *teflón* M [U] 1960s (2 tech) **It** [teflon] M, pl. Ø, 1960s (3 tech) **Rm** *teflon* [teflon] N [U] 1960s (3 tech) → *teflonat* adj. **Rs** *teflon* [U] end20c (2 tech) → *-ovyï* adj. **Po** *teflon* M [U] mid20c (3) → *-owy* adj. **Cr** *teflon* M [U] end20c (3) **Bg** *teflon* M [U] 1970s (2 tech) → *-ov* adj.; *-iram* v. **Fi** [=E] mid20c (3) **Hu** [teflon] [U] 1970s (3) **Gr** *teflon* N [U] mid20c (5Fr)

telebanking *n.* 'a banking system whereby computerized transactions are effected by telephone'

Ge [te:lebeŋkiŋ] N [U] 1990s (1 tech, mod) **Du** [=E] C [U] 1980s (1 tech, mod) → *telebankieren* v.; *thuisbankieren* v. **Nw** - < *telebank; telegiro* **Fr** - < *télébanque* **It** [telebankiŋ(g)] M, pl. Ø, 1990s (1 tech) **Rs** (0) **Po** [telebankink] M [U] end20c (1 tech) **Hu** [telebanking] [U] end20c (1 tech, mod) **Gr** <E>/*telebanking* N [U] 1990s (1 tech, mod)

telemarketing *n.* +2 'marketing through TV'

Ge [=E] N [U] 1990s (1 tech, rare) **Nw** [telema:rketiŋ] M [U] 1980s (1) < *telemarkedsføring* **It** [=E] M [U] 1990s (1 tech) **Rm** [=E] N [U] 1990s (1 mod) **Rs** *telemarketing* M [U] 1990s (1 tech, mod) **Cr** (0) **Bg** *telemarketing* M [U] 1990s (1 jour, mod) **Hu** [=E] [U] end20c (1 tech, mod) **Gr** <=E>/*telemarketing* N [U] 1980s (2)

teleprompter *n.* 'a device beside a television or cinema camera that slowly unrolls a speaker's script out of sight of the audience'

Ge [=E] M, pl. Ø, 1980s (1 tech) **Fr** *(télé)prompteur* M, end20c (4) **Sp** [teleprónter] M, end20c (1 tech) = *autocue* **Rs** *teleprompter* M, pl. -y, 1990s (1 tech) **Po** [teleprompter] M, end20c (1 tech) **Hu** [teleprompter] pl. Ø, mid20c (1 tech)

teleshopping *n.* +2 'advertising by television, ordering by telephone'

This term is so recent that it is difficult to judge its geographical distribution and usage value – it is likely to expand, and to become more common rapidly, possibly together with the two preceding items, in the course of modern communication.

Ge [te:ləʃopiŋ] N [U] 1980s (1 tech, mod) **Du** [=E] C [U] 1980s (1 tech) → *teleshoppen* [te:leʃɔpən] v. **Nw** - < *TV- shopping* **Ic** - < *sjónvarpsverslun* **Fr** *téléshopping* [teleʃopiŋ] M, 1990s (1 tech, ban) < *téléachat* **It** - < *video-shopping* **Rm** [=E] N [U] 1990s (1 mod) **Rs** *teleshopping* M [U] 1990s (1 tech, mod) **Po** - < *trsl* *telezakupy* **Cr** (0) **Bg** *teleshop* M [U] 1990s (3 mod) **Hu** [teleʃopiŋ] [U] end20c (1 tech, mod) → *teleshop, TV-shop*

telex *n.* 1 'an international system of telegraphy with printed messages transmitted and received by teleprinters', +2 'a document transmitted by telex'

This term, a blend of *teletype* and *exchange*, was coined for the new method in 1932. In recent years, the system has lost much ground to ↑*fax* and ↑*e-mail* – so the term may be on its way to obsolescence. Since the form is not distinctively English, its status as an anglicism is doubtful.
Ge [=E] M/N [U] 1960s (3) → *-en* v. **Du** [te:lɛks] C [U] 1940s (3) = *telexsysteem* **Nw** <=E>/*teleks* [tɛ:leks] M, pl. *-er*, 1940s (3 tech) **Ic** [=E] N [U] 1970s (2 tech) **Fr** *télex* M, mid20c, 1(3) **Sp** [teleks] M, 1970s (2 tech) **It** [teleks] M, pl. Ø, 1960s (3 tech) **Rm** [=E] N, 1960s, via Fr (3) → *-ist*, *ist* M/F **Rs** *teleks* M [U] end20c, 1(2 tech); pl. *-y*, +2(2 tech) **Po** *teleks*/ <=E> M, mid20c (3) **Cr** *teleks* M, pl. *-i*, mid20c (2 tech) **Bg** *teleks* M [U] 1970s (2 tech) **Fi** *teleksi* 20c (3 tech) = *kaukokirjoitin* **Hu** [=E] pl. *-ek*, 20c (3) → *-ez* v. **Al** *teleks* M, pl. *-e*, 1970s (3) **Gr** <=E>/*telex* N [U] end20c (2 tech)

telpher *n.* 'a system for transporting goods etc. by electrically driven trucks or cable cars'
Rs *tel'fer* M [U] mid20c (1 tech) **Bg** *telfer* M [U]/pl. *-al-i*, mid20c (1 tech)

temple block *n.* 'a percussion instrument consisting of a hollow block of wood which is struck with a stick'
It [tempel blɔk] M, pl. Ø, 1960s (1 tech)

temper *v.* +1 'heat glass or steel'
Ge *tempern* end19c (3 tech) **Bg** *temperovam* beg20c (3 tech) **Hu** *temperál* [tempera:l] 20c (3 tech) → *-ás* n.; *-t* adj.

tender[1] (2) *n.* 'an offer, esp. one in writing to execute work or supply goods at a fixed price'
Du [=E] C, 1940s (1 tech) **It** [=E] M, pl. Ø, 20c (1 tech) **Rs** *tender* M, pl. *-y*, end20c (1 tech) **Hu** [tender] pl. *-ek*, 20c (3 tech) **Al** *tender* M, pl. *-a*, 1992 (1)

tender[2] (3) *n.* 2 'a vessel attending a larger one to supply stores, convey passengers, orders, etc.', 3 'a special truck closely coupled to a steam locomotive to carry fuel, water, etc.'
The almost universal distribution of this term is due to the English dominance in early railway terminology; however, it has become obsolescent or obsolete in Romance languages in particular.
Ge [tenda] M, pl. Ø, mid19c, 2(3 tech) 3(3 tech) **Du** [=E] C, mid19c (3 tech) **Nw** [=E] M, pl. *-e*, 19c (1 tech) **Fr** <=E> M, mid19c, 3(1 obs) **Sp** <=E>/*ténder* [tender] M, end19c (1 tech, obs) **It** [tender] M, pl. Ø, mid19c (1 tech, obs) < *carro, scorta* **Rm** [tender] N, beg20c, via Fr/Ge, 3(3 tech) **Rs** *tender* M, pl. *-y*, beg20c (1 tech) **Po** [-er] M, beg20c (1 arch) **Cr** *tender* M, pl. *-i*, beg20c, 3(3 tech) **Bg** *tender* M, pl. *-al-i*, beg20c, 3(1 tech) **Fi** *tenderi* 19c, 3(3 tech) = *hiilivaunu* **Hu** [tender] pl. Ø, 19c (3 arch) **Al** *tender* M, pl. *-a*, beg20c (2)

tennis[1] *n.* 'a game in which two or four players strike a ball with rackets over a net stretched across a court'
The designation for the sport, popular since the late nineteenth century, is universally English. Note that the compound ↑*lawn tennis*, once fairly widespread, is now much more restricted.
Ge [=E] N [U] 19c (3) **Du** [=E] N [U] 19c (3) **Nw** [=E] M [U] beg20c (3) **Ic** *tennis* [tʰɛn:ɪs] M [U] end19c, via Da (2) **Fr** [tenis] M, end19c (3) → *-man* M; *tenniswoman* F **Sp** *tenis* M [U] end19c (3) → *-ista* M; *-ístico* adj. **It** [=E] M [U] beg19c (3) **Rm** *tenis* [=E] N [U] beg20c, via Fr (3) **Rs** *tenis* M [U] beg20c (3) → *-ist* M; *-istka* F; *-ka* F; *-nyĭ* adj. **Po** *tenis* M [U] beg20c (3) → *-ista* M; *-istka* F; *-owy* adj. **Cr** [=E] M [U] beg20c (3) → *-ač* M; *-ki* adj. **Bg** *tenis* M/cp[1] [U] beg20c (2) → *-ist* M; *-istka* F **Fi** [ten:is] 19c (3) **Hu** *tenisz* [=E] [U] beg19c (3) → *-ező* n.; *-ezik* v. **Al** *tenis* M [U] end19c (3) **Gr** *tenis* N [U] end19c (2) → *tenistas* M; *tenistria* F

tennis[2] *n.* 'an item of clothing or a type of shoe'
Fr [tenis] F, 1960s (3) **Sp** *tenis* M/F, end20c (3) **Rm** *tenis* [=E] M, 1960s (3) **Po** *tenis* M [U] mid20c (1 tech) **Bg** - < *teniska* F

tent-fly *n.* 1 'a flap at the entrance to a tent', 2 'a flysheet'
Du - < 1: *tentluifeln* **Po** *tent* M, mid20c, 1(1 tech) **Cr** (0) **Bg** - < *tenta* F, pl. *-ti*, mid20c, 2(3 tech)

terminal *n.* 2 'a terminus for trains etc.', +2a 'a terminus for (un)loading', +2b 'a terminus for buses going to/from an airport', 3 'a departure and arrival building for air passengers', 5 'an apparatus for transmission of messages between a user and a computer'
Ge [=E] M/N, pl. *-s*, 1970s, +2a(1 tech); 1970s, 3(1 coll); N, pl. *-s*, 1980s, 5(1 tech) **Du** [=E] C, 1960s (2 tech) **Nw** [tærmina:l] M, pl. *-er*, mid20c, 1970s, +2b,5(3 tech) **Ic** [=E/tʰɛrmina(t)l] M, pl. *-ar*, mid/end20c, +2b,3(1) 5(1 tech) < 5: creat *útstöð* **Fr** [terminal] M, 1950s, 3(3/4) 1980s, 5(3/4) **Sp** [terminal] F, mid20c, +2b,3(3); M, end20c, 5(3/4) **It** [terminal] M, pl. Ø, 1960s (3) → *-ista* n. **Rm** [terminal] N, 1970s, via Fr, 2,+2a,3,5(3 tech) **Rs** *terminal* M, pl. *-y*, mid20c, +2a,5(1 tech) **Po** [terminal] M, end20c, +2b,3(1 coll) 5(1 tech) **Cr** *terminal* M, pl. *-i*, end20c, 3,5(1 tech) **Bg** *terminal* M, pl. *-al-i*, mid20c, 3(2); end20c, 5(2 tech) **Fi** *terminaali* mid20c, +2a,3(3) **Hu** *terminál* [termina:l] pl. *-ok*, 20c, 2,3(3); 1980s, +2a,5(2 > 3 tech) **Al** *terminal* M, pl. *-ë*, end20c, 3,5(3) **Gr** <=E>/*terminal* N, pl. *-s*, end20c, 5(1 tech) = trsl *termatiko*

terrier *n.* 'a small dog of various breeds originally used for turning out foxes etc. from their earths'
This term spread with other names for breeds of dogs, although its form does not appear to indicate whether a loanword is from English, from French, or from English with French transmission. Various breeds of terriers are also known by a British qualification such as *Yorkshire terrier* (which are not all listed as separate entries).
Ge [teriər] M, pl. Ø, 19c (3) **Du** *terriër* [tɛriər] C, beg20c (5) **Nw** [tærjer] M, pl. *-e*, end19c (3) **Ic** [=E] M, 20c (0) **Fr** (4) **Sp** (5Fr) **It** [terrjer/teriɛ] M, pl. Ø, 18c (3) **Rm** *terier* [terjɛr] M, end19c (5Fr)

Rs *ter'er* M, pl. *-y*, beg20c (3) **Po** *terier* [-er] M, beg20c, via Fr (3) → *-ek* M **Cr** *terijer* M, pl. *-i*, beg20c (3) **Bg** *terier* M, pl. *-al-i*, beg20c, via Fr (2 tech) **Fi** *terrieri* 19c (3) **Hu** [terrier] pl. *-ek*, end19/beg20c (3) **Gr** *terie* N, 20c, via Fr (2)

Terylene *n.* (^TM) 'synthetic polyester used as a textile fibre'

Ge [teryle:n] N [U] mid20c (3 tech) **Nw** [terile:n] M [U] 1950s (2) **Ic** *terelín/terelyn(e)/terylene* [th ɛ:relin] N [U] 1960s (2) **Fr** (0) **Sp** [terilene] M, mid20c (1 tech) **It** *terilene* [terilene] M [U] 1940s (3 tech) **Rm** *terilenă/terilen* [terilenə/terilen] F/N [U] 1950s, via Fr (1 tech) **Rs** *terilen* M [U] mid20c (2 tech) **Po** *terylen* [terilen] M [U] mid20c (1 tech) **Cr** *terilen* M [U] mid20c (1 tech) **Bg** *terilen* M [U] mid20c (1 tech, obs) **Fi** *teryleeni* mid20c (3) **Hu** *terilén* [terile:n] [U] mid20c (3) **Gr** *terylini* F [U] mid20c (3 tech)

test *n.* 1 'a trial of a person's or thing's qualities', 3 'a minor examination, esp. in school', +3a 'a multiple-choice test'

Ge [=E] M, pl. *-sl-e*, mid19c/beg20c, 1,3,+3a(3) **Du** [=E] C, pl. *-sl-en*, beg20c, 1(3) = *toets* **Nw** [=E] M, pl. *-er*, mid19c, 1,3(3) **Ic** [=E] N, pl. Ø, 1970s, 1,3(1 coll) < *próf* **Fr** [=E] M, end19c, 1(3) < +3a: *QCM questionnaire à choix multiple* → *testeur* M; *testable* adj.; *testabilité* n. **Sp** [=E/tes] M, pl. *-s*, beg20c, 1,3(2) **It** [test] M, pl. Ø, end19c, 1,3(3) +3a(2) **Rm** [=E] N, 1960s, via Fr, 1,3,+3a(3) **Rs** *test* M, pl. *-y*, beg20c, 3,+3a(2) → *ovyǐ* adj. **Po** M, beg20c, 1,3,+3a(3) → *teścik* M; *-owy* adj. **Cr** *test* M, pl. *-ovi*, mid20c, 1,3 (2) → *-iran* adj. **Bg** *test* M, pl. *-al-ove*, mid20c (2) → *-ov* adj.; *-uvane* N **Fi** *testi* 19c, 1,3(3) < *koe* **Hu** *teszt* [=E] pl. *-ek*, beg20c, 1(3); 1960s, 3,+3a(3) **Al** *test* M, pl. *-e*, 1960s, 1,3 (1 reg) **Gr** *test* N, beg20c, 1,3(2) → *testaki* N

test *v.* 1 'make trial of', +5 'find out attitudes by investigation, a poll etc.'

Ge [testən] 1950s (3) **Du** *testen* [testə(n)] 1940s (3) **Nw** *teste* [teste] mid20c, 1(3) **Ic** *testa* [th esta] 1970s, 1(1 coll) < *prófa* **Fr** *tester* 20c (2) **Sp** *testar* (3 tech) **It** *testare* [testare] 1980s, via Fr (3) → *-ato* part. **Rm** *testa* [testa] mid20c, via Fr (3) → *-are* F **Rs** *testirovat'* 20c (2) → *-irovanie* N **Po** *testować* [testovatç] mid20c (3) → *prze*-v. **Cr** *testirati* mid 20c (3) **Bg** *testuvam/testvam* 20c, 1(3) **Fi** *testata* mid20c (3) **Hu** *tesztel* [testel] 1960s (3) → *-ő* n. **Al** *testëroj* mid20c (3) **Gr** *testaro* mid/end20c, 1(3 coll)

test case *n.* 'a case setting a precedent for other cases involving the same question of law'

Du [=E] M, pl. *-s*, 20c (1 tech)

test drive *n.* 'a drive taken to determine the qualities of a motor vehicle with a view to regular use'

Gr <=E>/*test draiv* N, pl. *-s*, 1990s (1 tech, mod)

tester *n.* 1 'a person or thing that tests'

Whereas the noun and verb ↑*test* are almost universal, the derived noun is, unsurprisingly, less widespread; it is applied to persons who professionally test the quality of products (*Which*), and less often to apparatuses.

Ge [testa] M, pl. Ø, 1960s (3) **Nw** [tester] (3) ← *teste* v. **Fr** *tester* M, 1950s (1 tech, ban) < *testeur* **Sp** *tíster*/ <=E> M, end20c (1 tech_ELEC) **It** [tester] M, pl. Ø, 1940s (1 tech) = *prova ricevitore* **Rm** [tester] N, 20c, via Fr (3 tech) **Rs** *tester* M, pl. *-y*, mid20c (1 tech) **Po** [-er] M, end20c (1 jour) **Bg** *tester* M, pl. *-al-i*, end20c (1 tech) **Hu** - < *tesztelő*

texter* *n.* 'a writer of advertisements, lyrics, etc.'

Ge [teksta] M, pl. Ø, beg20c (3) **Rm** - < *textier*

text marker *n.* 'a felt pen in a fluorescent colour, used to mark certain passages in a written text'

Ge *Textmarker* [=E] M, end20c, 1970s (2) > *Leuchtmarker* **Du** *tekstmarker* [=E] C, pl. *-s* (2) = *accentueerstift* **Nw** - < rend *markørpenn, markørtusj* **Po** - < *marker* **Cr** [=E] (0) **Hu** - < trsl *szövegkiemelő*

thank you *phr.* 'a polite formula acknowledging a gift or service or an offer accepted or refused'

Rs *senkyu* end20c (1 coll, fac) **Bg** *tenkyu* mid20c (2 coll/fac)

think-tank *n.* 'a body of experts providing advice and ideas on specific national and commercial problems'

Ge [=E] M, pl. *-s*, 1980s (1 jour, rare) < rend *Denkfabrik* **Du** [=E] C, 1980s (1 jour, rare) < trsl *denktank* **Nw** [=E] M, pl. *-s*, 1970s (1 rare) = trsl *tenketank* **Sp** [=E] M, 1980s (1 jour) = *gabinete de estrategia* **It** [=E] M, pl. Ø, 1980s (1 jour, rare) **Rm** [sinktenk] N, end20c (1 jour, rare)

thinner *n.* 'a volatile liquid used to dilute paint etc.'

Ge - < trsl *Verdünner* **Du** [θɪnər/ tɪnər/sɪnər] C, 1980s (1 tech) **Nw** - < trsl *tynner* **Ic** - < trsl *þynnir* **Rm** *tiner* [tiner] N [U] 1980s (1 tech) **Fi** *tinneri* beg20c (3)

thomas slag* *n.* 'a fertilizer'

Ge *Thomasschlacke* beg20c (3 tech+5) **Du** *thomasslakkenmeel* (5) **Nw** *thomasslagg/thomasfosfat* 20c (1+5 tech) **Rs** *tomasshlak* M [U] mid20c (1 tech) **Po** *tomasyna* [tomasina] F [U] mid20c (1 tech) → *tomasynowski* adj. **Bg** *tomasshlak* M [U] mid20c, via Rs (3 tech) **Fi** *thomas*-cp¹ [=E] (3 tech)

thrill *n.* +1a 'an event etc. causing a nervous tremor of excitement in films etc.'

Ge [=E] M, pl. *-s*, 1980s (1 jour, rare) **Du** [=E] C, 1980s (1 jour, rare, you) **Nw** (0) **Ic** *þrill* [=E] N [U] mid20c (1 coll)

thriller *n.* 1 'a sensational story, film, etc.', +2 an exciting event'

Although the /θr-/ presents serious phonetic problems, this word is almost universally known, in contrast to the rare ↑*thrill*. This is no doubt a consequence of the frequent use of ∼ for films (advertisements and reviews). The word is recorded for the beginning of the twentieth century but became popular only from the 1950s.

Ge [srila] M, pl. Ø, mid20c, 1(2 coll) **Du** [=E/trɪlər] C, 1940s, 1(2) **Nw** [trɪler] M, pl. *-e*, 1940s, 1(2) **Ic**

ʒriller [θrɪl:er] M, pl. *-ar*, 1970s, 1(2 coll) = *tryllir* **Fr** <=E> M, 1930s, 1(1 coll) **Sp** <=E> M, pl. *-s*, 1970s, 1(1 tech) **It** [trɪller] M, pl. Ø, 1950s, 1(2) **Rm** [srɪlər/trɪler] N, 1970s, 1(1 jour, mod) **Rs** *trɪller* M, pl. *-y*, end20c, 1(1 jour, mod) **Po** [triler] M, end20c (1 tech) **Cr** *triler* M, pl. *-i*, mid20c, 1(1 tech) **Bg** *trɪlŭr* M, pl. *-al-i*, end20c (2 mod) **Fi** *trilleri* mid20c, 1(2) **Hu** [=E/tr-] pl. *-ek/Ø*, end20c, 1(2 jour, mod) **Gr** *thriler* N (2)

ticker *n.* (US) 3 'a tape machine'
 Ge [=E] M, pl. Ø, 1970s (1 jour) **Du** *tikker* [=E] C, 1940s (3) **Rs** *tɪker* M, pl. *-y*, end20c (1 tech)

ticket *n.* 1a 'a written or printed piece of paper or card entitling the holder to enter a place, participate in an event, travel by public transport, etc.', 2 'an official notification of a traffic offence etc.', +8 'a sum of money which must be paid to receive public health service or buy medicines', +9 'coupons for low price meals for employees of a firm or institution', +10 'a receipt for bettings' (horse racing)
 This word is competing with native equivalents and the earlier French *billet* (which is – or was – almost universal throughout Europe). In consequence, ~ started being used for air travel etc. and is now becoming more frequent in advertising and in English+English compounds (like ↑*job-ticket*).

Ge [=E] N, pl. *-s*, 19c, 1a(2 coll, mod); 1970s, 2(1 mod, rare) < *Fahr-/Flug-/Eintrittskarte* < 2: *Strafzettel* **Du** [=E/ticæt] N/C, beg20c (2) < *kaartje* **Nw** (0) < *billett* **Fr** <=E> M, 18c (2) → *ticson* **Sp** [tɪket/tɪke] M, pl. *-s*, beg20c, 1a(2) = *billete* → *tickero, tiquetero* n.; *ticar* v. **It** [tɪket] M, pl. Ø, 1970s, 1a, +8(2); 1980s, +9(2 tech); end19c, +10(2 tech) **Rm** *tichet* [tɪket] N, end 19c, via Fr, 1a(3) < *bilet* **Cr** *tiket* 20c, 1a(2) **Hu** *tikett* [tɪkett] pl. *-ek/Ø*, end19/beg20c (1 arch, rare) < *belép-tijegy/menetjegy* **Gr** *tikẹto* N, 19c, via Fr, 1a(1 arch)

tie-break *n.* 'a means of deciding a winner from competitors who have tied' (tennis, volleyball)
 Ge [=E] M/N, pl. *-s*, 1980s (1 tech) **Du** *tiebreak* [=E] C, 1970s (1 tech) **Nw** [=E] N/M, pl. Ø, 20c (1 tech) **Fr** M, 1970s (1 tech, ban) > *échange décisif/manche décisive/jeu décisif* **Sp** [=E/taibrek] M, end20c (1 tech) = *muerte súbita* **It** [tai brɛk] M, pl. Ø, 1980s (2 tech) **Rm** [=E] N, 20c (1 tech) **Rs** *taï-breïk* M [U] end20c (1 tech) **Po** M [U] end20c (1 tech) **Cr** [=E] M [U] end20c (1 tech) **Bg** *taïbrek* M, [U] mid20c (1 tech) **Fi** [=E] 1970s (1 tech) **Gr** <=E> [=E] N, pl. Ø/-s, end20c (1 tech)

tiffany *n./cp¹* +2 'a decorative art forming designs from pieces of coloured glass'
 (Named after L.C. Tiffany, 1848–1933)
 Ge [=E]/[tɪfani:] [U] 1930s? (2) **Nw** [=E] cp¹, 20c (1

tech) **Po** N [U] mid20c (1 tech)

tilt *n.* +6 'the end of a game in pin-ball machines caused by moving the apparatus too violently'
 Du [=E] C [U] 1970s (2) **Nw** [=E] M [U] 1970s (3 coll, obs) **Fr** [tilt] M, 1960s (2 mod) **It** [tilt] M [U] 1950s (3 tech, coll) **Fi** *tiltti* end20c (2)

time *n.* 5 'a point of time, esp. in hours and minutes', +20 'the moment at which half of the game is over' (footb.)
 Ic *tæm* [=E] N [U] mid/end20c, 5(1 sla); < +20: *hálfleik-ur* **Rs** *taïm* M, pl. *-y*, beg20c, +20(3) **Cr** (0)

time *v.* 1 'choose the time or occasion for', 2 'do at a chosen or correct time'
 Ge [taimən] 1970s, 1(1 coll) **Du** *timen* [tajmən] 1950s, 1(2) **Nw** [taime] 1950s, 1(2) → *timing* **Ic** [tʰai:ma] end20c (1 sla)

time *interj.* 'a signal to take up the game again' (esp. tennis)
 Du [=E] 1970s (1 tech) **Fr** [tajm] 20c (1 tech, ban) < *reprise* **Rm** *taïm/time* [=E] 1970s (1 tech, rare) **Rs** (0) **Bg** *taïm* 20c (1 tech) **Gr** [=E] 20c (1 tech)

timekeeper *n.* 1 'a person who records time, esp. of workers or in a game'
 It [=E] M, pl. Ø, 1960s (1 tech) < *cronometrista*

time-out *phr.* 1 'a brief intermission in a game', 2 (= time-off) 'time for recreation'
 As a sports term, this word is widely known only to people interested in volleyball, chess, etc.; the general absence of calques is remarkable.

Ge [=E] N, pl. *-s*, 1980s, 1(1 tech) < trsl *Auszeit* **Du** *time-out* [=E] C, 1980s (1 tech) **Nw** [=E] M, pl. *-er/-s*, 1(1 tech) **Ic** [=E] N [U] mid/end20c, 1(1 tech) **Fr** [=E] 1980s (1 tech, ban) > *arrêt de jeu* **Sp** - < trsl *tiemp (muerto)* **It** [taimaut] M, pl. Ø, 1960s, 1(2 tech) **Rm** *taim-aut/time-out* [=E] N, 1970s (1 tech, rare) **Rs** *taïm-aut* M, mid20c (2 tech) **Po** <=E> M, uninfl., end20c, 1(1 tech) **Cr** *tajmaut* M [U] end20c (1 tech) **Bg** *taïm-aut* M, pl. *-al-i*, mid20c, 1(1 tech) **Fi** - < trsl *aikalisä* **Gr** *taïm aut* N, 1980s (1 tech), 2(2)

timer *n.* 1 'a person or device that measures or records time taken', 2 'an automatic mechanism for activating a device etc. at a pre-set time', +3 'a diary'
 This word is particularly widespread as the term for a mechanism giving a signal, or starting a process, at a time previously selected; the fashionable use for 'diary' is infrequent and of uncertain permanence.

Ge [=E] M, pl. Ø, 1970s, 2(2 tech) +3(1 mod) **Du** [=E] C, 1980s, 2(2) **Nw** [=E] M, pl. *-e*, 1960s, 1(1 rare) 2(2 tech) **Fr** 2(0) **It** [=E] M, pl. Ø, 1930s, 2(3 tech) **Rm** [=E] N, end20c, 2(1 tech) **Rs** *taïmer* M, pl. *-y*, end20c, 2(1 tech) **Cr** *tajmer* M, pl. *-i*, mid20c, 2(2 tech) **Bg** *taïmer* M, pl. *-al-i*, end20c, 2(1>2 tech) **Fi** [=E/tai-meri] end20c, 2(2) < rend *ajastin*

time-sharing *n.* 1 'the operation of a computer system by several users for different operations at one time', 2 'the use of a holiday home at agreed times by several joint owners'

The two meanings are both technical and not too well known, although both concepts are likely to become more important in due course; the compound is supported by similar combinations in ↑*car-*~ and ↑*job-*~.

Ge [tɑimʃeːriŋ] N [U] 1980s (1 tech) **Du** [=E] C, 1980s (1 tech) **Nw** <=E>/*time-share* [=E] M [U] 1980s, 2(1 tech) **Fr** [tajmʃɛriŋ] M, 1970s, 1(1 obs, ban) < *partage du temps/temps partagé* **Sp** <=E> M [U] end

20c, 1,2(1 tech, rare) = 1: trsl *(trabajo en) tiempo compartido*; 2: *multipropiedad*/trsl *tiempo compartido* **It** [=E] M [U] 1980s, 1(1 tech) **Rm** (o) **Rs** *tɑimsher* M [U] 1990s, 2(1 mod/jour_ECON) → *-nyi* adj. **Cr** [=E] M [U] end20c, 1(1 tech) **Hu** [tɑimʃeːring] [U] 1980s, 1(1 tech) **Gr** <=E> [=E] N [U] 1990s, 1(1 tech) 2(1 mod) = 1: rend *dhiamerismos khronu*

timing *n.* 1 'the way an action or process is timed', +3 'the right time'

This word is mainly used as a fashionable expression for 'the right time' alternating with (rather than replacing) native terms. The spread from the Northwest into other parts of Europe is clearly reflected in the grid.

Ge [=E] N [U] 1960s, +3(1 coll) **Du** [=E] C [U] 1960s (2) **Nw** [=E/tɑimiŋ] M [U] 1960s, +3(2) **Ic** [tʰaːimiŋ(k)] F [U] end20c, 1(1 coll) **Fr** [tajmiŋ] M, beg20c (1 mod, ban) < *calendrier, minutage* **Sp** [tɑimin] M [U] end20c, 1(1 mod) **It** [tɑimiŋ(g)] M, pl. Ø, 1970s, 1(1 tech, jour) **Rm** [=E] N, end20c, 1(1 rare) **Rs** *tɑiming* M [U] 1995, +3(1 jour) **Po** [-nk] M [U] end20c, 1(1 tech) **Cr** *tɑjming* M [U] end20c, 1(1 tech) **Bg** *tɑiming* M [U] end20c, +3(1 tech_SPORT) **Gr** *tɑiming* N [U] 1990s, +3(1 coll)

timothy grass *n.* 'fodder grass' (named after Timothy Hanson who introduced it in Carolina c.1720)

Ge *Timotheegras* (o arch) **Du** *timot(h)eegras* [timoteːrɑs] N [U] end18c (name +5) **Nw** *timotei* [timutæi] M [U] 19c (3) **Ic** *tímóte(i)gras* N [U] end19c (1+5 arch) **Fr** *timothy* M, 19c (1 arch) < *fléole des prés* **Rm** *timoftică/timoftă/simoftică* timofti 19c (1 tech) **Rs** - < trsl *timofeevka* **Po** *tymotka* [timotka] F, mid20c (1 tech) **Fi** *timotei* 19c (5La) **Hu** <=E> [=E/timoti] [U] beg19c (1 tech, arch, rare) = trsl *Thimoteus füve*

tip *v.* 2 'name as the likely winner of a race or contest etc.', +4 'guess', +4a 'participate in the pools', +5 'empty the gravel from a cart, truck, etc.' (road work)
Ge *tippen* beg20c (3) **Du** *tippen* [tɪpə(n)] 1950s, 2,

+4(4 coll) **Nw** *tippe* [tɪpe] beg20c, 2, +4(3) → *tipping* M/F **Ic** *tippa* [tʰɪhpa] 1970s, via Da, +4,+4a(2 coll); beg20c, via Da, +5(2 tech, arch) **Cr** *tipovati* mid20c, 2,+4(3) **Hu** *tippel* [tɪppel] beg20c, 2, +4(3) → *-ö* n.

tip *n.* 1 'a small money present, esp. for a service given', 2 'a piece of private or special information', +4 'a set of members in a pools or lottery', +5 'the job of spreading the gravel' (road work)

This term was taken over with other words relating to horse-racing in the nineteenth century (a piece of advice as to the expected winner). The word quickly spread to other forms of gambling and to more general contexts – but remained restricted to the Germanic North-west. (Cf. ↑*tip* v. and ↑*tipper*).

Ge [=E] M, pl. *-s*, 1870s, 2(3 coll) **Du** [=E] C, beg20c, 2(3 coll) **Nw** *tips/tipp* [=E] N, pl. Ø, beg20c, 1,2(3) → *tipse* v.; *tippe* v. **Ic** *tips* [tʰɪ(h)ps/tʰɪfs] N [U] 1960s, 1,2(1 coll); *tipp* [tʰɪhp] N [U] 1970s, via Da, +4(2 coll); *tipp(ur)* M [U] beg20c, via Da, +5(2 tech, arch) → *tipsa* v. **Hu** *tipp* [tɪpp] pl. *-ek*, beg20c, 2, +4(3)

tipper* *n.* 1 'a participant in a pools or lottery', 2 'a man who spreads the gravel' (road work)

Ge [tɪpɐ] M, pl. Ø, 1950s, 1(3) **Nw** [tɪper] M, pl. *-e*, 1920s, 2(3) **Ic** *tippari* [tʰɪhparɪ] M, pl. *-ar*, 1970s, 1(2 coll); *tippmaður* M, beg20c, via Da, 2(2+5 tech, arch) **Hu** - < *tippelő*

tip-top *adj./n.* 'highest excellence; the very best'

Although recorded from the late nineteenth century onwards, this term became really popular (largely losing its 'Englishness') from the mid-twentieth century – but not spreading to Southern Europe in general.

Ge *tipptopp* adj., uninfl., end19c (3) **Du** *tip-top* [=E] adv./predic. adj., beg20c (3) **Nw** *tipp topp* [=E] beg20c (3) **Ic** *tipptopp* [tʰɪhp tʰɔhp] adj./cp¹, uninfl., end19c, via Da (2 coll) **Fr** (o) **Rm** *tip-top* [=E] adj. uninfl., beg20c, via Ge (3) **Rs** *tip-top* adj., uninfl., mid20c (1 coll) **Po** <=E> M, uninfl., beg20c (2) **Cr** *tip-top* beg20c (2) **Bg** *tip-top* adj., uninfl., mid20c (2 coll) **Hu** *tipp-topp* [=E] end19/beg20c (3)

tissue *n./cp*² 3 'a disposable piece of thin soft absorbent paper for wiping, drying, etc.'

Ge [tɪsuː] N/cp², pl. *-s*, 1970s (1 mod, rare) **Du** [=E] M, 1980s (2 mod) **Nw** (o) **Ic** <=E>/*tissjú* [=E] N, pl. Ø, mid20c (2 coll) **Sp** <=E>/*tisú* M, pl. *-s*, 1970s (1 tech, rare)

toast[1] (1) *n.* 1 'bread in slices browned on both sides by radiant heat'

This word has largely replaced native terms and paraphrases denoting 'roasted bread' – except where it is uncommon to toast bread. The corresponding verb is (expectedly) much rarer, as is the appliance (↑*toaster*).

Ge [to:st] **M**, pl. *-s/-e*, beg19c
(2)   **Du** [to:st] **C**, beg19c (3) <
toost   **Nw** [=E] **M** [U] mid19c
(1) < *ristet brød*   **Ic** - < *ristað
braunð*   **Fr** [tost] **M**, end19c
(2)   **Sp** [tost] end19c (o>1 jour)
< *tostada*   **It** [tɔst] **M** [U] 1930s

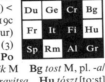

(3) = 1: *pane tostato*   **Rm** [tost] **N**, end20c (1)   **Rs** *tost*
M, pl. *-y*, mid20c (2)   **Po** *tost* [tost] **M**, mid20c (2) →
-owy adj.   **Cr** *tost* **M** [U] mid20c (2)   **Bg** *tost* **M** [U]/
pl. *-al-ove*, end20c (1 mod)   **Fi** <=E>/*tousti* mid20c
(2 coll) < *paahtoleipä*   **Hu** [to:st] [U] 20c (Ø>1 writ) <
pirítós   **Al** *tost* **M** [U] 1990s (1)   **Gr** *tost* **N**, mid
20c (2)

toast² (2)   *n.* 2b 'a salute, or a call to drink or an
instance of drinking in honour of someone'
    The historical relation to ↑*toast¹* is uncertain and
apparently not felt to be relevant in the borrowing
process; the word is less frequent than its homonym
– and the derived verb is found even more seldom.

Ge [to:st] **M**, pl. *-s*, end18c (2)
Du [to:st] **C**, beg19c (3) < *toost*
Nw [=E] **M**, pl. *-er*, mid19c (Ø) <
skål(tale)   **Fr** [tost] **M**, end19c
(2)   **Sp** [tost] mid19c (o>1 jour)
Rm [toast] **N**, beg19c, via Fr (3)
Rs *tost* **M**, pl. *-y*, mid19c (3)   **Po**
[toast] **M**, mid19c (3) → *toaścik* **M**   **Bg** *tost* **M**, pl. *-al
-ove*, beg20c, via Rs (3) > *nazdravitsa*   **Hu** *tószt* [to:st]
[U] 19c (3) < *pohárköszöntő* → *-oz* v.

toast¹ (1)   *v.* 'cook or brown by radiant heat'
Ge [to:stn] 1960s (2)   **Du** - < *roosteren*   **Nw** (o) <
riste   **Sp** *tostar* (5La)   **It** *tostare* (5La)   **Cr** *tostirati*
mid20c (2)   **Fi** *toustata* mid20c (2 coll)   **Hu** [=E] 19c
(Ø tech, arch)

toast² (2)   *v.* 4 'drink to the health or in honour of
someone'
Ge [to:stən] 19c (2 obs)   **Du** [to:stə(n)] 1940s
(3)   **Rm** *toasta* [toasta] mid19c, via Fr (3)   **Po** - <
wznieść toast   **Hu** *tósztoz* [to:stoz] 1930s (3) <
pohárköszöntőt mond

toaster   *n.* 'an electrical device for making toast'
    The electric appliance was invented in the USA in
1913, and the word apparently spread with the item,
but became widely used on (parts of) the Continent
only from the 1950s.

Ge [to:sta] **M**, pl. Ø, 1960s (2)
Du [=E] **C**, 1990s (1 jour, you) <
broodrooster   **Nw** (o) < *brødris-
ter*   **Fr** *toaster/toasteur* 1960s (1)
< *grille-pain*   **Sp** - < *tostadora*
It - < *tostapane*   **Rm** (o) = *prăji-
tor de pâine*   **Rs** *toster* **M**, pl. *-y*,

end20c (1 tech, mod)   **Po** *toster* [toster] **M**, end20c (1
tech) < *opiekacz*   **Cr** *toster* **M**, pl. *-i*, end20c (1
tech)   **Bg** *toster* **M**, pl. *-al-i*, mid20c (2)   **Gr** *tostiera*
F, mid20c (3)

toboggan   *n.* 1 'a long light narrow sledge', +2 'a
flyover, a chute'

    This term comes from Algonquian via Canadian
French, but gained international currency through
English mediation in the twentieth century. Note the
distribution of the non-English sense +2.
Ge [=E] **M**, pl. *-s*, beg20c, 1(Ø/1 tech, rare)   **Du** [=E/
to:bogan] **C**, beg20c, 1(2 tech)   **Nw** [=E] **M**, pl. *-er*,
beg20c, 1(1 tech)   **Fr** <=E> **M**, end19c (2)   **Sp** *to-
bogàn* **M**, beg20c, 1,+2(3)   **It** *toboga/taboga* [toboga/
ta-] **M**, pl. Ø, 1900s, 1(3)   **Rm** *tobogan* [tobogan] **N**,
mid20c, via Fr, +2(3)   **Rs** *toboggan* **M**, pl. *-y*, mid20c,
1(2 tech)   **Po** *tobogan* [tobogan] **M**, mid20c, 1(2)
Cr *tobogan* **M**, pl. *-i*, mid20c, 1(1 tech)   **Bg** *tobogan*
M, pl. *-al-i*, mid20c, 1(1 tech)   **Hu** *tobogán* [toboga:n]
pl. Ø, end19/beg20c, 1(3 tech); mid20c, +2(3 tech)
Gr *tobogan* **N**, 20c, 1(Ø/1 tech)

toddy   *n.* 1 'a drink of spirits with hot water and sugar
or spices', 2 'the sap of some kinds of palm, fermented
to produce arrack', +3 'cold grog without sugar'
    One of the numerous nineteenth-century English
drinks which is almost totally forgotten – in contrast
to the other mixed drink transmitted through Indian
English, ↑*punch*.
Ge [=E] **M** [U] 19c, 2,+3(Ø/1 arch)   **Du** 19c, 2(Ø);
[=E] **C**, pl. -'*s*, end18c, +3(1 arch)   **Nw** <=E>/*toddi*
[=E] **M** [U] mid19c, 1,2(2)   **Ic** *toddý* [tʰot:i] **N** [U]
mid19c, via Da, 1(2)   **Fr** <=E> **M**, 19c, 2(1 tech)   **It**
[tɔdi] **M**, pl. Ø, 19/20c, 2(1 arch)   **Sp** [todi] **M**, 2(1
tech, rare)   **It** [=E] **M** [U] 19c, 2(Ø/1 arch)   **Hu** [=E]
[U] 19c, 2(1 tech, arch)

toe-loop*   *n.* 'a jump in ice/roller skating'
Ge [tu:lup] **M**, pl. *-s*, 1980s (1 tech)   **Du** (Ø)   **Nw**
[tu:lup] **M**, pl. *-s*, end20c (1 tech)   **It** [tulup] **M**, pl. Ø,
end20c (1 tech)   **Rm** *tulup* [tulup] **N**, 1980s (1 tech)
Rs *tulup* **M**, pl. *-y*, mid20c (3 tech)   **Bg** *tulup* **M**, pl.
-al-i, mid20c (1 tech)   **Gr** *tulup* **N**, end20c (1 tech)

toffee   *n./cp²* 1 'a kind of firm and hard sweet softening when sucked or chewed, made by boiling sugar,
butter etc.'
    This word appears to have remained largely a for-
eignism (applied to imported sweets thus named) or
not to have been adopted at all; how successfully it
competes with native equivalents is difficult to determine.

Ge [=E] **N**, pl. *-s*, 1930s (1 tech)
Du [=E/tofe:] **C**, 1940s (2>3)   **Nw**
[=E] **M** [U] 20c (1 tech)   **Ic** *toffi*
[=E] *cp²*, mid20c (2) < *kara-
mella*   **Fr** (o)   **Sp** [tofi/tofe] **M**,
pl. *-s*, mid20c (1 tech)   **It** [tɔffi:]

M, pl. Ø, 1950s (1)   **Rs** *toffi* **N**,
uninfl., 1990s (1 tech)   **Po** *tofi* **M/N**, uninfl., mid20c
(3)   **Cr** [=E] **M** [U] mid20c (1)   **Bg** *tofi/*<=E> **N**, pl.
-ta, 1990s (1 mod)   **Fi** [tof:e:] beg20c (2)

token   *n.* 1 'a thing serving as a symbol, reminder etc.'
Du [to:kən] **N**, 1980 (1 tech)   **Nw** [=E] attrib., 1990s
(1 tech, rare)   **Rm** [=E] **N** [U] 1980s (1 tech)

tomahawk   *n.* 1 'a North American Indian axe with
a stone or iron head, esp. one used as a weapon'
    This term has remained a foreignism, but is widely

known through James Fenimore Cooper's novels and various travelogues. The early adoption is indicated by obvious spelling pronunciations pointing to borrowing from written sources.

Ge [t̪omahak] M, pl. *-s*, 19c (Ø)   **Du** (Ø)   **Nw** [=E] M, pl. *-er*, mid19c (Ø)   **Ic** *tómahok* N, pl. Ø, mid20c (Ø) < *striðsöxi*   **Fr** *tomawak*/*tomahawk* beg20c (0)   **Sp** <=E>/*tomawak* [=E] M, beg20c (Ø)   **It** [tomaho:k/t̪omawak] M [U] beg19c (Ø) < *ascia di guerra*   **Rm** [t̪omahok] N, 20c (1 tech/Ø)   **Rs** *tomagavk* M, pl. *-i*, end19c (Ø)   **Po** [tomahavk] M, beg20c (Ø)   **Cr** *t̪omahavk* M, pl. *-i*, beg20c (2)   **Bg** *tomakhavka* F, pl. *-ki*, beg20c (Ø)   **Hu** [t̪omahavk] pl. *-ok*/Ø, beg19c (Ø)   **Gr** *t̪omakhok* N, 20c (Ø)

Tommy   *n.* 1 'a nickname for a British private soldier', +2 'any Briton'

Ge [=E] M, pl. *-(ie)s*, beg20c, 1(1 arch) +2(2)   **Du** 1(Ø)   **Nw** [=E] M, 20c, 1(1 arch)   **Sp** [=E] M, pl. *-ies*, beg20c, 1(Ø)   **It** [t̪ommi] M, pl. Ø, 1900s, 1(1 arch)   **Rs** *Tommi* M, uninfl., beg20c, 1(Ø)   **Bg** *tomi* C, pl. *-ta*, mid20c, 1(Ø)   **Hu** <=E>/*tomi* [=E] pl. *-k*, end19/beg20c, 1(1 arch)

tom-tom   *n.* 2 'a tall drum beaten with the hands and used in jazz bands etc.'

Ge [=E] N, pl. *-s*, 20c (3)   **Nw** *tamtam* [t̪amtam] M, pl. *-er*, 20c (3 tech)   **Ic** [=E] N, end20c (1 tech)   **Fr** (5)   **It** *tam tam* (5)   **Rm** *tam-tam* (5Fr)   **Rs** *tamt̪am* pl. *-y*, end20c (1 tech/5Fr)   **Po** *tam-tam* (5Ind)   **Cr** (0)   **Bg** *tamt̪am* (5Fr)   **Hu** *tamtam* [t̪amtam] pl. Ø, 20c (3)   **Gr** *tamt̪am* N, 20c (5Fr)

toner   *n.* 1 'a chemical bath for toning a photographic print', 2 'a powder used in xerographic copying processes'

Ge [t̪o:na] M [U] 1970s, 2(1 tech)   **Du** [t̪o:nər] C, 1980s, 2(1 tech)   **Nw** [t̪u:ner] M, pl. *-e*, 1980s, 2(3)   **Ic** [=E] M [U] end20c, 2(1 tech)   **Fr** M, 1980s, 2(1 tech, ban) < *encre*   **Sp** [t̪oner] M, pl. *-Ø*, end20c, 2(1 tech <2 tech)   **It** [t̪oner] M, pl. Ø, 1980s, 2(2 tech)   **Rm** [t̪onər] N, pl. *-e*, 1970s, 2(1 tech)   **Rs** *t̪oner* M [U] end20c, 2(1 tech)   **Po** [toner] M, end20c (1 mod)   **Cr** [t̪oner] M [U] end20c, 2(1 tech)   **Bg** *t̪oner* M [U] end20c, 2(1 tech)   **Hu** [t̪o:ner] M [U] 1970s, 2(1 tech >2 tech)   **Gr** <=E>/*t̪oner* N, end20c, 2(1 tech) = *melani se skoni*

tonic   *n.* +1a 'an invigorating cosmetic fluid', 2 'anything serving to invigorate', 3 'tonic water'

Ge [=E] N [U] 1960s, +1a,3(1 mod)   **Du** [=E] C, 1950s, 3(2)   **Nw** [=E] M [U] 1960s, +1a(1 tech); mid20c, 3(2)   **Ic** *t̪ónik* [t̪hou:nɪk] N [U] mid20c, +1a(1), 3(2) < +1a: rend *andlitsvatn*   **Fr** M, 1970s, 3(1 mod)   **Sp** *t̪ónico* +1a(4); (*agua*) *t̪ónica* 3(3)   **It** [t̪onik] M [U] 1960s, 3(1) < 1a: *tonico*; 3: *acqua tonica*   **Rm** [t̪onik] N, 1970s, via Fr, +1a(3) < 3: *apǎ tonicǎ*   **Rs** *t̪onik* M [U] end20c (2 mod)   **Po** *tonik* M, end20c, +1a,3(2)   **Cr** *t̪onik* M [U] end20c, 3(3)   **Bg** *t̪onik* M, pl. *-al-nitsi*, 1970s, 2,3(2)   **Fi** [=E] mid20c, 3(2)   **Hu** <=E>/*tonik* [t̪onik] pl. Ø, 1970s, +1a(5Gr/La) 3(3)   **Al** *tonik* M, pl. *-ë*, +1a,3(1 you)   **Gr** *t̪onik* N [U] end20c, 3(2)

top[1] (1)   *n.* 2a 'the highest rank or place', 4a 'a (sleeveless) blouse, jumper', +14 'the charts' (music)

Ge [=E] N/M, pl. *-s*, 1970s, 4a(1 tech)   **Du** [=E] C, pl. *-en*, 1910s, 2a(5); *topje* 1970s, 4a(4)   **Nw** *topp* [=E] M, pl. *-er* (4)   **Ic** *toppur* [t̪hɔhpɣr] M, pl. *-ar*, 2a(5); end20c, 4a(4 mod); *topp-* cp[1], 1960s, +14(4)   **Sp** M, pl. *-s*, 1990s (2)   **It** [t̪ɔp] M [U]/pl. Ø, 1960s, 2a(2 tech, mod) 4a(2 tech)   **Rm** [=E] N, pl. *-uri*, 1970s, 2a,+14(2 jour, mod)   **Rs** *top* M, pl. *-y*, end20c, 4a(1 mod)   **Po** M, end20c, 2a,+14(2 you); *topka* F, end20c, 4a(1 mod)   **Cr** *top* M, end20c, 2a(2) 4a(1)   **Fi** *toppi* mid20c, 4a(2)   **Hu** [=E] [U] end20c, 2a(1 tech COMPUT); 1990s, 4a(2 mod); 1970s, +14(1 writ, mod)   **Al** *top* M [U] 1990s, 2a,+14(1)   **Gr** *top* N, 4a(2); usu. pl., +14(1 tech)

top[2] (2)   *n.* 10 'a platform round the head of each of the lower masts of a sailing ship' (naut.)

Ge *Topp* M, pl. *-s/-e*, 19c (3 tech)   **Du** (5)   **Nw** (5)   **Rs** *top* M, pl. *-y*, 19c (1 tech)   **Po** M, mid20c (1 tech)   **Cr** (0)   **Bg** *top* M, pl. *-al-ove*, beg20c (1 tech)

top   *adj.*/*cp*[1] 2 'highest in degree or importance'

Ge [=E] uninfl., 1970s (3)   **Du** [=E] adj./cp[1], 1970s (4) → *topper* n.   **Nw** *topp* [=E] beg20c (4)   **Ic** *topp-* [t̪hɔhp] cp[1], mid/end20c (3 coll)   **Fr** adj./cp[1], uninfl., mid20c (1)   **Sp** [top] cp[1], 1970s   **It** [t̪ɔp] cp[1], 1960s (2)   **Rm** [=E] cp[1], 1980s (1 jour)   **Rs** *top* cp[1], 1990s (1 jour)   **Po** *top* uninfl., end20c (2 coll, jour)   **Cr** [=E] end20c (2)   **Bg** *top* cp[1], 1990s (2 jour)   **Hu** [=E] cp[1], 1970s (3)   **Al** *top* 1990s (1 mod)   **Gr** *top* adj./cp[1], end20c (2 coll)

top class*   *n.* 'the highest class offered to passengers in planes etc.'

Du [=E] C [U] end20c (1 tech)   **It** [t̪ɔp klas] F, pl. Ø, 1980s (1 tech)

top-down   *adj.* 1 'proceeding from the general to the particular, or from the top downwards'

Ge [=E] uninfl., 1980s (1 tech, rare)   **Du** [=E] end20c (1 tech)   **Nw** [=E] cp[1], end20c (1 tech)   **It** [t̪ɔp daun] adj./adv., uninfl., 1980s (1 tech)   **Fi** [=E] uninfl., adj./adv., 1980s (1 tech)

topfit*   *adj.* 'in excellent physical or mental condition'

Ge [=E] 1960s (2)   **Du** [=E] 1980s (3>2)

topless*   *n.* +2a 'a bathing costume without a top'

This word is variously used as an adjective or as a noun for a 'topless swimming-suit'. The idea is mainly 'Western', so that the absence of the loanword can mean that the concept is expressed by native equivalents (trsl in Norwegian and remarkably free in German, French) – or that there is no need for the word, at least for local use; *monokini* is also marginally used.

Nw - < trsl *toppløs (badedrakt)*   **Sp** [toples/tople̞s] M, 1970s (2)   **It** [t̪ɔples] M, pl. Ø, 1960s (2)   **Rm** *toples*/*-less* [=E] F [U] 1990s (1 jour, mod)   **Rs** *t̪oples* M, pl. *-y*, end20c (1 mod) < creat *kupal'nyi kostyum bez verkha*   **Po** *toples*/<=E> [-les] M, mid20c (2)   **Cr** *t̪oples* M, pl. *-i*, mid20c (2)   **Bg** - < *monokini*   **Hu** [t̪ople̞ss] pl. Ø, end20c (2 mod)   **Gr** *t̪oples* N, end20c (1 jour, mod)

topless   *adj.* 2b 'bare-breasted'
Ge (o) < creat *oben ohne* **Du**
[=E] 1970s (2)   **Nw** (o) < trsl
toppløs   **Ic** *topplaus* [tʰɔhplœys]
1970s (4)   **Fr** (o) < creat *sein*
nu   **It** - < creat *a seno nudo* **Sp**
[toples/toplḙs] 1970s (2)   **Rm** *to-*
plesl-less [=E] uninfl., 1990s (1
jour, mod)   **Rs** (o)   **Po** *toples*/<=E> [-les] uninfl.,
mid20c (2)   **Cr** *toples* mid20c (2)   **Bg** *toples* uninfl.,
end20c (1 mod, jour)   **Fi** [=E] end20c (1) < trsl *yläo-*
saton   **Hu** [topless] pl. Ø, end20c (2 mod)   **Gr** *toples*
uninfl., 1960s (2) = creat *ghymnostithi*

top management   *n.* 'the highest ranking members
of a board of directors or the people in charge of
running a business, regarded collectively'
Ge [=E] N, 1980s? (2 tech)   **Du** [=E] N [U] (1
tech)   **Nw** - < rend *toppledelse*   **It** [tɔp mḙnidʒment]
M, pl. Ø, 1980s (1 tech)   **Bg** *top mḙnidzhmǔnt* M [U]
1990s (1 tech)

top manager*   *n.* 'a member of the board of directors of a business'
Ge [=E] N, 1980s? (2 tech)   **Du** *topmanager* [=E] C,
pl. *-s*, end20c (2 tech)   **It** [top mḙnadʒer/man-] M, pl.
Ø, 1980s (1 tech)   **Bg** *top mḙnidzhǔr* M, pl. *-ri*, 1990s
(2 tech)

topmodel*   *n.* 'a female model for fashion shows
etc.'
Ge [=E] N, pl. *-s*, 1970s (2 tech)   **Nw** *toppmodell* 20c
(4) < *supermodell*   **Ic** *toppmódel* [tʰɔhpmou:tel] N, pl.
Ø, end20c (2)   **Fr** <=E>/*top-modèle* M, 1990s (1
mod)   **Sp** *top model* [top mode̯l] M/F, 1990s (2 tech)
It [topmode̯l] F, pl. Ø, 1980s (2 tech, jour)   **Rm** [top-
mode̯l] N, pl. *-e*, 1990s (1 mod)   **Rs** *topmode̯l'* F, pl. *-i*,
end20c (1 tech)   **Po** *topmodelka* F, end20c
(2 coll)   **Cr** (o)   **Bg** *topmodel* M, pl. *-al-i*, end20c (2
mod) → *-ka* F   **Hu** [topmode̯l] pl. *-ek*, end20c (2
mod)   **Al** *topmodel* M, pl. *-e*, end20c (1 mod)   **Gr**
topmode̯l N, pl. *-s*, 1980s (2 mod)

topper   *n.* +4 'a short ladies' jacket'
Ge [=E] M, pl. Ø, 1960s (1 tech, obs)   **Du** [=E] C,
1940s (1 rare, obs)

top rate   *n.* 'the highest interest rates which banks
apply to their clients' (banking)
Du [=E] C, pl. *-s*, end20c (1 tech)   **It** [=E] M, pl. Ø,
1980s (1 tech)

topsail   *n.* +3 'a kind of sail'
Ge - < *Toppsegel* (5)   **Du** - < *topzeil* (5)   **Nw** (o) <
toppseil (5)   **Ic** - < trsl *toppsegl*   **Rs** *topsel'* M, pl. *-i*,
mid20c (1 tech/5Da)   **Po** *topsel* [topsel] M, mid20c (1
tech)   **Cr** (o)   **Bg** *topsel* M, pl. *-al-i*, 20c, via Rs (3
tech)

top secret   *adj.* 'of the highest secrecy'
This word is largely colloquial and journalese, and
restricted to Western languages; native equivalents are
available in all languages and preferred in neutral use.
Ge [=E] 1960s (1 coll)   **Du** [=E] 1970s (2)   **Nw** [=E]
1950s (1)   **Ic** [=E] uninfl., end20c (o)   **Fr** [tɔp sǝkrɛ]
1960s (1+5)   **Sp** [=E/top sḙkret] 1960s (1>2)   **It** [tɔp

sḙkrit/-kret] uninfl., 1960s (2 coll,
jour)   **Rm** [topsekret] 1990s (1
jour)   **Rs** (o)   **Po** - < *największy*
sekret   **Cr** (o)   **Bg** - < trsl
svrŭkh sekretno   **Hu** [top si:kret]
end20c (1>2)   **Al** *top sekret*
1970s (1 you)   **Gr** (o)

topspin   *n.* 'a fast forward spinning motion imparted
to a ball in (table) tennis by hitting it upward and
forward'
Ge [=E] M [U] 1980s (1 tech, rare)   **Du** [=E] C [U]
1950s (1 tech)   **Nw** *toppspinn* (4)   **Ic** [=E] end20c (1
tech)   **Sp** [=E] M [U] end20c (1 tech, rare) < *golpe*
liftado   **It** [tɔpspin] M, pl. Ø, mid20c (1 tech)   **Rm**
<=E>/*topsin* [tops(p)in] N [U] 1960s (1 tech)   **Rs** (o)
Cr [=E] M [U] end20c (1 tech)   **Bg** *topspin* M [U]
end20c (1 tech)

top ten   *n.* 1 'the first ten records in the charts', +2 'the
ten best players in the world' (tennis)
Ge *Top Ten* pl., 1980s, 1(1 tech, jour)   **Du** *top-tien*
pl., end20c, 1(3+5)   **Nw** [=E] 1960s (1 tech)   **Ic** *topp*
tíu uninfl., 1960s, 1(3+5)   **Sp** M, end20c (1 jour)   **It**
[=E] M/F, pl., end20c, +2(1 jour)   **Rm** (o)   **Rs** *top*
ten, end20c (1 tech, jour)   **Po** - < *pierwszych dziesięciu*
Cr - < rend *top-lista*   **Bg** *top ten* end20c, 1(1 jour) <
trsl *top deset*   **Fi** [=E] 20c, 1(1 you)   **Hu** <=E>/*top*
10 [U] end20c (1 writ, jour)   **Al** *topten* 1992, 1(you)
Gr *top ten* pl., end20c (1 tech, you)

top weight*   *n.* 1 'the highest weight assigned to a
horse in a handicap race', 2 'the horse'
It [=E] M, pl. Ø, 1900s (1 tech)

Tory   *n.* 2 'a member of the Conservative Party'
Although the political persuasions of the British
Tories are well-known in Continental Europe, the
term does not seem to have been applied to local
conditions (except for a few metaphorical cases) and
is therefore generally classified as a foreignism.
Ge [to:ri] M, pl. *-(ie)s*, 19c (Ø)   **Du** (Ø)   **Nw** [=E]
M, pl. *-er/-ies*, mid19c (Ø)   **Fr** (Ø)   **Sp** [tori] M, pl.
-ies, mid19c (Ø)   **It** [tɔri] M, pl. Ø/-s, 18c (Ø)   **Rm**
[=E] M [U] beg20c (1)   **Rs** *tori* M, uninfl., pl., mid19c
(Ø)   **Po** *torys* [toris] M, mid19c (Ø)   **Cr** *tori* M, 19c
(Ø) → *-jevac* M   **Bg** *tori* M, pl. Ø, end19c (Ø)   **Fi**
[=E] 19c (Ø)   **Hu** *tory* [=E] pl. *-k*, beg19c (Ø)   **Gr**
(Ø)

total loss*   *n.* 'a heavily damaged car'
Du [total lɔs] 1970s (2)

touch   *n.* 4a 'a musician's manner of playing keys or
strings', 4c 'an artist's or writer's style of workman-
ship, writing, etc.', 5a 'a distinguishing quality or trait,
style, a characteristic feature', 5b 'a special skill or
proficiency', 10 'the part of the field outside the side
limits' (footb.)
This fashionable word is certainly one of the 'un-
necessary' words in modish or facetious uses; note the
survival (?) of an older football term in two Balkanic
languages.
Ge [tatʃ] M [U] 1960s, 5a(1 jour, mod)   **Du** [=E] C,
pl. *-es*, 1970s, 5a,10(1 mod/obs) **Nw** [tøtʃ] M/N, pl. Ø,

5a(2) **Ic** [=E] N [U] 1970s,
4a,4c, 5b(1 sla) **Fr** 5a(o) **Sp**
5a(o) **Rm** - < *tuşă* (5Fr) **Bg**
tŭch M [U]/pl. *-al-ove*, beg20c,
10(2 tech) **Hu** *taccs* [tatʃ] [U]
19c, 10(3) < *partvonal* **Gr** *tats*
N [U] end20c, 5a(1 mod, jour,
coll)

touchy *adj.* 1 'apt to take offence, oversensitive'
Nw [=E] end20c (1 coll) **Ic** [=E] uninfl., 1970s (1 sla)

tough *adj.* 2 'able to endure; persistent (in negotia-
tions)' (of persons), 3 'difficult', +6 'cool, bold,
stately'
Another term which is popular in informal youth
language – but restricted to the Germanic north-west.
Note that meanings in loanwords are more restricted
(and more informal) than in most
English usages.
Ge *tough/taff* [taf] 1980s, 2(1 coll)
Du [=E] 1990s, 2(1 mod) **Nw**
toff [tøf] mid20c (3) → *tøffe* v.
Ic *töffe* [tʰœf:] uninfl., beg20c (2
coll) → *töffari* M

tourism *n.* 'the organization and operation of (esp.
foreign) holidays, esp. as a commercial enterprise'
Ge *Tourismus* (3/5La) **Du** *toerisme* 19c (3) **Nw**
turisme [tʉrisme] M [U] 1930s (3) → *turist* M **Fr**
tourisme M, 19c (3) **Sp** *turismo* M, end19c
(3) **Rm** *turism* (5) **Bg** *turizŭm* M [U] end19c, via
Fr (2) **Fi** *turismi* 20c (3) **Hu** *turizmus* [tʉrizmuʃ]
[U] 20c (3/5Fr) **Al** *turizëm* M, pl. *-e*, end19c
(3) **Gr** *turismos* M, 20c (5Fr)

tourist *n.* 1 'a person making a visit or a tour as a
holiday; a traveller, esp. abroad'
Although this word is clearly from English (first
recorded in 1780), a fact supported by its spread
through Britons travelling the Continent in the nineteenth century, the form is ambiguous as to English or
French provenance – or mediation.
Ge [tuːrist] M, pl. *-en*, 19c, via Fr (3) → *-istik* F; *-ismus*
M; *-istisch* adj. **Du** *toerist* [tuːrist] C, end19c (3) →
toerisme n.; *toeristisch* adj. **Nw** *turist* [tʉrist] M, pl.
-er, 19c (3) **Ic** *túristi* [tʰuːrɪstɪ] M, pl. *-ar*, end19c (5Fr)
< *ferðamaður* **Fr** *touriste* [turist] M/F, beg19c (3) →
tourisme n.; *touristique* adj. **Sp** *turista* M/F, end 19c
(3) → *turístico* **It** *turista* [turista] M/F, pl. *-i/-e*,
beg19c, via Fr (3) → *turismo* M; *turistico* adj. **Rm**
turist,-ă [turist, -ə] M/F, mid19c, via Fr (3) → *-ism* N;
-istic adj. **Rs** *turist* M, pl. *-y*, beg20c (3) → *-ka* F;
-icheskii adj.; *turizm* M **Po** (5Fr) **Cr** *turist* M, pl. *-i*,
beg20c (3) **Bg** *turist*, M, pl. *-i*, beg20c (2) → *-icheski*
adj.; *-ka* F; *turizŭm* M **Fi** *turisti* 20c(3) **Hu** *turista*
[tuːriʃta] pl. *-ák*, 19c, via Ge(3) **Al** *turist* M, pl. *-a*,
beg20c (3) **Gr** *turistas* M, *turistria* F, 20c, via Fr(3)

tower *n.* +2a 'a control tower on an airport'
Ge [=E] M, pl. Ø, 1970s (1 mod) < *Kontrollturm* **Nw**
(o) < *tårn* **Hu** [tauer] pl. Ø, 20c (1 tech) < *(irányító)-
torony*

town *n.* 1a 'an urban area with a name, defined

boundaries, and local government, being larger than
a village and usu. not created a city', 2b 'the central
business or shopping area in a neighbourhood'
Ic [=E] N, 1970s (1 sla)

tracer *n.* 3 'an artificially produced radioactive iso-
tope capable of being followed through the body by
the radiation it produces'
This word illustrates the impact of English/Amer-
ican technology in modern medicine which does not
yet extend to the east of Europe in general – and the
adaptation of Romance languages 'reclaiming' a word
formed on a Romance base.
Ge [treːsa] M, pl. Ø, 1980s (1 tech) **Du** [treːsər] C,
1950s (1 tech) **Nw** [=E] M, pl. *-e*, 1960s (1 tech) **Fr**
- < trsl *traceur* **Sp** - < *trazador* **Rm** - < *trasor* **Rs**
(o) **Cr** [trejser] M [U] mid20c (1 tech)

track *n.* 4a 'a racecourse for horses, dogs, etc.', 4b 'a
section of tape or disk', 5b 'a section of a gramophone
record, cassette tape, compact disc, etc., containing
one song', 6b 'the path travelled by a ship, aircraft,
etc.'
Ge [trak/=E] M, pl. *-s*, beg20c, 6b(1 rare); 1960s, 4a(1
tech, rare); 1970s, 5b(1 tech, you) **Du** [=E] C, 1970s,
5b(1 mod/tech); *trek* 6b(5) **Nw** (o) **Rs** *trek* M, pl.
-i, beg20c, 4a(1 tech) **Po** [-e-] M, beg20c, 4a(1 tech)
Cr *trek* M, pl. *-ovi*, beg20c, 4a(1 tech) **Bg** *trek* M, pl.
-al-ove, 1990s, 4b(1 tech)

tracking *n.* 1 'the formation of a conducting path
over the surface of an insulating material' (electr.)
Du [=E] C [U] end20c (1 tech) **Fr** (o ban) < *aligne-
ment des pales* **It** [trɛkiŋ(g)] M, pl. Ø (1 tech)

trade mark *n.* 1 'a device, word, or words, secured
by legal registration or established by use as representing a company, product, etc.', 2 'a distinctive characteristic etc., a typical feature, a hallmark'
This term was widespread in Europe during the late
nineteenth century and the beginning of the twentieth
century, as a consequence of English predominance in
trade and industry, but was replaced by calques in
most languages quite soon. The metaphorical extension to include general features (e.g. of a person's
character) is not yet well established.
Ge [treːtmark] F/N [U] end19c,
1(1 tech, obs); 1980s, 2(1 jour) <
1: *Warenzeichen* **Du** [=E] N,
beg20c (1 tech) = *handelsmerk*
Nw (o) < *varemerke* **Ic** - < 1:
vörumerki **Fr** - < rend (*nom de*)
marque **Sp** <=E> M, end20c,

1(o> 1 tech) < trsl *marca comercial*; rend *marca
registrada* **It** [trɛdmark/treid mark] M, pl. Ø,
end19c, 1(1 tech) < rend *marchio di fabbrica* **Rm**
[=E] N, 20c, 1(1 tech) < *marcă comercială* **Rs** *treīd
mark* M, pl. *-i*, mid20c, 1(1 tech) **Po** [-t mark] M,
uninfl., beg20c, 1(1 tech) **Cr** [trejdmark] M [U]
beg20c, 1(1 tech) **Bg** - < rend *zapazena marka* **Fi**
- < trsl *kauppamerkki* **Hu** [treːdmaːrk] pl. Ø, end19c
(1 arch) < *védjegy* **Gr** <=E> [=E] N, 20c, 1(o
tech)

trailer *n.* 1a 'the rear section of an articulated lorry', 1c 'a platform for transporting a boat etc.', 1d 'a caravan', +1e 'a single-axle carrier for horses, etc.', 2 'a series of brief extracts from a film used to advertise it in advance'

English usage is divided between British English and American English; it appears significant for the dominance of British English on the Continent that the 'American' sense 'caravan' has a very marginal distribution (in Icelandic slang only).

Ge [trɛːla] M, pl. Ø, 1980s, 1c, +1e(1 tech, rare) 2(1 tech)   **Du** [=E] C, 1950s, 2(1 tech); 1940s, 1a,c(1 tech)   **Nw** [=E/trailer] M, pl. *-e*, mid20c, 1a(3) 2(1 tech)   **Ic** [=E] M, pl. *-ar*, 1970s, 1d(1 coll) 2(1 tech) < creat 1d: *hjólhýsi*   **Sp** [trailer] M, pl. *-s*, 1950s, 1a,2(2)   **It** [trailer] M, pl. Ø, 1940s, 1c, +1e,2(1 tech)   **Rm** *trailă/ treiler* [trajlə(r)/trejler] N, pl. *-e*, 1970s, 1a,1c (2,3 tech)   **Rs** *trejler* M, pl. *-y*, end20c, 1c(2)   **Cr** *trejler* M, pl. *-i*, end20c, 1a(1 tech)   **Fi** *traileri* [treileri] 1980s, 1c(2)   **Hu** *tréler* [trɛːler] pl. Ø, 1960s, 1a,c(1 tech, arch) < *utánfutó*   **Gr** *trejler* N, 1990s, 1c(1 tech) 2(2 mod, jour)

train *v.* 2 (trans., intrs.) 'teach/undergo physical exercise'

Ge *trainieren* [trɛːniːrən] 19c (3)   **Du** *trainen* [trɛːinə(n)] 19c (3)   **Nw** *trene* [trɛːne] 19c (3)   **Sp** - < *entrenar*   **Rm** - < *antrena*   **Rs** *trenirovat'* → *trenirovat'sya*; *trenirovka* F   **Po** *trenować* [trenovatç] mid19c (3) → *roz-* v.; *trenowanie* N,   **Cr** *trenirati* beg20c (3)   **Bg** *treniram* beg20c (3) → *-nirovka* F; *-nirovüchen* adj.   **Fi** *treenata* beg20c (3 coll)   **Hu** *tréningez* [trɛːningez] 19c (3); *treníroz* [treniːroz] via Ge, 19c (3)

trainee *n.* +1a 'a student trained in a business firm after graduating from university'

Ge [treːniː] M, pl. *-s*, 1970s (1 tech)   **Du** [=E] C, 1970s (1 tech)   **Nw** [=E] M, pl. *-s*, 1970s (1 tech)

trainer *n.* +2a 'a person who trains sportsmen'

This word, as applied to sports coaches, is widespread esp. in Germanic and Slavic languages, whereas Romance languages prefer calques coined on a formally similar basis. In the well-established family of loanwords on *train-* the individual items appear to support each other.

Ge [treːna] M, pl. Ø, mid19c (2)   **Du** [treːnər] C, beg20c (2) → *trainster*   **Nw** *trener* [treːner] M, pl. *-e*, end19c (3) → *trene* v.   **Fr** (0 ban) < *entraîneur*   **Sp** (0) < *entrenador*   **It** [trainer/trejner] M, pl. Ø, end19c (2 tech) < *allenatore*, ↑*coach*   **Rm** [=E] M, 1970s (0/1 rare) < *antrenor*   **Rs** *trener* M, pl. *-y*, mid19c (3) → *-stvo* N; *-skiĭ* adj.   **Po** *trener* [trener] M, mid19c (3) → *-ka* F; *-stwo* N [U]; *-ski* adj.   **Cr** *trener* M, pl. *-i*, end19c (3) → *-ka*, F; *-ski* adj.   **Bg** *trenyor* M, pl. *-i*, beg20c (3) → *-ka* F; *-ski* adj.; *-stvam* v.   **Hu** *tréner* [treːner] pl. *-ek*, 19c (3) < *edző*   **Al** *trajner* M, pl. *-ë*, beg20c (3)

training *n.* 1 'the act or process of teaching or learn-

ing a skill, discipline, etc.', 2 'the state of being physically fit as a result of undergoing physical training', +3 'a track suit'

This word is even more widespread, but note the reluctant adoption in the South (in French and Romanian it is used only in a typical shortening of a compound).

Ge [treːniŋ] N [U] mid19c, 1(2); *Trainingsanzug* cp[1]/M, 20c, +3 (3+5)   **Du** [treːniŋg] C, beg20c, 1(2) → *trainen* v.   **Nw** *trening* [treːniŋ] M, pl. *-er*, end19c, 1(3) ← *trene* v.,   **Fr** [treniŋ] M, mid19c, 1(1 tech, ban) +3(1) < 1: *entraînement*   **Sp** [treiniŋ] M [U] end20c, 1,2(1 jour) < 1: *entrenamiento*   **It** [treiniŋ(g)/treniŋ(g)] M [U] 1970s, 1(2) < *allenamento*   **Rm** *trening* [trening] N, pl. *-uri*, mid20c, +3(3)   **Rs** *trening* [-nk] M [U] end20c, 1(2)   **Po** *trening* [trenink] M, beg20c, 1(3) → *re-* M, *-owy* adj.   **Cr** *trening* M, pl. *-zi*, beg20c, 1(3)   **Bg** *trening* M [U] end20c, 1(1 tech_{PSYCHOL}, mod); mid20c, 2(2)   **Fi** *treeni* beg20c, 1(3)   **Hu** *tréning* [treːniŋ] pl. Ø, 19c, 1,2(3) < 1,2: *edzés*; +3: trsl *-ruha*   **Al** *trening* M, pl. *-e*, beg20c, 1,2(3) → *tréningez*

tram *n.* 1 'an electrically powered passenger vehicle running on rails laid in a public road' (cf. ↑*tramway*)

First borrowed in the full form ↑*tramway*, the word was shortened to *tram* in various languages, some of which retain both the short and long forms. Note the general absence of calques, in conspicuous contrast to *railway*.

Ge [tram] F/N, pl. *-s*, mid19c (1 reg/obs) < *Straßenbahn*   **Du** *tram/trem* [=E] C, pl. *-s/-men*, mid19c (3) → *tremmen/trammen* v.   **Nw** (0)   **Fr** *tram/tramway* M, end19c (2) → *traminot*   **It** [tram] M, pl. Ø, mid19c (3)   **Rm** - < *tramvai*   **Rs** *metrotram* cp[1], pl. *-y*, end20c (1 tech/mod)   **Cr** [tram] M, beg20c (3)   **Hu** [tram] M, pl. Ø, 19c (1 rare) < *villamos*   **Gr** *tram* N, 19/ beg20c, via Fr (2)

tramp *v.* +5 'hitchhike'

Ge [trempən] 1950s (3) → *-er* M   **Du** - < ↑*liften*   **Nw** *trampe* [trampe] mid20c (1 obs)   **Fr** (0)   **Po** (0)

tramp *n.* 1 'an itinerant vagrant or beggar', 6 'an ocean tramp, a merchant ship, esp. a steamer, running on no regular line or route'

Ge [tremp] M, pl. *-s*, 1940s, 1(Ø); cp[1], beg20c, 6(1 tech)   **Du** [=E] C, 1940s, 1(2) 6(1 tech)   **Nw** [=E/tramp] M, pl. *-er*, mid20c, 1(Ø) 6(1 tech)   **Fr** [trămp] M, 20c, 6(1 tech)   **Sp** [tramp] M, 1980s, 6(1 tech, rare)   **It** [tremp] M, pl. Ø, mid20c, 6(1 tech)   **Rm** [tramp] M, pl. *-e/uri*, 1950s, 6(1 tech)   **Po** [tramp] M, mid20c, 1(2) 6(1 tech) → *-ek* M; *-ka* F; *-owy* adj.   **Cr** *tramp* M, pl. *-ovi*, mid20c, 1(1 tech)   **Bg** *tramp* M, pl. *-al-ove*, mid20c,

6(1 tech) → *-ov* adj. **Fi** *tramppi* beg20c, 6(3) **Hu** [tremp] pl. *-ek*, 20c, 1(Ø) **Al** - < *tramper*

tramping   *n.* 1b 'going on foot, esp. a distance', +7 'tramp shipping'

Nw [trampiŋ] M/F [U] mid20c, 1b(1 obs) **Fr** [trãm-piŋ] M, 20c, +7(1 tech, ban) > *transport maritime à la demande* **Rm** [tramping] N [U] 1950s, +7(1 tech) **Po** [-a-] M, end20c, 1b(1 mod) **Bg** - < +7: *trampovo plavane* **Fi** *trampata* beg20c, 1b(3)

tramway   *n.* 1b 'a tramcar system', +1c 'a tramcar' (cf. ↑*tram*)

Ge [tramve:] F/M, pl. *-s*, mid19c (1 reg/obs) < *Straßenbahn* **Nw** (0) < *trikk* **Fr** [tramwɛ] end19c (2) **Sp** <=E> M, mid19c (1 jour, arch); *tranvía* F, end19c, via Fr (3) **It** *tramvai/tranvai/tranvia* [tramvai/tramvia] M, pl. Ø, mid19c (1 rare) **Rm** *tramvai* [tramvaj] N, pl. *-e*, end19c, via Fr, 1b(3); → *tramvaist* M **Rs** *tramvai* M, pl. *-ai*, beg20c (3) → *-nyi* adj. **Po** *tramwaj* [tramvai] M, beg20c (3) → *-arz* M; *-arka* F; *-ik* M; *-owy* adj.; *-arski* adj. **Cr** *tramvaj* M, pl. *-i*, beg20c (3) → *-ac* M; *-ka* F; *-ski* adj. **Bg** *tramvai* M, pl. *-vaya/-vai*, beg20c, via Rs, +1c(3) → *-en* adj.; *-dzhiya* M; *-dzhiika* F **Hu** [tramve:] pl. Ø, 19c (1 rare) < *tram, villamos* **Al** *tramvaj* M, pl. *-ë*, beg20c, via Rs (3) **Gr** *tramvai* N, 19/beg20c, via Fr (1 obs) → *tramvaghieris* M

trance   *n.* 1b 'a hypnotic or cataleptic state', 2 'such a state as entered into by a medium', 3 'a state of extreme exaltation or rapture; ecstasy'

Ge [trãns(ə)] F, pl. *-n*, end19c, via Fr, 1b(3) **Du** [trans] C, end19c, 1b(3) **Nw** *transe* [transe/traŋse] M, pl. *-er*, beg20c, 2(2 tech) 3(2 coll) **Ic** *trans* [tʰrans] M/N [U] beg20c, 2(2 tech) 3(2 coll) **Fr** 1b(4) **Sp** 1b,2(5) **It** [trans] F [U] mid19c (3) **Rm** *transă* [transə] F, pl. *-e*, beg20c (5Fr) **Rs** *trans* M [U] beg20c, 1b(2) **Po** *trans* [trans] M [U] beg20c (2) **Cr** *trans* M [U] mid20c, 1b(3) **Bg** *trans* M [U] beg20c, 1b,2(2) → *-ov* adj. **Fi** *transsi* 19c, 1b(3) **Hu** *transz* [trans] [U] 19c, via Fr? (3) **Al** *trans* M [U] 20c (3) **Gr** *trans* F/ N [U] end20c (2)

tranquillizer   *n.* 'a drug used to diminish anxiety'
The adoption of the English form is the exception; more commonly, a Romance suffix replaces the English one, or the term is translated.

Ge *Tranquil(l)izer* [treŋkvilaiza] M, pl. Ø, 1960s (1 tech) < *Beruhigungsmittel* **Du** *tranquillizer* [=E] 1960s (1 tech) **Nw** [=E] 20c (1 tech) < *beroligende middel* **Ic** - < *róandi(lyf)* **Fr** - < trsl *tranquillisant* **Sp** - < trsl *tranquilizante* **It** - < *tranquillante* **Rm** - < *tranchilizant* **Rs** - < *trankvilizator* **Po** *trenkwilizator* (5La) **Cr** *trankvilajzer* M, pl. *-i*, mid20c (1 tech) **Bg** - < *trankvilizator* **Hu** - < *trankvilláns* (5La)

transceiver   *n.* 'a combined radio transmitter and receiver'

Du [=E] C, pl. *-s*, end20c (1 tech) **It** [=E] M, pl. Ø, 1980s (1 tech) **Rm** *transiver* [transiver] N, end20c (1

tech) **Rs** *transiver* M, pl. *-y*, 1990s (1 tech) **Cr** (0) **Bg** *transiver* M, pl. *-al- i*, 1990s (1 tech)

transient   *n.* 2 'a brief current etc.' (electr.)

It *transiente* [tranzijɛnte] M/adj., pl. *-i*, 20c (3) < *transitorio* **Rm** *tranzient* adj., 20c (1 tech) **Po** *transjenty* [transienti] pl., mid20c (1 tech)

transmitter   *n.* 2 'a set of equipment used to generate and transmit electromagnetic waves carrying messages, signals, etc.', 3 'a neurotransmitter' (biol.)

Ge [transmita] M, pl. Ø, beg20c, 2(1 tech, rare); 1980s, 3(1 tech, rare) **Du** *transmittor*, 2(5); *transmitter* [transmitər] C, 1980s, 3(1 tech) **Nw** [transmiter] M, pl. *-e*, 20c, 2,3(1 tech) **Ic** - < 2: *sendir, senditæki* **Fr** - < 2: *transmetteur* **Sp** - < *transmisor* **Rm** - < 2: *transmițător* **Rs** *transmitter* M, pl. *-y*, beg20c, 2(1 tech) **Po** 2(5La) **Cr** [=E] M, pl. *-i*, mid20c, 2(1 tech) **Bg** *transmiter* M, pl. *-al-i*, mid20c, 2(1 tech) **Hu** *transzmitter* [transmitter] pl. Ø, 20c, 3(1 tech) **Al** - < *transmetues*

transporter   *n.* 2 'a vehicle used to transport other vehicles or large pieces of machinery etc. by road'

Ge *Transporter* [=E] M, pl. Ø, 1960s (3) **Du** [trans-] C, pl. *-s*, mid20c (3) **Fr** (4) **It** [=E] M, pl. Ø, 1980s? (1 tech) **Rm** *transportor* (5Fr) **Rs** *transportër* pl. *-y*, mid20c (2 tech/5Fr) **Po** (5La) **Cr** (0) **Hu** (5Fr) **Al** *transportier* M, pl. *-ë* < *mjet transportues*

trap   *n.* 7b 'a device for preventing the passage of steam, gases, or odours'

Ge *Traps* [traps] M, pl. *-e*, beg20c (1 tech)

trapper   *n.* 1 'a person who traps wild animals, esp. to obtain furs'
Widely known as a term of nineteenth-century North American history (popularized through novels of James Fenimore Cooper), the term was apparently never applied to European conditions.

Ge [trapa] M, pl. Ø, 19c (Ø) **Du** (Ø) **Nw** [=E/ traper] M, pl. *-e*, beg20c (Ø) **Fr** *trappeur* M, mid19c (Ø) < *coureur des bois* **It** (Ø), 19c (Ø) **Rm** *trapeur* [trapœr] M, pl. *-i*, 20c, via Fr (Ø/ 3) **Po** *traper* [traper] M, beg20c (Ø) → *-stwo* N; *-ski* adj. **Cr** *traper* M, pl. *-i*, mid20c (Ø/2) **Bg** *traper* M, pl. *-i*, beg20c (Ø) **Hu** [trapper] pl. *-ek*, 19c/20c (Ø) **Al** *traper* M, pl. *-e*, end19c (1 reg)

trash   *n.* +6 'a style of music'

Ge [=E] 1990s (1 you, mod) **Du** [=E] C, 1990s (1 you, mod) **Nw** *thrash/trash* [=E] M [U] 1980s (1 tech) **Sp** [=E] M [U] end20c (1 you, mod) **Rs** *trésh* M [U] 1990s (1 you, mod) **Po** [treʃ] M, uninfl., end20 (1 you, mod) **Cr** (0) **Bg** *trash* M [U] end20c (1 you, mod/tech) **Fi** [=E] 1990s (1 you, mod) **Gr** *trash* F [U] 1990s (1 tech, you, mod)

traveller's cheque   *n.* 'a cheque for a fixed amount that may be cashed on signature, usu. internationally'
This word has spread tremendously in the past few years; 'absences' are due to the predominance of calques (mainly in the west) and the fact that the item is not (yet) well-known.

Ge *Travellerscheck* [=E] M, pl. *-s*, 1970s (1 tech) < rend *Reisescheck* **Du** *travellerscheque* [=E] C, 1970s

(1 mod) = *reischeque* **Nw** (o) < rend *reisesjekk* **Ic** - < rend *ferðatékki* **Fr** *traveller's (chèque)* [travlœr] M, 1960s (1 tech, ban) > rend *chèque de voyage, chèque-voyage* **Sp** [trabelertʃek] M, 1960s (1 tech) < rend *cheque de viaje* **It** [treveler̜ʃek/tʃek] M, pl. Ø/-s, 1930s (2 tech) **Rm** [=E] N, pl. -*uri*, 1990s (1 tech) **Rs** *trevler-chek* M, pl. -*i*, end2oc (1 tech) **Po** <=E> M, end2oc (1 tech) < rend *czeki podróne* **Cr** *treveler-ček* M, pl. -*ovi*, mid2oc (1 tech) **Bg** *travel chek* M, pl. -*ove*, end2oc (1 tech, sla) < *pŭtnicheski chek* **Fi** - < rend *matkašekki* **Hu** [trevelers tʃek] pl. -*ek*/Ø, 1980s (1>2 writ, jour, mod) < rend *utazási csekk* **Al** - < rend *çek udhëtues* **Gr** *traveller's (tsek)* [tra-] N, 1990s (1 tech)

travelling matte* *n.* 'a filming technique used for superimposing an action on a different background' (cinematogr.)
It [treveliŋ met] M, pl. Ø, 1960s (1 tech)

travelling (shot)* *n.* 'a sequence in a film taken during movement'
Fr *travelling* [travliŋ] M, 1920s (2 tech) **Sp** *travelling/travelín* [travelin] M, 1950s (2 tech) **Rm** *travling/travelling* [travliŋ] N, pl. -*uri*, 1950s (1 tech)

trawl *v.* 1a 'fish with a trawl'
Nw *tråle* [troːle] 1930s (3) → *tråler* M **Ic** *trolla* [tʰrolːa] end19c (3a) < *toga* **Rm** *traula* [trawla] 2oc (5Rm) **Po** *trałować* [trawovat͡ɕ] mid2oc (1 tech) **Cr** *travlirati* beg2oc (3) **Fi** *troolata* end19c (3)

trawler *n.* 1 'a boat used for trawling'
This word appears to have spread with the nineteenth-century British fishing and shipbuilding industries which typically restricted it to Germanic and Slav languages (with German and Russian transmission involved).
Ge [troːla] M, pl. Ø, end19c (2 tech) **Du** [=E] C, 1910s (2 tech) = *treiler* → *trawlen* v. **Nw** *tråler* [troːler] M, pl. -*e*, end19c (3) **Ic** *trollari* [tʰrɔːlari] M, pl. -*ar*, end19c (1 obs) < creat *togari; botnvörpungur* **Sp** [=E] M, pl. -*s*, 1920s (1 tech, rare) **It** [troːler] M, pl. Ø, 1930s (1 tech) **Rm** *trauler* [trawlər] N, pl. -*e*, 1950s (3 tech) **Rs** *trauler* M, pl. -*y*, end19c (2 tech) **Po** *trauler* <=E> [trawler] mid2oc (2) **Cr** *troler* M, pl. -*i*, 2oc (3 tech) **Bg** *trauler* M, pl. -*al-i*, mid2oc, via Rs (3 tech); *tralr* beg2oc (3 tech) **Fi** *troolari* 19c (3 tech)

trawler-yacht* *n.* 'a kind of ship'
It [trɔːler jaːt] M, pl. Ø, 1980s (1 tech)

trawl (net) *n.* 2 'a large wide-mouthed fishing-net dragged by a boat along the bottom of the sea'
Ge *Trawl* [=E] N, pl. -*s*, end19c (1 tech) **Du** *trawlnet* [troːlnɛt] N, end19c (2 tech+5) = *trawl* → *trawlen* v.; *trawler* n. **Nw** *tråI* [trɔːl] M, pl. -*er*, end19c (3) → *tråle* v.; *tråler* M **Ic** *troll* [tʰrɔːl] N, pl. Ø, end19c (3) > creat *botnvarpa* **It** [trɔːl nɛt] M, pl. Ø, 1930s (1 tech) **Rm** *traul* [trawl] N, pl. -*e*, 1960s (3 tech) →

traulare **Rs** *tral* M, pl. -*y*, mid2oc (2 tech) **Po** (o) **Cr** *travla* F, pl. -*e*, beg2oc (1 tech) **Bg** *tral* M, pl. -*al* -*ove*, beg2oc, via Rs (3 tech) → -*ya* v. **Fi** *trooli* 19c (3) **Al** *tral* M, pl. -*e*, mid2oc (1 tech)

treatment *n.* +3a 'a laid-down schedule for a film or TV show', +3b 'a phase of elaboration and exposé of a cinematographic subject'
Ge [=E] N, pl. -*s*, 1960s (1 tech, rare) **It** [=E] M, pl. Ø, 1940s (1 tech) < trsl *trattamento, sceneggiatura*

trekkie *n.* 'a Star Trek fan'
Ge [=E] M, pl. -*s*, 1980s (1 sla) **Ic** *trekkari* [tʰrɛhkarı] M, pl. -*ar*, end2oc (2 you) **Sp** [treki] M, pl. -*s*, end2oc (Ø/1 tech) **Fi** [=E] end2oc (1 mod) = rend *trekkari*

trekking *n.* +1a 'a long-distance walk', +3 'a touristic expedition'
Ge [=E] N [U] 1980s, +3(1 tech) **Du** [=E] C, 1990s, via Afrikaans (2 tech) **Nw** [=E] M [U] 1980s (1 tech) **Fr** M, 1970s (1 tech) **Sp** [trekin] M [U] 1980s (1 tech) **It** [trɛkkiŋ(g)] M [U] 1970s, +3(1 tech, mod) **Rs** *trekking* M [U] end2oc, +3(1 tech) **Po** [-nk] M [U] (1 tech) **Cr** *treking* M [U] (1 tech) **Bg** *treking* M [U] end2oc, +3(1 tech, mod) **Gr** <=E>/*treking* N [U] 1990s, +1a(1 tech) = *pezoporia*

trench (coat) *n.* 2 'a loose belted raincoat'
The coat was originally worn by officers in the trenches during the first World War, but quickly spread to non-military contexts from the 1920s onwards; some of the shortened forms may point to French transmission, but may also be independent.
Ge [trɛntʃkoːt] M, pl. -*s*, 1930s (2); *Trench* 1970s (1 tech, rare) **Du** [=E] C, 1940s (2) **Nw** [=E] M, pl. -*erl-s*, mid2oc (1 tech) **Ic** *trenchkápa* [tʰrɛns-] F, pl. -*ur*, end2oc (1+5) < *rykfrakki* **Fr** *trench-(coat)* 1920s (1 obs) **Sp**

trench [=E] M/F, end2oc (1 tech) < *trinchera* **It** *trench/*<=E> [trɛntʃkot] M, pl. Ø, 1930s (2 tech) **Rm** *trenci/trencicot* [trɛntʃ/trɛntʃ kot/=E] N, pl. -*uri*, 1930s (3) **Po** *trencz* [trɛnʃ] M, mid2oc (3) → -*yk* M; -*owy* adj. **Cr** *trenčkot* M, pl. -*ovi*, mid2oc (3) **Bg** *trenchkot* M, pl. -*al-i*, beg2oc (1 arch) **Fi** *trenssi (takki)* mid2oc (2) **Hu** *trencskó(t)* [trɛntʃkoː(t)] pl. Ø, 1920s (3 obs) **Gr** *trents kot* N, mid2oc (1)

trend *n.* 1 'a general direction and tendency (esp. of events, fashion, or opinion etc.)'
Although adopted early, this word made it into the core vocabulary only in the Germanic North West and neighbouring languages – where it often remained restricted to technical registers; cf. the much less widespread currency of ↑ ~ *setter* and ↑ ~ *y*.
Ge [trɛnt] M, pl. -*s*, beg2oc (3) **Du** [trɛnt] C, 1940s (3) **Nw** [=E] M, pl. -*er*, mid2oc (2) **Ic** [=E] N [U] 1980s (1 sla) **It** [trɛnd] M [U] 1930s (2 tech) **Rm** [=E] N, pl. -*uri*, 1970s (o>1 tech) **Rs** *trend* M, pl. -*y*, end2oc (1 mod) **Po** [-t] M, mid2oc (2) **Cr** *trend* M, pl. -*ovi*,

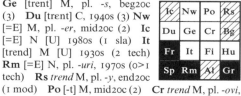

mid20c (2)   **Bg** *trend* M, pl. *-al-ove*, end20c (1 tech ᴇᴄᴏɴ)   **Fi** *trendi* mid20c (3)   **Hu** [trend] pl. Ø, beg20c (3 tech)   **Al** *trend* M, pl. *-e*, mid20c (1 reg)   **Gr** - < mean *tasi*

trendsetter   *n.* 'a person who leads the way in fashion etc.'

Ge [trɛntseta] M, pl. Ø, 1970s (1 mod)   **Du** [trɛnt-sɛtər] C, 1960s (2 mod) → *trendsetten* v.   **Nw** [=E] M, pl. *-e*, 1970s (1) → *trendsettende* adj.   **Ic** [=E] end20c (0)   **Cr** *trend setter* M, pl. *-i*, end20c (2)   **Fi** *trendsetteri* end20c (1 you)

trendy   *adj.* 'fashionable; following fashionable trends'

Ge [=E] uninfl., 1980s (1 mod) > *trendig*   **Du** [trɛndi] 1980s (1 mod) = *modieus*   **Nw** [=E] 1970s (1 mod)   **Ic** [=E] uninfl., end20c (1 sla)   **It** [=E] uninfl., mid20c (1 mod)   **Po** (0)   **Fi** - < creat *trendikäs*   **Gr** <=E>/*trendi*/-*i*, 1990s (1 jour, mod)

trial   *n.* 4 'a sports match to test the ability of players eligible for selection to a team', 5 'a test of individual ability on a motorcycle over rough ground'

Ge [=E] N, pl. *-s*, 1970s, 5(1 tech, rare)   **Du** [=E] C, 1950s (1 tech)   **Nw** [=E] M, pl. *-er*, 1970s (1 tech)   **Sp** [trial] M, 1970s, 5(2 tech) → *trialerom, trialeraf, trialsín*   **It** [trial/trajal] M, pl. Ø, 1970s (2 tech)   **Rm** [=E] N, pl. *-uri*, 1970s, 4(1 tech)

trial and error   *phr.* 'repeated (usu. varied and unsystematic) attempts or experiments continued until one is successful'

Ge [=E] [U] 1970s (1 tech)   **Du** [trajlənd ɛrər] 1980s (1 tech)   **Nw** (0)   **Sp** - < trsl *ensayo y error*   **Bg** - < trsl *proba i greshka*

trick   *n./cp¹* 1 'an action or scheme undertaken to fool, outwit, or deceive', 2 'an optical or other illusion', 3 'a special technique', 4b 'an unusual action learnt by an animal'

This English loanword is among the earliest borrowings in many Continental languages; interestingly enough, some have an almost homophonous word from (not via) French of the same meaning (*truc*).

Ge [=E] M, pl. *-s*, beg19c, 1,3,4b(3)   **Du** [trɪk] C, 1980s (2) < *truc(je)* → *tricky* adj.   **Nw** <=E>/*triks*/ *trikk* [=E] N, pl. Ø, beg20c (3)   **Ic** *trikk* [tʰrɪhk] N, pl. Ø, mid20c (2 coll); *trix* [tʰrɪxs] N, pl. Ø, 1930s, via Da, 1,3(2 coll) → *trixa* v.   **Fr** [trik] M, end18c, 1(1 tech)   **Sp** - < *truco* (5Fr)   **It** - < *trucco* (5Fr)   **Rm** - < *truc* (5Fr/It)   **Rs** - < *tryuk* (5Fr)   **Po** *trik/* <=E> M, beg20c (2) → *-owy* adj.   **Cr** *trik* M, pl. *-ovi*, end19c (3)   **Bg** *trik* M, pl. *-al-ove*, beg20c, 1,2,3(2) → *-ov* adj.   **Fi** *trikki* N/cp¹, beg20c, 1,2(3)   **Hu** (5Fr)   **Al** *trik* M, pl. *-e*, beg20c (1 reg)   **Gr** *trik* N, beg20c, 1,2,3(2)

trick   *v.* 2 'cheat; treat deceitfully so as to deprive'   **Ge** *(aus)tricksen* 1970s (3 coll) → *Trickser* M,   **Nw** *trikse* [trɪkse] beg20c (3)

trickfilm*   *n.* 'an animated cartoon, a cartoon film'

Ge [=E] M, pl. *-e*, 1960s (3)   **Du** - < *tekenfilm, cartoon*   **Po** (0)   **Cr** [=E] M, pl. *-ovi*, mid20c (2)   **Bg**

---

trikfilm M, pl. *-al-i*, mid20c (3)   **Hu** *trükkfilm* [trykk-film] pl. *-ek*, 1960s (5Fr+3)

tricky   *adj.* 2 'crafty or deceitful'

Ge <=E>/*trickig* [=E/-ıg] 1970s (1 you)   **Du** [=E] end20c (1 you)   **Nw** [=E] 1980s (1 rare)   **Ic** [tʰrɪhci] end20c (1 sla)

trifle   *n.* +3b 'a dessert made of macaroons, sherry, fruit, and whipped cream'

Ic *tri(f)fli* [tʰrɪflɪ] N [U] beg20c, via Da (2)   **It** [=E] M, pl. Ø, 20c (1 rare)

trigger   *n./cp¹* 2 'an event, occurrence, etc., that sets off a chain reaction' (electr., med.)

Ge [=E] M, pl. Ø, end20c (1 tech)   **Du** *trigger*-[trɪgər-] cp¹, 1980s (1 tech)   **Nw** [=E] M, pl. *-e*, 20c (1 tech)   **Fr** <=E> M, 20c (1 tech)   **It** [=E] M, pl. Ø, 1960s (1 tech)   **Rm** [trigər] M, pl. *-e*, 1980s (1 tech)   **Rs** *trigger* M, pl. *-y*, mid20c (1 tech)   **Bg** *triger* M, pl. *-al-i*, mid20c (1 tech)   **Hu** [trigger] pl. Ø, 20c (1 tech)

trike   *n.* 'a tricycle; a three-wheeled motor-bike'

For the children's toy native words (some possibly calqued as German *Dreirad*) are common; the English word was adopted from the 1980s for the motor-bike, but the word is as rare as the thing.

Ge [=E] N, pl. *-s*, 1980s (1 mod, rare)   **Du** [=E] C, 1980s (1 tech)   **Sp** [traik] M, pl. *-s*, end20c (1 tech)   **It** - < *triciclo*   **Gr** *traik* N, pl. Ø/-*s*, end20c (1 tech, mod) < *ghuruna*

trim   *v.* 1 'make neat or of the required size or form, esp. by cutting away irregular or unwanted parts; shear (a dog)', 4 'adjust the balance of (a ship or aircraft) by the arrangement of its cargo etc.', 5 'arrange (sails) to suit the wind', +8 'transport coal', +9 'train (a dog)', +10 (refl) 'become/remain fit', +11 'undertake physical exercise in order to keep fit'

At least three different meanings – not felt to be related in the receiving languages – have been borrowed at different times and in different contexts: the early loans are typically related to ships and to dogs, whereas the most recent (and most popular in German) relating to physical exercise is confined to the Germanic languages and may be a Continental innovation.

Ge *trimmen*, beg20c, 1,+9(3) 4,5, +8(3 tech); 1970s, +10(3)   **Du** *trimmen* [trɪmə(n)] 1940s, 1(3 tech); 1960s, 5(3 tech); 1960s, +10(1 tech); beg20c [trɛ mə(n)] 1940s, +8(3 tech) = *trimmen*   **Nw** *trimme* [trɪme]

beg20c, 1,+9(3); 19c, 5(3 tech); beg20c, +8(3 tech); 1960s, +11(3) → *trimmer* M; *trimming* M   **Ic** *trimma* [tʰrɪm:a] 1970s, 4(3 tech) +11(3)   **Cr** *trimovati* 20c, 5(1 tech)   **Fi** *trimmata* 19c, 1,4,5(3)   **Hu** *trimmel* [trimmel] 1930s, 5(3 tech) 1(3) → *-és* n.

trim   *adj./n.* 2 'in good order' (naut.), +6 'the position of a ship in water', +7 'unused filming material', +8 'the act of becoming or keeping fit by physical exercise'

Ge *Trimm* M [U] beg20c, +6(3 tech) → *-ung* F **Du** [trɪm] N [U] 1960s, 2,+6,+7(3 tech) **Nw** [=E] M [U] beg20c, 2, +8(3) **Ic** *trimm* [tʰrɪm:] N [U] 1970s, +8(3) **Fr** [trim] M, 20c, +6(1 tech, ban) > *assiette* **It** [trim] M, pl. Ø, 1930s, +6,+8(1 tech, rare) **Po** *trym* M, end20c, +6(1 tech) **Cr** [trim] M, mid20c, +6(1 tech) **Hu** *trimm* [=E] [U] 20c, +6(3 tech)

trimmer[1] (1)   *n.* 3 'an instrument for clipping etc.', 5 'a small capacitator (etc.) used to tune a radio set' (electr.)

Ge [trɪ̱ma] M, pl. Ø, 1980s, 3(1 tech); 1960s, 5(1 tech) **Du** [trɪ̱mər] C, 1960s, 5(1 tech) 3(1 tech, obs) **Nw** [=E] M, pl. *-e*, 20c, 3(3 tech) **Fr** [trimœr] M, 19c, 3(1 tech); 20c, 5(1 tech) **Sp** [trɪmer] M, end20c, 3(0>1 tech) **Rm** *trimer* [trɪ̱mer] N, pl. *-e*, 1960s, 5(1 tech) **Rs** *trɪ̱mmer* M, pl. *-y*, mid20c, 5(1 tech) **Po** *trymer* [trimer] M, end20c, 5(1 tech) **Cr** *trɪ̱mer* M, pl. *-i*, end20c, 5(1 tech) **Bg** *trɪ̱mer* M, pl. *-al-i*, mid20c, 5(1 tech) **Al** *trimer* M, pl. *-ë(r)*, end20c, 5(1 tech)

trimmer[2] (1)   *n.* +7a 'a device for improving a ship's balance'

Fr *trimer* [trimœr] M, end19c (1 tech) **Rs** *trɪ̱mmer* M, mid20c (1 tech) **Po** *trymer* [-er] M, end20c (1 tech) **Fi** *trimmeri* mid20c (3)

trimmer[3] (1)   *n.* +8 'a worker loading coals', +9 'a person trying to keep fit'

Ge [trɪ̱ma] M, pl. Ø, end19c, +8(3 tech, arch); 1970s, +9(1 obs) **Du** *tremmer* [trɛ̱mər] C, beg20c (3 tech) = *trimmer* **Nw** [trɪ̱mmer] M, pl. *-e*, 1960s, +9(3) **Ic** *trimmari* [tʰrɪm:arɪ] M, pl. *-ar*, 1970s, +9(3) **Rs** *trɪ̱mmer* M, pl. *-y*, mid20c, +8(1 tech) **Po** *trymer* [-er] M, mid20c, +8(1 tech)

trimming   *n.* +4 'a sports activity to keep fit', +5 'shearing a dog'

Ge [trɪ̱mɪŋ] N [U] 1980s, +4(3) **Nw** [trɪ̱mɪŋ] M/F [U] 1960s (3) **Sp** [trɪmɪn] M, end20c, +5(0>1 tech) **Rs** *trɪ̱mmɪng* M [U] end20c, +5(1 tech) **Po** (0) **Fi** - < +5: *trimmaus* **Hu** - < +5: *trimmelés*

trip   *v.* 7a 'have a hallucinatory experience caused by a drug, esp. LSD', +8 'be enthusiastic or diligent'

Du *trippen* 1970s, 7a(1 tech) **Nw** *trippe* [tri̱ːpe] 1970s, 7a(1 tech) **Ic** *trippa* [tʰrɪhpa] 1970s (1 sla) **Sp** *tripar* (3 sla)

trip   *n./cp*[2] 1 'a journey or excursion made for pleasure', 4 'a drug-induced experience, esp. from taking LSD', +6 'enthusiasm'

Although recorded from the nineteenth century this word has remained remarkably restricted – not just in its common 'travel' sense, but also (more surprisingly?) in its usage in the language of drug addicts.

Ge [=E] M, pl. *-s*, 19c, 1(2); 1960s, 4(1 sla) **Du** [=E] C, 1910s, 1(2); 1960s, 4(2) → *trippen* v.; *trippy* adj. **Nw** *tripp* [=E] M, pl. *-er*, 19c, 1(3); <=E> 1970s, 4, +6(1 sla) **Ic** *tripp* [tʰrɪhp] N [U] 1970s, 4, +6(1 sla) **Fr** [trip] M, 1970s, 4(2) < *voyage* **Sp** [trip] M, end20c, 1,+6(0>1 jour); *trip/tripi* M, pl. *-s*, 1970s, 4(2

sla) = *viaje* → *tripar* v., *tripante*, *triposo* adj. **It** [trip] M, pl. Ø, 1960s, 4(2 sla, you) < mean *viaggio* **Po** [=E] F [U] end20c, +6(1 sla) **Cr** [=E] M [U] end20c, 4(2) **Bg** *trip* M, pl. *-al-ove*, end20c, 4(1 tech) **Fi** *trippi* beg20c, 1(2); end20c, 4(2) **Hu** [=E] [U] end20c, 4(2 tech) **Gr** *trip* N, end20c, 4(1 sla) → *tripaki* N

trolley   *n./cp*[1] 3 'a wheel attached to a pole etc. used for collecting current from an overhead electric wire to drive a vehicle', 4b ↑ 'a trolleybus'

Du [=E] C, pl. *-s* (1 tech) **Nw** cp[1] in *trolleybus* **Fr** *trolley* [trɔlɛ] M, 1920s (2) **Sp** <=E>/*trole* [trole] M, 1920s (2 tech) → *trolebús* **It** [trɔli] M, pl. Ø, end19c (1 tech) < *pantografo* **Po** *trolej* 20c, 3(1 tech) **Cr** *trola* 20c, 3 (1 tech) **Bg** *trolei̯* M, pl. *-eyal-ei*, mid20c, via Rs, 4b(3 coll) **Hu** *troli* [=E] pl. *-k*, beg20c (3) **Gr** *trolei* 20c (3)

troll(e)y-bar*   *n.* 'a small table or stand on wheels or castors for use in serving food'

Fr *trolley* [trɔlɛ] M, 20c (1 tech, ban) < *chariot* **Hu** - < *mozgóbár* **Gr** *trolei bar* N, end20c (1 tech)

trolleybus   *n.* 1 'a bus powered by electricity obtained from an overhead cable by means of a trolley-wheel' (cf. ↑*trolley*)

Ge [trɔ̱libus] M, pl. *-se*, beg20c (1 tech, reg) < *O-bus* **Du** [trɔ̱lɪbys] C, pl. *-sen*, beg20c (1 tech+5) **Nw** *trolleybuss* [trɔ̱libus] M, pl. *-er*, beg20c (1 obs) < *strømbuss* **Fr** <=E>/*trolley* [trɔlɛ] M, 1920s (2) **Sp** *trolebús* M, mid20c (3 arch/obs) **It** [trɔllibus] M, pl. Ø, end19c (1 obs) < *filobus* M **Rm** *troleibuz* [trolejbu̱z] N, pl. *-e*, mid20c, via Fr (3) **Rs** *trolei̯bus* M, pl. *-y*, mid20c (2 tech) **Po** *trolejbus* [troleibus] M, mid20c (2) → *-ik* M; *-owy* adj. **Cr** *trolejbus* M, pl. *-i*, mid20c (2) → *-ni* adj. **Bg** *trolei̯bus/trolei̯* M, pl. *-sal-si*; *-leyal-lei*, mid20c, via Rs (2/3 coll) → *-en* adj. **Hu** *troli(busz)* [trɔli(bus)] pl. *-ok*, 1930s (3) **Al** *trolejbus* M, pl. *-ë*, mid20c (3) **Gr** *troleibas* N, 1950s (1 obs) < *trolei* N

trotter   *n.* 1 'a horse bred or trained for trotting'

Fr *trotteur* 19c (3) **It** [trɔ̱tter] M, pl. Ø, end19c (1 tech)

trouble   *n.* 1 'difficulty or distress', 2a 'inconvenience, bother', 3 'a cause of annoyance or concern'

Ge [trabel] M [U] 1970s, 1(1 you) **Du** [=E] C, pl. *-s*/*trubbels*, 1990s (1 mod) > *troebel* **Nw** *trøbbel* [trøbel] N [U] beg20c, 1(3) → *trøble* v.; *trøblete* adj. **Ic** [tʰrɔ̱p:ul] N [U] mid/end20c (1 coll) **Fr** (5)

troublemaker   *n.* 'a person who habitually causes trouble'

Ge [trablme:ka] M, pl. Ø, 1970s (1 coll, jour) **Du** [=E] C, 1990s (1 mod) **Nw** [=E] M, pl. *-e*, 1960s (1) < *bråkmaker* **Ic** [=E] M, mid/end20c (0)

troubleshooter   *n.* +1a 'a specialist called in an emergency'

Note that in German this term is sometimes identified with ↑*troublemaker* and misunderstood as someone raising trouble.

Ge [=E] M, pl. Ø, 1970s (1 coll, jour)   **Du** [=E] C, 1970s (1 tech, coll) → *-shooting* n.   **Nw** [=E/trøbel] M, pl. *-e*, 1970s (1)

trousers   *n.* 1 'an outer garment reaching from the waist usu. to the ankles, divided into two parts to cover the legs'

Rs *trauzery* pl., 1980s (1 sla)

truck   *n.* 2 'a big lorry', +8 'a pivoted chassis of a railway or lorry', +9 'a forklift truck'

Apart from technical uses, this term appears to be making headway as a fashionable expression for a big lorry (as it is in Britain as against *lorry*); lorry-drivers also tend to prefer to be called ↑ 'truckers' in German and Dutch, but the term is apparently restricted to these two languages so far.

Ge [trak] M, pl. *-s*, 1980s, 2(1 mod)   **Du** [trʏk] C, beg20c, 2(2); end19c, +8(2 tech); 1960s, +9(2) = 2, +8: *vrachtwagen*; +9: *heftruck*   **Nw** [=E] M, pl. *-er*, mid20c, 2(1 rare) +9(2) → *trucke* v.   **Ic** *trukkur* [tʰrʏhkʏr] M, pl. *-ar*, mid20c, 2(3)   **Sp** <=E> M, mid20c, 2, +9(0)   **It** [trak] M, pl. Ø, end20c, 2(1) **Rm** *truc* [truk] N, pl. *-uri*, mid20c, via Fr/Ge, +8(2 tech)   **Po** <=E> M, end20c, 2(1 tech)   **Cr** *trak* (0)   **Fi** *trukki* beg20c, +9(3)   **Hu** [trak] pl. Ø, 20c, 2(1 tech_MILIT); +8(1 tech)

trucker   *n.* 'a long-distance lorry driver'

Ge [traka] M, pl. *-s*, 1980s (1 mod)   **Du** [trʏkər] C, 1970s (2 coll)   **Nw** (0)   **Cr** *traker* (0)

truck (system)*   *n.* 'the payment of workers in the form of goods or vouchers'

Ge [traksyste:m] N [U] end19c (1 tech, obs+5)   **Du** *truck(garage)-stelsen* C/N [U] beg20c (1 tech+5)   **Nw** [=E+Nw] N, pl. *-er*, 20c (1 tech, obs+5)   **It** [=E] M [U] end19c (1 obs)   **Rm** *truck* [=E] N [U] 20c (1 tech)   **Cr** *trak-sistem* M [U] 20c (1 tech)   **Hu** *truck-rendszer* [trakrendser] [U] 20c (1 tech, arch+5)

truism   *n.* 'an obviously true or hackneyed statement'

This word, as an early loan in French, was apparently handed on to other languages, while only a few borrowed it anew at a later stage. The concept is expressed by native equivalents in the other languages (German *Binsenweisheit* etc.)

Ge (0)   **Du** *truïsme* [trʏɪsme] N, pl. *-n*, 1940s (3 tech) = *truism*   **Nw** *truisme* [trʉɪsme] M, pl. *-r*, beg20c (3 tech)   **Fr** *truisme* M, mid19c (3)   **Sp** *truismo* M, end20c (1 rare)   **It** *truismo* [truɪzmo] M, pl. *-i*, 1910s (3) **Rm** [truɪsm] N, pl. *-e*, beg20c, via Fr (3)   **Rs** *tryuizm* M [U] beg20c (2)   **Po** *truizm* [tru-] M, beg20c (3)   **Bg** *truizŭm* M [U] beg20c (1 tech)   **Fi** *truismi* 19c (3)   **Al** *truizëm* M [U] beg20c (1 reg)

trust   *n.* 8c 'an organized association of several companies for the purpose of reducing or defeating competition etc.'

Ge [trast, -ö-] M, pl. *-s*, beg19c (2 tech)   **Du** [=E] C,

beg20c (1 tech)   **Nw** [=E] M, pl. *-er*, beg20c (2 tech)   **Fr** M, end19c (2 ban) > *fiducie* → *truster* v.; *trusteur* M   **Sp** [trust] M, pl. *-s*, end19c (2 tech) → *trustero* M, *trustear* v.   **It** [=E/trast] M, pl. Ø, beg20c (2 tech)   **Rm** [trust] N, pl. *-uri*, beg20c, via Fr (3)   **Rs** *trest* M, pl. *-y*, mid20c (1 tech) → *trestovskiĭ* adj.   **Po** M, beg20c (1 tech)   **Cr** *trust* M, pl. *-ovi*, mid20c (1 tech)   **Bg** *trŭst* M, pl. *-al-ove*, beg20c (2 tech) → *-ov* adj.   **Fi** [=E] beg20c (Ø)   **Hu** *tröszt* [trɔst] pl. *-ök*, end19c, via Ge (3 obs)   **Al** *trust* M, pl. *-e*, mid20c (3)   **Gr** *trast* N [U] end20c (1 tech)

T-shirt   *n.* 'a short-sleeved casual top'

This term is first recorded in F. Scott Fitzgerald (1920). The piece of clothing was popularized by M. Brando in the film version of *A Streetcar Named Desire* and became really widespread in international fashion from the 1970s onwards: it comes as a surprise that it is not (yet) recorded for some languages (a few have calques).

Ge [tiːʃört] N, pl. *-s*, 1970s (2)   **Du** [=E] N, 1970s (2)   **Nw** [=E] M, pl. *-s*, 1970s (1) < trsl *t-skjorte*   **Ic** [=E] N, pl. Ø, end20c (0) < *(T-)bolur*   **Fr** <=E> M, 1950s (2)   **Sp** [tiʃert] M, pl. *-s*, end20c (1 jour, mod)   **It** <=E>/*tee-shirt* [tiʃœrt] F, pl. Ø/-s, 1960s (2>3) **Rm** [=E] N, pl. *-uri* end20c (1 mod) < *tricou*   **Rs** (0); *tishotka* F, pl. *-i*, end20c (1 you)   **Po** [tiʃert] M, 1980s (1 you)   **Cr** [tiʃert] M, end20c (1)   **Bg** *tishŭrt* M, pl. *-al-i*, 1990s (1 mod); *-ka* F, pl. *-ki* (3 mod) < *teniska*   **Fi** - < trsl *t-paita*   **Hu** [tiːʃərt] pl. *-ök*, 1970s (1 tech, jour >2) < *póló*   **Al** *tishërt* M, pl. *-ë*, 1980s (1 you)   **Gr** <=E>/*tisert* N, end20c (2)

tub   *n.* 4 'a bath', 5b 'a stout roomy boat for rowing practice'

Ge 4(0 arch)   **Du** [tɑp] C, end19c, 4(1 rare); 1960s, 5b(1 tech)   **Nw** (0)   **Fr** <=E> M, end19c, 4(1 rare) **Po** [tup] M, beg20c, 4(1 obs)

tubbing*   *n.* 'the lining of mine shafts with wooden or iron casing'

Ge <u/ü> [=E/y] M, pl. *-s*, beg20c (1 tech)   **Sp** *tubing* M, 20c (1 tech)   **Rs** *tyubing* M [U] mid20c (1 tech)   **Po** *tubing* [tubiŋk] M, mid20c (1 tech)   **Cr** (0)   **Bg** *tyubing* M [U] 20c, via Rs (1 tech) → *-ov* adj.   **Hu** *tübbing* [tʏbbiŋ] [U] 1950s, via Rs (1 tech)

tube   *n.* 2 'a soft metal or plastic cylinder sealed at one end and having a screw cap at the other, for holding a semi-liquid substance ready for use (toothpaste etc.)', 4a 'an underground railway system, esp. the one in London'

Ge [tuːbə] F, pl. *-n*, 19c, 2 (3)   **Du** [tyːbə] (5Fr)   **Nw** [tuːbe] M, pl. *-r*, beg20c (3/5)   **Ic** *túpa* [tʰuːpa] F, pl. *-ur*, beg20c, 2(5Da) 4a(Ø)   **Fr** (5)   **It** - < 2: *tubetto* (5La)   **Rm** *tub* [tub] N, pl. *-uri*, beg20c (5Fr/It)   **Rs** *tyubik* M, pl. *-i*, beg20c, 2(3)   **Cr** *tuba* F, pl. *-e*, beg20c (3)   **Bg** *tuba* F, pl. *-bi*, beg20c, via Ge, 2(5Fr)   **Hu** (5La)   **Al** *tubet* M, pl. *-e*, beg20c, via It (2)

tubeless* *n.* 'a tyre characterized by the absence of an inner tube'
Du [=E] C, 20c (1 tech) **Fr** *pneu tubeless* mid20c (1 tech) **It** [tju̯bles/tub-] M, pl. Ø, 1960s (2 tech)

tubing *n.* +3 'a tube which conducts oil out of an oil ditch'
Sp [tubin] M, 20c (1 tech) **It** [tju̯bin(g)] M, pl. Ø, 1980s (1 tech)

tufting* *n.* 'a process in carpet production'
Ge [=E] N [U] 1960s (1 tech, rare) **Cr** [=E] M [U] mid20c (1 tech)

tumbler *n.* 1 'a drinking glass with no handle or foot', 3 'a tumble-dryer, a machine for drying washing in a heated rotating drum', 6 'an electrical switch worked by pushing a small sprung lever'
Ge [=E] M, pl. Ø, 1960s, 3(1 tech, rare) **Du** [tʌmblər] C, 1970s, 3(1 tech, rare) = *tuimeldroger* < *droogtrommel* **Nw** (o) < 3: *tørketrommel* **It** [tam-bler] M, pl. Ø, 1980s, 1(1 tech) **Rs** *tumbler* M, pl. -*y*, mid20c, 6(1 tech) **Hu** *tömbler* [tømbler] pl. Ø, mid20c, 6(1 tech, arch)

tune *n.* +2 'a melody played at the beginning and end of a TV programme'
Du [tju:n] C, 1970s (2)

tune *v.* 1 'put (a musical instrument) in tune', 2a,b 'adjust a radio receiver to the particular frequency of the required signals', 3 'adjust (an engine, etc.) to run efficiently'
Ge [tju:nən] 1970s, 20c (1 tech, mod) **Du** *tunen* [tju̯nə(n)] M, 1970s (2) < *opvoeren* **Nw** [tju:ne] 20c, 2a,b(1 tech) **Ic** *tjúna* [tʰju:na] end20c (1 tech) < *stilla* **Hu** *tuningol* [tu̯ningol] 20c, 3(1 tech_SPORT)

tuner *n.* 2 'a device for tuning a radio receiver', 3 'an electric device for tuning a guitar etc.', +4 'FM radio'
Ge [tju:na] M, pl. Ø, 1960s, 2(1 tech) +4(1 tech) **Du** [=E] C, 1970s (2 tech) **Nw** [=E] M, pl. -*e*, end20c, 2,+4(1 tech) **Ic** [=E] M, pl. -*ar*, end20c, 3(1 tech) **Fr** [tynœʀ] M, 1960s, 2,+4(2 ban) < *syntoniseur* **It** [=E] M, pl. Ø, 1980s, 2(1 tech) < *sintonizzatore* **Rs** *tyuner* M, pl. -*y*, end20c, 2,+4(1 tech/mod) **Po** [=E, tuner] end20c, 2(2) **Cr** [tju̯ner] M, pl. -*i*, end20c, 2(1 tech) **Bg** *tuner* M, pl. -*al/-i*, mid20c, 2(1 tech) **Hu** [tiu̯:ner] pl. Ø, mid20c, 2+4(1 tech, writ) **Gr** <=E>/ *tju̯ner* [tj-] N, end20c, +4(0 tech)

tuning *n.* +2 'the alteration of a motorcar for greater speed and a more sporty appearance'
Ge [=E] N [U] 1970s (1 tech, mod) **Fr** [tyniŋ] M, mid20c (1 tech, ban) > *accord* **Hu** *tuningolás* [tu̯ning-gola:ʃ] [U] 20c (1 tech_SPORT)

tunnel *n.* 1, 2 'an artificial underground passage built by humans or animals'
This term became universally adopted in the nineteenth century (partly through the mediation of French and German); it is now without competing native terms, and is generally no longer felt as an anglicism.

Ge *Tunnel/Tunell* (reg) [tunəl/tunel] M, pl. Ø/-s, beg19c, via Fr? (3) → *(unter)tunneln* **Du** [tynəl] C, mid19c (3) **Nw** [tʉnel/tu̯nel] M, pl. -*er*, mid19c (3) **Fr** <=E> M, mid19c (3) → *tunnelier* M **Sp** *túnel* M, mid19c (3) **It** [tunnel] M, pl. Ø, mid19 (3) = *galleria* **Rm** *tunel* [tunel] N, pl. -*uri/-e*, mid19c, via Fr (3) → *tunelist* M **Rs** *tunnel'* M, pl. -*i*, mid19c (3) → -*nyĭ* adj. **Po** *tunel* [tunel] M, mid19c (3) → -*owy* adj. **Cr** *tunel* M, pl. -*i*, beg20c (3) → -*ski* adj. **Bg** *tunel* M, pl. -*al/-i*, end20c, via Ge (2) → -*en* adj.; -*dzhiya* M; -*dzhiĭski* adj. **Fi** *tunneli* 19c (3) **Hu** [tunnel] pl. -*ek/Ø*, end19c, via Ge (3 arch) **Al** *tunel* M, pl. -*e*, 20c (3) **Gr** *tunel* N, beg20c (2)

Tupperware *n./cp¹* 'tupperware, a range of plastic containers for food' (orig.ᵀᴹ)
Formed from the name of the inventor, Earl S. Tupper, the term became widely known in Western Europe from the 1970s on, and quickly became generic.

Ge [tupa va:rə] [U] 1980s (3) → *eintuppern* v. **Du** *tupperware* [typər-/=E] C [U] 1980s (2) → *tupperware-party* n. **Nw** *Tupperware* [=E/tu̯pervare] 1970s (1 tech, mod) **Ic**ᵀᴹ only **Fr** [typɛʀwaʀ] M, 1980s (1 tech) **Sp** [tuperbare] M [U] 1960s (1 < 2 tech) **It**ᵀᴹ only **Fi**ᵀᴹ only **Gr** *tu̯per* N, mid20c (2)

turf *n.* 1a 'a layer of grass etc. with earth and matted roots, as the surface of grassland', 3a 'horse-racing', 3b 'the racecourse for horse racing'
This word was adopted with the import of horse racing – and its frequency has declined with the decline of interest (native equivalents also becoming more widely used); French and German acted as mediators for a few European languages.

Ge [turf] M [U] end19c, 3a,b(1 obs) **Du** [tʏrf] C [U] beg20c, 3a,b(1 tech) **Nw** (o) **Fr** [tyrf] M, mid19c, 3b(1 obs) → *turfiste* M/F **Sp** <=E> M [U] mid20c, 1a,3a(1 tech) **It** [tœrf] M [U]/pl. Ø, end19c, 1a(1 obs) 3b(1 tech) **Rm** [turf] N, end19c, via Fr, 3a,b(3 tech) → *turfist* M **Rs** *torf* M [U] via Ge, 1a(3) **Po** [turf] M [U] mid19c, 3a,b(1 obs) **Hu** [tərf] [U] beg 19c, via Ge, 1a,3b(1 rare) 3a(2 obs)

turn *v.* +1b 'become entangled or knotted (of ropes, fishing gear, etc.)', (naut.) +31 'introduce someone to cannabis'
Ic *törna* [tʰœrna] 1970s, +31(1 sla); *turna* [tʰʏrtna] 1970s (orig. from OE) +31(4 sla); *törnast* mid20c, +1b(2 tech) → *törnaður* adj.

turn *n./cp²* 8 'an opportunity or obligation etc. that comes successively to each of several persons etc.', +8a 'a burst of work or other activity', +18 'a sailing trip', +19 'an aerobatic curve', +20 'a drug-induced trance'
Ge *Törn* M, pl. -*s*, 1960s, +18(3 tech); *Turn*, 1940s, +19(1 tech); 1980s, +20(1 sla) **Nw** *törn* [tørn] M, pl. -*er*, 19c, 8, +8a(3) **Ic** *törn* [tʰærtn] F, pl. *tarnir* (freq. cp²) beg20c, via Da, 8,+8a(3 coll) **Rs** *turné* + 18(5Fr) **Hu** [=E] [U] end20c, +20(1 tech)

turnip *n.* 2 'the white globular root of a plant, used as a vegetable'

The fact that this word was borrowed from English may come as a surprise; it appears to have been more widespread a hundred years ago, since when native terms have come to be preferred in some languages.

Ge (o arch) **Nw** *turnips* [tʉːr-nips] M, pl. *er*, beg20c (3) **Ic** *turnips* N, mid19c, via Da (1 obs) < *næpa* **Fr** *turnep/turneps* M, end19c (1 tech) **Rs** *turneps* M, pl. *-y*, beg20c (2) **Po** *turnips* [tur-] M, beg20c (1 tech) **Fi**

turnipsi 19c (3) **Hu** [tu̱rnip] [U] beg19c (1 tech, arch)

turn on *v.* +2 'excite, enthuse', +3 'become intoxicated with drugs'

Ge *antörnen*, 1970s, +2(1 you) +3(1 sla) **Nw** *tørne* ["tø̱ːrne] 1970s, +2(2 coll)

turnover *n.* 1 'the act or an instance of turning over', 2 'the amount of money taken in a business', 3 'the number of people entering and leaving employment etc.'

Nw [=E/-oːver-] M, pl. *-s*, 1960s, 3(1 tech) **Fr** [tœRnɔvœR] M, 1990s, 3(tech, jour) **It** [turno̱ver] M, pl. Ø, 1970s, 1(1 tech) 2(2 tech_ECON) 3(2 tech, jour)

turtleneck *n.* 1 'a high close-fitting neck on a knitted garment'

Du [=E] C, 1980s (1 tech) **Nw** [=E] 1980s (1 rare) < *høyhals* **Gr** <=E>/*tertl nek* N, 1990s (1 tech, mod) < *zivago*

TV *abbrev./cp¹* 'television' (cf. ↑*television*)

The abbreviation has obvious advantages for titles and headlines, but is more restricted than might be expected; pronunciation varies between English and native ones. By contrast, the full form *television* is treated as a Latinism in all languages here investigated.

Ge cp¹ [teː fa̱u] N [U] 1980s (3 jour) < *Fernsehen* **Du** [teːveː] C, 1970s (3) **Nw** [te̱ːve] M, pl. *-er*, 1960s (3) **Ic** [=E] N [U] end20c (o sla) < *sjónvarp* **Fr** [teve] F, 1960s (2) **Sp** [teu̱be] F, 1970s (2) **It** [teve] (2 reg) **It** *tv/tivù* [tivu̱] F, pl. Ø, 1950s (3) **Rm** *TV(R)* [te ve̱ (re)] N [U] 1960s (5) < *televiziune* **Rs** *teve̱* 1980s (1 coll) **Po** [=E] N [U] 1980s (1 coll) **Cr** [teve] F [U] end20c (2 coll) < *televizija* **Bg** *tv/* <=E> [te̱ ve/ti vi̱] 1990s (2 jour/coll) **Fi** [teːveː] 1960s (3) **Hu** [te̱ːveː] pl. *-k*, 1960s (3) **Al** [të vë] 1960s (3) **Gr** *tv/ti vi̱* F [U] 1980s (1 jour, coll)

tweed *n.* 1 'a rough-surfaced woollen cloth, usu. of mixed flecked colours, originally produced in Scotland'

This term is one of the most widespread early adoptions illustrating the dominance of English textiles.

Ge [twiːt] M [U] beg20c (2) **Du** [twiːt] N [U] 1940s (2 tech) **Nw** [tviːd] M [U] end19c (2) **Ic** *tweed/tvíd* [tʰviːt] N [U] end19c (2) **Fr** [twid] M, mid19c (2) **Sp** [twid] M, pl. *-s*, 1920s (1 tech) **It** [twiːd] M [U] end19c (2 tech) **Rm** [=E] N [U] 1960s (2 tech) **Rs** *tvid* M [U] mid20c (2) → *-ovyi̱* adj. **Po** [twit] M,

mid20c (2) → *-owy* adj. **Cr** *tvid* M [U] mid20c (2) **Bg** *tu̱id* M [U] mid20c (1 tech) **Fi** [tveːd] 19c (2) **Hu** [=E] [U] beg20c (3 tech) → cp¹ **Gr** *tu̱id* N [U] beg20c (2 tech)

tweeter *n.* 'a loudspeaker designed to reproduce high frequencies'

Ge [=E] M, pl. Ø (1 tech, rare) **Du** [=E] C, pl. *-s* (1 tech) **Fr** [twitœR] M, mid20c (1 tech, ban) > *haut parleur d'aigus, tuiteur* **Sp** <=E> M, end20c (1 tech, rare) **It** [twi̱ter] M, pl. Ø (1 tech)

twen* *n.* 'a (esp. male) person between 20 and 29'

This word was coined in German by the fashion industry to create an equivalent to ↑*teenager* – and never spread abroad, except to Dutch. It is now obsolescent, and is mainly used facetiously, if at all. It is often quoted as the typical case of a pseudo-anglicism made from English lexical material but not recorded in English itself (and not borrowed into it!).

Ge [tven] M, pl. *-s*, 1960s (2 mod > 2 obs) **Du** [twɛn] C, 1960s (2) → *twenny* n., *twennie* n.

twill *n.* 'a fabric so woven as to have a surface of diagonal parallel ridges'

Ge [=E] M, pl. *-sl-e*, 1930s (2/3 tech) **Nw** <=E>/*tvill* [=E] M [U] 20c (1 tech) **Sp** [=E] M, 1980s (1 tech) **Hu** [=E] [U] beg20c (1 tech, arch)

twinset *n.* 'a matching combination of jumper and cardigan'

This word was popular from the 1960s onwards in Western Europe – although the combination of two pieces had of course been used before; the term did not spread to the east, and it is difficult to see why it should. (There is also a German coinage *triset* which is rare and does not seem to have spread to other languages)

Ge [tvi̱nset] N/M, pl. *-s*, 1960s (2 tech) **Du** [=E] C, 1970s (2 tech) **Nw** [=E] N, pl. Ø, 20c (1 rare) < *kardigansett* **Fr** [twinsɛt] M, 1950s (1) **Sp** [=E] M, pl. *-s*, end20c (1 tech) **It** [twi̱n set] M, pl. Ø, 1960s (2 tech) **Cr** *(tvin) set* M, pl. *-ovi*, mid20c (1 tech)

twist (1) *v.* 10 'dance the twist'

Ge [tvi̱sten] 1960s (1 obs) **Du** [=E] 1960s (4 obs) **Nw** *twiste* [tvi̱ste] 1960s (1 obs) **Ic** *tvista* [tʰvi̱sta] 1960s (2 coll, arch) **Rs** *tvistovat'* mid20c (1 obs) **Po** - < *tanczyc' twista* **Cr** *tvi̱stati* mid20c (3) **Fi** *twistata* 1960s (1 obs) **Hu** *tw-/tvisztel* [tvi̱stel] 1960s (2 obs)

twist¹ (1) *n.* 12 'the act of twisting' (gymnastics), 15 'a dance with a twisting movement of the body'

Ge [tvist] M [U] 1960s, 15(1 obs) **Du** [twɪst] C [U] 1960s (2 obs) **Nw** [tvist] M [U] 1960s, 15(1 obs) **Ic** *tvist* [tʰvɪst] N [U] 1960s, 15(2 coll, arch) **Fr** [=E] M, 1960s (1 obs) **Sp** [=E] M, 1960s (1 obs) **It** [=E] M [U] 1960s (2 obs) **Rm** [=E] N, pl. *-uri*, 1960s (1 obs) **Rs**

tvist M [U] mid20c (1 obs)   **Po** [=E/tvist] M [U] mid20c, 15(1 obs) → *-owy* adj.   **Cr** *tvist* M [U] mid20c, 15(1 obs)   **Bg** *tsvist* M, pl. *-a/-ove*, 20c, 12(1 tech); *tuist* M [U] 1960s, 15 (1 obs)   **Fi** [=E] 1960s (1 obs)   **Hu** <=E>/*tviszt* [=E] [U] 1960s (2 obs)   **Al** *tuist* M [U] mid20c, 15(2)   **Gr** *tuist* N [U] 1960s (1 obs)

twist² (1)   *n.* +3a 'cotton waste' (used for wiping oil from machines, etc.), 7 'a fine strong silk', +7b 'a cotton thread or fabric used as a warp in weaving and embroidering'

At least three homonyms were borrowed into European languages: the meaning of a mixed drink is obsolete in Britain and has been for some time on the Continent (and is therefore not documented here); the nineteenth-century borrowing for 'a fine strong silk' is still very much alive, its distribution nicely illustrating the economic influence of Britain; and a short-lived dance of the 1960s, the term more widely attested throughout Europe, but now obsolete as a consequence of changing fashions.

Ge [tvist] M [U] beg19c, 7(2)   **Du** *twist* end19c, 7(4)   **Nw** [tvist] M [U] mid19c, +3a, 7(2)   **Ic** *tvistur* [tʰvɪstʏr] M [U] 17c, +7b(3); beg20c, +3a(3)

two-step   *n.* 'a round dance in march or polka time'

The name of the dance spread quickly in the 1920s, but did not affect Eastern and Southern Europe; the dance is largely obsolescent – which means that the loanword is rarely found and very unlikely to spread any further.

Ge [=E] M [U] 1920s (1 obs)   **Du** [=E] C, end19c (1

tech)   **Nw** [=E] M [U] 20c (1 obs)   **Ic** *tústep* [tʰus-tɛhp] N [U] beg/mid20c, via Da (1 obs)   **Fr** [tustɛp] M, beg20c (1 obs)   **Sp** [=E/tueste(p)] M, pl. *-s*, beg20c (1 arch)   **It** [=E] M, pl. Ø, 1940s (1 obs)   **Rs** *tustep* M [U] beg20c (1 obs)   **Cr** [=E] M [U] beg20c (1 obs)   **Fi** [=E] 1920s (1 obs)   **Hu** [=E] [U] beg20c (1 obs)

tycoon   *n.* 'a business magnate'

This word originated as a foreignism, the address to the great shogun in Japan in the nineteenth century, but came quickly to be applied to important people in business. It has marginal status in a few mainly Central European languages in journalese writing.

Ge [=E] M, pl. *-s/-e*, 1960s (1 mod)   **Du** [=E] C, pl. *-conen*, 1980s (1 mod)   **Nw** (0)   **Sp** (0)   **It** [=E] M, pl. Ø, 1970s (1 mod/ jour)   **Cr** *tajkun* M, pl. *-i*, end20c (1)

typhoon   *n.* 'a tropical storm in the western Pacific'

The etymology of this word is multiple, merging Greek, Arabic, Persian, Indian, and Chinese sources. This makes it difficult to establish on what basis individual lexemes are based, and to determine the English component in the process of transmission.

Ge *Taifun* M, pl. *-e*, beg19c (3)   **Du** *tyfoon* [ti:fo:n] C, 19c (3) > *taifoen*   **Nw** *tyfon* [tyfu:n] M, pl. *-er*, 19c (3)   **Fr** *typhon* [tifõ] M, 19c (3)   **Sp** *tifón* M, 19c (3/ 5Fr)   **It** *tifone* (5Port/Arab/Gr)   **Rm** *taifun* [tajfun] N, pl. *-uri*, end19c, via Ge (3); *tifon* [tifon] M, pl. *-i*, end19c, via Fr (3 arch); *tifone* [tifone] M, pl. *-i*, mid19c, via It (3 arch)   **Rs** *taifun* M, pl. *-y*, 19c (3)   **Po** (5Ge)   **Cr** *tajfun* M, pl. *-i*, 19c (3)   **Bg** *taifun* M, pl. *-a/-i*, beg20c (2)   **Fi** *taifun* 19c, via Ge (3)   **Hu** *tájfun* [ta:ifun] pl. Ø, beg19c, via Ge/Port (3/5Gr)   **Al** *tajfun* M, pl. *-e*, end19c (3)   **Gr** *tyfonas* M, 20c (3)

U

UFO *n.* 1 'an unidentified flying object', +2 (metaph.) 'a person who is unable to see reality; an idiot'

The acronym is opaque in Continental languages; it is normally pronounced according to national conventions. The thing is widely referred to by the name of one particular type of UFO – the ↑*Flying Saucer* (which is also frequent in calqued forms).
Ge [u̲:fo:] N, pl. *-s*, 1950s, 1(3) < *Fliegende Untertasse* **Du** *UFO/ufo* [y̲:fo:] C, pl. *-'s*, 1960s, 1(2) **Nw** [u̲:fo] M, pl. *-er*, 1950s, 1(3) **Ic** [=E/uf:ou] end20c, 1(1) < *fljúgandi furðuhlutur* **Fr** - < trsl *OVNI = objet volant non identifié → ufologie* F **Sp** [u̲fo] M, pl. *-s*, 1970s, 1(1) < *OVNI (Objeto Volador No Identificado) → ufólogo/ufología* **It** [u̲fo] M, pl. Ø, 1960s, 1(3) < trsl *oggeto volante non identificato, disco volante → ufologia* n.; *ufologo* n. **Rm** [ufo] N, 1970s, 1(2) < trsl *OZN* **Rs** 1(0) < trsl *NLO → ufologiya* F **Po** [ufo] N, end20c, 1(2) **Cr** *ufo* M, end20c, 1(1) < trsl *neidentificiram leteći objekt (leteći tanjur)* **Bg** - < 1: trsl *NLO (neidentifitsiran letyasht obekt)* **Fi** [u:εf:o:/ufo] 1950s, 1(2) **Hu** [ufo̲:] pl. *-k*, 1980s, 1(3) **Al** *UFO* F, pl. Ø, 1980s, 1(3) **Gr** *ufo* N, end20c, 1(2) +2(2 coll)

ullage *n.* 2 'loss by evaporation or leakage'
Du [y̲lɔзə] C, 1940s (1 tech) **Rm** *ulaj* [ula3] N [U] 1960s, via Fr? (2 tech) **Po** *ulaż* [ula3] M, mid20c (1 tech)

ulster[1] (1) *n.* 'a long loose overcoat of rough cloth'
The words for the dress and for the cloth were widely adopted from the nineteenth century onwards, but appear to have become obsolescent in most languages (revival of fashion terms never to be excluded).
Ge [ulsta] M, pl. Ø, end19c (1 tech, obs) **Du** [y̲lstər] C, end19c (2 tech) **Nw** [u̲lster] M, pl. *-e*, beg20c (1 obs) **Ic** *úlster/ulster* [ulster] M, pl. *-ar* (freq. as cp[1]) beg20c (2 arch, mod) **Fr** [ylstɛʀ] M, end19c (1 tech) **Sp** [u̲lster] M, beg20c (1 jour, arch) **It** [u̲lster] M, pl. Ø, 1870s (1 arch) **Rm** [u̲lster] N, pl. *-e*, mid20c, via Fr? (2 tech) **Rs** (0) **Po** *ulster* [ulster] M, mid20c (1 tech) **Cr** *u̲lster* M, pl. *-i*, beg20c (1 tech) (3) **Hu** *ulszter* [u̲lster] pl. *-ek/Ø*, end19c/beg20c (1 tech, arch)

ulster[2] (1) *n.* +2 'a type of cloth'

Ge [ulsta] M [U] end19c (1 tech, obs) **Nw** (0) **Ic** [ulster] N [U] beg20c (2) **Fr** [ylstɛʀ] M, end19c (1 tech) **It** [ulster] M, pl. Ø, 1870s (1 arch) **Rs** (0) **Po** *ulster* [ulster] M [U] mid20c (1 tech) **Cr** *u̲lster* M [U] beg20c (1 tech)

u(ltra)p(ast)e(urization)* *n.* 'partial sterilization of milk'
Sp *uperización* **It** *uperizzazione* F, 1970s → *uperizzare* v.; *uperizzatore* n.

umpire *n.* 1 'a person chosen to enforce the rules and settle disputes in various sports'
Ge [=E] M, end19c (0 arch) **Du** [ʏm-] C, pl. *-s*, beg20c (1 tech_{TENNIS})

Uncle Sam *n.* 'a nickname for the USA'
Ge [=E] M [U] beg20c (1 obs) **Du** (Ø) **Nw** <=E>/*onkel Sam* [=E] [U] 20c (1) **Ic** - < trsl *Sámur frændi* **Fr** (0) **Sp** - < trsl *Tio Sam* **It** - < trsl *zio Sam* **Rs** - < trsl *dyadyushka Sém* **Cr** - < trsl *Ujak Sam* **Bg** - < trsl *Chicho Sam* **Hu** [=E] [U] 20c (0)

under- *cp*[1] +1a 'a team in which members do not exceed a certain age' (sports)
It [a̲nder/u̲nder] F/adj., pl. Ø, 1950s (3) e.g. *la nazionale under 21*

undercover *cp*[1] 2 'engaged in spying, esp. by working with or among those to be observed'
Ge +*Agent* [=E] cp[1], 1980s (1 mod) < *verdeckter Ermittler, V-Mann* **Du** *undercover* [yndər-/=E] 1980s (1 tech) **Nw** [=E] cp[1], 1980s (1) **Rm** - < trsl *sub acoperire*

undercut *n.* +5 'a blow to the adversary's ribs' (box.)
Du [ʏndəkʏt] C, pl. *-s* (1 tech) **It** [a̲nderkat] M, pl. Ø, 1930s (1 tech)

underdog *n.* 1 'a competitor thought to have little chance of winning a fight or contest', +3 'a person not treated according to their desert'
Ge [a̲ndadɔk] M, pl. *-s*, 1960s, +3(1 coll) **Du** [ʏndərdɔk] C, 1960s, +3(1 coll) **Nw** [=E] M, pl. *-s/-er*, 20c, 1(1) **Rs** *anderdog* M, pl. *-i*, end20c, +3(1 coll) **Po** [=E] N, pl. *-s*, 1970s, 1, +3(1 jour)

underground *n./cp*[1/2] 1 'an underground railway', 2 'secret, hidden', 3 'unconventional, experimental', +3a 'a subculture with an alternative lifestyle to the socially accepted (sometimes connected with drugs)', +3b 'a school concentrating on taboo topics' (film, music, literature, etc.), +4 'a style of popmusic', +5 'the underworld'

The wide adoption of the term – for which native terms were available in all the languages concerned – appears to be remarkable; even calques are less frequent than might have been expected.

Ge I (Ø); [=E] M [U] 1960s, +3b(I tech) = +3b: trsl *Unter-grund* **Du** I(Ø); [yndər-/=E] C, 1960s, +3b(I tech) **Nw** [=E] M/ cp¹ [U] end20c, +3a(I tech); - < I: *undergrum* = 3b: *undergrunns-* **Ic** [=E] N [U] mid20c I(Ø) +3a(I sla); [=E] cp¹, 1970s, 2,3(I sla) < 2,3: trsl *neðanjarðar-* **Fr** cp² [=E] end20c (I tech); [ɛ̃dœʀgrund] N, 1960s, +3b(I obs) **Sp** [andergraun/ undergraun] 1960s (I tech) **It** [=E] M [U] 1970s, +3a(I tech); [andergraund] uninfl., 1970s (I tech) **Rm** [=E] N, 1970s, 3,+3b(2 tech); [=E] N [U] 1990s, +3a(0>I writ) **Rs** *andergraund/andegraund* M [U] 1990s, 2,+3b(I jour) +3a(I you) **Po** [andergraunt] M [U] mid20c, +3a(2 mod); [-er-] uninfl., end 20c, 2,3(I tech) **Cr** [=E] adj., end20c, 2(I tech) = trsl *podzemni* **Bg** *ŭndŭrgraund* M [U] 1980s, 3(I youмusic) +4(I tech, you) +5(3 sla, you) **Hu** [andergraund] [U] 20c, +3a(I coll, jour, mod); [=E] end20c, 2(I tech) +3b(I mod) < 2, +3b: *földalatti* **Gr** <=E>/adergraud N [U] end20c, +3a,b(I tech)

understatement *n.* I 'expression in greatly or unduly restrained terms'

Ge [andaste:tment] N, pl. -s, 1950s (I coll) < *Untertreibung* **Du** [yndər-/=E] N, 1960s (I coll, jour) **Nw** [=E] N, pl. -s, mid20c (I coll) **Ic** [=E] N, pl. Ø, mid/ end20c (I sla) = *úrdráttur* **It** [=E] M, pl. Ø, 1950s (I coll) **Po** (0) **Fi** [=E] (0) **Hu** [andersteitment] pl. Ø, end20c (I tech)

unfair *adj.* I 'not honest', 2 'not according to the rules'

The distribution of this term is far more limited than that of ↑*fair*, native forms of negation being normally preferred outside the Germanic languages, which have *un-* in identical function.

Ge [unfe:r] beg20c (3) → *-ness* F **Du** [ynfe:r] 1940s (2) = *onspor-tief, oneerlijk* **Nw** [=E] beg20c (2) < *usportslig* **Ic** [=E] end20c, I(I sla) **Po** (0) **Cr** *unfer* mid20c (3) **Hu** [anfer] end19c/ beg20c (2)

unisex *n./cp¹* '(hairstyle, dress, etc.) designed to be suitable for both sexes'

Ge [u:niseks] uninfl., 1970s (I mod) **Du** *uniseks* [y:nisɪks] C [U] 1960s (I tech) **Nw** [u:niseks] 1960s (I obs) **Ic** <=E>/*únísex* [=E/u:nisɛks] cp¹, uninfl.,

1970s (I mod, obs) **Fr** *unisexe* 1960s (4) **Sp** [uni-seks] uninfl., 1970s (I jour); *unisexo* (4) **It** [unisɛks] M/adj. [U] 1960s (2 mod) **Rm** [uniseks] adj., uninfl., 1980s (I mod) **Rs** *uniseks* adj., uninfl., 1980s (I mod/ you) **Po** [uniseks] M, uninfl., end20c (I mod) **Bg** *uniseks* adj., uninfl., 1980s (I mod) **Cr** *uniseks* M [U] end20c (I tech) **Fi** [uniseks] 1970s (I mod) **Hu** *uniszex* [uniseks] adj., 1970s → n. **Gr** <=E> [juni-seks] adj., uninfl., mid20c (2)

unit *n.* Ia 'an individual, thing, person, or group regarded as single and complete'

Du [jynɪt] F/M, 1950s (2) **Nw** (0) **Hu** [=E/unit] pl. Ø, mid20c (I tech)

update *n.* 2 'a set of updated information' (esp. in computing)

Ge [=E] N, pl. -s, end20c (I tech/mod) **Du** [yp-] C, pl. -s, end20c (I tech) **Bg** *ŭpdeĭt* M [U] 1990s (I tech, mod) **Gr** <=E> [=E] N, pl. -s, end20c (I tech)

upper *n.* 'a stimulant drug, esp. an amphetamine'

Ic [œhparɪ] M, pl. -ar, 1970s (I sla)

upper class *n./cp¹* I 'the aristocracy', +2 'belonging to the upper (price) range' (of products, services)

Ge [=E] F [U] 1970s, I(Ø>I mod); 1980s, +2(I mod) **Du** [ypər-/=E] (Ø) **Nw** I(0) **Ic** [=E] cp¹, mid/end20c, I(0) < *yfirstéttar-* **Sp** I(0) **It** [aper klas] F, pl. Ø, end20c (I jour, mod) **Rm** (0)

uppercut *n.* 'an upwards blow delivered with the arm bent' (box.)

Ge [apakat] M, pl. -s, beg20c (I tech, obs) < *Aufwärts-haken* **Du** [ypər-/=E] C, mid20c (I tech) **Nw** [=E] M, pl. -er/-s, 1930s (I tech) **Ic** [=E] N [U] mid20c (I tech) **Fr** [ypɛʀkyt] beg20c (I tech) **It** [upperkut/=E] M, pl. Ø, 1910s (2 tech) < *rend montante* **Rm** *upercut* [uperkut] N, beg20c, via Fr? (2 tech) → *upercuta* v. **Rs** *apperkot* M [U] beg20c (I tech) **Po** *aperkut/uper-kut* [aperkut/uperkut] M, beg20c (I tech) **Cr** *aperkat* M, pl. -i, beg20c (I tech) **Bg** *ŭperkut/ŭperkŭt* M, pl. -al-i, beg/mid20c (I tech) **Hu** [=E/əpperkət] [U] beg20c (I tech, arch) **Al** *aperkat* M, pl. -e, mid20c (I rare) **Gr** *aperkat* N, 20c (I tech)

upper ten* *n.* 'the upper class'

Ge [apaten] pl. -s, end19c (I arch) < trsl *die oberen Zehntausend* **Du** [ypərtɛn] C [U] beg20c (2 rare) **Nw** [=E] 20c (I obs) **Hu** - < trsl *felső tízezer*

ups and downs *phr.* +3 'variations in health and spirits'

Du *ups end downs* [yps ən dauns] pl., 1980s (2) **Nw** [=E] 20c (I) **Ic** [=E/œhp(ɪn) o: tau:n(ɪn)] 1970s (I sla)

up to date *adj.* 'meeting or according to the latest requirements, knowledge, or fashion; modern'

The fashionable adoption of this term by those who want to be up to date is in progress and difficult to judge.

Ge [aptude:t] uninfl., mid20c (2) **Du** [yp-/ =E] uninfl., 1970s (2) → *updaten* v.; *updater* n., *updating* n., *update* n. **Nw** [=E] 20c (I)

Ic [=E] uninfl., end20c (0)   **Fr** (0)   **It** [ap tu de͟it] uninfl., 1920s (1 mod, rare)   **Rm** [=E] 1970s (0>1 tech)   **Rs** *ap-tu-de͟it*, uninfl., 1990s (1 coll, mod)   **Hu** [a͟ptode:t] beg20c (1 rare)   **Gr** <=E> [=E] 1990s (1 coll, mod)

used   *adj.* 'second-hand' (of clothes, vehicles, etc.)

Ge [=E] uninfl., 1980s (1 rare, mod)   **Gr** <=E> [=E] uninfl., 1980s (1 writ/2 coll)

user   *n.* 1 'a person who uses a computer', 2 'a drug addict'

Ge [ju͟:za] M, pl. Ø, 1980s, 1(1 tech); 1970s, 2(1 sla, rare)   **Du** - < trsl *gebruiker* **Nw** - < 1: *bruker*; 2: *misbruker* **Ic** - < 1: trsl *notandi*; 2: *-neytandi* M/cp[2]   **Fr** (0 ban) < *usager*   **Rm** [=E] M, end1980s, 1(1 tech, sla) < trsl *utilizator*   **Rs** *yu͟zer* M, pl. *-y*, 1995, 1(1 tech, sla) 1980s, 1,2(1 tech) < 1: *felhasználó* pl. Ø/-s, end20c, 2(1 sla)

Hu [iu͟:ser] pl. Ø, **Gr** <=E͟> [=E] M,

vamp *n.* 'a woman who uses sexual attraction to exploit men'
Ge [vemp] M, pl. -s, beg20c (2 obs) **Du** [=E] C, 1940s (2) = *vampier* **Nw** [vamp] M, pl. -er, beg20c (3) → *vampete* adj. **Fr** [vãp] F, beg20c (1 obs) → *vamper* v. **Sp** [bamp] F, 1970s (1 jour) < *vampi*/*vampiresa* **It** [vamp] F, pl. Ø, 1930s (3 coll) **Rm** *vampă* [vampə] F, mid20c, via Fr (3) **Rs** *vamp* F, pl. -y, mid20c (1 jour) **Po** *wamp* M, mid20c (3) **Cr** *vamp* F, pl. -ovi, mid20c (2) **Bg** *zhena-vamp* F/cp², pl. *zheni-vamp*, mid20c (5+2) **Fi** *vamppi* beg20c (3) **Hu** [vamp] pl. Ø, beg20c (3 obs) **Gr** *vab* F, mid20c (2 obs)

van *n.* 1 'a covered vehicle for conveying goods etc.', +1a 'a large (eight-seater) car', +1b 'a covered vehicle for racehorses'
Ge [ven] M, pl. -s, 1990s, +1a (1 tech, mod) = *Großraumlimousine* **Nw** [=E] M, pl. -s, 1970s (2 mod) **Ic** *van* [va:n] M, mid/end20c, 1(1 tech) < rend *sendi(ferða)bíll* **Fr** (0) **It** [van] M, pl. Ø, 1980s (1 tech) **Rm** [van] N, beg20c, via Fr, +1b(3 tech, rare) **Po** <=E> M, end20c (1 coll)

VAT *abbrev.* 'Value Added Tax'
National terms/acronyms are expected for the tax. The English term is itself calqued on German *Mehrwertsteuer*, so the borrowing into Polish comes as a surprise – there may be a euphemistic function in employing a non-transparent foreign acronym.
Du - < *BTW* (= creat *Belasting over de toegevoegde waarde*) **Nw** (0) < *moms* **Ic** - < *virðisaukaskattur*/VSK **Fr** - < trsl *TVA* (*taxe à la valeur ajoutée*) **Sp** - < trsl *IVA* **It** - < trsl *IVA* (*imposta sul valore aggiunto*) **Rm** - < rend *TVA* (*taxă pe valoarea adăugată*) **Rs** - < rend *NDS* **Po** [vat] end20c (2 mod) **Cr** - < creat *PDV* (*porez na dodanu vrijednost*) **Bg** - < rend *DDS* (*Danŭk dobavena stoĭnost*) **Fi** - < creat *ALV* (*arvonlisävero*) **Hu** - < rend *áfa* **Gr** (0) < trsl *FPA*

Vauxhall* *n.* 'a railway station'
This meaning was coined in Russian, when an English Vauxhall (amusement park) opened close to a station of the first railway line in Russia near St. Petersburg. In the course of time, the name for this fair was transferred to the station building close by and finally became a generic term for railway stations in general. The use spread to Poland (then under Russian rule), but it is now used only as a street name in Warsaw.
Rs *vokzal* M, pl. -y, mid19c (3) **Po** *foksal* [foksal] M, end19c (1 arch) **Cr** (0)

verdict *n.* 2 'a decision'
Ge *Verdikt* N, 19c (5La) **Du** [vərdɪkt] N, pl. -en, beg19c (1 tech, rare) **Nw** (0) **Fr** [vɛrdikt] M, end18c (3) **Sp** *veredicto* M, 19c (3) **It** *verdetto* [verdetto] M, pl. -i, 17c (3) **Rm** [verdikt] N, mid19c, via Fr (3) **Rs** *verdikt* M, pl. -y, beg20c (1 tech) **Po** *werdykt* [verdikt] M, beg20c (3) **Cr** (0) **Bg** *verdikt* M, pl. -al-i, end19c (1 tech, arch) **Hu** *verdikt* [verdikt] pl. -ek, mid18c (3) **Al** *verdikt* M, pl. -e, 20c (1 tech)

VHS *abbrev.* 'Video Home System'
Ge [fauha:es] N [U] 1980s (3 tech) **Du** [ve:ha:ɪs] 1980s (3 tech) **Nw** [ve:ho:es] 1980s (3 tech) **Ic** *VHS* [vaf: hau:ɛs:] uninfl., 1980s (2 tech) **Fr** [veaʃɛs] 1980s (1 tech) **Sp** [ube atʃ e ese] M [U] end20c (1 tech) **It** [vu-akka-esse] end20c (1) **Rm** [ve haʃ es] 1990s (1 tech, writ, rare) **Rs** [ve ha es] end20c (1 tech) **Po** [fau ha es] end20c (2) **Cr** (0) **Bg** <=E> [ve ha es/ vi:ejtʃ es] end20c (1 tech, mod) **Fi** [ve:ho:es] 1980s (3) **Hu** [ve:ha:eʃ] [U] end20c (2 tech) **Gr** <=E> [=E] N [U] 1980s (2 tech)

video art* *n.* 'a form of art using television to produce abstract or figurative works of art'
Ge [=E] F [U] 1980s (1 tech) **It** [video art] F, pl. Ø, 1980s (1 tech)

videoclip *n.* 'a short video film on a pop music item' (cf. ↑*clip*)
Ge [=E] M, pl. -s, 1980s (1 mod) **Du** [=E] C, 1980s (2) **Nw** (*musikk-*)*video* [vi:deu] M, pl. -er, 1980s (3) **Ic** - < rend *tónlistarmyndband; (músik) vídeó* **Fr** *videoclip* [=E] M (1 tech, ban) > (*bande*) *promo* **Sp** [bideoklip] M, pl. -s, 1980s (1>2) **It** [=E] M, pl. Ø, 1980s (1>2 tech) **Rm** [=E] N, 1990s (1 mod) **Rs** *videoklip* M, pl. -y, end20c (2 mod) **Po** *video-clip* [=E] M, end20c (1 mod) **Bg** (*video*)*klip* M, pl. -al-ove, 1980s (2) **Hu** *videoklip* [=E] M, pl. -ek, 1980s (2 mod) **Al** *videoklip* M, pl. -e, 1992 (1 mod) **Gr** *videoklip* N, pl. Ø/-s, 1980s (2)

video game *n.* 'a game played by electronically

manipulating images produced by a computer program on a television screen'
Du *videogame* [=E] C, pl. *-s*, end20c (1 tech)   **Nw** - < trsl *videospill*   **Fr** - < trsl *jeu vidéo*   **It** [=E/gem] M, pl. *Ø/-s* (1 tech) = trsl *videogioco*   **Po** - < *gra na wideo*   **Bg** - < trsl *videoigra*   **Hu** Ø < trsl *videojáték* (3+5)   **Gr** <=E> [=E] N, pl. *-s* (1 tech, you)

video recorder   *n.* 'an apparatus for recording and playing videotapes'
Ge [vi:deorekorda] M, pl. Ø, 1970s (3)   **Du** [=E] C, 1970s (3)   **Nw** (0) < *videospiller, video*   **Ic** *vídeó (tæki)* [vi:de.ou-] N, pl. Ø, 1980s (2) = creat *myndbandstæki*   **Sp** (0) < *vídeo* M   **It** [=E/-re] M, pl. Ø, 1960s (1 tech) < trsl *videoregistratore*   **Rm** [videorekorder] N, 1980s (3) < *video*   **Rs** *vjdeo* N, uninfl., 1980s (3) = *videomagnitofon, vjdik*   **Po** *wideo* [video] N, uninfl., end20c (2)   **Cr** [videorekorder] M, pl. *-i*, end20c (3)   **Bg** *video(rekorder)* N, pl. *videa(-ri)*, 1980s (2)   **Hu** <=E>/ *-rekorder* [videorekorder] pl. *-ek*, 1980s (1 tech>2) < *képmagnó video*   **Al** *video* F/ N, pl. Ø, 1990 (2)   **Gr** *vjdeo* N, 1980s (2)

videotape   *n.* 2 'a video cassette', 3 'a recording made on such tape'
Ge - < *Videokassette*   **Du** [=E] C, pl. *-s*, end20c (1 tech)   **Nw** [vi:deuteip] M, pl. *-er*, end20c (1 tech) < *videobånd, -kassett*   **Fr** - < *bande vidéo*   **Sp** [=E] M, 1970s (0>1 tech)   **It** [=E] M, pl. Ø, 1970s (1 tech) > *videonastro*   **Po** - < *kaseta wideo*   **Cr** *videotejp* end20c (1 tech)   **Bg** - < trsl *videokaseta*   **Hu** [=E] pl. *-ek*, end20c (1 tech, writ) < *videokazetta*   **Al** - < *videokasetë*

videotex(t)   *n.* 'any electronic information system, esp. teletext or viewdata'
Ge (5La)   **Du** [=E] C [U] end20c (1 tech)   **Nw** [vi:deuteks(t)] M [U] 1980s (1 tech/5La?)   **Fr** *vidéotexte* [videotɛkst] M, 1980s (1 tech)   **Sp** [=E] M, 1980s (1 tech)   **It** [videoteks(t)] M, pl. Ø, 1980s (1 tech)   **Hu** [=E] pl. Ø, end20c, (1 tech)

VIP   *abbrev./n.* 1 'very important person', +2 'an airport checkpoint for VIPs'
   Although this term was coined in 1933 and has been used as a loanword at least from the 1960s onwards, its status (accepted? facetious?) and its form (to be pronounced as a word?, as individual letters – and, if so, according to national or English conventions?) appear to be largely unsettled. The item is relatively well-known in the combination *VIP-Lounge*.
Ge [vip/vi:aipi:] M, pl. *-s*, 1960s, 1(1 mod)   **Du** *VIP/vip* [vip] C, 1950s (1 coll)   → *viproom* n.   **Nw** [vip/ve:i:pe:] M, pl. *-er*, 1960s (3 fac, mod)   **Ic** <=E> / *vippi* [=E/vɪhpɪ] M, pl. *-ar*, mid/end20c, 1(1/2 coll)   **Fr** *veipe/ viajpi* M [U] 1960s (1 fac)   **Sp** [bip] M, pl. *-s*, 1960s (2)   **It** [vip] M/F, pl. Ø, 1960s (2 mod)   **Rm** [vip] N/ M/F, 1990s (1 coll, mod)   **Rs** *vi-aĭ-pĭ* M/F, uninfl., 1990s (1 mod)   **Po** [vip] M, end20c (1 coll)   **Cr** [vip] M, pl. *-ovi*, end20c (1)   **Bg** <=E>/*VIP* [vip] M [U]

Ic	Nw	Po	Rs
Du	Ge	Cr	Bg
Fr	It	Fi	Hu
Sp	Rm	Al	Gr

mid20c, +2(3 tech) → *-adzhiya* M   **Fi** [vip:1] 1960s (2 obs)   **Hu** [vip] [U] 20c (2>3)   **Al** *VIP* [U] 1995 (1)   **Gr** [vip] pl. *-s*, 1(2)

visiting professor   *n.* 'an academic spending some time at another institution'
Ge (0) < rend *Gastprofessor*   **Du** - < rend *gasthoogleraar*   **Nw** (0) < rend *gjesteprofessor*   **Ic** - < trsl *gistikennari*, rend *gestaprófessor*   **Fr** - < rend *professeur invité*   **Sp** - < trsl *profesor visitante*   **It** [vistin(g) professor] M, pl. Ø/-s, end20c (1 tech)   **Rm** (0) < rend *profesor invitat*   **Rs** (0)   **Po** [-profesor] M, end20c (1 tech) < rend *profesor wizytujcy*   **Cr** - < rend *gost profesor*   **Bg** - < trsl *gost-profesor*   **Hu** - < trsl *vendégprofesszor*   **Al** - < *profesor i ftuar*   **Gr** - < trsl *episkeptis kathighitis*

voice recorder   *n.* 'a device for recording voices and conversations, esp. in the cockpit of a plane'
Ge *Voice-Recorder* [=E] M, pl. Ø, end20c (1 tech)   **Du** [=E] C, pl. *-s*, end20c (1 tech)   **Nw** [=E] M, pl. *-e*, 20c (1 tech) = *taleregistrator*

volley   *n.* 3,4 'the return or kick of a ball before it touches the ground' (tennis and footb.)
Ge [voli] M, pl. *-s*, end19c (1 tech) > *Flugball* → *volley* adv.   **Du** [voli] C, 1940s (1 tech) → *volleyen* v.   **Nw** [=E] M, pl. *-er*, 1970s (1 tech)   **Fr** *vollée* F, end19c (4 tech)   **Sp** - < mean *volea*   **It** - < *volée, colpo al volo*   **Rm** *voleu* [volew] N, beg20c (5Fr)   **Rs** *volleĭ* M, pl. *-lei*, beg20c (1 tech)   **Po** [volej] M, beg20c (1 tech)   **Cr** *volej* M, pl. *-i*, beg20c (1 tech)   **Bg** *vole* N [U] mid20c (5Fr)   **Hu** [voli] [U] end19c (1 tech, arch) < *röpte*   **Gr** *vole* N, beg20c, via Fr (1 tech)

volleyball   *n.* 1 'a game for two teams of six hitting a large ball by hand over a net', +2 'the ball used'
Ge [volibal] M [U] 1950s (2+5) → *-er* M   **Du** *volleybal* [voli-] N [U] 1950s (2 tech+5) → *-en* v.   **Nw** [=E+Nw] M [U] 1930s (2+5)   **Ic** - < 1: rend *blak*   **Fr** *volley-ball/volley* M, 1920s (2) → *volleyer* v.; *volleyeur/ volleyeuse* M/F   **Sp** <=E>/*volibol/voleibol* M [U] 1960s (2>3) > *balonvolea*   **It** [volleibɔ:l] M [U] 1920s (2 tech) < trsl *pallavolo*   **Rm** *volei/volei-bal* [volejbal] N, 1920s, 1(3); - < +2: rend *minge de volei (-bal)* → *voleibalist* M/F; *voleibalistic* adj.   **Rs** *voleĭbol* M [U] 20c (3) → *-nyĭ* adj.; *-istka* F   **Po** - < *siatkówka*   **Cr** [volibol] M [U] 20c (1 tech)   **Bg** *voleĭbol* M [U] beg20c, 1(2); *valibol* (1 arch) → *-en* adj.; *-ist* M; *-istka* F   **Fi** [vol:ei] cp[1], mid20c (2)   **Hu** [volibal] [U] 1950s/60s (1 arch) < *röplabda*   **Al** *volejboll* M [U] 1940s, 1(3)   **Gr** *volei(bol)* N [U] 20c (2) > rend *petosferisi* → *voleibolistas* M; *voleibolistria* F

volume   *n.* 3a 'quantity or power of sound'
Ge (0)   **Du** (5Fr)   **Nw** - < mean *volum*   **Ic** [=E] N [U] 1970s (1 tech)   **Sp** - < mean *volumen*   **It** (5La)   **Rm** - < mean *volum*   **Cr** *volumen* M [U] mid20c (3)   **Fi** *volyymi*   **Hu** [E] [U] end20c (1 tech, writ)   **Al** - < mean *volum*   **Gr** <=E> 20c (1 writ)

voucher   *n./cp[1]* 1 'a document which can be used instead of money, for goods or services'
Ge [=E] M/cp[1], pl. Ø, 1970s (1 tech)   **Du** [fu:ʃe:] C, 1970s (1 tech)   **Nw** [=E] M, pl. *-e/-s*, 1970s (1 tech)

Ic [=E] M, pl. -*ar*, 1960s (1 tech)
Fr (o ban) < *bon d'échange, coupon* **Sp** [=E] M, 1970s (1 tech, rare) **It** [v̲autʃer] M, pl. Ø, 1970s (1 tech) < *coupon, buono* **Rm** [=E] N, end20c (1 tech) **Rs** *v̲au-cher* M, pl. -*y*, end20c (2 tech) → -*nyĭ* adj. **Po** [-er] M, end20c (1 tech) **Cr** *v̲aučer* M, pl. -*i*, end20c (1 tech) **Bg** *v̲aucher* M, pl. -*al-ĭ*, end20c (2 tech) **Fi** [=E] mid20c (1 rare) < *kuponki* **Hu** <=E>/*vócser* [v̲o:tʃer] pl. Ø, 1960s (1 tech > 2) **Gr** <=E>/*v̲autser* N, pl. Ø/-*s*, end20c (2 tech)

VSOP *abbrev.* 1 'Very Special Old Pale' (brandy etc.), +2 'of very good quality'
Ge [vi̲:eso:pi̲:/fa̲ueso:pe̲:] 1970s, 1(3 tech, rare) **Du** [ve:ɛso:pe:] 1970s, 1(1 tech) **Nw** [ve̲:esu:pe̲] 20c, 1(1 tech) **Ic** [vaf:ɛs: o: pʰje:] mid/end20c (2 tech) **It** [vu-ɛsse- ɔ- pi̲/viɛsse ɔ pi] mid20c, 1(1 tech) < *stravecchio* **Rm** <=E> 20c (1 tech, writ) **Rs** <=E> end20c, 1(1 tech, rare) **Po** [vauesope/=E] mid20c, 1(1 tech) **Cr** (o) **Hu** [ve̲:eso:pe:] 20c, 1(1 tech, writ) **Gr** (1 writ)

W

wad *n.* 1 'a lump or bundle of soft material used esp. to keep things apart or in place or to stuff up an opening'
It [wad] M, pl. Ø, 1960s (1 tech)

waders *n.* 2 'high waterproof boots, or a waterproof garment for the legs and body, worn in fishing etc.'
Nw - < trsl *vadere* **Ic** - < *vöðlur* **Fr** [wedœrs] pl., 1970s (1 tech) > *bottes pantalon* **It** [wader] M, pl. Ø, 1960s (1 tech) **Po** *wadery* [vaderi] pl., end20c (1 tech)

wagon *n.* 2 'a railway vehicle used for goods, esp. an open truck', +2a 'a railway vehicle used for people', +7 'a tramway wagon'

This word is one of the most widespread loanwords of nineteenth-century English railway terms, but since it was predominantly transmitted through French, it has largely lost its Englishness (acquiring nasalized pronunciation and end-stress in some languages).

Ge *Waggon* [vagón/õ] M, pl. *-s*, 19c, via Fr, 2, +2a(3) **Du** [wə:xon] C, mid19c (1 arch) **Nw** [vagon/vagon] M, pl. *-er*, mid19c (1 arch) **Fr** [vagõ] M, mid19c (3) **Sp** *vagón* M, pl. *-s*, mid19c, via Fr (3) **It** *vagone* [vagone] M, pl. *-i*, beg19c, via Fr (3) **Rm** *vagon* [vagon] N, mid19c, via Fr (3) **Rs** *vagon* M, pl. *-y*, end19c, via Ge (3) → *-nyĭ* adj. **Po** [vagon] M, mid19c, 2,+2a,+7(3) → *-ik* M; *-ownia* F; *-owy* adj. **Cr** *vagon* M, pl. *-i*, 19c/20c, 2(3) **Bg** *vagon* N, pl. *-al/-i*, end19c, via Fr, 2,+2a(3) → *-en* adj. **Hu** *vagon* [vagon] pl. *-ok*, 19c, 2,+2a(3) **Al** *vagon* M, pl. *-ë*, mid19c (3) **Gr** *vaghoni* N, 19c, via It (3)

Ic	Nw	Po	Rs
Du	Ge	Cr	Bg
Fr	It	Fi	Hu
Sp	Rm	Al	Gr

wagonette *n.* 'a four-wheeled horse-drawn pleasure vehicle, usu. open, with facing side seats'
It [wegonet] F, pl. Ø, 20c (1 tech)

wa(h)-wa(h) *n./cp¹* 'an effect achieved on brass instruments by alternately applying and removing a mute' (mus.)
Nw [=E] M/cp¹, 20c (1 tech) **It** [wa wa] F, pl. Ø, 1960s (1 tech)

walkie-talkie *n.* 1 'a two-way radio carried on the person'
Ge [=E] N, pl. *-s*, 1960s (2 tech) **Du** [=E] C, 1950s (1 tech) > *portofoon* **Nw** [=E] M, pl. *-r/-s*, mid20c (2) **Ic** [=E] 1960s (0) < trsl *labb-rabb* **Fr** <=E>/*talkie-walkie* [tokiwoki] M, 1940s (1) **Sp** [=E/gwolki tolki/gwalki talki] M, pl. *-s*, 1970s (1<2) **It** [wɔ:(l)ki tɔ:(l)ki] M [U] 1940s (2 tech) **Rm** <=E>/*talkie-walkie* [=E] N, 1970s (1 coll) **Rs** *voki-toki* N, uninfl., end20c (2 tech, coll) **Po** [wokitoki] N, uninfl., end20c (2) **Cr** *voki-toki* M, pl. *-ji*, end20c (2) **Bg** *uoki-toki* N, pl. *-ta*, end20c (1 tech, coll) **Fi** [=E] mid20c (2) **Hu** <=E>/*talkie-walkie* [=E] pl. Ø/-k, 1970s (2) **Gr** *ghuoki-toki/*[=E] N, mid20c (2)

Ic	Nw	Po	Rs
Du	Ge	Cr	Bg
Fr	It	Fi	Hu
Sp	Rm	Al	Gr

Walkman *n.* (orig.^TM) 'a type of personal stereo' (cf. ↑*discman*)

This term is an excellent illustration for a modern product name becoming generic in a very short time (obviously because it was felt to be descriptively adequate); only Norwegian, Icelandic and French appear to have produced calques which successfully compete with the loanword. The word *watchman* coined on the same pattern for a portable TV set does not appear to have caught on.

Ge [vɔ:kmen] M, pl. *-s/-men*, 1980s (2) **Du** [=E] C, pl. *-men/-s*, 1980s (2) **Nw** [=E] M, pl. *-er*, 1980s (2) = *lommedisco* **Ic** [=E] M, 1980s (1 tech) < rend *vasadiskó* **Fr** <=E> M, 1980s (2 ban) < *baladeur* **Sp** [walman/wolman] M, pl. Ø/-s, 1980s (2) **It** [wɔlkmɛn] M, pl. Ø, 1980s (2) **Rm** [=E] N, 1980s (2 you) **Rs** *vokmén/uolkmén* M, pl. *-y*, 1980s (2) **Po** [wokmen] M, end20c (2) **Cr** *vokmen* M, pl. *-i*, end20c (2) **Bg** *uokmen* M, pl. *-al-i*, 1980s (2) **Hu** [vɔ:kmen] pl. *-ek*, 1980s (2) **Gr** <=E>/*ghuokman* N, 1980s (2)

Ic	Nw	Po	Rs
Du	Ge	Cr	Bg
Fr	It	Fi	Hu
Sp	Rm	Al	Gr

walkover *n.* 1 'an easy victory', +2 'a race contested by one competitor only'
Ge (0 arch) **Du** [=E] C, 1940s (1 tech) **Nw** [=E] M, pl. *-e*, 20c, 1,+2(1 tech) **Fr** [walkvœr] M, mid19c, +2(1 tech, ban) > *forfait* **It** [wɔlkover] M [U] end19c (1 tech) **Rm** [=E] N [U] 20c, +2(1 tech, rare) **Po** *walkower* [valkover] M, beg20c, +2(3) **Hu** [=E] [U] end19/beg20c, +2(1 tech)

Ic	Nw	Po	Rs
Du	Ge	Cr	Bg
Fr	It	Fi	Hu
Sp	Rm	Al	Gr

Wall Street *n.* 'the American financial world or money market'

The proper name has apparently become generic in

a few languages in which it now can also refer to local conditions. The term is of course universally known as a foreignism.

Ge (Ø) **Du** *Wallstreet* [=E] C, 1940s (1 tech) **Nw** (Ø) **Ic** [=E] 20c (Ø) **Fr** (Ø) **Sp** (Ø) **It** [wɔl striːt] M [U] 20c (Ø) **Rm** (Ø) **Rs** *Uoll- strit* F [U] 20c (Ø) **Po** [=E] M [U] mid20c (1) **Cr** [=E] M [U] mid20c (2) **Bg** *Uolstrüt* M [U] 20c (Ø) **Fi** (Ø) **Hu** [=E] [U] 20c (1 tech) **Al** *Uoll Strit* M, 20c (1 jour) **Gr** <=E>/*Ghuol Strit* F [U] 20c (Ø)

war game *n.* 1 'a military exercise testing or improving tactical knowledge' etc., 2 'a battle etc. conducted with toy soldiers'

Du [=E] C, pl. -*s*, 1(1 tech) **Nw** [=E] N, pl. -*s*, 1980s, 1,2(1 tech) **Fr** - < *jeu de guerre* **It** [wor geim/worgɛm] M, pl. Ø/-*s*, 1970s (1 tech) **Bg** - < trsl *voenna igra*

warm(ing)-up *n.* 1 'preparing for a contest', 3 'becoming enthusiastic'

Ge *warm-up* [vɔrmap] N, pl. -*s*, 1980s, 1(1 tech, rare) **Du** [wa:mɪŋ ʏp] C, 1970s, 1(2) **Nw** - < trsl *oppvarming* **Ic** - < trsl *upphitun* F **Fr** - < *échauffement* **Sp** *warmup* M, end20c, 1(1 tech, jour, rare) **It** [wa̱rm ap] M, pl. Ø, end20c (1 tech) **Rm** - < rend *îm cǎlzine* **Cr** - < trsl *nerijavnje*

warm-up *n.* +2 'a preparatory feature preceding a TV broadcast, advertisement, etc.'

Ge [vɔrmap] N, pl. -*s*, 1980s (1 tech, rare) **Du** - < trsl *opwarmen* **Nw** - < trsl *oppvarming* **Sp** (0) **It** [=E] M, pl. Ø, end20c (2>3 tech) **Fi** (0)

warrant *n.* 2a 'a written authorization, money voucher, travel document, etc.'

Du [=E] C, pl. -*s*, end20c (1 tech) **Sp** [=E/ba̱ran] M, pl. -*s*, end20c (1 tech_ECON) **It** [=E] M, pl. Ø, 1860s (1 tech) **Hu** [wa̱rrant] [U] 20c (1 tech)

wash and go *phr.* (orig.[TM]) 'together'

Ge [vɔ̱ʃentgoː] 1990s (1 tech, mod) **Du** [=E] 1990s (2 mod) **Nw** [=E] 1990s (1 fac) **Rs** *vosh énd gou* 1990s (1 tech, mod) **Po** end20c (2) **Cr** (0) **Fi**[TM] only **Hu** [va̱ʃ end goː] 1990s (2 jour, mod) **Gr** <=E> [=E] 1990s (1 tech, writ)

wash-and-wear *phr.* 'easily and quickly laundered' (of a garment)

Ge [=E] 1960s (1 mod) **It** [wa̱ʃ ɛnd wea̱r] adj., pl. Ø, 1960s (1 jour, mod)

washboard *n.* 1 'a board of ribbed wood or a sheet of corrugated zinc on which clothes are scrubbed when washing'

It [wa̱ʃbɔrd] M, pl. Ø, 1960s (1 tech)

washed out *adj.* 1 'faded by washing'

Ge cp[1] [=E] 1970s (1 tech, you)

water *n.* +12 'a lavatory with the means for flushing the pan with water'

Nw [va̱:ter] N, pl. -*e*, beg20c (1 arch) < ↑*WC, toalett, do* **It** [va̱ter] M, pl. Ø, 1960s (3)

water closet *n.* 1 'a lavatory with the means for flushing the pan with water' (cf. ↑*WC*.)

Ge *(Wasser)Klosett* N, 19c (1 obs) < *Klo* **Du** - < *WC* **Nw** *klosett* [klose̱t] N/M, pl. -*er*, 19c (1 obs) <

WC, toalett, do **It** [wɔter klɔsit] M, pl. Ø, 1900s (1 tech) **Bg** *va̱terklozet* M, pl. -*al-i*, beg20c, via Rs (1 arch) **Hu** [wa̱:ter-klozet] pl. -*ek*, beg20c (1 arch) < *WC* **Gr** - < *WC*

watergate *n.* see ↑*-gate*

waterline *n.* 1 'the line along which the surface of water touches a ship's side'

Rs *vaterli̱niya* F, pl. -*nii*, beg20c (3 tech) **Po** *waterlinia* [vaterlinia] F, beg20c (1 tech) **Cr** (0) **Bg** *va̱terliniya* F, pl. -*nii*, beg20c, via Rs (3 tech)

water polo *n.* 'a game played by swimmers with a ball like a football'

The sport was known from the early twentieth century; it is not quite clear how far the English word served as a model for native equivalents, which are more frequent than in other ball games. Since the second element is not particularly English-looking, identification of the item as a loanword depends on the retention of *water*.

Ge - < *Wasserball* **Du** *water-polo* [U] end19c (5+3) **Nw** (0) < trsl *vannpolo* **Fr** [vatɛrpɔlo] M, end19c (1) → *waterpoliste* **Sp** [waterpo̱lo/b-] M [U] beg20c (1 tech) → *waterpolista* n. **It** [wɔter polo] M [U] 1910s

(1 tech) < *pallanuoto* → *waterpoliste* **Rm** [=E] N [U] beg20c (1 obs) < rend *polo (pe apǎ)* N, uninfl., beg20c (1 tech) < trsl *vodnoje po̱lo* → *vaterpo̱list* M; -*ka* F **Po** [vaterpolo] N, uninfl., beg20c (1 tech) **Cr** *vaterpo̱lo* M [U] beg20c (3) **Bg** *vaterpolo* N [U] mid20c, via Rs (3 tech) < creat *vodna topka* → -*polist* M **Fi** - < trsl *vesipolo* **Hu** *vizipó̱ló* 20c (5+3) < trsl *vizilabda* **Al** *vaterpo̱lo* F [U] mid20c (1 reg) **Gr** [=E] N [U] beg20c (2) = *ydhatosferisi* < *po̱lo*

waterproof *adj.* 'impervious to water' (of dress, shoes, etc.)

Ge [=E] uninfl., 1970s (1 coll) < *wasserdicht* **Du** *waterproef* (5) = *waterdicht* **Nw** [=E] 20c (1 rare) < *vanntett* **Ic** - < rend *vatnsheldur* **Fr** [watɛrpruf] 19c (1) < *imperméabil* **Sp** [=E] uninfl., end20c (1 tech) **It** [wɔterpruːf] uninfl., mid19c (1 tech) < *impermeabile* **Rm** (0) < *impermeabil* **Rs** [wo̱terpruf] adj., uninfl., beg20c (1 tech) **Cr** [=E] adj., uninfl., mid20c (1 tech) **Hu** [=E] 19c (1 tech, arch) < *vízhatlan* **Gr** - < trsl *adhiavrokho*

waterproof *n.* +2 'a raincoat'

The noun was widely borrowed to refer to a typically British type of raincoat, but was largely replaced by native equivalents; it is now obsolete or obsolescent on the Continent – and not very common in Britain. By contrast, the adjective has been at least partly revived as a modish alternative to native terms which are available in all languages. Other -*proof* compounds do not appear to have caught on at all.

Ge [va̱:tapruːf] M, pl. -*s*, end19c

(1 arch)   **Du** [wa:tərpru:f] C [U] 19c (1 rare) = *water-proof*   **Fr** [watɛrpruf] M, 19c (1 arch) < *imperméable*   **Sp** [=E] M, beg20c (0 < 1 jour, obs) < *impermeable*   **It** - < *impermeabil*   **Rm** - < *impermeabil*   **Po** (0)   **Hu** [=E] [U] 19c (1 arch)

watt   *n.* 1 'the SI unit of power, equivalent to one joule per second'

The name of the Scottish engineer James Watt (1736–1819) is connected with the steam engine and the electric bulb (not invented by him); the unit named after him is probably the best known among the more technical scientific terms, as a loanword widely pronounced according to national conventions.
Ge [vat] N [U] 19c (3)   **Du** [vat] C, end19c (2 tech) → *wattage* n.   **Nw** [vat] M, pl. Ø, 19c (2)   **Ic** *vatt* [vaht] N, pl. *vött*, beg20c, via Da (2)   **Fr** [wat] M, end19c (2)   **Sp** (0) < *vatio* end19c (3)   **It** [vat] M, pl. Ø/-*s*, end19c (3) → *wattmetro/wattometro* n.; *wattora* n.; *wattorametro* n.; *wattsecondo* n.   **Rm** [vat] M, end19c (3)   **Rs** *vatt* M, pl. -*y*, beg20c (3)   **Po** *wat* [vat] M, beg20c (3) → -*owy* adj.; *pod-+ -ny* adj.   **Cr** *vat* M, pl. -*i*, beg20c (3)   **Bg** *vat* M, pl. -*a*, beg20c, via Rs (3) → -*ov* adj.   **Fi** [vat:i] 19c (3)   **Hu** [vatt] [U] end19/beg20c (3) → -*os* adj./cp[1]   **Al** *vat* M, pl. Ø, end19c (3)   **Gr** *vat* N (2)

wattman   *n.* 'a tram driver'

This term illustrates the spread of a nineteenth-century pseudo-anglicism; whereas it is now obsolescent in French, which coined it, the word survives in common use in two Balkan languages.
Fr [watman] M, end19c (1 arch)   **Rm** *vatman* [vatman] M, end19c, via Fr (3) → *vătmăniţă* F   **Bg** *vatman* M, pl. -*i*, beg20c, via Fr (3) → -*ka* F; -*ski* adj.

wave   *n.* +10 'a kind of pop music popular in the 1980s, connected with a bleak, mostly black clothing style', +11 'a new wave fan', +12 'a hair-style', +13 'a wave produced by fans in football stadiums by raising their hands' (cf. ↑*New Wave*)
Ge (*New*) *Wave* [(nju:) weif] M/N [U] 1980s, +10(1 you, mod, obs)   **Du** [=E] C, 1980s, +10, +13(1 tech)   **Nw** *New Wave* [=E] M [U] 1970s, +10(1 tech, obs) = +10: rend *nyveiv*; +13: - < *bølgen*   **Sp** *New Wave* [nju weif] [U] 1980s, +10(1 you, mod, obs)   **It** *New Wave* [=E] F [U] 1980s, +10,+11, +12(1 tech)   **Rs** *veiv* M [U] 1980s, +10, +11(2 you)   **Po** [-f] F [U] end20c, +10(1 you)   **Cr** (0)   **Bg** *ueif* M, pl. -*ove*, 1980s, +10,+11,+12(3 you) → -*ka* F; -*adzhiya* M; -*che* N   **Hu** *New Wave* [=E] [U] 1980s, +10(1 jour, you, mod) < trsl *újhullám*   **Gr** <=E>/(*niu*)*ghueiv* F/ N [U] 1980s, +10,+12(1 tech)

waver   *n.* 'a fan of the New Wave style of pop music, dressing all in black'
Ge *Waver* [weifa] M/F, pl. -*s*/Ø, 1980s (1 you, obs)   **Du** *waver* [=E] 1980s (1 obs)

way of life   *n.* 'the principles or habits governing all one's actions'

Ge [ve:oflaif] M [U] 1960s (1 jour) < *Lebensweise*   **Du** [=E] C [U] 1970s (1 tech) < *levensstijl*   **Nw** (0) < *livsstil*   **Ic** [=E] uninfl., end20c (0) < *lífsstíll*   **Sp** [weioflaif] M [U] 1960s (1 jour) < trsl *modo de vida*   **It** - < trsl *stile di vita*   **Rm** - < trsl *stil de viaţă*   **Rs** - < trsl *stil' zhizni*   **Bg** - < trsl *nachin na zhivot*   **Fi** - < trsl *elämäntapa*   **Al** - < *mënyrë jetese*   **Gr** [=E] (0> 1 mod)

WC   *abbrev.* 1 'water closet'

The term was originally adopted in its full form *water closet* in a few languages in the nineteenth century but was soon superseded by the abbreviation which was easier to pronounce (and less straightforward), by a shortened form *Klosett* etc. (with French stress), or by the older French loanword *toilet*. The full history of these alternatives needs investigation. In German *Klosett* was in turn shortened to *Klo*, which in colloquial use superseded the older forms.
Ge [ve:tse:] N, pl. -*s*, beg20c (3) < *Klo(sett)*   **Du** [ve:se:] C, pl. -'*s*, beg20c (3)   **Nw** [ve:se:] N, pl. -*er*, beg20c (3) < *toalett*; > *klosett*, ↑*water*   **Ic** [vaf: sjɛ:] 20c (1) = *VS* (*vatnssalerni*)   **Fr** [vese/dublovese] M, pl., end19c (1 obs) → *waters* M   **Sp** [uveθé] M, 1970s (1 fac)   **It** [vi tʃi] M, pl. Ø, 1900s (3) < *vater*   **Rm** *vece/veceu* [vetʃe/vetʃew] N, mid20c (3) = *closet* > *clo*   **Rs** *WC* beg20c (1 writ)   **Po** [wuce] N, pl. -*ty*, mid19c (1 coll)   **Cr** [vece] M, pl. -*ovi*, beg20c (3)   **Bg** <=E> [vetse] beg20c (1 writ/3 coll) < *toaletna*   **Fi** [ve:se:] 19c (3) → *vessa* 20c (3 coll)   **Hu** [vetse] pl. -*k*, end19c/beg20c (3)   **Al** *wc* [vëcë] F, uninfl., mid20c (3)   **Gr** <=E> (1 writ); [vese] N, beg20c (5Fr)

-wear   *cp[2]/n.* 2 'things worn; fashionable or suitable clothing'

This element has been overused by the fashion industry (at least in German), sparking off some (often ironic) purist reactions; nevertheless, the use appears to be expanding without having produced hybrid compounds so far.
Ge [ve:r] N [U] 1980s (1 mod)   **Nw** [=E] [U] 1990s (1 mod)   **Fr** cp[2], 1980s (1 mod)   **It** [we:r] cp[2], 1980s (1 mod)   **Hu** (0 writ)   **Gr** [=E] cp[2] (1 you, mod)

Wedgwood   *n.* 'ceramic ware made by J. Wedgwood, English potter d. 1795, and his successors'
Ge *Wedgwood(ware)* [vetʃwut-] beg19c (Ø/1 tech)   **Du** *wedg(e)wood* [=E] N [U] mid19c (1 tech)   **Nw** [=E] mid19c (1 tech)   **Fr** (0)   **It** [=E] 19c (Ø_NAME)   **Rm** (Ø)   **Rs** *vedzhvud* M [U] 19c (1 tech)   **Po** *wedgwood* [=E] beg20c (1 tech)   **Gr** <=E> [=E] 20c (1 tech)

weekend   *n.* 1 'Saturday and Sunday'

This word is surprisingly widespread (and appears still to be spreading). A few languages (German, Spanish, Finnish) use practically only calques, which have so far barred the adoption of the English word, even though this is occasionally found in advertising, youth language, and facetious uses.
Ge [vi:kent] N, pl. -*s*, 1930s (0) < trsl *Wochenende*   **Du** [vi:kɛnt] N, pl. -*s*/-*en*, 1940s (2) > *weekeinde* (5) → *weeke(i)nden* v.; *weekender* n.   **Nw** [=E] M, pl.

-er/-s, mid20c (2) < *helg*; > trsl
ukeslutt **Fr** *week-end* M,
beg20c (2) **Sp** [wi̯kend] M, pl.
-s, beg20c (1) < trsl *fin de sema-
na* **It** [wikе̯nd] M, pl. Ø, 1900s
(3) = *fine settimana* **Rm** [=E] N,
mid20c (2) **Rs** *uikе́nd* M, pl. *-y*,
mid20c (2) **Po** [wikent] M, beg20c (2) → *-owanie* N;
-owiec M; *-owicz* M; v.: *-owy* adj. **Cr** *vi̯kend* M, pl. *-i*,
mid20c (3) **Bg** *uikе̯nd* M, pl. *-al-i*, end20c (2) **Fi** - <
trsl *viikonloppu* **Hu** *víkend* [vi̯:kend] pl. *-ek*, 1920s (3)
→ *-ez* v. **Al** *uikе̯nd* M, pl. *-e*, 1980s (3) **Gr** <=E>
[=E] N, pl. Ø/-*s*, 1990s (1 mod); *ghuikе̯d* N, end20c, via
Fr (1 mod)

welfare state   *n.* 1a 'a system whereby the state un-
dertakes to protect the health and well-being of its
citizens'

In Italy, this term has recently (1995–97) seen a
remarkable revival; it is often found in the short
form *welfare*, frequent as a euphemistic political
catch phrase.
Ge - < trsl *Wohlfahrtsstaat* **Nw** - < trsl *veferds-
stat* **Sp** [=E] M [U] end20c (1 tech) **It** [wе̯lfea
stei̯t] M, pl. Ø, 1950s (1 tech) **Hu** - < trsl *jóléti állam*

wellington   *n.* 1 'a waterproof rubber or plastic
boot', +2 'a sherry', +3 'a kind of biscuit'

The boot is named after Arthur Wellesley, first duke
of Wellington (1769–1852); the term is generic in
British English, mostly used in plural form and often
shortened to *welly*. It is likely that the term was more
widespread in European languages in the nineteenth
century but survives only marginally today. The origin of the names for the sherry and the biscuit is
opaque.
Du [=E] C, 1980s, 1(2 tech); 1950s, +2,+3(1 tech) **It**
[=E] M, pl. *-s*, 1940s, 1(1 obs) **Rs** *vellington* M, pl. *-y*,
mid20c, 1(1 tech) **Po** [velington] M, mid20c, 1(1 coll)

Wellingtonia   *n.* 'a Californian conifer'
Sp <=E>/*velintonia* F (1 tech) **It** [wellingtо̯nia] F,
1970s (1 tech)

wellness   *n.* 'fitness, well- being'

This word appears to be very recent (from American English). It was soon adopted by health-conscious Germans but had no chance of spreading any
further (and may in fact not be permanent).
Ge [vе̯lnes] F [U] 1990s (1 mod)

welter(weight)   *n./cp[1]* 'a weight in certain sports
(e.g. boxing, wrestling) intermediate between light-
weight and middleweight'

This boxing term (fixed in 1896) is widespread, but
known to specialists only; mainly eastern languages
appear to prefer native equiva-
lents.
Ge +*gewicht* [vе̯lta] cp[1], 1930s
(3 tech) **Du** *weltergewicht*
[vɪltər-] cp[1], 1950s (1 tech+5)
Nw *weltervekt* [=E] M/cp[1],
1930s (1 tech) **Ic** - < *velti-
vigt* **Fr** [vɛltɛʀ/w-] M, beg20c

(1 tech) **Sp** [wе̯lter] adj./M, beg20c (1 tech) **It**
[v[ɛ]lter] adj./M, pl. Ø, 1930s (2 tech) **Rm** *welter*
[=E] N [U] mid20c (1 tech, rare) < *semimijlocie* **Rs**
(0) **Po** [velter] M, end20c (1 tech) **Cr** *vе̯lter* M [U]
mid20c (1 tech) **Bg** - < creat *polusredna kategoriya* **Hu** [vе̯lter-] cp[1] [U] end19/beg20c (1 tech, obs)
< *váltósúly*

West End   *n.* +2 'a well-to-do part of a city'

With prevailing west winds, 'Westends' of cities
tend to be least polluted and are traditionally preferred by the well-to-do outside Britain, too. Since
the term is, then, meaningful in Continental contexts,
there was a reason for its (limited) adoption, whereas
in other languages it has remained a foreignism.
Ge [vе̯stent] N [U] mid20c (2) **Nw** (Ø) < *vest-
kant* **Rs** *uest е́nd* M [U] mid20c (Ø) **Po** (Ø) **Cr**
(Ø) **Bg** *Uе̯stend* (Ø) **Hu** [=E] [U] 20c (Ø>1)

Western   *n.* 'a film, television drama, or novel about
cowboys in western North America'
Ge [vе̯stan] M, pl. Ø/-*s*, mid20c (2) **Du** [vе̯stərn] C,
1960s (2>3) **Nw** [vе̯stern] M, pl. *-er/-s*, 1950s (2) **Ic**
- < *vestri* **Fr** [wɛstɛʀn] M, 1920s (2) **Sp** [wе̯sten] M,
pl. *-s*, mid20c (2) < rend *película del Oeste* **It** [wes-
tern] M, pl. Ø, 1940s (3) **Rm** [western] N, mid20c
(2) **Rs** *vе̯stern* M, pl. *-y*, mid20c (2) **Po** *western*
[western/vestern] M, mid20c (2) **Cr** *vе̯stern* M, pl. *-i*,
mid20c (2) **Bg** *uе̯stûrn* M, pl. *-al-i*, mid20c (2) **Fi**
[vesterni] mid20c (2) = rend *länkkäri* **Hu** *western*
[vе̯stern] pl. *-ek*, 1930s (2>3) → cp[1] **Al** *uestе̯rn* M,
pl. Ø, 1980s (1 reg) **Gr** *ghuе̯stern* N, mid20c (2)

westerner   *n.* +2 'a hero of a Western film'
Ge [vе̯stana] M, pl. Ø, 1970s (1 tech, rare) **Hu** - <
westernhős (3+5)

wet gel   *n.* 'a kind of hair cosmetic which gives the
hair a wet look'
Ge [vе̯tge:l] N, pl. *-e*, 1980s (2 tech) **Nw** - < *våtgele*?

wetsuit   *n.* 'a close-fitting rubber garment worn for
warmth in water sports'
Du [wе̯tsu:t] C, 1970s (1 tech) **Nw** (0) < *våtdrakt*
Ic - < trsl *blautbúningur* **Fi** - < trsl *märkäpuku*

weymouth pine   *n./cp[1/2]* 'the tree'
Ge *Weymouths-/Weimutskiefer* [wе̯:muts-] cp[1], 19c (1
tech+5) **Nw** *weymouthfuru* [vе̯imut-] 20c (1
tech) **Fr** *(pin de Lord) Weymouth* 20c (1 tech) **Po**
wejmutka [veimutka] F, mid20c (1 tech)

whaleboat   *n.* 'a long narrow double-bowed boat of
a kind used for whaling'

This shipping term has a unique eastern distribution – other languages having been supplied with a
word before *whaleboat* was
borrowed; Bulgarian then reborrowed from Russian.
Rs *vel'bоt* M, pl. *-y*, beg20c (1
tech) **Po** *welbot* [velbot] M,
beg20c (1 tech) **Cr** (0) **Bg** *vеl-
bot* M, pl. *-al-i*, beg20c, via Rs (3
tech)

whig   *n.* 1 'a member of the British reforming and
constitutional party', +4 'a liberal-progressive party'

Nw (Ø)   **Sp** [=E] M, pl. -*s*, mid19c (1 tech)   **It** [wig] M/adj., pl. Ø, beg18c, 1(1 tech); end20c, +4(1 jour) **Po** *wig* [vig] M, mid19c (Ø)   **Bg** *Vigi* pl., 19c, via Rs, 1(Ø)   **Hu** (Ø)

whipcord   *n.* 2 'a closely woven worsted fabric'
    Ge [=E] M [U] 1930s (1 tech)   **Du** *whipcord* [=E] N [U] 1940s (1 tech)   **Nw** [=E] M [U] mid20c (1 tech)   **Fr** <=E> M, end19c (1 tech)

whirlpool   *n.* (orig.^{TM}) +2 'a swimming pool with an artificial whirlpool used for massage'
    Ge [vø̱rlpu:l] M, pl. -*s*, 1980s (2 tech)   **Du** [=E] C, 1980s (1 jour, mod) < *bubbelbad*   **Ic** - < *nuddpottur*   **It** - < *idromassaggio* **Hu** [və̱rlpu:l] [U] 1990s (1 writ, jour,^{TM} only) < *hullámfür-dő*   **Gr** <=E> [=E] N, pl. Ø/-*s*, 1980s (1 mod) = *ydromasaz*

whisk(e)y   *n.* 2 'a spirit distilled esp. from malted barley.'
    Ge [viski] M [U] end18c (2)   **Du** [vɪski] C [U] beg19c (2) → *whiskytje* n.   **Nw** [=E] M [U] mid19c (2)   **Ic** *viski* [vɪsci] N [U] end19c (2)   **Fr** [wiski] M, end19c (2)   **Sp** [wi̱ski] M, pl. -*s*, mid19c (2) → *w(h)isquería* **It** [wiski] M [U] beg19c (3)   **Rm** [=E] N, end19c (2); *vizichi* [viziki] N [U] 1970s (3 fac); *visic* [visi̱k] N, 20c (3 ban)   **Rs** *vi̱ski* N, uninfl., beg20c (2)   **Po** <=E> N, uninfl., beg20c (2)   **Cr** *viski* M [U] beg20c (3) **Bg** *ui̱ski* N, pl. -*ta*, mid20c (2); *vi̱ski* end19c/end20c (1 obs/2 coll)   **Fi** <=E>/*viski* [=E] 18c (1)   **Hu** [vi̱ski] pl. -*k*/ Ø, 17c/18c (2)   **Al** *uiski* M, uninfl., 1970s (2) **Gr** *ui̱ski* N, 20c (2)

whist   *n.* 'a card-game usu. for two pairs of players'
    Ge [vist] N [U] mid19c (1 arch)   **Du** [vɪst] N [U] beg19c (2)   **Nw** [=E] M [U] mid19c (2)   **Ic** *vist* [vɪst] F [U] 19c, via Da (3)   **Fr** [wist] M, 18c (1 arch)   **Sp** [wist] M, end19c (1 tech)   **It** [wist] M, pl. Ø, 18c (1 tech)   **Rm** [=E] N, mid19c (2); *vist* N (3 arch)   **Rs** *vist* M [U] mid19c (1 tech) → -*ovat'* v.   **Po** *wist* [vist] M, mid19c (1 arch)   **Cr** *vist* M [U] beg20c (1 arch)   **Bg** *vist* M [U] beg20c, via Rs (3)   **Fi** [=E] 19c (2)   **Hu** [vist] [U] 19c (1 arch)   **Gr** *uist* N [U] beg20c (1 tech, obs)

white spirit   *n.* 'light petroleum as a solvent'
    Nw [va̱itspri:t/=E] M [U] mid20c (2)   **Ic** [=E/vai̱t-sprɪht] N [U] (1 tech)   **Fr** <=E>/*white* [wajtspirit/wit] M [U] 1930s (1 tech)   **Sp** [=E] M [U] 20c (0) **Rm** [=E] N [U] mid20c (1 tech) > *solvent nafta* **Rs** *va̱it spirit* M [U] mid20c (2 tech)

who's who   *n.* 'a reference book with facts about notable persons'
    An annual register of celebrities first appeared under this name in London in 1849. It was frequently imitated abroad (where similar books were published with the title translated), but the term has hardly become generic. When found, it is more often a quotation word or used facetiously.
    Ge [=E] N [U] 1970s (1 tech, coll) > trsl *Wer ist wer*   **Du** [=E] 1980s (2 tech) = *wie is wie*   **Nw** (0)

Ic (0) **Fr** [wuizwu] M, 1960s (1 tech)   **Sp** [=E] M [U] beg20c (0>1 tech) < trsl *Quién es quién* **It** [=E] M [U] 1900s (Ø) < trsl *chi è (chi)*   **Rm** [=E] 1980s (0> 1 mod)   **Rs** (0) < trsl *kto est' kto*   **Po** <=E> M [U] end20c (1 tech) < trsl *kto jest kto*   **Cr** [=E] M [U] end20c (1 tech)   **Bg** <=E>/*khu is khu* 1990s (1 mod, jour_{NAME}) < rend *koĭ koĭ e*   **Fi** [=E] mid20c (1 tech) < trsl *kuka on kuka* **Hu** [hu̱:z hu:] [U] 1970s/80s (1 jour, mod>2) = trsl *ki-kicsoda*   **Gr** (0)

wicket   *n.* 1a 'a set of three stumps with the bails in position defended by the batsman' (cricket)
    Du [=E] C, pl. -*s* (1 tech)   **It** [wi̱kit] M, pl. Ø, 1940s (1 tech)

wigwam   *n.* 'a North American Indian's domed hut or tent of skins, mats, or bark on poles'
    Ge [vi̱gvam] M, pl. -*s*, 19c (Ø)   **Du** [vɪ̱xvam] (Ø)   **Nw** [vi̱gvam] M, pl. -*er*, end19c (Ø)   **Fr** [wig-wam] M, 19c (Ø)   **Sp** M, 20c (Ø/1 tech)   **It** [wigwam] M, pl. Ø, beg19c (Ø)   **Rm** [=E/vi̱gvam] N, beg20c (Ø/ 2 tech)   **Rs** *vigva̱m* M, pl. -*y*, beg20c (Ø)   **Po** [vig-vam] M, beg20c (2)   **Cr** *vigvam* M, pl. -*ovi*, mid20c (3) **Bg** *vigva̱m* M, pl. -*al-i*, beg20c, via Rs (Ø/3 mod)   **Hu** *vigvam* [vi̱gvam] pl. Ø/-*ok*, end19c (Ø)

wild card   *n.* 2 'a character that will match any character or sequence of characters in a file name' (comput.), 3 'an extra player or team chosen to enter a competition at the selector's discretion' (sport)
    Ge [=E] F, pl. -*s*, 1980s (1 tech, rare)   **Du** [wa̱jlt ka:t] C, 1980s (1 tech)   **Nw** [=E] N/M, pl. -*s*, 1980s, 2(1 tech); 3(0) < *joker*   **Ic** [=E] N, pl. Ø, end20c, 2(1 tech) < rend *algildisstafur*   **Fr** - < 2: *jo-ker*   **Sp** [=E/wa̱idkard] M, pl. -*s*, end20c, 3(1 jour); 2: - < *comodín*   **It** [=E] F, pl. Ø, end20c, 3(1 tech)   **Rm** [=E] N, end20c, 3(0>1 tech) **Po** - < *dzika karta*   **Cr** (0)   **Bg** *ua̱ild kard* M, pl. -*dal -ove*, 1990s (1 tech)   **Fi** - < trsl *villikortti*   **Hu** [va̱ild ka̱:rd] [U] 1980s, 2(1 tech)   **Gr** <=E> [=E] F, pl. -*s*, end20c, 2(1 tech)

Wild West   *n./cp[1]* 'the western USA in a time of lawlessness in its early history'
    Ge - < trsl *der Wilde Westen, Wildwest-*   **Du** *wild-west* [vɪlt vest] cp[1], mid20c (2)   **Nw** [=E/vi̱l vest] M, beg20c (1 obs) < *det ville Vesten, vill vest*   **Ic** - < trsl *villta vestrið*   **Fr** - < *Far West*   **Sp** - < rend *(lejano) Oeste, Far West*   **It** - < *Far West*   **Rm** (0) < rend *vestul sălbatic*   **Rs** - < trsl *dikiĭ zapad*   **Po** (0) < trsl *Dziki Zachód*   **Cr** *vi̱ldvest* M [U] mid20c (2)   **Bg** - < trsl *Diviyat Zapad*   **Fi** [=E] 20c = trsl *villi Länsi*   **Hu** [va̱ild vest] [U] 20c (0) < trsl *vadnyugat*   **Gr** [=E] (Ø) = trsl *aghria dhisi*

winch   *n.* 1 'the crank of wheel or axle', 2 'a windlass'
    Ge *Winsch* [vɪnʃ] F, pl. -*en*, 1900s, 2(3 tech)   **Du** [=E] C, pl. -*es*/-*en*, 2(1 tech) = *lier*   **Nw** *vinsj* [vinʃ] M, pl.

-er, 1920s, 2(3 tech)   **Fr** [wintʃ] M, mid20c (1 tech)   **Sp** <=E>/*winche* M, 20c, 2(1 tech)   **Cr** *vinč* M, pl. *-evi*, mid20c, 2(3 tech)   **Fi** *vinssi* 2(5Sw)

Winchester   *n.* 1 'a breech-loading repeating rifle'   **Ge** (o arch)   **Du** [=E] C, pl. *-s* (1 tech)   **Sp** [=E] M, end19c (1 tech)   **It** [wintʃester] M, pl. Ø, 1940s (2 tech)   **Po** [vintʃester] M, mid20c (1 tech)   **Bg** *vinchester* M, pl. *-al-i*, beg20c (3 tech)   **Hu** [vi̯ntʃester] pl. Ø/-*ek*, mid20c (2 tech, obs)

windbreaker   *n.* 'a kind of wind-resistant outer jacket'   **Du** [=E] C, pl. *-s*, end20c (1 mod)   **Nw** [=E] M, pl. *-el-s*, 1980s (1 mod) < *vindjakke*   **Hu** - < rend *széldzseki*

windglider   *n.* (TM) 'a type of windsurfing class/board'   **Ge** [vi̯ntglai̯da] M, pl. Ø, 1980s (1 tech, rare)   **Du** *windglijder* [wi̯ndɤlɛidər] C, 1980s (1 arch, rare, obs)   **Nw** [=E/vin-] M, pl. *-e*, 1980s (1 tech)   **Rm** (o)

windjammer   *n.* 'a merchant sailing ship'   **Ge** [vi̯ntjama] M, pl. Ø, 19c (3 tech)   **Du** [vi̯ndjamər] C, 1950s (3 tech)

windsurf   *n.* 'sailboard'   **Sp** [winsu̯rf] M [U] end20c (1 tech)   **It** [wi̯nd sœrf] M, pl. Ø, 1980s (2 tech)   **Bg** *ui̯ndsŭrf* M, pl. *-al- ove*, 1980s (3 tech)

windsurfer   *n.* 1 'a surf board', 2 'a person who windsurfs' (cf. ↑*surfer*)

This word is an infrequent alternative to ↑*surfer, wind* ~ being considered as pleonastic; languages which have both terms prefer the shorter form. The same applies to *-ing*.

Ge [vi̯ntsørfa] M, pl. Ø, 1970s (5+1 tech)   **Du** [=E] C, 1970s, 2(2)   **Nw** [=E] M, pl. *-e*, 1970s, 2(1 tech) < 1: *seilbrett*; 2: *brettsei-ler*   **Ic** - < 1: rend *seglbretti*   **Fr** (o) < rend *véliplanchiste*   **It** [wind sœrfer] M, pl. Ø, 1980s, 2(1 tech) < *windsurfista*   **Rm** [=E] M, 1980s (o>1 tech); *windsurf* [=E] 1980s, 1(o>1 tech) < *surfer*   **Rs** (o)   **Po** - < *windserwowiec* M   **Cr** *vindsu̯rfer* M, pl. *-i*, end20c, 2(1 tech)   **Bg** - < 1: (*ui̯nd*)*sŭrf*; 2: *sŭrfist*   **Hu** - < *szörföző, széllovas, hullámlovas*

windsurfing   *n.* 'the sport of riding on water on a sailboard' (cf. ↑*surfing*)   **Ge** [vi̯ntsørfiŋ] N [U] 1970s (1 tech) < *Surfen*   **Du** [=E] C [U] 1960s (2) < *plankzeilen*   **Nw** [=E] M/F [U] 1970s (1 tech) < *brettseiling*   **Fr** *windsurf* (o) < rend *planche a voile*   **Sp** *windsurfl* <=E> M [U] 1970s (1 tech) → *windsurfero* n.; *windsurfista* n.   **It** [windsœrfiŋ(g)] M, pl. Ø, 1980s (1 tech)   **Rm** [=E] N [U] 1970s (o>1 tech) < *(wind)surf*   **Rs** *vindsȇrfing* M [U] 1970s (1 tech)   **Po** [-serfink] M [U] end20c (2) → *-owy* adj.   **Cr** [vindserfing] M [U] end20c (2)   **Bg** *ui̯ndsŭrfing* M [U] end20c (2) < *sŭrf*   **Hu** - < *szörfözés, széllovaglás, hullámlovaglás*   **Gr** *ghuindserfing* N [U] 1980s (2) > *istiosanidha*

wishbone   *n.* +3 'part of a sailboard'

Fr *wish(bone)* [wiʃ] M, 1980s (1 tech, ban) < *bôme double*   **Rm** [=E] N, 1970s (1 tech)

wishful thinking   *n.* 'a belief founded on wishes rather than facts'   **Ge** - < rend *Wunschdenken*   **Du** [=E] N [U] (1) < rend *wensdenken*   **Nw** - < *ønsketenkning*

woofer   *n.* 'a loudspeaker designed to reproduce low frequencies'   **Ge** [=E] M, pl. Ø, 1960s (1 tech, rare)   **Du** [=E] C, pl. *-s*, mid20c (1 tech)   **Nw** [=E] M, pl. *-el-s*, 20c (1 tech)   **Fr** [wufœr] M, mid20c (1 tech, ban) > *haut parleur de graves, boumeur*   **Sp** [bu̯fer] M, 1980s (1 tech) = *altavoz de graves*   **It** [wu̯:fer] M, pl. Ø, 1960s (1 tech)

woolmark   *n.* (TM) 'an indication that a product is made of wool'   **Ge** - < rend *Wollsiegel*   **Nw** (TMonly)   **Rm** [=E] N, end20c (1 tech, writ)   **Po** [-ark] M [U] end20c (1 tech)   **Cr** [vulmark] M [U] end20c (1 tech)   **Hu** [vulma:rk] [U] 20c (1 tech, writ, jour,TM)

Worcester Sauce   *n.* 'a pungent sauce first made in Worcester'

This word was borrowed, with various culinary terms, into north-west and central European languages (mediated by German?) it was apparently first pronounced as spelt, but this un-English pronunciation has now become a hallmark of a genteel lack of education.

Ge [vu̯sta/vortʃesta zo:sə] F, pl. *-en*, 19c (1 tech+5Fr)   **Du** *worcestersaus* [wo̯rsɛstər-] C, 1970s (1 tech+5)   **Nw** *worcestersaus* [vu̯:ster-/vo̯:rtʃester-] M [U] 20c (1 tech)   **Ic** [vɔrsjɛster sou:sa] F [U] mid20c (1+5)   **Fr** (o)   **Sp** - < trsl *salsa worcestershire/salsa worcester* F, end20c (1 tech, rare)   **It** [wu̯ster sɔ:s/wo-/wortʃester/ - sɛster] F [U] mid20c (1) < trsl *salsa Worcester*   **Rm** (o)   **Cr** *vorčester* M [U] beg20c (1 tech)   **Fi** [=E] (Ø)   **Hu** [vu̯ster-/vo̯rtʃester-so̯:s]/*-mártás* [-ma̯:rta:ʃ] [U] end19/beg20c (1 tech >3)   **Gr** <=E> [=E] F, end20c (1 tech); *sa̯ltsa Worcester* F (5+1 tech)

word processor   *n.* 'a purpose-built computer system for electronically storing text entered from a keyboard, incorporating corrections, and providing a printout'   **Ge** [=E] M, pl. *-en*, 1980s (1 tech)   **Du** - < *tekstverwerker*   **Nw** - < *tekstbehanlings(program)*   **Fr** - < creat *(logiciel de) traitement de texte*   **Sp** - < rend *procesador de textos*   **It** [wə̯rd prouse̯sor] M, pl. Ø, 1980s (1 tech)   **Bg** *protse̯sor* M, pl. *-al-i*, 1980s (3 tech)   **Hu** [=E] pl. *-ok*, end20c (1 tech)

workaholic   *n.* 'a person addicted to working'   Coined in 1971 in American English on the basis of *alc+oholic*, this word was widely accepted among facetious derivatives in *o-laholic* (as in English itself).

This fashion appears to be obsolescent by 1995. Note the procedure in Russian, Polish, Bulgarian where the first element 'work' is translated independently.

Ge [vɔrkahǫlik] M, pl. -*s*, 1980s (1 coll) **Du** [=E] C, 1970s (1 coll) **Nw** (0) < *arbeidsnarkoman* **Ic** [=E] M, end20c (1 coll) < rend *vinnusjúklingur* **Fr** (0) **Sp** (0) < trsl *trabajólico* **Rm** (0) **Rs** - < trsl *trudogolik* M,

end20c **Po** [werkoxolik] M, end20c (1 mod) < trsl *pracoholik* → *workoholizm* M **Cr** [vorkahǫlik] M, pl. -*ci*, end20c (1) **Bg** - < trsl *rabotokholik* M, end20c **Fi** - < rend *työnarkomaani* **Gr** <=E> end20c (0>1 jour)

workout *n.* 'a session of physical exercise or training'
Ge [vǫrkaut] M, pl. -*s*, 1990s (1 rare, mod) **Nw** [=E] M [U] 1980s (1 rare) < *trening* **Fr** (0) **Gr** <=E> [=E]/*ghuorkaut* N [U] 1990s (1 tech, mod)

workshop *n.* 2a 'a meeting for concerted discussion or activity; a small conference'
  This term was adopted in fashionable academic jargon and is hardly ever met outside university contexts or business training; native equivalents are rarely used.
Ge [vǫrkʃop] M, pl. -*s*, 1970s (1 tech) = mean *Werkstatt* **Du** [=E] C, 1970s (2 tech) **Nw** [=E] M, pl. -*er*/-*s*, 1960/70s (2) = *gruppearbeid*; mean *verksted* **Ic** [=E]

uninfl., end20c (1 tech) **Fr** (Ø ban) < *atelier* > *bourse professionnelle, rencontre interprofessionnelle* **Sp** - < *taller* **It** [wǫrkʃop] M, pl. Ø, end20c (1 tech) **Rm** [=E] 1970s (1 tech>2) **Rs** (0) **Po** <=E> M, end20c (1 tech) **Cr** [vǫrkʃop] M, pl. -*ovi*, end20c (1 tech) **Bg** *uŭrkshop* M, pl. -*al-ove*, 1990s (0>1 jour) **Fi** [=E] 1970s (2 tech) **Hu** [vǫrkʃop] pl. -*ok*, end20c (1 tech>2)

workstation *n.* 1 'the location of a stage in a manufacturing process', 2 'a computer terminal or the desk etc. where it is located'
Du [=E] C, pl. -*s*, end20c (1 tech) **Nw** - < 2: trsl *arbeidsstasjon* **Fr** - < trsl *station (de travail)* **Sp** [=E] F, pl. -*s*, end20c, 2 (1 tech) = trsl *estación de trabajo* **It** [wǫrk steiʃon/stęʃon] F, pl. Ø, end20c (1

tech) **Fi** - < trsl *työasema* **Gr** <=E> [=E] N, pl. Ø/ -*s*, end20c (1 tech)

World Cup *n.* 'a competition between football or other sporting teams from various countries'
Ge [=E] M, pl. -*s*, 1960s (1 tech>2) < *Weltcup* **Du** - < trsl *wereldcup* **Nw** [=E] M, pl. -*er*, 1960s/70s (2) = *verdenscup* **Ic** - < *heimsbikarkeppni* **Fr** - < trsl *coupe du monde* **Sp** - < trsl *copa del mundo* **It** [=E] F, pl. Ø, mid20c (1 tech) < trsl *coppa del mondo* **Rm** (0) < rend *cupa mondială* **Rs** - < rend *kubok mira* **Po** - < rend *puchar świata* **Cr** - < trsl *svjetski kup* **Bg** - < trsl *svetovnata kupa* (5+3) **Hu** - < trsl *világkupa* **Al** - < *kupë botërore/kupa e botës* **Gr** (1 writ) < trsl *pagosmio kypelo*

would-be *adj.* 'desiring or aspiring to be' (often derog.)
Ge - < cp[1] *möchte-gern* **Du** [wʊd bi] beg20c (1 tech) **Nw** (0)

wow *interj.* 'expressing astonishment or admiration'
Ge [va:u] 1980s (1 coll) **Du** *wauw* [=E] (3) **Nw** [=E] 1980s (1 coll, mod) **Ic** *vá* [vau:] mid20c (3 you) **Sp** *guau* 1980s (2 you) **It** [=E] 1980s (1 coll, you) **Rm** *uau* [waw] end20c (2 you) **Po** end20c (1 you) **Fi** *vau* mid20c (3 you) **Gr** <=E>/*ghuau* 1980s (1 coll, rare)

wrestling *n.* +1a 'a show contest in which two opponents grapple and try to throw each other to the ground, with acrobatical elements' (sports)
Ge [=E] N [U] 1980s (2 tech) **Du** [=E] C [U] 1980s (1 tech) < *worstelen* **Nw** [=E] M [U] end20c (1 tech) **Gr** <=E> [=E] N [U] end20c (1 tech/Ø)

WYSIWYG *n.* 'what you see is what you get' denoting the representation of text on-screen in a form exactly corresponding to its appearance on a printout' (comput.)
Ge [=E] N? [U] 1990s (1 tech, rare) **Du** [=E] 1990s (1 tech) **Nw** [=E] 1990s (1 tech) **Fr** [wiziwig] M, 1990s (1 tech, ban) < *tel écran -tel écrit* **It** [=E] [U] end20c (1 tech, rare) **Rm** [=E/ visivig] N, 1990s (1 tech, rare)

Bg (0) **Fi** [=E] 1980s (1 tech) **Hu** [vi:sivig] [U] end20c (1 tech, writ) **Gr** <=E> [=E] N [U] end20c (1 tech)

Y

yacht   *n.* 1 'a light sailing vessel, esp. one equipped for racing', 2 'a larger usu. power-driven vessel equipped for cruising'
Ge *Jacht* [jaxt] F, pl. *-en*, 19c, 1(5Du); <=E> 1980s, 2(1 mod)   **Du** *jacht* (5)   **Nw** [=E/jakt] M, pl. *-er*, mid19c (1 tech)   **Ic** *jagt/jakt* [jaxt] F, pl. *-ir*, 17c, 1(5Da/Ge arch) < *skúta*   **Fr** [jɔt] M, 16c, 1,2(2) → *yachtman, -woman; yachting*   **Sp** *yate* M, mid19c (3)   **It** [jɔːt] M, pl. Ø, beg19c (3)   **Rm** <=E>/*iaht* [jaht] N, end19c, via Ge? (3)   **Rs** *yakhta* F, 18c, via Ge (3) → *-smen* M; *-klub* M   **Po** *jacht* [jaht] M, 18c, via Ge (2) → *-owy* adj.   **Cr** *jahta* F, pl. *-e*, 19/20c (3)   **Bg** *yakhta* F, pl. *-ti*, 19/20c, via Rs (5Du/3) → *yakhtsmen* M; *-klub* M   **Fi** *jahti* 19c, 1(3)   **Hu** *jacht* [jaxt] pl. *-ok*, 17c (3/5Du) → cp¹   **Al** *jaht* M, pl. *-e*, mid19c (3)   **Gr** *ghiot* N, 19/beg20c (2)

yachting   *n.* 'sailing or cruising on a yacht'
It [jatiŋ(g)] M, pl. Ø, 1900s (1 tech)   **Cr** *jahting* 20c (1 tech)   **Gr** *ghioting* N [U] end20c (1 mod)

yachtsman   *n.* 'a person who sails a yacht'
Fr [jotman] M, 19c (1 obs)   **Sp** (0)   **It** [jatsmɛn] M, pl. Ø, 1900s (1 tech)   **Bg** *yakhtsmen* M, pl. *-i*, mid20c, via Rs (3 tech)

Yale (lock)   *n.* (™) 'a type of lock for doors etc.'
The lock was named after its American inventor, Linus Yale (1821–68).
Du *yale-*[je:l-] cp¹, beg20c (1 tech) in *yaleslot* → *yalesleutel* n.   **Nw** *yalelås* [=E] 20c (2+5)   **Ic** (™ only)   **It** (™ only)   **Rm** *yală/ială* [jalə] F, mid20c (2>3)   **Po** [jale] N, uninfl., mid20c (1 coll)

yam   *n.* 'the edible starchy tuber of a plant of the genus Dioscorea'
Ge *Jamswurzel/Yamswurzel* [jams-] F, beg20c (Ø, 3 tech +5)   **Du** [jam] C, pl. *-men*, end19c (1 tech)   **Nw** *jams* [jams] M, pl. Ø, 20c? (Ø)   **Fr** *igname* (5)   **Rs** *yams* M [U] mid20c (1 tech)   **Po** <=E>/*jam* [jam] M, end20c (1 tech)   **Fi** *jamssi* 19c, via Ge (3)   **Hu** *jamszgyökér* (5)

Yankee   *n.* 1 'an inhabitant of the USA; an American'
European languages have adopted the British use (late eighteenth century) referring to an US American (not specifically a northerner). Although technically a foreignism, the word is recorded for all languages tested and universally known, mostly with pejorative connotations. Note the very different periods of adoption.

Ge [jɛŋki] M, pl. *-s*, end19c (2 coll, pej)   **Du** (Ø)   **Nw** [=E/jaŋki] M, pl. *-r*, mid19c (1 rare, obs)   **Ic** *janki* [jaʃcɪ] M, pl. *-ar*, mid20c (1 reg) < *kani*   **Fr** <=E> end18c (Ø)   **Sp** <=E>/*yanki/yanqui* M, pl. *-s*, mid19c (2<3 coll, pej)   **It** [jɛŋki/janki] M, pl. Ø, beg19c (2 coll, fac)   **Rm** *yankeu* [jankɛw] M, end19c, via Fr (2)   **Rs** *yanki* M, uninfl., end19c (2)   **Po** *jankes* [jankes] M, beg20c (2 coll) → *-ki* adj.   **Cr** *Jenki* M, pl. *-ji*, beg20c (2)   **Bg** *yanki* C, pl. Ø, beg20c (2 coll, jour)   **Fi** *jenkki* 19c (3)   **Hu** *jenki* [jɛnki] pl. *-k*, 19c (2 coll, pej)   **Al** *janki* M, pl. Ø, beg20c (3)   **Gr** *Janki* M, pl. *-s* (1/Ø); *Jankis* M (3/Ø)

yard   *n.* 1 'a unit of linear measure equal to 3 feet'
Ge (Ø)   **Du** (Ø)   **Nw** (Ø)   **Sp** *yarda* F (Ø/3 obs)   **It** [jard] F, pl. Ø, mid18c (1 tech)   **Po** *jard* [jart] M, beg20c (2)   **Bg** *yard* M, pl. *-a*, end19c (Ø)   **Fi** *jaardi* (Ø)   **Hu** *jard* [jaːrd] [U] 20c (Ø)   **Gr** *ghiardha* F (Ø)

yawl   *n.* 'a two-masted fore-and-aft sailing-boat with the mizzen-mast stepped far aft'
Ge *Jolle* F, pl. *-n* (5)   **Du** *jol* (5)   **Nw** [jo:l] M, pl. *-er*, 20c (1 tech)   **Ic** *jolla* [jol:a] F, pl. *-ur*, 17c, via Da (5Ge)   **Fr** [jol] M, 19c (1 tech)   **Sp** <=E>/*yola* F, end19c, via Fr (3 tech)   **It** [jɔːl] M, pl. Ø, end19c (1 tech); *iolla/jolla* [jɔlla] F, pl. *-e*, end19c (3)   **Rm** *iolă* [jolə] F, end19c, via Fr (3 tech)   **Rs** (5Du)   **Po** (5Ge)   **Cr** *jola* F, pl. *-e*, mid20c (1 tech)   **Bg** *yal* M/*yola* F, pl. *-a/-ove/-li*, beg20c (5Ge)   **Fi** *jolla* 20c (3)   **Hu** (5Du)

yearling   *n.* 'a racehorse in the calendar year after the year of foaling'
Ge *-* < trsl *Jährling*   **Fr** [jœrliŋ] M, 19c (1 tech)   **Sp** M, beg20c (1 tech)   **It** [jɔrliŋ(g)] M, pl. Ø, end19c (1 tech)   **Rm** [=E] M, beg20c (1 tech, rare)

yes   *interj* +3 'an expression of satisfaction when something went well'
Du [jɛs] 1970s (1 coll)   **Nw** [=E] end20c (1 coll)   **Ic** [jɛs:] mid20c (1 coll)   **Sp** (0)   **Rm** (0)   **Rs** (0)   **Po** (0) **Cr** (0)   **Bg** *yes* end20c (1 coll, you)   **Fi** [jes:] 1970s (1 coll)   **Hu** [jes] 20c (Ø)   **Gr** (0)

yes-man   *n.* 'a weakly acquiescent person, an obsequious subordinate'
Nw *-* < trsl *ja-mann*   **It** [jes mɛn] M, pl. Ø, 1970s (1 tech)   **Gr** <=E> [=E] M, end20c (1 tech)

yorkshire (terrier)   *n.* 'a small long-haired bluegrey and tan kind of terrier'
Ge [=E] M, pl. Ø (1 tech)   **Du** [=E] C, pl. *-s* (1 tech)   **Nw** [joːr)kʃertærjer] M, pl. *-e*, 20c (1 tech)

Fr [jɔʀʃœʀ] M, end19c (1 tech)
Sp [jorsai]/*yorkie* [jorki] M, pl.
-*s*, end20c (1 tech)   **It** [jorkʃər
(terrier)] M, pl. Ø, 1930s (1
tech)   **Po** [-er] M, end20c (1
coll)   **Bg** *yorkshirski terier* M,
pl. -*ra*/-*ri*, 20c (3 tech)

young enterprise   *n.* 'a newly established firm'
  Rm [=E] end20c (0>1 mod)   **Po** N, uninfl., end20c (1
jour)

youngster   *n.* 1 'a child or young person', +1a 'a
young sportsman', +1b 'a young horse'
  Ge [=E] M, pl. Ø/-*s*, 1960s, 1(1 coll, rare) +1a(1 tech,
rare); end19c, +1b(1 tech, arch)   **Nw** (0)   **Rs** (0)

youth hostel   *n.* 'a place where holidaymakers can
put up cheaply at night'
  Ge - < trsl *Jugendherberge*   **Du** (Ø)   **Nw** - < trsl
ungdomsherberge   **Ic** - < *farfuglaheimili*   **Fr** - < trsl
auberge de jeunesse   **Sp** - < rend *albergue juvenil*   **It** -
< trsl *ostello della gioventù*   **Po** - < rend *schronisko
mtodzieżowe*   **Hu** [=E] pl. -*ek*, 1980s (1 writ, mod) <
ifjúsági szálló   **Gr** <=E> [=E] N, pl. Ø/-*s*, end20c (2)
< trsl *xenonas neotitos*

yo-yo   *n.* 1 'a toy consisting of a pair of discs with a
deep groove between them in which a string is attached and wound, which can be spun alternately
downward and upward by its weight and momentum
as the string unwinds and rewinds'
  Ge *Jo-Jo*/*Yo-Yo* [jo:jo:] N, pl. -*s*, 1930s (3)   **Du** *jojo*
(5Fr) = *klimtol*   **Nw** *jojo* [juju] M, pl. -*er*, mid20c (3)

Ic *jójó* [jou:jou] N, pl. Ø, mid20c (3); [jojo] M, pl. -*s*,
1930s (3)   **Fr** *yoyo* M, pl. -*s*, 20c (2)   **It** [jojo] M, pl.
Ø, 1930s (3)   **Rm** [=E] N, 20c (3)   **Po** *jo-jo* [jojo] N,
mid20c (2 coll)   **Cr** *jo-jo* M [U] mid20c (3)   **Fi** *jojo*
1960s (3)   **Hu** *jojó* [=E] pl. Ø, 1930s (3)   **Gr** [jojo] N,
20c (3)

yuppie   *n.* 1 'a young middle-class professional person working in a city'
  This acronym (for 'young urban professional' + -
i.e., as in ↑*hippie, yippie*) was fashionable in 1988–92,
but appears to be obsolescent. It sparked off a great
number of similar facetious formations which have
not had any currency abroad – but a few pseudo-
anglicisms are recorded from around 1990 (in German
yuffies 'young urban failures' etc., all *ad hoc* and long
forgotten).
  Ge [jupi/japi] M, pl. -*(ie)s*, 1980s
(1 mod)   **Du** <=E>/*yup* [jyp(i)]
C, 1980s (1 coll/fac)   **Nw** *yap*/
japp [jap] M, pl. -*er*, 1980s (3) →
jappe v.; *jappete* adj.   **Ic** - < *uppi*
Fr <=E>/*yuppy* [jupi/jœpi] M/F,
1980s (1 mod)   **Sp** [jupi] M, pl.

-*ies*, 1980s (2) → *yupismo*   **It** [juppi] M/F, pl. Ø/-*s*,
1980s (1 mod)   **Rs** *yuppi*/*yappi* M, uninfl., 1980s (1
jour/mod)   **Po** [jupi] M, pl. -*ies*, 1990s (1 tech)   **Cr**
jupi M, pl. -*ji*, end20c (1 tech)   **Bg** *yupi*/*yapi* M, pl. -*ta*,
1990s (1 mod)   **Fi** <=E>/*juppi* [=E] 1980s (1)   **Hu**
[juppi] pl. Ø, 1980s (1 fac, rare)   **Gr** *japi* M, pl. -*s* (1
mod); *japis* M (3 mod)

Z

zapping *n.* 2b 'switching TV programmes by remote control'
Ge [=E] N [U] 1980s (1 mod) → *zappen* v. **Du** - → *zappen* v.; *zapper* n. **Nw** [sapiŋ] M/F [U] 1980s (1 mod) → *zappe* v. **Fr** [zapiŋ] M, 1980s (1 mod) → *zapper* v. → *zappeur* M **Sp** [Өapin] M [U] 1980s (2 tech) > *zapeo* → *zapear* v. **It** [dzappiŋ(g)] M [U] 1990s (2) **Rm** [=E] N [U] 1990s (1 jour, mod) **Rs** *zapping* M [U] end20c (1 tech) **Gr** *zaping* N [U] 1990s (1 mod)

zip *n./cp¹* 3a 'a fastening device of two flexible strips with interlocking projections closed or opened by pulling a slide along them'

The word *zipper* was coined as a trade-name in American English in 1925 and has long become generic (*zip* being preferred in British English); both forms are recorded as loanwords, but do not seem to compete successfully with native equivalents (although these tend to be longer and clumsier). The fact that *zipper* is (marginally) recorded only for German underlines the traditional dominance of British English (rather than American English) in most domains on the Continent.

Ge *Zip(p)* M, pl. -*s*, 1980s (1 reg, rare) < *Reißverschluß* **Nw** (0) < *glidelås* **Fr** [zip] M, 1970s (1) < *fermeture éclair* → *zipper* v. **It** [zip] M, pl. Ø, 1930s (3) < *cerniera lampo, chiusura lampo* **Cr** [=E] M, pl. -*ovi*, end20c (2) **Bg** *tsip* M, pl. -*al-ove*, mid20c, via Czech (3) **Hu** *cipzár* [tsipza:r] cp¹, pl. -*ak*, 1930s (3)

zombie *n.* 1 'a dull or apathetic person', 2 'a corpse said to be revived by witchcraft'
Ge [tsombi] M, pl. -*s*, 1980s, 1(1 you) 2(1 tech) **Du** [zombi] C, 1970s (1 you) **Nw** [=E] M, pl. -*r*, 1980s, 1,2(1 you) **Ic** [sompi] M, pl. -*ar*, end20c, 2(1 tech) **Fr** <=E>/*zombi* [zõbi] M, mid19c (1) **Sp** <=E>/*zombi* [Өombi] end20c, 1(2 coll) 2(1 tech) **It** <=E>/*zombi* [dzombi] M, pl. Ø, 1970s (1 coll) **Rm** *zombi* M, end20c, 2(1 jour) **Rs** *zombi* M, uninfl., end20c (1 coll/jour/you)

→ -*irovanie* N; -*irovat'* v. **Cr** *zombi* M, pl. -*ji*, end20c (1 tech) **Bg** *zombi* C, pl. -*ta*, 1990s, 1(1 tech) → -*ram* v.; -*byasal* adj. **Fi** [=E] end20c (1) **Hu** [zombi] pl. -*k*, 20c, 1(2) **Gr** *zobi* N, 1980s, 1(1 coll, you) 2(2)

zoning *n.* 'dividing towns up into functional zones'
Du [zo:niŋ] C, 1940s (1 tech, rare) < *zone-indeling, zonering* **Fr** [zoniŋ] M, 1980s (1 tech, ban) < *zonage* **Sp** - < *zonificación* **It** [dzoning(g)] M, pl. Ø, 1930s (1 tech) < *zonizzazione* **Rm** - < *zonare, zonificare*

zoom *v.* 2a,b 'cause (an aeroplane) to mount at high speed and a steep angle', 3a 'close up rapidly from a long shot to a close-up', 3b 'cause (a lens or camera) to do this'

Whereas the noun is almost universally available (as a widely known term from photography and photocopying machines) the derived verb is (unsurprisingly) much less common, thus clearly suggesting which is derived from which.

Ge [zu:mən] 1970s, 3a(1 tech) **Du** *uitzoomen/inzoomen* [œyt-zu:mən] 1960s, 3a(2) **Nw** *zoome* [su:me/su:me] 1970s, 3a,b(1 tech) **Ic** [sum:a] end20c, 3a,b(2 tech) **It** *zumare/zoomare* [dzumare] 1910s, 2a,b(3tech); 1950s, 3a,b(3) **Rm** - < *rend a face zoom, a da un zoom* 1980s (3 tech) **Cr** *zumirati* end20c, 3a(2) **Bg** *zumiram* (3) **Fi** *zoomata* [tsu:mata] end20c, 3a(2) **Hu** *zoomol* [zu:mol] 20c (1 tech) **Gr** *zumaro* 3a,b(3 tech, coll) < *estiazo*

zoom *n./cp¹* 2 'a zooming camera shot', +3 'a lens allowing a camera to zoom', +4 'a facility on a xeroxing machine'
Ge [=E] N [U] 1970s, +3,+4(1 tech) → *zoomen* v. **Du** *zoomlens* [zu:m-] cp¹, C, 1960s, +3(1 tech) → *zoomen* v. **Nw** [=E/su:m] M, pl. -*er*, 1960s, +3(2) **Ic** <=E> [sum:] N [U] end20c, 2,+4(2 tech); *summlinsa* F, pl. -*ur*, end20c, +3(2+5) **Fr** [zum] 1950s, +3,+4(1 tech) **Sp** [Өum] M, 1970s, +3,+4(1 tech) **It** [dzum] M, pl. Ø, 1960s, +3(2 tech) +4(1) **Rm** [=E] N [U] 1970s, +3,+4 (1 tech) **Rs** *zum* M [U] end20c, +3,+4(1 tech) **Po** [zum] M [U] end20c, +3(1 tech) **Cr** *zum* M, end20c, +3(1 tech) **Bg** *zum* M [U] end20c, +3,+4(1 tech) **Fi** *zoomi* [tsu:mi] end20c, +3(2) **Hu** [zu:m] n./cp¹ [U] mid20c, +3(1 tech) +4(1 tech) < +3: *gumiobjektiv* → -*os* adj. **Gr** *zum* N, end20c, +3,+4(1 tech)